T0215003

Lecture Notes in Computer Science   **9634**

Commenced Publication in 1973
Founding and Former Series Editors:
Gerhard Goos, Juris Hartmanis, and Jan van Leeuwen

Editorial Board

David Hutchison, UK
Josef Kittler, UK
Friedemann Mattern, Switzerland
Moni Naor, Israel
Bernhard Steffen, Germany
Doug Tygar, USA

Takeo Kanade, USA
Jon M. Kleinberg, USA
John C. Mitchell, USA
C. Pandu Rangan, India
Demetri Terzopoulos, USA
Gerhard Weikum, Germany

Advanced Research in Computing and Software Science

Subline of Lecture Notes in Computer Science

Subline Series Editors

Giorgio Ausiello, *University of Rome 'La Sapienza', Italy*
Vladimiro Sassone, *University of Southampton, UK*

Subline Advisory Board

Susanne Albers, *TU Munich, Germany*
Benjamin C. Pierce, *University of Pennsylvania, USA*
Bernhard Steffen, *University of Dortmund, Germany*
Deng Xiaotie, *City University of Hong Kong*
Jeannette M.Wing, *Microsoft Research, Redmond, WA, USA*

More information about this series at http://www.springer.com/series/7407

Bart Jacobs · Christof Löding (Eds.)

Foundations of Software Science and Computation Structures

19th International Conference, FOSSACS 2016
Held as Part of the European Joint Conferences
on Theory and Practice of Software, ETAPS 2016
Eindhoven, The Netherlands, April 2–8, 2016
Proceedings

Editors
Bart Jacobs
Radboud University Nijmegen
Nijmegen
The Netherlands

Christof Löding
RWTH Aachen University
Aachen
Germany

ISSN 0302-9743   ISSN 1611-3349 (electronic)
Lecture Notes in Computer Science
ISBN 978-3-662-49629-9   ISBN 978-3-662-49630-5 (eBook)
DOI 10.1007/978-3-662-49630-5

Library of Congress Control Number: 2016932745

LNCS Sublibrary: SL1 – Theoretical Computer Science and General Issues

© Springer-Verlag Berlin Heidelberg 2016
This work is subject to copyright. All rights are reserved by the Publisher, whether the whole or part of the material is concerned, specifically the rights of translation, reprinting, reuse of illustrations, recitation, broadcasting, reproduction on microfilms or in any other physical way, and transmission or information storage and retrieval, electronic adaptation, computer software, or by similar or dissimilar methodology now known or hereafter developed.
The use of general descriptive names, registered names, trademarks, service marks, etc. in this publication does not imply, even in the absence of a specific statement, that such names are exempt from the relevant protective laws and regulations and therefore free for general use.
The publisher, the authors and the editors are safe to assume that the advice and information in this book are believed to be true and accurate at the date of publication. Neither the publisher nor the authors or the editors give a warranty, express or implied, with respect to the material contained herein or for any errors or omissions that may have been made.

Printed on acid-free paper

This Springer imprint is published by Springer Nature
The registered company is Springer-Verlag GmbH Berlin Heidelberg

ETAPS Foreword

Welcome to the proceedings of ETAPS 2016, which was held in Eindhoven, located in "the world's smartest region," also known as the Dutch Silicon Valley. Since ETAPS' second edition held in Amsterdam (1999), ETAPS returned to The Netherlands this year.

ETAPS 2016 was the 19th instance of the European Joint Conferences on Theory and Practice of Software. ETAPS is an annual federated conference established in 1998, consisting of five constituting conferences (ESOP, FASE, FoSSaCS, TACAS, and POST) this year. Each conference has its own Programme Committee and its own Steering Committee. The conferences cover various aspects of software systems, ranging from theoretical computer science to foundations to programming language developments, analysis tools, formal approaches to software engineering, and security. Organizing these conferences in a coherent, highly synchronized conference program, enables attendees to participate in an exciting event, having the possibility to meet many researchers working in different directions in the field, and to easily attend the talks of various conferences. Before and after the main conference, numerous satellite workshops took place and attracted many researchers from all over the globe.

The ETAPS conferences received 474 submissions in total, 143 of which were accepted, yielding an overall acceptance rate of 30.2 %. I thank all authors for their interest in ETAPS, all reviewers for their peer-reviewing efforts, the Program Committee members for their contributions, and in particular the program co-chairs for their hard work in running this intensive process. Last but not least, my congratulations to all the authors of the accepted papers!

ETAPS 2016 was greatly enriched by the unifying invited speakers Andrew Gordon (MSR Cambridge and University of Edinburgh, UK), and Rupak Majumdar (MPI Kaiserslautern, Germany), as well as the conference-specific invited speakers (ESOP) Cristina Lopes (University of California at Irvine, USA), (FASE) Oscar Nierstrasz (University of Bern, Switzerland), and (POST) Vitaly Shmatikov (University of Texas at Austin, USA). Invited tutorials were organised by Lenore Zuck (Chicago) and were provided by Grigore Rosu (University of Illinois at Urbana-Champaign, USA) on software verification and Peter Ryan (University of Luxembourg, Luxembourg) on security. My sincere thanks to all these speakers for their inspiring and interesting talks!

ETAPS 2016 took place in Eindhoven, The Netherlands. It was organized by the Department of Computer Science of the Eindhoven University of Technology. It was further supported by the following associations and societies: ETAPS e.V., EATCS (European Association for Theoretical Computer Science), EAPLS (European Association for Programming Languages and Systems), and EASST (European Association of Software Science and Technology). The local organization team consisted of Mark van den Brand, Jan Friso Groote (general chair), Margje Mommers, Erik Scheffers, Julien Schmaltz, Erik de Vink, Anton Wijs, Tim Willemse, and Hans Zantema.

The overall planning for ETAPS is the main responsibility of the Steering Committee, and in particular of its Executive Board. The ETAPS Steering Committee consists of an Executive Board and representatives of the individual ETAPS conferences, as well as representatives of EATCS, EAPLS, and EASST. The Executive Board consists of Gilles Barthe (Madrid), Holger Hermanns (Saarbrücken), Joost-Pieter Katoen (chair, Aachen and Twente), Gerald Lüttgen (Bamberg), Vladimiro Sassone (Southampton), and Tarmo Uustalu (Tallinn). Other members of the Steering Committee are: Parosh Abdulla (Uppsala), David Basin (Zurich), Giuseppe Castagna (Paris), Marsha Chechik (Toronto), Javier Esparza (Munich), Jan Friso Groote (Eindhoven), Reiko Heckel (Leicester), Marieke Huisman (Twente), Bart Jacobs (Nijmegen), Paul Klint (Amsterdam), Jens Knoop (Vienna), Kim G. Larsen (Aalborg), Axel Legay (Rennes), Christof Löding (Aachen), Matteo Maffei (Saarbrücken), Pasquale Malacaria (London), Tiziana Margaria (Limerick), Andrzej Murawski (Warwick), Catuscia Palamidessi (Palaiseau), Frank Piessens (Leuven), Jean-Francois Raskin (Brussels), Mark Ryan (Birmingham), Julia Rubin (Massachussetts), Don Sannella (Edinburgh), Perdita Stevens (Edinburgh), Gabriele Taentzer (Marburg), Peter Thiemann (Freiburg), Luca Vigano (London), Igor Walukiewicz (Bordeaux), Andrzej Wąsowski (Copenhagen), and Hongseok Yang (Oxford).

I sincerely thank all ETAPS Steering Committee members for all their work in making the 19th edition of ETAPS a success. Moreover, thanks to all speakers, attendees, organizers of the satellite workshops, and Springer for their support. Finally, a big thanks to Jan Friso and his local organization team for all their enormous efforts enabling ETAPS to take place in Eindhoven!

January 2016

Joost-Pieter Katoen
ETAPS SC Chair
ETAPS e.V. President

Preface

This volume contains the papers presented at the 19th International Conference on Foundations of Software Science and Computation Structures (FoSSaCS 2016) held in Eindhoven, The Netherlands, during April 4–7, 2016, as part of the European Joint Conferences on Theory and Practice of Software (ETAPS). The conference is dedicated to foundational research with a clear significance for software science and brings together research on theories and methods to support the analysis, integration, synthesis, transformation, and verification of programs and software systems.

The 24 members of the Program Committee (PC) selected 31 papers out of 85 submissions. Each submission was reviewed by at least three PC members, with the help of external experts. After a three-day rebuttal phase, the selection was made based on discussions via the EasyChair conference management system.

We wish to thank all authors who submitted to FoSSaCS 2016, all the PC members for their excellent work, and the external reviewers for their thorough evaluation of the submissions. In addition, we would like to thank the ETAPS organization for providing an excellent environment for FoSSaCS and other conferences and workshops.

January 2016

Christof Löding
Bart Jacobs

Organization

Program Committee

Achim Blumensath	TU Darmstadt, Germany
Thomas Brihaye	Université de Mons, France
Arnaud Carayol	Université Paris Est, France
Stéphane Demri	ENS Cachan, France
Maribel Fernandez	King's College London, UK
Nate Foster	Cornell University, USA
Marco Gaboardi	University of Dundee, UK
Masahito Hasegawa	Kyoto University, Japan
Chris Heunen	University of Oxford, UK
Jan Hoffmann	Carnegie Mellon University, USA
Bart Jacobs	Radboud University Nijmegen, The Netherlands
Radha Jagadeesan	DePaul University, USA
Bartek Klin	University of Warsaw, Poland
Naoki Kobayashi	University of Tokyo, Japan
Manfred Kufleitner	University of Stuttgart, Germany
Orna Kupferman	Hebrew University of Jerusalem, Israel
Paul Levy	University of Birmingham, UK
Christof Löding	RWTH Aachen University, Germany
Matteo Mio	ENS Lyon, France
Sylvain Salvati	Université de Bordeaux, France
Olivier Serre	Université Paris Diderot, France
Colin Stirling	The University of Edinburgh, UK
Nikos Tzevelekos	Queen Mary University of London, UK
Daniele Varacca	Université Paris Est Créteil, France

Contents

Types

Comprehensive Parametric Polymorphism: Categorical Models and Type Theory

Neil Ghani[1], Fredrik Nordvall Forsberg[1]($\boxtimes$), and Alex Simpson[2]

[1] Department of Computer and Information Sciences, University of Strathclyde, Glasgow, UK
{neil.ghani,fredrik.nordvall-forsberg}@strath.ac.uk
[2] Faculty of Mathematics and Physics, University of Ljubljana, Ljubljana, Slovenia
alex.simpson@fmf.uni-lj.si

Abstract. This paper combines reflexive-graph-category structure for relational parametricity with fibrational models of impredicative polymorphism. To achieve this, we modify the definition of fibrational model of impredicative polymorphism by adding one further ingredient to the structure: *comprehension* in the sense of Lawvere. Our main result is that such *comprehensive* models, once further endowed with reflexive-graph-category structure, enjoy the expected consequences of parametricity. This is proved using a type-theoretic presentation of the category-theoretic structure, within which the desired consequences of parametricity are derived. The formalisation requires new techniques because equality relations are not available, and standard arguments that exploit equality need to be reworked.

1 Introduction

According to Strachey [26], a polymorphic program is *parametric* if it applies the same uniform algorithm at all instantiations of its type parameters. Reynolds [23] proposed *relational parametricity* as a mathematical model of parametric polymorphism. Relational parametricity is a powerful mathematical tool with many useful consequences; see [13,21,27] for numerous examples.

The polymorphic lambda-calculus, $\lambda 2$, (a.k.a. System F) was introduced independently by Girard [11] and Reynolds [22]. It serves as a model type theory for (impredicative) polymorphism, and thus provides a significant testing ground for ideas on relational parametricity. In this paper we address the question:

> What is the fundamental category-theoretic structure needed to model relational parametricity for $\lambda 2$, which is both (i) minimal, in assuming as little structure as possible; but (ii) strong enough to ensure the expected consequences of parametricity hold?

It is perhaps surprising that this question does not yet have an established answer. On the one hand, category-theoretic models for $\lambda 2$ were developed many years ago by Seely [25]. They are studied systematically as $\lambda 2$ *fibrations* in Jacobs [15]. On the other, the fundamental category-theoretic structure

© Springer-Verlag Berlin Heidelberg 2016
B. Jacobs and C. Löding (Eds.): FOSSACS 2016, LNCS 9634, pp. 3–19, 2016.
DOI: 10.1007/978-3-662-49630-5_1

needed to model relational parametricity is also known. The crucial ingredient is the notion of *reflexive graph category* which appeared implicitly in Ma and Reynolds [19], was used explicitly by O'Hearn and Tennent [20], and Robinson and Rosolini [24], and reached maturity in the *parametricity graphs* of Dunphy and Reddy [7,8].

To obtain minimal structure for relational parametricity for $\lambda 2$, it is natural to combine the structure of $\lambda 2$ fibrations with that of parametricity graphs. This results in the notion of $\lambda 2$ *parametricity graph*, which we define in Sect. 3. Sadly, $\lambda 2$ parametricity graphs enjoy the expected properties of parametricity only in the special case that the underlying category is *well-pointed*. (Similar observations, for different but related notions of model, are made in [6–8].) Since well-pointedness rules out many categories of interest in semantics (e.g., functor categories) this limits the generality of the theory.

One way of circumventing the restriction to well-pointed categories was proposed by Birkedal and Møgelberg [6], who developed a more elaborate category-theoretic structure, which overcomes the limitation by modelling Plotkin and Abadi's logic for parametricity [21]. This method of modelling the combination of $\lambda 2$ with an extraneous logic has been refined and simplified by Hermida [12]. Nonetheless, it does not enjoy the simplicity in conception of combining the structure of category-theoretic models of $\lambda 2$ with that of parametricity graphs.

To obtain our minimal structure, we retain the original idea of combining parametricity graphs with category-theoretic models of $\lambda 2$. However, we implement this in a perhaps unexpected way. *We modify the notion of $\lambda 2$ model.* We ask for $\lambda 2$ fibrations to additionally satisfy Lawvere's *comprehension* property. Not only are the resulting *comprehensive $\lambda 2$ fibrations* natural in their own right as models of $\lambda 2$, but, when combined with parametricity-graph structure to form *comprehensive $\lambda 2$ parametricity graphs*, they do indeed enjoy all expected consequences of parametricity.

Sections 2 and 3 define comprehensive $\lambda 2$ fibrations and comprehensive $\lambda 2$ parametricity graphs respectively. In Sect. 4, we present a type theory $\lambda 2\mathbf{R}$, corresponding to our category-theoretic structure, which provides a simple system for reasoning about parametricity. The type theory $\lambda 2\mathbf{R}$ is similar to Dunphy's System P [7], and Abadi, Cardelli and Curien's System R [1], to which it is compared in Sect. 7.

In Sect. 5, we develop the technical machinery needed to reason in $\lambda 2\mathbf{R}$. A key obstacle is that the system does not include *equality relations*. This means that graph relations, which are a crucial ingredient in standard arguments involving relational parametricity, are not in general definable. In Sect. 5, we instead identify two forms of *pseudograph* relations, whose subtle interrelationship allows us to establish the consequences we need. One kind of pseudograph relation is immediately definable using the *fibrational* structure built into the notion of parametricity graph. The other type of pseudograph requires *opfibrational* structure. We use an impredicative encoding to show that opfibrational structure is definable in $\lambda 2\mathbf{R}$, and hence always present in comprehensive $\lambda 2$ parametricity graphs. In Sect. 6, we finally apply the technical machinery and establish that the expected consequences of relational parametricity are indeed derivable in $\lambda 2\mathbf{R}$, and hence hold in comprehensive $\lambda 2$ parametricity graphs.

In summary, the main contributions of this work are:

(i) The definition of *comprehensive* $\lambda\mathbf{2}$ *fibrations* as models of $\lambda\mathbf{2}$.
(ii) The definition of a new category-theoretic notion of model of relational parametricity, obtained by combining parametricity graphs and comprehensive $\lambda\mathbf{2}$ fibrations into *comprehensive* $\lambda\mathbf{2}$ *parametricity graphs*.
(iii) The extraction of $\lambda\mathbf{2R}$ as the type theory intrinsic to comprehensive $\lambda\mathbf{2}$ parametricity graphs.
(iv) The derivation of the expected consequences of parametricity in $\lambda\mathbf{2R}$, and hence in comprehensive $\lambda\mathbf{2}$ parametricity graphs. This requires novel techniques: establishing the *opfibration* property of comprehensive $\lambda\mathbf{2}$ parametricity graphs, and the use of *pseudograph* relations.

In the category-theoretic parts of the paper, we assume familiarity with fibred category theory, for which Jacobs [15] is our main reference. Nevertheless, a substantial portion of the paper is presented in purely type-theoretic terms, and may be read without reference to the accompanying category-theoretic material.

2   Comprehensive $\lambda\mathbf{2}$ Fibrations

In Fig. 1, we recall the polymorphic λ-calculus $\lambda\mathbf{2}$. We use $x, y, \ldots$ to range over term variables, and $\alpha, \beta, \ldots$ to range over type variables. Our presentation has four judgements: $\boxed{\Gamma \; \mathsf{ctxt}}$, stating that Γ is a well-formed context; $\boxed{\Gamma \vdash A \; \mathsf{type}}$, stating that A is a well-formed type in context Γ; $\boxed{\Gamma \vdash t : A}$, stating that the term t has type A in context Γ; and judgemental equality $\boxed{\Gamma \vdash t_1 = t_2 : A}$. We assume β and η-equalities for both term abstraction, λ, and type abstraction, Λ. Equality is also assumed to be a congruence relation, although the rules guaranteeing this have been omitted from Fig. 1 for brevity.

A minor departure from many presentations of $\lambda\mathbf{2}$ is that we interleave type variables and term variables in a single context. This approach is not only natural, but indeed standard when $\lambda\mathbf{2}$ is considered in the context of dependent type theory; for example, when derived as an instance of a pure type system [3]. Since there is no dependency of $\lambda\mathbf{2}$ types on term variables, such interleaving is syntactically vacuous. Nevertheless, we shall see below that its presence does have semantic implications.

We next recall the standard category-theoretic notion of $\lambda\mathbf{2}$ *fibration*, which models $\lambda\mathbf{2}$. We directly restrict the definition to the *split* case to circumvent coherence issues that would otherwise arise, cf. [15].

Definition 1 ($\lambda\mathbf{2}$ fibration). A $\lambda\mathbf{2}$ *fibration* is a split fibration $p : \mathbb{T} \to \mathbb{C}$, where the base category $\mathbb{C}$ has finite products, and the fibration:

(i) is fibred cartesian closed;
(ii) has a split generic object U [15, Definition 5.2.1] — we write Ω for pU;
(iii) and has fibred-products along projections $X \times \Omega \longrightarrow X$ in $\mathbb{C}$.

Context formation rules:

$$\frac{}{\cdot \text{ ctxt}} \qquad \frac{\Gamma \text{ ctxt}}{\Gamma, \alpha \text{ ctxt}} \ (\alpha \notin \Gamma) \qquad \frac{\Gamma \text{ ctxt} \qquad \Gamma \vdash A \text{ type}}{\Gamma, x : A \text{ ctxt}} \ (x \notin \Gamma)$$

Type formation rules:

$$\frac{}{\Gamma \vdash \alpha \text{ type}} \ (\alpha \in \Gamma) \qquad \frac{\Gamma \vdash A \text{ type} \qquad \Gamma \vdash B \text{ type}}{\Gamma \vdash A \to B \text{ type}} \qquad \frac{\Gamma, \alpha \vdash A \text{ type}}{\Gamma \vdash \forall \alpha.\, A \text{ type}}$$

Term typing rules:

$$\frac{}{\Gamma \vdash x : A} \ (x : A \in \Gamma) \qquad \frac{\Gamma, x : A \vdash t : B}{\Gamma \vdash \lambda x.\, t : A \to B} \qquad \frac{\Gamma \vdash s : A \to B \qquad \Gamma \vdash t : A}{\Gamma \vdash st : B}$$

$$\frac{\Gamma, \alpha \vdash t : A}{\Gamma \vdash \varLambda \alpha.\, t : \forall \alpha.\, A} \qquad \frac{\Gamma \vdash t : \forall \alpha.\, A \qquad \Gamma \vdash B \text{ type}}{\Gamma \vdash t[B] : A[\alpha \mapsto B]}$$

Judgemental equality:

$$\frac{}{\Gamma \vdash (\lambda x.\, t)u = t[x \mapsto u] : B} \qquad \frac{}{\Gamma \vdash t = \lambda x.\, tx : A \to B} \ (x \notin \Gamma)$$

$$\frac{}{\Gamma \vdash (\varLambda \alpha.\, t)[U] = t[\alpha \mapsto U] : A[\alpha \mapsto U]} \qquad \frac{}{\Gamma \vdash t = \varLambda \alpha.\, t[\alpha] : \forall \alpha.\, A} \ (\alpha \notin \Gamma)$$

Fig. 1. The type system $\lambda 2$

Moreover, the reindexing functors given by the splitting are required to preserve the above-specified structure in fibres on the nose.

The above definition differs slightly from [15, Definition 8.4.3(b)] in that we do not include fibred coproducts in condition (iii). These are not needed to model $\lambda 2$, and their existence is anyway derivable in parametric models.

In a $\lambda 2$ fibration, we write $\mathbb{T}_X$ for the fibre category over X. We also use X as a subscript when referring to structure in $\mathbb{T}_X$; e.g., $\mathbf{1}_X$ is the specified terminal object in $\mathbb{T}_X$, and $\Rightarrow_X$ is the exponential structure in $\mathbb{T}_X$. Given $f : X \longrightarrow Y$ in $\mathbb{C}$, we write f^* for the reindexing functor $\mathbb{T}_Y \to \mathbb{T}_X$, and $A^*f : f^*A \longrightarrow A$ for the specified cartesian lifting of f relative to A. We also write $\prod_\Omega$ for the specified right adjoint, given by (iii), to reindexing functors $\pi_1^* : \mathbb{T}_X \to \mathbb{T}_{X \times \Omega}$.

We recall in outline the semantic interpretation of $\lambda 2$ in a $\lambda 2$ fibration $\mathbb{T} \to \mathbb{C}$. A context $\Theta = \alpha_1, \dots, \alpha_n$ of type variables is interpreted as the n-fold product $[\![\Theta]\!] = \Omega^n$ in $\mathbb{C}$. A type A in type-variable context Θ is then interpreted as an object $[\![A]\!]_\Theta$ of $\mathbb{T}$ over $[\![\Theta]\!]$, defined by induction on the structure of A, using cartesian closure for function types, fibred products for universal types, and the reindexing $(\pi_i)^* U$ of the generic object along the projection $\pi_i : \Omega^n \longrightarrow \Omega$ to interpret α_i over $[\![\Theta]\!]$. Finally, the interpretation of a term $\Gamma \vdash t : A$ is obtained by splitting Γ into its component contexts: Θ of type variables, and Δ of term variables. Then $\Delta = x_1 : A_1, \ldots, x_m : A_m$ is interpreted as the product $[\![\Delta]\!]_\Theta = [\![A_1]\!]_\Theta \times \cdots \times [\![A_m]\!]_\Theta$ in the fibre over $[\![\Theta]\!]$, and t is interpreted as a morphism $[\![t]\!]_\Gamma : [\![\Delta]\!]_\Theta \longrightarrow [\![A]\!]_\Theta$ in $\mathbb{T}_{[\![\Theta]\!]}$.

In the above outline, one sees that the structure of a $\lambda 2$ fibration fits uneasily alongside our mixed contexts of interleaved type and term variables, since these have to be separated to define the semantic interpretation. In *dependent* type theory, where no such separation is possible, a more direct semantic interpretation is achieved using Lawvere's *comprehension* property [18] to model the process of context extension [14]. It is natural to apply the same idea to $\lambda 2$.

Definition 2 (Comprehensive $\lambda 2$ fibration). A $\lambda 2$ fibration $p : \mathbb{T} \to \mathbb{C}$ is *comprehensive* if it enjoys the *comprehension* property [15, Definition 10.4.7]: the terminal-object functor $X \mapsto 1_X : \mathbb{C} \to \mathbb{T}$ has a specified right adjoint $K : \mathbb{T} \to \mathbb{C}$.

Requiring a *specified* right adjoint maintains consistency with our policy of working with split fibrational structure. Given A in $\mathbb{T}_X$, we write $\kappa_A : KA \longrightarrow X$ for the 'projection' map obtained by applying p to the counit $1_{KA} \longrightarrow A$ in $\mathbb{T}$.

To show that comprehensive $\lambda 2$ fibrations permit a direct, inductive-on-syntax semantic interpretation, we present the interpretation of $\lambda 2$ types in detail. A context Γ ctxt is interpreted as an object $[\![\Gamma]\!]$ of $\mathbb{C}$; and a type $\Gamma \vdash A$ type is interpreted as an object $[\![A]\!]_\Gamma$ in $\mathbb{T}_{[\![\Gamma]\!]}$. These are defined by mutual induction, together with maps $\pi_\Gamma^\alpha : [\![\Gamma]\!] \longrightarrow \Omega$ for every context Γ containing α.

$$[\![\cdot]\!] = \mathbf{1} \qquad\qquad [\![\alpha]\!]_\Gamma = (\pi_\Gamma^\alpha)^* U \qquad\qquad \pi_{\Gamma,\alpha}^\alpha = \pi_2$$

$$[\![\Gamma, \alpha]\!] = [\![\Gamma]\!] \times \Omega \quad [\![A \to B]\!]_\Gamma = [\![A]\!]_\Gamma \Rightarrow_{[\![\Gamma]\!]} [\![B]\!]_\Gamma \quad \pi_{\Gamma,\beta}^\alpha = \pi_\Gamma^\alpha \circ \pi_1 \ (\beta \neq \alpha)$$

$$[\![\Gamma, x : A]\!] = K[\![A]\!]_\Gamma \qquad [\![\forall \alpha. A]\!] = \prod_\Omega [\![A]\!]_{\Gamma, \alpha} \qquad \pi_{\Gamma, x:A}^\alpha = \pi_\Gamma^\alpha \circ \kappa_{[\![A]\!]_\Gamma}$$

Having made the above definitions, a term $\Gamma \vdash t : A$ is interpreted as a global element $[\![t]\!]_\Gamma : 1_{[\![\Gamma]\!]} \longrightarrow [\![A]\!]_\Gamma$ in $\mathbb{T}_{[\![\Gamma]\!]}$. The definition, which we omit, is a straightforward induction on the derivation of $\Gamma \vdash t : A$.

The appropriateness of comprehensive $\lambda 2$ fibrations as a notion of model for $\lambda 2$ is supported by soundness and completeness results.

Theorem 3 (Soundness for $\lambda 2$). *If $\Gamma \vdash t_1 = t_2 : A$ then, in every comprehensive $\lambda 2$ fibration, we have $[\![t_1]\!]_\Gamma = [\![t_2]\!]_\Gamma$.*

Theorem 4 (Full completeness for $\lambda 2$). *There exists a comprehensive $\lambda 2$ fibration satisfying:*

(i) *for every type $\Gamma \vdash A$ type, every global point $1_{[\![\Gamma]\!]} \longrightarrow [\![A]\!]_\Gamma$ is the denotation $[\![t]\!]_\Gamma$ of some term $\Gamma \vdash t : A$; and*
(ii) *for all terms $\Gamma \vdash t_1, t_2 : A$ satisfying $[\![t_1]\!]_\Gamma = [\![t_2]\!]_\Gamma$, we have $\Gamma \vdash t_1 = t_2 : A$.*

Theorem 3 is proved by a routine induction on equality derivations, and Theorem 4 by construction of a syntactic model, which has the requisite properties.

3   Comprehensive $\lambda 2$ Parametricity Graphs

Reflexive graph categories are studied in [7,8,16,19,24] as a simple category-theoretic structure for modelling relational parametricity. A *reflexive graph category* consists of a pair of categories, $\mathbb{V}$, the *vertex category*, and $\mathbb{E}$, the *edge category*, together with functors $\nabla_1, \nabla_2 : \mathbb{E} \to \mathbb{V}$ and $\Delta : \mathbb{V} \to \mathbb{E}$ satisfying $\nabla_1 \Delta = \mathrm{id}_{\mathbb{V}} = \nabla_2 \Delta$. Informally, one thinks of $\mathbb{E}$ as a category whose objects are binary 'relations' between objects of $\mathbb{V}$. Then ∇_1, ∇_2 are 'projection' functors, and Δ maps an object to its 'identity relation'.

We shall be guided by the following general thesis. *A model of relational parametricity, irrespective of the type theory for which it is considered, should form a reflexive graph category, in the (2-)category of structure-preserving functors between models of the type theory in question.* This thesis is supported by the following considerations. Endowing the edge category $\mathbb{E}$ with the categorical structure needed to interpret types corresponds to giving types a *relational interpretation*. The preservation of this structure by the projection functors ∇_1, ∇_2 means that the relational interpretation commutes with the usual non-relational interpretation of types. The preservation of structure by Δ, in combination with the identity property discussed later, corresponds to Reynolds' *identity extension* property [23].

In the context of the present paper, we need to specialise the above recipe to (comprehensive) $\lambda 2$ fibrations. A *morphism* from one (comprehensive) $\lambda 2$ fibration $p' : \mathbb{T}' \to \mathbb{C}'$ to another $p : \mathbb{T} \to \mathbb{C}$ is given by a pair of functors, $H : \mathbb{T}' \to \mathbb{T}$ and $L : \mathbb{C}' \to \mathbb{C}$ such that $pH = Lp'$, and such that H, L preserve all other specified structure (including the choice of cartesian morphisms in the splitting) on the nose. By a *reflexive graph of (comprehensive) $\lambda 2$ fibrations*, we thus mean a pair of (comprehensive) $\lambda 2$ fibrations with functors between them:

$$
\begin{array}{ccc}
\mathcal{R}(\mathbb{T}) & \xrightleftharpoons[\hspace{3cm}]{\nabla_1^{\mathrm{T}},\ \Delta^{\mathrm{T}},\ \nabla_2^{\mathrm{T}}} & \mathbb{T} \\[4pt]
{\scriptstyle p^{\mathcal{R}}}\Big\downarrow & & \Big\downarrow{\scriptstyle p} \\[4pt]
\mathcal{R}(\mathbb{C}) & \xrightleftharpoons[\nabla_1^{\mathrm{C}},\ \Delta^{\mathrm{C}},\ \nabla_2^{\mathrm{C}}]{} & \mathbb{C}
\end{array}
\tag{1}
$$

where each of the three pairs $\nabla_1^{\mathrm{T}}, \nabla_1^{\mathrm{C}}$ and $\nabla_2^{\mathrm{T}}, \nabla_2^{\mathrm{C}}$ and $\Delta^{\mathrm{T}}, \Delta^{\mathrm{C}}$ is a morphism of (comprehensive) $\lambda 2$ fibrations, and where each of the triples $\nabla_1^{\mathrm{T}}, \nabla_2^{\mathrm{T}}, \Delta^{\mathrm{T}}$ and $\nabla_1^{\mathrm{C}}, \nabla_2^{\mathrm{C}}, \Delta^{\mathrm{C}}$ is a reflexive graph category. We emphasise that $p^{\mathcal{R}} : \mathcal{R}(\mathbb{T}) \to \mathcal{R}(\mathbb{C})$, in (1), is an arbitrary (comprehensive) $\lambda 2$ fibration fitting into the diagram. The notation $\mathcal{R}(\cdot)$ is merely mnemonic, and does not imply that $\mathcal{R}(\mathbb{T})$ is obtained using a particular construction from $\mathbb{T}$.

One needs to add further conditions to the above structure to ensure that the objects of $\mathcal{R}(\mathbb{T})$ behave sufficiently like relations. In [19], this was addressed by requiring the fibre category $\mathcal{R}(\mathbb{T})_{1_{\mathcal{R}(\mathbb{C})}}$, over the terminal object, to coincide with a particular category of *logical relations* over $\mathbb{T}_{1_C}$. As well as only being applicable if $\mathbb{T}_{1_C}$ has (sufficient) finite limits, this requirement also has the weakness that it says nothing about other fibres of $p^{\mathcal{R}}$. As a result, the structure is too weak to imply consequences of parametricity in general, see [6, 24] for discussion. To remedy this, we instead need axiomatic structure for a category of relations, in a form that is suitable for being imposed fibrewise on $p^{\mathcal{R}}$. This is provided by Dunphy and Reddy's notion of *parametricity graph* [7, 8], which we now recall.

A reflexive graph category $\nabla_1, \nabla_2 : \mathbb{E} \to \mathbb{V}$, $\Delta : \mathbb{V} \to \mathbb{E}$ is said to be *relational* if the functor $\langle \nabla_1, \nabla_2 \rangle : \mathbb{E} \to \mathbb{V} \times \mathbb{V}$ is faithful. This property allows one to think of morphisms in $\mathbb{E}$ as pairs of *relation-preserving* maps from $\mathbb{V}$. Accordingly, we call objects of $\mathbb{E}$ *relations*, we write $R : A \leftrightarrow B$ to mean an object R of $\mathbb{E}$ with $\nabla_1 R = A$ and $\nabla_2 R = B$, and we write $f \times g : R \longrightarrow S$ to mean that there is a (necessarily unique) map $h : R \longrightarrow S$ in $\mathbb{E}$ with $\nabla_1 h = f$ and $\nabla_2 h = g$. A reflexive graph category satisfies the *identity property* if, for every $h : \Delta A \longrightarrow \Delta B$ in $\mathbb{E}$, it holds that $\nabla_1 h = \nabla_2 h$. This allows one to think of ΔA as an identity relation on A (although, cf. Sect. 5 for caveats). In a relational reflexive graph category, the identity property is equivalent to the fullness of the functor Δ. A *parametricity graph* is a relational reflexive graph category with the identity property, for which the functor $\langle \nabla_1, \nabla_2 \rangle : \mathbb{E} \to \mathbb{V} \times \mathbb{V}$ is a fibration. The fibration property supports the following definition mechanism. Let $R : A \leftrightarrow B$ be a relation in $\mathbb{E}$. Then, given morphisms $f : A' \longrightarrow A$ and $g : B' \longrightarrow B$ in $\mathbb{V}$, reindexing produces an *inverse image* relation $[f \times g]^{-1} R : A' \leftrightarrow B'$.[1]

The main category-theoretic definition of this paper is a fibrewise adaptation of parametricity graph to the context of comprehensive $\lambda 2$ fibrations.

Definition 5 ((Comprehensive) $\lambda 2$ parametricity graph). A *(comprehensive) $\lambda 2$ parametricity graph* is a reflexive graph of (comprehensive) $\lambda 2$ fibrations, as in (1), that satisfies, for all objects W of $\mathcal{R}(\mathbb{C})$ and X of $\mathbb{C}$:

(Relational) The functor $\langle \nabla_1^{\mathbb{T}}, \nabla_2^{\mathbb{T}} \rangle \restriction_{\mathcal{R}(\mathbb{T})_W} : \mathcal{R}(\mathbb{T})_W \to \mathbb{T}_{\nabla_1^{\mathbb{C}} W} \times \mathbb{T}_{\nabla_2^{\mathbb{C}} W}$ is faithful.
(Identity property) The functor $\Delta^{\mathbb{T}} \restriction_{\mathbb{T}_X} : \mathbb{T}_X \to \mathcal{R}(\mathbb{T})_{\Delta^{\mathbb{C}} X}$ is full.
(Fibration) $\langle \nabla_1^{\mathbb{T}}, \nabla_2^{\mathbb{T}} \rangle \restriction_{\mathcal{R}(\mathbb{T})_W} : \mathcal{R}(\mathbb{T})_W \to \mathbb{T}_{\nabla_1^{\mathbb{C}} W} \times \mathbb{T}_{\nabla_2^{\mathbb{C}} W}$ is a cloven fibration.

Moreover, for every $\phi : W' \longrightarrow W$ in $\mathcal{R}(\mathbb{C})$, we require the commuting square

$$
\begin{array}{ccc}
\mathcal{R}(\mathbb{T})_W & \xrightarrow{\;(p^{\mathcal{R}})^* \phi\;} & \mathcal{R}(\mathbb{T})_{W'} \\
\Big\downarrow{\scriptstyle \langle \nabla_1^{\mathbb{T}}, \nabla_2^{\mathbb{T}} \rangle \restriction_{\mathcal{R}(\mathbb{T})_W}} & & \Big\downarrow{\scriptstyle \langle \nabla_1^{\mathbb{T}}, \nabla_2^{\mathbb{T}} \rangle \restriction_{\mathcal{R}(\mathbb{T})_{W'}}} \\
\mathbb{T}_{\nabla_1^{\mathbb{C}} W} \times \mathbb{T}_{\nabla_2^{\mathbb{C}} W} & \xrightarrow[{\;p^*(\nabla_1^{\mathbb{C}} \phi) \times p^*(\nabla_2^{\mathbb{C}} \phi)\;}]{} & \mathbb{T}_{\nabla_1^{\mathbb{C}} W'} \times \mathbb{T}_{\nabla_2^{\mathbb{C}} W'}
\end{array}
$$

(where the notation distinguishes reindexing functors determined by p and $p^{\mathcal{R}}$) to give a cleavage-preserving fibred functor from $\langle \nabla_1^{\mathbb{T}}, \nabla_2^{\mathbb{T}} \rangle \restriction_{\mathcal{R}(\mathbb{T})_W}$ to $\langle \nabla_1^{\mathbb{T}}, \nabla_2^{\mathbb{T}} \rangle \restriction_{\mathcal{R}(\mathbb{T})_{W'}}$.

---

[1] We use $(\cdot)^{-1}$ rather than $(\cdot)^*$ for reindexing to emphasise that we are in a relational setting: $\langle \nabla_1, \nabla_2 \rangle$ is a preorder fibration since it is faithful.

This definition could by strengthened by asking for the parametricity-graph fibrations to be split instead of merely cloven. Such a strengthening does not affect any of the results in the sequel, and may seem natural given our use of split fibrations in all previous definitions. Nevertheless, our choice of definition reflects the fact that the weaker cloven assumption is all that is needed to avoid coherence issues arising in the semantic interpretation of the type theory $\lambda 2\mathbf{R}$ introduced in Sect. 4 below.

It is Definition 5, with the comprehension property included, that provides our answer to the question highlighted in the introduction. (The definition without comprehension is included for comparison purposes only.)

4   A Type System for Relational Reasoning

We define a type system $\lambda 2\mathbf{R}$, suggested by the structure of comprehensive $\lambda 2$ parametricity graphs. This system is similar, in many respects, to System R of Abadi, Cardelli and Curien [1] and System P of Dunphy [7], to which we shall compare it in Sect. 7.

The rules for $\lambda 2\mathbf{R}$ are given by Fig. 1 (it extends $\lambda 2$) in combination with Fig. 2. The latter adds three new judgements: $\boxed{\Theta \text{ rctxt}}$ says that Θ is a well-defined *relational context*; $\boxed{\Theta \vdash A_1 R A_2 \text{ rel}}$ says that R is a *relation* between types A_1 and A_2, in relational context Θ; and $\boxed{\Theta \vdash (t_1 : A_1)R(t_2 : A_2)}$ is a *relatedness judgement*, asserting that $t_1 : A_1$ is related to $t_2 : A_2$ by the relation R.

Relations, in Fig. 2, are built up from a collection of *relation variables* $\rho, \ldots$, which, for clarity, we choose to keep disjoint from type and term variables. In the rules, we make use of three operations $(\cdot)_1$, $(\cdot)_2$ and $\langle \cdot \rangle$, defined in Fig. 3, which implement reflexive graph structure on syntax. The $(\cdot)_i$ operations project a relational context to a typing context, whereas the $\langle \cdot \rangle$ operation acts in the other direction. In the definition of the latter, we associate a distinct relation variable ρ^α to every type variable α. Lemma 7 below states how these operations relate typing and relational judgements.

The rules for building relational contexts and relations, in Fig. 2, require some explanation. In adding an assertion $\alpha \rho \beta$ to a relational context Θ, all variables α, β, ρ need to be sufficiently fresh. However, the formulation of $\lambda 2\mathbf{R}$ is such that variables on the left-hand side of relations are always manipulated separately from variables on the right. Thus, for example, α is sufficiently fresh in $\alpha \rho \beta$, as long as α does not already occur on the left side $(\Theta)_1$ of Θ. A similar separation principle applies also with respect to the term variables x_1, x_2 in assertions $(x_1 : A_1)R(x_2 : A_2)$. The separation principle means that one needs to be cautious in interpreting assertions of the form $\alpha \rho \alpha$ and $(x : A)R(x : A)$. In such assertions, even though the same variable appears on the left and right, the correct intuition is that these are really two distinct variables. We have chosen not to underline this distinction by requiring the variables to be syntactically different, since doing so would add unnecessary syntactic clutter to the system; for example, it would complicate the definition of the $\langle \cdot \rangle$ operation. Instead, we

Relational context formation rules:

$$\frac{}{\cdot \ \mathsf{rctxt}} \qquad \frac{\Theta \ \mathsf{rctxt}}{\Theta, \alpha\rho\beta \ \mathsf{rctxt}} \ (\rho \notin \Theta, \alpha \notin \Theta_1, \beta \notin \Theta_2)$$

$$\frac{\Theta \ \mathsf{rctxt} \qquad \Theta \vdash A_1 R A_2 \ \mathsf{rel}}{\Theta, (x_1 : A_1) R (x_2 : A_2) \ \mathsf{rctxt}} \ (x_1 \notin \Theta_1, x_2 \notin \Theta_2)$$

Relation formation rules:

$$\frac{}{\Theta \vdash \alpha\rho\beta \ \mathsf{rel}} \ (\alpha\rho\beta \in \Theta) \qquad \frac{\Theta \vdash A_1 R A_2 \ \mathsf{rel} \qquad \Theta \vdash B_1 S B_2 \ \mathsf{rel}}{\Theta \vdash (A_1 \to B_1)(R \to S)(A_2 \to B_2) \ \mathsf{rel}}$$

$$\frac{\Theta, \alpha\rho\beta \vdash A_1 R A_2 \ \mathsf{rel}}{\Theta \vdash (\forall \alpha. \, A_1)(\forall \alpha\rho\beta. \, R)(\forall \beta. \, A_2) \ \mathsf{rel}}$$

$$\frac{\Theta \vdash B_1 R B_2 \ \mathsf{rel} \qquad \Theta_1 \vdash t_1 : A_1 \to B_1 \qquad \Theta_2 \vdash t_2 : A_2 \to B_2}{\Theta \vdash A_1 ([t_1 \times t_2]^{-1} R) A_2 \ \mathsf{rel}}$$

Relatedness rules:

$$\frac{}{\Theta \vdash (x_1 : A_1) R (x_2 : A_2)} \ ((x_1 : A_1) R (x_2 : A_2) \in \Theta)$$

$$\frac{\Theta, (x_1 : A_1) R (x_2 : A_2) \vdash (t_1 : B_1) S (t_2 : B_2)}{\Theta \vdash (\lambda x_1. \, t_1 : A_1 \to B_1)(R \to S)(\lambda x_2. \, t_2 : A_2 \to B_2)}$$

$$\frac{\Theta \vdash (s_1 : A_1 \to B_1)(R \to S)(s_2 : A_2 \to B_2) \qquad \Theta \vdash (t_1 : A_1) R (t_2 : A_2)}{\Theta \vdash (s_1 \, t_1 : B_1) S (s_2 \, t_2 : B_2)}$$

$$\frac{\Theta, \alpha\rho\beta \vdash (t_1 : A_1) R (t_2 : A_2)}{\Theta \vdash (\Lambda\alpha. \, t_1 : \forall \alpha. \, A_1)(\forall \alpha\rho\beta. \, R)(\Lambda\beta. \, t_2 : \forall \beta. \, A_2)}$$

$$\frac{\Theta \vdash (t_1 : \forall \alpha. \, A_1)(\forall \alpha\rho\beta. \, R)(t_2 : \forall \beta. \, A_2) \qquad \Theta \vdash B_1 S B_2 \ \mathsf{rel}}{\Theta \vdash (t_1[B_1] : A_1[\alpha \mapsto B_1]) R[\alpha\rho\beta \mapsto B_1 S B_2](t_2[B_2] : A_2[\beta \mapsto B_2])}$$

$$\frac{\Theta \vdash (t_1 \, u_1 : B_1) R (t_2 \, u_2 : B_2)}{\Theta \vdash (u_1 : A_1)([t_1 \times t_2]^{-1} R)(u_2 : A_2)} \qquad \frac{\Theta \vdash (u_1 : A_1)([t_1 \times t_2]^{-1} R)(u_2 : A_2)}{\Theta \vdash (t_1 \, u_1 : B_1) R (t_2 \, u_2 : B_2)}$$

$$\frac{\Theta \vdash (t_1 : A_1) R (t_2 : A_2) \qquad \Theta_1 \vdash t_1 = s_1 : A_1 \qquad \Theta_2 \vdash t_2 = s_2 : A_2}{\Theta \vdash (s_1 : A_1) R (s_2 : A_2)}$$

Parametricity rule:

$$\frac{\langle \Gamma \rangle \vdash (s : A)\langle A \rangle(t : A)}{\Gamma \vdash s = t : A}$$

Fig. 2. The type system $\lambda 2\mathbf{R}$

The operations $(-)_i$ (for $i \in \{0, 1\}$) on relational contexts:

$$(\cdot)_i = \cdot$$
$$(\Theta, \alpha_1 \rho \alpha_2)_i = (\Theta)_i, \alpha_i$$
$$(\Theta, (x_1 : A_1) R (x_2 : A_2))_i = (\Theta)_i, x_i : A_i$$

The operation $\langle - \rangle$ on contexts and types:

$$\langle \cdot \rangle = \cdot \qquad\qquad\qquad \langle \alpha \rangle = \rho^\alpha$$
$$\langle \Gamma, \alpha \rangle = \langle \Gamma \rangle, \alpha \, \rho^\alpha \alpha \qquad\qquad \langle A \to B \rangle = (\langle A \rangle \to \langle B \rangle)$$
$$\langle \Gamma, x : A \rangle = \langle \Gamma \rangle, (x : A) \langle A \rangle (x : A) \qquad \langle \forall \alpha. \, A \rangle = \forall \alpha \, \rho^\alpha \alpha. \, \langle A \rangle$$

Fig. 3. Syntactic reflexive graph structure

rely on left and right positioning to make the necessary distinctions. This is crucial in the definition of the substitution operations on relations. There are two such operations: $R[\alpha \rho \beta \mapsto ASB]$ substitutes, in the relation R, the type A for all left occurrences of α, the type B for all right occurrences of β (which may itself be α), and the relation S for all occurrences of ρ; similarly, $S[x \mapsto s, y \mapsto t]$ substitutes, in the relation S, the term s for all left occurrences of x, and the term t for all right occurrences of y (which may itself be x). Note that relations can indeed contain terms and (hence) type variables, due to the $[t_1 \times t_2]^{-1} R$ construction, where we consider t_1 as occurring on the left, and t_2 on the right.

Lemma 6 (Substitution lemma)

(i) If $\Theta \vdash A_1 R A_2$ rel and $\Theta, \alpha_1 \rho \alpha_2 \vdash (t_1 : B_1) S (t_2 : B_2)$ then
$\Theta \vdash (t_1[\alpha_1 \mapsto A_1] : B_1[\alpha_1 \mapsto A_1]) S[\alpha_1 \rho \alpha_2 \mapsto A_1 R A_2](t_2[\alpha_2 \mapsto A_2] : B_2[\alpha_2 \mapsto A_2])$.

(ii) If $\Theta \vdash (t_1 : A_1) R (t_2 : A_2)$ and $\Theta, (x_1 : A_1) R (x_2 : A_2) \vdash (s_1 : B_1) S (s_2 : B_2)$ then $\Theta \vdash (s_1[x_1 \mapsto t] : B_1) S[x_1 \mapsto t_1, x_2 \mapsto t_2](s_2[x_2 \mapsto t_2] : B_2)$.

The relatedness rules of Fig. 2 include the expected rules for relations $R \to S$ and $\forall \alpha \rho \beta. \, R$, which mimic the analogous type constructions in $\lambda 2$. The rules for $[t_1 \times t_2]^{-1} R$ implement its intended interpretation as an inverse image construction. In addition, a further rule expresses an extensionality principle for relations with respect to judgemental equality. Such an intermixing of relatedness judgements with equality judgements is legitimised by statement (i) of the lemma below.

Lemma 7

(i) If $\Theta \vdash (t_1 : A_1) R (t_2 : A_2)$ then $(\Theta)_i \vdash t_i : A_i$.
(ii) If $\Gamma \vdash t : A$ then $\langle \Gamma \rangle \vdash (t : A) \langle A \rangle (t : A)$.

Statement (ii) of the lemma asserts that all terms enjoy the characteristic relation-preservation property of relational parametricity. By the extensionality rule, it follows that $\Gamma \vdash s = t : A$ implies $\langle \Gamma \rangle \vdash (s : A)\langle A \rangle(t : A)$. That is, equal terms are *parametrically related*. Since parametric relatedness captures a form of behavioural equivalence, we can ask also for the converse implication to hold. This is implemented by the *parametricity rule* in Fig. 2. This rule, in the general form given, is derivable from its empty-context version: $\vdash (s : A)\langle A \rangle(t : A)$ implies $\vdash s = t : A$. Thus the parametricity rule is equivalent to asking for the relational interpretation of a closed type to act as an identity relation between closed terms—a weak version of Reynold's *identity extension* property [23]. We discuss the relational interpretation of open types in Sect. 5.

We outline the semantic interpretation of $\lambda \mathbf{2R}$. Given a comprehensive $\lambda \mathbf{2}$ parametricity graph, the contexts, types and terms of $\lambda \mathbf{2}$ are interpreted in the comprehensive $\lambda \mathbf{2}$ fibration $p : \mathbb{T} \to \mathbb{C}$, as in Sect. 2. In addition, we interpret a relational context Θ as an object $[\![\Theta]\!]$ of $\mathcal{R}(\mathbb{C})$, and a syntactic relation $\Theta \vdash A R B$ rel as a semantic relation $[\![R]\!]_\Theta : [\![A]\!]_{(\Theta)_1} \leftrightarrow [\![B]\!]_{(\Theta)_2}$ in $\mathcal{R}(\mathbb{T})_{[\![\Theta]\!]}$. The definitions of $[\![\Theta]\!]$ and $[\![R]\!]_\Theta$ interpret context extension, function space and universal quantification using the structure of the comprehensive $\lambda \mathbf{2}$ fibration $p^{\mathcal{R}} : \mathcal{R}(\mathbb{T}) \to \mathcal{R}(\mathbb{C})$, where relation variables $\alpha \rho \beta$ are interpreted using the generic object of $p^{\mathcal{R}}$. For the inverse-image relation $\Theta \vdash A_1([t_1 \times t_2]^{-1}R)A_2$ rel, we have that $[\![t_1]\!]_{(\Theta)_1}$ and $[\![t_2]\!]_{(\Theta)_2}$ determine maps $[\![A_1]\!]_{(\Theta)_1} \longrightarrow [\![B_1]\!]_{(\Theta)_1}$ and $[\![A_2]\!]_{(\Theta)_2} \longrightarrow [\![B_2]\!]_{(\Theta)_2}$ in $\mathbb{T}_{[\![(\Theta)_1]\!]}$ and $\mathbb{T}_{[\![(\Theta)_2]\!]}$ respectively. The fibration property of $\langle \nabla_1^{\mathbb{T}}, \nabla_2^{\mathbb{T}} \rangle \upharpoonright_{\mathcal{R}(\mathbb{T})_{[\![\Theta]\!]}}$ then gives $[\![[t_1 \times t_2]^{-1}R]\!] : [\![A_1]\!]_{(\Theta)_1} \leftrightarrow [\![A_2]\!]_{(\Theta)_2}$ as the inverse image of $[\![R]\!] : [\![B_1]\!]_{(\Theta)_1} \leftrightarrow [\![B_2]\!]_{(\Theta)_2}$ along these maps.

In the above semantic interpretation, the comprehension property is needed in order to interpret a relational context Θ as an object $[\![\Theta]\!]$ of $\mathcal{R}(\mathbb{C})$, and essential use is made of this in the definition of $[\![[t_1 \times t_2]^{-1}R]\!]$. Were the comprehension property of models dropped, it would be possible to rejig the semantics to interpret a restricted calculus with inverse-image relations definable only in relational contexts containing no term variables, but not full $\lambda \mathbf{2R}$.

The semantics is supported by soundness and completeness theorems.

Theorem 8 (Soundness for $\lambda \mathbf{2R}$). *In every comprehensive $\lambda \mathbf{2}$ parametricity graph:*

(i) if $\Gamma \vdash t_1 = t_2 : A$ then $[\![t_1]\!]_\Gamma = [\![t_2]\!]_\Gamma$; and
(ii) if $\Theta \vdash (t_1:A_1)R(t_2:A_2)$ then $[\![t_1]\!]_{(\Theta)_1} \times [\![t_2]\!]_{(\Theta)_2} : 1_{[\![\Theta]\!]} \longrightarrow [\![R]\!]_\Theta$.

Theorem 9 (Full completeness for $\lambda \mathbf{2R}$). *There exists a comprehensive $\lambda \mathbf{2}$ parametricity graph satisfying the following.*

(i) For every type $\Gamma \vdash A$ type, every global point $1_{[\![\Gamma]\!]} \longrightarrow [\![A]\!]_\Gamma$ is the denotation $[\![t]\!]_\Gamma$ of some term $\Gamma \vdash t : A$.
(ii) For all terms $\Gamma \vdash t_1, t_2 : A$ satisfying $[\![t_1]\!]_\Gamma = [\![t_2]\!]_\Gamma$, we have $\Gamma \vdash t_1 = t_2 : A$.
(iii) For every relation $\Theta \vdash A_1 R A_2$ type, every global point $1_{[\![\Theta]\!]} \longrightarrow [\![R]\!]_\Theta$ arises as $[\![t_1]\!]_{(\Theta)_1} \times [\![t_2]\!]_{(\Theta)_2}$ for terms t_1, t_2 such that $\Theta \vdash (t_1:A_1)R(t_2:A_2)$.

Theorem 8 is proved by induction on derivations. We highlight that the soundness of the parametricity rule follows from the identity property of comprehensive $\lambda \mathbf{2}$ parametricity graphs. Theorem 9 is proved by a term model construction.

5   Direct-Image and Pseudograph Relations

As already discussed, the parametricity rule of Fig. 2 interprets the relation $\langle A \rangle$ as an identity relation when A is a closed type. When A contains type variables, however, this interpretation is not available. Consider an open type $\alpha \vdash A(\alpha)$ type (where we write $A(\alpha)$ to highlight the occurrences of α in A). Then we have $\alpha\rho\alpha \vdash A(\alpha)(\langle A \rangle(\rho))A(\alpha)$ rel. However, the independent handling of left and right variables in $\lambda \mathbf{2R}$ (forced by the semantic correspondence with comprehensive $\lambda \mathbf{2}$ parametricity graphs), means that the latter relation is equivalent to $\alpha\rho\beta \vdash A(\alpha)(\langle A \rangle(\rho))A(\beta)$ rel; i.e., it is a family (indexed by relations ρ) of relations between different types. Indeed, the distinctness of left and right type variables means $\lambda \mathbf{2R}$ has no facility for formulating relations between open types and themselves. In particular, $\lambda \mathbf{2R}$ contains no mechanism for defining identity relations on open types. Nonetheless, the relation $\langle A \rangle$ can act as a kind of *pseudo-identity* relation for type A where the parametricity rule can establish equalities from $\langle A \rangle$-relatedness *in relational contexts of the form* $\langle \Gamma \rangle$.

Graphs of functions are ubiquitous in standard arguments involving relational parametricity. Since we have only pseudo-identity relations, we correspondingly have only *pseudographs* available in $\lambda \mathbf{2R}$. Suppose $\Gamma \vdash f : A \to B$. Define:

$$gr_*(f) := [f \times \mathsf{id}_B]^{-1} \langle B \rangle$$

Clearly $\langle \Gamma \rangle \vdash A \, gr_*(f) \, B$ rel. Its defining property is that $(x : A) \, gr_*(f) \, (y : B)$ holds if and only if $(fx : B)\langle B \rangle(y : B)$. Mathematically, there is, however, another natural pseudograph relation, for f, between A and B. This is the relation $gr_!(f)$ defined by $(x : A)gr_!(f)(y : B)$ if there exists $w : A$ such that $(x : A)\langle A \rangle(w : A)$ and $y = fw$. Since, by (ii) of Lemma 7, f maps $\langle A \rangle$-related values to $\langle B \rangle$-related values, $gr_!(f) \subseteq gr_*(f)$. However, because $\langle A \rangle$ and $\langle B \rangle$ are not identity relations, there is no need for this inclusion to be an equality. We shall need to make use of *both* forms of pseudograph relation to derive the standard consequences of parametricity. In order to do so, we must first provide a definition of $gr_!(f)$ in $\lambda \mathbf{2R}$ itself, and establish formal analogues of the informal observations above.

The main construction we need is that of *direct-image relations* $[t_1 \times t_2]_! R$, dual to inverse-image relations. This is achieved using an impredicative encoding.

Theorem 10 (Direct-image relations). *Using the definition*

$$[t_1 \times t_2]_! R := [i_{B_1} \times i_{B_2}]^{-1} (\forall \alpha \rho \alpha. ([(-\circ t_1) \times (-\circ t_2)]^{-1}(R \to \rho)) \to \rho)$$

where i_B *abbreviates* $\lambda b. \Lambda \alpha. \lambda t. t\, b : B \to \forall \alpha. (B \to \alpha) \to \alpha$ *and* $(-\circ t_j)$ *abbreviates* $\lambda(v_j : B_j \to \alpha).\lambda(x_j : A_j).v_j(t_1 x_j)$, $\lambda \mathbf{2R}$ *supports the derived rules below.*

$$\frac{\Theta_1 \vdash t_1 : A_1 \to B_1 \qquad \qquad}{\Theta \vdash A_1 R A_2 \text{ rel} \quad \Theta_2 \vdash t_2 : A_2 \to B_2} \qquad \frac{\Theta \vdash (u_1 : A_1)R(u_2 : A_2)}{\Theta \vdash (t_1 u_1 : B_1)([t_1 \times t_2]_! R)(t_2 u_2 : B_2)}$$

$$\frac{\Theta \vdash A_1 R A_2 \text{ rel}}{\Theta \vdash B_1([t_1 \times t_2]_! R)B_2 \text{ rel}}$$

$$\frac{\Theta \vdash C_1 Q C_2 \text{ rel} \quad \Theta_1 \vdash v_1 : B_1 \to C_1 \quad \Theta_2 \vdash v_2 : B_2 \to C_2}{\Theta \vdash (u_1 : B_1)([t_1 \times t_2]_! R)(u_2 : B_2) \quad \Theta \vdash (v_1 \circ t_1 : A_1 \to C_1)(R \to Q)(v_2 \circ t_2 : A_2 \to C_2)}$$
$$\frac{}{\Theta \vdash (v_1 \, u_1 : C_1)Q(v_2 \, u_2 : C_2)}$$

In fact, these rules are derivable without use of the parametricity rule of $\lambda 2\mathbf{R}$.

It is now straightforward to define the second form of pseudograph relation discussed above. Suppose that $\Gamma \vdash f : A \to B$ and define $\langle \Gamma \rangle \vdash A \, gr_!(f) \, B$ rel by:

$$gr_!(f) := [\mathrm{id}_A \times f]_! \langle A \rangle.$$

To understand the relationship between the two pseudograph relations we introduce some notation. Given R and S such that $\Theta \vdash ARB$ rel and $\Theta \vdash ASB$ rel, let $\Theta \vdash R \subseteq S$ abbreviate $\Theta, (x : A)R(y : B) \vdash (x : A)S(y : B)$.

Lemma 11. *If $\Gamma \vdash f : A \to B$ then:*

(i) $\langle \Gamma \rangle \vdash gr_!(f) \subseteq gr_*(f)$; and
(ii) $\langle \Gamma \rangle \vdash (s{:}A) \, gr_*(f) \, (t{:}B)$ iff $\Gamma \vdash f \, s = t{:}B$ iff $\langle \Gamma \rangle \vdash (s{:}A) \, gr_!(f) \, (t{:}B)$.

We comment that, in spite of item (ii), the converse inclusion to (i) does not hold in general. Property (ii) applies only in context $\langle \Gamma \rangle$, and thus implies nothing about what happens if further relational assumptions are added.

Theorem 10 has a semantic analogue: direct image relations correspond to opfibrational structure on comprehensive $\lambda 2$ parametricity graphs.

Theorem 12. *In any comprehensive $\lambda 2$ parametricity graph, for every object W of $\mathcal{R}(\mathbb{C})$, the functor $\langle \nabla_1^{\mathbb{T}}, \nabla_2^{\mathbb{T}} \rangle \restriction_{\mathcal{R}(\mathbb{T})_W} : \mathcal{R}(\mathbb{T})_W \to \mathbb{T}_{\nabla_1^{\mathbb{C}} W} \times \mathbb{T}_{\nabla_2^{\mathbb{C}} W}$ is an opfibration.*

6   Consequences of Parametricity

System $\lambda 2\mathbf{R}$ is strong enough to prove the familiar consequences of parametricity.

Theorem 13 (Consequences of Parametricity). *System $\lambda 2\mathbf{R}$ proves:*

(i) The unit (terminal) type can be encoded as $\mathbf{1} = \forall \alpha. \, \alpha \to \alpha$.
(ii) The product of A and B can be encoded as $A \times B = \forall \alpha. \, (A \to B \to \alpha) \to \alpha$.
(iii) The empty (initial) type can be encoded as $\mathbf{0} = \forall \alpha. \, \alpha$.
(iv) The sum of A and B can be encoded as $A{+}B = \forall \alpha. \, (A \to \alpha) \to (B \to \alpha) \to \alpha$.
(v) Existential types can be encoded as $\exists \alpha. \, T(\alpha) = \forall \alpha. \, (\forall \beta. \, (T(\beta) \to \alpha)) \to \alpha$.
(vi) The type $\forall \alpha. \, (T(\alpha) \to \alpha) \to \alpha$ is the carrier of the initial T-algebra for all functorial type expressions $T(\alpha)$.
(vii) The type $\exists \alpha. \, (\alpha \to T(\alpha)) \times \alpha$ is the carrier of the final T-coalgebra for all functorial type expressions $T(\alpha)$.

This result for $\lambda 2\mathbf{R}$ implies that analogous category-theoretic properties (which we do not state for lack of space) hold for comprehensive $\lambda 2$ parametricity graphs.

The proofs of (i)–(vii) follow the usual ones, see, e.g., [21], but with graph relations replaced by pseudographs. Pseudograph relations of the form $gr_*(f)$ suffice in all proofs with the exception of the verification of final coalgebras, where

$gr_!(f)$ is used. In this section, we explain how this difference in the treatment of initial algebras and final coalgebras arises. For lack of space, we focus on the use of pseudograph relations only, and omit the (standard) supporting arguments.

Suppose $\Gamma, \alpha \vdash T$ type. We write $T(\alpha)$ to highlight the occurrences of α in T, and $T(A)$ for the substitution $T[\alpha \mapsto A]$. If α occurs only positively in T (i.e., not on the left-hand side of an odd number of arrows) then it is standard that T defines an endofunctor on types. If $\Gamma' \vdash f : A \to B$, where Γ' extends Γ, then we use the notation $\Gamma' \vdash T(f) : T(A) \to T(B)$ for the functorial action of T. This action preserves identities and composition up to judgemental equality. In addition, the corresponding relational substitution preserves pseudo-identity relations; i.e., $\langle T \rangle(\langle A \rangle)$ (by which we mean the substitution $\langle T \rangle[\alpha \rho^\alpha \alpha \mapsto \langle A \rangle]$) syntactically coincides with $\langle T(A) \rangle$. Also, the functorial action lifts to relations: if $\Theta \vdash (f : A \to B)(R \to S)(f' : A' \to B')$, where Θ extends $\langle \Gamma \rangle$, then:

$$\Theta \vdash (T(f) : T(A) \to T(B))(\langle T \rangle(R) \to \langle T \rangle(S))(T(f') : T(A') \to T(B')).$$

Using these facts (which assert that T is a reflexive-graph functor [8]) one establishes the following properties of the action of $\langle T \rangle$ on pseudograph relations.

Lemma 14. *Suppose α occurs positively in Γ, $\alpha \vdash T$ type and $\Gamma' \vdash f : A \to B$, where Γ' extends Γ.*

(i) $\langle \Gamma' \rangle \vdash \langle T \rangle(gr_*(f)) \subseteq gr_*(T(f))$.
(ii) $\langle \Gamma' \rangle \vdash gr_!(T(f)) \subseteq \langle T \rangle(gr_!(f))$.

Our proof of this lemma closely mirrors the proof of the Graph Lemma in [9], which exploits the fact that *graph relations* can be defined either using inverse image, analogously to $gr_*(f)$, or using direct image, analogously to $gr_!(f)$.

We now explain how Lemma 14 bears on the proofs of the universal properties of initial algebras and final coalgebras. Given T as above, standard constructions produce a T-algebra and a T-coalgebra that can be shown to be weakly initial and weakly final respectively, without invoking parametricity. The parametricity rule is used to establish the uniqueness part of the universal property. In the initiality and finality arguments, one is led to consider T-algebra and T-coalgebra homomorphisms respectively:

$$
\begin{array}{ccc}
T(A) & \xrightarrow{T(h)} & T(B) \\
{\scriptstyle a}\downarrow & & \downarrow{\scriptstyle b} \\
A & \xrightarrow{h} & B
\end{array}
\qquad\qquad
\begin{array}{ccc}
T(A) & \xrightarrow{T(h')} & T(B) \\
{\scriptstyle a'}\uparrow & & \uparrow{\scriptstyle b'} \\
A & \xrightarrow{h'} & B
\end{array}
$$

where the diagrams are given by terms, in a context Γ' extending Γ, which commute up to judgemental equality. Lemma 14 allows one to prove the following crucial properties as consequences of the commutativity of the above diagrams.

$$\langle \Gamma' \rangle \vdash (a : T(A) \to A)\left(\langle T \rangle(gr_*(h)) \to gr_*(h)\right)(b : T(B) \to B)$$
$$\langle \Gamma' \rangle \vdash (a' : A \to T(A))\left(gr_!(h') \to \langle T \rangle(gr_!(h'))\right)(b' : B \to T(B))$$

It is the orientation of the function relations above that necessitates the use of a different type of pseudograph relation in each case. Modulo this subtlety, the remaining proofs of initiality and finality proceed as usual, cf. [21].

7   Related and Further Work

System R of [1] and System P of [7] share with λ**2R** the property of having a syntax in which function space and universal quantification are basic constructions on relations. Indeed λ**2R** is especially similar to System P, which also has the inverse-image-relation constructor $[t_1 \times t_2]^{-1} R$. The most significant difference is that, in System P, the formation rule for this construction is restricted: the terms t_1, t_2 are not allowed to contain free term variables. However, they are permitted to contain so-called *indeterminates*, which, in the semantics of System P, range over *global elements* in models. This device allows System P to be used to establish consequences of parametricity in *well-pointed* models [7]. In λ**2R**, our general arguments for consequences of parametricity make essential use of the possibility for t_1 and t_2 to contain free term variables. As already observed in Sect. 4, the comprehension property of our models is crucial to the semantic interpretation of inverse-image relations in such cases.

System R of [1] departs from λ**2R** (and System P) in two main ways. The first is that, in System R, every type A has an associated *identity relation* A^*.[2] A key rule of System R (written in our notation) is that $\Theta \vdash x \, A^* \, x$, whenever $x : A$ appears anywhere in relational context Θ. This rule breaks the independence between left and right variables in the relational judgements of λ**2R**. (For example, property (i) of Lemma 7 fails.) The second difference is that System R has an explicit syntax for defining graph relations, rather than the inverse-image construct of λ**2R** (and System P), which would be more general in that context. Due to the presence of both identity and graph relations, the arguments, in System R, for consequences of parametricity proceed along standard lines [1]. However, System R currently lacks a corresponding semantic story of the kind we have used in this paper in justification of λ**2R**.

In fact, the interplay between models and syntax could be pushed much further than in the present paper. By adding primitive product types to λ**2** and λ**2R**, one can strengthen our full completeness results by obtaining syntactic categories that are initial in an appropriate 2-category of strict structure-preserving morphisms of models. It would be more natural, however, to broaden both the notion of model, by replacing splittings of fibrations with cleavages, and the notion of morphism, by permitting non-strict structure preservation. With such a relaxation, coherence issues arise, but one would expect to obtain (pseudo-) initiality of the syntactic model of λ**2R** (without any need to extend the syntax with products).

For lack of space we have not presented any concrete models in this paper. In fact, any instance of the more elaborate axiomatic structure from [6] can

---

[2] In System P, every type A is itself a relation, which, although called an "identity relation" in [7], has the properties of the relation $\langle A \rangle$ in the present paper.

be reconstrued (albeit in a nontrivial way) as a comprehensive $\lambda 2$ parametricity graph. So our minimal structure at least generalises the known models of parametricity. However, we do not know whether our structure encompasses any genuinely new models of relational parametricity that truly exploit the (potential) added generality of our approach.

The results of the present paper should be contrasted with those of other recent work by first two authors and colleagues [9,10]. In this paper, we have axiomatised category-theoretic structure modelling relational parametricity for the specific type theory $\lambda 2$, where the resulting structure encompasses both 'syntactic' and 'semantic' models. In contrast, [9,10] axiomatise the category-theoretic structure required on a 'semantic' model for Reynolds' original set-theoretic definition of relational parametricity [23] to generalise to the model. Interestingly, the category-theoretic notion of bifibration occurs both as a central ingredient in the axiomatisation of [9,10], and, in the guise of direct-image relations, as a vital tool in the present paper. A novelty in the present paper is that the bifibrational structure is derived rather than assumed.

From a type-theoretic perspective, one advantage of the approach followed in this paper is that the passage from the original type theory ($\lambda 2$) to the relational version ($\lambda 2R$) appears not to depend on specific properties of the former, other than that essential use is made of judgemental equality in the formulation of the parametricity rule. We believe that this potential flexibility may be useful for transferring our methods to dependent type theories, where parametricity is an active area of study [2,4,5,17].

The proof-relevant setting of dependent type theory, however, requires modifications to our semantic framework. In particular the *relational* property of parametricity graphs must be relaxed. Ongoing work on a higher-dimensional, proof-relevant form of parametricity may show how to remove this requirement.

Acknowledgements. We thank Bob Atkey, Claudio Hermida, Rasmus Møgelberg and the anonymous reviewers for helpful discussions and comments. This research was supported by EPSRC grants GR/A11731/01, EP/E016146/1, EP/K023837/1 and EP/M016951/1.

References

1. Abadi, M., Cardelli, L., Curien, P.-L.: Formal parametric polymorphism. Theor. Comput. Sci. **121**(1&2), 9–58 (1993)
2. Atkey, R., Ghani, N., Johann, P.: A relationally parametric model of dependent type theory. In: Jagannathan, S., Sewell, P. (eds.), POPL, pp. 503–515. ACM (2014)
3. Barendregt, H.: Introduction to generalized type systems. J. Funct. Program. **1**(2), 125–154 (1991)
4. Bernardy, J.-P., Coquand, T., Moulin, G.: A presheaf model of parametric type theory. In: Ghica, D.R. (ed.), MFPS, ENTCS, pp. 17–33. Elsevier (2015)
5. Bernardy, J.-P., Jansson, P., Paterson, R.: Proofs for free. J. Funct. Program. **22**, 107–152 (2012)

6. Møgelberg, E.: Categorical models for Abadi and Plotkin's logic for parametricity. Math. Struct. Comput. Sci. **15**, 709–772 (2005)
7. Dunphy, B.: Parametricity as a notion of uniformity in reflexive graphs. Ph.D. thesis, University of Illinois (2002)
8. Dunphy, B., Reddy, U.: Parametric limits. In: LICS, pp. 242–251 (2004)
9. Ghani, N., Johann, P., Nordvall Forsberg, F., Orsanigo, F., Revell, T.: Bifibrational functorial semantics of parametric polymorphism. In: Ghica, D.R. (ed.) MFPS, ENTCS, pp. 67–83. Elsevier (2015)
10. Ghani, N., Nordvall Forsberg, F., Orsanigo, F.: Parametric polymorphism — universally. In: de Paiva, V., de Queiroz, R., Moss, L.S., Leivant, D., de Oliveira, A. (eds.) WoLLIC 2015. LNCS, vol. 9160, pp. 81–92. Springer, Heidelberg (2015)
11. Girard, J.-Y.: Interprétation fonctionelle et élimination des coupures dans l'arithmétique d'ordre supérieur. Ph.D. thesis, University of Paris VII (1972)
12. Hermida, C.: Fibrational relational polymorphism (2006). http://maggie.cs.queensu.ca/chermida/papers/FibRelPoly.pdf
13. Hermida, C., Reddy, U., Robinson, E.: Logical relations and parametricity – a Reynolds programme for category theory and programming languages. ENTCS **303**, 149–180 (2014)
14. Jacobs, B.: Comprehension categories and the semantics of type dependency. Theor. Comput. Sci. **107**(2), 169–207 (1993)
15. Jacobs, B.: Categorical Logic and Type Theory. Elsevier, Amsterdam (1999)
16. Kinoshita, Y., O'Hearn, P.W., Power, J., Takeyama, M., Tennent, R.D.: An axiomatic approach to binary logical relations with applications to data refinement. In: Abadi, M., Ito, T. (eds.) Theoretical Aspects of Computer Software. LNCS, vol. 1281, pp. 191–212. Springer, Heidelberg (1997)
17. Krishnaswami, N.R., Dreyer, D.: Internalizing relational parametricity in the extensional calculus of constructions. In: Ronchi, S., Rocca, D. (eds.) CSL, pp. 432–451 (2013)
18. Lawvere, F.W.: Equality in hyperdoctrines and comprehension schema as an adjoint functor. Appl. Categorical Algebra **17**, 1–14 (1970)
19. Ma, Q., Reynolds, J.C.: Types, abstraction, and parametric polymorphism, part 2. In: Brookes, S., Main, M., Melton, A., Mislove, M., Schmidt, D. (eds.) Mathematical Foundations of Programming Semantics. LNCS, vol. 598, pp. 1–40. Springer, Heidelberg (1991)
20. O'Hearn, P.W., Tennent, R.D.: Parametricity and local variables. J. ACM **42**(3), 658–709 (1995)
21. Plotkin, G., Abadi, M.: A logic for parametric polymorphism. In: Bezem, M., Groote, J.F. (eds.) Typed Lambda Calculi and Applications. LNCS, vol. 664, pp. 361–375. Springer, Heidelberg (1993)
22. Reynolds, J.: Towards a theory of type structure. In: Robinet, B. (ed.) Programming Symposium. LNCS, vol. 19, pp. 408–425. Springer, Heidelberg (1974)
23. Reynolds, J.: Types, abstraction and parametric polymorphism. In: Mason, R.E.A. (ed.), Information Processing, pp. 513–523 (1983)
24. Robinson, E.P., Rosolini, G.: Reflexive graphs and parametric polymorphism. In: LICS, pp. 364–371. IEEE Computer Society (1994)
25. Seely, R.A.G.: Categorical semantics for higher order polymorphic lambda calculus. J. Symbolic Logic **52**, 969–989 (1987)
26. Strachey, C.: Fundamental concepts in programming languages. High. Order Symbolic Comput. **13**(1–2), 11–49 (2000)
27. Wadler, P.: Theorems for free! In: Stoy, J.E. (ed.) FPCA, pp. 347–359. ACM (1989)

Guarded Dependent Type Theory
with Coinductive Types

Aleš Bizjak[1]([✉]), Hans Bugge Grathwohl[1], Ranald Clouston[1],
Rasmus E. Møgelberg[2], and Lars Birkedal[1]

[1] Aarhus University, Aarhus, Denmark
{abizjak,hbugge,ranald.clouston,birkedal}@cs.au.dk
[2] IT University of Copenhagen, Copenhagen, Denmark
mogel@itu.dk

Abstract. We present guarded dependent type theory, gDTT, an extensional dependent type theory with a 'later' modality and clock quantifiers for programming and proving with guarded recursive and coinductive
types. The later modality is used to ensure the productivity of recursive
definitions in a modular, type based, way. Clock quantifiers are used for
controlled elimination of the later modality and for encoding coinductive
types using guarded recursive types. Key to the development of gDTT are
novel type and term formers involving what we call 'delayed substitutions'.
These generalise the applicative functor rules for the later modality considered in earlier work, and are crucial for programming and proving with
dependent types. We show soundness of the type theory with respect to a
denotational model.

1 Introduction

Dependent type theory is useful both for programming, and for proving properties
of elements of types. Modern implementations of dependent type theories such as
Coq [17], Nuprl [11], Agda [21], and Idris [8], have been used successfully in many
projects. However, they offer limited support for programming and proving with
coinductive types.

One of the key challenges is to ensure that functions on coinductive types
are well-defined; that is, productive with unique solutions. Syntactic guarded
recursion [12], as used for example in Coq [13], ensures productivity by requiring
that recursive calls be nested directly under a constructor, but it is well known
that such syntactic checks exclude many valid definitions, particularly in the
presence of higher-order functions.

To address this challenge, a *type-based* approach to guarded recursion, more
flexible than syntactic checks, was first suggested by Nakano [20]. A new modality, written ▷ and called 'later' [2], allows us to distinguish between data we
have access to now, and data which we will get later. This modality must be
used to guard self-reference in type definitions, so for example *guarded streams*
of natural numbers are described by the guarded recursive equation

$$\mathsf{Str}_{\mathbb{N}}^{g} \simeq \mathbb{N} \times {\triangleright}\mathsf{Str}_{\mathbb{N}}^{g}$$

asserting that stream heads are available now, but tails only later.

© Springer-Verlag Berlin Heidelberg 2016
B. Jacobs and C. Löding (Eds.): FOSSACS 2016, LNCS 9634, pp. 20–35, 2016.
DOI: 10.1007/978-3-662-49630-5_2

Types defined via guarded recursion with ▷ are not standard coinductive types, as their denotation is defined via models based on the *topos of trees* [5]. More pragmatically, the bare addition of ▷ disallows productive but *acausal* [16] functions such as the 'every other' function that returns every second element of a stream. Atkey and McBride proposed *clock quantifiers* [3] for such functions; these have been extended to dependent types [7,19], and Møgelberg [19, Theorem 2] has shown that they allow the definition of types whose denotation is precisely that of standard coinductive types interpreted in set-based semantics. As such, they allow us to program with real coinductive types, while retaining productivity guarantees.

In this paper we introduce the extensional guarded dependent type theory gDTT, which provides a framework where guarded recursion can be used not just for programming with coinductive types but also for coinductive reasoning.

As types depend on terms, one of the key challenges in designing gDTT is coping with elements that are only available later, i.e., elements of types of the form ▷A. We do this by generalising the applicative functor structure of ▷ to the dependent setting. Recall the rules for applicative functors [18]:

$$\frac{\Gamma \vdash t : A}{\Gamma \vdash \mathsf{next}\ t : \triangleright A} \qquad \frac{\Gamma \vdash f : \triangleright(A \to B) \qquad \Gamma \vdash t : \triangleright A}{\Gamma \vdash f \circledast t : \triangleright B} \tag{1}$$

The first rule allows us to make later use of data that we have now. The second allows, for example, functions to be applied recursively to the tails of streams.

Suppose now that f has type ▷$(\Pi x : A.B)$, and t has type ▷A. What should the type of $f \circledast t$ be? Intuitively, t will eventually reduce to some value $\mathsf{next}\ u$, and so the resulting type should be ▷$(B[u/x])$, but if t is an open term we may not be able to perform this reduction. This problem occurs in coinductive reasoning: if, e.g., A is $\mathsf{Str}^g_{\mathbb{N}}$, and B a property of streams, in our applications f will be a (guarded) coinduction assumption that we will want to apply to the tail of a stream, which has type ▷$\mathsf{Str}^g_{\mathbb{N}}$.

We hence must introduce a new notion, of *delayed substitution*, similar to let-binding, allowing us to give $f \circledast t$ the type

$$\triangleright [x \leftarrow t].B$$

binding x in B. Definitional equality rules then allow us to simplify this type when t has form $\mathsf{next}\ u$, i.e., ▷$[x \leftarrow \mathsf{next}\ u].B \equiv$ ▷$(B[u/x])$. This construction generalises to bind a list of variables. Delayed substitution is essential to many examples, as shown in Sect. 3, and surprisingly the applicative functor termformer $\circledast$, so central to the standard presentation of applicative functors, turns out to be *definable* via delayed substitutions, as shown in Sect. 2.

Contributions. The contributions of this paper are:

– We introduce the extensional guarded dependent type theory gDTT, and show that it gives a framework for programming and proving with guarded recursive

and coinductive types. The key novel feature is the generalisation of the 'later' type-former and 'next' term-former via *delayed substitutions*;
- We prove the soundness of gDTT via a model similar to that used in earlier work on guarded recursive types and clock quantifiers [7,19].

We focus on the design and soundness of the type theory and restrict attention to an extensional type theory. We postpone a treatment of an intensional version of the theory to future work (see Sects. 7 and 8).

In addition to the examples included in this paper, we are pleased to note that a preliminary version of gDTT has already proved crucial for formalizing a logical relations adequacy proof of a semantics for PCF using guarded recursive types by Paviotti et. al. [22].

Note that for space reasons many details appear only in the technical report version of this paper [6].

2 Guarded Dependent Type Theory

gDTT is a type theory with base types unit $\mathbf{1}$, booleans $\mathbf{B}$, and natural numbers $\mathbf{N}$, along with Π-types, Σ-types, identity types, and universes. For space reasons we omit all definitions that are standard to such a type theory; see e.g. Jacobs [15]. Our universes are à la Tarski, so we distinguish between types and terms, and have terms that represent types; they are called *codes* of types and they can be recognised by their circumflex, e.g., $\widehat{\mathbf{N}}$ is the code of the type $\mathbf{N}$. We have a map El sending codes of types to their corresponding type. We follow standard practice and often omit El in examples, except where it is important to avoid confusion.

$\vdash_\Delta \kappa$	valid clock	$\Gamma \vdash_\Delta A \equiv B$	type equality
$\Gamma \vdash_\Delta$	well-formed context	$\Gamma \vdash_\Delta t \equiv u : A$	term equality
$\Gamma \vdash_\Delta A$ type	well-formed type	$\vdash_\Delta \xi : \Gamma \xrightarrow{\kappa} \Gamma'$	delayed substitution
$\Gamma \vdash_\Delta t : A$	typing judgment		

Fig. 1. Judgements in gDTT.

We fix a countable set of *clock variables* $\mathrm{CV} = \{\kappa_1, \kappa_2, \cdots\}$ and a single *clock constant* κ_0, which will be necessary to define, for example, the function hd in Sect. 5. A *clock* is either a clock variable or the clock constant; they are intuitively temporal dimensions on which types may depend. A *clock context* $\Delta, \Delta', \cdots$ is a finite *set* of *clock variables*. We use the judgement $\vdash_\Delta \kappa$ to express that either κ is a clock variable in the set Δ or κ is the clock constant κ_0. All judgements, summarised in Fig. 1, are parametrised by clock contexts. Codes of types inhabit *universes* $\mathcal{U}_\Delta$ parametrised by clock contexts similarly. The universe $\mathcal{U}_\Delta$ is only well-formed in clock contexts Δ' where $\Delta \subseteq \Delta'$. Intuitively, $\mathcal{U}_\Delta$ contains codes of types that can vary only along dimensions in Δ. We have *universe inclusions* from $\mathcal{U}_\Delta$ to $\mathcal{U}_{\Delta'}$ whenever $\Delta \subseteq \Delta'$; in the examples we will not write these explicitly. Note that we do not have $\widehat{\mathcal{U}_\Delta} : \mathcal{U}_{\Delta'}$, i.e., these universes do not form a hierarchy. We could additionally have an orthogonal hierarchy of universes, i.e. for each clock context Δ a hierarchy of universes $\mathcal{U}_\Delta^1 : \mathcal{U}_\Delta^2 : \cdots$.

All judgements are closed under clock weakening and clock substitution. The former means that if, e.g., $\Gamma \vdash_\Delta t : A$ is derivable then, for any clock variable $\kappa \notin \Delta$, the judgement $\Gamma \vdash_{\Delta,\kappa} t : A$ is also derivable. The latter means that if, e.g., $\Gamma \vdash_{\Delta,\kappa} t : A$ is derivable and $\vdash_\Delta \kappa'$ then the judgement $\Gamma[\kappa'/\kappa] \vdash_\Delta t[\kappa'/\kappa] : A[\kappa'/\kappa]$ is also derivable, where clock substitution $[\kappa'/\kappa]$ is defined as obvious.

The rules for guarded recursion can be found in Figs. 2 and 3; rules for coinductive types are postponed until Sect. 4. Recall the 'later' type former $\triangleright$, which expresses that something will be available at a later time. In gDTT we have $\overset{\kappa}{\triangleright}$ for each clock κ, so we can delay a type along different dimensions. As discussed in the introduction, we generalise the applicative functor structure of each $\overset{\kappa}{\triangleright}$ via *delayed substitutions*, which allow a substitution to be delayed until its substituent is available. We showed in the introduction how a type with a single delayed substitution $\overset{\kappa}{\triangleright} [x \leftarrow t].A$ should work. However if we have a term f with more than one argument, for example of type $\overset{\kappa}{\triangleright}(\Pi(x : A).\Pi(y : B).C)$, and wish to type an application $f \circledast t \circledast u$ (where $\circledast$ is the applicative functor operation $\circledast$ for clock κ) we may have neither t nor u available now, and so we need sequences of delayed substitutions to define the type $\overset{\kappa}{\triangleright}[x \leftarrow t, y \leftarrow u].C$. Our concrete examples of Sect. 3 will show that this issue arises in practice. We therefore define sequences of delayed substitutions ξ. The new raw types, terms, and delayed substitutions of gDTT are given by the grammar

$$A, B ::= \cdots \mid \overset{\kappa}{\triangleright} \xi A \qquad t, u ::= \cdots \mid \mathsf{next}^\kappa \xi.t \mid \widehat{\triangleright}^\kappa t \qquad \xi ::= \cdot \mid \xi\,[x \leftarrow t].$$

Note that we just write $\overset{\kappa}{\triangleright}A$ where its delayed substitution is the empty $\cdot$, and that $\overset{\kappa}{\triangleright}\xi.A$ binds the variables substituted for by ξ in A, and similarly for next.

The three rules DS-EMP, DS-CONS, and TF-$\triangleright$ are used to construct the type $\overset{\kappa}{\triangleright}\xi.A$. These rules formulate how to generalise these types to arbitrarily long delayed substitutions. Once the type formation rule is established, the introduction rule TY-NEXT is the natural one.

With delayed substitutions we can *define* $\circledast$ as

$$f \circledast t \triangleq \mathsf{next}^\kappa \begin{bmatrix} g \leftarrow f \\ x \leftarrow t \end{bmatrix}.g\,x.$$

Using the rules in Fig. 2 we can derive the following typing judgement for $\circledast$

$$\frac{\Gamma \vdash_\Delta f : \overset{\kappa}{\triangleright}\xi.\Pi(x : A).B \qquad \Gamma \vdash_\Delta t : \overset{\kappa}{\triangleright}\xi.A}{\Gamma \vdash_\Delta f \circledast t : \overset{\kappa}{\triangleright}\xi[x \leftarrow t].B} \ \text{Ty-}\circledast$$

When a term has the form $\mathsf{next}^\kappa \xi\,[x \leftarrow \mathsf{next}^\kappa \xi.u]\,.t$, then we have enough information to perform the substitution in both the term and its type. The rule

TmEq-Force applies the substitution by equating the term with the result of an actual substitution, $\text{next}^\kappa \xi.t[u/x]$. The rule TyEq-Force does the same for its type. Using TmEq-Force we can derive the basic term equality

$$(\text{next}^\kappa \xi.f) \circledast_\kappa (\text{next}^\kappa \xi.t) \equiv \text{next}^\kappa \xi.(ft).$$

typical of applicative functors [18].

It will often be the case that a delayed substitution is unnecessary, because the variable to be substituted for does not occur free in the type/term. This is what TyEq-▷-Weak and TmEq-Next-Weak express, and with these we can justify the simpler typing rule

$$\frac{\Gamma \vdash_\Delta f : \overset{\kappa}{\triangleright}\xi.(A \to B) \qquad \Gamma \vdash_\Delta t : \overset{\kappa}{\triangleright}\xi.A}{\Gamma \vdash_\Delta f \circledast_\kappa t : \overset{\kappa}{\triangleright}\xi.B}$$

In other words, delayed substitutions on the type are not necessary when we apply a non-dependent function.

Further, we have the applicative functor identity law

$$(\text{next}^\kappa \xi.\lambda x.x) \circledast_\kappa t \equiv t.$$

This follows from the rule TmEq-Next-Var, which allows us to simplify a term $\text{next}^\kappa \xi\,[y \leftarrow t]\,.y$ to t.

Sometimes it is necessary to switch the order in the delayed substitution. Two substitutions can switch places, as long as they do not depend on each other; this is what TyEq-▷-Exch and TmEq-Next-Exch express.

Rule TmEq-Next-Comm is not used in the examples of this paper, but it implies the rule $\text{next}^\kappa \xi\,[x \leftarrow t]\,.\text{next}^\kappa x \equiv \text{next}^\kappa t$, which is needed in Paviotti's PhD work.

2.1   Fixed Points and Guarded Recursive Types

In gDTT we have for each clock κ valid in the current clock context a fixed-point combinator fix^κ. This differs from a traditional fixed-point combinator in that the type of the recursion variable is not the same as the result type; instead its type is *guarded* with $\overset{\kappa}{\triangleright}$. When we define a term using the fixed-point, we say that it is defined by *guarded recursion*. When the term is intuitively a proof, we say we are proving by *Löb induction* [2].

Guarded recursive types are defined as fixed-points of suitably guarded functions on universes. This is the approach of Birkedal and Møgelberg [4], but the generality of the rules of gDTT allows us to define more interesting dependent guarded recursive types, for example the predicates of Sect. 3.

We first illustrate the technique by defining the (non-dependent) type of guarded streams. Recall from the introduction that we want the type of guarded streams, for clock κ, to satisfy the equation $\text{Str}_A^\kappa \equiv A \times \overset{\kappa}{\triangleright}\text{Str}_A^\kappa$.

The type A will be equal to $\text{El}(B)$ for some code B in some universe $\mathcal{U}_\Delta$ where the clock variable κ is not in Δ. We then define the *code* S_A^κ of Str_A^κ in the

Universes

$$\frac{\Delta' \subseteq \Delta \qquad \Gamma \vdash_\Delta}{\Gamma \vdash_\Delta \mathcal{U}_{\Delta'} \text{ type}} \text{ Univ} \qquad\qquad \frac{\Gamma \vdash_\Delta A : \mathcal{U}_{\Delta'}}{\Gamma \vdash_\Delta \mathsf{El}(A) \text{ type}} \text{ El}$$

Delayed substitutions:

$$\frac{\Gamma \vdash_\Delta \qquad \vdash_\Delta \kappa}{\vdash_\Delta \cdot : \Gamma \xrightarrow{\kappa} \cdot} \text{ DS-Emp} \qquad\qquad \frac{\vdash_\Delta \xi : \Gamma \xrightarrow{\kappa} \Gamma' \qquad \Gamma \vdash_\Delta t : \vartriangleright\xi.A}{\vdash_\Delta \xi[x \leftarrow t] : \Gamma \xrightarrow{\kappa} \Gamma', x : A} \text{ DS-Cons}$$

Typing rules:

$$\frac{\Gamma, \Gamma' \vdash_\Delta A \text{ type} \qquad \vdash_\Delta \xi : \Gamma \xrightarrow{\kappa} \Gamma'}{\Gamma \vdash_\Delta \vartriangleright\xi.A \text{ type}} \text{ Tf-}\vartriangleright \qquad\qquad \frac{\vdash_{\Delta'} \kappa \qquad \Gamma \vdash_\Delta A : \vartriangleright\mathcal{U}_{\Delta'}}{\Gamma \vdash_\Delta \vartriangleright^\kappa A : \mathcal{U}_{\Delta'}} \text{ Ty-}\vartriangleright$$

$$\frac{\Gamma, \Gamma' \vdash_\Delta t : A \qquad \vdash_\Delta \xi : \Gamma \xrightarrow{\kappa} \Gamma'}{\Gamma \vdash_\Delta \mathsf{next}^\kappa \xi.t : \vartriangleright\xi.A} \text{ Ty-Next} \qquad\qquad \frac{\vdash_\Delta \kappa \qquad \Gamma, x : \vartriangleright A \vdash_\Delta t : A}{\Gamma \vdash_\Delta \mathsf{fix}^\kappa x.t : A} \text{ Ty-Fix}$$

Fig. 2. Overview of the new typing rules involving ▷ and delayed substitutions.

universe $\mathcal{U}_{\Delta,\kappa}$ to be $S_A^\kappa \triangleq \mathsf{fix}^\kappa X.B \,\widehat{\times}\, \vartriangleright^\kappa X$, where $\widehat{\times}$ is the code of the (simple) product type. Via the rules of gDTT we can show $\mathsf{Str}_A^\kappa \simeq A \times \vartriangleright\mathsf{Str}_A^\kappa$ as desired.

The head and tail operations, $\mathsf{hd}^\kappa : \mathsf{Str}_A^\kappa \to A$ and $\mathsf{tl}^\kappa : \mathsf{Str}_A^\kappa \to \vartriangleright\mathsf{Str}_A^\kappa$ are simply the first and the second projections. Conversely, we construct streams by pairing. We use the suggestive cons^κ notation which we define as

$$\mathsf{cons}^\kappa : A \to \vartriangleright\mathsf{Str}_A^\kappa \to \mathsf{Str}_A^\kappa \qquad\qquad \mathsf{cons}^\kappa \triangleq \lambda\,(a : A)\left(as : \vartriangleright\mathsf{Str}_A^\kappa\right).\langle a, as\rangle$$

Defining guarded streams is also done via guarded recursion, for example the stream consisting only of ones is defined as $\mathsf{ones} \triangleq \mathsf{fix}^\kappa x.\mathsf{cons}^\kappa 1\, x$.

The rule TyEq-El-▷ is essential for defining guarded recursive types as fixed-points on universes, and it can also be used for defining more advanced guarded recursive dependent types such as covectors; see Sect. 3.

2.2   Identity Types

gDTT has standard extensional identity types $\mathsf{Id}_A(t, u)$ (see, e.g., Jacobs [15]) but with two additional type equivalences necessary for working with guarded dependent types. We write $r_A t$ for the reflexivity proof $\mathsf{Id}_A(t, t)$. The first type equivalence is the rule TyEq-▷. This rule, which is validated by the model of Sect. 6, may be thought of by analogy to type equivalences often considered in homotopy type theory [24], such as

$$\mathsf{Id}_{A \times B}(\langle s_1, s_2\rangle, \langle t_1, t_2\rangle) \equiv \mathsf{Id}_A(s_1, t_1) \times \mathsf{Id}_B(s_2, t_2). \tag{2}$$

There are two important differences. The first is that (2) is (using univalence) a propositional type equality, whereas TyEq-▷ specifices a definitional type equality. This is natural in an extensional type theory. The second difference is that

Definitional type equalities:

$$\triangleright^{\kappa}\xi\,[x \leftarrow t]\,.A \equiv \triangleright^{\kappa}\xi.A \qquad\qquad (\text{TyEq-}\triangleright\text{-Weak})$$

$$\triangleright^{\kappa}\xi\,[x \leftarrow t, y \leftarrow u]\,\xi'.A \equiv \triangleright^{\kappa}\xi\,[y \leftarrow u, x \leftarrow t]\,\xi'.A \qquad\qquad (\text{TyEq-}\triangleright\text{-Exch})$$

$$\triangleright^{\kappa}\xi\,[x \leftarrow \mathsf{next}^{\kappa}\,\xi.t]\,.A \equiv \triangleright^{\kappa}\xi.A[t/x] \qquad\qquad (\text{TyEq-Force})$$

$$\mathsf{El}(\hat{\triangleright}^{\kappa}\,(\mathsf{next}^{\kappa}\,\xi.t)) \equiv \triangleright^{\kappa}\xi.\,\mathsf{El}(t) \qquad\qquad (\text{TyEq-El-}\triangleright)$$

$$\mathsf{Id}_{\triangleright^{\kappa}\xi.A}(\mathsf{next}^{\kappa}\,\xi.t, \mathsf{next}^{\kappa}\,\xi.s) \equiv \triangleright^{\kappa}\xi.\mathsf{Id}_A(t, s) \qquad\qquad (\text{TyEq-}\triangleright)$$

Definitional term equalities:

$$\mathsf{next}^{\kappa}\,\xi\,[x \leftarrow t]\,.u \equiv \mathsf{next}^{\kappa}\,\xi.u \qquad\qquad (\text{TmEq-Next-Weak})$$

$$\mathsf{next}^{\kappa}\,\xi\,[x \leftarrow t]\,.x \equiv t \qquad\qquad (\text{TmEq-Next-Var})$$

$$\mathsf{next}^{\kappa}\,\xi\,[x \leftarrow t, y \leftarrow u]\,\xi'.v \equiv \mathsf{next}^{\kappa}\,\xi\,[y \leftarrow u, x \leftarrow t]\,\xi'.v \qquad\qquad (\text{TmEq-Next-Exch})$$

$$\mathsf{next}^{\kappa}\,\xi.\,\mathsf{next}^{\kappa}\,\xi'.u \equiv \mathsf{next}^{\kappa}\,\xi'.\,\mathsf{next}^{\kappa}\,\xi.u \qquad\qquad (\text{TmEq-Next-Comm})$$

$$\mathsf{next}^{\kappa}\,\xi\,[x \leftarrow \mathsf{next}^{\kappa}\,\xi.t]\,.u \equiv \mathsf{next}^{\kappa}\,\xi.u[t/x] \qquad\qquad (\text{TmEq-Force})$$

$$\mathsf{fix}^{\kappa}\,x.t \equiv t[\mathsf{next}^{\kappa}\,(\mathsf{fix}^{\kappa}\,x.t)\,/x] \qquad\qquad (\text{TmEq-Fix})$$

Fig. 3. New type and term equalities in gDTT. Rules TyEq-$\triangleright$-Weak and TmEq-Next-Weak require that A and u are well-formed in a context without x. Rules TyEq-$\triangleright$-Exch and TmEq-Next-Exch assume that exchanging x and y is allowed, i.e., that the type of x does not depend on y and vice versa. Likewise, rule TmEq-Next-Comm assumes that exchanging the codomains of ξ and ξ' is allowed and that none of the variables in the codomains of ξ and ξ' appear in the type of u.

there are terms going in both directions in (2), whereas we would have a term of type $\mathsf{Id}_{\triangleright^{\kappa}\xi.A}(\mathsf{next}^{\kappa}\xi.t, \mathsf{next}^{\kappa}\xi.u) \to \triangleright^{\kappa}\xi.\mathsf{Id}_A(t, u)$ without the rule TyEq-$\triangleright$.

The second novel type equality rule, which involves clock quantification, will be presented in Sect. 4.

3   Examples

In this section we present some example terms typable in gDTT. Our examples will use a term, which we call pη, of type $\Pi(s, t : A \times B).\mathsf{Id}_A(\pi_1 t, \pi_1 s) \to \mathsf{Id}_B(\pi_2 t, \pi_2 s) \to \mathsf{Id}_{A \times B}(t, s)$. This term is definable in any type theory with a strong (dependent) elimination rule for dependent sums. The second property we will use is that $\mathsf{Str}_A^{\kappa} \equiv A \times \triangleright\mathsf{Str}_A^{\kappa}$. Because hd^{κ} and tl^{κ} are simply first and second projections, pη also has type $\Pi(xs, ys : \mathsf{Str}_A^{\kappa})\,.\mathsf{Id}_A(\mathsf{hd}^{\kappa}xs, \mathsf{hd}^{\kappa}ys) \to \mathsf{Id}_{\triangleright\mathsf{Str}_A^{\kappa}}(\mathsf{tl}^{\kappa}xs, \mathsf{tl}^{\kappa}ys) \to \mathsf{Id}_{\mathsf{Str}_A^{\kappa}}(xs, ys)$.

zipWith$^{\kappa}$ *Preserves Commutativity.* In gDTT we define the zipWith$^{\kappa}$ function which has the type $(A \to B \to C) \to \mathsf{Str}_A^{\kappa} \to \mathsf{Str}_B^{\kappa} \to \mathsf{Str}_C^{\kappa}$ by

$$\mathsf{zipWith}^{\kappa} f \triangleq \mathsf{fix}^{\kappa}\phi.\lambda xs, ys.\mathsf{cons}^{\kappa}\,(f\,(\mathsf{hd}^{\kappa}xs)\,(\mathsf{hd}^{\kappa}ys))\,(\phi \circledast_{\kappa} \mathsf{tl}^{\kappa}xs \circledast_{\kappa} \mathsf{tl}^{\kappa}ys).$$

We show that commutativity of f implies commutativity of $\mathsf{zipWith}^\kappa f$, i.e., that

$$\Pi(f : A \to A \to B).\,(\Pi(x, y : A).\mathsf{Id}_B(f\,x\,y, f\,y\,x)) \to$$
$$\Pi(xs, ys : \mathsf{Str}_A^\kappa).\mathsf{Id}_{\mathsf{Str}_B^\kappa}(\mathsf{zipWith}^\kappa f\,xs\,ys, \mathsf{zipWith}^\kappa f\,ys\,xs)$$

is inhabited. The term that inhabits this type is

$$\lambda f.\lambda c.\mathsf{fix}^\kappa\phi.\lambda xs, ys.\mathsf{p}\eta\ (c\,(\mathsf{hd}^\kappa xs)\,(\mathsf{hd}^\kappa ys))\ (\phi \circledast_\kappa \mathsf{tl}^\kappa xs \circledast_\kappa \mathsf{tl}^\kappa ys).$$

Here, ϕ has type $\stackrel{\kappa}{\triangleright}(\Pi(xs, ys : \mathsf{Str}_A^\kappa).\mathsf{Id}_{\mathsf{Str}_B^\kappa}(\mathsf{zipWith}^\kappa f\,xs\,ys, \mathsf{zipWith}^\kappa f\,ys\,xs))$ so to type the term above, we crucially need delayed substitutions.

An Example with Covectors. The next example is more sophisticated, as it involves programming and proving with a data type that, unlike streams, is dependently typed. Indeed the generalised later, carrying a delayed substitution, is necessary to type even elementary programs. *Covectors* are the potentially infinite version of vectors (lists with length). To define guarded covectors we first need guarded co-natural numbers. The definition in gDTT is $\mathsf{CoN}^\kappa \triangleq \mathsf{El}\left(\mathsf{fix}^\kappa X.(\widehat{1} \,\widehat{+}\, \widehat{\triangleright}^\kappa X)\right)$; this type satisfies $\mathsf{CoN}^\kappa \equiv 1 + \stackrel{\kappa}{\triangleright} \mathsf{CoN}^\kappa$. Using CoN^κ we can define the type family of covectors $\mathsf{CoVec}_A^\kappa\,n \triangleq \mathsf{El}(\widehat{\mathsf{CoVec}}_A^\kappa\,n)$, where

$$\widehat{\mathsf{CoVec}}_A^\kappa \triangleq \mathsf{fix}^\kappa\left(\phi : \stackrel{\kappa}{\triangleright}(\mathsf{CoN}^\kappa \to \mathcal{U}_{\Delta,\kappa})\right).\lambda(n : \mathsf{CoN}^\kappa).\mathsf{case}\,n\,\mathsf{of}$$
$$\mathsf{inl}\,u \Rightarrow \widehat{1}$$
$$\mathsf{inr}\,m \Rightarrow A\,\widehat{\times}\,\widehat{\triangleright}^\kappa(\phi \circledast_\kappa m).$$

We will not distinguish between CoVec_A^κ and $\widehat{\mathsf{CoVec}}_A^\kappa$. As an example of covectors, we define ones of type $\Pi(n : \mathsf{CoN}^\kappa).\mathsf{CoVec}_\mathbb{N}^\kappa\,n$ which produces a covector of any length consisting only of ones:

$$\mathsf{ones} \triangleq \mathsf{fix}^\kappa\phi.\lambda(n : \mathsf{CoN}^\kappa).\mathsf{case}\,n\,\mathsf{of}\,\{\mathsf{inl}\,u \Rightarrow \mathsf{inl}\,\langle\rangle; \mathsf{inr}\,m \Rightarrow \langle 1, \phi \circledast_\kappa m\rangle\}.$$

Although this is one of the simplest covector programs one can imagine, it does not type-check without the generalised later with delayed substitutions.

The map function on covectors is defined as

$$\mathsf{map}\ :\ (A \to B) \to \Pi(n : \mathsf{CoN}^\kappa).\,\mathsf{CoVec}_A^\kappa\,n \to \mathsf{CoVec}_B^\kappa\,n$$
$$\mathsf{map}\,f \triangleq \mathsf{fix}^\kappa\phi.\lambda(n : \mathsf{CoN}^\kappa).\mathsf{case}\,n\,\mathsf{of}$$
$$\mathsf{inl}\,u \Rightarrow \lambda(x : 1).x$$
$$\mathsf{inr}\,m \Rightarrow \lambda\left(p : A \times \stackrel{\kappa}{\triangleright}[n \leftarrow m].(\mathsf{CoVec}_A^\kappa\,n)\right).\langle f\,(\pi_1 p), \phi \circledast_\kappa m \circledast_\kappa (\pi_2 p)\rangle.$$

It preserves composition: the following type is inhabited

$$\Pi(f : A \to B)(g : B \to C)(n : \mathsf{CoN}^\kappa)(xs : \mathsf{CoVec}_A^\kappa\,n).$$
$$\mathsf{Id}_{\mathsf{CoVec}_C^\kappa\,n}(\mathsf{map}\,g\,n\,(\mathsf{map}\,f\,n\,xs), \mathsf{map}\,(g \circ f)\,n\,xs)$$

by the term

$$\lambda(f : A \to B)(g : B \to C).\text{fix}^\kappa \phi.\lambda(n : \text{CoN}^\kappa).\text{case } n \text{ of}$$
$$\text{inl } u \Rightarrow \lambda(xs : 1).\text{r}_1 xs$$
$$\text{inr } m \Rightarrow \lambda(xs : \text{CoVec}_A^\kappa(\text{inr } m)).\text{p}\eta \, (\text{r}_C g(f(\pi_1 xs))) \, (\phi \circledS m \circledS \pi_2 xs).$$

4 Coinductive Types

As discussed in the introduction, guarded recursive types on their own disallow productive but acausal function definitions. To capture such functions we need to be able to remove $\overset{\kappa}{\triangleright}$. However such eliminations must be controlled to avoid trivialising $\overset{\kappa}{\triangleright}$. If we had an unrestricted elimination term $\text{elim} : \overset{\kappa}{\triangleright}A \to A$ every type would be inhabited via fix^κ, making the type theory inconsistent.

However, we may eliminate $\overset{\kappa}{\triangleright}$ provided that the term does not depend on the clock κ, i.e., the term is typeable in a context where κ does not appear. Intuitively, such contexts have no temporal properties along the κ dimension, so we may progress the computation without violating guardedness. Figure 4 extends the system of Fig. 2 to allow the removal of clocks in such a setting, by introducing *clock quantifiers* $\forall \kappa$ [3,7,19]. This is a binding construct with associated term constructor $\Lambda \kappa$, which also binds κ. The elimination term is *clock application*. Application of the term t of type $\forall \kappa.A$ to a clock κ is written as $t[\kappa]$. One may think of $\forall \kappa.A$ as analogous to the type $\forall \alpha.A$ in polymorphic lambda calculus; indeed the basic rules are precisely the same, but we have an additional construct $\text{prev } \kappa.t$, called 'previous', to allow removal of the later modality $\overset{\kappa}{\triangleright}$.

Typing this new construct $\text{prev } \kappa.t$ is somewhat complicated, as it requires 'advancing' a delayed substitution, which turns it into a context morphism (an actual substitution); see Fig. 5 for the definition. The judgement $\rho :_\Delta \Gamma \to \Gamma'$ expresses that ρ is a context morphism from context $\Gamma \vdash_\Delta$ to the context $\Gamma' \vdash_\Delta$. We use the notation $\rho[t/x]$ for extending the context morphism by mapping the variable x to the term t. We illustrate this with two concrete examples.

First, we can indeed remove later under a clock quantier:

$$\text{force} : \forall \kappa. \overset{\kappa}{\triangleright} A \to \forall \kappa.A \qquad\qquad \text{force} \triangleq \lambda x.\text{prev } \kappa.x[\kappa].$$

The type is correct because advancing the empty delayed substitution in $\overset{\kappa}{\triangleright}$ turns it into the identity substitution ι, and $A\iota \equiv A$. The β and η rules (Fig. 6) ensure that force is the inverse to the canonical term $\lambda x.\Lambda \kappa.\text{next}^\kappa x[\kappa]$ of type $\forall \kappa.A \to \forall \kappa. \overset{\kappa}{\triangleright} A$.

Second, we may see an example with a non-empty delayed substitution in the term $\text{prev } \kappa.\text{next}^\kappa \lambda n.\text{succ } n \circledS \text{next}^\kappa 0$ of type $\forall \kappa.\mathbb{N}$. Recall that $\circledS$ is syntactic sugar and so more precisely the term is

$$\text{prev } \kappa.\text{next}^\kappa \begin{bmatrix} f \leftarrow \text{next}^\kappa \lambda n.\text{succ } n \\ x \leftarrow \text{next}^\kappa 0 \end{bmatrix} . f\, x. \tag{3}$$

$$\frac{\Gamma \vdash_\Delta \quad \Gamma \vdash_{\Delta,\kappa} A \text{ type}}{\Gamma \vdash_\Delta \forall \kappa.A \text{ type}} \text{ TF-}\forall \qquad \frac{\Delta' \subseteq \Delta \quad \Gamma \vdash_\Delta t : \forall \kappa.\mathcal{U}_{\Delta',\kappa}}{\Gamma \vdash_\Delta \widehat{\forall} t : \mathcal{U}_{\Delta'}} \text{ TY-}\forall\text{-CODE}$$

$$\frac{\Gamma \vdash_\Delta \quad \Gamma \vdash_{\Delta,\kappa} t : A}{\Gamma \vdash_\Delta \Lambda \kappa.t : \forall \kappa.A} \text{ TY-}\Lambda \qquad \frac{\vdash_\Delta \kappa' \quad \Gamma \vdash_\Delta t : \forall \kappa.A}{\Gamma \vdash_\Delta t[\kappa'] : A[\kappa'/\kappa]} \text{ TY-APP}$$

$$\frac{\Gamma \vdash_\Delta \quad \Gamma \vdash_{\Delta,\kappa} t : \stackrel{\kappa}{\triangleright}\xi.A}{\Gamma \vdash_\Delta \text{prev } \kappa.t : \forall \kappa.(A(\text{adv}_\Delta^\kappa(\xi)))} \text{ TY-prev}$$

Fig. 4. Overview of the new typing rules for coinductive types.

$$\frac{\vdash_{\Delta,\kappa} \cdot : \Gamma \stackrel{\kappa}{\to} \cdot \quad \Gamma \vdash_\Delta}{\text{adv}_\Delta^\kappa(\cdot) \triangleq \iota :_{\Delta,\kappa} \Gamma \to \Gamma}$$

$$\frac{\vdash_{\Delta,\kappa} \xi[x \leftarrow t] : \Gamma \stackrel{\kappa}{\to} \Gamma', x : A \quad \Gamma \vdash_\Delta}{\text{adv}_\Delta^\kappa(\xi[x \leftarrow t]) \triangleq \text{adv}_\Delta^\kappa(\xi)[(\text{prev } \kappa.t)[\kappa]/x] :_{\Delta,\kappa} \Gamma \to \Gamma, \Gamma', x : A}$$

Fig. 5. Advancing a delayed substitution.

Advancing the delayed substitution turns it into the substitution mapping the variable f to the term (prev $\kappa.\text{next}^\kappa \lambda n.\text{succ } n)[\kappa]$ and the variable x to the term (prev $\kappa.\text{next}^\kappa 0)[\kappa]$. Using the β rule for prev, then the β rule for $\forall \kappa$, this simplifies to the substitution mapping f to $\lambda n.\text{succ } n$ and x to 0. With this we have that the term (3) is equal to $\Lambda \kappa.((\lambda n.\text{succ } n) 0)$ which is in turn equal to $\Lambda \kappa.1$.

An important property of the term prev $\kappa.t$ is that κ is *bound* in t; hence prev $\kappa.t$ has type $\forall \kappa.A$ instead of just A. This ensures that substitution of terms in types and terms is well-behaved and we do not need the explicit substitutions used, for example, by Clouston et al. [9] where the unary type-former $\Box$ was used in place of clocks. This binding structure ensures, for instance, that the introduction rule TY-Λ closed under substitution in Γ.

The rule TMEQ-$\forall$-FRESH states that if t has type $\forall \kappa.A$ and the clock κ does not appear in the *type* A, then it does not matter to which clock t is applied, as the resulting term will be the same. In the polymorphic lambda calculus, the corresponding rule for universal quantification over types would be a consequence of relational parametricity.

We further have the construct $\widehat{\forall}$ and the rule TY-$\forall$-CODE which witness that the universes are closed under $\forall \kappa$.

To summarise, the new raw types and terms, extending those of Sect. 2, are

$$A, B ::= \cdots \mid \forall \kappa.A \qquad t, u ::= \cdots \mid \Lambda \kappa.t \mid t[\kappa] \mid \widehat{\forall} t \mid \text{prev } \kappa.t$$

Finally, we have the equality rule TYEQ-$\forall$-ID analogous to the rule TYEQ-$\triangleright$. Note that, as in Sect. 2.2, there is a canonical term of type $\text{Id}_{\forall \kappa.A}(t, s) \to \forall \kappa.\text{Id}_A(t[\kappa], s[\kappa])$, but, without this rule, no term in the reverse direction.

4.1   Derivable Type Isomorphisms

The encoding of coinductive types using guarded recursive types crucially uses a family of type isomorphisms commuting $\forall \kappa$ over other type formers [3,19]. By a type isomorphism $A \cong B$ we mean two well-typed terms f and g of types $f : A \to B$ and $g : B \to A$ such that $f(g\,x) \equiv x$ and $g(f\,x) \equiv x$. The first type isomorphism is $\forall \kappa.A \cong A$ whenever κ is not free in A. The terms $g = \lambda x.\Lambda \kappa.x$ of type $A \to \forall \kappa.A$ and $f = \lambda x.x[\kappa_0]$ of type $A \to \forall \kappa.A$ witness the isomorphism. Note that we used the clock constant κ_0 in an essential way. The equality $f(g\,x) \equiv x$ follows using only the β rule for clock application. The equality $g(f\,x) \equiv x$ follows using by the rule TMEQ-$\forall$-FRESH.

The following type isomorphisms follow by using β and η laws for the constructs involved.

- If $\kappa \notin A$ then $\forall \kappa.\Pi(x : A).B \cong \Pi(x : A).\forall \kappa.B$.
- $\forall \kappa.\Sigma\,(x : A)\,B \cong \Sigma\,(y : \forall \kappa.A)\,(\forall \kappa.B[y[\kappa]/x])$.
- $\forall \kappa.A \cong \forall \kappa.\overset{\kappa}{\triangleright} A$.

There is an important additional type isomorphism witnessing that $\forall \kappa$ commutes with binary sums; however unlike the isomorphisms above we require equality reflection to show that the two functions are inverse to each other up to definitional equality. There is a canonical term of type $\forall \kappa.A + \forall \kappa.B \to \forall \kappa.(A + B)$ using just ordinary elimination of coproducts. Using the fact that we encode binary coproducts using Σ-types and universes we can define a term com^+ of type $\forall \kappa.(A + B) \to \forall \kappa.A + \forall \kappa.B$ which is a inverse to the canonical term. In particular com^+ satisfies the following two equalities which will be used below.

$$\mathsf{com}^+ (\Lambda \kappa.\mathsf{inl}\ t) \equiv \mathsf{inl}\ \Lambda \kappa.t \qquad \mathsf{com}^+ (\Lambda \kappa.\mathsf{inr}\ t) \equiv \mathsf{inr}\ \Lambda \kappa.t. \tag{4}$$

5   Example Programs with Coinductive Types

Let A be a type with code $\widehat{A}$ in clock context Δ and κ a fresh clock variable. Let $\mathsf{Str}_A = \forall \kappa.\mathsf{Str}_A^\kappa$. We can define head, tail and cons functions

$$\begin{aligned}
\mathsf{hd} &: \mathsf{Str}_A \to A & \mathsf{hd} &\triangleq \lambda xs.\mathsf{hd}^{\kappa_0}\,(xs[\kappa_0]) \\
\mathsf{tl} &: \mathsf{Str}_A \to \mathsf{Str}_A & \mathsf{tl} &\triangleq \lambda xs.\mathsf{prev}\ \kappa.\mathsf{tl}^\kappa(xs[\kappa]) \\
\mathsf{cons} &: A \to \mathsf{Str}_A \to \mathsf{Str}_A & \mathsf{cons} &\triangleq \lambda x.\lambda xs.\Lambda \kappa.\mathsf{cons}^\kappa x\,(\mathsf{next}^\kappa\,(xs[\kappa])).
\end{aligned}$$

With these we can define the *acausal* 'every other' function eo^κ that removes every second element of the input stream. It is acausal because the second element of the output stream is the third element of the input. Therefore to type the function we need to have the input stream always available, so clock quantification must be used. The function eo^κ of type $\mathsf{Str}_A \to \mathsf{Str}_A^\kappa$ is defined as

$$\mathsf{eo}^\kappa \triangleq \mathsf{fix}^\kappa \phi.\lambda\,(xs : \mathsf{Str}_A)\,.\mathsf{cons}^\kappa(\mathsf{hd}\ xs)\,(\phi \circledast \mathsf{next}^\kappa\,((\mathsf{tl}\,(\mathsf{tl}\ xs)))).$$

Definitional type equalities:

$$\frac{\Gamma \vdash_\Delta \quad \Delta' \subseteq \Delta \quad \Gamma \vdash_{\Delta,\kappa} t : \mathcal{U}_{\Delta',\kappa}}{\Gamma \vdash_\Delta \mathsf{El}(\widehat{\forall}\, \Lambda\kappa.t) \equiv \forall\kappa.\, \mathsf{El}(t)} \;\; \text{TyEq-}\forall\text{-el}$$

$$\frac{\Gamma \vdash_\Delta \quad \Gamma \vdash_{\Delta,\kappa} A \text{ type} \quad \Gamma \vdash_\Delta t : \forall\kappa.A \quad \Gamma \vdash_\Delta s : \forall\kappa.A}{\Gamma \vdash_\Delta \forall\kappa.\mathsf{Id}_A(t[\kappa], s[\kappa]) \equiv \mathsf{Id}_{\forall\kappa.A}(t,s)} \;\; \text{TyEq-}\forall\text{-id}$$

Definitional term equalities:

$$\frac{\Gamma \vdash_\Delta \quad \vdash_\Delta \kappa' \quad \Gamma \vdash_{\Delta,\kappa} t : A}{\Gamma \vdash_\Delta (\Lambda\kappa.t)[\kappa'] \equiv t[\kappa'/\kappa] : A[\kappa'/\kappa]} \;\; \text{TmEq-}\forall\text{-}\beta \qquad \frac{\kappa \notin \Delta \quad \Gamma \vdash_\Delta t : \forall\kappa.A}{\Gamma \vdash_\Delta \Lambda\kappa.t[\kappa] \equiv t : \forall\kappa.A} \;\; \text{TmEq-}\forall\text{-}\eta$$

$$\frac{\kappa \notin \Delta \quad \Gamma \vdash_\Delta A \text{ type} \quad \Gamma \vdash_\Delta t : \forall\kappa.A \quad \vdash_\Delta \kappa' \quad \vdash_\Delta \kappa''}{\Gamma \vdash_\Delta t[\kappa'] \equiv t[\kappa''] : A} \;\; \text{TmEq-}\forall\text{-fresh}$$

$$\frac{\Gamma \vdash_\Delta \quad \vdash_{\Delta,\kappa} \xi : \Gamma \stackrel{\kappa}{\rightarrow} \Gamma' \quad \Gamma, \Gamma' \vdash_{\Delta,\kappa} t : A}{\Gamma \vdash_\Delta \mathsf{prev}\, \kappa.\, \mathsf{next}^\kappa \xi.t \equiv \Lambda\kappa.t(\mathsf{adv}_\Delta^\kappa(\xi)) : \forall\kappa.(A(\mathsf{adv}_\Delta^\kappa(\xi)))} \;\; \text{TmEq-prev-}\beta$$

$$\frac{\Gamma \vdash_\Delta \quad \Gamma \vdash_{\Delta,\kappa} t : \stackrel{\kappa}{\triangleright}A}{\Gamma \vdash_{\Delta,\kappa} \mathsf{next}^\kappa\,((\mathsf{prev}\,\kappa.t)[\kappa]) \equiv t : \stackrel{\kappa}{\triangleright}A} \;\; \text{TmEq-prev-}\eta$$

Fig. 6. Type and term equalities involving clock quantification.

The result is a *guarded* stream, but we can easily strengthen it and define eo of type $\mathsf{Str}_A \rightarrow \mathsf{Str}_A$ as eo $\triangleq \lambda xs.\Lambda\kappa.\mathsf{eo}^\kappa xs$.

We can also work with covectors (not just guarded covectors as in Sect. 3). This is a dependent coinductive type indexed by conatural numbers which is the type $\mathsf{CoN} = \forall\kappa.\,\mathsf{CoN}^\kappa$. It is easy to define $\overline{0}$ and $\overline{\mathsf{succ}}$ as $\overline{0} \triangleq \Lambda\kappa.\mathsf{inl}\,\langle\rangle$ and $\overline{\mathsf{succ}} \triangleq \lambda n.\Lambda\kappa.\mathsf{inr}\,(\mathsf{next}^\kappa\,(n[\kappa]))$. Next, we can define a transport function $\mathsf{com}^{\mathsf{CoN}}$ of type $\mathsf{com}^{\mathsf{CoN}} : \mathsf{CoN} \rightarrow 1 + \mathsf{CoN}$ satisfying

$$\mathsf{com}^{\mathsf{CoN}}\overline{0} \equiv \mathsf{inl}\,\langle\rangle \qquad \mathsf{com}^{\mathsf{CoN}}(\overline{\mathsf{succ}}n) \equiv \mathsf{inr}\,n. \tag{5}$$

This function is used to define the type family of covectors as $\mathsf{CoVec}_A\, n \triangleq \forall\kappa.\,\mathsf{CoVec}_A^\kappa\, n$ where $\mathsf{CoVec}_A^\kappa : \mathsf{CoN} \rightarrow \mathcal{U}_{\Delta,\kappa}$ is the term

$$\mathsf{fix}^\kappa\phi.\lambda\,(n : \mathsf{CoN})\,.\mathsf{case}\,\mathsf{com}^{\mathsf{CoN}}n\,\mathsf{of}\,\left\{ \mathsf{inl}\,\_ \Rightarrow \widehat{1}; \mathsf{inr}\,n \Rightarrow A \widehat{\times} \widehat{\stackrel{\kappa}{\triangleright}}\,(\phi \circledast (\mathsf{next}^\kappa n)) \right\}.$$

Using term equalities (4) and (5) we can derive the type isomorphisms

$$\mathsf{CoVec}_A\,\overline{0} \equiv \forall\kappa.1 \cong 1$$

$$\mathsf{CoVec}_A\,(\overline{\mathsf{succ}}n) \equiv \forall\kappa\left(A \times \stackrel{\kappa}{\triangleright}(\mathsf{CoVec}_A^\kappa\,n)\right) \cong A \times \mathsf{CoVec}_A\,n \tag{6}$$

which are the expected properties of the type of covectors.

A simple function we can define is the tail function

$$\mathsf{tl} : \mathsf{CoVec}_A(\overline{\mathsf{succ}}n) \rightarrow \mathsf{CoVec}_A \qquad \mathsf{tl} \triangleq \lambda v.\mathsf{prev}\,\kappa.\pi_2\,(v[\kappa])\,.$$

Note that (6) is needed to type tl. The map function of type

$$\mathsf{map} : (A \to B) \to \Pi(n : \mathsf{CoN}).\, \mathrm{CoVec}_A\, n \to \mathrm{CoVec}_B\, n$$

is defined as $\mathsf{map}f \triangleq \lambda n.\lambda xs.\Lambda\kappa.\mathsf{map}^\kappa f\, n\ (xs[\kappa])$ where map^κ is

$$\mathsf{map}^\kappa : (A \to B) \to \Pi(n : \mathsf{CoN}).\, \mathrm{CoVec}^\kappa_A\, n \to \mathrm{CoVec}^\kappa_B\, n$$

$$\mathsf{map}^\kappa = \lambda f.\mathsf{fix}^\kappa\phi.\lambda n.\mathsf{case}\,\mathsf{com}^{\mathsf{CoN}}n\ \mathsf{of}$$

$$\mathsf{inl}\ \_ \Rightarrow \lambda v.v$$

$$\mathsf{inr}\ n \Rightarrow \lambda v.\, \langle f(\pi_1 v), \phi \circledast_\kappa (\mathsf{next}^\kappa n) \circledast_\kappa \pi_2(v)\rangle.$$

5.1   Lifting Guarded Functions

In this section we show how in general we may lift a function on guarded recursive types, such as addition of guarded streams, to a function on coinductive streams. Moreover, we show how to lift proofs of properties, such as the commutativity of addition, from guarded recursive types to coinductive types.

Let Γ be a context in clock context Δ and κ a fresh clock. Suppose A and B are types such that $\Gamma \vdash_{\Delta,\kappa} A$ type and $\Gamma, x : A \vdash_{\Delta,\kappa} B$ type. Finally let f be a function of type $\Gamma \vdash_{\Delta,\kappa} f : \Pi(x : A).B$. We define $\mathfrak{L}(f)$ satisfying the typing judgement $\Gamma \vdash_\Delta \mathfrak{L}(f) : \Pi(y : \forall\kappa.A).\forall\kappa.\, (B\,[y[\kappa]\,/x])$ as $\mathfrak{L}(f) \triangleq \lambda y.\Lambda\kappa.f\,(y[\kappa])$.

Now assume that f' is another term of type $\Pi(x : A).B$ (in the same context) and that we have proved $\Gamma \vdash_{\Delta,\kappa} p : \Pi(x : A).\mathsf{Id}_B(f\,x, f'\,x)$. As above we can give the term $\mathfrak{L}(p)$ the type $\Pi(y : \forall\kappa.A).\forall\kappa.\mathsf{Id}_{B[y[\kappa]/x]}(f(y[\kappa]), f'(y[\kappa]))$. which by using the type equality TyEq-$\forall$-Id and the η rule for $\forall$ is equal to the type $\Pi(y : \forall\kappa.A).\mathsf{Id}_{\forall\kappa.B[y[\kappa]/x]}(\mathfrak{L}(f)\,y, \mathfrak{L}(f')\,y)$. So we have derived a property of lifted functions $\mathfrak{L}(f)$ and $\mathfrak{L}(f')$ from the properties of the guarded versions f and f'. This is a standard pattern. Using Löb induction we prove a property of a function whose result is a "guarded" type and derive the property for the lifted function.

For example we can lift the zipWith function from guarded streams to coinductive streams and prove that it preserves commutativity, using the result on guarded streams of Sect. 3.

6   Soundness

gDTT can be shown to be sound with respect to a denotational model interpreting the type theory. The model is a refinement of Bizjak and Møgelberg's [7] but for reasons of space we leave the description of a full model of gDTT for future work. Instead, to provide some intuition for the semantics of delayed substitutions, we just describe how to interpret the rule

$$\frac{x : A \vdash B \, \mathsf{type} \qquad \vdash t : \triangleright A}{\vdash \triangleright[x \leftarrow t].B \, \mathsf{type}} \qquad (7)$$

in the case where we only have one clock available.

The subsystem of gDTT with only one clock can be modelled in the category $\mathcal{S}$, known as the topos of trees [5], the presheaf category over the first infinite ordinal ω. The objects X of $\mathcal{S}$ are families of sets $X_1, X_2, \ldots$ indexed by the positive integers, together with families of *restriction functions* $r_i^X : X_{i+1} \rightarrow X_i$ indexed similarly. There is a functor $\blacktriangleright : \mathcal{S} \rightarrow \mathcal{S}$ which maps an object X to the object

$$1 \overset{!}{\longleftarrow} X_1 \overset{r_1^X}{\longleftarrow} X_2 \overset{r_2^X}{\longleftarrow} X_3 \longleftarrow \cdots$$

where ! is the unique map into the terminal object.

In this model, a closed type A is interpreted as an object of $\mathcal{S}$ and the type $x : A \vdash B \, \mathsf{type}$ is interpreted as an indexed family of sets $B_i(a)$, for a in A_i together with maps $r_i^B(a) : B_{i+1}(a) \rightarrow B_i(r_i^A(a))$. The term t in (7) is interpreted as a morphism $t : 1 \rightarrow \triangleright A$ so $t_i(*)$ is an element of A_i (here we write $*$ for the element of 1).

The type $\vdash \triangleright[x \leftarrow t].B \, \mathsf{type}$ is then interpreted as the object X, defined by

$$X_1 = 1 \qquad\qquad X_{i+1} = B_i(t_{i+1}(*)).$$

Notice that the delayed substitution is interpreted by substitution (reindexing) in the model; the change of the index in the model (B_i is reindexed along $t_{i+1}(*)$) corresponds to the delayed substitution in the type theory. Further notice that if B does not depend on x, then the interpretation of $\vdash \triangleright[x \leftarrow t].B \, \mathsf{type}$ reduces to the interpretation $\triangleright B$, which is defined to be $\blacktriangleright$ applied to the interpretation of B.

The above can be generalised to work for general contexts and sequences of delayed substitutions, and one can then validate that the definitional equality rules do indeed hold in this model.

7   Related Work

Birkedal et al. [5] introduced dependent type theory with the $\triangleright$ modality, with semantics in the topos of trees. The guardedness requirement was expressed using the syntactic check that every occurrence of a type variable lies beneath a $\triangleright$. This requirement was subsequently refined by Birkedal and Møgelberg [4], who showed that guarded recursive types could be constructed via fixed-points of functions on universes. However, the rules considered in these papers do not allow one to apply terms of type $\triangleright(\Pi(x : A).B)$, as the applicative functor construction $\circledast$ was defined only for simple function spaces. They are therefore less expressive for both programming (consider the covector **ones**, and function **map**, of Sect. 3) and proving, noting the extensive use of delayed substitutions in our example proofs. They further do not consider coinductive types, and so are restricted to causal functions.

The extension to coinductive types, and hence acausal functions, is due to Atkey and McBride [3], who introduced *clock quantifiers* into a simply typed setting with guarded recursion. Møgelberg [19] extended this work to dependent types and Bizjak and Møgelberg [7] refined the model further to allow clock synchronisation.

Clouston et al. [9] introduced the logic $Lg\lambda$ to prove properties of terms of the (simply typed) guarded λ-calculus, $g\lambda$. This allowed proofs about coinductive types, but not in the integrated fashion supported by dependent type theories. Moreover it relied on types being "total", a property that in a dependently typed setting would entail a strong elimination rule for $\triangleright$, which would lead to inconsistency.

Sized types [14] have been combined with copatterns [1] as an alternative type-based approach for modular programming with coinductive types. This work is more mature than ours with respect to implementation and the demonstration of syntactic properties such as normalisation, and so further development of gDTT is essential to enable proper comparison. One advantage of gDTT is that the later modality is useful for examples beyond coinduction, and beyond the utility of sized types, such as the guarded recursive domain equations used to model program logics [23].

8   Conclusion and Future Work

We have described the dependent type theory gDTT. The examples we have detailed show that gDTT provides a setting for programming and proving with guarded recursive and coinductive types.

In future work we plan to investigate an intensional version of the type theory and construct a prototype implementation to allow us to experiment with larger examples. Preliminary work has suggested that the path type of cubical type theory [10] interacts better with the new constructs of gDTT than the ordinary Martin-Löf identity type.

Finally, we are investigating whether the generalisation of applicative functors [18] to apply over *dependent* function spaces, via delayed substitutions, might also apply to examples quite unconnected to the later modality.

Acknowledgements. This research was supported in part by the ModuRes Sapere Aude Advanced Grant and DFF-Research Project 1 Grant no. 4002-00442, both from The Danish Council for Independent Research for the Natural Sciences (FNU). Aleš Bizjak was supported in part by a Microsoft Research PhD grant.

References

1. Abel, A., Pientka, B.: Wellfounded recursion with copatterns: A unified approach to termination and productivity. In: ICFP, pp. 185–196 (2013)
2. Appel, A.W., Melliès, P.A., Richards, C.D., Vouillon, J.: A very modal model of a modern, major, general type system. In: POPL, pp. 109–122 (2007)

3. Atkey, R., McBride, C.: Productive coprogramming with guarded recursion. In: ICFP, pp. 197–208 (2013)
4. Birkedal, L., Møgelberg, R.E.: Intensional type theory with guarded recursive types qua fixed points on universes. In: LICS, pp. 213–222 (2013)
5. Birkedal, L., Møgelberg, R.E., Schwinghammer, J., Støvring, K.: First steps in synthetic guarded domain theory: step-indexing in the topos of trees. LMCS 8(4) (2012)
6. Bizjak, A., Grathwohl, H.B., Clouston, R., Møgelberg, R.E., Birkedal, L.: Guarded dependent type theory with coinductive types (2016). http://arxiv.org/abs/1601.01586
7. Bizjak, A., Møgelberg, R.E.: A model of guarded recursion with clock synchronisation. In: MFPS (2015)
8. Brady, E.: Idris, a general-purpose dependently typed programming language: design and implementation. J. Funct. Program. **23**(5), 552–593 (2013)
9. Clouston, R., Bizjak, A., Grathwohl, H.B., Birkedal, L.: Programming and reasoning with guarded recursion for coinductive types. In: FoSSaCS (2015)
10. Cohen, C., Coquand, T., Huber, S., Mörtberg, A.: Cubical type theory: a constructive interpretation of the univalence axiom, unpublished (2015)
11. Constable, R.L., Allen, S.F., Bromley, H.M., Cleaveland, W.R., Cremer, J.F., Harper, R.W., Howe, D.J., Knoblock, T.B., Mendler, N.P., Panangaden, P., Sasaki, J.T., Smith, S.F.: Implementing Mathematics with the Nuprl Proof Development System. Prentice-Hall Inc, Upper Saddle River, NJ, USA (1986)
12. Coquand, T.: Infinite objects in type theory. In: TYPES, pp. 62–78 (1993)
13. Giménez, E.: Codifying guarded definitions with recursive schemes. In: TYPES, pp. 39–59 (1995)
14. Hughes, J., Pareto, L., Sabry, A.: Proving the correctness of reactive systems using sized types. In: POPL, pp. 410–423 (1996)
15. Jacobs, B.: Categorical Logic and Type Theory. Studies in Logic and the Foundations of Mathematics, vol. 141. North Holland, Amsterdam (1999)
16. Krishnaswami, N.R., Benton, N.: Ultrametric semantics of reactive programs. In: LICS, pp. 257–266 (2011)
17. The Coq development team: the coq proof assistant reference manual. LogiCal Project (2004). version 8.0. http://coq.inria.fr
18. McBride, C., Paterson, R.: Applicative programming with effects. J. Funct. Program. **18**(1), 1–13 (2008)
19. Møgelberg, R.E.: A type theory for productive coprogramming via guarded recursion. In: CSL-LICS (2014)
20. Nakano, H.: A modality for recursion. In: LICS, pp. 255–266 (2000)
21. Norell, U.: Towards a practical programming language based on dependent type theory. Ph.D. thesis, Chalmers University of Technology (2007)
22. Paviotti, M., Møgelberg, R.E., Birkedal, L.: A model of PCF in guarded type theory. In: MFPS (2015)
23. Svendsen, K., Birkedal, L.: Impredicative concurrent abstract predicates. In: Shao, Z. (ed.) ESOP 2014 (ETAPS). LNCS, vol. 8410, pp. 149–168. Springer, Heidelberg (2014)
24. The Univalent Foundations Program: Homotopy Type Theory: Univalent Foundations of Mathematics, Institute for Advanced Study (2013). http://homotopytypetheory.org/book

Dependent Types
and Fibred Computational Effects

Danel Ahman[1]([⊠]), Neil Ghani[2], and Gordon D. Plotkin[1]

[1] LFCS, University of Edinburgh, Edinburgh, Scotland, UK
d.ahman@ed.ac.uk, gdp@inf.ed.ac.uk
[2] MSP Group, University of Strathclyde, Glasgow, Scotland, UK
neil.ghani@strath.ac.uk

Abstract. We study the interplay between dependent types and general computational effects. We define a language with both value types and terms, and computation types and terms, where types depend only on value terms. We use computational Σ-types to account for type-dependency in the sequential composition of computations. Our language design is justified by a natural class of categorical models. We account for both algebraic and non-algebraic effects. We also show how to extend the language with general recursion, using continuous families of cpos.

1 Introduction

While dependent types have proven very useful on their own, for both programming and theorem proving, one also seeks a general way to combine them with computational effects, such as I/O, state, continuations, or recursion, so as to write more practical, concise, or clearer programs. However, despite the study of each of the two fields being well advanced, their combination presents difficulties, as recognised already by Moggi [25].

One puzzling problem is what to make of a type $A(M)$ if M can raise an effect. We do not know a general denotational semantics for such types, though there may be one (there is one for local names [28]). Pragmatically, the situation depends on the nature of the computational effects considered. For effects not requiring interaction with the program runtime, such as local names [28] or general recursion [7], one need not restrict M, as computing $A(M)$ then only depends on static information. However, this does not work well in general, as some effects, e.g., I/O, do crucially depend on interaction with the program runtime, and so then will the computation of $A(M)$. As one consequence, extending a coarse-grained language, e.g., Moggi's computational lambda calculus [24], with dependent types seems not to give a general solution, as the natural elimination rule for Π-types produces types of the form $A(M)$ (and cf. Levy [20, Sect. 12.4.1]).

D. Ahman—This work was funded by a University of Edinburgh PhD scholarship and by the scholarship program Kristjan Jaak, which is funded and managed by Archimedes Foundation in collaboration with the Estonian Ministry of Education and Research.

© Springer-Verlag Berlin Heidelberg 2016
B. Jacobs and C. Löding (Eds.): FOSSACS 2016, LNCS 9634, pp. 36–54, 2016.
DOI: 10.1007/978-3-662-49630-5_3

A natural move to try to solve these problems is to allow types to depend only on value terms. This is the route we take in this paper and it does lead to a natural general semantics. While at first such a choice might seem limiting, we recover dependency on the statically available information about computational effects by inspecting the structure of thunked computations.

To ensure that types depend only on values, we make a clear distinction between values and computations, using separate classes of value types A and computation types $\underline{C}$, as in Call-By-Push-Value (CBPV) [20] and the Enriched Effect Calculus (EEC) [9]. Then the variables in types range only over value types, as desired. However, a further problem then arises: the usual typing rule

$$\frac{\Gamma \vdash M : FA \quad \Gamma, x : A \vdash N(x) : \underline{C}(x)}{\Gamma \vdash M \text{ to } x \text{ in } N(x) : \underline{C}(x)} (*)$$

for sequential composition of computations is not correct as x may occur freely in $\underline{C}(x)$ in the conclusion. An evident move here is to prohibit x from occurring freely in $\underline{C}$, as, e.g., advocated by Levy [20, Sect. 12.4.1] and Brady [5]. However, this seems too restrictive: to make the most of dependent types, it is desirable for the type of an effectful program to depend on values produced by preceding computations. As an example, consider combining monadic parsing [16] with dependent types and applying it to the parsing of well-typed syntax. Then it is natural to decompose the parsing of function applications into a parser for the function and a parser for the argument, where the type of the latter crucially depends on the domain of the type of the parsed function.

The approach we take is to keep the restricted form of (*), but to also introduce *computational Σ-types* $\Sigma x : A.\underline{C}(x)$, whose use is inspired by the algebraic treatment of computational effects [31]. To explain these, suppose computation types denote algebras for the algebraic theory of boolean-valued read-only store [35, Sect. III.A]. Now let us consider the composite effectful program

$$((\text{return } 2) ? (\text{return } 3)) \text{ to } x \text{ in } M(x)$$

where $x : \text{Nat} \vdash M(x) : \underline{C}(x)$. Here we see that, after looking up the bit with ?, this program either evaluates as $M(2)$, which has type $\underline{C}(2)$, or as $M(3)$, which has type $\underline{C}(3)$. So the whole computation yields an element of the coproduct of algebras $\underline{C}(2) + \underline{C}(3)$. This pattern also recurs with other computational effects, and dependency on value types other than natural numbers: hence the computational Σ-types. These types enable us to type sequential composition by "closing-off" the free variable x in $\underline{C}(x)$: using the hypothesis of (*) we derive

$$\Gamma, x : A \vdash \langle x, N(x) \rangle : \Sigma x : A.\underline{C}(x)$$

using the introduction rule for computational Σ-types, and then derive

$$\Gamma \vdash M \text{ to } x \text{ in } \langle x, N(x) \rangle : \Sigma x : A.\underline{C}(x)$$

using the restricted form of (*).

We aim to put these ideas together at a *foundational* level, comparable with the levels at which the two fields have been studied separately. In contrast, the existing work on combining dependent types with first-class computational effects has concerned only *particular* kinds of effects (e.g., [7,26,28,37]). Other authors have used dependent types in existing languages to *represent* effects using DSLs (e.g., [5,13,23]). There has, however, been no work combining dependent types with *general, first class* computational effects.

In Sect. 2, we define a small dependently-typed language with computational effects, combining features from Martin-Löf type theory (MLTT) [22] and computational languages separating values and computations, such as CBPV or EEC. The language design we propose is justified in Sect. 3 in terms of a sound and complete interpretation in a class of categorical models naturally combining (i) comprehension categories arising from the semantics of dependent types; and (ii) adjunctions arising from the semantics of computational effects. In Sect. 4, we extend the language and its semantics with algebraic effects. In Sect. 5, we extend the language and its semantics with general recursion.

2   A Dependently-typed Effectful Language

We now define the syntax and equational theory of our dependently-typed effectful language, making a clear distinction between values and computations, at both type and term levels: the value fragment of our language is based on MLTT; the computational fragment is greatly influenced by CBPV and EEC.

Variables. We assume two countable sets: of *value variables*, ranged over by $x, y, \ldots$; and of *computation variables*, ranged over by $z, \ldots$. The former are treated as in MLTT: they are intuitionistic, and enjoy structural rules of weakening and contraction. The latter, on the other hand, are treated linearly, as in EEC, and play a crucial role in the elimination rule for computational Σ-types.

Types. Our *value types* $A, B, \ldots$ are given as in MLTT, except for the type $U\underline{C}$ of thunks, familiar from CBPV. To keep the presentation simple and focussed on the computational fragment of our language, we omit value sum types and general inductive types, both of which can be easily added. Our *computation types* $\underline{C}, \underline{D}, \ldots$ generalise those of CBPV and EEC. The grammar of types is

$$A ::= \mathsf{Nat} \mid 1 \mid \Sigma x : A.B \mid \Pi x : A.B \mid \mathsf{Id}_A(V, W) \mid U\underline{C} \qquad \underline{C} ::= FA \mid \Sigma x : A.\underline{C} \mid \Pi x : A.\underline{C}$$

Here, FA is the type of computations returning values of type A. The computational Σ- and Π-types are the natural dependently-typed generalisations of EEC's computational tensor and function types: $!A \otimes \underline{C}$, $A \to \underline{C}$. Rules defining well-formed value contexts $\vdash \Gamma$ and types $\Gamma \vdash A$, $\Gamma \vdash \underline{C}$ are given in Fig. 1.

Terms. We let $V, W, \ldots$ to range over *value terms*. These are given as in MLTT, except for thunked computations **thunk** M, familiar from CBPV. Compared to CBPV, we include both value functions and complex values to accommodate pure programs on which the types of our language could depend. Regarding effectful programs, we further distinguish between *computation terms*, ranged over by $M, N, \ldots$ and *homomorphism terms*, ranged over by $K, L, \ldots$. We decorate our terms with certain type-annotations, so that we can later define the denotational semantics on raw syntax — a standard approach in the literature [15,36]. We omit these annotations in informal discussion. The grammar of terms is

$$V ::= x \mid \mathsf{zero} \mid \mathsf{succ}\, V \mid \mathsf{rec}_{x.A}(V_z, y_1.y_2.V_s, W) \mid \star \mid \lambda x : A.V \mid V(W)_{(x:A).B} \mid$$
$$\langle V, W \rangle_{(x:A).B} \mid \mathsf{fst}_{(x:A).B} V \mid \mathsf{snd}_{(x:A).B} V \mid \mathsf{thunk}\, M \mid$$
$$\mathsf{refl}\, V \mid \mathsf{ind}_A(x_1.x_2.x_3.B, y.W, V_1, V_2, V_p)$$

$$M ::= \mathsf{return}\, V \mid M \text{ to } x : A \text{ } \mathsf{in}_{\underline{C}}\, N \mid \mathsf{force}_{\underline{C}} V \mid \lambda x : A.M \mid M(V)_{(x:A).\underline{C}} \mid$$
$$\langle V, M \rangle_{(x:A).\underline{C}} \mid M \text{ to } \langle x : A, z : \underline{C} \rangle \text{ } \mathsf{in}_{\underline{D}}\, K$$

$$K ::= z \mid K \text{ to } x : A \text{ } \mathsf{in}_{\underline{C}}\, M \mid \lambda x : A.K \mid K(V)_{(x:A).\underline{C}} \mid$$
$$\langle V, K \rangle_{(x:A).\underline{C}} \mid K \text{ to } \langle x : A, z : \underline{C} \rangle \text{ } \mathsf{in}_{\underline{D}}\, L$$

Well-formed value types

$$\frac{\vdash \Gamma}{\Gamma \vdash \mathsf{Nat}} \qquad \frac{\vdash \Gamma}{\Gamma \vdash 1} \qquad \frac{\Gamma, x : A \vdash B}{\Gamma \vdash \Sigma x : A.B} \qquad \frac{\Gamma, x : A \vdash B}{\Gamma \vdash \Pi x : A.B} \qquad \frac{\Gamma \vdash V : A \quad \Gamma \vdash W : A}{\Gamma \vdash \mathsf{Id}_A(V, W)} \qquad \frac{\Gamma \vdash \underline{C}}{\Gamma \vdash U\underline{C}}$$

Well-formed value contexts   **Well-formed computation types**

$$\frac{}{\vdash \cdot} \qquad \frac{\vdash \Gamma \quad x \notin Vars(\Gamma) \quad \Gamma \vdash A}{\vdash \Gamma, x : A} \qquad\qquad \frac{\Gamma \vdash A}{\Gamma \vdash FA} \qquad \frac{\Gamma, x : A \vdash \underline{C}}{\Gamma \vdash \Sigma x : A.\underline{C}} \qquad \frac{\Gamma, x : A \vdash \underline{C}}{\Gamma \vdash \Pi x : A.\underline{C}}$$

Fig. 1. Well-formed contexts and types.

Our *computation terms* share many similarities with those in CBPV, but additionally include the introduction and elimination rules for computational Σ-types, given by pairing $\langle V, M \rangle$ and pattern-matching M to $\langle x, z \rangle$ in K, whose syntax is similar to that for computational tensor types $!A \otimes \underline{C}$ in EEC.

As with the linear terms in EEC, our *homomorphism terms* contain computation variables z used linearly. From an operational perspective, the typing rules for homomorphism terms ensure that a computation bound to z always happens first in a well-typed term containing it. So, when eliminating a pair $\langle V, M \rangle$, M always happens before the rest of K in the compound term $\langle V, M \rangle$ to $\langle x, z \rangle$ in K, thus preserving the intended left-to-right evaluation order. This use of computation variables ensures that homomorphism terms denote algebra homomorphisms in the examples based on Eilenberg-Moore algebras of monads, or on algebraic effects [31]: hence the name. Similar forms of linearity are also present in CBPV with stacks [20, Sect. 2.3.4]; indeed, homomorphism terms can be viewed as a programmer-friendly syntax for dependently-typed stack terms.

Well-typed value terms $\Gamma \vdash V : A$, well-typed computation terms $\Gamma \vdash M : \underline{C}$, and well-typed homomorphism terms $\Gamma \mid z : \underline{C} \vdash K : \underline{D}$ are defined in Fig. 2.

The linear use of computation variables is also reminiscent of recent work on combining dependent and linear types in languages with distinguished intuitionistic and linear fragments [19,38]. That work is designed to capture the

Type conversion rules

$$\frac{\Gamma \vdash V : A \quad \Gamma \vdash A = B}{\Gamma \vdash V : B} \qquad \frac{\Gamma \vdash M : \underline{C} \quad \Gamma \vdash \underline{C} = \underline{D}}{\Gamma \vdash M : \underline{D}} \qquad \frac{\Gamma \mid z : \underline{C} \vdash K : \underline{D_1} \quad \Gamma \vdash \underline{D_1} = \underline{D_2}}{\Gamma \mid z : \underline{C} \vdash K : \underline{D_2}}$$

Well-typed value terms

$$\frac{\vdash \Gamma \quad x : A \in \Gamma}{\Gamma \vdash x : A} \qquad \frac{\Gamma \vdash M : \underline{C}}{\Gamma \vdash \mathtt{thunk}\ M : U\underline{C}} \qquad \frac{\vdash \Gamma}{\Gamma \vdash \star : 1} \qquad \frac{\vdash \Gamma}{\Gamma \vdash \mathtt{zero} : \mathsf{Nat}} \qquad \frac{\Gamma \vdash V : \mathsf{Nat}}{\Gamma \vdash \mathtt{succ}\ V : \mathsf{Nat}}$$

$$\frac{\Gamma, x : \mathsf{Nat} \vdash A \quad \Gamma \vdash V_z : A[\mathtt{zero}/x] \quad \Gamma, y_1 : \mathsf{Nat}, y_2 : A[y_1/x] \vdash V_s : A[\mathtt{succ}\ y_1/x] \quad \Gamma \vdash W : \mathsf{Nat}}{\Gamma \vdash \mathtt{rec}_{x.A}(V_z, y_1.y_2.V_s, W) : A[W/x]}$$

$$\frac{\Gamma \vdash V : A \quad \Gamma, x : A \vdash B \quad \Gamma \vdash W : B[V/x]}{\Gamma \vdash \langle V, W \rangle_{(x:A).B} : \Sigma x : A.B} \qquad \frac{\Gamma \vdash V : \Sigma x : A.B}{\Gamma \vdash \mathtt{fst}_{(x:A).B} V : A} \qquad \frac{\Gamma \vdash V : \Sigma x : A.B}{\Gamma \vdash \mathtt{snd}_{(x:A).B} V : B[\mathtt{fst}_{(x:A).B} V/x]}$$

$$\frac{\Gamma, x : A \vdash V : B}{\Gamma \vdash \lambda x : A.V : \Pi x : A.B} \qquad \frac{\Gamma \vdash V : \Pi x : A.B \quad \Gamma \vdash W : A}{\Gamma \vdash V(W)_{(x:A).B} : B[W/x]} \qquad \frac{\Gamma \vdash V : A}{\Gamma \vdash \mathtt{refl}\ V : \mathsf{Id}_A(V, V)}$$

$$\frac{\Gamma, x_1 : A, x_2 : A, x_3 : \mathsf{Id}_A(x_1, x_2) \vdash B \quad \Gamma, y : A \vdash W : B[y/x_1, y/x_2, \mathtt{refl}\ y/x_3] \quad \Gamma \vdash V_1 : A \quad \Gamma \vdash V_2 : A \quad \Gamma \vdash V_p : \mathsf{Id}_A(V_1, V_2)}{\Gamma \vdash \mathtt{ind}_A(x_1.x_2.x_3.B, y.W, V_1, V_2, V_p) : B[V_1/x_1, V_2/x_2, V_p/x_3]}$$

Well-typed computation terms

$$\frac{\Gamma \vdash V : A}{\Gamma \vdash \mathtt{return}\ V : FA} \qquad \frac{\Gamma \vdash M : FA \quad \Gamma \vdash \underline{C} \quad \Gamma, x : A \vdash N : \underline{C}}{\Gamma \vdash M\ \mathtt{to}\ x : A\ \mathtt{in}_{\underline{C}}\ N : \underline{C}} \qquad \frac{\Gamma, x : A \vdash M : \underline{C}}{\Gamma \vdash \lambda x : A.M : \Pi x : A.\underline{C}}$$

$$\frac{\Gamma \vdash M : \Pi x : A.\underline{C} \quad \Gamma \vdash V : A}{\Gamma \vdash M(V)_{(x:A).\underline{C}} : \underline{C}[V/x]} \qquad \frac{\Gamma \vdash V : A \quad \Gamma, x : A \vdash \underline{C} \quad \Gamma \vdash M : \underline{C}[V/x]}{\Gamma \vdash \langle V, M \rangle_{(x:A).\underline{C}} : \Sigma x : A.\underline{C}}$$

$$\frac{\Gamma \vdash M : \Sigma x : A.\underline{C} \quad \Gamma \vdash \underline{D} \quad \Gamma, x : A \mid z : \underline{C} \vdash K : \underline{D}}{\Gamma \vdash M\ \mathtt{to}\ \langle x : A, z : \underline{C} \rangle\ \mathtt{in}_{\underline{D}}\ K : \underline{D}} \qquad \frac{\Gamma \vdash V : U\underline{C}}{\Gamma \vdash \mathtt{force}_{\underline{C}}\ V : \underline{C}}$$

Well-typed homomorphism terms

$$\frac{\Gamma \vdash \underline{C}}{\Gamma \mid z : \underline{C} \vdash z : \underline{C}} \qquad \frac{\Gamma \mid z_1 : \underline{C} \vdash K : \Sigma x : A.\underline{D_1} \quad \Gamma \vdash \underline{D_2} \quad \Gamma, x : A \mid z_2 : \underline{D_1} \vdash L : \underline{D_2}}{\Gamma \mid z_1 : \underline{C} \vdash K\ \mathtt{to}\ \langle x : A, z_2 : \underline{D_1} \rangle\ \mathtt{in}_{\underline{D_2}}\ L : \underline{D_2}}$$

$$\frac{\Gamma \vdash V : A \quad \Gamma, x : A \vdash \underline{D} \quad \Gamma \mid z : \underline{C} \vdash K : \underline{D}[V/x]}{\Gamma \mid z : \underline{C} \vdash \langle V, K \rangle_{(x:A).\underline{D}} : \Sigma x : A.\underline{D}} \qquad \frac{\Gamma \vdash \underline{C} \quad \Gamma, x : A \mid z : \underline{C} \vdash K : \underline{D}}{\Gamma \mid z : \underline{C} \vdash \lambda x : A.K : \Pi x : A.\underline{D}}$$

$$\frac{\Gamma \mid z : \underline{C} \vdash K : FA \quad \Gamma \vdash \underline{D} \quad \Gamma, x : A \vdash M : \underline{D}}{\Gamma \mid z : \underline{C} \vdash K\ \mathtt{to}\ x : A\ \mathtt{in}_{\underline{D}}\ M : \underline{D}} \qquad \frac{\Gamma \mid z : \underline{C} \vdash K : \Pi x : A.\underline{D} \quad \Gamma \vdash V : A}{\Gamma \mid z : \underline{C} \vdash K(V)_{(x:A).\underline{D}} : \underline{D}[V/x]}$$

Fig. 2. Well-typed terms.

adjunction models of intuitionistic linear logic [3]; in contrast, our language is designed to capture the computational nature of certain adjunctions.

Equations. We equip our language with an equational theory, consisting of equations between well-formed types, written $\Gamma \vdash A = B$ and $\Gamma \vdash \underline{C} = \underline{D}$; and well-typed terms, written $\Gamma \vdash V = W : A$, $\Gamma \vdash M = N : \underline{C}$ and $\Gamma \mid z : \underline{C} \vdash K = L : \underline{D}$. The equations between types consist of reflexivity equations for Nat and 1, and congruence rules for all the other type formers. We omit the equations between value terms as they are standard from MLTT with natural numbers and intensional identity types [15,22]. The rules for equations between computation and homomorphism terms are given in Fig. 3. We leave the well-typedness assumptions about the constituent terms implicit, and omit type conversion, equivalence, and congruence rules. Many of the equations in Fig. 3 are familiar from EEC, modulo the dependent-typing. Compared to other computational languages, such as [24], standard equations that may seem missing from the theory, such as associativity of sequential composition, are in fact derivable.

Equations involving thunking and forcing

$$\Gamma \vdash \mathtt{thunk}\,(\mathtt{force}_{\underline{C}}\,V) = V : U\underline{C} \qquad \Gamma \vdash \mathtt{force}_{\underline{C}}\,(\mathtt{thunk}\,M) = M : \underline{C}$$

Equations between well-typed computation terms

$$\Gamma \vdash \mathtt{return}\,V\,\mathtt{to}\,x\!:\!A\,\mathtt{in}_{\underline{C}}\,M = M[V/x] : \underline{C} \qquad \Gamma \vdash M\,\mathtt{to}\,x\!:\!A\,\mathtt{in}_{\underline{C}}\,K[\mathtt{return}\,x/z] = K[M/z] : \underline{C}$$

$$\Gamma \vdash \langle V, M \rangle\,\mathtt{to}\,\langle x\!:\!A, z\!:\!\underline{C}\rangle\,\mathtt{in}_{\underline{D}}\,K = K[V/x, M/z] : \underline{D} \qquad \Gamma \vdash (\lambda x\!:\!A.M)(V)_{(x:A).\underline{C}} = M[V/x] : \underline{C}[V/x]$$

$$\Gamma \vdash M\,\mathtt{to}\,\langle x\!:\!A, z_2\!:\!\underline{C}\rangle\,\mathtt{in}_{\underline{D}}\,K[\langle x, z_2 \rangle/z_1] = K[M/z_1] : \underline{D} \qquad \Gamma \vdash M = \lambda x\!:\!A.M(x)_{(x:A).\underline{C}} : \Pi x\!:\!A.\underline{C}$$

Equations between well-typed homomorphism terms

$$\Gamma \mid z_1\!:\!\underline{C} \vdash K\,\mathtt{to}\,x\!:\!A\,\mathtt{in}_{\underline{D}}\,L[\mathtt{return}\,x/z_2] = L[K/z_2] : \underline{D}$$

$$\Gamma \mid z_1\!:\!\underline{C} \vdash \langle V, K \rangle\,\mathtt{to}\,\langle x\!:\!A, z_2\!:\!\underline{D}_1\rangle\,\mathtt{in}_{\underline{D}_2}\,L = L[V/x, K/z_2] : \underline{D}_2$$

$$\Gamma \mid z_1\!:\!\underline{C} \vdash K\,\mathtt{to}\,\langle x\!:\!A, z_3\!:\!\underline{D}_1\rangle\,\mathtt{in}_{\underline{D}_2}\,L[\langle x, z_3 \rangle/z_2] = L[K/z_2] : \underline{D}_2$$

$$\Gamma \mid z_1\!:\!\underline{C} \vdash (\lambda x\!:\!A.K)(V)_{(x:A).\underline{D}} = K[V/x] : \underline{D}[V/x]$$

$$\Gamma \mid z_1\!:\!\underline{C} \vdash K = \lambda x\!:\!A.K(x)_{(x:A).\underline{D}} : \Pi x\!:\!A.\underline{D}$$

Fig. 3. Fragment of the equational theory.

Some meta-theory. The substitution of value terms for value variables has a straightforward mutually recursive definition. We write $A[V/x]$ for the substitution of V for x in A. The substitution of computation and homomorphism terms for computation variables is also routine, recursing only in the sub-terms where linearly used computation variables can appear. We write $K[M/z]$ for the substitution of M for z in K. Then, standard weakening and substitution rules for value variables are admissible for all judgments of our language. In addition, further substitution rules for computation variables are admissible for judgments $\Gamma \mid z\!:\!\underline{C} \vdash K\!:\!\underline{D}$ and $\Gamma \mid z\!:\!\underline{C} \vdash K = L : \underline{D}$, covering the substitution of both computation and homomorphism terms for computation variables.

3   Denotational Semantics

The denotational semantics of our language is based on standard fibred category theory. To make our work more accessible, we recall some preliminaries of this theory and suggest [18] for more details. Fibred category theory provides a natural framework for developing the semantics of dependently-typed languages, where: (i) functors model type-dependency; (ii) split fibrations model substitution; and (iii) closed comprehension categories model Σ- and Π-types. The ideas we develop can also be expressed in terms of other models of dependent types, such as categories with families, or categories with attributes [15, 27].

3.1   Fibred Category Theory Preliminaries

Fibrations. Given a functor $p : \mathcal{E} \longrightarrow \mathcal{B}$, a morphism $g : A \longrightarrow B$ is called a *Cartesian lifting* of $f : X \longrightarrow Y$ if $p(g) = f$ and for all $i : C \longrightarrow B$ and $j : p(C) \longrightarrow X$, such that $p(i) = f \circ j$ in $\mathcal{B}$, there exists a unique $h : C \longrightarrow A$ over j such that $g \circ h = i$. The functor $p : \mathcal{E} \longrightarrow \mathcal{B}$ is called a *fibration* if for every B in $\mathcal{E}$ and $f : X \longrightarrow p(B)$ in $\mathcal{B}$ there exists a Cartesian lifting $g : A \longrightarrow B$ of f in $\mathcal{E}$. A morphism $f : A \longrightarrow B$ in $\mathcal{E}$ is called *vertical* if $p(A) = p(B) = X$ and $p(f) = \mathsf{id}_X$. For any X in $\mathcal{B}$, we write $\mathcal{E}_X$ for the *fibre over* X, i.e., for the subcategory of $\mathcal{E}$ consisting of objects over X and vertical morphisms. A fibration is called *cloven* if it comes with a choice of Cartesian liftings. We write $\overline{f}(B) : f^*(B) \longrightarrow B$ for the chosen Cartesian lifting of $f : X \longrightarrow p(B)$. In cloven fibrations, every $\mathcal{B}$-morphism $f : X \longrightarrow Y$ determines a *reindexing functor* $f^* : \mathcal{E}_Y \longrightarrow \mathcal{E}_X$, satisfying $(\mathrm{id}_X)^* \cong \mathrm{id}_{\mathcal{E}_X}$ and $(g \circ f)^* \cong f^* \circ g^*$. A cloven fibration is said to be *split* if these two isomorphisms are identities.

Given split fibrations $p : \mathcal{V} \longrightarrow \mathcal{B}$ and $q : \mathcal{C} \longrightarrow \mathcal{B}$, a *split fibred functor* $F : p \longrightarrow q$ is given by a functor $F : \mathcal{V} \longrightarrow \mathcal{C}$, such that $q \circ F = p$ and F preserves the chosen Cartesian morphisms on-the-nose. Given two split fibred functors $F, G : p \longrightarrow q$, a *split fibred natural transformation* $\alpha : F \Rightarrow G$ is given by a natural transformation $\alpha : F \Rightarrow G$, in which every component of α is vertical. A *split fibred adjunction* $F \dashv U : q \longrightarrow p$ is given by split fibred functors $F : p \longrightarrow q$ and $U : q \longrightarrow p$, together with split fibred natural transformations $\eta : \mathrm{id}_{\mathcal{V}} \longrightarrow U \circ F$ and $\varepsilon : F \circ U \longrightarrow \mathrm{id}_{\mathcal{C}}$, subject to the standard unit-counit laws for adjunctions.

Comprehension categories. A *(split) comprehension category with unit* is given by a (split) fibration $p : \mathcal{E} \longrightarrow \mathcal{B}$, together with a comprehension-admitting terminal object functor $1 : \mathcal{B} \longrightarrow \mathcal{E}$, i.e., 1 has a right adjoint $\{-\} : \mathcal{E} \longrightarrow \mathcal{B}$; it is said to be *full* when the functor $A \overset{\pi_{(-)}}{\mapsto} p(\varepsilon_A^{1 \dashv \{-\}}) : \mathcal{E} \longrightarrow \mathcal{B}^{\rightarrow}$ is full and faithful. For all A in $\mathcal{E}$, the $\mathcal{B}$-morphism $\pi_A : \{A\} \longrightarrow p(A)$ is called a *projection map*. The corresponding reindexing functor $\pi_A^* : \mathcal{E}_{p(A)} \longrightarrow \mathcal{E}_{\{A\}}$ is called the *weakening functor*. For every comprehension category with unit $p : \mathcal{E} \longrightarrow \mathcal{B}$, we have an isomorphism $\mathcal{E}_{p(A)}(1_{p(A)}, A) \cong \{g : p(A) \longrightarrow \{A\} \mid \pi_A \circ g = \mathrm{id}_{p(A)}\}$, for all A in $\mathcal{E}$. As a notational convention, we write $\mathsf{s}(f) : p(A) \longrightarrow \{A\}$ for the section corresponding to the global element $f : 1_{p(A)} \longrightarrow A$, given by $\{f\} \circ \eta_A^{1 \dashv \{-\}}$.

A comprehension category with unit $p : \mathcal{E} \longrightarrow \mathcal{B}$ is said to have *dependent products* (resp. *weak dependent sums*) when the weakening functors π_A^* have right adjoints Π_A (resp. left adjoints Σ_A), for all A in $\mathcal{E}$, satisfying the Beck-Chevalley condition: for all Cartesian morphisms $f : A \longrightarrow B$, the canonical natural transformation $(p(f))^* \circ \Pi_B \longrightarrow \Pi_A \circ \{f\}^*$ (resp. $\Sigma_A \circ \{f\}^* \longrightarrow (p(f))^* \circ \Sigma_B$) is an isomorphism. A comprehension category with unit $p : \mathcal{E} \longrightarrow \mathcal{B}$ is said to have *strong dependent sums* when it has weak dependent sums, s.t. for all B in $\mathcal{E}_{\{A\}}$, the morphism $\{\overline{\pi_A}(\Sigma_A B) \circ \eta_B^{\Sigma_A \dashv \pi_A^*}\} : \{B\} \longrightarrow \{\Sigma_A B\}$ is an isomorphism.

Split closed comprehension categories. In order to define fibred adjunction models in Sect. 3.2, we use a particularly well-behaved class of comprehension categories (from the perspective of interpreting type theory), namely, those that are split and closed. A *split closed comprehension category* (SCCompC) is a split full comprehension category with unit $p : \mathcal{E} \longrightarrow \mathcal{B}$, where the base category $\mathcal{B}$ has a terminal object; the fibred terminal objects are preserved on-the-nose by reindexing; and which has dependent products and strong dependent sums, for which the isomorphisms in the Beck-Chevalley conditions are identities.

Natural numbers. A SCCompC $p : \mathcal{E} \longrightarrow \mathcal{B}$ is said to support *weak natural numbers* if there exists an object $\mathbb{N}$ in $\mathcal{E}_1$ and vertical morphisms $\mathsf{zero} : 1_1 \longrightarrow \mathbb{N}$, $\mathsf{succ} : \mathbb{N} \longrightarrow \mathbb{N}$, s.t. for all X in $\mathcal{B}$, A in $\mathcal{E}_{\{!_X^*(\mathbb{N})\}}$, $h_z : 1_X \longrightarrow (\mathsf{s}(!_X^*(\mathsf{zero})))^*(A)$ in $\mathcal{E}_X$ and $h_s : 1_{\{A\}} \longrightarrow \pi_A^*(\{!_X^*(\mathsf{succ})\}^*(A))$ in $\mathcal{E}_{\{A\}}$, there exists $h : 1_{\{!_X^*(\mathbb{N})\}} \longrightarrow A$ in $\mathcal{E}_{\{!_X^*(\mathbb{N})\}}$, satisfying $(\mathsf{s}(!_X^*(\mathsf{zero})))^*(h) = h_z$ and $\pi_A^*(\{!_X^*(\mathsf{succ})\}^*(h)) = h_s$.

We present $\mathbb{N}$ axiomatically rather than using weak initial algebras since our language and its models do not assume coproducts. Moreover, discussing the semantics of inductive types and their fibred induction principles in full generality [10] would digress too much from our central theme.

Identity types. Following the axiomatic presentation given by Warren [39], a SCCompC $p : \mathcal{E} \longrightarrow \mathcal{B}$ is said to support *identity types*, if, for all A in $\mathcal{E}$, there exists an object Id_A in $\mathcal{E}_{\{\pi_A^*(A)\}}$, and $\mathbf{r}_A : 1_{\{A\}} \longrightarrow \delta_A^*(\mathsf{Id}_A)$ in $\mathcal{E}_{\{A\}}$, such that for all B in $\mathcal{E}_{\{\mathsf{Id}_A\}}$ and $f : 1_{\{A\}} \longrightarrow (\mathsf{s}(\mathbf{r}_A))^*(\{\overline{\delta_A}(\mathsf{Id}_A)\}^*(B))$ in $\mathcal{E}_{\{A\}}$, there exists $\mathbf{i}_{A,B}(f) : 1_{\{\mathsf{Id}_A\}} \longrightarrow B$ in $\mathcal{E}_{\{\mathsf{Id}_A\}}$, satisfying $(\mathsf{s}(\mathbf{r}_A))^*(\{\overline{\delta_A}(\mathsf{Id}_A)\}^*(\mathbf{i}_{A,B}(f))) = f$. These identity types are also required to satisfy a split Beck-Chevalley condition: for all Cartesian morphisms $f : A \longrightarrow B$, we must have $\{f'\}^*(\mathsf{Id}_B) = \mathsf{Id}_A$ in $\mathcal{E}_{\{\pi_A^*(A)\}}$, where $f' : \pi_A^*(A) \longrightarrow \pi_B^*(B)$ is the unique mediating morphism over $\{f\}$, arising from $\overline{\pi_B}(B) : \pi_B^*(B) \longrightarrow B$ being a Cartesian morphism. As in [18, Sect. 9.3.5], the *diagonal morphisms* δ_A arise from pullback squares of the form

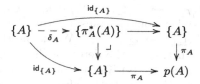

3.2   Interpretation of Our Language in Fibred Adjunction Models

A *fibred adjunction model* is given by a SCCompC $p : \mathcal{V} \longrightarrow \mathcal{B}$, a split fibration $q : \mathcal{C} \longrightarrow \mathcal{B}$, and a split fibred adjunction $F \dashv U : q \longrightarrow p$, such that p supports identity types and weak natural numbers (in the sense of Sect. 3.1), and q supports split dependent products and sums with respect to p as depicted in

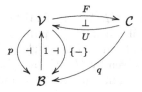

The split dependent products and sums in q, with respect to p, are defined as left and right adjoints to the weakening functors $\pi_A^* : \mathcal{C}_{p(A)} \longrightarrow \mathcal{C}_{\{A\}}$, required to satisfy the analogues of the split Beck-Chevalley conditions from Sect. 3.1.

Given a SCCompC $p : \mathcal{V} \longrightarrow \mathcal{B}$ that supports identity types and weak natural numbers, we can always pick the identity adjunction $\mathrm{id}_{\mathcal{V}} \dashv \mathrm{id}_{\mathcal{V}} : \mathcal{V} \longrightarrow \mathcal{V}$ to construct a corresponding "effect-free" fibred adjunction model. Further, we can construct a restricted form of adjunction models (without identity types) from models of EEC with weak natural numbers [9], i.e., from $\mathcal{D}$-enriched adjunctions $F_{\mathrm{EEC}} \dashv U_{\mathrm{EEC}} : \mathcal{E} \longrightarrow \mathcal{D}$, where $\mathcal{D}$ is Cartesian closed and has a weak NNO, $\mathcal{E}$ is $\mathcal{D}$-enriched and has all $\mathcal{D}$-tensors and -cotensors. These models are based on a computational variant $q : \mathsf{s}(\mathcal{D}, \mathcal{E}) \longrightarrow \mathcal{D}$ of the the simple fibration

$p : \mathsf{s}(\mathcal{D}) \longrightarrow \mathcal{D}$ [18, Theorem 10.5.5]. In particular, the objects of $\mathsf{s}(\mathcal{D}, \mathcal{E})$ are pairs $(X, \underline{C})$ of a $\mathcal{D}$-object X and a $\mathcal{E}$-object $\underline{C}$; and the morphisms $(X, \underline{C}) \longrightarrow (Y, \underline{D})$ are pairs (f, g) of morphisms, with $f : X \longrightarrow Y$ in $\mathcal{D}$ and $g : X \otimes \underline{C} \longrightarrow \underline{D}$ in $\mathcal{E}$.

Interpretation. Following Streicher [36] and Hoffmann [15], we define the interpretation of our language in fibred adjunction models by first giving a *partial interpretation function* $[\![-]\!]$ on raw syntax and then proving that $[\![-]\!]$ is defined on well-formed expressions. We do so because of the well-known issue in interpreting dependently-typed languages: as the derivations of judgments are not unique, due to the type conversion rules, defining the interpretation on the derivations would require simultaneously proving that the definition is coherent.

If defined, $[\![-]\!]$ maps a context Γ to an object $[\![\Gamma]\!]$ in $\mathcal{B}$; a pair of a context Γ and a value type A to an object $[\![\Gamma; A]\!]$ in $\mathcal{V}_{[\![\Gamma]\!]}$; a pair of a context Γ and computation type $\underline{C}$ to an object $[\![\Gamma; \underline{C}]\!]$ in $\mathcal{C}_{[\![\Gamma]\!]}$; a pair of a context Γ and a value term V to an object A and a morphism $[\![\Gamma; V]\!] : 1_{[\![\Gamma]\!]} \longrightarrow A$ in $\mathcal{V}_{[\![\Gamma]\!]}$; a pair of a context Γ and a computation term M to an object $\underline{C}$ in $\mathcal{C}_{[\![\Gamma]\!]}$ and a morphism $[\![\Gamma; M]\!] : 1_{[\![\Gamma]\!]} \longrightarrow U(\underline{C})$ in $\mathcal{V}_{[\![\Gamma]\!]}$; and a triple of a context Γ, a computation type $\underline{C}$ and a homomorphism term K to an object $\underline{D}$ and a morphism $[\![\Gamma; \underline{C}; K]\!] : [\![\Gamma; \underline{C}]\!] \longrightarrow \underline{D}$ in $\mathcal{C}_{[\![\Gamma]\!]}$. We define these different cases of $[\![-]\!]$ simultaneously by induction on the depth of the argument expressions. In the definition, it is convenient to use Kleene equality $\simeq$ where two sides of an equation are equal if either they are both defined and equal or they are both undefined. For contexts, $[\![-]\!]$ is defined as

$$[\![\cdot]\!] \simeq 1 \qquad\qquad [\![\Gamma, x:A]\!] \simeq \{[\![\Gamma; A]\!]\} \quad \text{if } x \notin Vars(\Gamma)$$

For types, we illustrate the definition of $[\![-]\!]$ with the following example cases:

$$[\![\Gamma; \mathsf{Nat}]\!] \simeq \mathop{!}^*_{[\![\Gamma]\!]}(\mathbb{N}) \qquad [\![\Gamma; \mathsf{Id}_A(V, W)]\!] \simeq (\langle \mathsf{s}([\![\Gamma; V]\!]), \mathsf{s}([\![\Gamma; W]\!])\rangle)^*(\mathsf{Id}_{[\![\Gamma; A]\!]})$$
$$[\![\Gamma; \Sigma x:A.\underline{C}]\!] \simeq \Sigma_{[\![\Gamma; A]\!]}([\![\Gamma, x:A; \underline{C}]\!]) \qquad [\![\Gamma; \Pi x:A.\underline{C}]\!] \simeq \Pi_{[\![\Gamma; A]\!]}([\![\Gamma, x:A; \underline{C}]\!])$$

where the pairing morphism $\langle \mathsf{s}([\![\Gamma; V]\!]), \mathsf{s}([\![\Gamma; W]\!])\rangle : [\![\Gamma]\!] \longrightarrow \{\pi^*_{[\![\Gamma; A]\!]}([\![\Gamma; A]\!])\}$ is the unique mediating morphism into the pullback square from Sect. 3.1, for $\mathsf{s}([\![\Gamma; V]\!])$ and $\mathsf{s}([\![\Gamma; W]\!])$. We also note that $[\![\Gamma; \mathsf{Id}_A(V, W)]\!]$ is conditional on the codomains of the morphisms given by $[\![\Gamma; V]\!]$ and $[\![\Gamma; W]\!]$ being equal to $[\![\Gamma; A]\!]$.

For terms, we present the definition only for homomorphism terms, given by

$$[\![\Gamma; \underline{C}; z]\!] \simeq [\![\Gamma; \underline{C}]\!] \xrightarrow{\mathsf{id}_{[\![\Gamma; \underline{C}]\!]}} [\![\Gamma; \underline{C}]\!]$$

$$[\![\Gamma; \underline{C}; K \text{ to } x:A \text{ in}_{\underline{D}} M]\!] \simeq [\![\Gamma; \underline{C}]\!] \xrightarrow{[\![\Gamma; \underline{C}; K]\!]} F([\![\Gamma; A]\!]) \xrightarrow{[\![\Gamma, x:A; M]\!]^\dagger} [\![\Gamma; \underline{D}]\!]$$

$$[\![\Gamma; \underline{C}; \langle V, K \rangle_{(x:A).\underline{D}}]\!] \simeq [\![\Gamma; \underline{C}]\!] \xrightarrow{[\![\Gamma; \underline{C}; K]\!]} \mathsf{s}([\![\Gamma; V]\!])^*([\![\Gamma, x:A; \underline{D}]\!]) \xrightarrow{\mathsf{s}([\![\Gamma; V]\!])^*(\eta^{\Sigma \dashv \pi^*}_{[\![\Gamma, x:A; \underline{D}]\!]})}$$
$$\mathsf{s}([\![\Gamma; V]\!])^*(\pi^*_{[\![\Gamma; A]\!]}(\Sigma_{[\![\Gamma; A]\!]}([\![\Gamma, x:A; \underline{D}]\!]))) \xrightarrow{=} \Sigma_{[\![\Gamma; A]\!]}([\![\Gamma, x:A; \underline{D}]\!])$$

$$[\![\Gamma; \underline{C}; K \text{ to } \langle x:A, z:\underline{D}_1 \rangle \text{ in}_{\underline{D}_2} L]\!] \simeq [\![\Gamma; \underline{C}]\!] \xrightarrow{[\![\Gamma; \underline{C}; K]\!]} \Sigma_{[\![\Gamma; A]\!]}([\![\Gamma, x:A; \underline{D}_1]\!]) \xrightarrow{[\![\Gamma, x:A; \underline{D}_1; L]\!]} [\![\Gamma; \underline{D}_2]\!]$$

$$[\![\Gamma; \underline{C}; \lambda x:A.K]\!] \simeq [\![\Gamma; \underline{C}]\!] \xrightarrow{\lambda[\![\Gamma, x:A; \underline{C}; K]\!]} \Pi_{[\![\Gamma; A]\!]}\underline{D}$$

$$[\![\Gamma; \underline{C}; K(V)_{(x:A).\underline{D}}]\!] \simeq [\![\Gamma; \underline{C}]\!] \xrightarrow{=} \mathsf{s}([\![\Gamma; V]\!])^*(\pi^*_{[\![\Gamma; A]\!]}([\![\Gamma; \underline{C}]\!])) \xrightarrow{\mathsf{s}([\![\Gamma; V]\!])^*(\pi^*_{[\![\Gamma; A]\!]}([\![\Gamma; \underline{C}; K]\!]))}$$
$$\mathsf{s}([\![\Gamma; V]\!])^*(\pi^*_{[\![\Gamma; A]\!]}(\Pi_{[\![\Gamma; A]\!]}([\![\Gamma, x:A; \underline{D}]\!]))) \xrightarrow{\mathsf{s}([\![\Gamma; V]\!])^*(\epsilon^{\pi^* \dashv \Pi}_{[\![\Gamma, x:A; \underline{D}]\!]})} \mathsf{s}([\![\Gamma; V]\!])^*([\![\Gamma, x:A; \underline{D}]\!])$$

where the vertical morphisms $[\![\Gamma, x : A; M]\!]^{\dagger}$, $[\![[\Gamma, x : A, \underline{D}_1; L]\!]]$ and $\lambda[\![\Gamma; \underline{C}; K]\!]$ are derived using the adjunctions involved in the definition of fibred adjunction models. Similarly to [15, 36], we make some of the cases of the definition (implicitly) conditional on the denotations of sub-terms having a particular form, based on the type-annotations with which we have decorated our terms.

Theorem 1 (Soundness). *The partial interpretation function $[\![-]\!]$ is defined on well-formed contexts, well-formed types and well-typed terms. In addition, the interpretation identifies types and terms that are equal in the equational theory.*

Similarly to [15, 36], the proof of soundness relies on lemmas relating weakening and substitution in the syntax to reindexing in fibred adjunction models.

The classifying model. We now show that the interpretation of our language in fibred adjunction models is complete by constructing its classifying model.

First, in the classifying fibred adjunction model the objects of $\mathcal{B}$ are given by equivalence classes of well-formed value contexts Γ. The morphisms $\Gamma_1 \longrightarrow \Gamma_2$ are given by equivalence classes of tuples of value terms $\mathbf{V} = (V_1, \ldots, V_m)$, where $\Gamma_2 = y_1 : B_1, \ldots, y_m : B_m$ and $\Gamma_1 \vdash V_i : B_i[V_1/y_1, \ldots, V_{i-1}/y_{i-1}]$, for all $1 \leq i \leq m$.

Next, the objects of the total category $\mathcal{V}$ are given by equivalence classes of value types $\Gamma \vdash A$ and its morphisms $\Gamma_1 \vdash A \longrightarrow \Gamma_2 \vdash B$ by equivalence classes of tuples of value terms $(\mathbf{V}, V)$, where $\mathbf{V}$ are typed as in $\mathcal{B}$, and V is typed as $\Gamma_1, x : A \vdash V : B[\mathbf{V}/\Gamma_2]$. The objects and morphisms of $\mathcal{C}$ are defined similarly: as equivalence classes of computation types $\Gamma \vdash \underline{C}$; and as equivalence classes of tuples of terms $(\mathbf{V}, K)$, where K is typed as $\Gamma_1 \mid z : \underline{C} \vdash K : \underline{D}[\mathbf{V}/\Gamma_2]$. The fibrations p and q are defined by context projections, i.e., by $p(\Gamma \vdash A) = \Gamma$.

The various adjunctions involved in the definition of fibred adjunction models are defined in terms of their syntactic counterparts. For example, the split fibred adjunction $F \dashv U : q \longrightarrow p$ is defined using the types FA and $U\underline{C}$, given by

$$F(\Gamma \vdash A) = \Gamma \vdash FA \qquad F(\mathbf{V}, V) = (\mathbf{V}, z \text{ to } y : A \text{ in}_{FB[\mathbf{V}/\Gamma_2]} \text{ return } V[y/x])$$
$$U(\Gamma \vdash \underline{C}) = \Gamma \vdash U\underline{C} \qquad U(\mathbf{V}, K) = (\mathbf{V}, \text{thunk } K[\text{force}_{\underline{C}} \, x/z])$$

The identity types and natural numbers are also given in terms of their syntactic counterparts: the object $\mathsf{Id}_{\Gamma \vdash A}$ in $\mathcal{V}_{\{\pi^*_{\Gamma \vdash A}(\Gamma \vdash A)\}}$ is $\Gamma, x : A, y : A \vdash \mathsf{Id}_A(x, y)$.

Proposition 1. *The above definitions, based on the syntax of our language, constitute a fibred adjunction model, called the classifying model of our language.*

Finally, we can use this result to prove the completeness of the interpretation.

Theorem 2 (Completeness). *If two types or two terms of our language are identified in all fibred adjunction models, they are equal in the equational theory.*

3.3 Fibred Adjunction Models Based on the Families Fibration

We now discuss some examples of fibred adjunction models based on the pro-
totypical model of dependent types, the families fibration $p : \mathsf{Fam}(\mathcal{D}) \longrightarrow \mathsf{Set}$.
The objects of $\mathsf{Fam}(\mathcal{D})$ are given by pairs (X, A) of a set X and an X-indexed
family of $\mathcal{D}$-objects $A : X \longrightarrow ob(\mathcal{D})$; the morphisms $(X, A) \longrightarrow (Y, B)$ are pairs
$(f, \{g_x\}_{x \in X})$ of a function $f : X \longrightarrow Y$ and a X-indexed family of $\mathcal{D}$-morphisms
$\{g_x : A(x) \longrightarrow B(f(x))\}_{x \in X}$. The functor p is defined by first projection, i.e.
by $p(X, A) = X$. In fact, p is a split fibration: the reindexing functors f^* are
defined by pre-composition, i.e. by $f^*(Y, B) = (X, B \circ f)$ for all $f : X \longrightarrow Y$. In
our examples, we take $\mathcal{D}$ to be Set. In this case, p is a SCCompC [18, Sect. 10.5].
The examples we discuss below are instances of the following general result,
building on the fact that adjunctions can be lifted to families fibrations [18,
Example 1.8.7(i)].

Theorem 3. *Given $F \dashv U : \mathcal{E} \longrightarrow \mathsf{Set}$, such that $\mathcal{E}$ has both set-indexed products and coproducts, the fibrations $p : \mathsf{Fam}(\mathsf{Set}) \longrightarrow \mathsf{Set}$ and $q : \mathsf{Fam}(\mathcal{E}) \longrightarrow \mathsf{Set}$,
together with the pointwise lifting of $F \dashv U$, determine a fibred adjunction model.*

In Theorem 3, the set-indexed products and coproducts in $\mathcal{E}$ are assumed to
exist in order to define the dependent products and dependent sums in q as

$$\Pi_{(X,A)}(\textstyle\coprod_{x \in X} A(x), \underline{C}) = (X, x \mapsto \textstyle\prod_{a \in A(x)} \underline{C}(x, a))$$
$$\Sigma_{(X,A)}(\textstyle\coprod_{x \in X} A(x), \underline{C}) = (X, x \mapsto \textstyle\coprod_{a \in A(x)} \underline{C}(x, a))$$

The lifting $\hat{F} \dashv \hat{U}$ of $F \dashv U$ is defined by composition, i.e., $\hat{F}(X, A) = (X, F \circ A)$.
  The first collection of examples we discuss are based on Eilenberg-Moore
algebras (EM-algebras) for a monad (T, η, μ) on Set. As standard, we write Set^T
for the category of EM-algebras. Its objects are given by pairs (X, α) of a set X
and a function $\alpha : TX \longrightarrow X$ such that $\alpha \circ T(\alpha) = \alpha \circ \mu_X$ and $\alpha \circ \eta_X = \mathrm{id}_X$;
its morphisms $(X, \alpha) \longrightarrow (Y, \beta)$ are given by functions $f : X \longrightarrow Y$ such that
$\beta \circ T(f) = f \circ \alpha$. There is a canonical EM-adjunction $F^T \dashv U^T : \mathsf{Set}^T \longrightarrow \mathsf{Set}$.
  We note that Set^T has both set-indexed products and coproducts: Set^T is
complete [4, Theorem 4.3.1] and, assuming the axiom of choice (AC), Set^T is also
cocomplete [4, Theorem 4.3.5]. We note that, without assuming AC, it would
suffice to assume that Set^T has reflexive coequalizers for it to be cocomplete, as
first observed by Linton [21]. The set-indexed products in Set^T are defined from
the set-indexed products in Set by $\prod_{i \in I}(X_i, \alpha_i) = (\prod_{i \in I} X_i, \langle \alpha_i \circ T(\mathsf{proj}_i) \rangle_{i \in I})$.
As shown by Linton [21], the set-indexed coproduct $\coprod_{i \in I}(X_i, \alpha_i)$ can be defined
as the reflexive coequalizer $e : F^T(\coprod_{i \in I} X_i) \longrightarrow \coprod_{i \in I}(X_i, \alpha_i)$ of the diagram

$$F^T(\textstyle\coprod_{i \in I} X_i) \xrightarrow{\ F^T([\mathsf{inj}_i \circ \eta_{X_i}]_{i \in I})\ } F^T(\textstyle\coprod_{i \in I} TX_i) \underset{\mu_{\coprod_{i \in I} X_i} \circ F^T([T(\mathsf{inj}_i)]_{i \in I})}{\overset{F^T([\mathsf{inj}_i \circ \alpha_i]_{i \in I})}{\rightrightarrows}} F^T(\textstyle\coprod_{i \in I} X_i)$$

Corollary 1. *Given a monad (T, η, μ) on* Set, *the EM-adjunction $F^T \dashv U^T$ and the families fibration $p :$ Fam(Set) $\longrightarrow$ Set determine a fibred adjunction model.*

A particularly well-behaved collection of fibred adjunction models arises from the algebraic treatment of computational effects [31], namely, from monads arising from countable Lawvere theories. These are exactly the monads on Set that are of countable rank [33, Theorem 2.8]. As discussed in [17], such monads combine easily, in terms of combining the operations and equations of the corresponding countable Lawvere theories. We recall that every countable Lawvere theory $\mathcal{L}$ induces a category Mod($\mathcal{L}$, Set) of models of $\mathcal{L}$ in Set, with an associated forgetful functor $U_\mathcal{L} :$ Mod($\mathcal{L}$, Set) $\longrightarrow$ Set [33]. As Set is locally countably presentable [1], $U_\mathcal{L}$ has a left adjoint $F_\mathcal{L}$, inducing an equivalence of categories between Mod($\mathcal{L}$, Set) and Set$^{T_\mathcal{L}}$, for $T_\mathcal{L} = U_\mathcal{L} \circ F_\mathcal{L}$. Importantly for us, Mod($\mathcal{L}$, Set) is both complete and cocomplete, e.g., because $T_\mathcal{L}$ has countable rank and Set is complete and cocomplete, see [4, Theorem 4.3.6]. Therefore, Mod($\mathcal{L}$, Set) has set-indexed products and set-indexed coproducts and we get:

Corollary 2. *For any countable Lawvere theory $\mathcal{L}$, the adjunction $F_\mathcal{L} \dashv U_\mathcal{L}$ and the families fibration $p :$ Fam(Set) $\longrightarrow$ Set determine a fibred adjunction model.*

Finally, we present two computationally motivated examples arising from Theorem 3 and decompositions of monads (T, η, μ) on Set into adjunctions other than $F^T \dashv U^T$. In particular, we consider the continuations monad $R^{R^{(-)}}$ and the global state monad $((-) \times S)^S$. These monads can be decomposed into the adjunctions $R^{(-)} \dashv R^{(-)} :$ Set$^{\mathrm{op}} \longrightarrow$ Set and $(-) \times S \dashv (-)^S :$ Set $\longrightarrow$ Set, where Set^{op} inherits set-indexed products and set-indexed coproducts trivially from Set.

Corollary 3. *The adjunctions $R^{(-)} \dashv R^{(-)}$ and $(-) \times S \dashv (-)^S$ together with the families fibration $p :$ Fam(Set) $\longrightarrow$ Set determine fibred adjunction models.*

4 Extending the Language with Algebraic Effects

Until now we have have not said how computational effects, such as I/O, state, exceptions, etc., arise in our language and how programmers can program with them. In this section, we make the source of computational effects explicit, by drawing ideas from the algebraic treatment of computational effects [31].

4.1 Algebraic Effects in the Syntax

We begin by assuming we are given a *collection of typed operation symbols*

$$\mathsf{op} : (x_{\mathsf{in}} : I) \longrightarrow O$$

where we call $\cdot \vdash I$ the *input type* and $x_{\mathsf{in}} : I \vdash O$ the *output type* of op. We restrict I and O to be *pure value types*, i.e., value types that do not contain U.

We add such operation symbols to our language by extending the syntax of computation terms: for each operation symbol $\mathsf{op} : (x_{\mathsf{in}} : I) \longrightarrow O$, we add algebraic operations $\mathsf{op}_V^{\underline{C}}(x.M)$, for all $\underline{C}$, and a generic effect genop_V, typed as

$$\frac{\Gamma \vdash V : I \quad \Gamma \vdash \underline{C} \quad \Gamma, x{:}O[V/x_{\mathsf{in}}] \vdash M : \underline{C}}{\Gamma \vdash \mathsf{op}_V^{\underline{C}}(x.M) : \underline{C}} \qquad \frac{\Gamma \vdash V : I}{\Gamma \vdash \mathsf{genop}_V : F(O[V/x_{\mathsf{in}}])}$$

These operations and generic effects are in 1-to-1 correspondence, as in [30].

The operation symbols we consider can also come equipped with a *collection of equations*, describing their intended computational behaviour. We extend our language with the corresponding equations between computation terms.

Note that we allow the output types of operation symbols to depend on input values. This additional type-dependency is useful for giving more concise representations of collections of standard, simply-typed operations. For example, we can use a boolean-indexed type family and two operation symbols

$$\mathsf{lookup} : (x_{\mathsf{in}} : \mathsf{Bool}) \longrightarrow (\mathsf{if}\ x_{\mathsf{in}}\ \mathsf{then}\ \mathsf{Nat}\ \mathsf{else}\ \mathsf{Bool})$$
$$\mathsf{update} : (x_{\mathsf{in}} : \Sigma x{:}\mathsf{Bool}.(\mathsf{if}\ x\ \mathsf{then}\ \mathsf{Nat}\ \mathsf{else}\ \mathsf{Bool})) \longrightarrow 1$$

as a concise syntax for the four operations of global state with two locations:

$$\mathsf{lookup}_{\mathsf{tt}} : 1 \longrightarrow \mathsf{Nat} \quad \mathsf{update}_{\mathsf{tt}} : \mathsf{Nat} \longrightarrow 1 \quad \mathsf{lookup}_{\mathsf{ff}} : 1 \longrightarrow \mathsf{Bool} \quad \mathsf{update}_{\mathsf{ff}} : \mathsf{Bool} \longrightarrow 1$$

In order to make the computation terms $\mathsf{op}_V^{\underline{C}}(x.M)$ behave like algebraic operations, we extend our language with a *general algebraicity equation*:

$$\frac{\mathsf{op} : (x_{\mathsf{in}} : I) \longrightarrow O \quad \Gamma \vdash V : I \quad \Gamma, x{:}O[V/x_{\mathsf{in}}] \vdash M : \underline{C} \quad \Gamma \mid z{:}\underline{C} \vdash K : \underline{D}}{\Gamma \vdash K[\mathsf{op}_V^{\underline{C}}(x.M)/z] = \mathsf{op}_V^{\underline{D}}(x.K[M/z]) : \underline{D}} (**)$$

Using $(**)$, we can easily prove equations familiar from languages with algebraic effects, e.g. the algebraicity equation for sequential composition from [34, Sect. 3.3]:

$$\Gamma \vdash \mathsf{op}_V^{FA}(x.M)\ \mathsf{to}\ y{:}A\ \mathsf{in}_{\underline{C}}\ N = \mathsf{op}_V^{\underline{C}}(x.(M\ \mathsf{to}\ y{:}A\ \mathsf{in}_{\underline{C}}\ N)) : \underline{C}$$

We omit handlers of algebraic effects [32] from this paper as a full account, in which the equational properties of handlers are derived from those of homomorphism terms, i.e., from $(**)$, involves extending our language with a further computation type former $\langle A, \{V_{\mathsf{op}}\}_{\mathsf{op}} \rangle$ for user-defined algebras. To make handlers first-class, one extends the language with the type $\underline{C} \multimap \underline{D}$ of homomorphisms, familiar from EEC. We will report on this extension separately elsewhere.

4.2 Algebraic Effects in the Semantics

Following the definition of algebraic operations for a monad in terms of its EM-algebras [30, Sect. 6], we say that a *fibred adjunction model supports algebraic operations* if for all $\mathsf{op} : (x_{\mathsf{in}} : I) \longrightarrow O$, there exist vertical morphisms

$$[\![\mathsf{op}]\!]_{\underline{C}} : \Sigma_{!^*_{q(\underline{C})}([\![I]\!])}(\Pi_{\{!_{\overline{q(\underline{C})}}([\![I]\!])\}^*([\![O]\!])}(\pi^*_{\{!_{\overline{q(\underline{C})}}([\![I]\!])\}^*([\![O]\!])}(\pi^*_{!^*_{q(\underline{C})}([\![I]\!])}(U(\underline{C}))))) \longrightarrow U(\underline{C})$$

that are natural in $\underline{C}$. When combining this naturality with the fact that U is a split fibred functor, it can be shown that the $[\![\text{op}]\!]_{\underline{C}}$'s are preserved by reindexing. If the given collection of operation symbols also comes with associated equations, these vertical morphisms are additionally required to satisfy these equations.

The classifying model from Sect. 3.2 can be straightforwardly extended: for any $\Gamma = x_1:A_1,\ldots,x_n:A_n$ and $\Gamma\vdash \underline{C}$, the vertical morphisms $[\![\text{op}]\!]_{\Gamma\vdash\underline{C}}$ are

$$[\![\text{op}]\!]_{\Gamma\vdash\underline{C}} = \big(x_1,\ldots,x_n,\text{thunk }(\text{op}^{\underline{C}}_{\text{fst }x'}(x.\text{force}_{\underline{C}}((\text{snd}\,x')\,x))))\big)$$

where x' has type $\Sigma x_{\text{in}}:I.\Pi x:O.U\underline{C}$. The naturality of these is proved by using the equations describing the interaction between thunking and forcing, in combination with the general algebraicity equation $(**)$ from Sect. 4.1.

Finally, we note how algebraic operations can be characterised in the fibred adjunction models based on the families fibration and EM-algebras of a monad.

Proposition 2. *The fibred adjunction models from Sect. 3.3, based on the EM-algebras of a monad (T,η,μ) on* Set, *support algebraic operations if for all operations* op : $(x_{\text{in}}:I) \longrightarrow O$ *there exists a family of natural transformations*

$$\Big\{\ [\![\text{op}]\!]_i : (U^T(-))^{[\![O]\!](\langle\star,i\rangle)} \longrightarrow U^T(-)\ \Big\}_{i\in[\![I]\!](\star)} (*)$$

5   Extending the Language with General Recursion

We now show how to extend our language with general recursion, considering it as a computational effect to keep the MLTT fragment of our language effect-free.

5.1   Recursion in the Syntax

We start by extending our language with a new computation term, the *fixed point operation* $\mu x:U\underline{C}.M$. The corresponding typing rule is given by

$$\frac{\Gamma,x:U\underline{C} \vdash M:\underline{C}}{\Gamma \vdash \mu x : U\underline{C}.M:\underline{C}}$$

We also extend the language's equational theory with unfolding of fixed points:

$$\Gamma \vdash \mu x:U\underline{C}.M = M[\text{thunk }(\mu x:U\underline{C}.M)/x] : \underline{C}$$

Finally, we also alter the definition of identity types $\text{Id}_{A_{\text{disc}}}(V,W)$, restricting them to be over *discrete value types*, to be able to interpret this extended language in models based on continuous families of cpos. These discrete types are

$$A_{\text{disc}}, B_{\text{disc}} ::= \ \text{Nat}\mid \Sigma x:A_{\text{disc}}.B_{\text{disc}}\mid 1\mid \Pi x:A.B_{\text{disc}}\mid \text{Id}_{A_{\text{disc}}}(V,W)$$

5.2   Domain-Theoretic Semantics for Recursion

We build the denotational semantics for the language with recursion around the $SCCompC$ of continuous families $p : \mathsf{CFam}(\mathcal{CPO}) \longrightarrow \mathcal{CPO}$ [18, Sect. 10.6].

Compared to [18], we use ω-complete partial orders instead of directed-complete partial orders, because the former constitute a locally countably presentable category, whereas the latter do not [1, Example 1.14(4)]; and we need local presentability for fibred adjunction models based on the algebraic treatment of computational effects. An overview of the relevant domain theory can be found in [11,29].

We recall that the objects of $\mathsf{CFam}(\mathcal{CPO})$ are pairs (X, A) of a cpo X and a continuous functor $A : X \longrightarrow \mathcal{CPO}^{\mathrm{EP}}$ (a *continuous family*), treating X as a category and valued in the category of embedding-projection pairs. The morphisms $(X, A) \longrightarrow (Y, B)$ are pairs $(f, \{g_x\}_{x \in |X|})$ of a continuous function $f : X \longrightarrow Y$ and a family of continuous functions $\{g_x : A(x) \longrightarrow B(f(x))\}_{x \in |X|}$, satisfying

$$x_1 \sqsubseteq_X x_2 \implies B(f(x_1 \sqsubseteq_X x_2))^e \circ g_{x_1} \sqsubseteq_{B(f(x_2))} A(x_1) \ g_{x_2} \circ A(x_1 \sqsubseteq_X x_2)^e$$
$$\langle x_n \rangle \text{ incr. } \omega\text{-chain} \implies g_{\bigvee_n x_n} = \bigvee_n \left(B(f(x_n \sqsubseteq_X \textstyle\bigvee_n x_n))^e \circ g_{x_n} \circ A(x_n \sqsubseteq_X \textstyle\bigvee_n x_n)^p \right)$$

The dependent products and strong dependent sums are defined by using the cpo-indexed products $\prod_X A$ and coproducts $\coprod_X A$ in $\mathcal{CPO}$, which are given by

$$\coprod_X A = \left(\coprod_{x \in |X|} |A(x)|, \langle x_1, a_1 \rangle \sqsubseteq \langle x_2, a_2 \rangle \text{ iff } x_1 \sqsubseteq_X x_2 \text{ and } A(x_1 \sqsubseteq_X x_2)^e(a_1) \sqsubseteq a_2 \right)$$
$$\textstyle\prod_X A = \left(\{f : X \longrightarrow \coprod_X A \mid \mathsf{fst} \circ f = \mathsf{id}_X \}, f_1 \sqsubseteq f_2 \text{ iff } \forall x \in |X|. \ f_1(x) \sqsubseteq_{\coprod_X A} f_2(x) \right)$$

For identity types, we require A to be a continuous family of discrete cpos, matching the changes we made in the syntax of our language, and then define

$$\mathsf{Id}_{(X,A)} = \left(\{\pi^*_{(X,A)}(X, A)\}, \langle x, a, a' \rangle \mapsto \coprod_{\{* \mid a = a'\}} 1 \right)$$

The discreteness of A is necessary for $\langle x, a, a' \rangle \mapsto \coprod_{\{* \mid a = a'\}} 1$ to constitute a continuous functor: if A would not be discrete, then from $\langle x_1, a_1, a_1' \rangle \sqsubseteq \langle x_2, a_2, a_2' \rangle$ and $a_1 = a_1'$ it would not follow that $a_2 = a_2'$, and vice versa, which we need for defining the embedding-projection pair between $\coprod_{\{* \mid a_1 = a_1'\}} 1$ and $\coprod_{\{* \mid a_2 = a_2'\}} 1$.

For modeling computation terms involving recursion, we assume a $\mathcal{CPO}$-enriched monad (T, η, μ) on $\mathcal{CPO}$, such that its EM-algebras are pointed and the morphisms between them are strict; or equivalently, we assume that the given monad supports a least zero-ary algebraic operation, in the sense of [30, Sect. 6]. For modeling computational Σ-types, we further assume that $\mathcal{CPO}^T$ has reflexive coequalizers. We can then model our computation types in the split fibration $q : \mathsf{CFam}(\mathcal{CPO}^T) \longrightarrow \mathcal{CPO}$, defined analogously to p above. Monads satisfying these conditions arise naturally from the algebraic treatment of computational effects: from $\mathcal{CPO}$-enriched countable Lawvere theories [17] with a least constant.

The dependent products and sums in q, with respect to p, are defined using the cpo-indexed products and coproducts in $\mathcal{CPO}^T$. First, the cpo-indexed product $\prod_X \underline{C}$ in $\mathcal{CPO}^T$ is directly inherited from $\mathcal{CPO}$, being defined on the carrier $\prod_X (U^T \circ \underline{C})$. On the other hand, analogously to Sect. 3.3, the cpo-indexed coproduct $\coprod_X \underline{C}$ cannot be defined simply by taking $\coprod_X (U^T \circ \underline{C})$ as the carrier. Instead, we construct $\coprod_X \underline{C}$ as the reflexive coequalizer for a diagram similar to the one used in Sect. 3.3, with the difference that here we would use the free algebras over cpo-indexed coproducts rather than over set-indexed coproducts.

Despite having a more complex categorical definition, the cpo-indexed coproducts in $\mathcal{CPO}^T$ have the same universal property as those in $\mathcal{CPO}$. We first recall Jacobs's remark [18, Sect. 10.6] that $\coprod_X A$ results from applying the Grothendieck construction to A. By a result of Gray [12], $\coprod_X A$ can also be understood as the oplax colimit of A in $\mathcal{CPO}$. In $\mathcal{CPO}^T$, the situation is analogous:

Proposition 3. $\coprod_X \underline{C}$ *is the oplax colimit of* $\underline{C} : X \longrightarrow (\mathcal{CPO}^T)^{EP}$ *in* $\mathcal{CPO}^T$.

Similarly to Sect. 3.3, the split fibred adjunction $F \dashv U : q \longrightarrow p$ is defined from $F^T \dashv U^T$ by post-composition, i.e., by setting $F(X, A) = (X, F^T \circ A)$, where $F^T \circ A$ is a continuous functor because of the $\mathcal{CPO}$-enrichment of F^T and the limit-colimit coincidences in $\mathcal{CPO}^{EP}$ and $(\mathcal{CPO}^T)^{EP}$. U is defined analogously.

We interpret our language as discussed in Sect. 3.2, except for recursion:

$$[\![\Gamma; \mu x : U\underline{C}.M]\!] = (\mathsf{id}_{[\![\Gamma]\!]}, \{x \in |1| \mapsto \mu(g_\gamma)\}_{\gamma \in |[\![\Gamma]\!]|}) : ([\![\Gamma]\!], \gamma \mapsto 1) \longrightarrow ([\![\Gamma]\!], U^T \circ [\![\Gamma; \underline{C}]\!])$$

where we use the least fixed points of the family of continuous functions $\{g_\gamma : U^T([\![\Gamma; \underline{C}]\!])(\gamma) \longrightarrow U^T([\![\Gamma; \underline{C}]\!])(\gamma)\}_{\gamma \in |[\![\Gamma]\!]|}$, determined by a vertical morphism $([\![\Gamma]\!], U^T \circ [\![\Gamma; \underline{C}]\!]) \longrightarrow ([\![\Gamma]\!], U^T \circ [\![\Gamma; \underline{C}]\!])$ we derive from $[\![\Gamma, x : U\underline{C}; M]\!]$. The least fixed points of g_γ's are guaranteed to exist because our assumptions about $\mathcal{CPO}^T$ make every $U^T \circ [\![\Gamma; \underline{C}]\!]$ into a continuous family of pointed cpos.

Theorem 4. *Given a monad (T, η, μ) on $\mathcal{CPO}$ satisfying the conditions given in this section, the fibred adjunction model built from p :* CFam$(\mathcal{CPO}) \longrightarrow \mathcal{CPO}$ *and $F^T \dashv U^T$ is a model of the equational theory extended with fixed point unfolding.*

Finally, we note that the other obvious candidate cod : $\mathcal{CPO}^{\rightarrow} \longrightarrow \mathcal{CPO}$, even if made split [8,14], is not a SCCompC, because of [18, Theorem 10.5.5] and:

Proposition 4. $\mathcal{CPO}$ *is not locally Cartesian closed.*

In particular, the condition that every base change functor has to have a right adjoint fails because some of these functors do not preserve all colimits, e.g., given a non-empty cpo X, the pullback of the epimorphism $n \mapsto n : \mathbb{N}_= \longrightarrow \mathbb{N}_\omega$ in $\mathcal{CPO}/\mathbb{N}_\omega$ along the constant map $x \mapsto \omega : X \longrightarrow \mathbb{N}_\omega$ is not an epimorphism.

6   Conclusions and Future Work

We addressed the problem of finding a mathematically natural combination of dependent types and computational effects. We were motivated by: (i) the success similar foundations have had in driving the study of computational effects in the simply-typed setting; and (ii) the success of dependently-typed programming in generating a number of concrete attempts to combine dependent types with computational effects. Our solution is mathematically natural, combining comprehension categories, arising from the semantics of dependent types, with adjunctions, arising from the semantics of computational effects. It is also general, covering a variety of algebraic and non-algebraic effects, and can be extended to accommodate general recursion. For future work, a natural next step is to investigate operational semantics, leading towards an implementation.

We are also working on a fibred generalisation of Atkey's parametrised notions of computation [2], aiming at a semantic account of the effects in Idris [5,6].

References

1. Adamek, J., Rosicky, J.: Locally Presentable and Accessible Categories. London Mathematical Society Lecture Note Series. Cambridge University Press, Cambridge (1994)
2. Atkey, R.: Algebras for parameterised monads. In: Kurz, A., Lenisa, M., Tarlecki, A. (eds.) CALCO 2009. LNCS, vol. 5728, pp. 3–17. Springer, Heidelberg (2009)
3. Benton, P.N.: A mixed linear and non-linear logic: proofs, terms and models. In: Pacholski, L., Tiuryn, J. (eds.) CSL 1994. LNCS, vol. 933. Springer, Heidelberg (1995)
4. Borceux, F.: Handbook of Categorical Algebra. Categories and Structures, vol. 2. Cambridge University Press, Cambridge (1994)
5. Brady, E.: Programming and reasoning with algebraic effects and dependent types. In: Morrisett, G., Uustalu, T. (eds.) Proceedings of 18th International Conference on Functional Programming, ICFP 2013, pp. 133–144. ACM (2013)
6. Brady, E.: Resource-dependent algebraic effects. In: Hage, J., McCarthy, J. (eds.) TFP 2014. LNCS, vol. 8843, pp. 18–33. Springer, Heidelberg (2015)
7. Casinghino, C., Sjöbergberg, V., Weirich, S.: Combining proofs and programs in a dependently typed language. In: Sewell, P. (ed.) Proceedings of 41st Annual Symposium on Principles of Programming Languages, POPL 2014, pp. 33–45. ACM (2014)
8. Clairambault, P., Dybjer, P.: The biequivalence of locally cartesian closed categories and martin-löf type theories. In: Ong, L. (ed.) Typed Lambda Calculi and Applications. LNCS, vol. 6690, pp. 91–106. Springer, Heidelberg (2011)
9. Egger, J., Møgelberg, R.E., Simpson, A.: The enriched effect calculus: syntax and semantics. J. Log. Comput. 24(3), 615–654 (2014)
10. Ghani, N., Johann, P., Fumex, C.: Indexed induction and coinduction, fibrationally. Logical Methods Comput. Sci. 9(3:6), 1–31 (2013). doi:10.2168/LMCS-9(3:6)2013
11. Gierz, G., Hofmann, K.H., Keimel, K., Lawson, J.D., Mislove, M., Scott, D.S.: Continuous Lattices and Domains. Cambridge University Press, Cambridge (2003)
12. Gray, J.W.: The categorical comprehension scheme. In: Gray, J.W. (ed.) Category Theory, Homology Theory and Their Applications III. Lecture Notes in Mathematics, vol. 99, pp. 242–312. Springer, Heidelberg (1969)
13. Hancock, P., Setzer, A.: Interactive programs in dependent type theory. In: Clote, P.G., Schwichtenberg, H. (eds.) CSL 2000. LNCS, vol. 1862, pp. 317–331. Springer, Heidelberg (2000)
14. Hofmann, M.: On the interpretation of type theory in locally cartesian closed. In: Pacholski, L., Tiuryn, J. (eds.) CSL 1994. LNCS, vol. 933, pp. 427–441. Springer, Heidelberg (1995)
15. Hofmann, M.: Syntax and semantics of dependent types. In: Pitts, A.M., Dybjer, P. (eds.) Semantics and Logics of Computation, pp. 79–130. Cambridge University Press, Cambridge (1997)

16. Hutton, G., Meijer, E.: Monadic parsing in Haskell. J. Funct. Program. **8**(4), 437–444 (1998)
17. Hyland, M., Plotkin, G., Power, J.: Combining effects: sum and tensor. Theor. Comput. Sci. **357**(1–3), 70–99 (2006)
18. Jacobs, B.: Categorical Logic and Type Theory. Studies in Logic and the Foundations of Mathematics, vol. 141. North Holland, Amsterdam (1999)
19. Krishnaswami, N.R., Pradic, P., Benton, N.: Integrating linear and dependent types. In: Walker, D. (ed.) Proceedings of 42nd Annual Symposium on Principles of Programming Languages, POPL 2015, pp. 17–30. ACM (2015)
20. Levy, P.B.: Call-By-Push-Value: A Functional/Imperative Synthesis. Semantics Structures in Computation, vol. 2. Springer, Heidelberg (2004)
21. Linton, F.: Coequalizers in categories of algebras. In: Eckmann, B. (ed.) Seminar on Triples and Categorical Homology Theory. Lecture Notes in Mathematics, vol. 80, pp. 75–90. Springer, Heidelberg (1969)
22. Martin-Löf, P.: An intuitionisitc theory of types, predicative part. In: Rose, E., Shepherdson, J.C. (eds.) Proceedings of Logic Colloquium 1973, pp. 73–118. North-Holland (1975)
23. McBride, C.: Functional pearl: Kleisli arrows of outrageous fortune. J. Funct. Program. (To appear)
24. Moggi, E.: Computational lambda-calculus and monads. In: Parikh, R. (ed.) Proceedings of 4th Annual Symposium on Logic in Computer Science, LICS 1989, pp. 14–23. IEEE (1989)
25. Moggi, E.: Notions of computation and monads. Inf. Comput. **93**(1), 55–92 (1991)
26. Nanevski, A., Morrisett, G., Birkedal, L.: Hoare type theory, polymorphism and separation. J. Funct. Program. **18**(5–6), 865–911 (2008)
27. Pitts, A.M.: Categorical logic. In: Abramsky, S., Gabbay, D.M., Maibaum, T.S.E. (eds.) Handbook of Logic in Computer Science. Algebraic and Logical Structures, vol. 5, pp. 39–128. Oxford University Press, Oxford (2000). chap. 2
28. Pitts, A.M., Matthiesen, J., Derikx, J.: A dependent type theory with abstractable names. In: Mackie, I., Ayala-Rincon, M. (eds.) Proceedings of 9th Workshop on Logical and Semantic Frameworks, with Applications, LSFA 2014. ENTCS, vol. 312, pp. 19–50. Elsevier (2015)
29. Plotkin, G.: Pisa notes (on domain theory) (1983)
30. Plotkin, G., Power, J.: Semantics for algebraic operations. In: Brookes, S., Mislove, M. (eds.) Proceedings of 17th Conference on the Mathematical Foundations of Programming Semantics, MFPS XVII. ENTCS, vol. 45, pp. 332–345. Elsevier (2001)
31. Plotkin, G., Power, J.: Notions of computation determine monads. In: Nielsen, M., Engberg, U. (eds.) FOSSACS 2002. LNCS, vol. 2303, pp. 342–356. Springer, Heidelberg (2002)
32. Plotkin, G.D., Pretnar, M.: Handling algebraic effects. Logical Methods Comput. Sci. **9**(4:23), 1–36 (2013). doi:10.2168/LMCS-9(4:23)2013
33. Power, J.: Countable Lawvere theories and computational effects. In: Seda, A.K., Hurley, T., Schellekens, M., an Airchinnigh, M.M., Strong, G.(eds.) Proceedings of 3rd Irish Conference on the Mathematical Foundations of Computer Science and Information Technology, MFCSIT 2004. ENTCS, vol. 161, pp. 59–71. Elsevier (2006)
34. Pretnar, M.: The Logic and Handling of Algebraic Effects. Ph.D. thesis, School of Informatics, University of Edinburgh (2010)

35. Staton, S.: Instances of computational effects: an algebraic perspective. In: Kupferman, O. (ed.) Proceedings of 28th Annual Symposium on Logic in Computer Science, LICS 2013, pp. 519–519. IEEE, June 2013
36. Streicher, T.: Semantics of Type Theory. Birkhäuser, Boston (1991)
37. Swamy, N., Weinberger, J., Schlesinger, C., Chen, J., Livshits, B.: Verifying higher-order programs with the Dijkstra monad. In: Flanagan, C. (ed.) Proceedings of 34th Conference on Programming Language Design and Implementation, PLDI 2013, pp. 387–398. ACM (2013)
38. Vákár, M.: A categorical semantics for linear logical frameworks. In: Pitts, A. (ed.) FOSSACS 2015. LNCS, vol. 9034, pp. 102–116. Springer, Heidelberg (2015)
39. Warren, M.A.: Homotopy Theoretic Aspects of Constructive Type Theory. Ph.D. thesis, Department of Philosophy, Carnegie Mellon University (2008)

Game Semantics for Bounded Polymorphism

James Laird[(⊠)]

Department of Computer Science, University of Bath, Bath, UK
`jiml@cs.bath.ac.uk`

Abstract. We describe a denotational, intensional semantics for programs with polymorphic types with bounded quantification, in which phenomena such as inheritance between stateful objects may be represented and studied. Our model is developed from a game semantics for unbounded polymorphism, by establishing dinaturality properties of generic strategies, and using them to give a new construction for interpreting subtyping constraints and bounded quantification. We use this construction to give a denotational semantics for a programming language with general references and an expressive polymorphic typing system. We show that full abstraction fails in general in this model, but that it holds for all terms at a rich collection of bounded types.

1 Introduction

By combining subtype and parametric polymorphism, type systems with bounded quantification increase the expressive power of both: they may be used to write programs which are generic, but range over a constrained set of types (a program of type $\forall X \leq S.T$ may be instantiated only with a subtype of S). They have been used to develop formal theories of key aspects of object oriented languages such as *inheritance* [6]. Our aim is to develop an *intensional* denotational semantics for subtyping and bounded polymorphism — i.e. a formal semantic account of the constraints on behaviour which can be expressed in such a system. This allows for models which combine bounded polymorphism with computational effects (in particular, state) and, potentially, for semantics-based subtyping theories which capture aspects of program behaviour.

Previous denotational models of bounded quantification have been based on an *extensional* interpretation of polymorphism — for instance by interpreting subtyping as inclusion of *partial equivalence relations* [5] or as a relation between games [8], so that bounded quantification corresponds to a product or intersection over all instances satisfying the bound. This has generated valuable insights into the theory of subtyping and polymorphism, but it is not clear how it may be extended to include computational effects (for example). We take an alternative, more intrinsically *intensional* approach by constructing an interpretation of bounded quantification without first specifying a subtyping relation, beyond the requirement that it gives rise to coercion morphisms between objects: we will subsequently show how to interpret subtyping judgements as such coercions.

© Springer-Verlag Berlin Heidelberg 2016
B. Jacobs and C. Löding (Eds.): FOSSACS 2016, LNCS 9634, pp. 55–70, 2016.
DOI: 10.1007/978-3-662-49630-5_4

Technically, our model is based on the game semantic framework for generic call-by-name polymorphism described in [15] and reviewed and updated in Sect. 2, which develops earlier notions of variable game [1,12] with a new interpretation of quantification as a relation between question and answer moves. In Sect. 3, we extend this framework by showing that context games correspond to mixed variance functors on games, and generic strategies to (composable) *dinatural* transformations between them. In Sect. 4, we use these properties to construct an interpretation of subtyping environments and bounded quantification. The basic idea is to represent a bounded quantification $\forall X \leq S.T(X^-, X^+)$ as an unbounded quantification $\forall X.T(S \times X, X)$, so that negative occurrences of type variables may be coerced into their bounding types by right projection: defining the composition of strategies with free, constrained variables requires precisely the dinaturality properties established in the previous section.

In Sect. 5 we give a semantics for a stateful programming language with a second-order typing system based on Cardelli and Wegner's *Bounded Fun* [6], and its extensively studied fragment, System $F_\leq$ ("F-sub") [7,9] (an extension of the second-order λ-calculus, System F [11,17] with bounded quantification). However, these are pure type theories: the language we study is (in essence) a conservative extension of the metalanguage with general references, and its games model, originally defined (and proposed as a semantic basis for object oriented programs) by Abramsky, Honda and McCusker [3]. Finally, we show that full abstraction does not hold in our model (arguably, due to an expressive deficit in the language and typing system) but holds for a significant fragment determined by a simple constraint on types.

2 Second Order Game Semantics

Our games model is based on a semantics of unbounded "System F - style" polymorphism which is essentially equivalent to that defined in [13,15], with some minor differences in the representation of games (up to these, our model of bounded quantification is a conservative extension). Here we recall and modify the key definitions, referring to [15] for details and proofs.

A *"n-context game"* as defined in [13] is a Hyland-Ong arena — a set of moves partitioned between two players, with a binary *enabling relation* defining a directed, bipartite acyclic graph — with a further partitioning of moves into sets of *questions*, *answers*, and *i-holes* for $i \in \{1, \ldots, n\}$ into which other arenas may be instantiated, and a *scoped question answer/relation* — a ternary relation on moves — $q \triangleright_m a$ means a can answer q within the scope of m — such that Player questions are scoped by Player moves and answered by Opponent moves, and Opponent moves are scoped by Opponent moves and answered by Player moves.

In the following, we will work within a *universal* set of moves in which enabling, labelling of moves and the question/answer relation are determined by a fixed representation — so a context arena may be specified simply by giving a set of moves within this universe (although this is not essential for our model of bounded quantification, it facilitates some constructions).

Definition 1. *Let $\mathcal{A}$ be the set $\mathbb{N} \cup \{l, r\} \cup \{\forall_i \mid i \in \mathbb{N}\}$. Define the universal set of moves $\mathcal{U}$ to be $\{w \bullet_n \mid w \in \mathcal{A}^* \wedge n \in \mathbb{N} \backslash \{0\}\}$ — i.e. a move is a word over $\mathcal{A}$ followed by a terminal symbol $\bullet_n$ for some $n \geq 1$.*

Say that a sequence $w \in \mathcal{A}^*$ is *positive* if it contains an even number of occurrences of the symbol l, and *negative* otherwise. If w is positive, then $w \bullet_i$ is an *Opponent* move, otherwise it is a *Player* move. (Given $X \subseteq \mathcal{U}$, X^+ is the set of Opponent moves and X^- the set of Player moves in X.)

Definition 2. *We define the* enabling relation *$\vdash \subseteq \mathcal{U} \times \mathcal{U}$: $m \vdash n$ if there exist sequences u, v, w with v, w not containing l, such that $m = u \cdot v$ and $n = u \cdot lw$.*

This is evidently a directed, bipartite acyclic graph on $\mathcal{U}$. Source nodes (Opponent moves containing no occurrence of l) are called initial moves.

Definition 3. *Moves are partitioned into* questions, answers, *and* i-holes *as follows:*

- *If $m = v \bullet_i$ where v contains no occurrences of $\forall_i$, then m is an i-hole move.*
- *Otherwise, $m = u \forall_i \cdot v \bullet_i$, for some unique v which contains no occurrences of $\forall_i$. Then m is a* question *if v is negative, and an* answer *if v is positive.*

The (ternary) scoped question/answer relation on moves is defined as follows:

- *$q \triangleright_m a$ if there exists t, u, v, w such that u contains no occurrences of l and u, v, w contain no occurrences of $\forall_i$, and $m = t \forall_i \cdot u$, $q = t \forall_i \cdot v \bullet_i$ and $a = \forall_i \cdot w \bullet_i$.*

Definition 4. *A* game *is a subset $A \subseteq \mathcal{U}$ such that if $u \bullet_i \in A$ is a hole move then u contains no occurrences of $\forall_j$ for $j \leq i$, and if $u \sqsubseteq m \in A$ then $m = u \bullet_i$.*

A is a n-context game if $H_A(i)$ (the set of i-hole moves in A) is empty for $i > n$.

2.1 Examples

Given a n-context game A and element $a \in \mathcal{A}$, we write $a.A$ for $\{am \mid m \in A\}$.

- We denote the empty game (the empty set of moves) by 1.
- For each $i \leq n$, $\{\bullet_i\}$ (or just $\bullet_i$) is the n-context game containing the single (Opponent hole) move $\bullet_i$, corresponding to a free type variable.
- For any indexing set $I \subseteq \mathbb{N}$, the disjoint union $\bigcup_{i \in I} i.A$ corresponds to an indexed product or record type.
- Let $A \Rightarrow B$ denote the game $l.A \cup r.B$ (the disjoint union of A and B, with the initial moves of B becoming enablers for the initial moves of A, and the moves of A switched between Player and Opponent.
- If A is a n-context game, $\forall_n.A$ is a $n-1$-context game; the Opponent i-hole moves of A become questions, scoped by the O-initial moves of A, and the Player i-holes of A become their answers.

In this way, we can interpret an (unbounded) second-order type (in which variables and their binders are represented as occurrences of $\bullet$ and $\forall$ with de Bruijn-style indices) directly as a game in which the moves correspond to the paths through the syntax tree of the type from the root to a leaf node (bound or free variable).

For example, suppose A and B are n-context games. The game $\forall_{n+1}((A \Rightarrow \bullet_{n+1}) \Rightarrow (B \Rightarrow \bullet_{n+1}) \Rightarrow \bullet_{n+1})$ (corresponding to the System F type $\forall X_{n+1}.(A \rightarrow X_{n+1}) \Rightarrow (B \rightarrow X_{n+1}) \rightarrow X_{n+1})$ consists of the initial Opponent question $\forall_{n+1}rr\bullet_{n+1}$, which enables and scopes its two (Player) answers $\forall_{n+1}rlr\bullet_{n+1}$ and $\forall_{n+1}lr\bullet_{n+1}$, and the moves $\forall_{n+1}ll.A$ and $\forall_{n+1}rll.B$, of which the moves of the form $\forall_{n+1}llm$ and $\forall_{n+1}rllm$ where m is initial in A or B respectively, are enabled by $\forall_{n+1}rlr\bullet_{n+1}$ and $\forall_{n+1}lr\bullet_{n+1}$, respectively. In other words, this is the *lifted sum* game [16], used to define a computational monad, and thus a call-by-value semantics in [2], which we will extend with bounded polymorphism.

2.2   Legal Sequences and Strategies

Interaction in the game may be seen as alternately choosing leaf nodes of this syntax tree, according to rules we now describe. Define the *pending question prefix* of a sequence of moves t over a 0-context arena A (if any):

- pending(sq) = sq, if q is a question,
- pending(sa) = pending(s'), if a is an answer, and pending(s) = $s'q$.

Definition 5. *A legal sequence t on A is a finite sequence of moves in A, alternating between Opponent and Player moves, equipped with a unique justification pointer from each non-initial move to a preceding move which enables it, such that:*

- *If $sqs'a \sqsubseteq t$, where q is the pending question in sqs' then there exists a move m in s which hereditarily justifies both q and a, such that $q \vartriangleright_m a$ (the* bracketing *condition).*

t is single threaded *if it contains at most one initial move, in which case any pointers from moves enabled by (and therefore justified by) the initial move are considered* implicit.

A *strategy* for a 0-context game A is a non-empty, even-prefix-closed, even-branching set of single-threaded legal sequences on A. For each n, we define a category $\mathcal{G}(n)$ in which objects are n-context games and morphisms from A to B are strategies on $\forall_1 \ldots \forall_n(A \Rightarrow B)$ (we will also write $\mathcal{G}(0)$ as just $\mathcal{G}$). To define composition in $\mathcal{G}(n)$, we use the following generalised notion of restriction on justified sequences: given a partial function $f : A \rightarrow B$ we may derive a function on sequences over B — $f^* : \mathcal{U}^* \rightarrow \mathcal{U}^*$ applies f pointwise to the moves on which it is defined, and omits moves on which it is not defined. This extends to justified sequences: $f(n)$ points to $f(m)$ in $f^*(s)$ iff $f(m)$ and $f(n)$ are both defined and n points to m in s. Where f is evident from the context, we shall write $s{\upharpoonright}B$ for $f^*(s)$.

Let $\sigma^\dagger$ be the least set of legal sequences containing σ and closed under interleaving. The composition of $\sigma : A \to B$ with $\tau : B \to C$ is defined: $\sigma; \tau = \{s \in L_{\forall(A \Rightarrow C)} \mid \exists t \in A + B + C. t {\upharpoonright} \forall(A \Rightarrow B) \in \sigma^\dagger \wedge t {\upharpoonright} \forall(B \Rightarrow C) \in \tau \wedge s = t {\upharpoonright} \forall(A \Rightarrow C)\}$. The identity on A is the set of copycat sequences $\{t \in L_{\forall(A \Rightarrow A)} \mid \forall s \sqsubseteq^E t. s {\upharpoonright} A^+ = s {\upharpoonright} A^-\}$.

For any n-context games A and B, $A \times B = 0.A \cup 1.B$ is a Cartesian product of A and B in $\mathcal{G}(n)$, and $A \Rightarrow B$ is an internal hom (so $\mathcal{G}(n)$ is a Cartesian closed category). For each n, if A is a n-context game, and B is a $n + 1$ context game, there is an evident isomorphism between the arenas $\forall_{n+1}(A \Rightarrow B)$ and $A \Rightarrow \forall_{n+1}B$, yielding an evident natural correspondence between $\mathcal{G}(n + 1)(J_{n+1}(A), B)$ and $\mathcal{G}(n)(A, \forall_{n+1}.B)$ — i.e. the inclusion $J_{n+1} : \mathcal{G}(n) \to \mathcal{G}(n + 1)$ has $\forall_{n+1}$ as its *right adjoint* [15].

2.3 Instantiation

Let A be a n-context game, and B and C be i-context games, with $i \leq n$. The *instantiation* of B and C into the (negative and positive) i-holes of A (respectively) is defined $A(B, C)_i =:$

$$A \backslash H_A(i) \cup \{w \cdot m \mid w \bullet_i \in H_A(i)^- \wedge m \in B\} \cup \{w \cdot m \mid w \bullet_i \in H_A(i)^+ \wedge m \in C\}.$$

This operation behaves as one would expect for a substitution[1]: e.g. if $A = \bullet_1 \Rightarrow \bullet_1 \Rightarrow \bullet_1$ then $A(B, C)_1 = B \Rightarrow B \Rightarrow C$. Moreover, each morphism in $\mathcal{G}(n)(A, B)$ corresponds to a *generic* family of morphisms from $A(C, C)$ to $B(C, C)$ for each n-context game C. These are defined (as in [15]) using the notion of instantiation of a game into strategy by playing *copycat* between the arenas plugged into the holes. Suppose t is a legal sequence on $\forall(A(C, C)_i \Rightarrow B(C, C)_i)$, such that $t {\upharpoonright} \forall(A \Rightarrow B)$ is a legal sequence, and $sa \sqsubseteq t {\upharpoonright} \forall(A \Rightarrow B)$, where $a = v \bullet_i$ is a Player answer in $\forall(A \Rightarrow B)$ corresponding to a i-hole move in $A \Rightarrow B$. As t is *well bracketed*, $\mathsf{pending}(s) = s'q$ where $q = u \bullet_i$ is an Opponent question in $\forall(A \Rightarrow B)$ corresponding to an i-hole move in $A \Rightarrow B$. So we may define $t {\upharpoonright} (\mathsf{pending}(s), sa)$ to be the projection of t onto $\forall(C \Rightarrow C)$ of moves which are suffixes of u and v (and hereditarily justified by q and a, respectively).

Definition 6. *Given a strategy $\sigma : A \to B$, let $\sigma[C]_i : A(C, C)_i \to B(C, C)_i$ be the set of sequences $t \in L_{\forall(A(C,C)_i \Rightarrow B(C,C)_i)}$ such that $t {\upharpoonright} \forall(A \Rightarrow B) \in \sigma$ and if $sa \sqsubseteq^E t$, where a is a Player i-hole move in $A \Rightarrow B$, then $t {\upharpoonright} (\mathsf{pending}(s), sa)) \in \mathsf{id}_C$.*

As shown in [15], the $\mathcal{G}(n)$ may be organised as an indexed cartesian closed category of context games, in which the J_n and $\forall_i$ form an indexed adjunction. Here we note the following result from *loc. cit.*.

Lemma 1. $\_[C]_i$ *is an endofunctor on $\mathcal{G}(n)$, such that* $\_[C]_i \cdot \_[D]_i = \_[B(C, C)_i]_i$.

---

[1] The condition that i-hole moves contain no occurrence of $\forall_j$ for $j \leq i$ prevents "capture" of the holes.

3   Generic Strategies as Dinatural Transformations

In addition to the structure defined in [15], instantiation also acts on strategies as a (mixed variance) functor (which we will require in order to define our semantics of bounded quantification) in the following sense:

Definition 7. *Given an Opponent hole* $w\bullet_i \in H_A^+(i)$, *let* $p_{w\bullet_i}$ *be the partial projection on moves sending* $\forall lw \cdot n$ *to* $\forall ln$ *and* $\forall rw \cdot n$ *to* $\forall rn$, *so that it projects a move in* $\forall(A(B,C)_i \Rightarrow A(B',C')_i)$ *into* $\forall(C \Rightarrow C')$. *If* $m \in H_A^-(i)$ *is a Player hole move, then let* p_m *be the corresponding projection from* $\forall(A(B,C)_i \Rightarrow A(B',C')_i)$ *into* $\forall(B' \Rightarrow B)$.

Now, given morphisms $\sigma : B' \to B, \tau : C \to C'$ *in* $\mathcal{G}(n)$, *we may define* $A(\sigma,\tau)_i : A(B,C) \to A(B',C')$ *to be the set of even-length sequences* $t \in L_{\forall(A(B,C)\Rightarrow A(B',C'))}$ *such that for all even prefixes* $s \sqsubseteq t$, $s|\forall(A \Rightarrow A) \in \mathrm{id}_A$ *and for any hole move* $m \in H_i^+(A)$, $p_m^*(s) \in \sigma^\dagger$ *and for any* $m \in H_n^-(A)$, $p_m^*(s) \in \tau^\dagger$.

Proposition 1. *For any* n-*context game* A, $A(\_,\_)_i$ *is a functor from* $\mathcal{G}(n)^{op} \times \mathcal{G}(n)$ *to* $\mathcal{G}(n)$.

One might hope that for any generic n-context strategy $\sigma : A \to B$, the family $\{\sigma[C] : A(C,C)_i \to B(C,C)_i\}$ is a *dinatural transformation* [4] from $A(\_,\_)_i$ to $B(\_,\_)_i$ — i.e. that for any morphism $\tau : C \to D$, the following diagram commutes:

$$
\begin{array}{ccc}
& A(C,C) \xrightarrow{\sigma[C]} B(C,C) & \\
A(\tau,C) \nearrow & & \searrow D(C,\tau) \\
A(D,C) & & B(C,D) \\
A(C,\tau) \searrow & & \nearrow A(\tau,D) \\
& A(D,D) \xrightarrow{\sigma[D]} B(D,D) &
\end{array}
$$

However, this is not the case:

Proposition 2. $\sigma[\_]_i$ *is not a dinatural transformation from* $A(\_,\_)_i$ *to* $B(\_,\_)_i$ *in general.*

Proof. Take, for example, $A = \forall_1(\bullet_1 \Rightarrow \bullet_1)$, $B = \bullet_1 \Rightarrow \bullet_1$ and $\sigma : \forall_1(\bullet_1 \Rightarrow \bullet_1) \to (\bullet_1 \to \bullet_1)$ to be the counit of the adjunction $J_1 \dashv \forall_1$ (i.e. the copycat strategy between A and B). At any game, $\perp$ is the strategy containing only the empty sequence. Then $A(\perp,1); \sigma[1]; B(1,\perp) = \perp$, but $A(\bullet_1,\perp); \sigma[\bullet_1]; B(\perp,\bullet_i) \neq \perp$ (it contains a response to the initial move).

The generic strategies (in Hughes' model of System F) which do correspond to dinatural transaformations are characterized in [10], to which we refer for further discussion. Here we take an alternative approach by showing that $\sigma[\_]_i$ *is* dinatural with respect to a subcategory of *linear morphisms*.

Definition 8. *A morphism* $\sigma : A \to B$ *is* linear *if for every initial move m in B there is an initial move m' in A such that $msm' \in \sigma$ if and only if $s = \varepsilon$ (so every non-empty sequence $s \in \sigma$ contains exactly one initial move from A).*

It is easy to see that the composition of linear morphisms is linear, and so for each n we may form a subcategory $\mathcal{G}^L(n)$ of $\mathcal{G}(n)$ consisting of n-context games and linear morphisms, with an inclusion $J_L : \mathcal{G}^L(n) \to \mathcal{G}(n)$. Note that $\times$ is a cartesian product in $\mathcal{G}^L(n)$.

Proposition 3. $\sigma[\_]_i$ *is a dinatural transformation from* $A \cdot J_L$ *to* $B \cdot J_L$.

In other words, for any *linear* morphism $\tau : C \to D$ the dinaturality hexagon does commute. We prove this by defining the instantiation of τ directly into σ, i.e. $\sigma[\tau]_i : A(B,B)_i \to D(C,C)_i$ by replacing the identity on B with τ in Definition 6 and showing that $A(C,\tau)_i; \sigma[C]_i; D(\tau,C)_i$ and $A(\tau,B)_i; \sigma[B]_i; D(B,\tau)_i$ are both equal to $\sigma[\tau]_i$. Although the composition of dinatural transformations is not, in general, dinatural [4], by Proposition 1, those which arise by instantiation of generic strategies do compose.

4   Semantics of Bounded Quantification

We may now use the functors and dinatural transformations derived from instantiation to represent bounded quantification. A subtyping constraint of the form $X_i \leq T$, where X_i is a type variable, corresponds to the ability to subsume any term of type X_i into the type T. Thus, in an environment where such a constraint holds, *negative occurences* of X_i may be represented as the game $[\![T]\!] \times \bullet_i$, from which there is a canonical coercion (left projection) into $[\![T]\!]$. On the other hand, *positive occurrences* of X_i are simply represented as $\bullet_i$ (we can't, for example, decompose X_i into the bound T and an "unknown" extension). The difficulty is to define a notion of composition between morphisms by "unifying" this different treatment of positive and negative occurrences[2]. The key to doing so is the following operation:

Definition 9. *Let A be an $n-1$-context game. Given $\sigma : B(\bullet_n, A \times \bullet_n)_n \to C(A \times \bullet_n, \bullet_n)_n$, define $\hat{\sigma} : B(A \times \bullet_n, A \times \bullet_n)_n \to C(A \times \bullet_n, A \times \bullet_n)_n$ as follows: ($\delta : A \to A \times A = \langle A, A \rangle$).*

$$B(A \times \bullet_n, A \times \bullet_n)_n \xrightarrow{B(A \times \bullet_n, \delta \times \bullet_n)_n} B(A \times \bullet_n, A \times A \times \bullet_n)_n \xrightarrow{\sigma[A \times \bullet_n]_n}$$
$$C(A \times A \times \bullet_n, A \times \bullet_n)_n \xrightarrow{C(\delta \times \bullet_n, A \times \bullet_n)_n} C(A \times \bullet_n, A \times \bullet_n)_n$$

We illustrate by describing a setting corresponding to an environment containing a single constrained type variable. Given a $n-1$-context game A, we may define a category $\mathcal{G}_A$ in which objects are n-context games and morphisms from B to C

---

[2] Representing negative *and* positive occurrences of X_i as $A \times \bullet_i$ leads to a simple interpretation of composition, but to the failure of bounded universal quantification to be antitone in type bounds — i.e. we get a model of *"kernel* $F_\leq$*"* [6].

are the morphisms from $B(\bullet_n, A \times \bullet_n)$ to $C(A \times \bullet_n, \bullet_n)$ in $\mathcal{G}$. The composition of $\sigma \in \mathcal{G}_A(B, C)$ with $\tau \in \mathcal{G}_A(C, D)$ is the composition of $B(\pi_r, A \times \bullet); \widehat{\sigma} : B(\bullet_n, A \times \bullet_n) \to C(A \times \bullet_n, A \times \bullet_n)$ with $\widehat{\tau}; D(A \times \bullet_n, \pi_r) : C(A \times \bullet_n, A \times \bullet_n) \to D(A \times \bullet_n, \bullet_n)$ in $\mathcal{G}$. The identity on B in $\mathcal{G}_A$ is $B(\pi_r, \pi_r)$.

Lemma 2. *The operation* $\widehat{(\_)}$ *satisfies the following properties:*

1. $B\widehat{(\pi_r, \pi_r)} = B(A \times \bullet, A \times \bullet)$.
2. *For* $\sigma : B(\bullet, A \times \bullet) \to C(A \times \bullet, \bullet)$, $\sigma = B(\pi_r, A \times \bullet); \widehat{\sigma}; C(A \times \bullet, \pi_r)$.
3. *For* $\tau : C(\bullet, A \times \bullet) \to D(A \times \bullet, \bullet)$, $\widehat{\sigma}; \widehat{\tau} = B(\pi_r, A \times \bullet); \widehat{\sigma; \widehat{\tau}}; D(A \times \bullet, \pi_r)$.

Proposition 4. $\mathcal{G}_A$ *is a well-defined category.*

Proof. That $B(\pi_r, \pi_r)$ is an identity follows from Lemma 2 (1). For associativity of composition, suppose $\rho \in \mathcal{G}_A(B, C)$, $\sigma \in \mathcal{G}_A(C, D)$ and $\tau \in \mathcal{G}_A(D, E)$. Then $(\rho; \sigma); \tau = B(\pi_r, A \times \bullet); B(\pi_r, A \times \bullet); \widehat{\rho; \widehat{\sigma}}; C(A \times \bullet, \pi_r); \widehat{\tau}; D(\pi_r, A \times \bullet, \pi_r)$. By Lemma 2 (3), this is equal to $B(\pi_r, A \times \bullet); \widehat{\rho}; \widehat{\sigma}; \widehat{\tau}; E(\pi_r, A \times \bullet, \pi_r)$, which is similarly equal to $\rho; (\sigma; \tau)$.

We also have operations on $\mathcal{G}_A$ corresponding to bounded quantification and instantiation: let $\forall^A C = \forall. C(A \times \bullet, \bullet)$. Then for any 0-context game B, there is an evident isomorphism of arenas between $\forall (B \Rightarrow C(A \times \bullet, \bullet))$ and $D \Rightarrow \forall^A C$ yielding:

Proposition 5. *The inclusion* $J_A : \mathcal{G} \to \mathcal{G}_A$ *is left adjoint to* $\forall^A : \mathcal{G}_A \to \mathcal{G}$.

Definition 10. *Given a 0-context arena* D, *and a linear morphism* $c : D \to A$, *representing a coercion of* D *into* A, *we define the* bounded instantiation *functor sending* $\sigma : B \to C$ *to* $\sigma\{c, D\} : B(D, D) \to C(D, D)$:

$$B(D, D) \xrightarrow{B(D, \langle c, D \rangle)} B(D, A \times D) \xrightarrow{\sigma[D]} C(D \times A, D) \xrightarrow{C(\langle c, D \rangle, D)} C(D, D)$$

Proposition 6. $\_\{c, D\}$ *is a (Cartesian closed) functor from* $\mathcal{G}_A$ *to* $\mathcal{G}$.

We iterate these constructions to define categories of context games for representing types with multiple bounded free variables.

Definition 11. *A* bounding sequence *of context games* $A_1, \ldots, A_n$ *is one in which each* A_i *is a* $i-1$*-context game. Given such a sequence, we define categories* $\mathcal{G}(n)_{A_1, \ldots, A_i}$ *(and its subcategory* $\mathcal{G}(n)^L_{A_1, \ldots, A_i}$*) for each* $i \leq n$, *in which objects are* n*-context games and:*

- $\mathcal{G}(n)_\varepsilon = \mathcal{G}(n)$.
- *In* $\mathcal{G}(n)_{A_1, \ldots, A_{i+1}}$, *morphisms from* B *to* C *are the morphisms from* $B(\bullet_i, A_{i+1} \times \bullet_{i+1})_{i+1}$ *to* $C(A_{i+1} \times \bullet_{i+1}, \bullet_{i+1})$ *in* $\mathcal{G}(n)_{A_1, \ldots, A_i}$, *with the composition of* $\sigma : B \to C$ *with* $\tau : C \to D$ *defined to be the composition of* $B(\pi_r, A_{i+1} \times \bullet_{i+1})_{i+1}; \widehat{\sigma}_i$ *with* $\widehat{\tau}_i; C(A_{i+1} \times \bullet_i, \pi_r)$ *in* $\mathcal{G}(n)_{A_1, \ldots, A_i}$. *The identity on* B *is* $B(\pi_r, \pi_r)_1, \ldots, (\pi_r, \pi_r)_{i+1}$.

Proof (by induction) that each $\mathcal{G}_{A_1,\ldots,A_i}$ is a (Cartesian closed) category follows the proof of Proposition 4 above. For any bounding sequence $A_1,\ldots,A_n,B$ we have a right adjoint $\forall^B_{n+1}$: to the inclusion functor $J^B_{n+1} : \mathcal{G}(n)_{A_1,\ldots,A_n} \to \mathcal{G}(n+1)_{A_1,\ldots,A_n,B}$.

Definition 12. *For any $i < n$, i-context game C and $c \in \mathcal{G}(n)^L_{A_1,\ldots,A_{i-1}}(C, A_i)$, the instantiation functor $_-\{c, C\}_i$ from $\mathcal{G}(n)_{A_1,\ldots,A_i}$ to $\mathcal{G}(n)_{A_1,\ldots,A_{i-1}}$ sends D to $D(C,C)_{n+1}$ and $\sigma : D \to E$ to $D(C, \langle c, C\rangle)_i; \sigma[C]_i; E(\langle c, C\rangle, C)_i$. This lifts to a functor from $\mathcal{G}(n+1)_{A_1,\ldots,A_n}$ to $\mathcal{G}(n)_{A_1,\ldots,A_{i-1},A_{i+1}(A_i,A_i),\ldots,A_j(A_i,A_i)}$ for each $n \geq j > i$, since e.g. $D(A_j \times \bullet_j, \bullet_j)(C,C)_i = D(C,C)_i(A_j(C,C)_i \times \bullet_j, \bullet_j)$*

Instantiation preserves cartesian closed structure, and also commutes with the second-order structure, in the following sense:

Proposition 7. $_-\{c, C\}_i \cdot \forall^A_j = \forall^{A(C,C)}_j \cdot _-\{c, C\}_i$.

5 A Stateful Language with Bounded Quantification

So far, we have described subtyping constraints on variables, and bounded quantification, without explicitly defining or discussing the semantics of the subtyping relation on games, beyond the assumption that it yields a coercing linear morphism from a subtype to its supertype. In this sense, our semantics is somewhat independent of any particular notion of subtyping, which can be supplied either *intensionally*, by a formal system of derivations for subtyping judgments with their interpretation as coercing morphisms, or *extensionally*, arising from a relation on objects in our category with a corresponding notion of coercion (for example, Chroboczek's notion of subtyping for games [8]). Taking the former approach, our interpretation of subtyping constraints, bounded quantification and instantiation is sufficient to model typing systems such as Cardelli and Wegner's *Fun* [6] or System $\text{F}_\leq$[7]. However, since we also wish to describe the behaviour of (possibly side effecting) programs in this context, we define a stateful, call-by-value metalanguage, $\mathcal{L}_\leq$, with such a typing system. (The main difference with respect to $\text{F}_\leq$ as a typing system is the inclusion of explicit object (i.e. record) types: although record types can be encoded in $\text{F}_\leq$, the semantics of this encoding in our model is not faithful to the direct interpretation of such types as products).

In essence, $\mathcal{L}_\leq$ and its model are an extension with subtyping and bounded quantification of the metalanguage with general references, $\mathcal{L}$, defined with its games model by Abramsky, Honda and McCusker [3] (from which there is a simple translation into $\mathcal{L}_\leq$). Raw types of $\mathcal{L}_\leq$ are generated by the grammar:

$$S ::= \text{unit} \mid \text{nat} \mid S \to O \mid \forall X \leq O.O \qquad\qquad O ::= X \mid [l_1 : S_1, \ldots, l_n : S_n]$$

(where the l_i are drawn from an unbounded collection of labels). Type variables are restricted to range over the (concrete and variable) *object types* O, which are assigned to records containing (possibly side-effecting) methods typed according to the values they may return. We can wrap any method type S in an object type $[S]$ with a single field, for which we omit the label (corresponding to the lifting operation of the computational λ-calculus), and "thunk" an object type O as the method type $Q = \texttt{unit} \to O$. Judgments $\Sigma \vdash T$ (T is a well-formed type with free variables in Σ) are derived via the rules:

Table 1. Subtyping judgments for $\mathcal{L}_{\leq}$

$$\frac{}{\Sigma,X,\Sigma' \vdash X} \qquad \frac{}{\Sigma : B} \qquad \frac{\Sigma \vdash S_1,\ldots,\Sigma \vdash S_n}{\Sigma \vdash [l_1 : S_1,\ldots,l_n : S_n]} \qquad \frac{\Sigma \vdash S \quad \Sigma \vdash O}{\Sigma \vdash S \to O} \qquad \frac{\Sigma \vdash O \quad \Sigma, X \vdash P}{\Sigma \vdash \forall X \leq O.P}$$

$$\frac{|\Theta| \vdash T}{\Theta \vdash T \leq T} \qquad \frac{\Theta \vdash T \leq T' \quad \Theta \vdash T' \leq T''}{\Theta \vdash T \leq T''} \qquad \frac{\Theta \vdash S_1 \leq S'_1 \ldots \Theta \vdash S_m \leq S'_m \quad m \leq n}{\Theta \vdash [l_1 : S_1,\ldots,l_n : S_n] \leq [l_1 : S'_1,\ldots,l_m : S'_m]}$$

$$\frac{}{\Theta, X \leq O, \Theta' \vdash X \leq O} \qquad \frac{\Theta \vdash S' \leq S \quad \Theta \vdash O \leq O'}{\Theta \vdash S \to O \leq S' \to O'} \qquad \frac{\Theta \vdash O' \leq O \quad \Theta, X \leq O \vdash P \leq P'}{\Theta \vdash \forall X \leq O.P \leq \forall X \leq O'.P'}$$

Table 2. Typing judgments for $\mathcal{L}_{\leq}$

$$\frac{}{\Theta; \Gamma, x : S, \Gamma' \vdash x : S} \qquad \frac{\Theta; \Gamma \vdash M : O \quad \Theta \vdash O \leq O'}{\Theta; \Gamma \vdash M : O'}$$

$$\frac{\Theta; \Gamma, x : S \vdash M : O}{\Theta; \Gamma \vdash \lambda x^S.M : S \to O} \qquad \frac{\Theta; \Gamma \vdash M : S \to O \quad \Theta; \Gamma \vdash N : S}{\Theta; \Gamma \vdash M\,N : O}$$

$$\frac{\Theta; \Gamma \vdash M_1 : S_1,\ldots,\Theta; \Gamma \vdash M_1 : S_n}{\Theta; \Gamma \vdash \{l_1 = M_1,\ldots,l_n = M_n\} : [l_1 : S_1,\ldots,l_n : S_n]} \qquad \frac{\Theta; \Gamma \vdash M : [l_1 : S_1,\ldots,l_n : S_n]}{\Theta; \Gamma \vdash M.l_i : S_i}$$

$$\frac{\Theta, X \leq O; \Gamma \vdash M : P}{\Theta; \Gamma \vdash \Lambda X \leq O.M : \forall X \leq O.P} X \notin FV(\Gamma) \qquad \frac{\Theta; \Gamma \vdash M : \forall X \leq O.P \quad \Theta \vdash O' \leq O}{\Theta; \Gamma \vdash M\{O'\} : P[O'/X]}$$

A *subtyping context* is a sequence of subtyping assumptions $X_1 \leq O_1,\ldots,X_n \leq O_n$ such that $X_1,\ldots,X_{i-1} \vdash O_i$ for each $1 \leq i \leq n$. $|X_1 \leq O_1,\ldots,X_n \leq O_n|$ is the sequence $X_1,\ldots,X_n$. *Subtyping judgments* $\Theta \vdash T \leq T'$ — where $\Theta = X_1 \leq O_1,\ldots,X_n \leq O_n$ is a subtyping context and $|\Theta| \vdash T$ and $|\Theta| \vdash T'$ — are derived according to the rules in Table 1. Note that there is a $\leq$-greatest object type — the record type with no labels, for which we will write $\top$. So (as in $F_{\leq}$) we can represent unbounded quantification $\forall X.O$ as $\forall X \leq \top.O$. There is no greatest method type, however. Nor do we capture inclusion of values in the subtyping relation, but leave it as a possible extension. The point is that the distinction between subtyping as inclusion of values, versus extension of records, which is blurred in the pure type theory $F_{\leq}$, becomes necessarily more significant in a setting with side effects. We define the type $\texttt{var}[S]$ of variables storing values of type S to be the object type with two methods, $[\texttt{get} : S, \texttt{set} : S \to [\texttt{unit}]]$.

Typing judgments $\Theta; \Gamma \vdash M : T$ — where Θ is a subtyping context, Γ is a sequence of typing assumptions $x_1 : S_1, \ldots, x_n : S_n$ and T is a type such that $|\Theta| \vdash S_1, \ldots, S_n, T$ — are derived according to the rules in Table 2 extended with constants for arithmetic, conditional branching ($\mathtt{If0}_S : \mathtt{nat} \to [S \to [S \to [S]]]$) and reference declaration ($\mathtt{new}_S : \mathtt{var}[S]$).

The operational semantics of $\mathcal{L}_<$ is based on that given for $\mathcal{L}$ in [3]. We extend the language with an unbounded set of constants $a, b, \ldots$ representing location names, and define the *values* of this extended language by the grammar:

$$V ::= \mathtt{n} \mid a \mid a.\mathtt{set} \mid \{l_1 = M_1, \ldots, l_n = M_n\} \mid \lambda x.M \mid \Lambda X.M$$

An environment $\mathcal{E}$ is a pair of a set of location names, and a partial function from this to the set of values. The evaluation relation $\Downarrow$ between pairs $(M, \mathcal{S})$ of a closed term and environment and $(V, \mathcal{S}')$ of a value and environment is defined in Table 3.

Table 3. Operational semantics for $\mathcal{L}_\le$

$$\frac{}{V,\mathcal{S}\Downarrow V,\mathcal{S}} \qquad \frac{M,\mathcal{S}\Downarrow\mathrm{suc}(\mathrm{n}),\mathcal{S}'}{\mathrm{pred}(M),\mathcal{S}\Downarrow\mathrm{n},\mathcal{S}'}$$

$$\frac{M,\mathcal{S}\Downarrow 0,\mathcal{S}'}{\mathtt{If0}_S\, M,\mathcal{S}\Downarrow\{\lambda x.\{\lambda y.\{x\}\}\},\mathcal{S}'} \qquad \frac{M,\mathcal{S}\Downarrow\mathrm{suc}(n),\mathcal{S}'}{\mathtt{If0}_S\, M,\mathcal{S}\Downarrow\{\lambda x^S.\{\lambda y^S.\{y\}\}\},\mathcal{S}'}$$

$$\frac{M,\mathcal{S}\Downarrow\lambda x^S.M',\mathcal{S} \quad N,\mathcal{S}'\Downarrow U,\mathcal{S}'' \quad M'[U/x],\mathcal{S}''\Downarrow V,\mathcal{S}'''}{M\,N,\mathcal{S}\Downarrow V,\mathcal{S}'''}$$

$$\frac{M,\mathcal{S}\Downarrow\{l_1=N_1,\ldots,l_k=N_k\},\mathcal{S}' \quad N_i,\mathcal{S}'\Downarrow U,\mathcal{S}''}{M.l_i,\mathcal{S}\Downarrow U,\mathcal{S}''}$$

$$\frac{M,\mathcal{S}\Downarrow\Lambda X{\le}O.M',\mathcal{S}' \quad M'[P/X],\mathcal{S}'\Downarrow V,\mathcal{S}''}{M\{P\},\mathcal{S}\Downarrow V,\mathcal{S}''}$$

$$\frac{}{\mathtt{new},\mathcal{S}\Downarrow a,\mathcal{S}\cup\{a\}}\,a\notin\mathcal{S} \qquad \frac{M,\mathcal{S}\Downarrow a,\mathcal{S}'}{M.\mathtt{get},\mathcal{S}\Downarrow V,\mathcal{S}'}\,\mathcal{S}'(a)=V$$

$$\frac{M,\mathcal{S}\Downarrow a,\mathcal{S}'}{M.\mathtt{set},\mathcal{S}\Downarrow a.\mathtt{set},\mathcal{S}'} \qquad \frac{M,\mathcal{S}\Downarrow a.\mathtt{set},\mathcal{S}' \quad N,\mathcal{S}'\Downarrow V,\mathcal{S}''}{M\,N,\mathcal{S}\Downarrow\{()\},\mathcal{S}''[a\mapsto V]}$$

5.1 Denotational Semantics

The denotational semantics of $\mathcal{L}_\le$ extends the games interpretation of references [3] with our model of bounded quantification. We define the denotations of types and the subtyping relation first.

Following [2,3], we will interpret method types as *indexed families* of games. That is, we interpret types with n free variables in the category $\mathsf{Fam}(\mathcal{G}(n))$

(the coproduct completion of $\mathcal{G}(n)$) in which objects are set-indexed families of objects of $\mathcal{G}(n)$, and morphisms from $\{A_i \mid i \in I\}$ to $\{B_j \mid j \in J\}$ are pairs $(f : I \to J, \{\sigma_i : A_i \to A_{f(i)} \mid i \in I\}$ of a reindexing function and an indexed family of morphisms from $\mathcal{G}(n)$). $\mathsf{Fam}(\mathcal{G}(n))$ is Cartesian closed and has (small) coproducts [2]. Defining $\Sigma\{A_i \mid i \in I\} = \forall_{n+1}(\Pi_{i \in I} J_{n+1}(A_i) \Rightarrow \bullet_{n+1}) \Rightarrow \bullet_{n+1}$ (as already observed in Sect. 2, this is concretely the same as the "lifted sum" construction used to interpret $\mathcal{L}$ in [3]) we have [15]:

Proposition 8. *Inclusion of $\mathcal{G}^L(n)$ in $\mathsf{Fam}(\mathcal{G}(n))$ is right adjoint to Σ_-.*

This yields a strong monad on $\mathsf{Fam}(\mathcal{G}(n))$. Object types are interpreted as objects of $\mathcal{G}(n)$ and method types as objects of $\mathsf{Fam}(\mathcal{G}(n))$, as follows:

$$[\![\mathtt{nat}]\!]_n = \{1 \mid i \in \mathbb{N}\} \qquad\qquad [\![\mathtt{unit}]\!] = \{1\}$$
$$[\![[l_1 : S_1, \ldots, l_m : S_m]]\!]_n = \Pi_{i \leq m} \Sigma[\![S_i]\!]_n \qquad [\![S \to O]\!]_n = [\![S]\!]_n \Rightarrow \{[\![O]\!]_n\}$$
$$[\![X_i]\!]_n = \bullet_i \qquad\qquad [\![\forall X_{n+1} \leq O.P]\!]_n = \forall_n^{[\![O]\!]} [\![P]\!]_{n+1}$$

Subtyping contexts $X_1 \leq O_1, \ldots, X_n \leq O_n$ are interpreted as the corresponding bounding sequences $[\![O_1]\!]_0, \ldots, [\![O_n]\!]_{n-1}$, and *subtyping judgments* $\Theta \vdash T \leq T'$ are interpreted as linear coercing morphisms from T to T' in $\mathsf{Fam}(\mathcal{G}^L_{[\![\Theta]\!]})$. The key point here is that while $\Theta \vdash T \leq T'$ may have multiple derivations, they all correspond to the same morphism.

Table 4. Denotational semantics of subyping judgments

$$[\![\Theta \vdash T \leq T]\!] = \mathrm{id}_{[\![T]\!]}$$
$$[\![\Theta \vdash T \leq T'']\!] = [\![\Theta \vdash T \leq T']\!]; [\![\Theta \vdash T' \leq T'']\!]$$
$$[\![\Theta, X \leq O, \Theta' \vdash X \leq O]\!] = J_{\Theta'}(\pi_l)$$
$$[\![\Theta \vdash [l_1 : S_1, \ldots, l_n : S_n] \leq [l_1 : T_1, \ldots, l_m : T_m]]\!] = \langle \pi_1; [\![\Theta \vdash S_1 \leq T_1]\!], \ldots, \pi_m; [\![\Theta \vdash S_m \leq T_m]\!]\rangle$$
$$[\![\Theta \vdash S \to O \leq S' \to O']\!] = [\![\Theta \vdash S' \leq S]\!] \to [\![\Theta \vdash O \leq O']\!]_\Theta$$
$$[\![\Theta \vdash \forall X_{n+1} \leq O.P \leq \forall X \leq O'.P']\!] = [\![P]\!][[\![\Theta \vdash O' \leq O]\!] \times \bullet_{n+1}]\{[\![\Theta, X_{n+1} \leq O \vdash P \leq P']\!]\}$$

Proposition 9. *For any derivable subtyping judgment $\Theta \vdash T \leq T'$, there is a unique morphism $[\![\Theta \vdash T \leq T']\!]$ satisfying the rules in Table 4.*

Proof. We define a notion of *canonical derivation* for subtyping judgments by replacing the transitivity and reflexivity rules with:

$$\frac{}{\Theta \vdash X \leq X} \qquad\qquad \frac{\Theta, X \leq O, \Theta' \vdash O \leq O'}{\Theta, X \leq O \vdash X \leq O'}$$

(This is essentially Curien and Ghelli's deterministic system for deriving subtyping judgments for $F_\leq$ [9].) We then prove that every derivation is denotationally equivalent to a canonical derivation.

5.2 Semantics of Terms

Terms in context are interpreted as morphisms in $\mathsf{Fam}(\mathcal{G}_{[\![\Theta]\!]})$ — terms of method type $\Theta; \Gamma \vdash M : S$ denote morphisms from $[\![\Gamma]\!]$ to $\Sigma[\![S]\!]$, and terms $\Theta; \Gamma \vdash M : O$

of object type denote morphisms from $[\![\Gamma]\!]$ to $[\![O]\!]$. The operations of $\mathcal{L}$ are interpreted as in the computational λ-calculus, and the constant **new** as the reference cell strategy defined in [3], while subsumption, universal quantification and instantiation are interpreted as follows:

$$[\![\Theta; \Gamma \vdash M : O']\!] = [\![\Theta; \Gamma \vdash M : O]\!]; [\![\Theta \vdash O \leq O']\!]$$
$$[\![\Theta; \Gamma \vdash M : \forall X \leq O.P]\!] = \forall_{[\![O]\!]_\Theta} [\![\Theta, X \leq O; \Gamma \vdash M : P]\!]$$
$$[\![\Theta; \Gamma \vdash M\{O'\} : P[O'/X]]\!] = [\![\Theta; \Gamma \vdash M : \forall X \leq O.P]\!] \{[\![\Theta \vdash O' \leq O]\!], [\![O']\!]_{|\Theta|}\}$$

As in the semantics of subtyping judgments, these rules show how to interpret each *derivation* of a typing judgment as a morphism. We need to show that any derivation for a given term in context yields the same denotation.

Proposition 10. *For any derivable typing judgment* $\Theta; \Gamma \vdash M : T$, *there is a unique morphism* $[\![\Theta; \Gamma \vdash M : T]\!]$.

Proof. This follows the proof in [5]. Use of the subsumption rule generates multiple derivations of the same typing judgment, which are shown to be equivalent by extending the language with a constant convert : $\forall X.[\forall Y \leq X.\underline{Y} \to X]$ (denoting the corresponding coercion), and replacing all uses of the subsumption rule with explicit coercions using convert. Using the (di)naturality properties of convert, we show that any two terms which correspond to the same term of $\mathcal{L}_\leq$ obtained by erasing all occurrences of convert have the same denotation.

We prove *soundness* of the operational rules using the properties of the computational λ-calculus, the equations relating the cell strategy to declaration, assignment and derefering in $\mathcal{L}$ [3] together with the properties of our semantics of bounded quantification (i.e. β-reduction for type-instantiation, which follows from Proposition 7).

Proposition 11. *If* $M, \_ \Downarrow V; \mathcal{S}$ *then* $[\![M]\!] \neq \bot$.

We prove *computational adequacy* using the approach described in [15]: defining an approximating semantics in which each cell can be accessed a bounded number of times, for which adequacy follows from the soundness of the operational rules by induction; this implies adequacy for the unbounded semantics by continuity.

Proposition 12 (Computational Adequacy). $[\![M]\!] \neq \bot$ *implies* $M \Downarrow$.

Let $\lesssim_T$ be the *observational preorder* at on closed terms of (closed) type T induced by the operational semantics — i.e. $M \lesssim_T N$ if and only if for all contexts $C[\_ : T]$, $C[M] \Downarrow$ implies $C[N] \Downarrow$. (Note that if $S \leq T$, terms may be observationally equivalent at type T but not at type S.) By a standard argument from adequacy:

Corollary 1. *If* $[\![M : T]\!] \subseteq [\![N : T]\!]$ *then* $M \lesssim_T N$.

6   Full Abstraction

We now consider how closely our model reflects the observational preorder and equivalence. First, we give a full abstraction result for a type-restricted fragment of the language. Define the *concretely bounded types* by the following grammar:

$$S :: B \mid S \to O \mid \forall X \leq [l_1 : S_1, \ldots, l_n : S_n].O \qquad O ::= X \mid [l_1 : S, \ldots, l_n : S]$$

That is, we require that quantification bounds are not type variables. This is a significant constraint — it prevents the inheritance between variable types from being represented directly as a subtyping assumption — but leaves an expressive typing system.

Proof that every finite strategy over a concretely bounded type is definable as a term closely follows the decomposition argument given in [15] for unbounded polymorphism (System F) with general references. The reason for the restriction on types is that we can eliminate negatively occuring concretely bounded quantifiers by instantiating them with a type which extends their bound with a single method of type unit — i.e. given a strategy $\sigma : [\![\forall X \leq [l_1 : T_1, \ldots, l_n : T_n].O]\!] \to [\![T]\!]$, we can find a strategy $\sigma' : [\![O[[l_1 : T_1, \ldots, l_n : T_n, l' : \text{unit}]/X]\!]\!] \to [\![T]\!]$ such that if σ' is the denotation of a term $x : [O[[l_1 : T_1, \ldots, l_n : T_n, l' : \text{unit}]/X]\!] \vdash M : T$, then σ is the denotation of $y : \forall X \leq [l_1 : T_1, \ldots, l_n : T_n] \vdash M[y\{[l_1 : T_1, \ldots, l_n : T_n, l' : \text{unit}]/x]$. Using this property, in conjunction with the decomposition argument given in [15], we may show that:

Proposition 13. *For any concretely bounded type T, context Γ and subtyping context Θ, each finite strategy $\sigma : [\![\Gamma]\!]_\Theta \to [\![T]\!]_\Theta$ is the denotation of a term $\Theta; \Gamma \vdash M : T$.*

This is sufficient to establish full abstraction at concretely bounded types, following the argument from finite definability in [3]. For any strategy σ, let $\text{comp}(\sigma)$ be the *complete plays* (sequences with no unanswered questions) of σ.

Theorem 1. *For any terms $M, N : T$, where T is a concretely bounded type, $M \lesssim_T N$ if and only if $\text{comp}([\![M]\!]) \subseteq \text{comp}([\![N]\!])$.*

Finally, we give a counterexample showing that full abstraction does not hold at all types. Consider the strategy consisting of prefixes of the sequence:

$$
\begin{array}{ccccc}
\forall_1^\top (\forall_2^{\bullet_1}.\Sigma & (\bullet_2 & \Rightarrow & \bullet_2)) & \Rightarrow & \Sigma 1) \\
& & & & & O_Q \\
P_Q & & & & & \\
O_A & & & & & \\
& O_A & & P_Q & & \\
& & & & & P_A
\end{array}
$$

This strategy is not the denotation of any term $X \leq \top; x : S \vdash M : [\text{unit}]$, where $S(X) = \forall Y \leq X.[\underline{Y} \to Y]$. Informally, if M calls x then it must instantiate it with a subtype of X — in the absence of further subtyping assumptions this must be X itself, giving an object of type $[\underline{X} \to X]$. But M cannot use such a method, as X is unbounded and does not occur anywhere else among its types. Formally, we observe that:

Lemma 3. *For any term* $x : S \vdash M : O$, *where* X *does not occur in* Γ, O
$$[\![\Gamma, x : S \vdash M : O]\!] = [\![\Gamma, x : S \vdash M[\Lambda Y.[\bot]/x] : O]\!]$$

From this we may derive a counterexample to full abstraction. Let $T = \forall X \leq \top.[(S \to [\text{unit}]) \to [\text{unit}]]$ and consider the terms $M = \lambda f^T.f\{\top\}\Lambda Y.[\bot]$ and $N = \lambda f^T.f\{\top\}\Lambda Y.[\lambda y^{\underline{Y}}.(y())]$ of type T. Evidently, $M \lesssim_T N$, moreover the inclusion of $[\![M]\!]$ in $[\![N]\!]$ in the games model at this type is strict — they are separated by playing against the strategy defined above.

Proposition 14. M_1 *and* M_2 *are observationally equivalent at* $T \to [\text{unit}]$.

Proof. It is sufficient to show that for any term $V = \Lambda X.\lambda x.M : T$, $V\{\top\}$ $\Lambda Y.\lambda y^Y.y$ is equivalent to $V\{\top\}\Lambda Y.\lambda y^Y.\bot$. This follows from Lemma 3, since M is (denotationally and thus observationally) equivalent to $M[\Lambda Y.[\bot]/x]$.

Arguably, this example shows up an expressive deficit in $\mathcal{L}_\leq$ (and similar type theories for bounded quantification such as $F_\leq$): it does not allow the *extension* of a variable type X with further methods to create a new subtype of X — in the absence of further assumptions, the only subtype of X is X itself, even though X represents an object which could be extended with new fields.

7   Further Directions

Avenues for further research include:

- Our model for bounded quantification has some quite general aspects, being based on a model of unbounded quantification in which morphisms correspond to composable dinatural transformations. A systematic account of this construction, and its coherence properties remains to be given.
- $\mathcal{L}_\leq$ could be seen as a more general system with polymorphism at value (method) types, extending the unbounded case [14]. Subtyping for such types is based on inclusion of their values, sucggesting that quantifiecation is bounded *below* (e.g. by the empty type).
- Extension of the full abstraction result to all types, by allowing the extension of a variable type with further methods. This would appear to require the capacity to declare new method labels, suggesting a role for *nominal games*.
- An open problem is to give a directly defined subtyping relation on games which captures all subtyping judgments of $\mathcal{L}_\leq$ (or $F_\leq$ itself). This appears feasible, notwithstanding the undecidability of subtyping in $F_\leq$ (which extends readily to $\mathcal{L}_\leq$), since such a relation need not precisely coincide with subtyping in $F_\leq$— for example, the types $\top$ and $S \Rightarrow \top$ are syntactically distinct, but semantically equivalent.

Acknowledgements. Research supported by EPSRC grant EP/K037633/1.

References

1. Abramsky, S., Jagadeesan, R.: A game semantics for generic polymorphism. Ann. Pure Appl. Logic **133**(1), 3–37 (2004)
2. Abramsky, S., McCusker, G.: Call-by-value games. In: Nielsen, M., Thomas, W. (eds.) CSL 1997. LNCS, vol. 1414, pp. 1–17. Springer, Heidelberg (1998)
3. Abramsky, S., Honda, K., McCusker, G.: A fully abstract games semantics for general references. In: Proceedings of the 13th Annual Symposium on Logic in Computer Science, LICS 1998, IEEE Press (1998)
4. Bainbridge, E.S., Freyd, P.J., Scedrov, A., Scott, P.J.: Functorial polymorphism. Theor. Comput. Sci. **70**(1), 35–64 (1990)
5. Bruce, K., Longo, G.: A modest model of records, inheritance and bounded quantification. Inf. Comput. **87**(1/2), 196–240 (1990)
6. Cardelli, L., Wegner, P.: On understanding types, data abstraction and polymorphism. Comput. Surv. **17**(4), 471–522 (1985)
7. Cardelli, L., Mitchell, J.C., Martini, S., Scedrov, A.: An extension of System F with subtyping. Inf. Comput. **109**(1–2), 4–56 (1994)
8. Chroboczek, J.: Game semantics and subtyping. In: Proceedings of the Fifteenth Annual Symposium on Logic in Computer Science, pp. 192–203. IEEE press (2000)
9. Curien, P.-L., Ghelli, G.: Coherence of subsumption, minimum typing and typechecking in F. Math. Struct. Comput. Sci. **2**(1), 55–91 (1992)
10. de Lataillade, J.: Dinatural terms in System F. In: Proceedings of the 24th Annual Symposium on Logic in Computer Science, LICS 2009, IEEE Press (2009)
11. Girard, J.-Y.: Linear logic. Theor. Comput. Sci. **50**, 1–102 (1987)
12. Hughes, D.: Games and definability for System F. In: Proceedings of the Twelfth International Syposium on Logic in Computer Science, LICS 1997, IEEE Computer Society Press (1997)
13. Laird, J.: Game semantics for a polymorphic programming language. In: Proceedings of LICS 2010, IEEE Press (2010)
14. Laird, J.: Game semantics for call-by-value polymorphism. In: Abramsky, S., Gavoille, C., Kirchner, C., Meyer auf der Heide, F., Spirakis, P.G. (eds.) ICALP 2010. LNCS, vol. 6199, pp. 187–198. Springer, Heidelberg (2010)
15. Laird, J.: Game semantics for a polymorphic programming language. J. ACM **60**(4) (2013)
16. McCusker, G.: Games and full abstraction for a functional metalanguage with recursive types. Ph.D. thesis, Imperial College London, Published by Cambridge University Press (1996)
17. Reynolds, J.C.: Towards a theory of type structure. In: Robinet, B. (ed.) Programming Symposium. Lecture Notes in Computer Science, vol. 19, pp. 408–425. Springer, Heidelberg (1974)

Recursion and Fixed-Points

Join Inverse Categories as Models of Reversible Recursion

Holger Bock Axelsen and Robin Kaarsgaard[(✉)]

DIKU, Department of Computer Science, University of Copenhagen,
Copenhagen, Denmark
{funkstar,robin}@di.ku.dk

Abstract. Recently, a number of reversible functional programming languages have been proposed. Common to several of these is the assumption of totality, a property that is not necessarily desirable, and certainly not required in order to guarantee reversibility. In a categorical setting, however, faithfully capturing partiality requires handling it as additional structure. Recently, Giles studied inverse categories as a model of partial reversible (functional) programming. In this paper, we show how additionally assuming the existence of countable joins on such inverse categories leads to a number of properties that are desirable when modelling reversible functional programming, notably morphism schemes for reversible recursion, a †-trace, and algebraic ω-compactness. This gives a categorical account of reversible recursion, and, for the latter, provides an answer to the problem posed by Giles regarding the formulation of recursive data types at the inverse category level.

1 Introduction

Reversible computing, that is, the study of computations that exhibit both forward and backward determinism, originally grew out of the thermodynamics of computation. Landauer's principle states that computations performed by some physical system (thermodynamically) dissipate heat when information is erased, but that no dissipation is entailed by information-preserving computations [28]. This has motivated a long study of diverse reversible computation models, such as logic circuits [15], Turing machines [4,6], and many forms of restricted automata models [27,31]. Reversibility concepts are important in quantum computing, but are increasingly seen to be of interest in other areas as well, including high-performance computing [33], process calculi [13], and even robotics [34,35].

In this paper we concern ourselves with the categorical underpinnings of functional reversible programming languages. At the programming language level, reversible languages exhibit interesting program properties, such as easy program inversion [40]. Now, most reversible languages are stateful, giving them a fairly straightforward semantics interpretation. While functional programs are usually easier to reason about at the meta-level, they do not have the concept of state that imperative languages do, making their semantics interesting objects of study.

© Springer-Verlag Berlin Heidelberg 2016
B. Jacobs and C. Löding (Eds.): FOSSACS 2016, LNCS 9634, pp. 73–90, 2016.
DOI: 10.1007/978-3-662-49630-5_5

Further, many reversible functional programming languages (such as Theseus [25] and the Π-family of combinator calculi [7]) come equipped with a tacit assumption of totality, a property that is neither required [4] nor necessarily desirable as far as guaranteeing reversibility is concerned. Shedding ourselves of the "tyranny of totality," however, requires us to handle partiality explicitly as additional categorical structure.

One approach which does precisely that is inverse categories, as studied by Cockett & Lack [9] as a specialization of restriction categories, which have recently been suggested and developed by Giles [16] as models of reversible (functional) programming. In this paper, we will argue that assuming ever slightly more structure on these inverse categories, namely the presence of *countable joins* of parallel morphisms [17], gives rise to a number of additional properties useful for modelling reversible functional programming, notably two different notions of reversible recursion, and an account of recursive data types (via algebraic ω-compactness with respect to structure-preserving functors), which are not present in the general case. This is done by adopting two different, but complementary, views on inverse categories with countable joins as enriched categories – as **CPO**-categories, and as (specifically Σ**Mon**-enriched) strong unique decomposition categories [18,23].

Overview. The necessary background on restriction and inverse categories is presented in Sect. 2. In Sect. 3 we show that inverse categories with countable joins are **CPO**-enriched, which allows us to demonstrate the existence of (reversible!) fixed points of both morphism schemes and structure-preserving functors. In Sect. 4 we show that inverse categories with countable joins and a join-preserving disjointness tensor are unique decomposition categories equipped with a uniform †-trace. Sect. 5 gives conclusions and directions for future work.

2   Background

This section gives an introduction to restriction and inverse categories (with joins), dagger categories, and categories of partial maps as they will be used in the remainder of this text. Unless otherwise stated, the material described in this section can be found in standard texts on restriction and inverse category theory (*e.g.*, Cockett & Lack [9–11], Giles [16], Guo [17]).

We begin by recalling the definition of *restriction structures* and *restriction categories*.

Definition 1 (Cockett & Lack, 2002). *A restriction structure on a category consists of an operator $\overline{(\cdot)}$ on morphisms mapping each morphism $f : A \to B$ to a morphism $\overline{f} : A \to A$ (the restriction idempotent of f) such that*

(i) $f \circ \overline{f} = f$ *for all morphisms $f : A \to B$,*
(ii) $\overline{f} \circ \overline{g} = \overline{g} \circ \overline{f}$ *whenever $dom(f) = dom(g)$,*
(iii) $\overline{\overline{f} \circ \overline{g}} = \overline{f} \circ \overline{g}$ *whenever $dom(f) = dom(g)$, and*
(iv) $\overline{h} \circ f = \overline{h \circ f} \circ f$ *whenever $cod(f) = dom(h)$.*

A category with a restriction structure is called a restriction category.

As a trivial example, any category can be equipped with a restriction structure given by setting $\overline{f} = 1_A$ for every morphism $f : A \to B$. However, there are also many useful and nontrivial examples of restriction categories (see, *e.g.*, Cockett & Lack [9, Sect. 2.1.3]), the canonical one being the category **Pfn** of sets and partial functions. In this category, the restriction idempotent $\overline{f} : A \to A$ for a partial function $f : A \to B$ is given by the partial identity function

$$\overline{f}(x) = \begin{cases} x & \text{if } f \text{ is defined at } x, \\ \text{undefined} & \text{otherwise.} \end{cases}$$

Since we take restrictions as additional structure, we naturally want a notion of functors that preserve this structure.

Definition 2. *A functor $F : \mathscr{C} \to \mathscr{D}$ between restriction categories $\mathscr{C}$ and $\mathscr{D}$ is a restriction functor if $\overline{F(f)} = F(\overline{f})$ for all morphisms f of $\mathscr{C}$.*

A morphism $f : A \to B$ of a restriction category is said to be *total* if $\overline{f} = 1_A$. Given a restriction category $\mathscr{C}$, we can form the category Total($\mathscr{C}$), consisting of all objects and only the total morphisms of $\mathscr{C}$, which embeds in $\mathscr{C}$ via a faithful restriction functor. Further, a restriction category in which every restriction idempotent splits is called a *split restriction category*, and, by way of the Karoubi envelope, every restriction category $\mathscr{C}$ can be embedded in a split restriction category Split($\mathscr{C}$) via a fully faithful restriction functor. Restriction categories with restriction functors form a category, **rCat**.

A useful feature of restriction categories, and one we will exploit throughout this article, is that hom-sets can be equipped with a partial order (often called the natural partial order), defined as follows:

Proposition 1. *In a restriction category $\mathscr{C}$, every hom-set $\mathrm{Hom}_{\mathscr{C}}(A, B)$ can be equipped with the structure of a partial order where we let $f \leq g$ iff $g \circ \overline{f} = f$. Further, every restriction functor F is locally monotone on this order, in the sense that $f \leq g$ implies $F(f) \leq F(g)$.*

In **Pfn**, this corresponds to the usual partial order on partial functions: For $f, g : A \to B$, $f \leq g$ if, for all $x \in A$, f is defined at x implies that g is defined at x and $f(x) = g(x)$.

A natural question to ask is when this partial order has a least element: A sufficient condition for this is when the restriction category has a *restriction zero*.

Definition 3. *A restriction category $\mathscr{C}$ has a restriction zero object 0 iff for all objects A and B, there exists a unique morphism $0_{A,B} : A \to B$ that factors through 0 and satisfies $\overline{0_{A,A}} = 0_{A,A}$.*

If such a restriction zero object exists, it is unique up to (total) isomorphism. When a given restriction category has such a restriction zero, the zero map $0_{A,B} : A \to B$ is precisely the least element of $\mathrm{Hom}_{\mathscr{C}}(A, B)$.

Moving on to inverse categories, in order to define these we first need the notion of a partial isomorphism:

Definition 4. *In a restriction category $\mathscr{C}$, we say that a morphism $f : A \to B$ is a* partial isomorphism *if there exists a unique morphism $f^\circ : B \to A$ of $\mathscr{C}$ (the* partial inverse *of f) such that $f^\circ \circ f = \overline{f}$ and $f \circ f^\circ = \overline{f^\circ}$.*

Definition 5. *A restriction category $\mathscr{C}$ is said to be an* inverse category *if all morphisms of $\mathscr{C}$ are partial isomorphisms.*

In this manner, if we accept an intuition of restriction categories as "categories with partiality," inverse categories are "groupoids with partiality" – and, indeed, the category **PInj** of sets and partial injective functions is *the* canonical example of an inverse category. In fact, the Wagner-Preston representation theorem (see, *e.g.*, Lawson [29]) for inverse monoids can be extended to show that every locally small inverse category can be faithfully embedded in **PInj** (see Heunen [21] for the general case, or Cockett & Lack [9] for the special case of small categories).

The analogy with groupoids goes even further; similar to how we can construct a groupoid Core($\mathscr{C}$) by taking only the isomorphisms of $\mathscr{C}$, every restriction category $\mathscr{C}$ has a subcategory Inv($\mathscr{C}$) that is an inverse category, and has as morphisms only the partial isomorphisms of $\mathscr{C}$. Inverse categories with restriction functors form a category, **invCat**.

More generally, inverse categories are *dagger categories* (sometimes also called *categories with involution*):

Definition 6. *A category $\mathscr{C}$ is said to be a* dagger category *if it is equipped with a contravariant endofunctor $(-)^\dagger : \mathscr{C} \to \mathscr{C}^{\mathrm{op}}$ such that $1_A^\dagger = 1_A$ for all objects A, and $f^{\dagger\dagger} = f$ for all morphisms f.*

Proposition 2. *Every inverse category $\mathscr{C}$ is a dagger category with the dagger functor given by $A^\dagger = A$ on objects, and $f^\dagger = f^\circ$ on morphisms.*

As is conventional, we will call $f^\dagger$ the *adjoint* of f, and say that f is *self-adjoint* if $f = f^\dagger$, and *unitary* if $f^\dagger = f^{-1}$. In inverse categories, unitary morphisms thus correspond precisely to (total) isomorphisms. For the remainder of this text, we will use this induced dagger-structure when refering to the partial inverse of a morphism (and write, *e.g.*, $f^\dagger$ rather than f°).

A useful feature of this definition of inverse categories is that we do not need an additional notion of an "inverse functor" as a functor that preserves partial inverses; restriction functors suffice.

Definition 7. *A functor $F : \mathscr{C} \to \mathscr{D}$ between dagger categories is a* dagger preserving *if $F(f)^\dagger = F(f^\dagger)$ for all morphisms f of $\mathscr{C}$.*

Proposition 3. *Every restriction functor $F : \mathscr{C} \to \mathscr{D}$ between inverse categories $\mathscr{C}$ and $\mathscr{D}$ is dagger preserving.*

That this holds can be seen from the fact that the property of being a partial isomorphism is defined purely in terms of composition and restriction idempotents, both of which are preserved by restriction functors.

2.1   Joins and Compatibility

Given that hom-sets of restriction (and, by extension, inverse) categories are partially ordered, one may wonder when this partial order has joins. It turns out, however, that it does not in the general case, and that only very simple restriction categories have joins for arbitrary parallel morphisms. However, we *can* define a meaningful notion of joins for parallel morphisms if this operation is not required to be total, but only be defined for *compatible* morphisms. For restriction categories, this compatibility relation is defined as follows:

Definition 8. *Parallel morphisms* $f, g : A \to B$ *of a restriction category* $\mathscr{C}$ *are said to be* restriction compatible *if* $g \circ \overline{f} = f \circ \overline{g}$; *if this is the case, we write* $f \smile g$. *By extension, a set* $S \subseteq \mathrm{Hom}_{\mathscr{C}}(A, B)$ *is restriction compatible if all morphisms of* S *are pairwise restriction compatible.*

This compatibility relation can be extended to apply to inverse categories by requiring that morphisms be compatible in both directions:

Definition 9. *Parallel morphisms* $f, g : A \to B$ *of an inverse category* $\mathscr{C}$ *are said to be* inverse compatible *if* $f \smile g$ *and* $f^{\dagger} \smile g^{\dagger}$; *if this is the case, we write* $f \asymp g$. *A set* $S \subseteq \mathrm{Hom}_{\mathscr{C}}(A, B)$ *is inverse compatible if all morphisms of* S *are pairwise inverse compatible.*

The familiar reader will notice that this definition differs in its statement from Guo's [17, p. 98], who defined $f \asymp g$ in an inverse category $\mathscr{C}$ if $f \smile g$ holds in both $\mathscr{C}$ and $\mathscr{C}^{\mathrm{op}}$ (relying on the observation that inverse categories are simultaneously restriction categories and *corestriction* categories). To avoid working explicitly with corestriction categories, however, we will use this equivalent definition instead.

We define restriction categories with (countable) joins as follows:

Definition 10 (Guo, 2012). *A restriction category* $\mathscr{C}$ *is a (countable)* join restriction category *if it has a restriction zero object, and satisfies that for all (countable) restriction compatible subsets* S *of all hom sets* $\mathrm{Hom}_{\mathscr{C}}(A, B)$, *there exists a morphism* $\bigvee_{s \in S} s$ *such that*

(i) $s \leq \bigvee_{s \in S} s$ *for all* $s \in S$, *and* $s \leq t$ *for all* $s \in S$ *implies* $\bigvee_{s \in S} s \leq t$;
(ii) $\overline{\bigvee_{s \in S} s} = \bigvee_{s \in S} \overline{s}$;
(iii) $f \circ \left(\bigvee_{s \in S} s \right) = \bigvee_{s \in S} (f \circ s)$ *for all* $f : B \to X$; *and*
(iv) $\left(\bigvee_{s \in S} s \right) \circ g = \bigvee_{s \in S} (s \circ g)$ *for all* $g : Y \to A$.

In addition, we say that a restriction functor that preserves all thus constructed joins is a *join restriction functor*.

As a concrete example, **Pfn** has joins of all restriction compatible sets; here, $f \smile g$ iff whenever f and g are both defined at some point x, $f(x) = g(x)$, and the join of a set of restriction compatible partial functions F is given by

$$\left(\bigvee_{f \in F} f \right) (x) = \begin{cases} f'(x) & \text{if there exists an } f' \in F \text{ such that } f' \text{ is defined at } x, \\ \text{undefined} & \text{otherwise.} \end{cases}$$

Notice that the compatibility relation ensures precisely that the result is a partial function.

This, finally, allows us to define join inverse categories by narrowing the definition above to only require the existence of joins of inverse compatible (sets of) morphisms:

Definition 11. *An inverse category $\mathscr{C}$ is a (countable) join inverse category if it has a restriction zero object, and Definition 10 is satisfied for all (countable) inverse compatible subsets S of all $\mathrm{Hom}_{\mathscr{C}}(A, B)$.*

Analogously to **Pfn**, the category **PInj** is a join inverse category with joins given precisely as in **Pfn**, since the additional requirement that $f^{\dagger} \smile g^{\dagger}$ ensures that the resulting partial function is injective.

2.2 Categories of Partial Maps

Categories of partial maps provide a synthetic approach to partiality in a categorical setting, and was first introduced by Robinson and Rosolini [32] in 1988. To form a category of partial maps, we consider a *stable system of monics*: In a category $\mathscr{C}$, a collection $\mathcal{M}$ of monics of $\mathscr{C}$ is said to be a stable system of monics if it contains all isomorphisms of $\mathscr{C}$ and is closed under composition and pullbacks (in the sense that the pullback m' of an $m : X \to B$ in $\mathcal{M}$ along any $f : A \to B$ exists and $m' \in \mathcal{M}$). Given such a stable system of monics $\mathcal{M}$ in a category $\mathscr{C}$, we can form the category of partial maps as follows:

Proposition 4. *Given a category $\mathscr{C}$ and a stable system of monics $\mathcal{M}$ of $\mathscr{C}$, we form the category of partial maps $\mathrm{Par}(\mathscr{C}, \mathcal{M})$ by choosing the objects to be the objects of $\mathscr{C}$, and placing a morphism $(m, f) : A \to B$ for every pair (m, f) where $m : A' \to A \in \mathcal{M}$ and $f : A' \to B$ is a morphism of $\mathscr{C}$, as in*

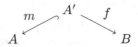

factored out by the equivalence relation $\cdot \sim \cdot$ in which $(m, f) \sim (m', f')$ if there exists an isomorphism $\alpha : A' \to A''$ such that $m' \circ \alpha = m$ and $f' \circ \alpha = f$. Composition of morphisms $(m, f) : A \to B$ and $(m', g) : B \to C$ is given by $(m \circ m'', g \circ f') : A \to C$ where m'' and f' arise from the pullback

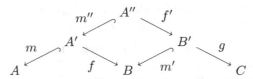

where $m'' \circ m \in \mathcal{M}$ precisely by $\mathcal{M}$ closed under composition and pullbacks.

Categories of partial maps are prime examples of restriction categories; in fact, of split restriction categories. Further, it can be shown that every restriction category $\mathscr{C}$ embeds fully and faithfully and in a restriction preserving manner into a category of partial maps [9].

3   As CPO-categories

In the present section, we will show that inverse categories with countable joins are intrinsically **CPO**-enriched. This observation leads to two properties that are highly useful for modelling reversible functional programming, namely the existence of fixed points for both morphism schemes for recursion (that is, continuous endomorphisms on hom-objects) and for locally continuous functors. The former can be applied to model reversible recursive functions, and the latter to model recursive data types [3]. Further, we will show that the partial inverse of the fixed point of a morphism scheme for recursion can be computed as the fixed point of an *adjoint* morphism scheme, giving a style of recursion similar to the reversible functional programming language RFUN [39].

Recall that a category $\mathscr{C}$ is **CPO**-enriched (or simply a **CPO**-category) if all $\mathrm{Hom}_{\mathscr{C}}(A, B)$ are pointed ω-complete partial orders (*i.e.*, they have a least element and satisfy that each ω-chain has a supremum), and composition is monotone, continuous and strict. To begin, we will need the lemma below.

Lemma 1. *Let $\mathscr{C}$ be an inverse category and $f, g : A \to B$ be parallel morphisms of $\mathscr{C}$. If $f \leq g$ then $f \asymp g$.*

This lemma allows us to show **CPO**-enrichment of join inverse categories:

Theorem 1. *Every inverse category $\mathscr{C}$ with countable joins is **CPO**-enriched.*

Proof. Let A, B be objects of $\mathscr{C}$, and let $\{f_i\}_{i \in \omega}$ be an ω-chain in $\mathrm{Hom}_{\mathscr{C}}(A, B)$ with respect to the canonical partial ordering. By Lemma 1, all f_i and f_j for $i, j \in \omega$ of this chain are inverse compatible, so the set $F = \{f_i \mid i \in \omega\}$ is an inverse compatible subset of $\mathrm{Hom}_{\mathscr{C}}(A, B)$. But then we can form the supremum of $\{f_i\}_{i \in \omega}$ by

$$\sup\{f_i\}_{i \in \omega} = \bigvee_{f \in F} f$$

which is the supremum of this chain directly by definition of the join.

Let $f, g : A \to B$ and $F = \{f_i \mid i \in \omega\}$. Monotony of compositions holds in all restriction categories, not just inverse categories with countable joins: Supposing $f \leq g$ then $g \circ \overline{f} = f$, and for $h : B \to X$,

$$h \circ g \circ \overline{h \circ f} = h \circ g \circ \overline{h \circ g \circ \overline{f}} = h \circ g \circ \overline{h \circ g} \circ \overline{f} = h \circ g \circ \overline{f} = h \circ f$$

so $h \circ f \leq h \circ g$ in $\mathrm{Hom}_{\mathscr{C}}(A, X)$; the argument is analogous for postcomposition. That composition is continuous follows directly by definition of joins, as we have

$$h \circ \sup\{f_i\}_{i \in \omega} = h \circ \bigvee_{f \in F} f = \bigvee_{f \in F} (h \circ f) = \sup\{h \circ f_i\}_{i \in \omega}$$

for all $h : B \to X$, and analogously for postcomposition. That composition is strict follows by the fact that the zero map $0_{A,B} : A \to B$ is least in $\mathrm{Hom}_{\mathscr{C}}(A, B)$, and that $g \circ 0_{A,B} = 0_{A,X}$ for all $g : B \to X$ by the universal mapping property of the zero object, and likewise for postcomposition.   □

Recall that a functor $F : \mathscr{C} \to \mathscr{D}$ between **CPO**-categories is *locally continuous* iff each $F_{A,B} : \mathrm{Hom}_{\mathscr{C}}(A, B) \to \mathrm{Hom}_{\mathscr{D}}(\mathrm{FA}, \mathrm{FB})$ is monotone and continuous. Note that since all restriction functors preserve the partial order on hom-sets, and since suprema are defined in terms of joins, join restriction functors are in particular locally continuous.

3.1   Reversible Fixed Points of Morphism Schemes

In the following, let $\mathscr{C}$ be an inverse category with countable joins. We will use the term *morphism scheme* to refer to a monotone and continuous function $f : \mathrm{Hom}_{\mathscr{C}}(A, B) \to \mathrm{Hom}_{\mathscr{C}}(X, Y)$ – note that such schemes are morphisms of **CPO** and not of the inverse category $\mathscr{C}$, so they are specifically *not* required to have inverses. Enrichment in **CPO** then has the following immediate corollary by Kleene's fixed point theorem:

Corollary 1. *Every morphism scheme of the form* $\mathrm{Hom}_{\mathscr{C}}(A, B) \xrightarrow{f} \mathrm{Hom}_{\mathscr{C}}(A, B)$ *has a least fixed point* $\mathrm{fix}\, f : A \to B$ *in* $\mathscr{C}$.

Proof. Define $\mathrm{fix}\, f = \sup\{f^n(0_{A,B})\}$; that this is the least fixed point follows by Kleene's fixed point theorem, as $0_{A,B}$ is least in $\mathrm{Hom}_{\mathscr{C}}(A, B)$. $\qquad\square$

Morphism schemes on their own are useful for modelling parametrized reversible functions, *i.e.*, functions that take other functions *given at compile-time* as parameters to produce new, first-order reversible functions. Since higher-order reversible functional programming is yet to be well-understood, parametrized functions (as implemented in, *e.g.*, Theseus [25]) allow for a higher degree of abstraction and code reuse, as we know it from higher-order functional irreversible programming. With this in mind, recursive reversible functions can be seen as least fixed points of self-parametrized functions.

Given that we can thus model reversible recursive functions via least fixed points of morphism schemes, a prudent question to ask is if the inverse of a least fixed point can be computed as the least fixed point of another morphism scheme. We will answer this in the affirmative, but to do this, we need to show that the induced dagger functor is locally continuous.

Lemma 2. *The canonical dagger functor* $\dagger : \mathscr{C}^{\mathrm{op}} \to \mathscr{C}$ *is locally continuous.*

Proof. Let $f, g : A \to B$. For monotony, suppose $f \le g$, *i.e.*, $g \circ \overline{f} = f$. Then

$$g^{\dagger} \circ \overline{f^{\dagger}} = g^{\dagger} \circ f \circ f^{\dagger} = g^{\dagger} \circ g \circ \overline{f} \circ f^{\dagger} = \overline{g} \circ \overline{f} \circ f^{\dagger} = \overline{g \circ \overline{f}} \circ f^{\dagger}$$
$$= \overline{f} \circ f^{\dagger} = f^{\dagger} \circ f \circ f^{\dagger} = f^{\dagger} \circ \overline{f^{\dagger}} = f^{\dagger}$$

so $f^{\dagger} \le g^{\dagger}$ as well, as desired. For continuity, let $\{f_i\}_{i \in \omega}$ be an ω-chain in $\mathrm{Hom}_{\mathscr{C}}(A, B)$, and let $F = \{f_i \mid i \in \omega\}$ be the corresponding set for this chain. Since $f \le \bigvee_{f \in F} f$ for each $f \in F$ by Definition 11, we have $f^{\dagger} \le \left(\bigvee_{f \in F} f\right)^{\dagger}$ for all $f \in F$ by monotony of $\dagger$, and so

$$\sup\{f_i^\dagger\}_{i\in\omega} = \bigvee_{f\in F} f^\dagger \;\leq\; \left(\bigvee_{f\in F} f\right)^\dagger = \sup\{f_i\}_{i\in\omega}^\dagger$$

by Definition 11. In the other direction, we have $f^\dagger \leq \bigvee_{f\in F} f^\dagger$ for all $f \in F$
by Definition 11, so by monotony of $\dagger$, $f = f^{\dagger\dagger} \leq \left(\bigvee_{f\in F} f^\dagger\right)^\dagger$ for all $f \in F$.
But then $\bigvee_{f\in F} f \leq \left(\bigvee_{f\in F} f^\dagger\right)^\dagger$ by Definition 11, and so by monotony of $\dagger$, we
finally get

$$\sup\{f_i\}_{i\in\omega}^\dagger = \left(\bigvee_{f\in F} f\right)^\dagger \;\leq\; \left(\bigvee_{f\in F} f^\dagger\right)^{\dagger\dagger} = \bigvee_{f\in F} f^\dagger = \sup\{f_i^\dagger\}_{i\in\omega}$$

as desired.   □

With this lemma, we are able to show that the inverse of a least fixed point
of a morphism scheme can be computed as the least fixed point of an adjoint
morphism scheme:

Theorem 2. *Every*
morphism scheme of the form $\mathrm{Hom}_\mathscr{C}(A, B) \xrightarrow{f} \mathrm{Hom}_\mathscr{C}(A, B)$ *has an adjoint mor-*
phism scheme $\mathrm{Hom}_\mathscr{C}(B, A) \xrightarrow{f_\ddagger} \mathrm{Hom}_\mathscr{C}(B, A)$ *such that* $(\mathrm{fix}\ f)^\dagger = \mathrm{fix}\ f_\ddagger$.

Proof. Let $\iota_{A,B} : \mathrm{Hom}_\mathscr{C}(A, B) \to \mathrm{Hom}_\mathscr{C}(B, A)$ denote the family of functions
defined by $\iota_{A,B}(f) = f^\dagger$; each of these are monotone and continuous by Lemma 2,
and an isomorphism (with inverse $\iota_{B,A}$) by $f^{\dagger\dagger} = f$. Given a morphism scheme
$f : \mathrm{Hom}_\mathscr{C}(A, B) \to \mathrm{Hom}_\mathscr{C}(A, B)$, we define $f_\ddagger = \iota_{A,B} \circ f \circ \iota_{B,A}$ – this is monotone
and continuous since it is a (monotone and continuous) composition of monotone
and continuous functions. But since

$$f_\ddagger^n = (\iota_{A,B} \circ f \circ \iota_{B,A})^n = \iota_{A,B} \circ f^n \circ \iota_{B,A}$$

by $\iota_{B,A}$ an isomorphism with inverse $\iota_{A,B}$, and since $0_{A,B}^\dagger = 0_{B,A}$ by the universal mapping property of the zero object, we get

$$\mathrm{fix}\ f_\ddagger = \sup\{f_\ddagger^n(0_{B,A})\} = \sup\{(\iota_{A,B} \circ f^n \circ \iota_{B,A})(0_{B,A})\} = \sup\{f^n(0_{B,A}^\dagger)^\dagger\}$$
$$= \sup\{f^n(0_{A,B})^\dagger\} = \sup\{f^n(0_{A,B})\}^\dagger = (\mathrm{fix}\ f)^\dagger$$

as desired.   □

In modelling recursion in reversible functional programming, this theorem
states precisely that the partial inverse of a recursive reversible functions is,
itself, a recursive reversible function, and that it can be obtained by inverting
the function body and replacing recursive calls with recursive calls to the thus
constructed inverse: Coincidentally, this is *precisely* the inverse semantics of
recursive reversible functions in RFUN [39].

3.2   Algebraic ω-compactness for Free!

A pleasant property of **CPO**-categories is that algebraic ω-compactness – the property that every locally continuous functor has a canonical fixed point – is relatively easy to check for, thanks to the fixed point theorem due to Adámek [3] and Barr [5]:

Theorem 3 (Adámek & Barr). *Let $\mathscr{C}$ be a* **CPO***-category with an initial object. If $\mathscr{C}$ has colimits of ω-sequences of embeddings, then $\mathscr{C}$ is algebraically ω-compact over* **CPO***.*

Canonical fixed points of functors are of particular interest in modelling functional programming, since they can be used to provide interpretations for recursive data types. In the following, we will couple this theorem with a join-completion theorem for restriction categories to show that every inverse category can be faithfully embedded in an algebraically ω-compact inverse category with joins. That this succeeds rests on the following lemmas:

Lemma 3. *If an inverse category $\mathscr{C}$ embeds faithfully in a restriction category $\mathscr{D}$, it also embeds faithfully in $\mathrm{Inv}(\mathscr{D})$.*

Proof. We notice that Inv : **rCat** $\to$ **invCat** is right adjoint to the forgetful functor U : **invCat** $\to$ **rCat**, with each component of the counit $\epsilon : U \circ \mathrm{Inv} \to 1_{\mathbf{rCat}}$ given by the faithful inclusion functor $\epsilon_{\mathscr{C}} : U(\mathrm{Inv}(\mathscr{C})) \to \mathscr{C}$ (that this is an adjunction follows by an argument entirely analogous to Core : **Cat** $\to$ **Grpd** being right adjoint to U : **Grpd** $\to$ **Cat**). That faithful restriction functors are preserved follows readily since restriction functors preserve partial isomorphisms, and every restriction functor out of an inverse category factors through Inv-inclusion by this adjunction. $\square$

Lemma 4. *The functor* Inv : **rCat** $\to$ **invCat** *takes join restriction categories to join inverse categories (and preserves join restriction functors).*

The latter of these lemmas was shown by Guo [17, Lemma 3.1.27]. To ease presentation of the completion theorem for join restriction categories due to Cockett and Guo [8,17], we make the following notational shorthand:

Convention 12. *For a restriction category $\mathscr{C}$, let $\overline{\mathscr{C}}$ denote the category of presheaves* **Set**$^{\mathrm{Total}(\mathrm{Split}(\mathscr{C}))^{\mathrm{op}}}$.

Note in particular that $\overline{\mathscr{C}}$ is cocomplete and all colimits are stable under pullback (since colimits in $\overline{\mathscr{C}}$ are constructed object-wise in **Set**).

Theorem 4 (Cockett & Guo). *Every restriction category $\mathscr{C}$ can be faithfully embedded in a join restriction category of the form* $\mathrm{Par}(\overline{\mathscr{C}}, \widehat{\mathcal{M}_{gap}})$.

The stable system of monics $\widehat{\mathcal{M}_{\mathbf{gap}}}$ relates to the join-completion for restriction categories via $\mathcal{M}$-gaps (see Cockett [8] or Guo [17, Sect. 3.2.2] for details). We can now show the algebraic ω-compactness theorem for restriction categories:

Theorem 5. *If $\mathscr{C}$ is a restriction category then* $\mathrm{Par}(\overline{\mathscr{C}}, \widehat{\mathcal{M}_{gap}})$ *is algebraically* ω-*compact for* **CPO***; so for join restriction functors.*

Proof. Let $\mathscr{C}$ be a restriction category. By Theorem 4, $\mathrm{Par}(\overline{\mathscr{C}}, \widehat{\mathcal{M}_{\mathrm{gap}}})$ is join restriction category. By Adámek & Barr's fixed point theorem and the fact that join restriction categories are **CPO**-enriched (by Theorem 1) and have a restriction zero object (which is specifically initial) by definition, it suffices to show that $\mathrm{Par}(\overline{\mathscr{C}}, \widehat{\mathcal{M}_{\mathrm{gap}}})$ has colimits of ω-diagrams of embeddings. Let $D : \omega \to \mathrm{Par}(\overline{\mathscr{C}}, \widehat{\mathcal{M}_{\mathrm{gap}}})$ be such a diagram of embeddings. This corresponds to the diagram

$$
\begin{array}{ccccccc}
& m_0 & A & f_0 & m_1 & B & f_1 \\
D(0) & & & & D(1) & & & D(2) \cdots
\end{array}
$$

in $\overline{\mathscr{C}}$. Since $\overline{\mathscr{C}}$ is cocomplete, this diagram has a colimiting cocone $\alpha : D \Rightarrow$ colim D such that

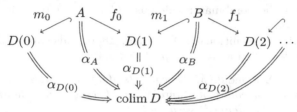

commutes. Further, since colimits in $\overline{\mathscr{C}}$ are constructed object-wise in **Set**, this colimit is stable under pullbacks, so composition in $\mathrm{Par}(\overline{\mathscr{C}}, \widehat{\mathcal{M}_{\mathrm{gap}}})$, corresponding to pullbacks in $\overline{\mathscr{C}}$, commutes with this colimit. Thus, the family of morphisms $\{(m_i, \alpha_{D(i+1)} \circ f_i)\}_{i \in \omega}$ is a colimiting cocone for D in $\mathrm{Par}(\overline{\mathscr{C}}, \widehat{\mathcal{M}_{\mathrm{gap}}})$. $\qquad\square$

Finally, using this machinery, we can show how this theorem extends to inverse categories.

Corollary 2. *Every inverse category can be faithfully embedded in a join inverse category that is algebraically ω-compact for join restriction functors.*

Proof. Let $\mathscr{C}$ be an inverse category. Since $U(\mathscr{C})$ is the exact same category viewed as a restriction category, $U(\mathscr{C})$ embeds faithfully in $\mathrm{Par}(\overline{\mathscr{C}}, \widehat{\mathcal{M}_{\mathrm{gap}}})$, which is a join restriction category by Theorem 4, and algebraically ω-compact by Theorem 5. But then it follows by Lemma 3 that $\mathscr{C}$ embeds faithfully in $\mathrm{Inv}(\mathrm{Par}(\overline{\mathscr{C}}, \widehat{\mathcal{M}_{\mathrm{gap}}}))$, which is a join inverse category by Lemma 4, and is algebraically ω-compact for join restriction functors (which are specifically locally monotone and continuous) since fixed points of functors are (total) isomorphisms, so preserved in $\mathrm{Inv}(\mathrm{Par}(\overline{\mathscr{C}}, \widehat{\mathcal{M}_{\mathrm{gap}}}))$. $\qquad\square$

4   As Unique Decomposition Categories

A complementary view on inverse categories with countable joins is as unique decomposition categories, a kind of category introduced by Haghverdi [18] equipped with a partial sum operation on Hom-sets via enrichment in the category of Σ-monoids (shown to be symmetric monoidal by Hoshino [23]). Unique decomposition categories (including Hoshino's *strong* unique decomposition categories [23] which we will employ here) are specifically traced monoidal categories [26] if they satisfy certain conditions. This is desirable when modelling functional programming, as traces can be used to model notions of feedback [1] and recursion [19,20,24].

Here, we will show that inverse categories with countable joins and a join-preserving *disjointness tensor* (due to Giles [16]) are strong unique decomposition categories, and satisfy the conditions required to be equipped with a trace. We extend this result further to show that the trace is a †-trace [37], and thus has pleasant inversion properties (the trace in **PInj** is well studied, *cf.* [2,18,22]). This is particularly interesting given that the reversible programming language Theseus [25] and the combinator calculus Π^0 [7] both rely on a †-trace for reversible recursion.

We begin with the definition of a Σ-monoid [18] (see also Manes & Benson [30] where these are described as *positive partial monoids*):

Definition 13. *A Σ-monoid (M, Σ) consists of a nonempty set M and a partial operator Σ defined on countable families in M (say that a family $\{x_i\}_{i \in I}$ is summable if $\sum_{i \in I} x_i$ is defined) such that*

(i) if $\{x_i\}_{i \in I}$ is a countable family in M and $\{I_j\}_{j \in J}$ is a countable partitioning of I, then $\{x_i\}_{i \in I}$ is summable iff all $\{x_i\}_{i \in I_j}$ and $\sum_{i \in I_j} x_i$ are summable for all $j \in J$, and in this case

$$\sum_{j \in J} \sum_{i \in I_j} x_i = \sum_{i \in I} x_i \,,$$

(ii) any family $\{x_i\}_{i \in I}$ in M where I is singleton is summable with $\sum_{i \in I} x_i = x_j$ if $I = \{j\}$.

The class of Σ-monoids with homomorphisms preserving partial sums forms a category, $\Sigma\mathbf{Mon}$. As such, a category $\mathscr{C}$ is enriched in $\Sigma\mathbf{Mon}$ if all hom-sets of $\mathscr{C}$ are Σ-monoids, and composition distributes over partial addition.

Lemma 5. *Every inverse category with countable joins is $\Sigma\mathbf{Mon}$-enriched.*

Proof (Sketch). In an inverse category $\mathscr{C}$, defining

$$\sum_{i \in I} s_i = \bigvee_{s \in \{s_i | i \in I\}} s$$

for a countable family $\{s_i\}_{i \in I}$ of some hom-set $\mathrm{Hom}_{\mathscr{C}}(A, B)$, summability coincides with inverse compatibility. That the axioms of Σ-monoids are satisfied follows straightforwardly by Definition 11. $\square$

Haghverdi defines unique decomposition categories in the following way:

Definition 14 (Haghverdi). *A unique decomposition category $\mathscr{C}$ is a symmetric monoidal category enriched in $\Sigma\mathbf{Mon}$ such that for all finite index sets I and all $j \in I$, there are* quasi-injections $\iota_j : X_j \to \oplus_{i \in I} X_i$ *and* quasi-projections $\rho_j : \oplus_{i \in I} X_i \to X_j$ *satisfying*

(i) $\rho_k \circ \iota_j = 1_{X_k}$ if $j = k$, and $0_{X_j, X_k}$ otherwise, and
(ii) $\Sigma_{i \in I} \iota_i \circ \rho_i = 1_{\oplus_{i \in I} x X_i}$.

This definition is strengthened by Hoshino:

Definition 15 (Hoshino). *A strong unique decomposition category is a symmetric monoidal category enriched in $\Sigma\mathbf{Mon}$ satisfying that the identity on the monoidal unit I is $0_{I,I}$, and $1_X \oplus 0_{Y,Y} + 0_{X,X} \oplus 1_Y = 1_{X \oplus Y}$ for all X and Y.*

An elementary result is that strong unique decomposition categories are unique decomposition categories, with their quasi injections and projections given by $\iota_1 = (1_A \oplus 0_{0,B}) \circ u_r^{-1} : A \to A \oplus B$ and $\rho_1 = u_r \circ (1_A \oplus 0_{B,0}) : A \oplus B \to A$, and analogously for ι_2 and ρ_2 (thus extending to any finite index set).

As such, (strong) unique decomposition categories rely on a sum-like monoidal tensor – in the context of inverse categories, such a one can be found in Giles' definition of a disjointness tensor [16, Definition 7.2.1].

Definition 16 (Giles). *An inverse category $\mathscr{C}$ with a restriction zero object 0 is said to have a* disjointness tensor *if it is equipped with a symmetric monoidal restriction functor $- \oplus - : \mathscr{C} \times \mathscr{C} \to \mathscr{C}$ such that*

(i) the restriction zero 0 is the tensor unit, and
(ii) the morphisms given by $\text{II}_1 = (1_A \oplus 0_{0,B}) \circ u_r^{-1} : A \to A \oplus B$ and $\text{II}_2 = (0_{0,B} \oplus 1_A) \circ u_l^{-1} : A \to B \oplus A$ are jointly epic, and their partial inverses $\text{II}_1^\dagger : A \oplus B \to A$ and $\text{II}_2^\dagger : B \oplus A \to A$ are jointly monic,

where $u_l : 0 \oplus A \to A$ and $u_r : A \oplus 0 \to A$ denote the left respectively the right unitor of the symmetric monoidal tensor.

Though not required from this definition, since we are working exclusively with join inverse categories, we make the additional assumption that the disjointness tensor is a join restriction functor. Since Giles' definition already demands that the zero object be the monoidal unit, and even defines II_i precisely like Hoshino's definition of ι_i (one can similarly see that $\text{II}_i^\dagger = \rho_i$), we can show the following:

Theorem 6. *Every inverse category with countable joins and a join-preserving disjointness tensor is a strong unique decomposition category.*

Proof. By Lemma 5, any inverse category with countable joins (and a join-preserving disjointness tensor) is enriched in $\Sigma\mathbf{Mon}$, so it suffices to show that the (specifically symmetric monoidal) disjointness tensor satisfies Definition 15. That $1_{I,I} = 0_{I,I}$ follows by $1_{0,0} = 0_{0,0}$ for the (restriction) zero 0, and $1_X \oplus 0_{Y,Y} + 0_{X,X} \oplus 1_Y = 1_{X \oplus Y}$ by the definition of partial sums as joins and the additional requirement that the disjointness tensor preserves joins. □

Due to the $\Sigma\mathbf{Mon}$-enrichment on unique decomposition categories, the trace can be constructed as a denumerable sum of morphisms, provided that morphisms of a certain form are always summable, *cf.* [18, Proposition 4.0.11] and [23, Corollary 5.4]:

Theorem 7 (Haghverdi, Hoshino). *Let $\mathscr{C}$ be a (strong) unique decomposition category such that for every X, Y, and U and every $f : X \oplus U \to Y \oplus U$, the sum $f_{11} + \sum_{n=0}^{\infty} f_{21} \circ f_{22}^n \circ f_{12}$ exists, where $f_{ij} = \rho_j \circ f \circ \iota_i$. Then $\mathscr{C}$ has a uniform trace given by*

$$Tr_{X,Y}^{U}(f) = f_{11} + \sum_{n=0}^{\infty} f_{21} \circ f_{22}^n \circ f_{12}.$$

In a join inverse category, we say that parallel morphisms $f, g : A \to B$ are *inverse disjoint* if $\overline{f} \circ \overline{g} = 0_{A,A}$ and $\overline{f^{\dagger}} \circ \overline{g^{\dagger}} = 0_{B,B}$.

Lemma 6. *In an inverse category, the following hold:*

(i) All inverse disjoint morphisms are inverse compatible,
(ii) $g \smile g'$ and $f \smile f'$ implies $g \circ f \smile g' \circ f'$ when $\mathrm{dom}(g) = \mathrm{cod}(f)$, and
(iii) $\overline{g \circ f} = \overline{g \circ f \circ \overline{f}}$ when $\mathrm{dom}(g) = \mathrm{cod}(f)$.

This lemma allows us to show the existence of all trace sums: The core idea is to use part (ii) of this lemma until we get morphisms that are immediately disjoint by (iii), so inverse compatible by (i).

Lemma 7. *In a join inverse category with a disjointness tensor, all morphisms of the forms f_{11} or $f_{21} \circ f_{22}^n \circ f_{12}$ for any $n \in \mathbb{N}$ and some $f : X \oplus U \to Y \oplus U$ are pairwise inverse compatible.*

Recall that a $\dagger$-category with a trace is said to have a $\dagger$-*trace* (see, *e.g.*, Selinger [37]) if $\mathrm{Tr}_{X,Y}^{U}(f)^{\dagger} = \mathrm{Tr}_{Y,X}^{U}(f^{\dagger})$ for every morphism $f : X \oplus U \to Y \oplus U$.

Theorem 8. *Every inverse category $\mathscr{C}$ with countable joins and a join-preserving disjointness tensor has a uniform $\dagger$-trace.*

Proof. By Theorem 6, $\mathscr{C}$ is a (strong) unique decomposition category, and by Lemma 7 it has all trace sums, so it follows that $\mathscr{C}$ has a uniform trace. To see that this is a $\dagger$-trace, let $f : X \oplus U \to Y \oplus U$ be a morphism of $\mathscr{C}$. We notice that

$$(f_{ij})^{\dagger} = (\rho_j \circ f \circ \iota_i)^{\dagger} = (\amalg_j^{\dagger} \circ f \circ \amalg_i)^{\dagger} = \amalg_i^{\dagger} \circ f^{\dagger} \circ \amalg_j^{\dagger\dagger} = \amalg_i^{\dagger} \circ f^{\dagger} \circ \amalg_j = (f^{\dagger})_{ji}$$

and so $(f_{11})^{\dagger} = (f^{\dagger})_{11}$ and

$$(f_{21} \circ f_{22}^n \circ f_{12})^{\dagger} = (f_{12})^{\dagger} \circ (f_{22}^n)^{\dagger} \circ (f_{21})^{\dagger} = (f^{\dagger})_{21} \circ (f_{22}^{\dagger})^n \circ (f^{\dagger})_{12}$$

which gives us

$$\mathrm{Tr}_{X,Y}^U(f)^\dagger = \left(f_{11} + \sum_{n\in\omega} f_{21} \circ f_{22}^n \circ f_{12}\right)^\dagger = \left(f_{11} \vee \bigvee_{n\in\omega} f_{21} \circ f_{22}^n \circ f_{12}\right)^\dagger$$

$$= (f_{11})^\dagger \vee \left(\bigvee_{n\in\omega} f_{21} \circ f_{22}^n \circ f_{12}\right)^\dagger = (f_{11})^\dagger \vee \bigvee_{n\in\omega} (f_{12})^\dagger \circ (f_{22}^n)^\dagger \circ (f_{21})^\dagger$$

$$= (f^\dagger)_{11} \vee \bigvee_{n\in\omega} (f^\dagger)_{21} \circ (f^\dagger)_{22}^n \circ (f^\dagger)_{12} = \mathrm{Tr}_{Y,X}^U(f^\dagger)$$

by definition of the partial sum as join (Lemma 5), and by $(\bigvee_{f\in F} f)^\dagger = \bigvee_{f\in F} f^\dagger$ by Lemma 2. □

5 Conclusion

We have shown that inverse categories with countable joins carry with them a few key properties that are highly useful for modelling partial reversible functional programming. Notably, we have shown that any inverse category with countable joins is **CPO**-enriched – from this view, we gathered that morphism schemes have fixed points, and that the partial inverses of such fixed points can be computed as fixed points of adjoint morphism schemes. This gave us a model of recursion à la RFUN.

Further, we were able to show that any inverse category can be embedded in an inverse category with joins, in which all join restriction functors have canonical fixed points. Finally, we showed that the presence of a join-preserving disjointness tensor on an inverse category with countable joins gives us a strong unique decomposition category, and in turn, a uniform †-trace: a model of recursion à la Theseus and Π^0.

Restriction categories have recently been considered as enriched categories by Cockett & Garner [12], though their approach relied on enrichments based on *weak double categories* rather than monoidal categories, as it is otherwise usually done (including in this paper). Further, fixed points in categories with a notion of partiality have previously been considered, notably by Fiore [14] who also relied on order-enrichment, though his work was in categories of partial maps directly. Finally, Giles [16] has shown the construction of a trace in inverse categories recently, relying instead on the presence of countable *disjoint sums* rather than joins (whether or not this approach leads to a †-trace is unspecified). It should also be noted that the trace in the canonical inverse category **PInj** has seen study independent of unique decomposition and restriction categories, notably by Hines [22] and Abramsky, Haghverdi, and Scott [2].

As regards future work, since an inverse category with countable joins and a disjointness tensor is †-traced, it can be embedded in a †-compact closed category via the Int-construction [26,38]. It may be of interest to consider †-compact closed categories generated in this manner, as we suspect these will be inverse categories as well (notably, Int(**PInj**) is [22]) – and could provide, *e.g.*, an alternative treatment of projectors as restriction idempotents, and isometries as restriction monics (see also Selinger [36]).

Additionally, while our focus in this article has been on inverse categories, we conjecture that many of these results can be generalized to restriction categories.

Acknowledgments. We thank the anonymous reviewers for their useful comments. An abstract of this paper was presented at the *27th Nordic Workshop on Programming Theory* held in Reykjavík, Iceland in October, 2015. The research was partly funded by the *Danish Council for Independent Research | Natural Sciences* under the *Foundations of Reversible Computing* project. We also acknowledge the support given by *COST Action IC1405 Reversible computation.*

References

1. Abramsky, S.: Retracing some paths in process algebra. In: Montanari, U., Sassone, V. (eds.) CONCUR 1996. LNCS, vol. 1119, pp. 1–17. Springer, Heidelberg (1996)
2. Abramsky, S., Haghverdi, E., Scott, P.: Geometry of interaction and linear combinatory algebras. Math. Struct. Comput. Sci. **12**(5), 625–665 (2002)
3. Adámek, J.: Recursive data types in algebraically ω-complete categories. Inf. Comput. **118**, 181–190 (1995)
4. Axelsen, H.B., Glück, R.: What do reversible programs compute? In: Hofmann, M. (ed.) FOSSACS 2011. LNCS, vol. 6604, pp. 42–56. Springer, Heidelberg (2011)
5. Barr, M.: Algebraically compact functors. J. Pure Appl. Algebra **82**(3), 211–231 (1992)
6. Bennett, C.H.: Logical reversibility of computation. IBM J. Res. Dev. **17**(6), 525–532 (1973)
7. Bowman, W.J., James, R.P., Sabry, A.: Dagger traced symmetric monoidal categories and reversible programming. In: Proceedings of RC 2011, pp. 51–56. Ghent University (2011). http://www.cs.indiana.edu/~sabry/papers/cat-rev.pdf
8. Cockett, J.R.B., Guo, X.: Join restriction categories and the importance of being adhesive (2007). http://www.mat.uc.pt/~categ/ct2007/slides/cockett.pdf, presentation at Category Theory 2007
9. Cockett, J.R.B., Lack, S.: Restriction categories I: categories of partial maps. Theoret. Comput. Sci. **270**(1–2), 223–259 (2002)
10. Cockett, J.R.B., Lack, S.: Restriction categories II: partial map classification. Theoret. Comput. Sci. **294**(1–2), 61–102 (2003)
11. Cockett, J.R.B., Lack, S.: Restriction categories III: colimits, partial limits and extensivity. Math. Struct. Comput. Sci. **17**(4), 775–817 (2007)
12. Cockett, R., Garner, R.: Restriction categories as enriched categories. Theoret. Comput. Sci. **523**, 37–55 (2014)
13. Cristescu, I., Krivine, J., Varacca, D.: A compositional semantics for the reversible π-calculus. In: LICS 2013, pp. 388–397. IEEE Computer Society (2013)
14. Fiore, M.P.: Axiomatic Domain Theory in Categories of Partial Maps. Ph.D. thesis, University of Edinburgh (1994)
15. Fredkin, E., Toffoli, T.: Conservative logic. Int. J. Theor. Phys. **21**(3–4), 219–253 (1982)
16. Giles, B.G.: An Investigation of some Theoretical Aspects of Reversible Computing. Ph.D. thesis, University of Calgary (2014)
17. Guo, X.: Products, Joins, Meets, and Ranges in Restriction Categories. Ph.D. thesis, University of Calgary (2012)

18. Haghverdi, E.: A Categorical Approach to Linear Logic, Geometry of Proofs and Full Completeness. Ph.D. thesis, Carlton University and University of Ottawa (2000)
19. Hasegawa, M.: Models of Sharing Graphs. Ph.D. thesis, University of Edinburgh (1997)
20. Hasegawa, M.: Recursion from cyclic sharing: traced monoidal categories and models of cyclic lambda calculi. In: de Groote, P., Hindley, J.R. (eds.) TLCA 1997. LNCS, vol. 1210, pp. 196–213. Springer, Heidelberg (1997)
21. Heunen, C.: On the functor ℓ^2. In: Coecke, B., Ong, L., Panangaden, P. (eds.) Computation, Logic, Games and Quantum Foundations. LNCS, vol. 7860, pp. 107–121. Springer, Heidelberg (2013)
22. Hines, P.M.: The Algebra of Self-Similarity and its Applications. Ph.D. thesis, University of Wales, Bangor (1998)
23. Hoshino, N.: A representation theorem for unique decomposition categories. In: Berger, U., Mislove, M. (eds.) MFPS XXVIII. Electronic Notes in Theoretical Computer Science, vol. 286, pp. 213–227. Elsevier (2012)
24. Hyland, M.: Abstract and concrete models for recursion. In: Grumberg, O., Nipkow, T., Pfaller, C. (eds.) Proceedings of the NATO Advanced Study Institute on Formal Logical Methods for System Security and Correctness, pp. 175–198. IOS Press (2008)
25. James, R.P., Sabry, A.: Theseus: a high level language for reversible computing, work-in-progress report at RC 2014 (2014). https://www.cs.indiana.edu/~sabry/papers/theseus.pdf
26. Joyal, A., Street, R., Verity, D.: Traced monoidal categories. Math. Proc. Camb. Philos. Soc. **119**(3), 447–468 (1996)
27. Kutrib, M., Wendlandt, M.: Reversible limited automata. In: Durand-Lose, J., Nagy, B. (eds.) MCU 2015. LNCS, vol. 9288, pp. 113–128. Springer, Heidelberg (2015)
28. Landauer, R.: Irreversibility and heat generation in the computing process. IBM J. Res. Dev. **5**(3), 183–191 (1961)
29. Lawson, M.V.: Inverse Semigroups: The Theory of Partial Symmetries. World Scientific, Singapore (1998)
30. Manes, E.G., Benson, D.B.: The inverse semigroup of a sum-ordered semiring. Semigroup Forum **31**(1), 129–152 (1985)
31. Morita, K.: Two-way reversible multihead automata. Fundamenta Informaticae **110**(1–4), 241–254 (2011)
32. Robinson, E., Rosolini, G.: Categories of partial maps. Inf. Comput. **79**, 95–130 (1988)
33. Schordan, M., Jefferson, D., Barnes, P., Oppelstrup, T., Quinlan, D.: Reverse code generation for parallel discrete event simulation. In: Krivine, J., Stefani, J.B. (eds.) RC 2015. LNCS, vol. 9138, pp. 95–110. Springer, Heidelberg (2015)
34. Schultz, U.P., Bordignon, M., Støy, K.: Robust and reversible execution of self-reconfiguration sequences. Robotica **29**(1), 35–57 (2011)
35. Schultz, U.P., Laursen, J.S., Ellekilde, L., Axelsen, H.B.: Towards a domain-specific language for reversible assembly sequences. In: Krivine, J., Stefani, J.B. (eds.) RC 2015. LNCS, vol. 9138, pp. 111–126. Springer, Heidelberg (2015)
36. Selinger, P.: Idempotents in dagger categories. In: Selinger, P. (ed.) QPL 2006. Electronic Notes in Theoretical Computer Science, vol. 210, pp. 107–122. Elsevier (2008)

37. Selinger, P.: A survey of graphical languages for monoidal categories. In: Coecke, B. (ed.) New Structures for Physics. Lecture Notes in Physics, vol. 813, pp. 289–355. Springer, Heidelberg (2011)
38. Selinger, P.: Finite dimensional Hilbert spaces are complete for dagger compact closed categories. Logical Methods Comput. Sci. 8(3), 1–12 (2012)
39. Yokoyama, T., Axelsen, H.B., Glück, R.: Towards a reversible functional language. In: De Vos, A., Wille, R. (eds.) RC 2011. LNCS, vol. 7165, pp. 14–29. Springer, Heidelberg (2012)
40. Yokoyama, T., Glück, R.: A reversible programming language and its invertible self-interpreter. In: Proceedings of the Partial Evaluation and Program Manipulation, pp. 144–153. ACM (2007)

A Coalgebraic View of Bar Recursion and Bar Induction

Venanzio Capretta[1] and Tarmo Uustalu[2]([envelope])

[1] School of Computer Science, University of Nottingham, Nottingham, UK
venanzio.capretta@nottingham.ac.uk
[2] Institute of Cybernetics, Tallinn University of Technology, Tallinn, Estonia
tarmo@cs.ioc.ee

Abstract. We reformulate the bar recursion and induction principles in terms of recursive and wellfounded coalgebras. Bar induction was originally proposed by Brouwer as an axiom to recover certain classically valid theorems in a constructive setting. It is a form of induction on non-wellfounded trees satisfying certain properties. Bar recursion, introduced later by Spector, is the corresponding function definition principle.

We give a generalization of these principles, by introducing the notion of barred coalgebra: a process with a branching behaviour given by a functor, such that all possible computations terminate.

Coalgebraic bar recursion is the statement that every barred coalgebra is recursive; a recursive coalgebra is one that allows definition of functions by a coalgebra-to-algebra morphism. It is a framework to characterize valid forms of recursion for terminating functional programs. One application of the principle is the tabulation of continuous functions: Ghani, Hancock and Pattinson defined a type of wellfounded trees that represent continuous functions on streams. Bar recursion allows us to prove that every *stably* continuous function can be tabulated to such a tree, where by stability we mean that the modulus of continuity is its own modulus. Coalgebraic bar induction states that every barred coalgebra is wellfounded; a wellfounded coalgebra is one that admits proof by induction.

1 Introduction

Bar induction is a reasoning principle formulated by L. E. J. Brouwer [9,23].

He argued that it is justified in a constructive view of mathematics. Some classical theorems that are not otherwise provable in intuitionistic mathematics, follow from bar induction.

Intuitively, it posits a link between termination and induction. It says that if processes of a certain class always terminate, then the class admits a form of wellfounded induction.

Specifically, here is the original formulation of bar induction. Assume:

- Q is a decidable predicate on lists of natural numbers and Q is a *bar* (for every stream σ there exists a natural n such that the list of the first n elements of σ satisfies Q);

© Springer-Verlag Berlin Heidelberg 2016
B. Jacobs and C. Löding (Eds.): FOSSACS 2016, LNCS 9634, pp. 91–106, 2016.
DOI: 10.1007/978-3-662-49630-5_6

– R is another predicate on lists of naturals, such that Q implies R (every list satisfying Q also satisfies R) and is *inductive* (for every list l, if every extension of l by one element satisfies R, then l also satisfies R);

Then the empty list satisfies R.

In this statement, streams must be interpreted as *choice sequences*, that is, infinite sequences of natural numbers not necessarily given by an effective rule. Kleene proved that bar induction implies that not all streams are computable [16]. Recently, Nakata, Bezem and one of us (Uustalu) [17] proved some interesting consequences of the principle on the relationships between some temporal operators (some of them mixed inductive/coinductive) on branching processes.

Later, Spector [19] formulated the principle of *bar recursion* that allows definition of higher-order functionals (see also [10] and Chap. 5 of [4]); he exploited the principle to give a proof of consistency of mathematical analysis. Berardi, Bezem and Coquand [5] reformulated Spector's principle and results; their version was termed modified bar recursion by Berger and Oliva [6], who also gave an analysis of the relation between the different variations.

We offer a reformulation and generalization of the principle in terms of coalgebras. Coalgebras are useful to model branching computational processes and types of infinite data. In previous work [7,8] we studied the notions of *recursive* and *wellfounded coalgebras*, useful to analyze recursive functions in total functional programming and induction proofs of their properties.

Now we formulate a new notion of *barred coalgebra*, which characterizes processes whose computations always terminate, or data structures whose paths are all finite. We then state two principles as modern versions of Brouwer's.

Coalgebraic bar recursion states that every barred coalgebra is recursive. This allows us to define total recursive functions on a structure if we know that all its paths are finite. We give one application to continuous functions on streams. Ghani, Hancock and Pattinson [13] defined a type of inductive trees that represent continuous functions on streams by tabulating the outputs in their leaves. We restrict our attention to *stably* continuous functions, where stability means that the modulus of continuity is also continuous with itself as the modulus. We show that bar recursion implies that all stably continuous functions on streams can be tabulated.

Coalgebraic bar induction states that every barred coalgebra is wellfounded. This allows us to reason about the process by a form of induction. The original form of bar induction is an instantiation of this version.

We do not claim that the principles should be accepted always and in full generality. Instead, we view them as plausible assumptions encapsulating powerful function definition and reasoning devices that need to be justified depending on the exact setting where they are invoked.

The paper is organized as follows. In Sect. 2, we introduce coalgebraic bar recursion. In Sect. 3, we apply it to tabulation of stably continuous stream functions. Coalgebraic bar induction is introduced and compared to Brouwer's principle in Sect. 4.

2   Bar Recursion

In previous work with Vene [7], we contributed to the study of *recursive coalgebras*, introduced by Osius [18] and further elaborated by Paul Taylor [20–22]. More recently, Adámek, Milius and colleagues [2,3] have made additional significant contributions.

Definition 1. *A coalgebra (A, α) of an endofunctor F on a category $\mathcal{C}$ is called recursive if for every algebra (C, γ) there exists a unique map $f : A \to C$ (a coalgebra-to-algebra morphism) making the following diagram commute:*

This is a useful notion in total functional programming: It guarantees that every structured recursive diagram (that is, a coalgebra-to-algebra morphism diagram) based on it is a definite description of a function.

In the definition, unique existence of a mediating morphism is demanded upfront. No "more intrinsic" property of the coalgebra is invoked to guarantee unique constructibility of the solution.

We are interested in coalgebras of functors that can be viewed as tree generators with a good notion of a path. A special class of set functors, called *container functors* [1] (they are closely related to *polynomial functors* [12]), give tree types that work for us.

Definition 2. *A* container *is given by a set S of shapes and an S-indexed family of positions for every shape. It defines a set functor $[\![S, P]\!]$ by*

$$[\![S, P]\!]\, X = \Sigma s : S.\, P\, s \to X.$$

We use containers to describe "branching types" of trees. A container (S, P) says that there are S many "types" of branching nodes and that nodes of type $s : S$ have $P\, s$ many children. The sets of wellfounded and non-wellfounded trees with branching type (S, P) are described as the inductive type $\mu X.\, [\![S, P]\!]\, X$ (the initial algebra) and the coinductive type $\nu X.\, [\![S, P]\!]\, X$ (the final coalgebra). For the first of these to have any elements at all, there must be at least one shape with no positions.

We demand that inhabitedness of $P\, s$ is decidable for all $s : S$.

A coalgebra (A, α) is a process with a set of states A and a transition function $\alpha : A \to [\![S, P]\!]\, A$ that generates a shape and new states in every position. Unfolding α takes a given initial state $a : A$ to a non-wellfounded tree. This is the unique coalgebra morphism from (A, α) to the final coalgebra.

Recursiveness of the coalgebra is equivalent to this tree unfolding being actually wellfounded for every initial state $a : A$, which in other words is to say that the unique coalgebra morphism to the final coalgebra factors through the initial algebra. (This was observed by Adámek, Lücke and Milius [2], who also called this condition the halting property.)

We suggest a classically equivalent, but constructively weaker condition. This is that, for every initial state $a : A$, every *path* in the tree unfolding of α takes one from the root to a leaf in a finite number of steps.[1]

We need first some additional definitions to formalize what we mean by paths of an element of the coalgebra.

For every state a, we define the set $\mathsf{Path}_\alpha\, a$ of paths starting from it. At each stage, the path chooses a position through which to proceed. Notation: We define types and families by rules; sets of rules written with a single rule line are inductive definitions, sets of rules written with a double rule line are coinductive definitions.

$$\dfrac{\alpha\, a = (s, h) \quad \neg P\, s}{\mathsf{end} : \mathsf{Path}_\alpha\, a} \qquad \dfrac{\alpha\, a = (s, h) \quad p : P\, s \quad \pi : \mathsf{Path}_\alpha\, (h\, p)}{p \prec \pi : \mathsf{Path}_\alpha\, a}$$

The first rule states that, if we reached a shape with no positions, then we are at a leaf of the tree and the path ends. The second rule states that we can construct a path by choosing a position in the present shape and continuing from the new state given by the transition in that position. This definition is coinductive, so the path may continue forever.

Alternatively, we could define paths as functions from $\mathbb{N}$; but this would exclude finite paths, which would have to be extended by iterating a distinguished element. The coinductive presentation is therefore more natural and avoids some coding. The status of general coinductive types in constructivism is unclear. However, paths and also tree unfoldings of coalgebras of containers can be coded with inductive and function types. So we are justified in using them.

Next we inductively define finiteness of a path. A path π is considered finite ($\pi \downarrow$) if it reaches a positionless shape after a finite number of steps. The definition mirrors that of paths, but it is inductive.

$$\dfrac{\alpha\, a = (s, h) \quad \neg P\, s}{\mathsf{end} \downarrow} \qquad \dfrac{\alpha\, a = (s, h) \quad p : P\, s \quad \pi : \mathsf{Path}_\alpha\, (h\, p) \quad \pi \downarrow}{p \prec \pi \downarrow}$$

Definition 3. *A* barred coalgebra *is a coalgebra α whose all paths are finite:*

$$\forall a : A.\, \forall \pi : \mathsf{Path}_\alpha\, a.\ \pi \downarrow.$$

Note that the simpler condition that the coalgebra has no infinite paths, although classically equivalent, is constructively weaker than finiteness of all paths. Adopting this condition instead would make coalgebraic bar induction too strong; it would not follow from Brouwer's formulation anymore. Assuming decidability of inhabitation of $P\, s$, the difference of the two conditions is exactly Markov's principle.

---

[1] In our constructive setting, it might in fact be more appropriate to take the name 'halting' for this condition that considers individual runs one by one rather than the whole entirety of evolutions of the process at once.

We are now ready to formulate a coalgebraic version of the principle of bar recursion. It says that finiteness of all paths of a coalgebra implies that we can define functions by recursion. Classically this is provable, but constructively it is just a plausible extra axiom.

COALGEBRAIC BAR RECURSION: Every barred coalgebra is recursive.

$$\alpha \text{ barred} \Rightarrow \alpha \text{ recursive}$$

The converse implication does not need to be assumed: it is provable.

Proposition 1. *Every recursive coalgebra of a container functor is barred.*

$$\alpha \text{ recursive} \Rightarrow \alpha \text{ barred}$$

Proof. Assume that a coalgebra $\alpha : A \to [\![S, P]\!] A$ is recursive. Then we have the unique coalgebra-to-algebra morphism $f : A \to \mu X. [\![S, P]\!] X$. For an element $a : A$, finiteness of all paths from a is proved by structural induction on $f\,a$. $\square$

We will not define Spector's bar recursion here. (Instead we will discuss Brouwer's bar induction in detail in Sect. 4.) But it corresponds to instances of coalgebraic bar recursion for $S = 1 + 1$ and $P(\text{inl} *) = 0$, $P(\text{inr} *) = A$, with A some fixed set. This means that $[\![S, P]\!] X \cong 1 + (A \to X)$. The typical case is $A = \mathbb{N}$, but Spector also considered general A. This allowed him to interpret the general axiom of countable choice.

3 Continuous Functions on Streams

We illustrate the coalgebraic bar recursion principle by applying it to continuous functions on streams.

A function on streams is continuous if it only uses a finite initial segment of its input stream to determine its result.

Ghani, Hancock and Pattinson [13] defined an inductive type of trees for representing continuous functions on streams. When applied to a stream, a function can either immediately return a result, or read the next element of the stream and continue the computation. In the tree representation, an immediate return is modelled by a leaf containing the output value, a reading operation is modelled by a node that branches according to the input value.

The statement that all continuous functions can be represented as trees in this manner is not provable constructively without additional assumptions. Ghani, Hancock and Pattinson give a proof of a negative version of this statement: If a function has no tree representation, then it cannot be continuous.

We will show that, assuming coalgebraic bar recursion, the positive statement of representability becomes provable for what we call stably continuous functions. Stability is a natural condition, requiring that the modulus of continuity is also continuous, with itself as its modulus.

Let $\mathbb{S}_A$ be the type of streams (infinite sequences) of elements of type A. The equivalence relation $=_n$, for n a natural number, identifies streams that coincide on the first n elements:

$$\sigma_1 =_n \sigma_2 \quad \text{if and only if} \quad \forall i < n. \, \sigma_1(i) = \sigma_2(i).$$

Definition 4. *A function* $f : \mathbb{S}_A \to B$ *from streams of elements of type* A *to results of type* B *is* continuous *if*

$$\forall \sigma : \mathbb{S}_A.\ \exists n : \mathbb{N}.\ \forall \sigma' : \mathbb{S}_A.\ \sigma' =_n \sigma \to f\,\sigma' = f\,\sigma.$$

So a function f is continuous on a stream σ if the value of f only depends on the first n elements of σ, for some n. It is continuous globally if it is continuous on every stream.

This definition corresponds to $\mathbb{S}_A$ being assigned the prodiscrete and B the discrete topology. This is what is appropriate for our purposes here. It can feel limited. For $B = \mathbb{S}_A$, for instance, not even the identity function is continuous, but then with the trees considered here it cannot be tabulated either.[2]

For other purposes, other choices can be appropriate. Brouwer's continuity principle states that all functions of type $\mathbb{S}_\mathbb{N} \to \mathbb{N}$ are continuous. It seems justified by a computational view of functions as programs: a terminating program computes its result in a finite number of steps; during the computation it can only read a finite number of entries from the stream. This principle can be generalized to functions $A \to B$ where A and B are assigned their "native" topologies (whereby stream types must get product topologies). However, Escardó recently discovered that the continuity principle is inconsistent in type theory [11], so the principle cannot be added safely to current type-theoretic foundations. The intuitive reason is that adding the principle adds new functions to the system and some of those are problematic. Various strands of research are investigating weaker and more refined versions of the principle that may be safe.

For our goals, it is important that a continuous function has an explicit *modulus of continuity*, the mapping that gives the length of the initial segment of the stream needed for the computation, and that this modulus is stable, that is, it makes consistent choices for streams that have the same initial segment.

Definition 5. *A* modulus of continuity *for a function* $f : \mathbb{S}_A \to B$ *is a function* $m_f : \mathbb{S}_A \to \mathbb{N}$ *such that*

$$\forall \sigma, \sigma' : \mathbb{S}_A.\ \sigma' =_{m_f\,\sigma} \sigma \to f\,\sigma' = f\,\sigma.$$

The modulus is stable *if*

$$\forall \sigma, \sigma' : \mathbb{S}_A.\ \sigma' =_{m_f\,\sigma} \sigma \to m_f\,\sigma' = m_f\,\sigma.$$

So a modulus of continuity is stable if and only if it is its own modulus of continuity. Stability is a reasonable assumption in the computational view of functions:

– If, to compute $f\,\sigma$, we only need to read the first $m_f\,\sigma$ elements of σ; and
– σ' coincides with σ on the first $m_f\,\sigma$ elements;

---

[2] In a different work [14], Hancock, Pattinson and Ghani used a mixed inductive/coinductive type to tabulate stream processors, i.e., continuous functions $f : \mathbb{S}_A \to \mathbb{S}_B$ where both $\mathbb{S}_A$ and $\mathbb{S}_B$ are given the prodiscrete topology.

- then we only need the first $m_f \, \sigma$ elements of σ' to compute $f \, \sigma'$ (which is equal to $f \, \sigma$);
- so it is reasonable to expect that $m_f \, \sigma' = m_f \, \sigma$.

However, given a possibly non-stable modulus, it is not in general possible to construct another modulus which is stable. In the case that the original modulus is continuous, there is an algorithm to stabilize it.

Given a non-stable but continuous modulus m, we construct a new stable modulus $\bar{m}$ for the same function. We do it by truncating every stream at an appropriate point, dictated by m, and filling in the rest of it with a fixed stream. If A is inhabited, so we know an element, we can repeat that element in a constant stream σ_0. For every σ and every index $i : \mathbb{N}$, let $\sigma|_i$ be its truncation at position i, that is, the list $[\sigma(0), \ldots, \sigma(i - 1)]$. Let $n_i = m \, (\sigma|_i \mathbin{+\!\!+} \sigma_0)$. (The notation $\mathbin{+\!\!+}$ denotes prepending a list to a stream and also to a path.) We now define the result of the new modulus $\bar{m}$ on σ:

$$\bar{m} \, \sigma = n_k \quad \text{where } k = \min\{i \mid n_i \leq i\}.$$

Continuity of m guarantees that $\bar{m}$ is well defined: k always exists. In fact we know that there is a j such that, if $\sigma' =_j \sigma$, then $m \, \sigma' = m \, \sigma$. In particular, if we choose $\sigma' = \sigma|_i \mathbin{+\!\!+} \sigma_0$ where $i = \max(j, m \, \sigma)$, we have:

$$n_i = m \, \sigma' = m \, \sigma \leq i.$$

So, since there is at least one i such that $n_i \leq i$, there is a minimal one k.

In Ghani, Hancock and Pattinson's work [13], a continuous function $f : \mathbb{S}_A \to B$ is represented by a wellfounded tree, an element of the inductive type $\mathsf{SF}_{A,B}$ given by the rules

$$\frac{b : B}{\mathsf{write} \, b : \mathsf{SF}_{A,B}} \qquad \frac{g : A \to \mathsf{SF}_{A,B}}{\mathsf{read} \, g : \mathsf{SF}_{A,B}}$$

The idea is that an element of $\mathsf{SF}_{A,B}$ is a tabulation of all the values of a function as leaves in a tree whose finite paths have to be matched against the input stream. The application of a tabulation gives us a continuous function:

$$
\begin{aligned}
&\mathsf{apply} : \mathsf{SF}_{A,B} \to \mathbb{S}_A \to B \\
&\mathsf{apply} \, (\mathsf{write} \, b) \, s = b \\
&\mathsf{apply} \, (\mathsf{read} \, g) \, (a \prec s) = \mathsf{apply} \, (g \, a) \, s
\end{aligned}
$$

The operator apply is defined by structural recursion on its tree argument.

Is there an inverse transformation, that is, a tabulation operator assigning a tree to every continuous function,

$$\mathsf{tabulate} : (\mathbb{S}_A \to B) \to \mathsf{SF}_{A,B}?$$

Classically, we can prove that this function exists, but the proof is not constructive. Intuitively, the algorithm to obtain the tabulation should be the following. Let $f : \mathbb{S}_A \to B$ be continuous. Then we can define:

$$
\begin{array}{ll}
\mathsf{tabulate} \, f = \mathsf{write} \, b & \text{if } f \text{ "must be" constantly } b \\
\mathsf{tabulate} \, f = \mathsf{read} \, (\lambda a.\mathsf{tabulate} \, (\lambda\sigma.f \, (a \prec \sigma))) & \text{otherwise.}
\end{array}
$$

It is of course undecidable whether f is constant. But if the function is continuous constructively, we also have a modulus for it and can check whether the modulus is 0 on some fixed stream (we assume A to be inhabited, so we can construct one). This a sufficient condition for constancy.

However, it is not constructively provable that this algorithm generates a wellfounded tree. If the modulus is stable, we can prove that the paths of the recursive calls generated by the second equation for f are always finite. But this is not enough to conclude that the a priori non-wellfounded tabulation tree is wellfounded.

Ghani, Hancock and Pattinson proved a negative version of the statement: they did not construct a tabulation operator, but proved that, if a function cannot be tabulated, then it is not continuous.

With bar recursion, we can conclude the positive statement, using stable continuity. We provide two distinct proofs. The first proof is local: for every stably continuous function it constructs a barred coalgebra and uses it to generate the tabulation tree. The second proof is global: it constructs a single barred coalgebra on the set of all stably continuous functions and uses it to define a tabulation operation.

3.1 Individual Tabulations

First we show how to tabulate a single stably continuous function by associating an individual barred coalgebra to it. Let $f : \mathbb{S}_A \to B$ be a function with a stable modulus of continuity $m : \mathbb{S}_A \to \mathbb{N}$. We will assume that A is inhabited and has a distinguished element, which we can repeat in a stream σ_0.

We construct a coalgebra on the functor $FX = B + (A \to X)$ with carrier the set of lists of elements of A:

$$\alpha_f : \mathsf{List}_A \to B + (A \to \mathsf{List}_A)$$
$$\alpha_f\, l = \begin{cases} \mathsf{inl}\,(f\,(l +\!\!+ \sigma_0)) & \text{if } m\,(l +\!\!+ \sigma_0) \leq \mathsf{length}\, l \\ \mathsf{inr}\,(\lambda a.\, l +\!\!+ [a]) & \text{otherwise.} \end{cases}$$

The coalgebra checks whether the list l is sufficient to determine the result given by f: if the modulus of continuity on a stream starting with l is at most the length of l, then we know that f will depend only on it. In this case, the coalgebra terminates with the value given by f. Else, it branches into new processes for all elements of A, lengthening the list by appending the element at the end.

Observe that the functor F is a container with shapes $B + 1$, a shape for each possible leaf in B, and a single shape for the continuation. The shapes in B have no positions: the coalgebra terminates. The single continuation shape has positions for all possible input elements, so the set of positions is A. The paths in $\mathsf{Path}_\alpha\, l$ are sequences of position choices, so in this case they are sequences of elements of A. Any such path π can be padded out to a stream of elements of A by appending σ_0 to it: $\mathsf{pad}\,\mathsf{end} = \sigma_0$, $\mathsf{pad}\,(a \prec \pi) = a \prec \mathsf{pad}\,\pi$.

Lemma 1. α_f *is a barred coalgebra.*

Proof. Given l : List_A and π : $\mathsf{Path}_\alpha\, l$, we prove that $\pi \downarrow$ by induction on $m\,\sigma_{l,\pi} - \mathsf{length}\,l$ where $\sigma_{l,\pi} = l \mathbin{+\!\!+} \mathsf{pad}\,\pi$.

- If $m\,\sigma_{l,\pi} - \mathsf{length}\,l = 0$, then $m\,\sigma_{l,\pi} \leq \mathsf{length}\,l$, so $\sigma_{l,\pi} =_{m\,\sigma_{l,\pi}} l \mathbin{+\!\!+} \sigma_0$. By stability, $m\,(l \mathbin{+\!\!+} \sigma_0) = m\,\sigma_{l,\pi} \leq \mathsf{length}\,l$. Therefore $\alpha_f\,l = \mathsf{inl}\,(f\,(l \mathbin{+\!\!+} \sigma_0))$ and $\pi = \mathsf{end}$. In this case obviously the path is finite.
- Otherwise, if $m\,\sigma_{l,\pi} - \mathsf{length}\,l > 0$, then $m\,\sigma_{l,\pi} > \mathsf{length}\,l$. It is impossible that $m\,(l \mathbin{+\!\!+} \sigma_0) \leq \mathsf{length}\,l$ because, if it were, then also $m\,\sigma_{l,\pi} = m\,(l \mathbin{+\!\!+} \sigma_0) \leq \mathsf{length}\,l$ by stability. So $\alpha_f\,l = \mathsf{inr}\,(\lambda a.\,l \mathbin{+\!\!+} [a])$ and $\pi = a \prec \pi'$ for some a : A and π' : $\mathsf{Path}_\alpha\,(l \mathbin{+\!\!+} [a])$.
  Note that $\sigma_{l \mathbin{+\!\!+} [a],\pi'} = \sigma_{l,\pi}$, so $m\,\sigma_{l \mathbin{+\!\!+} [a],\pi'} - \mathsf{length}\,(l \mathbin{+\!\!+} [a]) = m\,\sigma_\pi - \mathsf{length}\,l - 1$. Therefore $\pi' \downarrow$ by the induction hypothesis and so $\pi \downarrow$.   □

We can now invoke bar induction on this coalgebra to tabulate f.

Theorem 1. *The coalgebraic bar induction principle implies that there exists an element* $\mathsf{tabulate}_f$: $\mathsf{SF}_{A,B}$ *such that* $\mathsf{apply}\,(\mathsf{tabulate}_f)\,\sigma = f\,\sigma$ *for every* σ : $\mathbb{S}_A$.

Proof. If we apply the coalgebraic bar recursion principle to the statement of Lemma 1, we obtain that α_f is a recursive coalgebra.

Notice that $\mathsf{SF}_{A,B}$ is the carrier of the initial algebra of the functor F:

$$\mathsf{SF}_{A,B} = \mu X.\, B + (A \to X).$$

The copair of the two constructors $[\mathsf{write}, \mathsf{read}]$ is the actual algebra.

We can apply the defining property of recursive coalgebras to deduce that there exists a unique function tab making the following diagram commute.

$$
\begin{array}{ccc}
\mathsf{List}_A & \xrightarrow{\;\;\alpha_f\;\;} & B + (A \to \mathsf{List}_A) \\[2pt]
{\scriptstyle\mathsf{tab}}\Big\downarrow & & \Big\downarrow{\scriptstyle F\,\mathsf{tab}} \\[2pt]
\mathsf{SF}_{A,B} & \xleftarrow[\;[\mathsf{write},\mathsf{read}]\;]{} & B + (A \to \mathsf{SF}_{A,B}).
\end{array}
$$

We can now define the Ghani, Hancock and Pattinson representation of f by

$$
\begin{aligned}
\mathsf{tabulate}_f &: \mathsf{SF}_{A,B} \\
\mathsf{tabulate}_f &= \mathsf{tab}\,[].
\end{aligned}
$$

Its correctness can be checked simply by observing that, in general,

$$\mathsf{apply}\,(\mathsf{tab}\,l)\,\sigma = f\,(l \mathbin{+\!\!+} \sigma).$$ □

3.2 Global Tabulation

The second way to use coalgebraic bar recursion for tabulation is to define a coalgebra on the set of all stably continuous functions:

$$\mathcal{F} = \{(f,m) \mid m : \mathbb{S}_A \to \mathbb{N} \text{ is a stable modulus of } f : \mathbb{S}_A \to B\}.$$

We use the same functor as for the individual coalgebras of the previous section: $FX = B + (A \to X)$. The algebra simply tests whether a function must be constant: if it has to be, it returns its value, otherwise it branches. It does so by checking that the modulus is 0 for σ_0; it must be then be 0 for all streams by stability.

$$\alpha : \mathcal{F} \to B + (A \to \mathcal{F})$$

$$\alpha(f, m) = \begin{cases} \mathsf{inl}\,(f\,\sigma_0) & \text{if } m\,\sigma_0 = 0 \\ \mathsf{inr}\,(\lambda a.\,(f_a, m_a)) & \text{otherwise} \end{cases}$$

where

$$f_a\,\sigma = f\,(a \prec \sigma) \quad \text{and} \quad m_a\,\sigma = m\,(a \prec \sigma) - 1.$$

In the branching case, the coalgebra reads an element of the input, a, and returns the function f_a obtained by shifting f by a. The modulus m_a of f_a is one less than the modulus of f, as we do not count the prepended element a.

Lemma 2. *The coalgebra α is barred.*

Proof. Let $\pi : \mathsf{Path}_\alpha\,(f, m)$ be a path of the coalgebra. We prove that $\pi \downarrow$ by induction on $m\,\sigma_\pi$ where $\sigma_\pi = \mathsf{pad}\,\pi$.

- If $m\,\sigma_\pi = 0$, then also $m\,\sigma_0 = 0$ by stability. So $\alpha(f, m) = \mathsf{inl}\,(f\,\sigma_0)$ and $\pi = \mathsf{end}$.
- If $m\,\sigma_\pi > 0$, then also $m\,\sigma_0 > 0$ by stability. So $\alpha(f, m) = \mathsf{inr}\,(\lambda a.\,(f_a, m_a))$. It must then be that $\pi = a \prec \pi'$ for some $a : A$ and $\pi' : \mathsf{Path}_\alpha\,(f_a, m_a)$. If we then compute the modulus of the stream associated to the tail of the path, we obtain

$$m_a\,\sigma_{\pi'} = m\,(a \prec \sigma_{\pi'}) - 1 = m\,\sigma_\pi - 1.$$

Therefore $\pi' \downarrow$ by the induction hypothesis, so $\pi \downarrow$. $\qquad\qquad\square$

We can now invoke bar induction on this coalgebra to construct a global tabulation operator.

Theorem 2. *The coalgebraic bar induction principle implies that there exists a function $\mathsf{tabulate} : \mathcal{F} \to \mathsf{SF}_{A,B}$ such that, for every continuous function with stable modulus $(f, m) : \mathcal{F}$ and every stream $\sigma : \mathbb{S}_A$, we have*

$$\mathsf{apply}\,(\mathsf{tabulate}\,(f, m))\,\sigma = f\,\sigma.$$

Proof. Applying the coalgebraic bar induction principle to the result of Lemma 2, we obtain that $(\mathcal{F}, \alpha)$ is a recursive coalgebra. In particular, the following diagram has a unique solution.

$$\begin{array}{ccc} \mathcal{F} & \xrightarrow{\quad\alpha\quad} & B + (A \to \mathcal{F}) \\ {\scriptstyle\mathsf{tabulate}}\Big\downarrow & & \Big\downarrow{\scriptstyle F\,\mathsf{tabulate}} \\ \mathsf{SF}_{A,B} & \xleftarrow[{[\mathsf{write},\mathsf{read}]}]{} & B + (A \to \mathsf{SF}_{A,B}). \end{array}$$

The operator $\mathsf{tabulate}$ maps every function to a correct tabulation tree for it. We prove this by induction on $m\,\sigma_0$:

– If $m\,\sigma_0 = 0$, then, by commutativity of the diagram, definition of α and continuity,

$$
\begin{aligned}
\mathsf{apply}\,(\mathsf{tabulate}\,(f,m))\,\sigma &= \mathsf{apply}\,([\mathsf{write},\mathsf{read}]\,(F\,\mathsf{tabulate}\,(\alpha\,(f,m))))\,\sigma \\
&= \mathsf{apply}\,([\mathsf{write},\mathsf{read}]\,(\mathsf{inl}\,(f\,\sigma_0)))\,\sigma \\
&= \mathsf{apply}\,(\mathsf{write}\,(f\,\sigma_0))\,\sigma \\
&= f\,\sigma_0 = f\,\sigma.
\end{aligned}
$$

– If $m\,\sigma_0 > 0$, then, writing $\sigma = a \prec \sigma'$, by commutativity of the diagram, the definition of α and the induction hypothesis,

$$
\begin{aligned}
\mathsf{apply}\,(\mathsf{tabulate}\,(f,m))\,\sigma &= \mathsf{apply}\,([\mathsf{write},\mathsf{read}]\,(F\,\mathsf{tabulate}\,(\alpha\,(f,m))))\,\sigma \\
&= \mathsf{apply}\,([\mathsf{write},\mathsf{read}]\,(\mathsf{inr}\,(\lambda a.\,\mathsf{tabulate}\,(f_a,m_a))))\,\sigma \\
&= \mathsf{apply}\,(\mathsf{read}\,(\lambda a.\,\mathsf{tabulate}\,(f_a,m_a)))\,(a \prec \sigma') \\
&= \mathsf{apply}\,(\mathsf{tabulate}\,(f_a,m_a))\,\sigma' \\
&= f_a\,\sigma' = f\,(a \prec \sigma') = f\,\sigma. \qquad \square
\end{aligned}
$$

We finish this discussion of tabulation of continuous functions on streams by noting that we need bar recursion for tabulation because our notion of (stable) continuity of a function (which is the standard notion of continuity) is path-based. It considers one stream (choice sequence) at a time and requires that reaching an answer takes a finite number of steps. Alternatively, we could define continuity in a way that considers the entirety of possible evolutions of the choice process at once. This would result in a stronger notion of continuity and then a continuous function could be tabulated without assumptions like bar recursion.

Concretely, we could define continuity as a predicate on $\mathbb{S}_A \to B$ inductively as follows.

$$
\frac{\forall \sigma, \sigma' : \mathbb{S}_A.\, f\,\sigma = f\,\sigma'}{f \text{ continuous}} \qquad \frac{\forall a : A.\,(\lambda \sigma.\, f\,(a \prec \sigma)) \text{ continuous}}{f \text{ continuous}}
$$

Tabulation would be immediate by structural recursion on the proof of continuity (and not exciting at all).

4   Bar Induction

We now want to give a coinductive account of the traditional formulation of bar induction. For this purpose, the notion of *wellfounded coalgebra* will be useful. Intuitively, it is a coalgebra that admits proofs of properties of its elements by induction. This notion was introduced by Taylor [20–22], who proved that, under weak reasonable assumptions, recursiveness and wellfoundedness of a coalgebra are equivalent. (In a previous article [8], we gave a review of the topic and extended it to the dual case or corecursive vs. antifounded algebras.)

Our formulation uses the *next-time operator* by Jacobs [15] on subobjects (subsets) of the carrier of a coalgebra. Let (A, α) be a coalgebra of a functor F that preserves pullbacks along monos on a category with pullbacks along monos. (These requirements are satisfied by container functors.)

Definition 6. *Let $j : U \hookrightarrow A$ be a subobject of the carrier of the coalgebra. The next-time subobject, $\mathsf{nt}_\alpha\, j : \mathsf{nt}_\alpha\, U \hookrightarrow A$ is defined by the following pullback.*

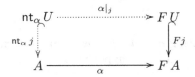

The idea of this definition is that, if U is a subset of A, then $\mathsf{nt}_\alpha\, U$ is the subset of A consisting of the elements that, after an α transition, fall into U.

In particular, suppose F is a container functor, $F = [\![S, P]\!]$. If $a : A$, then $\alpha\, a : F\, A$ has the form (s, h) with $s : S$ and $h : P\, s \to A$. We have that $a \in \mathsf{nt}_\alpha\, U$ if, for all $p : P\, s$, $h\, p \in U$.

$$\mathsf{nt}_\alpha\, U = \{a : A \mid \forall p : P\, s.\ h\, p \in U \text{ where } (s, h) = \alpha\, a\}$$

Definition 7. *The coalgebra (A, α) is wellfounded if, for every subobject $j : U \hookrightarrow A$, if $\mathsf{nt}_\alpha\, U$ factors through U, then j is an isomorphism. In diagram form this says that*

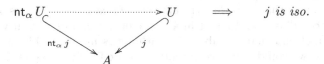

In simpler terms, the coalgebra is wellfounded, if $\mathsf{nt}_\alpha\, U \subseteq U$ implies $A \subseteq U$.

Intuitively, the defining property of wellfounded coalgebras is a generalization of the familiar induction principle associated to initial algebras. We want to prove that all elements of A are in the subset U. And we do this by showing that, if all "components" of an element $a : A$ (given by $\alpha\, a$) are in U, so is a.

We introduce the following principle.

COALGEBRAIC BAR INDUCTION: Every barred coalgebra is wellfounded.

$$\alpha \text{ barred} \Rightarrow \alpha \text{ wellfounded}$$

This principle says that, if all paths of a coalgebra are finite, then we can prove its properties by induction.

The converse implication holds without extra assumptions.

Proposition 2. *Every wellfounded coalgebra is barred.*

$$\alpha \text{ wellfounded} \Rightarrow \alpha \text{ barred}$$

Proof. Assume that α is wellfounded and take U to be the subset of those elements of A whose all paths are finite:

$$U = \{a : A \mid \forall \pi : \mathsf{Path}_\alpha\, a.\ \pi \downarrow\}.$$

We then have that

$$\mathsf{nt}_\alpha\, U = \{a : A \mid \forall p : P\, s.\ \forall \pi' : \mathsf{Path}_\alpha\, (h\, p).\, \pi' \downarrow \text{ where } (s, h) = \alpha\, a\}.$$

Suppose $a \in \mathsf{nt}_\alpha\, U$; we want to prove that $a \in U$. So assume $\pi : \mathsf{Path}_\alpha\, a$; we will show that this path is finite. Suppose $\alpha\, a = (s, h)$. If $\pi = \mathsf{end}$, as $\neg P\, s$, then we conclude immediately that $\pi \downarrow$. If $\pi = p \prec \pi'$ for some $p : P\, s$ and $\pi' : \mathsf{Path}_\alpha\, (h\, p)$, then we know by assumption that $\pi' \downarrow$ and consequently $\pi \downarrow$.

We proved that $\mathsf{nt}_\alpha\, U \subseteq U$; therefore, by wellfoundedness of α, we have that $A \subseteq U$. So all paths are finite.   □

The traditional formulation of bar induction from Brouwer is about predicates on lists of natural numbers.

Brouwer's Bar Induction:

- Let Q be a *decidable* predicate on lists of natural numbers. Assume that Q is a *bar*: $\forall \sigma : \mathbb{S}_\mathbb{N}.\ \exists n : \mathbb{N}.\ Q\, (\sigma|_n)$.
- Let R be a predicate on lists of naturals. Assume that Q implies R and R is *inductive*: $\forall l : \mathsf{List}_\mathbb{N}.\ (\forall p : \mathbb{N}.\ R\, (l + [p])) \to R\, l$.
- Then $R\, []$ holds.

We can assume that Q and R are suffix closed: $\forall l : \mathsf{List}_\mathbb{N}.\ \forall p : \mathbb{N}.\ Q\, l \to Q\, (l + [p])$ and similarly for R. Indeed, if they are not, we can use their suffix closures. We can define $\hat{Q}\, l$ to hold if $\exists n \leq \mathsf{length}\, l.\ Q\, (l|_n)$ and similarly for $\hat{R}$. The new predicates $\hat{Q}$ and $\hat{R}$ still satisfy the assumptions of the principle and $\hat{R}\, [] \leftrightarrow R\, []$. Also, since Q is decidable, Q being a bar implies that it is also a "tight" bar: $\forall \sigma : \mathbb{S}_\mathbb{N}.\ \exists n : \mathbb{N}.\ (\forall m : \mathbb{N}.\ m < n \to \neg Q\, (\sigma|_m)) \wedge Q\, (\sigma|_n)$.

Instead of $\mathbb{N}$, one could consider other sets in Brouwer's bar induction. The case of $\mathbb{B}$ is known as the fan "theorem" (Brouwer thought that fan theorem and bar induction were theorems, but both are just plausible axioms; the fan theorem is a positive version of weak König's lemma). In principle one could replace $\mathbb{N}$ with any fixed set, but the question is how justified this is from the constructive point of view. $\mathbb{N}$ is special in that it is a set that can be traversed by an infinite process.

The traditional form of bar induction follows from the coalgebraic version.

Theorem 3. *Coalgebraic bar induction implies Brouwer's bar induction.*

Proof. Given Q and R satisfying the assumptions of Brouwer's bar induction, we define a coalgebra structure of the functor $F\, X = 1 + (\mathbb{N} \to X)$ on the set $\mathsf{List}_\mathbb{N}$.

$$\alpha : \mathsf{List}_\mathbb{N} \to 1 + (\mathbb{N} \to \mathsf{List}_\mathbb{N})$$

$$\alpha\, l = \begin{cases} \mathsf{inl}\, * & \text{if } Q\, l \\ \mathsf{inr}\, (\lambda p.\, l + [p]) & \text{otherwise.} \end{cases}$$

The function α is welldefined, since Q is decidable. From the assumption that Q is a bar, we conclude that α is barred. Indeed, let $\pi : \mathsf{Path}_\alpha\, l$ for some list l; we must prove that π is finite. We consider the stream $\sigma = l +\!\!+ \mathsf{pad}\,\pi$ (using, e.g., 0 as the distinguished element of $\mathbb{N}$ for padding). Since Q is decidable and a bar, σ must have a shortest finite prefix $\sigma|_n$ satisfying Q. If $n < \mathsf{length}\,l$, then $\sigma|_n$ is a proper prefix of l. This forces that $\pi = \mathsf{end}$, since suffix-closedness of Q gives us that $Q\,l$. If $n \geq \mathsf{length}\,l$, then $l +\!\!+ \pi = \sigma|_n +\!\!+ \mathsf{end}$. Either way, π is finite.

Thus we can apply coalgebraic bar induction and learn that α is wellfounded.

Let $U = \{l : \mathsf{List}_\mathbb{N} \mid R\,l\}$. (In type theory we can use the dependent pair type $\Sigma l : \mathsf{List}_\mathbb{N}.\, R\,l$.) We will prove that $\mathsf{nt}_\alpha\, U \subseteq U$ from where by wellfoundedness of α it will follow that $\mathsf{List}_\mathbb{N} \subseteq U$.

By definition

$$\mathsf{nt}\,U = \{l : \mathsf{List}_\mathbb{N} \mid \alpha\,l \in 1 + (\mathbb{N} \to U)\}$$

We prove that if $l \in \mathsf{nt}\,U$, then $l \in U$, by cases:

- If $Q\,l$ holds, then $\alpha\,l = \mathsf{inl}\,*$. Since Q implies R, we also have $R\,l$, that is, $l \in U$.
- If $Q\,l$ does not hold, then $\alpha\,l = \mathsf{inr}\,(\lambda p.\, l +\!\!+ [p])$ with $l +\!\!+ [p] \in U$ for every $p : \mathbb{N}$. By the assumption that R is inductive, we can derive that $l \in U$.

Therefore, since α is wellfounded, we can deduce that $\mathsf{List}_\mathbb{N} \subseteq U$, that is, $\forall l : \mathsf{List}_\mathbb{N}.\, R\,l$.

In particular, $R\,[]$, as desired. □

From Brouwer's bar induction, coalgebraic bar induction follows for the functor $F\,X = 1 + (\mathbb{N} \to X)$.

Theorem 4. *Brouwer's bar induction implies coalgebraic bar induction for* $F\,X = 1 + (\mathbb{N} \to X)$.

Proof. Given any set A with a barred coalgebra structure $\alpha : A \to 1 + (\mathbb{N} \to A)$ and a subset U of A satisfying the assumption $\mathsf{nt}_\alpha\, U \subseteq U$ of coalgebraic bar induction.

We define a function $\searrow\, : A \to \mathsf{List}_\mathbb{N} \to 1 + A$ by

$$a \searrow [] = \mathsf{inr}\,a$$

$$a \searrow (l +\!\!+ [p]) = \begin{cases} \mathsf{inl}\,* & \text{if } a \searrow l = \mathsf{inl}\,* \\ \mathsf{inl}\,* & \text{if } a \searrow l = \mathsf{inr}\,a' \text{ and } \alpha\,a' = \mathsf{inl}\,* \\ \mathsf{inr}\,(f\,p) & \text{if } a \searrow l = \mathsf{inr}\,a' \text{ and } \alpha\,a' = \mathsf{inr}\,f \end{cases}$$

For any $a : A$, we define $Q_a\,l$ to hold, if $a \searrow l = \mathsf{inl}\,*$, and $R_a\,l$ to hold, if $a \searrow l = \mathsf{inl}\,*$ or $a \searrow l = \mathsf{inr}\,a'$ and $a' \in U$.

It is immediate that, for any $a : A$, Q_a is decidable and $\forall l : \mathsf{List}_\mathbb{N}.\, Q_a\,l \to R_a\,l$. Moreover, as α is barred, Q_a is also a bar.

From $\mathsf{nt}_\alpha\, U \subseteq U$, it also follows that R_a is inductive for all $a : A$.

Hence, for any given $a : A$, we can apply Brouwer's bar induction, and conclude that $R_a\,[]$. Since $a \searrow [] = \mathsf{inr}\,a$, this means that $a \in U$. □

Coalgebraic bar induction follows from Brouwer's bar induction also for general container functors $[\![S, P]\!]$ for which $\Sigma s : S.\,P\,s$ is isomorphic to a decidable subset of $\mathbb{N}$. This is proved by "approximate" branchings of type $[\![S, P]\!]$ with branchings of type $FX = 1 + (\mathbb{N} \to X)$.

5 Conclusions

The explicit use of bar recursion and bar induction makes it possible to encapsulate non-constructive aspects of arguments about non-wellfounded trees and stream functions.

In this paper, we have defined coalgebraic versions of bar recursion and bar induction. We find that this perspective has at least two benefits. First, we can speak of the ingredients involved in bar recursion and bar induction using the terminology of modern theoretical computer science, especially coalgebra. Second, we can avoid unnecessary coding when we want to deal with types of trees with multiple types of branching nodes, with different numbers of children.

The notion of barred coalgebra neatly fills a useful position in the range of properties that a coalgebra may satisfy. In reasoning about the total correctness of programs, it is usual to give a proof of termination for all computations and then prove by induction that some invariant holds. This application of wellfounded induction is classically justified from termination, but is not constructively valid. Bar induction is the missing principle that provides the link. Since coalgebraic methods are becoming standard tools in programming and reasoning about correctness, we hope that the coalgebraic formulation of bar recursion will establish itself as a useful tool in functional programming and type theory.

Directly applying the traditional forms of bar induction and bar recursion in concrete cases often requires a lot of encoding, namely making all nodes to be of the same type with the same number of children, which also makes all paths infinite, all this artificially; termination is then characterized by a predicate with the bar property. Our formulation is more liberal and requires no encoding: nodes of different branching degrees are allowed and termination is simply modelled by leaves.

Acknowledgements. Capretta is grateful to the School of Computer Science that gave him a sabbatical semester. Uustalu was supported by the ERDF funded Estonian national CoE project EXCS and ICT national programme project Coinduction (the latter paid also Capretta's visit to Tallinn), the Estonian Science Foundation grant no. 9475 and the Estonian Ministry of Education and Research institutional research grant no. IUT-3313.

References

1. Abbott, M., Altenkirch, T., Ghani, N.: Containers: constructing strictly positive types. Theoret. Comput. Sci. **342**(1), 3–27 (2005)
2. Adámek, J., Lücke, D., Milius, S.: Recursive coalgebras of finitary functors. Theoret. Inform. Appl. **41**(4), 447–462 (2007)

3. Adámek, J., Milius, S., Moss, L.S., Sousa, L.: Well-pointed coalgebras. Log. Methods Comput. Sci. **9**(3), article 2 (2013)
4. Barendregt, H.P., Dekkers, W., Statman, R.: Lambda Calculus with Types: Perspectives in Logic. Cambridge University Press, Cambridge (2013)
5. Berardi, S., Bezem, M., Coquand, T.: On the computational content of the axiom of choice. J. Symb. Log. **63**(2), 600–622 (1998)
6. Berger, U., Oliva, P.: Modified bar recursion. Math. Struct. Comput. Sci. **16**(2), 163–183 (2006)
7. Capretta, V., Uustalu, T., Vene, V.: Recursive coalgebras from comonads. Inf. Comput. **204**(4), 437–468 (2006)
8. Capretta, V., Uustalu, T., Vene, V.: Corecursive algebras: a study of general structured corecursion. In: Oliveira, M.V.M., Woodcock, J. (eds.) SBMF 2009. LNCS, vol. 5902, pp. 84–100. Springer, Heidelberg (2009)
9. Dummett, M.: Elements of Intuitionism, 2nd edn. Oxford Science Publications, Oxford (2000)
10. Escardó, M.H., Oliva, P.: Selection functions, bar recursion and backward induction. Math. Struct. Comput. Sci. **20**(2), 127–168 (2010)
11. Escardó, M.H., Xu, C.: The inconsistency of a Brouwerian continuity principle with the Curry-Howard interpretation. In: Altenkirch, T. (ed.) 13th International Conference on Typed Lambda Calculi and Applications, TLCA 2015, Leibniz International Proceedings in Informatics, vol. 38, pp. 153–164. Dagstuhl Publishing, Saarbrücken (2015)
12. Gambino, N., Hyland, M.: Wellfounded trees and dependent polynomial functors. In: Berardi, S., Coppo, M., Damiani, F. (eds.) TYPES 2003. LNCS, vol. 3085, pp. 210–225. Springer, Heidelberg (2004)
13. Ghani, N., Hancock, P., Pattinson, D.: Continuous functions on final coalgebras. Electron. Notes Theoret. Comput. Sci. **164**(1), 141–155 (2006)
14. Hancock, P., Pattinson, D., Ghani, N.: Representations of stream processors using nested fixed points. Log. Methods Comput. Sci. **5**(3), article 9 (2009)
15. Jacobs, B.: The temporal logic of coalgebras via Galois algebras. Math. Struct. Comput. Sci. **12**(6), 875–903 (2002)
16. Kleene, S., Vesley, R.: The Foundations of Intuitionistic Mathematics: Especially in Relation to Recursive Functions. North-Holland, Amsterdam (1965)
17. Nakata, K., Uustalu, T., Bezem, M.: A proof pearl with the fan theorem and bar induction. In: Yang, H. (ed.) APLAS 2011. LNCS, vol. 7078, pp. 353–368. Springer, Heidelberg (2011)
18. Osius, G.: Categorical set theory: a characterization of the category of sets. J. Pure Appl. Algebra **4**(1), 79–119 (1974)
19. Spector, C.: Provably recursive functionals of analysis: a consistency proof of analysis by an extension of principles in current intuitionistic mathematics. In: Dekker, F.D.E. (ed.) Recursive Function Theory: Proceedings of Symposia in Pure Mathematics. vol. 5, pp. 1–27. American Mathematical Society, Providence, RI (1962)
20. Taylor, P.: Intuitionistic sets and ordinals. J. Symb. Logic **61**(3), 705–744 (1996)
21. Taylor, P.: Towards a unified treatment of induction, I: The general recursion theorem. Manuscript (1996)
22. Taylor, P.: Practical Foundations of Mathematics. Cambridge Studies in Advanced Mathematics. Cambridge University Press, Cambridge (1999)
23. Troelstra, A.: Choice Sequences. Clarendon Press, Oxford (1977)

A New Foundation for Finitary Corecursion

The Locally Finite Fixpoint and Its Properties

Stefan Milius[1], Dirk Pattinson[2], and Thorsten Wißmann[1]([✉])

[1] Friedrich-Alexander-Universität Erlangen-Nürnberg, Erlangen, Germany
thorsten.wissmann@fau.de
[2] The Australian National University, Canberra, Australia

Abstract. This paper contributes to a theory of the behaviour of "finite-state" systems that is generic in the system type. We propose that such systems are modeled as coalgebras with a finitely generated carrier for an endofunctor on a locally finitely presentable category. Their behaviour gives rise to a new fixpoint of the coalgebraic type functor called *locally finite fixpoint* (LFF). We prove that if the given endofunctor preserves monomorphisms then the LFF always exists and is a subcoalgebra of the final coalgebra (unlike the rational fixpoint previously studied by Adámek, Milius and Velebil). Moreover, we show that the LFF is characterized by two universal properties: 1. as the final locally finitely generated coalgebra, and 2. as the initial fg-iterative algebra. As instances of the LFF we first obtain the known instances of the rational fixpoint, e.g. regular languages, rational streams and formal power-series, regular trees etc. And we obtain a number of new examples, e.g. (realtime deterministic resp. non-deterministic) context-free languages, constructively S-algebraic formal power-series (and any other instance of the generalized powerset construction by Silva, Bonchi, Bonsangue, and Rutten) and the monad of Courcelle's algebraic trees.

1 Introduction

Coalgebras capture many types of state based system within a uniform and mathematically rich framework [39]. One outstanding feature of the general theory is *final semantics* which gives a fully abstract account of system behaviour. For example, coalgebraic modelling of deterministic automata (without a finiteness restriction on state sets) yields the set of all formal languages as a final model, and restricting to *finite* automata one precisely obtains the regular languages [38]. This correspondence has been generalized to locally finitely presentable categories [8,20], where *finitely presentable* objects play the role of finite sets, leading to the notion of *rational fixpoint* that provides final semantics to all models with finitely presentable carrier [30]. It is known that the rational fixpoint is fully abstract (identifies all behaviourally equivalent states) as long as finitely presentable objects agree with finitely generated objects in the base category

---

S. Milius and T. Wißmann—Supported by Deutsche Forschungsgemeinschaft (DFG) under project MI 717/5-1.

© Springer-Verlag Berlin Heidelberg 2016
B. Jacobs and C. Löding (Eds.): FOSSACS 2016, LNCS 9634, pp. 107–125, 2016.
DOI: 10.1007/978-3-662-49630-5_7

[12, Proposition 3.12]. While this is the case in some categories (e.g. sets, posets, graphs, vector spaces, commutative monoids), it is currently unknown in other base categories that are used in the construction of system models, for example in idempotent semirings (used in the treatment of context-free grammars [43]), in algebras for the stack monad (used for modelling configurations of stack machines [23]); or it even fails, for example in the category of finitary monads on sets (used in the categorical study of algebraic trees [7]), or Eilenberg-Moore categories for a monad in general (the target category of generalized determinization [41], in which the above examples live). Coalgebras over a category of Eilenberg-Moore algebras over Set in particular provide a paradigmatic setting: automata that describe languages beyond the regular languages consist of a finite state set, but their transitions produce side effects such as the manipulation of a stack. These can be described by a monad, so that the (infinite) set of system states (machine states plus stack content) is described by a free algebra (for that monad) that is generated by the finite set of machine states. This is formalized by the generalized powerset construction [41] and interacts nicely with the coalgebraic framework we present.

Technically, the shortcoming of the rational fixpoint is due to the fact that finitely presentable objects are not closed under quotients, so that the rational fixpoint itself may fail to be a subcoalgebra of the final coalgebra and so identifies too little behaviour. The main conceptual contribution of this paper is the insight that also in cases where finitely presentable and finitely generated do not agree, the *locally finite fixpoint* provides a fully abstract model of finitely generated behaviour. We give a construction of the locally finite fixpoint, and support our claim both by general results and concrete examples: we show that under mild assumptions, the locally finite fixpoint always exists, and is indeed a subcoalgebra of the final coalgebra. Moreover, we give a characterization of the locally finite fixpoint as the initial iterative algebra. We then instantiate our results to several scenarios studied in the literature.

First, we show that the locally finite fixpoint is universal (and fully abstract) for the class of systems produced by the generalized powerset construction over Set: every determinized finite-state system induces a unique homomorphism to the locally finite fixpoint, and the latter contains precisely the finite-state behaviours.

Applied to the coalgebraic treatment of context-free languages, we show that the locally finite fixpoint yields precisely the context-free languages, and realtime deterministic context-free languages, respectively, when modelled using algebras for the stack monad of [23]. For context-free languages weighted in a semiring S, or equivalently for constructively S-algebraic power series [36], the locally finite fixpoint comprises precisely those, by phrasing the results of Winter et al. [44] in terms of the generalized powerset construction. Our last example shows the applicability of our results beyond categories of Eilenberg-Moore algebras over Set, and we characterize the monad of Courcelle's algebraic trees over a signature [7,16] as the locally finite fixpoint of an associated functor (on a category of monads), solving an open problem of [7].

The work presented here is based on the third author's master thesis in [45]. Most proofs are omitted; they can be found in the full version [33] of our paper.

2   Preliminaries and Notation

Locally Finitely Presentable Categories. A *filtered colimit* is the colimit of a diagram $\mathcal{D} \to \mathcal{C}$ where $\mathcal{D}$ is filtered (every finite subdiagram has a cocone in $\mathcal{D}$) and *directed* if $\mathcal{D}$ is additionally a poset. *Finitary functors* preserve filtered (equivalently directed) colimits. Objects $C \in \mathcal{C}$ are *finitely presentable* (fp) if the hom-functor $\mathcal{C}(C, -)$ preserves filtered (equivalently directed) colimits, and *finitely generated* (fg) if $\mathcal{C}(C, -)$ preserves directed colimits of monos (i.e. colimits of directed diagrams where all connecting morphisms are monic). Clearly any fp object is fg, but not vice versa. Also, fg objects are closed under strong epis (quotients) which fails for fp objects in general. A cocomplete category is *locally finitely presentable* (lfp) if the full subcategory $\mathcal{C}_{fp}$ of finitely presentable objects is essentially small, i.e. is up to isomorphism only a set, and every object $C \in \mathcal{C}$ is a filtered colimit of a diagram in $\mathcal{C}_{fp}$. We refer to [8,20] for further details.

It is well known that the categories of sets, posets and graphs are lfp with finitely presentable objects precisely the finite sets, posets, graphs, respectively. The category of vector spaces is lfp with finite-dimensional spaces being fp. Every finitary variety is lfp (i.e. an equational class of algebras induced by finite-arity operations or equivalently the Eilenberg-Moore category for a finitary Set-Monad, see Sect. 4.1 later). The finitely generated objects are the finitely generated algebras, and finitely presentable objects are algebras specified by finitely many generators and relations. This includes the categories of groups, monoids, (idempotent) semirings, semi-modules, etc. Every lfp category has mono/strong epi factorization [8, Proposition 1.16], i.e. every f factors as $f = m \cdot e$ with m mono (denoted by $\rightarrowtail$), e strong epi (denoted by $\twoheadrightarrow$), and we call the domain $\mathsf{Im}(f)$ of e the *image* of f. Any strong epi e has the diagonal fill-in property, i.e. $m \cdot g = h \cdot e$ with m mono and e strong epi gives a unique d such that $m \cdot d = h$ and $g = d \cdot e$.

Coalgebras. If $H : \mathcal{C} \to \mathcal{C}$ is an endofunctor, *H-coalgebras* are pairs (C, c) with $c : C \to HC$, and C is the *carrier* of (C, c). Homomorphisms $f : (C, c) \to (D, d)$ are maps $f : C \to D$ such that $Hf \cdot c = d \cdot f$. This gives a category denoted by $\mathsf{Coalg}H$. If its final object exists then this final H-coalgebra $(\nu H, \tau)$ represents a canonical domain of behaviours of H-typed systems, and induces for each (C, c) a unique homomorphism, denoted by $c^{\dagger}$, giving semantics to the system (C, c). The final coalgebra always exists provided $\mathcal{C}$ is lfp and H is finitary. The forgetful functor $\mathsf{Coalg}H \to \mathcal{C}$ creates colimits and reflects monos and epis. A morphism f in $\mathsf{Coalg}H$ is *mono-carried* (resp. *epi-carried*) if the underlying morphism in $\mathcal{C}$ is monic (resp. epic). Strong epi/mono factorizations lift from $\mathcal{C}$ to $\mathsf{Coalg}H$ whenever H preserves monos yielding epi-carried/mono-carried factorizations. A *directed union of coalgebras* is the colimit of a directed diagram in $\mathsf{Coalg}H$ where all connecting morphisms are mono-carried.

The Rational Fixpoint. For $\mathcal{C}$ lfp and $H : \mathcal{C} \to \mathcal{C}$ finitary let $\mathsf{Coalg}_{fp}H$ denote the full subcategory of $\mathsf{Coalg}H$ of coalgebras with fp carrier, and $\mathsf{Coalg}_{lfp}H$ the full subcategory of $\mathsf{Coalg}H$ of coalgebras that arise as filtered colimits of coalgebras with fp carrier [30, Corollary III.13]. The coalgebras in $\mathsf{Coalg}_{lfp}H$ are called *lfp coalgebras* and for $\mathcal{C} = \mathsf{Set}$ those are precisely the locally finite coalgebras (i.e. those coalgebras where every element is contained in a finite subcoalgebra). The final lfp coalgebra exists and is the colimit of the inclusion $\mathsf{Coalg}_{\mathsf{fp}}H \hookrightarrow \mathsf{Coalg}H$, and it is a fixpoint of H (see [6]) called the *rational fixpoint* of H. Here are some examples: the rational fixpoint of a polynomial set functor associated to a finitary signature Σ is the set of rational Σ-trees [6], i.e. finite and infinite Σ-trees having, up to isomorphism, finitely many subtrees only, and one obtains rational weighted languages for Noetherian semirings S for a functor on the category of S-modules [12], and rational λ-trees for a functor on the category of presheaves on finite sets [2] or for a related functor on nominal sets [34]. If the classes of fp and fg objects coincide in $\mathcal{C}$, then the rational fixpoint is a subcoalgebra of the final coalgebra [12, Theorem 3.12]. This is the case in the above examples, but not in general, see [12, Example 3.15] for a concrete example where the rational fixpoint does not identify behaviourally equivalent states. Conversely, even if the classes differ, the rational fixpoint can be a subcoalgebra, e.g. for any constant functor.

Iterative Algebras. If $H : \mathcal{C} \to \mathcal{C}$ is an endofunctor, an H-algebra $(A, a : HA \to A)$ is *iterative* if every *flat equation morphism* $e : X \to HX + A$ where X is an fp object has a unique *solution*, i.e. if there exists a unique $e^{\dagger} : X \to A$ such that $e^{\dagger} = [a, \mathrm{id}_A] \cdot (He^{\dagger} + \mathrm{id}_A) \cdot e$. The rational fixpoint is also characterized as the initial iterative algebra [6] and is the starting point of the coalgebraic approach to Elgot's iterative theories [18] and to the iteration theories of Bloom and Ésik [3, 4, 6, 11].

3   The Locally Finite Fixpoint

The locally finite fixpoint can be characterized similarly to the rational fixpoint, but with respect to coalgebras with finitely generated (not finitely presentable) carrier. We show that the locally finite fixpoint always exists, and is a subcoalgebra of the final coalgebra, i.e. identifies all behaviourally equivalent states. As a consequence, the locally finite fixpoint provides a fully abstract notion of finitely generated behaviour. From now on, we rely on the following:

Assumption 3.1. *Throughout the rest of the paper we assume that $\mathcal{C}$ is an lfp category and that $H : \mathcal{C} \to \mathcal{C}$ is finitary and preserves monomorphisms.*

As for the rational fixpoint, we denote the full subcategory of $\mathsf{Coalg}H$ comprising all coalgebras with finitely generated carrier by $\mathsf{Coalg}_{\mathsf{fg}}H$ and have the following notion of locally finitely generated coalgebra.

Definition 3.2. *A coalgebra $X \xrightarrow{x} HX$ is called* locally finitely generated (lfg) *if for all $f : S \to X$ with S finitely generated, there exist a coalgebra $p : P \to HP$ in $\mathsf{Coalg}_{\mathsf{fg}}H$, a coalgebra morphism $h : (P, p) \to (X, x)$ and some $f' : S \to P$ such that $h \cdot f' = f$. $\mathsf{Coalg}_{\mathsf{lfg}}H \subseteq \mathsf{Coalg}H$ denotes the full subcategory of lfg coalgebras.*

Equivalently, one can characterize lfg coalgebras in terms of subobjects and subcoalgebras, making it a generalization of of *local finiteness* in Set, i.e. the property of a coalgebra that every element is contained in a finite subcoalgebra.

Lemma 3.3. $X \xrightarrow{x} HX$ *is an lfg coalgebra iff for all fg subobjects* $S \stackrel{f}{\rightarrowtail} X$, *there exist a subcoalgebra* $h : (P, p) \rightarrowtail (X, x)$ *and a mono* $f' : S \rightarrowtail P$ *with* $h \cdot f' = f$, *i.e.* S *is a subobject of* P.

Proof. ($\Rightarrow$) Given some mono $f : S \rightarrowtail X$, factor the induced h into some strong epi-carried and mono-carried homomorphisms and use that fg objects are closed under strong epis. ($\Leftarrow$) Factor $f : S \to X$ into an epi and a mono $g : \mathsf{Im}(f) \rightarrowtail X$ and use the diagonal fill-in property for g. □

Evidently all coalgebras with finitely generated carriers are lfg. Moreover, lfg coalgebras are precisely the filtered colimits of coalgebras from $\mathsf{Coalg}_{\mathsf{fg}}H$.

Proposition 3.4. *Every filtered colimit of coalgebras from* $\mathsf{Coalg}_{\mathsf{fg}}H$ *is lfg.*

Proof (Sketch). One first proves that directed unions of coalgebras from $\mathsf{Coalg}_{\mathsf{fg}}H$ are lfg. Now given a filtered colimit $c_i : X_i \to C$ where X_i are coalgebras in $\mathsf{Coalg}_{\mathsf{fg}}H$, one epi-mono factorizes every colimit injection: $c_i = (X_i \xrightarrow{e_i} T_i \xrightarrow{m_i} C)$. Using the diagonalization of the factorization one sees that the T_i form a directed diagram of subobjects of C. Furthermore C is the directed union of the T_i and therefore an lfg coalgebra as desired. □

Proposition 3.5. *Every lfg coalgebra* (X, x) *is a directed colimit of its subcoalgebras from* $\mathsf{Coalg}_{\mathsf{fg}}H$.

Proof. Recall from [8, ProofIofTheorem 1.70] that X is the colimit of the diagram of all its finitely generated subobjects. Now the subdiagram given by all subcoalgebras of X is cofinal. Indeed, this follows directly from the fact that (X, x) is an lfg coalgebra: for every subobject $S \rightarrowtail X$, S fg, we have a subcoalgebra of (X, x) in $\mathsf{Coalg}_{\mathsf{fg}}H$ containing S. □

Corollary 3.6. *The lfg coalgebras are precisely the filtered colimits, or equivalently directed unions, of coalgebras with fg carrier.*

As a consequence, a coalgebra is final in $\mathsf{Coalg}_{\mathsf{lfg}}F$ if there is a unique morphism from every coalgebra with finitely generated carrier.

Proposition 3.7. *An lfg coalgebra* L *is final in* $\mathsf{Coalg}_{\mathsf{lfg}}H$ *iff for every for every coalgebra* X *in* $\mathsf{Coalg}_{\mathsf{fg}}H$ *there exists a unique coalgebra morphism from* X *to* L.

The proof is analogous to [30, Theorem 3.14]; the full argument can be found in [33]. Cocompleteness of $\mathcal{C}$ ensures that the final lfg coalgebra always exists.

Theorem 3.8. *The category* $\mathsf{Coalg}_{\mathsf{lfg}}H$ *has a final object, and the final lfg coalgebra is the colimit of the inclusion* $\mathsf{Coalg}_{\mathsf{fg}}H \hookrightarrow \mathsf{Coalg}_{\mathsf{lfg}}H$.

Proof. By Corollary 3.6, the colimit of the inclusion $\mathsf{Coalg}_{\mathsf{fg}}H \hookrightarrow \mathsf{Coalg}_{\mathsf{lfg}}H$ is the same as the colimit of the entire $\mathsf{Coalg}_{\mathsf{lfg}}H$. And the latter is clearly the final object of $\mathsf{Coalg}_{\mathsf{lfg}}H$. □

This theorem provides a construction of the final lfg coalgebra collecting precisely the behaviours of the coalgebras with fg carriers. In the following we shall show that this construction does indeed identify precisely behaviourally equivalent states, i.e. the final lfg coalgebra is always a subcoalgebra of the final coalgebra. Just like fg objects are closed under quotients – in contrast to fp objects – we have a similar property of lfg coalgebras:

Lemma 3.9. *Lfg coalgebras are closed under strong quotients, i.e. for every strong epi carried coalgebra homomorphisms $X \twoheadrightarrow Y$, if X is lfg then so is Y.*

The failure of this property for lfp coalgebras is the reason why the rational fixpoint is not necessarily a subcoalgebra of the final coalgebra and in particular the rational fixpoint in [12, Example 3.15] is an lfp coalgebra for which the property fails.

Theorem 3.10. *The final lfg H-coalgebra is a subcoalgebra of the final H-coalgebra.*

Proof. Let (L, ℓ) be the final lfg coalgebra. Consider the unique coalgebra morphism $L \to \nu H$ and take its factorization:

$$\mathrm{id} \left(\begin{array}{c} \dashrightarrow \\ \dashleftarrow \end{array} \right. (L, \ell) \underset{i^\dagger}{\overset{e}{\rightrightarrows}} (I, i) \overset{m}{\rightarrowtail} (\nu H, \tau) \;, \quad \text{with } e \text{ strong epi in } \mathcal{C}.$$

By Lemma 3.9, I is an lfg coalgebra and so by finality of L we have the coalgebra morphism $i^\dagger$ such that $\mathrm{id}_L = i^\dagger \cdot e$. It follows that e is monic and therefore an iso. □

In other words, the final lfg H-coalgebra collects precisely the finitely generated behaviours from the final H-coalgebra. We now show that the final lfg coalgebra is a fixpoint of H which hinges on the following:

Lemma 3.11. *For any lfg coalgebra $C \overset{c}{\to} HC$, the coalgebra $HC \overset{Hc}{\longrightarrow} HHC$ is lfg.*

Proof. Consider $f : S \to HC$ with S finitely generated. As $\mathcal{C}$ is lfp we know that HC is the colimit of its fg subobjects, and so $f : S \to HC$ factors through some subobject $\mathrm{in}_q : Q \rightarrowtail HC$ with Q fg and $f = \mathrm{in}_q \cdot f'$. On the other hand, (C, c) is lfg, i.e. the directed union of its subcoalgebras from $\mathsf{Coalg}_{\mathsf{fg}}H$. Then, since H is finitary and mono-preserving, $HC \overset{c}{\to} HHC$ is also a directed union and the morphism $\mathrm{in}_q : Q \to HC$ factors through some $HP \overset{Hp}{\longrightarrow} HHP$ with $(P, p) \in \mathsf{Coalg}_{\mathsf{fg}}H$ via $\mathrm{in}_p : (P, p) \rightarrowtail (C, c)$, i.e. $H\mathrm{in}_p \cdot q = \mathrm{in}_q$. Finally, we can construct a coalgebra with fg carrier

$$Q + P \overset{[q,p]}{\longrightarrow} HP \overset{H\mathrm{inr}}{\longrightarrow} H(Q + P)$$

and a coalgebra homomorphism $H\mathrm{in}_p \cdot [q, p] : Q + P \to HC$. In the diagram

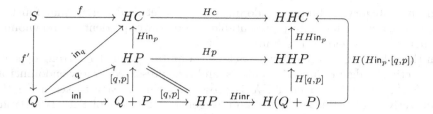

every part trivially commutes, so $Hin_p \cdot [q, p]$ is the desired homomorphism. $\square$

So with a proof in virtue to Lambek's Lemma [28, Lemma 2.2], we obtain the desired fixpoint:

Theorem 3.12. *The carrier of the final lfg H-coalgebra is a fixpoint of H.*

We denote the above fixpoint by $(\vartheta H, \ell)$ and call it the *locally finite fixpoint* (LFF) of H. In particular, the LFF always exists under Assumption 3.1, providing a finitary corecursion principle.

Remark 3.13. As we mentioned in the introduction the rational fixpoint of the finitary functor H is the initial iterative algebra for H. A similar algebraic characterization is possible for the LFF. One simply replaces the fp object X in the definition of a flat equation morphism by an fg object to obtain the notion of an fg-iterative algebra.

Theorem 3.14. *The LFF is the initial fg-iterative H-algebra.*

For details, see the full version [33] of our paper or [45].

Relation to the Rational Fixpoint. There are examples, where the rational fixpoint is not a subcoalgebra of the final coalgebra. In categories, where fp and fg objects coincide, the rational fixpoint and the LFF coincide as well (cf. the respective colimit-construction in Sect. 2 and Theorem 3.8). In this section we will see, under slightly stronger assumptions, that fg-carried coalgebras are quotients of fp-carried coalgebras, and in particular the locally finite fixpoint is a quotient of the rational fixpoint: namely its image in the final coalgebra.

Assumption 3.15. *In addition to Assumption 3.1, assume that in the base category $\mathcal{C}$, every finitely presentable object is a strong quotient of a finitely presentable strong epi projective object and that the endofunctor H also preserves strong epis.*

The condition that every fg object is the strong quotient of a strong epi projective often is phrased as *having enough strong epi projectives* [14]. This assumption is apparently very strong but still is met in many situations:

Example 3.16

- In categories in which all (strong) epis are split, every object is projective and any endofunctor preserves epis, e.g. in Set or Vec_K.

- In the category of finitary endofunctors $\mathsf{Fun}_f(\mathsf{Set})$, all polynomial functors are projective. The finitely presentable functors are quotients of polynomial functors H_Σ, where Σ is a finite signature.
- In the Eilenberg-Moore category Set^T for a finitary monad T, strong epis are surjective T-algebra homomorphisms, and thus preserved by any endofunctor. In Set^T, every free algebra TX is projective; this is easy to see using the projectivity of X in Set. Every finitely generated object of Set^T is a strong quotient of some free algebra TX with X finite. For more precise definitions, see Sect. 4.1 later.

Proposition 3.17. *Every coalgebra in* $\mathsf{Coalg}_{\mathsf{fg}} H$ *is a strong quotient of a coalgebra with finitely presentable carrier.*

Theorem 3.18. *ϑH is the image of the rational fixpoint ϱH in the final coalgebra.*

Proof. Consider the factorization $(\varrho H, r) \overset{e}{\twoheadrightarrow} (B, b) \overset{m}{\rightarrowtail} (\nu H, \tau)$. Since ϱH is the colimit of all fp carried H-coalgebras it is an lfg coalgebra by Proposition 3.4 using that fp objects are also fg. Hence, by Lemma 3.9 the coalgebra B is lfg, too. By Proposition 3.7 it now suffices to show that from every $(X, x) \in \mathsf{Coalg}_{\mathsf{fg}} H$ there exists a unique coalgebra morphism into (B, b). Given (X, x) in $\mathsf{Coalg}_{\mathsf{fg}} H$, it is the quotient $q : (P, p) \twoheadrightarrow (X, x)$ of an fp-carried coalgebra by Proposition 3.17. Hence, we obtain a unique coalgebra morphism $p^\dagger : (P, p) \to (\varrho H, r)$. By finality of νH, we have $m \cdot e \cdot p^\dagger = x^\dagger \cdot q$ (with $x^\dagger : (X, x) \to (\nu H, \tau)$). So the diagonal fill-in property induces a homomorphism $(X, x) \to (B, b)$, being the only homomorphism $(X, x) \to (B, b)$ by the finality of νH and because m is monic. $\square$

4   Instances of the Locally Finite Fixpoint

We will now present a number of instances of the LFF. First note, that all the known instances of the rational fixpoint (see e.g. [6,12,30] are also instances of the locally finite fixpoint, because in all those cases the fp and fg objects coincide. For example, the class of regular languages is the rational fixpoint of $2 \times (-)^\Sigma$ on Set. In this section, we will study further instances of the LFF that are most likely not instances of the rational fixpoint and which – to the best of our knowledge – have not been characterized by a universal property yet:

1. Behaviours of finite-state machines with side-effects as considered by the generalized powerset construction (cf. Sect. 4.1), particularly the following.
   (a) Deterministic and ordinary context-free languages obtained as the behaviours of deterministic and non-deterministic stack-machines, respectively.
   (b) Constructively S-algebraic formal power series, i.e. the "context-free" subclass of weighted languages with weights from a semiring S, yielded from weighted context-free grammars.
2. The monad of Courcelle's algebraic trees.

4.1   Generalized Powerset Construction

The determinization of a non-deterministic automaton using the powerset construction is an instance of a more general framework, described by Silva, Bonchi, Bonsangue, and Rutten [41] based on an observation by Bartels [10] (see also Jacobs [26]). In that *generalized powerset construction*, an automaton with side-effects is turned into an ordinary automaton by internalizing the side-effects in the states. The LFF interacts well with this construction, because it precisely captures the behaviours of finite-state automata with side effects. The notion of side-effect is formalized by a monad, which induces the category, in which the LFF is considered.

In the following we assume that readers are familiar with monads and Eilenberg-Moore algebras (see e.g. [29] for an introduction). For a monad T on $\mathcal{C}$ we denote by $\mathcal{C}^T$ the category of Eilenberg-Moore algebras. Recall from [8, Corollary 2.75] that if $\mathcal{C}$ is lfp (in most of our examples $\mathcal{C}$ is Set) and T is finitary then $\mathcal{C}^T$ is lfp, too, and for every fp object X the free Eilenberg-Moore algebra TX is fp in $\mathcal{C}^T$. In all the examples we consider below, the classes of fp and fg objects either provably differ or it is still unknown whether these classes coincide.

Example 4.1. In Sects. 4.4 and 4.5 we are going to make use of Moggi's exception monad transformer (see e.g. [15]). Let us recall that for a fixed object E, the finitary functor $(-) + E$ together with the unit $\eta_X = \mathrm{inl} : X \to X + E$ and multiplication $\mu_X = \mathrm{id}_X + [\mathrm{id}_E, \mathrm{id}_E] : X + E + E \to X + E$ form a finitary monad, the *exception monad*. Its algebras are E-pointed objects, i.e. objects X, together with a morphism $E \to X$, and homomorphisms are morphisms preserving the pointing. So the induced Eilenberg-Moore category is just the slice category $\mathcal{C}^{(-)+E} \cong E/\mathcal{C}$.

Now, given any monad T we obtain a new monad $T(- + E)$ with obvious unit and multiplication. An Eilenberg-Moore algebra for $T(- + E)$ consists of an Eilenberg-Moore algebra for T and an E-pointing, and homomorphisms are T-algebra homomorphisms preserving the pointing [25].

Now an automaton with side-effects is modelled as an HT-coalgebra, where T is a finitary monad on $\mathcal{C}$ providing the type of side-effect. For example, for $HX = 2 \times X^\Sigma$, where Σ is an input alphabet, $2 = \{0, 1\}$ and T the finite powerset monad on Set, HT-coalgebras are non-deterministic automata. However, the coalgebraic semantics using the final HT-coalgebra does not yield the usual language semantics of non-deterministic automata. To obtain this one considers the final coalgebra of a lifting of H to $\mathcal{C}^T$. Denote by $U : \mathcal{C}^T \to \mathcal{C}$ the canonical forgetful functor.

Definition 4.2. *For a functor $H : \mathcal{C} \to \mathcal{C}$ and a monad $T : \mathcal{C} \to \mathcal{C}$, a lifting of H is a functor $H^T : \mathcal{C}^T \to \mathcal{C}^T$ such that $H \cdot U = U \cdot H^T$.*

If such a (not necessarily unique) lifting exists, the generalized powerset construction transforms an HT-coalgebra into a H^T-coalgebra on $\mathcal{C}^T$: For a coalgebra $x : X \to HTX$, HTX carries an Eilenberg-Moore algebra, and one uses freeness of the Eilenberg-Moore algebra TX to obtain a canonical T-algebra homomorphism $x^\sharp : (TX, \mu^T) \to H^T(TX, \mu^T)$. The *coalgebraic language seman-tics* of (X, x) is then given by $X \xrightarrow{\eta_X} TX \xrightarrow{x^{\sharp\dagger}} \nu H^T$, i.e. by composing the unique coalgebra morphism induced by $x^\sharp$ with η_X. This construction yields a func-tor $T' : \mathsf{Coalg}(HT) \to \mathsf{Coalg}H^T$ mapping coalgebras $X \xrightarrow{x} HTX$ to $x^\sharp$ and homomorphisms f to Tf (see e.g. [12, ProofofLemma 3.27] for a proof).

Now our aim is to show that the LFF of H^T characterizes precisely the coalgebraic language semantics of all fp-carried HT-coalgebras. As the right adjoint U preserves monos and is faithful, we know that H^T preserves monos, and as T is finitary, filtered colimits in $\mathcal{C}^T$ are created by the forgetful functor to $\mathcal{C}$, and we therefore see that H^T is finitary. Thus, by Theorem 3.8, ϑH^T exists and is a subcoalgebra of νH^T. By [37] and [10, Corollary 3.4.19], we know that νH^T is carried by νH equipped with a canonical algebra structure.

Now let us turn to the desired characterization of ϑH^T. Formally, the coalge-braic language semantics of all fp-carried HT-coalgebras is collected by forming the colimit $k : K \to HK$ of the diagram $\mathsf{Coalg}_{\mathsf{fg}}HT \xrightarrow{T'} \mathsf{Coalg}H^T \xrightarrow{U} \mathsf{Coalg}H$. This coalgebra K is not yet a subcoalgebra of νH (for $\mathcal{C} = \mathsf{Set}$ that means, not all behaviourally equivalent states are identified in K), but taking its image in νH we obtain the LFF:

Proposition 4.3. *The image (I, i) of the unique coalgebra morphism $k^\dagger : K \to \nu H^T$ is precisely the locally finite fixpoint of the lifting H^T.*

One can also directly take the union of all desired behaviours, for $\mathcal{C} = \mathsf{Set}$:

Theorem 4.4. *The locally finite fixpoint of the lifting H^T comprises precisely the images of determinized HT-coalgebras:*

$$\vartheta H^T = \bigcup_{\substack{x:X \to HTX \\ X \text{ finite}}} x^{\sharp\dagger}[TX] = \bigcup_{\substack{x:X \to HTX \\ X \text{ finite}}} x^{\sharp\dagger} \cdot \eta_X^T[X] \subseteq \nu H^T. \tag{1}$$

This result suggests that the locally finite fixpoint is the right object to consider in order to represent finite behaviour. We now instantiate the general theory with examples from the literature to characterize several well-known notions as LFF.

4.2   The Languages of Non-deterministic Automata

Let us start with a simple standard example. We already mentioned that non-deterministic automata are coalgebras for the functor $X \mapsto 2 \times \mathcal{P}_{\mathsf{f}}(X)^\Sigma$. Hence they are HT-coalgebras for $H = 2 \times (-)^\Sigma$ and $T = \mathcal{P}_{\mathsf{f}}$ the finite powerset monad on Set. The above generalized powerset construction then instantiates as the usual powerset construction that assigns to a given non-deterministic automaton its determinization.

Now note that the final coalgebra for H is carried by the set $\mathcal{L} = \mathcal{P}(\Sigma^*)$ of all formal languages over Σ with the coalgebra structure given by $o : \mathcal{L} \to 2$ with

$o(L) = 1$ iff L contains the empty word and $t : \mathcal{L} \to \mathcal{L}^\Sigma$ with $t(L)(s) = \{w \mid sw \in L\}$ the left language derivative. The functor H has a canonical lifting H^T on the Eilenberg-Moore category of $\mathcal{P}_f$, viz. the category of join semi-lattices. The final coalgebra νH^T is carried by all formal languages with the join semi-lattice structure given by union and $\emptyset$ and with the above coalgebra structure. Furthermore, the coalgebraic language semantics of $x : X \to HTX$ assigns to every state of the non-deterministic automaton X the language it accepts. Observe that join semi-lattices form a so-called *locally finite variety*, i.e. the finitely presentable algebras are precisely the finite ones. Hence, Theorem 4.4 states that the LFF of H^T is precisely the subcoalgebra of νH^T formed by all languages accepted by finite NFA, i.e. regular languages.

Note that in this example the LFF and the rational fixpoint coincide since both fp and fg join semi-lattices are simply the finite ones. Similar characterizations of the coalgebraic language semantics of finite coalgebras follow from Theorem 4.4 in other instances of the generalized powerset construction from [41] (cf. e.g. the treatment of the behaviour of finite weighted automata in [12]).

We now turn to examples that, to the best of our knowledge, cannot be treated using the rational fixpoint.

4.3   The Behaviour of Stack Machines

Push-down automata are finite state machines with infinitely many configurations. It is well-known that deterministic and non-deterministic pushdown automata recognize different classes of context-free languages. We will characterize both as instances of the locally finite fixpoint, using the results from [23] on stack machines, which can push or read *multiple* elements to or from the stack in a single transition, respectively.

That is, a transition of a stack machine in a certain state consists of reading an input character, going to a successor state based on the stack's topmost elements and of modifying the topmost elements of the stack. These stack operations are captured by the stack monad.

Definition 4.5 (Stack monad, [22, Proposition 5]). *For a finite set of stack symbols Γ, the* stack monad *is the submonad T of the store monad $(- \times \Gamma^*)^{\Gamma^*}$ for which the elements $\langle r, t \rangle$ of $TX \subseteq (X \times \Gamma^*)^{\Gamma^*} \cong X^{\Gamma^*} \times (\Gamma^*)^{\Gamma^*}$ satisfy the following restriction: there exists k depending on r, t such that for every $w \in \Gamma^k$ and $u \in \Gamma^*$, $r(wu) = r(w)$ and $t(wu) = t(w)u$.*

Note that the parameter k gives a bound on how may of the topmost stack cells the machine can access in one step.

Using the stack monad, stack machines are HT-coalgebras, where $H = B \times (-)^\Sigma$ is the Moore automata functor for the finite input alphabet Σ and the set B of all predicates mapping (initial) stack configurations to output values from 2, taking only the topmost k elements into account: $B = \{p \in 2^{\Gamma^*} \mid \exists k \in \mathbb{N}_0 : \forall w, u \in \Gamma^*, |w| \geq k : p(wu) = p(w)\} \subseteq 2^{\Gamma^*}$.

The final coalgebra νH is carried by B^{Σ^*} which is (modulo power laws) a set of predicates, mapping stack configurations to formal languages. Goncharov et al. [23] show that H lifts to Set^T and conclude that finite-state HT-coalgebras match the intuition of *deterministic* pushdown automata without spontaneous transitions. The languages accepted by those automata are precisely the *real-time deterministic context-free languages*; this notion goes back to Harrison and Havel [24]. We obtain the following, with γ_0 playing the role of an initial symbol on the stack:

Theorem 4.6. *The locally finite fixpoint of H^T is carried by the set of all maps $f \in B^{\Sigma^*}$ such that for any fixed $\gamma_0 \in \Gamma$, $\{w \in \Sigma^* \mid f(w)(\gamma_0) = 1\}$ is a real-time deterministic context-free language.*

Proof. By [23, Theorem 5.5], a language L is a real-time deterministic context-free language iff there exists some $x : X \to HTX$, X finite, with its determinization $x^\sharp : TX \to HTX$ and there exist $s \in X$ and $\gamma_0 \in \Gamma$ such that $f = x^{\sharp\dagger} \cdot \eta_X^T(s) \in B^{\Sigma^*}$ and $f(w)(\gamma_0) = 1$ for all $w \in \Sigma^*$. The rest follows by (1).   □

Just as for pushdown automata, the expressiveness of stack machines increases when equipping them with non-determinism. Technically, this is done by considering the *non-deterministic stack monad T'*, i.e. T' denotes a submonad of the non-deterministic store monad $\mathcal{P}_f(- \times \Gamma^*)^{\Gamma^*}$, as described in [23, Sect. 6]. In the non-deterministic setting, a similar property holds, namely that the determinized HT'-coalgebras with finite carrier describe precisely the context-free languages [23, Theorem 6.5]. Combine this with (1):

Theorem 4.7. *The locally finite fixpoint of $H^{T'}$ is carried by the set of all maps $f \in B^{\Sigma^*}$ such that for any fixed $\gamma_0 \in \Gamma$, $\{w \in \Sigma^* \mid f(w)(\gamma_0) = 1\}$ is a context-free language.*

4.4   Context-Free Languages and Constructively S-Algebraic Power Series

One generalizes from formal (resp. context-free) languages to weighted formal (resp. context-free) languages by assigning to each word a weight from a fixed semiring. More formally, a weighted language – a.k.a. *formal power series* – over an input alphabet X is defined as a map $X^* \to S$, where S is a semiring. The set of all formal power series is denoted by $S\langle\!\langle X \rangle\!\rangle$. Ordinary formal languages are formal power series over the boolean semiring $\mathbb{B} = \{0, 1\}$, i.e. maps $X^* \to \{0, 1\}$.

An important class of formal power series is that of *constructively S-algebraic* formal power series. We show that this class arises precisely as the LFF of the standard functor for deterministic Moore automata $H = S \times (-)^\Sigma$, but on an Eilenberg-Moore category of a Set monad. As a special case, constructively $\mathbb{B}$-algebraic series are the context-free weighted languages and are precisely the LFF of the automata functor in the category of idempotent semirings.

The original definition of constructively S-algebraic formal power series goes back to Fliess [19], see also [17]. Here, we use the equivalent coalgebraic characterization by Winter et al. [44].

Let $S\langle X \rangle \subseteq S\langle\!\langle X \rangle\!\rangle$ the subset of those maps, that are 0 for all but finitely many $w \in X^*$. If S is commutative, then $S\langle - \rangle$ yields a finitary monad and thus also $T = S\langle - + \Sigma\rangle$ by Example 4.1. The algebras for $S\langle -\rangle$ are associative S-algebras (over the commutative semiring S), i.e. S-modules together with a monoid structure that is a module morphism in both arguments. The algebras for T are Σ-pointed S-algebras. The following notions are special instances of S-algebras.

Example 4.8. For $S = \mathbb{B} = \{0,1\}$, one obtains idempotent semirings as $\mathbb{B}$-algebras, for $S = \mathbb{N}$ semirings, and for $S = \mathbb{Z}$ ordinary rings.

Winter et al. [44, Proposition 4] show that the final H-coalgebra is carried by $S\langle\langle \Sigma \rangle\rangle$ and that constructively S-algebraic series are precisely those elements of $S\langle\langle \Sigma \rangle\rangle$ that arise as the behaviours of those coalgebra $c : X \to HS\langle X\rangle$ with finite X, after determinizing them to some $c^{\sharp} : S\langle X\rangle \to HS\langle X\rangle$ (see [44, Theorem 23]).

However, this determinization is not directly an instance of the generalized powerset construction. We shall show that the same behaviours can be obtained by using the standard generalized powerset construction with an appropriate lifting of H to T-algebras. Having an S-algebra structure on A and a Σ-pointing $j : \Sigma \to A$ we need to define another S-algebra structure and Σ-pointing on $HA = S \times A^{\Sigma}$. While the S-module structure is just point-wise, we need to take care when multiplying two elements from HA. To this end we first we define the operation $[-, -] : S \times A^{\Sigma} \to A$ by

$$[o, \delta] := i(o) + \sum_{b \in \Sigma} \big(j(b) \cdot \delta(b) \big),$$

where $i : S \to A$ is the canonical map with $i(s) = s \cdot 1$ with 1 the neutral element of the monoid on A. The idea is that $[o, \delta]$ acts like a state with output o and derivation δ. The multiplication on $HA = S \times A^{\Sigma}$ is then defined by

$$(o_1, \delta_1) * (o_2, \delta_2) := \big(o_1 \cdot o_2, a \mapsto \delta_1(a) \cdot [o_2, \delta_2] + i(o_1) \cdot \delta_2(a) \big). \tag{2}$$

The Σ-pointing is the obvious: $a \mapsto (0, \varrho_a)$ where $\varrho_a(a) = 1$ and $\varrho_a(b) = 0$ for $a \neq b$.

Lemma 4.9. *For any $w \in A$ in Set^T and any H^T-coalgebra structure $c : A \to H^T A$, w and $[c(w)]$ are behaviourally equivalent in Set.*

Given a coalgebra $c : X \to HS\langle X\rangle$, Winter et al. [44, Proposition 14] determinize c to some $\hat{c} = \langle \hat{o}, \hat{\delta} \rangle : S\langle X\rangle \to HS\langle X\rangle$ with the property that for any $v, w \in S\langle X\rangle$,

$$\hat{o}(v * w) = \hat{o}(v) \cdot \hat{o}(w) \quad \text{and} \quad \hat{\delta}(v * w, a) = \hat{\delta}(v, a) * w + \hat{o}(v) * \hat{\delta}(w, a), \tag{3}$$

and such that $\hat{c}$ is a S-module homomorphism. However, the generalized powerset construction w.r.t. T yields a coalgebra $c^{\sharp} : S\langle X + \Sigma\rangle \to HS\langle X + \Sigma\rangle$. The above property, together with Lemma 4.9 and (2) implies that $\hat{c}$ and $c^{\sharp}$ are essentially the same coalgebra structures:

Lemma 4.10. *In* Set, $u \in (S\langle X \rangle, \hat{c})$ *and* $S\langle \mathsf{inl} \rangle(u) \in (S\langle X + \Sigma \rangle, c^{\sharp})$ *are behaviourally equivalent.*

It follows that $\hat{c}^{\dagger} = c^{\sharp\dagger} \cdot S\langle \mathsf{inl} \rangle$ and thus their images in νH are identical. Hence, a formal power series is constructively S-algebraic iff it is in the image of some $c^{\sharp\dagger} \cdot S\langle \mathsf{inl} \rangle$, and by (1), iff it is in the locally finite fixpoint of H^T.

4.5 Courcelle's Algebraic Trees

For a fixed signature Σ of so called *givens*, a *recursive program scheme* (or *rps*, for short) contains mutually recursive definitions of new operations $\varphi_1, \ldots, \varphi_k$ (with respective arities $n_1, \ldots, n_k$). The recursive definition of φ_i may involve symbols from Σ, operations $\varphi_1, \ldots, \varphi_k$ and n_i variables $x_1, \ldots, x_{n_i}$. The (uninterpreted) solution of an rps is obtained by unravelling these recursive definitions, producing a possibly infinite Σ-tree over $x_1, \ldots, x_{n_i}$ for each operation φ_i. Figure 1 shows an rps over the signature $\Sigma = \{\star/0, \times/2, +/2\}$ and its solution. In general, an *algebraic Σ-tree* is a Σ-tree which is definable by an rps over

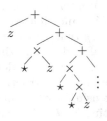

Fig. 1. Solution of $\varphi(z) = z + \varphi(\star \times z)$

Σ (see Courcelle [16]). Generalizing from a signature to a finitary endofunctor $H : \mathcal{C} \to \mathcal{C}$ on an lfp category, Adámek et al. [7] describe an rps as a coalgebra for a functor $\mathcal{H}_{\mathsf{f}}$ on $H/\mathsf{Mnd}_{\mathsf{f}}(\mathcal{C})$, in which objects are finitary H-pointed monads on $\mathcal{C}$, i.e. finitary monads M together with a natural transformation $H \to M$. They introduce the *context-free* monad C^H of H, which is an H-pointed monad that is a subcoalgebra of the final coalgebra for $\mathcal{H}_{\mathsf{f}}$ and which is the monad of Courcelle's algebraic Σ-trees in the special case where $\mathcal{C} = \mathsf{Set}$ and H is a polynomial functor associated to a signature Σ. We will prove that this monad is the LFF of $\mathcal{H}_{\mathsf{f}}$, and thereby we characterize it by a universal property – solving the open problem in [7].

The setting is again an instance of the generalized powerset construction, but this time with $\mathsf{Fun}_{\mathsf{f}}(\mathcal{C})$ as the base category in lieu of Set. Let $\mathcal{C}$ be an lfp category in which the coproduct injections are monic and consider a finitary, mono-preserving endofunctor $H : \mathcal{C} \to \mathcal{C}$. Denote by $\mathsf{Fun}_{\mathsf{f}}(\mathcal{C})$ the category of finitary endofunctors on $\mathcal{C}$. Then H induces an endofunctor $H \cdot (-) + \mathsf{Id}$ on $\mathsf{Fun}_{\mathsf{f}}(\mathcal{C})$, denoted $\dot{H}$ and mapping an endofunctor V to the functor $X \mapsto HVX + X$. This functor $\dot{H}$ gets precomposed with a monad on $\mathsf{Fun}_{\mathsf{f}}(\mathcal{C})$ as we now explain.

Proposition 4.11 (Free monad, [5,9]). *For a finitary endofunctor H, free H-algebras $\varphi_X : HF^H X \to F^H X$ exist for all $X \in \mathcal{C}$. F^H itself is a finitary monad on $\mathcal{C}$, more specifically it is the free monad on H.*

For example, if H is a polynomial functor associated to a signature Σ, then $F^H X$ is the usual term algebra that contains all finite Σ-trees over the set of generators X. Proposition 4.11 implies that $H \mapsto F^H$ is the object assignment of a monad on $\mathsf{Fun}_{\mathsf{f}}(\mathcal{C})$. The Eilenberg-Moore category of $F^{(-)}$ is easily seen to be $\mathsf{Mnd}_{\mathsf{f}}(\mathcal{C})$, the category of finitary monads on $\mathcal{C}$. Here, fp and fg objects differ, see [45, Sect. 5.4.1] for a proof.

Similarly as in the case of context-free languages, we will work with the monad $E^{(-)} = F^{H+(-)}$, so we get H-pointed finitary monads as the $E^{(-)}$-algebras. This category is equivalent to a slice category: the universal property induced by $F^{(-)}$ states, that for any finitary monad B the natural transformations $H \to B$ are in one-to-one correspondence with monad morphisms $F^H \to B$; so the category $H/\mathsf{Mnd_f}(\mathcal{C})$ of finitary H-pointed monads on $\mathcal{C}$ is isomorphic to the slice category $F^H/\mathsf{Mnd_f}(\mathcal{C})$. This finishes the description of the base category and we now lift the functor $\dot{H}$ to this category.

Consider an H-pointed monad $(B, \beta : H \to \mathcal{C}) \in H/\mathsf{Mnd_f}(\mathcal{C})$. By [21], the endofunctor $H \cdot B + \mathrm{Id}$ carries a canonical monad structure. Furthermore, we have an obvious pointing $\mathrm{inl} \cdot H\eta^B : H \to H \cdot B + \mathrm{Id}$. By [32], this defines an endofunctor on H-pointed monads, $\mathcal{H_f} : H/\mathsf{Mnd_f}(\mathcal{C}) \to H/\mathsf{Mnd_f}(\mathcal{C})$, which is a lifting of $\dot{H}$. In order to verify that $\mathcal{H_f}$ is finitary, we first need to know how filtered colimits look in $H/\mathsf{Mnd_f}(\mathcal{C})$.

Lemma 4.12. *The forgetful* $U : \mathsf{Mnd_f}(\mathcal{C}) \to \mathsf{Fun_f}(\mathcal{C})$ *creates filtered colimits.*

Clearly, the canonical projection functor $H/\mathsf{Mnd_f}(\mathcal{C}) \to \mathsf{Mnd_f}(\mathcal{C})$ creates filtered colimits, too. Therefore, filtered colimits in the slice category $H/\mathsf{Mnd_f}(\mathcal{C})$ are formed on the level of $\mathsf{Fun_f}(\mathcal{C})$, i.e. object-wise. The functor $\dot{H}$ is finitary on $\mathsf{Fun_f}(\mathcal{C})$ and thus also its lifting $\mathcal{H_f}$ is finitary. So all requirements from Assumption 3.1 are met: we have a finitary endofunctor $\mathcal{H_f}$ on the lfp category $H/\mathsf{Mnd_f}(\mathcal{C})$, and by [7, Corollary 2.20] $\mathcal{H_f}$ preserves monos since H does. By Theorem 3.8, $\mathcal{H_f}$ has a locally finite fixpoint.

Remark 4.13. The final $\mathcal{H_f}$-coalgebra is not of much interest, but that of a related functor. $\mathcal{H_f}$ generalizes to a functor $\mathcal{H} : H/\mathsf{Mnd_c}(\mathcal{C}) \to H/\mathsf{Mnd_c}(\mathcal{C})$ on H-pointed countably accessible[1] monads. For any object $X \in \mathcal{C}$, the finitary endofunctor $H(-) + X$ has a final coalgebra; call the carrier TX. Then T is a monad [1], is countably accessible [7] and is the final $\mathcal{H}$-coalgebra [32].

Adámek et al. [7] characterize a (guarded) recursive program scheme as a natural transformation $V \to H \cdot E^V + \mathrm{Id}$ with V fp (in $\mathsf{Fun_f}(\mathcal{C})$), or equivalently, via the generalized powerset construction w.r.t. the monad $E^{(-)}$ as an $\mathcal{H_f}$-coalgebra on the carrier E^V (in $\mathsf{Mnd_f}(\mathcal{C})$). These $\mathcal{H_f}$-coalgebras on carriers E^V where $V \in \mathsf{Fun_f}(\mathcal{C})$ is fp form the full subcategory $\mathsf{EQ} \subseteq \mathsf{Coalg}\mathcal{H_f}$. They show two equivalent ways of constructing the monad of Courcelle's algebraic trees for the case $\mathcal{C} = \mathsf{Set}$: as the image of $\mathsf{EQ}_{\mathrm{colim}}$ in the final coalgebra T of Remark 4.13, and as the colimit of EQ_2, where EQ_2 is the closure of EQ under strong quotients. We now provide a third characterization, and show that the monad of Courcelle's algebraic trees is the locally finite fixpoint of $\mathcal{H_f}$.

To this end it suffices to show that EQ_2 is precisely the diagram of $\mathcal{H_f}$-coalgebras with an fg carrier. This is established with the help of the following two technical lemmas. We now assume that $\mathcal{C} = \mathsf{Set}$.

---

[1] A colimit is *countably filtered* if its diagram has for every countable subcategory a cocone. A functor is *countably accessible* if it preserves countably filtered colimits.

Lemma 4.14. $\mathcal{H}_f$ *maps strong epis to morphisms carried by strong epi natural transformations.*

We have the following variation of Proposition 3.17:

Lemma 4.15. *Any $\mathcal{H}_f$-coalgebra $b : (B, \beta) \to \mathcal{H}_f(B, \beta)$, with B fg, is the strong quotient of a coalgebra from* EQ.

The proof of Lemma 4.15 makes use of Lemma 4.14 as well as the following properties:

- The fp objects in $\mathsf{Fun}_f(\mathsf{Set})$ are the quotients of polynomial functors.
- The polynomial functors are projective. That means that for a polynomial functor P and any natural transformation $n : K \to L$ with surjective components we have the following property: for every $f : P \to L$ there exists $f' : P \to K$ with $n \cdot f' = f$.
- Any fg object in $H/\mathsf{Mnd}_f(\mathsf{Set})$ is the quotient of some E^V with V fp in $\mathsf{Fun}_f(\mathsf{Set})$ and thus also of some E^P with P a polynomial functor.

Note that the last property holds because $H/\mathsf{Mnd}_f(\mathsf{Set})$ is an Eilenberg-Moore category and E^V is the free Eilenberg-Moore algebra on the fp object V. It follows from Lemma 4.15 that $\mathsf{Coalg}_{fg}\mathcal{H}_f$ is the same category as EQ_2; thus their colimits in $\mathsf{Coalg}\mathcal{H}_f$ are isomorphic and we conclude:

Theorem 4.16. *The locally finite fixpoint of $\mathcal{H}_f$: $H_\Sigma/\mathsf{Mnd}_f(\mathsf{Set}) \to H_\Sigma/\mathsf{Mnd}_f(\mathsf{Set})$ is the monad of Courcelle's algebraic trees, sending a set to the algebraic Σ-trees over it.*

5 Conclusions and Future Work

We have introduced the locally finite fixpoint of a finitary mono-preserving endofunctor on an lfp category. We proved that this fixpoint is characterized by two universal properties: it is the final lfg coalgebra and the initial fg-iterative algebra for the given endofunctor. And we have seen many instances where the LFF is the domain of behaviour of finite-state and finite-equation systems. In particular all previously known instances of the rational fixpoint are also instances of the LFF, and we have obtained a number of interesting further instances not captured by the rational fixpoint.

On a more technical level, the LFF solves a problem that sometimes makes the rational fixpoint hard to apply. The latter identifies behaviourally equivalent states (i.e. is a subcoalgebra of the final coalgebra) if the classes of fp and fg objects coincide. This condition, however, may be false or unknown (and sometimes non-trivial to establish) in a given lfp category. But the LFF always identifies behaviourally equivalent states.

There are a number of interesting topics for future work concerning the LFF. First, it should be interesting to obtain further instances of the LFF, e.g. analyzing the behaviour of tape machines [23] may perhaps lead to a description of the recursively enumerable languages by the LFF. Second, syntactic descriptions of the LFF are of interest. In works such as [12,35,40,42] Kleene type theorems and axiomatizations of the behaviour of finite systems are studied. Completeness of an axiomatization is then established by proving that expressions modulo axioms form the rational fixpoint. It is an interesting question whether the theory of the LFF we presented here may be of help as a tool for syntactic descriptions and axiomatizations of further system types.

As we have mentioned already the rational fixpoint is the starting point for the coalgebraic study of iterative and iteration theories. A similar path could be followed based on the LFF and this should lead to new coalgebraic iteration/recursion principles, in particular in instances such as context-free languages or constructively S-algebraic formal power series.

Another approach to more powerful recursive definition principles are abstract operational rules (see [27] for an overview). It has been shown that certain rule formats define operations on the rational fixpoint [13,31], and it should be investigated whether a similar theory can be developed based on the LFF.

Finally, in the special setting of Eilenberg-Moore categories one could base the study of finite systems on *free* finitely generated algebras (rather than all fp or all fg algebras). Does this give a third fixpoint capturing behaviour of finite state systems with side effects besides the rational fixpoint and the LFF? And what is then the relation between the three fixpoints? Also the parallelism in the technical development between rational fixpoint and LFF indicates that there should be a general theory that is parametric in a class of "finite objects" and that allows to obtain results about the rational fixpoint, the LFF and other possible "finite behaviour domains" as instances.

References

1. Aczel, P., Adámek, J., Milius, S., Velebil, J.: Infinite trees and completely iterative theories: a coalgebraic view. Theoret. Comput. Sci. **300**, 1–45 (2003)
2. Adámek, J., Milius, S., Velebil, J.: Semantics of higher-order recursion schemes. Log. Methods Comput. Sci. **7**(1:15), 43 (2011)
3. Adámek, J., Milius, S., Velebil, J.: Equational properties of iterative monads. Inf. Comput. **208**, 1306–1348 (2010)
4. Adámek, J., Milius, S., Velebil, J.: Elgot theories: a new perspective of the equational properties of iteration. Math. Struct. Comput. Sci. **21**(2), 417–480 (2011)
5. Adámek, J.: Free algebras and automata realizations in the language of categories. Comment. Math. Univ. Carolin. **015**(4), 589–602 (1974)
6. Adámek, J., Milius, S., Velebil, J.: Iterative algebras at work. Math. Struct. Comput. Sci. **16**(6), 1085–1131 (2006)
7. Adámek, J., Milius, S., Velebil, J.: On second-order iterative monads. Theoret. Comput. Sci. **412**(38), 4969–4988 (2011)
8. Adámek, J., Rosický, J.: Locally Presentable and Accessible Categories. Cambridge University Press, New York (1994)
9. Barr, M.: Coequalizers and free triples. Math. Z. **116**, 307–322 (1970)

10. Bartels, F.: On generalized coinduction and probabilistic specification formats: Distributive laws in coalgebraic modelling. Ph.D. thesis, Vrije Universiteit Amsterdam.(2004)

11. Bloom, S.L., Ésik, Z.: Iteration Theories: The Equational Logic of Iterative Processes. EATCS Monographs on Theoretical Computer Science. Springer, Heidelberg (1993)

12. Bonsangue, M., Milius, S., Silva, A.: Sound and complete axiomatizations of coalgebraic language equivalence. ACM Trans. Comput. Log. 14((1: 7)), 52.(2013)

13. Bonsangue, M.M., Milius, S., Rot, J.: On the specification of operations on the rational behaviour of systems. In: Luttik, B., Reniers, M.A. (eds.) Proceedings of Combined Workshop on Expressiveness in Concurrency and Structural Operational Semantics (EXPRESS/SOS'12), Electronic Proceedings of Theoretical Computer Science, vol. 89, pp. 3–18.(2012)

14. Borceux, F.: Handbook of Categorical Algebra: Volume 1, Basic Category Theory. Encyclopedia of Mathematics and its Applications. Cambridge University Press, Cambridge (1994)

15. Cenciarelli, P., Moggi, E.: A syntactic approach to modularity in denotational semantic. In: Proceedings of 5th CTCS. CWI Technical report.(1993)

16. Courcelle, B.: Fundamental properties of infinite trees. Theoret. Comput. Sci. 25, 95–169 (1983)

17. Droste, M., Kuich, W., Vogler, H.: Handbook of Weighted Automata, 1st edn. Springer Publishing Company, Berlin (2009)

18. Elgot, C.: Monadic computation and iterative algebraic theories. In: Rose, H.E., Sheperdson, J.C. (eds.) Logic Colloquium 1973, vol. 80, pp. 175–230. North-Holland Publishers, Amsterdam (1975)

19. Fliess, M.: Sur divers produits de séries formelles. Bulletin de la Société Mathématique de France 102, 181–191 (1974)

20. Gabriel, P., Ulmer, F.: Lokal präsentierbare Kategorien. Lecture Notes in Mathematics, vol. 221. Springer, Heidelberg (1971)

21. Ghani, N., Lüth, C., Marchi, F.D.: Monads of coalgebras: rational terms and term graphs. Math. Struct. Comput. Sci. 15, 433–451 (2005)

22. Goncharov, Sergey: Trace Semantics via Generic Observations. In: Heckel, Reiko, Milius, Stefan (eds.) CALCO 2013. LNCS, vol. 8089, pp. 158–174. Springer, Heidelberg (2013)

23. Goncharov, Sergey, Milius, Stefan, Silva, Alexandra: Towards a Coalgebraic Chomsky Hierarchy. In: Diaz, Josep, Lanese, Ivan, Sangiorgi, Davide (eds.) TCS 2014. LNCS, vol. 8705, pp. 265–280. Springer, Heidelberg (2014)

24. Harrison, M.A., Havel, I.M.: Real-time strict deterministic languages. SIAM J. Comput. 1(4), 333–349 (1972)

25. Hyland, M., Plotkin, G., Power, J.: Combining effects: sum and tensor. Theoret. Comput. Sci. 357(1–3), 70–99 (2006)

26. Jacobs, Bart: A Bialgebraic Review of Deterministic Automata, Regular Expressions and Languages. In: Futatsugi, Kokichi, Jouannaud, Jean-Pierre, Meseguer, José (eds.) Algebra, Meaning, and Computation. LNCS, vol. 4060, pp. 375–404. Springer, Heidelberg (2006)

27. Klin, B.: Bialgebras for structural operational semantics: an introduction. Theoret. Comput. Sci. 412(38), 5043–5069 (2011)

28. Lambek, J.: A fixpoint theorem for complete categories. Math. Z. 103, 151–161 (1968)

29. MacLane, S.: Categories for the Working Mathematician. Graduate Texts in Mathematics, 2nd edn. Springer, New York.(1998)

30. Milius, S.: A sound and complete calculus for finite stream circuits. In: Proceedings of 25th Annual Symposium on Logic in Computer Science (LICS 2010), pp. 449–458.(2010)

31. Milius, S., Bonsangue, M.M., Myers, R.S., Rot, J.: Rational operation models. Electron. Notes Theoret. Comput. Sci. 298, 257–282. In: Mislove, M. (ed.) Proceedings of 29th conference on Mathematical Foundations of Programming Science (MFPS XXIX).(2013)

32. Milius, S., Moss, L.S.: The category theoretic solution of recursive program schemes. Theoret. Comput. Sci. **366**, 3–59 (2006)

33. Milius, S., Pattinson, D., Wißmann, T.: A new foundation for finitary corecursion: the locally finite fixpoint and its properties (2015).. http://arxiv.org/abs/1601.01532

34. Milius, S., Wißmann, T.: Finitary corecursion for the infinitary lambda calculus. In: Proceedings of 6th Conference on Algebra and Coalgebra in Computer Science, CALCO 2015. Leibniz International Proceedings in Informatics.(2015)

35. Myers, R.: Rational coalgebraic machines in varieties: Languages, completeness and automatic proofs. Ph.D. thesis, Imperial College London, Department of Computing.(2011)

36. Petre, I., Salomaa, A.: Algebraic systems and pushdown automata. In: Droste, M., Kuich, W., Vogler, H. (eds.) Handbook of Weighted Automata. Monographs in Theoretical Computer Science. An EATCS Series, pp. 257–289.. Springer, Heidelberg (2009)

37. Plotkin, G., Turi, D.: Towards a mathematical operational semantics. In: Proceedings of 12th LICS Conference, pp. 280–291. IEEE Computer Society Press.(1997)

38. Rutten, J.J.M.M.: Automata and Coinduction. In: Sangiorgi, Davide, de Simone, Robert (eds.) CONCUR 1998. LNCS, vol. 1466, pp. 194–218. Springer, Heidelberg (1998)

39. Rutten, J.: Universal coalgebra: a theory of systems. Theoret. Comput. Sci. **249**(1), 3–80 (2000)

40. Silva, A., Bonchi, F., Bonsangue, M.M., Rutten, J.J.M.M.: Quantitative kleene coalgebras. Inf. Comput. **209**(5), 822–849 (2011)

41. Silva, A., Bonchi, F., Bonsangue, M.M., Rutten, J.: Generalizing determinization from automata to coalgebras. Log. Meth. Comput. Sci. **9**(1), 1–27 (2013)

42. Silva, A., Bonsangue, M.M., Rutten, J.: Non-deterministic Kleene coalgebras. Log. Meth. Comput. Sci. 6(3: 23), 39.(2010)

43. Winter, J., Bonsangue, M., Rutten, J.: Coalgebraic characterizations of context-free languages. Log. Meth. Comput. Sci. **9**(3), 1–39 (2013)

44. Winter, J., Bonsangue, M.M., Rutten, J.J.: Context-free coalgebras. J. Comput. Syst. Sci. **81**(5), 911–939 (2015)

45. Wißmann, T.: The locally finite fixpoint and its properties. Master's thesis, Friedrich-Alexander Universität Erlangen-Nürnberg (April 2015). http://thorsten-wissmann.de/theses/ma-wissmann.pdf

Fixed-Point Elimination in the Intuitionistic Propositional Calculus

Silvio Ghilardi[1], Maria João Gouveia[2], and Luigi Santocanale[3]([✉])

[1] Dipartimento di Matematica, Università degli Studi di Milano, Milan, Italy
[2] CEMAT-CIÊNCIAS, Universidade de Lisboa, 1749-016 Lisboa, Portugal
[3] LIF, CNRS UMR 7279, Aix-Marseille Université, Marseille, France
luigi.santocanale@lif.univ-mrs.fr

Abstract. It is a consequence of existing literature that least and greatest fixed-points of monotone polynomials on Heyting algebras—that is, the algebraic models of the Intuitionistic Propositional Calculus—always exist, even when these algebras are not complete as lattices. The reason is that these extremal fixed-points are definable by formulas of the **IPC**. Consequently, the μ-calculus based on intuitionistic logic is trivial, every μ-formula being equivalent to a fixed-point free formula. We give in this paper an axiomatization of least and greatest fixed-points of formulas, and an algorithm to compute a fixed-point free formula equivalent to a given μ-formula. The axiomatization of the greatest fixed-point is simple. The axiomatization of the least fixed-point is more complex, in particular every monotone formula converges to its least fixed-point by Kleene's iteration in a finite number of steps, but there is no uniform upper bound on the number of iterations. We extract, out of the algorithm, upper bounds for such n, depending on the size of the formula. For some formulas, we show that these upper bounds are polynomial and optimal.

1 Introduction

In [23] the author proved that, for each formula $\phi(x)$ of the Intuitionistic Propositional Calculus, there exists a number $n \geq 0$ such that $\phi^n(x)$—the formula obtained from ϕ by iterating n times substitution of ϕ for the variable x—and $\phi^{n+2}(x)$ are equivalent in Intuitionistic Logic. This result has, as an immediate corollary, that a syntactically monotone formula $\phi(x)$ converges both to its least fixed-point and to its greatest fixed-point in at most n steps. Using a modern notation based on μ-calculi [3], we have $\mu_x.\phi(x) = \phi^n(\bot)$ and $\nu_x.\phi(x) = \phi^n(\top)$. These identities also show that a μ-calculus based on Intuitionistic Logic is trivial, every μ-formula being equivalent to a fixed-point free formula.

Ruitenberg's work [23] leaves open how to extract or estimate the least number $\rho(\phi)$ such that $\phi^{\rho(\phi)}(x) = \phi^{\rho(\phi)+2}(x)$. Yet, our motivations stem from the theory of extremal fixed-points and μ-calculi [3]. In principle, being able to compute or bound Ruitenberg's number $\rho(\phi)$ might end up in an over-approximation of the closure ordinal of ϕ—the least k such that $\mu_x.\phi(x) = \phi^k(\bot)$. For the analogous problem with the greatest fixed-point, we shall see that the least number k such that $\nu_x.\phi(x) = \phi^k(\top)$ is bounded by 1, while $\rho(\phi)$ might be arbitrarily large.

© Springer-Verlag Berlin Heidelberg 2016
B. Jacobs and C. Löding (Eds.): FOSSACS 2016, LNCS 9634, pp. 126–141, 2016.
DOI: 10.1007/978-3-662-49630-5_8

Later in [20], the author gave an independent proof that least fixed-points of monotone formulas are definable within Intuitionistic Logic. His proof relies on semantics methods and on the coding of Intuitionistic Logic into Grzegorczyk's Logic; the proof was further refined in [21] to encompass the standard coding of Intuitionistic Logic into its modal companion, the logic **S4**. Curiously, no mention of greatest fixed-points appears in these works.

Another relevant source for this paper stem from the discovery that **IPC** has uniform interpolants [22], often named *bisimulation quantifiers*. Together with the deduction property of **IPC**, they give the category of (finitely generated) Heyting algebras—that is, the algebraic models of the Intuitionistic Propositional Calculus—a rather strong structure, axiomatized and studied in [14,15]. It is possible to argue that in every category with similar properties the extremal fixed-points of monotone formulas are definable. This is possible by using quantified formulas analogous to the one used in [9, Sect. 3] to argue that **PDL** lacks the uniform interpolation property. In this paper we exploit this idea and the existential bisimulation quantifiers to characterize greatest fixed-points in the Intuitionistic Propositional Calculus.

A μ-calculus is a prototypical kind of computational logic, obtained from a base logic or algebraic system by addition of distinct forms of iteration so to increase expressivity. This paper is part of a line of research whose goal is to understand, under a unified perspective, why alternation-depth hierarchies of μ-calculi are degenerate or trivial. A μ-calculus adds to an underlying logical-algebraic system formal lgfps of formula-terms whose semantic monotonicity can be witnessed at the syntactic level. When addition of extremal fixed-points is iterated, formula-terms with nested extremal fixed-points are generated. The alternation-depth hierarchy [3, Sect. 2.6] of a μ-calculus measures the complexity of a formula-term as a function of the nesting of the different types of fixed-points, with respect to a fixed class of models. It is well known that fixed-points that are unguarded can be eliminated in the propositional modal μ-calculus [18]. We can rephrase this fact by saying that the alternation-depth hierarchy of the μ-calculus over distributive lattices is trivial, every μ-term being equivalent to a fixed-point free term. A goal of [12] was to understand closely this result and to generalize it. We were able to exhibit equational classes of lattices $\mathcal{D}_n$—with $\mathcal{D}_0$ the class of distributive lattices—where the extremal fixed-points can be uniformly computed by iterating a formula-term $n+1$ times from the bottom/top of the lattice; moreover, we showed that these uniform upper bounds are optimal. The reasons for the degeneracy of the hierarchy can be ultimately found in the structural theory of lattices.

As we show in this paper, the situation is quite different when the base for the μ-calculus is Intuitionistic Logic, with its standard models the Heyting algebras. Several ingredients contribute to the existence of a closure ordinal of each formula and to its finiteness. Among them, *strongness* of the monotone polynomials on Heyting algebras. This means that a monotone polynomial $f : H \longrightarrow H$ over a Heyting algebra H can be considered as a functor enriched over H, when H is consider as a closed category [16]. For some polynomials, existence and finiteness of the closure ordinal is a consequence of being *inflating* (or expanding) and, on the syntactic level, to a restriction to the use of conjunction that determines a notion of disjunctive formula. As far as the greatest fixed-point is concerned, monotone formulas uniformly converge to it after one step. A key ingredient of the algorithm we present is creation of least fixed-points via the *Rolling* equation (cf. Lemma 1), a fact already used in [10]. For Intuitionistic Logic and Heyting algebras, where formula-terms can be semantically antitone (i.e. contravariant), existing greatest fixed-points create least fixed-points. The most striking difference with the case of distributive lattices (and with the case of the varieties $\mathcal{D}_n$) is the absence of a finite uniform upper bound on the closure ordinals, the rate of convergence to the least fixed-point crucially depending on the shape of the formula.

As emphasized in [19] for the propositional modal μ-calculus, once a formula is known to be equivalent to some other formula of smaller complexity, we should also be able to effectively compute this second formula. Thus, the fact that the alternation hierarchy is trivial for μ-calculi based on the **IPC** should not be the end of the story. The main contribution of this paper is to achieve an effective transformation of an intuitionisitc μ-formula into an equivalent fixed-point free intuitionisitc formula. The size of the formula might exhibit an exponential grow during this transformation. Yet, this is mainly due, as usual, to the need of precompiling a formula into an equivalent one in some kind of conjunctive normal form. We might use sharing in substitutions—or introduce the appropriate formalism for approximants to least fixed-points—so that, if we are given an already precompiled formula, then its least fixed-point w.r.t. the variable x is only polynomially bigger than the original formula. For these formulas, we instantiate this claim by explicitly giving a way of computing $f(\phi)$ such that $\mu_x.\phi(x) = \phi^{f(\phi)}(\bot)$, so that $f(\phi)$ is an upper bound to the closure ordinal of ϕ. In some cases we are able to show that $f(\phi)$ is optimal, by exhibiting some formula $\phi(x)$ such that $\phi^{f(\phi)-1}(\bot) < \mu_x.\phi(x)$.

The paper is structured as follows. We recall in Sect. 2 some elementary facts from fixed-point theory. In Sect. 3 we recall the Intuitionistic Propositional Calculus and introduce the Intuitionistic Propositional μ-Calculus. In Sect. 4 we argue that monotone polynomials are strong and exhibit the interactions between least fixed-points and strong functions. In Sect. 5 we use the existential bisimulation quantifier to argue that monotone polynomials converge to their greatest fixed-point in one step. Section 6 is the core of our paper, where we show ho to eliminate a least fixed-point from a formula. Together with the result in the previous Section, this leads to a procedure to eliminate off the fixed-points from a **IPC**$_\mu$ formula. Finally, in Sect. 7, we show how upper bounds to closure ordinals can be extracted from the procedure elimination of the least fixed-points. In Sect. 8 we present our final remarks.

2   Notation and Elementary Concepts

Let P and Q be posets. A function $f : P \longrightarrow Q$ is *monotone* if $x \le y$ implies $f(x) \le f(y)$, for each $x, y \in P$. If $f : P \longrightarrow P$ is a monotone endofunction, then $x \in P$ is a *prefixed-point* of f if $f(x) \leq x$; we denote by Pre_f the set of prefixed points of f. Whenever Pre_f has a least element, we denote it by $\mu.f$. Therefore, $\mu.f$ denotes the *least prefixed-point* of f, whenever it exists. If $\mu.f$ exists, then it is a fixed-point of f, necessarily the least one. The notions of least prefixed-point and of least fixed-point coincide on complete lattices or when the least fixed-point is computed by iterating from the bottom of a lattice; for our purposes they are interchangeable, so we shall abuse of language and refer to $\mu.f$ as the least fixed-point of f. Dually (and abusing again of language), the *greatest fixed-point* of f shall be denoted by $\nu.f$.

Let us mention few elementary facts from fixed-point theory.

Lemma 1. *Let P, Q be posets, $f : P \longrightarrow Q$ and $g : Q \longrightarrow P$ be monotone functions. If $\mu.(g \circ f)$ exists, then $\mu.(f \circ g)$ exists as well and is equal to $f(\mu.(g \circ f))$.*

As we do not work in complete lattices (so we are not ensured that least fixed-points exist) we express the above statement via the equality

$$\mu.(f \circ g) := f(\mu.(g \circ f)) \,, \tag{Roll}$$

where the colon emphasizes existence: if the least fixed-point in the expression on the right *exists*, then this expression is the least fixed-point of $f \circ g$. Analogous notations will be used later. We endow the product of two posets P and Q with the coordinatewise ordering. Therefore a function $f : P \times Q \longrightarrow R$ is monotone if, as a function of two variables, it is monotone in each variable. To deal with least fixed-points of functions of many variables, we use the standard notation: for example, if $f : P \times P \longrightarrow P$ is the monotone function $f(x, y)$, then, for a fixed $p \in P$, $\mu_x.f(x, p)$ denotes the least fixed-point of $f(x, p)$. Let us recall that the correspondence $p \mapsto \mu_x.f(x, p)$—noted $\mu_x.f(x, y)$—is again monotone.

Lemma 2. *If P is a poset and $f : P \times P \longrightarrow P$ is a monotone mapping, then*

$$\mu_x.f(x, x) := \mu_x.\mu_y.f(x, y) \,. \tag{Diag}$$

Lemma 3. *If P and Q are posets and $\langle f, g \rangle : P \times Q \longrightarrow P \times Q$ is a monotone function, then $\mu.\langle f, g \rangle := \langle \mu_1, \mu_2 \rangle$, where*

$$\mu_1 = \mu_x.f(x, \mu_y.g(x, y)) \quad and \quad \mu_2 = \mu_y.g(\mu_1, y) \,. \tag{Bekic}$$

3   The Intuitionistic Propositional μ-Calculus

Formulas of the Intuitionistic Propositional Calculus are generated according to the following grammar:

$$\phi \;\Rightarrow\; x \mid \top \mid \phi \wedge \phi \mid \bot \mid \phi \vee \phi \mid \phi \rightarrow \phi \,, \tag{1}$$

where x ranges over a countable set $\mathbb{X}$ of propositional variables. For the **IPC**, the formulation of the consequence relation $\vdash_{\mathbf{LJ}}$ (relating a set of formulas to a formula) goes back to Gentzen's work on the system **LJ** [13]. It is well known that Intuitionistic Logic is sound and complete w.r.t. the class of its algebraic models, the Heyting algebras.

Definition 1. *A* Heyting algebra *H is a bounded lattice (with least element $\perp$ and greatest element $\top$) equipped with a binary operation $\rightarrow$ such that the following equations hold in H:*

$$x \wedge (x \rightarrow y) = x \wedge y, \qquad x \wedge (y \rightarrow x) = x, \qquad (2)$$
$$x \rightarrow x = \top, \qquad x \rightarrow (y \wedge z) = (x \rightarrow y) \wedge (x \rightarrow z).$$

We can define on any Heyting algebra a partial order by saying that $x \leq y$ holds when $x \vee y = y$. We identify formulas of the **IPC** with terms of the theory of Heyting algebras, constructed therefore from variables and using the signature $\langle \top, \wedge, \perp, \vee, \rightarrow \rangle$. For ϕ such a formula-term, H a Heyting algebra, and $v : \mathbb{X} \longrightarrow H$ a valuation of the propositional variables in H, let us write $[\![\phi]\!]_v$ for the result of evaluating the formula in H, starting from the variables. The soundness and completeness theorem of the **IPC** over Heyting algebras—see e.g. [6]—can then be stated as follows: *if Γ is a finite set of formula-terms and ϕ is a formula-term, then $\Gamma \vdash_{\mathbf{LJ}} \phi$ holds if and only if $\bigwedge_{\gamma \in \Gamma} [\![\gamma]\!]_v \leq [\![\phi]\!]_v$ holds, in every Heyting algebra H and for every valuation of the propositional variables $v : \mathbb{X} \longrightarrow H$.* Given this theorem, we shall often abuse of notation and write $\leq$ in place of $\vdash_{\mathbf{LJ}}$, and the equality symbol $=$ to denote logical equivalence of formulas.

We aim at studying extremal fixed-points on Heyting algebras. To this end, we formalize the Intuitionistic Propositional μ-Calculus.

An occurrence of a variable x is *positive* in a formula-term ϕ if, in the syntax tree of ϕ, the path from the root to the leaf labeled by this variable contains an even number of nodes labeled by subformulas $\psi_1 \rightarrow \psi_2$ immediately followed by a node labeled by the subformula ψ_1. If, on this path the number of those nodes is odd, then we say that this occurrence of x is *negative* in ϕ. A variable x is positive in a formula ϕ if each occurrence of x is positive in ϕ. A variable x is negative in a formula ϕ if each occurrence of x is negative in ϕ. If we add to the previous grammar (1) the following productions:

$$\phi \Rightarrow \mu_x.\phi, \qquad\qquad \phi \Rightarrow \nu_x.\phi,$$

subject to the restriction that x is positive in ϕ, we obtain then a grammar for the formulas of **IPC**$_\mu$, the Intuitionistic Propositional μ-Calculus. The semantics of these formulas is the expected one. Let ϕ be a formula of **IPC**$_\mu$, and let x be positive in ϕ. Let us denote by $\mathbb{X}_\phi$ the set of variables having an occurrence in ϕ. If $v : \mathbb{X}_\phi \setminus \{x\} \longrightarrow H$ is a valuation of all the variables of ϕ but x in a *complete* Heyting algebra, then the function $[\![\phi]\!]_v$, defined by

$$h \mapsto [\![\phi]\!]_{v,h/x},$$

is monotone, so $\mu_x.\phi$ (resp., $\nu_x.\phi$) is to be evaluated over the least fixed-point (resp., the greatest fixed-point) of this function. A sequent calculus for **IPC**$_\mu$ is presented in [7, Sect. 2].

Let us say that a formula ϕ of **IPC**$_\mu$ is fixed-point free if it is a formula of **IPC**, that is, it does not contain either of the symbols μ, ν.

Proposition 1. *Every formula ϕ of $\mathbf{IPC}_\mu$ is equivalent to a fixed-point free formula ϕ'.*

Proof. Clearly, the statement holds if we can show that it holds whenever $\phi = \mu_x.\psi$ or $\phi = \nu_x.\psi$, where ψ is a fixed-point free formula. For a natural number $n \geq 0$, let $\psi^n(x)$ denote the formula obtained by substituting x for ψ n times. Ruitenburg [23] proves that, for each intuitionisitic formula ψ, there exists a number $n \geq 0$ such that the formulas $\psi^n(x)$ and $\psi^{n+2}(x)$ are equivalent. If x is positive in ψ, then instantiating x with $\bot$, leads to the equivalence $\psi^{n+1}(\bot) \equiv \psi^n(\bot)$, exhibiting $\psi^n(\bot)$ as the least fixed-point of ψ. Similarly, $\psi^n(\top)$ is the greatest fixed-point of ψ. $\square$

While it is an obvious step to derive the previous Proposition from Ruitenburg's result, there has been no attempt (as far as we know) to compute an upper bound on $n \geq 0$ such that $\psi^n(x)$ and $\psi^{n+2}(x)$ are equivalent. Nor is such an n necessarily a tight upper bound for convergence of a formula to its least or greatest fixed-point.

4   Strong Monotone Functions and Fixed-Points

If H is a Heyting algebra and $f : H \longrightarrow H$ is a monotone function, then we say that f is *strong* if

$$x \wedge f(y) \leq f(x \wedge y), \qquad \text{for any } x, y \in H.$$

The interplay between fixed-points and this class of functions has already been emphasized, mainly in the context of categorical proof-theory and semantics of functional programming languages with inductive data types [7,8].

Lemma 4. *A monotone $f : H \longrightarrow H$ is strong if and only if any of the following equivalent conditions holds in H:*

$$x \wedge f(y) \leq f(x \wedge y), \tag{3}$$
$$f(x \rightarrow y) \leq x \rightarrow f(y), \tag{4}$$
$$x \rightarrow y \leq f(x) \rightarrow f(y). \tag{5}$$

The proof of these equivalences is usual in categorical algebra [17] and therefore it is omitted here.

Definition 2. *Let H be a Heyting algebra. We say that a function $f : H \longrightarrow H$ is* monotone polynomial *if there exist a formula ϕ of the $\mathbf{IPC}$, a variable x positive in ϕ, and a valuation $v : \mathbb{X}_\phi \setminus \{x\} \longrightarrow H$ such that, for each $h \in H$, we have $f(h) = [\![\phi]\!]_{v,h/x}$.*

Proposition 2. *Every monotone polynomial f on a Heyting algebra is strong.*

Proof. Recall that the replacement Lemma holds in the **IPC**: $z \leftrightarrow w \vdash_{\mathbf{LJ}} \phi(z) \leftrightarrow \phi(w)$. Substituting x for z and $x \wedge y$ for w, and considering that $x \rightarrow y \vdash_{\mathbf{LJ}} x \leftrightarrow$

$(x \wedge y)$, we derive that $x \to y \vdash_{\mathbf{LJ}} \phi(x) \leftrightarrow \phi(x \wedge y)$. Assuming that u is positive in $\phi(u)$, we have $\phi(x) \leftrightarrow \phi(x \wedge y) \vdash_{\mathbf{LJ}} \phi(x) \to \phi(x \wedge y) \vdash_{\mathbf{LJ}} \phi(x) \to \phi(y)$, whence $x \to y \vdash_{\mathbf{LJ}} \phi(x) \to \phi(y)$. The last relation immediately implies that Eq. (4) from Lemma 4 holds, when $\mathfrak{f}$ is a monotone polynomial. $\qquad\square$

It can be shown that the relation $\mathfrak{f}(x) \wedge y = \mathfrak{f}(x \wedge y) \wedge y$ holds (for any x, y and) for *any* polynomial on a Heyting algebra. The analogous remark for Boolean algebras is credited to Peirce, in view of the iteration rule for existential graphs of type Alpha, see [11].

Proposition 3. *If $\mathfrak{f}$ is a strong monotone function on H and $a \in H$, then*

$$\mu.a \to \mathfrak{f} := a \to \mu.\mathfrak{f}, \qquad\qquad \mu.a \wedge \mathfrak{f} := a \wedge \mu.\mathfrak{f}. \qquad (6)$$

Proof. Let us argue first that first equation holds. To this end, let us set $\mathfrak{f}^a(x) =_{\mathtt{def}} a \to \mathfrak{f}(x)$. From $\mathfrak{f} \le \mathfrak{f}^a$ we have $\mathtt{Pre}_{\mathfrak{f}^a} \subseteq \mathtt{Pre}_\mathfrak{f}$. Thus, if $p \in \mathtt{Pre}_{\mathfrak{f}^a}$, then $\mu_x.\mathfrak{f}(x) = \mathfrak{f}(\mu_x.\mathfrak{f}(x)) \le \mathfrak{f}(p)$ and $a \to \mu.\mathfrak{f} \le a \to \mathfrak{f}(p) = \mathfrak{f}^a(p) \le p$. That is, $a \to \mu.\mathfrak{f}$ is below any element of $\mathtt{Pre}_{\mathfrak{f}^a}$. To obtain the proposition, we need to argue that $a \to \mu.\mathfrak{f}$ belongs to $\mathtt{Pre}_{\mathfrak{f}^a}$. To this end, we notice that $\{ a \to p \mid p \in \mathtt{Pre}_\mathfrak{f} \} \subseteq \mathtt{Pre}_{\mathfrak{f}^a}$, since if $\mathfrak{f}(p) \le p$, then $\mathfrak{f}^a(a \to p) = a \to \mathfrak{f}(a \to p) \le a \to \mathfrak{f}(p) \le a \to p$, where we used the fact that $\mathfrak{f}$ is strong, thus (4) holds.

Let us come now to the second equation, for which we set $\mathfrak{f}_a(x) =_{\mathtt{def}} a \wedge \mathfrak{f}(x)$. Suppose $a \wedge \mathfrak{f}(p) \le p$, so $\mathfrak{f}(p) \le a \to p$. Then $\mathfrak{f}(a \to p) \le a \to \mathfrak{f}(p) \le a \to p$, using (4), whence $\mu.\mathfrak{f} \le a \to p$ and $a \wedge \mu.\mathfrak{f} \le p$. Thus we are left to argue that $a \wedge \mu.\mathfrak{f}$ is a prefixed-point of $\mathfrak{f}_a$. Yet, this is true for an arbitrary prefixed-point p of $\mathfrak{f}$: $a \wedge \mathfrak{f}(a \wedge p) \le a \wedge \mathfrak{f}(p) \le a \wedge p$. $\qquad\square$

Corollary 1. *For each $n \ge 1$ and each collection $\mathfrak{f}_i$, $i = 1, \dots, n$ of monotone polynomials, we have the following distribution law:*

$$\mu_x. \bigwedge_{i=1,\dots,n} \mathfrak{f}_i(x) := \bigwedge_{i=1,\dots,n} \mu_x.\mathfrak{f}_i(x). \qquad (7)$$

Proof. For $n = 1$ there is nothing to prove. We suppose therefore that the statement holds for every collection of size $n \ge 1$, and prove it holds for a collection of size $n + 1$. We have

$$\mu_x.(\mathfrak{f}_{n+1}(x) \wedge \bigwedge_{i=1,\dots,n} \mathfrak{f}_i(x)) := \mu_x.\mu_y.(\mathfrak{f}_{n+1}(y) \wedge \bigwedge_{i=1,\dots,n} \mathfrak{f}_i(x)), \qquad \text{by (Diag)},$$

$$:= \mu_x.((\mu_y.\mathfrak{f}_{n+1}(y)) \wedge \bigwedge_{i=1,\dots,n} \mathfrak{f}_i(x)), \qquad \text{by (6)},$$

$$:= (\mu_y.\mathfrak{f}_{n+1}(y)) \wedge \mu_x.(\bigwedge_{i=1,\dots,n} \mathfrak{f}_i(x)), \qquad \text{again by (6)},$$

$$:= (\mu_y.\mathfrak{f}_{n+1}(y)) \wedge \bigwedge_{i=1,\dots,n} \mu_x.\mathfrak{f}_i(x), \qquad \text{by the IH.} \qquad\square$$

The elimination of greatest fixed-points is easy for strong monotone functions (we are thankful to the referee for pointing out the following fact, which greatly simplifies our original argument):

Proposition 4. *If* $f : L \longrightarrow L$ *is any strong monotone function on a bounded lattice* L, *then* $f^2(\top) = f(\top)$. *Thus* $f(\top)$ *is the greatest fixed-point of* f.

Proof. Indeed, we have $f(\top) = f(\top) \wedge f(\top) \leq f(f(\top) \wedge \top) = f^2(\top)$. □

5   A Digression on Fixpoints and Bisimulation Quantifiers

The connection between extremal fixed-points and bisimulation quantifiers, as emphasized in [9], was a main motivation to tackle this research. Although in the end our computations are independant on that, we nevertheless want to have a closer look to the topic (the content of this section is not needed afterwards).

It was discovered in [22] that **IPC** has the uniform interpolation property. As made clear from the title of [22], this property amounts to an internal existential and universal quantification. This result was further refined in [15] to show that any morphism between finitely generated Heyting algebras has a left and a right adjoint. We shall be interested in Heyting algebras $H[x]$ of polynomials with coefficients from H, and to (the left and right adjoints to) the inclusion of H into $H[x]$. The algebra of polynomials $H[x]$ is formally defined as the coproduct (in the category of Heyting algebras) of H with the free Heyting algebra on one generator. The universal property gives that if $h_0 \in H$, then there exists a unique morphism $[\![\cdot]\!]_{h_0/x} : H[x] \longrightarrow H$ such that $[\![x]\!]_{h_0/x} = h_0$ and $[\![h]\!]_{h_0/x} = h$, for each $h \in H$. Thus, for $f \in H[x]$ and $h \in H$, we can define $f(h) = [\![f]\!]_{h/x}$. It follows from [15] that if H is finitely generated, then the inclusion $i_x : H \longrightarrow H[x]$ has both adjoints $\exists_x, \forall_x : H[x] \longrightarrow H$, with $\exists_x \dashv i_x \dashv \forall_x$. In particular, we shall use the unit relation for $\exists_x$:

$$f \leq i_x(\exists_x(f)), \qquad \text{for all } f \in H[x].$$

Identifying $h \in H$ with $i_x(h) \in H[x]$, we can read the above inequality as $f \leq \exists_x.f$. We can identify a monotone polynomial, as defined in Definition 2, as an element $f \in H[x]$ such that $[\![f]\!]_{h_0/x} \leq [\![f]\!]_{h_1/x}$ whenever $h_0 \leq h_1$.

Proposition 5. *If* f *is a monotone polynomial on a finitely generated Heyting algebra, then*

$$\nu.f := \exists_x.(x \wedge (x \rightarrow f(x))). \tag{8}$$

Proof. By the unit relation $x \wedge x \rightarrow f(x) \leq \exists_x.(x \wedge x \rightarrow f(x))$. Recall that evaluation at $p \in H$ is a Heyting algebra morphism, thus it is monotone. Therefore, if $p \in H$ is a postfixed-point of f, then by evaluating the previous inequality at p, we have

$$p = p \wedge p \rightarrow f(p) \leq \exists_x.(x \wedge x \rightarrow f(x)),$$

so that $\exists_x.(x \wedge x \rightarrow \mathfrak{f}(x))$ is greater than any postfixed-point of $\mathfrak{f}$. Let us show that $\exists_x.(x \wedge x \rightarrow \mathfrak{f}(x))$ is also a postfixed-point. To this end, it will be enough to argue that $x \wedge x \rightarrow \mathfrak{f}(x) \leq \mathfrak{f}(\exists_x.(x \wedge x \rightarrow \mathfrak{f}(x)))$ in $H[x]$. We compute as follows:

$$
\begin{aligned}
x \wedge x \rightarrow \mathfrak{f}(x) &\leq \mathfrak{f}(x) \wedge x \rightarrow \mathfrak{f}(x) \\
&\leq \mathfrak{f}(x \wedge x \rightarrow \mathfrak{f}(x)), &&\text{since } \mathfrak{f} \text{ is strong, by (3),} \\
&\leq \mathfrak{f}(\exists_x.(x \wedge x \rightarrow \mathfrak{f}(x))), &&\text{since } \mathfrak{f} \text{ is monotone.} \quad \square
\end{aligned}
$$

In a similar fashion, we can prove that if $\mathfrak{f}$ is a monotone polynomial on a finitely generated Heyting algebra, then $\mu.\mathfrak{f} := \forall_x.((\mathfrak{f}(x) \rightarrow x) \rightarrow x)$. As an application, we give an alternative proof of Proposition 4:

Corollary 2. *If $\mathfrak{f}$ is a monotone polynomial on a Heyting algebra H, then*

$$
\nu.\mathfrak{f} := \mathfrak{f}(\top). \tag{9}
$$

Proof. It is easy to see that if $\mathfrak{f}$ is a monotone polynomial on a finitely generated Heyting algebra, then $\exists_x.\mathfrak{f} = \mathfrak{f}(\top)$. Thus we have

$$
\nu.\mathfrak{f} = \exists_x.(x \wedge (x \rightarrow \mathfrak{f}(x))) = \exists_x.(x \wedge \mathfrak{f}(x)) = \top \wedge \mathfrak{f}(\top) = \mathfrak{f}(\top).
$$

Therefore, if ϕ is a formula-term whose variables are among set $x, y_1, \ldots, y_n$, then the equation $\phi^2(\top) = \phi(\top)$ holds in the free Heyting algebra on the set $\{\, y_1, \ldots, y_n \,\}$. Consequently, the equation $\mathfrak{f}(\top) = \mathfrak{f}^2(\top)$ holds in H, making $\mathfrak{f}(\top)$ into the greatest fixed-point of $\mathfrak{f}$. $\square$

6 The Elimination Procedure

In this Section we present our main result, a procedure that both axiomatizes and eliminates least fixed-points of the form $\mu_x.\phi(x)$ with ϕ fixed-point free. Together with the axiomatization of greatest fixed-points given in Sect. 5, the procedure can be extended to a procedure to construct a fixed-point free formula ψ equivalent to a given formula χ of the **IPC**$_\mu$.

Definition 3. *An occurrence of the variable x is* strongly positive *in a formula-term ϕ if there is no subformula ψ of ϕ of the form $\psi_0 \rightarrow \psi_1$ such that x is located in ψ_0. A formula-term ϕ is* strongly positive *in the variable x if every occurrence of x is strongly positive in ϕ. An occurrence of a variable x is* weakly negative *in a formula-term ϕ if it is not strongly positive. A formula-term ϕ is* weakly negative *in the variable x if every occurrence of x is weakly negative in ϕ.*

Observe that a variable might be neither strongly positive nor weakly negative in a formula-term. A second key concept for the elimination is the following notion of disjunctive formula.

Definition 4. *The set of formula-terms that are* disjunctive in the variable x *is generated by the following grammar:*

$$
\phi \;\Rightarrow\; x \mid \beta \vee \phi \mid \phi \vee \beta \mid \alpha \rightarrow \phi \mid \phi \vee \phi, \tag{10}
$$

where α and β are formulas with no occurrence of the variable x. A formula-term ϕ is in normal form *(w.r.t. x) if it is a conjunction of formula-terms ϕ_i, $i \in I$, so that each ϕ_i either does not contain the variable x, or it is disjunctive in x.*

Notice that disjunctive formula-terms are strongly positive in x. Due to Eq. (2) and since the usual distributive laws hold in Heyting algebras, we have the following Lemma.

Lemma 5. *Every strongly positive formula-term is equivalent to a formula-term in normal form.*

In order to compute the least fixed-point $\mu_x.\phi$, we take the following steps:

1. We rename all the weakly negative occurrences of x in ϕ to a fresh variable y, so $\phi(x) = \psi(x, x/y)$ with ψ strongly positive in x and weakly negative in y.
2. We compute a normal form of $\psi(x, y)$, so this formula is equivalent to a conjunction $\bigwedge_{i \in I} \psi_i(x, y)$ with each ψ_i disjunctive in x or not containing the variable x.
3. *Strongly positive elimination.* For each $i \in I$: if x has an occurrence in ψ_i, we compute then a formula ψ_i' equivalent to the least fixed-point $\mu_x.\psi_i(x, y)$ and observe that ψ_i' is weakly negative in y; otherwise, we let $\psi_i' = \psi_i$.
4. *Weakly negative elimination.* The formula $\bigwedge_{i \in I} \psi_i'(y)$ is weakly negative in y; we compute a formula χ equivalent to $\mu_y. \bigwedge_i \psi_i'(y)$ and return it.

The correction of the procedure relies on the following chain of equivalences:

$$\mu_x.\phi(x) = \mu_y.\mu_x.\psi(x, y) = \mu_y.\mu_x. \bigwedge_{i \in I} \psi_i(x, y), \qquad \text{where we use (Diag)}$$

$$= \mu_y. \bigwedge_{i \in I} \mu_x.\psi_i(x, y) = \mu_y. \bigwedge_{i \in I} \psi_i'(y) = \chi, \qquad \text{where we have used (7).}$$

6.1   Strongly positive Elimination

We tackle here the problem of computing the least fixed-point $\mu_x.\phi$ of a formula-term ϕ which is *disjunctive* in x. Recall that the formulas α and β appearing in a parse tree as leaves—according to the grammar (10)—do not contain the variable x. We call such a formula α a *head subformula* of ϕ, and such a β a *side subformula* of ϕ, and thus we put:

$$\mathsf{Head}(\phi) =_{\mathbf{def}} \left\{ \alpha \mid \alpha \text{ is a head subformula of } \phi \right\},$$
$$\mathsf{Side}(\phi) =_{\mathbf{def}} \left\{ \beta \mid \beta \text{ is a side subformula of } \phi \right\}.$$

Recall that a monotone function $f : P \longrightarrow P$ is *inflating* if $x \leq f(x)$.

Lemma 6. *The interpretation of a strongly positive disjunctive formula ϕ as a function of x is inflating.*

The key observation needed to prove Proposition 6 is the following Lemma on monotone inflating functions. In the statement of the Lemma we assume that P is a join-semilattice, and that $f \vee g$ is the pointwise join of the two functions f and g.

Lemma 7. *If $f, g : P \longrightarrow P$ are monotone inflating functions, then $\mathbf{Pre}_{f \vee g} = \mathbf{Pre}_{f \circ g}$. Consequently, for any monotone function $h : P \longrightarrow P$, we have*

$$\mu.(f \vee g \vee h) :=: \mu.((f \circ g) \vee h). \tag{11}$$

Proof. Observe firstly that $\mathbf{Pre}_{f \vee g} = \mathbf{Pre}_f \cap \mathbf{Pre}_g$. If $p \in \mathbf{Pre}_{f \circ g}$, then $f(p) \leq f(g(p)) \leq p$ and $g(p) \leq f(g(p)) \leq p$, showing that $p \in \mathbf{Pre}_{f \vee g}$. Conversely, if $p \in \mathbf{Pre}_{f \vee g}$, then p is a fixed point of both f and g, since these functions are inflating. It follows that $f(g(p)) = f(p) = p$, showing $p \in \mathbf{Pre}_{f \circ g}$.

We have argued that $\mathbf{Pre}_{f \vee g}$ coincides with $\mathbf{Pre}_{f \circ g}$; this implies that $\mathbf{Pre}_{(f \circ g) \vee h} = \mathbf{Pre}_{f \vee g \vee h}$ and, from this equality, Eq. (11) immediately follows.   □

To ease reading of the next Proposition and of its proof, let us put

$$[\alpha] \, \phi =_{\mathbf{def}} \alpha \rightarrow \phi.$$

Proposition 6. *If ϕ is a disjunctive formula-term, then*

$$\mu.\phi = \left[\bigwedge_{\alpha \in \mathsf{Head}(\phi)} \alpha \right] \left(\bigvee_{\beta \in \mathsf{Side}(\phi)} \beta \right). \tag{12}$$

Proof. For ψ, χ formula-terms, let us write $\psi \sim \chi$ when $\mu.\psi = \mu.\chi$. We say that a disjunctive formula ψ is reduced (w.r.t. ϕ) if either it is x, or it is of the form $\beta \vee x$ (or $x \vee \beta$) for some $\beta \in \mathsf{Side}(\phi)$, or of the form $[\alpha] \, x$ for some $\alpha \in \mathsf{Head}(\phi)$. A set Φ of disjunctive formulas is *reduced* if every formula in Φ is reduced.

We shall compute a reduced set of disjunctive formulas Φ_k such that $\phi \sim \bigvee \Phi_k$. Thus let $\Phi_0 = \{ \phi \}$. If Φ_i is not reduced, then there is $\phi_0 \in \Phi_i$ which is not reduced, thus of the form (a) $\beta \vee \psi$ (or $\psi \vee \beta$) with $\psi \neq x$, or (b) $[\alpha] \, \psi$ with $\psi \neq x$, or (c) $\psi_1 \vee \psi_2$. According to the case (ℓ), with $\ell \in \{ a, b, c \}$, we let Φ_{i+1} be $(\Phi_i \setminus \{ \phi_0 \}) \cup \Psi_\ell$ where Ψ_ℓ is as follows:

$$\Psi_a = \{ \beta \vee x, \psi \}, \qquad \Psi_b = \{ [\alpha] \, x, \psi \}, \qquad \Psi_c = \{ \psi_1, \psi_2 \}.$$

By Lemma 7, we have $\bigvee \Phi_i \sim \bigvee \Phi_{i+1}$. Morever, for some $k \geq 0$, Φ_k is reduced and $\Phi_k \subseteq \{ [\alpha] \, x \mid \alpha \in \mathsf{Head}(\phi) \} \cup \{ \beta \vee x \mid \beta \in \mathsf{Side}(\phi) \} \cup \{ x \}$. Consequently

$$\mu_x.\phi(x) = \mu_x. \bigvee \Phi_k \leq \mu_x.(x \vee \bigvee_{\alpha \in \mathsf{Head}(\phi)} [\alpha] \, x \vee \bigvee_{\beta \in \mathsf{Side}(\phi)} \beta \vee x). \tag{13}$$

On the other hand, if $\alpha \in \mathsf{Head}(\phi)$, then $\phi(x) = \psi_1(x, [\alpha] \, \psi_2(x))$ for some disjunctive formulas ψ_1 and ψ_2, so

$$[\alpha] \, x \leq [\alpha] \, \psi_2(x) \leq \psi_1(x, [\alpha] \, \psi_2(x)) = \phi(x)$$

and, similarly, $\beta \vee x \leq \phi(x)$, whenever $\beta \in \mathsf{Side}(\phi)$. It follows that

$$x \vee \bigvee_{\alpha \in \mathsf{Head}(\phi)} [\alpha] \, x \vee \bigvee_{\beta \in \mathsf{Side}(\phi)} \beta \vee x \leq \phi(x),$$

whence, by taking the least fixed-point in both sides of the above inequality, we derive equality in (13). Finally, in order to obtain (12), we compute as follows:

$$\mu_x.(x \vee \bigvee_{\alpha \in \mathsf{Head}(\phi)} [\alpha] \, x \vee \bigvee_{\beta \in \mathsf{Side}(\phi)} \beta \vee x)$$

$$= \mu_x.([\alpha_1] \dots [\alpha_n] \, x \vee (x \vee \bigvee_{\beta \in \mathsf{Side}(\phi)} \beta \vee x))$$

by Lemma 7, with $\mathsf{Head}(\phi) = \{\, \alpha_1, \dots, \alpha_n \,\}$,

$$= \mu_x.\left(\left[\bigwedge_{\alpha \in \mathsf{Head}(\phi)} \alpha \right] x \vee (x \vee \bigvee_{\beta \in \mathsf{Side}(\phi)} \beta \vee x) \right),$$

since $[\alpha_1] \dots [\alpha_n] \, x = \left[\bigwedge_{i=1,\dots,n} \alpha_i \right] x$,

$$= \mu_x.\left(\left[\bigwedge_{\alpha \in \mathsf{Head}(\phi)} \alpha \right] (x \vee \bigvee_{\beta \in \mathsf{Side}(\phi)} \beta \vee x) \right), \qquad \text{by Lemma 7,}$$

$$= \left[\bigwedge_{\alpha \in \mathsf{Head}(\phi)} \alpha \right] \mu_x.(x \vee \bigvee_{\beta \in \mathsf{Side}(\phi)} \beta \vee x), \qquad \text{by Proposition 3,}$$

$$= \left[\bigwedge_{\alpha \in \mathsf{Head}(\phi)} \alpha \right] (\bigvee_{\beta \in \mathsf{Side}(\phi)} \beta).$$

$$\square$$

6.2 Weakly Negative Elimination

If ϕ is weakly negative in x then we can write

$$\phi(x) = \psi_0(\psi_1(x), \dots, \psi_n(x)), \tag{14}$$

for formula-terms $\psi_0(y_1, \dots, y_n)$ and $\psi_i(x)$, $i = 1, \dots, n$, such that: (a) all the variables y_i are negative in ψ_0; (b) for $i = 1, \dots, n$, x is negative ψ_i.

Proposition 7. *Let $\langle \nu_1, \dots, \nu_n \rangle$ be a collection of formula-terms denoting the greatest solution of the system of equations $\{\, y_i = \psi_i(\psi_0(y_1, \dots, y_n)) \mid i = 1, \dots, n \,\}$. Then $\psi_0(\nu_1, \dots, \nu_n)$ is a formula equivalent to $\mu_x.\phi(x)$.*

Proof. Let $v : \mathbb{X} \setminus \{\, x, y_1, \dots, y_n \,\} \longrightarrow H$ be a partial valuation into an Heyting algebra H, put $\mathfrak{f}_0 = [\![\psi_0]\!]_v$ and, for $i = 1, \dots, n$, $\mathfrak{f}_i = [\![\psi_i]\!]_v$. Then $\mathfrak{f}_0$ is a monotone function from $[H^{op}]^n$ to H. Here H^{op} is the poset with the same elements as H but with the opposite ordering relation. Similarly, for $1 \leq i \leq n$, $\mathfrak{f}_i : H \longrightarrow H^{op}$. If we let $\bar{\mathfrak{f}} = \langle \mathfrak{f}_i \mid i = 1, \dots, n \rangle \circ \mathfrak{f}_0$, then $\bar{\mathfrak{f}} : [H^{op}]^n \longrightarrow [H^{op}]^n$. We exploit next the fact that $(\cdot)^{op}$ is a functor, so that $f^{op} : P^{op} \longrightarrow Q^{op}$ is the same monotone function as f, but considered as having distinct domain and codomain. Then, using (Roll), we can write

$$\mu.(\mathfrak{f}_0 \circ \langle \mathfrak{f}_i \mid i = 1, \ldots, n \rangle) = \mathfrak{f}_0(\langle \mathfrak{f}_i \mid i = 1, \ldots, n \rangle \circ \mathfrak{f}_0)$$
$$= \mathfrak{f}_0(\mu.\bar{\mathfrak{f}}) = \mathfrak{f}_0(\nu.\bar{f}^{op}), \tag{15}$$

since the least fixed-point of f in P^{op} is the greatest fixed-point of f^{op} in P. That is, if we consider the function $\langle \mathfrak{f}_i \mid i = 1, \ldots, n \rangle \circ \mathfrak{f}_0$ as sending a tuple of elements of H (as opposite to H^{op}) to another such a tuple, then Eq. (15) proves that a formula denoting the least fixed-point of ϕ is constructible out of formulas for the greatest solution of the system mentioned in the statement of the Proposition. $\qquad\square$

As far as computing the greatest solution of the system mentioned in the Proposition, this can be achieved by using the Bekic elimination principle, see Lemma 3. This principle implies that solutions of systems can be constructed from solutions of linear systems, i.e. from usual parametrized fixed-points. In our case, as witnessed by Eq. (9), these parametrized greatest fixed-points are computed by substituting $\top$ for the fixed-point variable. In the next Section we shall give a more explicit description, by means of approximants, of the least fixed-point of a weakly negative formula ϕ.

7   Upper Bounds on Closure Ordinals

Recall that Ruitenburg's result [23] implies that a monotone formula converges to its (parametrized) least fixed-point by iterating the formula n times from $\bot$, for some $n \geq 0$. That is, we can always substitute $\mu_x.\phi(x)$ for some equivalent $\phi^n(\bot)$. We show, in this Section, how to extract, from the procedure just seen, upper bounds for such a number n.

Proposition 8. *If ϕ is a disjunctive formula and n is the cardinality of the set* Head(ϕ), *then*

$$\mu_x.\phi(x) = \phi^{n+1}(\bot). \tag{16}$$

Proof. We have seen, in the proof of Propositon 6, that $[\alpha]\, x \leq \phi(x)$ for any $\alpha \in$ Head(ϕ) and, similarly, $\beta \vee x \leq \phi(x)$ for any $\beta \in$ Side(ϕ). Thus we have

$$\bigvee_{\beta \in \mathsf{Side}(\phi)} \beta = \bigvee_{\beta \in \mathsf{Side}(\phi)} \beta \vee \bot \leq \phi(\bot).$$

Let Head$(\phi) = \{\alpha_1, \ldots, \alpha_n\}$. Supposing that $[\alpha_i] \ldots [\alpha_1] (\bigvee_{\beta \in \mathsf{Side}(\phi)} \beta) \leq \phi^{i+1}(\bot)$, then

$$[\alpha_{i+1}][\alpha_i] \ldots [\alpha_1] (\bigvee_{\beta \in \mathsf{Side}(\phi)} \beta) \leq [\alpha_{i+1}] (\phi^{i+1}(\bot)) \leq \phi(\phi^{i+1}(\bot)) = \phi^{i+2}(\bot).$$

Whence

$$\mu_x.\phi(x) = \left[\bigwedge_{i=1,\ldots,n} \alpha_i\right] (\bigvee_{\beta \in \mathsf{Side}(\phi)} \beta) = [\alpha_n] \ldots [\alpha_1] (\bigvee_{\beta \in \mathsf{Side}(\phi)} \beta) \leq \phi^{n+1}(\bot).$$

$\qquad\square$

The upper bound given in (16) is optimal: if we let $\phi_n(x) =_{\text{def}} b \vee \bigvee_{i=1,\dots,n} a_i \rightarrow x$ and consider the Heyting algebra of downsets of $\langle P(\{1,\dots,n\}), \subseteq \rangle$, then, interpreting b as $\{\emptyset\}$ and a_i as $\{s \subseteq \{1,\dots,n\} \mid i \notin s\}$, ϕ_n converges exactly after $n+1$ steps.

In order to tackle convergence of weakly negative formulas, we mention some general statements, where we assume that all the posets have a least element.

Lemma 8. *Convergence for* Roll*). Let $f : P \longrightarrow Q$ and $g : Q \longrightarrow P$ be monotone functions. If $\mu.(f \circ g) = (f \circ g)^n(\bot)$, then $\mu.(g \circ f) = (g \circ f)^{n+1}(\bot)$.*

Lemma 9. *Convergence for* Diag*. Let $f : P \times P \longrightarrow P$ be a monotone function. For each $p \in P$, put $g_p(y) = f(p,x)$ and $h(x) = \mu_y.g_x(y)$. Suppose that, for each $p \in P$, $h(p) = \mu_y.f(p,y) = g_p^n(\bot)$ and that $\mu_x.h(x) = h^m(\bot)$. Then $\mu_x.f(x,x) = f^{nm}(\bot,\bot)$.*

For our purposes, the following Lemma provides more accurate upper bounds than Lemma 9.

Lemma 10. *Let $f,g : H \longrightarrow H$ be strong monotone mappings. If $\mu.f = f^n(\bot)$ and $\mu.g = g^m(\bot)$, then $\mu.f \wedge g = (f \wedge g)^{n+m-1}(\bot)$.*

For the Bekic property we have a similar statement, bounding convergence of $\langle f, g \rangle$ by $(n+1)(m+1) - 1$, with m and n being bounds on convergence of $\mu_y.g(x,y)$ and $\mu_x.f(x,\mu_y.g(x,y))$, respectively. While in general this bound is optimal, the relevant observation is, for our purposes, the following Lemma.

Lemma 11. *Let $\{x_i = f_i(x_1,\dots,x_k) \mid i = 1,\dots,k\}$ be a monotone system of equations P on some poset with least element $\bot$. Suppose that all the functions generated under substitution from $\{f_1,\dots,f_k\} \cup \{\bot\}$ converge to their parametrized least fixed-point in one step. Then the least solution of this system of equations is obtained by iterating k times $\langle f_1,\dots,f_k \rangle$ from $(\bot,\dots,\bot) \in P^k$.*

Proposition 9. *Let $\phi(x)$ be a weakly negative formula, so that we have a decomposition of the form (14). Then $\phi(x)$ converges at its least fixed-point in at most $n+1$ steps.*

Proof. Applying Lemma 11, we have

$$\nu.(\langle \psi_i \mid i = 1,\dots,n \rangle \circ \psi_0) = (\langle \psi_i \mid i = 1,\dots,n \rangle \circ \psi_0)^n(\top). \qquad (17)$$

Considering that

$$\mu.\phi = \mu.(\psi_0 \circ \langle \psi_i \mid i = 1,\dots,n \rangle) = \psi_0(\nu.(\langle \psi_i \mid i = 1,\dots,n \rangle \circ \psi_0))$$

we can use (17) and Lemma 8 to deduce that

$$\mu.\phi = (\psi_0 \circ \langle \psi_i \mid i = 1,\dots,n \rangle)^{n+1}(\bot). \qquad \square$$

It is possible to combine Propositions 8 and 9 with Lemma 8 to obtain upper bounds for all formulas. Yet, mainly due to the exponential blow-up in computing an equivalent normal-form of a given formula, that is, step 2 of the procedure described in Sect. 6, these bounds turn out to be exponential functions of the size of the formula. It is possible on the other hand to pinpoint fragments of the $\mathbf{IPC}_\mu$ for which we still have polynomial bounds. For example, if we define a formula-term to be weakly disjunctive if it is generated by the grammar (10), with the difference that we allow x to have weakly negative occurrences in α and β, then bounds are polynomials of order 2.

8   Conclusions

As mentioned in the Introduction, a main motivation for the research described in this paper was to provide in-depth answers to the question of why alternation-depth hierarchies in μ-calculi collapse or are trivial. Until now, the authors dealt with trivial alternation-depth hierarchies. The tools and ideas so far developed still need to be tested when a hierarchy does not completely collapse at its lowest level. In particular, and given the closeness of Intuitionistic Logic with Modal Logic based on transitive frames, it becomes appealing to investigate further connections with existing work on the subject [1, 2, 10, 24].

Compared to other works, such as [20, 21], we definitely took an algebraic and constructive approach to the problem of showing definability of least fixed-points within the **IPC**. Witnessing the fruitfulness of our approach, the algebra made the goal of computing upper bounds of closure ordinals of the monotone functions denoted by intuitionisitc formulas an accessible task. Let us notice on the way that our work leads to an obvious *decision procedure*, based on any decision procedure for **IPC**, for the Intuitionistic Propositional μ-Calculus. This logic, already studied on the side of proof theory and of game semantics [7], should also be of interest in verification, for example when transition systems come with some ordering and upward or downward closed properties are defined by μ-formulas, see [5].

Overall, we believe that understanding extremal fixed-points and more in general fixed-points in an intuitionisitc setting—where sparse but surprising results are known, see for [4] example—is still in quest for an elementary but solid theory to be developed. The present paper is a contribution toward this goal.

References

1. Alberucci, L., Facchini, A.: The modal μ-calculus hierarchy on restricted classes of transition systems. J. Symb. Log. **74**(4), 1367–1400 (2009)
2. Alberucci, L., Facchini, A.: On modal μ-calculus and Gödel-Löb logic. Studia Logica **91**(2), 145–169 (2009)
3. Arnold, A., Niwiński, D.: Rudiments of μ-calculus. Elsevier, Amsterdam (2001)
4. Bauer, A., Lumsdaine, P.L.: On the Bourbaki-Witt principle in toposes. Math. Proc. Cambridge Philos. Soc. **155**, 87–99 (2013)
5. Bertrand, N., Schnoebelen, P.: Computable fixpoints in well-structured symbolic model checking. Formal Meth. Syst. Des. **43**(2), 233–267 (2013)

6. Bezhanishvili, N., de Jongh, D.: Intuitionistic Logic. Technical report, Institute for Logic, Language and Computation, Universiteit van Amsterdam, p. 25 (2006)
7. Clairambault, P.: Strong functors and interleaving fixpoints in game semantics. RAIRO - Theory Inf. Appl. **47**(1), 25–68 (2013)
8. Cockett, J.R.B., Spencer, D.: Strong categorical datatypes II: a term logic for categorical programming. Theory Comput. Sci. **139**(1&2), 69–113 (1995)
9. D'Agostino, G., Hollenberg, M.: Logical questions concerning the mu-calculus: interpolation. Lyndon Los-Tarski. J. Symb. Log. **65**(1), 310–332 (2000)
10. D'Agostino, G., Lenzi, G.: On the μ-calculus over transitive and finite transitive frames. Theory Comput. Sci. **411**(50), 4273–4290 (2010)
11. Dau, F.: Some notes on proofs with alpha graphs. In: Schärfe, H., Hitzler, P., Øhrstrøm, P. (eds.) ICCS 2006. LNCS (LNAI), vol. 4068, pp. 172–188. Springer, Heidelberg (2006)
12. Frittella, S., Santocanale, L.: Fixed-point theory in the varieties $\mathcal{D}_n$. In: Höfner, P., Jipsen, P., Kahl, W., Müller, M.E. (eds.) RAMiCS 2014. LNCS, vol. 8428, pp. 446–462. Springer, Heidelberg (2014)
13. Gentzen, G.: Untersuchungen über das logische Schließen. I. Mathematische Zeitschrift **39**(1), 176–210 (1935)
14. Ghilardi, S., Zawadowski, M.: Sheaves, Games, and Model Completions: A Categorical Approach to Nonclassical Propositional Logics, 1st edn. Springer Publishing Company, Heidelberg (2011)
15. Ghilardi, S., Zawadowski, M.W.: Model completions, r-Heyting categories. Ann. Pure Appl. Log. **88**(1), 27–46 (1997)
16. Kelly, G.: Basic Concepts of Enriched Category Theory. Lecture Notes in Mathematics, vol. 64. Cambridge University Press, Cambridge (1982). Republished on In: Reprints in Theory and Applications of Categories, vol. 10, pp. 1–13 (2005)
17. Kock, A.: Strong functors and monoidal monads. Archiv der Mathematik XXIII **23**(1), 113–120 (1972)
18. Kozen, D.: Results on the propositional mu-calculus. Theory Comput. Sci. **27**, 333–354 (1983)
19. Lehtinen, K., Quickert, S.: Deciding the first levels of the modal mu alternation hierarchy by formula construction. In: Kreutzer, S. (ed.) 24th EACSL Annual Conference on Computer Science Logic, CSL September 7–10, 2015, Berlin, Germany, vol. 41, pp. 457–471. LIPIcs, Schloss Dagstuhl - Leibniz-Zentrum fuer Informatik (2015)
20. Mardaev, S.I.: Least fixed points in Grzegorczyk's Logic and in the intuitionistic propositional logic. Algebra Log. **32**(5), 279–288 (1993)
21. Mardaev, S.I.: Convergence of positive schemes in our and S4 and Int. Algebra Log. **33**(2), 95–101 (1994)
22. Pitts, A.M.: On an interpretation of second order quantification in first order intuitionistic propositional logic. J. Symb. Log. **57**(1), 33–52 (1992)
23. Ruitenburg, W.: On the period of sequences $(a^n(p))$ in intuitionistic propositional calculus. J. Symb. Log. **49**(3), 892–899 (1984)
24. Visser, Albert: Löb's logic meets the μ-calculus. In: Middeldorp, Aart, Oostrom, Vincent, Raamsdonk, Femke, Vrijer, Roel (eds.) Processes, Terms and Cycles: Steps on the Road to Infinity. LNCS, vol. 3838, pp. 14–25. Springer, Heidelberg (2005)

Verification and Program Analysis

A Theory of Monitors
(Extended Abstract)

Adrian Francalanza$^{(\boxtimes)}$

CS, ICT, University of Malta, Msida, Malta
`adrian.francalanza@um.edu.mt`

Abstract. We develop a behavioural theory for *monitors* — software entities that passively analyse the runtime behaviour of systems so as to infer properties about them. First, we extend the monitor language and instrumentation relation of [17] to handle piCalculus process monitoring. We then identify contextual behavioural preorders that allow us to relate monitors according to criteria defined over monitored executions of piCalculus processes. Subsequently, we develop alternative monitor preorders that are more tractable, and prove full-abstraction for the latter alternative preorders with respect to the contextual preorders.

1 Introduction

Monitors (execution montors [32]) are software entities that are *instrumented* to execute along side a program so as determine properties about it, inferred from the *runtime analysis* of the exhibited (program) execution; this basic monitor form is occasionally termed (sequence) *recognisers* [28]. In other settings, monitors go further and either *adapt* aspects of the monitored program [7,11,22] or *enforce* predefined properties by modifying the observable behaviour [4,15,28]. Monitors are central to software engineering techniques such as monitor-oriented programming [16] and fail-fast design patterns [8] used in fault-tolerant systems [19,34]; they are also used exten sively in runtime verification [27], a lightweight verification technique that attempts to mitigate state explosion problems associated with full-blown verification methods such as model checking.

Monitoring setups typically consist of three components: apart from the program being monitored, P, there is the *monitor* itself, M, and the *instrumentation*, the mechanism composing the monitor with the program, $P \triangleleft M$. The latter gives rise to a software composition relation that has seldom been studied in its own right. This paper investigates compositional reasoning techniques for monitors performing *detections* (recognisers), composed using the instrumentation relation employed in [17], for programs expressed as piCalculus processes [29,31], a well-studied concurrency model. We set out to develop monitor preorders

$$M_1 \sqsubseteq M_2 \tag{1}$$

The research was supported by the UoM research fund CPSRP05-04 and the research grant COST-STSM-ECOST-STSM-IC1201-170214-038253.

© Springer-Verlag Berlin Heidelberg 2016
B. Jacobs and C. Löding (Eds.): FOSSACS 2016, LNCS 9634, pp. 145–161, 2016.
DOI: 10.1007/978-3-662-49630-5_9

stating that, when instrumented in the *context* of an *arbitrary* process P, if $P \triangleleft M_1$ exhibits certain properties, then $P \triangleleft M_2$ exhibits them as well. Within this setup, we formalise the possible instrumentation properties one may require from an instrumented (monitored) process, and show how these give rise to different monitoring preorders.

Example 1. Consider the monitors M_1 and M_2 below. M_1 monitors for output actions on channel a with a payload that is not in the set C. Apart from detecting the same outputs on channel a, M_2 also detects outputs with payload b on channels that are not in D (the $+$ construct acts as an external choice [23]).

$$M_1 = \text{match } a!x.\text{if } x \notin C \text{ then } \checkmark$$
$$M_2 = (\text{match } a!x.\text{if } x \notin C \text{ then } \checkmark) + (\text{match } y!b.\text{if } y \notin D \text{ then } \checkmark)$$

One can argue that M_2 is related to M_1, i.e., $M_1 \sqsubseteq M_2$, since all the detections raised by M_1 are also raised by M_2. However, under different criteria, the two monitors would not be related. Consider the case where $a \in D$ (or $b \in C$): for a process P exhibiting action $a!b$, monitor M_2 may non-deterministically *fail to detect* this behaviour; by contrast, M_1 *always* detects the behaviour $a!b$ and, in this sense, M_2 does not preserve all the properties of M_1. Monitors are also expected to *interfere minimally* with the execution of the analysed process, giving rise to other criteria for relating monitors, as we will see in the sequel. ∎

There are various reasons why such preorders are useful. For a start, they act as notions of *refinement*: they allow us to formally specify properties that are expected of a monitor M by expressing them in terms of a monitor description, Spec_M, and then requiring that $\text{Spec}_M \sqsubseteq M$ holds. Moreover, our preorders provide a formal understanding for when it is valid to *substitute one monitor implementation for another* while preserving elected monitoring properties. We consider a general model that allows monitors to behave non-deterministically; this permits us to study the cases where non-determinism is either tolerated or considered erroneous. Indeed, there are settings where determinism is unattainable (*e.g.*, distributed monitoring [18,33]). Occasionally, non-determinism is also used to expresses under-specification in program refinement.

Although formal and intuitive, the preorders alluded to in (1) turn out to be hard to establish. One of the principal obstacles is the universal quantification over all possible processes for which the monitoring properties should hold. We therefore develop alternative characterisations for these preorders, $M_1 \leq M_2$, that do not rely on this universal quantification over process instrumentation. We show that such relations are sound wrt. the former monitor preorders, which serves as a semantic justification for the alternative monitor preorders. More importantly, however, it also allows us to use the more tractable alternative relations as a proof technique for establishing inequalities in the original preorders. We also show that these characterisations are complete, thereby obtaining full-abstraction for these alternative preorders.

The rest of the paper is structured as follows. Section 2 briefly overviews our process model whereas Sect. 3 introduces our monitor language together with the instrumentation relation. In Sect. 4 we formalise our monitor preorder relations

Syntax

$$P, Q \in \text{PROC} ::= u!v.P \quad \textit{(output)} \qquad \mid u?x.P \qquad\qquad\quad \textit{(input)}$$
$$\mid \text{nil} \quad\;\; \textit{(nil)} \qquad\qquad \mid \text{if } u = v \text{ then } P \text{ else } Q \quad \textit{(conditional)}$$
$$\mid \text{rec } X.P \quad \textit{(recursion)} \qquad \mid X \qquad\qquad\qquad \textit{(process var.)}$$
$$\mid P \,\|\, Q \quad\;\;\, \textit{(parallel)} \qquad\quad \mid \text{new } c.P \qquad\qquad \textit{(scoping)}$$

Semantics

$$\text{pOut} \frac{}{I \rhd c!d.P \xrightarrow{c!d} P} \qquad\qquad \text{pIn} \frac{}{I \rhd c?x.P \xrightarrow{c?d} P[d/x]}$$

$$\text{pThn} \frac{}{I \rhd \text{if } c = c \text{ then } P \text{ else } Q \xrightarrow{\tau} P} \qquad \text{pEls} \frac{c \sharp d}{I \rhd \text{if } c = d \text{ then } P \text{ else } Q \xrightarrow{\tau} Q}$$

$$\text{pRec} \frac{}{I \rhd \text{rec } X.P \xrightarrow{\tau} P[\text{rec } X.P/X]} \qquad \text{pPar} \frac{I \rhd P \xrightarrow{\mu} P'}{I \rhd P \,\|\, Q \xrightarrow{\mu} P' \,\|\, Q}$$

$$\text{pCom} \frac{I, d \rhd P \xrightarrow{c!d} P' \quad I, d \rhd Q \xrightarrow{c?d} Q'}{I, d \rhd P \,\|\, Q \xrightarrow{\tau} P' \,\|\, Q'} \qquad \text{pRes} \frac{I, d \rhd P \xrightarrow{\mu} P' \quad d \sharp \mu}{I \rhd \text{new } d.P \xrightarrow{\mu} \text{new } d.P'}$$

$$\text{pCls} \frac{I \rhd P \xrightarrow{c!d} P' \quad I \rhd Q \xrightarrow{c?d} Q' \quad d \sharp I}{I \rhd P \,\|\, Q \xrightarrow{\tau} \text{new } d.(P' \,\|\, Q')} \qquad \text{pOpn} \frac{I, d \rhd P \xrightarrow{c!d} P'}{I \rhd \text{new } d.P \xrightarrow{c!d} P'}$$

Fig. 1. piCalculus syntax and semantics

wrt. this instrumentation. We develop our alternative preorders in Sect. 5, where we also establish the correspondence with the other preorders. Section 6 concludes.

2   The Language

Figure 1 presents our process language, a standard version of the piCalculus. It has the usual constructs and assumes separate denumerable sets for channel names $c, d, a, b \in \text{CHANS}$, variables $x, y, z \in \text{VARS}$ and process variables, $X, Y \in \text{PVARS}$, and lets identifiers u, v range over the sets, $\text{CHANS} \cup \text{VARS}$. The input construct, $c?x.P$, the recursion construct, $\text{rec } X.P$, and the scoping construct, $\text{new } c.P$, are *binders* where the free occurrences of the variable x, the process variable X, and the channel c resp., are bound in the guarded body P. We write $\mathbf{fv}(P), \mathbf{fV}(P), \mathbf{fn}(P), \mathbf{bV}(P), \mathbf{bv}(P)$ and $\mathbf{bn}(P)$ for the *resp.* free/bound variables, process variables and names in P. We use standard syntactic conventions *e.g.*, we identify processes up to renaming of bound names and variables (alpha conversion). For arbitrary syntactic objects o, o', we write $o \sharp o'$ when the free *names* in o and o' are disjoint *e.g.*, $P \sharp Q$ means $\mathbf{fn}(P) \cap \mathbf{fn}(Q) = \emptyset$.

The operational semantics of the language is defined by the Labelled Transition System (LTS) shown in Fig. 1. LTS judgements are of the form

$$I \triangleright P \xrightarrow{\mu} P'$$

where $I \subseteq$ CHANS denotes an *interface* of names *known* (or shared) by both the process and an implicit observer (with which interactions occur), P is a closed term, and $\mathbf{fn}(P) \subseteq I$. We write I, c as a shorthand for $I \cup \{c\}$ where $c \notin I$, and generally assume a version of the Barendregt convention whereby $\mathbf{bn}(P) \sharp I$.[1] For arbitrary names c, d, actions $\mu \in \mathrm{ACT}_\tau$ range over *input* actions, $c?d$, *output* actions, $c!d$, and a distinguished *silent* action, τ ($\alpha \in \mathrm{ACT}$ ranges over *external* actions, that exclude τ). The rules in Fig. 1 are fairly standard, using I for book-keeping purposes relating to free/bound names (we elide symmetric rules for pPAR, pCOM and pCLS); implicitly, $c, d \in I$ in rule pOUT and $c \in I$ in rule pIN (but d is not necessarily in I). We use $s, t \in \mathrm{ACT}^*$ to denote *traces of external actions*. Although actions do not include explicit information relating to extruded names, this may be retrieved using I as shown in Definition 1; the absence of action name binding (as in [24,31]) simplifies subsequent handling of traces. The evolution of I after a transition is determined exclusively by the *resp.* action of the transition, defined as $\mathbf{aftr}(I, \mu)$ in Definition 1; note that both the process (through outputs) and the implicit observer (through inputs) may extend I.

Definition 1 (Extruded Names and Interface Evolution)

$$\mathbf{ext}(I, \tau) \stackrel{def}{=} \emptyset \qquad \mathbf{ext}(I, c!d) \stackrel{def}{=} \{d\} \setminus I \qquad \mathbf{ext}(I, c?d) \stackrel{def}{=} \emptyset$$

$$\mathbf{aftr}(I, \tau) \stackrel{def}{=} I \qquad \mathbf{aftr}(I, c!d) \stackrel{def}{=} I \cup \{d\} \qquad \mathbf{aftr}(I, c?d) \stackrel{def}{=} I \cup \{d\}$$

We lift the functions in Definition 1 to traces, *e.g.*, $\mathbf{aftr}(I, s)$, in the obvious way and denote successive transitions $I \triangleright P \xrightarrow{\mu_1} P_1$ and $\mathbf{aftr}(I, \mu_1) \triangleright P_1 \xrightarrow{\mu_2} P_2$ as $I \triangleright P \xrightarrow{\mu_1} \mathbf{aftr}(I, \mu_1) \triangleright P_1 \xrightarrow{\mu_2} P_2$. We write $I \triangleright P \xrightarrow{\mu}$ to denote $\nexists P' \cdot I \triangleright P \xrightarrow{\mu} P'$ and $I \triangleright P \xRightarrow{s} Q$ to denote $I_0 \triangleright P_0 \xrightarrow{\mu_1} I_1 \triangleright P_1 \xrightarrow{\mu_2} I_2 \triangleright P_2 \ldots \xrightarrow{\mu_n} P_n$ where $P_0 = P$, $P_n = Q$, $I_0 = I$, $I_i = \mathbf{aftr}(I_{i-1}, \mu_i)$ for $i \in 1..n$, and s is equal to $\mu_1 \ldots \mu_n$ after filtering τ labels.

Example 2. Consider $P_{\mathrm{sv}} = \mathrm{rec}\, X.c?x.\mathrm{new}\, d.x!d.X$, modelling the idiomatic server that repeatedly waits for requests on c and answers back on the inputted channel with a *fresh* channel. We can derive the following behaviour *wrt.* $I = \{c\}$:

$$I \triangleright P_{\mathrm{sv}} \xRightarrow{c?a} I, a \triangleright \mathrm{new}\, d.a!d.P_{\mathrm{sv}} \xRightarrow{a!d}$$

$$I, a, d \triangleright P_{\mathrm{sv}} \xRightarrow{c?a} I, a, d \triangleright \mathrm{new}\, d.a!d.P_{\mathrm{sv}} \xRightarrow{a!d'} I, a, d, d' \triangleright P_{\mathrm{sv}}$$

Above, bound outputs/inputs [31] are manifested as interface extensions. ∎

3   Monitor Instrumentation

Monitors, $M, N \in$ MON, are syntactically defined by the grammar of Fig. 2. They may reach either of *two* verdicts, namely detection, $\checkmark$, or termination, end, denoting an inconclusive verdict. Our setting is a mild generalisation to that in [17]

---

[1] The rules in Fig. 1 still check explicitly for this; see rules pRES, pCLS and pOPN.

Syntax

$$p, q \in \text{PAT} ::= u?v \quad \textit{(input pattern)} \qquad | \; u!v \quad \textit{(output pattern)}$$
$$w \in \text{VERD} ::= \text{end} \quad \textit{(termination)} \qquad | \; \checkmark \quad \textit{(detection)}$$

$$
\begin{aligned}
M, N \in \text{MON} ::= \; & w && \textit{(verdict)} && | \; p.M && \textit{(pattern match)} \\
| \; & M + N && \textit{(choice)} && | \; \text{if } u = v \text{ then } M \text{ else } N && \textit{(branch)} \\
| \; & \text{rec } X.M && \textit{(recursion)} && | \; X && \textit{(monitor var.)}
\end{aligned}
$$

Monitor Semantics

$$\text{MVER} \frac{}{\; w \xrightarrow{\alpha} w \;} \qquad \text{MPAT} \frac{\text{match}(p, \alpha) = \sigma}{p.M \xrightarrow{\alpha} M\sigma} \qquad \text{MCHL} \frac{M \xrightarrow{\mu} M'}{M + N \xrightarrow{\mu} M'}$$

$$\text{MREC} \frac{}{\text{rec } X.M \xrightarrow{\tau} M[\text{rec } X.M/X]} \qquad \text{MCHR} \frac{N \xrightarrow{\mu} N'}{M + N \xrightarrow{\mu} N'}$$

$$\text{MTHN} \frac{}{\text{if } c = c \text{ then } M \text{ else } N \xrightarrow{\tau} M} \qquad \text{MELS} \frac{c \, \sharp \, d}{\text{if } c = d \text{ then } M \text{ else } N \xrightarrow{\tau} N}$$

Instrumented System Semantics

$$\text{IMON} \frac{I \triangleright P \xrightarrow{\alpha} P' \quad M \xrightarrow{\alpha} M'}{I \triangleright P \triangleleft M \xrightarrow{\alpha} P' \triangleleft M'} \qquad \text{IASYP} \frac{I \triangleright P \xrightarrow{\tau} P'}{I \triangleright P \triangleleft M \xrightarrow{\tau} P' \triangleleft M}$$

$$\text{ITER} \frac{I \triangleright P \xrightarrow{\alpha} P' \quad M \nrightarrow \quad M \nrightarrow}{I \triangleright P \triangleleft M \xrightarrow{\alpha} P' \triangleleft \text{end}} \qquad \text{IASYM} \frac{M \xrightarrow{\tau} M'}{I \triangleright P \triangleleft M \xrightarrow{\tau} P \triangleleft M'}$$

Fig. 2. Monitor syntax, semantics and Instrumentation Semantics

since monitors need to reason about communicated names so as to adequately monitor for piCalculus processes. They are thus equipped with a pattern matching construct (used to observe external actions) and a name-comparison branching construct. The remaining constructs, *i.e.*, external branching and recursion, are standard. Note that, whereas the syntax allows for monitors with free occurrences of monitor variables, monitors are always closed wrt. (value) variables, whereby the outermost occurrence of a variable acts as a binder. *E.g.*, in the monitor $(x?c.x!y.\text{if } y = d \text{ then end else } \checkmark)$ pattern $x?c$ binds variable x in the continuation whereas pattern $x!y$ binds variable y.

The monitor semantics is defined in terms of an LTS (Fig. 2), modeling the analysis of the visible runtime execution of a process. Following [15,17,30], in rule MVER verdicts are able to analyse *any* external action but transition to the *same* verdict, *i.e.*, verdicts are *irrevocable*. By contrast, pattern-guarded monitors only transition when the action matches the pattern, binding pattern variables to the resp. action names, $\text{match}(p, \alpha) = \sigma$, and substituting them in the continuation, $M\sigma$; see rule MPAT. The remaining transitions are unremarkable.

A *monitored system*, $P \triangleleft M$, consists of a process, P, instrumented with a monitor, M, analysing its (external) behaviour. Figure 2 defines the instrumentation semantics for configurations, $I \triangleright P \triangleleft M$, *i.e.*, systems augmented with an interface I, where again we assume P is closed and $\mathbf{fn}(P) \subseteq I$. The LTS semantics follows [7, 17] and relies on the *resp.* process and monitor semantics of Figs. 1 and 2. In rule iMON, if the process exhibits the external action α *wrt.* I, and the monitor can analyse this action, they transition in lock-step in the instrumented system while exhibiting *same* action. If, however, a process exhibits an action that the monitor cannot analyse, the action is manifested at system level while the monitor is *terminated*; see rule iTER. Finally, iAsyP and iAsyM allow monitors and processes to transition independently *wrt.* internal moves, *i.e.*, our instrumentation forces process-monitor synchronisation for *external* actions only, which constitute our *monitorable* actions. We note that, as is expected of recognisers, the process drives the behaviour of a monitored system: if the process cannot α-transition, the monitored system cannot α-transition either.

Example 3. Recall P_{sv} from Example 2. Using the semantics of Fig. 2, one can derive the monitored execution leading to a detection below, when composed with the monitor $M_1 = (c?y.y!z.\text{if } z = c \text{ then end else } \checkmark)$, subject to $I' = \{c, a\}$:

$$I' \triangleright P_{\mathrm{sv}} \triangleleft M_1 \xRightarrow{c?a \cdot a!d} P_{\mathrm{sv}} \triangleleft \checkmark$$

Contrastingly, for the same I', monitoring with $M_2 = (y!z.\text{if } y = a \text{ then end else } \checkmark)$ does not lead to a detection for the same trace, because the first action, $c?a$ (an input) cannot pattern match with the output pattern, $y!z$. In fact, rule iTER terminates the monitor after transition $c?a$, so as to avoid erroneous detections.

$$
\begin{aligned}
I' \triangleright P_{\mathrm{sv}} \triangleleft M_2 &\xrightarrow{\tau} c?x.\text{new } d.x!d.P_{\mathrm{sv}} \triangleleft M_2 \\
&\xrightarrow{c?a} \text{new } d.a!d.P_{\mathrm{sv}} \triangleleft \text{end} \xRightarrow{a!d} P_{\mathrm{sv}} \triangleleft \text{end}
\end{aligned}
\tag{2}
$$

For illustrative purposes, consider $N = c?y.\text{if } y = c \text{ then end else } y!z.c?z.\checkmark$, another monitor. We have the following (dissected) transition sequence for $I = \{c\}$:

$$
\begin{aligned}
I \triangleright P_{\mathrm{sv}} \triangleleft N \;\; &\xrightarrow{\tau} \cdot \xrightarrow{c?a} \;\; I, a \triangleright (\text{new } d.a!d.P_{\mathrm{sv}}) \triangleleft \text{if } a = c \text{ then end else } a!z.c?z.\checkmark \tag{3} \\
&\xrightarrow{\tau} \;\; I, a \triangleright (\text{new } d.a!d.P_{\mathrm{sv}}) \triangleleft a!z.c?z.\checkmark \tag{4} \\
&\xrightarrow{a!d} \;\; (I, a, d) \triangleright P_{\mathrm{sv}} \triangleleft c?d.\checkmark \tag{5} \\
&\xrightarrow{\tau} \cdot \xrightarrow{c?b} \;\; (I, a, d, b) \triangleright \text{new } d'.b!d'.P_{\mathrm{sv}} \triangleleft \text{end} \tag{6} \\
&\xrightarrow{b!d'} \;\; (I, a, d, b, d') \triangleright P_{\mathrm{sv}} \triangleleft \text{end} \tag{7}
\end{aligned}
$$

In (3) the server (asynchronously) unfolds (pREC and iAsyP) and inputs on c the fresh name a (pIN); the monitor can analyse $c?a$ (mPAT where $\mathrm{match}(c?y, c?a) = \{y \mapsto a\}$), transitioning accordingly (iMON) while learning the fresh name a

for future monitoring. At this stage, the instrumentation temporarily *stalls* the process, even though it can produce the (scope extruding) output $a!d$. More precisely, although the monitor cannot presently analyse $a!d$, the rule ιTER — which terminates the monitor execution — *cannot* be applied, since the monitor can silently transition and potentially become capable of analysing the action. This is indeed the case, (4) using MELS, resulting in the second monitoring transition, (5) using ιMON, where the monitor learns the second fresh name d, this time originating from the monitored process. After another unfolding, the process is ready to input on c again. However, the monitor cannot match $c?b$ ($\mathsf{match}(c?d, c?b)$ is undefined) and since the monitor cannot silently transition either, it is terminated (ιTER) while still allowing the process to proceed, (6). In (7), verdicts allow monitored processes to execute without any hindrance. ∎

Example 3 highlights two conflicting instrumentation requirements. On the one hand, monitors should *interfere minimally* with the execution of a monitored process where, observationally, a monitored process should behave like the original one. On the other hand, instrumentation must also ensure *bona fide detections*, e.g., in (2) and (6), terminating monitoring when the observed process behaviour does not correspond, (through rule ιTER). But in order to do this while avoiding premature termination, instrumentation needs to allow for monitor internal computation, e.g., (4). Unfortunately, the premise caveat $M \not\xrightarrow{\tau}$ in rule ιTER — necessary to prevent premature terminations — allows monitors to affect (indirectly) process behaviour. For instance the monitor Ω below:

$$\Omega = \mathsf{rec}\, X.(\mathsf{if}\ c{=}c\,\mathsf{then}\ X\ \mathsf{else}\ X) \qquad \Omega' = \mathsf{if}\ c{=}c\,\mathsf{then}\ \Omega\ \mathsf{else}\ \Omega \qquad (8)$$

is divergent, i.e., $\Omega \xrightarrow{\tau} \Omega' \xrightarrow{\tau} \Omega \xrightarrow{\tau} \ldots$, and unresponsive, i.e., $\forall \alpha \cdot \Omega \not\xrightarrow{\alpha}$ and $\Omega' \not\xrightarrow{\alpha}$. As a result, it suppresses *every* process external behaviour when instrumented: for arbitrary $I \triangleright P$ we can show $I \triangleright P \triangleleft \Omega \not\xrightarrow{\alpha}$ and $I \triangleright P \triangleleft \Omega' \not\xrightarrow{\alpha}$ for any α, since rules ιMON and ιTER cannot be applied. We revisit this point in Sect. 4. We conclude with the property stating that verdicts are irrevocable.

Theorem 1 (Definite Verdicts). $I \triangleright P \triangleleft w \xRightarrow{s} Q \triangleleft M$ *implies* $M = w$

4 Monitor Preorders

We can use the formal setting presented in Sect. 3 to develop the monitor preorders discussed in the Introduction. We start by defining the monitoring predicates we expect to be preserved by the preorder; a number of these predicates rely on *computations* and *detected* computations, defined below.

Definition 2 (Detected Computations). *The transition sequence*

$$I \triangleright P \triangleleft M \xRightarrow{s} I_0 \triangleright P_0 \triangleleft M_0 \xrightarrow{\tau} I_1 \triangleright P_1 \triangleleft M_1 \xrightarrow{\tau} I_2 \triangleright P_2 \triangleleft M_2 \xrightarrow{\tau} \ldots$$

is called an s-computation if it is maximal *(i.e., either it is infinite or it is finite and* cannot be extended further *using τ-transitions). An s-computation is called* detected *(or a detected computation along s) iff $\exists n \in \mathbb{N} \cdot M_n = \checkmark$.* ∎

One criteria for comparing monitors considers the verdicts reached after observing a *specific execution trace* produced by the process under scrutiny. The semantics of Sect. 3 assigns a *passive role* to monitors, prohibiting them from influencing the branching execution of the monitored process. Definition 2 thus differentiates between detected computations, identifying them by the visible trace that is dictated by the process (over which the monitor should not have any control).

Example 4. Consider $P = $ new $d.(d! \| d?.c!a \| d?.c!b)$, $I = \{c, b, a\}$ and monitors:

$$M_1 = c!a.\checkmark + c!b.\checkmark \qquad\qquad M_2 = c!a.\checkmark + c!b.\mathsf{end} \qquad M_3 = c!a.\checkmark$$
$$M_4 = c!a.\checkmark + c!b.\checkmark + c!b.\mathsf{end} \qquad M_5 = c!a.\checkmark + c!b.\checkmark + c!a.\mathsf{end} + c!b.\mathsf{end}$$

Configurations $I \triangleright M_i \triangleleft P$ for $i \in 1..5$ exhibit detecting computations along $s = c!a.\epsilon$. For trace $t = c!b.\epsilon$, configurations $I \triangleright M_j \triangleleft P$ for $j \in \{1, 4, 5\}$ detect t-computations as well, whereas the *resp.* configurations with M_2 and M_3 *do not.* Although the configuration with M_1 *always* detects along t, those with M_4 and M_5 may fail to detect it along such a trace. Similarly, configuration with M_1 and M_4 deterministically detect along trace s, but $I \triangleright M_5 \triangleleft P$ does not. ∎

Example 4 suggests two types of computation detections that a monitor may exhibit.

Definition 3 (Potential and Deterministic Detection). M potentially detects *for $I \triangleright P$ along trace s, denoted as $\mathsf{pd}(M, I, P, s)$, iff there exists a detecting s-computation from $I \triangleright P \triangleleft M$. M deterministically detects for $I \triangleright P$ along trace s, denoted as $\mathsf{dd}(M, I, P, s)$, iff all s-computation from $I \triangleright P \triangleleft M$ are detecting.* ∎

Remark 1. If a monitored process cannot produce trace s, i.e., $I \triangleright P \not\xrightarrow{s}$, then $\mathsf{pd}(M, I, P, s)$ is trivially false and $\mathsf{dd}(M, I, P, s)$ is trivially true for any M. ∎

The detection predicates of Definition 3 induce the following monitor preorders (and equivalences), based on the *resp.* detection capabilities.

Definition 4 (Potential and Deterministic Detection Preorders)

$$M \sqsubseteq_{pd} N \quad \overset{def}{=} \quad \forall I, P, s \cdot \mathsf{pd}(M, I, P, s) \ \textit{implies} \ \mathsf{pd}(N, I, P, s)$$
$$M \sqsubseteq_{dd} N \quad \overset{def}{=} \quad \forall I, P, s \cdot \mathsf{dd}(M, I, P, s) \ \textit{implies} \ \mathsf{dd}(N, I, P, s)$$

$M \cong_{pd} N$ *and* $M \cong_{dd} N$ *are the kernel equivalences induced by the resp. preorders, i.e.,* $M \cong_{pd} N \overset{def}{=} (M \sqsubseteq_{pd} N$ *and* $N \sqsubseteq_{pd} M)$, *and similarly for* $M \cong_{dd} N$. *We write* $M \sqsubset_{pd} N$ *in lieu of* $(M \sqsubseteq_{pd} N$ *and* $N \not\sqsubseteq_{pd} M)$ *and similarly for* $M \sqsubset_{dd} N$. ∎

Example 5. Recall the monitors defined in Example 4. It turns out that

$$M_2 \quad \cong_{pd} \quad M_3 \quad \sqsubset_{pd} \quad M_5 \quad \cong_{pd} \quad M_4 \quad \cong_{pd} \quad M_1 \qquad (9)$$
$$M_5 \quad \sqsubset_{dd} \quad M_2 \quad \cong_{dd} \quad M_3 \quad \cong_{dd} \quad M_4 \quad \sqsubset_{dd} \quad M_1 \qquad (10)$$

Note that, whereas M_5 can *potentially* detect more computations that M_2 and M_3, (9), it can *deterministically* detect less computations than these monitors (10); in fact, M_5 cannot deterministically detect *any* computation. ∎

As opposed to prior work on monitors [2,10,15], the detection predicates in Definition 3 consider monitor behaviour within an instrumented system. Apart from acting as a continuation for the study in [17], this setup also enables us to formally justify subtle monitor orderings, Example 6, and analyse peculiarities brought about by the instrumentation relation, Example 7.

Example 6. Using the shorthand $\tau.M$ for $\operatorname{rec} X.M$ where $X \notin \mathbf{fV}(M)$, we have:

$$\checkmark \cong_{\mathsf{pd}} \tau.\checkmark \qquad \text{but} \qquad \checkmark \sqsubseteq_{\mathsf{dd}} \tau.\checkmark$$

For process $P = \Omega$, defined as in (8), predicate $\mathsf{dd}(\checkmark, I, P, \epsilon)$ holds trivially, but predicate $\mathsf{dd}(\tau.\checkmark, I, P, \epsilon)$ *does not*, due of the non-detecting ϵ-computation $I \rhd \Omega \lhd \tau.\checkmark \xrightarrow{\tau} \cdot \xrightarrow{\tau} \Omega \lhd \tau.\checkmark \xrightarrow{\tau} \cdot \xrightarrow{\tau} \dots$, refuting the inequality $\checkmark \sqsubseteq_{\mathsf{dd}} \tau.\checkmark$. ∎

Example 7. Recalling the divergent monitor Ω from (8), we have:

$$(\mathsf{end} \quad \cong_{\mathsf{dd}} \quad c!a.\mathsf{end}) \quad \sqsubseteq_{\mathsf{dd}} \quad c!a.\checkmark \quad \sqsubseteq_{\mathsf{dd}} \quad \Omega \quad \sqsubseteq_{\mathsf{dd}} \quad \checkmark \tag{11}$$

$$\Omega + \mathsf{end} \quad \sqsubseteq_{\mathsf{dd}} \quad (\Omega \quad \cong_{\mathsf{dd}} \quad \Omega + \checkmark \quad \cong_{\mathsf{dd}} \quad \operatorname{rec} X.(\tau.X + \checkmark)) \tag{12}$$

$$\Omega + c!a.\checkmark \quad \sqsubseteq_{\mathsf{pd}} \quad \Omega + \checkmark \quad \text{but} \quad \Omega + c!a.\checkmark \quad \cong_{\mathsf{dd}} \quad \Omega + \checkmark \tag{13}$$

In (11), *every* computation starting with monitor $\checkmark$ is trivially detected. Monitor Ω limits all computations to ϵ-computations, *i.e.*, irrespective of $I \rhd P$, configuration $I \rhd P \lhd \Omega$ exhibits no s-computations for any s where $|s| > 0$, rendering $\mathsf{dd}(\Omega, I, P, s)$ for $|s| > 0$ vacuously true (see Remark 1). By contrast, $\mathsf{dd}(c!a.\checkmark, I, P, s)$ holds only whenever $s = c!a.t$ (for arbitrary t) and $I \rhd P \xrightarrow{s}$.

In (12), monitor $\Omega + \mathsf{end}$ does not deterministically detect *any* computation: when composed with an arbitrary $I \rhd P$, it clearly can never reach a detection, but it can neither prohibit the process from producing visible actions, as in the case of Ω (see rules MVER, MCHR and IMON). Monitor $\Omega + \checkmark$ can either behave like Ω or transition to $\checkmark$ after one external action observed; in both cases, it deterministically detects all s-computation where $|s| > 0$. The monitor $\operatorname{rec} X.(\tau.X + \checkmark)$ first silently transitions to $(\tau.\operatorname{rec} X.(\tau.X + \checkmark)) + \checkmark$ and then either transitions back to the original state or else transitions to $\checkmark$ with an external action; in either case, when composed with any process $I \rhd P$, it also deterministically detects all s-computation for $|s| > 0$.

In (13), although monitor $\Omega + c!a.\checkmark$ potentially detects less computations than $\Omega + \checkmark$ (e.g., for $I = \{c, a, b\}$, $P = c!b.\mathsf{nil}$ and $s = c!b.\epsilon$, the predicate $\mathsf{pd}(\Omega + \checkmark, I, P, s)$ holds but $\mathsf{pd}(\Omega + c!a.\checkmark, I, P, s)$ *does not*), both deterministically detect the same computations, *i.e.*, all s-computation where $|s| > 0$. Specifically, if a process being monitored, say $I \rhd P$, can produce an action other than $c!a$, the instrumentation with monitor $\Omega + c!a.\checkmark$ restrains such an action, since the monitor *cannot* transition with that external action (it can only transition with $c!a$) but, at the same time, it can τ-transition (see rules IMON and ITRM). ∎

The preorders in Definition 4 are not as discriminating as one might expect.

Example 8. Consider the monitor $M_{any} = x?y.\checkmark + x!y.\checkmark$.

$$M_{any} \cong_{pd} M_{any} + \Omega \quad \text{and} \quad M_{any} \cong_{dd} M_{any} + \Omega \tag{14}$$
$$c!a.end \cong_{pd} c!a.end + c!a.\Omega \quad \text{and} \quad c!a.end \cong_{dd} c!a.end + c!a.\Omega \tag{15}$$

Intuitively, M_{any} potentially and deterministically detects any s-computation when $|s| > 0$. It turns out that $M_{any} + \Omega$ produces the same potential and deterministic detections, yielding the *resp.* equalities in (14). In (15), neither monitor produces *any* potential or deterministic detections and they are thus equivalent according to the *resp.* kernel equivalences of Definition 4.   ∎

There are however settings where the equalities established in Example 8 are deemed too coarse. *E.g.*, in (15), whereas monitor $c!a.end$ is innocuous when instrumented with a process, monitor $c!a.end + c!a.\Omega$ may potentially change the observed behaviour of the process under scrutiny after the action $c!a$ is emitted (by suppressing external actions, as explained in Example 7); a similar argument applies for the monitors in (14). We thus define a third monitor predicate called *transparency* [5,15,28], stating that whenever a monitored process *cannot* perform an external action, it must be because the (unmonitored) process is unable to perform that action (*i.e.*, the monitoring does not prohibit that action).

Definition 5 (Transparency Preorder). *M is transparent for $I \triangleright P$ wrt. trace s, denoted as tr(M, P, I, s), iff $\left(I \triangleright P \triangleleft M \xRightarrow{s} Q \triangleleft N \text{ and } \mathbf{aftr}(I, s) \triangleright (Q \triangleleft N) \not\xRightarrow{\alpha} \right)$ implies $\mathbf{aftr}(I, s) \triangleright Q \not\xRightarrow{\alpha}$. We define the induced preorder as expected:*

$$M \sqsubseteq_{tr} N \overset{def}{=} \forall I, P, s \cdot tr(M, I, P, s) \text{ implies } tr(N, I, P, s) \qquad \blacksquare$$

Although the preorders in Definitions 4 and 5 are interesting in their own right, we define the following relation as the finest monitor preorder in this paper.

Definition 6 (Monitor Preorder)

$$M \sqsubseteq N \overset{def}{=} M \sqsubseteq_{pd} N \text{ and } M \sqsubseteq_{dd} N \text{ and } M \sqsubseteq_{tr} N \qquad \blacksquare$$

Example 9. We have $M_{any} \not\sqsubseteq M_{any} + \Omega$ because $M_{any} \not\sqsubseteq_{tr} M_{any} + \Omega$, since $\neg tr(M_{any} + \Omega, I, P, s)$ for $I = \{c, a\}$, $P = c!a.c!a.nil$ and $s = c!a.\epsilon$. Similarly, we also have $c!a.end \not\sqsubseteq c!a.end + c!a.\Omega$.   ∎

Inequalities from the preorders of Definitions 4 and 5 are relatively easy to repudiate. For instance, we can use P, I and t from Example 4 as counter examples to show that $pd(M_5, I, P, t)$ and $\neg pd(M_3, I, P, t)$, thus *disproving* $M_5 \sqsubseteq_{pd} M_3$. However, it is much harder to show that an inequality from these preorders holds because we need to consider monitor behaviour wrt. *all* possible processes, interfaces and traces. As shown in Examples 6, 7 and 8, this often requires intricate reasoning in terms of the three LTSs defined in Figs. 1 and 2.

5   Characterisation

We define alternative monitor preorders for which positive statements about their inequalities are easier to establish. The new preorders are defined exclusively in terms of the monitor operational semantics of Fig. 2, as opposed to how they are affected by arbitrary processes as in Definition 6 (which considers also the process and instrumentation LTSs). We show that the new preorders coincide with those in Sect. 4. Apart from equipping us with an easier mechanism for determining the inequalities of Sect. 4, the correspondence results provide further insight into the properties satisfied by the preorders of Definitions 4 and 5.

We start with the potential-detection preorder. We first define a restricted monitor LTS that disallows idempotent transitions from verdicts, $w \xrightarrow{\alpha} w$: these are redundant when considering the monitor operational semantics in isolation. Note, however, that we can still used rule MVER, e.g., to derive $\checkmark + M \xrightarrow{\alpha}_r \checkmark$.

Definition 7 (Restricted Monitor Semantics). *A derived monitor transition,* $M \xrightarrow{\mu}_r N$, *is the least relation satisfying the conditions* $M \xrightarrow{\mu} N$ *and* $M \neq w$. $M \xLongrightarrow{s}_r N$ *denotes a transition sequence in the restricted LTS.* ∎

We use the restricted LTS to limit the detecting transition sequences on the left of the implication of Definition 8. However, we permit these transitions to be matched by transition sequences in the original monitor LTS, so as to allow the monitor to the right of the inequality to match the sequence with a *prefix* of visible actions (which can then be padded by $\checkmark \xrightarrow{\alpha} \checkmark$ transitions as required).

Definition 8 (Alternative Potential Detection Preorder)

$$M \preceq_{pd} N \overset{\text{def}}{=} \forall s \cdot M \xLongrightarrow{s}_r \checkmark \quad implies \quad N \xLongrightarrow{s} \checkmark$$

Theorem 2 (Potential-Detection Preorders). $M \sqsubseteq_{pd} N$ *iff* $M \preceq_{pd} N$

Example 10. By virtue of Theorem 2, to show that $\Omega + c!a.\checkmark \sqsubseteq_{pd} \Omega + \checkmark$ from (13) of Example 7 holds, we only need to consider $\Omega + c!a.\checkmark \xLongrightarrow{c!a}_r \checkmark$, which can be matched by $\Omega + \checkmark \xLongrightarrow{c!a} \checkmark$. Similarly, to show $(x!a.\text{if } x = c \text{ then } \checkmark \text{ else end}) \sqsubseteq_{pd} \checkmark$, we only need to consider $(x!a.\text{if } x = c \text{ then } \checkmark \text{ else end}) \xLongrightarrow{c!a}_r \checkmark$, matched by $\checkmark \xrightarrow{c!a} \checkmark$. ∎

For the remaining characterisations, we require two divergence judgements.

Definition 9 (Divergence and Strong Divergence)

- $M \uparrow$ denotes that M diverges, *meaning that it can produce an infinite transition sequence of τ-actions* $M \xrightarrow{\tau} M' \xrightarrow{\tau} M'' \xrightarrow{\tau} \ldots$
- $M \Uparrow$ denotes that M strongly diverges, *meaning that it cannot produce finite transition sequence of τ-actions* $M \xrightarrow{\tau} M' \xrightarrow{\tau} \ldots M'' \nrightarrow$. ∎

Lemma 1. $M \xrightarrow{\tau}$ *implies* $M \neq w$

The alternative preorder for deterministic detections, Definition 11 below, is based on three predicates describing the behaviour of a monitor M along a trace s. The predicate $\mathsf{blk}(M, s)$ describes the potential for M to *block* before it can complete trace s. Predicate $\mathsf{fl}(M, s)$ describes the potential for *failing* after monitoring trace s, i.e., an s-derivative of M reaches a non-detecting state from which no further τ actions are possible, or it diverges (implicitly, by Lemma 1, this also implies that the monitors along the diverging sequences are never detecting). Finally $\mathsf{nd}(M, s)$ states the existence of a non-detecting s-derivative of M.

Definition 10 (Monitor Block, Fail and Non-Detecting)

$$\mathsf{blk}(M, s) \stackrel{def}{=} \exists s_1, \alpha, s_2, N \cdot s = s_1 \alpha s_2 \text{ and } M \stackrel{s_1}{\Longrightarrow} N \stackrel{\tau}{\not\rightarrow} \text{ and } N \stackrel{\alpha}{\not\rightarrow}$$

$$\mathsf{fl}(M, s) \stackrel{def}{=} \exists N \cdot M \stackrel{s}{\Longrightarrow} N \text{ and } ((N \neq \checkmark \text{ and } N \stackrel{\tau}{\not\rightarrow}) \text{ or } N \uparrow)$$

$$\mathsf{nd}(M, s) \stackrel{def}{=} \exists N \cdot M \stackrel{s}{\Longrightarrow} N \text{ and } N \neq \checkmark$$

Note that $\mathsf{blk}(M, s)$ implicitly requires $|s| \geq 1$ for the predicate to hold. ■

Corollary 1. $\mathsf{blk}(M, s)$ *implies* $\forall t \cdot \mathsf{blk}(M, st)$

Definition 11 (Alternative Deterministic Detection Preorder)

$$M \preceq_{dd} N \stackrel{def}{=} \forall s \cdot \begin{cases} \mathsf{blk}(N, s) & implies & \mathsf{blk}(M, s) \text{ or } \mathsf{fl}(M, s) \\ \mathsf{fl}(N, s) & implies & \mathsf{blk}(M, s) \text{ or } \mathsf{fl}(M, s) \\ \mathsf{nd}(N, s) & implies & \mathsf{nd}(M, s) \text{ or } \mathsf{blk}(M, s) \end{cases}$$

We write $M \simeq_{dd} N$ to denote the kernel equality ($M \preceq_{dd} N$ and $N \preceq_{dd} M$). ■

Theorem 3 (Deterministic-Detection Preorders). $M \sqsubseteq_{dd} N$ *iff* $M \preceq_{dd} N$

Example 11. Consider $M = c?a.\mathsf{end} + x!b.\mathsf{end}$ and $N = c?a.\mathsf{end}$. By virtue of Theorem 3, to determine $M \sqsubseteq_{dd} N$ we prove $M \preceq_{dd} N$ as follows:

1. We have $\mathsf{blk}(N, s)$ whenever $s = \alpha s'$ and $\alpha \neq c?a$. We have two subcases:
   - If $\mathsf{match}(x!b, \alpha)$ is undefined, we show $\mathsf{blk}(M, \alpha s')$ by first showing that $\mathsf{blk}(M, \alpha \epsilon)$ and then generalising the result for arbitrary s' using Corollary 1.
   - If $\exists \sigma \cdot \mathsf{match}(x!b, \alpha) = \sigma$, we show $\mathsf{fl}(M, \alpha s')$ by first showing $\mathsf{fl}(M, \alpha \epsilon)$ and then generalising the result for arbitrary s' using Theorem 1.
2. For any s, we have $\mathsf{fl}(N, c?a.s)$: we can show $\mathsf{fl}(M, c?a.s)$, again using Theorem 1 to alleviate the proof burden.
3. For any s, we have $\mathsf{nd}(N, c?a.s)$: the required proof is analogous to the previous case. ■

Example 12. Due to full abstraction (*i.e.*, completeness), we can alternatively disprove $\checkmark \sqsubseteq_{dd} \tau.\checkmark$ from Example 6 by showing that $\checkmark \not\preceq_{dd} \tau.\checkmark$: we can readily argue that whereas $\mathsf{nd}(\tau.\checkmark, \epsilon)$, we *cannot* show either $\mathsf{nd}(\checkmark, \epsilon)$ or $\mathsf{blk}(\checkmark, \epsilon)$. ■

Example 13. Recall the equalities $\Omega \cong_{dd} \Omega + \checkmark \cong_{dd} \mathsf{rec} X.(\tau.X + \checkmark)$ claimed in (12) of Example 7. It is arguably easier to determine these equalities by considering only the monitor LTSs to show that $\Omega \simeq_{dd} \Omega + \checkmark \simeq_{dd} \mathsf{rec} X.(\tau.X + \checkmark)$ since:

1. For any $s \neq \epsilon$ we have $\neg \mathsf{blk}(\Omega, s)$, $\neg \mathsf{blk}(\Omega + \checkmark, s)$ and $\neg \mathsf{blk}(\mathrm{rec}\,X.(\tau.X + \checkmark), s)$.
2. We only have $\mathsf{fl}(\Omega, \epsilon)$, $\mathsf{fl}(\Omega + \checkmark, \epsilon)$ and $\mathsf{fl}(\mathrm{rec}\,X.(\tau.X + \checkmark), \epsilon)$.
3. Similarly, we only have $\mathsf{nd}(\Omega, \epsilon)$, $\mathsf{nd}(\Omega + \checkmark, \epsilon)$ and $\mathsf{nd}(\mathrm{rec}\,X.(\tau.X + \checkmark), \epsilon)$. ∎

Remark 2. The alternative preorder in Definition 11 can be optimised further using refined versions of the predicates $\mathsf{fl}(M, s)$ and $\mathsf{nd}(M, s)$ that are defined in terms of the restricted monitor transitions of Definition 7, as in the case of Definition 3. ∎

The alternative transparency preorder, Definition 13 below, is defined in terms of *divergence refusals* which, in turn, rely on strong divergences from Definition 9. Intuitively, divergence refusals are the set of actions that cannot be performed whenever a monitor reaches a strongly divergent state following the analysis of trace s. These actions turn out to be those that are suppressed on a process when instrumented with the *resp.* monitor.

Definition 12 (Divergence Refusals)

$$dref(M, s) \stackrel{def}{=} \left\{ \alpha \mid \exists N \cdot M \stackrel{s}{\Longrightarrow} N \text{ and } N \Uparrow \text{ and } N \stackrel{\alpha}{\nRightarrow} \right\}$$

Definition 13 (Alternative Transparency Preorder)

$$M \preceq_{tr} N \stackrel{def}{=} \forall s \cdot dref(N, s) \subseteq dref(M, s)$$

Theorem 4 (Transparency Preorders). $M \sqsubseteq_{tr} N$ *iff* $M \preceq_{tr} N$

Example 14. Recall monitors $c!a.\mathsf{end}$ and $c!a.\mathsf{end} + c!a.\Omega$ from (15) of Example 8. The inequality $c!a.\mathsf{end} + c!a.\Omega \sqsubseteq_{tr} c!a.\mathsf{end}$ follows trivially from Theorem 4, since $\forall s \cdot dref(c!a.\mathsf{end}, s) = \emptyset$. The symmetric case, $c!a.\mathsf{end} \sqsubseteq_{tr} c!a.\mathsf{end} + c!a.\Omega$, can also be readily repudiated by plying Theorem 4. Since $dref((c!a.\mathsf{end} + c!a.\Omega), c!a.\epsilon) = \textsc{Act}$ (and $dref(c!a.\mathsf{end}, c!a.\epsilon) = \emptyset$) we trivially obtain a violation of the set inclusion requirements of Definition 13. ∎

Example 15. Recall again $\Omega + \checkmark$ and $\mathrm{rec}\,X.(\tau.X + \checkmark)$ from (12). We can differentiate between these monitors from a transparency perspective, and Theorem 4 permits us to do this with relative ease. In fact, whereas $dref((\Omega + \checkmark), \epsilon) = \textsc{Act}$ (since $\Omega + \checkmark \stackrel{\tau}{\longrightarrow} \Omega$ and $dref(\Omega, \epsilon) = \textsc{Act}$) we have $dref((\mathrm{rec}\,X.(\tau.X + \checkmark)), \epsilon) = \emptyset$; for all other traces $|s| \geq 1$ we obtain empty divergence refusal sets for both monitors. We thus can positively conclude that $\Omega + \checkmark \sqsubseteq_{tr} \mathrm{rec}\,X.(\tau.X + \checkmark)$ while refuting $\mathrm{rec}\,X.(\tau.X + \checkmark) \sqsubseteq_{tr} \Omega + \checkmark$. ∎

Definition 14 (Alternative Monitor Preorder)

$$M \preceq N \stackrel{def}{=} M \preceq_{pd} N \text{ and } M \preceq_{dd} N \text{ and } M \preceq_{tr} N$$ ∎

Theorem 5 (Full Abstraction). $M \sqsubseteq N$ *iff* $M \preceq N$

6 Conclusion

We have presented a theory for (recogniser) monitors that allows us to substitute a monitor M_1 in a monitored process $P \lhd M_1$ by another monitor M_2 while guaranteeing the preservation of a number of monitoring properties relating to (behaviour) detection and monitor interference. The theory is *compositional*, since it enables us to ensure the preservation of properties by analysing the *resp.* monitors M_1 and M_2 *in isolation*, without needing to consider the process being monitored, P (which may be arbitrarily complex). To the best of our knowledge, it is the first monitor theory of its kind and could be used to alleviate efforts for proving monitors correct *e.g.*, [26]. The concrete contributions are:

1. The definition of three monitor preorders, each requiring the preservation of different monitoring properties: Definitions 3, 4 and 5.
2. The characterisation of these preorders in terms of alternative preorders that are more tractable, Theorems 2, 3 and 4.

Related and Future Work. The instrumentation relation we consider is adopted from [17] and embodies *synchronous* instrumentation (where the external actions constituted the monitorable actions). Synchronous instrumentation is the most prevalent method used in monitoring tools (*e.g.*, [1,9,14,25]) because it carries benefits such as timely detections. There are however variants such as asynchronous instrumentation (*e.g.*, [12,20]) as well as hybrid variations (*e.g.*, [6,7,9,30]). Our theory should be applicable, at least in part, to these variants.

In runtime verification, three-verdict monitors [2,10,15,17] are often considered, where detections are partitioned into acceptances and rejections. The monitors studied here express generic detections only; they are nevertheless maximally expressive for branching-time properties [17]. They also facilitate comparisons with other linear-time preorders (see below). We also expect our theory to extend smoothly to settings with acceptances and rejections.

Our potential and deterministic detection preorders are reminiscent of the classical may and must preorders of [13,23] and, more recently (for the deterministic detection preorder), of the subcontract relations in [3,21]. However, these relations differ from ours in a number of respects. For starters, the monitor instrumentation relation of Fig. 2 assigns monitors a *passive* role whereas the parallel composition relation composing processes (servers in [3,21]) with tests (clients in [3,21]) invites tests to *interact* with the process being probed. Another important difference is that testing preorders typically relate processes, whereas our preorders are defined over the adjudicating entities *i.e.*, the monitors. The closest work in this regard is that of [3], where the authors develop a must theory for clients. Still, there are significant discrepancies between this must theory and our deterministic detection preorder (further to the differencies between the detected (monitored) computations of Definition 2 and the successful computations under tests of [3,13,23] as outlined above — success in the compliance relation of [21] is even more disparate). Concretely, in our setting we have equalities such as $c!a.\checkmark \cong_{\mathsf{dd}} c!a.\checkmark + c!b.\mathsf{end}$ (see (10) of Example 6), which would not hold in the setting of [3] since their client preorder is sensitive to external choices ($\sqsubseteq_{dd}$ is not because monitored executions are distinguished by their visible trace). The two relations are in fact incomparable, since divergent processes are bottom elements in the client must preorder of [3], but they are not in $\sqsubseteq_{dd}$. In fact, we have $\Omega \not\sqsubseteq_{dd} \Omega + \text{end}$ in (12) of Example 7 or, more clearly, $\Omega \not\sqsubseteq_{dd} \Omega + \alpha.\text{end}$; at an intuitive level, this is because the instrumentation relation of Fig. 2 prioritises silent actions over external actions that cannot be matched by the monitor.

Transparency is usually a concern for enforcement monitors whereby the visible behaviour of a monitored process should not be modified unless it violates some specified property [5,15,28]. We adapted this concept to recognisers, whereby the process behaviour should never be suppressed by the monitor.

To our knowledge, the only body of work that studies monitoring for the piCalculus is [5,11,22], and focusses on synthesising adaptation/enforcement monitors from session types. The closest to our work is [5]: their definitions of monitor correctness are however distinctly different (e.g., they are based on branching-time equivalences) and their decomposition methods for decoupling the monitor analysis from that of processes rely on static type-checking.

Acknowledgements. The paper benefited from discussions with Luca Aceto, Giovanni Bernardi, Matthew Hennessy and Anna Ingólfsdóttir.

References

1. Barringer, H., Falcone, Y., Havelund, K., Reger, G., Rydeheard, D.E.: Quantified event automata: Towards expressive and efficient runtime monitors. In: Giannakopoulou, D., Méry, D. (eds.) FM 2012. LNCS, vol. 7436, pp. 68–84. Springer, Heidelberg (2012)
2. Bauer, A., Leucker, M., Schallhart, C.: Runtime verification for LTL and TLTL. TOSEM **20**(4), 14 (2011)
3. Bernardi, G., Hennessy, M.: Mutually testing processes. LMCS **11**(2:1), 1–23 (2015)
4. Bielova, N., Massacci, F.: Do you really mean what you actually enforced? Edited automata revisited. Int. J. Inf. Secur. **10**(4), 239–254 (2011)
5. Bocchi, L., Chen, T.-C., Demangeon, R., Honda, K., Yoshida, N.: Monitoring networks through multiparty session types. In: Beyer, D., Boreale, M. (eds.) FORTE 2013 and FMOODS 2013. LNCS, vol. 7892, pp. 50–65. Springer, Heidelberg (2013)
6. Cassar, I., Francalanza, A.: On synchronous and asynchronous monitor instrumentation for actor systems. FOCLASA **175**, 54–68 (2014)
7. Kane, A., Chowdhury, O., Datta, A., Koopman, P.: A case study on runtime monitoring of an autonomous research vehicle (ARV) system. In: Bartocci, E., et al. (eds.) RV 2015. LNCS, vol. 9333, pp. 102–117. Springer, Heidelberg (2015). doi:10.1007/978-3-319-23820-3_7
8. Cesarini, F., Thompson, S.: Erlang Programming. O'Reilly, Sebastopol (2009)
9. Chen, F., Roşu, G.: MOP: An efficient and generic runtime verification framework. In: OOPSLA, pp. 569–588. ACM, (2007)
10. Cini, C., Francalanza, A.: An LTL proof system for runtime verification. In: Baier, C., Tinelli, C. (eds.) TACAS 2015. LNCS, vol. 9035, pp. 581–595. Springer, Heidelberg (2015)

11. Coppo, M., Dezani-Ciancaglini, M., Venneri, B.: Self-adaptive monitors for multiparty sessions. In: PDP, pp. 688–696. IEEE Computer Society (2014)
12. D'Angelo, B., Sankaranarayanan, S., Sánchez, C., Robinson, W., Finkbeiner, B., Sipma, H.B., Mehrotra, S., Manna, Z.: LOLA: Runtime monitoring of synchronous systems. In: TIME, IEEE (2005)
13. De Nicola, R., Hennessy, M.C.B.: Testing equivalences for processes. TCS **34**(1–2), 83–133 (1984)
14. Decker, N., Leucker, M., Thoma, D.: jUnit^{RV}–adding runtime verification to junit. In: Brat, G., Rungta, N., Venet, A. (eds.) NFM 2013. LNCS, vol. 7871, pp. 459–464. Springer, Heidelberg (2013)
15. Falcone, Y., Fernandez, J.-C., Mounier, L.: What can you verify and enforce at runtime? STTT **14**(3), 349–382 (2012)
16. Formal Systems Laboratory. Monitor Oriented Programming. University of Illinois at Urbana Champaign. http://fsl.cs.illinois.edu/index.php/Monitoring-Oriented_Programming
17. Kane, A., Chowdhury, O., Datta, A., Koopman, P.: A case study on runtime monitoring of an autonomous research vehicle (ARV) system. In: Bartocci, E., et al. (eds.) RV 2015. LNCS, vol. 9333, pp. 102–117. Springer, Heidelberg (2015). doi:10.1007/978-3-319-23820-3_7
18. Francalanza, A., Gauci, A., Pace, G.J.: Distributed system contract monitoring. JLAP **82**(5–7), 186–215 (2013)
19. Francalanza, A., Hennessy, M.: A theory for observational fault tolerance. JLAP **73**(1–2), 22–50 (2007)
20. Francalanza, A., Seychell, A.: Synthesising correct concurrent runtime monitors. FMSD **46**(3), 226–261 (2015)
21. Castagna, G., Gesbert, N., Padovani, L.: A theory of contracts for web services. ACM Trans. Program. Lang. Syst. **31**(5), 1–61 (2009)
22. Giusto, C.D., Perez, J.A.: Disciplined structured communications with disciplined runtime adaptation. Sci. Comput. Program. **97**(2), 235–265 (2015)
23. Hennessy, M.: Algebraic Theory of Processes. MIT Press, Cambridge (1988)
24. Hennessy, M.: A Distributed Pi-Calculus. Cambridge University Press, Cambridge (2007)
25. Kim, M., Viswanathan, M., Kannan, S., Lee, I., Sokolsky, O.: Java-MaC: A runtime assurance approach for Java programs. FMSD **24**(2), 129–155 (2004)
26. Kane, A., Chowdhury, O., Datta, A., Koopman, P.: A case study on runtime monitoring of an Autonomous Research Vehicle (ARV) system. In: Bartocci, E., et al. (eds.) RV 2015. LNCS, vol. 9333, pp. 102–117. Springer, Heidelberg (2015). doi:10.1007/978-3-319-23820-3_7
27. Leucker, M., Schallhart, C.: A brief account of runtime verification. JLAP **78**(5), 293–303 (2009)
28. Ligatti, J., Bauer, L., Walker, D.: Edit automata: enforcement mechanisms for run-time security policies. Int. J. Inf. Secur. **4**(1–2), 2–16 (2005)
29. Milner, R.: Communication and Concurrency. Prentice-Hall Inc, Upper Saddle River (1989)
30. Roşu, G., Havelund, K.: Rewriting-based techniques for runtime verification. Autom. Softw. Engg. **12**(2), 151–197 (2005)
31. Sangiorgi, D., Walker, D.: PI-Calculus: A Theory of Mobile Processes. Cambridge University Press, Cambridge (2001)
32. Schneider, F.B.: Enforceable security policies. ACM Trans. Inf. Syst. Secur. **3**(1), 30–50 (2000)

33. Sen, K., Vardhan, A., Agha, G., Rosu, G.: Efficient decentralized monitoring of safety in distributed systems. In: ICSE, pp. 418–427. IEEE (2004)
34. Verissimo, P., Rodrigues, L.: Distributed Systems for System Architects. Kluwer Academic Publishers, Norwell (2001)

Contextual Approximation
and Higher-Order Procedures

Ranko Lazić and Andrzej S. Murawski(✉)

DIMAP and Department of Computer Science, University of Warwick, Coventry, UK
a.murawski@warwick.ac.uk

Abstract. We investigate the complexity of deciding contextual approximation (refinement) in finitary Idealized Algol, a prototypical language combining higher-order types with state. Earlier work in the area established the borderline between decidable and undecidable cases, and focussed on the complexity of deciding approximation between terms in normal form.

In contrast, in this paper we set out to quantify the impact of locally declared higher-order procedures on the complexity of establishing contextual approximation in the decidable cases. We show that the obvious decision procedure based on exhaustive β-reduction can be beaten. Further, by classifying redexes by levels, we give tight bounds on the complexity of contextual approximation for terms that may contain redexes up to level k, namely, $(k-1)$-EXPSPACE-completeness. Interestingly, the bound is obtained by selective β-reduction: redexes from level 3 onwards can be reduced without losing optimality, whereas redexes up to order 2 are handled by a dedicated decision procedure based on game semantics and a variant of pushdown automata.

1 Introduction

Contextual approximation (refinement) is a fundamental notion in programming language theory, facilitating arguments about program correctness [14] as well as supporting formal program development [5]. Intuitively, a term M_1 is said to *contextually approximate* another term M_2, if substituting M_1 for M_2 in any context will not lead to new observable behaviours. Being based on universal quantification over contexts, contextual approximation is difficult to establish directly. In this paper, we consider the problem of contextual approximation in a higher-order setting with state. Contextual reasoning at higher-order types is a recognised challenge and a variety of techniques have been proposed to address it, such as Kripke logical relations [3] or game models [2]. In this work, we aim to understand the impact of locally defined higher-order procedures on the complexity of establishing contextual approximation. Naturally, one would expect the complexity to grow in the presence of procedures and it should grow as the type-theoretic order increases. We shall quantify that impact by providing tight

Research supported by EPSRC (EP/J019577/1, EP/M011801/1).

© Springer-Verlag Berlin Heidelberg 2016
B. Jacobs and C. Löding (Eds.): FOSSACS 2016, LNCS 9634, pp. 162–179, 2016.
DOI: 10.1007/978-3-662-49630-5_10

complexity bounds for contextual approximation in our higher-order framework. The results demonstrate that, from the complexity-theoretic point of view, it is safe to inline procedures only down to a certain level. Below that level, however, it is possible to exploit compositionality to arrive at better bounds than those implied by full inlining.

The vehicle for our study is Idealized Algol [1,13], the protypical language for investigating the combination of local state with higher-order procedures. In order to avoid obviously undecidable cases, we restrict ourselves to its finitary variant IA_f, featuring finite base types and no recursion (looping is allowed, though). Both semantic and syntactic methods were used to reason about Idealized Algol [1,12] in the past. In particular, on the semantic front, there exists a game model that captures contextual approximation (in the sense of inequational full abstraction) via complete-play inclusion. Earlier work in the area [6,9,11] used this correspondence to map out the borderline between decidable and undecidable cases within IA_f. The classification is based on type-theoretic order: a term is of order i if its type is of order at most i and all free variables have order less than i. We write IA_i for the set of IA_f-terms of order i. It turns out that contextual approximation is decidable for terms of all orders up to 3, but undecidable from order 4 onwards. The work on decidability has also established accurate complexity bounds for reasoning about contextual approximation between terms in β-normal form as well as terms with the simplest possible β-redexes, in which arguments can only be of base type. For order-3 terms, the problem can be shown EXPTIME-complete [11], while at orders $0, 1, 2$ it is PSPACE-complete [10]. In this paper, we present a finer analysis of the decidable cases and consider arbitrary β-redexes. In particular, functions can be used as arguments, which corresponds to the inlining of procedures.

We evaluate the impact of redexes by introducing a notion of their level: the level of a β-redex $(\lambda x.M)N$ will be the order of the type of $\lambda x.M$. Accordingly, we can split IA_i into sublanguages IA_i^k, in which terms can contain redexes of level up to k. IA_i^0 is then the normal-form case and IA_i^1 is the case of base-type arguments. Obviously, the problem of contextually approximating IA_i^k $(i \leq 3, k \geq 2)$ terms can be solved by β-reduction (and an appeal to the results for IA_i^0), but this is known to result in a k-fold exponential blow-up, thus implying a $(k+1)$-EXPTIME upper bound for IA_3^k. This bound turns out to be suboptimal. One could lower it by reducing to IA_i^1 instead, which would shave off a single exponential, but this is still insufficient to arrive at the optimal bound. It turns out, however, that reducing IA_3^k terms to IA_3^2 (all redexes up to order 3 are eliminated) does not lead to a loss of optimality. To work out the accurate bound for the IA_3^2 case, one cannot apply further β-reductions, though. Instead we devise a dedicated procedure based on game semantics and pushdown automata. More specifically, we introduce a variant of visibly pushdown automata [4] with ϵ-transitions and show how to translate IA_3^2 into such automata so that the accepted languages are faithful representations of the term's game semantics [1]. The translation can be performed in exponential time and, crucially, the automata correspoding to IA_3^2-terms satisfy a boundedness property: the stack symbols pushed on the stack during ϵ-moves can only form contiguous segments of exponential length with respect to the term size. This allows us to solve the corresponding inclusion problem in exponential space with respect to the original term size. Consequently, we can show that IA_3^2 contextual approximation is in EXPSPACE.

The above result then implies that program approximation of IA_3^k-terms is in $(k-1)$-EXPSPACE. Furthermore, we can prove matching lower bounds for IA_1^k. The table below summarises the complexity results. The results for $k \geq 2$ are new.

	$k = 0$	$k = 1$	$k \geq 2$
IA_1^k	PSPACE-complete [10]	PSPACE-complete [10]	$(k-1)$-EXPSPACE-complete
IA_2^k	PSPACE-complete [10]	PSPACE-complete [10]	$(k-1)$-EXPSPACE-complete
IA_3^k	EXPTIME-complete [11]	EXPTIME-complete [11]	$(k-1)$-EXPSPACE-complete

2   Idealized Algol

We consider a finitary version IA_f of Idealized Algol with active expressions [1]. Its types are generated by the following grammar.

$$\theta ::= \beta \mid \theta \to \theta \qquad \beta ::= \mathsf{com} \mid \mathsf{exp} \mid \mathsf{var}$$

IA_f can be viewed as a simply-typed λ-calculus over the base types $\mathsf{com}, \mathsf{exp}, \mathsf{var}$ (of commands, expressions and variables respectively) augmented with the constants listed below

$$\mathbf{skip} : \mathsf{com} \qquad i : \mathsf{exp} \quad (0 \leq i \leq max) \qquad \mathbf{succ} : \mathsf{exp} \to \mathsf{exp} \qquad \mathbf{pred} : \mathsf{exp} \to \mathsf{exp}$$

$$\mathbf{ifzero}_\beta : \mathsf{exp} \to \beta \to \beta \to \beta \qquad \mathbf{seq}_\beta : \mathsf{com} \to \beta \to \beta \qquad \mathbf{deref} : \mathsf{var} \to \mathsf{exp}$$

$$\mathbf{assign} : \mathsf{var} \to \mathsf{exp} \to \mathsf{com} \qquad \mathbf{cell}_\beta : (\mathsf{var} \to \beta) \to \beta$$

$$\mathbf{while} : \mathsf{exp} \to \mathsf{com} \to \mathsf{com} \qquad \mathbf{mkvar} : (\mathsf{exp} \to \mathsf{com}) \to \mathsf{exp} \to \mathsf{var}$$

where β ranges over base types and $\mathsf{exp} = \{0, \cdots, max\}$. Other IA_f-terms are formed using λ-abstraction and application

$$\frac{\Gamma \vdash M : \theta \to \theta' \quad \Gamma \vdash N : \theta}{\Gamma \vdash MN : \theta'} \qquad \frac{\Gamma, x : \theta \vdash M : \theta'}{\Gamma \vdash \lambda x^\theta . M : \theta \to \theta'}$$

using the obvious rules for constants and free identifiers. Each of the constants corresponds to a different programming feature. For instance, the sequential composition of M and N (typically denoted by $M; N$) is expressed as $\mathbf{seq}_\beta MN$, assignment of N to M ($M := N$) is represented by $\mathbf{assign} MN$ and $\mathbf{cell}_\beta(\lambda x.M)$ amounts to creating a local variable x visible in M (**new** x **in** M). **mkvar** is the so-called bad-variable constructor that makes it possible to construct terms of type var with prescribed read- and write-methods. $\mathbf{while} MN$ corresponds to **while** M **do** N. We shall write Ω_β for the divergent constant that can be defined using **while** 1 **do** **skip**.

The operational semantics of IA_f, based on call-by-name evaluation, can be found in [1]; we will write $M \Downarrow$ if M reduces to **skip**. We study the induced contextual approximation.

$$M_{A \times B} = M_A + M_B \qquad M_{A \Rightarrow B} = M_A + M_B$$
$$\lambda_{A \times B} = [\lambda_A, \lambda_B] \qquad \lambda_{A \Rightarrow B} = [\overline{\lambda}_A, \lambda_B]$$
$$\vdash_{A \times B} = \vdash_A + \vdash_B \qquad \vdash_{A \Rightarrow B} = \vdash_B + (I_B \times I_A) + (\vdash_A \cap (M_A \times M_A))$$

$\overline{\lambda}_A$ reverses the ownership of moves in A while preserving their kind.

Fig. 1. Constructions on arenas

Definition 1. *We say that $\Gamma \vdash M_1 : \theta$ contextually approximates $\Gamma \vdash M_2 : \theta$ if, for any context $C[-]$ such that $C[M_1], C[M_2]$ are closed terms of type* com, *we have $C[M_1] \Downarrow$ implies $C[M_2] \Downarrow$. We then write $\Gamma \vdash M_1 \precsim M_2$.*

Even though the base types are finite, $\mathsf{IA_f}$ contextual approximation is not decidable [9]. To obtain decidability one has to restrict the order of types, defined by:

$$\mathsf{ord}(\beta) = 0 \qquad \mathsf{ord}(\theta \to \theta') = \max(\mathsf{ord}(\theta) + 1, \mathsf{ord}(\theta')).$$

Definition 2. *Let $i \geq 0$. The fragment IA_i of $\mathsf{IA_f}$ consists of $\mathsf{IA_f}$-terms $x_1 : \theta_1, \cdots, x_n : \theta_n M : \theta$ such that $\mathsf{ord}(\theta_j) < i$ for any $j = 1, \cdots, n$ and $\mathsf{ord}(\theta) \leq i$.*

Contextual approximation is known to be decidable for IA_1, IA_2 and IA_3 [11], but it is undecidable for IA_4 [9].

Definition 3. – *The* level *of a β-redex $(\lambda x^\theta.M)N$ is the order of the type of $\lambda x^\theta.M$.*
– *A term has* degree k *if all redexes inside it have level at most k.*
– *IA_i^k is the subset of IA_i consisting of terms whose degree is at most k.*

β-reduction can be used to reduce the degree of a term by one at an exponential cost.

Lemma 1. *Let $d \geq 1$. A λ-term M of degree d can be reduced to a term M' of degree $d - 1$ with a singly-exponential blow-up in size.*

3   Games

Game semantics views computation as an exchange of moves between two players, called O and P. It interprets terms as strategies for P in an abstract game derived from the underlying types. The moves available to players as well as the rules of the game are specified by an arena.

Definition 4. *An* arena *is a triple $A = \langle M_A, \lambda_A, \vdash_A \rangle$, where*

– *M_A is a set of* moves;
– *$\lambda_A : M_A \to \{O, P\} \times \{Q, A\}$ is a function indicating to which player (O or P) a move belongs and of what kind it is (question or answer);*

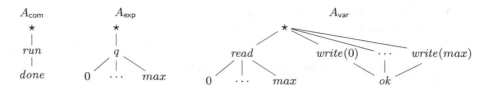

Fig. 2. Arenas for base types

- $\vdash_A \subseteq (M_A + \{\star\}) \times M_A$ *is the so-called* enabling *relation, which must satisfy the following conditions:*
  - *If $\star$ enables a move then it is an O-question without any other enabler. A move like this is called* initial *and we shall write I_A for the set containing all initial moves of A.*
  - *If one move enables another then the former must be a question and the two moves must belong to different players.*

Arenas used to interpret the base types of $\mathsf{IA_f}$ are shown in Fig. 2: the moves at the bottom are answer-moves. Product and function-space arenas can be constructed as shown in Fig. 1. Given an $\mathsf{IA_f}$-type θ, we shall write $[\![\theta]\!]$ for the corresponding arena obtained compositionally from A_{com}, A_{exp} and A_{var} using the $\Rightarrow$ construction. Given arenas, we can play games based on a special kind of sequences of moves. A *justified sequence* s in an arena A is a sequence of moves in which every move $m \notin I_A$ must have a pointer to an earlier move n in s such that $n \vdash_A m$. n is then said to be the *justifier* of m. It follows that every justified sequence must begin with an O-question.

Given a justified sequence s, its O-view $\llcorner s \lrcorner$ and P-view $\ulcorner s \urcorner$ are defined as follows, where o and p stand for an O-move and a P-move respectively:

$$\llcorner \epsilon \lrcorner = \epsilon \quad \llcorner so \lrcorner = \llcorner s \lrcorner o \qquad\qquad \llcorner so \overset{\frown}{t} p \lrcorner = \llcorner s \lrcorner o \overset{\frown}{\,} p$$
$$\ulcorner \epsilon \urcorner = \epsilon \quad \ulcorner so \urcorner = o \quad \text{(if } o \text{ is initial)} \quad \ulcorner sp \urcorner = \ulcorner s \urcorner p \quad \ulcorner sp \overset{\frown}{t} o \urcorner = \ulcorner s \urcorner p \overset{\frown}{\,} o.$$

A justified sequence s satisfies *visibility* condition if, in any prefix tm of s, if m is a non-initial O-move then its justifier occurs in $\llcorner t \lrcorner$ and if m is a P-move then its justifier is in $\ulcorner t \urcorner$. A justified sequence satisfies the *bracketing* condition if any answer-move is justified by the latest unanswered question that precedes it.

Definition 5. *A justified sequence is a* play *iff O- and P-moves alternate and it satisfies bracketing and visibility. We write P_A for the set of plays in an arena A. A play is* single-threaded *if it contains at most one occurrence of an initial move.*

The next important definition is that of a strategy. Strategies determine unique responses for P (if any) and do not restrict O-moves.

Definition 6. *A* strategy *in an arena A (written as $\sigma : A$) is a non-empty prefix-closed subset of* single-threaded *plays in A such that:*

$[\![\mathbf{skip}]\!] : [\![\mathsf{com}]\!]$ *run done*

$[\![i]\!] : [\![\mathsf{exp}]\!]$ $q\,i$

$[\![\mathbf{succ}]\!] : [\![\mathsf{exp}]\!]_1 \Rightarrow [\![\mathsf{exp}]\!]$ $q\,q_1\,\sum_{i=0}^{max} i_1\,((i+1)\bmod max)$

$[\![\mathbf{pred}]\!] : [\![\mathsf{exp}]\!]_1 \Rightarrow [\![\mathsf{exp}]\!]$ $q\,q_1\,\sum_{i=0}^{max} i_1\,((i-1)\bmod max)$

$[\![\mathbf{ifzero}_\beta]\!] : [\![\mathsf{exp}]\!]_3 \Rightarrow [\![\beta]\!]_2 \Rightarrow [\![\beta]\!]_1 \Rightarrow [\![\beta]\!]$

$$\sum_{q\vdash_{[\![\beta]\!]} a} q\,q_3\,0_3\,q_1\,a_1\,a + \sum_{q\vdash_{[\![\beta]\!]} a} q\,q_3\,(\sum_{i=1}^{max} i_3)\,q_2\,a_2\,a$$

$[\![\mathbf{seq}_\beta]\!] : [\![\mathsf{com}]\!]_2 \Rightarrow [\![\beta]\!]_1 \Rightarrow [\![\beta]\!]$ $\sum_{q\vdash_{[\![\beta]\!]} a} q\,run_2\,done_2\,q_1\,a_1\,a$

$[\![\mathbf{deref}]\!] : [\![\mathsf{var}]\!]_1 \Rightarrow [\![\mathsf{exp}]\!]$ $q\,read_1\,\sum_{i=0}^{max} i_1\,i$

$[\![\mathbf{assign}]\!] : [\![\mathsf{var}]\!]_2 \Rightarrow [\![\mathsf{exp}]\!]_1 \Rightarrow [\![\mathsf{com}]\!]$ $run\,q_1\,\sum_{i=0}^{max} i_1\,write(i)_2\,ok_2\,done$

$[\![\mathbf{cell}_\beta]\!] : ([\![\mathsf{var}]\!]_{1,1} \Rightarrow [\![\beta]\!]_1) \Rightarrow [\![\beta]\!]$

$$\sum_{q\vdash_{[\![\beta]\!]} a} q\,q_1\,(read_{1,1}\,0_{1,1})^*(\sum_{i=0}^{max} write(i)_{1,1}\,ok_{1,1}(read_{1,1}\,i_{1,1})^*)^*a_1 a$$

$[\![\mathbf{mkvar}]\!] : ([\![\mathsf{exp}]\!]_{2,1} \Rightarrow [\![\mathsf{com}]\!]_2) \Rightarrow [\![\mathsf{exp}]\!]_1 \Rightarrow [\![\mathsf{var}]\!]$

$$read\,q_1\,(\sum_{i=0}^{max} i_1\,i) + \sum_{i=0}^{max} write(i)\,run_2\,(q_{2,1}\,i_{2,1})^*\,done_2\,ok$$

$[\![\mathbf{while}]\!] : [\![\mathsf{exp}]\!]_2 \Rightarrow [\![\mathsf{com}]\!]_1 \Rightarrow [\![\mathsf{com}]\!]$ $run\,q_2\,(\sum_{i=1}^{max} i_2\,run_1\,done_1\,q_2)^*\,0_2\,done$

Fig. 3. Strategies for constants. Only complete plays are specified.

(i) whenever $sp_1, sp_2 \in \sigma$ and p_1, p_2 are P-moves then $p_1 = p_2$;

(ii) whenever $s \in \sigma$ and $so \in P_A$ for some O-move o then $so \in \sigma$.

We write $\mathsf{comp}\,(\sigma)$ for the set of non-empty complete plays in σ, i.e. plays in which all questions have been answered.

An IA_f term $\Gamma \vdash M : \theta$, where $\Gamma = x_1 : \theta_1, \cdots, x_n : \theta_n$, is interpreted by a strategy (denoted by $[\![\Gamma \vdash M : \theta]\!]$) in the arena $[\![\Gamma \vdash \theta]\!] = [\![\theta_1]\!] \times \cdots \times [\![\theta_n]\!] \Rightarrow [\![\theta]\!]$. The denotations are calculated compositionally starting from strategies corresponding to constants and free identifiers [1]. The latter are interpreted by identity strategies that copy moves across from one occurrence of the same arena to the other, subject to the constraint that the interactions must be plays. Strategies corresponding to constants are given in Fig. 3, where the induced complete plays are listed. We use subscripts to indicate the origin of moves. Let $\sigma : A \Rightarrow B$ and $\tau : B \Rightarrow C$. In order to compose the strategies, one first defines an auxiliary set $\sigma^\dagger$ of (not necessarily single-threaded) plays on $A \Rightarrow B$ that are special interleavings of plays taken from σ (we refer the reader to [1] for details). Then $\sigma; \tau : A \Rightarrow C$ can be obtained by synchronising $\sigma^\dagger$ and τ on B-moves and erasing them after the synchronisation. The game-semantic interpretation captures contextual approximation as follows.

Theorem 1 [1]. $\Gamma \vdash M_1 \precsim M_2$ if and only if $\mathsf{comp}\,[\![\Gamma \vdash M_1]\!] \subseteq \mathsf{comp}\,[\![\Gamma \vdash M_2]\!]$.

Remark 1. $\sigma^\dagger$ is an interleaving of plays in σ that must itself be a play in $P_{A \Rightarrow B}$. For instance, only O is able to switch between different copies of σ and this can only happen after P plays in B. We shall discuss two important cases in detail, namely, $B = [\![\beta]\!]$ and $B = [\![\beta_k \to \cdots \to \beta_1 \to \beta]\!]$.

– If $B = [\![\beta]\!]$ then a new copy of σ can be started only after the previous one is completed. Thus $\sigma^\dagger$ in this case consists of iterated copies of σ.

– If $B = [\![\beta_k \rightarrow \cdots \rightarrow \beta_1 \rightarrow \beta]\!]$ then, in addition to the above scenario, a new copy of σ can be started by O each time P plays q_i (question from β_i). An old copy of σ can be revisited with a_i, which will then answer some unanswered occurrence of q_i. However, due to the bracketing condition, this will be possible only after all questions played after that q_i have been answered, i.e. when all copies of σ opened after q_i are completed. Thus, in this particular case, $\sigma^\dagger$ contains "stacked" copies of σ. Consequently, we can capture $X = \{ \epsilon \} \cup \mathsf{comp}\,(\sigma^\dagger)$ in this case by equation

$$X = \{\varepsilon\} \cup \bigcup\{ q\,A_0\,q_{i_1}\,X\,a_{i_1}\,A_1 \ldots q_{i_m}\,X\,a_{i_m}\,A_m\,a\,X \mid$$
$$q A_0 q_{i_1} a_{i_1} A_1 \ldots q_{i_m} a_{i_m} A_m a \in \mathsf{comp}\,(\sigma)\}$$

where A_j's stand for (possibly empty and possibly different) segments of moves from A. Note that, in a play of σ, q_i will always be followed by a_i.

4   Upper Bounds

We shall prove that contextual approximation of IA_3^2 terms can be decided in exponential space. Thanks to Lemma 1, this will imply that approximation of IA_3^k $(k \geq 2)$ terms is in $(k-1)$-EXPSPACE. In Sect. 5 we will show that these bounds are tight.

This shows that by firing redexes of level higher than 3 we do not lose optimal complexity. However, if redexes of order 2 were also executed (i.e. first-order procedures were inlined), the problem would be reduced to IA_3^1 and the implied bound would be 2-EXPTIME, which turns out suboptimal. In what follows, we show that contextual approximation of IA_3^2 terms is in EXPSPACE. To that end, we shall translate the terms to automata that represent their game semantics. The alphabet of the automata will consist of moves in the corresponding games. Recall that each occurrence of a base type in a type contributes distinct moves. In order to represent their origin faithfully, we introduce a labelling scheme based on subscripts.

First we discuss how to label occurrences of base types in types. Let Θ be a type of order at most 3. Then $\Theta \equiv \Theta_m \rightarrow \cdots \rightarrow \Theta_1 \rightarrow \beta$ and Θ_i's are of order at most 2. Consequently, for each $1 \leq i \leq m$, we have $\Theta_i \equiv \Theta_{i,m_i} \rightarrow \cdots \rightarrow \Theta_{i,1} \rightarrow \beta_i$ and $\Theta_{i,j}$'s are of order at most 1. Thus, we have $\Theta_{i,j} \equiv \beta_{i,j,m_{i,j}} \rightarrow \cdots \rightarrow \beta_{i,j,1} \rightarrow \beta_{i,j}$. Note that the above decomposition assigns a sequence of subscripts to each occurrence of a base type in Θ. Observe that $\mathsf{ord}(\Theta) = 3$ if and only if some occurrence of a base type gets subscripted with a triple. Next we are going to employ the subscripts to distinguish base types in IA_3 typing judgments.

Definition 7. *A third-order typing template* Ψ *is a sequence* $x_1 : \theta_1, \cdots, x_n : \theta_n, \theta$, *where* $\mathsf{ord}(\theta_i) \leq 2$ $(1 \leq i \leq n)$ *and* $\mathsf{ord}(\theta) \leq 3$.

To label $\theta_1, \cdots, \theta_n, \theta$ we will use the same labelling scheme as discussed above but, to distinguish θ_i's from θ and from one another, we will additionally use superscripts x_i for the former. The labelling scheme will also be used to identify moves in the corresponding game. Recall that the game corresponding to a third-order typing template will have moves from $M_{[\![\theta_1]\!]} + \cdots + M_{[\![\theta_n]\!]} + M_{[\![\theta]\!]}$. The super- and subscripts will identify their origin in a unique way.

Example 1. Let $\Psi \equiv x_1 : (\mathsf{com} \to \mathsf{exp}) \to \mathsf{var}, x_2 : \mathsf{com} \to \mathsf{exp} \to \mathsf{var}, ((\mathsf{com} \to \mathsf{exp}) \to \mathsf{var}) \to \mathsf{com}$. Here is the labelling scheme for Ψ: $x_1 : (\mathsf{com}_{1,1}^{x_1} \to \mathsf{exp}_1^{x_1}) \to \mathsf{var}^{x_1}$, $x_2 : \mathsf{com}_2^{x_2} \to \mathsf{exp}_1^{x_2} \to \mathsf{var}^{x_2}$, $((\mathsf{com}_{1,1,1} \to \mathsf{exp}_{1,1}) \to \mathsf{var}_1) \to \mathsf{com}$. In the corresponding games, among others, we will thus have moves $run_{1,1}^{x_1}$, $run_2^{x_2}$, $q_1^{x_2}$, $read^{x_2}$, $run_{1,1,1}$ as well as run.

Our representation of game semantics will need to account for justification pointers. Due to the well-bracketing condition, pointers from answers need not be represented explicitly. Moreover, because of the visibility condition, in our case we only need to represent pointers from moves of the shapes $q_{i,j}^x$ and $q_{i,j,k}$. Such pointers must point at some moves of the form q_i^x and $q_{i,j}$ respectively. In order to represent a pointer we are going to place a hat symbol above both the source and target of the pointer, i.e. we shall also use "moves" of the form $\widehat{q_{i,j}^x}, \widehat{q_{i,j,k}}$ (sources) and $\widehat{q_i^x}, \widehat{q_{i,j}}$ (targets) - the latter hatted moves will only be used if the former exist in the sequence. Similarly to [8], we shall represent a single play by *several* sequences of (possibly hatted) moves under the following conditions:

- whenever a target-move of the kind discussed above is played, it may or may not be hatted in the representing sequences of moves,
- if a target-move is hatted, all source-moves pointing at the target move are also hatted,
- if a target-move is not hatted, no source-moves pointing at the move are hatted.

Note that this amounts to representing all pointers for a selection of possible targets, i.e. none, one or more (including all). Because the same $\,\widehat{}\,$-symbol is used to encode each pointer, in a single sequence there may still be ambiguities as to the real target of a pointer. However, among the representing plays we will also have plays representing pointers only to single targets, which suffice to recover pointer-related information. This scheme works correctly because only pointers from P-moves need to be represented and the strategies are deterministic (see the discussion at the end of Sect. 3 in [11]).

Example 2. The classic examples of terms that do need explicit pointers are the Kierstaad terms $\vdash K_1, K_2 : ((\mathsf{com}_{1,1,1} \to \mathsf{com}_{1,1}) \to \mathsf{com}_1) \to \mathsf{com}$ defined by $K_i \equiv \lambda f^{(\mathsf{com} \to \mathsf{com}) \to \mathsf{com}}.f(\lambda x_1^{\mathsf{com}}.f(\lambda x_2^{\mathsf{com}}.x_i))$. To represent the corresponding strategies the following sequences of moves will be used (among others).

- K_1: $q\, q_1\, q_{1,1}\, q_1\, q_{1,1}\, q_{1,1,1}$ (zero targets), $q\, q_1\, \widehat{q_{1,1}}\, q_1\, q_{1,1}\, \widehat{q_{1,1,1}}$ (one target),
  $q\, q_1\, q_{1,1}\, q_1\, \widehat{q_{1,1}}\, q_{1,1,1}$ (one target), $q\, q_1\, \widehat{q_{1,1}}\, q_1\, \widehat{q_{1,1}}\, \widehat{q_{1,1,1}}$ (two targets).
- K_2: $q\, q_1\, q_{1,1}\, q_1\, q_{1,1}\, q_{1,1,1}$ (zero targets), $q\, q_1\, \widehat{q_{1,1}}\, q_1\, q_{1,1}\, q_{1,1,1}$ (one target),
  $q\, q_1\, q_{1,1}\, q_1\, \widehat{q_{1,1}}\, \widehat{q_{1,1,1}}$ (one target), $q\, q_1\, \widehat{q_{1,1}}\, q_1\, \widehat{q_{1,1}}\, \widehat{q_{1,1,1}}$ (two targets).

To represent strategies corresponding to IA_3^2-terms we are going to define an extension of visibly pushdown automata [4]. The alphabet will be divided push-, pop- and no-op-letters corresponding to possibly hatted moves. Additionally, we will use ϵ-transitions that can modify stack content, albeit using a distinguished stack alphabet.

Definition 8. *Let $\Psi = x_1 : \theta_1, \cdots, x_m : \theta_m, \theta$ be a third-order typing template and let $\mathcal{M} = M_{\llbracket \theta_1 \rrbracket} + \cdots + M_{\llbracket \theta_n \rrbracket} + M_{\llbracket \theta \rrbracket}$. Below we shall refer to the various components of $\mathcal{M}$ using subscripts and superscripts according to the labelling scheme introduced earlier, also using q and a for questions and answers respectively. We define the sets $\Sigma_{\mathrm{push}}, \Sigma_{\mathrm{pop}}, \Sigma_{\mathrm{noop}}$ as follows.*

- *$\Sigma_{\mathrm{push}} = \{q_{i,j,k}, \widehat{q_{i,j,k}} \mid q_{i,j,k} \in \mathcal{M}\} \cup \{q_{i,j}^{x_h}, \widehat{q_{i,j}^{x_h}} \mid q_{i,j}^{x_h} \in \mathcal{M}\}$*
- *$\Sigma_{\mathrm{pop}} = \{a_{i,j,k} \mid a_{i,j,k} \in \mathcal{M}\} \cup \{a_{i,j}^{x_h} \mid a_{i,j}^{x_h} \in \mathcal{M}\}$*
- *$\Sigma_{\mathrm{noop}} = (\mathcal{M} \setminus (\Sigma_{\mathrm{push}} \cup \Sigma_{\mathrm{pop}})) \cup \{\widehat{q_{i,j}} \mid q_{i,j,k} \in \mathcal{M}\} \cup \{\widehat{q_i^{x_h}} \mid q_{i,j}^{x_h} \in \mathcal{M}\}$*

Σ_{push} and Σ_{pop} contain exclusively P- and O-moves respectively, while we can find both kinds of moves in Σ_{noop}. Let us write $\Sigma_{\mathrm{noop}}^O, \Sigma_{\mathrm{noop}}^P$ for subsets of Σ_{noop} consisting of O- and P-moves respectively. The states of our automata will be partitioned into states at which O is to move (O-states) and whose at which P should reply (P-states). Push-moves and ϵ-transitions are only available at P-states, while pop-transitions belong to O-states. No-op transitions may be available from any kind of state. Further, to reflect determinacy of strategies, P-states allow for at most one executable outgoing transition, which may be labelled with an element of Σ^P (push or no-op) or be silent (noop, push or pop).

Definition 9. *Let Ψ be a third-order typing template. A Ψ-automaton $\mathcal{A}$ is a tuple $(Q, \Sigma, \Upsilon, \delta, i, F)$ such that*

- *$Q = Q^O + Q^P$ is a finite set of states partitioned into O-states and P-states,*
- *$\Sigma = \Sigma^O + \Sigma^P$ is the finite transition alphabet obtained from Ψ as above, partitioned into O- and P-letters, where $\Sigma^O = \Sigma_{\mathrm{pop}} + \Sigma_{\mathrm{noop}}^O$ and $\Sigma^P = \Sigma_{\mathrm{push}} + \Sigma_{\mathrm{noop}}^P$,*
- *$\Upsilon = \Upsilon^\Sigma + \Upsilon^\epsilon$ is a finite stack alphabet partitioned into Σ-symbols and ϵ-symbols,*
- *$\delta = \delta_{\mathrm{pop}}^O + \delta_{\mathrm{noop}}^O + \delta^P$ is a transition function consisting of $\delta_{\mathrm{pop}}^O : Q^O \times \Sigma_{\mathrm{pop}} \times \Upsilon_\Sigma \rightharpoonup Q^P$, $\delta_{\mathrm{noop}}^O : Q^O \times \Sigma_{\mathrm{noop}}^O \rightharpoonup Q^P$ and $\delta^P : Q^P \rightharpoonup (\Sigma_{\mathrm{push}} \times Q^O \times \Upsilon_\Sigma) + (\Sigma_{\mathrm{noop}}^P \times Q^O) + Q^P + (Q^P \times \Upsilon_\epsilon) + (\Upsilon_\epsilon \rightharpoonup Q^P)$,*
- *$i \in Q^O$ is an initial state, and*
- *$F \subseteq Q^O$ is a set of final states.*

Ψ-automata are to be started in the initial state with empty stack. They will accept by final state, but whenever this happens the stack will be empty anyway. Clearly, they are deterministic. The set of words derived from runs will be referred to as the trace-set of $\mathcal{A}$, written $\mathcal{T}(\mathcal{A})$. We write $\mathcal{L}(\mathcal{A})$ for the subset of $\mathcal{T}(\mathcal{A})$ consisting of accepted words only. The Ψ-automata to be constructed will satisfy an additional run-time property called *P-liveness*: whenever the automaton reaches a configuration $(q, \gamma) \in Q^P \times \Upsilon$ from (i, ϵ), δ^P will provide a unique executable transition.

Remark 2. In what follows we shall reason about IA_3^2 terms by structural induction. The base cases are the constants and identifiers $\Gamma, f : \theta \vdash f : \theta$, where $\mathsf{ord}(\theta) \leq 2$. For inductive cases, we split the rule for application into linear application and contraction.

$$\frac{\Gamma \vdash M : \theta \to \theta' \quad \Delta \vdash N : \theta}{\Gamma, \Delta \vdash MN : \theta'} \; \mathsf{ord}(\theta \to \theta') \leq 2 \qquad \qquad \frac{\Gamma, x : \theta, y : \theta \vdash M : \theta'}{\Gamma, x : \theta \vdash M[x/y] : \theta'}$$

Note that the restriction on $\theta \to \theta'$ is consistent with the fact that the level of redexes cannot exceed 2 and free identifiers have types of order at most 2. The relevant λ-abstraction rule is

$$\frac{\Gamma, x : \theta \vdash M : \theta'}{\Gamma \vdash \lambda x^\theta . M : \theta \to \theta'} \; \mathsf{ord}(\theta \to \theta') \leq 3.$$

This stems from the fact that we are considering IA_3.

Lemma 2. *Let* $x_1 : \theta_1, \cdots, x_m : \theta_m \vdash M : \theta$ *be an* IA_3^2-*term and let* $\sigma = [\![x_1 : \theta_1, \cdots, x_m : \theta_m \vdash M : \theta]\!]$. *There exists a P-live* $(x_1 : \theta_1, \cdots, x_m : \theta_m, \theta)$-*automaton* $\mathcal{A}_M$, *constructible from* M *in exponential time, such that* $\mathcal{T}(\mathcal{A}_M)$ *and* $\mathcal{L}(\mathcal{A}_M)$ *represent respectively* σ *and* $\mathsf{comp}\,(\sigma)$ *(in the sense of our representation scheme).*

Proof. Translation by structural induction in IA_3^2. The base cases corresponding to the special constants can be resolved by constructing finite automata, following the description of the plays in Fig. 3. For free identifiers, automata of a similar kind have already been constructed as part of the translation of normal forms in [11]. We revisit them below to show which moves must be marked to represent pointers.

Let θ be a second-order type. Then $x : \theta \vdash x : \theta$ is interpreted by the identity strategy, which has complete plays of the form $\sum_{q \vdash a} q q^x X a^x a$, where X is given by the context-free grammar below. When writing $\sum_{q \vdash a}$, we mean summing up over all pairs of moves of the indicated shape available in the associated arena $\mathcal{M}$ such that $q \vdash_{\mathcal{M}} a$. Below we also use the condition $\exists q.q_i \vdash q$ to exclude moves of the form q_i that do not enable any other questions (such moves are never targets of justification pointers).

$$X \to \quad \epsilon \quad | \quad \left(\textstyle\sum_{q_i \vdash a_i} q_i^x q_i Y_i^* a_i a_i^x \right) X \quad | \quad \left(\textstyle\sum_{\substack{q_i \vdash a_i \\ \exists q.q_i \vdash q}} \widehat{q_i^x} q_i (\widehat{Y_i})^* a_i a_i^x \right) X$$

$$Y_i \to \quad \textstyle\sum_{q_{i,j} \vdash a_{i,j}} q_{i,j} q_{i,j}^x X a_{i,j}^x a_{i,j} \qquad \widehat{Y_i} \quad \to \quad \textstyle\sum_{q_{i,j} \vdash a_{i,j}} q_{i,j} \widehat{q_{i,j}^x} X a_{i,j}^x a_{i,j}$$

To capture X, we can construct $\mathcal{A}_x$ as in [11], by pushing return addresses when reading $q_{i,j}^x, \widehat{q_{i,j}^x}$ and popping them at $a_{i,j}^x$. Note that this simply corresponds to interpreting recursion in the grammar.

λ-abstraction and contraction are interpreted by renamings of the alphabet, so it remains to consider the hardest case of (linear) application. The rule simply corresponds to composition: in any cartesian-closed category $[\![\Gamma, \Delta \vdash MN : \theta']\!]$ is equal (up to currying) to $[\![\Delta \vdash N : \theta]\!]; [\![\vdash \lambda x^\theta . \lambda \Gamma . M x : \theta \to (\Gamma \to \theta')]\!]$. Note that in our case $\operatorname{ord}(\theta) \leq 1$, i.e. Remark 1 will apply and the strategy for MN can be obtained by running the strategy for M, which will call copies of N, whose interleavings will obey the stack discipline. To model the interaction, let us consider the moves on which the automata will synchronise. Since $\operatorname{ord}(\theta) \leq 1$, the moves that will interact will be of the form q, a, q_i, a_i from N's point of view and $q_k, a_k, q_{k,i}, a_{k,i}$ from M's viewpoint for some k. Thus, given $\mathcal{A}_M = (Q_M, \Sigma_M, \Upsilon_M, i_M, \delta_M, F_M)$ and $\mathcal{A}_N = (Q_N, \Sigma_N, \Upsilon_N, i_N, \delta_N, F_N)$, we let $\mathcal{A}_{MN} = (Q_{MN}, \Sigma_{MN}, \Upsilon_{MN}, i_M, \delta_{MN}, F_M)$, where

$$
\begin{aligned}
Q_{MN} &= Q_M + (Q_M^O \times Q_N) \\
\Sigma_{MN} &= (\Sigma_M \setminus \{q_k, a_k, q_{k,i}, a_{k,i}\}) + (\Sigma_N \setminus \{q_0, a_0, q_1, a_1\}) \\
\Upsilon_{MN}^{\Sigma_{MN}} &= \Upsilon_M + \Upsilon_N \\
\Upsilon_{MN}^{\epsilon} &= \Upsilon_M^{\epsilon} + \Upsilon_N^{\epsilon} + Q_M^O
\end{aligned}
$$

The decomposition of Σ_{MN} into push-, pop- and noop-letters is inherited from the constituent automata. We specify the transition function δ_{MN} below using derivation rules referring to transitions in $\mathcal{A}_M$ and $\mathcal{A}_N$. A push-transition reading x and pushing γ will be labelled with $\xrightarrow{x/\gamma}$. Dually, $\xrightarrow{x,\gamma}$ will represent a pop. $\widetilde{x}$ stands for any transition involving x, where x could also be ϵ.

– $\mathcal{A}_M$'s non-interacting transitions are copied over to $\mathcal{A}_{MN}$.

$$
\frac{s \xrightarrow{\widetilde{x}}_{\mathcal{A}_M} s'}{s \xrightarrow{\widetilde{x}}_{\mathcal{A}_{MN}} s'} \quad x \in (\Sigma_M \setminus \{q_k, a_k, q_{k,i}, a_{k,i}\}) + \{\epsilon\}
$$

– M calls N (left) and N returns from the call (right).

$$
\frac{s \xrightarrow{q_k}_{\mathcal{A}_M} s' \quad i_N \xrightarrow{q}_{\mathcal{A}_N} t}{s \xrightarrow{\epsilon}_{\mathcal{A}_{MN}} (s', t)} \qquad \frac{s' \xrightarrow{a_k}_{\mathcal{A}_M} s'' \quad t \xrightarrow{a}_{\mathcal{A}_N} f \in F_N}{(s', t) \xrightarrow{\epsilon}_{\mathcal{A}_{MN}} s''}
$$

– N's non-interacting transitions are copied over while keeping track of $\mathcal{A}_M$'s state.

$$
\frac{t \xrightarrow{\widetilde{x}}_{\mathcal{A}_N} t'}{(s, t) \xrightarrow{\widetilde{x}}_{\mathcal{A}_{MN}} (s, t')} \quad s \in Q_M^O, \ x \in (\Sigma_N \setminus \{q_0, a_0, q_1, a_1\}) \cup \{\epsilon\}
$$

– N calls its argument (left) and the argument returns (right).

$$
\frac{s \xrightarrow{q_{k,i}}_{\mathcal{A}_M} s' \quad t \xrightarrow{q_i}_{\mathcal{A}_N} t'}{(s, t) \xrightarrow{\epsilon/t'}_{\mathcal{A}_{MN}} s'} \qquad \frac{s' \xrightarrow{a_{k,i}}_{\mathcal{A}_M} s'' \quad t' \xrightarrow{a_i}_{\mathcal{A}_N} t''}{s' \xrightarrow{\epsilon, t'}_{\mathcal{A}_{MN}} (s'', t'')}
$$

Note that the interaction involves moves that are not used to represent pointers, i.e. whenever pointers are represented they remain the same as they were in the original strategies, which is consistent with the definition of composition. The states in Q_{MN} are divided into O- and P-states as follows: $Q_{MN}^O = Q_M^O + (Q_M^O \times Q_N^O)$ and $Q_{MN}^P = Q_M^P + (Q_M^O \times Q_N^P)$. The correctness of the construction follows from the fact that it is a faithful implementation of legal interactions (see, e.g., [7]), as discussed in Remark 1. P-liveness follows from the fact the constituent strategies are P-live and that the construction simulates interaction sequences, including infinite chattering.   □

Our next step will be to analyse the shape of reachable configurations of $\mathcal{A}_M$. We aim to understand how many elements of Υ_ϵ can occur consecutively on the stack.

Definition 10. *Suppose $(q, \gamma) \in Q \times (\Upsilon_\Sigma \cup \Upsilon_\epsilon)^*$. The ϵ-density of γ is defined to be the length of the longest segment in γ consisting solely of consecutive elements from Υ_ϵ.*

While the size of stacks corresponding to IA_3^2 terms is unbounded (consider, for instance, $x : \theta \vdash x : \theta$ with $\theta = (\mathsf{com} \to \mathsf{com}) \to \mathsf{com}$), ϵ-density turns out to be bounded. We shall prove that it is exponential with respect to the size of the original term. This will be crucial to obtaining our upper bound. The main obstacle to proving this fact is the case of composition MN. As discussed in Remark 1, M "stacks up" copies of N and we would first like to obtain a bound on the number of nested calls to N that are not separated by a move from Σ_{push} (such moves block the growth of ϵ-density). For this purpose, we go back to plays and analyse sequences in which the relevant questions are pending: a *pending question* is one that has been played but remains unanswered. Observe that sequences of pending questions are always alternating. We will not be interested in the specific questions but only in their kinds, as specified by the table below.

Question	q	q_i, q^x	$q_{i,j}, q_i^x$	$q_{i,j,k}, q_{i,j}^x$
Kind	0	1	2	3

Definition 11. *Let s be a play. We define $\mathsf{pend}(s)$ to be the sequence from $\{0, 1, 2, 3\}^*$ obtained from s by restricting it to pending questions and replacing each question with the number corresponding to its kind.*

Thus, any non-empty even-length play s, $\mathsf{pend}(s)$ will match the expression $0(12 + 32)^*(1 + 3)$. We say that the (12)-*potential* of s is equal to k if k is the largest k such that $\mathsf{pend}(s) = \cdots (12)^k \cdots$. In other words, the (12)-potential of a play is the length of the longest segment $(12)^k$ in $\mathsf{pend}(s)$.

Lemma 3. *Let $\Gamma \vdash M : \theta$ be an IA_3^2-term. Then the (12)-potential of any play in $[\![\Gamma \vdash M]\!]$ is bounded and the bound b_M is exponential in the size of M.*

Lemma 3 is a key technical result needed to establish the following boundedness property that is satisfied by automata representing IA_3^2-terms.

Lemma 4. *Let $\Gamma \vdash M : \theta$ be an IA_3^2-term and consider $\mathcal{A}_M$ constructed in Lemma 2. There exists a bound d_M, exponential in the size of M, such that the ϵ-density of configurations reachable by $\mathcal{A}_M$ is bounded by d_M.*

Next we derive a bound on plays witnessing failure of contextual approxima-tion in IA_3^2. Consider IA_3^2-terms $\Gamma \vdash M_1, M_2 : \theta$ and let $\sigma_i = [\![\Gamma \vdash M_i : \theta]\!]$ for $i = 1, 2$. Given a play, let its *height* be the maximum number of pending ques-tions from Σ_{push} occurring in any of its prefixes. Note that, for plays from σ_i, this will be exactly the maximum number of symbols from Υ_Σ that will appear on the stack of $\mathcal{A}_{M_i}$ at any point of its computation.

Lemma 5. *There exists a polynomial p such that if $\mathsf{comp}\,\sigma_1 \setminus \mathsf{comp}\,\sigma_2$ is not empty then it contains a play of height $p(n_1 + n_2)$, where n_1, n_2 are the numbers of states in $\mathcal{A}_{M_1}$ and $\mathcal{A}_{M_2}$ respectively.*

Theorem 2. *For IA_3^2-terms $\Gamma \vdash M_1, M_2 : \theta$, one can decide $\Gamma \vdash M_1 \precsim M_2$ in exponential space.*

Proof. Note that this boils down to testing emptiness of $\mathsf{comp}\,\sigma_1 \setminus \mathsf{comp}\,\sigma_2$. By Lemma 5, it suffices to guess a play whose height is polynomial in the size of $\mathcal{A}_{M_1}$, $\mathcal{A}_{M_2}$, i.e. exponential with respect to term size. Moreover, by Lemma 4, the ϵ-density of the corresponding configurations of $\mathcal{A}_{M_1}$ and $\mathcal{A}_{M_2}$ will also be exponential. Thus, in order to check whether a candidate s is accepted by $\mathcal{A}_{M_1}$ and rejected by $\mathcal{A}_{M_2}$, we will only need to consider stacks of exponential size wrt M_1, M_2. Consequently, the guess can be performed on the fly and verified in exponential space. Because NEXPSPACE=EXPSPACE, the result follows.

Corollary 1. *For $k \geq 2$, contextual approximation of IA_3^k-terms is in $(k-1)$-EXPSPACE.*

5 Lower Bounds

Here we show that contextual approximation of IA_1^k-terms is $(k-1)$-EXPSPACE-hard for $k \geq 2$. Note that this matches the upper bound shown for IA_3^k-terms and will allow us to conclude that contextual approximation in $\mathsf{IA}_1^k, \mathsf{IA}_2^k$ and IA_3^k is $(k-1)$-EXPSPACE-complete. Our hardness results will rely on nesting of function calls and iteration afforded by higher-order types. Below we introduce the special types and terms to be used.

Let $k, n \in \mathbb{N}$. Define the type $\overline{n}$ by $\overline{0} = \mathsf{com}$ and $\overline{n+1} = \overline{n} \to \overline{n}$. Note that $\mathsf{ord}(\overline{n}) = n$. Also, let $\mathsf{Exp}(k, n)$ be defined by $\mathsf{Exp}(0, n) = n$ and $\mathsf{Exp}(k+1, n) = 2^{\mathsf{Exp}(k,n)}$. Given $k \geq 2$, consider the term $\mathsf{twice}_k = \lambda x^{\overline{k-1}}.\lambda y^{\overline{k-2}}.x(xy) : \overline{k}$.

Definition 12. *Let $k \geq 2$. Writing $M^n N$ as shorthand for $\underbrace{M(M \cdots (M\,N) \cdots)}_{n}$,*

let us define a family of terms $\{\mathsf{nest}_{n,k}\}$ with $f : \overline{1}, x : \overline{0} \vdash \mathsf{nest}_{n,k} : \overline{0}$ by taking $\mathsf{nest}_{n,k} \equiv (\mathsf{twice}_k^n\, g_{k-1})g_{k-2} \cdots g_1 g_0$, where $g_0 \equiv x$, $g_1 \equiv f$ and $g_i \equiv \mathsf{twice}_i$ for $i > 1$.

The terms have several desirable properties, summarised below.

Lemma 6. *Let $k \geq 2$. $\mathsf{nest}_{n,k}$ belongs to IA_2^k, has polynomial size in n and is β-reducible to $f^{\mathsf{Exp}(k-1,n)}x$.*

Note that the nested applications of f in $f^{\mathsf{Exp}(k-1,n)}x$ are akin to generating a stack of height $\mathsf{Exp}(k-1,n)$. We shall exploit this in our encodings. Note that, by substituting $\lambda c^{\mathsf{com}}.c;c$ for f in $f^{\mathsf{Exp}(k-1,n)}x$, we obtain a term that *iterates* x as many as $\mathsf{Exp}(k,n)$ times, i.e. $\mathsf{Exp}(k-1,n)$-fold nesting is used to simulate $\mathsf{Exp}(k,n)$-fold iteration.

Simulating Turing Machines. Let w be an input word. Let $n = |w|$, $l = \mathsf{Exp}(k-1,n)$ and $N = \mathsf{Exp}(k,n)$. We shall consider a deterministic Turing machine T running in $SPACE(l)$ and $TIME(N)$ and simulate T's behaviour on w. This suffices to establish $SPACE(l)$-hardness.

We start off with the description of an encoding scheme for configurations of T. We shall represent them as strings of length l over an alphabet Σ_T, to be specified later. We shall write Config_T for the subset of $(\Sigma_T)^l$ corresponding to configurations. The encoding of the initial configuration will be denoted by c_{init} and we shall write Accept_T for the set of representations of accepting configurations. Given $c \in \mathsf{Config}_T$, we write $\mathsf{next}(c)$ for the representation of the successor of c according to T's transition function. Let us introduce a number of auxiliary languages that will play an important role in the simulation. We write c^R for the reverse of c.

Definition 13. *Let $\Sigma_T^{\#} = \Sigma_T + \{\#\}$. We define the languages $\mathcal{L}_0, \mathcal{L}_1 \subseteq (\Sigma_T)^*$ and $\mathcal{L}_2, \mathcal{L}_3, \mathcal{L}_4 \subseteq (\Sigma_T^{\#})^*$ as follows.*

$$\mathcal{L}_0 = \{c_{init}\} \qquad \mathcal{L}_1 = \mathsf{Accept}_T \qquad \mathcal{L}_2 = \{c^R \,\#\, \mathsf{next}(c) \mid c \in \mathsf{Config}_T\}$$
$$\mathcal{L}_3 = \{c \,\#\, \mathsf{next}(c)^R \mid c \in \mathsf{Config}_T\} \qquad \mathcal{L}_4 = \{c \,\#\, d^R \mid c \in \mathsf{Config}_T, d \neq \mathsf{next}(c)\}$$

Lemma 7. *There exists a representation scheme for configurations of T such that Σ_T is polynomial in the size of T, w and the following properties hold.*

1. *There exist deterministic finite-state automata $\mathcal{A}_0, \mathcal{A}_1$, constructible from T, w in polynomial time, such that $L(\mathcal{A}_0) \cap (\Sigma_T)^l = \mathcal{L}_0$ and $L(\mathcal{A}_1) \cap (\Sigma_T)^l = \mathcal{L}_1$.*
2. *For any $i = 2, 3, 4$, there exists a deterministic pushdown automaton $\mathcal{A}_i$, constructible from T, w in polynomial time, such that $L(\mathcal{A}_i) \cap ((\Sigma_T)^l \#(\Sigma_T)^l) = \mathcal{L}_i$. Moreover, transitions of the automata are given by three transition functions $\delta_{\mathrm{push}} : Q^{\mathrm{push}} \times \Sigma_T \to Q^{\mathrm{push}} \times \Upsilon$, $\delta_{\mathrm{noop}} : Q^{\mathrm{push}} \times \{\#\} \to Q^{\mathrm{pop}}$ and $\delta_{\mathrm{pop}} : Q^{\mathrm{pop}} \times \Sigma_T \times \Upsilon \to Q^{\mathrm{pop}}$, the initial state belongs to Q^{push} and the automaton accepts by final state. I.e., the automata will process elements of $(\Sigma_T)^l \#(\Sigma_T)^l$ by performing push-moves first, then a noop move for $\#$ and, finally, pop-moves.*

Remark 3. Note that in the above lemma we had to use intersection with $(\Sigma_T)^l$ (resp. $(\Sigma_T)^l \#(\Sigma_T)^l$) to state the correctness conditions with respect to Config_T, because the automata will not be able to count up to l. However, in our argument, we are going to use the nesting power of IA_1^k to run their transition functions for suitably many steps (l and $2l+1$ respectively).

The significance of the languages $\mathcal{L}_0, \mathcal{L}_1, \mathcal{L}_2, \mathcal{L}_3, \mathcal{L}_4$ stems from the fact that they are building blocks of two other languages, $\mathcal{L}_5$ and $\mathcal{L}_6$, which are closely related to the acceptance of w by T.

Lemma 8. *Consider the languages* $\mathcal{L}_5, \mathcal{L}_6 \subseteq (\Sigma_T^\#)^*$ *defined by* $\mathcal{L}_5 = \{c_{init} \# c_1^R \# d_1 \# \cdots c_N^R \# d_N \# f^R \mid c_j \in \mathsf{Config}_T, f \in \mathsf{Accept}_T, \forall_i \mathsf{next}(c_i) = d_i\}$ *and* $\mathcal{L}_6 = \{c_1 \# d_1^R \# \cdots c_N \# d_N^R \mid c_j \in \mathsf{Config}_T, \exists_i \mathsf{next}(c_i) \neq d_i\}$. *Then* T *accepts* w *if and only if* $\mathcal{L}_5 \not\subseteq \mathcal{L}_6$.

Proof. Note that if T accepts w then the sequence of (representations of the) configurations belonging to the accepting run, in which every other representation is reversed, gives rise to a word that belongs to $\mathcal{L}_5$ but not to $\mathcal{L}_6$.

Conversely, if a word $c_{init} \# c_1^R \# d_1 \# \cdots c_N^R \# d_N \# f^R \in \mathcal{L}_5$ does not belong to $\mathcal{L}_6$ then $c_1 = \mathsf{next}(c_{init})$, $c_{i+1} = \mathsf{next}(d_i)$ $(i = 1, \cdots, N-1)$ and $f = \mathsf{next}(d_N)$. Thus, the word actually represents an accepting run on w. □

Our hardness argument consists in translating the above lemma inside IA_1^k. To that end, we shall show how to capture $\mathcal{L}_2, \mathcal{L}_3, \mathcal{L}_4$ and, ultimately, $\mathcal{L}_5$ and $\mathcal{L}_6$, using IA_1^k terms. We shall work under the assumption that $\Sigma_T^\# = \{0, \cdots, max\}$. Note, though, that the results can be adapted to any $max > 0$ by encoding $\Sigma_T^\#$ as sequences of exp-values. Similarly, using multiple exp-valued variables, IA-terms can store values that are bigger than max. We shall take advantage of such storage implicitly (e.g. for state values or stack elements), but the number of extra variables needed for this purpose will remain polynomial.

Definition 14. *We shall say that an* IA*-term* $z : \mathsf{exp} \vdash M : \mathsf{com}$ *captures* $L \subseteq (\Sigma_T^\#)^*$ *if* $\mathsf{comp}(\llbracket z \vdash M \rrbracket) = \{run\, q^z\, (a_1)^z\, q^z\, (a_2)^z \cdots q^z\, (a_k)^z\, done \mid a_1 a_2 \cdots a_k \in L\}$.

Example 3. The term $z : \mathsf{exp} \vdash M_\# : \mathsf{com}$, where $M_\# \equiv$ if $z = \#$ then **skip** else Ω, captures $\{\#\}$. In our constructions we often write [condition] to stand in for the assertion if (condition) then **skip** else Ω.

Lemma 9. *There exist* IA_1^k-*terms* $z : \mathsf{exp} \vdash M_0, M_1 : \mathsf{com}$, *constructible from* T, w *in polynomial time, capturing* $\mathcal{L}_0, \mathcal{L}_1$ *respectively.*

Lemma 10. *There exists an* IA_1^k-*term* $z : \mathsf{exp} \vdash M_2 : \mathsf{com}$, *constructible from* T, w *in polynomial time, which captures* $\mathcal{L}_2$.

Thanks to the last two lemmas we are now ready to capture $\mathcal{L}_5$.

Lemma 11. *There exists an* IA_1^k-*term* $z : \mathsf{exp} \vdash M_5 : \mathsf{com}$, *constructible in polynomial time from* T, w, *which captures* $\mathcal{L}_5$.

Proof. Note that a word from $\mathcal{L}_5$ contains $N = \mathsf{Exp}(k, n)$ segments from $\mathcal{L}_2$. To account for that, it suffices to use N copies of $M_\#; M_2$. However, for a polynomial-time reduction, we need to do that succinctly. Recall that $\mathsf{nest}_{n,k}$ gives us l-fold nesting of functions, where $l = \mathsf{Exp}(k-1, n)$. Consequently, N-fold iteration can be achieved by l-fold nesting of $\lambda c^{\mathsf{com}}.c; c$. Thus, we can take

$$M_5 \equiv M_0; \mathsf{nest}_{n,k}[\lambda c^{\mathsf{com}}.c; c/f, (M_\#; M_2)/x]; M_\#; M_1.$$

To complete the hardness argument (by restating Lemma 8 using IA_1^k terms), we also need to capture $\mathcal{L}_6$. Because of the existential clause in its definition we need to use a slightly different capture scheme.

Lemma 12. *There exists an* IA_1^k-*term* $z : \mathsf{exp}, FLAG : \mathsf{var} \vdash M_6' : \mathsf{com}$, *constructible in polynomial time from* T, w, *such that* $\mathsf{comp}\,([\![z, FLAG \vdash M_6']\!]) = \{run\,q^z\,(a_1)^z\,q^z\,(a_2)^z \cdots q^z\,(a_k)^z\,done \mid a_1 a_2 \cdots a_k \;\in\; \mathcal{L}_3\} \cup \{run\,q^z\,(a_1)^z\,q^z\,(a_2)^z \cdots q^z\,(a_k)^z\,write(1)^{FLAG}\,ok^{FLAG}\,done \mid a_1 a_2 \cdots a_k \in \mathcal{L}_4\}.$

Lemma 13. *There exists an* IA_1^k-*term* $z : \mathsf{exp} \vdash M_6 : \mathsf{com}$, *constructible in polynomial time from* T, w, *which captures* $\mathcal{L}_6$.

Proof. It suffices to run M_6' for $N + 1$ steps and check whether the flag was set:

$$M_6 \equiv \mathbf{new}\; FLAG\; \mathbf{in}\; (FLAG := 0;\, \mathsf{nest}_{n,k}[\lambda c^{\mathsf{com}}.c;\, c/f,\, (M_6';M_\#)/x];\, M_6';\, [!FLAG = 1])$$

Theorem 3. *Contextual approximation between* IA_1^k *terms is* $(k - 1)$-*EXPSPACE-hard.*

Proof. By Lemmas 8, 11 and 13, for any Turing machine T running in $SPACE(\mathsf{Exp}(k-1, n))$ and $TIME(\mathsf{Exp}(k, n))$ and an input word w, there exist IA_1^k-terms $x : \mathsf{exp} \vdash M_5, M_6$, constructible from T, w in polynomial time, such that T accepts w if and only if M_5 does not approximate M_6. This implies $(k - 1)$-EXPSPACE-hardness. □

6 Conclusion

We have shown that contextual approximation in $\mathsf{IA}_1^k, \mathsf{IA}_2^k, \mathsf{IA}_3^k$ is $(k - 1)$-EXPSPACE-complete. The algorithm that leads to these optimal bounds reduces terms to IA_3^2 (with possibly $(k - 2)$-fold exponential blow-up) and we use a dedicated EXPSPACE procedure for IA_3^2 exploiting game semantics and decision procedures for a special kind of pushdown automata. In particular, the results show that untamed β-reduction would yield suboptimal bounds, but selective β-reduction of redexes up to level 3 does not jeopardise complexity. The bounds above apply to open higher-order terms, i.e. IA_i $(i > 0)$ terms, for which the problem of contextual approximation is difficult to attack due to universal quantification over contexts.

Our work also implies bounds for contextual approximation of IA_0^k terms, i.e. closed terms of base type. Conceptually, this case is much easier, because it boils down to testing termination. In this case our techniques can be employed to obtain better upper bounds for IA_0^k than those for IA_1^k $((k - 1)$-EXPSPACE). For a start, like for IA_1^k, we can reduce IA_0^k terms (at $(k - 2)$-fold exponential cost) to IA_0^2. Then termination in IA_0^2 can be checked in exponential *time* by constructing pushdown automata via Lemma 2 and testing them for emptiness (rather than inclusion). Since emptiness testing of pushdown automata can be performed in polynomial time and the automata construction in Lemma 2 costs a single exponential, this yields an EXPTIME upper bound for termination in IA_0^2. Consequently, termination in IA_0^k $(k \geq 2)$ can be placed in $(k - 1)$-EXPTIME, though it is not clear to us whether this bound is optimal. For completeness, let us just mention that termination in IA_0^0 and IA_0^1 is PSPACE-complete due to presence of variables and looping (membership follows from the corresponding upper. bounds for contextual equivalence).

Another avenue for future work is $\mathsf{IA}_1^k, \mathsf{IA}_2^k, \mathsf{IA}_3^k$ contextual equivalence. Of course, our upper bounds for approximation also apply to contextual equivalence, which amounts to two approximation checks. However, one might expect better bounds in this case given that our hardness argument leans heavily on testing inclusion.

Finally, one should investigate how our results can be adapted to the call-by-value setting. An educated guess would be that, in the analogous fragment of ML, the reduction of redexes up to order 3 (rather than 2) should be suppressed in order to obtain accurate complexity estimates.

References

1. Abramsky, S., McCusker, G.: Linearity, sharing, state: a fully abstract game semantics for Idealized Algol with active expressions. In: O'Hearn, P.W., Tennent, R.D. (eds.) Algol-Like Languages, pp. 297–329. Birkhaüser, Boston (1997)
2. Abramsky, S., McCusker, G.: Game semantics. In: Schwichtenberg, H., Berger, U. (eds.) Logic and Computation, Proceedings of the 1997 Marktoberdorf Summer School. Springer-Verlag (1998)
3. Ahmed, A., Dreyer, D., Rossberg, A.: State-dependent representation independence.In: Proceedings of POPL, pp. 340–353. ACM (2009)
4. Alur, R., Madhusudan, P.: Visibly pushdown languages. In: Proceedings of STOC 2004, pp. 202–211 (2004)
5. Colvin, R., Hayes, I.J., Strooper, P.A.: Calculating modules in contextual logic program refinement. Theory Pract. Logic Program. **8**(01), 1–31 (2008)
6. Ghica, D.R., McCusker, G.: Reasoning about idealized ALGOL using regular languages. In: Welzl, E., Montanari, U., Rolim, J.D.P. (eds.) ICALP 2000. LNCS, vol. 1853, p. 103. Springer, Heidelberg (2000)
7. Harmer, R.: Games and full abstraction for non-deterministic languages. Ph.D. thesis, University of London (2000)
8. Hopkins, D., Murawski, A.S., Ong, C.-H.L.: A fragment of ML decidable by visibly pushdown automata. In: Aceto, L., Henzinger, M., Sgall, J. (eds.) ICALP 2011, Part II. LNCS, vol. 6756, pp. 149–161. Springer, Heidelberg (2011)
9. Murawski, A.S.: On program equivalence in languages with ground-type references. In: Proceedings of IEEE Symposium on Logic in Computer Science, pp. 108–117. Computer Society Press (2003)
10. Murawski, A.S.: Games for complexity of second-order call-by-name programs. Theor. Comput. Sci. **343**(1/2), 207–236 (2005)
11. Murawski, A.S., Walukiewicz, I.: Third-order idealized algol with iteration is decidable. In: Sassone, V. (ed.) FOSSACS 2005. LNCS, vol. 3441, pp. 202–218. Springer, Heidelberg (2005)
12. Pitts, A.M.: Operational semantics and program equivalence. In: Barthe, G., Dybjer, P., Pinto, L., Saraiva, J. (eds.) APPSEM 2000. LNCS, vol. 2395, pp. 378–412. Springer, Heidelberg (2002)

13. Reynolds, J.C.: The essence of Algol. In: de Bakker, J.W., van Vliet, J.C. (eds.) Algorithmic Languages, pp. 345–372. North Holland, Amsterdam (1978)
14. Turon, A., Dreyer, D., Birkedal, L.: Unifying refinement and hoare-style reasoning in a logic for higher-order concurrency. In: Proceedings of ICFP 2013, pp. 377–390 (2013)

A Theory of Slicing for Probabilistic Control Flow Graphs

Torben Amtoft[1]([⊠]) and Anindya Banerjee[2]

[1] Kansas State University, Manhattan, KS, USA
tamtoft@ksu.edu
[2] IMDEA Software Institute, Madrid, Spain
anindya.banerjee@imdea.org

Abstract. We present a theory for slicing probabilistic imperative programs—containing random assignment and "observe" statements—represented as control flow graphs whose nodes transform probability distributions. We show that such a representation allows direct adaptation of standard machinery such as data and control dependence, postdominators, relevant variables, *etc.* to the probabilistic setting. We separate the specification of slicing from its implementation: first we develop syntactic conditions that a slice must satisfy; next we prove that any such slice is semantically correct; finally we give an algorithm to compute the least slice. A key feature of our syntactic conditions is that they involve two disjoint slices such that the variables of one slice are *probabilistically independent* of the variables of the other. This leads directly to a proof of correctness of probabilistic slicing.

1 Introduction

The task of program slicing [12,14] is to remove the parts of a program that are irrelevant in a given context. This paper addresses slicing of probabilistic imperative programs which, in addition to the usual control structures, contain "random assignment" and "observe" statements. The former assign random values from a given distribution to variables. The latter remove undesirable combinations of values, a feature which can be used to bias the variables according to real world observations. The excellent survey by Gordon *et al.* [6] depicts many applications of probabilistic programs.

Program slicing of deterministic imperative programs is increasingly well understood [1,3,5,10,11]. A basic notion is that if the slice contains a program point which depends on some other program points then these also should be included in the slice; here "depends" typically encompasses data dependence and control dependence. However, Hur *et al.* [7] recently demonstrated that in the presence of random assignments and observations, standard notions of data and

---

A. Banerjee—Research supported by the US National Science Foundation (NSF). Any opinion, findings, and conclusions or recommendations expressed in this material are those of the authors and do not necessarily reflect the views of NSF.

© Springer-Verlag Berlin Heidelberg 2016
B. Jacobs and C. Löding (Eds.): FOSSACS 2016, LNCS 9634, pp. 180–196, 2016.
DOI: 10.1007/978-3-662-49630-5_11

control dependence no longer suffice for semantically correct (backward) slicing. They develop a denotational framework in which they prove correct an algorithm for program slicing. In contrast, this paper shows how *classical notions of dependence can be extended to give a semantic foundation for the (backward) slicing of probabilistic programs.* The paper's key contributions are:

- A formulation of probabilistic slicing in terms of probabilistic control flow graphs (Sect. 3) that allows direct adaptation of standard machinery such as data and control dependence, postdominators, relevant variables, *etc.* to the probabilistic setting. We also provide a novel operational semantics of probabilistic control flow graphs (Sect. 4): written $(v, D) \Rightarrow (v', D')$, the semantics states that as "control" moves from node v to node v' in the CFG, the probability distribution D transforms to distribution D'.
- Syntactic conditions for correctness (Sect. 5) that in a non-trivial way extend classical work on program slicing [5], and whose key feature is that they involve *two* disjoint slices; in order for the first to be a correct final result of slicing, the other must contain any "observe" nodes sliced away and all nodes on which they depend. We show that the variables of one slice are *probabilistically independent* of the variables of the other, and this leads directly to the correctness of probabilistic slicing (Sect. 6).
- An algorithm, with running time at most cubic in the size of the program, that computes the best possible slice (Sect. 7) in that it is contained in any other (syntactic) slice of the program.

Our approach separates the specification of slicing from algorithms to compute the best possible slice. The former is concerned with defining what is a correct syntactic slice, such that the behavior of the sliced program is equivalent to that of the original. The latter is concerned with how to compute the best possible syntactic slice; this slice is automatically a semantically correct slice—no separate proof is necessary.

A program's behavior is its final probability distribution; we demand equality modulo a constant factor so as to allow the removal of "observe" statements that do not introduce any bias in the final distribution. This will be the case if the variables tested by "observe" statements are independent, in the sense of probability theory, of the variables relevant for the final value.

Full proofs of all results appear in the accompanying technical report [2].

2   Motivating Examples

Probabilistic Programs. Whereas in deterministic languages, a variable has only one value at a given time, we consider a language where a variable may have many different values at a given time, each with a certain probability. (Determinism is a special case where one value has probability one, and all others have probability zero.) We assume, to keep our development simple, that each possible value is an integer. A more general development, somewhat orthogonal to the aims of this paper, would allow real numbers and would require us to employ measure theory (as explained in [9]); we conjecture that much will extend naturally (with summations becoming integrals).

Similarly to [6], probabilities are introduced by the construct $x := \mathtt{Random}(\psi)$ which assigns to variable x a value with probability given by the random distribution ψ which in our setting is a mapping from $\mathbb{Z}$ (the set of integers) to $[0,1]$ such that $\sum_{z \in \mathbb{Z}} \psi(z) = 1$. A program phrase transforms a distribution into another distribution, where a distribution assigns a probability to each possible store. This was first formalized by Kozen [8] in a denotational setting. As also in [6], we shall use the construct $\mathtt{Observe}(B)$ to "filter out" values which do not satisfy the boolean expression B. That is, the resulting distribution assigns zero probability to all stores not satisfying B, while stores satisfying B keep their probability.

The Examples. Slicing amounts to picking a set Q of "program points" (satisfying certain conditions as we shall soon discuss) and then removing nodes not in Q (as we shall formalize in Sect. 4.6). The examples all use a random distribution ψ_4 over $\{0,1,2,3\}$ where $\psi_4(0) = \psi_4(1) = \psi_4(2) = \psi_4(3) = \frac{1}{4}$ whereas $\psi_4(i) = 0$ for $i \notin \{0,1,2,3\}$. The examples all consider whether it is correct to let Q contain exactly $x := \mathtt{Random}(\psi_4)$ and $\mathtt{Return}(x)$, and thus slice into a program P_x with straightforward semantics: after execution, the probability of each possible store is given by the distribution Δ' defined as $\Delta'(\{x \mapsto i\}) = \frac{1}{4}$ if $i \in \{0,1,2,3\}$; otherwise $\Delta'(\{x \mapsto i\}) = 0$.

Example 1. *Consider the program $P_1 \overset{def}{=} 1: x := \mathtt{Random}(\psi_4); 2: y := \mathtt{Random}(\psi_4); 3: \mathtt{Observe}(y \geq 2); 4: \mathtt{Return}(x)$. The distribution produced by the first two assignments will assign probability $\dfrac{1}{4} \cdot \dfrac{1}{4} = \dfrac{1}{16}$ to each possible store $\{x \mapsto i, y \mapsto j\}$ with $i,j \in \{0,1,2,3\}$. In the final distribution D_1, a store $\{x \mapsto i, y \mapsto j\}$ with $j < 2$ is impossible, and for each $i \in \{0,1,2,3\}$ there are thus only two possible stores that associate x with i: the store $\{x \mapsto i, y \mapsto 2\}$, and the store $\{x \mapsto i, y \mapsto 3\}$. Restricting to the variable x that is ultimately returned,*

$$D_1(\{x \mapsto i\}) = \sum_{j=2}^{3} D_1(\{x \mapsto i, y \mapsto j\}) = \frac{1}{16} + \frac{1}{16} = \frac{1}{8}$$

if $i \in \{0,1,2,3\}$ (otherwise, $D_1(\{x \mapsto i\}) = 0$). We see that the probabilities in D_1 do not add up to 1 which reflects that the purpose of an $\mathtt{Observe}$ statement is to cause undesired parts of the "local" distribution to "disappear" (which may give certain branches more relative weight than other branches). We also see that D_1 equals Δ' except for a constant factor: $D_1 = 0.5 \cdot \Delta'$. That is, Δ' gives the same relative distribution over the values of x as D_1 does. (An alternative way of phrasing this is that "normalizing" the "global" distribution, as done in [6], gives the same result for P_x as for P_1.) We shall therefore say that P_x is a correct slice of P_1.

Thus the $\mathtt{Observe}$ statement is irrelevant to the final relative distribution of x. This is because y and x are *independent* in D_1, as formalized in Definition 3.

Example 2. *Consider the program* $P_2 \stackrel{def}{=}$ *1:* $x := \mathtt{Random}(\psi_4)$*; 2:* $y :=$ $\mathtt{Random}(\psi_4)$*; 3:* $\mathtt{Observe}(x+y \geq 5)$*; 4:* $\mathtt{Return}(x)$*. Here the final distribution* D_2 *allows only 3 stores:* $\{x \mapsto 2,\ y \mapsto 3\})$*,* $\{x \mapsto 3,\ y \mapsto 2\})$ *and* $\{x \mapsto 3,\ y \mapsto 3\})$*, all with probability* $\dfrac{1}{16}$*, and hence* $D_2(\{x \mapsto 2\}) = \dfrac{1}{16}$ *and* $D_2(\{x \mapsto 3\}) = \dfrac{1}{8}$*. Thus the program is biased towards high values of* x*; in particular we cannot write* D_2 *in the form* $c\Delta'$*. Hence it is* incorrect *to slice* P_2 *into* P_x*.*

In this example, x and y are *not* independent in D_2; this is as expected since the $\mathtt{Observe}$ statement in P_2 depends on something (the assignment to x) on which the returned variable x also depends.

Example 3. *Consider the program* $P_3 \stackrel{def}{=} x := \mathtt{Random}(\psi_4); (\mathbf{if}\ x \geq 2\ \ z :=$ $\mathtt{Random}(\psi_4);\ \mathtt{Observe}(z \geq 3)); \mathtt{Return}(x)$*.* P_3 *is biased towards returning low values of* x*, with the final distribution* D_3 *given by* $D_3(\{x \mapsto i\}) = \frac{1}{4}$ *when* $i \in \{0,1\}$ *and* $D_3(\{x \mapsto i\}) = D_3(\{x \mapsto i,\ z \mapsto 3\}) = \frac{1}{16}$ *when* $i \in \{2,3\}$*. Hence it is* incorrect *to slice* P_3 *into* P_x*.*

The $\mathtt{Observe}$ statement cannot be removed: it is *control dependent* on the assignment to x, on which the returned x also depends.

The discussion so far suggests the following tentative correctness condition for the set Q picked by slicing:

– Q is "closed under dependency", *i.e.*, if a program point in Q depends on another program point then that program point also belongs to Q;
– Q is part of a "slicing pair": any $\mathtt{Observe}$ statement that is sliced away belongs to a set Q_0 that is also closed under dependency and is disjoint from Q.

The above condition will be made precise in Definition 9 (Sect. 5) which contains a further requirement, necessary since an $\mathtt{Observe}$ statement may be encoded as a potentially non-terminating loop, as the next example illustrates.

Example 4. *Consider the program* $P_4 \stackrel{def}{=} x := \mathtt{Random}(\psi_4);\ y := \mathtt{Random}(\psi_4);$ $(\mathbf{if}\ x \geq 2\ \ (\mathbf{while}\ y \leq 5\ \mathbf{do}\ y := E)); \mathtt{Return}(x)\ \ where\ E\ is\ an\ arithmetic$ *expression. If* E *is "*$y+1$*" then the loop terminates and* y*'s final value is 6. In the resulting distribution* D'*, for* $i \in \{0,1,2,3\}$ *we have* $D'(\{x \mapsto i\}) = D'(\{x \mapsto i,\ y \mapsto 6\}) = \frac{1}{4} = \Delta'(\{x \mapsto i\})$*. Thus it is correct to slice* P_4 *into* P_x*.*

*   *But if* E *is "*$y-1$*" then the program will not terminate when* $x \geq 2$ *(and hence the conditional encodes* $\mathtt{Observe}(x < 2)$*). Thus the resulting distribution* D_4 *is given by* $D_4(\{x \mapsto i\}) = \frac{1}{4}$ *when* $i \in \{0,1\}$ *and* $D_4(\{x \mapsto i\}) = 0$ *when* $i \notin \{0,1\}$*. Thus it is incorrect to slice* P_4 *into* P_x*. Indeed, Definition 9 rules out such a slicing.*

3   Control Flow Graphs

This section precisely defines the kind of CFGs we consider, as well as some key concepts that are mostly standard (see, *e.g.*, [3,10]). However, we also introduce a notion (Definition 1) specific to our approach.

Figure 1 depicts, with the nodes numbered, the CFGs corresponding to the programs P_3 and P_4 from Examples 3 and 4. We see that a node can be labeled with an assignment $x := E$ (x a program variable and E an arithmetic expression), with a random assignment $x := \text{Random}(\psi)$ (we shall assume that the probability distribution ψ contains no program variables though it would be straightforward to allow it as in [7]), with $\text{Observe}(B)$ (B is a boolean expression), or (though not part of these examples) with Skip. Also, there are branching nodes with *two* outgoing edges. Finally, there is a unique End node $\text{Return}(x)$ to which there must be a path from all other nodes but which has no outgoing edges, and a special node Start (which may have any label and is numbered 1 in the examples) from which there is a path to all other nodes.

We let $Def(v)$ be the variable occurring on the left hand side if v is a (random) assignment, and let $Use(v)$ be the variables occurring in the right hand side of an assignment, in a boolean expression used in an Observe node or in a branching node, or as the sole variable in a End node. We demand that all variables be defined before they are used.

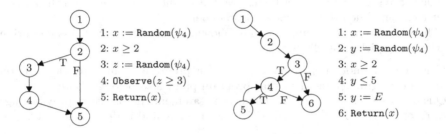

Fig. 1. The CFGs for P_3 (left) and P_4 (right) from Examples 3 and 4.

We say that v_1 **postdominates** v if v_1 occurs on all paths from v to End; if also $v_1 \neq v$, v_1 is a **proper postdominator** of v. And we say that v_1 is the **first proper postdominator** of v if whenever v_2 is another proper postdominator of v then all paths from v to v_2 contain v_1. It is easily shown that for any v with $v \neq$ End, there is a unique first proper postdominator of v, called $1PPD(v)$. In Fig. 1(right), $1PPD(1) = 2$, while also nodes 3 and 6 are proper postdominators.

We say that v_2 is **data dependent** on v_1, written $v_1 \xrightarrow{dd} v_2$, if there exists $x \in Use(v_2) \cap Def(v_1)$, and there exists a non-trivial path π from v_1 to v_2 such that $x \notin Def(v)$ for all nodes v that are interior in π. In Fig. 1(left), $1 \xrightarrow{dd} 2$. A set of nodes Q is **closed under data dependence** if whenever $v_2 \in Q$ and $v_1 \xrightarrow{dd} v_2$ then also $v_1 \in Q$. We say that x is **(Q-)relevant** in v, written $x \in rv_Q(v)$, if there exists $v' \in Q$ such that $x \in Use(v')$, and a path π from v to v' such that $x \notin Def(v_1)$ for all $v_1 \in \pi \setminus \{v'\}$. In Fig. 1(left), $rv_{\{4,5\}}(4) = \{x, z\}$ but $rv_{\{4,5\}}(3) = \{x\}$.

Next, a concept we have discovered useful for the subsequent development:

Definition 1. With v' a postdominator of v, and Q a set of nodes, we say that v ***stays outside Q until*** v' iff whenever π is a path from v to v' where v' occurs only at the end, π will contain no node in Q except possibly v'.

In Fig. 1(right), node 4 stays outside $\{1, 6\}$ until 6 but does not stay outside $\{1, 5, 6\}$ until 6. It turns out that if v stays outside Q until v' and Q is closed under data dependence then v has the same Q-relevant variables as v'. Moreover, if Q satisfies certain additional properties, the distribution at v' (of the relevant variables) will equal the distribution at v.

4   Semantics

In this section we shall define the meaning of the CFGs introduced in the previous section, in terms of an operational semantics that manipulates distributions which assign probabilities to stores (Sect. 4.1). Section 4.2 defines what it means for sets of variables to be independent wrt. a given distribution. To prepare for the full semantics (Sect. 4.5) we define a one-step reduction (Sect. 4.3) from which we construct a reduction which allows multiple steps but only a bounded number of iterations (Sect. 4.4). The semantics also applies to sliced programs and hence (Sect. 4.6) provides the meaning of slicing.

4.1   Stores and Distributions

Let $\mathcal{U}$ be the universe of variables. A store s is a partial mapping from $\mathcal{U}$ to $\mathbb{Z}$. We write $s[x \mapsto z]$ for the store s' that is like s except $s'(x) = z$, and write $dom(s)$ for the domain of s. We write $\mathcal{S}(R)$ for the set of stores with domain R, and also write $\mathcal{F}$ for $\mathcal{S}(\mathcal{U})$. If $s_1 \in \mathcal{S}(R_1)$ and $s_2 \in \mathcal{S}(R_2)$ with $R_1 \cap R_2 = \emptyset$, we may define $s_1 \oplus s_2$ with domain $R_1 \cup R_2$ the natural way. With R a subset of $\mathcal{U}$, we say that s_1 agrees with s_2 on R, written $s_1 \stackrel{R}{=} s_2$, iff $R \subseteq dom(s_1) \cap dom(s_2)$ and for all $x \in R$, $s_1(x) = s_2(x)$. We assume that there is a function $[\![\ ]\!]$ such that $[\![E]\!]s$ is the integer result of evaluating E in store s and $[\![B]\!]s$ is the boolean result of evaluating B in store s (the free variables of E, B must be in $dom(s)$).

A distribution D (we shall later also use the letter Δ) is a mapping from $\mathcal{F}$ to non-negative reals with $\sum D < \infty$ where $\sum D$ is a shorthand for $\sum_{s \in \mathcal{F}} D(s)$. Thanks to our assumption that values are integers, and since $\mathcal{U}$ can be assumed finite, $\mathcal{F}$ is a countable set and thus $\sum D$ is well-defined even without measure theory. If $\sum D \leq 1$, implying $D(s) \leq 1$ for all s, we say that D is a probability distribution. We define $D_1 + D_2$ by stipulating $(D_1 + D_2)(s) = D_1(s) + D_2(s)$, and for $c \geq 0$ we define cD by stipulating $(cD)(s) = cD(s)$. We write $D_1 \leq D_2$ iff $D_1(s) \leq D_2(s)$ for all s, and say that $D = 0$ iff $D(s) = 0$ for all s. We assume there is a designated initial distribution, $D_\mathcal{I}$, such that $\sum D_\mathcal{I} = 1$ ($D_\mathcal{I}$ may be arbitrary as all variables must be defined before they are used).

As suggested by the calculation in Example 1, we have

Definition 2. For partial store s with domain R, let $D(s) = \sum_{s_0 \in \mathcal{F} \ | \ s \stackrel{R}{=} s_0} D(s_0)$.

Observe that $D(\emptyset) = \sum D$. Say that D_1 **agrees with** D_2 on R, written $D_1 \stackrel{R}{=} D_2$, if $D_1(s) = D_2(s)$ for all $s \in \mathcal{S}(R)$. If $D_1 \stackrel{R'}{=} D_2$ and $R \subseteq R'$ then $D_1 \stackrel{R}{=} D_2$.

4.2 Probabilistic Independence

Some variables of a distribution D may be independent of others. Formally:

Definition 3 (independence). Let R_1 and R_2 be disjoint sets of variables. We say that R_1 and R_2 are **independent** in D iff for all $s_1 \in \mathcal{S}(R_1)$ and $s_2 \in \mathcal{S}(R_2)$, we have $D(s_1 \oplus s_2) \sum D = D(s_1)D(s_2)$.

To motivate the definition, first observe that if $\sum D = 1$ it amounts to the well-known definition of probabilistic independence; next observe that if $\sum D > 0$, it is equivalent to the well-known definition for "normalized" probabilities:

$$\frac{D(s_1 \oplus s_2)}{\sum D} = \frac{D(s_1)}{\sum D} \cdot \frac{D(s_2)}{\sum D}$$

Trivially, R_1 and R_2 are independent in D if $D = 0$ or $R_1 = \emptyset$ or $R_2 = \emptyset$.

Example 5. *In Example 1, $\{x\}$ and $\{y\}$ are independent in D_1. This is since for $i \in \{0,1,2,3\}$ and $j \in \{2,3\}$ we have $D_1(\{x \mapsto i,\ y \mapsto j\}) = \dfrac{1}{16}$ so that $D_1(\{x \mapsto i\}) = \dfrac{1}{8}$, $D_1(\{y \mapsto j\}) = \dfrac{1}{4}$, and $\sum D_1 = \dfrac{1}{2}$; we thus have the desired equality $D_1(\{x \mapsto i,\ y \mapsto j\}) \sum D_1 = \dfrac{1}{32} = D_1(\{x \mapsto i\}) \cdot D_1(\{y \mapsto j\})$.*
*   And the equality holds trivially if $i \notin \{0,1,2,3\}$ or $j \notin \{2,3\}$ since then $D_1(\{x \mapsto i,\ y \mapsto j\}) = 0$ and either $D_1(\{x \mapsto i\}) = 0$ or $D_1(\{y \mapsto j\}) = 0$.*

Example 6. *In Example 2, $\{x\}$ and $\{y\}$ are not independent in D_2. This is since $D_2(\{x \mapsto 3,\ y \mapsto 3\}) \sum D_2 = \frac{3}{256}$ while $D_2(\{x \mapsto 3\})D_2(\{y \mapsto 3\}) = \frac{4}{256}$.*

4.3 One-Step Reduction

If v has label $\texttt{Branch}(B)$, with v_1 (v_2) the successor taken when B is true (false), we define

- $(v, D) \xrightarrow{T} (v_1, D_1)$ where $D_1(s)$ equals $D(s)$ when $[\![B]\!]s$ but is 0 otherwise;
- $(v, D) \xrightarrow{F} (v_2, D_2)$ where $D_2(s)$ is 0 when $[\![B]\!]s$ but equals $D(s)$ otherwise.

Thus $D = D_1 + D_2$. Given v such that v has exactly one successor v', the one step reduction $(v, D) \to (v', D')$ is given by defining $D'(s')$ as follows:

Skip	$x := E$	$x := \texttt{Random}(\psi)$	$\texttt{Observe}(B)$
$D(s')$	$\sum_{s \in \mathcal{F}\ \mid\ s' = s[x \mapsto [\![E]\!]s]} D(s)$	$\sum_{s \in \mathcal{F}\ \mid\ s' \stackrel{\mathcal{U}\setminus\{x\}}{=} s} \psi(s'(x))D(s)$	$\begin{cases} D(s') \text{ if } [\![B]\!]s' \\ 0 \text{ otherwise} \end{cases}$

If $(v, D) \to (v', D')$ then $\sum D' \le \sum D$ with equality if v is not an $\texttt{Observe}$ node.

4.4   Multi-step Reduction and Loops

The key semantic relation is of the form $(v, D) \Rightarrow (v', D')$ where v' postdominates v, saying that distribution D transforms to distribution D' as "control" moves from v to v' along paths that may contain multiple branches and even loops but which do *not* contain v' until the end. To define that relation, we need an auxiliary relation of the form $(v, D) \overset{k}{\Rightarrow} (v', D')$ where k is a non-negative integer that bounds the number of times control is allowed to move "away" from the End node; if $k = 1$ then we only take into account paths that for each step get closer to the End node, but if $k = 2$ we also allow paths with one cycle, etc. ($k = 0$ corresponds to "$\perp$" in denotational semantics.) Our goal is to let D' be a function of v, D, v' and k, and we do so by a definition that is inductive first in k, and next on the length of the longest acyclic path from v to v' (proving properties of the relation will involve a case analysis on the various clauses).

Definition 4. ($\overset{k}{\Rightarrow}$)   Given v and v' where v' postdominates v, and given k and D, $(v, D) \overset{k}{\Rightarrow} (v', D')$ holds when D' is defined as follows:

1. if $k = 0$ then $D' = 0$;
2. otherwise, if $v' = v$ then $D' = D$;
3. otherwise, if with $v'' = 1PPD(v)$ we have $v' \neq v''$, we recursively first find D'' with $(v, D) \overset{k}{\Rightarrow} (v'', D'')$ and next find D' with $(v'', D'') \overset{k}{\Rightarrow} (v', D')$;
4. otherwise, if v has exactly one successor, which must be v', we let D' be such that $(v, D) \rightarrow (v', D')$;
5. otherwise, if v has two successors with $(v, D) \overset{T}{\rightarrow} (v_1, D_1)$ and $(v, D) \overset{F}{\rightarrow} (v_2, D_2)$ (thus v' postdominates v_1 and v_2), we recursively find D_1' and D_2' such that $(v_1, D_1) \overset{k_1}{\Rightarrow} (v', D_1')$ and $(v_2, D_2) \overset{k_2}{\Rightarrow} (v', D_2')$, and let $D' = D_1' + D_2'$. Here k_i ($i = 1, 2$) is given as follows: if the longest acyclic path from v_i to v' is shorter than the length of the longest acyclic path from v to v' then $k_i = k$, otherwise $k_i = k - 1$.

Example 7. *Consider the CFG for* P_4 *(Fig. 1(right)) with* E *chosen as "$y + 1$" and with* D_k *such that* $(1, D_\mathcal{I}) \overset{k}{\Rightarrow} (6, D_k)$. *If* $i \in \{0, 1\}$ *and* $j \in \{0, 1, 2, 3\}$ *then for all* $k \geq 1$ *we have* $D_k(\{x \mapsto i, \ y \mapsto j\}) = \dfrac{1}{16}$ *and thus* $D_k(\{x \mapsto i\}) = \dfrac{1}{4}$. *But if* $i \in \{2, 3\}$ *then we have* $D_k(\{x \mapsto i, \ y \mapsto 6\}) = 0$ *if* $k \leq 3$; $D_4(\{x \mapsto i, \ y \mapsto 6\}) = \frac{1}{16}$ *(for* y *initially 3)*; $D_5(\{x \mapsto i, \ y \mapsto 6\}) = \frac{2}{16}$; $D_6(\{x \mapsto i, \ y \mapsto 6\}) = \frac{3}{16}$; *and* $D_k(\{x \mapsto i, \ y \mapsto 6\}) = \frac{4}{16}$ *if* $k \geq 7$.

Note also that for $k > 0$, $(4, D) \overset{k}{\Rightarrow} (4, D')$ *only holds if* $D' = D$, *since the only path from 4 to 4 where 4 does not occur until the end is the empty path. Still, the cycle between nodes 4 and 5 is taken into account. For if* $(4, D) \overset{k}{\Rightarrow} (6, D')$ *then* $D' = D_1' + D_2$ *where* $D = D_1 + D_2$ *(*D_2 *is* D *restricted to states where* $y > 5$*) and* D_1' *is such that for some* D_1'', $(5, D_1) \overset{k-1}{\Rightarrow} (4, D_1'')$ *and* $(4, D_1'') \overset{k-1}{\Rightarrow} (6, D_1')$.

D' *is a monotone function of* D *and of* k:

Lemma 1 (monotonicity). *If $(v, D_1) \overset{k_1}{\Rightarrow} (v', D_1')$ and $(v, D_2) \overset{k_2}{\Rightarrow} (v', D_2')$ with $k_1 \leq k_2$ and $D_1 \leq D_2$ then $D_1' \leq D_2'$. If $(v, D) \overset{k}{\Rightarrow} (v', D')$ then $\sum D' \leq \sum D$.*

Equality between $\sum D'$ and $\sum D$ can fail due to Observe nodes (*cf.* Examples 1–3), or due to infinite loops (*cf.* Example 4) which cause k to be eventually zero.

4.5   Top-Level Semantics

Definition 5. ($\Rightarrow$) Given (v, D), and v' which postdominates v, $(v, D) \Rightarrow (v', D')$ holds when D' is defined as follows: with D_k (for $k \geq 0$) the unique distribution such that $(v, D) \overset{k}{\Rightarrow} (v', D_k)$, let $D' = \lim_{k \to \infty} D_k$ (the limit is taken pointwise).

Observe by Lemma 1 that $D_{k_1} \leq D_{k_2}$ when $k_1 \leq k_2$; for each s we thus have $D_0(s) \leq D_1(s) \leq \ldots \leq D_k(s) \leq D_{k+1}(s) \leq \ldots$ and hence it is well-defined to let $D'(s) = \lim_{k \to \infty} D_k(s)$. Also at top-level, monotonicity holds:

Lemma 2. *If $(v, D) \Rightarrow (v', D')$ then $\sum D' \leq \sum D$.*

Example 8. *Continuing Example 7, we see that the limit D' is given as follows: $D'(\{x \mapsto i, \ y \mapsto j\}) = \frac{1}{16}$ if $i \in \{0, 1\}$, $j \in \{0, 1, 2, 3\}$; $D'(\{x \mapsto i, \ y \mapsto j\}) = \frac{1}{4}$ if $i \in \{2, 3\}, j = 6$; and $D'(\{x \mapsto i, \ y \mapsto j\}) = 0$ otherwise.*

We may define the meaning of a CFG with End node Return(x) as $\lambda v. D'(\{x \mapsto v\})$ where D' is such that $(\text{Start}, D_I) \Rightarrow (\text{Return}(x), D')$.

4.6   Semantics of Slicing

A *slice set* is a set of nodes (which must satisfy certain conditions, *cf.* Definition 9). Slicing amounts to ignoring nodes not in the slice set:

Definition 6. ($\Longrightarrow$) Given a slice set Q, we define the semantics of the CFG that results from slicing wrt. Q as follows:

Let $(v, \Delta) \overset{k}{\Longrightarrow} (v', \Delta')$ be defined as $(v, D) \overset{k}{\Rightarrow} (v', D')$ (Definition 4), except that whenever $v \notin Q \cup \{\text{End}\}$ then v is labeled Skip and the successor of v becomes $1PPD(v)$. And let $(v, \Delta) \Longrightarrow (v', \Delta')$ be defined by letting $\Delta' = \lim_{k \to \infty} \Delta_k$ where for each $k \geq 0$, Δ_k is the unique distribution such that $(v, \Delta) \overset{k}{\Longrightarrow} (v', \Delta_k)$.

5   Conditions for Slicing

With Q the slice set, we now develop conditions for Q that ensure semantic correctness. It is standard to require Q to be closed under data dependence, and additionally also under some kind of "control dependence". In this section we first elaborate on the latter condition after which we study the extra conditions needed in our probabilistic setting. Eventually, Definition 9 gives conditions that involve not only Q but also another slice set Q_0 containing all Observe nodes to be sliced away. As stated in Proposition 1, these conditions are sufficient to establish probabilistic independence of Q and Q_0. This in turn is crucial for establishing the correctness of slicing, as stated in Theorem 1 (Sect. 6).

Weak Slice Sets. Danicic *et al.* [5] show that various kinds of control dependence can all be elegantly expressed within a general framework whose core is the following notion:

Definition 7 (next observable). With Q a set of nodes, v' is a **next observable** in Q of v iff $v' \in Q \cup \{End\}$, and v' occurs on all paths from v to a node in $Q \cup \{End\}$.

A node v can have at most one next observable in Q. It thus makes sense to write $v' = next_Q(v)$ if v' is a next observable in Q of v. We say that Q **provides next observables** iff $next_Q(v)$ exists for all nodes v. If $v' = next_Q(v)$ then v' is a postdominator of v, and if $v \in Q \cup \{End\}$ then $next_Q(v) = v$.

In the CFG for P_3 (Fig. 1), letting $Q = \{1, 3, 5\}$, node 5 is a next observable in Q of 4: all paths from 4 to a node in Q will contain 5. But no node is a next observable in Q of 2: node 3 is not since there is a path from 2 to 5 not containing 3, and node 5 is not since there is a path from 2 to 3 not containing 5. Therefore Q cannot be the slice set: node 1 can have only one successor in the sliced program but we have no reason to choose either of the nodes 3 and 5 over the other as that successor. This motivates the following definition:

Definition 8 (weak slice set). We say that Q is a **weak slice set** iff it provides next observables, and is closed under data dependence.

While the importance of "provides next observable" was recognized already in [1,11], Danicic *et al.* were the first to realize that it is *the* key property (together with data dependence) to ensure semantically correct slicing. They call the property "weakly committing" (thus our use of "weak") and our definition differs slightly from theirs in that we always consider End an "observable".

It is easy to see that the empty set, as well as the set of all nodes, is a weak slice set. Moreover, if Q_1, Q_2 are weak slice sets, so is $Q_1 \cup Q_2$.

Adapting to the Probabilistic Setting. The key challenge in slicing probabilistic programs is, as already motivated through Examples 1–4, to handle Observe nodes. In Sect. 2 we hinted at some tentative conditions a slice set Q must satisfy; we can now phrase them more precisely:

1. Q must be a weak slice set that contains End, and
2. there exists another weak slice set Q_0 such that (a) Q and Q_0 are disjoint and (b) all Observe nodes belong to either Q or Q_0.

For programs P_1, P_2, the control flow is linear and hence all nodes have a next observable (so a node set that is closed under data dependence is a weak slice set).

For P_1 we may choose $Q = \{1, 4\}$ and $Q_0 = \{2, 3\}$ as they are disjoint, and both closed under data dependence. Hence we may use $\{1, 4\}$ as a slice set; from Definition 6 we see that the resulting slice is 1: $x := \texttt{Random}(\psi_4)$; 2: $\texttt{Skip}$; 3: $\texttt{Skip}$; 4: $\texttt{Return}(x)$, which is obviously equivalent to P_x as defined in Sect. 2.

Next consider the program P_2 where Q should contain 4 and hence (by data dependence) also contain 1. Now assume, in order to remove the $\texttt{Observe}$ node (and produce P_x), that Q does not contain 3. Then Q_0 must contain 3, and (as Q_0 is closed under data dependence) also 1. But then Q and Q_0 are not disjoint, which contradicts our requirements. Thus Q does contain 3, and hence also 2. That is, $Q = \{1, 2, 3, 4\}$. We see that the only possible slicing is the trivial one.

Any slice for P_3 will also be trivial. From $5 \in Q$ we infer (by data dependence) that $1 \in Q$. Assume, to get a contradiction, that $4 \notin Q$. Then $4 \in Q_0$, and for node 2 to have a next observable in Q_0 we must also have $2 \in Q_0$ which by data dependence implies $1 \in Q_0$ which as $1 \in Q$ contradicts Q and Q_0 being disjoint. Thus $4 \in Q$ which implies $3 \in Q$ (by data dependence) and $2 \in Q$ (as otherwise 2 has no next observable in Q).

For P_4, it is plausible that $Q = \{1, 6\}$ and $Q_0 = \emptyset$, since for all $v \neq 1$ we would then have $6 = next_Q(v)$. From Definition 6 we see that after removing unreachable nodes, the resulting slice is: 1: $x := \texttt{Random}(\psi_4)$; 2: $\texttt{Skip}$; 3: $\texttt{Skip}$; 6: $\texttt{Return}(x)$. Yet, in Example 4 we saw that this is in general *not* a correct slice of P_4. This reveals a problem with our tentative correctness conditions; they do not take into account that $\texttt{Observe}$ nodes may be "encoded" as infinite loops. To repair that, we demand that just like all $\texttt{Observe}$ nodes must belong to either Q or Q_0, also all cycles must touch either Q or Q_0. With this requirement, it is no longer possible that Q contains only nodes 1 and 6. For if so, then Q_0 would have to contain node 4 or node 5 since these two nodes form a cycle. But then, in order for node 3 to have a next observable in Q_0, it must be the case that Q_0 contains node 3, and hence (by data dependence) also node 1 which contradicts Q and Q_0 being disjoint. Thus we have motivated the following definition.

Definition 9 (slicing pair). Let Q, Q_0 be sets of nodes. (Q, Q_0) is a **slicing pair** iff (a) Q, Q_0 are both weak slice sets with $\texttt{End} \in Q$; (b) Q, Q_0 are disjoint; (c) all $\texttt{Observe}$ nodes are in $Q \cup Q_0$; and (d) all cycles contain at least one element of $Q \cup Q_0$.

If (Q, Q_0) is a slicing pair then $rv_Q(v) \cap rv_{Q_0}(v) = \emptyset$ for all nodes v. For, if $x \in rv_Q(v) \cap rv_{Q_0}(v)$ then a definition of x, known to exist, would be in $Q \cap Q_0$ which is empty. Moreover, the Q-relevant variables are probabilistically independent (as defined in Definition 3) of the Q_0-relevant variables, as stated by the following preservation result which is one of the main contributions of this paper in that it gives a syntactic condition for probabilistic independence:

Proposition 1 (Independence). *Let (Q, Q_0) be a slicing pair. Assume that $(v, D) \overset{k}{\Rightarrow} (v', D')$ where v' postdominates v. If $rv_Q(v)$ and $rv_{Q_0}(v)$ are independent in D then $rv_Q(v')$ and $rv_{Q_0}(v')$ are independent in D'.*

6   Slicing and Its Correctness

We can now precisely phrase the desired correctness result:

Theorem 1. *Given a CFG with* End *of the form* Return(x), *and let* (Q, Q_0) *be a slicing pair. Let* D' *and* Δ' *be the unique distributions such that* (Start$, D_{\mathcal{I}}) \Rightarrow$ (End$, D'$) *and* (Start$, D_{\mathcal{I}}) \Longrightarrow$ (End$, \Delta'$) *where the latter denotes slicing wrt.* Q *(cf. Sect. 4.6). Then there exists a real number c with $0 \leq c \leq 1$ such that for all v, $D'(\{x \mapsto v\}) = c\Delta'(\{x \mapsto v\})$.*

This follows from a more general proposition (allowing an inductive proof) stated below, with $v = $ Start so that (from the requirement that a variable must be defined before it is used) R and R_0 are both empty (and thus independent), with $v' = $ End $= $ Return(x) so that $R' = \{x\}$, and with $\Delta = D = D_{\mathcal{I}}$.

Proposition 2. *Let* (Q, Q_0) *be a slicing pair. Let* v' *postdominate* v, *with* $R = rv_Q(v)$, $R' = rv_Q(v')$, *and* $R_0 = rv_{Q_0}(v)$. *Assume that* D *is such that* R *and* R_0 *are independent in* D, *and that* Δ *is such that* $D \stackrel{R}{=} \Delta$. *Let* D' *and* Δ' *be the unique distributions such that* $(v, D) \Rightarrow (v', D')$ *and* $(v, \Delta) \Longrightarrow (v', \Delta')$. *Then there exists a real number c with $0 \leq c \leq 1$ such that $D' \stackrel{R'}{=} c\Delta'$.*

Moreover, $c = 1$ if v stays outside Q_0 until v' (since then the conditions for a slicing pair guarantee that no observe nodes, or infinite loops, are sliced away).

That is, for the relevant variables, the final distribution is the same in the sliced program as in the original program, except for a constant factor c such that $\sum D' = c \sum \Delta'$.

To prove Proposition 2, we need a similar result that involves k and where the proof of sequential composition (case 3 in Definition 4) employs Proposition 1 to ensure that the independence property still holds after the first reduction, so that we can apply the induction hypothesis to the second reduction.

7   Computing the (Least) Slice

There always exists at least one slicing pair, with Q the set of all nodes and with Q_0 the empty set; in that case, the sliced program is the same as the original. Our goal, however, is to find a slicing pair (Q, Q_0) where Q is as small as possible while including the End node. This section describes an algorithm BSP for doing so. The running time of our algorithms is measured in terms of n, the number of nodes in the graph. Note that the number of edges is at most $2n$ and thus in $O(n)$. Our algorithms use a boolean table DD* such that DD*(v, v') is true iff $v \stackrel{dd^*}{\rightarrow} v'$ where $\stackrel{dd^*}{\rightarrow}$ is the reflexive and transitive closure of $\stackrel{dd}{\rightarrow}$. Given DD*, it is easy to ensure that sets are closed under data dependence, and we shall do that in an incremental way: there exists an algorithm DD^{close} which given a node set Q_0 that is closed under data dependence, and a node set Q_1, returns the least set Q containing Q_0 and Q_1 that is closed under data dependence.

```
PN?(Q)                                      LWS(Q_0)
    F ← Q ∪ {End};                              Q ← DD^close(∅, Q_0); C ← PN?(Q);
    foreach v ∈ V                               while C ≠ ∅
        if v ∈ F                                    Q ← DD^close(Q, C);
            N[v] ← v                                 C ← PN?(Q)
        else                                    return Q
            N[v] ← ⊥;
    C ← ∅;                                   BSP()
    while F ≠ ∅ ∧ C = ∅                          W ← the set of essential nodes;
        F' ← ∅;                                  foreach v ∈ W ∪ {End}
        foreach edge from v ∉ Q                      Q_v ← LWS({v});
                     to v' ∈ F                   Q ← ∅; F ← Q_End;
            if N(v) = ⊥                          while F ≠ ∅
                N(v) ← N(v');                        Q ← Q ∪ F; F ← ∅;
                F' ← F' ∪ {v}                        foreach v ∈ W
            else if N(v) ≠ N(v')                         if Q_v ∩ Q ≠ ∅
                C ← C ∪ {v};                                W ← W \ {v}; F ← F ∪ Q_v;
        F ← F'                                   Q_0 ← ⋃_{v∈W} Q_v;
    return C                                     return (Q, Q_0)
```

Fig. 2. Algorithms for: checking if a set provides next observables (PN?); finding the least weak slice set containing a given set (LWS); finding the best slicing pair (BSP).

Computing the Least Weak Slice. In Fig. 2(upper right) we define a function LWS which constructs the least weak slice set that contains a given set; it works by successively adding nodes to the set until it is closed under data dependence, and provides next observables.

To check the latter, we employ a function PN? as defined in Fig. 2(left): given Q, it does a backward breadth-first search from $Q \cup \{End\}$ to find the first node (if any) from which two nodes in that set are reachable without going through Q; such a node must be included in any superset providing next observables.

Lemma 3. *Given Q, the function PN? runs in time $O(n)$ and returns C such that (a) if C is empty then Q provides next observables, and (b) if C is non-empty then $C \cap Q = \emptyset$ and all supersets of Q that provide next observables contain C.*

Lemma 4. *Given Q_0, the function LWS returns Q such that Q is a weak slice set and $Q_0 \subseteq Q$. Moreover, if Q' is a weak slice set with $Q_0 \subseteq Q'$, then $Q \subseteq Q'$. Finally, given DD*, LWS runs in time $O(n^2)$.*

Computing the Best Slicing Pair. We now develop an algorithm BSP which given a CFG returns a slicing pair (Q, Q_0) with Q as small as possible. From Definition 9 we know that each Observe node has to be put either in Q or in Q_0, and also that at least one node from each cycle has to be put either in Q or in Q_0. Especially the latter requirement may suggest that our algorithm will have to explore a huge search space, but fortunately it is sufficient to consider only the node(s) with minimal *height*. Here node v's height, denoted $H(v)$, is the length of the shortest path(s) from v to End. This motivates

Definition 10. A node v is **essential** if either (a) v is an Observe node, or (b) v belongs to a cycle π where $H(v) \leq H(v_1)$ for all $v_1 \in \pi$.

For disjoint weak slice sets (Q, Q_0) with End $\in Q$ to be a slicing pair, it is sufficient and necessary that each essential node be placed either in Q or in Q_0.

Lemma 5 (Sufficient). *Let Q and Q_0 be disjoint weak slice sets with End $\in Q$, and assume that all essential nodes are in $Q \cup Q_0$. Then (Q, Q_0) is a slicing pair.*

Lemma 6 (Necessary). *Let (Q, Q_0) be a slicing pair. If v is essential then $v \in Q \cup Q_0$.*

Fig. 2 (lower right) presents the algorithm BSP that computes the best slicing pair (Q, Q_0). The idea is to built Q incrementally, initially containing only End, and then add v whenever v is essential but cannot be placed in Q_0 as then Q and Q_0 would overlap. That BSP produces the *best slicing pair* is captured by

Proposition 3. *The algorithm BSP returns (on a given CFG) Q and Q_0 such that (Q, Q_0) is a slicing pair, and if (Q', Q_0') is a slicing pair then $Q \subseteq Q'$.*

After analyzing the running times, we get:

Theorem 2. *For a given CFG, there is an algorithm that in time $O(n^3)$ computes a slicing pair (Q, Q_0) where $Q \subseteq Q'$ for any other slicing pair (Q', Q_0').*

Also the algorithm given in [5] for computing (their version of) weak slices runs in cubic time. We do not expect that there exists an algorithm with lower asymptotic complexity, since we need to compute data dependencies which is known to involve computing a transitive closure.

Illustrating the Algorithms. First consider the program P_1 from Example 1 where the non-trivial true entries of DD* are $(1, 4)$ (since $1 \xrightarrow{dd} 4$) and $(2, 3)$, and where 3 is the only essential node. BSP thus computes LWS($\{4\}$) and LWS($\{3\}$). When running LWS on $\{4\}$, initially $Q = \{1, 4\}$ which is also the final value of Q since PN?($\{1, 4\}$) returns $\emptyset$ (after a sequence of iterations where F is first $\{1, 4\}$ and next $\{3\}$ and next $\{2\}$ and finally $\emptyset$). Thus $Q_4 = \{1, 4\}$ and similarly we get $Q_3 = \{2, 3\}$. When the members of $W = \{3\}$ are first examined in the BSP algorithm, we have $Q = Q_4$ and thus $Q_3 \cap Q = \emptyset$. Hence the while loop terminates with $Q = \{1, 4\}$ and subsequently we get $Q_0 = Q_3 = \{2, 3\}$.

Next consider the CFG for P_4 (Fig. 1) with E containing only y free. Here $\xrightarrow{dd}$ is given as follows: $1 \xrightarrow{dd} 3$, $1 \xrightarrow{dd} 6$, $2 \xrightarrow{dd} 4$, $2 \xrightarrow{dd} 5$, $5 \xrightarrow{dd} 4$, and $5 \xrightarrow{dd} 5$. Since $H(4) = 1$ and $H(5) = 2$, node 4 is the only essential node. BSP thus has to compute LWS($\{6\}$) and LWS($\{4\}$):

- LWS($\{6\}$): initially, $Q = \{1, 6\}$ which is also the final value of Q since PN?($\{1, 6\}$) returns $\emptyset$ (after a sequence of iterations where F is first $\{1, 6\}$ and next $\{3, 4\}$ and next $\{2, 5\}$ and finally $\emptyset$). Thus $Q_6 = \{1, 6\}$.

– LWS($\{4\}$): initially, $Q = \{2, 4, 5\}$. In PN? we initially thus have $F = \{2, 4, 5, 6\}$ which causes the first iteration of the while loop to put 3 in C so that $\{3\}$ is eventually returned. Since $1 \xrightarrow{dd} 3$ holds, the next iteration of LWS will have $Q = \{1, 2, 3, 4, 5\}$ on which PN? will return $\emptyset$. Thus $Q_4 = \{1, 2, 3, 4, 5\}$.

When the members of $W = \{4\}$ are first examined in the BSP algorithm, we have $Q = Q_6$ and thus $Q_4 \cap Q = \{1\} \neq \emptyset$. Hence Q will equal $Q_6 \cup Q_4 = \{1, 2, 3, 4, 5, 6\}$ and as W is now empty, the loop will terminate and we get $Q_0 = \emptyset$.

8 Extensions and Future Work

Section 7 presented an algorithm for computing the least syntactic slice. But there may exist even smaller slices that are still semantically correct: recall Example 4 where the only correct syntactic slice is the program itself (as shown in Sect. 7) but where a much smaller slice may be semantically correct for certain instantiations of the generic "E". Similarly, a node labeled Observe(B) can be safely discarded if B always evaluates to *true*. For example, the CFG with textual representation $1 : x := \text{Random}(\psi_4)$; $2 : y := 7$; $3 : \text{if } x \geq 2 \ (4 : \text{Observe}(y = 7))$; $5 : \text{Return}(x)$ is semantically equivalent to the CFG containing only nodes 1 and 5. But the former has no smaller syntactic slice, since if (Q, Q_0) is a slicing pair with $5 \in Q$ (and thus $1 \in Q$) then $Q = \{1, 2, 3, 4, 5\}$ as we now show. If $4 \in Q_0$ then $3 \in Q_0$ (as Q_0 provides next observables) and thus $1 \in Q_0$ which contradicts $Q \cap Q_0 = \emptyset$. Hence (as 4 must belong to $Q \cup Q_0$) $4 \in Q$; but then $2 \in Q$ (by data dependence) and $3 \in Q$ (as Q provides next observables).

Simple analyses like constant propagation may improve the precision of slicing even in a deterministic setting, but the probabilistic setting gives an extra opportunity: after an Observe(B) node, we know that B holds. As richly exploited in [7], a simple syntactic transformation often suffices to get the benefits of that information, as we illustrate on the program from [7, Fig. 4] whose CFG (in slightly modified form) is depicted in Fig. 3. In our setting, if (Q, Q_0) with $18 \in Q$ is the best slicing pair, then Q will contain everything except nodes 12, 13, 14, as can be seen as follows: $16, 17 \in Q$ by data dependence; $15 \in Q$ as Q provides next observables; $6, 7, 8, 9 \in Q$ by data dependence; $3, 4, 5 \in Q$ as Q provides next observables; $1, 2 \in Q$ by data dependence; also $10 \in Q$ as otherwise $10 \in Q_0$ and thus also $9 \in Q_0$ which contradicts $Q \cap Q_0 = \emptyset$.

Alternatively, suppose we insert a node 11 labeled $g := 0$ between nodes 10 and 12. This clearly preserves the semantics, but allows a much smaller slice: choose $Q = \{11, 15, 16, 17, 18\}$ and $Q_0 = \{1, 2, 3, 4, 5, 6, 7, 8, 9, 10\}$. This is much like what is arrived at (through a more complex process) in [7, Fig. 15].

Future work involves exploring a larger range of examples, and investigating useful techniques for computing slices that are smaller than the least syntactic slice yet semantically correct. (Of course it is in general undecidable to compute the least semantically correct slice.) We have recently augmented our theory such that we can ignore loops that are known (by some means) to always terminate.

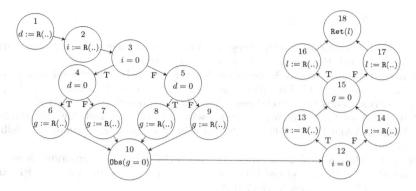

Fig. 3. The program from [7, Fig. 4] (modified).

That is, for a slicing pair (Q, Q_0), a cycle which cannot go on forever (or does it with probability zero) does not need to contain a node from $Q \cup Q_0$.

9   Conclusion and Related Work

We have developed a theory for the slicing of probabilistic imperative programs. We have used and extended techniques from the literature [1,3,10,11] on the slicing of deterministic imperative programs. These frameworks, some of which have been partly verified by mechanical proof assistants [4,13], were recently coalesced by Danicic *et al.* [5] who provided solid semantic foundations to the slicing of a large class of deterministic programs. Our extension of that work is non-trivial in that we need to capture probabilistic independence as done in Proposition 1 which requires *two* slice sets rather than just one.

We were directly inspired by Hur *et al.* [7] who point out the challenges involved in the slicing of probabilistic programs, and present an algorithm which constructs a semantically correct slice. The paper does not state whether it is in some sense the least possible slice; neither does it address the complexity of the algorithm. While Hur *et al.*'s approach differs from ours, for example it is based on a denotational semantics for a structured language (we expect the two semantics to coincide for CFGs of structured programs), it is not surprising that their correctness proof also has probabilistic independence (termed "decomposition") as a key notion. Our theory separates specification and implementation which we believe provides for a cleaner approach. But as mentioned in Sect. 8, they incorporate powerful optimizations that we do not (yet) allow.

Acknowledgements. Thanks to Gordon Stewart for comments on earlier drafts.

References

1. Amtoft, T.: Slicing for modern program structures: a theory for eliminating irrelevant loops. Inf. Process. Lett. **106**(2), 45–51 (2008)
2. Amtoft, T., Banerjee, A.: A theory of slicing for probabilistic control flow graphs. Technical Report CIS TR 2015-1, Kansas State University, July 2015. http://people.cis.ksu.edu/~tamtoft/Papers/Amt+Ban:ProbSlice-2015/long.pdf
3. Ball, T., Horwitz, S.: Slicing programs with arbitrary control flow. In: Fritzson, P.A. (ed.) AADEBUG 1993. LNCS, vol. 749, pp. 206–222. Springer, Heidelberg (1993)
4. Blazy, S., Maroneze, A., Pichardie, D.: Verified validation of program slicing. In: Proceedings of the 2015 Conference on Certified Programs and Proofs, CPP 2015, pp. 109–117. ACM, New York (2015)
5. Danicic, S., Barraclough, R.W., Harman, M., Howroyd, J.D., Kiss, Á., Laurence, M.R.: A unifying theory of control dependence and its application to arbitrary program structures. Theor. Comput. Sci. **412**(49), 6809–6842 (2011)
6. Gordon, A.D., Henzinger, T.A., Nori, A.V., Rajamani, S.K.: Probabilistic programming. In: Dwyer, M.B., Herbsleb, J. (eds.) ICSE, Future of Software Engineering track, FOSE 2014, pp. 167–181. ACM, New York (2014)
7. Hur, C.-K., Nori, A.V., Rajamani, S.K., Samuel, S.: Slicing probabilistic programs. In: Pingali, K. (ed.) Proceedings of the 35th ACM SIGPLAN Conference on Programming Language Design and Implementation, PLDI 2014, pp. 133–144. ACM, New York (2014)
8. Kozen, D.: Semantics of probabilistic programs. J. Comput. Syst. Sci. **22**, 328–350 (1981)
9. Panangaden, P.: Labelled Markov Processes. Imperial College Press, London (2009)
10. Podgurski, A., Clarke, L.A.: A formal model of program dependences and its implications for software testing, debugging, and maintenance. IEEE Trans. Softw. Eng. **16**(9), 965–979 (1990)
11. Ranganath, V.P., Amtoft, T., Banerjee, A., Hatcliff, J., Dwyer, M.B.: A new foundation for control dependence and slicing for modern program structures. ACM Trans. Program. Lang. Syst. (TOPLAS), **29**(5), Aug 2007. (A special issue with extended versions of selected papers from the 14th European Symposium on Programming (ESOP'05))
12. Tip, F.: A survey of program slicing techniques. J. Program. Lang. **3**, 121–189 (1995)
13. Wasserrab, D.: From Formal Semantics to Verified Slicing. Ph.D. thesis, Karlsruher Institut für Technologie (2010)
14. Weiser, M.: Program slicing. IEEE Trans. Softw. Eng. **10**(4), 352–357 (1984)

Verification of Parameterized Communicating Automata via Split-Width

Marie Fortin and Paul Gastin[✉]

LSV, ENS Cachan, CNRS, Université Paris-Saclay, 94235 Cachan, France
mfortin@ens-cachan.fr, gastin@lsv.ens-cachan.fr

Abstract. We study verification problems for distributed systems communicating via unbounded FIFO channels. The number of processes of the system as well as the communication topology are not fixed a priori. Systems are given by parameterized communicating automata (PCAs) which can be run on any communication topology of bounded degree, with arbitrarily many processes. Such systems are Turing powerful so we concentrate on under-approximate verification. We extend the notion of split-width to behaviors of PCAs. We show that emptiness, reachability and model-checking problems of PCAs are decidable when restricted to behaviors of bounded split-width. Reachability and emptiness are EXP-TIME-complete, but only polynomial in the size of the PCA. We also describe several concrete classes of bounded split-width, for which we prove similar results.

Keywords: Parameterized distributed systems · Model checking · Split-width · Message sequence charts

1 Introduction

We study verification problems for parameterized communicating automata (PCAs), which model distributed systems consisting of arbitrarily many identical processes, distributed on some communication topology. Each process runs a copy of the same finite automaton, that can send and receive messages from other processes through FIFO channels. Though the system may contain unboundedly many processes, we assume that each process may only communicate with a bounded number of other processes.

PCAs were introduced in [5] to study logical characterizations of parameterized systems. They extend communicating finite-state machines [8]. While the latter assume a fixed and known communication topology, a PCA can be run on *any* communication topology of bounded degree. Communicating finite-state machines are already Turing equivalent, and thus their verification is undecidable. The fact that PCAs can be run on arbitrarily large topologies induces other sources of undecidability. For instance, a Turing machine can be simulated on grid topologies by a PCA *performing a bounded number of actions on each process*. Thus, some restrictions on the topologies are necessary. Yet, even when

© Springer-Verlag Berlin Heidelberg 2016
B. Jacobs and C. Löding (Eds.): FOSSACS 2016, LNCS 9634, pp. 197–213, 2016.
DOI: 10.1007/978-3-662-49630-5_12

fixing a simple class of topologies such as pipelines, and imposing rendez-vous synchronization, reachability of PCAs is undecidable [7].

In order to regain decidability, we focus on under-approximate verification. The idea is to restrict the verification problems to meaningful classes C of finite behaviors. Typically, we are interested in the following problem: given a PCA S, is there a topology T and a behavior in C over T on which S reaches some local/global state? Our aim is to study under-approximation classes C for which verification problems of PCAs becomes decidable. Even when we cannot cover all behaviors of a system with a decidable class, under-approximate verification is still very useful to detect bugs. Usually, the classes C_i are parameterized and cover more and more behaviors when the parameter i increases.

The behaviors of PCAs are described by finite message sequence charts (MSC) [18], that is, graphs describing the communications between the different processes. Each node of the graph corresponds to an action performed by some process (sending or receiving a message), and the dependencies between the different actions are indicated by the edges of the graph. For model-checking, the specifications of our systems are typically given as monadic second order logic (MSO) or propositional dynamic logic (PDL) formulas over MSCs.

It is known that for any MSO definable class of bounded degree graphs, having a decidable MSO theory is equivalent to having bounded tree-width [9]. This applies to classes of MSCs, and characterizes decidability of MSO model-checking. However, showing a bound on tree-width is in general difficult. In the case of MSCs over a *fixed* architecture, an alternative notion called split-width has been introduced [1,2]. Split-width is equivalent to tree-width on MSCs, but easier to use. It provides means to define uniform decision procedures, applying to many well-studied restrictions of communicating finite-state machines [10].

Following this approach, we generalize the definition of split-width, and we extend existing results over fixed architectures to the parameterized case. The idea of split-width is to decompose an MSC into atomic pieces, that is, pairs of matching send and receive events. This is done using two operations: splitting some edges between consecutive events of a same process, and dividing the resulting graph into disjoint components. Intuitively, an MSC has bounded split-width when this can be done while splitting a bounded number of edges at each step, on a bounded number of processes.

We show that emptiness and reachability of PCAs restricted to MSCs of bounded split-width are decidable. These problems are EXPTIME-complete but only polynomial in the size of the PCA. Our decision procedures are based on an interpretation of MSCs of bounded split-width into binary trees, and reductions to tree automata verification problems.

In the extended version [16] we also prove that model-checking restricted to bounded split-width is decidable. For MSO specifications, it has non-elementary complexity. However, the under-approximate model-checking is respectively EXPTIME-complete and 2-EXPTIME complete for CPDL (PDL with converse) and ICPDL (PDL with converse and intersection). In all cases, the problem is still polynomial in the size of the PCA.

Further, we give several examples of concrete classes of MSCs with bounded split-width, including existentially bounded or context-bounded behaviors, for which we show similar decidability and complexity results. Our approach based on split-width is generic since it can be easily adapted to other under-approximation classes.

Related Work. Various models of parameterized systems have been considered in the literature. In several cases, the assumptions of the model are sufficient to get decidability results without additional restrictions on the behaviors. Examples include token-passing systems [3,15], models with a global store without locking [14], message-passing systems communicating synchronously via broadcast [12,13], or rendez-vous [4]. An important distinction between the latter and PCAs is that PCAs use point-to-point communication: a process can distinguish between its neighbors, and specify the recipients of its messages. This makes the model more expressive, but also leads to undecidability.

The emptiness and model-checking problems for PCAs have been considered in [6,7], respectively. Both papers assume rendez-vous synchronization, and a fixed class of topologies: pipelines, rings, or trees. Several notions of *contexts* are introduced, and decision procedures are described for the corresponding classes of context-bounded behaviors.

In the present paper, we also address context-bounded verification, but for unbounded FIFO channels and arbitrary topologies of bounded tree-width. In the general case of bounded split-width, we do not assume any restriction on the topology, but a bound on split-width already implies a bound on the tree-width of the communication topology.

Communicating finite-state machines (over fixed topologies) have been more extensively studied, and several restrictions are known to bring back decidability. Our work generalizes some of them to the parameterized setting, namely, context bounds (introduced in [19] for multi-stack concurrent systems), existential bounds [17], and bounded split-width [2].

Split-width was first introduced for multi-pushdown systems [11], and then generalized to communicating multi-pushdown systems [2].

Outline. In Sect. 2, we define topologies, PCAs, and MSCs. In Sect. 3, we introduce split-width. In Sect. 4, we give several examples of classes of bounded split-width, and state our results for the reachability problems of those classes. In Sect. 5, we present in more details the decision procedures leading to these results. In Sect. 6, we briefly present how they can be extended to decide model-checking problems, and discuss possible extensions of our model. Most proofs are omitted and can be found in the full version of the paper [16].

2   Parameterized Communicating Automata

We describe our formal model for communicating systems: we introduce topologies, MSCs, and parameterized communicating automata. Our definitions are taken from [5], except that we abstract away idle processes.

Topologies. We model distributed systems consisting of an unbounded number of processes. Each process is equipped with a bounded number of interfaces, through which it can communicate with other processes. A topology is a graph, describing the connections between the different processes (each of which is represented by a node in the graph, see example on the right). Throughout the paper, we assume a *fixed* nonempty finite set $\mathcal{N} = \{a, b, \ldots\}$ of *interface names* (or, simply, *interfaces*).

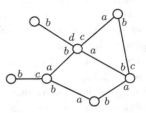

Definition 1. *A* topology *over* $\mathcal{N}$ *is a pair* $\mathcal{T} = (P, \longmapsto)$ *where* P *is the nonempty finite set of* processes *and* $\longmapsto \subseteq P \times \mathcal{N} \times \mathcal{N} \times P$ *is the* edge relation. *We write* $p \xmapsto{a\ b} q$ *for* $(p, a, b, q) \in \longmapsto$, *which means that the* a-interface of p is connected the b-interface of q. *We require that, whenever* $p \xmapsto{a\ b} q$, *the following hold:*

(a) $p \neq q$ *(there are no self loops),*

(b) $q \xmapsto{b\ a} p$ *(adjacent processes are mutually connected), and*

(c) *for all* $a', b' \in \mathcal{N}$ *and* $q' \in P$ *such that* $p \xmapsto{a'\ b'} q'$, *we have* $a = a'$ *iff* $q = q'$ *(an interface is connected to at most one process, and two distinct interfaces are connected to distinct processes).*

Message Sequence Charts. The possible behaviors of our systems are depicted as message sequence charts. A message sequence chart consists of a set of processes, and, for each process, of a sequence of events. Each event corresponds to an action of the process (sending or receiving a message through a given interface), and matching send and receive events are connected by a message edge. Events are labeled with elements of $\Sigma \stackrel{\text{def}}{=} \{a? \mid a \in \mathcal{N}\} \cup \{a! \mid a \in \mathcal{N}\}$, according to the type of action they execute.

Definition 2. *A* pre-message sequence chart (pre-MSC) *over the set of interfaces* $\mathcal{N}$ *is a tuple* $M = (P, E, \rightarrow, \lhd, \pi, \lambda)$, *where*

– P *and* E *are nonempty finite sets of* processes *and* events, *respectively.*
– $\pi : E \rightarrow P$ *is a surjective map determining the* location *of an event. For* $p \in P$, *we let* $E_p \stackrel{\text{def}}{=} \{e \in E \mid \pi(e) = p\}$.
– $\lambda : E \rightarrow \Sigma$ *associates with each event the type of action that it executes. We let* $E_? \stackrel{\text{def}}{=} \{e \in E \mid \exists a \in \mathcal{N}.\lambda(e) = a?\}$, *and* $E_! \stackrel{\text{def}}{=} \{e \in E \mid \exists a \in \mathcal{N}.\lambda(e) = a!\}$.

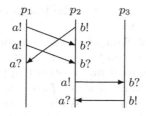

Fig. 1. An MSC with 3 processes

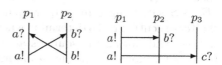

Fig. 2. pre-MSCs that are not MSCs

- $\rightarrow$ *is a union* $\bigcup_{p \in P} \rightarrow_p$, *where each* $\rightarrow_p \subseteq E_p \times E_p$ *is the direct-successor relation of some total order on* E_p.
- $\lhd \subseteq E_! \times E_?$ *defines a bijection from* $E_!$ *to* $E_?$. *Moreover, for each* $(e, f) \in \lhd$, $\pi(e) \neq \pi(f)$.

Given such a pre-MSC, we define $\mathcal{T}_M \overset{\text{def}}{=} (P, \{(p, a, b, q) \in P \times \mathcal{N}^2 \times P \mid \exists (e, f) \in E_p \times E_q. (e \lhd f \wedge \lambda(e) = a! \wedge \lambda(f) = b?)$ or $(f \lhd e \wedge \lambda(e) = a? \wedge \lambda(f) = b!)\})$.

Not all pre-MSCs correspond to actual behaviors of systems (Fig. 2). To define MSCs, we additionally require that the events are coherently ordered, and that communications are compatible with some topology and follow a FIFO policy.

Definition 3. *A* message sequence chart (MSC) *over* $\mathcal{N}$ *is a pre-MSC* $M = (P, E, \rightarrow, \lhd, \pi, \lambda)$ *such that the relation* $\leq \overset{\text{def}}{=} (\rightarrow \cup \lhd)^*$ *is a partial order, and:*

- $\mathcal{T}_M$ *as defined above is a topology, called the* observable topology *of* M.
- *For all* $e_1 \lhd e_2$, $f_1 \lhd f_2$ *s.t.* $\pi(e_i) = \pi(f_i)$, *we have* $e_1 \leq f_1$ *iff* $e_2 \leq f_2$ *(FIFO).*

An MSC M is called *compatible* with a topology $\mathcal{T}$ when $\mathcal{T}_M$ is a subgraph of $\mathcal{T}$. Intuitively, an MSC is compatible with a topology $\mathcal{T}$ when it can be interpreted as a behavior over $\mathcal{T}$, in which some processes may be inactive or may not use all their interfaces. We denote by MSC the set of all MSCs over $\mathcal{N}$, and by MSC$_{\mathcal{T}}$ the set of all MSCs compatible with a topology $\mathcal{T}$.

Example 4. An example MSC is depicted in Fig. 1. The vertical lines represent the succession of events on a given process, and $\lhd$-edges are depicted by arrows.

Parameterized Communicating Automata. The idea is that each process of a topology runs one and the same automaton, whose transitions are labeled with actions of the form $a!m$, which emits a message m through interface a, or $a?m$, which receives m from interface a. The acceptance condition of a parameterized communicating automaton is given as a boolean combination of conditions of the form "at least n processes end in state s", written $\langle \#(s) \geq n \rangle$.

Definition 5. *A* parameterized communicating automaton (PCA) *over* $\mathcal{N}$ *is a tuple* $\mathcal{S} = (S, \iota, Msg, \Delta, F)$ *where* S *is the finite set of* states, $\iota \in S$ *is the* initial state, Msg *is a nonempty finite set of* messages, $\Delta \subseteq S \times (\Sigma \times Msg) \times S$ *is the* transition relation, *and* F *is the* acceptance condition, *a finite boolean combination of statements of the form* $\langle \#(s) \geq n \rangle$, *with* $s \in S$ *and* $n \in \mathbb{N}$.

The *size* $|F|$ of the acceptance condition of $\mathcal{S}$ is defined as the length of its encoding, where all integer values are written in binary.

Let $M = (P, E, \rightarrow, \lhd, \pi, \lambda)$ be an MSC. A run of $\mathcal{S}$ on M will be a mapping $\rho : E \rightarrow S$ satisfying some requirements. Intuitively, $\rho(e)$ is the local state of $\pi(e)$ after executing e. To determine when ρ is a run, we define another mapping, $\rho^- : E \rightarrow S$, denoting the source state of a transition: whenever $f \rightarrow e$, we let $\rho^-(e) = \rho(f)$; moreover, if e is $\rightarrow$-minimal, we let $\rho^-(e) = \iota$. With this, we say that ρ is a run of $\mathcal{S}$ on M if, for all $(e, f) \in \lhd$, there is a message $m \in Msg$ such that $(\rho^-(e), (\lambda(e), m), \rho(e)) \in \Delta$, and $(\rho^-(f), (\lambda(f), m), \rho(f)) \in \Delta$. A run ρ is accepting if it satisfies the acceptance condition. In particular, ρ satisfies $\langle \#(s) \geq n \rangle$ when $|\{e \in E \mid e$ is $\rightarrow$-maximal and $\rho(e) = s\}| \geq n$.

The set of MSCs that allow for an accepting run is denoted by $L(\mathcal{S})$. Given a topology $\mathcal{T}$, we let $L_{\mathcal{T}}(\mathcal{S}) = L(\mathcal{S}) \cap \mathsf{MSC}_{\mathcal{T}}$.

Remark 6. We could add labels from a finite alphabet to the events of MSCs and to the transitions of PCAs. Such labels can be handled similarly to the λ-labeling, and all our results can easily be adapted to this setting. Similarly, allowing internal transitions for PCAs would not add any technical difficulties.

Verification Problems. The *non-emptiness problem* asks, given a PCA $\mathcal{S}$, whether its language $L(\mathcal{S})$ is non empty; or in other words, whether $L_{\mathcal{T}}(\mathcal{S}) \neq \varnothing$ for some topology $\mathcal{T}$. The *(local) reachability problem* asks, given a PCA $\mathcal{S}$ and a state s of $\mathcal{S}$, whether there exists a run of $\mathcal{S}$ in which some process reaches the state s. It can be seen as a special instance of the non-emptiness problem, by modifying the acceptance condition of $\mathcal{S}$ to $\langle \#(s) \geq 1 \rangle$.

Notice that the non-emptiness problem $L_{\mathcal{T}}(\mathcal{S}) \neq \varnothing$ for a *fixed* topology $\mathcal{T}$ is already undecidable, since two finite automata connected by two queues can easily simulate a Turing machine. Furthermore, many decidable restrictions over fixed topologies remain undecidable in the parameterized case: for instance, bounding the number of contexts, or even of actions, performed by each process, or imposing rendez-vous synchronization (even when restricted to pipeline topologies [7]). The idea is that the unbounded number of processes can be used to construct a PCA whose behaviors are grid-like MSCs of arbitrary height and width (see Figs. 3 and 4). It is then easy to encode runs of a Turing machine: the unbounded horizontal direction encodes the tape of the machine, and the vertical direction its evolution with time.

In the remaining of the paper, we will study several decidable underapproximations of the problem. For a family $(\mathcal{C}_i)_i$ of classes of MSCs (for the concrete families studied in Sect. 4, the index i is a tuple of integers), we define the problem $\mathcal{C}$-NONEMPTINESS as follows (and similarly, $\mathcal{C}$-REACHABILITY):

> *Input:* i in unary, a set of interfaces $\mathcal{N}$, a PCA $\mathcal{S}$ over $\mathcal{N}$
> *Question:* $L(\mathcal{S}) \cap \mathcal{C}_i \neq \varnothing$?

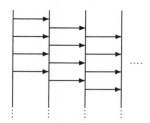
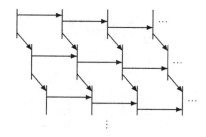

Fig. 3. Undecidability with pipelines and rendez-vous synchronization

Fig. 4. Undecidability with a bounded number of actions on each process, using grid topologies

3   Split-Width

In this section, we introduce the notion of split-width, and state our decidability result for MSCs of bounded split-width. The main motivation behind split-width is that it allows to design generic decision procedures that apply to many under-approximation classes, instead of having to develop for each class a specific decision procedure with its complexity. Several examples of classes of MSCs that are captured with split-width will be given in Sect. 4.

The idea of split-width is to decompose an MSC into *atomic* pieces consisting of a pair of matching send and receive events, using two operations: *split* (removing some process edges of the MSC), and *divide* (separating the resulting graph into two independent parts). This is described below as a two-player game. First, we introduce the notion of split MSC (an MSC missing process edges).

Definition 7. *A* split (pre-)MSC *is a tuple* $M = (P, O, E, \rightarrow, \dashrightarrow, \lhd, \pi, \lambda)$, *where* $(P, E, \rightarrow \cup \dashrightarrow, \lhd, \pi, \lambda)$ *is a (pre-)MSC,* $\dashrightarrow \cap \rightarrow = \varnothing$, $O \subseteq P$ *is the set of* open processes *of* M, *and every split process is open, i.e.,* $\{p \in P \mid (E_p)^2 \cap \dashrightarrow \neq \varnothing\} \subseteq O$.

The $\dashrightarrow$ edges are called *elastic*, and the $\rightarrow$ edges *rigid*. Processes of $P \setminus O$ are called *closed*. The intuition is that an open process of M is a process that may be missing some of its events or process edges, and an elastic edge represents a missing part of a process between two events. Any MSC can be seen as a split MSC, by taking O and $\dashrightarrow$ empty.

A *block* of a split (pre-)MSC M is a maximal connected component of $(E, \rightarrow)$ on some *open* process. In particular, M has exactly $|O| + |\dashrightarrow|$ blocks.

Several split MSCs are depicted in Fig. 5. Elastic edges are represented by red dotted lines. Open processes are indicated by dotted lines at their extremities. For instance, M' has one open process with 3 blocks, and M_2' has 2 open processes, with resp. 1 and 2 blocks.

We call *splitting* an edge of M the action of making elastic some rigid edge $e \rightarrow f$ of M. The resulting split MSC is $M' = (P, O \cup \{\pi(e)\}, E, \rightarrow \setminus \{(e, f)\}, \dashrightarrow \cup$

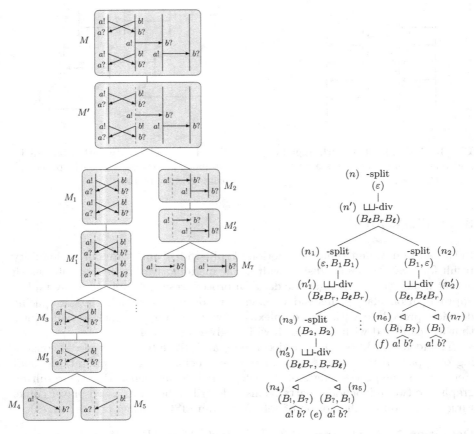

Fig. 5. A split decomposition of width 4 (Color figure online)

Fig. 6. 4-DST associated with the decomposition of Fig. 5 (Color figure online)

$\{(e, f)\}, \vartriangleleft, \pi, \lambda)$. For instance in Fig. 5, M' is obtained by splitting two process edges of M.

We say that M can be *divided* into $M_1 = (P_1, O_1, E_1, \rightarrow_1, \dashrightarrow_1, \pi_1, \lambda_1)$ and $M_2 = (P_2, O_2, E_2, \rightarrow_2, \dashrightarrow_2, \pi_2, \lambda_2)$ when M_1 and M_2 are split (pre)-MSCs, and $E = E_1 \uplus E_2$, $\rightarrow = \rightarrow_1 \uplus \rightarrow_2$, $\vartriangleleft = \vartriangleleft_1 \uplus \vartriangleleft_2$, $\pi = \pi_1 \uplus \pi_2$, $\lambda = \lambda_1 \uplus \lambda_2$, and for $i \in \{1, 2\}$, $O_i = O \cap P_i$ and $\dashrightarrow_i \subseteq (\rightarrow \cup \dashrightarrow)^+$. For instance, in Fig. 5, M' can be divided into M_1 and M_2. A *connected component* of M is a split MSC $M_1 = (P_1, O_1, E_1, \rightarrow_1, \dashrightarrow_1, \pi_1, \lambda_1)$ such that E_1 is a connected component of $(E, \rightarrow \cup \vartriangleleft)$. Then, either $M = M_1$ or M can be divided into M_1 and some M_2.

Split-Game. Let M be a split MSC with at most k blocks. A *split-game with budget* k on M is a two player game in which the existential player (Eve) tries to prove that M has split-width at most k, while the universal player (Adam) tries to disprove it. Eve begins by trying to disconnect M by splitting some of its process edges, with the condition that the resulting split MSC M' has at most k blocks. Adam then chooses a connected component M'' of M', and the game resumes on M''. Eve wins a play if it ends in an *atomic* MSC, i.e. a pair of matching send and receive events. She loses if she cannot disconnect a non-atomic MSC without introducing more than k blocks.

The *split-width* of an MSC M is the minimal k such that Eve wins the split-game with budget k on M. It is defined identically for pre-MSCs. We denote by SW_k the set of MSCs of split-width at most k.

Example 8. Eve wins the split-game with budget 4 on M (see Fig. 5). She starts by splitting two process edges of M, which results in the split MSC M' with three blocks. M' has two connected components, M_1 and M_2, providing two choices for Adam. If he chooses M_2, Eve wins by cutting the only remaining process edge: both connected components of the resulting M_2' are atomic. If he chooses M_1, Eve split the middle process edge on the first process, which creates two more blocks, and results in a total of four blocks. M_1' has two isomorphic connected components, so Adam's choices are all equivalent. Eve can then cut the two remaining process edges while still respecting her budget of four blocks.

Shuffle and Merge. One can also give a bottom-up description of split-width. The duals of the split and divide operations are called respectively *merge* ($\curlywedge$) and *shuffle* ($\sqcup\!\sqcup$). $\curlywedge(M)$ is the set of split MSCs that can be obtained by making some elastic edges of M rigid, and/or closing some of its open processes. $M_1 \sqcup\!\sqcup M_2$ is the set of split MSCs M such that M can be divided into M_1 and M_2.

An MSC has split-width at most k when it can be obtain by combining atomic MSCs with shuffle and merge operations, while keeping the number of blocks at most k at each step.

Remark 9. The notion of open and closed processes is new. Our bound on the number of blocks (i.e. the number of open processes plus the number of elastic edges) replaces the bound on the number of elastic edges only that was used in [1,2] for the split-width of MSCs over fixed architectures. When the topology $\mathcal{T}$ is fixed, the two definitions are equivalent since the number of open processes is already bounded by the number of processes in $\mathcal{T}$. This is no longer true in the parameterized case. For instance, the families of MSCs defined in Figs. 3 and 4 can be decomposed into atomic pieces while using only two elastic edges, but this introduces an unbounded number of open processes. In fact, they embed a grid, hence they should have unbounded width.

Remark 10. For MSCs, split-width is equivalent to tree-width and clique-width: there are linear bounds between the three measures (the proof is an easy adaptation from the non-parameterized case [10]). The motivation for introducing split-width rather than using existing measures on graphs is that it allows to take into account the specificities of MSCs, and is thus both simpler to understand and to use. In particular, using tree-width or clique-width would result in more involved automata constructions in Sect. 5.

Notice also that a bound on the split-width of an MSC M induces a bound on the tree-width of the observable topology $\mathcal{T}_M$ (See Theorem 20).

Decidability. The non-emptiness problem becomes decidable when restricted to MSCs of bounded split-width. Roughly, the proof goes as follows. First, we show that trees representing Eve's winning strategies can be abstracted by trees over a *finite* alphabet (that depends only on the bound k on split-width). Then, we reduce the verification problems for PCAs to emptiness problems on tree automata. The details for these constructions will be given in Sect. 5. The proof is inspired from the non-parameterized case [2], and we show that the complexity remains the same in our setting.

Theorem 11. SW-NonEmptiness *is* Exptime-*complete, and only polynomial in the number of states and transitions of the input PCA.*

4   Classes of Bounded Split-Width

The decision procedures based on split-width are generic and apply to various classes of MSCs (the main condition being that MSCs in the class have bounded split-width). When the topology is fixed, this covers many well-studied restrictions [10]. In this section, we give two examples of such classes that can be generalized to the parameterized setting: existentially bounded MSCs, and context-bounded MSCs. We also define a further extension of context-bounded MSCs, called *tile-bounded* MSCs, and show that it is equivalent to bounded split-width.

Existentially Bounded MSCs. M is called *existentially k-bounded* when there exists a linearization $\leq_{\mathrm{lin}}$ of its events (i.e. a total order extending $\leq$) such that there are at most k *process or message edges* going out of any prefix of the linearization: for all $g \in E$,

$$\left|\left\{(e,f) \in E^2 \mid (e \lhd f \vee e \to f) \wedge e \leq_{\mathrm{lin}} g <_{\mathrm{lin}} f\right\}\right| \leq k.$$

In the case of MSCs over a fixed topology, this is equivalent to bounding the number of pending messages at each prefix of the linearization, which is the usual definition of existentially bounded. This is no longer the case when considering topologies with an unbounded number of processes. For instance, the MSC of Fig. 3 is not existentially k-bounded. It is possible to find a linearization for which every prefix has at most one pending message, but it is not possible to simultaneously bound the number of non-terminated processes.

We denote by EB_k the set of all existentially k-bounded MSCs over $\mathcal{N}$.

Lemma 12. *An existentially k-bounded MSC has split-width at most $k + 2$.*

Proof. Eve's strategy is as follows. She successively isolates the first events of the linearization by splitting the process edges originating from them, until a pair of matching send/receive events is disconnected. Adam chooses the remaining component, and Eve continues as before. In the split MSC obtained by isolating the first events $e_1 <_{\text{lin}} \ldots <_{\text{lin}} e_i$ of the linearization and removing the disconnected messages, each block either consists of a single e_j $(1 \leq j \leq i)$, or only contains events that occur after e_i in the linearization, and is the last block on some open process. Blocks of the first kind are necessarily send events whose matching receive event occurs after e_i, hence they correspond to pending messages at e_i. Now consider a block of the second kind, and let f be its first event. Then f must occur after e_i in the linearization (otherwise, its block would be of the first kind). Moreover, since its process is open, there must be some $e \in \{e_1, \ldots, e_i\}$ such that $e \to f$ in the initial MSC. Hence, each block of the second kind correspond to a pending process edge at e_i (the edge $e \to f$). Thus, there are in total at most k blocks. Eve introduces at most two extra blocks when splitting a process edge. Hence she wins with budget $k + 2$. □

Eve's winning strategy results in a tree that is word-like [2,10], i.e., at every binary node, one of the subtree is small (bounded size). Hence, we can use word automata instead of tree automata, resulting in a better complexity for the verification problems.

Theorem 13. EB-NONEMPTINESS *is* PSPACE-*complete.*

Context-Bounded MSCs. A context is an interval of events on a process, in which only one interface is accessed, and in a single direction (send or receive). More formally, let $M = (P, E, \to, \lhd, \pi, \lambda)$ be an MSC. A *context* of M is a subset $c = \{e_1, \ldots, e_n\}$ of E such that $e_1 \to \cdots \to e_n$ and $\lambda(e_i) = \lambda(e_j)$ for all i, j.

An MSC M is k-*context bounded* when for all $p \in P$, there are contexts $c_1, \ldots, c_i$ with $i \leq k$ such that $E_p = c_1 \uplus \ldots \uplus c_i$. The class of k-context bounded MSCs has unbounded split-width. Actually, this is even the case for MSCs having a bounded number of events on every process (see Fig. 4). However, we obtain a bound on split-width when we additionally require that the topology has bounded tree-width.

Lemma 14. *If M is a k-context-bounded MSC and $\mathcal{T}_M$ has tree-width at most h, then M has split-width at most $k(h + 1) + 2$.*

We denote by $\mathsf{CB}_{k,h}$ the set of all k-context bounded MSCs over topologies of tree-width at most h.

Theorem 15. CB-NONEMPTINESS *is* EXPTIME-*complete, and polynomial in the number of states and transitions of the input PCA.*

Tile-Bounded MSCs. We can generalize the notion of contexts introduced above to *tiles*, which are independant parts of an MSC involving a *bounded* number of processes. In some sense, this section gives the link between fixed and parameterized topologies, when it comes to conditions ensuring decidability. Intuitively, an MSC with split-width at most k over an arbitrary topology (involving arbitrarily many processes) can be decomposed in tiles involving at most some fixed number (k) of processes. Moreover, each tile has bounded split-width and each process intersects at most some fixed number of tiles.

A k-*tile* is a split MSC T of split-width at most k and having only open processes. In particular, T has at most k blocks, hence at most k processes.

Let $M = (P, E, \to, \lhd, \pi, \lambda)$ be an MSC. A (k, ℓ)-*tile-decomposition* of M is a sequence $T_1, \ldots, T_n$ of k-tiles such that $M \in \mathcal{M}(T_1 \sqcup\!\sqcup \ldots \sqcup\!\sqcup T_n)$ and every process $p \in P$ is part of at most ℓ tiles. An MSC is called (k, ℓ)-*tile-bounded* when it admits some (k, ℓ)-*tile-decomposition*.

Example 16. A $(5, 3)$-decomposition with three tiles is depicted on the right. The first and the last process intersect with one tile, the middle one with 3 tiles and the other two processes intersect with two tiles. Tiles T_1 and T_3 have split-width exactly 5 (note that the first process is counted as open in T_1). Tile T_2 tile has split-width 4.

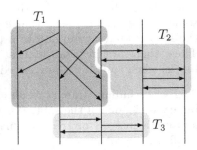

Example 17. A k-context bounded MSC M (see page 11) admits a $(2k+2, 2|\mathcal{N}|)$-tile-decomposition. The tile decomposition is given by defining, for each pair of processes (p, q) connected in $\mathcal{T}_M$, a tile $T_{p,q}$ induced by the contexts of p in which it sends to q, and the contexts of q in which it receives from p. Notice that a tile needs not be a connected graph. In particular, each tile has at most $2k$ blocks, and can be decomposed by disconnecting one by one its messages, which introduces at most 2 extra blocks. Each process of M takes part in at most $2|\mathcal{N}|$ tiles, one for each type $(a!, a?, \ldots)$ of contexts it has.

We obtain the same results as for context-bounded MSCs. We denote by $\mathsf{TB}_{k,\ell,h}$ the set of (k, ℓ)-tile-bounded MSCs M such that $\mathcal{T}_M$ has tree-width at most h.

Lemma 18. *Let* $M \in \mathsf{TB}_{k,\ell,h}$. *Then* M *has split-width at most* $2k^2\ell^2(h + 1)$.

Theorem 19. TB-NONEMPTINESS *is* EXPTIME-*complete, and polynomial in the number of states and transitions of the input PCA.*

In fact, such bounds are equivalent to bounding split-width, as shown by the theorem below.

Theorem 20. *Let* $M \in \mathsf{SW}_k$. *Then* $\mathcal{T}_M$ *has tree-width at most* $k - 1$, *and* M *is* $(k^2 + 2k, 3|\mathcal{N}|^k)$-*tile-bounded.*

5   Tree Interpretation

We present the decision procedures leading to our complexity results. The general idea is to encode MSCs of bounded split-width into binary trees over a finite alphabet, and reduce our verification problems to problems on tree automata.

Split-Terms. The encoding of MSCs of bounded split-width into trees is based on the bottom-up description of split-width. Recall that an MSC has split-width at most k if it can be constructed by combining through shuffles and merges split MSCs with at most k blocks, the starting points being atomic MSCs. This construction can be described by a *split-term*, that is, a term over the following grammar: $s ::= a! \lhd b? \mid \Lambda(s) \mid s \sqcup s$ (with $a, b \in \mathcal{N}$).

However, since the merge and shuffle operations are ambiguous, a split-term may correspond to several MSCs. The next step is to disambiguate these operations by adding labels to the nodes of split-terms, describing respectively how the blocks of the children are shuffled, or which blocks are merged and which processes are closed.

Compared to the non-parameterized case [1,2], the difficulty is that the number of processes may grow arbitrarily along the DST, instead of being fixed from the beginning – and we still need to use labels from a bounded domain. The solution comes from the distinction between open and closed processes, and the fact that the number of *open* processes stays bounded. Merge and shuffle operations only act on open processes: a merge makes some elastic edges rigid (which are all located on open processes, by definition), and/or closes some open processes. Similarly, a shuffle of two split MSCs M_1 and M_2 may only combine some pairs of *open* processes of M_1 and M_2 by shuffling their blocks and adding elastic edges between them. It simply takes the disjoint union of closed processes.

Thus, the disambiguated labels will focus on open processes. The idea is to describe how many blocks each process has after the operation, and the origin of each block.

A k-*disambiguated split-term* (k-*DST*) is a split-term in which each internal node is labeled by a tuple of words $(w_p)_{1 \leq p \leq m}$ such that $\sum_{p=1}^{m} |w_p| \leq k$, and

- For a $\sqcup$-node, the word $w_p \in \{B_\ell, B_r\}^+$ describes the composition of some open process, where B_ℓ stands for a block coming from the left child, and B_r stands for a block coming from the right child (see for instance the label of n' in Fig. 6 which describes the origin of the 3 blocks of the open process of M' in Fig. 5).
- For a Λ-node, the word $w_p \in \{B_i \mid 1 \leq i \leq k\}^*$ describes how the blocks of the p-th open process of its child are merged: B_i stands for a block resulting from the merge of i consecutive blocks of the child. We use $w_p = \varepsilon$ to indicate that process p is closed, merging all its blocks if any. For instance, in Figs. 5 and 6 the label (B_2, B_2) of node n_3 indicates that on both process of M'_3, the two blocks are merged in M_3.
- For a $\lhd$-node, $m \leq 2$ and the word $w_p \in \{B_!, B_?\}$ indicates that the p-th open process consists of the send (resp. receive) event. If $m = 2$ then $w_1 \neq w_2$. For instance, n_7 is labeled $(B_!)$, which means that in M_7 the process of the send event is open whereas the process of the receive event is closed.

We denote by DST^k the set of all k-DSTs. A k-DST is called *valid* when the label of each node is coherent with the number of processes and blocks appearing in the label of its child/children. For instance, we cannot have $w_p = B_2 B_1$ at a $\wedge$-node if its child does not have 3 blocks on process p.

A valid k-DST t can be associated with a unique split pre-MSC (which is not necessarily a split MSC) $M_t = (P, O, E, \rightarrow, \dashrightarrow, \lhd, \pi, \lambda)$, defined as follows. E is the set of leaves of t, and λ associates with a leaf e its label. We let $e \lhd f$ whenever e and f are respectively the left and right children of a same $\lhd$-node.

To determine whether two leaves e and f are connected by a $\rightarrow$-edge, we proceed as follows. We track the block associated with leaf e, until reaching a $\wedge$-node n in which it is merged with the block on its right (see example in green in Fig. 6). Similarly, we track the block associated with leaf f, until reaching a $\wedge$-node n' in which it is merged with the block on its left (in blue in Fig. 6). We set $e \rightarrow f$ if $n = n'$ and the blocks coincide. Similarly, we let $e \dashrightarrow f$ when no merge ever occurs on the right of the block of e or on the left of the block of f, and at the root, the block of f is located just after the block of e.

We identify processes with connected components of $(E, \rightarrow \cup \dashrightarrow)$. To determine whether the process of an event e is open or closed, we walk up the tree remembering the process of e, until reaching a $\wedge$-node in which it is closed, or the root (in which case it is open).

For example, in Figs. 5 and 6 the split pre-MSC associated with the k-DST starting in node n_i (resp. n_i') is M_i (resp. M_i').

The next lemma states that the conditions for M_t to be an MSC can be checked by a tree automaton. We denote by $\mathsf{DST}^k_{\mathsf{msc}}$ the set of all valid k-DSTs t such that M_t is an MSC.

Lemma 21. *One can construct in space polynomial in k and $|\mathcal{N}|$ a deterministic bottom-up tree automaton $\mathcal{A}^k_{\mathsf{msc}}$ with $2^{\mathcal{O}(|\mathcal{N}|k^4)}$ states s.t. $L(\mathcal{A}^k_{\mathsf{msc}}) = \mathsf{DST}^k_{\mathsf{msc}}$.*

From PCAs to Tree Automata. Given a PCA, we can construct a tree automaton that accepts a tree $t \in \mathsf{DST}^k_{\mathsf{msc}}$ iff M_t is accepted by the PCA.

Lemma 22. *Let $\mathcal{S} = (S, \iota, Msg, \Delta, F)$ be a PCA, and $k \in \mathbb{N}$. There is a bottom-up tree automaton $\mathcal{A}^k_{\mathcal{S}}$ of size $|S|^{\mathcal{O}(k|F|^2)}$ such that $L(\mathcal{A}^k_{\mathcal{S}}) \cap \mathsf{DST}^k_{\mathsf{msc}} = \{t \in \mathsf{DST}^k_{\mathsf{msc}} \mid M_t \in L(\mathcal{S})\}$. It can be constructed in space polynomial in k and $|F|$, and logarithmic in $|S|$ and $|\Delta|$.*

Proof. $\mathcal{A}^k_{\mathcal{S}}$ guesses a run of $\mathcal{S}$ on M_t, and inductively checks that it is a valid accepting run. To do so, it remembers the states of $\mathcal{S}$ before and after each block in the split MSC associated with the current subtree, that is, a pair (ρ^-, ρ^+) of partial functions from $[k]$ to S. (The blocks are numbered according to their position in the concatenation $w_1 w_2 \ldots w_m$ of the words in the label of the current node.) In addition, for each $s \in S$ appearing in F, $\mathcal{A}^k_{\mathcal{S}}$ remembers the number n_s of closed processes that ends in state s, up to the maximal n such that $\langle \#(s) \geq n \rangle$ appears in F. A state is accepting if it satisfies F.

At leaves, $\mathcal{A}^k_{\mathcal{S}}$ remembers the type of action executed (in Σ), and at a $\lhd$-node of the form $a! \lhd b?$, it guesses a message m and transitions $p \xrightarrow{a!m} p'$ and

$q \xrightarrow{b?m} q'$ of $\mathcal{S}$. The functions ρ^- and ρ^+ of the $\lhd$-node are initialized accordingly. For instance, after reading $a!$ $\lhd_{(B_!, B_?)}$ $b?$ and guessing the transitions, $\mathcal{A}^k_\mathcal{S}$ goes to the state where $\rho^-(1) = p, \rho^+(1) = p', \rho^-(2) = q, \rho^+(2) = q'$ and ρ^-, ρ^+ are undefined elsewhere. After reading $a!$ $\lhd_{(B_?)}$ $b?$, $\mathcal{A}^k_\mathcal{S}$ checks that $p = \iota$ and increments $n_{p'}$, and moves to state $\rho^-(1) = q, \rho^+(1) = q'$.

The functions ρ^- and ρ^+ are updated at each $\sqcup\!\sqcup$- and $\wedge\!\wedge$-node according to the renaming of the blocks. At a $\wedge\!\wedge$-node, $\mathcal{A}^k_\mathcal{S}$ checks than whenever two blocks b and $b+1$ are merged, $\rho^+(b) = \rho^-(b+1)$. It also checks that each process being closed starts in ι, and increments the counter n_s of its end state s (unless it has already reached its maximal value). □

We then have $L(\mathcal{S}) \cap \mathsf{SW}_k \neq \varnothing$ iff $L(\mathcal{A}^k_\mathcal{S} \cap \mathcal{A}^k_{\mathsf{msc}}) \neq \varnothing$, which leads to an algorithm in time polynomial in $|S|$ and exponential in k, $|\mathcal{N}|$ and $|F|$ to decide the non-emptiness of $L(\mathcal{S}) \cap \mathsf{SW}_k$. This proves the upperbound of Theorem 11.

Classes of Bounded Split-With. The above decision procedure can be adapted for any class $\mathcal{C}$ of MSCs of split-width at most k, provided we can construct an automaton $\mathcal{A}_\mathcal{C}$ that accepts only encodings of MSCs in $\mathcal{C}$, and at least one encoding for each $M \in \mathcal{C}$. Under those assumptions, and given a PCA $\mathcal{S}$, deciding whether $L(\mathcal{S}) \cap \mathcal{C} = \varnothing$ e.g. reduces to deciding whether $L(\mathcal{A}^k_\mathcal{S} \cap \mathcal{A}^k_{\mathsf{msc}} \cap \mathcal{A}_\mathcal{C}) = \varnothing$.

This applies in particular to existentially bounded MSCs, and context- or tile-bounded MSCs over topologies of bounded tree-width. The construction of $\mathcal{A}_\mathcal{C}$ is in all three cases based on the proof that $\mathcal{C}$ has split-width at most k.

Note that this would also apply for instance to any class of bounded split-width that is recognized by a PCA.

6 Further Results

Model-Checking. The results presented in Sects. 3 and 5 can be generalized to model-checking problems (details can be found in [16]). Our most general decidability result states that the model-checking of PCAs against Monadic Second-Order (MSO) formulas is decidable. The idea is to construct, for a given specification φ, a tree automaton $\mathcal{A}^k_\varphi$ that accepts a valid k-DST t iff M_t satisfies φ. The bounded split-width model-checking problem then reduces to testing whether $L(\mathcal{A}^k_\mathcal{S} \cap \mathcal{A}^k_{\neg\varphi} \cap \mathcal{A}^k_{\mathsf{msc}}) = \varnothing$, and similarly for the other classes.

However, when the specification φ is given by an MSO formula, the construction of $\mathcal{A}^k_\varphi$ is non-elementary. Towards a better complexity, we study model checking against PDL specifications. PDL is both expressive (it subsumes most if not all temporal logics), easy to use and understand, and enjoys a very good complexity. We show that model-checking against PDL formulas is Exptime-complete, i.e., not harder than non-emptiness and reachability. It remains in Exptime when we extend PDL with converse (CPDL), and is 2-Exptime-complete for ICPDL (PDL with converse and intersection). A summary of our results is given in Fig. 7.

	$\mathcal{C}_k = \mathsf{EB}_k$	$\mathcal{C}_{(k,h)} = \mathsf{CB}_{k,h}$	$\mathcal{C}_k = \mathsf{SW}_k$	$\mathcal{C}_{(k,\ell,h)} = \mathsf{TB}_{k,\ell,h}$
$\mathcal{C}$-REACHABILITY				
$\mathcal{C}$-NONEMPTINESS	PSPACE-c		EXPTIME-c	
$\mathcal{C}$-CPDL-SAT/MC				
$\mathcal{C}$-ICPDL-SAT/MC	EXPSPACE-c		2-EXPTIME-c	
$\mathcal{C}$-MSO-SAT/MC		Non-elementary		

Fig. 7. Complexity results. All problems are only polynomial in the number of states and transitions of the input PCA.

Multi-pushdown Processes. Our model could be extended by adding one or several stacks to processes, similarly to what is done in the case of fixed architectures [2]. We could also allow several FIFO channels between any pair of processes. This means relaxing the definition of topologies to allow loops or multiple edges, and similarly adapt the definition of MSCs. The definition of split-width and k-DSTs is the same, except that at $\lhd$-nodes, the send and receive events may be placed on the same process. Our decision procedures remain correct, with an additional check by $\mathcal{A}_{\mathsf{msc}}^k$ of the LIFO conditions on the stacks. The results on existentially-bounded MSCs, context-bounded MSCs, or tile decompositions are also still valid.

References

1. Aiswarya, C., Gastin, P.: Reasoning about distributed systems: WYSIWYG (invited talk). In: FSTTCS 2014, LIPIcs, vol. 29, pp. 11–30. Leibniz-Zentrum für Informatik (2014)
2. Aiswarya, C., Gastin, P., Narayan Kumar, K.: Verifying communicating multi-pushdown systems via split-width. In: Cassez, F., Raskin, J.-F. (eds.) ATVA 2014. LNCS, vol. 8837, pp. 1–17. Springer, Heidelberg (2014)
3. Aminof, B., Jacobs, S., Khalimov, A., Rubin, S.: Parameterized model checking of token-passing systems. In: McMillan, K.L., Rival, X. (eds.) VMCAI 2014. LNCS, vol. 8318, pp. 262–281. Springer, Heidelberg (2014)
4. Aminof, B., Kotek, T., Rubin, S., Spegni, F., Veith, H.: Parameterized model checking of rendezvous systems. In: Baldan, P., Gorla, D. (eds.) CONCUR 2014. LNCS, vol. 8704, pp. 109–124. Springer, Heidelberg (2014)
5. Bollig, B.: Logic for communicating automata with parameterized topology. In: CSL-LICS 2014. ACM (2014)
6. Bollig, B., Gastin, P., Kumar, A.: Parameterized communicating automata: Complementation and model checking. In: FSTTCS 2014, LIPIcs, vol. 29, pp. 625–637 (2014)
7. Bollig, B., Gastin, P., Schubert, J.: Parameterized verification of communicating automata under context bounds. In: Ouaknine, J., Potapov, I., Worrell, J. (eds.) RP 2014. LNCS, vol. 8762, pp. 45–57. Springer, Heidelberg (2014)
8. Brand, D., Zafiropulo, P.: On communicating finite-state machines. J. ACM **30**(2), 323–342 (1983)
9. Courcelle, B., Engelfriet, J.: Graph Structure and Monadic Second-Order Logic - A Language-Theoretic Approach. Encyclopedia of mathematics and its applications, vol. 138. Cambridge University Press, Cambridge (2012)

10. Cyriac, A.: Verification of Communicating Recursive Programs via Split-width. Ph.D. thesis, ENS Cachan (2014). http://www.lsv.ens-cachan.fr/~cyriac/download/Thesis_Aiswarya_Cyriac.pdf
11. Cyriac, A., Gastin, P., Kumar, K.N.: MSO decidability of multi-pushdown systems via split-width. In: Koutny, M., Ulidowski, I. (eds.) CONCUR 2012. LNCS, vol. 7454, pp. 547–561. Springer, Heidelberg (2012)
12. Delzanno, G., Sangnier, A., Zavattaro, G.: Parameterized verification of ad hoc networks. In: Gastin, P., Laroussinie, F. (eds.) CONCUR 2010. LNCS, vol. 6269, pp. 313–327. Springer, Heidelberg (2010)
13. Delzanno, G., Sangnier, A., Zavattaro, G.: On the power of cliques in the parameterized verification of ad hoc networks. In: Hofmann, M. (ed.) FOSSACS 2011. LNCS, vol. 6604, pp. 441–455. Springer, Heidelberg (2011)
14. Durand-Gasselin, A., Esparza, J., Ganty, P., Majumdar, R.: Model checking parameterized asynchronous shared-memory systems. In: Kroening, D., Păsăreanu, C.S. (eds.) CAV 2015. LNCS, vol. 9206, pp. 67–84. Springer, Heidelberg (2015)
15. Emerson, E.A., Namjoshi, K.S.: On reasoning about rings. Int. J. Found. Comput. Sci. **14**(4), 527–550 (2003)
16. Fortin, M., Gastin, P.: Verification of parameterized communicating automata via split-width. Technical report, LSV, ENS Cachan (2016). http://www.lsv.ens-cachan.fr/~gastin/mes-publis.php
17. Genest, B., Kuske, D., Muscholl, A.: A Kleene theorem and model checking algorithms for existentially bounded communicating automata. Inf. Comput. **204**(6), 920–956 (2006)
18. ITU-TS Recommendation Z.120anb: Formal Semantics of Message Sequence Charts (1998)
19. Qadeer, S., Rehof, J.: Context-bounded model checking of concurrent software. In: Halbwachs, N., Zuck, L.D. (eds.) TACAS 2005. LNCS, vol. 3440, pp. 93–107. Springer, Heidelberg (2005)

Automata, Logic, Games

Robust Equilibria in Mean-Payoff Games

Romain Brenguier[✉]

University of Oxford, Oxford, UK
romain.brenguier@cs.ox.ac.uk

Abstract. We study the problem of finding robust equilibria in multi-player concurrent games with mean payoff objectives. A (k,t)-robust equilibrium is a strategy profile such that no coalition of size k can improve the payoff of one its member by deviating, and no coalition of size t can decrease the payoff of other players. While deciding whether there exists such equilibria is undecidable in general, we suggest algorithms for two meaningful restrictions on the complexity of strategies. The first restriction concerns memory. We show that we can reduce the problem of the existence of a memoryless robust equilibrium to a formula in the (existential) theory of reals. The second restriction concerns randomisation. We suggest a general transformation from multiplayer games to two-player games such that pure equilibria in the first game correspond to winning strategies in the second one. Thanks to this transformation, we show that the existence of robust equilibria can be decided in polynomial space, and that the decision problem is PSPACE-complete.

1 Introduction

Games are intensively used in computer science to model interactions in computerised systems. Two player antagonistic games have been successfully used for the synthesis of reactive systems. In this context, the opponent acts as a hostile environment, and winning strategies provide controllers that ensure correctness of the system under any scenario. In order to model complex systems in which several rational entities interact, multiplayer concurrent games come into the picture. Correctness of the strategies can be specified with different solution concepts, which describe formally what is a "good" strategy. In game theory, the fundamental solution concept is Nash equilibrium [15], where no player can benefit from changing its own strategy. The notion of robust equilibria refines Nash equilibria in two ways: 1. a robust equilibrium is *resilient*, i.e. when a "small" coalition of player changes its strategy, it can not improve the payoff of one of its participants; 2. it is *immune*, i.e. when a "small" coalition changes its strategy, it will not lower the payoff of the non-deviating players. The size of what is considered a small coalition is determined by a bound k for resilience and another t for immunity. When a strategy is both k-resilient and t-immune, it is called a (k,t)-robust equilibrium. We also generalise this concept to the notion

---

R. Brenguier—Work supported by ERC Starting Grant inVEST (279499) and EPSRC grant EP/M023656/1.

© Springer-Verlag Berlin Heidelberg 2016

B. Jacobs and C. Löding (Eds.): FOSSACS 2016, LNCS 9634, pp. 217–233, 2016.
DOI: 10.1007/978-3-662-49630-5_13

(k, t, r)-robust equilibrium, where if t players are deviating, the others should not have their payoff decrease by more than r.

Example. In the design of network protocols, when many users are interacting, coalitions can easily be formed and resilient strategies are necessary to avoid deviation. It is also likely that some clients are faulty and begin to behave unexpectedly, hence the need for immune strategies.

As an example, consider a program for a server that distributes files, of which a part is represented in Fig. 1. The functions listen and send_files will be run in parallel by the server. Some choices in the design of these functions have not been fixed yet and we wish to analyse the robustness of the different alternatives.

This program uses a table clients to keep track of the clients which are connected. Notice that the table has fixed size 2, which means that if 3 clients try to connect at the same time, one of them may have its socket overwritten in the table and will have to reconnect later to get the file. We want to know what strategy the clients should use and how robust the protocol will be: can clients exploit the protocol to get their files faster than the normal usage, and how will the performance of the over clients be affected.

We consider different strategies to chose between the possible alternatives in the program of Fig. 1. The strategy that chooses alternatives 1 and 3 does not give 1-resilient equilibria even for just two clients: Player 1 can always reconnect just after its socket was closed, so that clients[0] points to player 1 once again. In this way, he can deviate from any profile to never have to wait for the file. Since the second player could do the same thing, no profile is 1-resilient (nor 1-immune). For the same reasons, the strategy 2, 3 does not give 1-resilient equilibria. The strategy 1, 4 does not give 1-resilient equilibria either, since player 1 can launch a new connection after player 2 to overwrite clients[1].

The strategy 2, 4 is the one that may give the best solution. We modelled the interaction of this program as a concurrent game for a situation with 2 potential clients in Fig. 2. The labels represent the content of the table clients: 0 means no connection, 1 means connected with player 1 and 2 connected with player 2; and the instruction that the function send_files is executing. Because the game is quite big we represent only the part where player 1 connects before player 2 and the rest of the graph can be deduced by symmetry. The actions of the players are either to wait (action w) or to connect (action ch or ct). Symbol * means any possible action. Note that in the case both player try to connect at the same time we simulate a matching penny game in order to determine which one will be treated first, this is the reason why we have two different possible actions to connect (ch for "head" and ct for "tail"). Clients have a positive reward when we send them the file they requested, this corresponds for Player i to states labelled with send(i).

If both clients try to connect in the same slot, we use a matching penny game to decide which request was the first to arrive. For a general method to transform a game with continuous time into a concurrent game, see [6, Chap. 6].

```
clients = new socket[2];

void listen() {
  while(true) {
    Socket socket = serverSocket.accept();
    if(clients[0].isConnected())
    //// Two possible alternatives:
    | 1) clients[1] = socket;
    | 2) if(socket.remoteSocketAddress()
         != clients[0].remoteSocketAddress())
    |       clients[1] = socket;
    else
       clients[0] = socket;
  } }

void send_files() {
  while(true) {
    if(clients[0].isConnected()) {
      send(clients[0]);
      clients[0].close();
    }
    //// Two possible alternatives :
    | 3) else if(clients[1].isConnected()) {
    | 4) if(clients[1].isConnected()) {
      send(clients[1]);
      clients[1].close();
} } }
```

Fig. 1. Example of a server program.   **Fig. 2.** Example of a concurrent game generated from the program of Fig. 1.

Related Works and Comparison with Nash Equilibria and Secure Equilibria. Other solution concepts have been proposed as concepts for synthesis of distributed systems, in particular Nash equilibrium [4,18,19], subgame perfect equilibria [10,17], and secure equilibria [12]. A subgame perfect equilibria is a particular kind of Nash equilibria, where at any point in the game, if we forget the history the players are still playing a Nash equilibrium. In a secure equilibria, we ask that no player can benefit or keep the same reward while reducing the payoff of other players by changing its own strategy. However these concepts present two weaknesses: 1. There is no guarantee when two (or more) users deviate together. It can happen on a network that the same person controls several devices (a laptop and a phone for instance) and can then coordinate there behaviour. In that case, the devices would be considered as different agents and Nash equilibria offers no guarantee. 2. When a deviation occurs, the strategies of the equilibrium can punish the deviating user without any regard for payoffs of the others. This can result in a situation where, because of a faulty device, the protocol is totally blocked. By comparison, finding resilient equilibria with k greater than 1, ensures that clients have no interest in forming coalitions (up to size k), and finding immune equilibria with t greater than 0 ensures that other clients will not suffer from some agents (up to t) behaving differently from what was expected.

Note that the concept of robust equilibria for games with LTL objectives is expressible in logics such as strategy logic [13] or ATL* [2]. However, satisfiability in these logic is difficult: it is 2EXPTIME-complete for ATL* and undecidable for strategy logic in general (2EXPTIME-complete fragments exist [14]). Moreover, these logics cannot express equilibria in quantitative games such as mean-payoff.

Contributions. In this paper, we study the problem of finding robust equilibria in multiplayer concurrent games. This problem is undecidable in general (see Sect. 2.3). In Sect. 3, we show that if we look for stationary (but randomised) strategies, then the problem can be decided using the theory of reals. We then turn to the case of pure (but memoryful) strategies. In Sect. 4, we describe a generic transformation from multiplayer games to two-player games. The resulting two-player game is called the *deviator game*. We show that pure equilibria in the original game correspond to winning strategies in the second one. In Sect. 5, we study quantitative games with mean-payoff objectives. We show that the game obtained by our transformation is equivalent to a multidimensional mean-payoff game. We then show that this can be reduced to a value problem with linear constraints in multidimensional mean-payoff games. We show that this can be solved in polynomial space, by making use of the structure of the deviator game. In Sect. 7, we prove the matching lower bound which shows the robustness problem is PSPACE-complete. Due to space constraints, most proofs have been omitted from this paper; they can be found in the long version of this paper [7].

2   Definitions

2.1   Weighted Concurrent Games

We study concurrent game as defined in [2] with the addition of weights on the edges.

Concurrent Games. A *weighted concurrent game* (or simply a *game*) $\mathcal{G}$ is a tuple $\langle \mathsf{Stat}, s_0, \mathsf{Agt}, \mathsf{Act}, \mathsf{Tab}, (w_A)_{A \in \mathsf{Agt}} \rangle$, where: Stat is a finite set of *states* and $s_0 \in \mathsf{Stat}$ is the *initial state*; Agt is a finite set of *players*; Act is a finite set of *actions*; a tuple $(a_A)_{A \in \mathsf{Agt}}$ containing one action a_A for each player A is called a *move*; $\mathsf{Tab} : \mathsf{Stat} \times \mathsf{Act}^{\mathsf{Agt}} \to \mathsf{Stat}$ is the *transition function*, it associates with a given state and a given move, the resulting state; for each player $A \in \mathsf{Agt}$, $w_A : \mathsf{Stat} \mapsto \mathbb{Z}$ is a *weight function* which assigns to each agent an integer weight.

In a game $\mathcal{G}$, whenever we arrive at a state s, the players simultaneously select an action. This results in a move a_{Agt}; the next state of the game is then $\mathsf{Tab}(s, a_{\mathsf{Agt}})$. This process starts from s_0 and is repeated to form an infinite sequence of states.

An example of a game is given in Fig. 2. It models the interaction of two clients A_1 and A_2 with the program presented in the introduction. The weight functions for this game are given by $w_{A_1} = 1$ in states labelled by send(1) and $w_{A_1} = 0$ elsewhere, similarly $w_{A_2} = 1$ in states labelled by send(2).

History and Plays. A *history* of the game $\mathcal{G}$ is a finite sequence of states and moves ending with a state, i.e. an word in $(\mathsf{Stat} \cdot \mathsf{Act}^{\mathsf{Agt}})^* \cdot \mathsf{Stat}$. We write h_i the i-th state of h, starting from 0, and $\mathsf{move}_i(h)$ its i-th move, thus $h = h_0 \cdot \mathsf{move}_0(h) \cdot h_1 \cdots \mathsf{move}_{n-1}(h) \cdot h_n$. The length $|h|$ of such a history is $n+1$. We write $\mathsf{last}(h)$ the last state of h, i.e. $h_{|h|-1}$. A *play* ρ is an infinite sequence of states and moves, i.e. an element of $(\mathsf{Stat} \cdot \mathsf{Act}^{\mathsf{Agt}})^\omega$. We write $\rho_{\leq n}$ for the prefix of ρ of length $n+1$, i.e. the history $\rho_0 \cdot \mathsf{move}_0(\rho) \cdots \mathsf{move}_{n-1}(\rho) \cdot \rho_n$.

The *mean-payoff* of weight w along a play ρ is the average of the weights along the play: $\mathsf{MP}_w(\rho) = \liminf_{n \to \infty} \frac{1}{n} \sum_{0 \leq k \leq n} w(\rho_k)$. The *payoff* for agent $A \in \mathsf{Agt}$ of a play ρ is the mean-payoff of the corresponding weight: $\mathsf{payoff}_A(\rho) = \mathsf{MP}_{w_A}(\rho)$. Note that it only depends on the sequence of states, and not on the sequence of moves. The *payoff vector* of the run ρ is the vector $p \in \mathbb{R}^{\mathsf{Agt}}$ such that for all players $A \in \mathsf{Agt}$, $p_A = \mathsf{payoff}_A(\rho)$; we simply write $\mathsf{payoff}(\rho)$ for this vector.

Strategies. Let $\mathcal{G}$ be a game, and $A \in \mathsf{Agt}$. A *strategy* for player A maps histories to probability distributions over actions. Formally, a strategy is a function $\sigma_A \colon (\mathsf{Stat} \cdot \mathsf{Act}^{\mathsf{Agt}})^* \cdot \mathsf{Stat} \to \mathcal{D}(\mathsf{Act})$, where $\mathcal{D}(\mathsf{Act})$ is the set of probability distributions over Act. For an action $a \in \mathsf{Act}$, we write $\sigma_A(a \mid h)$ the probability assigned to a by the distribution $\sigma(h)$. A *coalition* $C \subseteq \mathsf{Agt}$ is a set of players, its size is the number of players it contains and we write it $|C|$. A strategy $\sigma_C = (\sigma_A)_{A \in C}$ for a coalition $C \subseteq \mathsf{Agt}$ is a tuple of strategies, one for each player in C. We write σ_{-C} for a strategy of coalition $\mathsf{Agt} \setminus C$. A *strategy profile* is a strategy for Agt. We will write (σ_{-C}, σ'_C) for the strategy profile σ''_{Agt} such that if $A \in C$ then $\sigma''_A = \sigma'_A$ and otherwise $\sigma''_A = \sigma_A$. We write $\mathsf{Strat}_{\mathcal{G}}(C)$ for the set of strategies of coalition C. A strategy σ_A for player A is said *deterministic* if it does not use randomisation: for all histories h there is an action a such that $\sigma(a \mid h) = 1$. A strategy σ_A for player A is said *stationary* if it depends only on the last state of the history: for all histories h, $\sigma_A(h) = \sigma_A(\mathsf{last}(h))$.

Outcomes. Let C be a coalition, and σ_C a strategy for C. A history h is *compatible* with the strategy σ_C if, for all $k < |h| - 1$, $(\mathsf{move}_k(h))_A = \sigma_A(h_{\leq k})$ for all $A \in C$, and $\mathsf{Tab}(h_k, \mathsf{move}_k(h)) = h_{k+1}$. A play ρ is *compatible* with the strategy σ_C if all its prefixes are. We write $\mathsf{Out}_{\mathcal{G}}(s, \sigma_C)$ for the set of plays in $\mathcal{G}$ that are compatible with strategy σ_C of C and have initial state s, these paths are called *outcomes* of σ_C from s. We simply write $\mathsf{Out}_{\mathcal{G}}(\sigma_C)$ when $s = s_0$ and $\mathsf{Out}_{\mathcal{G}}$ is the set of plays that are compatible with some strategy. Note that when the coalition C is composed of all the players and the strategies are deterministic the outcome is unique.

An *objective* Ω is a set of plays and a strategy σ_C is said *winning* for objective Ω if all its outcomes belong to Ω.

Probability Measure Induced by a Strategy Profile. Given a strategy profile σ_{Agt}, the *conditional probability* of a_{Agt} given history $h \in (\mathsf{Stat} \cdot \mathsf{Act}^{\mathsf{Agt}})^*$.

Stat is $\sigma_{\mathsf{Agt}}(a_{\mathsf{Agt}} \mid h) = \prod_{A \in \mathsf{Agt}} \sigma_A(a_A \mid h)$. The probabilities $\sigma_{\mathsf{Agt}}(a_{\mathsf{Agt}} \mid h)$ induce a probability measure on the Borel σ-algebra over $(\mathsf{Stat} \cdot \mathsf{Act}^{\mathsf{Agt}})^\omega$ as follows: the probability of a basic open set $h \cdot (\mathsf{Stat} \cdot \mathsf{Act}^{\mathsf{Agt}})^\omega$ equals the product $\prod_{j=1}^n \sigma_{\mathsf{Agt}}(h_{j,A}^{\mathsf{Act}} \mid h_{\leq j})$ if $h_0 = s_0$ and $\mathsf{Tab}(h_j, h_{\mathsf{Agt},j}^{\mathsf{Act}}) = h_{j+1}$ for all $1 \leq j < n$; in all other cases, this probability is 0. By Carath?odory's extension theorem, this extends to a unique probability measure assigning a probability to every Borel subset of $(\mathsf{Stat} \cdot \mathsf{Act}^{\mathsf{Agt}})^\omega$, which we denote by $\mathrm{Pr}^{\sigma_{\mathsf{Agt}}}$. We denote by $\mathrm{E}^{\sigma_{\mathsf{Agt}}}$ the expectation operator that corresponds to $\mathrm{Pr}^{\sigma_{\mathsf{Agt}}}$, that is $\mathrm{E}^{\sigma_{\mathsf{Agt}}}(f) = \int f \, \mathrm{d}\,\mathrm{Pr}^{\sigma_{\mathsf{Agt}}}$ for all Borel measurable functions $f \colon (\mathsf{Stat} \cdot \mathsf{Act}^{\mathsf{Agt}})^\omega \mapsto \mathbb{R} \cup \{\pm\infty\}$. The expected payoff for player A of a strategy profile σ_{Agt} is $\mathsf{payoff}_A(\sigma_{\mathsf{Agt}}) = \mathrm{E}^{\sigma_{\mathsf{Agt}}}(\mathsf{MP}_{w_A})$.

2.2 Equilibria Notions

We now present the different solution concepts we will study. Solution concepts are formal descriptions of "good" strategy profiles. The most famous of them is Nash equilibrium [15], in which no single player can improve the outcome for its own preference relation, by only changing its strategy. This notion can be generalised to consider coalitions of players, it is then called a resilient strategy profile. Nash equilibria correspond to the special case of 1-resilient strategy profiles.

Resilience [3]. Given a coalition $C \subseteq \mathsf{Agt}$, a strategy profile σ_{Agt} is C-*resilient* if for all agents A in C, A cannot improve her payoff even if all agents in C change their strategies, i.e. σ_{Agt} is said C-resilient when:

$$\forall \sigma_C' \in \mathsf{Strat}_{\mathcal{G}}(C). \ \forall A \in C. \ \mathsf{payoff}_A(\sigma_{-C}, \sigma_C') \leq \mathsf{payoff}_A(\sigma_{\mathsf{Agt}})$$

Given an integer k, we say that a strategy profile is k-resilient if it is C-resilient for every coalition C of size k.

Immunity [1]. Immune strategies ensure that players *not* deviating are not too much affected by deviation. Formally, a strategy profile σ_{Agt} is *(C, r)-immune* if all players not in C, are not worse off by more than r if players in C deviates, i.e. when:

$$\forall \sigma_C' \in \mathsf{Strat}_{\mathcal{G}}(C). \ \forall A \in \mathsf{Agt} \setminus C. \ \mathsf{payoff}_A(\sigma_{\mathsf{Agt}}) - r \leq \mathsf{payoff}_A(\sigma_{-C}, \sigma_C')$$

Given an integer t, a strategy profile is said *(t, r)-immune* if it is (C, r)-immune for every coalition C of size t. Note that t-immunity as defined in [1] corresponds to $(t, 0)$-immunity.

Robust Equilibrium [1]. Combining resilience and immunity, gives the notion of robust equilibrium: a strategy profile is a (k, t, r)-*robust equilibrium* if it is both k-resilient and (t, r)-immune.

The aim of this article is to characterise robust equilibria in order to construct the corresponding strategies, and precisely describe the complexity of the following decision problem for mean-payoff games.

Robustness Decision Problem. Given a game $\mathcal{G}$, integers k, t, rational r does there exist a profile σ_{Agt}, that is a (k, t, r)-robust equilibrium σ_{Agt} in $\mathcal{G}$?

2.3 Undecidability

We show that allowing strategies that can use both randomisation and memory leads to undecidability. The problem of existence of Nash equilibria has been shown to be undecidable if we put constraints on the payoffs in [19]. The proof was improved to involve only 3 players and no constraint on the payoffs for games with terminal-reward (the weights are non-zero only in terminal vertices of the game) [5]. This corresponds to the particular case where $k = 1$, $t = 0$ for the robustness decision problem. Therefore, the following is a corollary of [5, Theorem 13].

Theorem 1. *For randomised strategies, the robustness problem is undecidable even for 3 players, $k = 1$ and $t = 0$.*

To recover decidability, two restrictions are natural. In the next section, we will show that for randomised strategies with no memory, the problem is decidable. The rest of the article is devoted to the second restriction, which concerns pure strategies.

3 Stationary Strategies

We use the *existential theory of reals*, which is the set of all existential first-order sentences that hold in the ordered field $\mathfrak{R} := (\mathbb{R}, +, \cdot, 0, 1, \leq)$, to show that the robustness decision problem is decidable. The associated decision problem is in the **PSPACE** complexity class [11]. However, since the system of equation we produce is of exponential size, we can only show that the robustness problem for (randomised) stationary strategies is in **EXPSPACE**.

Encoding of Strategies. We encode a stationary strategy σ_A, by a tuple of real variables $(\varsigma_{s,a})_{s \in \mathsf{Stat}, a \in \mathsf{Act}} \in \mathbb{R}^{\mathsf{Stat} \times \mathsf{Act}}$ such that $\varsigma_{s,a} = \sigma_A(a \mid s)$ for all $s \in \mathsf{Stat}$ and $a \in \mathsf{Act}$. We then write a formula saying that these variables describe a correct stationary strategy. The following lemma is a direct consequence of the definition of strategy.

Lemma 1. *Let $(\varsigma_{s,a})_{s \in S, a \in \mathsf{Act}}$ be a tuple of real variables. The mapping $\sigma \colon s, a \mapsto \varsigma_s$ is a stationary strategy if, and only if, ς is a solution of the following equation:*

$$\mu(\varsigma) := \bigwedge_{s \in S} \left(\sum_{a \in \mathsf{Act}} \varsigma_{s,a} = 1 \wedge \bigwedge_{a \in \mathsf{Act}} \varsigma_{s,a} \geq 0 \right)$$

Payoff of a Profile. We now give an equation which links a stationary strategy profile and its payoff. For this we notice that a concurrent game where the stationary strategy profile has been fixed corresponds to a *Markov reward process* [16]. We recall that a Markov reward process is a tuple $\langle S, P, r \rangle$ where: 1. S is a set of states; 2. $P \in \mathbb{R}^{S \times S}$ is a transition matrix; 3. $r \colon S \mapsto \mathbb{R}$ is a reward function. The expected value is then the expectation of the average reward of r. This value for each state is described by a system of equations in [16, Theorem 8.2.6]. We reuse these equations to obtain Theorem 2. Details of the proof are in the appendix.

Theorem 2. *Let σ_{Agt} be a stationary strategy profile. The expectation for MP_w of σ_{Agt} from s is the component γ_s of the solution γ of the equation:*

$$\psi(\gamma, \sigma_{\mathsf{Agt}}, w) := \exists \beta \in \mathbb{R}^S . \bigwedge_{s \in S} \left(\gamma_s = \sum_{a_{\mathsf{Agt}} \in \mathsf{Act}^{\mathsf{Agt}}} \gamma_{\mathsf{Tab}(s, a_{\mathsf{Agt}})} \cdot \prod_{A \in \mathsf{Agt}} \sigma_A(a_A \mid s) \right)$$

$$\wedge \bigwedge_{s \in S} \left(\gamma_s + \beta_s = w(s) + \sum_{a_{\mathsf{Agt}} \in \mathsf{Act}^{\mathsf{Agt}}} \beta_{\mathsf{Tab}(s, a_{\mathsf{Agt}})} \cdot \prod_{A \in \mathsf{Agt}} \sigma_A(a_A \mid s) \right)$$

Optimal Payoff of a Deviation. We now want to keep the strategy profile fixed but also allow deviations and investigate what is the maximum payoff that a coalition can achieve by deviating. The system that is obtained is then a *Markov decision processes*. We recall that a Markov decision process (MDP) is a tuple $\langle S, A, P, r \rangle$, where: 1. S is a the non-empty, countable set of *states*. 2. A is a set of *actions*. 3. $P \colon S \times A \times S \mapsto [0, 1]$ is the *transition relation*. It is such that for each $s \in S \setminus S_{\exists}$ and $a \in A$, $\sum_{(s,a,s') \in S \times A \times S} P(s, a, s') = 1$. 4. $r \colon S \mapsto \mathbb{R}$ is the *reward function*. The *optimal value* is then maximal expectation that can be obtained by a strategy. The optimal values in such systems can be described by a linear program [16, Sect. 9.3]. We reuse this linear program to characterise optimal values against a strategy profile C. Details of the proof can be found in the appendix.

Theorem 3. *Let σ_{Agt} be a stationary strategy profile, C a coalition, s a state and w a weight function. The highest expectation $\mathsf{Agt} \setminus C$ can obtain for w in $\mathcal{G}$ from s: $\sup_{\sigma_{-C}} E^{\sigma_C, \sigma_{-C}}(\mathsf{MP}_w, s)$, is the smallest γ_s component of a solution of the system of inequation:*

$$\phi(\gamma, \sigma_C, w) := \bigwedge_{a_{-C} \in \mathsf{Act}^{\mathsf{Agt} \setminus C}} \bigwedge_{s \in S} \gamma_s \geq \sum_{a_C \in \mathsf{Act}^C} \gamma_{\delta(s, a_C, a_{-C})} \cdot \prod_{A \in C} \sigma_A(a_A \mid s)$$

$$\wedge \bigwedge_{a_{-C} \in \mathsf{Act}^{\mathsf{Agt} \setminus C}} \bigwedge_{s \in S} \gamma_s \geq w(s) - \beta_s + \sum_{a_C \in \mathsf{Act}^C} \left(\beta_{\delta(s, a_C, a_{-C})} \cdot \prod_{A \in C} \sigma_A(a_A \mid s) \right)$$

Expressing the Existence of Robust Equilibria. Putting these results together, we obtain the results. Intuitively, $\psi(\gamma, \sigma_{\mathsf{Agt}}, w_A)$ ensures that γ correspond to the payoff for σ_{Agt} of A, and $\phi(\gamma', \sigma_{-C}, w_A)$ makes γ' correspond to the payoff for a deviation of σ_C.

Theorem 4. *Let σ_{Agt} be a strategy profile.*

- *It is C-resilient if, and only if, it satisfies the formula:*

$$\rho(C, \sigma_{\mathsf{Agt}}) := \bigwedge_{A \in C} \exists \gamma, \gamma' . \left(\psi(\gamma, \sigma_{\mathsf{Agt}}, w_A) \wedge \phi(\gamma', \sigma_{-C}, w_A) \wedge (\gamma' \leq \gamma) \right)$$

- *It is C, r-immune if, and only if, it satisfies equation:*

$$\iota(C, \sigma_{\mathsf{Agt}}) := \bigwedge_{A \not\subseteq C} \exists \gamma, \gamma'. \ (\psi(\gamma, \sigma_{\mathsf{Agt}}, A) \wedge \phi(\gamma', \sigma_{-C}, -w_A) \wedge \gamma - r \leq -\gamma')$$

– *There is a robust equilibria if, and only if, the following equation is satisfiable:*

$$\exists \varsigma \in \mathbb{R}^{\mathsf{Agt} \times \mathsf{Stat} \times \mathsf{Act}}. \ \mu(\varsigma) \wedge \bigwedge_{C \subseteq \mathsf{Agt} || C | \leq k} \rho(C, \varsigma) \wedge \bigwedge_{C \subseteq \mathsf{Agt} || C | \leq t} \iota(C, \varsigma)$$

Theorem 5. *The robustness problem is in* EXPSPACE *for stationary strategies.*

Proof. By Theorem 4, the existence of a robust equilibria is equivalent to the satisfiability of a formula in the existential theory of reals. This formula can be of exponential size with respect to k and t, since a conjunction over coalitions of these size is considered. The best known upper bound for the theory of the reals in PSPACE [11], which gives the EXPSPACE upper bound for our problem.

4   Deviator Game

We now turn to the case of non-randomised strategies. In order to obtain simple algorithms for the robustness problem, we use a correspondence with zero-sum two-players game. Winning strategies has been well studied in computer science and we can make use of existing algorithms. We present the deviator game, which is a transformation of multiplayer game into a turn-based zero-sum game, such that there are strong links between robust equilibria in the first one and winning strategies in the second one. This is formalised in Theorem 6. Note that the proofs of this section are independent from the type of objectives we consider, and the result could be extended beyond mean-payoff objectives.

Deviator. The basic notion we use to solve the robustness problem is that of deviators. It identifies players that cause the current deviation from the expected outcome. A *deviator* from move a_{Agt} to a'_{Agt} is a player $D \in \mathsf{Agt}$ such that $a_D \neq a'_D$. We write this set of deviators: $\mathsf{Dev}(a_{\mathsf{Agt}}, a'_{\mathsf{Agt}}) = \{A \in \mathsf{Agt} \mid a_A \neq a'_A\}$. We extend the definition to histories and strategies by taking the union of deviator sets, formally $\mathsf{Dev}(h, \sigma_{\mathsf{Agt}}) = \bigcup_{0 \leq i < |h|} \mathsf{Dev}(\mathsf{move}_i(h), \sigma_{\mathsf{Agt}}(h_{\leq i}))$. It naturally extends to plays: if ρ is a play, then $\mathsf{Dev}(\rho, \sigma_{\mathsf{Agt}}) = \bigcup_{i \in \mathbb{N}} \mathsf{Dev}(\mathsf{move}_i(\rho), \sigma_{\mathsf{Agt}}(\rho_{\leq i}))$.

Intuitively, given an play ρ and a strategy profile σ_{Agt}, deviators represent the agents that need to change their strategies from σ_{Agt} in order to obtain the play ρ. The intuition is formalised in the following lemma.

Lemma 2. *Let ρ be a play, σ_{Agt} a strategy profile and $C \subseteq \mathsf{Agt}$ a coalition. Coalition C contains $\mathsf{Dev}(\rho, \sigma_{\mathsf{Agt}})$ if, and only if, there exists σ'_C such that $\rho \in \mathsf{Out}_{\mathcal{G}}(\rho_0, \sigma'_C, \sigma_{-C})$.*

4.1   Deviator Game

We now use the notion of deviators to draw a link between multiplayer games and a two-player game that we will use to solve the robustness problem. Given a concurrent game structure $\mathcal{G}$, we define the deviator game $\mathcal{D}(\mathcal{G})$ between two players called Eve and Adam. Intuitively Eve needs to play according to an equilibrium, while Adam tries to find a deviation of a coalition which will profit one of its player or harm one of the others. The states are in $\mathsf{Stat}' = \mathsf{Stat} \times 2^{\mathsf{Agt}}$; the second component records the deviators of the current history. The game starts in $(s_0, \varnothing)$ and then proceeds as follows: from a state (s, D), Eve chooses an action profile a_{Agt} and Adam chooses another one a'_{Agt}, then the next state is $(\mathsf{Tab}(s, a'_{\mathsf{Agt}}), D \cup \mathsf{Dev}(a_{\mathsf{Agt}}, a'_{\mathsf{Agt}}))$. In other words, Adam chooses the move that will apply, but this can be at the price of adding players to the D component when he does not follow the choice of Eve. The weights of a state (s, D) in this game are the same than that of s in $\mathcal{G}$. The construction of the deviator arena is illustrated in Fig. 3.

We now define some transformations between the different objects used in games $\mathcal{G}$ and $\mathcal{D}(\mathcal{G})$. We define projections π_{Stat}, π_{Dev} and π_{Act} from Stat' to Stat, from Stat' to 2^{Agt} and from $\mathsf{Act}^{\mathsf{Agt}} \times \mathsf{Act}^{\mathsf{Agt}}$ to $\mathsf{Act}^{\mathsf{Agt}}$ respectively. They are given by $\pi_{\mathsf{Stat}}(s, D) = s$, $\pi_{\mathsf{Dev}}(s, D) = D$ and $\pi_{\mathsf{Act}}(a_{\mathsf{Agt}}, a'_{\mathsf{Agt}}) = a'_{\mathsf{Agt}}$. We extend these projections to plays in a natural way, letting $\pi_{\mathsf{Out}}(\rho) = \pi_{\mathsf{Stat}}(\rho_0) \cdot \pi_{\mathsf{Act}}(\mathsf{move}_0(\rho)) \cdot \pi_{\mathsf{Stat}}(\rho_1) \cdot \pi_{\mathsf{Act}}(\mathsf{move}_1(\rho)) \cdots$ and $\pi_{\mathsf{Dev}}(\rho) = \pi_{\mathsf{Dev}}(\rho_0) \cdot \pi_{\mathsf{Dev}}(\rho_1) \cdots$. Note that for any play ρ, and any index i, $\pi_{\mathsf{Dev}}(\rho_i) \subseteq \pi_{\mathsf{Dev}}(\rho_{i+1})$, therefore $\pi_{\mathsf{Dev}}(\rho)$ seen as a sequence of sets of coalitions is increasing and bounded by Agt, its limit $\delta(\rho) = \cup_{i \in \mathbb{N}} \pi_{\mathsf{Dev}}(\rho_i)$ is well defined. Moreover to a strategy profile σ_{Agt} in $\mathcal{G}$, we can naturally associate a strategy $\kappa(\sigma_{\mathsf{Agt}})$ for Eve in $\mathcal{D}(\mathcal{G})$ such that for all histories h by $\kappa(\sigma_{\mathsf{Agt}})(h) = \sigma_{\mathsf{Agt}}(\pi_{\mathsf{Out}}(h))$.

The following lemma states the correctness of the construction of the deviator game, in the sense that it records the set of deviators in the strategy profile suggested by Adam with respect to the strategy profile suggested by Eve.

Lemma 3. *Let $\mathcal{G}$ be a game and σ_{Agt} be a strategy profile and $\sigma_{\exists} = \kappa(\sigma_{\mathsf{Agt}})$ the associated strategy in the deviator game.*

1. *If $\rho \in \mathsf{Out}_{\mathcal{D}(\mathcal{G})}(\sigma_{\exists})$, then $\mathsf{Dev}\ (\pi_{\mathsf{Out}}(\rho), \sigma_{\mathsf{Agt}}) = \delta(\rho)$.*
2. *If $\rho \in \mathsf{Out}_{\mathcal{G}}$ and $\rho' = ((\rho_i, \mathsf{Dev}(\rho_{\leq i}, \sigma_{\mathsf{Agt}})) \cdot (\sigma_{\mathsf{Agt}}(\rho_{\leq i}), \mathsf{move}_i(\rho)))_{i \in \mathbb{N}}$ then $\rho' \in \mathsf{Out}_{\mathcal{D}(\mathcal{G})}(\sigma_{\exists})$*

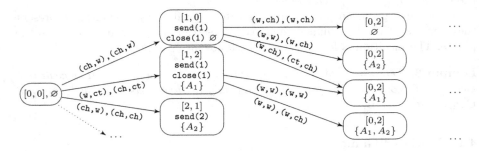

Fig. 3. Part of the deviator game construction for the game of Fig. 2. Labels on the edges correspond to the action of Eve and the action of Adam. Labels inside the states are the state of the original game and the deviator component.

4.2   Objectives of the Deviator Game

We now show how to transform equilibria notions into objectives of the deviator game. These objectives are defined so that winning strategies correspond to equilibria of the original game. First, we define an objective $\Omega(C, A, G)$ in the following lemma, such that a profile which ensures some quantitative goal $G \subseteq \mathbb{R}$ in $\mathcal{G}$ against coalition C corresponds to a winning strategy in the deviator game.

Lemma 4. *Let $C \subseteq \mathsf{Agt}$ be a coalition, σ_{Agt} be a strategy profile, $G \subseteq \mathbb{R}$ and A a player. We have that for all strategies σ'_C for coalition C, $\mathsf{payoff}_A(\sigma_{-C}, \sigma'_C) \in G$ if, and only if, $\kappa(\sigma_{\mathsf{Agt}})$ is winning in $\mathcal{D}(\mathcal{G})$ for objective $\Omega(C, A, G) = \{\rho \mid \delta(\rho) \subseteq C \Rightarrow \mathsf{payoff}_A(\pi_{\mathsf{Out}}(\rho)) \in G\}$.*

This lemma makes it easy to characterise the different kinds of equilibria, using objectives in $\mathcal{D}(\mathcal{G})$. For instance, we define a *resilience objective* where if there are more than k deviators then Eve has nothing to do; if there are exactly k deviators then she has to show that none of them gain anything; and if there are less than k then no player at all should gain anything. This is because if a new player joins the coalition, its size remains smaller or equal to k. Similar characterisations for immune and robust equilibria lead to the following theorem.

Theorem 6. *Let $\mathcal{G}$ be a concurrent game, σ_{Agt} a strategy profile in $\mathcal{G}$, $p = \mathsf{payoff}(\mathsf{Out}(\sigma_{\mathsf{Agt}}))$ the payoff profile of σ_{Agt}, k and t integers, and r a rational.*

- *The strategy profile σ_{Agt} is k-resilient if, and only if, strategy $\kappa(\sigma_{\mathsf{Agt}})$ is winning in $\mathcal{D}(\mathcal{G})$ for the resilience objective $\mathcal{R}e(k, p)$ where $\mathcal{R}e(k, p)$ is defined by: $\mathcal{R}e(k, p) = \{\rho \mid |\delta(\rho)| > k\} \cup \{\rho \mid |\delta(\rho)| = k \wedge \forall A \in \delta(\rho).\ \mathsf{payoff}_A(\pi_{\mathsf{Out}}(\rho)) \leq p(A)\} \cup \{\rho \mid |\delta(\rho)| < k \wedge \forall A \in \mathsf{Agt}.\ \mathsf{payoff}_A(\pi_{\mathsf{Out}}(\rho)) \leq p(A)\}$*
- *The strategy profile σ_{Agt} is (t, r)-immune if, and only if, strategy $\kappa(\sigma_{\mathsf{Agt}})$ is winning for the immunity objective $\mathcal{I}(t, r, p)$ $\mathcal{I}(t, r, p)$ is defined by: $\mathcal{I}(t, r, p) = \{\rho \mid |\delta(\rho)| > t\} \cup \{\rho \mid \forall A \in \mathsf{Agt} \setminus \delta(\rho).\ p(A) - r \leq \mathsf{payoff}_A(\pi_{\mathsf{Stat}}(\rho))\}$*
- *The strategy profile σ_{Agt} is a (k, t, r)-robust profile in $\mathcal{G}$ if, and only if, $\kappa(\sigma_{\mathsf{Agt}})$ is winning for the robustness objective $\mathcal{R}(k, t, r, p) = \mathcal{R}e(k, p) \cap \mathcal{I}(t, r, p)$.*

5   Reduction to Multidimensional Mean-Payoff Objectives

We first show that the deviator game reduces the robustness problem to a winning strategy problem in multidimensional mean-payoff games. We then solve this by requests to the polyhedron value problem of [9].

5.1   Multidimensional Objectives

Multidimensional Mean-Payoff Objective. Let $\mathcal{G}$ be a two-player game, $v \colon \mathsf{Stat} \mapsto \mathbb{Z}^d$ a multidimensional weight functions and $I, J \subseteq [\![1, d]\!]^1$ a partition of $[\![1, d]\!]$ (i.e. $I \uplus J = [\![1, d]\!]$). We say that Eve *ensures threshold* $u \in \mathbb{R}^d$

---

[1] We write $[\![i, j]\!]$ for the set of integers $\{k \in \mathbb{Z} \mid i \leq k \leq j\}$.

if she has a strategy $\sigma_\exists$ such that all outcomes ρ of $\sigma_\exists$ are such that for all $i \in I$, $\mathsf{MP}_{v_i}(\rho) \geq u_i$ and for all $j \in J$, $\overline{\mathsf{MP}}_{v_j}(\rho) \geq u_j$, where $\overline{\mathsf{MP}}_{v_j}(\rho) = \limsup_{n \to \infty} \frac{1}{n} \sum_{0 \leq k \leq n} v_j(\rho_k)$. That is, for all dimensions $i \in I$, the limit inferior of the average of v_i is greater than u_i and for all dimensions $j \in J$ the limit superior of v_j is greater than u_j.

We consider two decision problems on these games: 1. The *value problem*, asks given $\langle \mathcal{G}, v, I, J \rangle$ a game with multidimensional mean-payoff objectives, and $u \in \mathbb{R}^d$, whether Eve can ensure u. 2. The *polyhedron value problem*, asks given $\langle \mathcal{G}, v, I, J \rangle$ a game with multidimensional mean-payoff objectives, and $(\lambda_1, \ldots, \lambda_n)$ a tuple of linear inequations, whether there exists a threshold u which Eve can ensure and that satisfies the inequation λ_i for all i in $[\![1, d]\!]$. We assume that all linear inequations are given by a tuple $(a_1, \ldots, a_d, b) \in \mathbb{Q}^{d+1}$ and that a point $u \in \mathbb{R}^d$ satisfies it when $\sum_{i \in [\![1, d]\!]} a_i \cdot u_i \geq b$. The value problem was showed to be coNP-complete [20] while the polyhedron value problem is Σ_2P-complete [9]. Our goal is now to reduce our robustness problem to a polyhedron value problem for some well chosen weights.

In our case, the number d of dimensions will be equal to $4 \cdot |\mathsf{Agt}|$. We then number players so that $\mathsf{Agt} = \{A_1, \ldots, A_{|\mathsf{Agt}|}\}$. Let $W = \max\{|w_i(s)| \mid A_i \in \mathsf{Agt}, s \in \mathsf{Stat}\}$ be the maximum constant occurring in the weights of the game, notice that for all players A_i and play ρ, $-W - 1 < \mathsf{MP}_i(\rho) \leq W$. We fix parameters k, t and define our weight function $v \colon \mathsf{Stat} \mapsto \mathbb{Z}^d$. Let $i \in [\![1, |\mathsf{Agt}|]\!]$, the weights are given for $(s, D) \in \mathsf{Stat} \times 2^{\mathsf{Agt}}$ by:

1. if $|D| \leq t$ and $A_i \notin D$, then $v_i(s, D) = w_{A_i}(s)$;
2. if $|D| > t$ or $A_i \in D$, then $v_i(s, D) = W$;
3. if $|D| < k$, then for all $A_i \in \mathsf{Agt}$, $v_{|\mathsf{Agt}|+i}(s, D) = -w_{A_i}(s)$;
4. if $|D| = k$ and $A_i \in D$, then $v_{|\mathsf{Agt}|+i}(s, D) = -w_{A_i}(s)$;
5. if $|D| > k$ or $A_i \notin D$ and $|D| = k$, then $v_{|\mathsf{Agt}|+i}(s, D) = W$.
6. if $D = \varnothing$ then $v_{2 \cdot |\mathsf{Agt}|+i}(s, D) = w_{A_i}(s) = -v_{3 \cdot |\mathsf{Agt}|+i}(s, D)$;
7. if $D \neq \varnothing$ then $v_{2 \cdot |\mathsf{Agt}|+i}(s, D) = W = v_{3 \cdot |\mathsf{Agt}|+i}(s, D)$;

We take $I = [\![1, |\mathsf{Agt}|]\!] \cup [\![2 \cdot |\mathsf{Agt}| + 1, 3 \cdot |\mathsf{Agt}|]\!]$ and $J = [\![|\mathsf{Agt}| + 1, 2 \cdot |\mathsf{Agt}|]\!] \cup [\![3 \cdot |\mathsf{Agt}| + 1, 4 \cdot |\mathsf{Agt}|]\!]$. Intuitively, the components $[\![1, |\mathsf{Agt}|]\!]$ are used for immunity, the components $[\![|\mathsf{Agt}| + 1, 2 \cdot |\mathsf{Agt}|]\!]$ are used for resilience and components $[\![2 \cdot |\mathsf{Agt}| + 1, 4 \cdot |\mathsf{Agt}|]\!]$ are used to constrain the payoff in case of no deviation.

5.2 Correctness of the Objectives for Robustness

Let $\mathcal{G}$ be a concurrent game, ρ a play of $\mathcal{D}(\mathcal{G})$ and $p \in \mathbb{R}^{\mathsf{Agt}}$ a payoff vector. The following lemma links the weights we chose and our solution concepts.

Lemma 5. *Let ρ be a play, σ_{Agt} a strategy profile and $p = \mathsf{payoff}(\sigma_{\mathsf{Agt}})$.*

- *ρ satisfies objective $\delta(\rho) = \varnothing \Rightarrow \mathsf{MP}_{A_i}(\rho) = p_i$ if, and only if, $\mathsf{MP}_{2 \cdot v_{|\mathsf{Agt}|+i}}(\rho) \geq p(A_i)$ and $\overline{\mathsf{MP}}_{3 \cdot v_{|\mathsf{Agt}|+i}}(\rho) \geq -p(A_i)$.*
- *If ρ is an outcome of $\kappa(\sigma_{\mathsf{Agt}})$ then ρ satisfies objective $\mathcal{R}e(k, p)$ if, and only if, for all agents A_i, $\overline{\mathsf{MP}}_{v_{|\mathsf{Agt}|+i}}(\rho) \geq -p(A_i)$.*

- If ρ is an outcome of $\kappa(\sigma_{\mathsf{Agt}})$, then ρ satisfies objective $\mathcal{I}(t, r, p)$ if, and only if, for all agents A_i, $MP_{v_i}(\rho) \geq p(A_i) - r$.
- If ρ is an outcome of $\kappa(\sigma_{\mathsf{Agt}})$ with payoff(σ_{Agt}) $= p$, then play ρ satisfies objective $\mathcal{R}(k, t, r, p)$ if, and only if, for all agents A_i, $MP_{v_i}(\rho) \geq p(A_i) - r$ and $\overline{MP}_{v_{|\mathsf{Agt}|+i}}(\rho) \geq -p(A_i)$.

Putting together this lemma and the correspondence between the deviator game and robust equilibria of Theorem 6 we obtain the following proposition.

Lemma 6. *Let $\mathcal{G}$ be a concurrent game with mean-payoff objectives. There is a (k, t, r)-robust equilibrium in $\mathcal{G}$ if, and only if, for the multidimensional mean-payoff objective given by v, $I = [\![1, |\mathsf{Agt}|]\!] \cup [\![2 \cdot |\mathsf{Agt}| + 1, 3 \cdot |\mathsf{Agt}|]\!]$ and $J = [\![|\mathsf{Agt}| + 1, 2 \cdot |\mathsf{Agt}|]\!] \cup [\![3 \cdot |\mathsf{Agt}| + 1, 4 \cdot |\mathsf{Agt}|]\!]$, there is a payoff vector p such that Eve can ensure threshold u in $\mathcal{D}(\mathcal{G})$, where for all $i \in [\![1, |\mathsf{Agt}|]\!]$, $u_i = p(A_i) - r$, $u_{|\mathsf{Agt}|+i} = -p(A_i)$, $u_{2 \cdot |\mathsf{Agt}|+i} = p(A_i)$, and $u_{3 \cdot |\mathsf{Agt}|+i} = -p(A_i)$.*

5.3 Formulation of the Robustness Problem as a Polyhedron Value Problem

From the previous lemma, we can deduce an algorithm which works by querying the polyhedron value problem. Given a game $\mathcal{G}$ and parameters k, t, r, we ask whether there exists a payoff u that Eve ensured in the game $\mathcal{D}(\mathcal{G})$ with multidimensional mean-payoff objective given by v, I, J, and such that for all $i \in [\![1, |\mathsf{Agt}|]\!]$, $u_i + r = -u_{|\mathsf{Agt}|+i} = u_{2 \cdot |\mathsf{Agt}|+i} = -u_{3 \cdot |\mathsf{Agt}|+i}$. As we will show in Theorem 7 thanks to Lemma 6, the answer to this question is yes if, and only if, there is a (k, t, r)-robust equilibrium. From the point of view of complexity, however, the deviator game on which we perform the query can be of exponential size compared to the original game. To describe more precisely the complexity of the problem, we remark by applying the bound of [8, Theorem 22], that given a query, we can find solutions which have a small representation.

Lemma 7. *If there is a solution to the polyhedron value problem in $\mathcal{D}(\mathcal{G})$ then there is one whose encoding is of polynomial size with respect to $\mathcal{G}$ and the polyhedron given as input.*

We can therefore enumerate all possible solutions in polynomial space. To obtain an polynomial space algorithm, we must be able to check one solution in polynomial space as well. This account to show that queries for the value problem in the deviator game can be done in space polynomial with respect to the original game. This is the goal of the next section, and it is done by considering small parts of the deviator game called fixed coalition games.

6 Fixed Coalition Game

Although the deviator game may be of exponential size, it presents a particular structure. As the set of deviators only increases during any run, the game can be seen as the product of the original game with a directed acyclic graph (DAG). The nodes of this DAG correspond to possible sets of deviators, it is of exponential size but polynomial degree and depth. We exploit this structure to obtain a polynomial space algorithm for the value problem and thus also for the polyhedron value problem and the robustness problem. The idea is to compute winning states in one component at a time, and to recursively call the procedure for states that are successors of the current component. We will therefore consider one different game for each component.

We now present the details of the procedure. For a fixed set of deviator D, the possible successors of states of the component $\mathsf{Stat} \times D$ are the states in: $\mathsf{Succ}(D) = \{\mathsf{Tab}_{\mathcal{D}}((s, D), (m_{\mathsf{Agt}}, m'_{\mathsf{Agt}})) \mid s \in \mathsf{Stat}, m_{\mathsf{Agt}}, m'_{\mathsf{Agt}} \in \mathsf{Mov}(s)\} \setminus \mathsf{Stat} \times D\}$. Note that the size of $\mathsf{Succ}(D)$ is bounded by $|\mathsf{Stat}| \times |\mathsf{Tab}|$, hence it is polynomial. Let u be a payoff threshold, we want to know whether Eve can ensure u in $\mathcal{D}(\mathcal{G})$, for the multi-dimensional objective defined in Sect. 5.1. A winning path ρ from a state in $\mathsf{Stat} \times D$ is either: (1) such that $\delta(\rho) = D$; (2) or it reaches a state in $\mathsf{Succ}(D)$ and follow a winning path from there. Assume we have computed all the states in $\mathsf{Succ}(D)$ that are winning. We can stop the game as soon as $\mathsf{Succ}(D)$ is reached, and declare Eve the winner if the state that is reached is a winning state of $\mathcal{D}(\mathcal{G})$. This process can be seen as a game $\mathcal{F}(D, u)$, called the *fixed coalition game*.

In this game the states are those of $(\mathsf{Stat} \times D) \cup \mathsf{Succ}(D)$; transitions are the same than in $\mathcal{D}(\mathcal{G})$ on the states of $\mathsf{Stat} \times D$ and the states of $\mathsf{Succ}(D)$ have only self loops. The winning condition is identical to $\mathcal{R}(k, t, p)$ for the plays that never leave $(\mathsf{Stat} \times D)$; and for a play that reach some $(s', D') \in \mathsf{Succ}(D)$, it is considered winning Eve has a winning strategy from (s', D') in $\mathcal{D}(\mathcal{G})$ and losing otherwise.

In the fixed coalition game, we keep the weights previously defined for states of $\mathsf{Stat} \times D$, and fix it for the states that are not in the same D component by giving a high payoff on states that are winning and a low one on the losing ones. Formally, we define a multidimensional weight function v^f on $\mathcal{F}(D, u)$ by: 1. for all $s \in \mathsf{Stat}$, and all $i \in [\![1, 4 \cdot |\mathsf{Agt}|]\!]$, $v_i^f(s, D) = v_i(s, D)$. 2. if $(s, D') \in \mathsf{Succ}(D)$ and Eve can ensure u from (s, D'), then for all $i \in [\![1, 4 \cdot |\mathsf{Agt}|]\!]$, $v_i^f(s, D') = W$. 3. if $(s, D') \in \mathsf{Succ}(D)$ and Eve cannot ensure u from (s, D'), then for all $i \in [\![1, 4 \cdot |\mathsf{Agt}|]\!]$, $v_i^f(s, D') = -W - 1$.

Lemma 8. *Eve can ensure payoff* $u \in [\![-W, W]\!]^d$ *in* $\mathcal{D}(\mathcal{G})$ *from* (s, D) *if, and only if, she can ensure* u *in the fixed coalition game* $\mathcal{F}(D, p)$ *from* (s, D).

Using this correspondence, we deduce a polynomial space algorithm to check that Eve can ensure a given value in the deviator game and thus a polynomial space algorithm for the robustness problem.

Theorem 7. *There is a polynomial space algorithm, that given a concurrent game* $\mathcal{G}$, *tells if there is a* (k, t, r)-*robust equilibrium.*

Proof. We first show that there is a polynomial space algorithm to solve the value problem in $\mathcal{D}(\mathcal{G})$. We consider a threshold u and a state (s, D). In the fixed coalition game $\mathcal{F}(D, u)$, for each $(s', D') \in \mathsf{Succ}(D)$, we can compute whether it is winning by recursive calls. Once the weights for all $(s', D') \in \mathsf{Succ}(D)$ have been computed for $\mathcal{F}(D, u)$, we can solve the value problem in $\mathcal{F}(D, u)$. Thanks to Lemma 8 the answer to value problem in this game is yes exactly when Eve can ensure u from (s, D) in $\mathcal{D}(\mathcal{G})$. There is a coNP algorithm [20] to check the value problem in a given game, and therefore there also is an algorithm which uses polynomial space. The size of the stack of recursive calls is bounded by $|\mathsf{Agt}|$, so the global algorithm uses polynomial space.

We now use this to show that there is a polynomial space algorithm for the polyhedron value problem in $\mathcal{D}(\mathcal{G})$. We showed in Lemma 7, that if the polyhedron value problem has a solution then there is a threshold u of polynomial size that is witness of this property. We can enumerate all the thresholds that satisfy the size bound in polynomial space. We can then test that these thresholds satisfy the given linear inequations, and that the algorithm for the value problem answers yes on this input, in polynomial space thanks to the previous algorithm. If this is the case for one of the thresholds, then we answer yes for the polyhedron value problem. The correctness of this procedure holds thanks to Lemma 7.

We now use this to show that there is a polynomial space algorithm for the robustness problem. Given a game $\mathcal{G}$ and parameters (k, t, r), we define a tuple of linear equations, for all $i \in [\![1, |\mathsf{Agt}|]\!]$, $x_{2 \cdot |\mathsf{Agt}| + i} = x_i + r \wedge x_{2 \cdot |\mathsf{Agt}| + i} = -x_{|\mathsf{Agt}| + i} \wedge x_{2 \cdot |\mathsf{Agt}| + i} = -x_{3 \cdot |\mathsf{Agt}| + i}$ (each equation can be expressed by two inequations). Thanks to Lemma 6, there is a payoff which satisfies these constraints and which Eve can ensure in $\mathcal{D}(\mathcal{G})$ if, and only if, there is a (k, t, r)-robust equilibrium. Then, querying the algorithm we described for the polyhedron value problem in $\mathcal{D}(\mathcal{G})$ with our system of inequations, answers the robustness problem.

7 Hardness

In this section, we show a matching lower bound for the resilience problem. The lower bound holds for weights that are 0 in every states except on some terminal states where they can be 1. This is also called *simple reachability objectives*.

Theorem 8. *The robustness problem is* PSPACE-*complete.*

Note that we already proved PSPACE-membership in Theorem 7. We give the construction and intuition of the reduction to show hardness and leave the proof of correctness in the appendix. We encode QSAT formulas with n variable into a game with $2 \cdot n + 2$ players, such that the formula is valid if, and only if, there is n-resilient equilibria. We assume that we are given a formula of the form $\phi = \forall x_1.\exists x_2. \forall x_3.\exists x_n. C_1 \wedge \cdots \wedge C_k$, where each C_k is of the form $\ell_{1,k} \vee \ell_{2,k} \vee \ell_{3,k}$ and each $\ell_{j,k}$ is a literal (i.e. x_m or $\neg x_m$ for some m). We define the game $\mathcal{G}_\phi$ as illustrated by an example in Fig. 4. It has a player A_m for each positive literal x_m, and a player B_m for each negative literal $\neg x_m$. We add two extra players Eve and Adam. Eve is making choices for the existential quantification and Adam for the universal ones. When they chose a literal, the corresponding player can either go to a sink state $\bot$ or continue the game to the next quantification. Once a literal has been chosen for all the variables, Eve needs to chose a literal for each clause. The objective for Eve and the literal players is to reach $\bot$. The objective for Adam is to reach $\top$. We ask whether there is a $(n+1)$-resilient equilibrium.

To a history $h = \mathsf{Adam}_1 \cdot X_1 \cdot \mathsf{Eve}_2 \cdot X_2 \cdot \mathsf{Adam}_3 \cdots \mathsf{Eve}_m \cdot X_m$ with $X_i \in \{A_i, B_i\}$, we associate a valuation v_h, such that $v_h(x_i) = \mathsf{true}$ if $X_i = B_i$ and $v_h(x_i) = \mathsf{false}$ if $X_i = A_i$. Intuitively, Eve has to find a valuation that makes the formula hold, while Adam tries to falsify it.

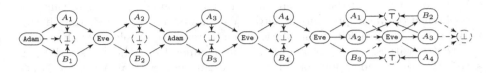

Fig. 4. Encoding of a formula $\phi = \forall x_1 . \exists x_2 . \forall x_3 . \exists x_4 . (x_1 \lor x_2 \lor \neg x_3) \land (\neg x_2 \lor x_3 \lor x_4)$. The dashed edges represent the strategies in the equilibrium of the players other than Eve.

References

1. Abraham, I., Dolev, D., Gonen, R., Halpern, J.: Distributed computing meets game theory: robust mechanisms for rational secret sharing and multiparty computation. In: Proceedings of the Twenty-Fifth Annual ACM Symposium on Principles of Distributed Computing, pp. 53–62. ACM (2006)
2. Alur, R., Henzinger, T.A., Kupferman, O.: Alternating-time temporal logic. J. ACM (JACM) **49**(5), 672–713 (2002)
3. Aumann, R.: Acceptable points in general cooperative n-person games. Top. Math. Econ. Game Theory Essays Honor Robert J Aumann **23**, 287–324 (1959)
4. Bouyer, P., Brenguier, R., Markey, N., Ummels, M.: Concurrent games with ordered objectives. In: Birkedal, L. (ed.) FOSSACS 2012. LNCS, vol. 7213, pp. 301–315. Springer, Heidelberg (2012)
5. Bouyer, P., Markey, N., Stan, D.: Mixed nash equilibria in concurrent terminal-reward games. In: 34th International Conference on Foundation of Software Technology and Theoretical Computer Science (FSTTCS 2014). Leibniz International Proceedings in Informatics (LIPIcs), Dagstuhl, Germany, vol. 29, pp. 351–363 (2014)
6. Brenguier, R.: Nash equilibria in concurrent games: application to timed games. Ph.D. thesis, Cachan, Ecole normale supérieure (2012)
7. Brenguier, R.: Robust equilibria in concurrent games. CoRR, http://arxiv.org/abs/1311.7683 (2015)
8. Brenguier, R., Raskin, J.-F.: Optimal values of multidimensional mean-payoff games (2014). https://hal.archives-ouvertes.fr/hal-00977352/
9. Brenguier, R., Raskin, J.-F.: Pareto curves of multidimensional mean-payoff games. In: Kroening, D., Păsăreanu, C.S. (eds.) CAV 2015. LNCS, vol. 9207, pp. 251–267. Springer, Heidelberg (2015)
10. Brihaye, T., Bruyère, V., De Pril, J.: Equilibria in quantitative reachability games. In: Ablayev, F., Mayr, E.W. (eds.) CSR 2010. LNCS, vol. 6072, pp. 72–83. Springer, Heidelberg (2010)

11. Canny, J.: Some algebraic and geometric computations in pspace. In: Proceedings of the Twentieth Annual ACM Symposium on Theory of Computing, pp. 460–467. ACM (1988)
12. Chatterjee, K., Henzinger, T.A., Jurdziński, M.: Games with Secure Equilibria'. In: de Boer, F.S., Bonsangue, M.M., Graf, S., de Roever, W.-P. (eds.) FMCO 2004. LNCS, vol. 3657, pp. 141–161. Springer, Heidelberg (2005)
13. Chatterjee, K., Henzinger, T.A., Piterman, N.: Strategy logic. Inform. Comput. 208(6), 677–693 (2010)
14. Mogavero, F., Murano, A., Perelli, G., Vardi, M.Y.: What makes ATL* decidable? A decidable fragment of strategy logic. In: Koutny, M., Ulidowski, I. (eds.) CONCUR 2012. LNCS, vol. 7454, pp. 193–208. Springer, Heidelberg (2012)
15. Nash Jr., J.F.: Equilibrium points in n-person games. Proc. Nat. Acad. Sci. USA 36(1), 48–49 (1950)
16. Puterman, M.L.: Markov decision processes: Discrete stochastic dynamic programming (1994)
17. Ummels, M.: The complexity of nash equilibria in infinite multiplayer games. In: Amadio, R.M. (ed.) FOSSACS 2008. LNCS, vol. 4962, pp. 20–34. Springer, Heidelberg (2008)
18. Ummels, M., Wojtczak, D.: The complexity of nash equilibria in simple stochastic multiplayer games. In: Albers, S., Marchetti-Spaccamela, A., Matias, Y., Nikoletseas, S., Thomas, W. (eds.) ICALP 2009, Part II. LNCS, vol. 5556, pp. 297–308. Springer, Heidelberg (2009)
19. Ummels, M., Wojtczak, D.: The Complexity of Nash Equilibria in Limit-Average Games. In: Katoen, J.-P., König, B. (eds.) CONCUR 2011. LNCS, vol. 6901, pp. 482–496. Springer, Heidelberg (2011)
20. Velner, Y., Chatterjee, K., Doyen, L., Henzinger, T.A., Rabinovich, A., Raskin, J.-F.: The complexity of multi-mean-payoff and multi-energy games. CoRR abs/1209.3234 (2012)

Quantifier Alternation for Infinite Words

Théo Pierron, Thomas Place$^{(\boxtimes)}$, and Marc Zeitoun

LaBRI, UMR 5800, University of Bordeaux, 33400 Talence, France
tplace@labri.fr

Abstract. We investigate the expressive power of the quantifier alternation hierarchy of first-order logic over words. This hierarchy includes the classes Σ_i (sentences having at most i blocks of quantifiers starting with an $\exists$) and $\mathcal{B}\Sigma_i$ (Boolean combinations of Σ_i sentences). So far, this expressive power has been effectively characterized for the lower levels only. Recently, a breakthrough was made over finite words, and decidable characterizations were obtained for $\mathcal{B}\Sigma_2$ and Σ_3, by relying on a decision problem called separation, and solving it for Σ_2.

The contribution of this paper is a generalization of these results to the setting of infinite words: we solve separation for Σ_2 and Σ_3, and obtain decidable characterizations of $\mathcal{B}\Sigma_2$ and Σ_3 as consequences.

Regular word languages form a robust class, as they can be defined either by operational, algebraic, or logical means: they are exactly those that can be defined equivalently by finite state machines (operational view), morphisms into finite algebras (algebraic view) and monadic second order ("MSO") sentences [4,5,8,27] (logical view). To understand the structure of this class in depth, it is natural to classify its languages according to their descriptive complexity. The problem is to determine how complicated a sentence has to be to describe a given input language. This is a decision problem parametrized by a fragment of MSO: given an input language, can it be expressed in the fragment? This problem is called *membership* (is the language a *member* of the class defined by the fragment?).

The seminal result in this field is the membership algorithm for first-order logic (FO) over finite words, which is arguably the most prominent fragment of MSO. This algorithm was obtained in two steps. McNaughton and Papert [10] observed that the languages definable in FO are exactly the *star-free languages*: those that may be expressed by a regular expression in which complement is allowed while the Kleene star is disallowed. Furthermore, an earlier result of Schützenberger [23] shows that star-free languages are exactly the ones whose syntactic monoid is aperiodic. The syntactic monoid is a finite algebra that can be computed from any input regular language, and aperiodicity can be formulated as an equation that has to be satisfied by all elements of this algebra. Therefore, Schützenberger's result makes it possible to decide whether a regular language is star-free (and therefore definable in FO by McNaughton-Papert's result).

Following this first result, the attention turned to a deeper question: given an FO-definable language, find the "simplest" FO-sentences that define it. The standard complexity measure for FO sentences is their quantifier alternation,

© Springer-Verlag Berlin Heidelberg 2016
B. Jacobs and C. Löding (Eds.): FOSSACS 2016, LNCS 9634, pp. 234–251, 2016.
DOI: 10.1007/978-3-662-49630-5_14

which counts the number of switches between blocks of $\exists$ and $\forall$ quantifiers. This measure is justified not only because it is intuitively difficult to understand a sentence with many alternations, but also because the nonelementary complexity of standard problems for FO [25] (*e.g*, satisfiability) is tied to quantifier alternation. In summary, we classify FO definable languages by counting the number of quantifier alternations needed to define them and we want to be able to decide the level of a given language (which amounts to solving membership for each level).

This leads to define the following fragments of FO: an FO sentence is Σ_i if its prenex normal form has at most i blocks of $\exists$ or $\forall$ quantifiers and starts with a block of existential ones. Note that Σ_i is not closed under complement (the negation of a Σ_i sentence is called a Π_i sentence). A sentence is $\mathcal{B}\Sigma_i$ if it is a Boolean combination of Σ_i sentences (cf. figure). Clearly, we have $\Sigma_i \subseteq \mathcal{B}\Sigma_i \subseteq \Sigma_{i+1}$, and these inclusions are known to be strict [3,26]: $\Sigma_i \subsetneq \mathcal{B}\Sigma_i \subsetneq \Sigma_{i+1}$.

Solving membership for levels of this hierarchy is a longstanding open problem. Following Schützenberger's approach, it was first investigated for languages of finite words. However, the question also makes sense for more complex structures, in particular for the most natural extension: infinite words. Schützenberger's result was first generalized to infinite words by Perrin [11], and a suitable algebraic framework for languages of infinite words was set up by Wilke [28]. Since a regular language of infinite words is determined by regular languages of finite words, finding a membership algorithm for languages of infinite words does not usually require to start over. Instead these algorithms are obtained by building on top of the algorithms for finite words, adding new arguments, specific to infinite words.

Regarding the hierarchy, membership is easily seen to be decidable for Σ_1. For $\mathcal{B}\Sigma_1$, the classical result of Simon [24] was generalized from finite to infinite words by Perrin and Pin [12]. For finite words, membership to Σ_2 is known to be decidable [1,15], a result lifted to infinite words in [2,7]. Following these results, the understanding of the hierarchy remained stuck for years until the framework was extended to new and more general problems than membership.

Rather than asking whether a language is definable in a fragment $\mathcal{F}$, these problems ask what is the best $\mathcal{F}$-definable "approximation" of this language (with respect to specific criteria). The simplest example is $\mathcal{F}$-*separation*, which takes *two* regular languages as input and asks whether there exists a third language *definable in* $\mathcal{F}$ that contains the first language and is disjoint from the second. Separation is more general than membership: asking whether a regular language is definable in $\mathcal{F}$ is the same as asking whether it can be $\mathcal{F}$-separated from its (also regular) complement. A consequence is that deciding these more general problems is usually more challenging than deciding membership. However, their investigation in the setting of finite words has also been very rewarding. A good illustration is the transfer result of [18], which states that for all i, decidability of separation for Σ_i entails decidability of membership for Σ_{i+1}. Combined with an algorithm for Σ_2-separation [18], this proved that Σ_3 has decidable membership. This result was strengthened in [16], which shows that Σ_3-separation is decidable as well, thus obtaining decidability of membership for Σ_4. Finally, in [18], it was shown that $\mathcal{B}\Sigma_2$ has decidable membership by using a generalization of separation for Σ_2 and analyzing an algorithm solving this generalization.

It remained open to know whether it was possible to generalize with the same success this new approach to the setting of infinite words. This is the investigation that we carry out in the paper. More precisely, we rely on the crucial notion of Σ_i-chains, designed in [18] for presenting and proving membership and separation algorithms for finite words. We generalize this concept to infinite words and successfully use it to prove that the following problems are decidable: Σ_2-separation, Σ_3-separation, and $\mathcal{B}\Sigma_2$ membership. This demonstrates that Σ_i-chains remain a suitable framework for presenting arguments in the setting of infinite words. On the other hand, new issues specific to infinite words arise, for example, we were not able to generalize the transfer result from Σ_i-separation to Σ_{i+1}-membership (as a consequence, membership for Σ_4 remains open). Note also that, for each problem, we pre-compute some information by using the corresponding algorithm designed in [16,18] for finite words. This means that the involved algorithms from [16,18] are used as subroutines of our algorithms.

It is worth noting that the decidability of the membership problem for $\mathcal{B}\Sigma_2$ over infinite words has been obtained independently in [9]. While the algorithm is essentially the same as our own, its proof is completely different.

We now present the problems in depth in Sect. 1, and we solve them in the rest of the paper. A detailed outline is provided at the end of Sect. 1. Due to lack of space, some proofs are postponed to the full version of this paper, see [13].

1   Presentation of the Problem

In this section, we first define the quantifier alternation hierarchy of first-order logic. Then, we present the membership problem and the separation problem.

1.1   The Quantifier Alternation Hierarchy of First-Order Logic

We fix a finite alphabet A. We denote by A^+ the set of all finite nonempty words, and by A^∞ the set of all infinite words over A. We use the term "word" for "finite word". We call *language* (resp. *language of infinite words*) a subset of A^+ (resp. of A^∞). If u is a word and v is a word (resp. an infinite word), we denote by uv the word (resp. the infinite word) obtained by concatenating u to the left of v. If u is a word, we denote by u^∞ the infinite word $uuuu\cdots$ obtained as the infinite concatenation of u with itself. If u is a word or an infinite word, we denote by $\mathsf{alph}(u)$ the *alphabet* of u, *i.e.*, the set of letters of u.

First-Order Logic. Any word or infinite word can be viewed as a logical structure made of a linearly ordered sequence of positions (finite for words and infinite for infinite words) labeled over alphabet A. In first-order logic "FO", one can quantify over these positions and use the following predicates.

- for each $a \in A$, a unary predicate P_a selecting all positions labeled with an a.
- a binary predicate '<' interpreted as the (strict) linear order over the positions.

Since any FO sentence may be interpreted both on words and infinite words, each sentence φ defines two objects: a language $L_+ = \{w \in A^+ \mid w \models \varphi\}$ and a language of infinite words $L_\infty = \{w \in A^\infty \mid w \models \varphi\}$. For example, the sentence $\exists x \exists y \ (x < y \wedge P_a(y))$ defines the language $A^+ a \cup A^+ a A^+$ and the language of infinite words $A^+ a A^\infty$. Thus, we may associate two classes of objects with FO: a class of languages (we speak of FO over words) and a class of languages of infinite words (we speak of FO over infinite words).

Quantifier Alternation. It is usual to classify FO sentences by counting the quantifier alternations inside their prenex normal form. Let $i \in \mathbb{N}$, a sentence is said to be Σ_i (resp. Π_i) if its prenex normal form has either:

- *exactly* $i - 1$ quantifier alternations (*i.e.*, exactly i quantifier blocks) starting with an $\exists$ (resp. $\forall$), or
- *strictly less* than $i - 1$ quantifier alternations (*i.e.*, strictly less than i blocks).

For example, the sentence $\exists x_1 \forall x_2 \forall x_3 \exists x_4 \ \varphi$, with φ quantifier-free, is Σ_3. Note that in general, the negation of a Σ_i sentence is not a Σ_i sentence – it is called a Π_i sentence. Hence, it is also usual to define $\mathcal{B}\Sigma_i$ sentences as those that are Boolean combinations of Σ_i and Π_i sentences.

As for full first-order logic, each level Σ_i, Π_i or $\mathcal{B}\Sigma_i$ defines two classes of objects: a class of languages and a class of languages of infinite words. Therefore, we obtain two hierarchies: a hierarchy of classes of languages and a hierarchy of classes of languages of infinite words, both of which are known to be strict [3,26].

1.2   Decision Problems

Our objective is to investigate the quantifier alternation hierarchy of first-order logic over infinite words. We rely on two decision problems in order to carry out this investigation: the membership problem and the separation problem. The input of these problems are *regular* languages of finite and infinite words. They are those languages that can be equivalently defined by monadic second-order logic, finite Büchi automata or finite Wilke algebras. We will use Wilke algebras, whose definition is recalled in Sect. 2. Both problems are parametrized by a level in the hierarchy and come therefore in two versions: a 'language' one and a 'language of infinite words' one. Let $\mathcal{F}$ be a level in the hierarchy.

Membership. The *membership problem* for level $\mathcal{F}$ is as follows:

For Finite Words	For Infinite words
IN A regular language L	**IN** A regular language of infinite words L
OUT Is L $\mathcal{F}$-definable ?	**OUT** Is L $\mathcal{F}$-definable ?

Separation. The separation problem is more general. Given three languages or three languages of infinite words K, L_1, L_2, we say that K *separates* L_1 from L_2 if $L_1 \subseteq K$ and $L_2 \cap K = \emptyset$. For $\mathcal{F}$ a level in the hierarchy, L_1 is said $\mathcal{F}$-*separable* from L_2 if there exists an $\mathcal{F}$-definable language or language of infinite words that separates L_1 from L_2. Note that when $\mathcal{F}$ is not closed under complement (*e.g.*, for $\mathcal{F} = \Sigma_i$), the definition is not symmetrical: L_1 may be $\mathcal{F}$-separable from L_2 while L_2 is not $\mathcal{F}$-separable from L_1. The separation problem for $\mathcal{F}$ is as follows:

For Finite Words	For Infinite words
IN Two regular languages L_1, L_2	**IN** Two regular languages of infinite words L_1, L_2
OUT Is L_1 $\mathcal{F}$-separable from L_2 ?	**OUT** Is L_1 $\mathcal{F}$-separable from L_2 ?

An important remark is that membership reduces to separation. A regular language of words or infinite words is definable in $\mathcal{F}$ iff it is $\mathcal{F}$-separable from its (also regular) complement: separation is a more general problem than membership.

Both problems have been extensively studied in the literature. Indeed, it has been observed that obtaining an algorithm for the membership or separation problem associated to a particular level $\mathcal{F}$ usually yields a deep insight on $\mathcal{F}$. This is well illustrated by the most famous result of this kind, Schützenberger's Theorem [10,23], which yields a membership algorithm for FO over words. The result was later generalized to FO over infinite words by Perrin [11]. These results and the techniques used to obtain them provide not only a way to decide whether a regular language of finite or infinite words is FO-definable, but also a generic method for constructing a defining FO sentence, when possible. Since these first results, many efforts have been devoted for obtaining membership and separation algorithms for each level in the hierarchy. An overview of the results is presented in the following table (omitted levels are open in all cases).

Membership Problem

	Words	Infinite words
FO	Solved [23,10]	Solved [11]
Σ_1	Solved [1]	Solved [14,12]
$\mathcal{B}\Sigma_1$	Solved [24]	Solved [12]
Σ_2	Solved [1,15]	Solved [7,2]
$\mathcal{B}\Sigma_2$	Solved [18]	**This paper**
Σ_3	Solved [18]	**This paper**
Σ_4	Solved [16]	**Open**

Separation Problem

	Words	Infinite words
FO	Solved [19]	Solved [19]
Σ_1	Solved (Folklore)	Solved (Folklore)
$\mathcal{B}\Sigma_1$	Solved [6,17]	Solved [20]
Σ_2	Solved [18]	**This paper**
$\mathcal{B}\Sigma_2$	**Open**	**Open**
Σ_3	Solved [16]	**This paper**
Σ_4	**Open**	**Open**

Our objective is to bridge the gap between the knownledge for languages and that for languages of infinite words. More precisely, we want to extend the results of [16,18] to the setting of infinite words, *i.e.*, to obtain membership algorithms for $\mathcal{B}\Sigma_2$, Σ_3 and Σ_4 as well as separation algorithms for Σ_2 and Σ_3. We were able to obtain these algorithms for Σ_2, Σ_3 and $\mathcal{B}\Sigma_2$ as stated in the next theorem. Note that the Σ_3-membership algorithm follows from its separation algorithm. We leave open the case of Σ_4-membership for languages of infinite words.

Theorem 1. *The following properties hold:*

(a) *the separation problem is decidable for Σ_2 over infinite words.*
(b) *the membership problem is decidable for $\mathcal{B}\Sigma_2$ over infinite words.*
(c) *the separation problem is decidable for Σ_3 over infinite words.*

Our proof of Theorem 1 consists in three algorithms, one for each item in the theorem. An important remark is that each of these three algorithms depends upon an algorithm of [18] or [16] solving the corresponding problem for finite words:

- We present all algorithms in a specific framework which is adapted from the one used in [18]. In particular, we reuse the key notion of "Σ_i-chain" (generalized to infinite words in a straightforward way).
- We actually reuse the algorithms for finite words of [16,18] as subprocedures in our algorithms for languages of infinite words.

The remainder of the paper is devoted to proving Theorem 1. In Sect. 2, we recall classical notions required for our definitions and proofs: the algebraic definition of regular languages of infinite words and logical preorders. In Sect. 3, we present the general framework that we use. In particular, we introduce a notion that will be at the core of all our algorithms: "Σ_i-chains" (which are adapted and reused from [18]). We then devote a section to each algorithm: Sect. 4 to Σ_2-separation, Sect. 5 to $\mathcal{B}\Sigma_2$-membership and Sect. 6 to Σ_3-separation.

2   Preliminaries

We recall some classical notions that we will need. First, we present the definition of regular languages of infinite words in terms of Wilke algebras. Then, we define the logical preorders that one may associate to each level Σ_i in the hierarchy.

2.1   Semigroups and Wilke Algebras

We briefly recall the definition of regular languages and languages of infinite words in terms of semigroups and Wilke algebras. For details, see [12].

Semigroups. A semigroup is a set S equipped with an associative operation $s \cdot t$ (often written st). In particular, A^+ equipped with concatenation is a semigroup. Given a *finite* semigroup S, it is easy to see that there is an integer $\omega(S)$ (denoted by ω when S is understood) such that for all s of S, s^ω is idempotent: $s^\omega = s^\omega s^\omega$.

Given a language L and a morphism $\alpha : A^+ \to S$, we say that L is *recognized* by α if there exists $F \subseteq S$ such that $L = \alpha^{-1}(F)$. It is well-known that a language is regular if and only if it may be recognized by a *finite* semigroup.

Wilke Algebras. A *Wilke algebra* is a pair (S_+, S_∞), where S_+ is a semigroup and S_∞ is a set. Moreover, (S_+, S_∞) is equipped with two additional products: a *mixed product* $S_+ \times S_\infty \to S_\infty$ mapping $s, t \in S_+, S_\infty$ to an element st of S_∞, and an *infinite product* $(S_+)^\infty \to S_\infty$ mapping an infinite sequence $s_1, s_2, \cdots \in (S_+)^\infty$ to an element $s_1 s_2 \cdots$ of S_∞. We require these products to satisfy all possible forms of associativity. For $s \in S_+$, we let s^∞ be the infinite product $sss \cdots \in S_\infty$. Note that (A^+, A^∞) is a Wilke algebra. See [12] for further details (we use a distinct notation from [12], where what we write s^ω, s^∞ is noted s^π, s^ω, respectively).

We say that (S_+, S_∞) is *finite* if both S_+ and S_∞ are. Note that even if a Wilke algebra is finite, it is not clear how to represent the infinite product, since the set of infinite sequences of S_+ is uncountable. However, it has been shown by Wilke [28] that the infinite product is fully determined by the mapping $s \mapsto s^\infty$. This makes it possible to finitely represent any finite Wilke algebra.

Morphisms of Wilke algebras are defined in the natural way. In particular, observe that any morphism of Wilke algebra $\alpha : (A^+, A^\infty) \to (S_+, S_\infty)$ defines two maps: a semigroup morphism $\alpha_+ : A^+ \to S_+$ and a map $\alpha_\infty : A^\infty \to S_\infty$ (when there is no ambiguity, we shall write $\alpha(w)$ to mean $\alpha_+(w)$ if $w \in A^+$ or $\alpha_\infty(w)$ if $w \in A^\infty$). Therefore, a morphism recognizes both languages (the languages $\alpha_+^{-1}(F_+)$ for $F_+ \subseteq S_+$) and languages of infinite words (the languages of infinite words $\alpha_\infty^{-1}(F_\infty)$ for $F_\infty \subseteq S_\infty$). A language of infinite words is regular iff it may be recognized by a morphism into a *finite* Wilke algebra.

Syntactic Morphisms. It is known that given any regular language (resp. language of infinite words) L, there exists a canonical morphism $\alpha_L : A^+ \to S$ (resp. $\alpha_L : (A^+, A^\infty) \to (S_+, S_\infty)$) recognizing L. This object is called the *syntactic morphism* of L. We refer the reader to [12] for the detailed definition of this object. In the paper we only use two properties of the syntactic morphism. The first is that given any regular language of infinite words L, one can compute its syntactic morphism from any representation of L. We state the second one below.

Fact 2. *Let $i \geqslant 1$ and let L be a regular language of infinite words. Then L is definable in $\mathcal{B}\Sigma_i$ iff so are all languages of words and infinite words recognized by its syntactic morphism.*

The proof of Fact 2 may be found in [12] (in fact, this holds for any class of languages of infinite words which forms a "variety" of languages of infinite words, not just for $\mathcal{B}\Sigma_i$). In view of this, the syntactic morphism is central for membership questions: deciding if a language is definable in $\mathcal{B}\Sigma_i$ amounts to deciding a property of its syntactic morphism. This is the approach used in our membership algorithm for $\mathcal{B}\Sigma_2$ (see Sect. 5).

Morphisms and Separation. When working on separation, we are given two input languages or languages of infinite words. It is convenient to consider a single recognizing object for both inputs rather than two separate objects. This is not restrictive: given two languages (resp. two languages of infinite words) and two associated recognizing morphisms, one can define and compute a single morphism that recognizes them both. For example, if $L_0 \subseteq A^\infty$ is recognized by $\alpha_0 : (A^+, A^\infty) \to (S_+, S_\infty)$ and $L_1 \subseteq A^\infty$ by $\alpha_1 : (A^+, A^\infty) \to (T_+, T_\infty)$, then L_0 and L_1 are both recognized by $\alpha : (A^+, A^\infty) \to (S_+ \times T_+, S_\infty \times T_\infty)$ with $\alpha(w) = (\alpha_0(w), \alpha_1(w))$.

Alphabet Compatible Morphisms. It will be convenient to work with morphisms that satisfy an additional property. A morphism $\alpha : (A^+, A^\infty) \to (S_+, S_\infty)$ is said to be *alphabet compatible* if for all $u, v \in A^+ \cup A^\infty$, $\alpha(u) = \alpha(v)$ implies $\mathsf{alph}(u) = \mathsf{alph}(v)$. Note that when α is alphabet compatible, for all $s \in S_+ \cup S_\infty$, $\mathsf{alph}(s)$ is well defined as the unique $B \subseteq A$ such that for all $u \in \alpha^{-1}(s)$, we have $\mathsf{alph}(u) = B$ (if s has no preimage then we simply set $\mathsf{alph}(s) = \emptyset$).

To any morphism $\alpha : (A^+, A^\infty) \to (S_+, S_\infty)$, we associate a morphism β, called the *alphabet completion* of α. The morphism β recognizes all languages of infinite words recognized by α and is alphabet compatible. If α is already alphabet compatible, then $\beta = \alpha$. Otherwise, observe that 2^A is a semigroup with union as the multiplication and $(2^A, 2^A)$ is therefore a Wilke algebra. Hence, we let β be the morphism: $\beta : (A^+, A^\infty) \to (S_+ \times 2^A, S_\infty \times 2^A)$ with $\beta(w) = (\alpha(w), \mathsf{alph}(w))$.

2.2   Logical Preorders

To each level Σ_i in the hierarchy, one may associate preorders on the sets of words and infinite words. The definition is based on the notion of quantifier rank. The *quantifier rank* of a first-order formula is the length of the longest sequence of nested quantifiers inside the formula. For example, the following sentence,

$$\exists x \; P_b(x) \wedge \neg(\exists y \; (y < x \wedge P_c(y)) \wedge (\forall y \exists z \; x < y < z \wedge P_b(y)))$$

has quantifier rank 3. It is well-known (and easy to show) that for a fixed k, there is a finite number of non-equivalent first-order sentences of rank less than k.

We now define the preorders. Note that while we define two preorders for each level Σ_i (one on A^+, one on A^∞), we actually use the same notation for both. Let $i \geqslant 1$ be a level in the hierarchy and $k \geqslant 1$ as a quantifier rank. Given two words $w, w' \in A^+$ (resp two infinite words $w, w' \in A^\infty$), we write $w \lesssim_i^k w'$ if and only if *any* Σ_i sentence of rank at most k satisfied by w is satisfied by w' as well. By contrapositive, since the negation of a Σ_i sentence is in Π_i, we have $w \lesssim_i^k w'$ iff any Π_i sentence of rank at most k satisfied by w' is also satisfied by w.

One may verify that $\lesssim_i^k$ is preorder. Moreover, it is immediate that the preorders get refined when k or i increase: $w \lesssim_i^{k+1} w'$ or $w \lesssim_{i+1}^k w'$ imply $w \lesssim_i^k w'$. Since a Π_{i+1} sentence is in Σ_i, $w \lesssim_{i+1}^k w'$ also implies $w' \lesssim_i^k w$.

Denote by $\cong_i^k$ the equivalence generated by $\lesssim_i^k$: $w \cong_i^k w'$ when $w \lesssim_i^k w'$ and $w' \lesssim_i^k w$. That is, $w \cong_i^k w'$ if and only if w, w' satisfy the same Σ_i sentences (or equivalently the same $\mathcal{B}\Sigma_i$ sentences, which are nothing but Boolean combinations of Σ_i sentences). The following fact sums up what we just observed.

Fact 3. *Let $k, i \geqslant 1$ and let u, v be two words or two infinite words, then*

(1) $u \lesssim_i^{k+1} v \Rightarrow u \lesssim_i^k v$,   (2) $u \cong_i^{k+1} v \Rightarrow u \cong_i^k v$ (3) $u \lesssim_{i+1}^k v \Rightarrow u \cong_i^k v$.

We finish the section with a few properties about the preorders $\lesssim_i^k$. The proofs are easy and omitted (they are obtained with standard Ehrenfeucht-Fraïssé arguments). We start with decomposition and composition lemmas.

Lemma 4 (Decomposition Lemma). *Let $i, k \geqslant 1$ and let u, v be two words or two infinite words such that $u \lesssim_i^k v$. Then for any decomposition $u = u_1 u_2$ of u, there exist v_1, v_2 such that $v = v_1 v_2$, $u_1 \lesssim_i^{k-1} v_1$ and $u_2 \lesssim_i^{k-1} v_2$.*

Lemma 5 (Composition Lemma). *Let $i, k \geqslant 1$, let u_1, v_1 be two words such that $u_1 \lesssim_i^k v_1$, and u_2, v_2 be either two words or two infinite words such that $u_2 \lesssim_i^k v_2$. Then $u_1 u_2 \lesssim_i^k v_1 v_2$ and $u_1^\infty \lesssim_i^k v_1^\infty$.*

The last composition that we state is specific to infinite words.

Lemma 6. *Let $i, k \geqslant 1$, $u \in A^+$ be a word and $v \in A^\infty$ be an infinite word such that $v \lesssim_i^k u^\infty$. Then for any $\ell \geqslant 2^k$, we have $u^\infty \lesssim_{i+1}^k u^\ell v$.*

In particular we will use the special case of Lemma 6 in which $i = 1$. In this case, one can verify that given $u \in A^+$ and $v \in A^\infty$, when $\mathsf{alph}(u) = \mathsf{alph}(v)$, we have $v \lesssim_1^k u^\infty$ for any $k \geqslant 1$. Hence we have the following corollary of Lemma 6.

Corollary 7. *Let $k \geqslant 1$, $u \in A^+$ be a word and let $v \in A^\infty$ be an infinite word such that $\mathsf{alph}(u) = \mathsf{alph}(v)$. Then for any $\ell \geqslant 2^k$, we have $u^\infty \lesssim_2^k u^\ell v$.*

3 Σ_i-Chains for Language of Infinite Words

All algorithms for infinite words of this paper are strongly related to the finite words algorithms of [16,18]. In particular, we adapt and reuse the key notion of "Σ_i-chain" which was introduced in [18]. The section is devoted to the presentation of this notion. First, we define Σ_i-chains. We then detail the link between Σ_i-chains and our decision problems, first for Σ_i, then for $\mathcal{B}\Sigma_i$.

Σ_i-Chains were initially introduced in [18] as a tool designed to investigate the separation problem over finite words for the logics Σ_i and $\mathcal{B}\Sigma_i$. A set of Σ_i-chains can be associated to any morphism $\alpha : A^+ \to S$ into a finite semigroup S. Intuitively, this set captures information about what Σ_i and $\mathcal{B}\Sigma_i$ can express about the languages recognized by α (including which ones are separable with Σ_i and $\mathcal{B}\Sigma_i$). The definition is based on the following classical lemma.

Lemma 8. *Let $i, k \geqslant 1$ and L_1, L_2 be two languages or two languages of infinite words. Then L_1 is **not** Σ_i-separable (resp. **not** $\mathcal{B}\Sigma_i$-separable) from L_2 iff for all $k \geqslant 1$, there exist $w_1 \in L_1$ and $w_2 \in L_2$ such that $w_1 \lesssim_i^k w_2$ (resp. $w_1 \cong_i^k w_2$).*

Lemma 8 states simple criteria equivalent to Σ_i- and $\mathcal{B}\Sigma_i$-separability. However, both criteria involve a quantification over all natural numbers. Therefore, it is not immediate that they can be decided. Indeed, since both A^+ and A^∞ are infinite sets, $\lesssim_i^k$ and $\cong_i^k$ are endlessly refined as k gets larger.

Σ_i-Chains are designed to deal with this issue. The separation problem takes two *regular* languages or languages of infinite words as input. Therefore, we have a single morphism that recognizes them both. For example, in the case of infinite words, we have $\alpha : (A^+, A^\infty) \to (S_+, S_\infty)$, with (S_+, S_∞) a finite Wilke algebra, that recognizes both inputs. Intuitively, S_+ and S_∞ are finite abstractions of A^+ and A^∞. Consequently, we may abstract the preorders $\lesssim_i^k$ on these two finite sets: this is what Σ_i-chains are. For example, we say that $(s,t) \in (S_\infty)^2$ is a Σ_i-chain (of length 2) for α if for all k, there exist $u, v \in A^\infty$ such that $\alpha(u) = s$, $\alpha(v) = t$ and $u \lesssim_i^k v$. For languages of infinite words recognized by α, it is then easy to adapt the two criteria of Lemma 8 to work directly with the Σ_i-chains associated to α. In other words, we reduce separation to the (still difficult) problem of computing the set of Σ_i-chains associated to a given input morphism.

Chains. Let us now define chains. Given a finite set S, a *chain over* S is simply a finite word over S (*i.e.*, an element of S^+). We shall only consider chains over S_+ and over S_∞, where S_+ and S_∞ are the two components of some Wilke algebra (S_+, S_∞). A remark about notation is in order: a word is usually denoted as the concatenation of its letters. However, since S_+ is a semigroup, this would be ambiguous: when $st \in (S_+)^+$, st could either mean a word with 2 letters s and t, or the product of s and t in S_+. To avoid confusion, we will write $(s_1, \dots, s_n)$ for a chain of length n. We denote chains by $\bar{s}, \bar{t}, \dots$ and sets of chains by $\mathcal{S}, \mathcal{T}, \dots$

If (S_+, S_∞) is a Wilke algebra, then for all $n \in \mathbb{N}$, $(S_+)^n$ is a semigroup when equipped with the componentwise multiplication $(s_1, \dots, s_n)(t_1, \dots, t_n) = (s_1 t_1, \dots, s_n t_n)$. Moreover, the pair $((S_+)^n, (S_\infty)^n)$ is a Wilke algebra (in which the mixed and infinite products are defined componentwise as well).

Σ_i-Chains. Fix $i \geqslant 1$ and $x \in \{+, \infty\}$. We associate a set of Σ_i-chains to any map $\beta : A^x \to S$ where S is a finite set. The set $\mathcal{C}_i[\beta] \subseteq S^+$ of Σ_i-*chains* for β is defined as follows. Let $\bar{s} = (s_1, \dots, s_n) \in S^+$ be a chain. We have $\bar{s} \in \mathcal{C}_i[\beta]$ if and only if for all $k \in \mathbb{N}$, there exist $w_1, \dots, w_n \in A^x$ such that:

$$w_1 \lesssim_i^k w_2 \lesssim_i^k \cdots \lesssim_i^k w_n \text{ and for all } j, \ \beta(w_j) = s_j.$$

We let $\mathcal{C}_{i,n}[\beta]$ be the restriction of this set to chains of length n: $\mathcal{C}_{i,n}[\beta] = \mathcal{C}_i[\beta] \cap S^n$.

Σ_i-Chains Associated to a Morphism. It follows from the definition of Σ_i-chains that one may associate a set $\mathcal{C}_i[\alpha]$ to any semigroup morphism $\alpha : A^+ \to S$. This set is exactly the set of Σ_i-chains associated to α as defined in [18].

Moreover, given a morphism $\alpha : (A^+, A^\infty) \to (S_+, S_\infty)$ into a finite Wilke algebra (S_+, S_∞), one may associate two sets of Σ_i-chains to α: one to the morphism $\alpha_+ : A^+ \to S_+$ ($\mathcal{C}_i[\alpha_+] \subseteq (S_+)^+$) and one to the map $\alpha_\infty : A^\infty \to S_\infty$ ($\mathcal{C}_i[\alpha_\infty] \subseteq (S_\infty)^+$). We may now link Σ_i-chains to the separation problem.

3.1 Σ_i-Chains and Separation for Σ_i

We now connect Σ_i-chains to the separation problem. We begin with the simplest connection, which is between Σ_i-chains of length 2 and separation for Σ_i.

Theorem 9. *Let $i \geqslant 1$, $x \in \{+, \infty\}$ and $\beta : A^x \to S$ a map into a finite set S. Given $F_1, F_2 \subseteq S$, $L_1 = \beta^{-1}(F_1)$ and $L_2 = \beta^{-1}(F_2)$, the following are equivalent*

1. *L_1 is **not** Σ_i-separable from L_2.*
2. *there exist $s_1 \in F_1$ and $s_2 \in F_2$ such that $(s_1, s_2) \in \mathcal{C}_{i,2}[\beta]$.*

Theorem 9 is a straightforward consequence of the statement for Σ_i in Lemma 8. In view of the theorem, our approach for the Σ_i-separation problem is as follows:

- for languages, we look for an algorithm computing $\mathcal{C}_{i,2}[\alpha]$ from an input morphism $\alpha : A^+ \to S$ into a finite semigroup S.
- for languages of infinite words, we look for an algorithm computing $\mathcal{C}_{i,2}[\alpha_\infty]$ from an input morphism $\alpha : (A^+, A^\infty) \to (S_+, S_\infty)$ into a finite Wilke algebra (S_+, S_∞). Typically, this algorithm involves computing $\mathcal{C}_{i,2}[\alpha_+]$ first, which can be achieved by reusing the first item, *i.e.*, the algorithm for word languages.

This approach is exactly the one used in [16,18] to solve separation for Σ_2 and Σ_3 over finite words: the following theorems are proven in these papers.

Theorem 10 (see [18]). *Given as input a morphism $\alpha : A^+ \to S$ into a finite semigroup S, one can compute the set $\mathcal{C}_{2,2}[\alpha]$ of Σ_2-chains of length 2 for α.*

Theorem 11 (see [16]). *Given as input a morphism $\alpha : A^+ \to S$ into a finite semigroup S, one can compute the set $\mathcal{C}_{3,2}[\alpha]$ of Σ_3-chains of length 2 for α.*

We generalize these two theorems in Sect. 4 (for Σ_2) and Sect. 6 (for Σ_3) for infinite words by presenting two new algorithms. These algorithms both take a morphism $\alpha : (A^+, A^\infty) \to (S_+, S_\infty)$ as input and compute the sets $\mathcal{C}_{2,2}[\alpha_\infty]$ and $\mathcal{C}_{3,2}[\alpha_\infty]$ respectively. The algorithms of Theorems 10 and 11 are reused as subprocedures in these new algorithms for languages of infinite words: computing $\mathcal{C}_{2,2}[\alpha_\infty]$ and $\mathcal{C}_{3,2}[\alpha_\infty]$ requires to first compute $\mathcal{C}_{2,2}[\alpha_+]$ and $\mathcal{C}_{3,2}[\alpha_+]$.

Remark 12. The algorithms of Theorems 10 and 11 both work with objects that are actually more general than Σ_i-chains: the Σ_2 algorithm works with "Σ_2-junctures" and the Σ_3 algorithm with an even more general notion: "$\Sigma_{2,3}$-trees". We do not present these more general notions because we do not need them outside of the algorithms of Theorems 10 and 11, which we use as black boxes.

3.2 Σ_i-Chains and Separation for $\mathcal{B}\Sigma_i$

We finish by presenting the connection between the separation problem for $\mathcal{B}\Sigma_i$ and Σ_i-chains. This time, the connection depends on the whole set of Σ_i-chains. More precisely, it depends on yet another notion called *alternation*.

Let $x \in \{+, \infty\}$ and $\beta : A^x \to S$ be a map into a finite set S. We say that a pair $(s, t) \in S^2$ is Σ_i-*alternating* for β iff for all $n \geqslant 1$, we have $(s, t)^n \in \mathcal{C}_i[\beta]$ (where by $(s, t)^n$, we mean the chain $(s, t, s, t, \ldots, s, t)$ of length $2n$).

Theorem 13. *Let $i \geqslant 1$, $x \in \{+, \infty\}$ and $\beta : A^x \to S$ a map into a finite set S. Given $F_1, F_2 \subseteq S$, $L_1 = \beta^{-1}(F_1)$ and $L_2 = \beta^{-1}(F_2)$, the following are equivalent:*

1. L_1 *is* **not** $\mathcal{B}\Sigma_i$-*separable from* L_2.
2. *there exist $s_1 \in F_1$ and $s_2 \in F_2$ such that (s_1, s_2) is Σ_i-alternating.*

The proof of Theorem 13 is based on the second part of Lemma 8. In view of the theorem, the separation problem for $\mathcal{B}\Sigma_i$ reduces to the computation of the Σ_i-alternating pairs, which is unfortunately open for $i \geqslant 2$, even on finite words.

Regarding membership however, Theorem 13 yields an immediate corollary. For $x \in \{+, \infty\}$ and $\beta : A^x \to S$ a map into a finite set S, we say that β has *bounded* Σ_i *-alternation* iff every Σ_i-alternating pair $(s, t) \in S^2$ for β satisfies $s = t$.

Corollary 14. *Let $i \geqslant 1$, $x \in \{+, \infty\}$ and $\beta : A^x \to S$ be a map into a finite set S. Then all sets $\beta^{-1}(F)$ for $F \subseteq S$ are $\mathcal{B}\Sigma_i$-definable if and only if β has bounded Σ_i-alternation.*

Combining Corollary 14 with Fact 2 yields a criterion for $\mathcal{B}\Sigma_i$-membership: a regular language of finite or infinite words is definable in $\mathcal{B}\Sigma_i$ iff its syntactic morphism has bounded Σ_i-alternation. This is used in [18] to obtain a (language) membership algorithm for $\mathcal{B}\Sigma_2$. More precisely, the following result is proved.

Theorem 15 (see [18]). *Given as input a morphism $\alpha : A^+ \to S$ into a finite semigroup S, one can decide whether α has bounded Σ_2-alternation or not.*

In Sect. 5 we obtain our algorithm for $\mathcal{B}\Sigma_2$-membership over infinite words by proving that given a morphism $\alpha : (A^+, A^\infty) \to (S_+, S_\infty)$ as input, one can decide whether α_∞ has bounded Σ_2-alternation or not. More precisely, we prove that α_∞ having bounded Σ_2-alternation is equivalent to two decidable properties of α. The first is that α_+ has bounded Σ_2-alternation (which we can decide by Theorem 15). The second is a simple equation that (S_+, S_∞) needs to satisfy.

4 A Separation Algorithm for Σ_2

In this section, we present an algorithm for the separation problem associated to Σ_2 over infinite words. As expected, this algorithm is based on the computation of Σ_2-chains of length 2 (see Theorem 9): we prove that given a morphism α into a finite Wilke algebra, one can compute $\mathcal{C}_{2,2}[\alpha_\infty]$.

For an *alphabet compatible* morphism $\alpha : (A^+, A^\infty) \to (S_+, S_\infty)$ into a finite Wilke algebra, we denote by $\mathrm{Calc}_{\Sigma_2}(\alpha)$ the set of all pairs:

$$(r_1(s_1)^\infty, \ r_2(s_2)^\omega t_2) \in S_\infty \times S_\infty$$

with $(r_1, r_2) \in \mathcal{C}_{2,2}[\alpha_+]$, $(s_1, s_2) \in \mathcal{C}_{2,2}[\alpha_+]$, $t_2 \in \alpha(A^\infty)$ and $\mathsf{alph}(s_1) = \mathsf{alph}(t_2)$. Note that this last condition is well defined since α is alphabet compatible. Recall that s_1^∞ is the infinite product $s_1 s_1 \ldots$, and s_2^ω the idempotent power of s_2 in S_+.

Proposition 16. *Let $\alpha : (A^+, A^\infty) \to (S_+, S_\infty)$ be an alphabet compatible morphism into a finite Wilke algebra (S_+, S_∞). Then, $\mathcal{C}_{2,2}[\alpha_\infty] = \mathrm{Calc}_{\Sigma_2}(\alpha)$.*

A consequence of Proposition 16 is that the separation problem is decidable for Σ_2 over infinite words. Indeed, recall that for any two regular languages of infinite words, one may compute a single alphabet compatible Wilke algebra morphism that recognizes them both. Therefore, it follows from Theorem 9 that deciding Σ_2-separation amounts to having an algorithm that computes $\mathcal{C}_{2,2}[\alpha_\infty]$ from α.

We obtain this algorithm from Proposition 16 since $\mathrm{Calc}_{\Sigma_2}(\alpha)$ may be computed, given α as input. Indeed, by Theorem 10, we already know that the set $\mathcal{C}_{2,2}[\alpha_+]$ can be computed from α. Hence, we obtain the desired corollary.

Corollary 17. *Over infinite words, the separation problem is decidable for Σ_2.*

An important remark is that we use Theorem 10 as a black box: we do not reprove that $\mathcal{C}_{2,2}[\alpha_+]$ may be computed from α_+. This is not an immediate result. In fact, the proof of [18] requires to use a framework that is more general than Σ_2-chains (that of "Σ_2-junctures") as well as arguments that are independent from those that we are going to use to prove Proposition 16.

It remains to prove Proposition 16. We illustrate the algorithm by proving the easier inclusion: $\mathcal{C}_{2,2}[\alpha_\infty] \supseteq \mathrm{Calc}_{\Sigma_2}(\alpha)$ (this proves correctness: all computed chains are indeed Σ_2-chains). The converse inclusion (corresponding to completeness: all Σ_2-chains are computed) is available in the long version of the paper.

Correctness Proof: $\mathcal{C}_{2,2}[\alpha_\infty] \supseteq \mathrm{Calc}_{\Sigma_2}(\alpha)$. Let $(r_1, r_2) \in \mathcal{C}_{2,2}[\alpha_+]$, $(s_1, s_2) \in \mathcal{C}_{2,2}[\alpha_+]$ and $t_2 \in \alpha(A^\infty)$ such that $\mathsf{alph}(s_1) = \mathsf{alph}(t_2)$. Our objective is to prove that $(r_1(s_1)^\infty, r_2(s_2)^\omega t_2) \in \mathcal{C}_{2,2}[\alpha_\infty]$. Let $k \geqslant 1$. By definition, we need to find two infinite words $w_1 \lesssim_2^k w_2$ such that $\alpha(w_1) = r_1(s_1)^\infty$ and $\alpha(w_2) = r_2(s_2)^\omega t_2$.

By hypothesis, we have four words $x_1, x_2, y_1, y_2 \in A^+$ such that $x_1 \lesssim_2^k x_2$, $y_1 \lesssim_2^k y_2$, $\alpha(x_1) = r_1$, $\alpha(x_2) = r_2$, $\alpha(y_1) = s_1$ and $\alpha(y_2) = s_2$. Moreover, we have an infinite word $z \in A^\infty$ such $\alpha(z) = t_2$ and $\mathsf{alph}(y_1) = \mathsf{alph}(z)$. Let $w_1 = x_1(y_1)^\infty$ and $w_2 = x_2(y_2)^{2^k \omega} z$. Observe that by definition, we have $\alpha(w_1) = r_1(s_1)^\infty$ and $\alpha(w_2) = r_2(s_2)^\omega t_2$. Therefore, it remains to prove that $w_1 \lesssim_2^k w_2$.

By Corollary 7, we obtain that $(y_1)^\infty \lesssim_2^k (y_1)^{2^k \omega} z$. Moreover, using $y_1 \lesssim_2^k y_2$ and $z \lesssim_2^k z$ together with Lemma 5, we obtain $(y_1)^{2^k \omega} z \lesssim_2^k (y_2)^{2^k \omega} z$. Therefore, by transitivity $(y_1)^\infty \lesssim_2^k (y_2)^{2^k \omega} z$. Finally, we use the fact that $x_1 \lesssim_2^k x_2$ and Lemma 5 to conclude that $x_1(y_1)^\infty \lesssim_2^k x_2(y_2)^{2^k \omega} z$, i.e., that $w_1 \lesssim_2^k w_2$. $\qquad\square$

5   A Membership Algorithm for $\mathcal{B}\Sigma_2$

We now present our membership algorithm for $\mathcal{B}\Sigma_2$ over infinite words. The algorithm is stated as a decidable characterization of $\mathcal{B}\Sigma_2$ over infinite words.

Theorem 18. *Let $L \subseteq A^\infty$ be regular and let $\alpha : (A^+, A^\infty) \to (S_+, S_\infty)$ be the alphabet completion of its syntactic morphism. The following are equivalent:*

1. *L is definable in $\mathcal{B}\Sigma_2$.*
2. *α_∞ has bounded Σ_2-alternation.*
3. *α_+ has bounded Σ_2-alternation and α satisfies the following equation:*

$$(st^\omega)^\infty = (st^\omega)^\omega st^\infty \text{ for all } s, t \in \alpha(A^+) \text{ such that } \mathsf{alph}(s) = \mathsf{alph}(t) \quad (1)$$

We know that Item 3 in Theorem 18 is decidable. Indeed, Theorem 15 states that whether α_+ has bounded Σ_2-alternation is decidable (note however that this is a difficult result of [18] whose proof is independent from that of Theorem 18). Moreover, verifying that (1) is satisfied may be achieved by checking all possible combinations. Therefore, we obtain the following corollary of Theorem 18.

Corollary 19. *The membership problem over infinite words is decidable for $\mathcal{B}\Sigma_2$.*

It now remains to prove Theorem 18. That 2) $\Rightarrow$ 1) is immediate from Corollary 14. The most difficult (and interesting) direction is 3) $\Rightarrow$ 2). Due to lack of space, it is proved in the long version of this paper. As we did in the previous section, we illustrate the theorem by proving the easier 1) $\Rightarrow$ 3) direction.

Proof of 1) $\Rightarrow$ 3). Let L be $\mathcal{B}\Sigma_2$-definable. In particular, this means that every language of finite or infinite words recognized by α is definable in $\mathcal{B}\Sigma_2$ (we know from Fact 2 that it is true for the syntactic morphism of L, so this is true as well for its alphabet completion α, as one can test the alphabet of a word in $\mathcal{B}\Sigma_2$).

Since every language recognized by α is definable in $\mathcal{B}\Sigma_2$, Corollary 14 entails that α_+ has bounded Σ_2-alternation. It remains to establish Eq. (1). For $s, t \in \alpha(A^+)$ such that $\mathsf{alph}(s) = \mathsf{alph}(t)$, let us show that $(st^\omega)^\infty = (st^\omega)^\omega st^\infty$.

Let k such that for any $r \in S_\infty$, $\alpha^{-1}(r)$ may be defined by a $\mathcal{B}\Sigma_2$ sentence of quantifier rank less than k (k exists since all these languages of infinite words are definable in $\mathcal{B}\Sigma_2$). By choice of k, for any two infinite words $u, v \in A^\infty$, we have $u \cong_2^k v \Rightarrow \alpha(u) = \alpha(v)$. Therefore, in order to conclude, it suffices to find two infinite words u, v of images $(st^\omega)^\infty$ and $(st^\omega)^\omega st^\infty$ and such that $u \cong_2^k v$.

By definition of s, t, we have words $x, y \in A^+$ such that $\alpha(x) = s$, $\alpha(y) = t$ and $\mathsf{alph}(x) = \mathsf{alph}(y)$. Let $u = (xy^{2^k\omega})^\infty$ and $v = (xy^{2^k\omega})^{2^k\omega}xy^\infty$. It is imediate that u and v have images $(st^\omega)^\infty$ and $(st^\omega)^\omega st^\infty$. It remains to prove that $u \cong_2^k v$.

We prove that $u \lesssim_2^k v$ and $v \lesssim_2^k u$. Observe that $\mathsf{alph}(xy^{2^k\omega}) = \mathsf{alph}(xy^\infty)$. Hence, we get $u \lesssim_2^k v$ from Corollary 7. Conversely, we know that $\mathsf{alph}((xy^{2^k\omega})^\infty) = \mathsf{alph}(y)$. Therefore, we may use Corollary 7 again to obtain $y^\infty \lesssim_2^k y^{2^k\omega}(xy^{2^k\omega})^\infty$. That $v \lesssim_2^k u$ is then immediate from this inequality by Lemma 5.

6 A Separation Algorithm for Σ_3

We present our algorithm for the separation problem associated to Σ_3 over infinite words. As for Σ_2, this algorithm is based on Theorem 9: we give a procedure computing $\mathcal{C}_{3,2}[\alpha_\infty]$ from an input morphism $\alpha : (A^+, A^\infty) \to (S_+, S_\infty)$.

However, in this case, this computation requires a new ingredient. This new ingredient is a generalization of Σ_i-chains that we call *mixed chains*.

Mixed Chains. Let $x \in \{+, \infty\}$ and $\beta : A^x \to S$ as a map into some finite set S. We define a set $\mathcal{M}[\beta] \subseteq S^3$. Let $\bar{s} = (s_1, s_2, s_3) \in S^3$ be a chain over S. We have $\bar{s} \in \mathcal{M}[\beta]$ if and only if for all $k \in \mathbb{N}$, there exist $w_1, w_2, w_3 \in A^x$ such that,

$$\beta(w_1) = s_1, \quad \beta(w_2) = s_2, \quad \beta(w_3) = s_3 \quad \text{and} \quad w_1 \lesssim_2^k w_2 \lesssim_3^k w_3$$

Note the definition involves both the preorder "$\lesssim_2^k$" associated to Σ_2 and the preorder "$\lesssim_3^k$" associated to Σ_3 (hence the name "mixed chains"). An important remark is that we will not present any algorithm for computing mixed chains. On the other hand, our algorithm for computing $\mathcal{C}_{3,2}[\alpha_\infty]$ from a morphism α is parametrized by the set of mixed chains $\mathcal{M}[\alpha_+]$. That $\mathcal{M}[\alpha_+]$ may be computed from α_+ is a very difficult result of [16], stated below.

Theorem 20 (see [16]). *Given as input a morphism $\alpha : A^+ \to S$ into a finite semigroup S, one can compute the set $\mathcal{M}[\alpha]$ of mixed chains for α.*

Remark 21. The presentation of Theorem 20 is different in [16]. It is proved that one can compute the set of "$\Sigma_{2,3}$-trees" associated to α. Essentially $\Sigma_{2,3}$-trees are trees of depth 3 whose nodes are labeled by elements of a finite set S and mixed chains are the special case when there is only a single branch in the tree.

We may now present our separation algorithm for Σ_3 over infinite words. Let $\alpha : (A^+, A^\infty) \to (S_+, S_\infty)$ be an alphabet compatible morphism into a finite Wilke algebra (S_+, S_∞). We define $\mathrm{Calc}_{\Sigma_3}(\alpha) \subseteq (S_\infty)^2$ as the set of all pairs

$$\left(r_2 (s_2 (t_2)^\omega)^\infty, \; r_3 (s_3 (t_3)^\omega)^\omega s_1 (t_1)^\infty \right)$$

with $(r_2, r_3) \in \mathcal{C}_{3,2}[\alpha_+]$, $(s_1, s_2, s_3) \in \mathcal{M}[\alpha_+]$, $(t_1, t_2, t_3) \in \mathcal{M}[\alpha_+]$ and $\mathsf{alph}(s_1) = \mathsf{alph}(t_1)$. Since we know from Theorem 20 that one may compute $\mathcal{M}[\alpha_+]$ from α, it is immediate from the definition that one may compute $\mathrm{Calc}_{\Sigma_3}(\alpha)$ from α.

Proposition 22. *Let $\alpha : (A^+, A^\infty) \to (S_+, S_\infty)$ be an alphabet compatible morphism into a finite Wilke algebra (S_+, S_∞). Then, $\mathcal{C}_{3,2}[\alpha_\infty] = \mathrm{Calc}_{\Sigma_3}(\alpha)$.*

As for Σ_2, Proposition 22 immediately yields an algorithm for Σ_3-separation over infinite words. Indeed, it provides an algorithm computing $\mathcal{C}_{3,2}[\alpha_\infty]$ from any alphabet compatible morphism α, which suffices to decide Σ_3-separation.

Corollary 23. *The separation problem over infinite words is decidable for Σ_3.*

It remains to prove Proposition 22. We proceed as for Σ_2. Again, we only prove the easier inclusion and postpone the other to the long version of this paper.

Proof of $\mathcal{C}_{3,2}[\alpha_\infty] \supseteq \mathbf{Calc}_{\Sigma_3}(\alpha)$. Let $(r_2, r_3) \in \mathcal{C}_{3,2}[\alpha_+]$, $(s_1, s_2, s_3) \in \mathcal{M}[\alpha_+]$ and $(t_1, t_2, t_3) \in \mathcal{M}[\alpha_+]$ be chains such that $\mathsf{alph}(s_1) = \mathsf{alph}(t_1)$. We have to prove that $(r_2(s_2(t_2)^\omega)^\infty, r_3(s_3(t_3)^\omega)^\omega s_1(t_1)^\infty) \in \mathcal{C}_{3,2}[\alpha_\infty]$. Let $k \geqslant 1$, we need to find two infinite words $w_2 \lesssim_3^k w_3$ such that $\alpha(w_2) = r_2(s_2(t_2)^\omega)^\infty$ and $\alpha(w_3) = r_3(s_3(t_3)^\omega)^\omega s_1(t_1)^\infty$. The definition gives words $x_2, x_3, y_1, y_2, y_3, z_1, z_2, z_3$ with:

- $\alpha(x_j) = r_j$, $\alpha(y_j) = s_j$, $\alpha(z_j) = t_j$
- $x_2 \lesssim_3^k x_3$, $y_1 \lesssim_2^k y_2 \lesssim_3^k y_3$ and $z_1 \lesssim_2^k z_2 \lesssim_3^k z_3$.

Moreover, as $\mathsf{alph}(s_1) = \mathsf{alph}(t_1)$, we have $\mathsf{alph}(y_1) = \mathsf{alph}(z_1)$. We define $w_2 = x_2(y_2(z_2)^{2^k\omega})^\infty$ and $w_3 = x_3(y_3(z_3)^{2^k\omega})^{2^k\omega}y_1 z_1^\infty$. It is immediate from this definition that $\alpha(w_2) = r_2(s_2(t_2)^\omega)^\infty$ and that $\alpha(w_3) = r_3(s_3(t_3)^\omega)^\omega s_1(t_1)^\infty$. It remains to prove that $w_2 \lesssim_3^k w_3$.

We first prove $y_1 z_1^\infty \lesssim_2^k (y_2(z_2)^{2^k\omega})^\infty$. Since $\mathsf{alph}(y_1) = \mathsf{alph}(z_1)$, we may use Corollary 7 to obtain $z_1^\infty \lesssim_2^k (z_1)^{2^k\omega}(y_1(z_1)^{2^k\omega})^\infty$. By Lemma 5 and transitivity,

$$y_1 z_1^\infty \lesssim_2^k (y_1(z_1)^{2^k\omega})^\infty \lesssim_2^k (y_2(z_2)^{2^k\omega})^\infty \tag{2}$$

We may now use (2) together with Lemma 6 to obtain that $(y_2(z_2)^{2^k\omega})^\infty \lesssim_3^k (y_2(z_2)^{2^k\omega})^{2^k\omega}y_1 z_1^\infty$. Using Lemma 5 and transitivity again, we obtain that

$$x_2(y_2(z_2)^{2^k\omega})^\infty \lesssim_3^k x_3(y_3(z_3)^{2^k\omega})^{2^k\omega}y_1 z_1^\infty$$

This exactly says that $w_2 \lesssim_3^k w_3$ which concludes the proof. $\qquad\square$

7   Conclusion

We proved that for languages of infinite words, the separation problem is decidable for Σ_2 and Σ_3 and that the membership problem is decidable for $\mathcal{B}\Sigma_2$. Note that using a theorem of [21], these results may be lifted to the variants of these logics whose signature has been enriched with a predicate "+1", that is interpreted as the successor relation. This means that over infinite words, separation is decidable for $\Sigma_2(<, +1)$ and $\Sigma_3(<, +1)$ and membership is decidable for $\mathcal{B}\Sigma_2(<, +1)$.

A gap remains between languages and languages of infinite words: we leave open the case of Σ_4-membership for languages of infinite words while it is known to be decidable for languages [16]. The language algorithm was based on two ingredients: (1) the decidability of Σ_3-separation [16] and (2) an effective reduction of Σ_{i+1}-membership to Σ_i-separation [18] (which is generic for all $i \geqslant 1$). In the setting of languages of infinite words, we are missing the second result and it is not clear whether a similar reduction exists.

250   T. Pierron et al.

Acknowledgements. This study has been carried out with financial support from the French State, managed by the French National Research Agency (ANR) in the frame of the "Investments for the future" Programme IdEx Bordeaux -CPU (ANR-10-IDEX-03-02).

References

1. Arfi, M.: Polynomial operations on rational languages. In: Brandenburg, F.J., Vidal-Naquet, G., Wirsing, M. (eds.) STACS'87. LNCS, vol. 247, pp. 198–206. Springer, Heidelberg (1987)
2. Bojańczyk, M.: The common fragment of ACTL and LTL. In: Amadio, R.M. (ed.) FOSSACS 2008. LNCS, vol. 4962, pp. 172–185. Springer, Heidelberg (2008)
3. Brzozowski, J.A., Knast, R.: The dot-depth hierarchy of star-free languages is infinite. J. Comput. Syst. Sci. **16**(1), 37–55 (1978)
4. Büchi, J.R.: Weak second-order arithmetic and finite automata. Math. Logic Q. **6**(1–6), 66–92 (1960)
5. Büchi, J.R.: On a decision method in restricted second order arithmetic. In: Logic, Methodology and Philosophy of Science (Proc. 1960 Internat. Congr.), pp. 1–11. Stanford Univ. Press, Stanford (1962)
6. Czerwiński, W., Martens, W., Masopust, T.: Efficient separability of regular languages by subsequences and suffixes. In: Fomin, F.V., Freivalds, R., Kwiatkowska, M., Peleg, D. (eds.) ICALP 2013, Part II. LNCS, vol. 7966, pp. 150–161. Springer, Heidelberg (2013)
7. Diekert, V., Kufleitner, M.: Fragments of first-order logic over infinite words. Theory Comput. Syst. **48**(3), 486–516 (2011)
8. Elgot, C.C.: Decision problems of finite automata design and related arithmetics. Trans. Am. Math. Soc. **98**(1), 21–51 (1961)
9. Kufleitner, M., Walter, T.: Level two of the quantifier alternation hierarchy over infinite words. CoRR, abs/1509.06207 (2015)
10. McNaughton, R., Papert, S.A.: Counter-Free Automata. MIT Press, Cambridge (1971)
11. Perrin, D.: Recent results on automata and infinite words. In: Chytil, M.P., Koubek, V. (eds.) MFCS 1984. LNCS, vol. 176, pp. 134–148. Springer, Heidelberg (1984)
12. Perrin, D., Pin, J.É.: Infinite Words. Elsevier, Amsterdam (2004)
13. Pierron, T., Place, T., Zeitoun, M.: Quantifier alternation for infinite words. CoRR, abs/1511.09011 (2015)
14. Pin, J.É.: Positive varieties and infinite words. In: Lucchesi, C.L., Moura, A.V. (eds.) LATIN 1998. LNCS, vol. 1380, pp. 76–87. Springer, Heidelberg (1998)
15. Pin, J.É., Weil, P.: Polynomial closure and unambiguous product. Theory Comput.Syst. **30**(4), 383–422 (1997)
16. Place, T.: Separating regular languages with two quantifier alternations. In: Proceedings of the 30th Annual ACM/IEEE Symposium on Logic in Computer Science (LICS 2015), pp. 202–213. IEEE (2015)
17. Place, T., van Rooijen, L., Zeitoun, M.: Separating regular languages by piecewise testable and unambiguous languages. In: Chatterjee, K., Sgall, J. (eds.) MFCS 2013. LNCS, vol. 8087, pp. 729–740. Springer, Heidelberg (2013)
18. Place, T., Zeitoun, M.: Going higher in the first-order quantifier alternation hierarchy on words. In: Esparza, J., Fraigniaud, P., Husfeldt, T., Koutsoupias, E. (eds.) ICALP 2014, Part II. LNCS, vol. 8573, pp. 342–353. Springer, Heidelberg (2014)

19. Place, T., Zeitoun, M.: Separating regular languages with first-order logic. In: 2014 Proceedings of the Joint Meeting of the 23rd EACSL Annual Conference on Computer Science Logic (CSL 2014), 29th Annual ACM/IEEE Symposium on Logic in Computer Science (LICS 2014), pp. 75:1–75:10. ACM, New York (2011)
20. Place, T., Zeitoun, M.: Separating ω-languages without quantifier alternation (2015) (Unpublished)
21. Place, T., Zeitoun, M.: Separation and the successor relation. In preparation, long version of [22] (2015)
22. Place, T., Zeitoun, M.: Separation and the successor relation. In: Mayr, E.W., Ollinger, N. (eds.) 32nd International Symposium on Theoretical Aspects of Computer Science (STACS 2015). Leibniz International Proceedings in Informatics (LIPIcs), vol. 30, pp. 662–675. Schloss Dagstuhl-Leibniz-Zentrum fuer Informatik, Dagstuhl (2015)
23. Schützenberger, M.P.: On finite monoids having only trivial subgroups. Inf. Control 8(2), 190–194 (1965)
24. Simon, I.: Piecewise testable events. In: Brakhage, H. (ed.) Automata Theory and Formal Languages. LNCS, vol. 33, pp. 214–222. Springer, Heidelberg (1975)
25. Stockmeyer, L.J., Meyer, A.R.: Word problems requiring exponential time (preliminary report). In: Proceedings of the Fifth Annual ACM Symposium on Theory of Computing, STOC 1973, pp. 1–9. ACM, New York (1973)
26. Thomas, W.: A concatenation game and the dot-depth hierarchy. In: Börger, E. (ed.) Computation Theory and Logic. LNCS, vol. 270, pp. 415–426. Springer, Heidelberg (1987)
27. Trakhtenbrot, B.A.: Finite automata and logic of monadic predicates. Dokl. Akad. Nauk SSSR **149**, 326–329 (1961). In Russian
28. Wilke, T.: An Eilenberg theorem for ∞-languages. In: Leach Albert, J., Monien, B., Rodríguez Artalejo, M. (eds.) ICALP 1991. LNCS, vol. 510, pp. 588–599. Springer, Heidelberg (1991)

Synchronizing Automata over Nested Words

Dmitry Chistikov[1]([✉]), Pavel Martyugin[2], and Mahsa Shirmohammadi[3]

[1] Max Planck Institute for Software Systems (MPI-SWS),
Kaiserslautern and Saarbrücken, Germany
dch@mpi-sws.org
[2] Institute of Mathematics and Computer Science,
Ural Federal University, Ekaterinburg, Russia
martuginp@gmail.com
[3] University of Oxford, Oxford, UK
mahsa.shirmohammadi@cs.ox.ac.uk

Abstract. We extend the concept of a synchronizing word from deterministic finite-state automata (DFA) to nested word automata (NWA): A well-matched nested word is called synchronizing if it resets the control state of any configuration, i.e., takes the NWA from all control states to a single control state.

We show that although the shortest synchronizing word for an NWA, if it exists, can be (at most) exponential in the size of the NWA, the existence of such a word can still be decided in polynomial time. As our main contribution, we show that deciding the existence of a short synchronizing word (of at most given length) becomes PSPACE-complete (as opposed to NP-complete for DFA). The upper bound makes a connection to pebble games and Strahler numbers, and the lower bound goes via small-cost synchronizing words for DFA, an intermediate problem that we also show PSPACE-complete. We also characterize the complexity of a number of related problems, using the observation that the intersection nonemptiness problem for NWA is EXP-complete.

1 Introduction

The concept of a synchronizing word for finite-state machines has been studied in automata theory for more than half a century [22, 25]. Given a deterministic finite automaton (DFA) $\mathcal{D}$ over an input alphabet Σ, a word w is called *synchronizing* for $\mathcal{D}$ if, no matter which state $q \in Q$ the automaton $\mathcal{D}$ starts from, the word w brings it to some specific state $\bar{q}$ that only depends on w but not on q. Put differently, a synchronizing word *resets* the state of an automaton. If the state of $\mathcal{D}$ is initially unknown to an observer, then feeding $\mathcal{D}$ with the input w effectively restarts $\mathcal{D}$, making it possible for the observer to rely on the knowledge of the current state henceforth.

In this paper we extend the concept of a synchronizing word to so-called *nested words*. This is a model that extends usual words by imparting a parenthetical structure to them: some letters in a word are declared *calls* and *returns*, which are then matched to each other in a uniquely determined "nesting"

© Springer-Verlag Berlin Heidelberg 2016
B. Jacobs and C. Löding (Eds.): FOSSACS 2016, LNCS 9634, pp. 252–268, 2016.
DOI: 10.1007/978-3-662-49630-5_15

(non-crossing) way. On the language acceptor level, this hybrid structure (linear sequence of letters with matched pairs) corresponds to a pushdown automaton where every letter in the input word is coupled with the information on whether the automaton should push, pop, or not touch the pushdown (the stack). Such machines were first studied by Mehlhorn [17] under the name of *input-driven pushdown automata* in 1980 and have recently received a lot of attention under the name of *visibly pushdown automata*. The latter term, as well as the model of nested words and *nested word automata* (in NWA the matching relation remains a separate entity, while in input-driven pushdown automata it is encoded in the input alphabet), is due to Alur and Madhusudan [1].

The tree-like structure created by matched pairs of letters occurs naturally in many domains; for instance, nested words mimic traces of programs with procedures (which have pairs of calls and returns), as well as documents in eXtensible Markup Language (XML documents, ubiquitous today, have pairs of opening and closing tags). This makes the nested words model very appealing; at the same time, nested words and NWA enjoy many nice properties of usual words and finite-state machines: for example, constructions of automata for operations over languages, and many decidability properties naturally carry over to nested words—a fact widely used in software verification (see, e.g., [6] and references therein). This suggests that the classic concept of a synchronizing word may have an interesting and meaningful extension in the realm of nested words.

Our Contribution and Discussion. Nested word automata are essentially an expressive subclass of pushdown automata and, as such, define infinite-state transition systems (although the number of *control states* is only finite, the number of *configurations*—incorporating the state of the pushdown store—is infinite). Finding the right definition for a *synchronizing nested word* becomes for this reason a question of relevance: in the presence of infinitely many configurations not all of them may even have equal-length paths to a single designated one (this phenomenon also arises, for instance, in weighted automata [5]). In fact, any nested word w, given as input to an NWA, changes the stack height in a way that does not depend on the initial control state (and can only depend on the initial configuration if w has unmatched returns). We thus choose to define synchronizing words as those that reset the control state of the automaton and leave the pushdown store (the stack) unchanged (Definition 1; cf. location-synchronization in [5]). Consider, for instance, an XML processor that does not keep a heap storage and invokes and terminates its internal procedures in lockstep with opening and closing tags in the input; our definition of a synchronizing word corresponds to an XML document that resets the local variables.

Building on this definition, we show that shortest synchronizing words for NWA can be exponential in the size of the automaton (Example 2), in contrast to the case of DFA: every DFA with n states, if it has a synchronizing word, also has one of length polynomial in n. The best known worst-case upper bound on the length of the shortest synchronizing word is $(n^3-n)/6$, due to Pin [20]; Černý proved in the 1960s [24] a worst-case lower bound of $(n-1)^2$ and conjectured that this is also a valid upper bound, but as of now there is a gap between his quadratic lower bound and the cubic upper bound of Pin (see [25] for a survey). In the case of nested words, the exponential comes from the repeated doubling phenomenon, typical for pushdown automata.

Although the length of a synchronizing word can be exponential, it turns out that the existence of such a word—the shortest of which, in fact, cannot be longer than exponential—can be decided in polynomial time (Theorem 3), akin to the DFA case. However, generalizing the definition in standard ways (synchronizing from a subset instead of all states, or to a subset of states instead of singletons) raises the complexity to exponential time (Theorem 4); for DFA, the complexity is polynomial space [21, 22]. The lower bounds are by reduction from the intersection nonemptiness problem, which is known to be complete for polynomial space in the case of DFA [14] and which we observe to be complete for exponential time over nested words (Lemma 5).

Our main technical contribution is characterizing the complexity of deciding existence of *short* synchronizing words, where the bound on the length is given as part of the input (written in binary). In the DFA case, this problem is **NP**-complete as shown by Eppstein [7], and for NWA it becomes **PSPACE**-complete (Theorem 6). We believe that both upper and lower bound techniques that we use to prove this result are of interest.

Specifically, for the upper bound (Sect. 4) we first encode unranked trees (which represent nested words) with ranked trees. This reduces the search for a short synchronizing nested word to the search for a tree that satisfies a number of local properties. These properties, in turn, can be captured as acceptance by a certain tree automaton of exponential size. We show that guessing an accepting computation for such a machine—which amounts to guessing an exponentially large tree—can be done in polynomial space. To do this, we rely on the concept of *(black) pebbling games*, developed in the theory of computational complexity for the study of deterministic space-bounded computation (see, e.g., [23, Chapter 10]). We simulate optimal strategies for trees in such games [15], whose efficiency is determined by *Strahler numbers* [11]. Previous use of this technique in formal language theory and verification is primarily associated with derivations of context-free grammars, see, e.g., [9, 10] and [11] for a survey. In this body of work, closest to ours are apparently arguments due to Chytil and Monien [3]. We believe that our key procedure—which can decide *bounded nonemptiness* of *succinct tree automata*—may be of use in other domains as well.

Finally, for the matching polynomial-space lower bound (Sect. 5) we construct a two-step reduction from the problem of existence of *carefully* synchronizing words for partial DFA, whose hardness is known [16]. We define an intermediate problem of *small-cost synchronization* for DFA, where every letter in the alphabet comes with a cost and the task is to decide existence of a synchronizing word whose total cost does not exceed the budget. We show that this natural problem is complete for polynomial space (this strengthens previous results from [5, 12], where costs could be state-dependent). After this, we basically simulate cost-equipped DFA with NWA, relying on the above-mentioned repeated doubling phenomenon. We find it noteworthy that this "counting" feature of nested words alone is a ground for hardness.

We mention without proof that some of our techniques naturally extend to (going via) tree automata over ranked trees.

2   Nested Words and Nested Word Automata

A *nested word* of length k over a finite alphabet Σ is a pair $u = (x, \nu)$, where $x \in \Sigma^k$ and ν is a *matching relation* of length k: a subset $\nu \subseteq \{-\infty, 1, \ldots, k\} \times \{1, \ldots, k, +\infty\}$ such that, first, if $\nu(i, j)$ holds, then $i < j$; second, for $1 \le i \le k$ the set $\mu(i) \stackrel{\text{def}}{=} \{j \mid \nu(i, j) \text{ or } \nu(j, i)\}$ contains at most one element; third, whenever $\nu(i, j)$ and $\nu(i', j')$, it cannot be the case that $i < i' \le j < j'$. We assume that $\nu(-\infty, +\infty)$ never holds.

If $\nu(i, j)$, the position i in the word u is said to be a *call*, and the position j a *return*. All positions from $\{1, \ldots, k\}$ that are neither calls nor returns are *internal*. A call (a return) i is *matched* if ν matches it to an element of $\{1, \ldots, k\}$, i.e., if $\mu(i) \cap \{1, \ldots, k\} \ne \emptyset$, and *unmatched* otherwise. We shall call a nested word *well-matched* if it has no unmatched calls and no unmatched returns.

Define a *nested word automaton* (an NWA) over the input alphabet Σ as a structure $\mathcal{A} = (Q, \Gamma, \delta, q_0, \gamma_0)$, where:

- Q is a finite non-empty set of control states,
- Γ is a finite non-empty set of stack symbols,
- $\delta = (\delta^{\text{call}}, \delta^{\text{int}}, \delta^{\text{ret}})$, where
  - $\delta^{\text{int}} \colon Q \times \Sigma \to Q$ is an internal transition function,
  - $\delta^{\text{call}} \colon Q \times \Sigma \to Q \times \Gamma$ is a call transition function,
  - $\delta^{\text{ret}} \colon \Gamma \times Q \times \Sigma \to Q$ is a return transition function,
- $q_0 \in Q$ is the initial control state, and
- $\gamma_0 \in \Gamma$ is the initial stack symbol.

A *configuration* of $\mathcal{A}$ is a tuple $(q, s) \in Q \times \Gamma^*$. We write $(q, s) \xrightarrow{u} (q', s')$ for a nested word u if the following conditions hold. First suppose $u = (x, \nu)$ has length 1, then:

- if 1 is an internal position, then $\delta^{\text{int}}(q, x) = q'$ and $s' = s$;
- if 1 is a call, then $\delta^{\text{call}}(q, x) = (q', \gamma)$ and $s' = s\gamma$ for some $\gamma \in \Gamma$;
- if 1 is a return, then:
  - either $\delta^{\text{ret}}(\gamma, q, x) = q'$ and $s = s'\gamma$,
  - or $\delta^{\text{ret}}(\gamma_0, q, x) = q'$ and $s = s' = \varepsilon$.

Now take as $\longrightarrow$ the reflexive transitive closure of the union of $\xrightarrow{u}$ over all nested words u of length 1; these input words on top of the arrow are concatenated accordingly.

Alternatively, nested words can be seen as words over an extended alphabet. Let $\langle\Sigma$ and $\Sigma\rangle$ be disjoint copies of Σ that contain letters of the form $\langle a$ and $a\rangle$, respectively, for each $a \in \Sigma$. Then any nested word over Σ is associated with a word over the *nested alphabet* $\langle \Sigma \cup \overset{\frown}{\Sigma} \cup \overset{\smile}{\Sigma} \rangle$. Conversely, every word w over this nested alphabet is unambiguously associated with a matching relation ν_w of length $|w|$ where positions with elements of $\langle \overset{\frown}{\Sigma}, \Sigma,$ and $\overset{\smile}{\Sigma} \rangle$ are calls, internal positions, and returns, respectively; the word w can thus be identified with a nested word $(\pi(w), \nu_w)$ where π projects letters back to Σ. The automaton $\mathcal{A}$ can then be viewed as an ε-free pushdown automaton over the nested alphabet $\langle \overset{\frown}{\Sigma} \cup \Sigma \cup \overset{\smile}{\Sigma} \rangle$ in which the direction of stack operations (i.e., whether the automaton pushes, pops, or does not touch the stack) is determined by whether the current position belongs to $\langle \overset{\frown}{\Sigma}, \Sigma,$ or $\overset{\smile}{\Sigma} \rangle$. Such automata are known under the names *input-driven pushdown automata* and *visibly pushdown automata*. A *path* (*run*, *computation*) of an automaton $\mathcal{A}$ over an input word $u = a_1 \ldots a_k$, where each $a_i \in \langle \overset{\frown}{\Sigma} \cup \Sigma \cup \overset{\smile}{\Sigma} \rangle$, is a sequence of configurations (p_i, s_i), $i = 0, \ldots, k$, with $(p_{i-1}, s_{i-1}) \overset{a_i}{\longrightarrow} (p_i, s_i)$ for all i. We will sometimes talk about words *accepted* by $\mathcal{A}$, in which case we implicitly assume that $\mathcal{A}$ comes equipped with a subset $Q^f \subseteq Q$; accepted are words u for which there exists a path $(q_0, \varepsilon) \overset{u}{\longrightarrow} (\bar{q}, s)$ with $\bar{q} \in Q^f$.

3   Synchronizing Words for NWA

Informally, we call a well-matched nested word u synchronizing for an NWA $\mathcal{A}$ if it takes $\mathcal{A}$ from all control states to some single control state. Note that the result of feeding any well-matched word to an NWA does not depend on the stack contents; furthermore, if $(q_1, s_1) \overset{u}{\longrightarrow} (q_2, s_2)$ and u is well-matched, then $s_1 = s_2$. This lets us extend the definition of $\longrightarrow$ to sets of states: we write $(Q_1, s) \overset{u}{\longrightarrow} (Q_2, s)$ if, first, the word u is well-matched, second, for all $q_1 \in Q_1$ there exists a $q_2 \in Q_2$ such that $(q_1, s) \overset{u}{\longrightarrow} (q_2, s)$, and, third, for every state $q_2 \in Q_2$ there exists a $q_1 \in Q_1$ such that $(q_1, s) \overset{u}{\longrightarrow} (q_2, s)$. If $Q_i = \{q_i\}$, we write (q_i, s) instead of $(\{q_i\}, s)$.

Definition 1. *A well-matched nested word u is* synchronizing *for an NWA $\mathcal{A} = (Q, \Gamma, \delta, q_0, \gamma_0)$ if there exists a control state $\bar{q} \in Q$ such that the relation $(Q, \varepsilon) \overset{u}{\longrightarrow} (\bar{q}, \varepsilon)$ holds.*

By the observation above, u is synchronizing if and only if there exists a $\bar{q} \in Q$ such that for all $q \in Q$ and for all $s \in \Gamma^*$ the relation $(q, s) \overset{u}{\longrightarrow} (\bar{q}, s)$ holds.

Remark. Definition 1 crucially relies on the nested structure of the input word, in that this structure determines the stack behaviour of the NWA. Extending this definition to the general case of pushdown automata (PDA) would face the difficulties outlined in the introduction; to the best of our knowledge, no such extension has been proposed to date. The term "synchronization" in the context of PDA is known to be used when referring to the agreement between the transitions taken by the automaton and an external structure [2]: in NWA, for example, input symbols and stack actions are synchronized (in this sense).

Example 2. Given $n \geq 1$, we construct an NWA $\mathcal{A}_n$ with $O(\log n)$ control states and $O(1)$ stack symbols such that the shortest synchronizing word for $\mathcal{A}_n$ has length exactly n.

Our construction is inductive. We first construct a family of *incomplete* NWA $\mathcal{B}_n$ with stack symbols $\{x, y\}$ and two designated states q_x and q_y. In $\mathcal{B}_n$, the shortest run from q_x to q_y is driven by some well-matched nested word w of length n, and along this run the state q_y is not visited. These NWA will be incomplete in the sense that their transition functions will only be partial; redirecting all missing transitions to the initial state in would make these NWA complete. For each n, given $\mathcal{B}_n$, we construct NWA $\mathcal{B}_{2n+4}$ and $\mathcal{B}_{2n+5}$ where the length of the shortest run between two new states in and out is exactly $2n + 4$ and $2n + 5$, respectively. The construction of $\mathcal{B}_{2n+4}$ is depicted in Fig. 1. Here the shortest run from in to out is over $\mathsf{call}(x) \cdot w \cdot \mathsf{ret}(x) \cdot \mathsf{call}(y) \cdot w \cdot \mathsf{ret}(y)$ and has length $2n + 4$; splitting the state q_z into two states, with internal transitions pointing from one to the other, gives us $\mathcal{B}_{2n+5}$. We call this transformation *doubling*. For all $n \geq 4$ the NWA $\mathcal{B}_n$ can be constructed by several doubling transformations starting from one of the automata $\mathcal{B}_0, \mathcal{B}_1, \mathcal{B}_2, \mathcal{B}_3$ (which are simply NWAs with $1, 2, 3, 4$ states). The size of $\mathcal{B}_n$ is $O(\log n)$.

For all $n \geq 2$, from the NWA $\mathcal{B}_{n-2}$ we construct an NWA $\mathcal{A}_n$ where the shortest synchronizing word has length exactly n. Figure 2 shows the sketch of the construction: there are two new letters $\#$ and $\mathcal{L}$ and a new absorbing state sync. From all states q of $\mathcal{B}_{n-2}$, the letter $\#$ resets the NWA to in whereas $\mathcal{L}$-transitions are all self-loops except in the state out where $\mathsf{out} \xrightarrow{\mathcal{L}} \mathsf{sync}$. All missing transitions are directed to the state in (note that even in the case of DFA, existence of synchronizing words in the presence of *partial* transition functions is **PSPACE**-complete [16]; it is thus of utmost importance that our NWA are complete). Observe that the shortest synchronizing word has length exactly n; it is $\# \cdot w \cdot \mathcal{L}$ where w is the shortest word that takes $\mathcal{B}_{n-2}$ from in to out.

Remark. Our Example 2 seems to use a "non-uniform" set of call, return, and internal symbols, but this is easily remedied by making some of the symbols indistinguishable. All call positions in the word are simply call, and all return positions are ret; in figures, the letter in parentheses is the pushed or popped stack symbol.

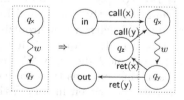

Fig. 1. Doubling transformation

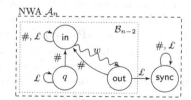

Fig. 2. NWA $\mathcal{A}_n$ based on $\mathcal{B}_{n-2}$

In decision problems that we study in this paper, the *size* of an automaton is proportional to $|\Gamma| \cdot |\Sigma| \cdot |Q|$.

Theorem 3. *If an NWA $\mathcal{A}$ has a synchronizing word, then it has one of length at most exponential in the size of $\mathcal{A}$. Moreover, the existence of a synchronizing word can be decided in time polynomial in the size of $\mathcal{A}$.*

This theorem extends a characterization of synchronizing automata from DFA: an NWA $\mathcal{A}$ has a synchronizing word if and only if for every pair of states p, q there exists a well-matched word u that synchronizes this pair, i.e., $(\{p, q\}, \varepsilon) \xrightarrow{u} (\bar{q}, \varepsilon)$ for some $\bar{q}$.

Theorem 4. *The following decision problems, with an NWA $\mathcal{A}$ part of the input, are* **EXP***-complete:*

(1) Given a subset $I \subseteq Q$, decide if there exists a well-matched nested word u such that $(I, \varepsilon) \xrightarrow{u} (\bar{q}, \varepsilon)$ for some state $\bar{q} \in Q$.

(2) Given a subset $F \subseteq Q$, decide if there exists a well-matched nested word u such that $(Q, \varepsilon) \xrightarrow{u} (F', \varepsilon)$ for some subset $F' \subseteq F$.

(3) Given subsets $I \subseteq Q$ and $F \subseteq Q$, decide if there exists a well-matched nested word u such that $(I, \varepsilon) \xrightarrow{u} (F', \varepsilon)$ for some subset $F' \subseteq F$.

The corresponding decision problems for DFA are **PSPACE**-complete [21, 22], where hardness is by a reduction from the DFA intersection nonemptiness problem (see [26] for a more refined complexity analysis). In the NWA case, the proofs are an easy adaptation of these arguments and are based on the following observation, which can be proved by a translation from tree automata or by a direct extension of Kozen's proof [14]:

Lemma 5. *The following problem is* **EXP***-complete: Given NWA $\mathcal{A}_1, \ldots, \mathcal{A}_m$, decide if there exists a well-matched word accepted by all $\mathcal{A}_i$.*

The following theorem is our main result.

Theorem 6. *The following problem* SHORT SYNCHRONIZING NESTED WORD *is* **PSPACE***-complete: Given an NWA $\mathcal{A}$ and an integer $\ell \geq 1$ written in binary, decide if $\mathcal{A}$ has a synchronizing word u of length at most ℓ.*

The corresponding decision problem for DFA is **NP**-complete [7]. (Note that deciding if the shortest synchronizing word has length exactly ℓ, a related but different problem, is **DP**-complete [18].) Since any DFA with a synchronizing word has one of length cubic in its size, it does not matter for DFA if ℓ is written in binary or in unary. In contrast, as our Example 2 shows, NWA may need an exponentially long word for synchronization; this explains the choice of the setting above. (In the alternative version, i.e., if ℓ is written in unary, the problem is **NP**-complete: the upper bound is a guess-and-check argument, and hardness already holds for DFA.)

4   Upper Bound of Theorem 6

In this section, we show that the following problem is in **PSPACE**: Given a nested word automaton $\mathcal{A}$ and an integer $\ell \geq 1$ written in binary, decide if there exists a synchronizing word for $\mathcal{A}$ of length at most ℓ. In fact, we can also adjust our arguments (see Subsect. 4.2) so that they give a **PSPACE** upper bound for another problem: Given a nested word automaton $\mathcal{A}$, two subsets of its control states $I, F \subseteq Q$, and an integer $\ell \geq 1$ written in binary, decide if there exists a well-matched word of length at most ℓ that takes all states in I to F.

The plan of the proof is as follows. We encode nested words using binary trees (Subsect. 4.1), so that runs of NWA correspond to computations of tree automata and synchronizing words to tuples of such computations (Subsect. 4.2). Thus the task of guessing a short synchronizing word is reduced to the task of guessing an accepting computation of a tree automaton on an unknown binary tree of potentially exponential size (Lemma 8); this is the same as guessing an exponentially large binary tree subject to local conditions. We prove that it's possible to solve this *bounded nonemptiness* problem in polynomial space, even if the tree automaton in question has exponentially many states and is only given in symbolic form (Subsect. 4.4); our solution relies on the concepts of pebble games and Strahler numbers (Subsect. 4.3).

4.1   Binary Tree Representation of Nested Words

In this subsection we describe a representation of nested words with binary trees used in the sequel. Because of space constraints, we only give a short summary.

Nested Words as Binary Trees. We denote the binary *tree representation* of a nested word u by $\mathsf{bin}(u)$. The explicit construction of $\mathsf{bin}(u)$ is not sophisticated, but we only describe the result. Nodes of $\mathsf{bin}(u)$ come in several different *types*. We did not attempt to minimize the number of these types; different representations are, of course, also possible.

Type	Degree	Notes
call-return binary	2	Associated with matched pair $\langle x_i, x_j \rangle$
auxiliary binary	2	*Corresponds* to positions $i < j$
call-return unary	1	Associated with matched pair $\langle x_i, x_j \rangle$
call-return leaf	0	Associated with matched pair $\langle x_i, x_j \rangle$, $j = i + 1$
internal leaf	0	Associated with internal letter x_i

We denote the set of types by Types; each type comes with a fixed degree, which is simply the number of children of a node. Note that auxiliary binary nodes are not associated with any letters in the nested word, although they do correspond to pairs of positions in it.

In general, execute the left-to-right depth-first traversal on the tree $\mathsf{bin}(u)$ and *spell* the letters associated with the nodes in the natural way. Specifically, at any call-return node v *associated* with $i < j$, spell "$\langle x_i$" when entering and "$x_j \rangle$" when leaving the subtree rooted at v; at any internal leaf associated with i, spell "x_i". The traversal of the entire tree $\mathsf{bin}(u)$ spells the word u, and every subtree spells some well-matched factor.

Claim 1. *For any nested word u of length ℓ its binary tree representation $\mathsf{bin}(u)$ has at most $2\ell - 1$ nodes. Moreover, if $\mathsf{bin}(u) = \mathsf{bin}(u')$, then $u = u'$.*

Trees as Terms over a Ranked Alphabet. We now switch the perspective a little and look at binary tree representations as terms. Indeed, pick the ranked alphabet

$$\mathcal{F} \subseteq \mathsf{Types} \times (\langle \Sigma \times \Sigma \rangle \cup \Sigma \cup \{\varepsilon\}) \tag{1}$$

as follows. All elements of $\mathcal{F}$ have *rank* 0, 1, or 2, according to their first (that is, Types-) component; the rank is simply the admissible number of children (i.e., the degree). The second component stores the associated letter or pair of letters, if any; the value ε corresponds to the undefined association mapping. Since the Types-component already determines whether the second component should carry a pair of call and return letters, a single letter, or ε, we only take valid combinations into $\mathcal{F}$.

As this term representation is essentially the same as the binary representation defined above, we shall denote it by the same symbol $\mathsf{bin}(u)$; that is, $\mathsf{bin}(u)$ is a term over $\mathcal{F}$ for any non-empty well-matched word u. In what follows, we will mostly refer to $\mathsf{bin}(u)$ as a tree but treat it as a term.

4.2 From Nested Word Automata to Tree Automata

From Runs of NWA to Runs of Tree Automata. Recall the definition of a *nondeterministic tree automaton* over a ranked alphabet $\mathcal{F}$ (see, e.g., [4]): such an automaton is a tuple $\mathcal{T} = (\mathcal{Q}, \mathcal{Q}^\mathsf{f}, \Delta)$ where $\mathcal{Q}$ is a finite set of states, $\mathcal{Q}^\mathsf{f} \subseteq \mathcal{Q}$ is a set of final states, and Δ is a set of transition rules. These rules have the form $f(q_1, \ldots, q_r) \mapsto q$ where $q, q_1, \ldots, q_r \in \mathcal{Q}$ and $r \geq 0$ is the rank of the symbol $f \in \mathcal{F}$; nondeterminism of $\mathcal{T}$ means that Δ can contain several rules with identical left-hand sides.

The semantics of tree automata is defined in the following manner. For any tree t over the ranked alphabet $\mathcal{F}$, we assign to any node v of t a state $q \in \mathcal{Q}$ inductively, phrasing it as "the subtree t_v rooted at v *evaluates* to the state q" (as the automaton is nondeterministic, the same subtree may evaluate to several different states). The inductive assertion is that if f is the label of v, the subtree t_v evaluates to q, and its principal subtrees evaluate to $q_1, \ldots, q_r$, then the transition $f(q_1, \ldots, q_r) \mapsto q$ appears in Δ. The entire tree t is *accepted* if the root of t evaluates to some final state $\bar{q} \in \mathcal{Q}^\mathsf{f}$.

Lemma 7. *For any NWA $\mathcal{A}$ with states Q and for all pairs $\bar{p}, \bar{q} \in Q$, there exists a tree automaton $\mathcal{T}(\bar{p}, \bar{q})$ over the ranked alphabet $\mathcal{F}$ as in (1) that has the following property: $\mathcal{T}(\bar{p}, \bar{q})$ accepts a tree $\mathrm{bin}(u)$ if and only if the NWA $\mathcal{A}$ has a run on u that starts in state $\bar{p}$ and ends in state $\bar{q}$. Moreover, $\mathcal{T}(\bar{p}, \bar{q})$ can be constructed from $\mathcal{A}$ in time polynomial in the size of $\mathcal{A}$.*

Synchronizing Words and Implicitly Presented Tree Automata. We can now return to the synchronizing word problem. Suppose $\mathcal{A}$ is an NWA with states Q; now a well-matched nested word u is a synchronizing word for $\mathcal{A}$ if and only if there is a state $\bar{q} \in Q$ such that for all i the tree $\mathrm{bin}(u)$ is accepted by the automaton $\mathcal{T}(q_i, \bar{q})$; here we assume $Q = \{q_1, \ldots, q_n\}$. The following statement rephrases this condition in terms of *products* of tree automata (the definition is standard; see, e.g., [4, Sect. 1.3]).

Lemma 8. *An NWA $\mathcal{A}$ with states $Q = \{q_1, \ldots, q_n\}$ has a synchronizing word of length at most ℓ iff there exists a state $\bar{q} \in Q$ such that the product automaton $\mathfrak{A}_{\bar{q}} = \mathcal{T}(q_1, \bar{q}) \times \ldots \times \mathcal{T}(q_n, \bar{q}) \times \mathcal{N}_\ell$ accepts some tree over $\mathcal{F}$. Here $\mathcal{N}_\ell$ is a tree automaton that only depends on ℓ and Σ and accepts the set of trees of the form $\mathrm{bin}(u)$ where the nested word u has length at most ℓ.*

Note that the set of states of $\mathfrak{A}_{\bar{q}}$, which we denote by $\mathfrak{Q}$, is, in general, exponential in the size of $\mathcal{A}$. Note, however, that (i) each state has a representation— as a tuple of n states of $\mathcal{T}(q_i, \bar{q})$ and a state of $\mathcal{N}_\ell$—polynomial in the size of $\mathcal{A}$ and ℓ and, moreover, that (ii) the following problems can be decided in **PSPACE** (and, in fact, in **P**, although we do not need to rely on this):

(a) given a state $\mathsf{q} \in \mathfrak{Q}$, decide if q is a final state of $\mathfrak{A}_{\bar{q}}$;
(b) given a symbol $f \in \mathcal{F}$ of rank r and states $\mathsf{q}, \mathsf{q}_1, \ldots, \mathsf{q}_r \in \mathfrak{Q}$, decide if $f(\mathsf{q}_1, \ldots, \mathsf{q}_r) \mapsto \mathsf{q}$ is a transition in $\mathfrak{A}_{\bar{q}}$.

We emphasize that the complexity bounds in these properties are given with respect to the size of $\mathcal{A}$ and ℓ, i.e., assuming that $\mathcal{A}$ and ℓ (and not $\mathfrak{A}_{\bar{q}}$!) are given as input. We will use these properties (i) and (ii) in Subsect. 4.4; for brevity, we shall simply say that $\mathfrak{A}_{\bar{q}}$ is *implicitly presented in polynomial space*.

Claim 2. *The automaton $\mathfrak{A}_{\bar{q}}$ from Lemma 8 is implicitly presented in polynomial space and does not accept any tree with more than $2\ell - 1$ nodes.*

The second part of the claim follows from Claim 1 in Subsect. 4.1.

4.3   Pebble Games and Strahler Numbers

In this subsection we recall a classic idea that we use in the proof of Lemma 9 in the following Subsect. 4.4. We believe that the involved concepts, albeit classic, deserve more attention from our community than they have hitherto received.

An instance of the (*black*) *pebble game* (see, e.g., [23, Chapter 10]) is defined on a directed acyclic graph, G. The game is one-player; the player sees the graph

G and has access to a supply of *pebbles*. The game starts with no pebbles on (vertices of) the graph. A *strategy* in the game is a sequence of moves of the following kinds:

(a) if all immediate predecessors of a vertex v have pebbles on them, put a pebble on (or move a pebble to) v;
(b) remove a pebble from a vertex v.

Note that for any source v of G, the pre-condition for the move of the first kind is always satisfied. The strategy is *successful* if during its execution every sink of G carries a pebble at least once; the strategy is said to *use* k pebbles if the largest number of pebbles on G during its execution is k. The (*black*) *pebbling number* of G, denoted $\mathsf{peb}(G)$, is the smallest k for which there exists a successful strategy for G using k pebbles.

The black pebbling number captures space complexity of deterministic computations [13,19]. Intuitively, think of G as a circuit, where sources are circuit inputs and sinks are circuit outputs; nodes with nonzero fan-in are gates that compute functions of their immediate predecessors. A strategy corresponds to computing the value of the circuit using auxiliary memory: *pebbling* a vertex (i.e., putting a pebble on it) corresponds to computing the value of the gate and storing it in memory; removing a pebble from the vertex corresponds to removing it from the memory. The pebbling number is thus (an abstraction of) the minimal amount of memory required to compute the value of the circuit.

Consider the case where the graph is a tree, $G = t$, with all edges directed towards the root; this corresponds to formulas, say arithmetic expressions [8]. For trees, the pebbling number can be computed inductively [15]: if t is a single-vertex tree, then $\mathsf{peb}(G) = 1$; suppose t has principal subtrees $t_1, \ldots, t_d$ and $\mathsf{peb}(t_1) \geq \mathsf{peb}(t_2) \geq \ldots \geq \mathsf{peb}(t_d)$, then $\mathsf{peb}(t) = \max(\mathsf{peb}(t_i) + i - 1)$ over $1 \leq i \leq d$. For binary trees (where all vertices have fan-in at most two, $d \leq 2$) the pebbling number (under different names) has been studied independently and rediscovered multiple times (although, to the best of our knowledge, no connection with the literature on pebbling games has ever been pointed out), see [8,11]. The value $\mathsf{peb}(t) - 1$ is usually called the *Strahler number* of the tree t and is also known, e.g., as the Horton–Strahler number and as tree dimension; this is the largest h such that t has a complete binary tree of height h as a minor.

In the sequel, we choose to talk about Strahler numbers but use the connection to pebble games. The key observation, following from the last characterization or from the recurrence above, is that the Strahler number of an m-node tree does not exceed $\lfloor \log_2(m+1) \rfloor - 1$ (this bound is tight). This value corresponds to the pebbling strategy that, before pebbling any vertex v of indegree 2, first (*i*) recurses into the subtree with the larger Strahler number; (*ii*) places (inductively) a pebble on its root and removes all other pebbles from this subtree; and then (*iii*) recurses into the other subtree. We will use this strategy in the following subsection.

4.4 Bounded Nonemptiness for Implicitly Presented Tree Automata

Here we combine the ideas from Subsects. 4.2 and 4.3 to prove the upper bound in Theorem 6.

Lemma 9. *For a tree automaton implicitly presented in polynomial space and a number m written in binary, one can decide in* **PSPACE** *if the automaton accepts some tree with at most m nodes.*

It is crucial that m constitute part of the input, because for *explicitly* presented tree automata the (non-)emptiness problem is **P**-complete, and an implicitly presented automaton can be exponentially big (this would give us an **EXP** upper bound, which is tight by Lemma 5 if no m is given). The upper bound on the size of the tree significantly shrinks the search space, so we refer to this problem as *bounded nonemptiness*. Assuming this lemma, the proof of the upper bound of Theorem 6 goes as follows.

Proof (upper bound of Theorem 6). Combine Lemmas 8 and 9 with the fact that the automaton $\mathfrak{A}_{\bar{q}}$ from the former is implicitly presented in polynomial space. Indeed, suppose an NWA $\mathcal{A}$ with states Q and an integer ℓ are given. By Lemma 8, a synchronizing word for $\mathcal{A}$ of length at most ℓ exists if and only if there exists a state $\bar{q} \in Q$ such that the tree automaton $\mathfrak{A}_{\bar{q}}$ accepts some tree over the ranked alphabet $\mathcal{F}$; recall that this is the alphabet defined by (1) in Subsect. 4.1. First note that the state $\bar{q}$ can be guessed in polynomial space. Then recall from Claim 2 in Subsect. 4.2 that $\mathfrak{A}_{\bar{q}}$ only accepts trees with at most $2\ell - 1$ nodes; thus deciding its emptiness reduces to deciding its *bounded emptiness*. Again by Claim 2, $\mathfrak{A}_{\bar{q}}$ is implicitly presented in polynomial space, and thus we can apply Lemma 9 with $m = 2\ell - 1$. This concludes the proof.   □

To prove Lemma 9, we design a decision procedure using the pebbling strategy for trees that we discussed in Subsect. 4.3.

Proof (of Lemma 9). Denote the tree automaton implicitly presented in polynomial space by $\mathfrak{A}_{\bar{q}}$, as above. We describe a procedure that guesses (with checks done on the fly) an accepting computation of $\mathfrak{A}_{\bar{q}}$. Since the number m is given in binary, we cannot afford to write down the entire accepted tree, as it could take up exponential space.

However, suppose that such a tree t exists and has $m' \le m$ nodes; we assume without loss of generality that $m = m'$. Consider some pebbling strategy for t, as defined in Subsect. 4.3. Our procedure will guess moves of this strategy on the fly and simulate them; it will also guess the tree t in lockstep. More precisely, we maintain the following invariant. Take any time step and any vertex v and denote by t_v the subtree of t rooted at v. If the pebbling strategy prescribes that v should have a pebble, then our procedure keeps in memory a pair $(\mathfrak{q}, k)$ where $\mathfrak{q} \in \mathfrak{Q}$ is a state of $\mathfrak{A}_{\bar{q}}$ that t_v evaluates to, and k is the total number of nodes in t_v. Note that any such pair $(\mathfrak{q}, k)$ takes up space polynomial in the size of the input: states of $\mathfrak{A}_{\bar{q}}$ have such representations by the assumptions of the lemma, and k never needs to grow higher than m.

We now describe how the moves of the strategy are simulated by our procedure. Suppose the strategy prescribes placing a pebble on a vertex v; by the rules of the pebble game, this means that all immediate predecessors $v_1, \ldots, v_d$ (if any) currently have pebbles on them. By our invariant, we already keep in memory corresponding pairs $(\mathfrak{q}_1, k_1), \ldots, (\mathfrak{q}_d, k_d)$. Our procedure now guesses the node v, i.e., its label $f \in \mathcal{F}$ in t. Then the procedure guesses a new state, $\mathfrak{q} \in \mathfrak{Q}$, verifies in polynomial space that $f(\mathfrak{q}_1, \ldots, \mathfrak{q}_d) \mapsto \mathfrak{q}$ is a transition in $\mathfrak{A}_{\bar{q}}$, and that $k = k_1 + \ldots + k_d + 1$ does not exceed m. If any check is failed, the procedure declares the current nondeterministic branch rejecting; if all the checks are passed, the procedure stores the pair $(\mathfrak{q}, k)$. Naturally, whenever a strategy prescribes removing a pebble from a vertex, the procedure simply erases the corresponding pebble from the memory (in fact, since t is a tree, we can assume that every pair $(\mathfrak{q}, k)$ is removed immediately after its use). At some point, the procedure guesses that the strategy can terminate; this means that the root of the tree t carries a pebble. The procedure picks some pair $(\mathfrak{q}, k)$ from the memory and verifies in polynomial space that the state $\mathfrak{q}$ is indeed final in $\mathfrak{A}_{\bar{q}}$. This signifies acceptance of t_v.

It remains to argue that the procedure only uses polynomial space. The tree t has m nodes, so, by the upper bound on Strahler numbers, the optimal strategy needs $\mathsf{peb}(t) \leq \lfloor \log_2(m+1) \rfloor$ pebbles, which is polynomial in the size of the input. If some guessed step requires more, the strategy cannot be optimal, and the procedure declares the branch rejecting. This completes the proof. □

The idea of the proof of Lemma 9 can be distilled in a different form: We can show that the *bounded emptiness* problem (are all trees up to a certain size rejected?) is in **PSPACE** for *succinct tree automata*. These are tree automata where the set of states, $\mathfrak{Q}$, can be exponentially large, but does not need to be written out explicitly, and the set of transitions and the set of final states are represented with Boolean circuits (or, alternatively, with logical formulas over an appropriate theory). The proof follows that of Lemma 9.

5   Lower Bound of Theorem 6

The matching lower bound for the SHORT SYNCHRONIZING NESTED WORD problem is established by a reduction from the *small-cost synchronizing word* problem, which we introduce and prove **PSPACE**-complete below.

5.1   Small-Cost Synchronizing Words in DFA

For a deterministic finite automaton (DFA) $\mathcal{D} = (Q, \Delta)$ over Σ, consider a function $\mathsf{cost} : \Sigma \to \mathbb{Z}_{>0}$ that assigns positive costs to letters $a \in \Sigma$. This function is naturally extended to finite words: $\mathsf{cost}(w \cdot a) = \mathsf{cost}(w) + \mathsf{cost}(a)$ where $w \in \Sigma^*$. The *small-cost synchronizing word* problem asks, given a DFA equipped with a cost function and a $\mathsf{budget} \in \mathbb{Z}_{>0}$ written in binary, whether the DFA has a synchronizing word w with $\mathsf{cost}(w) \leq \mathsf{budget}$.

Table 1. Summary of the transition function δ of the NWA $\mathcal{A}$ with $\Gamma = \{x, y, \mathcal{L}, \odot\}$ constructed from the DFA $\mathcal{D} = (Q, \Delta)$ over Σ. The table specifies the endpoint of all transitions: e.g., when $\mathcal{A}$ is at $q \in Q$ and reads call, it pushes x and stays at q.

State	Σ	#	call(γ)	ret(Γ)
$q \in Q$	$t_{q,a}$	p_q	$\gamma = x$ self-loop	self-loop
force	self-loop	p_q for some q	$\gamma = x$ self-loop	self-loop

For all $q \in Q$ and $a \in \Sigma$:

$t_{q,a}$	self-loop	p_q	$\gamma = \mathcal{L}$ in of pay(q, a)	self-loop
p_q	self-loop	p_q	$\gamma = \odot$ in of punish(q)	self-loop
$s \in$ pay(q, a)	self-loop	p_q	See gadget pay in Figure 4 (left) where: • missing transitions go to state err of the same pay(q, a) • from out, the transition ret($\mathcal{L}$) goes to $\Delta(q, a)$ • from err, the transition ret($\mathcal{L}$) goes to p_q	
$s \in$ punish(q)	self-loop	p_q	See gadget punish in Figure 4 (right) where: • missing transitions go to state in of the same punish(q) • from out, the transition ret($\odot$) goes to q	

Theorem 10. *The small-cost synchronizing word problem is* **PSPACE-complete**.

The upper bound is guess-and-check: any synchronizing word w with $\mathsf{cost}(w) \leq$ budget has $|w| \leq$ budget, since $\mathsf{cost}(a) \geq 1$ for all $a \in \Sigma$. The lower bound is by a reduction from the *careful synchronization* problem. Carefully synchronizing words [16] are a generalization of synchronizing words to finite-state automata with a partial transition function. Theorem 10 strengthens **PSPACE**-hardness results for similar models [5, 12]: the key difference is that in our setting the cost function can only depend on input letters and not on individual transitions.

5.2   Reduction to Short Synchronizing Nested Word

We prove the **PSPACE**-hardness of SHORT SYNCHRONIZING NESTED WORD by a reduction from the small-cost synchronizing word problem: given a DFA $\mathcal{D} = (Q, \Delta)$ over Σ, cost: $\Sigma \to \mathbb{Z}_{>0}$, and budget $\in \mathbb{Z}_{>0}$, we find an NWA $\mathcal{A}$ and a length ℓ such that $\mathcal{D}$ has a synchronizing word w with $\mathsf{cost}(w) \leq$ budget if and only if $\mathcal{A}$ has a synchronizing nested word of length at most ℓ.

The intuition behind the reduction is as follows. We encode the cost of each letter a in $\mathcal{D}$ with the length of a particular well-matched nested word $a \cdot w_a$ in $\mathcal{A}$; as a result, runs in $\mathcal{D}$ will be, in a sense, *simulated* by runs in $\mathcal{A}$. The nested word $a \cdot w_a$ is associated with a special gadget that we insert as a part of $\mathcal{A}$; we denote this gadget pay(q, a) (there is a separate copy for each $q \in Q$). The intention is that the length of a nested word read by $\mathcal{A}$ corresponds to the cost of some word read by $\mathcal{D}$. Obviously, there will be runs of $\mathcal{A}$ that have structure deviating from the form $a_1 \cdot w_{a_1} \cdots a_k \cdot w_{a_k}$; we call such deviations *cheating*. We will ensure that, along runs of interest, cheating is impossible: deviating transitions will lead to another set of gadgets, denoted punish(q), $q \in Q$. When

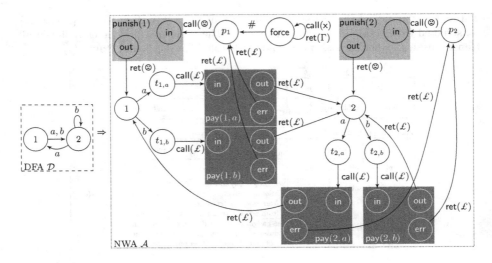

Fig. 3. An example of the reduction to the SHORT SYNCHRONIZING NESTED WORD. For $q \in \{1, 2\}$, all #-transitions from q and from all states of gadgets $\mathsf{pay}(q, a)$, $\mathsf{pay}(q, b)$, and $\mathsf{punish}(q)$ lead to p_q. All a, b-transitions in all states are self-loops, except in states $1, 2$. The NWA $\mathcal{A}$ has a synchronizing nested word of length $4 \cdot \mathsf{budget} + |w_{\mathsf{punish}}| + 1$ if and only if $\mathcal{D}$ has a synchronizing word with cost at most budget.

a run of $\mathcal{A}$ is *punished*, it is forced to read a very long nested word w_{punish}, which results in exceeding the length ℓ. On the technical level, this "forcing" means that all shorter continuations make no progress to the synchronization objective.

We now show how to construct the NWA $\mathcal{A}$ following this intuition; a small example is shown in Fig. 3. The set of states in $\mathcal{A}$ is $Q \cup \{\mathsf{force}\} \cup \bigcup_{q \in Q, a \in \Sigma} (\mathsf{pay}(q, a) \cup \{t_{q,a}\}) \cup \bigcup_{q \in Q} (\mathsf{punish}(q) \cup \{p_q\})$ where Q denotes, as above, the set of states of the DFA $\mathcal{D}$, and we abuse the notation by letting $\mathsf{pay}(q, a)$ and $\mathsf{punish}(q)$ refer to the sets of states of the corresponding gadgets. The set of stack symbols of $\mathcal{A}$ is $\Gamma = \{\mathsf{x}, \mathsf{y}, \mathcal{L}, \textcircled{\scriptsize\smile}\}$; the input letters are $\Sigma \cup \{\#\}$ where $\# \notin \Sigma$ (as in Remark on page 6, all call and return positions are assumed to have "fake" input letters call and ret). Table 1 describes transitions of $\mathcal{A}$.

It remains to define the gadgets $\mathsf{pay}(q, a)$ and $\mathsf{punish}(q)$. Recall that they need to let through runs on nested words w_a and w_{punish}; deviations are considered

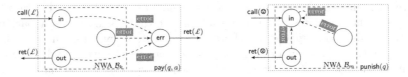

Fig. 4. Gadgets $\mathsf{pay}(q, a)$ (on the left) and punish (on the right) where $\mathcal{B}_k, \mathcal{B}_m$ are described in Example 2 with $k = 4 \cdot \mathsf{cost}(a) - 3$ and $m = |w_{\mathsf{punish}}| - 2$

cheating and are handled appropriately. We base the construction of $\mathsf{pay}(q,a)$ and $\mathsf{punish}(q)$ on the family of NWA $\mathcal{B}_n$ from Example 2; see Fig. 4. Each gadget has two designated local states in and out, and the shortest run from in to out is over the nested word that we denote by v_a (where $w_a = \mathsf{call} \cdot v_a \cdot \mathsf{ret}$) in $\mathsf{pay}(q,a)$ and by v_{punish} (where $w_{\mathsf{punish}} = \mathsf{call} \cdot v_{\mathsf{punish}} \cdot \mathsf{ret}$) in $\mathsf{punish}(q)$. We pick the parameter $k = |v_a|$ in $\mathcal{B}_k$ in such a way that $|a \cdot w_a| = |a \cdot \mathsf{call} \cdot v_a \cdot \mathsf{ret}| = 4 \cdot \mathsf{cost}(a)$; note that $k = 4 \cdot \mathsf{cost}(a) - 3 \geq 1$, since $\mathsf{cost}(a) \geq 1$. Our choice for m in $\mathcal{B}_m$ will be given below. Now recall that the NWA $\mathcal{B}_n$ in Example 2 had only partially defined transition functions; we make them complete by directing all missing transitions (shown as "errors" in Fig. 4) to in in punish and to new local states err in pay. Note that this includes missing transitions on call (they all push x to the stack) and missing transitions on ret (at every control state, there is a popping transition for each $\gamma \in \Gamma$). In contrast, on input # all transitions from $\mathsf{pay}(q,a)$ and $\mathsf{punish}(q)$ go to the state p_q.

In fact, every synchronizing word is forced to have at least one occurrence of #, otherwise the run starting from yet another state force cannot be synchronized with other runs. Therefore, every synchronizing word needs to have at least one occurrence of w_{punish}, and this determines our choice of ℓ and $|w_{\mathsf{punish}}|$. It is natural to pick $\ell = 1 + |w_{\mathsf{punish}}| + 4 \cdot \mathsf{budget}$; since we want to have $\ell < 2 \cdot |w_{\mathsf{punish}}|$, we need to make sure that $|w_{\mathsf{punish}}| > 4 \cdot \mathsf{budget} + 1$. We thus choose $m + 2 = |w_{\mathsf{punish}}| = 4 \cdot \mathsf{budget} + 2$ and $\ell = 8 \cdot \mathsf{budget} + 3$.

This completes the description of our reduction; we omit the proof of correctness because of space constraints. This reduction provides the lower bound in Theorem 6.

Acknowledgements. The authors are grateful to Michael Wehar for comments.

References

1. Alur, R., Madhusudan, P.: Adding nesting structure to words. J. ACM **56**(3), 16 (2009)
2. Caucal, D.: Synchronization of pushdown automata. In: Ibarra, O.H., Dang, Z. (eds.) DLT 2006. LNCS, vol. 4036, pp. 120–132. Springer, Heidelberg (2006)
3. Chytil, M.P., Monien, B.: Caterpillars and context-free languages. In: Choffrut, C., Lengauer, T. (eds.) STACS 90. LNCS, vol. 415, pp. 70–81. Springer, Heidelberg (1990)
4. Comon, H., Dauchet, M., Gilleron, R., Löding, C., Jacquemard, F., Lugiez, D., Tison, S., Tommasi, M.: Tree Automata Techniques and Applications, 12 October 2007. http://www.grappa.univ-lille3.fr/tata
5. Doyen, L., Juhl, L., Larsen, K.G., Markey, N., Shirmohammadi, M.: Synchronizing words for weighted and timed automata. In: 34th International Conference on Foundation of Software Technology and Theoretical Computer Science, FSTTCS, 15–17 December 2014, New Delhi, India, pp. 121–132 (2014)
6. Driscoll, E., Thakur, A., Reps, T.: OpenNWA: a nested-word automaton library. In: Madhusudan, P., Seshia, S.A. (eds.) CAV 2012. LNCS, vol. 7358, pp. 665–671. Springer, Heidelberg (2012)

7. Eppstein, D.: Reset sequences for monotonic automata. SIAM J. Comput. **19**(3), 500–510 (1990)

8. Ershov, A.P.: On programming of arithmetic operations. Commun. ACM **1**(8), 3–9 (1958)

9. Esparza, J., Ganty, P., Kiefer, S., Luttenberger, M.: Parikh's theorem: a simple and direct automaton construction. Inf. Process. Lett. **111**(12), 614–619 (2011)

10. Esparza, J., Ganty, P., Majumdar, R.: Parameterized verification of asynchronous shared-memory systems. In: Sharygina, N., Veith, H. (eds.) CAV 2013. LNCS, vol. 8044, pp. 124–140. Springer, Heidelberg (2013)

11. Esparza, J., Luttenberger, M., Schlund, M.: A brief history of Strahler numbers. In: Dediu, A.-H., Martín-Vide, C., Sierra-Rodríguez, J.-L., Truthe, B. (eds.) LATA 2014. LNCS, vol. 8370, pp. 1–13. Springer, Heidelberg (2014)

12. Fominykh, F.M., Martyugin, P.V., Volkov, M.V.: P(l)aying for synchronization. Int. J. Found. Comput. Sci. **24**(6), 765–780 (2013)

13. Hopcroft, J.E., Paul, W.J., Valiant, L.G.: On time versus space. J. ACM **24**(2), 332–337 (1977)

14. Kozen, D.: Lower bounds for natural proof systems. In: 18th Annual Symposium on Foundations of Computer Science, Providence, Rhode Island, USA, 31 October–1 November, pp. 254–266 (1977)

15. Lengauer, T., Tarjan, R.E.: The space complexity of pebble games on trees. Inf. Process. Lett. **10**(4/5), 184–188 (1980)

16. Martyugin, P.: Computational complexity of certain problems related to carefully synchronizing words for partial automata and directing words for nondeterministic automata. Theor. Comput. Syst. **54**(2), 293–304 (2014)

17. Mehlhorn, K.: Pebbling moutain ranges and its application of DCFL-recognition. In: Proceedings Automata, Languages and Programming, 7th Colloquium, Noordweijkerhout, The Netherland, July 14–18, pp. 422–435 (1980)

18. Olschewski, J., Ummels, M.: The complexity of finding reset words in finite automata. In: Hliněný, P., Kučera, A. (eds.) MFCS 2010. LNCS, vol. 6281, pp. 568–579. Springer, Heidelberg (2010)

19. Paterson, M.S., Hewitt, C.E.: Comparative schematology. In: Record of the Project MAC Conference on Concurrent Systems and Parallel Computation, pp. 119–127. ACM, MIT AI Memo AIM-201 (1970). http://hdl.handle.net/1721.1/5851

20. Pin, J.-É.: On two combinatorial problems arising from automata theory. North-Holland Math. Stud. **75**, 535–548 (1983)

21. Rystsov, I.K.: Polynomial complete problems in automata theory. Inf. Process. Lett. **16**(3), 147–151 (1983)

22. Sandberg, S.: Homing and synchronizing sequences. In: Broy, M., Jonsson, B., Katoen, J.-P., Leucker, M., Pretschner, A. (eds.) Model-Based Testing of Reactive Systems. LNCS, vol. 3472, pp. 5–33. Springer, Heidelberg (2005)

23. Savage, J.E.: Models of Computation - Exploring the Power of Computing. Addison-Wesley, Boston (1998)

24. Černý, J., Pirická, A., Rosenauerová, B.: On directable automata. Kybernetika **7**(4), 289–298 (1971)

25. Volkov, M.V.: Synchronizing automata and the Černý conjecture. In: Martín-Vide, C., Otto, F., Fernau, H. (eds.) LATA 2008. LNCS, vol. 5196, pp. 11–27. Springer, Heidelberg (2008)

26. Wehar, M.: Hardness results for intersection non-emptiness. In: Esparza, J., Fraigniaud, P., Husfeldt, T., Koutsoupias, E. (eds.) ICALP 2014, Part II. LNCS, vol. 8573, pp. 354–362. Springer, Heidelberg (2014)

On Freeze LTL with Ordered Attributes

Normann Decker[(✉)] and Daniel Thoma

Institute for Software Engineering and Programming Languages,
University of Lübeck, Lübeck, Germany
{decker,thoma}@isp.uni-luebeck.de

Abstract. This paper is concerned with Freeze LTL, a temporal logic
on data words with registers. In a (multi-attributed) data word each position carries a letter from a finite alphabet and assigns a data value to a
fixed, finite set of attributes. The satisfiability problem of Freeze LTL is
undecidable if more than one register is available or tuples of data values can be stored and compared arbitrarily. Starting from the decidable
one-register fragment we propose an extension that allows for specifying
a dependency relation on attributes. This restricts in a flexible way how
collections of attribute values can be stored and compared. This conceptual dimension is orthogonal to the number of registers or the available
temporal operators. The extension is strict. Admitting arbitrary dependency relations, satisfiability becomes undecidable. Tree-like relations,
however, induce a family of decidable fragments escalating the ordinal-
indexed hierarchy of fast-growing complexity classes, a recently introduced framework for non-primitive recursive complexities. This results
in completeness for the class $\mathbf{F}_{\epsilon_0}$. We employ nested counter systems and
show that they relate to the hierarchy in terms of the nesting depth.

1   Introduction

A central aspect in modern programming languages and software architectures
is dynamic and unbounded creation of entities. In particular object oriented
designs rely on instantiation of objects on demand and flexible multi-threaded
execution. Finite abstractions can hardly reflect these dynamics and therefore
infinite models are very valuable for specification and analysis. This motivates
us to study the theoretical framework of words over infinite alphabets. It allows
for abstracting, e.g., the internal structure and state of particular objects or
processes while still being able to capture the architectural design in terms of
interaction and relations between dynamically instantiated program parts.

These *data words*, as we consider them here, are finite, non-empty sequences
$w = (a_1, \mathbf{d}_1)(a_2, \mathbf{d}_2) \ldots (a_n, \mathbf{d}_n)$ where the i-th position carries a letter a_i from
a finite alphabet Σ. Additionally, for a fixed, finite set of *attributes* A a *data
valuation* $\mathbf{d}_i : A \to \Delta$ assigns to each attribute a *data value* from an infinite
domain Δ with equality.

This work was partially supported by EGIDE/DAAD-Procope (FREQS).

© Springer-Verlag Berlin Heidelberg 2016
B. Jacobs and C. Löding (Eds.): FOSSACS 2016, LNCS 9634, pp. 269–284, 2016.
DOI: 10.1007/978-3-662-49630-5_16

Freeze LTL. In formal verification, temporal logics are widely used for formulating behavioural specifications and, regarding data, the concept of storing values in registers for comparison at different points in time is very natural. This paper is therefore concerned with the logic *Freeze LTL* [8] that extends classical Linear-time Temporal Logic (LTL) by registers and was extensively studied during the past decade. Since the satisfiability problem of Freeze LTL is undecidable in general, we specifically consider the decidable fragment $\text{LTL}_1^\downarrow$ [7] that is restricted to a single register and future-time modalities. More precisely, we propose a generalisation of this fragment and study the consequences in terms of decidability and complexity.

Considering specification and modelling, the ability of comparing *tuples* of data values arbitrarily is a valuable feature. Unfortunately, this generically renders logics on data words undecidable (cf. related work below). We therefore extend Freeze LTL by a mechanism for carefully restricting the collections of values that can be compared in terms of a *dependency relation* on attributes. In general, this does not suffice to regain decidability of the satisfiability problem. Imposing, however, a *hierarchical* dependency structure such that comparison of attribute values is carried out in an ordered fashion, we obtain a strict hierarchy of decidable fragments parameterised by the maximal depth of the attribute hierarchy.

Before we exemplify this concept, let us introduce basic notation. Let Σ be a finite alphabet and $(A, \sqsubseteq)$ a finite set of attributes together with a reflexive and transitive relation $\sqsubseteq \subseteq A \times A$, i.e., a *quasi-ordering*, simply denoted A if $\sqsubseteq$ is understood. We call our logic $\text{LTL}_{qo}^\downarrow$ and define its *syntax* according to the grammar

$$\varphi ::= a \mid \neg\varphi \mid \varphi \wedge \varphi \mid X\varphi \mid \varphi U\varphi \mid \downarrow^x\varphi \mid \uparrow^x$$

for letters $a \in \Sigma$ and attributes $x \in A$. We further include common abbreviations such as disjunction, implication or the temporal operators release ($\varphi R \psi := \neg(\neg\varphi U \neg\psi)$), weak next ($\overline{X}\varphi := \neg X \neg\varphi$) and globally ($G \varphi := \text{false} R \varphi$). The restriction of $\text{LTL}_{qo}^\downarrow$ to a particular, fixed set of attributes $(A, \sqsubseteq)$ is denoted $\text{LTL}_{(A,\sqsubseteq)}^\downarrow$ (or simply $\text{LTL}_A^\downarrow$).

In the following, we explain the idea of our extension by means of an example. The formal semantics is defined in Sect. 2.

Example 1. Consider a system with arbitrarily many processes that can lock, unlock and use an arbitrary number of resources. A data word over the alphabet $\Sigma = \{\text{lock}, \text{unlock}, \text{use}, \text{halt}\}$ can model its behaviour in terms of an interleaving of individual actions and global signals. The corresponding data valuation can provide specific properties of an action, such as a unique identifier for the involved process and the resource. Let us use attributes $A = \{\text{pid}, \text{res}\}$ and interpret data values from Δ as IDs. Notice that this way, we do not assume a bound on the number of involved entities.

Consider now the property that locked resources must not be used by foreign processes and all locks must be released on system halt. To express this, we need to store both the process and resource ID for every *lock* action and verify that

	lock	lock	use	unlock	unlock		lock	lock	use	unlock	halt	unlock
(res)	1	2	2	2	1		1	3	3	3	9	1
(pid)	1	1	1	1	1		1	2	1	1	8	1

Fig. 1. The left word satisfies the formula from Example 1 whereas every strict prefix does not. The right word violates the property because at position 3 use holds and the value of res matches the one stored at position 2 but the whole valuation (3,1) differs from (3,2), so the check $\uparrow^{pid}$ fails. Moreover, halt occurs before (1,1) was observed again in combination with unlock.

a *use* involving the same resource also involves the same process. As mentioned earlier, employing a too liberal mechanism to store multiple data values at once breaks the possibility of automatic analysis. In our case, however, we do not need to refer to processes independently. It suffices to consider only resources individually and formulate that the particular process that locks a resource is the only one using it before unlocking. This *one-to-many* correspondence between processes and resources allows us to declare the attribute pid to be dependent on the attribute res and formulate the property by the formula

$$G(\text{lock} \rightarrow \downarrow^{pid}((\text{use} \wedge \uparrow^{res} \rightarrow \uparrow^{pid}) \wedge \neg\text{halt})U(\text{unlock} \wedge \uparrow^{pid})).$$

The *freeze quantifier* $\downarrow^{pid}$ stores the current value assigned to pid and also implicitly that of all its dependencies, res in this case. The *check operator* $\uparrow^x$, for an attribute $x \in A$, then verifies at some position that the current values of x and its dependencies coincide with the information that was stored earlier. Also, properties independent of the data can be verified within the same context, e.g., $\neg$halt for preventing a shut down as long as any resource is still locked. See Fig. 1 for example words.

Using this extended storing mechanism, we can select the values of the two attributes $(\downarrow^{pid})$ and identify and distinguish positions in a data word where both $(\uparrow^{pid})$, a particular one of them $(\uparrow^{res})$ or a global signal (e.g., halt) occurs. In contrast to other decidable fragments of Freeze LTL, we are thus able to store collections of values and can compare individual values across the hierarchy of attributes. This allows for reasoning on complex interaction of entities, also witnessed by the high, yet decidable, complexity of the logic.

Outline and Results. We define the semantics of $\text{LTL}^{\downarrow}_{qo}$ in Sect. 2 generalising Freeze LTL based on quasi-ordered attribute sets. We show that every fragment $\text{LTL}^{\downarrow}_A$ is undecidable unless A has a tree-like structure, formalised as what we call a *tree-quasi-ordering*.

Section 3 is devoted to *nested counter systems (NCS)* and an analysis of their coverability problem. We determine its non-primitive recursive complexity in terms of *fast-growing complexity classes* [20]. These classes $\mathbf{F}_\alpha$ are indexed by ordinal numbers α and characterise complexities by fast-growing functions from the extended Grzegorczyk hierarchy (details are provided in Sect. 3). We show that with increasing nesting level coverability in NCS exceeds every class $\mathbf{F}_\alpha$ for ordinals $\alpha < \epsilon_0$. By also providing a matching upper bound, we establish the following.

Theorem 2 (NCS). *The coverability problem in NCS is $\mathbf{F}_{\epsilon_0}$-complete.*

We consider the fragment $\text{LTL}^\downarrow_{tqo}$ in Sect. 4. It restricts the available dependency relations to tree-quasi-orderings. By reducing the satisfiability problem to NCS coverability, we obtain a precise characterisation of the decidability frontier in $\text{LTL}^\downarrow_{qo}$. Moreover, we transfer the lower bounds obtained for NCS to the logic setting. This leads us to a strict hierarchy of decidable fragments of $\text{LTL}^\downarrow_{tqo}$ parameterised by the depth of the attribute orderings and a completeness result for $\text{LTL}^\downarrow_{tqo}$.

Theorem 3 ($\text{LTL}^\downarrow_{qo}$). *The satisfiability problem of*

- *$\text{LTL}^\downarrow_A$ is decidable if and only if A is a tree-quasi-ordering.*
- *$\text{LTL}^\downarrow_{tqo}$ is $\mathbf{F}_{\epsilon_0}$-complete.*

Related Work. The *freeze* [13] mechanism was introduced as a natural form of storing and comparing (real-time) data at different positions in time [1] and since studied extensively in different contexts, e.g., [10,11,17]. In particular linear temporal logic employing the freeze mechanism over domains with only equality, i.e., data words, was considered in [8] and shown highly undecidable (Σ^1_1-hard). Therefore, several decidable fragments were proposed in the literature with complexities ranging from exponential [15] and double-exponential space [6] to non-primitive recursive complexities [7]. For the one-register fragment $\text{LTL}^\downarrow_1$ that we build on here, an $\mathbf{F}_\omega$ upper bound was given in [9]. Due to its decidability and expressiveness, it is called in [7] a "competitor" for the two-variable first-order logic over data words $\text{FO}^2(\sim, <, +1)$ studied in [3]. There, satisfiability was reduced to and from reachability in Petri nets in double-exponential time and polynomial time, respectively, for which recent results provide an $\mathbf{F}_{\omega^3}$ upper bound [16].

   Our main ambition is to incorporate means of storing and comparing collections of data values. The apparent extension of storing and comparing even only pairs generically renders logics on data words, even those with essential restrictions, undecidable [3,5,14]. This applies in particular to fragments of $\text{LTL}^\downarrow_1$ [6].

   The logic *Nested Data LTL (ND-LTL)* studied in [5] employs a navigation concept based on an *ordered* set of attributes. It inspired our extension of Freeze LTL but in contrast, data values in ND-LTL are not handled explicitly, resulting in incomparable expressiveness and different notions of natural restrictions. While ND-LTL also features a freeze-like mechanism, it does not contain an explicit check operator ($\uparrow$). Instead, data-aware variants of temporal operators such as $\text{U}^=$ express constraints (only) for position where the stored value is present. For example, an ND-LTL formula $\text{G}(\text{lock} \rightarrow \downarrow^{\text{pid}}(\neg\text{halt}\,\text{U}^=\text{unlock}))$ (in notation of this paper) requires that for every position satisfying lock there is a future position unlock with the same data value and that $\neg$halt holds (at least) on all those position in between that also carry this particular value. In contrast, $\text{G}(\text{lock} \rightarrow \downarrow^{\text{pid}}(\neg\text{halt}\,\text{U}(\text{unlock} \wedge \uparrow^{\text{pid}})))$ asserts that at *all* position in between ¬halt holds. Enforcing such constraints in ND-LTL typically requires an additional level of auxiliary attributes.

The future fragment ND-LTL$^+$ was shown decidable and non-primitive recursive on finite A-attributed data words for tree-(partial-)ordered attribute sets A. However, no upper complexity bounds were provided and the developments in this paper significantly raise the lower bounds (cf. Sect. 5). The influence of more general attribute orderings, in particular the precise decidability frontier in that dimension, was not investigated for ND-LTL and its fragments. Instead, the logic was shown undecidable by exploiting the combination of future- and past-time operators. Extending LTL$_1^\downarrow$ with past-time operators is also known to lead to undecidability. ND-LTL$^+$ stays decidable even on infinite words, which is not the case for LTL$_{tqo}^\downarrow$ since satisfiability of LTL$_1^\downarrow$ is already Π_1^0-complete [7].

2 Semantics and Undecidability of LTL$_{qo}^\downarrow$

By specifying dependencies between attributes from a set A in terms of a quasi-ordering $\sqsubseteq \subseteq A \times A$ the freeze mechanism can be used to store the values of multiple attributes at once. The essential intuition for our generalised storing mechanism can well be obtained from the special case of a linearly ordered attribute set $[k] = \{1, \ldots, k\}$ with the natural ordering $\leq$ for some natural number $k \in \mathbb{N}$. In fact, many of the technical developments in this paper concerning decidability and complexity are carried out within this setting but for concise presentation we only provide the most general formulation that captures also the undecidable case.

The valuations $\mathbf{d} \in \Delta^{[k]}$ in a $[k]$-attributed data word are essentially sequences (or vectors) $d_1 \ldots d_k$ where the x-th position carries the value $d_x = \mathbf{d}(x)$ of attribute $x \in [k]$. Note that Example 1 matches that setting when renaming res to 1 and pid to 2.

In a formula $\downarrow^x \varphi$ the subformula φ is evaluated in the context of the current value $\mathbf{d}(x)$ of the attribute $x \in A$ and the values $\mathbf{d}(y)$ of all smaller attributes $y \leq x$. Thus, the *prefix* $d_1 \ldots d_x$ of the value sequence at the current position is stored for later comparison. A check operator $\uparrow^y$ then compares the stored values $d_1 \ldots d_x$ to the values $d_1' \ldots d_y'$ at the current position: the check is successful if the latter sequence is a prefix of the former, i.e. $y \leq x$ and $d_1 \ldots d_y = d_1' \ldots d_y'$.

For the general setting of arbitrary (quasi-ordered) dependency relations $(A, \sqsubseteq)$, we lift the notion of the prefix of length x to the *restriction* of a valuation $\mathbf{d} : A \to \Delta$ to the *downward-closure* $\mathsf{cl}(x) = \{y \in A \mid y \sqsubseteq x\}$ of x in A. This restriction is defined as $\mathbf{d}|_x : \mathsf{cl}(x) \to \Delta$ with $\mathbf{d}|_x(y) = \mathbf{d}(y)$ for $y \sqsubseteq x$. We denote the set of all such partial data valuations by $\Delta_\perp^A = \{\mathbf{d} : \mathsf{cl}(x) \to \Delta \mid x \in A\}$.

Partial valuations $\mathbf{d}, \mathbf{d}' \in \Delta_\perp^A$ are compared in analogy to sequences: it must be possible to map one onto the other such that ordering is preserved and all values coincide. Formally, we define an equivalence relation $\simeq \subseteq \Delta_\perp^A \times \Delta_\perp^A$ by $\mathbf{d} \simeq \mathbf{d}'$ if and only if there is a bijection $h : \mathsf{dom}(\mathbf{d}) \to \mathsf{dom}(\mathbf{d}')$ such that, for all attributes $x \in \mathsf{dom}(\mathbf{d})$ we have $\mathbf{d}(x) = \mathbf{d}'(h(x))$ and, for all attributes $y \in \mathsf{dom}(\mathbf{d})$, $x \sqsubseteq y \Leftrightarrow h(x) \sqsubseteq h(y)$. Notice that this requires the domains of

d and **d'** to be isomorphic. In the definition presented next we therefore allow for restricting the stored valuation arbitrarily before it is matched against the current one. In the linear case this simply means truncating the stored sequence before comparison and intuitively it allows for removing unnecessary information from the context.

Semantics of $\mathbf{LTL}_{qo}^{\downarrow}$. For a non-empty data word $w = (a_1, \mathbf{d}_1) \ldots (a_n, \mathbf{d}_n) \in (\Sigma \times \Delta^A)^+$, an index $1 \leq i \leq n$ in w and a partial data valuation $\mathbf{d} \in \Delta_{\uparrow}^A$ the semantics of $\mathrm{LTL}_A^{\downarrow}$ formulae is defined inductively by

$$
\begin{aligned}
(w, i, \mathbf{d}) &\models a_i \\
(w, i, \mathbf{d}) &\models \neg\varphi &:&\Leftrightarrow& (w, i, \mathbf{d}) \not\models \varphi \\
(w, i, \mathbf{d}) &\models \varphi \wedge \psi &:&\Leftrightarrow& (w, i, \mathbf{d}) \models \varphi \text{ and } (w, i, \mathbf{d}) \models \psi \\
(w, i, \mathbf{d}) &\models \mathrm{X}\,\varphi &:&\Leftrightarrow& i+1 \leq n \text{ and } (w, i+1, \mathbf{d}) \models \varphi \\
(w, i, \mathbf{d}) &\models \varphi \mathrm{U}\psi &:&\Leftrightarrow& \exists_{i \leq k \leq n} : (w, k, \mathbf{d}) \models \psi \text{ and } \forall_{i \leq j < k} : (w, j, \mathbf{d}) \models \varphi \\
(w, i, \mathbf{d}) &\models \downarrow^x\varphi &:&\Leftrightarrow& (w, i, \mathbf{d}_i|_x) \models \varphi \\
(w, i, \mathbf{d}) &\models \uparrow^x &:&\Leftrightarrow& \exists_{y \in A} : \mathbf{d}|_y \simeq \mathbf{d}_i|_x.
\end{aligned}
$$

For formulae φ where every check operator $\uparrow^x$ is within the scope of some freeze quantifier $\downarrow^y$ the stored valuation is irrelevant and we write $w \models \varphi$ if $(w, 1, \mathbf{d}) \models \varphi$ for any valuation **d**.

Example 4. Consider a set of attributes $A = \{x_1, x_2, x_3, y_1, y_2\}$ with $x_1 \sqsubseteq x_2 \sqsubseteq x_3$ and $y_1 \sqsubseteq y_2$ (this is an example for a tree-quasi-ordering, see below), the formula $\downarrow^{x_3} \mathrm{X}(\uparrow^{y_2} \mathrm{U} \uparrow^{x_3})$ and a data word $w = (a_1, \mathbf{d}_1) \ldots (a_n, \mathbf{d}_n)$. The formula reads as: "Store the current values d_1, d_2, d_3 of x_1, x_2, x_3, respectively. Move on to the next position. Verify that the stored value d_1 appears in y_1 and that d_2 appears in y_2 until the values d_1, d_2, d_3 appear again in attributes x_1, x_2, x_3, respectively."

At the first position, the values $d_1 = \mathbf{d}_1(x_1)$, $d_2 = \mathbf{d}_1(x_2)$ and $d_3 = \mathbf{d}_1(x_3)$ are stored in terms of the valuation $\mathbf{d} = \mathbf{d}_1|_{x_3} : \{x_1, x_2, x_3\} \to \Delta$ since x_1, x_2, x_3 depend on x_3. Assume for the second position $\mathbf{d}_2(x_1) \neq \mathbf{d}_1(x_1) = d_1$. The formula $\uparrow^{x_3}$ is not satisfied at the second position in the context of **d** since the only attribute $p \in A$ such that $\mathrm{cl}(p)$ is isomorphic to $\{x_1, x_2, x_3\}$ is $p = x_3$. Then, however, any order preserving isomorphism needs to map $x_1 \in \mathrm{dom}(\mathbf{d})$ to $x_1 \in \mathrm{dom}(\mathbf{d}_2)$ since x_1 is the minimal element in both domains but $\mathbf{d}(x_1) \neq \mathbf{d}_2(x_1)$. The only way to not violate the formula is hence that $\mathbf{d}_2(y_1) = \mathbf{d}_1(x_1)$ and $\mathbf{d}_2(y_2) = \mathbf{d}_1(x_2)$. Then, we can choose $p = x_2$ and have $\mathbf{d}|_{x_2} \simeq \mathbf{d}_2|_{y_2}$ meaning that $\uparrow^{y_2}$ is satisfied.

Undecidability. For $\sqsubseteq = \{(x, x) \mid x \in A\}$ (identity) we obtain the special case where only single values can be stored and compared. If $|A| = 1$ we obtain the one-register fragment $\mathrm{LTL}_1^{\downarrow}$. On the other hand, if A contains three attributes x, y, z such that x and y are incomparable and $x \sqsubseteq z \sqsupseteq y$ then storing the value of z also stores the values of x and y. This amounts to storing and comparing the *set* $\{d_x, d_y\} \subset \Delta$ of values assigned to x and y. This is not precisely the same as storing the ordered *tuple* $(d_x, d_y) \in \Delta \times \Delta$ but together with the ability of storing and comparing x and y independently it turns out to be just as contagious considering decidability.

In [3] it is shown that the satisfiability problem of two-variable first-order logic over data words with two class relations is undecidable by reduction from *Post's correspondence problem*. We can adapt this proof and formulate the necessary conditions for a data word to encode a solution using only the attributes $x \sqsubseteq z \sqsupseteq y$. With ideas from [6] we can also omit using past-time operators. Moreover, this result can be generalised to arbitrary quasi-orderings that contain three attributes $x \sqsubseteq z \sqsupseteq y$.

The absence of such a constellation is formalised by the notion of a *tree-quasi-ordering* defined as a quasi-ordering where the downward-closure of every element is totally ordered. This precisely prohibits elements z that depend on two independent elements x and y. The definition describes in a general way a hierarchical, tree-like structure. Intuitively, a tree-quasi-ordering is (the reflexive and transitive closure of) a forest of strongly connected components.

Theorem 5 (Undecidability). *Let $(A, \sqsubseteq)$ be a quasi-ordered set of attributes that is* not *a tree-quasi-ordering. Then the satisfiability problem of $LTL_A^\downarrow$ is Σ_1^0-complete over A-attributed data words.*

As will be discussed in Sect. 4, tree-quasi-orderings represent not only necessary but also sufficient conditions for the logic to be decidable.

3   Nested Counter Systems

Nested counter systems (NCS) are a generalisation of counter systems similar to higher-order multi-counter automata as used in [2] and nested Petri nets [18]. In this section we establish novel complexity results for their coverability problem. A finite number of counters can equivalently be seen as a multiset $M = \{c_1 : n_1, \ldots, c_m : n_m\}$ over a set of counter names $C = \{c_1, \ldots, c_n\}$. We therefore define NCS in the flavor of [5] as systems transforming *nested multisets*.

Let $\mathfrak{M}(A)$ denote, for any set A, the set of all *finite multisets* of elements of A. For $k \in \mathbb{N}$ we write $[k]$ to denote the set $\{1, \ldots, k\} \subset \mathbb{N}$ with the natural linear ordering $\leq$. A *k-nested counter system (k-NCS)* is a tuple $\mathcal{N} = (Q, \delta)$ comprised of a finite set Q of *states* and a set $\delta \subseteq \bigcup_{i,j \in [k+1]} (Q^i \times Q^j)$ of *transition rules*. For $0 \leq i \leq k$ the set $\mathcal{C}_i$ of *configurations of level i* is inductively defined by $\mathcal{C}_k = Q$ and $\mathcal{C}_{i-1} = Q \times \mathfrak{M}(\mathcal{C}_i)$. The set of *configurations* of $\mathcal{N}$ is then $\mathcal{C}_\mathcal{N} = \mathcal{C}_0$. Every element of $\mathcal{C}_\mathcal{N}$ can, more conveniently, be presented as a term constructed over unary function symbols Q, constants Q and a binary operator $+$ that is associative and commutative. For example, the configuration $(q_0, \{(q_1, \emptyset) : 1, (q_1, \{(q_2, \emptyset) : 2\}) : 2, (q_1, \{(q_2, \emptyset) : 2, (q_3, \{(q_4, \emptyset) : 1\}) : 1\}) : 1\})$ can be represented by the term $q_0(q_1 + q_1(q_2 + q_2) + q_1(q_2 + q_2) + q_1(q_2 + q_2 + q_3(q_4)))$. The operational semantics of $\mathcal{N}$ is now defined in terms of the *transition relation* $\rightarrow \subseteq \mathcal{C}_\mathcal{N} \times \mathcal{C}_\mathcal{N}$ on configurations given by rewrite rules. For $((q_0, \ldots, q_i), (q_0', \ldots, q_j')) \in \delta$ and $i, j < k$ we let

$$q_0(X_1 + q_1(\ldots q_i(X_{i+1}) \ldots)) \rightarrow q_0'(X_1 + q_1'(\ldots q_j'(X_{j+1}) \ldots))$$

for any $X_h \in \mathfrak{M}(C_h)$ where $1 \leq h \leq k$ and $X_\ell = \emptyset$ for $i + 2 \leq \ell \leq j + 1$. For example, a rule $((q_0), (q_0'))$ changes the state q_0 in the example configuration above to q_0'. A rule $((q_0, q_1), (q_0, q_1, q_2'))$ adds a state q_2' non-deterministically as a direct child of one of the states q_1 resulting in one of the three configurations

$$q_0(q_1(q_2') + q_1(q_2 + q_2) + q_1(q_2 + q_2) + q_1(q_2 + q_2 + q_3(q_4))),$$
$$q_0(q_1 + q_1(q_2 + q_2 + q_2') + q_1(q_2 + q_2) + q_1(q_2 + q_2 + q_3(q_4))) \text{ and}$$
$$q_0(q_1 + q_1(q_2 + q_2) + q_1(q_2 + q_2) + q_1(q_2 + q_2 + q_3(q_4) + q_2')).$$

Moreover, a rule $((q_0, q_1, q_3), (q_0))$ would remove specifically and completely the sub-configuration $q_1(q_2 + q_2 + q_3(q_4))$ since it does not match any other one.

The remaining cases for transitions, where (1) $i < k = j$, (2) $i = k > j$ and (3) $i = k = j$, are defined as expected by rules

$$q_0(X_1 + q_1(\ldots q_i(X_{i+1})\ldots)) \rightarrow q_0'(X_1 + q_1'(\ldots q_{k-1}'(X_k + q_k')\ldots)) \quad (1)$$
$$q_0(X_1 + q_1(\ldots q_{k-1}(X_k + q_k)\ldots)) \rightarrow q_0'(X_1 + q_1'(\ldots q_j'(X_{j+1})\ldots)) \quad (2)$$
$$q_0(X_1 + q_1(\ldots q_{k-1}(X_k + q_k)\ldots)) \rightarrow q_0'(X_1 + q_1'(\ldots q_{k-1}'(X_k + q_k')\ldots)) \quad (3)$$

respectively, where for (1) we have $X_{i+2} = \ldots = X_k = \emptyset$. Note that these cases are exhaustive since the nesting depth of terms representing configurations from $\mathcal{C}_\mathcal{N}$ is at most k. As usual we denote by $\rightarrow^*$ the reflexive and transitive closure of $\rightarrow$. By $\preceq$ we denote the nested multiset ordering, i.e. $M' \preceq M$ iff M' can be obtained by removing elements (or nested multisets) from M. Given two configurations $C, C' \in \mathcal{C}_\mathcal{N}$ the *coverability problem* asks for the existence of a configuration $C'' \in \mathcal{C}_\mathcal{N}$ with $C'' \succeq C'$ and $C \rightarrow^* C''$.

To establish our complexity results on NCS we require some notions on ordinal numbers, ordinal recursive functions and respective complexity classes. We represent ordinals using the *Cantor normal form (CNF)*. An ordinal $\alpha < \epsilon_0$ is represented in CNF as a term $\alpha = \omega^{\alpha_1} + \ldots + \omega^{\alpha_k}$ over the symbol ω and the associative binary operator $+$ where $\alpha > \alpha_1 \geq \ldots \geq \alpha_k$. Furthermore, we denote *limit ordinals* by λ. These are ordinals such that $\alpha + 1 < \lambda$ for every $\alpha < \lambda$. We associate them with a *fundamental sequence* $(\lambda_n)_n$ with supremum λ defined by

$$(\alpha + \omega^{\beta+1})_n := \alpha + \overbrace{\omega^\beta + \ldots + \omega^\beta}^{n} \qquad \text{and} \qquad (\alpha + \omega^{\lambda'})_n := \alpha + \omega^{\lambda'_n}$$

for ordinals β and limit ordinals λ'. Then, ϵ_0 is the smallest ordinal α such that $\alpha = \omega^\alpha$. We denote the n-th exponentiation of ω as Ω_n, i.e. $\Omega_1 := \omega$ and $\Omega_{n+1} := \omega^{\Omega_n}$. Consequently, $(\Omega_n)_m < \Omega_n$ is the m-th element of the fundamental sequence of Ω_n. Given a monotone and expansive[1] function $h : \mathbb{N} \rightarrow \mathbb{N}$, a *Hardy hierarchy* is an ordinal-indexed family of functions $h^\alpha : \mathbb{N} \rightarrow \mathbb{N}$ defined by $h^0(n) := n$, $h^{\alpha+1}(n) := h^\alpha(h(n))$ and $h^\lambda(n) := h^{\lambda_n}(n)$. Choosing h as the incrementing function $H(n) := n + 1$, the *fast growing hierarchy* is the family of functions $F_\alpha(n)$ with $F_\alpha(n) := H^{\omega^\alpha}(n)$.

---

[1] A function $f : A \rightarrow A$ over an ordering $(A, \leq)$ is monotone if $a \leq a' \Rightarrow f(a) \leq f(a')$ and expansive if $a \leq f(a)$ for all $a, a' \in A$.

The hierarchy of *fast growing complexity classes* $\mathbf{F}_\alpha$ for ordinals α is defined in terms of the fast-growing functions F_α. We refer the reader to [20] for details and only remark that $\mathbf{F}_{<\omega}$ is the class of primitive recursive problems and problems in $\mathbf{F}_\omega, \mathbf{F}_{\omega^\omega}$ are solvable with resources bound by Ackermannian and Hyper-Ackermannian functions, respectively. The fact most relevant for our classification is that a basic $\mathbf{F}_\alpha$-complete problem is the termination problem of Minsky machines $\mathcal{M}$ where the sum of the counters is bounded by $F_\alpha(|\mathcal{M}|)$ [20].

Upper Bound. To obtain an upper bound for the coverability problem in k-NCS we reduce it to that in *priority channel systems (PCS)* [12]. PCS are comprised of a finite control and a fixed number of channels, each storing a string to which a letter can be appended (write) and from which the first letter can be read and removed (read). Every letter carries a priority and can be lost at any time and any position in a channel if its successor in the channel carries a higher or equal priority. PCS can easily simulate NCS by storing and manipulating an NCS configuration in a channel where a state q at level $i > 0$ in the NCS configuration is encoded by a letter $(q, k - i)$ with priority $k - i$. E.g., the 3-NCS configuration $q_0(q_1 + q_1(q_2 + q_2) + q_1(q_2 + q_2 + q_3(q_4)))$ can be encoded as a channel of the form $(q_1, 2)(q_1, 2)(q_2, 1)(q_2, 1)(q_1, 2)(q_2, 1)(q_2, 1)(q_3, 1)(q_4, 0)$ while q_0 is encoded in the finite control.

Taking the highest priority for the outermost level ensures that the lossiness of PCS corresponds to descending with respect to $\preceq$ for the encoded NCS configuration. Thus the coverability problem in NCS directly translates to that in PCS. The coverability (control-state reachability) problem in PCS with one channel and k priorities lies in the class $\mathbf{F}_{\Omega_{2k}}$ [12] and we thus obtain an upper bound for NCS coverability.

Proposition 6. *Coverability in k-NCS is in $\mathbf{F}_{\Omega_{2k}}$.*

Lower Bound. We can reduce, for any $k > 1$, the halting problem of $H^{(\Omega_k)_l}$-bounded Minsky machines to coverability in k-NCS with the number of states bounded by $l + c$, for some constant c. This yields the following characterisation (recall that $H^{(\Omega_{k+1})_l} = F_{(\Omega_k)_l}$).

Theorem 7. *Coverability in $(k + 1)$-NCS is $\mathbf{F}_{\Omega_k}$-hard.*

The idea is to construct a k-NCS $\mathcal{N} = (Q, \delta)$ that can simulate the evaluation of the Hardy function $H^\alpha(n)$ for $\alpha \leq (\Omega_k)_l$ in forward as well as backward direction. It can then compute a *budget* that is used for simulating the Minsky machine. Lower bounds for various models were obtained using this scheme for Turing machines [4,12] or Minsky machines [19,21].

The following construction uses $k + 1$ levels of which one can be eliminated later. We encode the ordinal parameter α of $H^\alpha(n)$ and its argument $n \in \mathbb{N}$ (unary) into a configuration

$$C_{\alpha,n} := \mathsf{main}(\mathsf{s}(M_\alpha) + \mathsf{c}(\overbrace{1 + \ldots + 1}^{n}))$$

using control-states $\mathsf{main}, \mathsf{s}, \mathsf{c}, \omega \in Q$ and configurations M_α defined by $M_0 := \emptyset$ and $M_{\omega^\alpha + \beta} := \omega(M_\alpha) + M_\beta$. For example, an ordinal $\alpha = \omega^\omega + \omega^2 + \omega^2 + 1$ is encoded by

$$M_\alpha = \{(\omega, \{(\omega, \{(\omega, \emptyset) : 1\}) : 1\}) : 1, (\omega, \{(\omega, \emptyset) : 2\}) : 2, (\omega, \emptyset) : 1\}$$

Note that we use shorthands for readability, e.g., ω^ω stands for ω^{ω^1} where 1 is again short for the ordinal ω^0. The construction has to fulfil the following two properties. As NCS do not feature a zero test exact simulation cannot be enforced but errors can be restricted to be "lossy".

Lemma 8. *For all configurations $C_{\alpha,n} \rightarrow^* C_{\alpha',n'}$ we have $H^\alpha(n) \geq H^{\alpha'}(n')$.*

The construction will, however, admit at least one run maintaining exact values.

Lemma 9. *If $H^\alpha(n) = H^{\alpha'}(n')$ then there is a run $C_{\alpha,n} \rightarrow^* C_{\alpha',n'}$.*

The main challenge is simulating a computation step from a limit ordinal to an element of its fundamental sequence, i.e., from $C_{\alpha+\lambda,n}$ to $C_{\alpha+\lambda_n,n}$ and conversely. Encoding the ordinal parameter using multisets loses the ordering of the addends of the respective CNF terms. Thus, instead of taking the last element of the CNF term we have to select the smallest element, with respect to $\preceq$, of the corresponding multiset. To achieve that, we extend NCS by two operations cp and min. Given some configuration $C = q_1(q_2(M)) \in \mathcal{C}_\mathcal{N}$ the operation $(q_1, q_2)\mathsf{cp}(q_1', q_2')$ copies M resulting in $C' = q_1'(q_2'(M_1) + q_2'(M_2))$ with $M_1, M_2 \preceq M$. Conversely, given the configuration C' the operation $(q_1', q_2')\mathsf{min}(q_1, q_2)$ results in C with $M \preceq M_1, M_2$.

Both operations can be implemented in a depth first search fashion using the standard NCS operations. Based on them the selection of a smallest element from a multiset can be simulated: all elements are copied (non-deterministically) one by one to an auxiliary set while enforcing a descending order. Applying the min operation in every step ensures that we either proceed indeed in descending order or make a "lossy" error. We guess, in each step, whether the smallest element is reached and in that case delete the source multiset. Thereby it is ensured, that the smallest element has been selected or, again, a "lossy" error occurs such that the selected element is now the smallest one. The additional level in the encoding of $C_{\alpha,n}$ enables us to perform this deletion step.

A similar idea to select a smallest ordinal from a multiset is used in [19]. However, we need to handle nested structures of variable size correctly whereas in this work the considered ordinals are below Ω_3. They are represented by a multiset of vectors of fixed length where the vectors can be compared and modified directly in order enforce the choice of a minimal one.

We now construct an NCS simulating an $H^\alpha(s)$-bounded Minsky machine $\mathcal{M}$ of size $s := |\mathcal{M}|$ analogously to the constructions in [4,12,21]. It starts in a configuration $C_{\alpha,s}$ to evaluate $H^\alpha(s)$. When it reaches $C_{0,n}$ for some $n \leq H^\alpha(s)$ it switches its control state and starts to simulate $\mathcal{M}$ using n as a budget for the sum of the two simulated counters. Zero tests can then be simulated by resets (deleting and creating multisets) causing a "lossy" error in case of an actually non-zero counter. When the simulation of $\mathcal{M}$ reaches a final state the NCS moves the current counter values back to the budged counter and performs a construction similar to the one above but now evaluating $H^\alpha(s)$ *backwards* until reaching $(C_{\alpha,s})'$, the initial configuration with a different control state. If $(C_{\alpha,s})'$ can be reached (or even covered) no "lossy" errors occurred and the Minsky machine $\mathcal{M}$ was thus simulated correctly regarding zero tests.

4   From $\mathrm{LTL}^{\downarrow}_{tqo}$ to NCS and Back

Theorem 5 established a necessary condition for $LTL^{\downarrow}_A$ to have a decidable satisfiability problem, namely that A is a tree-quasi-ordering. In the following we show that this is also sufficient. Let $\mathrm{LTL}^{\downarrow}_{tqo}$ denote the fragment of $\mathrm{LTL}^{\downarrow}_{qo}$ restricted to tree-quasi-ordered sets of attributes. The decidability and complexity results for NCS can be transferred to $\mathrm{LTL}^{\downarrow}_{tqo}$ to obtain upper and lower bounds for the satisfiability problem of the logic.

We show a correspondence between the nesting depth in NCS and the depths of the tree-quasi-ordered attribute sets that thus constitutes a semantic hierarchy of logical fragments. We provide the essential ideas in the following.

The *depth* of a finite tree-quasi-ordering A is the maximal length k of strictly increasing sequences $x_1 \sqsubset x_2 \sqsubset \ldots \sqsubset x_k$ of attributes in A. The first observation is that we can reduce satisfiability of any $\mathrm{LTL}^{\downarrow}_{tqo}$ formula over attributes A to satisfiability of an $\mathrm{LTL}^{\downarrow}_{[k]}$ formula where $[k] = \{1, \ldots, k\}$ is an initial segment of the natural numbers with natural *linear ordering* and k is the depth of A.

Proposition 10 ($\mathrm{LTL}^{\downarrow}_{tqo}$ to $\mathrm{LTL}^{\downarrow}_{[k]}$).   *For a tree-quasi-ordered attribute set A of depth k every $LTL^{\downarrow}_A$ formula can be translated to an equisatisfiable $LTL^{\downarrow}_{[k]}$ formula of exponential size.*

To reduce an arbitrary tree-quasi-ordering A of depth k we first remove maximal strongly connected components (SCC) in the graph of A and replace each of them by a single attribute. This does only affect the semantics of formulae φ if attributes are compared that did not have an isomorphic downward-closure in A. These cases can, however, be handled by additional constraints added to φ. Data words over a thus obtained *partially* ordered attribute set of depth k can now be encoded into words over the *linear* ordering $[k]$ of equal depth k. The idea is to encode a single position into a frame of positions in the fashion of [5,14]. That way a single attribute on every level suffices. Any formula can be transformed to operate on these frames instead of single positions at the cost of an at most exponential blow-up.

From $\mathrm{LTL}^{\downarrow}_{[k]}$ to NCS.   Given an $\mathrm{LTL}^{\downarrow}_{[k]}$ formula Φ we can now construct a $(k+1)$-NCS $\mathcal{N}$ and two configurations $C_{init}, C_{final} \in \mathcal{C}_{\mathcal{N}}$ such that Φ is satisfiable if and only if C_{final} can be covered from C_{init}.

The idea is to encode sets of *guarantees* into NCS configurations. These guarantees are subformulae of Φ and are guaranteed to be satisfiable. The constructed

$$
\begin{array}{c}
{}^{1}\{\varphi_1\}\ \checkmark \\
\diagup \quad \diagdown \\
{}^{2}\emptyset \qquad {}^{4}\{\varphi_2,\psi_2\}\ \checkmark \\
\mid \qquad \diagup \quad \diagdown \\
{}^{3}\emptyset \quad {}^{5}\{\psi_3\}\ \ {}^{6}\{\psi_3\}\ \checkmark
\end{array}
\qquad
\begin{array}{c}
{}^{7}\emptyset \\
\mid \\
{}^{8}\emptyset \\
\mid \\
{}^{9}\{a\}
\end{array}
\qquad \rightarrow^{*} \qquad
\begin{array}{c}
\{\varphi_1\}\ \checkmark \\
\diagup \quad \diagdown \\
\{\neg\uparrow^2\} \qquad \{\varphi_2\wedge\psi_2\}\ \checkmark \\
\mid \qquad \diagup \quad \diagdown \\
\{\uparrow^1\} \quad \{\psi_3\}\ \ \{\varphi_3,\uparrow^3\}\ \checkmark
\end{array}
\qquad
\begin{array}{c}
\{\downarrow^2\varphi_2\} \\
\mid \\
\{\neg b\} \\
\mid \\
\{a\}
\end{array}
$$

$$C \qquad\qquad\qquad\qquad\qquad\qquad\qquad\qquad C'$$

Fig. 2. Example of a guarantee forest of depth 3 maintained and modified by the NCS constructed for some $\mathrm{LTL}^{\downarrow}_{[3]}$ formula. Node enumeration (grey) is only for reference.

NCS can instantiate new guarantees and combine existing ones while maintaining the invariant that there is always a data word $w \in (\Sigma \times \Delta^{[k]})^+$ that satisfies all of them. To ensure the invariant, the guarantees are organised in a forest of depth k as depicted in Fig. 2.

All formulae φ contained in the same node v of this forest are moreover not only satisfied by the same word w but also with respect to a common valuation $\mathbf{d}_v \in \Delta^{[k]}$, i.e., $(w, 1, \mathbf{d}_v) \models \varphi$. Recall that valuations over linearly ordered attributes can be seen as sequences. The forest structure now represents the common-prefix relation between these valuations $\mathbf{d}_v$. For two nodes v, v' having a common ancestor at level $i \in [k]$ in the forest, the corresponding valuations $\mathbf{d}_v$, $\mathbf{d}_{v'}$ can be chosen such that they agree on attributes 1 to i. A uniquely marked branch in the forest further represents the valuation $\mathbf{d}_1$ at the first position in w. If a formula φ is contained in the marked node at level i in the forest then $(w, 1, \mathbf{d}_1|_i) \models \varphi$. In that case $(w, 1, \mathbf{d}) \models \downarrow^i \varphi$ holds for any $\mathbf{d} \in \Delta^{[k]}_{\bot}$ and the formula $\downarrow^i \varphi$ could be added to any of the nodes in the forest without violating the invariant. Similarly, for a marked node v at level i the formulae $\uparrow^i$ can be added to any node in the subtree with root v. Moreover, other atomic formulae, Boolean combinations, and temporal operators can also be added consistently. The NCS $\mathcal{N}$ can perform such modifications on the forest, represented by its configuration, by corresponding transitions.

Example 11. Consider the two guarantee forests depicted in Fig. 2 that are encoded in configurations C and C' of an NCS constructed for some $\mathrm{LTL}^{\downarrow}_{[3]}$ formula. The invariant is the existence of a word $w = (a, \mathbf{d})\dots$ and valuations $\mathbf{d}_v \in \Delta^{[i]}$ such that $(w, 1, \mathbf{d}_v)$ satisfies the formulae in a node v at level i. The forest structure relates these valuations to $\mathbf{d}$ (nodes marked by ✓) and each other. E.g., $(w, 1, \mathbf{d}|_1) \models \varphi_1$, $(w, 1, \mathbf{d}|_2) \models \varphi_2$ and there is $\mathbf{e}$ with $\mathbf{e}|_2 = \mathbf{d}|_2$ and $\mathbf{e}(3) \neq \mathbf{d}(3)$ s.t. $(w, 1, \mathbf{e}) \models \psi_3$. Let $v_1, \dots, v_9$ be the nodes of the forest (as enumerated in the figure). Several possible operations are exemplified by the transition between C and C'. The formula $\uparrow^3$ can be added to the node v_6 containing the formula φ_3 since that node is checked on level 3. Similarly, there is $\mathbf{d}_3$ for node v_3 such that $\mathbf{d}_3(1) = \mathbf{d}(1)$ and hence $(w, \mathbf{d}_3) \models \uparrow^1$. The formula $\uparrow^2$ cannot be added to the node v_2 since it is not below the checked node on level two. Consequently, the node can contain $\neg\uparrow^2$. Node v_4 on level

2 does already contain φ_2 and ψ_2, meaning they are both satisfied by w and a valuation $\mathbf{d}_4 \in \Delta^{[2]}$. Hence the same holds for their conjunction. Moreover, v_4 is checked and therefore $\mathbf{d}_4 = \mathbf{d}|_2$. This implies that $(w, \mathbf{d}') \models \downarrow^2 \varphi_2$ for any $\mathbf{d}'$ and that the formula can be added to any node in the tree, e.g. v_7.

Recall that we only need to consider subformulae of Φ and thus remain finite-state for representing nodes. More precisely, the number of states in $\mathcal{N}$ is exponential in the size of Φ since they encode sets of formulae.

A crucial aspect is how the NCS can consistently add formulae of the form $X \varphi$. This needs to be done for all stored guarantees at once but NCS do not have an atomic operation for modifying all states in a configuration. Therefore, the forest is copied recursively, processing each copied node. The NCS $\mathcal{N}$ can choose at any time to stop and remove the remaining nodes. That way it might loose guarantees but maintains the invariant since only processed nodes remain in the configuration. The forest of depth k itself could be maintained by a k-NCS but to implement the copy operation an additional level is needed.

The initial configuration C_{init} consists of a forest without any guarantees. In a setup phase, the NCS can add branches and formulae of the form $\overline{X}\varphi$ since they are all satisfied by any word of length 1. Once the formula Φ is encountered in the current forest the NCS can enter a specific target state q_{final}. A path starting in C_{init} and covering the configuration $C_{final} = q_{final}$ then constitutes a model of Φ and vice versa.

Theorem 12. *For tree-quasi-ordered attribute sets A with depth k satisfiability of $LTL_A^{\downarrow}$ can be reduced in exponential space to coverability in $(k + 1)$-NCS.*

From k-NCS to $\mathbf{LTL}_{[k]}^{\downarrow}$. Let $\mathcal{N} = (Q, \delta)$ be a k-NCS. We are interested in describing witnesses for coverability. It suffices to construct a formula $\Phi_{\mathcal{N}}$ that characterises precisely those words that encode a *lossy* run from a configuration C_{start} to a configuration C_{end}. We call a sequence $C_0 C_1 \ldots C_n$ of configurations $C_j \in \mathcal{C}_{\mathcal{N}}$ a lossy run from C_0 to C_n if there is a sequence of intermediate configurations $C'_0 \ldots C'_{n-1}$ such that $C_i \succeq C'_i \to C_{i+1}$ for $0 \le i < n$. Then C_{end} is coverable from C_{start} if and only if there is a lossy run from C_{start} to some $C_n \succeq C_{end}$.

A configuration of a k-NCS is essentially a tree of depth $k + 1$ and can be encoded into a $[k]$-attributed data word as a frame of positions, similar as done to prove Proposition 10. We use an alphabet Σ where every letter $a \in \Sigma$ encodes, among other information, a $(k+1)$-tuple of states from Q, i.e., a possible branch in the tree. Then a sequence of such letters represents a set of branches that form a tree. The data valuations represent the information which of the branches share a common prefix. Further, this representation is interlaced: it only uses odd positions. The even position in between are used to represent an exact copy of the structure but with distinct data values. We use appropriate $LTL_{[k]}^{\downarrow}$ formulae to express this shape. Figure 3 shows an example.

To be able to formulate the effect of transition rules without using past-time operators we encode lossy runs *reversed*. Given that a data word encodes

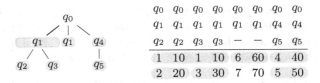

Fig. 3. Encoding of a 2-NCS configuration (l.) as [2]-attributed data word (r.). Instead of letters from Σ the encoded tuples of states from Q are displayed at every position.

a sequence $C_0 C_1 \ldots C_n$ of configurations as above we model the (reversed) control flow of the NCS $\mathcal{N} = (Q, \delta)$ by requiring that every configuration but for the last be annotated by some transition rule $t_j \in \delta$ for $0 \leq j < n$. The labelling is encoded into the letters from Σ and we impose that this transition sequence actually represents the reversal of a lossy run. That is, for every configuration C_j in the sequence (for $0 \leq j < n$) with annotated transition rule t_j there is a configuration C'_{j+1} (not necessarily in the sequence) such that $C_j \overset{t_j}{\leftarrow} C'_{j+1} \preceq C_{j+1}$.

For the transition t_j to be executed correctly (up to lossiness) we impose that every branch in C_j must have a corresponding branch in C_{j+1}. Yet, there may be branches in C_{j+1} that have no counterpart in C_j and were thus lost upon executing t_j. Shared data values are now used to establish a link between corresponding branches: for every even position in the frame that encodes C_j there must be an odd position in the consecutive frame (thus encoding C_{j+1}) with the same data valuation. To ensure that links are unambiguous we require that every data valuation occurs at most twice in the whole word. Depending on the effect of the current transition the letters of linked positions are related accordingly. E.g., for branches not affected at all by t_j the letters are enforced to be equal. This creates a chain of branches along the run that are identified: an odd position links forward to an even one, the consecutive odd position mimics it and links again forward.

Based on these ideas we can construct a formula satisfied precisely by words encoding a lossy run between particular configurations. The size of the formula is polynomial in the size of the NCS $\mathcal{N}$ and can be built by instantiating a set of patterns while iterating over the transitions and states of $\mathcal{N}$, requiring logarithmic space to control the iterations.

Theorem 13. *The coverability problem of k-NCS can be reduced in logarithmic space to $LTL^{\downarrow}_{[k]}$ satisfiability.*

5   Conclusion

By Theorem 12 together with Proposition 6 and Theorem 13 with Theorem 7 we can now characterise the complexity of $LTL^{\downarrow}_{tqo}$ fragments as follows.

Proposition 14. *Satisfiability of $LTL^{\downarrow}_A$ over a tree-quasi-ordered attribute set of depth k is in $\mathbf{F}_{\Omega_{2(k+1)}}$ and $\mathbf{F}_{\Omega_k}$-hard.*

Together with Theorem 5 this completes the proof of Theorem 3 stating that $\text{LTL}^{\downarrow}_{tqo}$ is the maximal decidable fragment of $\text{LTL}^{\downarrow}_{qo}$ and $\mathbf{F}_{\epsilon_0}$-complete. The result also shows that the complexity of the logic continues to increase strictly with the depth of the attribute ordering.

The logics ND-LTL$^{\pm}$ were shown to be decidable by reduction to NCS [5]. Our results thus provide a first upper bound for their satisfiability problem. Moreover, we derive significantly improved lower bounds by applying the construction to prove Theorem 13 analogously to ND-LTL^{+} and, with reversed encoding, to the past fragment ND-LTL^{-}. A subtle difference is that an additional attribute level is needed in order to express the global data-aware navigation needed to enforce the links between encoded configurations.

Corollary 15. *Satisfiability of ND-LTL$^{\pm}$ with $k + 1$ levels is in $\mathbf{F}_{\Omega_{2(k+1)}}$ and $\mathbf{F}_{\Omega_k}$-hard.*

PCS were proposed as a "master problem" for $\mathbf{F}_{\epsilon_0}$ [12] and indeed our upper complexity bounds for NCS rely on them. However, they are not well suited to prove our hardness results. This is due to PCS being based on sequences and the embedding ordering while NCS are only based on multisets and the subset ordering. In a sense, PCS generalise the concept of channels to multiple levels of nesting, whereas NCS generalise the concept of counters. Hence, we believe NCS are a valuable addition to the list of $\mathbf{F}_{\epsilon_0}$-complete models. They may serve well to prove lower bounds for formalisms that are like Freeze LTL more closely related to the concept of counting.

References

1. Alur, R., Henzinger, T.A.: A really temporal logic. J. ACM **41**(1), 181–204 (1994)
2. Björklund, H., Bojańczyk, M.: Shuffle expressions and words with nested data. In: Kučera, L., Kučera, A. (eds.) MFCS 2007. LNCS, vol. 4708, pp. 750–761. Springer, Heidelberg (2007)
3. Bojanczyk, M., David, C., Muscholl, A., Schwentick, T., Segoufin, L.: Two-variable logic on data words. ACM Trans. Comput. Log. **12**(4), 27 (2011)
4. Chambart, P., Schnoebelen, P.: The ordinal recursive complexity of lossy channel systems. In: LICS 2008, IEEE Symposium on Logic in Computer Science, IEEE Computer Society (2008)
5. Decker, N., Habermehl, P., Leucker, M., Thoma, D.: Ordered navigation on multi-attributed data words. In: Baldan, P., Gorla, D. (eds.) CONCUR 2014. LNCS, vol. 8704, pp. 497–511. Springer, Heidelberg (2014)
6. Demri, S., Figueira, D., Praveen, M.: Reasoning about data repetitions with counter systems. In: LICS 2013, ACM/IEEE Symposium on Logic in Computer Science, IEEE Computer Society (2013)
7. Demri, S., Lazic, R.: LTL with the freeze quantifier and register automata. ACM Trans. Comput. Log. **10**(3) (2009)
8. Demri, S., Lazic, R., Nowak, D.: On the freeze quantifier in constraint LTL: decidability and complexity. In: International Symposium on Temporal Representation and Reasoning (TIME 2005), IEEE Computer Society (2005)

9. Figueira, D.: Alternating register automata on finite words and trees. Log. Meth. Comput. Sci. **8**(1) (2012)

10. Fitting, M.: Modal logics between propositional and first-order. J. Log. Comput. **12**(6), 1017–1026 (2002)

11. Goranko, V.: Hierarchies of modal and temporal logics with reference pointers. J. Logic Lang. Inf. **5**(1), 1–24 (1996)

12. Haase, C., Schmitz, S., Schnoebelen, P.: The power of priority channel systems. Logical Meth. Comput. Sci. **10**(4) (2014)

13. Henzinger, T.A.: Half-order modal logic: how to prove real-time properties. In: ACM Symposium on Principles of Distributed Computing, ACM (1990)

14. Kara, A., Schwentick, T., Zeume, T.: Temporal logics on words with multiple data values. In: FSTTCS 2010, IARCS Annual Conference on Foundations of Software Technology and Theoretical Computer Science, LIPIcs, vol. 8, Schloss Dagstuhl - Leibniz-Zentrum für Informatik (2010)

15. Lazić, R.S.: Safely freezing LTL. In: Arun-Kumar, S., Garg, N. (eds.) FSTTCS 2006. LNCS, vol. 4337, pp. 381–392. Springer, Heidelberg (2006)

16. Leroux, J., Schmitz, S.: Reachability in vector addition systems demystified. In: LICS 2015, ACM/IEEE Symposium on Logic in Computer Science, IEEE Computer Society (2015)

17. Lisitsa, A., Potapov, I.: Temporal logic with predicate lambda-abstraction. In: International Symposium on Temporal Representation and Reasoning (TIME 2005), IEEE Computer Society (2005)

18. Lomazova, I.A., Schnoebelen, P.: Some decidability results for nested petri nets. In: Bjorner, D., Broy, M., Zamulin, A.V. (eds.) PSI 1999. LNCS, vol. 1755, pp. 208–220. Springer, Heidelberg (2000)

19. Rosa-Velardo, F.: Ordinal recursive complexity of unordered data nets. Technical report TR-4-14, Departamento de Sistemas Informáticos y Computación, Universidad Complutense de Madrid (2014)

20. Schmitz, S.: Complexity hierarchies beyond elementary. CoRR abs/1312.5686 (2013). http://arxiv.org/abs/1312.5686

21. Schnoebelen, P.: Revisiting Ackermann-Hardness for lossy counter machines and reset petri nets. In: Hliněný, P., Kučera, A. (eds.) MFCS 2010. LNCS, vol. 6281, pp. 616–628. Springer, Heidelberg (2010)

Regular Transformations of Data Words Through Origin Information

Antoine Durand-Gasselin[1] and Peter Habermehl[2][(✉)]

[1] Aix Marseille Université, CNRS, Centrale Marseille, LIF UMR 7279,
Marseille, France
`Antoine.Durand-Gasselin@centrale-marseille.fr`
[2] IRIF, Univ. Paris Diderot & CNRS, Paris, France
`Peter.Habermehl@liafa.univ-paris-diderot.fr`

Abstract. We introduce a class of transformations of finite data words generalizing the well-known class of regular finite string transformations described by MSO-definable transductions of finite strings. These transformations map input words to output words whereas our transformations handle data words where each position has a letter from a finite alphabet and a data value. Each data value appearing in the output has as origin a data value in the input. As is the case for regular transformations we show that our class of transformations has equivalent characterizations in terms of deterministic two-way and streaming string transducers.

1 Introduction

The theory of transformations of strings (or words) over a finite alphabet has attracted a lot of interest recently. Courcelle [8] defined finite string transformations in a logical way using Monadic second-order definable graph transductions. Then, a breakthrough was achieved in [9] where it was shown that these transformations are equivalent to those definable by deterministic two-way finite transducers on finite words. In [1] deterministic streaming string transducers (SST) on finite words were introduced. This model is one-way but it is equipped with string variables allowing to store words. It is equivalent [1] to the deterministic two-way finite transducers and to MSO-definable transformations. Interestingly, the motivation behind SST was the more powerful SDST model [2]. SDST work on data words, i.e. words composed of couples of letters from a finite alphabet and an infinite data domain. However, they do not have the same nice theoretical properties as SST, for example they are not closed under composition because SDST have data variables allowing to store data values and *compare* data values with each other. Furthermore, there is no equivalent logical characterization.

This work was supported in part by the VECOLIB project (ANR-14-CE28-0018) and by the PACS project (ANR-14-CE28-0002).
A. Durand-Gasselin—Part of this work was done while this author was at Technical University Munich.

© Springer-Verlag Berlin Heidelberg 2016
B. Jacobs and C. Löding (Eds.): FOSSACS 2016, LNCS 9634, pp. 285–300, 2016.
DOI: 10.1007/978-3-662-49630-5_17

In this paper, analogously to the case of string transformations of finite words, we obtain a class of transformations of finite data words which has an MSO characterization as well as equivalent characterizations in terms of deterministic two-way transducers and streaming transducers. To achieve this, we allow storing of data values in the transducers but not comparison.

As an example we consider the transformation taking a finite input word over $\{\#, a, b\}$ starting and finishing with a $\#$, together with associated data values from the integers, like $\left(\begin{smallmatrix}\#ab\#abb\#\\1\,2\,4\,5\,6\,7\,1\,4\end{smallmatrix}\right)$ and produces as output the word where (1) $\#$'s are left unchanged, and between successive $\#$'s (2) words w in $\{a, b\}^*$ are transformed into $w^R w$ where w^R denotes the reverse image of w, and (3) the data value associated to each a is the value of the first $\#$ and the value for b's is the value of the second $\#$. So, the output for the example word is $\left(\begin{smallmatrix}\#baab\#bbaabb\#\\1\,5\,1\,1\,5\,5\,4\,4\,5\,5\,4\,4\,4\end{smallmatrix}\right)$.

It is clear how a deterministic two-way transducer with the ability of storing data values can realize this transformation: it stores the first data value (1) in a *data variable* while outputting $\left(\begin{smallmatrix}\#\\1\end{smallmatrix}\right)$, then goes to the second $\#$, stores the corresponding data value (5) in a second data variable, and goes back one by one while producing $\left(\begin{smallmatrix}ba\\5\,1\end{smallmatrix}\right)$. Then, it turns around at the first $\#$, goes again to the second $\#$ producing $\left(\begin{smallmatrix}ab\\1\,5\end{smallmatrix}\right)$ and restarts the same process.

Now, to realize this transformation with a deterministic streaming string transducer one has to make with the fact that they can only go through the input word once from left to right. Nevertheless we will introduce a model which can realize the described transformation: in between two $\#'s$ it stores the so-far read string and its reverse in a *data word variable*. As the data value of the second $\#'$ is not known in the beginning it uses a *data parameter* p instead. For example, before the second $\#$, the stored word will be $\left(\begin{smallmatrix}baab\\p11p\end{smallmatrix}\right)$. When reading the second $\#$, it then replaces p everywhere by 5 and stores the result in another data word variable. The same repeats for the rest of the word until the end is reached and the output contained in a data word variable.

The same transformation can also be described logically. To define transformations on data words, a natural choice would be to use transducers with origin information and their corresponding MSO transductions studied in [6]. Basically, their semantics also takes into account information about the origin of a letter in the output, i.e. the position in the input from which it originates. Obviously, this can be generalized to data values by defining the data value of each output position as the data value in the input position from where the output originated. This definition is however not expressive enough to handle our example, since an input position can only be the origin of a bounded number of output positions but the data values attached to (unboundedly many) a's and b's between two successive $\#$'s come from the same two input positions.

Therefore, in this paper, we first introduce a logical characterization of word transformations with generalized origin information. Our logical characterization is an extension of classical MSO transductions with an additional functional MSO defined relation that maps each element of the interpretation (symbols of the output word) to an element of the interpreted structure (symbols of the input word). This generalization naturally defines transformations of data words;

the data value at a given position of the output is the data value carried at the corresponding position in the input. This suffices to define the previously described example transformation.

Interestingly, our class of transformations is captured by a natural model of deterministic two-way transducers extended with data variables whose values can neither be tested nor compared. By adding data word variables (as in streaming string transducers) containing data values and parameters, we then manage, while preserving determinism, to restrict that model to a one-way model. Data parameters are placeholders for data values which can be stored in data word variables and later replaced by concrete data values. We show that this one-way model can be captured by MSO to achieve the equivalence of all three models.

2 MSO Interpretations with MSO Origin Relation

2.1 Words, Strings and Data Words

For S a set of symbols, we denote by S^* the set of finite words (i.e. the set of finite sequences of elements of S) over S. Given a word w, we can refer to its length ($|w|$), its first symbol ($w[0]$), the symbol at some position $i < |w|$ in the word ($w[i]$), some of its subwords (e.g. $w[i{:}j]$ with $0 \le i \le j < |w|$, the subword between positions i and j) etc. In this paper, we only consider finite words.

An alphabet (typically denoted Σ or Γ) is a finite set of symbols. Furthermore, we use a (potentially infinite) set of *data values* called Δ. In the sequel, we use *string* to refer to a (finite) word over a finite alphabet and *data word* to refer to a word over the cartesian product of a finite alphabet and a set of data values. Since symbols of data words consist of a letter (from the finite alphabet) and a data value, we can naturally refer to the data value at some position in a data word, or the string corresponding to some data word. Conversely a string together with a mapping from its position to Δ forms a data word.

A string w (over alphabet Σ) is naturally seen as a directed node-labeled graph (rather than considering edges only connecting two successive positions, we take the transitive closure: thus the graph is a finite linear order). The graph is then seen as an interpreted relational structure whose domain is the positions of w, with a binary edge predicate $<$, and a monadic predicate for each letter of Σ. We denote $\mathcal{S}_\Sigma$ the signature consisting of $<_{/2}$ and $\sigma_{/1}$ for each $\sigma \in \Sigma$.

Any string over alphabet Σ is an interpretation over a finite domain of $\mathcal{S}_\Sigma$, conversely any interpretation of $\mathcal{S}_\Sigma$ is a string if (1) its domain is finite, (2) $<$ defines a linear order and (3) at every position exactly one monadic predicate holds. We remark that (2) and (3) can be expressed as monadic second order (MSO) sentences. Two interpretations are isomorphic iff they are the same string.

With this logic based approach we have a very simple classical characterization of regular languages: a language L over alphabet Σ is regular iff there exists an MSO sentence φ (over signature $\mathcal{S}_\Sigma$) such that the set of interpretations of $\mathcal{S}_\Sigma$ with finite domain satisfying φ is the set of strings in L.

2.2 MSO Interpretations

Using this model theoretic characterization of strings, we can define a class of transformations of strings. For the sake of clarity we consider transformations of strings over alphabet Σ to strings over alphabet Γ. We now define an MSO interpretation of $\mathcal{S}_\Gamma$ in $\mathcal{S}_\Sigma$, as $|\Gamma| + 2$ MSO formulas over signature $\mathcal{S}_\Sigma$: $\varphi_<$ with two free first-order variables and φ_{dom} and $(\varphi_\gamma)_{\gamma \in \Gamma}$ with one free first-order variable. Any interpretation $\mathcal{I}_\Sigma$ (of the signature $\mathcal{S}_\Sigma$) defines an interpretation of the structure $\mathcal{S}_\Gamma$: its domain is the set of elements of the domain of $\mathcal{I}_\Sigma$ satisfying φ_{dom} in $\mathcal{I}_\Sigma$, and the interpretation of the predicates over that domain is given by the truth value of each of the other MSO formulas.

An important remark is that if the interpretation $\mathcal{I}_\Sigma$ has finite domain, then so will the constructed interpretation of $\mathcal{S}_\Gamma$. Also, since we can express in MSO (over the signature $\mathcal{S}_\Gamma$) that the output structure is a string (with (2) and (3)), we can also express in MSO over the signature $\mathcal{S}_\Sigma$ that the output structure is a string, hence we can decide whether for any input string our MSO interpretation produces a string.

Above, we presented the core idea of Courcelle's definition [8] of MSO graph transductions. Courcelle further introduces the idea of interpreting the output structure in several copies of the input structures. To define such a transduction, we need to fix a *finite* set C of copies, the domain of the output structure will thus be a subset of the cartesian product of the domain of the input structure with the set of copies. The transduction consists of $|C|^2 + (|\Gamma| + 1)|C| + 1$ MSO formulas over the input structure:

- the sentence φ_{indom} that states whether the input structure is in the input domain of the transduction,
- formulas φ_{dom}^c (with one free first-order variable) for each c in C, each stating whether a node x in copy c is a node of the output structure,
- formulas φ_γ^c (also with one free first-order variable), for each $c \in C$ and each $\alpha \in \Gamma$ which states whether a node x in copy c is labelled by α,
- and formulas $\varphi_<^{c,d}$ (with two free first-order variables, namely x, y) that states whether there exists an edge from x in copy c to y in copy d.

The semantics of these transformations naturally provides a notion of origin: by definition a node of the output structure is a position x in the copy c of the input structure (such that $\varphi_{dom}^c(x)$ is true).

2.3 Transduction of Data Words

Data words cannot be represented as finite structures (over a finite signature) but they can be seen as strings together with a mapping of positions to data values.

To define a data word transduction, we take a string transduction that we extend with an MSO relation between positions in the input word and positions in the output word. Formally we extend the definition of MSO transduction with $|C|$ MSO formulas (with two free first-order variables) $\varphi_{orig}^c(x, y)$, which we call the origin formulas, stating that position x in copy c (in the output string) corresponds to position y in the input string. We further impose that for any input word in the domain of the transformation and any x and $c \in C$ such that x in copy c is in the output of the transformation, there exists exactly one y that validates $\varphi^c(x, y)$. We remark that this restriction can be ensured in MSO (over the input structure). Then, the data value at each output position is defined to be the data value at the corresponding input position.

We call MSOT the class of string transformations defined as MSO interpretations, and MSOT+O the class of data word transformation defined as MSO interpretations together with origin formulas. We remark that this definition of origin captures the usual origin information in the sense of [6] by fixing $\varphi^c_{orig}(x, y) \equiv (x = y)$.

2.4 The Running Example

Two copies suffice to define the transformation for the running example. For clarity, we do not represent the ordering relation $<$, but rather the successor relation.

φ_{indom} states the input word starts and ends with a #. $\varphi^1_{dom}(x)$ is true (every node in the first copy is part of the output), while $\varphi^2_{dom}(x) = \neg\#(x)$ tests the letter in the input at that position is not a #. The labeling formulas are the identity $(\varphi^1_a(x) = a(x),...)$ —the behaviour of the formula outside the output domain is considered irrelevant. $\varphi^{1,1}_<(x, y) = x < y$, and $\varphi^{2,2}_<(x, y)$ checks if there is a #-labeled position between position x and y (in the input): if so it ensures that $x < y$, if not it ensures $x > y$. $\varphi^{1,2}(x, y)$ and $\varphi^{1,2}(x, y)$ also distinguish cases whether there is a #-labeled position between x and y or not.

The origin information MSO formulas happen here to be the same for the two copies $\varphi^i(x, y)$ making cases on the letter x: if it is an a (resp. a b) it ensures y is the first #-labeled position before (resp. after) position x.

2.5 Properties

Defining word transformations through MSO interpretations yields some nice properties:

Theorem 1. *MSOT+O is closed under composition.*

Proof. MSOT is naturally closed under composition: given 2 mso transductions T_1 and T_2, (using C_1 and C_2 copies) we can define $T_1 \circ T_2$ as the MSO-interpretation T_1 of the MSO-interpretation T_2 of the original structure, which is an MSO-interpretation over $C_1 \times C_2$ copies.

In order to show the compositional closure of MSOT+O, it now suffices to define the origin information for the composition of two transductions T_1 and T_2 in MSOT+O. It is clear how to define formulas φ^c_{orig} that relate a position in the output with a position in the input, from the origin formulas of T_1 and T_2. We just need to show these origin formulas are functional; a fact that we easily derive from the functionality of the origin formulas of T_1 and T_2.

The (MSO)-typechecking problem of a transformation is defined as follows:

INPUT: Two MSO sentences $\varphi_{pre}, \varphi_{post}$ and an MSOT+O transformation T
OUTPUT: Does $w \models \varphi_{pre}$ imply that $T(w) \models \varphi_{post}$?

It consists in checking whether some property on the input implies a property on the output, those properties are here expressed in MSO.

Theorem 2. *MSO-typechecking of MSOT+O is decidable.*

Proof. An MSO formula can not reason about data values. Therefore it is sufficient to show that MSO-typechecking of MSOT is decidable. Since the output is defined as an MSO interpretation of the input, it is easy to convert an MSO formula on the output into an MSO formula on the input. We just need to check whether the input property implies that converted output property, on any input word, which is checking the universality of an MSO formula over finite strings.

2.6 MSO k-types

Since we present a generalisation of the classical MSO string transductions, the machine models that are expressively equivalent to our logical definition will be extensions of the classical machine models.

To show later that these logical transformations are captured by finite state machines, we use the notion of MSO k-types. We crucially use this notion (more precisely Theorem 3) to prove in Sect. 3 that we only need a finite number of data variables (Lemma 1) to store data values originating from the input.

Given a string w, we define its k-type as the set of MSO sentences of quantifier depth at most k (i.e. the maximum nesting of quantifiers is at most k) that hold for w. A crucial property is that the set of MSO k-types (which we denote Θ_k) is finite and defines an equivalence relation over strings which is a monoïd congruence of finite index. We refer the reader to [11] for more details.

These k-indexed congruences satisfy the following property: two k-equivalent strings will satisfy the same quantifier depth k MSO sentence.

We can extend this notion to MSO formulas with free first-order variables.

Theorem 3. *Given two strings w_1 and w_2 each with two distinguished positions x_1, y_1 and x_2, y_2. $(w_1, (x_1, y_1))$ and $(w_2, (x_2, y_2))$ satisfy the same MSO formulas with quantifier depth at most k and two free first order variables if:*

- *$w_1[x_1] = w_2[x_2]$ and $w_1[y_1] = w_2[y_2]$*
- *x_1, y_1 and x_2, y_2 occur in the same order in w_1 and w_2 (with the special case that if $x_1 = y_1$, then $x_2 = y_2$).*

– *The k-types of the two (strict) prefixes are the same, and the k-types of the two (strict) suffixes are the same, as well as the k-types of the two (strict) subwords between the two positions.*

Proof. Immediate with Ehrenfeucht-Fraïssé games.

3   Two-Way Transducers on Data Words

Two-way deterministic transducers on strings are known to be equivalent to MSO string transductions [9]. Since we process data words and output data words, we will naturally extend this model with a finite set of *data variables*. Notice that the data values in the input word do not influence the finite string part of the output. Therefore the transition function of the transducer may not perform any test on the values of those data variables. However the output word will contain some (if not all) data values of the input word, therefore the model may store some data value appearing in the input word in some variable, and when an output symbol is produced, this is done (deterministically) by combining some letter of the output alphabet together with the data value contained in some data variable.

We start by defining the classical two-way deterministic finite-state transducers (2dft) (with input alphabet Σ and output alphabet Γ) as a deterministic two-way automaton whose transitions are labeled by strings over Γ. The image of a string w by a 2dft A is defined (if w admits a run) as the concatenation of all the labels of the transitions along that run.

Definition 1. *A 2dft is a tuple $(\Sigma, \Gamma, Q, q_0, F, \delta)$ where:*

– *Σ and Γ are respectively the finite input and output alphabets ($\vdash, \dashv \notin \Sigma$)*
– *Q is the finite set of states, q_0 the initial state, and F the set of accepting states*
– *$\delta : Q \times (\Sigma \cup \{\vdash, \dashv\}) \to Q \times \{+1, -1\} \times \Gamma^*$ is the (two-way, Γ^*-labeled) transition function*

A (finite) run of a 2dft A over some string w is a finite sequence ρ of pairs of control states Q and positions in $[-1, |w|]$ (where -1 is supposed to be labeled by $\vdash$ and $|w|$ by $\dashv$), such that: $\rho(0) = (0, q_0)$, $\rho(|\rho|-1) \in \mathbb{N} \times F$ and at any position $k < |\rho| - 1$ in the run, if we denote $\rho(k) = (i_k, q_k)$ and $\rho(k+1) = i_{k+1}, q_{k+1}$, we have that $\delta(q_k, w(i_k)) = (q_{k+1}, i_{k+1} - i_k, u_{k+1})$ for some $u_{k+1} \in \Gamma^*$. Informally $+1$ corresponds to moving to the right in the input string and -1 to moving to the left. The output of A over w is simply the string $u_1 u_2 \ldots u_{|\rho|-1}$. We denote $T(A)$ the (partial) transduction from Σ^* to Γ^* defined by A.

Notice that not every input string admits a finite run (since the transducer might get stuck or loop), but if w admits a finite run, it is unique and has length at most $|Q|(|w|+2)$, as this run visits any position at most $|Q|$ times. Therefore a run can also be defined as a mapping from positions of $\vdash w \dashv$ to $Q^{\leq |Q|}$ (sequences of states of length at most $|Q|$).

The next theorem states the equivalence between transformations defined by this two-way machine model and the logical definition of string transformations.

Theorem 4 [9]. *Any string transformation from Σ^* to Γ^* defined by a 2dft can be defined as an MSO interpretation of Γ^* in Σ^* and vice versa.*

Now we define our two-way machine model, *two-way deterministic finite-state transducer with data variables* (2dftv) for data word transformations. We simply extend the 2dft by adding some data variables whose values are deterministically updated at each step of the machine.

Definition 2. *A 2dftv is a tuple $(\Sigma, \Gamma, \Delta, Q, q_0, F, V, \mu, \delta)$ where:*

- *Σ and Γ are respectively the input and output alphabets ($\vdash, \dashv \notin \Sigma$),*
- *Δ is the (infinite) data domain,*
- *Q is the finite set of states, q_0 the initial state, and F the set of accepting states,*
- *V a finite set of data variables with a designated variable curr $\in V$,*
- *$\mu : Q \times \Sigma \times (V \setminus \{curr\}) \to V$ is the data variable update function,*
- *$\delta : Q \times (\Sigma \cup \{\vdash, \dashv\}) \to Q \times \{+1, -1\} \times (\Gamma \times V)^*$ is the (two-way, $(\Gamma \times V)^*$-labeled) transition function.*

We can define the semantics of a 2dftv like the semantics of an 2dft by extending the notion of run. Here, a run is labeled by positions and states but also by a valuation of the variables, i.e. a partial function β which assigns to variables from V values from Δ. This partial function is updated in each step (while reading a symbol different from the endmarkers $\vdash$ or $\dashv$) according to μ and additionally to the variable *curr* the current data value in the input is assigned. The output is obtained by substituting the data variables appearing in the label of the transition relation by their value according to β which we suppose to be always defined (this can be checked easily). Then, naturally a 2dftv defines a transduction from words over $\Sigma \times \Delta$ to words over $\Gamma \times \Delta$.

We call 2DFTV the class of all data word transductions definable by a 2dftv.

Theorem 5. *MSOT+O is included in 2DFTV.*

The challenge to show the theorem is to be able to extend the MSOT to 2DFT proof from [9], so as to be able to also carry in data variables all the necessary data values needed in the output.

We recall the key features in the proof of [9]. First, 2dft's are explicitly shown to be composable [7], which gives regular look-around (the ability to test if the words to the left and to the right of the reading head are in some regular languages) for free: a first pass rewrites the input right-to-left and adds the regular look-ahead, and the second pass re-reverses that word while adding the regular look-back. It is then possible (by reading that regular look-around) to implement MSO-jumps. Given an MSO formula φ with 2 free variables, an MSO-jump φ from position x consists in directly going to a position y such that $\varphi(x, y)$ holds. Using MSO-jumps 2dft can then simulate MSO transformations.

We show thereafter how to extend such a 2dft that takes as input the (look-around enriched) string and produces its image, to a 2dftv. The proof is then in three steps: first we show that a finite number of data variables is needed, then we briefly describe how to update those data variables: each transition of the 2dft being possibly replaced by a "fetching" of exactly one data variable, and finally it is easy to see how to compose the preprocessing 2dft with that produced 2dftv.

To store only a finite number of data values, we will only store those which originate from a position on one side of the currently processed position and that are used on the other side of the currently processed position. The following lemma ensures a bound on the number of data variables.

Lemma 1. *Let w be a data word, x a position in w, and T a transducer. Denote k the quantifier depth of origin formulas. There are at most $|\Sigma||\Theta_k|^2$ positions $z > x$ such that there exists a position $y < x$ in some copy c such that $\varphi^c_{orig}(y, z)$ holds, i.e. that the data value carried by y in copy c is that of z.*

Proof. By contradiction, we use the pigeon hole principle. We can find two distinct positions z and z' such that the type of the subword between x and z and x and z' is the same, and the type of the suffix from z is the same as the type of the suffix from z'.

Let y a position, left of x where the data value of z is used, thus $\varphi^c_{orig}(y, z)$ holds. We apply Theorem 3 to $(w, (y, z))$ and $(w, (y, z'))$ and therefore $\varphi^c_{orig}(y, z')$ also holds, which contradicts the functionality of the relation φ_{orig}.   □

It seems appropriate to name our data variables using MSO types. The data variables are thus $\Sigma \times \Theta_k \times \Theta_k \times \{l, r\}$, $(\sigma, \tau_1, \tau_2, l)$ denoting the data variable containing the data value from the position y (in the input word which is labeled by σ), left (l) of current positions, such that the prefix up to y has type τ_1, and the subword between y and current position has type τ_2.

With an appropriate value of k' (greater than k) the knowledge of the k'-types of the prefix and suffix of the word from the currently processed position, informs us for each data variable whether it contains a value or not, whether it is used at the current position and most importantly to which data variable the value should be transfered when a transition to the right (or the left) is taken.

Notice that when the 2dft performs a transition to the right, four things can happen (only 2 and 3 are mutually exclusive):

1. A data value from a previous position was used for the last time and should be discarded
2. The current data value has been used earlier and will not be used later (and should be discarded)
3. The current data value may be used later and was not used before (and thus should be stored)
4. A data value from a next position is first used (and thus should be stored)

The challenging part is the case (4), as we would need to fetch the data value which we suddenly need to track. The new value is easily fetched through an MSO jump (to the right) which is a feature introduced by [9] allowing to jump to a position in the input specified by an MSO formula. In turn this jump is implemented (thanks to the look-around carried by the input word) as a one-way automaton that goes to the right until it reaches the position where the data value is, and a one-way automaton that goes (left) from that position back to the original position. The challenge is to be able to return to the current position. Thanks to our definition, we can also describe an MSO jump that allows the return: if we had to fetch a new data value, it is because it was *first* used at the position we want to jump back to. Such a position can easily be expressed uniquely with an MSO formula from the position we fetched our data value. We remark that we cannot fetch data values on a per-needed basis (an MSO jump to the position where the data is, is possible, but going back with an MSO-jump is not), which indicates we need data variables.

In the 2dft, any transition for which case (4) happens (this information is contained in the look-around) is replaced by two automata that go fetch (and back) that newly needed data value.

Finally we present how this conversion should work on our example. We need to consider 1-types. Θ_1 is 2^Σ: each characterizing exactly which letters are present in the word. This means hundreds of data variables, but at any point for this transformation, no more than 2 data values will be stored. So long as we read a's we should not have fetched the data value of the following $\#$-labeled position. When a b is read, we fetch that data value and then we can return back to our original position: it is the first position (after the last $\#$) in the word that contains a b.

4   One-Way Transducers

4.1   Streaming String Transducers with Data Variables and Parameters

We first define sstvp, i.e. streaming string transducers with data variables and data parameters. They have the features of streaming string transducers [1,2] extended with *data variables* and *data parameters*. Notice that in contrast to the streaming data-string transducers from [2] sstvp can not compare data values with each other.

Intuitively, sstvp read deterministically data words and compute an output data word. They are equipped with data variables which store data values, parameters which are placeholders for data values and data word variables containing data words which in addition to data values can also contain data parameters. These data parameters can be replaced by data values subsequently.

Definition 3. *A sstvp is a tuple* $(\Sigma, \Delta, \Gamma, Q, X, V, P, q_0, v_0, \delta, \Omega)$ *where:*

- Σ *and* Γ *are respectively the input and output alphabets,*
- Δ *is the (infinite) data domain,*
- Q *is the finite set of states and* $q_0 \in Q$ *the initial state,*
- X *is the finite set of data word variables,*

- V is the finite set of data variables with a designated variable $curr \in V$,
- P is the finite set of data parameters $(P \cap \Delta = \emptyset)$,
- $v_0 : X \to (\Gamma \times P)^*$ is a function representing the initial valuation of the data word variables.
- δ is a (deterministic) transition function: $\delta(q, \sigma) = (q', \mu_V, \mu_X, \mu_P)$ where:
  - $\mu_V : (V \setminus \{curr\}) \to V$ is the update function of data variables,
  - $\mu_X : X \to (X \cup (\Gamma \times (V \cup P)))^*$, is the update function of data word variables,
  - $\mu_P : P \times X \to P \cup V$ is the parameter assignment function (dependent on the data word variable).
- $\Omega : Q \to ((\Gamma \times V) \cup X)^*$ is the partial output function.

The streaming string transducers of [1,2] were defined by restricting updates to be *copyless*, i.e. each data word variable can appear only once in an update μ_X. Here, we relax this syntactic restriction along the lines of [5] by considering only 1-bounded sstvp's: informally, at any position the content of some data word variable may only occur once in the output. This allows to duplicate the value of some data word variable in two distinct data word variables, but the value of these variables can not be later combined. It is clear that this condition can be checked and a 1-bounded sstvp can be transformed into a syntactically copyless sstvp one [5].

Now, we define the semantics of sstvp. A valuation of data variables β_V for an sstvp is a partial function assigning data values to data variables. A valuation of data word variables β_X is a function assigning words over $\Gamma \times (\Delta \cup P)$ to data word variables. Then, a *configuration* of an sstvp consists of a control state and a valuation of data and word variables (β_V, β_X). The initial configuration is (q_0, β_V^0, v_0), where β_V^0 is the empty function. When processing a position i in the input word in some state q, first $curr$ is set to the data value at that position in the input, then the data word variables are updated according to μ_X, then the data words contained in data word variables are substituted according to μ_P and finally data variables are updated according to μ_V.

Formally, if $\delta(q, a) = (q', \mu_V, \mu_X, \mu_P)$, then from (q, β_V, β_X) at position i with a letter (a, d) one goes to $(q', \beta_V'', \beta_X''')$ where:

- $\beta_V'' = \beta_V' \cdot \mu_V$, where $\beta_V' = \beta_V[curr \mapsto d]$.
- $\beta_X' = \beta_X \cdot \mu_X$

$$\beta_X''(x) = \beta_X'(x)[v \leftarrow \beta_V'(v)]_{v \in V}$$

$$\beta_X'''(x) = \beta_X''(x) \left[p \leftarrow \begin{cases} \mu_P(x, p) \text{ if } \mu_P(x, p) \in P \\ \beta_V'(\mu_P(x, p)) \text{ if } \mu_P(x, p) \in V \end{cases} \right]$$

For each two data word variables x, x', we say that x at position i flows to x' at position $i + 1$ if $x \in \mu_X(x')$. The notion of flow can be easily extended by transitivity, the copylessness restriction forbids that the value of some data word variable at some position i flows more than once to some data word variable at position $j > i$. When reaching the end of the input word in a configuration (q, β),

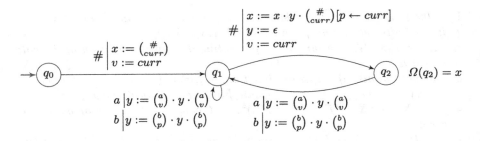

Fig. 1. The sstvp for the running example

a sstvp produces $\beta(\Omega(q))$ if $\Omega(q)$ is defined. Then, naturally a sstvp S defines a transduction from words in $\Sigma \times \Delta$ to words in $\Gamma \times \Delta$.

The sstvp for our running example is given in Fig. 1. All data word variables are initialized with the empty word. By convention, a variable which is not explicitly updated is unchanged. We omit these updates for readability.

Theorem 6. *Equivalence of two sstvp is decidable.*

To prove this theorem we can generalize the proof of decidability of equivalence of SST [2], a reduction to reachability in a non-deterministic one-counter machine. Given two transducers we choose non-deterministically an input string, and one conflicting position in each of the two images (of the transducers): either they are labeled by different letters, or with attached data value originating from two distinct positions in the input word. We keep track in the counter of the difference between the number of produced symbols which will be part of each output before the corresponding conflicting position. Therefore, if the counter reaches 0 at the last letter of the input, the two transducers are different.

We call SSTVP the class of all data word transductions definable by a sstvp.

4.2   From Two-Way to One-Way Transducers

Theorem 7. *2DFTV is included in SSTVP.*

Proof. (Sketch) We use ideas of [1] (based itself on Shepherdson's translation from 2DFA to DFA [10]) where two-way transducers are translated into streaming string transducers. As they translate two-way transducers to copyless streaming string transducers they have to go through an intermediate model called heap-based transducers. Since we relax the copylessness restriction to 1-boundedness we can directly translate 2dftv to sstvp. Furthermore, we have to take care of the contents of data variables of the 2dftv. For that purpose we use data variables and data parameters of the sstvp.

Since an sstvp does only one left-to-right pass on the input word, we cannot revisit any position. As we process a position we need to store all relevant information about that position possibly being later reprocessed by the two-way transducer. The two-way transducer may process a position multiple times (each time in a different state) each time with a different valuation of data variables and producing some different word: for each state, we need to store in an appropriate data word variable the corresponding production, the valuation of data variables being abstracted with data parameters. Notice that not all these data word variables will be used in the output. Given a 2dftv $A = (\Sigma, \Gamma, \Delta, Q, q_0, F, V, \mu, \delta)$, over which we assume all accepting runs end on the last symbol, we define an sstvp $B = (\Sigma, \Gamma, \Delta, Q', X, V', P, q_0', v_0, \delta', \Omega)$ as follows:

- $Q' = Q \times [Q \to (Q \times 2^V)]$

A state of the one-way transducer consists of a state of the two-way transducer and a partial mapping from states to a pair of a state and a set of variables. As a position $i+1$ is processed, the state of B contains the following information: in which state A first reaches position i and for each state q of A what would be the state of A when it reaches for the first time position $i+1$ had it started processing position i from state q: this part is the standard Shepherdson's construction. The function is partial, as from position i from some states A might never reach position $i + 1$ (getting stuck).

We remark that along the subrun from position i (in state q) to position $i+1$, the A might store some data values in some data variables. The set of data variables denotes the set of data variables the two-way transducer has updated along that run.

- $X = x_l \cup \{x_q \mid q \in Q\}$

At position i, variable x_l will store the word produced by A until it first reaches position i. Variable x_q will store the word produced from position i in state q until position $i + 1$ is first reached.

- $V' = V \cup \{v_q \mid v \in V, q \in Q\}$

At position $i + 1$, data variable v will contain the value of variable v of A as it first reaches position $i + 1$. Assume that B reaches position i in some state (q, f) with $f(q') = (q'', W)$, and $v \in W$. Then variable $v_{q'}$ will contain the last value stored in v when A processes from position i in state q' until it first reaches position $i + 1$.

- $P = \{p_{v,q} \mid v \in V, q \in Q\}$

At position i, parameter $p_{v,q}$ will be present only in data word variable x_q, representing that along the run of A the data value from data variable v at position i in state q was output before $i + 1$ was first reached. Such a symbol needs to be present in x_q, but the data value is not yet known, hence it is abstracted by the data parameter $p_{v,q}$.

It is then easy to see how to define q_0' and δ' so as to preserve these invariants. As B can not see $\dashv$, B must maintain the possible output in an extra variable, where it is supposed that the next symbol would be $\dashv$.

We now detail an example (see Fig. 2) so as to give an intuition how $\delta'(q, \sigma)$ is built: we will specifically focus on the value of x_{q_1}. We denote f the second component of q and we assume that $f(q_2) = (q_3, \{v_1, v_2\})$, $f(q_4) = (q_5, \{v_2, v_3\})$.

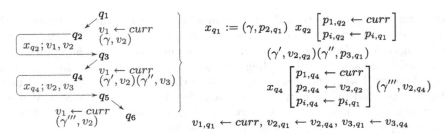

Fig. 2. An example to illustrate the transformation from A to B.

Furthermore, we assume that in A, $\delta(q_1, \sigma) = (q_2, -1, (\gamma, v_2))$ and $\delta(q_3, \sigma) = (q_4, -1, (\gamma', v_2)(\gamma'', v_3))$ and finally that $\delta(q_5, \sigma) = (q_6, +1, (\gamma''', v_2))$. Also reading σ in q_1 and q_3 assigns the current data value to v_1 (i.e. $\mu(q_1, \sigma, v_1) = \mu(q_3, \sigma, v_1) = curr$), other data variables are not modified (i.e. $\mu(q_1, \sigma, v_i) = \mu(q_3, \sigma, v_i) = v_i$).

By the aforementioned invariants, from state q_1, A will first reach the following position in state q_6 (from the σ-labeled position in state q_1, it first goes left, reaches it again in state q_3, goes left again, arrives in state q_5 and then moves to the right in state q_6).

If we abstract the data values, the content of the data word variable x_{q_1} will thus be $(\gamma, ?) x_{q_2} (\gamma', ?)(\gamma'', ?) x_{q_4} (\gamma''', ?)$. Now we detail data attached to the produced letters, and the parameter assignments in the data word variables:

γ will be given the data parameter p_{2,q_1}.

In x_{q_2}: since a data value is assigned to v_1 between q_1 and q_2, p_{1,q_1} should be substituted by that data value (which is $curr$) in x_{q_2}. Other parameters in x_{q_2} (which are all of the form p_{i,q_2}) are substituted by the corresponding p_{i,q_1}.

γ' will be given the data value v_{2,q_2} and (because v_3 has not been assigned a data value since q_1) γ'' will be assigned the data parameter p_{3,q_1}.

In x_{q_4}: as a data value was assigned to v_2 between q_2 to q_3, parameter p_{2,q_4} will be substituted by that value i.e. v_{2,q_2}; parameter p_{1,q_4} will be substituted by $curr$ and all other parameters (which are of the form p_{i,q_4}) will be assigned the corresponding data parameters p_{i,q_1}.

γ''' should be assigned data value v_{2,q_4}.

Therefore by reading a σ in B, we reach a state whose second component maps q_1 to $(q_6, \{v_1, v_2, v_3\})$, $v_{1,q_1} \leftarrow curr$, $v_{2,q_1} \leftarrow v_{2,q_4}$, $v_{3,q_1} \leftarrow v_{3,q_4}$.

4.3   From One-Way Transducers to MSO

In order to conclude that the three models of data word transformations are equivalent, it remains to show that our MSO transductions with MSO origin information capture all transformations defined by the one-way model.

Theorem 8. *SSTVP is included in MSOT+O.*

The proof is very similar to that of encoding finite state automata in MSO. Usually to show that MSO captures string transformations defined by a one-way model one defines an output graph with Γ-labeled edges and ϵ-edges. We directly give a proof that builds a (string) graph whose nodes are Γ-labeled.

Given an sstvp S we fix the set of copies C as the set of occurrences of symbols of Γ in the variable update function.

Since S is deterministic, we will write an MSO sentence φ that characterizes a run of a word in S. This formula will be of the form $\exists X_1, \ldots X_n \psi$, such that given a word w (in the domain of the transformation), there exists a unique assignment of the X_i such that ψ holds. These second order variables consist of:

- X_q for $q \in Q$: position $i \in X_q$ iff processing position i yielded state q.
- X_r for every word variable r: position $i \in X_r$ iff the content of variable r will flow in the output
- X_{r_1,r_2} for every pair of distinct word variables r_1, r_2: position $i \in X_{r_1,r_2}$ iff the content of variable r_1 will flow in the output before the content of the variable r_2 that will also flow in the output.

Our sequential machine model allows easily to write such a formula ψ. With the formula ψ, we can write formulas φ_{indom}, $(\varphi_{dom}^c)_{c \in C}$, $(\varphi_\gamma^c)_{c \in C}$, and $(\varphi_<^{c,d})_{c,d \in C}$. We remark that second order variables X_{r_1,r_2} have a unique valid assignment because of the (semantic) copylessness of sstvp. These variables are typically used to define $\varphi_<^{c,d}$.

To hint how to build formula $\varphi_{orig}^c(x, y)$ we state the following simple lemma about runs of sstvps.

Lemma 2. *Given an sstvp S, an input word w and position x that produces a symbol $\gamma \in \Gamma$ that will be part of the output.*

- *Either γ is produced with a data variable (namely v):*
  In this case, there exists a unique position $y \leq x$ where the data value curr was stored in some data variable and that data variable flows to data variable v at position x.
- *or γ is produced with a data parameter (namely p):*
  In this case, there exists a unique position z such that the data parameter attached to γ is some p_m at position z and that p_m is assigned a variable v_m (or curr) at position z. There exists a unique position $y \leq q$ such that at position y the data value curr was put in some data variable, which flows to a data variable v_m at position z.

The notion of "flow" is easily expressed with ψ and second order existential quantification. The copyless semantics of sstvps ensures that to each (output) symbols, exactly one data value (or equivalently a unique position from the input word) is assigned to. This allows to build MSO formulas φ_{orig}^c that have the desired functional property.

5   Conclusion

Finite string transformation have been generalized to infinite string transformations [5] and tree transformations [3,4]. It would be interesting to extend our results to these settings by adding data values and defining transformations via origin information. Furthermore, it would be interesting to study the pre-post condition checking problem along the lines of [2], i.e. the problem to check that given a transducer is it the case that each input satisfying a pre-condition defined via some automata-model is transformed into an output satisfying a similarly defined post-condition.

References

1. Alur, R., Černý, P.: Expressiveness of streaming string transducers. In: FSTTCS, vol. 8, pp. 1–12 (2010)
2. Alur, R., Černý, P.: Streaming transducers for algorithmic verification of single-pass list-processing programs. In: POPL, pp. 599–610 (2011)
3. Alur, R., D'Antoni, L.: Streaming tree transducers. In: Czumaj, A., Mehlhorn, K., Pitts, A., Wattenhofer, R. (eds.) ICALP 2012, Part II. LNCS, vol. 7392, pp. 42–53. Springer, Heidelberg (2012)
4. Alur, R., Durand-Gasselin, A., Trivedi, A.: From monadic second-order definable string transformations to transducers. In: 28th Annual ACM/IEEE Symposium on Logic in Computer Science, LICS, pp. 458–467. IEEE Computer Society (2013)
5. Alur, R., Filiot, E., Trivedi, A.: Regular transformations of infinite strings. In: Proceedings of the 27th Annual IEEE Symposium on Logic in Computer Science, LICS, pp. 65–74. IEEE Computer Society (2012)
6. Bojańczyk, M.: Transducers with origin information. In: Esparza, J., Fraigniaud, P., Husfeldt, T., Koutsoupias, E. (eds.) ICALP 2014, Part II. LNCS, vol. 8573, pp. 26–37. Springer, Heidelberg (2014)
7. Chytil, M., Jákl, V.: Serial composition of 2-way finite-state transducers and simple programs on strings. In: Salomaa, A., Steinby, M. (eds.) Automata, Languages and Programming. LNCS, vol. 52, pp. 135–147. Springer, London (1977)
8. Courcelle, B.: Monadic second-order definable graph transductions: a survey. Theoret. Comput. Sci. **126**(1), 53–75 (1994)
9. Engelfriet, J., Hoogeboom, H.J.: MSO definable string transductions and two-way finite-state transducers. ACM Trans. Comput. Log. **2**, 216–254 (2001)
10. Shepherdson, J.C.: The reduction of two-way automata to one-way automata. IBM J. Res. Dev. **3**(2), 198–200 (1959)
11. Thomas, W.: Ehrenfeucht games, the composition method, and the monadic theory of ordinal words. In: Mycielski, J., Rozenberg, G., Salomaa, A. (eds.) Structures in Logic and Computer Science. LNCS, vol. 1261, pp. 118–143. Springer, Heidelberg (1997)

Probabilistic and Timed Systems

Trace Refinement in Labelled Markov Decision Processes

Nathanaël Fijalkow$^{(\boxtimes)}$, Stefan Kiefer, and Mahsa Shirmohammadi

University of Oxford, Oxford, UK
{nathanael.fijalkow,stefan.kiefer,mahsa.shirmohammadi}@cs.ox.ac.uk

Abstract. Given two labelled Markov decision processes (MDPs), the trace-refinement problem asks whether for all strategies of the first MDP there exists a strategy of the second MDP such that the induced labelled Markov chains are trace-equivalent. We show that this problem is decidable in polynomial time if the second MDP is a Markov chain. The algorithm is based on new results on a particular notion of bisimulation between distributions over the states. However, we show that the general trace-refinement problem is undecidable, even if the first MDP is a Markov chain. Decidability of those problems was stated as open in 2008. We further study the decidability and complexity of the trace-refinement problem provided that the strategies are restricted to be memoryless.

1 Introduction

We consider labelled Markov chains (MCs) whose transitions are labelled with symbols from an alphabet L. Upon taking a transition, the MC emits the associated label. In this way, an MC defines a *trace-probability* function $Tr : L^* \to [0,1]$ which assigns to each finite trace $w \in L^*$ the probability that the MC emits w during its first $|w|$ transitions. Consider the MC depicted in Fig. 1 with initial state p_0. For example, see that if in state p_0, with probability $\frac{1}{4}$, a transition to state p_c is taken and c is emitted. We have, e.g., $Tr(abc) = \frac{1}{4} \cdot \frac{1}{4} \cdot \frac{1}{4}$. Two MCs over the same alphabet L are called *equivalent* if their trace-probability functions are equal.

The study of such MCs and their equivalence has a long history, going back to Schützenberger [19] and Paz [16]. Schützenberger and Paz studied *weighted* and *probabilistic* automata, respectively. Those models generalize labelled MCs, but the respective equivalence problems are essentially the same. It can be extracted from [19] that equivalence is decidable in polynomial time, using a technique based on linear algebra. Variants of this technique were developed, see e.g. [8, 20]. Tzeng [21] considered the path-equivalence problem for nondeterministic automata which asks, given nondeterministic automata A and B, whether each word has the same number of accepting paths in A as in B. He gives an NC algorithm[1] for deciding path equivalence which can be straightforwardly adapted to yield an NC algorithm for equivalence of MCs.

---

[1] The complexity class NC is the subclass of P containing those problems that can be solved in polylogarithmic parallel time (see e.g. [10]).

© Her Majesty the Queen in Right of the United Kingdom 2016
B. Jacobs and C. Löding (Eds.): FOSSACS 2016, LNCS 9634, pp. 303–318, 2016.
DOI: 10.1007/978-3-662-49630-5_18

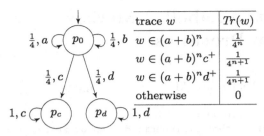

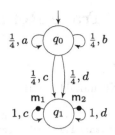

trace w	$Tr(w)$
$w \in (a+b)^n$	$\frac{1}{4^n}$
$w \in (a+b)^n c^+$	$\frac{1}{4^{n+1}}$
$w \in (a+b)^n d^+$	$\frac{1}{4^{n+1}}$
otherwise	0

Fig. 1. An MC with its trace-probability function. This MC, denoted by $\mathcal{C}(\mathcal{A})$, is also used in the reduction from universality of probabilistic automata to MC $\sqsubseteq$ MDP.

Fig. 2. An MDP where the choice of controller is relevant only in q_1. Two available moves m_1, m_2 are shown with small black circles.

More recently, the efficient decidability of the equivalence problem was exploited, both theoretically and practically, for the verification of probabilistic systems, see e.g. [12–15,17]. In those works, equivalence naturally expresses properties such as obliviousness and anonymity, which are difficult to formalize in temporal logic. The *inclusion problem* for two probabilistic automata asks whether for each word the acceptance probability in the first automaton is less than or equal to the acceptance probability in the second automaton. Despite its semblance to the equivalence problem, the inclusion problem is undecidable [6], even for automata of fixed dimension [3]. This is unfortunate, especially because deciding language inclusion is often at the heart of verification algorithms.

We study another "inclusion-like" generalization of the equivalence problem: trace refinement in labelled Markov decision processes (MDPs). MDPs extend MCs by nondeterminism; in each state, a controller chooses, possibly randomly and possibly depending on the history, one out of finitely many *moves*[2]. A move determines a probability distribution over the emitted label and the successor state. In this way, an MDP and a strategy of the controller induce an MC.

The *trace-refinement problem* asks, given two MDPs $\mathcal{D}$ and $\mathcal{E}$, whether for all strategies for $\mathcal{D}$ there is a strategy for $\mathcal{E}$ such that the induced MCs are equivalent. Consider the MDP depicted in Fig. 2 where in state q_1 there are two available moves; one move generates the label c with probability 1, the other move generates d with probability 1. A strategy of the controller that chooses the last generated label in the state q_1, either c or d, with probability 1, induces the same trace-probability function as the MC shown in Fig. 1; the MDP thus refines that MC. The described strategy needs one bit of memory to keep track of the last generated label. It was shown in [8] that the strategy for $\mathcal{E}$ may require *infinite memory*, even if $\mathcal{D}$ is an MC. The decidability of trace refinement was posed as an open problem, both in the introduction and in the conclusion of [8]. The authors of [8] also ask about the decidability of subcases, where $\mathcal{D}$ or $\mathcal{E}$ are restricted to be MCs. In this paper we answer all those questions. We show

---

[2] As in [8] we speak of moves rather than of actions, to avoid possible confusion with the label alphabet L.

that trace refinement is undecidable, even if $\mathcal{D}$ is an MC. In contrast, we show that trace refinement is decidable efficiently (in NC, hence in P), if $\mathcal{E}$ is an MC. Moreover, we prove that the trace-refinement problem becomes decidable if one imposes suitable *restrictions on the strategies* for $\mathcal{D}$ and $\mathcal{E}$, respectively. More specifically, we consider *memoryless* (i.e., no dependence on the history) and *pure memoryless* (i.e., no randomization and no dependence on the history) strategies, establishing various complexity results between NP and PSPACE.

To obtain the aforementioned NC result, we demonstrate a link between trace refinement and a particular notion of *bisimulation* between two MDPs that was studied in [11]. This variant of bisimulation is not defined between two states as in the usual notion, but between two *distributions* on states. An exponential-time algorithm that decides (this notion of) bisimulation was provided in [11]. We sharpen this result by exhibiting a coNP algorithm that decides bisimulation between two MDPs, and an NC algorithm for the case where one of the MDPs is an MC. For that we refine the arguments devised in [11]. The model considered in [11] is more general than ours in that they also consider continuous state spaces, but more restricted than ours in that the label is determined by the move.

The full version of the paper is available online [1].

2   Preliminaries

A trace over a finite set L of labels is a finite sequence $w = a_1 \cdots a_n$ of labels where the length of the trace is $|w| = n$. The empty trace ϵ has length zero. For $n \geq 0$, let L^n be the set of all traces with length n; we denote by L^* the set of all (finite) traces over L.

For a function $d : S \to [0,1]$ over a finite set S, define the *norm* $\|d\| := \sum_{s \in S} d(s)$. The *support* of d is the set $\mathsf{Supp}(d) = \{s \in S \mid d(s) > 0\}$. The function d is a *probability subdistribution* over S if $\|d\| \leq 1$; it is a *probability distribution* if $\|d\| = 1$. We denote by $\mathsf{subDist}(S)$ (resp. $\mathsf{Dist}(S)$) the set of all probability subdistributions (resp. distributions) over S. Given $s \in S$, the *Dirac distribution* on s assigns probability 1 to s; we denote it by d_s. For a non-empty subset $T \subseteq S$, the *uniform distribution* over T assigns probability $\frac{1}{|T|}$ to every element in T.

2.1   Labelled Markov Decision Processes

A *labelled Markov decision process* (MDP) $\mathcal{D} = \langle Q, \mu_0, \mathsf{L}, \delta \rangle$ consists of a finite set Q of states, an initial distribution $\mu_0 \in \mathsf{Dist}(Q)$, a finite set L of labels, and a finite probabilistic transition relation $\delta \subseteq Q \times \mathsf{Dist}(\mathsf{L} \times Q)$ where states are in relation with distributions over pairs of labels and successors. We assume that for each state $q \in Q$ there exists some distribution $d \in \mathsf{Dist}(\mathsf{L} \times Q)$ where $\langle q, d \rangle \in \delta$. The set of *moves* in q is $\mathsf{moves}(q) = \{d \in \mathsf{Dist}(\mathsf{L} \times Q) \mid \langle q, d \rangle \in \delta\}$; denote by $\mathsf{moves} = \bigcup_{q \in Q} \mathsf{moves}(q)$ the set of all moves.

For the complexity results, we assume that probabilities of transitions are rational and given as fractions of integers represented in binary.

We describe the behaviour of an MDP as a trace generator running in steps. The MDP starts in the first step in state q with probability $\mu_0(q)$. In each step, if the MDP is in state q the controller chooses $\mathsf{m} \in \mathsf{moves}(q)$; then, with probability $\mathsf{m}(a, q')$, the label a is generated and the next step starts in the successor state q'.

Given $q \in Q$, denote by $\mathsf{post}(q)$ the set $\{(a, q') \in \mathsf{Supp}(\mathsf{m}) \mid \mathsf{m} \in \mathsf{moves}(q)\}$. A *path* in $\mathcal{D}$ is a sequence $\rho = q_0 a_1 q_1 \ldots a_n q_n$ such that $(a_{i+1}, q_{i+1}) \in \mathsf{post}(q_i)$ for all $0 \leq i < n$. The path ρ has the last state $\mathsf{last}(\rho) = q_n$; and the generated trace after ρ is $a_1 a_2 \cdots a_n$, denoted by $\mathsf{trace}(\rho)$. We denote by $\mathsf{Paths}(\mathcal{D})$ the set of all paths in $\mathcal{D}$, and by $\mathsf{Paths}(w) = \{\rho \in \mathsf{Paths}(\mathcal{D}) \mid \mathsf{trace}(\rho) = w\}$ the set of all path generating w.

Strategies. A *randomized strategy* (or simply a strategy) for an MDP $\mathcal{D}$ is a function $\alpha : \mathsf{Paths}(\mathcal{D}) \to \mathsf{Dist}(\mathsf{moves})$ that, given a finite path ρ, returns a probability distribution $\alpha(\rho) \in \mathsf{Dist}(\mathsf{moves}(\mathsf{last}(\rho)))$ over the set of moves in $\mathsf{last}(\rho)$, used to generate a label a and select a successor state q' with probability $\sum_{\mathsf{m} \in \mathsf{moves}(q)} \alpha(\rho)(\mathsf{m}) \cdot \mathsf{m}(a, q')$ where $q = \mathsf{last}(\rho)$.

A strategy α is *pure* if for all $\rho \in \mathsf{Paths}(\mathcal{D})$, we have $\alpha(\rho)(\mathsf{m}) = 1$ for some $\mathsf{m} \in \mathsf{moves}$; we thus view pure strategies as functions $\alpha : \mathsf{Paths}(\mathcal{D}) \to \mathsf{moves}$. A strategy α is *memoryless* if $\alpha(\rho) = \alpha(\rho')$ for all paths ρ, ρ' with $\mathsf{last}(\rho) = \mathsf{last}(\rho')$; we thus view memoryless strategies as functions $\alpha : Q \to \mathsf{Dist}(\mathsf{moves})$. A strategy α is *trace-based* if $\alpha(\rho) = \alpha(\rho')$ for all ρ, ρ' where $\mathsf{trace}(\rho) = \mathsf{trace}(\rho')$ and $\mathsf{last}(\rho) = \mathsf{last}(\rho')$; we view trace-based strategies as functions $\alpha : \mathsf{L}^* \times Q \to \mathsf{Dist}(\mathsf{moves})$.

Trace-Probability Function. For an MDP $\mathcal{D}$ and a strategy α, the probability of a single path is inductively defined by $\mathsf{Pr}_{\mathcal{D},\alpha}(q) = \mu_0(q)$ and

$$\mathsf{Pr}_{\mathcal{D},\alpha}(\rho a q) = \mathsf{Pr}_{\mathcal{D},\alpha}(\rho) \cdot \sum_{\mathsf{m} \in \mathsf{moves}(\mathsf{last}(\rho))} \alpha(\rho)(\mathsf{m}) \cdot \mathsf{m}(a, q).$$

The *trace-probability* function $Tr_{\mathcal{D},\alpha} : \mathsf{L}^* \to [0, 1]$ is, given a trace w, defined by

$$Tr_{\mathcal{D},\alpha}(w) = \sum_{\rho \in \mathsf{Paths}(w)} \mathsf{Pr}_{\mathcal{D},\alpha}(\rho).$$

We may drop the subscript $\mathcal{D}$ or α from $Tr_{\mathcal{D},\alpha}$ if it is understood. We denote by $subDis_{\mathcal{D},\alpha}(w) \in \mathsf{subDist}(Q)$, the subdistribution after generating a traces w, that is

$$subDis_{\mathcal{D},\alpha}(w)(q) = \sum_{\rho \in \mathsf{Paths}(w):\mathsf{last}(\rho)=q} \mathsf{Pr}_{\mathcal{D},\alpha}(\rho).$$

We have:

$$Tr_{\mathcal{D},\alpha}(w) = \|subDis_{\mathcal{D},\alpha}(w)\| \tag{1}$$

A version of the following lemma was proved in [8, Lemma 1]:

Lemma 1. *Let $\mathcal{D}$ be an MDP and α be a strategy. There exists a trace-based strategy β such that $Tr_\alpha = Tr_\beta$.*

Here, by $Tr_\alpha = Tr_\beta$ we mean $Tr_\alpha(w) = Tr_\beta(w)$ for all traces $w \in \mathsf{L}^*$.

Labeled Markov Chains. A finite-state labeled Markov chain (MC for short) is an MDP where only a single move is available in each state, and thus controller's choice plays no role. An MC $\mathcal{C} = \langle Q, \mu_0, \mathsf{L}, \delta \rangle$ is an MDP where $\delta : Q \to \mathsf{Dist}(\mathsf{L} \times Q)$ is a probabilistic transition function. Since MCs are MDPs, we analogously define paths, and the probability of a single path inductively as follows: $\mathsf{Pr}_\mathcal{C}(q) = \mu_0(q)$ and $\mathsf{Pr}_\mathcal{C}(\rho a q) = \mathsf{Pr}_\mathcal{C}(\rho) \cdot \delta(q')(a, q)$ where $q' = \mathsf{last}(\rho)$. The notations $subDis_\mathcal{C}(w)$ and $Tr_\mathcal{C}$ are defined analogously.

2.2   Trace Refinement

Given two MDPs $\mathcal{D}$ and $\mathcal{E}$ with the same set L of labels, we say that $\mathcal{E}$ *refines* $\mathcal{D}$, denoted by $\mathcal{D} \sqsubseteq \mathcal{E}$, if for all strategies α for $\mathcal{D}$ there exists some strategy β for $\mathcal{E}$ such that $Tr_\mathcal{D} = Tr_\mathcal{E}$. We are interested in the problem $\mathsf{MDP} \sqsubseteq \mathsf{MDP}$, which asks, for two given MDPs $\mathcal{D}$ and $\mathcal{E}$, whether $\mathcal{D} \sqsubseteq \mathcal{E}$. The decidability of this problem was posed as an open question in [8]. We show in Theorem 2 that the problem $\mathsf{MDP} \sqsubseteq \mathsf{MDP}$ is undecidable.

We consider various subproblems of $\mathsf{MDP} \sqsubseteq \mathsf{MDP}$, which asks whether $\mathcal{D} \sqsubseteq \mathcal{E}$ holds. Specifically, we speak of the problem

- $\mathsf{MDP} \sqsubseteq \mathsf{MC}$ when $\mathcal{E}$ is restricted to be an MC;
- $\mathsf{MC} \sqsubseteq \mathsf{MDP}$ when $\mathcal{D}$ is restricted to be an MC;
- $\mathsf{MC} \sqsubseteq \mathsf{MC}$ when both $\mathcal{D}$ and $\mathcal{E}$ are restricted to be MCs.

We show in Theorem 2 that even the problem $\mathsf{MC} \sqsubseteq \mathsf{MDP}$ is undecidable. Hence we consider further subproblems. Specifically, we denote by $\mathsf{MC} \sqsubseteq \mathsf{MDP_m}$ the problem where the MDP is restricted to use only memoryless strategies, and by $\mathsf{MC} \sqsubseteq \mathsf{MDP_{pm}}$ the problem where the MDP is restricted to use only pure memoryless strategies. When both MDPs $\mathcal{D}$ and $\mathcal{E}$ are restricted to use only pure memoryless strategies, the trace-refinement problem is denoted by $\mathsf{MDP_{pm}} \sqsubseteq \mathsf{MDP_{pm}}$. The problem $\mathsf{MC} \sqsubseteq \mathsf{MC}$ equals the *trace-equivalence problem* for MCs: given two MCs $\mathcal{C}_1, \mathcal{C}_2$ we have $\mathcal{C}_1 \sqsubseteq \mathcal{C}_2$ if and only if $Tr_{\mathcal{C}_1} = Tr_{\mathcal{C}_2}$ if and only if $\mathcal{C}_2 \sqsubseteq \mathcal{C}_1$. This problem is known to be in NC [21], hence in P.

3   Undecidability Results

In this section we show:

Theorem 2. *The problem $\mathsf{MC} \sqsubseteq \mathsf{MDP}$ is undecidable. Hence a fortiori, $\mathsf{MDP} \sqsubseteq \mathsf{MDP}$ is undecidable.*

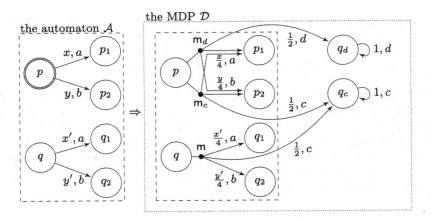

Fig. 3. Sketch of the construction of the MDP $\mathcal{D}$ from the probabilistic automaton $\mathcal{A}$, for the undecidability result of MC $\sqsubseteq$ MDP. Here, p is an accepting state whereas q is not. To read the picture, note that in p there is a transition to the state p_1 with probability x and label a: $\delta(p, a)(p_1) = x$.

Proof. To show that the problem MC $\sqsubseteq$ MDP is undecidable, we establish a reduction from the universality problem for probabilistic automata. A *probabilistic automaton* is a tuple $\mathcal{A} = \langle Q, \mu_0, \mathsf{L}, \delta, F \rangle$ consisting of a finite set Q of states, an initial distribution $\mu_0 \in \mathsf{Dist}(Q)$, a finite set L of letters, a transition function $\delta : Q \times \mathsf{L} \to \mathsf{Dist}(Q)$ assigning to every state and letter a distribution over states, and a set F of final states. For a word $w \in \mathsf{L}^*$ we write $dis_\mathcal{A}(w) \in \mathsf{Dist}(Q)$ for the distribution such that, for all $q \in Q$, we have that $dis_\mathcal{A}(w)(q)$ is the probability that, after inputting w, the automaton $\mathcal{A}$ is in state q. We write $\mathsf{Pr}_\mathcal{A}(w) = \sum_{q \in F} dis_\mathcal{A}(w)(q)$ to denote the probability that $\mathcal{A}$ accepts w. The *universality problem* asks, given a probabilistic automaton $\mathcal{A}$, whether $\mathsf{Pr}_\mathcal{A}(w) \geq \frac{1}{2}$ holds for all words w. This problem is known to be undecidable [16].

Let $\mathcal{A} = \langle Q, \mu_0, \mathsf{L}, \delta, F \rangle$ be a probabilistic automaton; without loss of generality we assume that $\mathsf{L} = \{a, b\}$. We construct an MDP $\mathcal{D}$ such that $\mathcal{A}$ is universal if and only if $\mathcal{C} \sqsubseteq \mathcal{D}$ where $\mathcal{C}$ is the MC shown in Fig. 1. The MDP $\mathcal{D}$ is constructed from $\mathcal{A}$ as follows; see Fig. 3.

Its set of states is $Q \cup \{q_c, q_d\}$, and its initial distribution is μ_0. (Here and in the following we identify subdistributions $\mu \in \mathsf{subDist}(Q)$ and $\mu \in \mathsf{subDist}(Q \cup \{q_c, q_d\})$ if $\mu(q_c) = \mu(q_d) = 0$.) We describe the transitions of $\mathcal{D}$ using the transition function δ of $\mathcal{A}$. Consider a state $q \in Q$:

– If $q \in F$, there are two available moves $\mathsf{m}_c, \mathsf{m}_d$; both emit a with probability $\frac{1}{4}$ and simulate the probabilistic automaton $\mathcal{A}$ reading the letter a, or emit b with probability $\frac{1}{4}$ and simulate the probabilistic automaton $\mathcal{A}$ reading the letter b. With the remaining probability of $\frac{1}{2}$, m_c emits c and leads to q_c and m_d emits d and leads to q_d. Formally, $\mathsf{m}_c(c, q_c) = \frac{1}{2}$, $\mathsf{m}_d(d, q_d) = \frac{1}{2}$ and $\mathsf{m}_c(e, q') = \mathsf{m}_d(e, q') = \frac{1}{4}\delta(q, e)(q')$ where $q' \in Q$ and $e \in \{a, b\}$.

- If $q \notin F$, there is a single available move m such that $\mathsf{m}(d, q_d) = \frac{1}{2}$ and $\mathsf{m}(e, q') = \frac{1}{4}\delta(q, e)(q')$ where $q' \in Q$ and $e \in \{a, b\}$.
- The only move from q_c is the Dirac distribution on (c, q_c); likewise the only move from q_d is the Dirac distribution on (d, q_d).

This MDP $\mathcal{D}$ "is almost" an MC, in the sense that a strategy α does not influence its behaviour until eventually a transition to q_c or q_d is taken. Indeed, for all α and for all $w \in \{a, b\}^*$ we have $subDis_{\mathcal{D},\alpha}(w) = \frac{1}{4^{|w|}} dis_{\mathcal{A}}(w)$. In particular, it follows $Tr_{\mathcal{D},\alpha}(w) = \|subDis_{\mathcal{D},\alpha}(w)\| = \frac{1}{4^{|w|}}\|dis_{\mathcal{A}}(w)\| = \frac{1}{4^{|w|}}$. Further, if α is trace-based we have:

$$
\begin{aligned}
Tr_{\mathcal{D},\alpha}(wc) &= \|subDis_{\mathcal{D},\alpha}(wc)\| && \text{by (1)} \\
&= subDis_{\mathcal{D},\alpha}(wc)(q_c) && \text{structure of } \mathcal{D} \\
&= \sum_{q \in F} subDis_{\mathcal{D},\alpha}(w)(q) \cdot \alpha(w, q)(\mathsf{m}_c) \cdot \frac{1}{2} && \text{structure of } \mathcal{D} \quad (2) \\
&= \frac{1}{4^{|w|}} \sum_{q \in F} dis_{\mathcal{A}}(w)(q) \cdot \alpha(w, q)(\mathsf{m}_c) \cdot \frac{1}{2} && \text{as argued above}
\end{aligned}
$$

We show that $\mathcal{A}$ is universal if and only if $\mathcal{C} \sqsubseteq \mathcal{D}$. Let $\mathcal{A}$ be universal. Define a trace-based strategy α with $\alpha(w, q)(\mathsf{m}_c) = \frac{1}{2\mathsf{Pr}_{\mathcal{A}}(w)}$ for all $w \in \{a, b\}^*$ and $q \in F$. Note that $\alpha(w, q)(\mathsf{m}_c)$ is a probability as $\mathsf{Pr}_{\mathcal{A}}(w) \geq \frac{1}{2}$. Let $w \in \{a, b\}^*$. We have:

$$
\begin{aligned}
Tr_{\mathcal{D},\alpha}(w) &= \frac{1}{4^{|w|}} && \text{as argued above} \\
&= Tr_{\mathcal{C}}(w) && \text{Figure 1}
\end{aligned}
$$

Further we have:

$$
\begin{aligned}
Tr_{\mathcal{D},\alpha}(wc) &= \frac{1}{4^{|w|}} \sum_{q \in F} dis_{\mathcal{A}}(w)(q) \cdot \alpha(w, q)(\mathsf{m}_c) \cdot \frac{1}{2} && \text{by (2)} \\
&= \frac{1}{4^{|w|}} \sum_{q \in F} dis_{\mathcal{A}}(w)(q) \cdot \frac{1}{\mathsf{Pr}_{\mathcal{A}}(w)} \cdot \frac{1}{4} && \text{definition of } \alpha \\
&= \frac{1}{4^{|w|+1}} && \mathsf{Pr}_{\mathcal{A}}(w) = \sum_{q \in F} dis_{\mathcal{A}}(w)(q) \\
&= Tr_{\mathcal{C}}(wc) && \text{Figure 1}
\end{aligned}
$$

It follows from the definitions of $\mathcal{D}$ and $\mathcal{C}$ that for all $k \geq 1$, we have $Tr_{\mathcal{D},\alpha}(wc^k) = Tr_{\mathcal{D},\alpha}(wc) = Tr_{\mathcal{C}}(wc) = Tr_{\mathcal{C}}(wc^k)$. We have $\sum_{e \in \{a,b,c,d\}} Tr_{\mathcal{D},\alpha}(we) = Tr_{\mathcal{D},\alpha}(w) = Tr_{\mathcal{C}}(w) = \sum_{e \in \{a,b,c,d\}} Tr_{\mathcal{C}}(we)$. Since for $e \in \{a, b, c\}$ we also proved that $Tr_{\mathcal{D},\alpha}(we) = Tr_{\mathcal{C}}(we)$ it follows that $Tr_{\mathcal{D},\alpha}(wd) = Tr_{\mathcal{C}}(wd)$. Hence, as above, $Tr_{\mathcal{D},\alpha}(wd^k) = Tr_{\mathcal{C}}(wd^k)$ for all $k \geq 1$. Finally, if $w \notin (a + b)^* \cdot (c^* + d^*)$ then $Tr_{\mathcal{D},\alpha}(w) = 0 = Tr_{\mathcal{C}}(w)$.

For the converse, assume that $\mathcal{A}$ is not universal. Then there is $w \in \{a,b\}^*$ with $\mathsf{Pr}_{\mathcal{A}}(w) < \frac{1}{2}$. Let α be a trace-based strategy. Then we have:

$$Tr_{\mathcal{D},\alpha}(wc) = \frac{1}{4^{|w|}} \sum_{q \in F} dis_{\mathcal{A}}(w)(q) \cdot \alpha(w,q)(\mathsf{m}_c) \cdot \frac{1}{2} \quad \text{by (2)}$$

$$\leq \frac{1}{4^{|w|}} \cdot \frac{1}{2} \cdot \sum_{q \in F} dis_{\mathcal{A}}(w)(q) \qquad \alpha(w,q)(\mathsf{m}_c) \leq 1$$

$$= \frac{1}{4^{|w|}} \cdot \frac{1}{2} \cdot \mathsf{Pr}_{\mathcal{A}}(w) \qquad \mathsf{Pr}_{\mathcal{A}}(w) = \sum_{q \in F} dis_{\mathcal{A}}(w)(q)$$

$$< \frac{1}{4^{|w|}} \cdot \frac{1}{2} \cdot \frac{1}{2} \qquad \text{definition of } w$$

$$= Tr_{\mathcal{C}}(wc) \qquad \text{Figure 1}$$

We conclude that there is no trace-based strategy α with $Tr_{\mathcal{D},\alpha} = Tr_{\mathcal{C}}$. By Lemma 1 there is *no* strategy α with $Tr_{\mathcal{D},\alpha} = Tr_{\mathcal{C}}$. Hence $\mathcal{C} \not\sqsubseteq \mathcal{D}$. □

A straightforward reduction from MDP $\sqsubseteq$ MDP now establishes:

Theorem 3. *The problem that, given two MDPs $\mathcal{D}$ and $\mathcal{E}$, asks whether $\mathcal{D} \sqsubseteq \mathcal{E}$ and $\mathcal{E} \sqsubseteq \mathcal{D}$ is undecidable.*

4   Decidability for Memoryless Strategies

Given two MCs $\mathcal{C}_1$ and $\mathcal{C}_2$, the (symmetric) trace-equivalence relation $\mathcal{C}_1 \sqsubseteq \mathcal{C}_2$ is polynomial-time decidable [21]. An MDP $\mathcal{D}$ under a memoryless strategy α induces a finite MC $\mathcal{D}(\alpha)$, and thus once a memoryless strategy is fixed for the MDP, its relation to another given MC in the trace-equivalence relation $\sqsubseteq$ can be decided in P. Theorems 4 and 5 provide tight complexity bounds of the trace-refinement problems for MDPs that are restricted to use only pure memoryless strategies. In Theorems 6 and 7 we establish bounds on the complexity of the problem when randomization is allowed for memoryless strategies.

4.1   Pure Memoryless Strategies

In this subsection, we show that the two problems $\mathsf{MC} \sqsubseteq \mathsf{MDP}_{\mathsf{pm}}$ and $\mathsf{MDP}_{\mathsf{pm}} \sqsubseteq \mathsf{MDP}_{\mathsf{pm}}$ are NP-complete and Π_2^p-complete.

Membership of $\mathsf{MC} \sqsubseteq \mathsf{MDP}_{\mathsf{pm}}$ in NP and $\mathsf{MDP}_{\mathsf{pm}} \sqsubseteq \mathsf{MDP}_{\mathsf{pm}}$ in Π_2^p are obtained as follows. Given an MC $\mathcal{C}$ and an MDP $\mathcal{D}$, the polynomial witness of $\mathcal{C} \sqsubseteq \mathcal{D}$ is a pure memoryless strategy α for $\mathcal{D}$. Once α is fixed, then $\mathcal{C} \sqsubseteq \mathcal{D}(\alpha)$ can be decided in P. Given another MDP $\mathcal{E}$, for all pure memoryless strategies β of $\mathcal{E}$ whether there exists a polynomial witness α for $\mathcal{E} \sqsubseteq \mathcal{D}$ such that $\mathcal{E}(\beta) \sqsubseteq \mathcal{D}(\alpha)$ can be decided in P.

The hardness results are by reductions from the *subset-sum problem* and a variant of the *quantified subset-sum* problem. Given a set $\{s_1, s_2, \cdots, s_n\}$

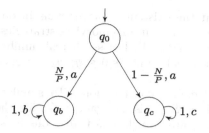

Fig. 4. The MC $\mathcal{C}$ in the reduction for NP-hardness of MC $\sqsubseteq$ MDP$_m$.

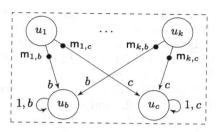

Fig. 5. The gadget G_u for the set $\{u_1, \cdots, u_k\}$.

of natural numbers and $N \in \mathbb{N}$, the subset-sum problem asks whether there exists a subset $S \subseteq \{s_1, \cdots, s_n\}$ such that $\sum_{s \in S} s = N$. The subset-sum problem is known to be NP-complete [7]. The quantified version of subset sum is a game between a *universal player* and an *existential player*. Given $k, N \in \mathbb{N}$, the game is played turn-based for k rounds. For each round $1 \leq i \leq k$, two sets $\{s_1, s_2, \cdots, s_n\}$ and $\{t_1, t_2, \cdots, t_m\}$ of natural numbers are given. In each round i, the universal player first chooses $S_i \subseteq \{s_1, \cdots, s_n\}$ and then the existential player chooses $T_i \subseteq \{t_1, \cdots, t_m\}$. The existential player wins if and only if

$$\sum_{s \in S_1} s + \sum_{t \in T_1} t + \cdots + \sum_{s \in S_k} s + \sum_{t \in T_k} t = N.$$

The quantified subset sum is known to be PSPACE-complete [9]. The proof therein implies that the variant of the problem with a fixed number k of rounds is Π_{2k}^p-complete.

To establish the NP-hardness of MC $\sqsubseteq$ MDP$_{\mathsf{pm}}$, consider an instance of subset sum, i.e., a set $\{s_1, \cdots, s_n\}$ and $N \in \mathbb{N}$. We construct an MC $\mathcal{C}$ and an MDP $\mathcal{D}$ such that there exists $S \subseteq \{s_1, \cdots, s_n\}$ with $\sum_{s \in S} s = N$ if and only if $\mathcal{C} \sqsubseteq \mathcal{D}$ when $\mathcal{D}$ uses only pure memoryless strategies.

The MC $\mathcal{C}$ is shown in Fig. 4. it generates traces in ab^+ with probability $\frac{N}{P}$ and traces in ac^+ with probability $1 - \frac{N}{P}$ where $P = s_1 + \cdots + s_n$.

For a set $\{u_1, \cdots, u_k\}$, we define a gadget G_u that is an MDP with $k + 2$ states: $u_1, \cdots, u_k$ and u_b, u_c; see Fig. 5. For all states u_i, two moves $\mathsf{m}_{i,b}$ and $\mathsf{m}_{i,c}$ are available, the Dirac distributions on (a, u_b) and (a, u_c). The states u_b, u_c emit only the single labels b and c. The MDP $\mathcal{D}$ is exactly the gadget G_s for $\{s_1, \cdots, s_n\}$ equipped with the initial distribution μ_0 where $\mu_0(s_i) = \frac{s_i}{P}$ for all $1 \leq i \leq n$. Choosing b in s_i simulates the membership of s_i in S by adding $\frac{s_i}{P}$ to the probability of generating ab^+.

Theorem 4. *The problem* MC $\sqsubseteq$ MDP$_{\mathsf{pm}}$ *is* NP-*complete.*

To establish the Π_2^p-hardness of MDP$_{\mathsf{pm}} \sqsubseteq$ MDP$_{\mathsf{pm}}$, consider an instance of quantified subset sum, i.e., $N \in \mathbb{N}$ and two sets $\{s_1, \cdots, s_n\}$ and $\{t_1, \cdots, t_m\}$.

We construct MDPs $\mathcal{E}_{univ}, \mathcal{E}_{exist}$ such that the existential player wins in one round if and only if $\mathcal{E}_{univ} \sqsubseteq \mathcal{E}_{exist}$ restricted to use pure memoryless strategies.

Let $P = s_1 + \cdots + s_n$ and $R = t_1 + \cdots + t_m$. Pick a small real number $0 < x < 1$ so that $0 < xP, xR, xN < 1$. Pick real numbers $0 \le y_1, y_2 \le 1$ such that $y_1 + xN = y_2 + xR$.

The MDPs $\mathcal{E}_{univ}$ and $\mathcal{E}_{exist}$ have symmetric constructions. To simulate the choice of the universal player, the MDP $\mathcal{E}_{univ}$ is the gadget G_s for the set $\{s_1, \cdots, s_n\}$ where two new states s_r, s_y are added. The transitions in s_r and s_y are the Dirac distributions on (a, s_b) and (a, s_c), respectively. The initial distribution μ_0 for $\mathcal{E}_{univ}$ is such that $\mu_0(s_y) = \frac{1}{2}y_1$ and $\mu_0(s_r) = 1 - \frac{1}{2}(xP + y_1)$, and $\mu_0(s_i) = \frac{1}{2}xs_i$ for all $1 \le i \le n$. Similarly, to simulate the counter-attack of the existential player, the MDP $\mathcal{E}_{exist}$ is the gadget G_t for $\{t_1, \cdots, t_m\}$ with two new states t_r, t_y. The transitions in t_r and t_y are the Dirac distributions on (a, t_b) and (a, t_c), respectively. The initial distribution μ'_0 is $\mu'_0(p_y) = \frac{1}{2}y_2$ and $\mu'_0(p_r) = 1 - \frac{1}{2}(xT + y_2)$, and $\mu'_0(t_j) = \frac{1}{2}xt_j$ for all $1 \le j \le m$. Choosing b in a set of states s_i by the universal player must be defended by choosing c in a right set of states t_j by existential player such that the probabilities of emitting ab^+ in MDPs are equal.

Theorem 5. *The problem* $\mathsf{MDP}_{pm} \sqsubseteq \mathsf{MDP}_{pm}$ *is* Π_2^p*-complete.*

4.2   Memoryless Strategies

In this subsection, we provide upper and lower complexity bounds for the problem $\mathsf{MC} \sqsubseteq \mathsf{MDP}_m$: a reduction to the existential theory of the reals and a reduction from nonnegative factorization of matrices.

A formula of the *existential theory of the reals* is of the form $\exists x_1 \ldots \exists x_m \, R(x_1, \ldots, x_n)$, where $R(x_1, \ldots, x_n)$ is a boolean combination of comparisons of the form $p(x_1, \ldots, x_n) \sim 0$, where $p(x_1, \ldots, x_n)$ is a multivariate polynomial and $\sim \in \{<, >, \le, \ge, =, \ne\}$. The validity of closed formulas (i.e., when $m = n$) is decidable in PSPACE [4,18], and is not known to be PSPACE-hard.

Theorem 6. *The problem* $\mathsf{MC} \sqsubseteq \mathsf{MDP}_m$ *is polynomial-time reducible to the existential theory of the reals, hence in* PSPACE.

Given a nonnegative matrix $M \in \mathbb{R}^{n \times m}$, a *nonnegative factorization* of M is any representation of the form $M = A \cdot W$ where $A \in \mathbb{R}^{n \times r}$ and $W \in \mathbb{R}^{r \times m}$ are nonnegative matrices (see [2,5,22] for more details). The *NMF problem* asks, given a nonnegative matrix $M \in \mathbb{R}^{n \times m}$ and a number $r \in \mathbb{N}$, whether there exists a factorization $M = A \cdot W$ with nonnegative matrices $A \in \mathbb{R}^{n \times r}$ and $W \in \mathbb{R}^{r \times m}$. The NMF problem is known to be NP-hard, but membership in NP is open [22].

Below, we present a reduction from the NMF problem to $\mathsf{MC} \sqsubseteq \mathsf{MDP}_m$. To establish the reduction, consider an instance of the NMF problem, i.e., a nonnegative matrix $M \in \mathbb{R}^{n \times m}$ and a number $r \in \mathbb{N}$. We construct an MC $\mathcal{C}$ and

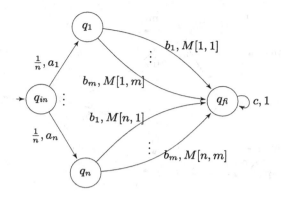

Fig. 6. The MC $\mathcal{C}$ of the reduction from NMF to MC $\sqsubseteq$ MDP$_\mathsf{m}$.

an MDP $\mathcal{D}$ such that the NMF instance is a yes-instance if and only if $\mathcal{C} \sqsubseteq \mathcal{D}$ where $\mathcal{D}$ is restricted to use only memoryless strategies.

We assume, without loss of generality, that M is a stochastic matrix, that is $\sum_{j=1}^{m} M[i,j] = 1$ for all rows $1 \leq i \leq n$. We know, by [2, Sect. 5], that there exists a nonnegative factorization of M with rank r if and only if there exist two stochastic matrices $A \in \mathbb{R}^{n \times r}$ and $W \in \mathbb{R}^{r \times m}$ such that $M = A \cdot W$.

The transition probabilities in the MC $\mathcal{C}$ encode the entries of matrix M. The initial distribution of the MC is the Dirac distribution on q_{in}; see Fig. 6. There are $n+m+1$ labels $a_1, \cdots, a_n, b_1, \cdots, b_m, c$. The transition in q_{in} is the uniform distribution over $\{(a_i, q_i) \mid 1 \leq i \leq n\}$. In each state q_i, each label b_j is emitted with probability $M[i,j]$, and a transition to q_{fi} is taken. In state q_{fi} only c is emitted. Observe that for all $1 \leq i \leq n$ and $1 \leq j \leq m$ we have $Tr_{\mathcal{C}}(a_i) = \frac{1}{n}$ and $Tr_{\mathcal{C}}(a_i \cdot b_j \cdot c^*) = \frac{1}{n} M[i,j]$.

The initial distribution of the MDP $\mathcal{D}$ is the uniform distribution over $\{p_1, \cdots, p_n\}$; see Fig. 7. In each p_i (where $1 \leq i \leq n$), there are r moves $\mathsf{m}_{i,1}, \mathsf{m}_{i,2}, \cdots, \mathsf{m}_{i,r}$ where $\mathsf{m}_{i,k}(a_i, \ell_k) = 1$ and $1 \leq k \leq r$. In each ℓ_k, there are m moves $\mathsf{m}'_{k,1}, \mathsf{m}'_{k,2}, \cdots, \mathsf{m}'_{k,m}$ where $\mathsf{m}'_{k,j}(b_j, p_{fi}) = 1$ where $1 \leq j \leq m$. In state p_{fi}, only c is emitted. The probabilities of choosing the move $\mathsf{m}_{i,k}$ in p_i and choosing $\mathsf{m}'_{k,j}$ in ℓ_k simulate the entries of $A[i,k]$ and $W[k,j]$.

Theorem 7. *The NMF problem is polynomial-time reducible to* MC $\sqsubseteq$ MDP$_\mathsf{m}$, *hence* MC $\sqsubseteq$ MDP$_\mathsf{m}$ *is NP-hard.*

Recall that it is open whether the NMF problem is in NP and whether the existential theory of the reals is PSPACE-hard. So Theorems 6 and 7 show that proving NP-completeness or PSPACE-completeness of MC $\sqsubseteq$ MDP$_\mathsf{m}$ requires a breakthrough in those areas.

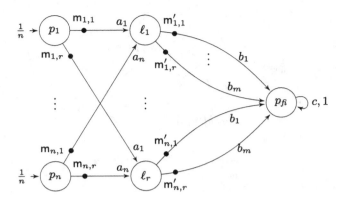

Fig. 7. The MDP $\mathcal{D}$ of the reduction from NMF to MC $\sqsubseteq$ MDP$_m$.

5   Bisimulation

In this section we show:

Theorem 8. *The problem* MDP $\sqsubseteq$ MC *is in* NC, *hence in* P.

We prove Theorem 8 in two steps: First, in Proposition 9 below, we establish a link between trace refinement and a notion of bisimulation between distributions that was studied in [11]. Second, we show that this notion of bisimulation can be decided efficiently (in NC, hence in P) if one of the MDPs is an MC. Proposition 9 then implies Theorem 8. Along the way, we prove that bisimulation between two MDPs can be decided in coNP, improving the exponential-time result from [11]. We rebuild a detailed proof from scratch, not referring to [11], as the authors were unable to verify some of the technical claims made in [11].

A *local strategy* for an MDP $\mathcal{D} = \langle Q, \mu_0, \mathsf{L}, \delta \rangle$ is a function $\alpha : Q \to$ Dist(moves) that maps each state q to a distribution $\alpha(q) \in$ Dist(moves(q)) over moves in q. We call α *pure* if for all states q there is a move m such that $\alpha(q)(\mathsf{m}) = 1$. For a subdistribution $\mu \in$ subDist(Q), a local strategy α, and a label $a \in \mathsf{L}$, define the *successor* subdistribution Succ(μ, α, a) with

$$\mathsf{Succ}(\mu, \alpha, a)(q') = \sum_{q \in Q} \mu(q) \cdot \sum_{\mathsf{m} \in \mathsf{moves}(q)} \alpha(q)(\mathsf{m}) \cdot \mathsf{m}(a, q')$$

for all $q' \in Q$. Let $\mathcal{D} = \langle Q_{\mathcal{D}}, \mu_0^{\mathcal{D}}, \mathsf{L}, \delta_{\mathcal{D}} \rangle$ and $\mathcal{E} = \langle Q_{\mathcal{E}}, \mu_0^{\mathcal{E}}, \mathsf{L}, \delta_{\mathcal{E}} \rangle$ be two MDPs over the same set L of labels. A *bisimulation* is a relation $\mathcal{R} \subseteq$ subDist$(Q_{\mathcal{D}}) \times$ subDist$(Q_{\mathcal{E}})$ such that whenever $\mu_{\mathcal{D}} \mathcal{R} \mu_{\mathcal{E}}$ then

- $\|\mu_{\mathcal{D}}\| = \|\mu_{\mathcal{E}}\|$;
- for all local strategies $\alpha_{\mathcal{D}}$ there exists a local strategy $\alpha_{\mathcal{E}}$ such that for all $a \in \mathsf{L}$ we have Succ$(\mu_{\mathcal{D}}, \alpha_{\mathcal{D}}, a) \mathcal{R}$ Succ$(\mu_{\mathcal{E}}, \alpha_{\mathcal{E}}, a)$;
- for all local strategies $\alpha_{\mathcal{E}}$ there exists a local strategy $\alpha_{\mathcal{D}}$ such that for all $a \in \mathsf{L}$ we have Succ$(\mu_{\mathcal{D}}, \alpha_{\mathcal{D}}, a) \mathcal{R}$ Succ$(\mu_{\mathcal{E}}, \alpha_{\mathcal{E}}, a)$.

As usual, a union of bisimulations is a bisimulation. Denote by $\sim$ the union of all bisimulations, i.e., $\sim$ is the largest bisimulation. We write $\mathcal{D} \sim \mathcal{E}$ if $\mu_0^{\mathcal{D}} \sim \mu_0^{\mathcal{E}}$. In general, the set $\sim$ is uncountably infinite, so methods for computing state-based bisimulation (e.g., partition refinement) are not applicable. The following proposition establishes a link between trace refinement and bisimulation.

Proposition 9. *Let $\mathcal{D}$ be an MDP and $\mathcal{C}$ be an MC. Then $\mathcal{D} \sim \mathcal{C}$ if and only if $\mathcal{D} \sqsubseteq \mathcal{C}$.*

We often view a subdistribution $d \in \mathsf{subDist}(Q)$ as a row vector $d \in [0,1]^Q$. For a local strategy α and a label a, define the *transition matrix* $\Delta_\alpha(a) \in [0,1]^{Q \times Q}$ with $\Delta_\alpha(a)[q,q'] = \sum_{m \in \mathsf{moves}(q)} \alpha(q)(m) \cdot m(a,q')$. Viewing subdistributions μ as row vectors, we have:

$$\mathsf{Succ}(\mu, \alpha, a) = \mu \cdot \Delta_\alpha(a) \tag{3}$$

In the following we consider MDPs $\mathcal{D} = \langle Q, \mu_0^{\mathcal{D}}, \mathsf{L}, \delta \rangle$ and $\mathcal{E} = \langle Q, \mu_0^{\mathcal{E}}, \mathsf{L}, \delta \rangle$ over the same state space. This is without loss of generality, since we might take the disjoint union of the state spaces. Since $\mathcal{D}$ and $\mathcal{E}$ differ only in the initial distribution, we will focus on $\mathcal{D}$.

Let $B \in \mathbb{R}^{Q \times k}$ with $k \geq 1$. Assume the label set is $\mathsf{L} = \{a_1, \ldots, a_{|\mathsf{L}|}\}$. For $\mu \in \mathsf{subDist}(Q)$ and a local strategy α we define a point $p(\mu, \alpha) \in \mathbb{R}^{|\mathsf{L}| \cdot k}$ such that

$$p(\mu, \alpha) = \begin{pmatrix} \mu\Delta_\alpha(a_1)B & \mu\Delta_\alpha(a_2)B & \cdots & \mu\Delta_\alpha(a_{|\mathsf{L}|})B \end{pmatrix}.$$

For the reader's intuition, we remark that we will choose matrices $B \in \mathbb{R}^{Q \times k}$ so that if two subdistributions $\mu_{\mathcal{D}}, \mu_{\mathcal{E}}$ are bisimilar then $\mu_{\mathcal{D}}B = \mu_{\mathcal{E}}B$. (In fact, one can compute B so that the converse holds as well, i.e., $\mu_{\mathcal{D}} \sim \mu_{\mathcal{E}}$ if and only if $\mu_{\mathcal{D}}B = \mu_{\mathcal{E}}B$.) It follows that, for subdistributions $\mu_{\mathcal{D}}, \mu_{\mathcal{E}}$ and local strategies $\alpha_{\mathcal{D}}, \alpha_{\mathcal{E}}$, if $\mathsf{Succ}(\mu_{\mathcal{D}}, \alpha_{\mathcal{D}}, a) \sim \mathsf{Succ}(\mu_{\mathcal{E}}, \alpha_{\mathcal{E}}, a)$ holds for all $a \in \mathsf{L}$ then $p(\mu_{\mathcal{D}}, \alpha_{\mathcal{D}}) = p(\mu_{\mathcal{E}}, \alpha_{\mathcal{E}})$. Let us also remark that for fixed $\mu \in \mathsf{subDist}(Q)$, the set $P_\mu = \{p(\mu, \alpha) \mid \alpha \text{ is a local strategy}\} \subseteq \mathbb{R}^{|\mathsf{L}| \cdot k}$ is a (bounded and convex) polytope. As a consequence, if $\mu_{\mathcal{D}} \sim \mu_{\mathcal{E}}$ then the polytopes $P_{\mu_{\mathcal{D}}}$ and $P_{\mu_{\mathcal{E}}}$ must be equal. In the next paragraph we define *"extremal"* strategies $\widehat{\alpha}$, which intuitively are local strategies such that $p(\mu, \widehat{\alpha})$ is a vertex of the polytope P_μ.

Let $v \in \mathbb{R}^{|\mathsf{L}| \cdot k}$ be a *column* vector; we denote column vectors in boldface. We view v as a "direction". Recall that d_q is the Dirac distribution on the state q. A pure local strategy $\widehat{\alpha}$ is *extremal in direction* v *with respect to* B if

$$p(d_q, \alpha)v \leq p(d_q, \widehat{\alpha})v \tag{4}$$
$$p(d_q, \alpha)v = p(d_q, \widehat{\alpha})v \quad \text{implies} \quad p(d_q, \alpha) = p(d_q, \widehat{\alpha}) \tag{5}$$

for all states $q \in Q$ and all pure local strategies α.

By linearity, if (4) and (5) hold for all pure local strategies α then (4) and (5) hold for all local strategies α. We say a local strategy $\widehat{\alpha}$ is *extremal with respect to B* if there is a direction v such that $\widehat{\alpha}$ is extremal in direction v with respect to B.

Proposition 10. *Let $\mathcal{D} = \langle Q, \mu_0, \mathsf{L}, \delta \rangle$ be an MDP. Let $B_1 \in \mathbb{R}^{Q \times k_1}$ and $B_2 \in \mathbb{R}^{Q \times k_2}$ for $k_1, k_2 \geq 1$. Denote by $\mathcal{V}_1, \mathcal{V}_2 \subseteq \mathbb{R}^Q$ the subspaces spanned by the columns of B_1, B_2, respectively. Assume $\mathcal{V}_1 \subseteq \mathcal{V}_2$. If a local strategy $\widehat{\alpha}$ is extremal with respect to B_1 then $\widehat{\alpha}$ is extremal with respect to B_2.*

In light of this fact, we may define that $\widehat{\alpha}$ be *extremal with respect to a column-vector space $\mathcal{V}$* if $\widehat{\alpha}$ is extremal with respect to a matrix B whose column space equals $\mathcal{V}$.

The following proposition describes a vector space $\mathcal{V}$ so that two subdistributions are bisimilar if and only if their difference (viewed as a row vector) is orthogonal to $\mathcal{V}$.

Proposition 11. *Let $\mathcal{D} = \langle Q, \mu_0, \mathsf{L}, \delta \rangle$ be an MDP. Let $\mathcal{V} \subseteq \mathbb{R}^Q$ be the smallest column-vector space such that*

- *$\mathbf{1} = (1 \; 1 \cdots 1)^T \in \mathcal{V}$ (where T denotes transpose) and*
- *$\Delta_{\widehat{\alpha}}(a)\boldsymbol{u} \in \mathcal{V}$ for all $\boldsymbol{u} \in \mathcal{V}$, all labels $a \in \mathsf{L}$ and local strategies $\widehat{\alpha}$ that are extremal with respect to $\mathcal{V}$.*

Then for all $\mu_{\mathcal{D}}, \mu_{\mathcal{E}} \in \mathsf{subDist}(Q)$, we have $\mu_{\mathcal{D}} \sim \mu_{\mathcal{E}}$ if and only if $\mu_{\mathcal{D}}\boldsymbol{u} = \mu_{\mathcal{E}}\boldsymbol{u}$ for all $\boldsymbol{u} \in \mathcal{V}$.

Proposition 11 allows us to prove the following theorem:

Theorem 12. *The problem that, given two MDPs $\mathcal{D}$ and $\mathcal{E}$, asks whether $\mathcal{D} \sim \mathcal{E}$ is in coNP.*

In the following, without loss of generality, we consider an MDP $\mathcal{D} = \langle Q, \mu_0^{\mathcal{D}}, \mathsf{L}, \delta \rangle$ and an MC $\mathcal{C} = \langle Q_{\mathcal{C}}, \mu_0^{\mathcal{C}}, \mathsf{L}, \delta \rangle$ with $Q_{\mathcal{C}} \subseteq Q$. We may view subdistributions $\mu_{\mathcal{C}} \in \mathsf{subDist}(Q_{\mathcal{C}})$ as $\mu_{\mathcal{C}} \in \mathsf{subDist}(Q)$ in the natural way. The following proposition is analogous to Proposition 11.

Proposition 13. *Let $\mathcal{D} = \langle Q, \mu_0^{\mathcal{D}}, \mathsf{L}, \delta \rangle$ be an MDP and $\mathcal{C} = \langle Q_{\mathcal{C}}, \mu_0^{\mathcal{C}}, \mathsf{L}, \delta \rangle$ be an MC with $Q_{\mathcal{C}} \subseteq Q$. Let $\mathcal{V} \subseteq \mathbb{R}^Q$ be the smallest column-vector space such that*

- *$\mathbf{1} = (1 \; 1 \cdots 1)^T \in \mathcal{V}$ (where T denotes transpose) and*
- *$\Delta_\alpha(a)\boldsymbol{u} \in \mathcal{V}$ for all $\boldsymbol{u} \in \mathcal{V}$, all labels $a \in \mathsf{L}$ and all local strategies α.*

Then for all $\mu_{\mathcal{D}} \in \mathsf{subDist}(Q)$ and all $\mu_{\mathcal{C}} \in \mathsf{subDist}(Q_{\mathcal{C}})$, we have $\mu_{\mathcal{D}} \sim \mu_{\mathcal{C}}$ if and only if $\mu_{\mathcal{D}}\boldsymbol{u} = \mu_{\mathcal{C}}\boldsymbol{u}$ for all $\boldsymbol{u} \in \mathcal{V}$.

Notice the differences to Proposition 11: there we considered all extremal local strategies (potentially exponentially many), here we consider all local strategies (in general infinitely many). However, we show that one can efficiently find few local strategies that span all local strategies. This allows us to reduce (in logarithmic space) the bisimulation problem between an MDP and an MC to the bisimulation problem between two MCs, which is equivalent to the trace-equivalence problem in MCs (by Proposition 9). The latter problem is known to be in NC [21]. Theorem 8 then follows with Proposition 9.

References

1. Full version. ArXiv CoRR: http://arxiv.org/abs/1510.09102 (2015)
2. Arora, S., Ge, R., Kannan, R., Moitra, A.: Computing a nonnegative matrix factorization - provably. In: STOC, pp. 145–162. ACM (2012)
3. Blondel, V.D., Canterini, V.: Undecidable problems for probabilistic automata of fixed dimension. Theor. Comput. Sci. **36**(3), 231–245 (2003)
4. Canny, J.: Some algebraic and geometric computations in PSPACE. In: STOC, pp. 460–467 (1988)
5. Cohen, J., Rothblum, U.: Nonnegative ranks, decompositions, and factorizations of nonnegative matrices. Linear Algebra Appl. **190**, 149–168 (1993)
6. Condon, A., Lipton, R.: On the complexity of space bounded interactive proofs (extended abstract). In: FOCS, pp. 462–467 (1989)
7. Cormen, T., Stein, C., Rivest, R., Leiserson, C.E.: Introduction to Algorithms, 2nd edn. McGraw-Hill Higher Education, New York (2001)
8. Doyen, L., Henzinger, T.A., Raskin, J.-F.: Equivalence of labeled Markov chains. Int. J. Found. Comput. Sci. **19**(3), 549–563 (2008)
9. Fearnley, J., Jurdzinski, M.: Reachability in two-clock timed automata is PSPACE-complete. Inf. Comput. **243**, 26–36 (2015)
10. Greenlaw, R., Hoover, H.J., Ruzzo, W.L.: Limits to Parallel Computation: P-completeness Theory. Oxford University Press, Oxford (1995)
11. Hermanns, H., Krčál, J., Křetínský, J.: Probabilistic bisimulation: naturally on distributions. In: Baldan, P., Gorla, D. (eds.) CONCUR 2014. LNCS, vol. 8704, pp. 249–265. Springer, Heidelberg (2014). Technical report at http://arxiv.org/abs/1404.5084
12. Kiefer, S., Murawski, A.S., Ouaknine, J., Wachter, B., Worrell, J.: Language equivalence for probabilistic automata. In: Gopalakrishnan, G., Qadeer, S. (eds.) CAV 2011. LNCS, vol. 6806, pp. 526–540. Springer, Heidelberg (2011)
13. Kiefer, S., Murawski, A.S., Ouaknine, J., Wachter, B., Worrell, J.: APEX: an analyzer for open probabilistic programs. In: Madhusudan, P., Seshia, S.A. (eds.) CAV 2012. LNCS, vol. 7358, pp. 693–698. Springer, Heidelberg (2012)
14. Li, L., Feng, Y.: Quantum Markov chains: description of hybrid systems, decidability of equivalence, and model checking linear-time properties. Inf. Comput. **244**, 229–244 (2015)
15. Ngo, T.M., Stoelinga, M., Huisman, M.: Confidentiality for probabilistic multi-threaded programs and its verification. In: Jürjens, J., Livshits, B., Scandariato, R. (eds.) ESSoS 2013. LNCS, vol. 7781, pp. 107–122. Springer, Heidelberg (2013)
16. Paz, A.: Introduction to Probabilistic Automata. Academic Press, Cambridge (1971)
17. Peyronnet, S., De Rougemont, M., Strozecki, Y.: Approximate verification and enumeration problems. In: Roychoudhury, A., D'Souza, M. (eds.) ICTAC 2012. LNCS, vol. 7521, pp. 228–242. Springer, Heidelberg (2012)
18. Renegar, J.: On the computational complexity and geometry of the first-order theory of the reals. Parts I-III. J. Symbolic Comput. **13**(3), 255–352 (1992)
19. Schützenberger, M.-P.: On the definition of a family of automata. Inf. Control **4**, 245–270 (1961)

20. Tzeng, W.: A polynomial-time algorithm for the equivalence of probabilistic automata. SIAM J. Comput. **21**(2), 216–227 (1992)
21. Tzeng, W.: On path equivalence of nondeterministic finite automata. Inf. Process. Lett. **58**(1), 43–46 (1996)
22. Vavasis, S.: On the complexity of nonnegative matrix factorization. SIAM J. Optim. **20**(3), 1364–1377 (2009)

Qualitative Analysis of VASS-Induced MDPs

Parosh Aziz Abdulla[1], Radu Ciobanu[2], Richard Mayr[2], Arnaud Sangnier[3], and Jeremy Sproston[4(✉)]

[1] Uppsala University, Uppsala, Sweden
[2] University of Edinburgh, Edinburgh, UK
[3] LIAFA, Univ Paris Diderot, Sorbonne Paris Cité, CNRS, Paris, France
[4] University of Turin, Turin, Italy
sproston@di.unito.it

Abstract. We consider infinite-state Markov decision processes (MDPs) that are induced by extensions of vector addition systems with states (VASS). Verification conditions for these MDPs are described by reachability and Büchi objectives w.r.t. given sets of control-states. We study the decidability of some qualitative versions of these objectives, i.e., the decidability of whether such objectives can be achieved surely, almost-surely, or limit-surely. While most such problems are undecidable in general, some are decidable for large subclasses in which either only the controller or only the random environment can change the counter values (while the other side can only change control-states).

1 Introduction

Markov decision processes (MDPs) [14,17] are a formal model for games on directed graphs, where certain decisions are taken by a strategic player (a.k.a. Player 1, or controller) while others are taken randomly (a.k.a. by nature, or the environment) according to pre-defined probability distributions. MDPs are thus a subclass of general 2-player stochastic games, and they are equivalent to 1.5-player games in the terminology of [10]. They are also called "games against nature".

A run of the MDP consists of a sequence of visited states and transitions on the graph. Properties of the system are expressed via properties of the induced runs. The most basic objectives are reachability (is a certain (set of) control-state(s) eventually visited?) and Büchi objectives (is a certain (set of) control-state(s) visited infinitely often?).

Since a strategy of Player 1 induces a probability distribution of runs of the MDP, the objective of an MDP is defined in terms of this distribution, e.g., if the probability of satisfying a reachability/Büchi objective is at least a given constant. The special case where this constant is 1 is a key example

P. A. Abdulla—Supported by UPMARC, Uppsala Programming for Multicore Architectures Research Center.

R. Mayr—Supported by EPSRC grant EP/M027651/1.

J. Sproston—Supported by the MIUR-PRIN project CINA and the EU ARTEMIS Joint Undertaking under grant agreement no. 332933 (HoliDes).

© Springer-Verlag Berlin Heidelberg 2016
B. Jacobs and C. Löding (Eds.): FOSSACS 2016, LNCS 9634, pp. 319–334, 2016.
DOI: 10.1007/978-3-662-49630-5_19

of a qualitative objective. Here one asks whether Player 1 has a strategy that achieves an objective surely (all runs satisfy the property) or almost-surely (the probability of the runs satisfying the property is 1).

Most classical work on algorithms for MDPs and stochastic games has focused on finite-state systems (e.g., [11,14,19]), but more recently several classes of infinite-state systems have been considered as well. For instance, MDPs and stochastic games on infinite-state probabilistic recursive systems (i.e., probabilistic pushdown automata with unbounded stacks) [13] and on one-counter systems [6,7] have been studied. Another infinite-state probabilistic model, which is incomparable to recursive systems, is a suitable probabilistic extension of Vector Addition Systems with States (VASS; a.k.a. Petri nets), which have a finite number of unbounded counters holding natural numbers.

Our Contribution. We study the decidability of probability-1 qualitative reachability and Büchi objectives for infinite-state MDPs that are induced by suitable probabilistic extensions of VASS that we call VASS-MDPs. (Most quantitative objectives in probabilistic VASS are either undecidable, or the solution is at least not effectively expressible in $(\mathbb{R}, +, *, \leq)$ [3]). It is easy to show that, for general VASS-MDPs, even the simplest of these problems, (almost) sure reachability, is undecidable. Thus we consider two monotone subclasses: 1-VASS-MDPs and P-VASS-MDPs. In 1-VASS-MDPs, only Player 1 can modify counter values while the probabilistic player can only change control-states, whereas for P-VASS-MDPs it is vice-versa. Still these two models induce infinite-state MDPs. Unlike for finite-state MDPs, it is possible that the value of the MDP, in the game theoretic sense, is 1, even though there is no single strategy that achieves value 1. For example, there can exist a family of strategies σ_ϵ for every $\epsilon > 0$, where playing σ_ϵ ensures a probability $\geq 1 - \epsilon$ of reaching a given target state, but no strategy ensures probability 1. In this case, one says that the reachability property holds limit-surely, but not almost-surely (i.e., unlike in finite-state MDPs, almost-surely and limit-surely do not coincide in infinite-state MDPs).

We show that even for P-VASS-MDPs, all sure/almost-sure/limit-sure reachability/Büchi problems are still undecidable. However, in the deadlock-free subclass of P-VASS-MDPs, the sure reachability/Büchi problems become decidable (while the other problems remain undecidable). In contrast, for 1-VASS-MDPs, the sure/almost-sure/limit-sure reachability problem and the sure/almost-sure Büchi problem are decidable.

Our decidability results rely on two different techniques. For the sure and almost sure problems, we prove that we can reduce them to the model-checking problem over VASS of a restricted fragment of the modal μ-calculus that has been proved to be decidable in [4]. For the limit-sure reachability problem in 1-VASS-MDP, we use an algorithm which at each iteration reduces the dimension of the considered VASS while preserving the limit-sure reachability properties.

Although we do not consider the class of qualitative objectives referring to the probability of (repeated) reachability being strictly greater than 0, we observe that reachability on VASS-MDPs in such a setting is equivalent to reachability on standard VASS (though this correspondence does not hold for repeated reachability).

Outline. In Sect. 2 we define basic notations and how VASS induce MDPs. In Sects. 3 and 4 we consider verification problems for P-VASS-MDP and 1-VASS-MDP, respectively. In Sect. 5 we summarize the decidability results (Table 1) and outline future work. Omitted proofs can be found in [2].

2 Models and Verification Problems

Let $\mathbb{N}$ (resp. $\mathbb{Z}$) denote the set of nonnegative integers (resp. integers). For two integers i, j such that $i \leq j$ we use $[i..j]$ to represent the set $\{k \in \mathbb{Z} \mid i \leq k \leq j\}$. Given a set X and $n \in \mathbb{N} \setminus \{0\}$, X^n is the set of n-dimensional vectors with values in X. We use $\mathbf{0}$ to denote the vector such that $\mathbf{0}(i) = 0$ for all $i \in [1..n]$. The classical order on $\mathbb{Z}^n$ is denoted $\leq$ and is defined by $\mathbf{v} \leq \mathbf{w}$ if and only if $\mathbf{v}(i) \leq \mathbf{w}(i)$ for all $i \in [1..n]$. We also define the operation $+$ over n-dimensional vectors of integers in the classical way (i.e., for $\mathbf{v}, \mathbf{v}' \in \mathbb{Z}^n$, $\mathbf{v} + \mathbf{v}'$ is defined by $(\mathbf{v} + \mathbf{v}')(i) = \mathbf{v}(i) + \mathbf{v}'(i)$ for all $i \in [1..n]$). Given a set S, we use S^* (respectively S^ω) to denote the set of finite (respectively infinite) sequences of elements of S. We now recall the notion of well-quasi-ordering (which we abbreviate as wqo). A quasi-order $(A, \preceq)$ is a wqo if for every infinite sequence of elements $a_1, a_2, \ldots$ in A, there exist two indices $i < j$ such that $a_i \preceq a_j$. For $n > 0$, $(\mathbb{N}^n, \leq)$ is a wqo. Given a set A with an ordering $\preceq$ and a subset $B \subseteq A$, the set B is said to be *upward closed* in A if $a_1 \in B$, $a_2 \in A$ and $a_1 \preceq a_2$ implies $a_2 \in B$.

2.1 Markov Decision Processes

A probability distribution on a countable set X is a function $f : X \mapsto [0,1]$ such that $\sum_{x \in X} f(x) = 1$. We use $\mathcal{D}(X)$ to denote the set of all probability distributions on X. We first recall the definition of Markov decision processes.

Definition 1 (MDPs). *A Markov decision process (MDP) M is a tuple $\langle C, C_1, C_P, A, \to, p \rangle$ where: C is a countable set of configurations partitioned into C_1 and C_P (that is $C = C_1 \cup C_P$ and $C_1 \cap C_P = \emptyset$); A is a set of actions; $\to \subseteq C \times A \times C$ is a transition relation; $p : C_P \mapsto \mathcal{D}(C)$ is a partial function which assigns to some configurations in C_P probability distributions on C such that $p(c)(c') > 0$ if and only if $c \xrightarrow{a} c'$ for some $a \in A$.*

Note that our definition is equivalent as seeing MDPs as games played between a nondeterministic player (Player 1) and a probabilistic player (Player P). The set C_1 contains the nondeterministic configurations (or configurations of Player 1) and the set C_P contains the probabilistic configurations (or configurations of Player P). Given two configurations c, c' in C, we write $c \to c'$ whenever there exists $a \in A$ such that $c \xrightarrow{a} c'$. We will say that a configuration $c \in C$ is a *deadlock* if there does not exist $c' \in C$ such that $c \to c'$. We use C_1^{df} (resp. C_P^{df}), to denote the configurations of Player 1 (resp. of Player P) which are not a deadlock (*df* stands here for deadlock free).

A *play* of the MDP $M = \langle C, C_1, C_P, A, \rightarrow, p \rangle$ is either an infinite sequence of the form $c_0 \xrightarrow{a_0} c_1 \xrightarrow{a_1} c_2 \cdots$ or a finite sequence $c_0 \xrightarrow{a_0} c_1 \xrightarrow{a_1} c_2 \cdots \xrightarrow{a_{k-1}} c_k$. We call the first kind of play an *infinite play*, and the second one a *finite play*. A play is said to be maximal whenever it is infinite or it ends in a deadlock configuration. These latter plays are called deadlocked plays. We use Ω to denote the set of maximal plays. For a finite play $\rho = c_0 \xrightarrow{a_0} c_1 \xrightarrow{a_1} c_2 \cdots \xrightarrow{a_{k-1}} c_k$, let $c_k = last(\rho)$. We use Ω_1^{df} to denote the set of finite plays ρ such that $last(\rho) \in C_1^{df}$.

A *strategy* for Player 1 is a function $\sigma : \Omega_1^{df} \mapsto C$ such that, for all $\rho \in \Omega_1^{df}$ and $c \in C$, if $\sigma(\rho) = c$ then $last(\rho) \rightarrow c$. Intuitively, given a finite play ρ, which represents the history of the game so far, the strategy represents the choice of Player 1 among the different possible successor configurations from $last(\rho)$. We use Σ to denote the the set of all strategies for Player 1. Given a strategy $\sigma \in \Sigma$, an infinite play $c_0 \xrightarrow{a_0} c_1 \xrightarrow{a_1} c_2 \cdots$ *respects* σ if for every $k \in \mathbb{N}$, we have that if $c_k \in C_1$ then $c_{k+1} = \sigma(c_0 \xrightarrow{a_0} c_1 \xrightarrow{a_1} c_2 \cdots c_k)$ and if $c_k \in C_P$ then $p(c_k)(c_{k+1}) > 0$. We define finite plays that respect σ similarly. Let $\mathtt{Plays}(M, c, \sigma) \subseteq \Omega$ be the set of all maximal plays of M that start from c and that respect σ.

Note that once a starting configuration $c_0 \in C$ and a strategy σ have been chosen, the MDP is reduced to an ordinary stochastic process. We define an event $\mathcal{A} \subseteq \Omega$ as a measurable set of plays and we use $\mathbb{P}(M, c, \sigma, \mathcal{A})$ to denote the probability of event $\mathcal{A}$ starting from $c \in C$ under strategy σ. The notation $\mathbb{P}^+(M, c, \mathcal{A})$ will be used to represent the maximal probability of event $\mathcal{A}$ starting from c which is defined as $\mathbb{P}^+(M, c, \mathcal{A}) = \sup_{\sigma \in \Sigma} \mathbb{P}(M, c, \sigma, \mathcal{A})$.

2.2   VASS-MDPs

Probabilistic Vector Addition Systems with States have been studied, e.g., in [3]. Here we extend this model with non-deterministic choices made by a controller. We call this new model VASS-MDPs. We first recall the definition of Vector Addition Systems with States.

Definition 2 (VASS). *For $n > 0$, an n-dimensional Vector Addition System with States (VASS) is a tuple $S = \langle Q, T \rangle$ where Q is a finite set of control states and $T \subseteq Q \times \mathbb{Z}^n \times Q$ is the transition relation labelled with vectors of integers.*

In the sequel, we will not always make precise the dimension of the considered VASS. Configurations of a VASS are pairs $\langle q, \mathbf{v} \rangle \in Q \times \mathbb{N}^n$. Given a configuration $\langle q, \mathbf{v} \rangle$ and a transition $t = \langle q, \mathbf{z}, q' \rangle$ in T, we will say that t is *enabled* at $\langle q'', \mathbf{v} \rangle$, if $q = q''$ and $\mathbf{v} + \mathbf{z} \geq \mathbf{0}$. Let then $En(q, \mathbf{v})$ be the set $\{t \in T \mid t \text{ is enabled at } \langle q, \mathbf{v} \rangle\}$. In case the transition $t = \langle q, \mathbf{z}, q' \rangle$ is enabled at $\langle q, \mathbf{v} \rangle$, we define $t(q, \mathbf{v}) = \langle q', \mathbf{v}' \rangle$ where $\mathbf{v}' = \mathbf{v} + \mathbf{z}$. An n-dimensional VASS S induces a labelled transition system $\langle C, T, \rightarrow \rangle$ where $C = Q \times \mathbb{N}^n$ is the set of configurations and the transition relation $\rightarrow \subseteq C \times T \times C$ is defined as follows: $\langle q, \mathbf{v} \rangle \xrightarrow{t} \langle q', \mathbf{v}' \rangle$ iff $\langle q', \mathbf{v}' \rangle = t(q, \mathbf{v})$. VASS are sometimes seen as programs manipulating integer variables, a.k.a. counters. When a transition of a VASS changes the i-th value of a vector $\mathbf{v}$, we will sometimes say that it modifies the value of the i-th counter. We show now in which manner we add probability distributions to VASS.

Definition 3 (VASS-MDP). *A VASS-MDP is a tuple $S = \langle Q, Q_1, Q_P, T, \tau \rangle$ where $\langle Q, T \rangle$ is a VASS for which the set of control states Q is partitioned into Q_1 and Q_P, and $\tau : T \mapsto \mathbb{N} \setminus \{0\}$ is a partial function assigning to each transition a weight which is a positive natural number.*

Nondeterministic (resp. probabilistic) choices are made from control states in Q_1 (resp. Q_P). The subset of transitions from control states of Q_1 (resp. control states of Q_P) is denoted by T_1 (resp. T_P). Hence $T = T_1 \cup T_P$ with $T_1 \subseteq Q_1 \times \mathbb{Z}^n \times Q$ and $T_P \subseteq Q_P \times \mathbb{Z}^n \times Q$. A VASS-MDP $S = \langle Q, Q_1, Q_P, T, \tau \rangle$ induces an MDP $M_S = \langle C, C_1, C_P, T, \rightarrow, p \rangle$ where: $\langle C, T, \rightarrow \rangle$ is the labelled transition system associated with the VASS $\langle Q, T \rangle$; $C_1 = Q_1 \times \mathbb{N}^n$ and $C_P = Q_P \times \mathbb{N}^n$; and for all $c \in C_P^{df}$ and $c' \in C$, if $c \rightarrow c'$, the probability of going from c to c' is defined by $p(c)(c') = (\sum_{\{t | t(c) = c'\}} \tau(t)) / (\sum_{t \in \text{En}(c)} \tau(t))$, whereas if $c \not\rightarrow c'$, we have $p(c)(c') = 0$. Note that the MDP M_S is well-defined: when defining $p(c)(c')$ in the case $c \rightarrow c'$, there exists at least one transition in $\text{En}(c)$ and consequently the sum $\sum_{t \in \text{En}(c)} \tau(t)$ is never equal to 0. Also, we could have restricted the weights to be assigned only to transitions leaving from a control state in Q_P since we do not take into account the weights assigned to the other transitions. A VASS-MDP is deadlock free if its underlying VASS is deadlock free.

Finally, as in [18] or [4], we will see that to gain decidability it is useful to restrict the power of the nondeterministic player or of the probabilistic player by restricting their ability to modify the counters' values and hence letting them only choose a control location. This leads to the two following definitions: a *P-VASS-MDP* is a VASS-MDP $\langle Q, Q_1, Q_P, T, \tau \rangle$ such that for all $\langle q, \mathbf{z}, q' \rangle \in T_1$, we have $\mathbf{z} = \mathbf{0}$ and a *1-VASS-MDP* is a VASS-MDP $\langle Q, Q_1, Q_P, T, \tau \rangle$ such that for all $\langle q, \mathbf{z}, q' \rangle \in T_P$, we have $\mathbf{z} = \mathbf{0}$. In other words, in a P-VASS-MDP, Player 1 cannot change the counter values when taking a transition and, in a 1-VASS-MDP, it is Player P which cannot perform such an action.

2.3   Verification Problems for VASS-MDPs

We consider qualitative verification problems for VASS-MDPs, taking as objectives control-state reachability and repeated reachability. To simplify the presentation, we consider a single target control-state $q_F \in Q$. However, our positive decidability results easily carry over to sets of target control-states (while the negative ones trivially do). Note however, that asking to reach a *fixed target configuration* like $\langle q_F, \mathbf{0} \rangle$ is a very different problem (cf. [3]).

Let $S = \langle Q, Q_1, Q_P, T, \tau \rangle$ be a VASS-MDP and M_S its associated MDP. Given a control state $q_F \in Q$, we denote by $[\![\lozenge q_F]\!]$ the set of infinite plays $c_0 \cdot c_1 \cdots$ and deadlocked plays $c_0 \cdots \cdots c_l$ of M_S for which there exists an index $k \in \mathbb{N}$ such that $c_k = \langle q_F, \mathbf{v} \rangle$ for some $\mathbf{v} \in \mathbb{N}^n$. Similarly, $[\![\square \lozenge q_F]\!]$ characterizes the set of infinite plays $c_0 \cdot c_1 \cdots$ of M_S for which the set $\{ i \in \mathbb{N} \mid c_i = \langle q_F, \mathbf{v} \rangle$ for some $\mathbf{v} \in \mathbb{N}^n \}$ is infinite. Since M_S is an MDP with a countable number of configurations, we know that the sets of plays $[\![\lozenge q_F]\!]$ and $[\![\square \lozenge q_F]\!]$ are measurable (for more details see for instance [5]), and are hence events for

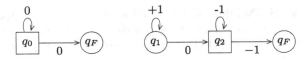

Fig. 1. Two 1-dimensional VASS-MDPs. The circles (resp. squares) are the control states of Player 1 (resp. Player P). All transitions have the same weight 1. From $\langle q_0, 0 \rangle$, the state q_F is reached almost-surely, but not surely, due to the possible run with an infinite loop at q_0 (which has probability zero). From $\langle q_1, 0 \rangle$, the state q_F can be reached limit-surely (by a family of strategies that repeats the loop at q_1 more and more often), but not almost-surely (or surely), since every strategy has a chance of getting stuck at state q_2 with counter value zero.

M_S. Given an initial configuration $c_0 \in Q \times \mathbb{N}^n$ and a control-state $q_F \in Q$, we consider the following questions:

1. The *sure reachability problem*: Does there exist a strategy $\sigma \in \Sigma$ such that $\mathtt{Plays}(M_S, c_0, \sigma) \subseteq [\![\Diamond q_F]\!]$?
2. The *almost-sure reachability problem*: Does there exist a strategy $\sigma \in \Sigma$ such that $\mathbb{P}(M_S, c_0, \sigma, [\![\Diamond q_F]\!]) = 1$?
3. The *limit-sure reachability problem*: Does $\mathbb{P}^+(M_S, c_0, [\![\Diamond q_F]\!]) = 1$?
4. The *sure repeated reachability problem*: Does there exist a strategy $\sigma \in \Sigma$ such that $\mathtt{Plays}(M_S, c_0, \sigma) \subseteq [\![\Box \Diamond q_F]\!]$?
5. The *almost-sure repeated reachability problem*: Does there exist a strategy $\sigma \in \Sigma$ such that $\mathbb{P}(M_S, c_0, \sigma, [\![\Box \Diamond q_F]\!]) = 1$?
6. The *limit-sure repeated reachability problem*: Does $\mathbb{P}^+(M_S, c_0, [\![\Box \Diamond q_F]\!]) = 1$?

Note that sure reachability implies almost-sure reachability, which itself implies limit-sure reachability, but not vice-versa, as shown by the counterexamples in Fig. 1 (see also [7]). The same holds for repeated reachability. For the sure problems, probabilities are not taken into account, and thus these problems can be interpreted as the answer to a two player reachability game played on the transition system of S. Such games have been studied for instance in [1,4,18]. Finally, VASS-MDPs subsume deadlock-free VASS-MDPs and thus decidability (resp. undecidability) results carry over to the smaller (resp. larger) class.

2.4   Undecidability in the General Case

It was shown in [1] that the sure reachability problem is undecidable for (2-dimensional) two player VASS. From this we can deduce that the sure reachability problem is undecidable for VASS-MDPs. We now present a similar proof to show the undecidability of the almost-sure reachability problem for VASS-MDPs.

For all of our undecidability results we use reductions from the undecidable control-state reachability problem for Minsky machines. A Minsky machine is a tuple $\langle Q, T \rangle$ where Q is a finite set of states and T is a finite set of transitions manipulating two counters, say x_1 and x_2. Each transition is a triple of the form $\langle q, x_i = 0?, q' \rangle$ (counter x_i is tested for 0) or $\langle q, x_i := x_i + 1, q' \rangle$ (counter x_i is incremented) or $\langle q, x_i := x_i - 1, q' \rangle$ (counter x_i is decremented) where $q, q' \in Q$.

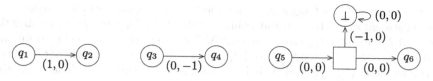

Fig. 2. Encoding $\langle q_1, x_1 := x_1 + 1, q_2 \rangle$ and $\langle q_3, x_2 := x_2 - 1, q_4 \rangle$ and $\langle q_5, x_1 = 0?, q_6 \rangle$

Configurations of a Minsky machine are triples in $Q \times \mathbb{N} \times \mathbb{N}$. The transition relation $\Rightarrow$ between configurations of the Minsky machine is then defined in the obvious way. Given an initial state q_I and a final state q_F, the control-state reachability problem asks whether there exists a sequence of configurations $\langle q_I, 0, 0 \rangle \Rightarrow \langle q_1, v_1, v_1' \rangle \Rightarrow \ldots \Rightarrow \langle q_k, v_k, v_k' \rangle$ with $q_k = q_F$. This problem is known to be undecidable [16]. W.l.o.g. we assume that Minsky machines are deadlock-free and deterministic (i.e., each configuration has always a unique successor) and that the only transition leaving q_F is of the form $\langle q_F, x_1 := x_1 + 1, q_F \rangle$.

We now show how to reduce the control-state reachability problem to the almost-sure and limit-sure reachability problems in deadlock-free VASS-MDPs. From a Minsky machine, we construct a deadlock-free 2-dimensional VASS-MDP for which the control states of Player 1 are exactly the control states of the Minsky machine. The encoding is presented in Fig. 2 where the circles (resp. squares) are the control states of Player 1 (resp. Player P), and for each edge the corresponding weight is 1. The state $\bot$ is an absorbing state from which the unique outgoing transition is a self loop that does not affect the values of the counters. This encoding allows us to deduce our first result.

Theorem 1. *The sure, almost-sure and limit-sure (repeated) reachability problems are undecidable problems for 2-dimensional deadlock-free VASS-MDPs.*

In the special case of 1-dimensional VASS-MDPs, the sure and almost-sure reachability problems are decidable [7].

2.5   Model-Checking μ-calculus on Single-Sided VASS

It is well-known that there is a strong connection between model-checking branching time logics and games, and in our case we have in fact undecidability results for simple reachability games played on a VASS and for the model-checking of VASS with expressive branching-time logics [12]. However for this latter point, decidability can be regained by imposing some restrictions on the VASS structure [4] as we will now recall. We say that a VASS $\langle Q, T \rangle$ is (Q_1, Q_2)-single-sided iff Q_1 and Q_2 represents a partition of the set of states Q such that for all transitions $\langle q, \mathbf{z}, q' \rangle$ in T with $q \in Q_2$, we have $\mathbf{z} = \mathbf{0}$; in other words only the transitions leaving a state from Q_1 are allowed to change the values of the counters. In [4], it has been shown that, thanks to a reduction to games played on a single-sided VASS with parity objectives, a large fragment of the μ-calculus called L_μ^{sv} has a decidable model-checking problem over single-sided

VASS. The idea of this fragment is that the "always" operator $\Box$ is guarded with a predicate enforcing the current control states to belong to Q_2. Formally, the syntax of L_μ^{sv} for (Q_1, Q_2)-single-sided VASS is given by the following grammar: $\phi ::= q \mid X \mid \phi \wedge \phi \mid \phi \vee \phi \mid \Diamond \phi \mid Q_2 \wedge \Box \phi \mid \mu X.\phi \mid \nu X.\phi$, where Q_2 stands for the formula $\bigvee_{q \in Q_2} q$ and X belongs to a set of variables $\mathcal{X}$. The semantics of L_μ^{sv} is defined as usual: it associates to a formula ϕ and to an environment $\varepsilon : \mathcal{X} \to 2^C$ a subset of configurations $[\![\phi]\!]_\varepsilon$. We use ε_0 to denote the environment which assigns the empty set to any variable. Given an environment ε, a variable $X \in \mathcal{X}$ and a subset of configurations C, we use $\varepsilon[X := C]$ to represent the environment ε' which is equal to ε except on the variable X, where we have $\varepsilon'(X) = C$. Finally the notation $[\![\phi]\!]$ corresponds to the interpretation $[\![\phi]\!]_{\varepsilon_0}$.

The problem of model-checking single-sided VASS with L_μ^{sv} can then be defined as follows: given a single-sided VASS $\langle Q, T \rangle$, an initial configuration c_0 and a formula ϕ of L_μ^{sv}, do we have $c_0 \in [\![\phi]\!]$?

Theorem 2 [4]. *Model-checking single-sided VASS wrt. L_μ^{sv} is decidable.*

3   Verification of P-VASS-MDPs

In [4] it is proved that parity games played on a single-sided deadlock-free VASS are decidable (this entails the decidability of model checking L_μ^{sv} over single-sided VASS). We will see here that in the case of P-VASS-MDPs, in which only the probabilistic player can modify the counters, the decidability status depends on the presence of deadlocks in the system.

3.1   Undecidability in Presence of Deadlocks

We point out that the reduction presented in Fig. 2 to prove Theorem 1 does not carry over to P-VASS-MDPs, because in that construction both players have the ability to change the counter values. However, it is possible to perform a similar reduction leading to the undecidability of verification problems for P-VASS-MDPs, the main difference being that we crucially exploit the fact that the P-VASS-MDP can contain deadlocks.

We now explain the idea behind our encoding of Minsky machines into P-VASS-MDPs. Intuitively, Player 1 chooses a transition of the Minsky machine to simulate, anticipating the modification of the counters values, and Player P is then in charge of performing the change. If Player 1 chooses a transition with a decrement and the accessed counter value is actually 0, then Player P will be in a deadlock state and consequently the desired control state will not be reached. Furthermore, if Player 1 decides to perform a zero-test when the counter value is strictly positive, then Player P is able to punish this choice by entering a deadlock state. Similarly to the proof of Theorem 1, Player P can test if the value of the counter is strictly greater than 0 by decrementing it. The encoding of the Minsky machine is presented in Fig. 3. Note that no outgoing edge of Player 1's states changes the counter values. Furthermore, we see that Player P

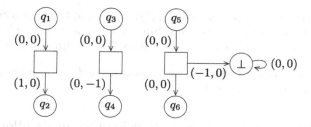

Fig. 3. Encoding $\langle q_1, x_1 := x_1 + 1, q_2 \rangle$ and $\langle q_3, x_2 := x_2 - 1, q_4 \rangle$ and $\langle q_5, x_1 = 0?, q_6 \rangle$

reaches the control state $\bot$ if and only if Player 1 chooses to take a transition with a zero-test when the value of the tested counter is not equal to 0. Note that, with the encoding of the transition $\langle q_3, x_2 := x_2 - 1, q_4 \rangle$, when Player P is in the control state between q_3 and q_4, it can be in a deadlock if the value of the second counter is not positive. In the sequel we will see that in P-VASS-MDP without deadlocks the sure reachability problem becomes decidable.

From this encoding we deduce the following result.

Theorem 3. *The sure, almost sure and limit sure (repeated) reachability problems are undecidable for 2-dimensional P-VASS-MDPs.*

3.2   Sure (repeated) Reachability in Deadlock-Free P-VASS-MDPs

Unlike in the case of general P-VASS-MDPs, we will see that the sure (repeated) reachability problem is decidable for deadlock-free P-VASS-MDPs. Let $S = \langle Q, Q_1, Q_P, T, \tau \rangle$ be a deadlock-free P-VASS-MDP, $M_S = (C, C_1, C_P, \rightarrow, p)$ its associated MDP and $q_F \in Q$ a control state. Note that because the P-VASS-MDP S is deadlock free, Player P cannot take the play to a deadlock to avoid the control state q_F, but he has to deal only with infinite plays. Since S is a P-VASS-MDP, the VASS $\langle Q, T \rangle$ is (Q_P, Q_1)-single-sided. In [1,18], it has been shown that control-state reachability games on deadlock-free single-sided VASS are decidable, and this result has been extended to parity games in [4]. This implies the decidability of sure (repeated) reachability in deadlock-free P-VASS-MDPs. However, to obtain a generic way of verifying these systems, we construct a formula of L_μ^{sv} that characterizes the sets of winning configurations and use then the result of Theorem 2. Let V_S^P be the set of configurations from which the answer to the sure reachability problem (with q_F as state to be reached) is negative, i.e., $V_S^P = \{c \in C \mid \nexists \sigma \in \Sigma \text{ s.t. } \mathtt{Plays}(M_S, c, \sigma) \subseteq [\![\Diamond q_F]\!]\}$ and similarly let $W_S^P = \{c \in C \mid \nexists \sigma \in \Sigma \text{ s.t. } \mathtt{Plays}(M_S, c, \sigma) \subseteq [\![\Box \Diamond q_F]\!]\}$. The next lemma relates these two sets with a formula of L_μ^{sv} (where Q_P corresponds to the formula $\bigvee_{q \in Q_P}$ and Q_1 corresponds to the formula $\bigvee_{q \in Q_1} q$).

Lemma 1. $-\ V_S^P = [\![\nu X.(\bigvee_{q \in Q \setminus \{q_F\}} q) \wedge (Q_1 \vee \Diamond X) \wedge (Q_P \vee (Q_1 \wedge \Box X))]\!].$
  $-\ W_S^P = [\![\mu Y.\nu X.((\bigvee_{q \in Q \setminus \{q_F\}} q) \wedge (Q_1 \vee \Diamond X) \wedge (Q_P \vee (Q_1 \wedge \Box X)) \vee (q_F \wedge Q_P \wedge \Diamond Y) \vee (q_F \wedge Q_1 \wedge \Box Y))]\!]$

We use $(Q_P \vee (Q_1 \wedge \Box X))$ instead of $(Q_P \vee \Box X)$ so that the formulae are in the guarded fragment of the μ-calculus. Since the two formulae belong to L_μ^{sv} for the (Q_P, Q_1)-single-sided VASS S, decidability follows directly from Theorem 2.

Theorem 4. *The sure reachability and repeated reachability problem are decidable for deadlock free P-VASS-MDPs.*

3.3   Almost-Sure and Limit-Sure Reachability in Deadlock-Free P-VASS-MDPs

We have seen that, unlike for the general case, the sure reachability and sure repeated reachability problems are decidable for deadlock free P-VASS-MDPs, with deadlock freeness being necessary to obtain decidability. For the corresponding almost-sure and limit-sure problems we now show undecidability, again using a reduction from the reachability problem for two counter Minsky machines, as shown in Fig. 4. The main difference with the construction used for the proof of Theorem 3 lies in the addition of a self-loop in the encoding of the transitions for decrementing a counter, in order to avoid deadlocks. If Player 1, from a configuration $\langle q_3, \mathbf{v} \rangle$, chooses the transition $\langle q_3, x_2 := x_2 - 1, q_4 \rangle$ which decrements the second counter, then the probabilistic state with the self-loop is entered, and there are two possible cases: if $\mathbf{v}(2) > 0$ then the probability of staying forever in this loop is 0 and the probability of eventually going to state q_4 is 1; on the other hand, if $\mathbf{v}(2) = 0$ then the probability of staying forever in the self-loop is 1, since the other transition that leaves the state of Player P and which performs the decrement on the second counter effectively is not available. Note that such a construction does not hold in the case of sure reachability, because the path that stays forever in the loop is a valid path.

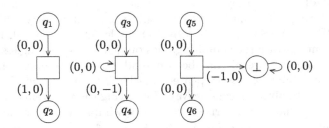

Fig. 4. Encoding $\langle q_1, x_1 := x_1 + 1, q_2 \rangle$ and $\langle q_3, x_2 := x_2 - 1, q_4 \rangle$ and $\langle q_5, x_1 = 0?, q_6 \rangle$

This allows us to deduce the following result for deadlock free P-VASS-MDPs.

Theorem 5. *The almost-sure and limit-sure (repeated) reachability problems are undecidable for 2-dimensional deadlock-free P-VASS-MDPs.*

4   Verification of 1-VASS-MDPs

In this section, we will provide decidability results for the subclass of 1-VASS-MDPs. As for deadlock-free P-VASS-MDPs, the proofs for sure and almost-sure problems use the decidability of L_μ^{sv} over single-sided VASS, whereas the technique used to show decidability of limit-sure reachability is different.

4.1   Sure Problems in 1-VASS-MDPs

First we show that, unlike for P-VASS-MDPs, deadlocks do not matter for 1-VASS-MDPs. The idea is that in this case, if the deadlock is in a probabilistic configuration, it means that there is no outgoing edge (because of the property of 1-VASS-MDPs), and hence one can add an edge to a new absorbing state, and the same can be done for the states of Player 1. Such a construction does not work for P-VASS-MDPs, because in that case deadlocks in probabilistic configurations may depend on the counter values, and not just on the current control-state.

Lemma 2. *The sure (resp. almost sure, resp. limit sure) (repeated) reachability problem for 1-VASS-MDPs reduces to the sure (resp. almost sure, resp. limit-sure) (repeated) reachability problem for deadlock-free 1-VASS-MDPs.*

Hence in the sequel we will consider only deadlock-free 1-VASS-MDPs. Let $S = \langle Q, Q_1, Q_P, T, \tau \rangle$ be a deadlock-free 1-VASS-MDP. For what concerns the sure (repeated) reachability problems we can directly reuse the results from Lemma 1 and then show that the complement formulae of the ones expressed in this lemma belong to L_μ^{sv} for the (Q_1, Q_P)-single-sided VASS $\langle Q, T \rangle$ (in fact the correctness of these two lemmas did not depend on the fact that we were considering P-VASS-MDPs). Theorem 2 allows us to retrieve the decidability results already expressed in [18] (for sure reachability) and [4] (for sure repeated reachability).

Theorem 6. *The sure (repeated) reachability problem is decidable for 1-VASS-MDPs.*

4.2   Almost-Sure Problems in 1-VASS-MDPs

We now move to the case of almost-sure problems in 1-VASS-MDPs. We consider a deadlock free 1-VASS-MDP $S = \langle Q, Q_1, Q_P, T, \tau \rangle$ and its associated MDP $M_S = \langle C, C_1, C_P, \rightarrow, p \rangle$. We will see that, unlike for P-VASS-MDPs, it is here also possible to characterize by formulae of L_μ^{sv} the two following sets: $V_{AS}^1 = \{ c \in C \mid \exists \sigma \in \Sigma$ such that $\mathbb{P}(M_S, c, \sigma, [\![\Diamond q_F]\!]) = 1 \}$ and $W_{AS}^1 = \{ c \in C \mid \exists \sigma \in \Sigma$ such that $\mathbb{P}(M_S, c, \sigma, [\![\Box \Diamond q_F]\!]) = 1 \}$, i.e. the set of configurations from which Player 1 has a strategy to reach the control state q_F, respectively to visit infinitely often q_F, with probability 1.

We begin with introducing the following formula of L_μ^{sv} based on the variables X and Y: $\mathtt{InvPre}(X, Y) = (Q_1 \wedge \Diamond(X \wedge Y)) \vee (\Diamond Y \wedge Q_P \wedge \Box X)$. Note that

$\text{InvPre}(X, Y)$ is a formula of L^{sv}_μ for the (Q_1, Q_P)-single-sided VASS $\langle Q, T \rangle$. Intuitively, this formula represents the set of configurations from which (i) Player 1 can make a transition to the set represented by the intersection of the sets characterized by the variables X and Y and (ii) Player P can make a transition to the set Y and cannot avoid making a transition to the set X.

Almost Sure Reachability. We will now prove that V^1_{AS} can be characterized by the following formula of L^{sv}_μ: $\nu X.\mu Y.(q_F \vee \text{InvPre}(X, Y))$. Note that a similar result exists for finite-state MDPs, see e.g. [9]; this result in general does not extend to infinite-state MDPs, but in the case of VASS-MDPs it can be applied. Before proving this we need some intermediate results.

We denote by E the set $[\![\nu X.\mu Y.(q_F \vee \text{InvPre}(X, Y))]\!]_{\varepsilon_0}$. Since $\nu X.\mu Y.(q_F \vee \text{InvPre}(X, Y))$ is a formula of L^{sv}_μ interpreted over the single-sided VASS $\langle Q, T \rangle$, we can show that E is an upward-closed set. We now need another lemma which states that there exists $N \in \mathbb{N}$ and a strategy for Player 1 such that, from any configuration of E, Player 1 can reach the control state q_F in less than N steps and Player P cannot take the play outside of E. The fact that we can bound the number of steps is crucial to show that $[\![\nu X.\mu Y.(q_F \vee \text{InvPre}(X, Y))]\!]_{\varepsilon_0}$ is equal to V^1_{AS}. For infinite-state MDPs where this property does not hold, our techniques do not apply.

Lemma 3. *There exists $N \in \mathbb{N}$ and a strategy σ of Player 1 such that for all $c \in E$, there exists a play $c \cdot c_1 \cdot c_2 \cdots \ldots$ in $\text{Plays}(M_S, c, \sigma)$ satisfying the three following properties: (1) there exists $0 \le i \le N$ such that $c_i \in [\![q_F]\!]$; (2) for all $0 \le j \le i$, $c_j \in E$; (3) for all $0 \le j \le i$, if $c_j \in C_P$ then for all $c'' \in C$ such that $c_j \to c''$, we have $c'' \in E$.*

This previous lemma allows us to characterize V^1_{AS} with a formula of L^{sv}_μ. The proof of the following result uses the fact that the number of steps is bounded, and also the fact that the sets described by closed L^{sv}_μ formulae are upward-closed. This makes the fixpoint iteration terminate in a finite number of steps.

Lemma 4. $V^1_{AS} = [\![\nu X.\mu Y.(q_F \vee \text{InvPre}(X, Y))]\!]$.

Since $\langle Q, T \rangle$ is (Q_1, Q_P)-single-sided and since the formula associated to V^1_{AS} belongs to L^{sv}_μ, from Theorem 2 we deduce the following theorem.

Theorem 7. *The almost-sure reachability problem is decidable for 1-VASS-MDPs.*

Almost Sure Repeated Reachability. For the case of almost sure repeated reachability we reuse the previously introduced formula $\text{InvPre}(X, Y)$. We can perform a reasoning similar to the previous ones and provide a characterization of the set W^1_{AS}.

Lemma 5. $W^1_{AS} = [\![\nu X.\text{InvPre}(X, \mu Y.(q_F \vee \text{InvPre}(X, Y)))]\!]$.

As previously, this allows us to deduce the decidability of the almost sure repeated reachability problem for 1-VASS-MDP.

Theorem 8. *The almost sure repeated reachability problem is decidable for 1-VASS-MDPs.*

4.3 Limit-Sure Reachability in 1-VASS-MDP

We consider a slightly more general version of the limit-sure reachability problem with a set $X \subseteq Q$ of target states instead of a single state q_F, i.e., the standard case corresponds to $X = \{q_F\}$.

We extend the set of natural numbers $\mathbb{N}$ to $\mathbb{N}_* = \mathbb{N} \cup \{*\}$ by adding an element $* \notin \mathbb{N}$ with $* + j = * - j = *$ and $j < *$ for all $j \in \mathbb{N}$. We consider then the set of vectors $\mathbb{N}_*^d$. The projection of a vector $\mathbf{v}$ in $\mathbb{N}^d$ by eliminating components that are indexed by a natural number k is defined by $proj_k(\mathbf{v})(i) = \mathbf{v}(i)$ if $i \neq k$ and $proj_k(\mathbf{v})(i) = *$ otherwise

Let Q_c represent control-states which are indexed by a color. The coloring functions $col_i : Q \to Q_c$ create colored copies of control-states by $col_i(q) = q_i$.

Given a 1-VASS-MDP $S = \langle Q, Q_1, Q_P, T, \tau \rangle$ of dimension d, an index $k \leq d$ and a color i, the colored projection is defined as:

$$Proj_k(S, d, i) = \langle col_i(Q), col_i(Q_1), col_i(Q_P), proj_{k,i}(T), \tau_{k,i} \rangle$$

where $proj_{k,i}(T) = \{proj_{k,i}(t) | t \in T\}$ is the projection of the set of transitions T and $proj_{k,i}(t) = \langle col_i(x), proj_k(\mathbf{z}), col_i(y) \rangle$ is the projection of transition $t = \langle x, \mathbf{z}, y \rangle$ obtained by removing component k and coloring the states x and y with color i. The transition weights carry over, i.e., $\tau_{k,i}(t') = \sum \{\tau(t) \,|\, proj_{k,i}(t) = t'\}$.

We define the functions $state : Q \times \mathbb{N}_*^d \to Q$ and $count : Q \times \mathbb{N}_*^d \to \mathbb{N}_*^d$ s.t for a configuration $c_i = \langle q, \mathbf{v} \rangle$, where $q \in Q$ and $\mathbf{v} \in \mathbb{N}_*^d$ we have that $state(q, \mathbf{v}) = q$ and $count(q, \mathbf{v}) = \mathbf{v}$. For any two configurations c_1 and c_2, we write $c_1 \prec c_2$ to denote that $state(c_1) = state(c_2)$, and there exists a nonempty set of indexes I where for every $i \in I$, $count(c_1)(i) < count(c_2)(i)$, whereas for every index $j \notin I$, $0 < j \leq d$, $count(c_1)(j) = count(c_2)(j)$.

Algorithm 1 reduces the dimension of the limit-sure reachability problem for 1-VASS-MDP by a construction resembling the Karp-Miller tree [15]. It takes as input a 1-VASS-MDP S of some dimension $d > 0$ with a set of target states X. It outputs a new 1-VASS-MDP S' of dimension $d-1$ and a new set of target states X' such that M_S can limit-surely reach X iff $M_{S'}$ can limit-surely reach X'. In particular, in the base case where $d-1 = 0$, the new system S' has dimension zero and thus induces a finite-state MDP $M_{S'}$, for which limit-sure reachability of X' coincides with almost-sure reachability of X', which is known to be decidable in polynomial time. Algorithm 1 starts by exploring all branches of the computation tree of S (and adding them to S' as the so-called initial *uncolored part*) until it encounters a configuration that is either (1) equal to, or (2) strictly larger than a configuration encountered previously on the same branch. In case (1) it just adds a back loop to the point where the configuration was encountered previously. In case (2), it adds a modified copy of S (identified by a unique color) to S'. This so-called colored subsystem is similar to S except that those counters that have strictly increased along the branch are removed. The intuition is that these counters could be pumped to arbitrarily high values and thus present no obstacle to reaching the target. Since the initial uncolored part is necessarily finite (by Dickson's Lemma) and each of the finitely many colored subsystems only has dimension $d - 1$ (since a counter is removed; possibly a different one in different colored subsystems), the resulting 1-VASS-MDP S' has dimension $d - 1$. The set of target states X' is defined as the union of all appearances of states in X in the uncolored part, plus all colored copies of states from X in the colored subsystems.

Algorithm 1. Reducing the dimension of the limit-sure reachability problem.

Require: $S = \langle Q, Q_1, Q_P, T, \tau \rangle$ 1-VASS-MDP, dimension $d > 0$, $c_0 = \langle q_0, \mathbf{v} \rangle \in Q \times \mathbb{N}^d$
    $X \subseteq Q$ - set of target states
Ensure: $S' = \langle Q', Q_1', Q_P', T', \tau' \rangle$; $c_0' = \langle q_0', \mathbf{0} \rangle$; $X' \subseteq Q'$; $\lambda : Q' \to ((Q \cup Q_c) \times \mathbb{N}_*^d)$
1: $Q' \leftarrow \varnothing$; $Q_1' \leftarrow \varnothing$; $Q_P' \leftarrow \varnothing$; $T' \leftarrow \varnothing$; $\tau' \leftarrow \varnothing$;
2: $\text{new}(q')$; $q_0' \leftarrow q'$; $\lambda(q') \leftarrow c_0$; $Q' \leftarrow \{q'\}$; $i \leftarrow 0$
3: **if** $state(\lambda(q')) \in Q_1$ **then** $Q_1' \leftarrow \{q'\}$ **else** $Q_P' \leftarrow \{q'\}$
4: $\text{ToExplore} \leftarrow \{q'\}$
5: **while** $\text{ToExplore} \neq \varnothing$ **do**
6:     Pick and remove a $q \in \text{ToExplore}$
7:     **if** $\exists q'$. q' is previously on the same branch as q and $\lambda(q') \prec \lambda(q)$ **then**
8:         get indexes I in which the counter is increasing
9:         pick and remove the first index k from I
10:         $i \leftarrow i + 1$; // increase color index
11:         $\text{new}(q'')$;
12:         $\lambda(q'') \leftarrow \langle col_i(state(\lambda(q))), proj_k(count(\lambda(q))) \rangle$
13:         **if** $state(\lambda(q)) \in Q_1$ **then** $Q_1' \leftarrow Q_1' \bigcup \{q''\}$ **else** $Q_P' \leftarrow Q_P' \bigcup \{q''\}$
14:         $T' \leftarrow T' \bigcup \{\langle q, \mathbf{0}, q'' \rangle\}$; $\tau'(\langle q, \mathbf{0}, q'' \rangle) = 1$;
15:         $Q_1' \leftarrow Q_1' \bigcup col_i(Q_1)$; $Q_P' \leftarrow Q_P' \bigcup col_i(Q_P)$; $T' \leftarrow T' \bigcup proj_{k,i}(T)$;
16:         $X' \leftarrow X' \bigcup col_i(X)$; $\tau' \leftarrow \tau' \cup \tau_{k,i}$
17:     **else**
18:         **for** every $t = \langle x, \mathbf{z}, y \rangle$ in T such that $t \in \text{En}(\lambda(q))$ **do**
19:             **if** $\exists q'$. q' is previously on the same branch as q and $t(\lambda(q)) = \lambda(q')$ **then**
20:                 $T' \leftarrow T' \bigcup \{\langle q, \mathbf{z}, q' \rangle\}$;
21:             **else**
22:                 $\text{new}(q')$; $\lambda(q') \leftarrow t(\lambda(q))$
23:                 $T' \leftarrow T' \bigcup \{\langle q, \mathbf{z}, q' \rangle\}$; $\tau'(\langle q, \mathbf{z}, q' \rangle) \leftarrow \tau(t)$
24:                 **if** $state(\lambda(q')) \in Q_1$ **then** $Q_1' \leftarrow Q_1' \bigcup \{q'\}$ **else** $Q_P' \leftarrow Q_P' \bigcup \{q'\}$
25:                 **if** $state(\lambda(q')) \in X$ **then** $X' \leftarrow X' \bigcup \{q'\}$
26:                 $\text{ToExplore} \leftarrow \text{ToExplore} \bigcup \{q'\}$
27:             **end if**
28:         **end for**
29:     **end if**
30: **end while**

Table 1. Decidability of verification problems for P-VASS-MDP, deadlock-free P-VASS-MDP and 1-VASS-MDP. A ✓ stands for decidable and a × for undecidable.

	P-VASS-MDP	df P-VASS-MDP	1-VASS-MDP
Sure reachability	× (Theorem 3)	✓ (Theorem 4)	✓ (Theorem 6)
Almost-sure reachability	× (Theorem 3)	× (Theorem 5)	✓ (Theorem 7)
Limit-sure reachability	× (Theorem 3)	× (Theorem 5)	✓ (Theorem 9)
Sure repeated reachability	× (Theorem 3)	✓ (Theorem 4)	✓ (Theorem 6)
Almost-sure repeated reachability	× (Theorem 3)	× (Theorem 5)	✓ (Theorem 8)
Limit-sure repeated reachability	× (Theorem 3)	× (Theorem 5)	Open

By Dickson's Lemma, the conditions on line 7 or line 19 of the algorithm must eventually hold on every branch of the explored computation tree. Thus, it will terminate.

Lemma 6. *Algorithm 1 terminates.*

The next lemma states the correctness of Algorithm 1. Let $S = \langle Q, Q_1, Q_P, T, \tau \rangle$ be 1-VASS-MDP of dimension $d > 0$ with initial configuration $c_0 = \langle q_0, \mathbf{v} \rangle$ and $X \subseteq Q$ a set of target states. Let $S' = \langle Q', Q'_1, Q'_P, T', \tau' \rangle$ with initial configuration $c'_0 = \langle q'_0, \mathbf{0} \rangle$ and set of target states $X' \subseteq Q'$ be the $(d-1)$ dimensional 1-VASS-MDP produced by Algorithm 1. As described above we have the following relation between these two systems.

Lemma 7. $\mathbb{P}^+(M_S, c_0, \llbracket \Diamond X \rrbracket) = 1$ *iff* $\mathbb{P}^+(M_{S'}, c'_0, \llbracket \Diamond X' \rrbracket) = 1$.

By applying the result of the previous lemma iteratively until we obtain a finite-state MDP, we can deduce the following theorem.

Theorem 9. *The limit-sure reachability problem for 1-VASS-MDP is decidable.*

5   Conclusion and Future Work

Table 1 summarizes our results on the decidability of verification problems for subclasses of VASS-MDP. The exact complexity of most problems is still open. Algorithm 1 relies on Dickson's Lemma for termination, and the algorithm deciding the model-checking problem of Theorem 2 additionally uses the Valk-Jantzen construction repeatedly. However, all these problems are at least as hard as control-state reachability in VASS, and thus EXPSPACE-hard [12].

The decidability of the limit-sure repeated reachability problem for 1-VASS-MDP is open. A hint of its difficulty is given by the fact that there are instances where the property holds even though a small chance of reaching a deadlock cannot be avoided from any reachable configuration. In particular, a solution would require an analysis of the long-run behavior of multi-dimensional random walks induced by probabilistic VASS. However, these may exhibit strange nonregular behaviors for dimensions ≥ 3, as described in [8] (Sect. 5).

References

1. Abdulla, P.A., Bouajjani, A., d'Orso, J.: Monotonic and downward closed games. J. Logic Comput. **18**(1), 153–169 (2008)
2. Abdulla, P.A., Ciobanu, R., Mayr, R., Sangnier, A., Sproston, J.: Qualitative analysis of VASS-induced MDPs. CoRR (2015). abs/1512.08824
3. Abdulla, P.A., Henda, N.B., Mayr, R.: Decisive Markov chains. Logical Meth. Comput. Sci. **3**(4) (2007)
4. Abdulla, P.A., Mayr, R., Sangnier, A., Sproston, J.: Solving parity games on integer vectors. In: D'Argenio, P.R., Melgratti, H. (eds.) CONCUR 2013 – Concurrency Theory. LNCS, vol. 8052, pp. 106–120. Springer, Heidelberg (2013)
5. Baier, C., Katoen, J.-P.: Principles of Model Checking. MIT Press, Cambridge (2008)
6. Brázdil, T., Brozek, V., Etessami, K.: One-counter stochastic games. In: FSTTCS 2010, LIPIcs, vol. 8, pp. 108–119. Schloss Dagstuhl - Leibniz-Zentrum für Informatik (2010)
7. Brázdil, T., Brozek, V., Etessami, K., Kučera, A., Wojtczak, D.: One-counter Markov decision processes. In: SODA 2010, pp. 863–874. SIAM (2010)
8. Brázdil, T., Kiefer, S., Kučera, A., Novotný, P.: Long-run average behaviour of probabilistic vector addition systems. In: LICS 2015, pp. 44–55. IEEE (2015)
9. Chatterjee, K., de Alfaro, L., Faella, M., Legay, A.: Qualitative logics and equivalences for probabilistic systems. Logical Meth. Comput. Sci. **5**(2) (2009)
10. Chatterjee, K., Jurdziński, M., Henzinger, T.A.: Simple stochastic parity games. In: Baaz, M., Makowsky, J.A. (eds.) CSL 2003. LNCS, vol. 2803, pp. 100–113. Springer, Heidelberg (2003)
11. Condon, A.: The complexity of stochastic games. Inf. Comput. **96**(2), 203–224 (1992)
12. Esparza, J., Nielsen, M.: Decidability issues for Petri nets - a survey. Bull. EATCS **52**, 244–262 (1994)
13. Etessami, K., Yannakakis, M.: Recursive Markov decision processes and recursive stochastic games. In: Caires, L., Italiano, G.F., Monteiro, L., Palamidessi, C., Yung, M. (eds.) ICALP 2005. LNCS, vol. 3580, pp. 891–903. Springer, Heidelberg (2005)
14. Filar, J., Vrieze, K.: Competitive Markov Decision Processes. Springer, New York (1997)
15. Karp, R., Miller, R.: Parallel program schemata. J. Comput. Syst. Sci. **3**(2), 147–195 (1969)
16. Minsky, M.L.: Computation: Finite and Infinite Machines. Prentice-Hall, Upper Saddle River (1967)
17. Puterman, M.L.: Markov Decision Processes. Wiley, New York (1994)
18. Raskin, J.-F., Samuelides, M., Begin, L.V.: Games for counting abstractions. In: AVoCS 2004, Electronic Notes in Theoretical Computer Science, vol. 128(6), pp. 69–85 (2005)
19. Shapley, L.S.: Stochastic games. Proc. Nat. Acad. Sci. **39**(10), 1095–1100 (1953)

Metric Temporal Logic with Counting

Shankara Narayanan Krishna[1]([✉]), Khushraj Madnani[1],
and Paritosh K. Pandya[2]

[1] Department of Computer Science and Engineering, IIT Bombay,
Mumbai 400 076, India
{krishnas,khushraj}@cse.iitb.ac.in
[2] School of Technology and Computer Science,
Tata Institute of Fundamental Research, Mumbai 400 005, India
pandya@tcs.tifr.res.in

Ability to count number of occurrences of events within a specified time interval is very useful in specification of resource bounded real time computation. In this paper, we study an extension of Metric Temporal Logic (MTL) with two different counting modalities called C and UT (until with threshold), which enhance the expressive power of MTL in orthogonal fashion. We confine ourselves only to the future fragment of MTL interpreted in a pointwise manner over finite timed words. We provide a comprehensive study of the expressive power of logic CTMTL and its fragments using the technique of EF games extended with suitable counting moves. Finally, as our main result, we establish the decidability of CTMTL by giving an equisatisfiable reduction from CTMTL to MTL. The reduction provides one more example of the use of temporal projections with oversampling introduced earlier for proving decidability. Our reduction also implies that MITL extended with C and UT modalities is elementarily decidable.

1 Introduction

Temporal logics provide constructs to specify qualitative ordering between events in time. But real time logics have the ability to specify quantitative timing constraints between events. Metric Temporal Logic MTL is amongst the best studied of real time logics. Its principal modality $a \cup_I b$ states that an event b should occur in future within a time distance lying within interval I. Moreover, a should hold continuously till then.

In many situations, especially those dealing with resource bounded computation, the ability to count the number of occurrences of events becomes important. In this paper, we consider an extension of MTL with two counting modalities C and UT (until threshold) which provide differing abilities to specify constraints on counts on events in time intervals. The resulting logic is called CTMTL. Modality $C_I^{\geq n} \phi$ states that the number of times formula ϕ holds in time interval I (measured relative to current time point) is at least n. This is a mild generalization of $C_{(0,1)}^{\geq n} \phi$ modality studied by Rabinovich [2] in context of continuous time MTL. The UT modality $\phi \cup_{I, \#\kappa \geq n} \psi$ is like MTL until but it additionally states that the number of time formula κ holds between now and time point

© Springer-Verlag Berlin Heidelberg 2016
B. Jacobs and C. Löding (Eds.): FOSSACS 2016, LNCS 9634, pp. 335–352, 2016.
DOI: 10.1007/978-3-662-49630-5_20

where ψ holds is at least n. Thus it extends U to simultaneously specify constraint on time and count of subformula. Constraining U by count of subformula was already explored for untimed LTL by Laroussini et al. [7]. But the combination of timing and counting seems new. The following example illustrates the use of these modalities.

Example 1. We specify some constraints to be monitored by exercise bicycle electronics.

- Two minutes after the start of exercise, the heartbeat (number of pulses in next 60 seconds) should be between 90 and 120. This can be stated as

$$\Box(st \Rightarrow (C^{\geq 90}_{[120,180]}pulse \wedge C^{<120}_{[120,180]}pulse))$$

- Here is one exerise routine: After start of exercise, *slow_peddling* should be done for 1 kilometre (marked by odometer giving 1000 pulses) and this should be achieved in interval 1 to 2 min. After this *fast_peddling* should be done for 3 min. This can be specified as

$$\Box(st \Rightarrow slowpeddle U_{[60,120],\#odo=1000}(\Box_{[0,180]}fastpeddle))$$

In specifying requirements over hybrid systems where count of events or mode changes are to be constrained by time intervals, our logic is quite relevant. In an HVAC case study, we have used these operators to specify properties such as no more than 3 switching on of motor are permitted in any one minute time interval. Similarly, in resource bounded computation, fairness constraints often need counting; e.g. "no more than 3 login attempted should be made in one minute". We believe that our operators are quite natural and useful in requirement modelling of real time systems.

The expressiveness and decidability properties of real time logics differ considerable based on nature of time. There has been considerable study of counting MTL in continuous time [3,12]. In this paper, we consider the case of pointwise time, i.e. CTMTL interpreted over finite timed words in a pointwise manner. We provide a comprehensive picture of expressiveness and decidability of CTMTL and its fragments in pointwise time and we find that this differs considerably when compared with continuous time.

As our first main result, we show that the C and the UT modalities both increase the expressive power of MTL but they are mutually incomparable. EF games are a classical technique used to study expressive power of logic. [10] have adapted EF games to MTL and shown a number of expressiveness results. In this paper, we further extend MTL EF games with counting moves corresponding to the C and UT modalities. We use the resulting EF theorem to characterise the expressive powers of several fragments of CTMTL.

One attraction of pointwise MTL over finite timed words is that its satisfiability is decidable [9] whereas continuous time MTL has undecidable satisfiability. As our second main result, we show that MTL extended with C and UT modalities also has decidable satisfiability. In order to prove this result, we give an equisatisfiable reduction from CTMTL to MTL. The reduction makes use of the notion of temporal projections modulo oversampling introduced earlier [4] where timed words satisfying original CTMTL formula have to be oversampled with additional time points to satisfy corresponding MTL formula. This result marks one more use of the technique of temporal projections. We note that our reduction can also be applied to MITL (with both U and S) extended with C and UT and it gives an equisatisfiable formula in MITL which is exponential in the size of original formula. Thus, we establish that CTMITL[U, S] has elementary satisfiability.

2   A Zoo of Timed Temporal Logics

In this section, we present the syntax and semantics of the various timed temporal logics we study in this paper. Let Σ be a finite set of propositions. A finite timed word over Σ is a tuple $\rho = (\sigma, \tau)$. σ and τ are sequences $\sigma_1 \sigma_2 \ldots \sigma_n$ and $t_1 t_2 \ldots t_n$ respectively, with $\sigma_i \in 2^\Sigma - \emptyset$, and $t_i \in \mathbb{R}_{\geq 0}$ for $1 \leq i \leq n$ and $\forall i \in dom(\rho)$, $t_i \leq t_{i+1}$, where $dom(\rho)$ is the set of positions $\{1, 2, \ldots, n\}$ in the timed word. An example of a timed word over $\Sigma = \{a, b\}$ is $\rho = (\{a, b\}, 0.3)(\{b\}, 0.7)(\{a\}, 1.1)$. ρ is strictly monotonic iff $t_i < t_{i+1}$ for all $i, i + 1 \in dom(\rho)$. Otherwise, it is weakly monotonic. The set of finite timed words over Σ is denoted $T\Sigma^*$.

The logic MTL extends linear temporal logic (LTL) by adding timing constraints to the "until" modality of LTL. We parametrize this logic by a permitted set of time intervals denoted by $I\nu$. The intervals in $I\nu$ can be open, half-open or closed, with end points in $\mathbb{N} \cup \{0, \infty\}$. Such an interval is denoted $\langle a, b \rangle$. For example, $[3, 7), [5, \infty)$. Let $t + \langle a, b \rangle = \langle t + a, t + b \rangle$.

Metric Temporal Logic. Given Σ, the formulae of MTL are built from Σ using boolean connectives and time constrained version of the modality U as follows: $\varphi ::= a (\in \Sigma) | true | \varphi \wedge \varphi | \neg \varphi | \varphi \mathsf{U}_I \varphi$ where $I \in I\nu$. For a timed word $\rho = (\sigma, \tau) \in T\Sigma^*$, a position $i \in dom(\rho)$, and an MTL formula φ, the satisfaction of φ at a position i of ρ is denoted $(\rho, i) \models \varphi$, and is defined as follows:

$\rho, i \models a \leftrightarrow a \in \sigma_i$ and $\rho, i \models \neg \varphi \leftrightarrow \rho, i \nvDash \varphi$

$\rho, i \models \varphi_1 \wedge \varphi_2 \leftrightarrow \rho, i \models \varphi_1$ and $\rho, i \models \varphi_2$

$\rho, i \models \varphi_1 \mathsf{U}_I \varphi_2 \leftrightarrow \exists j > i, \rho, j \models \varphi_2, t_j - t_i \in I$, and $\rho, k \models \varphi_1 \; \forall \; i < k < j$

ρ satisfies φ denoted $\rho \models \varphi$ iff $\rho, 1 \models \varphi$. Let $L(\varphi) = \{\rho \mid \rho, 1 \models \varphi\}$ denote the language of a MTL formula φ. Two formulae φ and ϕ are said to be equivalent denoted as $\varphi \equiv \phi$ iff $L(\varphi) = L(\phi)$. Additional temporal connectives are defined in the standard way: we have the constrained future eventuality operator $\Diamond_I a \equiv true \mathsf{U}_I a$ and its dual $\Box_I a \equiv \neg \Diamond_I \neg a$. We also define the next operator as $\mathsf{O}_I \phi \equiv \bot \mathsf{U}_I \phi$. Weak versions of operators are defined as $\Diamond_I^w a = a \vee \Diamond_I a, \Box_I^w a \equiv a \wedge \Box_I a$, $a \mathsf{U}_I^w b \equiv b \vee [a \wedge (a \mathsf{U}_I b)]$ if $0 \in I$, and $[a \wedge (a \mathsf{U}_I b)]$ if $0 \notin I$.

Theorem 1 [9]. *Satisfiability checking of* MTL *is decidable over finite timed words with non-primitive-recursive complexity.*

Metric Temporal Logic with Counting (CTMTL). We denote by CTMTL the logic obtained by extending MTL with the ability to count, by endowing it with two counting modalities C as well as UT.

Syntax of CTMTL: $\varphi ::= a(\in \Sigma)|true|\varphi \wedge \varphi|\neg\varphi|\varphi|C_I^{\geq n}\varphi|\varphi U_{I,\eta}\varphi$, where $I \in I\nu$, $n \in \mathbb{N} \cup \{0\}$ and η is a *threshold formula* of the form $\#\varphi \geq n$ or $\#\varphi < n$. The counting modality $C_I^{\geq n}\varphi$ is called the C modality, while $\varphi U_{I,\eta}\varphi$ is called the UT modality. Let $\rho = (\sigma, \tau) \in T\Sigma^*$, $i, j \in dom(\rho)$. Define

$$N^\rho[i, I](\varphi) = \{k \in dom(\rho) \mid t_k \in t_i + I \wedge \rho, k \models \varphi\}, \text{ and}$$
$$\rho[i, j](\varphi) = \{k \in dom(\rho) \mid i < k < j \wedge \rho, k \models \varphi\}.$$

Denote by $|N^\rho[i, I](\varphi)|$ and $|\rho[i, j](\varphi)|$ respectively, the cardinality of $N^\rho[i, I](\varphi)$ and $\rho[i, j](\varphi)$. $|N^\rho[i, I](\varphi)|$ is the number of points in ρ that lie in the interval $t_i + I$, and which satisfy φ, while $|\rho[i, j](\varphi)|$ is the number of points lying between i and j which satisfy φ. Define $\rho, i \models C_I^{\geq n}\varphi$ iff $|N^\rho[i, I](\varphi)| \geq n$. Likewise, $\rho, i \models \varphi_1 U_{I,\#\varphi \geq n}\varphi_2$ iff $\exists j > i$, $\rho, j \models \varphi_2$, $t_j - t_i \in I$, and $\rho, k \models \varphi_1$, $\forall i < k < j$ and $|\rho[i, j](\varphi)| \geq n$.

Remark: The classical until operator of MTL is captured in CTMTL since $\varphi U_I \psi \equiv \varphi U_{I,\#true \geq 0}\psi$. We can express $C_I^{\sim n}$ and $\#\varphi \sim n$ for $\sim \in \{\leq, <, >, =\}$ in CTMTL since $C_I^{<n}\varphi \equiv \neg C_I^{\geq n}\varphi$, $C_I^{>n}\varphi \equiv C_I^{\geq n+1}\varphi$, $C_I^{\leq n}\varphi \equiv \neg C_I^{\geq n+1}\varphi$ and $\#\varphi > n \equiv \#\varphi \geq n+1$, $\#\varphi \leq n \equiv \neg(\#\varphi > n+1)$. It can be shown that boolean combinations of threshold formulae are also expressible in CTMTL (see [6]). Thus, $aU_{(1,2),(\#d=3 \wedge \#C_{(0,1)}^{<2}b)} c$ is expressible in CTMTL. The *nesting depth* of a CTMTL formula is the maximum nesting of C, UT operators. Formally,

- $depth(\varphi_1 U_{I,\#\varphi_3 \sim n}\varphi_2) = max(depth(\varphi_1), depth(\varphi_2), depth(\varphi_3) + 1)$,
- $depth(C_I^{\geq n}\varphi) = depth(\varphi) + 1$, $depth(\varphi \wedge \psi) = max(depth(\varphi), depth(\psi))$,
- $depth(\neg\varphi) = depth(\varphi)$ and $depth(a) = 0$ for any $a \in \Sigma$.

For example, $depth(aU_{[0,2],\eta}C^{\geq 1}b)$ with $\eta = \#[aU_{(0,1),\#[C_{(0,1)}^{=2}a \wedge \Diamond_{(0,1),\#d=2}] \geq 1}c] < 7$ is 3. We obtain the following natural fragments of CTMTL as follows: We denote by CMTL, the fragment of CTMTL obtained by using the C modality and the U_I modality. Further, $C_{(0,u)}$MTL denotes the subclass of CMTL where the interval I in $C_I^{\sim n}\varphi$ is of the form $I = \langle 0, b\rangle$. When the interval is of the form $I = \langle 0, 1\rangle$, then we denote the class by $C_{(0,1)}$MTL. Note that $C_{(0,1)}$MTL is the class which allows counting in the next one unit of time. This kind of counting (unit counting in future and past) was introduced and studied in [2] in the continuous semantics. $C_{(0,1)}$MTL is the pointwise counterpart of this logic, with only future operators. Clearly, $C_{(0,1)}$MTL $\subseteq C_{(0,u)}$MTL $\subseteq$ CMTL $\subseteq$ CTMTL. Restricting CTMTL to the UT modality, we obtain the fragment TMTL. Restricting the C modality to $C_{(0,1)}$ or $C_{(0,u)}$ and also allowing the UT modality, one gets the fragments $C_{(0,1)}$TMTL and $C_{(0,u)}$TMTL respectively. If we disallow the C modality, restrict the intervals

I appearing in the formulae to non-punctual intervals of the form $\langle a, b \rangle$ $(a \neq b)$, and restrict threshold formulae η to be of the form $\#true \geq 0$, then we obtain MITL.

3   Expressiveness Hierarchy in the Counting Zoo

In this section, we study the expressiveness and hierarchy of the logics introduced in Sect. 2. The main results of this section are the following:

Theorem 2. MTL $\subset$ $C_{0,1)}$MTL $\subset$ $C_{(0,u)}$MTL $\subset$ TMTL $=$ $C_{(0,u)}$TMTL $\subset$ CTMTL. *Moreover,* CMTL *and* TMTL *are incomparable, and* $C_{(0,u)}$MTL $\subset$ CMTL.

While Theorem 2 shows that there is an expressiveness gap between classical MTL and CTMTL, we show later that both these logics are equisatisfiable. Given $\varphi \in$ CTMTL, we can construct a formula $\psi \in$ MTL such that φ is satisfiable iff ψ is. Note that our notion of equisatisfiability is a special one *modulo temporal projections*. If φ is over an alphabet Σ, ψ is constructed over a suitable alphabet $\Sigma' \supseteq \Sigma$ such that $L(\psi)$, when projected over to Σ gives $L(\varphi)$.

Theorem 3. *Satisfiability Checking of* CTMTL *is decidable over finite timed words.*

The rest of this paper is devoted to the proofs of Theorems 2 and 3. We establish Theorem 2 through Lemmas 1 to 4. To prove the separation between two logics, we define model-theoretic games.

3.1   CTMTL Games

Our games are inspired from the standard model-theoretic games [1,14]. The MTL games were introduced in [10]. We now extend these to CTMTL games.

Let (ρ_1, ρ_2) be a pair of timed words. We define a r-round k-counting pebble I_ν game on (ρ_1, ρ_2). The game is played on (ρ_1, ρ_2) by two players, the Spoiler and the Duplicator. The Spoiler will try to show that ρ_1 and ρ_2 are $\{r, k\}$-distinguishable by some formula in CTMTL[1] while the Duplicator will try to show that ρ_1, ρ_2 are $\{r, k\}$-indistinguishable in TMTL. Each player has r rounds and has access to a finite set of $\leq k$ pebbles from a box of pebbles $\mathcal{P}$ in each round of the game. Let I_ν be the set of permissible intervals allowed in the game.

A configuration of the game at the start of a round p is a pair of points (i_p, j_p) where $i_p \in dom(\rho_1)$ and $j_p \in dom(\rho_2)$. A configuration is called partially isomorphic, denoted $isop(i_p, j_p)$ iff $\sigma_{i_p} = \sigma_{j_p}$. Exactly one of the Spoiler or the Duplicator eventually wins the game. The initial configuration is (i_1, j_1), the

---

[1] ρ_1, ρ_2 are $\{r, k\}$-distinguishable iff there exists a CTMTL formula φ having $depth(\varphi) \leq r$ with max counting constant $\leq k$ in any threshold formula η or C modality in φ such that $\rho_1 \models \varphi$ and $\rho_2 \nvDash \varphi$ or vice-versa.

starting positions of both the words, before the first round. A 0-round game is won by the Duplicator iff $isop(i_1, j_1)$. The r round game is played by first playing one round from the starting position. Either the Spoiler wins the round, and the game is terminated or the Duplicator wins the round, and now the second round is played from this new configuration and so on. The Duplicator wins the game only if he wins all the rounds. The following are the rules of the game in any round. Assume that the current configuration is (i_p, j_p).

- If $isop(i_p, j_p)$ is not true, then Spoiler wins the game, and the game is terminated. Otherwise, the game continues as follows:
- The Spoiler chooses one of the words by choosing ρ_x, for $x \in \{1, 2\}$. Duplicator has to play on the other word ρ_y, where $x \neq y$. Then Spoiler plays either a $U_{I,\eta}$ round, by choosing an interval $I \in I_\nu$, and a number $c \leq k$ of counting pebbles to be used, or a $C_I^{\sim c}$ round by choosing an interval $I \in I_\nu$ and a number $c \leq k$ of counting pebbles to be used. The number c is obtained from $\eta = \#\varphi \geq c$ or $\eta = \neg(\#\varphi \geq c)$.

$U_{I,\eta}$ round: Given the current configuration as (i_p, j_p) with $isop(i_p, j_p)$, then
  - Spoiler chooses a position $i'_p \in dom(\rho_x)$ such that $i_p < i'_p$ and $(t_{i'_p} - t_{i_p}) \in I$.
  - The Duplicator responds by choosing $j'_p \in dom(\rho_y)$ in the other word such that $j_p < j'_p$ and $(t_{j'_p} - t_{j_p}) \in I$. If the Duplicator cannot find such a position, the Spoiler wins the round and the game. Otherwise, the game continues and Spoiler chooses one of the following three options.
  - $\Diamond$ Part: The round ends with the configuration $(i_{p+1}, j_{p+1}) = (i'_p, j'_p)$.
  - U Part: Spoiler chooses a position j''_p in ρ_y such that $j_p < j''_p < j'_p$. The Duplicator responds by choosing a position i''_p in ρ_x such that $i_p < i''_p < i'_p$. The round ends with the configuration $(i_{p+1}, j_{p+1}) = (i''_p, j''_p)$. If Duplicator cannot choose an i''_p, the game ends with Spoiler's win.
  - Counting Part: First, Spoiler chooses one of the two words to play in the counting part. In his chosen word, Spoiler keeps $c \leq k$ pebbles from $\mathcal{P}$ at c distinct positions between the points j_p and j'_p (or i_p and i'_p depending on the choice of the word). In response, the Duplicator also keeps c pebbles from $\mathcal{P}$ at c distinct positions between the points i_p and i'_p (or j_p and j'_p) in his word. Spoiler then chooses a pebbled position say i''_p (note that $i_p < i''_p < i'_p$) in the Duplicator's word. In response, Duplicator chooses a pebbled position j''_p (note that $j_p < j''_p < j'_p$) in the Spoiler's word, and the game continues from the configuration $(i_{p+1}, j_{p+1}) = (i''_p, j''_p)$. At the end of the round, the pebbles are returned to the box of pebbles $\mathcal{P}$.

$C_I^{\sim c} round$: Given the current configuration as (i_p, j_p) with $isop(i_p, j_p)$, Spoiler chooses an interval $I \in I_\nu$ as well as a number $c \leq k$. Spoiler then chooses one of the words to play (say ρ_1). From i_p, Spoiler places c pebbles from $\mathcal{P}$ in the points lying in the interval $t_{i_p} + I$. In response, Duplicator also places c pebbles from $\mathcal{P}$ in the points lying in $t_{j_p} + I$. Spoiler now picks a pebbled position j'_p in the word ρ_2, while Duplicator picks a pebbled position i'_p in the Spoiler's word. The round ends with the configuration (i'_p, j'_p). At the end of the round, the pebbles are returned to the box of pebbles $\mathcal{P}$.

Intuition on Pebbling: To give some intuition behind the pebbling, consider $\#\varphi \geq c$ or $C_I^{\geq c}\varphi$. The idea behind Spoiler keeping c pebbles on his word in the chosen interval I is to say that these are the c points where φ evaluates to true. Duplicator is expected to find c such points in his word. If Spoiler suspects that in the Duplicator's word, there are $< c$ positions in I where φ holds good, he picks up the appropriate pebble at the position where φ fails. However, any pebbled position in Spoiler's word will satisfy φ. In this case, Duplicator loses. Similarly, if we have $\neg(\#\varphi \geq c)$, or $C_I^{<c}\varphi$, then Spoiler chooses the word (say ρ_1) on which φ evaluates to true $\geq c$ times. Then Duplicator is on ρ_2. The idea is for Spoiler to find if there exist c or more positions in the interval I in ρ_1 where φ holds good, and if so, pebble those points. This is based on Spoiler's suspicion that there are at least c positions in I where φ evaluates to true, violating the formula. In response, Duplicator does the same on ρ_2. Spoiler will now pick any one of the c pebbles from ρ_2 and check for $\neg\varphi$. This is again based on Spoiler's belief that whichever c points Duplicator pebbles in ρ_2, $\neg\varphi$ will evaluate to true in at least one of them. If φ holds at all the c points in ρ_1, then Duplicator will lose on picking any pebble from ρ_1.

– We can restrict various moves according to the modalities provided by the logic. For example, in a TMTL$[\Diamond_I]$ game, the possible rounds are $\Diamond_I$ and $\Diamond_{I,\eta}$. A CMITL game has only U_I, $C_I^{\geq n}$ rounds, with I_ν containing only non-punctual intervals.

Game equivalence: $(\rho_1, i_1) \approx_{r,k,I_\nu} (\rho_2, j_1)$ iff for every r-round, k-counting pebble CTMTL game over the words ρ_1, ρ_2 starting from the configuration (i_1, j_1), the Duplicator always has a winning strategy.

Formula equivalence: $(\rho_1, i_1) \equiv_{r,k,I_\nu}^{\mathsf{CTMTL}} (\rho_2, j_1)$ iff for every CTMTL formula φ of depth $\leq r$ having max counting constant $\leq k$ in the C, UT modalities, $\rho_1, i_1 \models \varphi \iff \rho_2, j_1 \models \varphi$. The proof of Theorem 4 can be found in [6].

Theorem 4. $(\rho_1, i_1) \approx_{r,k,I_\nu} (\rho_2, j_1)$ *iff* $(\rho_1, i_1) \equiv_{r,k,I_\nu}^{\mathsf{CTMTL}} (\rho_2, j_1)$

We now use these games to show the separation between various logics. For brevity, from here on, we omit I_ν from the notations $\equiv_{r,k,I_\nu}^{\mathsf{CTMTL}}$, $\equiv_{r,k,I_\nu}^{\mathsf{CMTL}}$, $\equiv_{r,k,I_\nu}^{\mathsf{TMTL}}$ and $\equiv_{r,I_\nu}^{\mathsf{MTL}}$.

Lemma 1. CMTL − TMTL $\neq \emptyset$

Proof. Consider the formula $\varphi = C_{(1,2)}^{\geq 2} a \in$ CMTL. We show that for any choice of n rounds and k pebbles, we can find two words ρ_1, ρ_2 such that $\rho_1 \models \varphi, \rho_2 \not\models \varphi$, but $\rho_1 \equiv_{n,k}^{\mathsf{TMTL}} \rho_2$. Both ρ_1, ρ_2 are over $\Sigma = \{a\}$. Let $0 < \delta < \epsilon < \frac{1}{10^{10nk}}$ and $0 < \kappa < \frac{\epsilon - \delta}{2nk}$. Let l be the maximum constant in $\mathbb{N}$ appearing in the permissible intervals I_ν. Consider the word ρ_1 with $nl(k+1) = K$ unit intervals, with the following time stamps as depicted pictorially (Fig. 1) and in the table.

Thus, ρ_1 and ρ_2 differ only in the interval $(1,2)$: ρ_1 has two points in $(1,2)$, while ρ_2 has only one. Thus, $\rho_1 \models \varphi, \rho_2 \not\models \varphi$.

Points in	ρ_1	ρ_2
(0,1)	$x_1 = 0.5, z_1 = 0.6, y_1 = 0.8$ and $2nk$ points between z_1, y_1 that are κ apart from each other	$x_1' = 0.5, z_1' = 0.6, y_1' = 0.8$ and $2nk$ points between z_1', y_1' that are κ apart from each other
(1,2)	$x_2 = 1.8 - \epsilon, z_2 = 1.8 + \epsilon$	$x_2' = 1.8 - \epsilon$
(2,3)	$e = 2.4 + n\epsilon, y_2 = 2.7 + n\epsilon$ and $2nk$ points between e and y_2 that are κ apart from each other	$z_2' = 2.4 + n\epsilon, y_2' = 2.7 + n\epsilon$ and $2nk$ points between z_2' and y_2' that are κ apart from each other
$(i, i+1)$ $3 \leq i \leq K-1$	$x_i = i + 0.4 + (n-i)\epsilon$ $z_i = i + 0.8 + (n+i)\epsilon + \delta$ $y_i = i + 0.8 + (n+i+1)\epsilon$ and $2nk$ points between z_i, y_i that are κ apart from each other	$x_i' = i + 0.4 + (n-i)\epsilon$ $z_i' = i + 0.8 + (n+i)\epsilon + \delta$ $y_i' = i + 0.8 + (n+i+1)\epsilon$ and $2nk$ points between z_i, y_i that are κ apart from each other

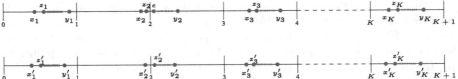

Fig. 1. Words showing $\mathsf{CMTL} - \mathsf{TMTL} \neq \emptyset$

Let $seg(i_p) \in \{0, 1, \ldots, K\}$ denote the left endpoint of the left closed, right open unit interval containing the point $i_p \in dom(\rho_1)$ or $dom(\rho_2)$. Our segments are $[0,1)$, $[1,2)$, $\ldots$, $[K, K+1)$. For instance, if the configuration at the start of the pth round is (i_p, j_p) with time stamps $(1.2, 3)$, then $seg(i_p) = 1, seg(j_p) = 3$. The following lemma says that in any round of the game, Duplicator can either achieve the same segment in both the words, or ensure that the difference in the segments is at most 1. Moreover, by the choice of the words, there are sufficiently many segments on the right of any configuration so that Duplicator can always duplicate Spoiler's moves for the remaining rounds, preserving the lag of one segment.

Copy-cat strategy. Consider the pth round of the game with configuration (i_p, j_p). If Duplicator can ensure that $seg(i_{p+1}) - seg(i_p) = seg(j_{p+1}) - seg(j_p)$, then we say that Duplicator has adopted a *copy-cat* strategy in the pth round. We prove the following proposition to argue Duplicator's win.

Proposition 1. *For an n round* TMTL *game over the words ρ_1, ρ_2, the* Duplicator *always has a winning strategy such that for any $1 \leq p \leq n$, if (i_p, j_p) is the initial configuration of the pth round, then $|seg(i_p) - seg(j_p)| \leq 1$. Moreover, when $|seg(i_p) - seg(j_p)| = 1$, then there are at least $(n-p)(l+1)$ segments to the right on each word after p rounds, for all $1 \leq p \leq n$.*

Proof. The initial configuration has time stamps $(0,0)$. We will play a (n,k)-TMTL game on ρ_1, ρ_2. Assume that the Spoiler chooses ρ_1 while the Duplicator chooses ρ_2. Since the interval $[1,2]$ is the only one different in both the words, it is interesting to look at the moves where the Spoiler chooses a point in interval $(1,2)$. We consider the two situations possible for Spoiler to land up in a point in interval $(1,2)$: he can enter interval $(1,2)$ from some point in interval $(0,1)$, or directly choose to enter interval $(1,2)$ from the initial configuration with time stamps $(0,0)$.

Situation 1: Consider the case when from the starting configuration (i_1, j_1) with time stamps $(0,0)$, Spoiler chooses a $U_{(1,2)\#a\sim c}$ move in ρ_1 and lands up at the point x_2 or z_2. In response, Duplicator has to come at the point x_2' in ρ_2'. If (i_1', j_1') has time stamps (x_2, x_2') and if Spoiler chooses to pebble between 0 and x_2, then Duplicator pebbles between 0 and x_2'; however, an identical configuration is obtained. Note that if Spoiler pebbles ρ_2, then Duplicator has it easy, since he will pebble the same positions in ρ_1. Let us hence consider obtaining the configuration (i_1', j_1') with time stamps (z_2, x_2'), and let Spoiler pebble ρ_1. Spoiler can keep a maximum of k pebbles in the points $x_1, \ldots, y_1, x_2$, while Duplicator keeps the same number of pebbles on the points $x_1', \ldots, y_1'$. In this case, Spoiler has to a pick a pebbled position from among $x_1', \ldots, y_1'$. In response, Duplicator will pick the same position from Spoiler's word and achieve an identical configuration. An interesting special case is when Spoiler keeps a single pebble at x_2 in ρ_1. In this case, Duplicator's best choice is to keep his pebble at x_1', so that the next configuration (i_2, j_2) is one with time stamps (x_2, x_1'). x_1' and x_2 are *topologically similar* in the sense that the distribution of points in subsequent segments have some nice properties as given below.

Topological Similarity of Words: Consider the $2nk+3$ points $x_j < z_j < p_j^1 < \cdots < p_j^{2nk} < y_j$ in ρ_1, and $x_{j-1}' < z_{j-1}' < q_{j-1}^1 < \ldots < q_{j-1}^{2nk} < y_{j-1}'$ in ρ_2, for $j \in \{2, 3, 4, \ldots, K\}$. Define a function f that maps points in ρ_1 to topologically similar points in ρ_2. $f : \{x_j, z_j, p_j^1, \ldots, p_1^{2nk}, y_j\} \to \{x_{j-1}', z_{j-1}', q_{j-1}^1, \ldots, q_{j-1}^{2nk}, y_{j-1}'\}$ by $f(x_j) = x_{j-1}', f(z_j) = z_{j-1}', f(y_j) = y_{j-1}', f(p_j^i) = q_{j-1}^i$. Let $g = f^{-1}$.

(a) The current configuration has timestamps $(x_2, x_1') = (x_2, f(x_2))$. For $j \geq 2$, if Spoiler chooses to move to any $p \in \{z_j, y_j, x_{j+2}\}$ from x_2, then Duplicator can move to $f(p)$ from $f(x_2)$ since, for any time interval I, it can be seen that $p - x_2 \in I$ iff $f(p) - f(x_1) \in I$. Moreover, if Spoiler chooses to move to x_3 from x_2, then Duplicator can move to z_2' from $f(x_2)$ since, $x_3 - x_2, z_2' - f(x_2) \in (0,1)$.

(b) We can extend (a) above as follows: Let the current configuration have timestamps $(p, f(p))$ or (x_3, z_2'). Then it can be seen that for any $q \in \{x_j, y_j, z_j\}$ and interval I, $q - p \in I$ iff $f(q) - f(p) \in I$, and $q - x_3 \in I$ iff $f(q) - z_2' \in I$.

The facts claimed in (a) and (b) are evident from the construction of the timed words. They show that from a configuration (i_p, j_p), such that $seg(i_p) - seg(j_p) \leq 1$, Duplicator can always achieve an intermediate configuration (i_p', j_p') in any $U_{I,\#a\sim c}$ such that $seg(i_p') - seg(j_p') \leq 1$. If Spoiler does not go for the until round or the counting round, then $(i_{p+1}, j_{p+1}) = (i_p', j_p')$. If Spoiler pebbles the points between i_p and i_p' (or j_p and j_p'), then Duplicator can always ensure that he pebbles points $f(P)$ in ρ_2 whenever Spoiler pebbles a set of points P in ρ_1. As a result, if Spoiler chooses a point $q = f(i) \in f(P)$ in ρ_2, then Duplicator can choose the point $g(q) = i \in P$ achieving the configuration $(i_{p+1}, j_{p+1}) = (g(q), q) = (i, f(i))$. By definition of f, g, we have $i_{p+1} - j_{p+1} \leq 1$. Note that Duplicator can also achieve an identical configuration if Spoiler moves ahead by several segments from i_p (thus, $i'_p >> i_p$), and pebbles a set of points that are also present between j_p and j'_p.

Situation 2: Starting from (i_1, j_1) with time stamps $(0,0)$, if the Spoiler chooses a $U_{(0,1),\#a \sim c}$ move and lands up at some point between x_1 and y_1, Duplicator will play copy-cat and achieve an identical configuration. Consider the case when Spoiler lands up at $y_1{}^2$. In response, Duplicator moves to y'_1. From configuration (i_2, j_2) with time stamps (y_1, y'_1), consider the case when Spoiler initiates a $U_{(1,2),\#a \sim c}$ and moves to $z_2 = 1.8 + \epsilon < 2$. In response, Duplicator moves to the point $z'_2 = 2.1 > 2$. A pebble is kept at the inbetween positions x_2, x'_2 respectively in ρ_1, ρ_2. When Spoiler picks the pebble in Duplicator's word, then we obtain the configuration (i_3, j_3) with time stamps (x_2, x'_2). If Spoiler does not get into the counting part/until part, the configuration obtained has time stamps (z_2, z'_2), with the lag of one segment $(seg(i_3) = 1, seg(j_3) = 2, seg(j_3)-seg(i_3)=1)$. We show in [6] that from (i_3, j_3) with time stamps either (x_2, x'_2) or (z_2, z'_2), Duplicator can either achieve an identical configuration, or achieve a configuration with a lag of one segment.

From situations (1), (2) in Proposition 1, we know that either Duplicator achieves an identical configuration, in which case there is no segment lag, or there is a lag of at most one segment. The length of the words are $lnk + nl = K$. If Spoiler always chooses bounded intervals (of length $\leq l$), then Duplicator respects his segment lag of 1, and the maximum number of segments that can be explored in either word is at most $nl < K$. In this case, after p rounds, there are at least $K - pl \geq nlk + nl - pl \geq (n - p)(l + 1)$ segments to the right of ρ_1 and $K - pl + 1$ segments to the right of ρ_2. If Spoiler chooses an unbounded interval in any round, then Duplicator can either enforce an identical configuration in both situations 1 and 2, or obtain one of the configurations with time stamps $(p, f(p))$, $f(p) \neq x'_2$, or (z_2, z'_2) or (x_2, x'_2), from where it is known that Duplicator wins.

Lemma 2. $MTL \subset C_{(0,1)}MTL \subset C_{(0,u)}MTL$

Proof. We show that the formula $\varphi = C_{(0,1)}^{=2}a \in C_{(0,1)}MTL$ cannot be expressed in MTL. Likewise, the formula $\varphi = C_{(0,2)}^{\geq 2}a \in C_{(0,u)}MTL$ cannot be expressed in $C_{(0,1)}MTL$. A detailed proof of these are given in [6].

Lemma 3. *(i)* $C_{(0,u)}MTL \subset TMTL = C_{(0,u)}TMTL = C_{(0,1)}TMTL$ *and*
(ii) $C_{(0,u)}MTL \subset CMTL$.

---

[2] The argument when Spoiler lands up at x_1 or a point in between x_1, y_1 is exactly the same.

Proof. (i) The first containment as well as the last two equalities follows from the fact that the counting modality $C_{(0,j)}^{\geq n} \varphi$ of $C_{(0,u)}MTL$ can be written in TMTL as $\Diamond_{(0,j),\#\varphi \geq n} true$. The strict containment of $C_{(0,u)}MTL$ then follows from Lemma 4. (ii) We know that $C_{(0,u)}MTL \subseteq CMTL$. This along with (i) and Lemma 1 gives the strict containment.

Lemma 4. $TMTL - CMTL \neq \emptyset$

Proof. Consider the formula $\varphi = \Diamond_{(0,1),\#a \geq 3}b \in TMTL$. We show that for any choice of n rounds and k pebbles, we can find two words ρ_1, ρ_2 such that $\rho_2 \models \varphi, \rho_1 \not\models \varphi$, but $\rho_1 \equiv_{n,k}^{CMTL} \rho_2$. The words can be seen in Fig. 2 and the details in [6].

Fig. 2. The red square represents a, the block of blue lines represents a block of b's. There are 3 a's in each unit interval of both ρ_1 and ρ_2. The difference is that ρ_1 has 3 blocks of b's in each unit interval, while ρ_2 has 4 blocks of b's in each unit interval except the last. Clearly, $\rho_2 \models \varphi, \rho_1 \not\models \varphi$ (Color figure online).

4 Satisfiability Checking of Counting Logics

In this section, we show that CTMTL has a decidable satisfiability checking. For this, given a formula in CTMTL we synthesize an equisatisfiable formula in MTL, and use the decidability of MTL. We start discussing some preliminaries. Let Σ, X be finite sets of propositions such that $\Sigma \cap X = \emptyset$.

1. (Σ, X)-*simple extensions.* A (Σ, X)-simple extension is a timed word $\rho' = (\sigma', \tau')$ over $X \cup \Sigma$ such that at any point $i \in dom(\rho')$, $\sigma'_i \cap \Sigma \neq \emptyset$. For $\Sigma = \{a, b\}, X = \{c, d\}$, $(\{a\}, 0.2)(\{b, c, d\}, 0.3)(\{b, d\}, 1.1)$ is a (Σ, X)-simple extension. However, $(\{a\}, 0.2)(\{c, d\}, 0.3)(\{b, d\}, 1.1)$ is not.

2. *Simple Projections.* Consider a (Σ, X)-simple extension ρ. We define the *simple projection* of ρ with respect to X, denoted $\rho \setminus X$ as the word obtained by erasing the symbols of X from each σ_i. Note that $dom(\rho) = dom(\rho \setminus X)$. For example, if $\Sigma = \{a, c\}$, $X = \{b\}$, and $\rho = (\{a, b, c\}, 0.2)(\{b, c\}, 1)(\{c\}, 1.3)$, then $\rho \setminus X = (\{a, c\}, 0.2)(\{c\}, 1)(\{c\}, 1.3)$. $\rho \setminus X$ is thus, a timed word over Σ. If the underlying word ρ is *not* a (Σ, X)-simple extension, then $\rho \setminus X$ is *undefined.*

3. (Σ, X)-*oversampled behaviours.* A (Σ, X)-oversampled behaviour is a timed word $\rho' = (\sigma', \tau')$ over $X \cup \Sigma$, such that $\sigma'_1 \cap \Sigma \neq \emptyset$ and $\sigma'_{|dom(\rho')|} \cap \Sigma \neq \emptyset$. Oversampled behaviours are more general than simple extensions since they allow occurrences of new points in between the first and the last position. These new points are called *oversampled points.*

All other points are called *action points*. For $\Sigma = \{a, b\}, X = \{c, d\}$, $(\{a\}, 0.2)(\{c, d\}, 0.3)(\{a, b\}, 0.7)(\{b, d\}, 1.1)$ is a (Σ, X)-oversampled behaviour, while $(\{a\}, 0.2)(\{c, d\}, 0.3)(\{c\}, 1.1)$ is not.

4. *Oversampled Projections.* Given a (Σ, X)-oversampled behaviour $\rho' = (\sigma', \tau')$, the oversampled projection of ρ' with respect to Σ, denoted $\rho' \downarrow X$ is defined as the timed word obtained by deleting the oversampled points, and then erasing the symbols of X from the action points. $\rho = \rho' \downarrow X$ is a timed word over Σ.

A *temporal projection* is either a simple projection or an oversampled projection. We now define *equisatisfiability modulo temporal projections*. Given MTL formulae ψ and ϕ, we say that ϕ is equisatisfiable to ψ *modulo temporal projections* iff there exist disjoint sets X, Σ such that (1) ϕ is over Σ, and ψ over $\Sigma \cup X$, (2) For any timed word ρ over Σ such that $\rho \models \phi$, there exists a timed word ρ' such that $\rho' \models \psi$, and ρ is a temporal projection of ρ' with respect to X, (3) For any behaviour ρ' over $\Sigma \cup X$, if $\rho' \models \psi$ then the temporal projection ρ of ρ' with respect to X is well defined and $\rho \models \phi$.

If the temporal projection used above is a simple projection, we call it *equisatisfiability modulo simple projections* and denote it by $\phi = \exists X.\psi$. If the projection in the above definition is an oversampled projection, then it is called *equisatisfiability modulo oversampled projections* and is denoted $\phi \equiv \exists \downarrow X.\psi$. Equisatisfiability modulo simple projections are studied extensively [5,11,13]. It can be seen that if $\varphi_1 = \exists X_1.\psi_1$ and $\varphi_2 = \exists X_2.\psi_2$, with X_1, X_2 disjoint, then $\varphi_1 \wedge \varphi_2 = \exists (X_1 \cup X_2).(\psi_1 \wedge \psi_2)$ [8].

As in the case of simple projections, equisatisfiability modulo oversampled projections are also closed under conjunctions when one considers the relativized formulae. For example, consider a formula $\varphi = \square_{(0,1)} a$ over $\Sigma = \{a, d\}$. Let $\psi_1 = \square_{(0,1)}(a \vee b) \wedge \Diamond_{(0,1)}(b \wedge \neg a)$ be a formula over the extended alphabet $\{a, b, d\}$ and $\psi_2 = \square(c \leftrightarrow \square_{(0,1)} a) \wedge c$ over the extended alphabet $\{a, c, d\}$. Note that $\varphi = \exists \downarrow \{b\}.\psi_1$ and $\varphi = \exists \downarrow \{c\}.\psi_2$ but $\varphi \wedge \varphi \neq \exists \downarrow \{b, c\}.(\psi_1 \wedge \psi_2)$ as the left hand side evaluates to φ which is satisfiable while the right hand side is unsatisfiable. This is due to the presence of a *non-action* point where only b holds. But this can easily be fixed by relativizing all the formulae over their respective action points. ψ_1 is relativized as $\lambda_1 = \square_{(0,1)}(act_1 \rightarrow (a \vee b)) \wedge \Diamond_{(0,1)}(act_1 \wedge b \wedge \neg a)$ and ψ_2 is relativized as $\lambda_2 = \square(act_2 \rightarrow (c \leftrightarrow \square_{(0,1)}(act_2 \rightarrow a))) \wedge act_2 \wedge c$ where $act_1 = b \vee d \vee a$ and $act_2 = a \vee c \vee d$. Now, $\varphi \wedge \varphi = \exists \downarrow \{b, c\}.(\lambda_1 \wedge \lambda_2)$. The relativized forms of ψ_1, ψ_2 are called their *Oversampled Normal Forms* with respect to Σ and denoted $ONF_\Sigma(\psi_1)$ and $ONF_\Sigma(\psi_2)$. Then it can be seen that $\varphi_1 \wedge \varphi_2 = \exists \downarrow \{b, d\}.[ONF_\Sigma(\psi_1) \wedge ONF_\Sigma(\psi_2)]$, and $\varphi_1 = \exists \downarrow \{b\}.ONF_\Sigma(\psi_1)$, $\varphi_2 = \exists \downarrow \{d\}.ONF_\Sigma(\psi_2)$. The formal definition of $ONF_\Sigma(\varphi)$ for a formula φ over $\Sigma \cup X$ can be found in [6]. Equisatisfiability modulo oversampled projections were first studied in [4] to eliminate non-punctual past from MTL over timed words. We use equisatifiability modulo simple projections to eliminate the C modality and oversampled projections to eliminate the UT modality from CTMTL.

Elimination of Counting Modalities from CTMTL. In this section, we show how to eliminate the counting constraints from CTMTL over strictly monotonic timed words. This can be extended to weakly monotonic timed words.

Given any CTMTL formula φ over Σ, we "flatten" the C, UT modalities of φ and obtain a flattened formula. As an example, consider the formula $\varphi = a\mathsf{U}_{[0,3]}(c \wedge \mathsf{C}^{=1}_{(2,3)} d\mathsf{U}_{(0,1),\#(d \wedge \mathsf{C}^{=1}_{(0,1)} e) \geq 1} \mathsf{C}^{\geq 2}_{(0,1)} e])$. Replacing the counting modalities with fresh witness propositions w_1, w_2, we obtain $\varphi_{flat} = [a\mathsf{U}_{[0,3]}(c \wedge w_1)] \wedge T$ where $T = T_1 \wedge T_2 \wedge T_3 \wedge T_4$, with $T_1 = \square^\mathsf{w}[w_1 \leftrightarrow \mathsf{C}^{=1}_{(2,3)} w_2]$, $T_2 = \square^\mathsf{w}[w_2 \leftrightarrow d\mathsf{U}_{(0,1),\#w_4 \geq 1} w_3]]$, $T_3 = \square^\mathsf{w}[w_4 \leftrightarrow (d \wedge \mathsf{C}^{=1}_{(0,1)} e)]$, and $T_4 = \square^\mathsf{w}[w_3 \leftrightarrow \mathsf{C}^{\geq 2}_{(0,1)} e]$. Each temporal projection T_i obtained after flattening contains either a C modality or a UT modality. In the following, we now show how to obtain equisatisfiable MTL formulae corresponding to each temporal projection.

Lemma 5. *The formula* $\mathsf{C}^{\geq n}_{(l,\infty)} b$ *is equivalent to* MTL *formula* $F_{(l,\infty)}(b \wedge F(b \wedge \ldots Fb)))$.

We now outline the steps followed to obtain an equisatisfiable formula in MTL, assuming $\mathsf{C}^{\geq n}_{(l,\infty)} b$ modalities have been eliminated using Lemma 5.

1. *Flattening*: Flatten χ obtaining χ_{flat} over $\Sigma \cup W$, where W is the set of witness propositions used, $\Sigma \cap W = \emptyset$.
2. *Eliminate Counting*: Consider, one by one, each temporal definition T_i of χ_{flat}. Let $\Sigma_i = \Sigma \cup W \cup X_i$, where X_i is a set of fresh propositions, $X_i \cap X_j = \emptyset$ for $i \neq j$.
   - If T_i is a temporal projection containing a C modality of the form $\mathsf{C}^{\sim n}_{(l,u)}$, or a UT modality of the form $x\mathsf{U}_{I,\#b \leq n} y$, then Lemma 6 synthesizes a formula $\zeta_i \in$ MTL over Σ_i such that $T_i \equiv \exists X_i.\zeta_i$.
   - If T_i is a temporal projection containing a UT modality of the form $x\mathsf{U}_{I,\#b \geq n} y$, Lemma 7 gives $\zeta_i \in$ MTL over Σ_i such that $ONF_\Sigma(T_i) \equiv \exists \downarrow X_i.\zeta_i$.
3. *Putting it all together*: The formula $\zeta = \bigwedge^k_{i=1} \zeta_i \in$ MTL is such that

$$\bigwedge^k_{i=1} ONF_\Sigma(T_i) \equiv \exists \downarrow X. \bigwedge^k_{i=1} \zeta_i \text{ where } X = \bigcup^k_{i=1} X_i.$$

Lemma 6. *1. Consider a temporal definition* $T = \square^\mathsf{w}[a \leftrightarrow \mathsf{C}^{\geq n}_{[l,u)} b]$, *built from* $\Sigma \cup W$. *Then we synthesize a formula* $\zeta \in$ MTL *over* $\Sigma \cup W \cup X$ *such that* $T \equiv \exists X.\zeta$.
2. Consider a temporal definition $T = \square^\mathsf{w}[a \leftrightarrow x\mathsf{U}_{I,\#b \leq n} y]$, *built from* $\Sigma \cup W$. *Then we synthesize a formula* $\zeta \in$ MTL *over* $\Sigma \cup W \cup X$ *such that* $T \equiv \exists X.\zeta$.

Proof. 1. Lets consider intervals of the form $[l, u)$. Our proof extends to all intervals $\langle l, u \rangle$. Consider $T = \square^\mathsf{w}[a \leftrightarrow \mathsf{C}^{\geq n}_{[l,u)} b]$. Let $\oplus$ denote addition modulo $n + 1$.

Intuitively, we run a global modulo $n+1$ counter B (encoded using propositional variables $b_0, \ldots, b_n \in X$) which is initialized to 0 and incremented modulo $n+1$ at every position in timed word where b occurs, else it remains same. This is enforced by (a) and (b) below. In any interval I, there are at least n bs iff counter takes all the values of the set $\{0, \ldots, n\}$ in interval I. This is checked in (c) below.

(a) *Construction of a* $(\Sigma \cup W, X)$- *simple extension.* We introduce a fresh set of propositions $X = \{b_0, b_1, \ldots, b_n\}$ and construct a simple extension $\rho' = (\sigma', \tau')$ from $\rho = (\sigma, \tau)$ as follows:
   - C1: $\sigma'_1 = \sigma_1 \cup \{b_0\}$. If $b_k \in \sigma'_i$ and if $b \in \sigma_{i+1}$, $\sigma'_{i+1} = \sigma_{i+1} \cup \{b_{k \oplus 1}\}$.
   - C2: If $b_k \in \sigma'_i$ and $b \notin \sigma_{i+1}$, then $\sigma'_{i+1} = \sigma_{i+1} \cup \{b_k\}$.
   - C3: σ'_i has exactly one symbol from X for all $1 \le i \le |dom(\rho)|$.

(b) *Formula specifying the above behaviour.* The variables in X help in counting the number of b's in ρ. $C1$ and $C2$ are written in MTL as follows:
   - $\delta_1 = \bigwedge_{k=0}^{n} \Box^w[(Ob \wedge b_k) \rightarrow Ob_{k \oplus 1}]$ and $\delta_2 = \bigwedge_{k=0}^{n} \Box^w[(O\neg b \wedge b_k) \rightarrow Ob_k]$

(c) *Marking the witness 'a' correctly at points satisfying* $C_{[l,u)}^{\ge n} b$. The index i of b_i at a chosen point gives the number of b's seen so far since the previous occurrence of b_0. From a point i, if the interval $[t_i + l, t_i + u)$ has k elements of X, then there must be k b's in $[t_i + l, t_i + u)$. To mark the witness a appropriately, we need to check the number of times b occurs in $[t_i + l, t_i + u]$ from the current point i. A point $i \in dom(\rho')$ is marked with witness a iff all variables of X are present in $[t_i + l, t_i + u)$, as explained in MTL by $\kappa = \Box^w[a \leftrightarrow (\bigwedge_{k=1}^{n} \Diamond_{[l,u)} b_k)]$.

   $\zeta = \delta_1 \wedge \delta_2 \wedge \kappa$ in MTL is equisatisfiable to T modulo simple projections.

2. The proof is similar to the above, details are in [6].

Lemma 7. *Consider a temporal definition* $T = \Box^w[a \leftrightarrow xU_{I, \#b \ge n} y]$, *built from* $\Sigma \cup W$. *Then we synthesize a formula* $\psi \in$ MTL *over* $\Sigma \cup W \cup X$ *such that* $ONF_\Sigma(T) \equiv \exists \downarrow X.\psi$ *where* $ONF_\Sigma(T)$ *is* T *relativized with respect to* Σ.

Proof. If I is of the form $\langle l, \infty \rangle$, then $xU_{\langle l, \infty \rangle, \#b \ge n} y \equiv xU_{\langle l, \infty \rangle} y \wedge xU_{\#b \ge n} y$. The untimed threshold formula $xU_{\#b \ge n} y$ can be straightforwardly rewritten in LTL (see [7]).

The case of bounded intervals is the most complex and requires oversampling. Timed word ρ is oversampled at every integer valued time point upto the maximum time stamp in ρ to give ρ'. All integer points are marked by a unique proposition from $C = \{c_0, \ldots c_u\}$ in a circular fashion with first point being marked as c_0. Each c_i is associated with a bounded counter B^i, which saturates at maximum value n (encoded using propositions $b_0^i, \ldots, b_n^i \in X$). This counter is reset to 0 at each occurrence of c_i and it is incremented each time a b occurs. This encoding is explained in (O1) and (O2) below and enforced by formula η given below. Let the resultant word after the markings be ρ'.

Now, by semantics, $\rho', j \models xU_{I, \#b \ge n} y$ iff for some $p > j$, $\rho', p \models y$, and x holds invariantly between j and p, and $\#b(\rho'[j, p]) \ge n$, i.e. number of times b holds between j and p is $\ge n$. This happens iff

– either (case i) there is a nearest previous integer point to p called α (marked c_i for some i) and there exist integers $g, h : 0 \leq g, h \leq n$ such that $\#b(\rho'[\alpha, p] \geq g$, and $\#b(\rho'[j, \alpha,] \geq h$ and $g + h \geq n$. This happens iff for some i and $0 \leq g, h \leq n$, we have $\rho', j \models x U_I(y \wedge B^i = g)$ and $\rho', j \models x \wedge \neg c_i U_{\#b \geq max(0,h)} c_i$ and $g + h \geq n$. This is encoded by the formula δ below.

– or, (case ii) j and p both lie inside a unit interval bounded by some $[c_{i-1}, c_i]$. In this case, untimed LTL formula $\rho', j \models (x \wedge (\neg \vee c_i)) U_{\#b=n} y)$ holds. Note that the formulae are not yet relativized, the relativized ones with details are given below.

(1) We consider the case when the interval I is bounded and left closed right open of the form $[l, u)$. Our reduction below can be adapted to other kinds of bounded intervals. Let $L = u - l$. Define $s \boxplus t = min(s + t, n)$, and $s \oplus t = (s + t) \bmod (u + 1)$.

– O1: $C = \{c_0, c_1, \ldots, c_u\}$. A point i of ρ is marked c_g iff $t_i \bmod u = g$. In the absence of such a point i (such that t_i is an integer value $k < t_{|dom(\rho)|}$), we add a new point i to $dom(\rho)$ with time stamp t'_i and mark it with c_g iff $t'_i \bmod u = g$. Let $\rho_c = (\sigma^c, \tau^c)$ denote the word obtained from ρ after this marking. O1 can be easily coded in MTL (say η_1).

– O2: $B = \cup_{i=0}^u B^i$, where $B^i = \{b_0^i, b_1^i, \ldots b_n^i\}$. All the points of ρ_c marked c_i are marked as b_0^i. Let p, q be two integer points such that p is marked c_i, q is marked $c_{i \oplus L}$, and no point between p, q is marked $c_{i \oplus L}$. p, q are L apart from each other. Let $p < r < q$ be such that $b_g^i \in \sigma_r^c$ for some g. If $c_{i \oplus L} \notin \sigma_{r+1}^c$ and $b \in \sigma_{r+1}^c$, then the point $r + 1$ is marked $b_{g \boxplus 1}^i$. If $c_{i \oplus L}, b \notin \sigma_{r+1}^c$, then the point $r + 1$ is marked b_g^i. Each B^i is a set of counters which are reset at c_i and counts the number of occurrences of b up to the threshold n between a c_i and the next occurrence of $c_{i \oplus L}$. Starting at a point marked c_i with counter b_0^i, the counter increments up to n on encountering a b, until the next $c_{i \oplus L}$. Further, we ensure that the counter B^i does not appear anywhere from $c_{i \oplus L}$ to the next c_i. Let the resultant word be ρ_b. Let ρ' be the word obtained after all the markings.

(2) *Formula for specifying above behaviour.* We give following MTL formulae to specify O2 . $\eta_2 = \bigwedge_{i=0}^u (\kappa_{2i}(1) \wedge \kappa_{2i}(2) \wedge \kappa_{2i}(3))$ encodes O2 where

$\eta_{2i}(1) = \Box^w(c_i \rightarrow b_0^i) \wedge \bigwedge_{k=0}^n \Box^w[(O(b \wedge \neg c_{i \oplus L}) \wedge b_k^i) \rightarrow O b_{k \boxplus 1}^i]$,

$\eta_{2i}(2) = \bigwedge_{k=0}^n \Box^w[(O(\neg b \wedge \neg c_{i \oplus L}) \wedge b_k^i) \rightarrow O b_k^i]$ and

$\eta_{2i}(3) = \bigwedge_{i=0}^u \Box^w[c_{i \oplus L} \rightarrow (\neg c_i \wedge \neg b^i) U c_i]$, where $b^i = \bigvee_{k=0}^u b_k^i$. Let $\eta = \eta_1 \wedge \eta_2$.

(3) *Marking the witness 'a' correctly at points satisfying $x U_{I, \#b \geq n} y$.* As explained above there are two possible cases: Let $act = \bigvee(\Sigma \cup W)$.

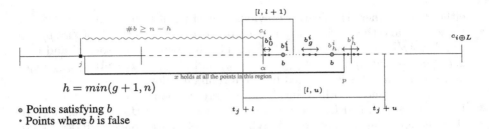

Fig. 3. Illustration of point j, p and the point α such that $t_\alpha = \lceil t_j + l \rceil$. α is marked with some c_i since it is an integer time point. The counting of b's is reset at c_i, starting with b_0^i, and continues till $c_{i \oplus L}$. h is the count of b's between α and p. To satisfy $\square(a \leftrightarrow x\mathsf{U}_{[l,u),\#b \geq n}y)$ at j, we check that the number of b's between j and α is $\geq n - h$ when b is not true at α, and is $\geq n - h - 1$ when b is true at α.

- Case(i): The formula is $\delta = \bigvee\limits_{0 \leq g, h \leq n \wedge g + h \geq n} \delta_1(g) \wedge \delta_2(h)$ where
  - $\delta_1(g) = (x \wedge \neg act)\mathsf{U}_I(y \wedge b_g)$ and
  - $\delta_2(h) = [\{(\neg act \vee x) \wedge \neg c_i\}\mathsf{U}_{\#b \geq h-1}(c_i \wedge b)] \vee [\{(\neg act \vee x) \wedge \neg c_i\}\mathsf{U}_{\#b \geq h}(c_i \wedge \neg b)]$
    for $h > 0$ and $\delta_2(0) = true$
- Case(ii): This formula takes care of the case when timestamps of points j and p have the same integral part. Thus $\lambda = (x \vee \neg act) \wedge \neg c)\mathsf{U}_{\#b \geq n}y$, where $c = \bigvee c_k$ captures the required condition. Note that this case is only applicable when the intervals are of the $\langle 0, u \rangle$. For other type of intervals we omit this case.

The formula $\zeta = \square^w(a \leftrightarrow \delta \vee \lambda)$ specifies the marking of witness correctly in ρ'.

Thus we obtain the MTL formula $\psi = \eta \wedge \zeta$. Thus, by above construction, we get a formula ψ such that $ONF_\Sigma(T) \equiv \exists \downarrow X.\psi$, where $X = C \cup B$.

5 Discussion and Related Work

Within temporal and real time logics, the notion of counting has attracted considerable interest. Laroussini *et al.* extended untimed LTL with threshold counting constrained until operator. They showed that the expressiveness of LTL is not increased by adding threshold counting but the logic becomes exponentially more succinct. Hirshfeld and Rabinovich introduced $\mathsf{C}_{(0,1)}$ operator in continuous timed QTL and showed that it added expressive power. They also showed that in continuous time, more general $\mathsf{C}_{\langle l,u \rangle}$ operator can be expressed with just $\mathsf{C}_{(0,1)}$. Building upon this, Hunter showed that MTL with $\mathsf{C}_{(0,1)}$ operator is expressively complete w.r.t. FO[<, +1]. Thus it can also express UT operator which is straightforwardly modelled in FO[<, +1].

In this paper, we have explored the case of MTL with counting operators over timed words interpreted in pointwise manner. We have shown that both C_I and UT operators add expressive power to MTL. Moreover, the two operators are independent in the sense that neither can be expressed in terms of the other and MTL. (We use prefixes C and T to denote a logic extended with C and UT operators respectively). We have also shown that $CMTL_{0,1} \subset CMTL_0 \subset CMTL_I \subset CTMTL$. Moreover, it is easy to show (see [6]) that CTMTL $\subset$ TPTL[1]. All these expressiveness results straightforwardly carry over to MTL over infinite timed words. Thus, pointwise semantics exhibits considerable complexity in expressiveness of operators as compared to continuous time semantics where all these logics are equally expressive. While this may arguably be considered a shortcoming of the pointwise models of timed behaviours, the pointwise models have superior decidability properties making them more amenable to algorithmic analysis. MTL already has undecidable satisfiability in continuous time whereas it has decidable satisfiability over finite timed words in pointwise semantics.

In this paper, we have shown that MTL extended with C and UT operators also has decidable satisfiability. The result is proved by giving an equisatisfiable reduction from CTMTL to MTL using the technique of oversampling projections. This technique was introduced earlier [4] and used to show that $MTL[U_I, S_{np}]$ with non-punctual past operator is also decidable in pointwise semantics. The current paper marks one more use of the technique of oversampling projections. A closer examination of our reduction from CTMTL to MTL shows that it can be used in presence of any other operator. Also, it does not introduce any punctual use of U_I in the reduced formula. The reduced formula is exponentially larger than the original formula (assuming binary encoding of integer constants). All this implies that $CTMTL[U_I, S_{np}]$ is also decidable over finite timed words. Thus, we significantly extend the frontier of decidable real time logics. Moreover, $CTMITL[U_{NS}, S_{NS}]$ can be equisatisfiably reduced to $MITL[U_{np}, S_{np}]$ and it is decidable with at most 2-EXPSPACE complexity. The exact complexity of satisfiability checking of CTMITL is open although EXPSPACE lowerbound trivially follows from MITL and counting LTL which are syntactic subsets.

In another line of work involving counting and projection, Raskin [13] extended MITL and event clock logic with ability to count by extending these logics with automaton operators and adding second order quantification. The expressiveness was shown to be that of recursive event clock automaton. These logics were able to count over the whole model rather than a particular timed interval. The resultant logic cannot specify constraints such as "within a time unit $(0, 1)$ the number of occurrences of a particular formula is k" but it can also incorporate modulo counting. Thus Raskin's logics and the CTMTL are expressively incomparable.

References

1. Etessami, K., Wilke, T.: An until hierarchy for temporal logic. In: LICS, pp. 108–117 (1996)
2. Hirshfeld, Y., Rabinovich, A.: An expressive temporal logic for real time. In: Královič, R., Urzyczyn, P. (eds.) MFCS 2006. LNCS, vol. 4162, pp. 492–504. Springer, Heidelberg (2006)

3. Hunter, P.: When is metric temporal logic expressively complete? In: CSL, pp. 380–394 (2013)
4. Krishna, S.N., Madnani, K., Pandya, P.K.: Partially punctual metric temporal logic is decidable. In: TIME, pp. 174–183 (2014)
5. Kini, D.R., Krishna, S.N., Pandya, P.K.: On construction of safety signal automata for $MITL[\mathcal{U}, \mathcal{S}]$ using temporal projections. In: Fahrenberg, U., Tripakis, S. (eds.) FORMATS 2011. LNCS, vol. 6919, pp. 225–239. Springer, Heidelberg (2011)
6. Krishna, S.N., Madnani, K., Pandya, P.K.: Metric temporal logic with counting (2015). CoRR, abs/1512.09032
7. Laroussinie, F., Meyer, A., Petonnet, E.: Counting LTL. In: TIME, pp. 51–58 (2010)
8. Madnani, K., Krishna, S.N., Pandya, P.K.: Partially punctual metric temporal logic is decidable (2014). http://arxiv.org/abs/1404.6965
9. Ouaknine, J., Worrell, J.: On the decidability of metric temporal logic. In: LICS, pp. 188–197 (2005)
10. Pandya, P.K., Shah, S.S.: On expressive powers of timed logics: comparing boundedness, non-punctuality, and deterministic freezing. In: Katoen, J.-P., König, B. (eds.) CONCUR 2011. LNCS, vol. 6901, pp. 60–75. Springer, Heidelberg (2011)
11. Prabhakar, P., D'Souza, D.: On the expressiveness of MTL with past operators. In: Asarin, E., Bouyer, P. (eds.) FORMATS 2006. LNCS, vol. 4202, pp. 322–336. Springer, Heidelberg (2006)
12. Rabinovich, A.: Complexity of metric temporal logics with counting and the Pnueli modalities. Theoret. Comput. Sci. **411**(22–24), 2331–2342 (2010)
13. Raskin, J.F.: Logics, automata and classical theories for deciding real time. Ph.D. thesis, Universite de Namur (1999)
14. Straubing, H.: Finite Automata, Formal Logic and Circuit Complexity. Birkhauser, Boston (1994)

Distributed Synthesis in Continuous Time

Holger Hermanns[1], Jan Krčál[1], and Steen Vester[2(✉)]

[1] Computer Science, Saarland University, Saarbrücken, Germany
{hermanns,krcal}@cs.uni-saarland.de
[2] Technical University of Denmark, Kongens Lyngby, Denmark
stve@dtu.dk

Abstract. We introduce a formalism modelling communication of distributed agents strictly in *continuous-time*. Within this framework, we study the problem of synthesising local strategies for individual agents such that a specified set of goal states is reached, or reached with at least a given probability. The flow of time is modelled explicitly based on continuous-time randomness, with two natural implications: First, the non-determinism stemming from interleaving disappears. Second, when we restrict to a subclass of *non-urgent* models, the quantitative value problem for two players can be solved in EXPTIME. Indeed, the explicit continuous time enables players to communicate their states by delaying synchronisation (which is unrestricted for non-urgent models). In general, the problems are undecidable already for two players in the quantitative case and three players in the qualitative case. The qualitative undecidability is shown by a reduction to decentralized POMDPs for which we provide the strongest (and rather surprising) undecidability result so far.

1 Introduction

Distributed self-organising and self-maintaining systems are posing interesting design challenges, and have been subject to many practical [33] as well as theoretical [28,29] investigations. Distributed systems interact in real time, and one very general way to reason about their timing behaviour is to assume that arbitrary continuous probability distributions govern the timing of local steps as well as of communication steps. We are interested in how foundational properties of such distributed systems differ from models where timing is abstracted. As principal means of communication we consider symmetric handshake communication, since it can embed other forms of communication faithfully [2,24] including asynchronous and input/output-separated communication.

As an example, consider the problem of leaking a secret from a sandboxed malware to an attacker. The behaviour of attacker and malware (and possibly other components) are prescribed in terms of states, private transitions, labelled synchronisation transitions, and delay transitions which model both local computation times and synchronisation times. The delays are governed by arbitrary continuous probability distributions over real time. Handshake synchronisation is assumed to take place if all devices able to do so agree on the same transition

© Springer-Verlag Berlin Heidelberg 2016
B. Jacobs and C. Löding (Eds.): FOSSACS 2016, LNCS 9634, pp. 353–369, 2016.
DOI: 10.1007/978-3-662-49630-5_21

label. Otherwise the components run fully asynchronously. The sandboxing can be thought of as restricting the set of labels allowed to occur on synchronisation transitions. The question we focus on is how to synthesise the component control strategies for malware and attacker so that they reach their target (of leaking the secret) almost surely or with at least a given probability p.

More precisely, we consider a parallel composition of n modules synchronizing via handshake communication. The modules are modelled by interactive Markov chains (IMCs) [16,18], a generalization of labelled transition systems and of continuous time Markov chains, equipped with a well-understood compositional theory. Each module may in each state enable private actions, as well as synchronisation actions. It is natural to view such a *distributed IMC* as a game with $n+1$ players, where the last player controls the interleaving of the modules. Each of the other n players controls the decisions in a single module, only based on its local timed history containing only transitions that have occurred within the module. On entering a state of its module, each player selects and commits to executing one of the actions enabled. A private action is executed immediately while a synchronisation action requires a CSP-style handshake [6], it is executed once all modules able to perform this action have committed to it.

For representing delay distributions, we make one decisive and one technical restriction. First, we assume that each distribution is continuous. This for instance disallows deterministic delays of, say, 3 time units. It is an important simplification assumed along our explorations of continuous-time distributed control. Second, we restrict to exponential distributions. This is a pure technicality, since (a) our results can be developed with general continuous distributions, at the price of excessive notational and technical overhead, and (b) exponential distributions can approximate arbitrary continuous distributions arbitrarily close [25]. Together, these assumptions enable us to work in a setting close to interactive Markov chains.

Apart from running in continuous time, the concepts behind distributed IMCs are rather common. Closely related are models based on probabilistic automata [32] or (partially observable) Markov decision processes [3,26]. In these settings, the power of the interleaving player $n+1$ is a matter of ongoing debate [7,8,27]. The problem is that without additional (and often complicated) assumptions this player is too powerful to be realistic, and can for instance leak information between the other players. This is a problem, e.g. in the security context, making model checking results overly pessimistic [13].

In sharp contrast to the discrete-time settings, in our distributed IMCs the interleaving player $n+1$ does not have decisive influence on the resulting game. The reason is that the interleaving player can only affect the order of transitions between two delays, but neither *which transitions* are taken nor what the different players *observe*. This is rooted in the common alphabet synchronisation and especially the continuous-time nature of the game: the probability of two local modules changing state at the same time instant is zero, except if synchronising.

Example 1. We consider the model displayed on the right where the delay transitions are labelled by some rate λ. It displays a very simplistic malicious *App* trying to communicate a secret to an outside *Attacker*, despite being sandboxed. Innocently looking action *login*, *logout* and *lookup* synchronise *App* and *Att*, while the unlabelled transitions denote some private actions of the respective module.

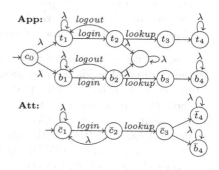

Initially, the *App* can only let time pass. The *Attacker* player has no other choice than committing to handshaking on action *login*. A race of the delay transitions will occur that at some point will lead to either state $(t_1, \bar{c}_1)$ or $(b_1, \bar{c}_1)$, with equal probability. Say in $(t_1, \bar{c}_1)$, the *App* player can only commit to action *login*. The synchronisation will happen immediately since the *Attacker* is committed to *login* already, leading to $(t_2, \bar{c}_2)$. Now the *App* player has either to commit to action *lookup* or *logout*. The latter will induce a deadlock due to a mismatch in players' commitments. Instead assuming the earlier, the state synchronously and immediately changes to $(t_3, \bar{c}_3)$. The *Attacker* player can now use its local timed history to decide which of the private actions to pick. Whatever it chooses, an interleaving of private actions of the two modules follows in zero time. Unless the reachability condition considers transient states such as $(t_3, \bar{t}_4)$ where no time is spent, the player resolving the interleaving has no influence on the outcome.

Now, assume the reachability condition is the state set $\{(t_4, \bar{t}_4), (b_4, \bar{b}_4)\}$. This corresponds to the *Attacker* player correctly determining the initial race of the *App*, and can be considered as a leaked secret. However, according to the explanations provided, it should be obvious that the probability of guessing correctly (by committing properly in state $\bar{c}_3$) is no larger than 0.5, just because the players are bound to decide only based on the local history. The crucial question is: is there an algorithm to compute such probabilities, in general?

Our Contribution. This paper is the first to explore distributed cooperative reachability games with continuous-time flow modelled explicitly. The formalism we study is based on interactive Markov chains, which in turn has been applied across a wide range of engineering domains. We aim at synthesising local strategies for the players to reach with at least a given probability a specified set of goal states. If this probability is 1 we call the problem *qualitative*, otherwise *quantitative*. We consider *existential* problems, asking for the existence of strategies with these properties, and *value* problems, asking for strategies approximating the given probability value arbitrarily closely. We have three main results:

1. We show that, under mild assumptions on the winning condition, in continuous-time distributed synthesis the interleaving player has no power.
2. In general, we establish that the quantitative problems are undecidable for two or more players, the qualitative value problem is undecidable for two or more players and the qualitative existence problem is EXPTIME-hard for two players and undecidable for three or more players.

3. However, when focusing on the subclass of 2-player *non-urgent* distributed IMCs, the quantitative value problem can be solved in exponential time. Non-urgency enables changing the decisions committed to after some time. Thus, it empowers the players to reach a distributed consensus about the next handshake to perform by observing the only information they jointly have access to: the advance of time.

The qualitative undecidability comes from a novel result about decentralised partially observable Markov decision processes (DEC-POMDP), a multi-player extensions of POMDP. While qualitative existence is decidable for POMDP [1], we show that qualitative existence is undecidable for DEC-POMDP already for 2 players. It is to the knowledge of the authors the strongest undecidability result for DEC-POMDPs with infinite horizon which is of its own interest. By a reduction from DEC-POMDP to distributed IMCs that adds one player, we get undecidability of qualitative existence for 3 or more players in distributed IMCs. Due to space constraints, full proofs can be found in [17].

2   Distributed Interactive Markov Chains

We denote by $\mathbb{R}$, $\mathbb{R}_{\geq 0}$, $\mathbb{N}$, and $\mathbb{N}_0$ the sets of real numbers, non-negative real numbers, positive integers, and non-negative integers, respectively. Furthermore, for a finite set X, we denote by $\Delta(X)$ the set of *discrete probability distributions* over X, i.e. functions $f : X \to [0, 1]$ such that $\sum_{x \in X} f(x) = 1$. Finally, for a tuple x from a product space $X_1 \times \cdots \times X_n$ and for $1 \leq i \leq n$, we use functional notation $x(i)$ to denote the ith element of the tuple.

We first give a definition of a (local) module based on the formalism of Interactive Markov Chains (IMC). Then we introduce (global) distributed IMC.

Definition 1 (IMC). *An* IMC *(module) is a tuple* $(S, Act, \hookrightarrow, \rightsquigarrow, s^{in})$ *where*

- *S is a finite set of states with an initial state s^{in},*
- *Act is a finite set of actions,*
- *$\hookrightarrow \subseteq S \times Act \times S$ is the action transition relation,*
- *$\rightsquigarrow \subseteq S \times \mathbb{Q}_{>0} \times S$ is the finite delay transition relation.*

We write $s \xrightarrow{a} s'$ when $(s, a, s') \in \hookrightarrow$ and $s \xrightarrow{\lambda} s'$ when $(s, \lambda, s') \in \rightsquigarrow$ (λ being the *rate* of the transition). We say that action a is *available* in s if $s \xrightarrow{a} s'$ for some s'.

Definition 2 Distributed IMC. *A* distributed IMC *is a tuple*

$$\mathcal{G} = ((S_i, Act_i, \hookrightarrow_i, \rightsquigarrow_i, s_i^{in}))_{1 \leq i \leq n}$$

of modules for players $Plr = \{1, ..., n\}$. *Furthermore, by* $Act = \bigcup_i Act_i$ *we denote the set of all actions, and by* $S = S_1 \times ... \times S_n$ *the set of (global) states.*

Intuitively, a distributed IMC moves in continuous-time from a (global) state to a (global) state using transitions with labels from $Label = Act \cup Plr$.

- An action transition with label $a \in Act$ corresponds to *synchronous* communication of all players in $\mathrm{Sync}(a) := \{j \in Plr \mid a \in Act_j\}$ and can only be taken when it is *enabled*, i.e. when all these players choose their local transitions with action a at the same time. It is called a *synchronisation* action if $|\mathrm{Sync}(a)| \geq 2$ and a *private* action if $|\mathrm{Sync}(a)| = 1$.
- A delay transition of any player $j \in Plr$ is taken *independently* by the player after a random delay, i.e. the set of players that synchronise over label j is $\mathrm{Sync}(j) = \{j\}$.

Formally, the (local) *choices of player* j range over $\mathcal{C}_j = \hookrightarrow_j \cup \{\bot\}$. When in (local) state s, the player may pick only a choice *available in* s. That is, either an action transition of the form $s \xrightarrow{a} s'$ or $\bot$ if there is no such action transition. We define *global choices* as $\mathcal{C} = \mathcal{C}_1 \times \cdots \times \mathcal{C}_n$. A global choice $\boldsymbol{c}$ induces the set $\mathrm{En}(\boldsymbol{c}) = \{a \in Act \mid \forall j \in \mathrm{Sync}(a) : \boldsymbol{c}(j) = (\cdot, a, \cdot)\}$ of actions *enabled* in $\boldsymbol{c}$.

To avoid that time stops by taking infinitely many action steps in zero time, we pose a standard assumption prohibiting cycles [14,15,19–21]: we require that for every action $a \in Act$ there is a player $j \in \mathrm{Sync}(a)$ such that the labelled transition system $(S_j, \hookrightarrow_j)$ does not have any cycle involving action a.

The behaviour of a distributed IMC is a *play*, an infinite sequence

$$\rho = \boldsymbol{s}_0 \boldsymbol{c}_0 \xrightarrow{a_1, t_1} \boldsymbol{s}_1 \boldsymbol{c}_1 \xrightarrow{a_2, t_2} \boldsymbol{s}_2 \boldsymbol{c}_2 \cdots$$

where each $\boldsymbol{s}_i \in S$ is the state after i moves, $\boldsymbol{c}_i \in \mathcal{C}$ is the choice of the players in the state $\boldsymbol{s}_i$, and $a_{i+1} \in Label$ and $t_{i+1} \in \mathbb{R}_{\geq 0}$ are the label and the absolute time of the next transition taken. By *Play* we denote the set of all plays. Which play is taken depends on the *strategies* of the players, on the *scheduler* which resolves interleaving of communication whenever multiple actions are enabled, and on the rules (involving randomness) given later.

2.1   Schedulers and Strategies

First we define strategies and schedulers basing their decision on the current local and global history, respectively. A *(global) history* is a finite prefix

$$h = \boldsymbol{s}_0 \boldsymbol{c}_0 \xrightarrow{a_1, t_1} \cdots \xrightarrow{a_i, t_i} \boldsymbol{s}_i$$

of a play ending with a state. For given h, we get the *local history* of player j as

$$\pi_j(h) = \boldsymbol{s}_0'(j)\boldsymbol{c}_0'(j) \xrightarrow{a_1', t_1'} \cdots \xrightarrow{a_\ell', t_\ell'} \boldsymbol{s}_\ell'(j)$$

where $vect \boldsymbol{s}_0' \boldsymbol{c}_0' \xrightarrow{a_1', t_1'} \cdots \xrightarrow{a_\ell', t_\ell'} \boldsymbol{s}_\ell'$ is the subsequence of h omitting all steps not visible for player j, i.e. all $\xrightarrow{a_m, t_m} \boldsymbol{s}_m \boldsymbol{c}_m$ with $j \notin \mathrm{Sync}(a_m)$. The set of all global histories is denoted by *Hist*; the set of local histories of player j by *Hist$_j$*.

Example 2. Consider again Example 1. Let *App* be controlled by player 1 and *Att* by player 2. For the following history we get corresponding local histories

$$h = (c_0, \bar{c}_1)(\bot, login) \xrightarrow{1, 0.42} (t_1, \bar{c}_1)(login, login) \xrightarrow{login, 0.42} (t_2, \bar{c}_2),$$

$$\pi_1(h) = c_0 \bot \xrightarrow{1, 0.42} t_1 \, login \xrightarrow{login, 0.42} t_2, \qquad \pi_2(h) = \bar{c}_1 \, login \xrightarrow{login, 0.42} \bar{c}_2$$

Note that the attacker can neither observe the Markovian transition nor the local state of the *App*. The *App* cannot observe the local state of the attacker either, but it can be deduced from the local history of the *App*.

A *strategy* for player j is a measurable function $\sigma : Hist_j \rightarrow \Delta(\mathcal{C}_j)$ that assigns to any local history h of player j a probability distribution over choices available in the last state of h. We say that a strategy σ for player j is *pure* if for all h we have $\sigma(h)(c) = 1$ for some c; and *memoryless* if for all h and h' with equal last local state we have $\sigma(h) = \sigma(h')$.

A *scheduler* is a measurable function $\delta : Hist \times C \rightarrow \Delta(Act) \cup \{\bot\}$ that assigns to any global history h and global choice c a probability distribution over actions enabled in c; or a special symbol $\bot$ again denoting that no action is enabled.

Example 3. The available local choices in $(t_2, \bar{c}_2)$, the last state of h from above, are $\{(t_2, lookup, t_3), (t_2, logout, t_1)\}$ for *App* and solely $\{(\bar{c}_2, lookup, \bar{c}_3)\}$ for *Att*. Let the strategy of *App* select either choice with equal probability. If $(t_2, lookup, t_3)$ is chosen, *lookup* is enabled and must be picked by the scheduler σ. If $(t_2, logout, t_1)$ is chosen, no action is enabled and δ must pick $\bot$, waiting for a delay transition.

2.2   Probability of Plays

Let us fix a *profile of strategies* $\boldsymbol{\sigma} = (\sigma_1, \ldots, \sigma_n)$ for individual players, and a scheduler δ. The play starts in the initial state $\boldsymbol{s_0} = (s_1^{in}, \ldots, s_n^{in})$ and inductively evolves as follows. Let the current history be $h = \boldsymbol{s_0}\boldsymbol{c_0} \xrightarrow{a_1, t_1} \cdots \xrightarrow{a_i, t_i} \boldsymbol{s_i}$.

- For the next choice $\boldsymbol{c_i}$, only players $P_i := \text{Sync}(a_i)$ involved in the last transition freely choose (we assume $P_0 := Plr$). Hence, independently for every $j \in P_i$, the choice $\boldsymbol{c_i}(j)$ is taken randomly according to $\sigma_j(\pi_j(h))$. All remaining players $j \notin P_i$ stick to the previous choice $\boldsymbol{c_i}(j) = \boldsymbol{c_{i-1}}(j)$ as for them, no observable event happened.
- After fixing $\boldsymbol{c_i}$, there are two types of transitions:
  1. If $\text{En}(\boldsymbol{c_i}) \neq \emptyset$, the next synchronization action $a_{i+1} \in \text{En}(\boldsymbol{c_i})$ is chosen randomly according to $\delta(h, \boldsymbol{c_i})$ and taken immediately at time $t_{i+1} := t_i$. The next state $\boldsymbol{s_{i+1}}$ satisfies for every $j \in Plr$:

$$\boldsymbol{s_{i+1}}(j) = \begin{cases} \text{target}(\boldsymbol{c_i}(j)) & \text{if } j \in \text{Sync}(a_{i+1}), \\ \boldsymbol{s_i}(j) & \text{if } j \notin \text{Sync}(a_{i+1}). \end{cases}$$

  where $\text{target}(\boldsymbol{c_i}(j))$ denotes the target of the transition chosen by player j. In other words, players involved in synchronisation move according to their choice, the remaining players stay in their previous states.
  2. If $\text{En}(\boldsymbol{c_i}) = \emptyset$, a local delay transition is taken after a random delay, chosen as follows. Each delay transition $\boldsymbol{s_i}(j) \xrightarrow{\lambda} \cdot$ outgoing from the current local state of any player j is assigned randomly a real-valued delay according to the exponential distribution with rate λ. This results in a collection of real numbers. The transition $\boldsymbol{s_i}(\ell) \xrightarrow{\lambda} s$ with the minimum delay d in

this collection is taken. Hence, $a_{i+1} := \ell$ (denoting that player ℓ moves), $t_{i+1} := t_i + d$, and the next state s_{i+1} satisfies for every $j \in Plr$:

$$s_{i+1}(j) = \begin{cases} s & \text{if } j \in \text{Sync}(a_{i+1}) = \{\ell\}, \\ s_i(j) & \text{if } j \notin \text{Sync}(a_{i+1}). \end{cases}$$

All these rules induce a probability measure $\text{Pr}^{\sigma,\delta}$ over the set of all plays by a standard cylinder construction.

2.3 Distributed Synthesis Problem

We study the following two fundamental reachability problems for distributed IMCs. Let $\mathcal{G}$ be a distributed IMC, $T \subseteq S$ be a target set of states, and p be a rational number in $[0, 1]$. Denoting by $\Diamond T$ the set of plays ρ that reach a state in T and stay there for a non-zero amount of time, we focus on:

Existence Does there exist a strategy profile σ s.t. for all schedulers δ,

$$\text{Pr}^{\sigma,\delta}(\Diamond T) \geq p \ ?$$

Value Can the value p be arbitrarily approached, i.e. do we have

$$\sup_{\sigma} \inf_{\delta} \text{Pr}^{\sigma,\delta}(\Diamond T) \geq p \ ?$$

We refer to the general problem with $p \in [0, 1]$ as *quantitative*. When we restrict to $p = 1$, we call the problem *qualitative*.

3 Schedulers Are Not that Powerful

The task of a scheduler is to choose among concurrently enabled transitions, thereby resolving the non-determinism conceptually caused by interleaving. In this section, we address the impact of the decisions of the scheduler. We show that despite having the ability to affect the order in which transitions are taken in the *global* play, the scheduler cannot affect what every player

observes *locally*. Thus, the scheduler affects neither the choices of any player nor what synchronisation occurs. As a result, for winning objectives that are closed under *local observation equivalence*, the scheduler cannot affect the probability of winning.

Example 4. Consider the distributed IMC to the right. After the delay transition is taken in C_1 and there is synchronisation on action a, the scheduler can choose whether there will be synchronisation on b or c first. However, it can only affect the interleaving, not any of the local plays.

For a play $\rho = s_0 c_0 \xrightarrow{a_1,t_1} s_1 c_1 \xrightarrow{a_2,t_2} s_2 c_2 \cdots$ we define the local play $\pi_j(\rho)$ of player j analogously to local histories. We define *local observation* equivalence $\sim$ over plays by setting $\rho \sim \rho'$ if $\pi_j(\rho) = \pi_j(\rho')$ for all $j \in Plr$. Let us stress that two local observation equivalent plays have exactly the same action and delay transitions happening at the same moments of time; only the order of action transitions happening at the same time can differ. Finally, we say that a set E of plays is *closed under local observation equivalence* if for any $\rho \in E$ and any ρ' such that $\rho \sim \rho'$ we have $\rho' \in E$. It is now possible to show the following.

Theorem 1. *Let E be a measurable set of plays closed under local observation equivalence. For any strategy profile σ and schedulers δ and δ' we have*

$$\mathrm{Pr}^{\sigma,\delta}(E) = \mathrm{Pr}^{\sigma,\delta'}(E).$$

As a result, for the rest of the paper we write $\mathrm{Pr}^{\sigma}(E)$ instead of $\mathrm{Pr}^{\sigma,\delta}(E)$ since the scheduler cannot affect the probability of the events we consider. Indeed, the reachability objectives defined in the previous section are closed under local observation equivalence.

Remark 1. The fact that interleaving does not have decisive impact in continuous time may seem natural and thus possibly unsurprising to experts. Yet, the result does not hold for many small variations of the setting we consider, e.g. neither for asymmetric communication nor when allowing cycles of action transitions.

4   Undecidability Results

In this section, we put distributed IMCs into context of other partial-observation models. As a result, we show that reachability quickly gets undecidable here.

Theorem 2. *For distributed IMCs we have that*

1. *the qualitative value, quantitative value, and quantitative existence problems are undecidable with $n \geq 2$ players; and*
2. *the qualitative existence problem is* ExpTime-*hard with $n = 2$ players and undecidable with $n \geq 3$ players.*

Theorem 2 is obtained by using two fundamental results. First, we provide a novel (and somewhat surprising) result for *decentralized POMDPs* (DEC-POMDPs) [3], an established multi-player generalization of POMDPs. We show that the qualitative existence problem for DEC-POMDPs is undecidable already for 2 players. This is, to the knowledge of the authors, currently the strongest known undecidability result for DEC-POMDPs. Second, we show that distributed IMCs are not only more expressive (w.r.t. reachability) than POMDPs but also more expressive than DEC-POMDPs. We show it by reducing reachability in DEC-POMDPs with n players to reachability in distributed IMCs with $n + 1$ players. Theorem 2 follows from these two results and from known results about POMDPs [4,12,26]. For an overview, see Table 1.

Table 1. Undecidability results for reachability. Unreferenced results are shown here.

	POMDPs	DEC-POMDPs	Distributed IMCs
Qual. Existence	Dec. [1]	Undec. for ≥ 2 players	Undec. for ≥ 3 players
Value	Undec. [12]	Undec. for ≥ 1 player [12]	Undec. for ≥ 2 players
Quant. Existence	Undec. [26]	Undec. for ≥ 1 player [26]	Undec. for ≥ 2 players
Value	Undec. [4]	Undec. for ≥ 1 player [4]	Undec. for ≥ 2 players

4.1 Decentralized POMDP (DEC-POMDP)

We start with a definition of the related formalism of decentralized POMDP [3].

Definition 3. *A DEC-POMDP is a tuple* $(S, Plr, (Act_i, \mathcal{O}_i)_{1 \leq i \leq n}, P, O, s^{in})$ *where*

- *S is a finite set of global states with initial state $s^{in} \in S$,*
- *$Plr = \{1, ..., n\}$ is a finite set of players,*
- *Act_i is a finite set of local actions of player i with $Act_i \cap Act_j = \emptyset$ if $j \neq i$,*
  (by $Act = Act_1 \times \cdots \times Act_n$ we denote the set of global actions),
- *$\mathcal{O}_i$ is a finite set of local observations for player i,*
  (by $\mathcal{O} = \mathcal{O}_1 \times \cdots \times \mathcal{O}_n$ we denote the set of global observations),
- *$P : S \times Act \to \Delta(S)$ is the transition function which assigns to a state and a global action a probability distribution over successor states, and*
- *$O : S \times Act \times S \to \Delta(\mathcal{O})$ is the observation function which assigns to every transition a probability distribution over global observations.*

In contrast to distributed IMCs that capture flow of time explicitly, DEC-POMDP is a discrete-time formalism. A DEC-POMDP starts in the initial state s^{in}. Assuming that the current state is s, one discrete step of the process works as follows. First, each player j chooses an action a_j. Then the next state s' is chosen according to the probability distribution $P(s, \boldsymbol{a})$ where $\boldsymbol{a} = (a_1, \ldots, a_n)$. Then, each player j receives an observation $o_j \in \mathcal{O}_j$ such that the observations $\boldsymbol{o} = (o_1, ..., o_n)$ are chosen with probability $O(s, \boldsymbol{a}, s')(\boldsymbol{o})$. Repeating this forever, we obtain a *play* which is an infinite sequence $\rho = s_0 \boldsymbol{a}_0 \boldsymbol{o}_0 s_1 \boldsymbol{a}_1 \boldsymbol{o}_1 \cdots$ where $s_0 = s^{in}$ and for all $i \geq 0$ it holds that $s_i \in S$, $\boldsymbol{a}_i \in Act$, and $\boldsymbol{o}_i \in \mathcal{O}$. Note that the players can only base their decisions on the sequences of observations they receive rather than the actual sequence of states which is not available to them. For a more complete coverage of DEC-POMDPs, see [3].

4.2 Reduction from DEC-POMDP

First we present the reduction from a DEC-POMDP $\mathcal{P}$ to a distributed IMC $\mathcal{G}$. In this subsection, we write $\Pr^\sigma_\mathcal{P}$ or $\Pr^\sigma_\mathcal{G}$ instead of $\Pr^\sigma$ to distinguish between the probability measure in the DEC-POMDP from the probability measure in the distributed IMC.

Proposition 1. *For a DEC-POMDP $\mathcal{P}$ with n players and a target set T of states of $\mathcal{P}$ we can construct in polynomial time a distributed IMC $\mathcal{G}$ with $n+1$ players and a target set T' of global states in $\mathcal{G}$ where:*

$$\exists \boldsymbol{\sigma} : \mathrm{Pr}^{\boldsymbol{\sigma}}_{\mathcal{G}}(\Diamond T) = p \quad \Longleftrightarrow \quad \exists \boldsymbol{\sigma}' : \mathrm{Pr}^{\boldsymbol{\sigma}'}_{\mathcal{P}}(\Diamond T') = p.$$

Proof (Proof Sketch). Let us fix n and $\mathcal{P} = (S, Plr, (Act_i)_{1 \leq i \leq n}, \delta, (\mathcal{O}_i)_{1 \leq i \leq n}, O)$ where $Plr = \{1, ..., n\}$. Further, let $Act_i = \{a_{i1}, ..., a_{im_i}\}$ and $\mathcal{O}_i = \{o_{i1}, ..., o_{i\ell_i}\}$ for player $i \in Plr$. The distributed IMC $\mathcal{G}$ has $n+1$ modules, one module for each player in $\mathcal{P}$ and the *main* module responsible for their synchronisation. Intuitively,

- the module of every player i stores the last local observation in its state space. Every step of $\mathcal{P}$ is modelled as follows: The player *outputs* to the main module the action it chooses and then *inputs* from the main module the next observation.
- The main module stores the global state in its state space. Every step of $\mathcal{P}$ corresponds to the following: The main module *inputs* the actions of all players one by one, then it randomly picks the new state and new observations according to the rules of $\mathcal{P}$ based on the actions collected. The observations are lastly *output* to all players, again one by one.

We construct the distributed IMC so that only the outputting player chooses what action to output whereas the inputting player accepts whatever comes. The construction of modules for player i is illustrated in Fig. 1 along with constructions for input and output. The interesting part is how an action from the set $\{a_1, ..., a_r\}$ is input in a state s. Instead of waiting in s, the player travels by delay transitions in a round-robin fashion through a cycle of r states, where in the i-th state, only the action a_i is available. Thus, the player has no influence and must input the action that comes. By this construction, the main module has at most one action transition in every state such that the player cannot influence anything; other modules get no insight by observing time and thus the players have the same power as in the DEC-POMDP. □

4.3   Undecidability of Qualitative Existence in DEC-POMDP

Next, we show that the qualitative existence problem for DEC-POMDPs even with $n \geq 2$ players is undecidable. The proof has similarities with ideas from

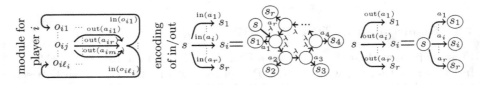

Fig. 1. Module for player i on the left. Input and output encoding to the right.

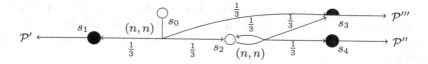

Fig. 2. Overall structure of $\mathcal{P}$ without details of $\mathcal{P}', \mathcal{P}''$ and $\mathcal{P}'''$.

[5] where it is shown that deciding existence of sure-winning strategies in safety games with 3 players and partial observation is undecidable. Using the randomness of DEC-POMDPs we show undecidability of the qualitative existence problem for reachability in 2-player DEC-POMDPs.

Theorem 3. *It is undecidable whether for a DEC-POMDP $\mathcal{P}$ with $n \geq 2$ players and a set T of target states in $\mathcal{P}$ if there exists a strategy profile σ such that $\mathrm{Pr}_{\mathcal{P}}^{\sigma}(\diamond T) = 1$.*

Proof (Proof Sketch). We do a reduction from the non-halting problem of a deterministic Turing machine M that starts with a blank input tape. From M we construct a DEC-POMDP $\mathcal{P}$ with two players $Plr = \{1, 2\}$ such that M does not halt if and only if players 1 and 2 have strategies $\sigma = (\sigma_1, \sigma_2)$ which ensure that the probability of reaching a target set T is 1. Figure 2 shows the overall structure of $\mathcal{P}$ without details of sub-modules $\mathcal{P}', \mathcal{P}''$ and $\mathcal{P}'''$.

Both players have two possible observations, black and white. We depict the observation of player 1 in the top-half and of player 2 in the bottom-half of every state. The play starts in s_0 and with probability 1, every player receives the black observation exactly once during the play. If the play goes to s_1 or s_4 the players will receive the observation at the same time and if the play goes to s_3 then player 2 will receive the observation in the step after player 1 does. The modules $\mathcal{P}', \mathcal{P}''$ and $\mathcal{P}'''$ are designed so that:

- In $\mathcal{P}'$, a target state is reached if and only if the sequence of actions played by both players encodes the initial configuration of M.
- In $\mathcal{P}''$, a target state is reached with probability 1 if and only if both players play the same infinite sequence of actions. Note that randomness is essential to build such a module.
- In $\mathcal{P}'''$, the target set is reached if and only if the sequences of actions played by player 1 and 2 encode two configurations C_1 and C_2 of M, respectively, such that C_1 is not an accepting configuration and C_2 is a successor configuration of C_1. This can be done since a finite automaton can be constructed that recognizes if one configuration is a successor of the other when reading both configurations at the same time. Note that it is possible because such configurations can only differ by a constant amount (the control state, the tape head position and in symbols in cells near the tape head).

It can be shown by induction that if there are strategies σ_1, σ_2 that ensure reaching T with probability 1 then every σ_i has to play the encoding of the jth configuration of M when it receives the black observation in the jth step. Further, it can be shown that these strategies do ensure reaching T with probability 1 if M does not halt on the empty input tape and do not ensure reaching T with probability 1 if M halts.   □

5   Decidability for Non-urgent Models

In this section, we turn our attention to a subclass of distributed IMCs, called *non-urgent*, that implies decidability for both the qualitative and quantitative value problems for 2 players.

Definition 4. *We call* $\mathcal{G} = ((S_i, Act_i, \hookrightarrow_i, \rightsquigarrow_i, s_{0i}))_{1 \leq i \leq n}$ non-urgent *if for every* $1 \leq j \leq n$:

1. *Every* $s \in S_j$ *is of one of the following forms:*
   (a) Synchronisation *state with at least one outgoing synchronisation action transition and exactly one outgoing delay transition which is a self-loop.*
   (b) Private *state with arbitrary outgoing delay transitions and private action transitions.*
2. *Player j has an action* $\varnothing_j \in Act_j$ *enabled in every synchronisation state from S_j that allows to "do nothing" and thus postpone the synchronisation. To this end,* $\varnothing_j$ *is also in* Act_k *for every other player $k \neq j$ but* $\varnothing_j$ *does not appear in* $\hookrightarrow_k$. *As a result, j does not take part in any synchronisation while choosing* $\varnothing_j$.

In a non-urgent distributed IMC, $s \in S$ is called a (global) *synchronisation state* if it is the initial state or all $s(j)$ are synchronisation states. We denote global synchronisation states by S'. All other global states $S \setminus S'$ are called *private*.

Example 5. Consider the non-urgent variant of Example 1 on the right. The "do nothing" actions are a natural concept; the only real modelling restriction is that one cannot model a communication time-out any more, the delay transitions from synchronisation states need to be self-loops.

Surprisingly, in this model, the secret can be leaked with probability 1 as follows. As before, the players reach the states $(t_2, \bar{c}_2)$ or $(b_2, \bar{c}_2)$ with equal probability. Now, the *App* player can arbitrarily postpone the *lookup* by committing to action $\varnothing_1$. Whenever the delay self-loop is taken, the player can re-decide to perform *lookup*. Since the self-loop is taken repetitively, the *App* player is flexible in choosing the timing of *lookup*. Thus, leaking the secret is simple,

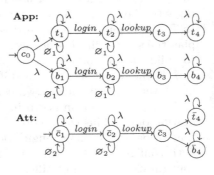

e.g. by performing *lookup* in an odd second when in t_2 and in an even second when in b_2.

For two players, we construct a general synchronisation scheme that (highly probably) shows the players the current global state after each communication.

Theorem 4. *The quantitative value problem for 2-player non-urgent distributed IMCs where the target set consists only of synchronisation states is in* ExpTime.

Being a special case, also the qualitative value problem is decidable. In essence, the problem becomes decidable because in the synchronisation states, the players can effectively exchange arbitrary information. This resembles the setting of [11]. The insight that observing global time provides an additional synchronization mechanism is not novel in itself, but it is obviously burdensome to formally capture in time-abstract models of asynchronous communication, and thus usually not considered. For distributed IMC, it still is non-trivial to develop; here it hinges on the non-urgency assumption. The results of [11] also indicate that for three or more players, additional constraints on the topology may be needed to obtain decidability.

In the rest of the section we prove Theorem 4, fixing a 2-player non-urgent distributed IMC $\mathcal{G} = ((S_i, Act_i, \hookrightarrow_i, \leadsto_i, s_{0i}))_{1 \leq i \leq 2}$, $p \in [0,1]$, and $T \subseteq S'$. We present the algorithm based on a reduction to a discrete-time Markov decision process and then discuss its correctness.

Markov decision process (MDP). An MDP is a tuple $\mathcal{M} = (S, A, P, s_0)$ where S is a finite set of states, A is a finite set of actions, $P : S \times A \to \Delta(S)$ is a partial probabilistic transition function, and s_0 is an initial state. An MDP is the special case of a DEC-POMDP with 1 player that has a unique observation for each state. A *play* in $\mathcal{M}$ is a sequence $\omega = s_0 s_1 \ldots$ of states such that $P(s_i, a_i)(s_{i+1}) > 0$ for some action a_i for every $i \geq 0$. A history is a prefix of a play. A *strategy* is a function π that to every history $h \cdot s$ assigns a probability distribution over actions such that if an action a is assigned a non-zero probability, then $P(s, a)$ is defined. A strategy π is *pure memoryless* if it assigns Dirac distributions to any history and its choice depends only on the last state of the history. When we fix a strategy π, we obtain a probability measure $\Pr^\pi$ over the set of plays. For further details, see [30].

The algorithm. It works by reduction to an MDP $\mathcal{M}_{\mathcal{G}} = (S', A, P, s_0)$ where

- $S' \subseteq S$ is the set of global synchronisation states;
- $A = \mathcal{C} \times \Sigma_1 \times \Sigma_2 \cup \{\bot\}$ where Σ_j is the set of pure memoryless strategies of player j in $\mathcal{G}$ that choose $\varnothing_j$ in every synchronisation state;
- For an arbitrary state (s_1, s_2), we define the transition function as follows:
  - For any $(c, \sigma_1, \sigma_2) \in A$, the transition $P((s_1, s_2), (c, \sigma_1, \sigma_2))$ is defined if c is available in (s_1, s_2) and the players agree in c on some action a, i.e. $En(c) = \{a\}$. If defined, the distribution $P((s_1, s_2), (c, \sigma_1, \sigma_2))$ assigns to any successor state (s_1', s_2') the probability that in $\mathcal{G}$ the state (s_1', s_2') is reached from (s_1, s_2) via states in $S \setminus S'$ by choosing c and then using the pure memoryless strategy profile (σ_1, σ_2).
  - To avoid deadlocks, the transition $P((s_1, s_2), \bot)$ is defined iff no other transition is defined in (s_1, s_2) and it is a self-loop, i.e. it assigns probability 1 to (s_1, s_2).

The MDP $\mathcal{M}_\mathcal{G}$ has size exponential in $|\mathcal{G}|$. Note that all target states T are included in S'. Slightly abusing notation, let $\diamond T$ denote the set of plays in $\mathcal{M}_\mathcal{G}$ that reach the set T. From standard results on MDPs [30], there exists an optimal pure memoryless strategy π^*, i.e. a strategy satisfying $\operatorname{Pr}^{\pi^*}(\diamond T) = \sup_\pi \operatorname{Pr}^\pi(\diamond T)$. Furthermore, such a strategy π^* and the value $v := \operatorname{Pr}^{\pi^*}(\diamond T)$ can be computed in time polynomial in $|\mathcal{M}_\mathcal{G}|$. Finally, the algorithm returns TRUE if $v \geq p$ and FALSE, otherwise.

Correctness of the algorithm Let us explain why the approach is correct.

Proposition 2. *The value of $\mathcal{G}$ is equal to the value of $\mathcal{M}_\mathcal{G}$, i.e.*

$$\sup_\sigma \operatorname{Pr}^\sigma(\diamond T) \quad = \quad \sup_\pi \operatorname{Pr}^\pi(\diamond T).$$

Proof Sketch. As regards the $\leq$ inequality, it suffices to show that any strategy profile σ can be mimicked by some strategy π. This is simple as π in $\mathcal{M}_\mathcal{G}$ has always knowledge of the global state. Much more interesting is the $\geq$ inequality. We argue that for any strategy π there is a sequence of local strategy profiles $\sigma^1, \sigma^2, \dots$ such that

$$\lim_{i \to \infty} \operatorname{Pr}^{\sigma^i}(\diamond T) = \operatorname{Pr}^\pi(\diamond T).$$

The crucial idea is that a strategy profile communicates correctly (with high probability) the current global state in a synchronisation state by *delaying* as follows. The time is divided into phases, each of $|S'_1| \cdot 2 |S'_2|$ slots (where S'_i are the synchronisation states of player i). We depict a phase by the table on the right where the time flows from top to bottom and from left to right (as reading a book). Players 1 and 2 try to synchronise in the row and column, respectively, corresponding to their current

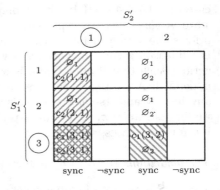

states (in circle) and in each slot take the choice $c_i(s_1, s_2)$ optimal given the current global state is (s_1, s_2); in the remaining slots they choose to do nothing. Since the players can change their choice only at random moments of time, their synchronising choice always stretches a bit into the successive silent slot (in a $\neg$sync column). The more we increase the size of each slot, the lower is the chance that a synchronisation choice of a player stretches to the next *synchronisation* slot. Thus, the lower is the chance of an erroneous synchronisation. We define the size of the slot to increase with i and also along the play so that for any fixed i the probability of at least one erroneous synchronisation is bounded by $\kappa_i < 1$ and for $i \to \infty$, we have $\kappa_i \to 0$. □

6   Discussion and Conclusion

This paper has introduced a foundational framework for modelling and synthesising distributed controllers interacting in continuous time via handshake communication. The continuous time nature of the model induces that the interleaving scheduler has in fact very little power. We studied cooperative reachability problems for which we presented a number of undecidability results, while for non-urgent models we established decidability of both quantitative and qualitative problems for the two-player case. In the framework considered, the restriction to exponential distributions is a technical vehicle, the results could have been developed in general continuous time, e.g. by using the model of stochastic automata [9].

Distributed IMCs can be considered as an attractive base model especially in the context of information flow and other security-related studies. This is because in contrast to the discrete time setting, the power of the interleaving scheduler is no matter of debate, it can leak no essential information.

From a more general perspective, distributed synthesis of control algorithms has received considerable attention in its entirety [22,28,29]. The asynchronous setting with handshake synchronisation has been considered in [23]. Notably, our assumption that players stay committed to a particular action choice for the time in between state changes implies the necessity to let the players explicitly solve distributed consensus problems. As done in [23], one can overcome this by letting local players pick sets of enabled actions (or letting them change choice with infinite speed), and then let some built-in magic pick a valid action from the intersection, implying that whenever possible a consensus is reached for sure. Such a change would however reintroduce the scheduler.

We should point out that distributed IMCs are not fully compositional: We are assuming a fixed vector of modules, and do not discuss that modules themselves may be vectors. Otherwise, we would face the phenomenon of auto-concurrency [10], where transitions with identical synchronisation actions might get enabled concurrently, despite not synchronising. This in turn would again re-introduce distinguishing power of the scheduler.

Distributed Markov chains [31] constitute another recent discrete-time approach where interleaving nondeterminism is tamed successfully via assumptions on the communication structure. The observation that continuous time reduces the power of the interleaving scheduler is not entirely new. Though not explicitly discussed, it underpins the model of probabilistic I/O automata (PIOA) [34] which uses I/O communication with input-enabledness and output-determinism. In that setting, output-determinism implies that local players have no decisive power, and hence a continuous time Markov chain arises. We can approximate I/O-based communication by distributed IMCs without the need for output-determinism. The approximation is linked to arbitrarily small but non-zero delays needed to cycle through synchronising action sets. A profound investigation of the continuous-time particularities of this and other synchronisation disciplines is considered an interesting topic for future work.

Acknowledgements. This work is supported by the EU 7th Framework Programme projects 295261(MEALS) and 318490 (SENSATION), by the Czech Science Foundation project P202/12/G061, the DFG Transregional Collaborative Research Centre SFB/TR 14 AVACS, and by the CDZ project 1023 (CAP).

References

1. Baier, C., Größer, M., Bertrand, N.: Probabilistic ω-automata. J. ACM **59**(1), 1 (2012)
2. Baier, C., Katoen, J.P.: Principles of Model Checking. MIT Press, Cambridge (2008)
3. Bernstein, D.S., Givan, R., Immerman, N., Zilberstein, S.: The complexity of decentralized control of Markov decision processes. Math. Oper. Res. **27**(4), 819–840 (2002)
4. Bertoni, A., Mauri, G., Torelli, M.: Some recursively unsolvable problems relating to isolated cutpoints in probabilistic automata. In: Degano, P., Gorrieri, R., Marchetti-Spaccamela, A. (eds.) ICALP 1997. LNCS, vol. 1256. Springer, Heidelberg (1997)
5. Berwanger, D., Kaiser, L.: Information tracking in games on graphs. J. Logic Lang. Inform. **19**(4), 395–412 (2010)
6. Brookes, S.D., Hoare, C.A.R., Roscoe, A.W.: A theory of communicating sequential processes. J. ACM **31**(3), 560–599 (1984)
7. Canetti, R., Cheung, L., Kaynar, D.K., Liskov, M., Lynch, N.A., Pereira, O., Segala, R.: Analyzing security protocols using time-bounded task-PIOAs. Discrete Event Dyn. Syst. **18**(1), 111–159 (2008)
8. Cheung, L., Lynch, N.A., Segala, R., Vaandrager, F.W.: Switched PIOA: parallel composition via distributed scheduling. Theoret. Comput. Sci. **365**(1–2), 83–108 (2006)
9. D'Argenio, P.R., Katoen, J.-P.: A theory of stochastic systems part I: stochastic automata. Inf. Comput. **203**(1), 1–38 (2005)
10. Droste, M., Gastin, P.: Asynchronous cellular automata for pomsets without autoconcurrency. In: Sassone, V., Montanari, U. (eds.) CONCUR 1996. LNCS, vol. 1119. Springer, Heidelberg (1996)
11. Genest, B., Gimbert, H., Muscholl, A., Walukiewicz, I.: Asynchronous games over tree architectures. In: Fomin, F.V., Freivalds, R., Kwiatkowska, M., Peleg, D. (eds.) ICALP 2013, Part II. LNCS, vol. 7966, pp. 275–286. Springer, Heidelberg (2013)
12. Gimbert, H., Oualhadj, Y.: Probabilistic automata on finite words: decidable and undecidable problems. In: Abramsky, S., Gavoille, C., Kirchner, C., Meyer auf der Heide, F., Spirakis, P.G. (eds.) ICALP 2010. LNCS, vol. 6199, pp. 527–538. Springer, Heidelberg (2010)
13. Giro, S., D'Argenio, P.R., Fioriti, L.M.F.: Distributed probabilistic input/output automata: Expressiveness, (un)decidability and algorithms. Theoret. Comput. Sci. **538**, 84–102 (2014)
14. Guck, D., Han, T., Katoen, J.-P., Neuhäußer, M.R.: Quantitative timed analysis of interactive markov chains. In: Goodloe, A.E., Person, S. (eds.) NFM 2012. LNCS, vol. 7226, pp. 8–23. Springer, Heidelberg (2012)
15. Hermanns, H., Johr, S.: May we reach it? Or must we? In what time? With what probability? In: MMB, pp. 125–140. VDE Verlag (2008)
16. Hermanns, H.: Interactive Markov Chains and The Quest for Quantified Quality. Lecture Notes in Computer Science, vol. 2428. Springer, New York (2002)

17. Hermanns, H., Vester, S., Krčál, J.: Distributed synthesis in continuous time. CoRR abs/1601.01587 (2016)
18. Hermanns, H., Katoen, J.-P.: The how and why of interactive markov chains. In: Boer, F.S., Bonsangue, M.M., Hallerstede, S., Leuschel, M. (eds.) FMCO 2009. LNCS, vol. 6286, pp. 311–338. Springer, Heidelberg (2010)
19. Hermanns, H., Krčál, J., Křetínský, J.: Compositional verification and optimization of interactive markov chains. In: D'Argenio, P.R., Melgratti, H. (eds.) CONCUR 2013 – Concurrency Theory. LNCS, vol. 8052, pp. 364–379. Springer, Heidelberg (2013)
20. Katoen, J.-P., Klink, D., Neuhäußer, M.R.: Compositional abstraction for stochastic systems. In: Ouaknine, J., Vaandrager, F.W. (eds.) FORMATS 2009. LNCS, vol. 5813, pp. 195–211. Springer, Heidelberg (2009)
21. Katoen, J.-P., Zapreev, I.S., Hahn, E.M., Hermanns, H., Jansen, D.N.: The ins and outs of the probabilistic model checker MRMC. Perform. Eval. 68(2), 90–104 (2011)
22. Madhusudan, P., Thiagarajan, P.S.: Distributed controller synthesis for local specifications. In: Orejas, F., Spirakis, P.G., van Leeuwen, J. (eds.) ICALP 2001. LNCS, vol. 2076, pp. 396–407. Springer, Heidelberg (2001)
23. Madhusudan, P., Thiagarajan, P.S.: A decidable class of asynchronous distributed controllers. In: Brim, L., Jančar, P., Křetínský, M., Kučera, A. (eds.) CONCUR 2002. LNCS, vol. 2421, pp. 145–160. Springer, Heidelberg (2002)
24. Milner, R.: Calculi for synchrony and asynchrony. Theoret. Comput. Sci. 25, 267–310 (1983)
25. Neuts, M.F.: Matrix-Geometric Solutions in Stochastic Models: An Algorithmic Approach. Courier Corporation, New York (1981)
26. Paz, A.: Introduction to Probabilistic Automata. Academic Press Inc., London (1971)
27. Pelozo, S.S., D'Argenio, P.R.: Security analysis in probabilistic distributed protocols via bounded reachability. In: Palamidessi, C., Ryan, M.D. (eds.) TGC 2012. LNCS, vol. 8191, pp. 182–197. Springer, Heidelberg (2013)
28. Pnueli, A., Rosner, R.: On the synthesis of an asynchronous reactive module. In: Ausiello, G., Dezani-Ciancaglini, M., Della Rocca, S.R. (eds.) ICALP. LNCS, vol. 372, pp. 652–671. Springer, Heidelberg (1989)
29. Pnueli, A., Rosner, R.: Distributed reactive systems are hard to synthesize. In: FOCS, pp. 746–757. IEEE Computer Society (1990)
30. Puterman, M.L.: Markov Decision Processes: Discrete Stochastic Dynamic Programming. John Wiley & Sons, New York (2009)
31. Saha, R., Esparza, J., Jha, S.K., Mukund, M., Thiagarajan, P.S.: Distributed markov chains. In: D'Souza, D., Lal, A., Larsen, K.G. (eds.) VMCAI 2015. LNCS, vol. 8931, pp. 117–134. Springer, Heidelberg (2015)
32. Segala, R.: Modeling and Verification of Randomized Distributed Real-Time Systems. Ph.D. thesis, Massachusetts Institute of Technology (1995)
33. Sinopoli, B., Sharp, C., Schenato, L., Schaffert, S., Sastry, S.S.: Distributed control applications within sensor networks. Proc. IEEE 91, 1235–1246 (2003)
34. Sue-Hwey, W., Smolka, S.A., Stark, E.W.: Composition and behaviors of probabilistic I/O automata. Theoret. Comput. Sci. 176(1–2), 1–38 (1997)

Proof Theory and Lambda Calculus

Unary Resolution: Characterizing PTIME

Clément Aubert[1], Marc Bagnol[2], and Thomas Seiller[3](✉)

[1] Department of Computer Science, Appalachian State University, Boone, USA
[2] Department of Mathematics and Statistics, University of Ottawa, Ottawa, Canada
[3] Department of Computer Science, University of Copenhagen, Copenhagen, Denmark
seiller@di.ku.dk

Abstract. We give a characterization of deterministic polynomial time computation based on an algebraic structure called the resolution semiring, whose elements can be understood as logic programs or sets of rewriting rules over first-order terms. This construction stems from an interactive interpretation of the cut-elimination procedure of linear logic known as the *geometry of interaction*.

This framework is restricted to terms (logic programs, rewriting rules) using only unary symbols, and this restriction is shown to be complete for polynomial time computation by encoding pushdown automata. Soundness w.r.t. PTIME is proven thanks to a saturation method similar to the one used for pushdown systems and inspired by the memoization technique.

A PTIME-completeness result for a class of logic programming queries that uses only unary function symbols comes as a direct consequence.

Keywords: Implicit complexity · Unary queries · Logic programming · Geometry of interaction · Proof theory · Pushdown automata · Saturation · Memoization

1 Introduction

Complexity theory classifies computational problems relatively to the amount of time or memory needed to solve them. Complexity classes are defined as sets of problems that can be solved by algorithms whose executions need comparable amounts of resources. For instance, the class PTIME is the set of predicates over binary words that can be decided by a Turing machine whose execution time is bounded by a polynomial in the size of its input.

One of the main motivations for an implicit computational complexity (ICC) theory is to find machine-independent characterizations of complexity classes. The aim is to characterize classes not *"by constraining the amount of resources a machine is allowed to use, but rather by imposing linguistic constraints on the*

This work was partly supported by the ANR-14-CE25-0005 Elica, the ANR-11-INSE-0007 Rever, the ANR-10-BLAN-0213 Logoi, the ANR-11-BS02-0010 Recré, the ANR 12 JS02 006 01 project Coquas and the European Union's Marie Skłodowska-Curie Individual Fellowship (H2020-MSCA-IF-2014) 659920 - ReACT.

© Springer-Verlag Berlin Heidelberg 2016
B. Jacobs and C. Löding (Eds.): FOSSACS 2016, LNCS 9634, pp. 373–389, 2016.
DOI: 10.1007/978-3-662-49630-5_22

way algorithms are formulated." [18, p. 90] This has been already achieved via different approaches, for instance by considering restricted programming languages or computational principles [12,37,38].

A number of results in this area also arose from proof theory, through the study of subsystems of linear logic [25]. More precisely, the Curry-Howard—or *proofs as programs*—correspondence expresses an isomorphism between formal proofs and typed programs. In this approach, once a formula Nat corresponding to the type of binary integers is set, proofs of the formula Nat ⇒ Nat *are* algorithms computing functions from integers to integers, via the cut-elimination procedure. By considering restricted subsystems, one allows *less* proofs of type Nat ⇒ Nat, hence *less* algorithms can be implemented, and the class of accepted proofs, or programs, may correspond[1] to some complexity class: elementary complexity [21, 29], polynomial time [11,36], logarithmic [19] and polynomial [24] space.

More recently, new methods for obtaining implicit characterizations of complexity classes based on the *geometry of interaction* (GoI) research program [27] have been developed. The GoI approach offers a more abstract and algebraic point of view on the cut-elimination procedure of linear logic. One works with a set of *untyped programs* represented as some geometric objects, e.g. graphs [20,40] or generalizations of graphs [42], bounded linear maps between Hilbert spaces (operators) [26,30,41], clauses (or "flows") [8,28]. This set of objects is then considered together with an abstract notion of execution, seen as an interactive procedure: a function does not process a static input, but rather communicate with it, asking for values, reading its answers, asking for another value, etc. (this interactive point of view on computation has proven crucial in characterizing logarithmic space computation [19]).

This method does not proceed by restricting a type system, but by imposing original conditions, of an algebraic nature, on the representation of programs. Note that one still benefits from the work in the typed case: for instance, the representation of words used here directly comes from their representation in linear logic. The first results in this direction were based on operator algebra [5, 6,31]. This paper considers a more syntactic flavor of the GoI interpretation, where untyped programs are represented in the so-called *resolution semiring* [8], a semiring based on the resolution rule [39] and a specific class of logic programs. This setting presents some advantages: it avoids the heavy structure of operator algebras theory, eases the discussions in terms of complexity (as first-order terms have natural notions of size, height, etc.) and offers a straightforward connection with complexity of logic programming [22]. Previous works in this direction led to characterizations of logarithmic space predicates LOGSPACE and CO-NLOG-SPACE [2,3], by considering restrictions on the height of variables.

The main contribution of this paper is a characterization of the class PTIME by studying a natural limitation, the restriction to *unary* function symbols. Pushdown automata are easily related to this simple restriction, for they can be represented as logical programs satisfying this "unarity" restriction. This implies the completeness of the model under consideration for polynomial time

---

[1] In an *extensional* correspondence: they can compute the same functions.

predicates. Soundness follows from a variation of the saturation algorithm for pushdown systems [13], inspired by S. Cook's memoization technique [17] for pushdown automata, that proves that any such unary logic program can be decided in polynomial time.

Compared to other ICC characterizations of PTIME, and in particular those coming from proof theory, this method has a simple formulation and provides an original point of view on this complexity class. It also constitutes the first characterization of a time-complexity class directly on the semantic side of the GoI interpretation. Nevertheless, the results presented here can be read independently of any knowledge of GoI.

An immediate consequence of this work is a PTIME-completeness result for a specific class of logic programming queries corresponding to unary flows.

1.1 Outline

Section 2.1 gives the formal definition of the resolution semiring; then representation of words and programs in this structure is briefly explained (Sect. 2.2). Section 2.3 introduce the restricted semiring that will be under study, the $Stack$ semiring. We believe the technical results presented in this section to be of importance, as they describe an algebraic restriction corresponding to Ptime and broaden previous algebraic restrictions for (CO-N)LOGSPACE.

The next two sections are respectively devoted to the completeness and soundness results for PTIME. Proving completeness needs to first review multi-head finite automata with pushdown stack, that characterize PTIME, and then to represent them as elements built from the $Stack$ semiring (Sect. 3). The soundness result is then obtained by "saturating" elements of the stack semiring, so that they become decidable with PTIME resources (Sect. 4).

PTIME-completeness of unary logic programming queries is then proved to be implied by this result (Sect. 5).

Sketched proofs are detailed in a technical report [4] and in the second author's Ph.D. thesis [8].

2 The Resolution Semiring

2.1 Flows and Wirings

We begin with some reminders on first-order terms and unification theory.

Notation 1 (terms). We consider first-order terms, written t, u, v, ..., built from variables and function symbols with assigned finite arity. Symbols of arity 0 will be called *constants*.

Sets of variables and of function symbols of any arity are supposed infinite. Variables will be noted in italics font (e.g. x, y) and function symbols in typewriter font (e.g. $\mathsf{c}, \mathsf{f}(\cdot), \mathsf{g}(\cdot, \cdot)$).

We distinguish a binary function symbol $\bullet$ (in infix notation) and a constant symbol $\star$. We will omit the parentheses for $\bullet$ and write $\mathsf{t} \bullet \mathsf{u} \bullet \mathsf{v}$ for $\mathsf{t} \bullet (\mathsf{u} \bullet \mathsf{v})$.

We write $\text{var}(t)$ the set of variables occurring in the term t and say that t is *closed* if $\text{var}(t) = \varnothing$. The *height* $h(t)$ of a term t is the maximal distance between its root and leaves; a variable occurrence's height in t is its distance to the root.

We will write θt for the result of applying the substitution θ to the term t and will call *renaming* a substitution α that bijectively maps variables to variables.

We focus on the resolution of equalities $t = u$ between terms, and hence need some definitions.

Definition 2 (Unification, Matching and Disjointness). *Two terms* t, u *are:*

- unifiable *if there exists a substitution* θ—*a* unifier *of t and u—such that* $\theta t = \theta u$. *If any other unifier of t and u is such that there exists a substitution that maps it to* θ, *we say* θ *is the* most general unifier *(MGU) of t and u;*
- matchable *if* t', u' *are unifiable, where* t', u' *are renamings of* t, u *such that* $\text{var}(t') \cap \text{var}(u') = \varnothing$;
- disjoint *if they are not matchable.*

A fundamental result of unification theory is that when two terms are unifiable, a MGU exists and is computable. More specifically, the problem of deciding whether two terms are unifiable is PTIME-complete [23, Theorem 1]. The notion of MGU allows to formulate the *resolution rule*, a key concept of logic programming defining the composition of Horn clauses (expressions of the form $H \dashv B_1, \dots, B_n$):

$$\frac{V \dashv T_1, \dots, T_n \qquad \text{var}(U) \cap \text{var}(V) = \varnothing}{\theta H \dashv \theta B_1, \dots, \theta B_m, U \qquad \theta \text{ is a MGU of } U \text{ and } V}{\theta H \dashv \theta B_1, \dots, \theta B_m, \theta T_1, \dots, \theta T_n} \text{ Res}$$

Note that the condition on variables implies that we are matching U and V rather than unifying them. In other words, the resolution rule deals with variables as if they were bounded.

From this perspective, "flows"—defined below—are a specific type of Horn clauses $H \dashv B$, with exactly one formula B at the right of $\dashv$ and all the variables of H already occurring in B. The product of flows will be defined as the resolution rule restricted to this specific type of clauses.

Definition 3 (Flow). *A flow is an ordered pair* f *of terms* $f := t \leftharpoonup u$, *with* $\text{var}(t) \subseteq \text{var}(u)$. *Flows are considered up to renaming: for any renaming* α, $t \leftharpoonup u = \alpha t \leftharpoonup \alpha u$.

A flow can be understood as a rewriting rule over the set of first-order terms, acting at the root. For instance, the flow $g(x) \leftharpoonup f(x)$ corresponds to "rewrite terms of the form $f(v)$ as $g(v)$".

Next comes the definition of the *product* of flows. From the term-rewriting perspective, this operation corresponds to composing two rules—when possible, i.e. when the result of the first rewriting rule allows the application of the second—into a single one. For instance, one can compose the flows $f_1 := \mathbf{h}(x) \multimap \mathbf{g}(x)$ and $f_2 := \mathbf{g}(\mathbf{f}(x)) \multimap \mathbf{f}(x)$ to produce the flow $f_1 f_2 = \mathbf{h}(\mathbf{f}(x)) \multimap \mathbf{f}(x)$. Notice by the way that this (partial) product is not commutative, as composing these rules the other way around is impossible, i.e. $f_2 f_1$ is not defined.

Definition 4 (Product of Flows). *Let $t \multimap u$ and $v \multimap w$ be two flows. Suppose we picked representatives of the renaming classes such that $var(u) \cap var(v) = \varnothing$.*

The product *of $t \multimap u$ and $v \multimap w$ is defined when u and v are unifiable, with MGU θ, as $(t \multimap u)(v \multimap w) := \theta t \multimap \theta w$.*

We now define wirings, which are just finite sets of flows and therefore correspond to logic programs. From the term-rewriting perspective they are just sets of rewriting rules. The definition of product of flows naturally lifts to wirings.

Definition 5 (Wiring). *A* wiring *is a finite set of flows. Their product is defined as $FG := \{fg \mid f \in F, g \in G, fg \text{ defined}\}$. The* resolution semiring $\mathcal{R}$ *is the set of all wirings.*

The set of wirings $\mathcal{R}$ indeed enjoys a structure of semiring[2]. We will use an *additive notation* for sets of flows to highlight this situation:

- The symbol $+$ will be used in place of $\cup$, and we write sets as sums of their elements: $\{f_1, \ldots, f_n\} := f_1 + \cdots + f_n$.
- We denote by 0 the empty set, i.e. the unit of the sum.
- The unit for the product is the wiring $I := x \multimap x$.

As we will always be working within $\mathcal{R}$, the term "semiring" will be used instead of "subsemiring of $\mathcal{R}$". Finally, let us extend the notion of height to flows and wirings, and recall the definition of nilpotency.

Definition 6 (Height). *The* height $h(f)$ *of a flow $f = t \multimap u$ is defined as $\max\{h(t), h(u)\}$. A* wiring's height *is defined as $h(F) = \max\{h(f) \mid f \in F\}$. By convention $h(0) = 0$.*

Definition 7 (Nilpotency). *A wiring F is* nilpotent—*written* $\mathbf{Nil}(F)$—*if and only if $F^n = 0$ for some n.*

That standard notion of nilpotency, coming from abstract algebra, has a specific reading in our case. In terms of logic programming, it means that all chains obtained by applying the resolution rule to the set of clauses we consider cannot be longer than a certain bound. From a rewriting point of view, it means that the set of rewriting rules is terminating with a uniform bound on the length of rewriting chains —again, we consider rewriting at the root of terms, while general term rewriting systems [7] allow for in-context rewriting.

---

[2] A *semiring* is a set R equipped with two operations $+$ (the sum) and $\times$ (the product), and an element $0 \in R$ such that: $(R, +, 0)$ is a commutative monoid; $(R, \times)$ is a *semigroup*; the product distributes over the sum; and the element 0 is absorbent, i.e. $0 \times r = r \times 0 = 0$ for all $r \in R$.

2.2   Representation of Words and Programs

This section explains and motivates the representation of words as flows. Studying their interaction with wirings from a specific semiring allows to define notions of program and accepted language. First, let us extend the binary function symbol $\bullet$, used to construct terms, to flows and then semirings.

Definition 8. *Let* $u \leftharpoonup v$ *and* $t \leftharpoonup w$ *be two flows. Suppose we have chosen representatives of their renaming classes that have disjoint sets of variables.*

We define $(u \leftharpoonup v) \bullet (t \leftharpoonup w) := u \bullet t \leftharpoonup v \bullet w$. *The operation is extended to wirings by* $(\sum_i f_i) \bullet (\sum_j g_j) := \sum_{i,j} f_i \bullet g_j$. *Then, given two semirings* $\mathcal{A}$ *and* $\mathcal{B}$, *we define the semiring* $\mathcal{A} \bullet \mathcal{B} := \{\sum_i F_i \bullet G_i | F_i \in \mathcal{A}, G_i \in \mathcal{B}\}$.

The operation indeed defines a semiring because for any wirings F, F', G and G', we have $(F \bullet G)(F \bullet G) = FF' \bullet GG'$. Moreover, we carry on the convention of writing $\mathcal{A} \bullet \mathcal{B} \bullet \mathcal{C}$ for $\mathcal{A} \bullet (\mathcal{B} \bullet \mathcal{C})$.

Notation 9. We write $t \leftrightharpoons u$ the sum $t \leftharpoonup u + u \leftharpoonup t$.

Definition 10 (Word Representation). *We fix for the rest of this paper an infinite set of constant symbols* P *(the* position constants*) and a finite alphabet* Σ *(we write* Σ^* *the set of words over* Σ*).*

Let $W = c_1 \cdots c_n \in \Sigma^*$ *and* $p = p_0, p_1, \dots, p_n$ *be pairwise distinct elements of* P. *Writing* $p_{n+1} = p_0$ *and* $c_{n+1} = c_0 = \star$, *we define the* representation *of* W *associated with* $p_0, p_1, \dots, p_n$ *as the following wiring, where* x *and* y *are two arbitrary but distinct variables:*

$$\bar{W}_p = \sum_{i=0}^{n} c_i \bullet r \bullet x \bullet y \bullet \text{HEAD}(p_i) \leftrightharpoons c_{i+1} \bullet 1 \bullet x \bullet y \bullet \text{HEAD}(p_{i+1})$$

Position constants $p_0, p_1, \dots, p_n$ represent memory cells storing the symbols $\star$, c_1, c_2, $\dots$. The representation of words is *dynamic*, i.e. we may think intuitively of *movement instructions* for an automaton reading the input, getting instructions to move from a symbol to the next (at the left, hence the 1) or the previous (to the right, hence the r). More details on this point of view will be given in the proof of Theorem 4. A term $c_i \bullet r$ (resp. $c_i \bullet 1$) at position p will be linked by flows of the representation to an element $c_{i+1} \bullet 1$ at position p_{i+1} (resp. $c_{i-1} \bullet r$ at position p_{i-1}).

Taking $c_{n+1} = c_0 = \star$ reflects the Church encoding of words and make the representation of the input circular. Flows representing the word $c_1 \cdots c_n$ can be pictured as follows:

The notion of *observation* will be the counterpart of a program in our construction. We first give a general definition, that will be instantiated later to particular classes of observations characterizing complexity classes. The important point is that observations cannot use any position constant, so that they interact the same way with all the representations $\bar{W}_p$ of a word W.

Definition 11 (Observation Semiring). *We define the semirings* $P^\perp$ *of flows that do not use the symbols in* P; *and* Σ_{1r} *the semiring generated by flows of the form* $c \bullet d \leftarrowtail c' \bullet d'$ *with* $c, c' \in \Sigma \cup \{\star\}$ *and* $d, d' \in \{1, r\}$.

We define the semiring of observations *as* $\mathcal{O} := (\Sigma_{1r} \bullet \mathcal{R}) \cap P^\perp$, *and the semiring of* observations over the semiring $\mathcal{A}$ *as* $\mathcal{O}[\mathcal{A}] := (\Sigma_{1r} \bullet \mathcal{A}) \cap P^\perp$.

The following property is a consequence of the fact that observations cannot use position constants [8, Theorem IV.5].

Theorem 1 (normativity). *Let* $\bar{W}_p$ *and* $\bar{W}_q$ *be two representations of a word* W *and* O *an observation. Then* $\mathbf{Nil}(O\bar{W}_p)$ *if and only if* $\mathbf{Nil}(O\bar{W}_q)$.

How a word can be accepted by an observation can now be safely defined: the following definition is independent of the specific choice of a representation.

Definition 12 (Accepted Language). *Let* O *be an observation. The* language accepted by O *is defined as* $\mathcal{L}(O) := \{W \in \Sigma^* \mid \forall p, \mathbf{Nil}(O\bar{W}_p)\}$.

A previous work [3] investigated the semiring of *balanced wirings*, that are defined as sets of balanced—or "height-preserving"—flows.

Definition 13 (Balance). *A flow* $f = t \leftarrowtail u$ *is balanced if for any variable* $x \in var(t) \cup var(u)$, *all occurrences of* x *in both* t *and* u *have the same height (recall notations p. 4). A balanced* wiring F *is a sum of balanced flows and the set of balanced wirings is written* $\mathcal{R}_b$.

A balanced observation is an element of $\mathcal{O}[\mathcal{R}_b \bullet \mathcal{R}_b]$.

This simple restriction was shown to characterize (non-deterministic) logarithmic space computation [3, Theorems 34-35], with a natural subclass of balanced wirings corresponding to the deterministic case. The balanced restriction won't be further considered, even if previous results on the nilpotency problem for balanced wirings [3, p. 54], [8, Theorem IV.12] are required to complete the detailed proof of Theorem 5 [4, 8].

2.3   The $\mathcal{S}tack$ Semiring

This paper deals with another restriction on flows, namely the restriction to *unary flows*, i.e. defined with unary function symbols only. The semiring of wirings composed only of unary flows is called the $\mathcal{S}tack$ semiring, and will be shown to give a characterization of polynomial time computation. Below are the needed definitions and results about this semiring, a more complete picture is in the second author's Ph.D. thesis [8].

Definition 14 (Unary Flows). *A* unary flow *is a flow built using only unary function symbols and a variable. The semiring* $\mathcal{S}tack$ *is the set of wirings of the form* $\sum_i t_i \leftarrowtail u_i$ *where the* $t_i \leftarrowtail u_i$ *are unary flows.*

Example 1 The flows $\mathtt{f}(\mathtt{f}(x)) \leftharpoondown \mathtt{g}(x)$ and $x \leftharpoondown \mathtt{g}(x)$ are both unary, while $x \bullet \mathtt{f}(x) \leftharpoondown \mathtt{g}(x)$ and $\mathtt{f}(\mathtt{c}) \leftharpoondown x$ are not.

The notion of *cyclic flow* is crucial to prove the characterization of polynomial time computation. It is complementary to the nilpotency property for elements of $\mathcal{S}tack$, i.e. a wiring in $\mathcal{S}tack$ will be either cyclic or nilpotent.

Definition 15 (Cyclicity). *A flow $t \leftharpoondown u$ is a* cycle *if t and u are matchable (Definition 2). A wiring F is* cyclic *if there is a k such that F^k contains a cycle.*

Remark 1. A flow f is a cycle iff $f^2 \neq 0$, which in turn implies $f^n \neq 0$ for all n in the case f is unary. This does not hold in general: $f = x \bullet \mathtt{c} \leftharpoondown \mathtt{d} \bullet x$ is a cycle as $f^2 = \mathtt{c} \bullet \mathtt{c} \leftharpoondown \mathtt{d} \bullet \mathtt{d} \neq 0$, but $f^3 = (x \bullet \mathtt{c} \leftharpoondown \mathtt{d} \bullet x)(\mathtt{c} \bullet \mathtt{c} \leftharpoondown \mathtt{d} \bullet \mathtt{d}) = 0$.

Theorem 2 (nilpotency). *A wiring $F \in \mathcal{S}tack$ is nilpotent iff it is acyclic.*

Proof (Sketch [8, Theorem II.52]). An immediate consequence of Remark 1 is that if F is acyclic, then it is not nilpotent. The converse is a consequence of a bound on the height of elements of F^n when F is acyclic [10]. From this, a contradiction can be obtained by realizing that manipulating bounded height terms built from a finite pool of symbols implies that one is wandering in a finite set and will eventually be cycling in it.   □

Example 2. The following nilpotent element of $\mathcal{S}tack$ illustrates how the nilpotency problem can be tricky to solve efficiently:

$$
\begin{aligned}
F := \quad & \mathtt{f}_1(x) \leftharpoondown \mathtt{f}_0(x) \\
+ & \mathtt{f}_0(\mathtt{f}_1(x)) \leftharpoondown \mathtt{f}_1(\mathtt{f}_0(x)) \\
+ & \mathtt{f}_0(\mathtt{f}_0(\mathtt{f}_1(x))) \leftharpoondown \mathtt{f}_1(\mathtt{f}_1(\mathtt{f}_0(x))) \\
+ & \mathtt{f}_0(\mathtt{f}_0(\mathtt{f}_0(x))) \leftharpoondown \mathtt{f}_1(\mathtt{f}_1(\mathtt{f}_1(x)))
\end{aligned}
$$

Taking the sequence $\mathtt{f}_x\mathtt{f}_y\mathtt{f}_z$ to be the integer $x + 2y + 4z$, this wiring implements a counter from 0 to 7 in binary notation, that resets to 0 when it reaches 8. It is clear with this intuition in mind that this wiring is cyclic. Indeed, an easy computation shows that $\mathtt{f}_0(\mathtt{f}_0(\mathtt{f}_0(x))) \leftharpoondown \mathtt{f}_0(\mathtt{f}_0(\mathtt{f}_0(x))) \in F^8$.

Lifting this example to the case of a counter from 0 to $2^n - 1$, gives a wiring for which the number of iterations needed to find a cycle is exponential in its size. This rules out a polynomial time decision procedure for the nilpotency problem that would simply compute iterations of a wiring until it finds a cycle.

Finally, let us define a new class of observations, based on the $\mathcal{S}tack$ semiring.

Definition 16 (Balanced Observation with Stack). *A balanced observation with stack is an element of the semiring $\mathcal{O}^{\mathsf{b+s}} := \mathcal{O}[\mathcal{S}tack \bullet \mathcal{R}_\mathsf{b}]$.*

3 Pushdown Automata and PTIME Completeness

Automata form a simple model of computation that can be extended in different ways. For instance, allowing multiple heads that can move in two directions on the input tape gives a model of computation equivalent to read-only Turing machines. If one adds moreover a "pushdown stack" one defines "pushdown automata", well-known to capture polynomial-time computation. PTIME-completeness of balanced observation with stacks will be attained by encoding pushdown automata: we recall briefly their definition and characterization of PTIME, before sketching how to represent them as observations.

Definition 17 (Pushdown Automata (2MFA+S)). *For $k \geqslant 1$, a pushdown automaton (formally, a 2-way k-head finite automaton with pushdown stack (2MFA+S(k))) is a tuple $M = \{S, i, A, B, \triangleright, \triangleleft, \boxdot, \sigma\}$ where:*

- *S is the finite set of states, with $i \in S$ the initial state;*
- *A is the input alphabet, B the stack alphabet;*
- *$\triangleright$ and $\triangleleft$ are the left and right endmarkers, $\triangleright, \triangleleft \notin A$;*
- *$\boxdot$ is the bottom symbol of the stack, $\boxdot \notin B$;*
- *σ is the transition relation, i.e. a subset of the product $(S \times (A_{\bowtie})^k \times B_{\boxdot}) \times (S \times \{-1, 0, +1\}^k \times \{pop, push(b)\})$ where $A_{\bowtie}$ (resp. $B_{\boxdot}$) denotes $A \cup \{\triangleright, \triangleleft\}$ (resp. $B \cup \{\boxdot\}$). The instruction -1 corresponds to moving the head one cell to the left, 0 corresponds to keeping the head on the current cell and $+1$ corresponds to moving it one cell to the right. Regarding the pushdown stack, the instruction pop means "erase the top symbol", while, for all $b \in B$, $push(b)$ means "write b on top of the stack".*

The automaton *rejects the input* if it loops, otherwise it *accepts*. This condition is equivalent to the standard way of defining acceptance and rejection by "reaching a final state" [35, Theorem 2]. Modulo another standard transformation, we restrict the transition relation so that at most one head moves at each transition.

We used in our previous work [3,6] the characterization of LOGSPACE and NLOGSPACE by 2-way k-head finite automata *without* pushdown stacks [43, pp. 223–225]. The addition of a pushdown stack improves the expressiveness of the machine model, as stated in the following theorem.

Theorem 3. *Pushdown automata characterize PTIME.*

Proof. Without reproving this classical result of complexity theory, we review the main ideas supporting it.

Simulating a PTIME Turing machine with a Pushdown automata amounts to designing an equivalent Turing machine whose movements of heads follow a regular pattern. That permits to seamlessly simulate their contents with a pushdown stack. A complete proof [16, pp. 9–11] as well as a precise algorithm [43, pp. 238–240] can be found in the literature.

Simulating a Pushdown automata with a Polynomial-time Turing Machine. cannot amount to simply simulate step-by-step the automaton with the Turing machine. The reason is that for any pushdown automaton, one can design a pushdown automaton that recognizes the same language but runs exponentially slower [1, p. 197]. That the pushdown automaton can accept its input after an exponential computation time is similar with the situation of the counter in Exmaple 2.

The technique invented by Alfred V. Aho et al. [1] and made popular by Stephen A. Cook consists in building a "memoization table" allowing the Turing machine to create shortcuts in the simulation of the pushdown automaton, decreasing drastically its computation time. In some cases, an automaton with an exponentially long run can even be simulated in linear time [17].

Let us now consider the proof of PTIME-*completeness* for the set of balanced observations with stacks. It relies on an encoding that is similar to the previously developed encoding of 2-way k-head finite automata (*without* pushdown stack) by flows [3, Sect. 4.1]. The only difference is the addition of a "plug-in" that allows to represent stacks in observations.

Remember that acceptance by observations is phrased in terms of nilpotency of the product $O\bar{W}_{\mathsf{p}}$ of the observation and the representation of the input (Definition 12). Hence the computation in this model is defined as an iteration: one computes by considering the sequence $O\bar{W}_{\mathsf{p}}, (O\bar{W}_{\mathsf{p}})^2, (O\bar{W}_{\mathsf{p}})^3, \ldots$ and the computation either ends at some point (i.e. accepts)—that is $(O\bar{W}_{\mathsf{p}})^n = 0$ for some integer n—or loops (i.e. rejects). This iteration represents a dialogue between the observation and its input: whereas an automaton is often thought of as manipulating some the "passive" data, in our setting, the observation and the word representation interact, taking turns in making the situation evolve.

Theorem 4. *If $L \in$ PTIME, then there exists a balanced observation with stack $O \in \mathcal{O}^{\mathsf{b+s}}$ such that $L = \mathcal{L}(O)$.*

Proof. Let $A = \Sigma$ be the input alphabet and M the 2MFA+S($k + 1$) that recognizes L. By Theorem 3, such a M exists, and its transition relation is encoded as a balanced observation with stack (Definition 16). More precisely, the automaton will be represented as an element O_M of $\mathcal{O}^{\mathsf{b+s}} = \mathcal{O}[\, \mathcal{S}tack \bullet \mathcal{R}_{\mathsf{b}}\,]$ which can be written as a sum of flows of the form

$$\mathsf{c}' \bullet \mathsf{d}' \bullet \sigma(x) \bullet \mathsf{q}' \bullet \mathrm{AUX}_k(y_1', \ldots, y_k') \bullet \mathrm{HEAD}(z') \hookleftarrow$$
$$\mathsf{c} \bullet \mathsf{d} \bullet \mathsf{s}(x) \bullet \mathsf{q} \bullet \mathrm{AUX}_k(y_1, \ldots, y_k) \bullet \mathrm{HEAD}(z)$$

with

- $\mathsf{c}, \mathsf{c}' \in \Sigma \cup \{\star\}$ and $\mathsf{d}, \mathsf{d}' \in \{1, \mathsf{r}\}$,
- σ a finite sequence of unary function symbols,
- s a unary function symbol,
- q, q' two constant symbols,
- AUX_k and HEAD two functions symbols of respective arity k and 1.

The intuition behind the encoding is that a configuration of a 2MFA+S($k + 1$) processing an input can be seen as a closed term

$$\texttt{c} \bullet \texttt{d} \bullet \tau(\square) \bullet \texttt{q} \bullet \texttt{AUX}_k(\texttt{p}_{i_1}, \, \ldots \, , \texttt{p}_{i_k}) \bullet \texttt{HEAD}(\texttt{p}_j)$$

where the $\texttt{p}_i$ are position constants representing the positions of the *main pointer* ($\texttt{HEAD}(\texttt{p}_j)$) and of the *auxiliary pointers* ($\texttt{AUX}_k(\texttt{p}_{i_1}, \, \ldots \, , \texttt{p}_{i_k})$); the symbol $\texttt{q}$ represents the state the automaton is in; $\tau(\square)$ represents the current stack; the symbol $\texttt{d}$ represents the direction of the next move of the main pointer; the symbol $\texttt{c}$ represents the symbol currently read by the main pointer.

When a configuration matches the right side of the flow, the transition is followed, leading to an updated configuration.

More precisely, the iterations of $O_M \bar{W}_\texttt{p}$, the product of the encoding of M with a word representation, is observed. Let us now explain how the basic operations of M are simulated:

Moving the Pointers. Looking back at the definition of the encoding of words (Definition 10) gives a new reading of the action of the representation of a word: it moves the main pointer in the required direction. From that perspective, the position holding the symbol $\star$ in Definition 10 allows to simulate the behavior of the endmarkers $\triangleright$ and $\triangleleft$.

On the other hand, the observation is not able to manipulate the position of pointers directly (remember observations are forbidden to use the position constants) but can change the direction symbol $\texttt{d}$, rearrange pointers (hence changing which one is the main pointer) and modify its state and the symbol $\texttt{c}$ accordingly. For instance, a flow of the form

$$\cdots \bullet \texttt{AUX}_k(x, \ldots, y_k) \bullet \texttt{HEAD}(y_1) \; \longleftarrow \; \cdots \bullet \texttt{AUX}_k(y_1, \ldots, y_k) \bullet \texttt{HEAD}(x)$$

encodes the instruction "swap the main pointer and the first auxiliary pointer".

Note however that our model has no built-in way to remember the values of the auxiliary pointers—it remembers only their *positions* as arguments of $\texttt{AUX}_k(\cdots)$—, but this can be implemented easily using additional states.

Handling the Stack. Given a unary function symbol $\underline{\texttt{b}}(\cdot)$ for each symbol b of the stack alphabet $B_\square$, reading the stack, pushing and popping elements are easily implemented:

$$\cdots \bullet x \bullet \cdots \; \longleftarrow \; \cdots \bullet \underline{\texttt{b}}(x) \bullet \cdots \qquad \text{(Read } b \text{ and pop it)}$$
$$\cdots \bullet \underline{\texttt{c}}(\underline{\texttt{b}}(x)) \bullet \cdots \; \longleftarrow \; \cdots \bullet \underline{\texttt{b}}(x) \bullet \cdots \qquad \text{(Read } b \text{ and push } c)$$

Changing the State. Given a constant $\texttt{q}$ for each state $\texttt{q}$ of M, updating the state amounts to picking the right $\texttt{q}$ and $\texttt{q}'$ in the flow representing the transition.

Acceptance and Rejection. The encoding of acceptance and rejection is slightly more delicate, as detailed in a previous article [5, Sect. 6.2.3.].

The basic idea is that acceptance in our model is defined as nilpotency, that is to say: the absence of loops. If no transition in the automaton can be fired, then no flow in our encoding can be unified, and the computation ends.

Conversely, a loop in the automaton will refrain the wiring from being nilpotent. Loops should be represented as a re-initialization of the computation, so that the observation performs forever the same computation when rejecting the input. Another encoding may interfere with the representation of acceptance as termination: an "in-place loop" triggered when reaching a particular state would make the observation cyclic, hence preventing the observation from being nilpotent *no matter the word representation processed*.

Indeed, the "loop" in Definition 17 of pushdown automata is to be read as "perform forever the same computation".   □

Observations resulting from encoding pushdown automata are sums of flows of a particular form (shown at the beginning of the preceding proof). However, using general observations with stack, not constrained in this way, does not increase the expressive power: the next section is devoted to prove that the language recognized by any observation with stack lies in PTIME.

4   Nilpotency in $\mathcal{S}tack$ and PTIME Soundness

We now introduce the *saturation* technique, which allows to decide nilpotency of $\mathcal{S}tack$ elements in polynomial time. This technique relies on the fact that in certain cases, the height of flows does not grow when computing their product. It adapts memoization [32] to our setting: we repeatedly extend the wiring by adding pairwise products of flows, allowing for more and more "transitions".

Remark 2. As pointed out by a reviewer of a previous version of this work, deciding the nilpotency of a unary flow is reminiscent of the problem of acyclicity for the configuration graph of a pushdown system (PDS) [13], a problem known to lie in PTIME [15]. However, our algorithm treats every state of the corresponding PDS as initial, and would detect cycles even in non-connected components: our problem is probably closer to the "uniform halting problem" [34], a problem known to be decidable [14, p. 10]. Whether this last problem, equivalent to deciding the *nœthériennité* of a finite system rewriting suffix words, is known to lie in PTIME, and if our Theorem 5 entails that bound, are both unknown to us.

Notation 18. Let τ and σ be sequences of unary function symbols. If $h\left(\tau(x)\right) \geq h\left(\sigma(x)\right)$ (reps. $h\left(\tau(x)\right) \leq h\left(\sigma(x)\right)$), we say that $\tau(x) \leftharpoonup \sigma(x)$ is *increasing* (resp. *decreasing*).

A wiring in $\mathcal{S}tack$ is *increasing* (resp. *decreasing*) if it contains only increasing (resp. *decreasing*) unary flows.

Lemma 1 (stability of height). *Let τ and σ be sequences of unary function symbols. If τ is decreasing and σ is increasing, then $h(\tau\sigma) \leq \max\{h(\tau), h(\sigma)\}$.*

With this lemma in mind, we can define a *shortcut* operation that augments an element of $Stack$ by adding new flows while keeping the maximal height unchanged. Iterating this operation, we obtain a *saturated* version of the initial wiring, containing shortcuts, shortcuts of shortcuts, etc. In a sense we are designing an *exponentiation by squaring* procedure for elements of $Stack$, the algebraic reading of memoization in our context.

Definition 19 (Saturation). *If $F \in Stack$ we define its increasing $F^\uparrow := \{f \in F | f$ is increasing$\}$ and decreasing $F^\downarrow := \{f \in F | f$ is decreasing$\}$ subsets. We set the shortcut operation $short(F) := F + F^\downarrow F^\uparrow$ and its least fixpoint, which we call the saturation of F: $satur(F) := \sum_{n \in \mathbb{N}} short^n(F)$ (where $short^n$ denotes the nth iteration of $short$).*

The point of this operation is that it is computable in PTIME (the fixpoint is reached in polynomial time) because of Lemma 1. This leads to a PTIME decision procedure for nilpotency of elements of $Stack$.

Theorem 5 (nilpotency is in PTIME). *Given any integer h, there is a procedure $\mathrm{NILP}_h(\cdot) \in$ PTIME that, given a $F \in Stack$ such that $h(F) \leq h$ as an input, accepts iff F is nilpotent.*

Proof (Sketch [8, Theorem IV.15]). This relies on the fact that $satur(\cdot)$ is computable in polynomial time and that the cyclicity of F and that of $satur(F)$ are related. More precisely F is cyclic iff either $satur(F)^\uparrow$ or $satur(F)^\downarrow$ is. Finally one has to see that the case of increasing or decreasing wirings is easy to treat by discarding the bottom of large stacks, which is harmless in that case.

The saturation technique can then be used to show that the language recognized by an observation with stack always belongs to the class PTIME. The important point in the proof is that, given an observation O and a representation $\bar{W}_p$ of a word W, one can produce in polynomial time an element of $Stack$ whose nilpotency is equivalent to the nilpotency of $O\bar{W}_p$.

Proposition 1. *Let $O \in \mathcal{O}^{b+s}$ be an observation with stack. There is a procedure $\mathrm{RED}_O(\cdot) \in$ FPTIME that, given a word W as an input, outputs a wiring $F \in Stack$ with $h(F) \leq h(O)$ such that F is nilpotent iff $O\bar{W}_p$ is for any choice of p.*

This is done essentially by remarking that the "balanced" part of the computation can never step outside a finite computation space, so that one can associate to each configuration a unary function symbol that is put on top of the stack.

Theorem 6 (soundness). *If $O \in \mathcal{O}^{b+s}$, then $\mathcal{L}(O) \in$ PTIME.*

5   Unary Logic Programming

In previous sections, we showed how the $Stack$ semiring captures polynomial time computation. As we already mentioned, the elements of this semiring correspond to a specific class of logic programs, so that our results have a reading in terms of complexity of logic programming [22] which we detail now.

Definition 20 (Data, Goal, Query). *A* unary query *is* $\mathbf{Q} = (D, P, G)$, *where:*

- *D is a set of closed unary terms (a* unary data*),*
- *P is a an element of $\mathcal{S}tack$ (a* unary program*),*
- *G is a closed unary term (a* unary goal*).*

We say that the query $\mathbf{Q}$ succeeds if $G \dashv$ can be derived combining $d \dashv$ with $d \in D$ and the elements of P by the resolution rule presented in Sect. 2.1, otherwise we say the query fails. The size $|\mathbf{Q}|$ of the query is defined as the total number of occurrences of symbols in it.

To apply the saturation technique directly, we need to represent all the elements of the unary query (data, program, goal) as elements of $\mathcal{S}tack$. This requires a simple encoding.

Definition 21 (Encoding Unary Queries). *We suppose that for any constant symbol c, we have a unary function symbol $\underline{\mathsf{c}}(\cdot)$. We also need two unary functions, $\mathrm{START}(\cdot)$ and $\mathrm{ACCEPT}(\cdot)$. To any unary data D we associate an element of $\mathcal{S}tack$: $[D] := \{\tau(\underline{\mathsf{c}}(x)) \leftharpoonup \mathrm{START}(x) | \tau(\mathsf{c}) \in D\}$ and to any unary goal $G = \tau(\mathsf{c})$ we associate $\langle G \rangle := \mathrm{ACCEPT}(x) \leftharpoonup \tau(\underline{\mathsf{c}}(x))$.*

Note that the program part P of the query needs not to be encoded as it is already an element of $\mathcal{S}tack$. Once a query is encoded, we can tell if it is successful or not using the language of the resolution semiring.

Lemma 2 (success). *A unary query $\mathbf{Q} = (D, P, G)$ succeeds if and only if $\mathrm{ACCEPT}(x) \leftharpoonup \mathrm{START}(x) \in \langle G \rangle P^n [D]$ for some n.*

The saturation technique then can be applied to unary queries adding to new shortcut rules which eventually allow to decide acceptance.

Lemma 3 (saturation of unary queries). *A unary query $\mathbf{Q} = (D, P, G)$ succeeds if and only if $\mathrm{ACCEPT}(x) \leftharpoonup \mathrm{START}(x) \in \boldsymbol{satur}([D] + P + \langle G \rangle)$.*

Theorem 7 (PTIME-completeness). *The* UQUERY *problem (given a unary query, is it successful?) is* PTIME-*complete.*

Proof. The lemma above, combined with the fact that $\boldsymbol{satur}(\cdot)$ is computable in polynomial time[3], ensures that the problem lies indeed in the class PTIME. The hardness part follows from a variation on the encoding presented in Sect. 3 and the reduction derived from Proposition 1.

Remark 3. We presented the result in a restricted form to stay in line with the previous sections. However, it should be clear to the reader that it would not be impacted if we allowed: non-closed goals and data; programs with no restriction on variables, e.g. $\mathtt{f}(x) \leftharpoonup \mathtt{g}(y)$; constants in the program part of the query.

---

[3] The bound on the running time of the procedure computing $\boldsymbol{satur}(\cdot)$ being exponential in the height, one needs to first process the query into an equivalent one using only terms of bounded height, which can easily be done in polynomial time.

Remark 4. In terms of complexity of logic programs, we are considering the *combined complexity* [22, p. 380]: every part of the query $\mathbf{Q} = (D, P, G)$ is variable. If for instance we fixed P and G (thus considering *data complexity*), we would have a problem that is still in PTIME, but it is unclear to us if it would be complete. Indeed, the encoding of Sect. 3 relies on a representation of inputs as plain programs, and on the fact that the evaluation process is a matter of interaction between programs rather than mere data processing.

6   Perspectives

Adding a "stack plugin" to observations extends modularly previous works [2, 3,5,6] and gives the perfect tool to characterize PTIME. This modularity was inspired by the classical addition of a stack to an automaton, allowing to switch from LOGSPACE to PTIME, and providing a decisive proof technique: memoization—or exponentiation by squaring in our context—implemented as saturation. The automata's qualitative constraint on memory is directly represented as a syntactic restriction on flows.

In this setting, evaluation is inspired by the interactive approach to the Curry-Howard correspondence—geometry of interaction—, which makes the complexity parametric in the program *and* the input. This mechanism of computation differs from automata's step-by-step evaluation, but that does not prevent the simulation of pushdown automata by unary logic program.

The mechanism of pre-computation of transitions, known as memoization, was adapted in a setting where logic programs are represented as algebraic objects. This *saturation technique* computes shortcuts in a logic program to decide its nilpotency in polynomial time. As it turns out, this is similar to the techniques employed to solve efficiently the problem of termination of pushdown systems.

More generally, this approach to complexity is based either on operator algebra [5,6,31] or unification theory [2,3,8]: it is emerging as a meeting point for computer science, logic and mathematics, and raises a number of perspectives.

A number of interrogations emerges naturally when considering the relations to proof theory. First, we could consider the Church encoding of other data types—trees for instance—and define "orthogonally" set of programs interacting with them, wondering what their computational nature is. In the distance, one may hope for a connection between our approach and ongoing work on higher order trees and model checking [33]; all alike, one could study the interaction between observations and one-way integers—briefly discussed in earlier work [3]—or non-deterministic data. Second, a still unanswered question of interest is to give proof-terms representation of captured programs, i.e. observations.

Finally, it should be possible to represent functional computation (and not only decision problems, i.e. to switch from PTIME to FPTIME), by considering a more general notion of observation that could express what an output is. In that perspective, a good place to start should be to show that light logics characterization results [9] can be recovered via our methods, which seems very likely but remains to be precisely investigated.

References

1. Aho, A.V., Hopcroft, J.E., Ullman, J.D.: Time and tape complexity of pushdown automaton languages. Inform. Control **13**(3), 186–206 (1968)
2. Aubert, C., Bagnol, M.: Unification and logarithmic space. In: Dowek, G. (ed.) RTA-TLCA 2014. LNCS, vol. 8560, pp. 77–92. Springer, Heidelberg (2014)
3. Aubert, C., Bagnol, M., Pistone, P., Seiller, T.: Logic programming and logarithmic space. In: Garrigue, J. (ed.) APLAS 2014. LNCS, vol. 8858, pp. 39–57. Springer, Heidelberg (2014)
4. Aubert, C., Bagnol, M., Seiller, T.: Memoization for unary logic programming: Characterizing ptime. Research Report RR-8796, INRIA (2015). https://hal.archives-ouvertes.fr/hal-01107377
5. Aubert, C., Seiller, T.: Characterizing co-NL by a group action. In: MSCS (FirstView), pp. 1–33, December 2014
6. Aubert, C., Seiller, T.: Logarithmic space and permutations. Inf. Comput. Spec. Issue Implicit Comput. Complex. (2015). doi:10.1016/j.ic.2014.01.018
7. Baader, F., Nipkow, T.: Term rewriting and all that. CUP, Cambridge (1998)
8. Bagnol, M.: On the Resolution Semiring. Ph.D. thesis, Aix-Marseille Université - Institut de Mathématiques de Marseille (2014). https://hal.archives-ouvertes.fr/tel-01215334
9. Baillot, P., Mazza, D.: Linear logic by levels and bounded time complexity. Theoret. Comput. Sci. **411**(2), 470–503 (2010)
10. Baillot, P., Pedicini, M.: Elementary complexity and geometry of interaction. Fund. Inform. **45**(1–2), 1–31 (2001)
11. Baillot, P., Terui, K.: Light types for polynomial time computation in lambda-calculus. In: LICS, pp. 266–275. IEEE Computer Society (2004)
12. Bellantoni, S.J., Cook, S.A.: A new recursion-theoretic characterization of the polytime functions. Comput. Complex. **2**, 97–110 (1992)
13. Carayol, A., Hague, M.: Saturation algorithms for model-checking pushdown systems. In: Ésik, Z., Fülöp, Z. (eds.), Proceedings 14th International Conference on Automata and Formal Languages, AFL 2014, Szeged, Hungary, May 27–29, 2014. EPTCS, vol. 151, pp. 1–24 (2014)
14. Caucal, D.: Récritures suffixes de mots. Research Report RR-0871, INRIA (1988). https://hal.inria.fr/inria-00075683
15. Caucal, D.: On the regular structure of prefix rewriting. In: Arnold, A. (ed.) CAAP '90. LNCS, vol. 431, pp. 87–102. Springer, Heidelberg (1990)
16. Cook, S.A.: Characterizations of pushdown machines in terms of time-bounded computers. J. ACM **18**(1), 4–18 (1971)
17. Cook, S.A.: Linear time simulation of deterministic two-way pushdown automata. In: IFIP Congress (1), pp. 75–80. North-Holland (1971)
18. Dal Lago, U.: A short introduction to implicit computational complexity. In: Bezhanishvili, N., Goranko, V. (eds.) ESSLLI 2010 and ESSLLI 2011. LNCS, vol. 7388, pp. 89–109. Springer, Heidelberg (2012)
19. Dal Lago, U., Schöpp, U.: Functional programming in sublinear space. In: Gordon, A.D. (ed.) ESOP 2010. LNCS, vol. 6012, pp. 205–225. Springer, Heidelberg (2010)
20. Danos, V.: La Logique Linéaire appliquée á l'étude de divers processus de normalisation (principalement du λ-calcul). Ph.D. thesis, Universit Paris VII (1990)
21. Danos, V., Joinet, J.B.: Linear logic and elementary time. Inf. Comput. **183**(1), 123–137 (2003)

22. Dantsin, E., Eiter, T., Gottlob, G., Voronkov, A.: Complexity and expressive power of logic programming. ACM Comput. Surv. **33**(3), 374–425 (2001)
23. Dwork, C., Kanellakis, P.C., Mitchell, J.C.: On the sequential nature of unification. J. Log. Program. **1**(1), 35–50 (1984)
24. Gaboardi, M., Marion, J.Y., Rocca Della Rocca, S.: An implicit characterization of pspace. ACM Trans. Comput. Log. **13**(2), 18:1–18:36 (2012)
25. Girard, J.Y.: Linear logic. Theoret. Comput. Sci. **50**(1), 1–101 (1987)
26. Girard, J.Y.: Geometry of interaction 1: Interpretation of system F. Stud. Logic Found. Math. **127**, 221–260 (1989)
27. Girard, J.Y.: Towards a geometry of interaction. In: Gray, J.W., Scedrov, A. (eds.) Proceedings of the AMS Conference on Categories, Logic and Computer Science. Categories in Computer Science and Logic, vol. 92, pp. 69–108. AMS (1989)
28. Girard, J.Y.: Geometry of interaction III: accommodating the additives. In: Girard, J.Y., Lafont, Y., Regnier, L. (eds.) Advances in Linear Logic, pp. 329–389. No. 222 in London Mathematical Society Lecture Note Series, CUP, June 1995
29. Girard, J.Y.: Light linear logic. In: Leivant, D. (ed.) Logic and Computational Complexity. LNCS, vol. 960, pp. 145–176. Springer, Heidelberg (1995)
30. Girard, J.Y.: Geometry of interaction V: Logic in the hyperfinite factor. Theoret. Comput. Sci. **412**(20), 1860–1883 (2011)
31. Girard, J.Y.: Normativity in logic. In: Dybjer, P., Lindström, S., Palmgren, E., Sundholm, G. (eds.) Epistemology versus Ontology. LEUS, vol. 27, pp. 243–263. Springer, Heidelberg (2012)
32. Glück, R.: Simulation of two-way pushdown automata revisited. In: Banerjee, A., Danvy, O., Doh, K.G., Hatcliff, J. (eds.) Festschrift for Dave Schmidt. EPTCS, vol. 129, pp. 250–258 (2013)
33. Grellois, C., Melliés, P.A.: Relational semantics of linear logic and higher-order model checking. In: Kreutzer, S. (ed.) CSL. LIPIcs, vol. 41, pp. 260–276. Schloss Dagstuhl - Leibniz-Zentrum fuer Informatik (2015). http://www.dagstuhl.de/dagpub/978-3-939897-90-3
34. Huet, G., Lankford, D.: On the uniform halting problem for term rewriting systems. Research Report RR-283, INRIA (1978). http://www.ens-lyon.fr/LIP/REWRITING/TERMINATION/Huet_Lankford.pdf
35. Ladermann, M., Petersen, H.: Notes on looping deterministic two-way pushdown automata. Inf. Process. Lett. **49**(3), 123–127 (1994)
36. Lafont, Y.: Soft linear logic and polynomial time. Theoret. Comput. Sci. **318**(1), 163–180 (2004)
37. Leivant, D.: Stratified functional programs and computational complexity. In: Van Deusen, M.S., Lang, B. (eds.) POPL, pp. 325–333. ACM Press (1993)
38. Neergaard, P.M.: A functional language for logarithmic space. In: Chin, W.-N. (ed.) APLAS 2004. LNCS, vol. 3302, pp. 311–326. Springer, Heidelberg (2004)
39. Robinson, J.A.: A machine-oriented logic based on the resolution principle. J. ACM **12**(1), 23–41 (1965)
40. Seiller, T.: Logique dans le facteur hyperfini : géometrie de l'interaction et complexité. Ph.D. thesis, Université de la Méditerranée (2012), https://hal.archives-ouvertes.fr/tel-00768403
41. Seiller, T.: A correspondence between maximal abelian sub-algebras and linear logic fragments. ArXiv preprint abs/1408.2125, to appear in MSCS (2014)
42. Seiller, T.: Interaction graphs: Graphings. ArXiv preprint abs/1405.6331 (2014)
43. Wagner, K.W., Wechsung, G.: Computational Complexity, Mathematics and its Applications. Springer, Heidelberg (1986)

Focused and Synthetic Nested Sequents

Kaustuv Chaudhuri[(✉)], Sonia Marin, and Lutz Straßburger

Inria & LIX/École polytechnique, Palaiseau, France
{kaustuv.chaudhuri,sonia.marin,lutz.strassburger}@inria.fr

Abstract. Focusing is a general technique for transforming a sequent proof system into one with a syntactic separation of non-deterministic choices without sacrificing completeness. This not only improves proof search, but also has the representational benefit of distilling sequent proofs into synthetic normal forms. We show how to apply the focusing technique to nested sequent calculi, a generalization of ordinary sequent calculi to tree-like instead of list-like structures. We thus improve the reach of focusing to the most commonly studied modal logics, the logics of the modal S5 cube. Among our key contributions is a focused cut-elimination theorem for focused nested sequents.

1 Introduction

The *focusing* technique has its origin in the foundations of logic programming [1,22] and is now increasingly relevant in *structural proof theory* because it improves proof search procedures [11,21] and because focused proofs have clearly identifiable and semantically meaningful *synthetic* normal forms [6,8,10,31]. The essential idea of focusing is to identify and coalesce the non-deterministic choices in a proof, so that a proof can be seen as an alternation of *negative* phases, where invertible rules are applied eagerly, and *positive* phases, where applications of the other rules are confined and controlled. This, in turn, lets us abstract from the usual unary and binary logical connectives by collapsing whole phases into *n*-ary *synthetic connectives*. The full theory of focusing was initially developed for the sequent calculus for linear logic [1], but it has since been extended to a wide variety of logics [11,19,27] and proof systems [4,7]. This generality suggests that the ability to transform a proof system into a focused form is a good indication of its syntactic quality, in a manner similar to how admissibility of cut shows that a proof system is syntactically consistent.

It is natural to ask whether the focusing technique works as well for modal logics. Traditionally, modal logics are specified in terms of Hilbert-style axiomatic systems, but such systems are not particularly suitable since axioms reveal none of the structure of logical reasoning. It is well known that certain modal logics, S5 in particular, are not representable in a variant of Gentzen's sequent calculus without sacrificing analyticity. There are two principal ways to overcome this problem. The first is based on *labeled proof systems* that reify the Kripke semantics—the frame conditions—directly as formulas in the sequents [24,29]. These "semantic formulas" are not subformulas of the end-sequent and they

© Springer-Verlag Berlin Heidelberg 2016
B. Jacobs and C. Löding (Eds.): FOSSACS 2016, LNCS 9634, pp. 390–407, 2016.
DOI: 10.1007/978-3-662-49630-5_23

cause the interpretation of sequents to fall outside the class of propositional modal formulas, and for this reason, such calculi are also called *external*.

The second way is to use so-called *internal* calculi, that enrich the sequent structure such that analyticity is preserved and such that every sequent has an interpretation that stays inside the modal language. Well-known examples are *hypersequents* [2] and *display calculi* [3]. A more recent development are *nested sequents* [5, 12, 14, 26], which generalize the notion of context from a list-like structure (familiar from Gentzen's sequent calculus) to a tree-like structure. Like ordinary sequents, nested sequents have a straightforward interpretation in the language of the logic, and enjoy cut admissibility (with a cut-elimination proof that stays wholly internal to the system) and hence the usual subformula property. Moreover, nested proof systems can be built *modularly* for every modal logic in the S5 cube, in both classical and intuitionistic variants [5, 20].

In this paper, we build a focused variant, with its concomitant benefits, for all modal logics of the classical S5 cube. For simplicity we use a polarized syntax [15] consisting of two classes of positive and negative formulas and a pair of *shift* connectives to move back and forth between the classes. Crucially, we interpret $\Diamond$ as positive and $\Box$ as negative, which differs from the polarity that would be assigned to these connectives if they were interpreted in terms of ? and !, respectively, from linear logic [25]. Our key technical contributions are: (1) a purely *internal* proof of cut-elimination for the focused nested calculus, given in terms of a traditional rewriting procedure to eliminate cuts (which shows that our system is compositional and suitably continuous), and (2) a proof of completeness of the focused system with respect to the non-focused system (and hence to the Kripke semantics) by showing that the focused system admits the rules of the non-focused system. It generalizes similar proofs of cut-elimination and focusing completeness for (non-nested) sequent calculi [11, 19].

To our knowledge there have been only two other attempts to apply the focusing technique to modal logics. The first uses a labeled system [23], using the work in [24] on geometric axioms to obtain systems that extend the basic modal logic K. The cut-elimination and completeness results in [23] are obtained externally as a reduction to LKF, a focused system for first-order logic [19]. Therefore, the polarities of the modalities are inherited from the associated quantifiers, i.e., $\Box$ is negative and $\Diamond$ is positive, similar to our setting. The second approach [18] also uses nested sequents, but in a restricted form, in which the tree-structure is reduced to a single branch. This efficiently simulates the standard sequent system for the modal logic K, but makes both modalities positive.

Our approach uses the full power of nested sequents. and is intended as a prototype for how similar focused systems may be built for other modal logic formalisms. After some preliminaries (Sect. 2), we start with a *weakly focused* proof system (Sect. 3), where negative rules may be applied everywhere, including in the middle of focused phases. From this system, we extract a *strongly focused* system (also Sect. 3) and a *synthetic* system (Sect. 4) where the logical content of the phases of focusing are abstracted from the level of formulas to the level of nested sequents. We also sketch the cut-elimination theorem for this synthetic variant. The synthetic design generalizes similar designs for the sequent calculus [6, 31].

d: $\Box A \supset \Diamond A$
t: $A \supset \Diamond A$
b: $A \supset \Box \Diamond A$
4: $\Diamond \Diamond A \supset \Diamond A$
5: $\Diamond A \supset \Box \Diamond A$

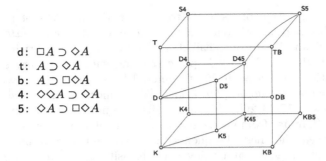

Fig. 1. Left: Some standard modal axioms   **Right:** Modal S5 cube

2 Modal Logics and the Nested Sequent Calculus KN

Classical modal logic is obtained from classical propositional logic by adding the modal connectives $\Box$ and $\Diamond$. Starting with a countable set of atoms $(a, b, \ldots)$, the formulas $(A, B, \ldots)$ of modal logic are given by the following grammar:

$$A, B, \ldots ::= a \mid \bar{a} \mid A \wedge B \mid A \vee B \mid \Box A \mid \Diamond A \tag{1}$$

To avoid excessive syntax, formulas are kept in negation-normal form, so the only formally negated formulas are the atoms. The negation $\bar{A}$ of an arbitrary formula A is given by the De Morgan laws: $\bar{\bar{A}} = A$, $\overline{A \wedge B} = \bar{A} \vee \bar{B}$ and $\overline{\Box A} = \Diamond \bar{A}$. We also define $A \supset B$ as $\bar{A} \vee B$, $A \equiv B$ as $(A \supset B) \wedge (B \supset A)$, $\top$ as $a \vee \bar{a}$, and $\bot$ as $a \wedge \bar{a}$ (for some atom a).

Modal logics are traditionally specified using Hilbert-style axiom schemata. The basic modal logic K, for instance, is obtained by adding the following k axiom to the ordinary Hilbert axioms for propositional logic.

$$\mathsf{k}: \Box(A \supset B) \supset (\Box A \supset \Box B) \tag{2}$$

To obtain the theorems of K, we then also add two inference rules of *modus ponens* and *necessitation*.

$$\mathsf{mp} \frac{A \quad A \supset B}{B} \qquad \mathsf{nec} \frac{A}{\Box A} \tag{3}$$

Stronger modal logics can be obtained by adding to K other axioms mentioning the modal connectives. In this paper, we consider the most common five axioms d, t, b, 4 and 5, which are shown on the left in Fig. 1. Picking subsets of these axioms lets us define thirty-two modal logics, but only fifteen of them are non-redundant. For example, the sets {b, 4} and {t, 5} both yield the modal logic S5. The fifteen distinct modal logics follow chains of extension from K to S5 and can be arranged as a pair of nested cubes depicted on the right in Fig. 1; this is sometimes called the S5 *cube* [13].

$$\text{id}\ \frac{}{\Gamma\{a,\bar{a}\}}\qquad \vee\ \frac{\Gamma\{A,B\}}{\Gamma\{A\vee B\}}\qquad \wedge\ \frac{\Gamma\{A\}\quad\Gamma\{B\}}{\Gamma\{A\wedge B\}}\qquad \Box\ \frac{\Gamma\{[A]\}}{\Gamma\{\Box A\}}\qquad \mathsf{k}^{\circ}\ \frac{\Gamma\{\Diamond A,[A,\Delta]\}}{\Gamma\{\Diamond A,[\Delta]\}}$$

$$\mathsf{d}^{\circ}\ \frac{\Gamma\{\Diamond A,[A]\}}{\Gamma\{\Diamond A\}}\qquad \mathsf{t}^{\circ}\ \frac{\Gamma\{\Diamond A,A\}}{\Gamma\{\Diamond A\}}\qquad \mathsf{b}^{\circ}\ \frac{\Gamma\{[\Delta,\Diamond A],A\}}{\Gamma\{[\Delta,\Diamond A]\}}$$

$$\mathsf{4}^{\circ}\ \frac{\Gamma\{\Diamond A,[\Diamond A,\Delta]\}}{\Gamma\{\Diamond A,[\Delta]\}}\qquad \mathsf{5}^{\circ}\ \frac{\Gamma\{\Diamond A\}\{\Diamond A\}}{\Gamma\{\Diamond A\}\{\emptyset\}}\ \ \mathrm{dp}(\Gamma\{\ \}\{\emptyset\})\geq 1$$

Fig. 2. Rules for $\mathsf{KN}+\mathsf{X}^{\circ}$. The first row constitutes KN.

Let us recall the notion of *nested sequents*, first defined by Kashima [14] and then independently rediscovered by Poggiolesi [26] (who called them *tree-hypersequents*) and Brünnler [5]. In Gentzen's one-sided sequent calculus, a sequent is just a multiset of formulas; nested sequents generalize this notion to a multiset of formulas and boxed sequents, resulting in a tree structure.

Definition 2.1. A *nested sequent* $(\Gamma,\Delta,\dots)$ is a finite multiset of formulas and *boxed sequents* of the form $[\Delta]$, where Δ is itself a nested sequent. In other words, nested sequents have the following grammar:

$$\Gamma,\Delta,\dots ::= A_1,\dots,A_m,[\Gamma_1],\dots,[\Gamma_n] \tag{4}$$

Both m and n may be 0, in which case the sequent is *empty*; when we need to be explicit, we will use the notation $\emptyset$ to stand for an empty sequent. As is usual in sequent calculi, we consider the comma to be associative and commutative.

Definition 2.2 (Corresponding Formulas). For any nested sequent Γ, a *corresponding formula*, written $\mathrm{fm}(\Gamma)$, gives an interpretation of Γ as a modal logic formula. Corresponding formulas obey the following equivalences: $\mathrm{fm}(\emptyset)\equiv\bot$, $\mathrm{fm}(A)\equiv A$, $\mathrm{fm}([\Gamma])\equiv\Box\mathrm{fm}(\Gamma)$, and $\mathrm{fm}(\Gamma_1,\Gamma_2)\equiv\mathrm{fm}(\Gamma_1)\vee\mathrm{fm}(\Gamma_2)$.

Definition 2.3 (Context). An *n-holed context* is like a nested sequent but contains n pairwise distinct numbered *holes* of the form $\{\ \}_i$ (for $1\leq i\leq n$) in place of formulas. (No hole can occur inside a formula.) We depict such a context as $\Gamma\{\ \}_1\cdots\{\ \}_n$. Given such a context and n nested sequents $\Delta_1,\dots,\Delta_n$, we write $\Gamma\{\Delta_1\}_1\cdots\{\Delta_n\}_n$ to stand for the nested sequent where the hole $\{\ \}_i$ (for $1\leq i\leq n$) in the context has been replaced by Δ_i, with the understanding that if Δ_i is empty then the hole is simply removed. Unless there is any ambiguity, we will omit the hole index subscripts in this paper to keep the notation light.

Definition 2.4. The *depth* of $\Gamma\{\ \}$, written $\mathrm{dp}(\Gamma\{\ \})$, is given inductively by: $\mathrm{dp}(\{\ \})=0$, $\mathrm{dp}(\Delta,\Gamma\{\ \})=\mathrm{dp}(\Gamma\{\ \})$, and $\mathrm{dp}([\Gamma\{\ \}])=\mathrm{dp}(\Gamma\{\ \})+1$.

Example 2.5. Let $\Gamma\{\ \}\{\ \}=A,[B,\{\ \},[\{\ \},C]$. For the sequents $\Delta_1=D$ and $\Delta_2=A,[C]$, we get: $\Gamma\{\Delta_1\}\{\Delta_2\}=A,[B,D,[A,[C]],C]$ and $\Gamma\{\emptyset\}\{\Delta_2\}=A,[B,[A,[C]],C]$. We also have that $\mathrm{dp}(\Gamma\{\ \}\{\Delta_1\})=1$ and $\mathrm{dp}(\Gamma\{\Delta_1\}\{\ \})=2$.

The basic modal logic K (as presented in [5]) is captured using nested sequents as the cut-free proof system KN shown in the first row in Fig. 2. The deductive system corresponding to each normal extension K + X, where X ⊆ {d, t, b, 4, 5} is a set of modal axioms (Fig. 1), can be obtained by adding the corresponding *diamond rules* X° ⊆ {d°, t°, b°, 4°, 5°} (final two rows of Fig. 2) to KN. The 5° rule has a side condition that the context in which the principal ◇-formula occurs has non-zero *depth*, i.e., that it does not occur at the root of the conclusion sequent.

To make the correspondence between extensions of K and the proof systems precise, we need the following additional notion:

Definition 2.6 (45-Closure). We say that X ⊆ {d, t, b, 4, 5} is *45-closed*, if:

– whenever 4 is derivable in K + X, 4 ∈ X
– whenever 5 is derivable in K + X, 5 ∈ X.

In this paper, we will always work with 45-closed axiom sets. The reason is that, for example, the axiom 4 is not provable (without cut) in KN + {t°, 5°} even though 4 is a theorem of the logic K + {t, 5} (which is S5). Note that this is not a real restriction, since for every logic in the modal cube (Fig. 1) there is a 45-closed set of axioms defining it (see [5] for details). We can now state the soundness, completeness, and cut-admissibility for KN and its extensions.

Theorem 2.7. *Let* cut *be the following rule:*

$$\text{cut} \frac{\Gamma\{A\} \quad \Gamma\{\bar{A}\}}{\Gamma\{\emptyset\}}$$

Let X ⊆ {d, t, b, 4, 5} *be 45-closed. For any formula A, the following are equivalent.*

1. *A is a theorem of* K + X.
2. *A is provable in* KN + X° + cut.
3. *A is provable in* KN + X°.

The proof that 1 ⟹ 2 ⟹ 3 ⟹ 1 can be found in [5].   □

3   The Focused Systems KNwF and KNF

The essence of the focusing technique [1] is to classify formulas into *positive* formulas, whose rules are not invertible, and *negative* whose rules are invertible. (As usual, we consider a rule to be invertible if whenever the conclusion of the rule is derivable then so are each of its premises.) Due to invertibility, when searching for a proof it is always safe to apply—reading from conclusion to premises—a rule for a negative formula, so these may be applied at any time. On the other hand, rules for positive formulas may require rules on other formulas to be applied first. For example, the KN sequent □ā, ◇a can only be proved by first applying the □ rule, showing that ◇-formulas are positive. A focused proof is one where the *decision* to apply a rule to a positive formula has to be explicitly taken, which then commits the proof to continue applying rules to this *focused* positive formula and its immediate positive descendants (and no other formula in the sequent), which drastically reduces the search space. The main theorem of focusing is that this strategy is complete, i.e., every theorem has a focused proof.

We will now build such a focused version of KN. To simplify the meta-theorems about this system, we will adopt a *polarized syntax* [15] where the positive and negative formulas are grouped together in different syntactic categories and explicitly mediated by *shift* connectives ($\uparrow$ and $\downarrow$). As already mentioned, $\Diamond$ is in the positive class, and its dual $\Box$ is in the negative class, unlike what would be expected if they were interpreted in terms of the linear logic modalities ? and ! respectively. One way of explaining this phenomenon is that the standard shallow rule k in sequent calculus (corresponding to the *promotion* rule of linear logic) realises two steps at once: accessing the formula under a $\Box$ and moving the $\Diamond$-formulas from the context next to that formula. These two steps are done by two different rules $\Box$ and k° in nested sequent systems like KN.

The rest of the formulas have ambiguous polarities and the choice does not alter the focusing result — some reasons to pick certain polarizations can be found in [11,19]. We arbitrarily assign all atoms to be positive (and their negations to be negative), and present the system in the strongest form, i.e., split the conjunctions and disjunctions into positive and negative versions. Thus, polarized formulas have the following grammar:

$$
\begin{array}{lll}
\text{positive:} & P, Q, \ldots ::= a \mid P \wedge Q \mid P \stackrel{\vee}{} Q \mid \Diamond P \mid {\downarrow} N \\
\text{negative:} & N, M, \ldots ::= \bar{a} \mid N \stackrel{\vee}{} M \mid N \wedge M \mid \Box N \mid {\uparrow} P
\end{array}
\tag{5}
$$

Each column in the grammar above defines a De Morgan dual pair; note that the negation of a positive formula is a negative formula, and vice versa. Units are definable similarly to the non-focused case, so we have $t^+ = a \stackrel{\vee}{} {\downarrow}\bar{a}$, $f^+ = a \wedge {\downarrow}\bar{a}$, and dually for f^-/t^-. When the polarity of a formula is not important, we write it as $A, B, \ldots$. A polarized nested sequent is the same as in the non-focused setting, with the difference that all formulas are polarized. Likewise, a polarized context is a polarized nested sequent where some formulas have been replaced by holes. In the rest of this paper, we will drop the adjective "polarized" and treat all constructs implicitly as polarized, unless otherwise indicated.

Definition 3.1 (Neutral). A formula is said to be *neutral* if it is a positive formula or a negated atom. A nested sequent is *neutral* if it is built from multisets of neutral formulas and boxed neutral sequents. A context $\Gamma\{ \} \cdots \{ \}$ is *neutral* if $\Gamma\{\emptyset\} \cdots \{\emptyset\}$ is neutral.

Definition 3.2. A *focused sequent* is of the form $\Gamma\{\langle P \rangle\}$ where $\Gamma\{ \}$ is a context and P is a positive formula. The formula P is called its *focus*. The notion of corresponding formula (Definition 2.2) is extended with $\mathrm{fm}(\langle P \rangle) \equiv \mathrm{fm}(P)$.

The inference rules of the focused system KNwF (w for "weak") are shown in the first three rows in Fig. 3 (the basic system for K). Then, for a set $X \subseteq \{d, t, b, 4, 5\}$, we write $X_f^\circ \subseteq \{k_f^\circ, t_f^\circ, b_f^\circ, 4_f^\circ, 5_f^\circ\}$ for the corresponding subset

$$\text{sto } \frac{\Gamma\{P\}}{\Gamma\{\uparrow P\}} \quad \text{rel } \frac{\Gamma\{N\}}{\Gamma\{\langle\downarrow N\rangle\}} \quad \text{dec } \frac{\Gamma\{P, \langle P\rangle\}}{\Gamma\{P\}}$$

$$\bar{\wedge} \frac{\Gamma\{A\} \quad \Gamma\{B\}}{\Gamma\{A \bar{\wedge} B\}} \quad \bar{\vee} \frac{\Gamma\{A, B\}}{\Gamma\{A \bar{\vee} B\}} \quad \Box \frac{\Gamma\{[A]\}}{\Gamma\{\Box A\}}$$

$$\text{id } \frac{}{\Gamma\{\bar{a}, \langle a \rangle\}} \quad \dot{\wedge} \frac{\Gamma\{\langle A\rangle\} \quad \Gamma\{\langle B\rangle\}}{\Gamma\{\langle A \dot{\wedge} B\rangle\}} \quad \dot{\vee}_1 \frac{\Gamma\{\langle A\rangle\}}{\Gamma\{\langle A \dot{\vee} B\rangle\}} \quad \dot{\vee}_2 \frac{\Gamma\{\langle B\rangle\}}{\Gamma\{\langle A \dot{\vee} B\rangle\}} \quad \mathsf{k}_f^\diamond \frac{\Gamma\{[\langle A\rangle, \Delta]\}}{\Gamma\{\langle \Diamond A\rangle, [\Delta]\}}$$

$$\mathsf{d}_f^\diamond \frac{\Gamma\{[\langle A\rangle]\}}{\Gamma\{\langle \Diamond A\rangle\}} \quad \mathsf{t}_f^\diamond \frac{\Gamma\{\langle A\rangle\}}{\Gamma\{\langle \Diamond A\rangle\}} \quad \mathsf{b}_f^\diamond \frac{\Gamma\{[\Delta], \langle A\rangle\}}{\Gamma\{[\Delta, \langle \Diamond A\rangle]\}}$$

$$\mathsf{4}_f^\diamond \frac{\Gamma\{[\langle \Diamond A\rangle, \Delta]\}}{\Gamma\{\langle \Diamond A\rangle, [\Delta]\}} \quad \mathsf{5}_f^\diamond \frac{\Gamma\{\emptyset\}\{\langle \Diamond A\rangle\}}{\Gamma\{\langle \Diamond A\rangle\}\{\emptyset\}} \quad \mathrm{dp}(\Gamma\{\ \}\{\emptyset\}) \geq 1$$

Fig. 3. Focused Rules for $\mathsf{KNF} + \mathsf{X}_f^\diamond$ and $\mathsf{KNwF} + \mathsf{X}_f^\diamond$. The first three rows constitute KNwF and KNF.

of the focused diamond rules in the last two rows. Observe that the rules for negative formulas are exactly the same as in the unfocused system, while the rules for positive formulas can only be applied if the principal formula is in focus. Mediating between ordinary and focused sequents are the rules dec ("decide"), that chooses a positive formula in the conclusion and focuses on a copy of it in the premise, and rel ("release") that drops the focus on a shifted formula. Since dec keeps the original positive formula in the context, there is no need to incorporate contraction in every positive rule, like in KN. The sto ("store") rule removes a shift in front of a positive formula and is used to produce neutral premises from non-neutral conclusions.

We define the system KNF to be a restriction of KNwF where the conclusion of the dec rule is required to be neutral, as well as the contexts surrounding the focus in all rules involving focused sequents. Thus, in KNF, the dec rule is only applicable when no other rule is applicable (no negative rule as there is no negative formula in a neutral sequent and no positive rule as there is no focus), and hence we sometimes call it *strongly focused*. We immediately have the following proposition:

Proposition 3.3. *Let $X \subseteq \{\mathsf{d}, \mathsf{t}, \mathsf{b}, 4, 5\}$. A formula A is provable in $\mathsf{KNF} + \mathsf{X}_f^\diamond$ if and only if it is provable in $\mathsf{KNwF} + \mathsf{X}_f^\diamond$.*

Proof. A derivation in $\mathsf{KNF} + \mathsf{X}_f^\diamond$ is by definition also a derivation in $\mathsf{KNwF} + \mathsf{X}_f^\diamond$. Conversely, to convert a derivation in $\mathsf{KNwF} + \mathsf{X}_f^\diamond$ into one in $\mathsf{KNF} + \mathsf{X}_f^\diamond$, we first have to replace all instances of id with a sequence of applications of $\{\Box, \bar{\wedge}, \dot{\wedge}, \mathsf{sto}\}$ followed (reading from conclusion upwards) by id, to ensure that the conclusion of the id rule is neutral. Then, the negative rules $\{\bar{\wedge}, \bar{\vee}, \Box\}$ can be permuted down by straightforward rule permutations to ensure that dec only applies to neutral sequents. $\square$

$$\text{weak}\ \frac{\Gamma\{\emptyset\}}{\Gamma\{\Delta\}} \qquad \text{weak}_f\ \frac{\Gamma\{\emptyset\}\{\langle P\rangle\}}{\Gamma\{\Delta\}\{\langle P\rangle\}} \qquad \text{cont}\ \frac{\Gamma\{\bar{a},\bar{a}\}}{\Gamma\{\bar{a}\}} \qquad \mathsf{k}^{[]}\ \frac{\Gamma\{[\Delta],[\Sigma]\}}{\Gamma\{[\Delta,\Sigma]\}}$$

Fig. 4. Structural rules.

$$\mathsf{d}^{[]}\ \frac{\Gamma\{[\ ]\}}{\Gamma\{\emptyset\}} \qquad \mathsf{t}^{[]}\ \frac{\Gamma\{[\Delta]\}}{\Gamma\{\Delta\}} \qquad \mathsf{b}^{[]}\ \frac{\Gamma\{[\Sigma,[\Delta]]\}}{\Gamma\{[\Sigma],\Delta\}} \qquad \mathsf{4}^{[]}\ \frac{\Gamma\{[\Delta],[\Sigma]\}}{\Gamma\{[[\Delta],\Sigma]\}} \qquad \mathsf{5}^{[]}\ \frac{\Gamma\{[\Delta]\}\{\emptyset\}}{\Gamma\{\emptyset\}\{[\Delta]\}}$$

Fig. 5. Structural modal rules for axioms $\mathsf{d},\mathsf{t},\mathsf{b},4,5$ (where $\mathrm{dp}(\Gamma\{\ \}\{[\Delta]\}) \geq 1$ in $\mathsf{5}^{[]}$)

In order to establish the soundness and completeness of KNwF, we use the obvious forgetful injection of the polarized syntax into the unpolarized syntax.

Definition 3.4 (Depolarization). If A is a polarized formula, then we write $\lfloor A\rfloor$ for the unpolarized formula obtained from A by erasing the shifts $\uparrow$ and $\downarrow$, collapsing $\bar{\wedge}$ and $\tilde{\wedge}$ into $\wedge$, and collapsing $\bar{\vee}$ and $\tilde{\vee}$ into $\vee$.

Theorem 3.5 (Soundness). *Let* $X \subseteq \{\mathsf{d},\mathsf{t},\mathsf{b},4,5\}$. *If a formula* A *is provable in* $\mathsf{KNF} + X_f^\circ$, *then* $\lfloor A\rfloor$ *is provable in* $\mathsf{KN} + X^\circ$.

Proof. By forgetting the polarity information, every $\mathsf{KNF} + X_f^\circ$ proof of A is transformed into a $\mathsf{KN} + X^\circ$ proof of $\lfloor A\rfloor$. $\square$

Completeness is considerably trickier. We use a technique pioneered by Laurent for linear logic [16] and proceed via cut-elimination in KNwF.

3.1   Cut Elimination

In this section we will show that a collection of cuts is admissible for $\mathsf{KNwF} + X_f^\circ$. As usual, a rule is said to be admissible if it is the case that whenever any instance of all its premises is derivable, so is the corresponding instance of the conclusion. In order to show the admissibility of the cut rules, it will be very useful to appeal to a collection of other admissible and invertible rules.

Lemma 3.6. *Let* $X \subseteq \{\mathsf{d},\mathsf{t},\mathsf{b},4,5\}$. *The rules* weak, weak$_f$, cont, *and* $\mathsf{m}^{[]}$ *(shown in Fig. 4) are admissible for* $\mathsf{KNwF} + X_f^\circ$. *Moreover, the rules* sto, $\square$, $\bar{\wedge}$, *and* $\bar{\vee}$ *are invertible for* $\mathsf{KNwF} + X_f^\circ$.

Proof. By straightforward induction on the height of the derivation. $\square$

Note that here we use contraction only on negated atoms because that is all that is needed in the cut-elimination proof below. One can indeed show that the general contraction rule on arbitrary sequents (and not just formulas) is admissible, but this requires a complicated argument for focused sequents. The corresponding result for KN is shown in [5].

Lemma 3.7. *Let* $X \subseteq \{\mathsf{d},\mathsf{t},\mathsf{b},4,5\}$. *If* X *is 45-closed, then any rule* $\mathsf{x}^{[]}$ *in* $X^{[]}$ *(shown in Fig. 5) is admissible for* $\mathsf{KNwF} + X_f^\circ$.

$$\text{cut}_1 \; \frac{\Gamma\{P\} \quad \Gamma\{\bar{P}\}}{\Gamma\{\emptyset\}} \qquad \text{cut}_2 \; \frac{\Gamma\{\langle P \rangle\} \quad \Gamma\{\bar{P}\}}{\Gamma\{\emptyset\}} \qquad \text{cut}_3 \; \frac{\Gamma\{\langle Q \rangle\}\{P\} \quad \Gamma\{\emptyset\}\{\bar{P}\}}{\Gamma\{\langle Q \rangle\}\{\emptyset\}}$$

Fig. 6. The various cuts in $\mathsf{KNwF} + \mathsf{X}_f^\circ$

Proof. Analogous to the corresponding lemma for KN in [5, Lemma 9]. The full proof can be found in [9, Lemma 3.7]. □

We are now ready to prove the admissibility of cuts. Specifically, we show all the cuts in Fig. 6 are simultaneously admissible. The cut_1 rule is our *standard cut* between ordinary nested sequents, while cut_2 defines a *principal cut* between a focus and its dual as cut formulas. Finally, cut_3 is a *commutative cut* for situations where the positive cut formula is not principal. Note that this collection of cuts is just sufficiently large to make the standard cuts admissible. It is easy to imagine many other cut-like rules, but it is not necessary—and may not even be possible—to admit them.

Definition 3.8. The *height* of a formula A, written $\text{ht}(A)$, is computed inductively as follows: $\text{ht}(a) = \text{ht}(\bar{a}) = 1$, $\text{ht}(A \star B) = \max(\text{ht}(A), \text{ht}(B)) + 1$ where $\star \in \{\bar{\wedge}, \bar{\wedge}, \bar{\vee}, \bar{\vee}\}$, and $\text{ht}(\bigcirc A) = \text{ht}(A) + 1$ where $\bigcirc \in \{\Diamond, \Box, \uparrow, \downarrow\}$. The *rank* of an instance of one of the cut rules is the height of its cut formula (the P in Fig. 6).

Lemma 3.9 (Cut Reduction). *Let* $\mathsf{X} \subseteq \{\mathsf{d}, \mathsf{t}, \mathsf{b}, 4, 5\}$ *be 45-closed. For every derivation*

$$\text{cut}_i \; \frac{\overset{\mathcal{D}_1}{\diagdown\diagup} \; \overset{\mathcal{D}_2}{\diagdown\diagup}}{\Gamma_0} \qquad\qquad (6)$$

in $\mathsf{KNwF} + \mathsf{X}_f^\circ + \{\text{cut}_1, \text{cut}_2, \text{cut}_3\}$, *where* $\mathcal{D}_1$ *and* $\mathcal{D}_2$ *are cut-free, there is a cut-free derivation of* Γ_0 *in* $\mathsf{KNwF} + \mathsf{X}_f^\circ$.

Proof. Let $\mathcal{D}_1$ always stand for the derivation with the positive cut formula. We proceed by lexicographic induction: the induction hypothesis may be applied whenever (1) the rank of the cut decreases, or (2) the rank stays the same and a cut_1 is replaced by a cut_2, or (3) the rank stays the same and the height of $\mathcal{D}_1$ decreases. The height of $\mathcal{D}_2$ does not matter for the induction. The proof is then given in terms of a terminating rewrite sequence, written with $\rightsquigarrow$.

Most cases of this rewrite are standard, so we show here only certain cases characteristic of focusing; the full list of cases can be found in [9, Lemma 3.9].

– The commutative cases are simple, relying on the invertibility of the negative rules (Lemma 3.7). Here we show the case of rel above a cut_3:

$$
\text{cut}_3 \dfrac{\text{rel}\, \dfrac{\Gamma\{N\}\{P\}}{\Gamma\{\langle\downarrow N\rangle\}\{P\}} \quad \overset{\mathcal{D}_2}{\triangle}}{\Gamma\{\langle\downarrow N\rangle\}\{\emptyset\}} \quad \rightsquigarrow \quad \text{rel}\,\dfrac{\text{cut}_1\,\dfrac{\overset{\mathcal{D}_1'}{\triangle}\,\Gamma\{N\}\{P\} \quad \text{weak}\,\dfrac{\overset{\mathcal{D}_2}{\triangle}\,\Gamma\{\emptyset\}\{\bar P\}}{\Gamma\{N\}\{\bar P\}}}{\Gamma\{N\}\{\emptyset\}}}{\Gamma\{\langle\downarrow N\rangle\}\{\emptyset\}}
$$

The resulting cut_2 can be reduced because it has a smaller height.

– The cases of dec with the cut formula being principal:

$$
\text{cut}_1\,\dfrac{\text{dec}\,\dfrac{\overset{\mathcal{D}_1'}{\triangle}\,\Gamma\{P,\langle P\rangle\}}{\Gamma\{P\}} \quad \overset{\mathcal{D}_2}{\triangle}\,\Gamma\{\bar P\}}{\Gamma\{\emptyset\}} \quad \rightsquigarrow \quad \text{cut}_2\,\dfrac{\text{cut}_3\,\dfrac{\overset{\mathcal{D}_1'}{\triangle}\,\Gamma\{P,\langle P\rangle\} \quad \overset{\mathcal{D}_2}{\triangle}\,\Gamma\{\bar P\}}{\Gamma\{\langle P\rangle\}} \quad \overset{\mathcal{D}_2}{\triangle}\,\Gamma\{\bar P\}}{\Gamma\{\emptyset\}}
$$

In the resulting derivation, we first reduce the upper cut_3, which is allowed because the height is smaller. Then, we reduce the lower cut, which is allowed because a cut_2 can be used to justify a cut_1 of the same rank.

– Finally, here is a characteristic case for the modal axioms, for the 4_f° rule:

$$
\text{cut}_2\,\dfrac{4^\circ\,\dfrac{\overset{\mathcal{D}_1'}{\triangle}\,\Gamma\{[\langle\Diamond P\rangle,\Delta]\}}{\Gamma\{\langle\Diamond P\rangle,[\Delta]\}} \quad \overset{\mathcal{D}_2}{\triangle}\,\Gamma\{\Box\bar P,[\Delta]\}}{\Gamma\{[\Delta]\}} \quad \rightsquigarrow \quad \text{cut}_2\,\dfrac{\overset{\mathcal{D}_1'}{\triangle}\,\Gamma\{[\langle\Diamond P\rangle,\Delta]\} \quad \Box\,\dfrac{4^{[]}\,\dfrac{\Box^{-1}\,\dfrac{\overset{\mathcal{D}_2}{\triangle}\,\Gamma\{\Box\bar P,[\Delta]\}}{\Gamma\{[\bar P],[\Delta]\}}}{\Gamma\{[[\bar P],\Delta]\}}}{\Gamma\{[\Box\bar P,\Delta]\}}}{\Gamma\{[\Delta]\}}
$$

The resulting cut_2 can be reduced because it has a smaller height. In the right branch, the $\Box^{-1}$ rule is the admissible inverse of the $\Box$ rule (Lemma 3.6) and the $4^{[]}$ rule is given by Lemma 3.7. $\square$

Theorem 3.10. *Let* $X \subseteq \{d, t, b, 4, 5\}$ *be 45-closed. If a sequent* Γ *is provable in* $\mathsf{KNF} + X_f^\circ + \{\text{cut}_1, \text{cut}_2, \text{cut}_3\}$, *then it is also provable in* $\mathsf{KNF} + X_f^\circ$.

Proof. Apply Lemma 3.9 to all cut instances in the derivation, starting with a topmost one. This gives us a cut-free proof in $\mathsf{KNwF} + X_f^\circ$, from which we get a cut-free proof in $\mathsf{KNF} + X_f^\circ$ using Proposition 3.3. $\square$

3.2 Completeness

We can now use Theorem 3.10 to show completeness of the focused systems $\mathsf{KNF} + X_f^\circ$ (and hence $\mathsf{KNwF} + X_f^\circ$) with respect to $\mathsf{KN} + X^\circ$. As an intermediate step, we consider a variant of KN that can deal with polarized formulas. Let KN' denote the system that is obtained from KN by adding the rules

$$
\text{rel}\,\dfrac{\Gamma\{N\}}{\Gamma\{\downarrow N\}} \qquad \text{sto}\,\dfrac{\Gamma\{P\}}{\Gamma\{\uparrow P\}}
$$

and by duplicating the rules for $\wedge$ and $\vee$ such that there is a variant for each of $\dot{\wedge}$ and $\bar{\wedge}$, and $\dot{\vee}$ and $\bar{\vee}$, respectively. We immediately have the following lemma:

Lemma 3.11. *A formula A is provable in* $\mathsf{KN'}+\mathsf{X}_f^\diamond$ *if and only if* $\lfloor A \rfloor$ *is provable in* $\mathsf{KN} + \mathsf{X}^\diamond$. ☐

We are now going to simulate $\mathsf{KN'} + \mathsf{X}_f^\diamond$ in $\mathsf{KNwF} + \mathsf{X}_f^\diamond$. For this, we need another property of KNwF:

Lemma 3.12 (Identity Reduction). *The following rule is derivable in* KNwF:

$$\mathsf{gid}\,\frac{}{\Gamma\{\langle P\rangle, \bar{P}\}}$$

Proof. By straightforward induction on the height of P. Details can be found in [9, Lemma 3.12]. ☐

Lemma 3.13 (Simulation). *Let* $\mathsf{X} \subseteq \{\mathsf{d}, \mathsf{t}, \mathsf{b}, 4, 5\}$ *and let A be a formula that is provable in* $\mathsf{KN'} + \mathsf{X}_f^\diamond$. *Then A is provable in* $\mathsf{KNwF} + \mathsf{X}_f^\diamond + \mathsf{cut}_1$.

Proof. We show that each rule in $\mathsf{KN'} + \mathsf{X}_f^\diamond$ is derivable in $\mathsf{KNwF} + \mathsf{X}_f^\diamond + \mathsf{cut}_1$. Then the lemma follows by replacing in the proof of A in $\mathsf{KN'}+\mathsf{X}_f^\diamond$ each instance of a rule by the corresponding derivation in $\mathsf{KNwF} + \mathsf{X}_f^\diamond$. For the rules sto, $\Box$, $\bar{\wedge}$, $\bar{\vee}$ this is trivial. We show below the cases for $\dot{\vee}$, $\mathsf{d}^\diamond$, and $4^\diamond$. The others are similar, and a full list can be found in [9, Lemma 3.13].

$$
\mathsf{cut}_1\,\frac{\mathsf{weak}\,\frac{\Gamma\{P,Q\}}{\Gamma\{P\dot{\vee}Q, P, Q\}} \qquad \mathsf{cut}_1\,\frac{\dot{\vee}\,\dfrac{\mathsf{gid}\,\dfrac{}{\Gamma\{P\dot{\vee}Q, \langle Q\rangle, P, \bar{Q}\}}}{\Gamma\{P\dot{\vee}Q, \langle P\dot{\vee}Q\rangle, P, \bar{Q}\}}}{\mathsf{dec}\,\dfrac{}{\Gamma\{P\dot{\vee}Q, P, \bar{Q}\}}}}{\Gamma\{P\dot{\vee}Q, P\}} \qquad \mathsf{dec}\,\frac{\dot{\vee}\,\dfrac{\mathsf{gid}\,\dfrac{}{\Gamma\{P\dot{\vee}Q, \langle P\rangle, \bar{P}\}}}{\Gamma\{P\dot{\vee}Q, \langle P\dot{\vee}Q\rangle, \bar{P}\}}}{\Gamma\{P\dot{\vee}Q, \bar{P}\}}}{\Gamma\{P\dot{\vee}Q\}}
$$

$$
\mathsf{cut}_1\,\frac{\Box\,\dfrac{\mathsf{sto}\,\dfrac{\Gamma\{\Diamond P, [P]\}}{\Gamma\{\Diamond P, [\uparrow P]\}}}{\Gamma\{\Diamond P, \Box\uparrow P\}} \qquad \mathsf{dec}\,\dfrac{\mathsf{d}_f^\diamond\,\dfrac{\mathsf{rel}\,\dfrac{\mathsf{dec}\,\dfrac{\mathsf{k}_f^\diamond\,\dfrac{\mathsf{gid}\,\dfrac{}{\Gamma\{\Diamond P, [\langle P\rangle, \bar{P}], \Diamond\downarrow\bar{P}\}}}{\Gamma\{\Diamond P, \langle \Diamond P\rangle, [\bar{P}], \Diamond\downarrow\bar{P}\}}}{\Gamma\{\Diamond P, [\bar{P}], \Diamond\downarrow\bar{P}\}}}{\Gamma\{\Diamond P, [\langle\downarrow\bar{P}\rangle], \Diamond\downarrow\bar{P}\}}}{\Gamma\{\Diamond P, \langle\Diamond\downarrow\bar{P}\rangle, \Diamond\downarrow\bar{P}\}}}{\Gamma\{\Diamond P, \Diamond\downarrow\bar{P}\}}}{\Gamma\{\Diamond P\}} \qquad \mathsf{cut}_1\,\dfrac{\Gamma\{\Diamond P, [\Diamond P, \Delta]\} \qquad \mathsf{dec}\,\dfrac{4_f^\diamond\,\dfrac{\mathsf{gid}\,\dfrac{}{\Gamma\{\Diamond P, [\langle\Diamond P\rangle, \Box\bar{P}, \Delta]\}}}{\Gamma\{\Diamond P, \langle\Diamond P\rangle, [\Box\bar{P}, \Delta]\}}}{\Gamma\{\Diamond P, [\Box\bar{P}, \Delta]\}}}{\Gamma\{\Diamond P, [\Delta]\}}
$$

Note that we make a crucial use of cut_1 and Lemma 3.12. ☐

Theorem 3.14 (Completeness). *Let* $\mathsf{X} \subseteq \{\mathsf{d}, \mathsf{t}, \mathsf{b}, 4, 5\}$ *be 45-closed. For any A, if $\lfloor A \rfloor$ is provable in* $\mathsf{KN} + \mathsf{X}^\diamond$, *then A is provable in* $\mathsf{KNF} + \mathsf{X}_f^\diamond$.

Proof. Suppose that we have a proof of $\lfloor A \rfloor$ in $\mathsf{KN} + \mathsf{X}^\diamond$. By Lemma 3.11, there is a proof of A in $\mathsf{KN'} + \mathsf{X}_f^\diamond$. Then, by Lemma 3.13, there is also a proof of A in $\mathsf{KNwF} + \mathsf{X}_f^\diamond + \mathsf{cut}_1$. Finally, using Theorem 3.10, we get a proof in $\mathsf{KNF} + \mathsf{X}_f^\diamond$. ☐

4   The Synthetic System

As already mentioned, the strongly focused system KNF is given as a restriction of KNwF where the dec rule is restricted to neutral contexts. However, the cut-elimination and admissibility theorems (3.9 and 3.10) were proved in the KNwF system and made essential use of the admissibility of weakening by arbitrary formulas, including negative formulas, and of the possibility of applying negative rules even within a positive phase. This freedom simplifies the proofs of the meta-theorems, and leaves them at least a recognizable variant of similar proofs in the non-focused system KN. Of course, thanks to Proposition 3.3, we also have a cut-elimination proof for $\mathsf{KNF} + \mathsf{X}_f^\diamond$, but this is not entirely satisfactory: it is not an internal proof, i.e., a sequence of cut reductions for $\mathsf{KNF} + \mathsf{X}_f^\diamond + \{\mathsf{cut}_1, \mathsf{cut}_2, \mathsf{cut}_3\}$ that stays inside the system.

One possible response to this issue might be to try to redo the cut-elimination using just $\mathsf{KNF} + \mathsf{X}_f^\diamond$, but this quickly gets rather complicated because we no longer have access to the weakening rules (Fig. 4) in the case where the weakened structure contains negative formulas. Indeed, published proofs of similar attempts for the sequent calculus usually solve this problem by adding additional cut rules, which greatly complicates the cut-elimination argument [11,19,28].

$$\preccurlyeq\bar{\vee}\ \frac{\Gamma \preccurlyeq M \quad \Delta \preccurlyeq N}{\Gamma, \Delta \preccurlyeq M \,\bar{\vee}\, N} \qquad \preccurlyeq\bar{\wedge}_1\ \frac{\Gamma \preccurlyeq M}{\Gamma \preccurlyeq M \,\bar{\wedge}\, N} \qquad \preccurlyeq\bar{\wedge}_2\ \frac{\Gamma \preccurlyeq N}{\Gamma \preccurlyeq M \,\bar{\wedge}\, N} \qquad \preccurlyeq\Box\ \frac{\Gamma \preccurlyeq N}{[\Gamma] \preccurlyeq \Box N}$$

$$\preccurlyeq\uparrow\ \frac{}{P \preccurlyeq \uparrow P} \qquad \preccurlyeq\mathsf{id}\ \frac{}{\bar{a} \preccurlyeq \bar{a}}$$

Fig. 7. Synthetic substructure matching

To avoid this complexity, it is better to consider the focused proof system in a *synthetic* form where the logical inference rules for the various connectives are composed as much as possible, so that the proof system itself contains exactly two logical rules: one for a positive and one for a negative *synthetic connective* [6,31]. This synthetic view moreover improves the concept of focusing itself by showing that a focused proof consists of: (1) a selection of a certain *substructure* (the generalization of *subformula*) of the principal formula, and (2) the *contextualization* of that substructure. For positive principal formulas, this contextualization is in the form of a *check* in the surrounding context for other structures, such as dual atoms or nested sequents. For negative principal formulas, on the other hand, contextualization amounts to *asserting* the presence of additional structure in the surrounding context. This design will become clear in the explicit formulation of the synthetic version of KNF—which we call KNS—in the rest of this section.

4.1   Synthetic Substructures

For any negative formula, there is a collection of corresponding nested sequents that represents one of the possible branches taken in a sequence of negative rules applied to the formula. This correspondence is formally given below.

Definition 4.1 (Matching). The nested sequence Γ *matches* the negative formula N, written $\Gamma \preccurlyeq N$, if it is derivable from the rules in Fig. 7.

For the system to follow, we will use two additional sequent-like structures that are not themselves neutral sequents.

Definition 4.2 (Extended Sequents)

- An *inversion sequent* is a structure of the form $\Gamma\{N\}$ where $\Gamma\{\ \}$ is a neutral sequent context.
- A *focused sequent* is a structure of the form $\Gamma\{\langle\Delta\rangle\}$ where $\Gamma\{\ \}$ is a neutral sequent context and Δ is a neutral sequent.

Note that in $\Gamma\{N\}$, there is exactly one occurrence of N as a top-level formula anywhere; likewise, in $\Gamma\{\langle\Delta\rangle\}$, there is a single occurrence of the sub-structure $\langle\Delta\rangle$. Hence, these extended sequent forms uniquely determine their decomposition into context (the $\Gamma\{\ \}$) and the extended entity (the N or the $\langle\Delta\rangle$).

Definition 4.3 (Corresponding Formula). A *corresponding formula* of a neutral or extended sequent Γ, denoted as $\mathrm{f\bar{m}}(\Gamma)$, is a negative formula satisfying:

$$\mathrm{f\bar{m}}(\Gamma, \Delta) \equiv \mathrm{f\bar{m}}(\Gamma) \mathbin{\bar{\vee}} \mathrm{f\bar{m}}(\Delta) \qquad \mathrm{f\bar{m}}(P) \equiv {\uparrow} P \qquad \mathrm{f\bar{m}}(N) \equiv N$$

$$\mathrm{f\bar{m}}([\Gamma]) \equiv \Box\mathrm{f\bar{m}}(\Gamma) \qquad \mathrm{f\bar{m}}(\langle\Delta\rangle) \equiv {\uparrow}\left(\overline{\mathrm{f\bar{m}}(\Delta)}\right)$$

where $N \equiv M$ stands for $({\uparrow}\bar{N} \mathbin{\bar{\vee}} M) \mathbin{\bar{\wedge}} ({\uparrow}\bar{M} \mathbin{\bar{\vee}} N)$.

The system KNS consists of the rules in the first two lines of Fig. 8. For a set $X \subseteq \{\mathsf{d}, \mathsf{t}, \mathsf{b}, 4, 5\}$, we write $X^{\langle\rangle} \subseteq \{\mathsf{d}^{\langle\rangle}, \mathsf{t}^{\langle\rangle}, \mathsf{b}^{\langle\rangle}, 4^{\langle\rangle}, 5^{\langle\rangle}\}$ for the corresponding structural rules in Fig. 8, and KNS+$X^{\langle\rangle}$ for the corresponding system. It becomes clearer that the duality between positive and negative synthetic rules amounts to a meta-quantification over substructures: the positive rule $\mathsf{pos}^{\langle\rangle}$ quantifies existentially over the substructures of $\bar{P}$ and pick one such Δ as a focus in the unique premise, while the negative rule quantifies universally, and so the rule actually consists of one premise for each way in which to prove $\Delta \preccurlyeq N$. Thus, for example, if N is $\bar{a} \mathbin{\bar{\wedge}} \Box(\bar{b} \mathbin{\bar{\vee}} {\uparrow} P)$, then we know that $\bar{a} \preccurlyeq N$ and $[\bar{b}, P] \preccurlyeq N$, so the rule instance in this case is:

$$\mathsf{neg}^{\langle\rangle} \frac{\Gamma\{\bar{a}\} \quad \Gamma\{[\bar{b}, P]\}}{\Gamma\{\bar{a} \mathbin{\bar{\wedge}} \Box(\bar{b} \mathbin{\bar{\vee}} {\uparrow} P)\}}$$

It is instructive to compare KNS $+ X^{\langle\rangle}$ with KNwF $+ X_{\mathsf{f}}^{\circ}$ (and hence also KNF $+ X_{\mathsf{f}}^{\circ}$). In the latter system, the focus $\langle \Diamond P \rangle$ is used to drive the modal rules

$$\text{pos}^{\langle\rangle} \frac{\Delta \preccurlyeq \bar{P} \quad \Gamma\{P, \langle\Delta\rangle\}}{\Gamma\{P\}} \qquad \text{neg}^{\langle\rangle} \frac{\{\Gamma\{\Delta\}\}_{\Delta \preccurlyeq N}}{\Gamma\{N\}}$$

$$\text{split}^{\langle\rangle} \frac{\Gamma\{\langle\Delta_1\rangle\} \quad \Gamma\{\langle\Delta_2\rangle\}}{\Gamma\{\langle\Delta_1, \Delta_2\rangle\}} \qquad \text{id}^{\langle\rangle} \frac{}{\Gamma\{\bar{a}, \langle\bar{a}\rangle\}} \qquad \text{rel}^{\langle\rangle} \frac{\Gamma\{\bar{P}\}}{\Gamma\{\langle P\rangle\}} \qquad \text{k}^{\langle\rangle} \frac{\Gamma\{[\Omega, \langle\Delta\rangle]\}}{\Gamma\{[\Omega], \langle[\Delta]\rangle\}}$$

....

$$\text{d}^{\langle\rangle} \frac{\Gamma\{[\langle\Delta\rangle]\}}{\Gamma\{\langle[\Delta]\rangle\}} \qquad \text{t}^{\langle\rangle} \frac{\Gamma\{\langle\Delta\rangle\}}{\Gamma\{\langle[\Delta]\rangle\}} \qquad \text{b}^{\langle\rangle} \frac{\Gamma\{[\Omega, \langle\Delta\rangle]\}}{\Gamma\{[\Omega, \langle[\Delta]\rangle]\}}$$

$$4^{\langle\rangle} \frac{\Gamma\{[\Omega, \langle[\Delta]\rangle]\}}{\Gamma\{[\Omega], \langle[\Delta]\rangle\}} \qquad 5^{\langle\rangle} \frac{\Gamma\{\langle[\Delta]\rangle\}\{\emptyset\}}{\Gamma\{\emptyset\}\{\langle[\Delta]\rangle\}} \; \text{dp}(\Gamma\{\emptyset\}\{\ \}) \geq 1$$

Fig. 8. Synthetic rules for $\mathsf{KNS} + \mathsf{X}^{\langle\rangle}$. The first two rows constitute KNS.

$\{\text{d}_f^{\diamond}, \text{k}_f^{\diamond}, \text{t}_f^{\diamond}, \text{b}_f^{\diamond}, 4_f^{\diamond}, 5_f^{\diamond}\}$. Such modal rules can be applied only a fixed number of times before $\langle\Diamond P\rangle$ needs to be reduced to $\langle P\rangle$, and logical rules or the identity to be used — which is necessary to finish the proof since foci can never be weakened. Thus, the analysis of P is forced to be interleaved with the modal rules for $\Diamond P$, as shown by the alternation of $\text{d}_f^{\diamond}$ and $\check{\vee}$ in the derivation on the left below. In $\mathsf{KNS}+\mathsf{X}^{\langle\rangle}$, in contrast, the $\text{pos}^{\langle\rangle}$ rule itself performs the analysis of P up front to produce a synthetic substructure; the modal rules $\{\text{k}^{\langle\rangle}, \text{d}^{\langle\rangle}, \text{t}^{\langle\rangle}, \text{b}^{\langle\rangle}, 4^{\langle\rangle}, 5^{\langle\rangle}\}$ then work entirely at the level of focused substructures, as in the derivation on the right below.

$$\text{k}_f^{\diamond} \frac{\text{id} \dfrac{}{\Diamond(p \,\check{\vee}\, \Diamond p), [[\,\langle p\rangle, \bar{p}]]}}{\check{\vee} \dfrac{\Diamond(p \,\check{\vee}\, \Diamond p), [\langle\Diamond p\rangle, [\bar{p}]]}{\text{k}_f^{\diamond} \dfrac{\Diamond(p \,\check{\vee}\, \Diamond p), [\langle p \,\check{\vee}\, \Diamond p\rangle, [\bar{p}]]}{\text{dec} \dfrac{\Diamond(p \,\check{\vee}\, \Diamond p), \langle\Diamond(p \,\check{\vee}\, \Diamond p)\rangle, [[\bar{p}]]}{\Diamond(p \,\check{\vee}\, \Diamond p), [[\bar{p}]]}}}}$$

$$\text{pos}^{\langle\rangle} \frac{[[\bar{p}]] \preccurlyeq \Diamond(p \,\check{\vee}\, \Diamond p) \qquad \text{k}^{\langle\rangle} \dfrac{\text{k}^{\langle\rangle} \dfrac{\text{id}^{\langle\rangle} \dfrac{}{\Diamond(p \,\check{\vee}\, \Diamond p), [[\,\langle\bar{p}\rangle, \bar{p}]]}}{\Diamond(p \,\check{\vee}\, \Diamond p), [\langle[\bar{p}]\rangle, [\bar{p}]]}}{\Diamond(p \,\check{\vee}\, \Diamond p), \langle[[\bar{p}]]\rangle, [[\bar{p}]]}}{\Diamond(p \,\check{\vee}\, \Diamond p), [[\bar{p}]]}$$

Thus, the modal rules of $\mathsf{KNS} + \mathsf{X}^{\langle\rangle}$ are properly seen as *structural* rules rather than logical rules.

4.2 Cut Elimination

Cut elimination for $\mathsf{KNS}+\mathsf{X}^{\langle\rangle}$ is achieved in a similar way to that for $\mathsf{KNwF}+\mathsf{X}_f^{\diamond}$.

Lemma 4.4 (Admissible Rules). *The rules* weak, weak$_f$, cont, $\text{m}^{[]}$ *(shown in Fig. 4), restricted to neutral and extended sequents (as appropriate) are admissible in* $\mathsf{KNS} + \mathsf{X}^{\langle\rangle}$. *Moreover, if* $\mathsf{X} \subseteq \{\text{d}, \text{t}, \text{b}, 4, 5\}$ *is 45-closed, then any rule* $\text{x}^{[]} \in \mathsf{X}^{[]}$ *(see Fig. 5) is admissible in* $\mathsf{KNS} + \mathsf{X}^{\langle\rangle}$.

Proof. By induction on the height of the derivation, analogous to the proofs of Lemmas 3.6 and 3.7. □

Note that we do not allow, e.g., weakening $\Gamma\{\langle\Delta\rangle\}\{\emptyset\}$ to $\Gamma\{\langle\Delta\rangle\}\{N\}$; the latter is, in fact, not even a well-formed KNS focused sequent. Like with KNwF,

$$\mathsf{cut}_1^{\langle\rangle} \frac{\Gamma\{P\} \quad \Gamma\{\bar P\}}{\Gamma\{\emptyset\}} \qquad \mathsf{cut}_2^{\langle\rangle} \frac{\Gamma\{\langle\Delta\rangle\} \quad \Gamma\{\Delta\}}{\Gamma\{\emptyset\}} \qquad \mathsf{cut}_3^{\langle\rangle} \frac{\Gamma\{\langle\Delta\rangle\}\{P\} \quad \Gamma\{\emptyset\}\{\bar P\}}{\Gamma\{\langle\Delta\rangle\}\{\emptyset\}}$$

Fig. 9. Synthetic variants of the cut rule (cf. Fig. 6)

we have three cut rules for KNS, which are shown in Fig. 9. We can now give the synthetic variant of the cut-elimination theorem.

Theorem 4.5. *Let* $\mathsf X \subseteq \{\mathsf d, \mathsf t, \mathsf b, 4, 5\}$ *be 45-closed. Each rule of* $\{\mathsf{cut}_1^{\langle\rangle}, \mathsf{cut}_2^{\langle\rangle}, \mathsf{cut}_3^{\langle\rangle}\}$ *is admissible in* $\mathsf{KNS} + \mathsf X^{\langle\rangle}$.

Proof. The idea of the proof is similar to that of Theorem 3.10, using a reduction similar to that of Lemma 3.9. However, in the synthetic case there is a complication because the inverse of the negative rule $\mathsf{neg}^{\langle\rangle}$ is not admissible in $\mathsf{KNS} + \mathsf X^{\langle\rangle}$. The cut reduction argument therefore has to work at the level of synthetic derivations. We show two illustrative examples here. The first is the case where the cut formula is principal in both derivations:

$$\mathsf{cut}_1^{\langle\rangle} \frac{\mathsf{pos}^{\langle\rangle}\dfrac{\Delta \preccurlyeq \bar P \quad \Gamma\{P, \langle\Delta\rangle\}}{\Gamma\{P\}} \quad \mathsf{neg}^{\langle\rangle}\dfrac{\left\{\begin{array}{c}\mathcal D_\Delta\\ \Gamma\{\Delta\}\end{array}\right\}_{\Delta \preccurlyeq \bar P}}{\Gamma\{\bar P\}}}{\Gamma\{\emptyset\}} \quad \rightsquigarrow \quad \mathsf{cut}_2^{\langle\rangle}\frac{\mathsf{cut}_3^{\langle\rangle}\dfrac{\Gamma\{P, \langle\Delta\rangle\} \quad \Gamma\{\bar P\}}{\Gamma\{\langle\Delta\rangle\}} \quad \begin{array}{c}\mathcal D_\Delta\\ \Gamma\{\Delta\}\end{array}}{\Gamma\{\emptyset\}}$$

The instance of $\mathsf{cut}_3^{\langle\rangle}$ can be reduced because the height is smaller, while that of $\mathsf{cut}_2^{\langle\rangle}$ can be reduced because a $\mathsf{cut}_2^{\langle\rangle}$ can justify a $\mathsf{cut}_1^{\langle\rangle}$ of the same rank. The other illustrative case is for permuting a $\mathsf{cut}_3^{\langle\rangle}$ past a $\mathsf{rel}^{\langle\rangle}$.

$$\mathsf{cut}_3^{\langle\rangle}\frac{\mathsf{rel}^{\langle\rangle}\dfrac{\mathsf{neg}^{\langle\rangle}\dfrac{\left\{\begin{array}{c}\mathcal D_\Delta\\ \Gamma\{\Delta\}\{P\}\end{array}\right\}_{\Delta \preccurlyeq \bar Q}}{\Gamma\{\bar Q\}\{P\}}}{\Gamma\{\langle Q\rangle\}\{P\}} \quad \begin{array}{c}\mathcal D_2\\ \Gamma\{\emptyset\}\{\bar P\}\end{array}}{\Gamma\{\langle Q\rangle\}\{\emptyset\}} \quad \rightsquigarrow \quad \mathsf{rel}^{\langle\rangle}\frac{\mathsf{neg}^{\langle\rangle}\dfrac{\left\{\begin{array}{c}\mathsf{cut}_1^{\langle\rangle}\dfrac{\begin{array}{c}\mathcal D_\Delta\\ \Gamma\{\Delta\}\{P\}\end{array} \quad \mathsf{weak}\dfrac{\begin{array}{c}\mathcal D_2\\ \Gamma\{\emptyset\}\{\bar P\}\end{array}}{\Gamma\{\Delta\}\{\bar P\}}}{\Gamma\{\Delta\}\{\emptyset\}}\end{array}\right\}_{\Delta \preccurlyeq \bar Q}}{\Gamma\{\bar Q\}\{\emptyset\}}}{\Gamma\{\langle Q\rangle\}\{\emptyset\}}$$

The instance of weak is justified by Lemma 4.4. The remainder of the cases of the proof have to be adjusted similarly. The full proof can be found in [9, Theorem 4.5]. $\square$

It is worth remarking that this cut-elimination proof did not have to mention any logical connectives, and was instead able to factorize all logical reasoning in terms of the matching. This means that the matching judgement can be modified at will without affecting the nature of the cut argument, as long as it leaves the structure of nested sequents untouched. This makes our result modular in yet another way, in addition to the modularity obtained by means of the structural rules for foci. Indeed, we can obtain a similarly synthetic version of identity reduction (Lemma 3.12).

Lemma 4.6 (Identity Reduction). *The following rule is derivable in* KNS.

$$\mathsf{sid}^{\langle\rangle} \frac{}{\Gamma\{\langle\Delta\rangle, \Delta\}}$$

Proof. By induction on the structure of the focus, $\langle\Delta\rangle$. The full proof can be found in [9, Lemma 4.6]. □

Showing $\mathsf{KNS} + \mathsf{X}^{\langle\rangle}$ sound and complete with respect to $\mathsf{KN} + \mathsf{X}^\circ$ is fairly straightforward and the details are omitted here. Soundness follows directly from replacing the KNS sequent $\Gamma\{\langle\Delta\rangle\}$ with the KNF sequent $\Gamma\{\langle\overline{\mathsf{fm}}(\Delta)\rangle\}$ and then interpreting the $\mathsf{KNS}+\mathsf{X}^{\langle\rangle}$ proof in $\mathsf{KNF}+\mathsf{X}^\circ_\mathsf{f}$, using matching derivation (Fig. 7) to determine how to choose between the two $\check{\mathsf{v}}$ rules. For completeness, we can follow the strategy of Lemma 3.13 nearly unchanged. However, like with the cut-elimination proof, we have to avoid appeals to weakening with negative formulas by using the synthetic form of $\mathsf{neg}^{\langle\rangle}$.

5 Perspectives

We have presented strongly focused and synthetic systems for all modal logics in the classical S5-cube. We used the formalism of nested sequents as carrier, but we are confident that something similar can be achieved for hypersequents, for example based on the work of Lellmann [17]. We chose nested sequents over hypersequents for two reasons. First, the formula interpretation of a nested sequent is the same for all logics in the S5-cube, which simplifies the presentation of the meta-theory. Second, due to the close correspondence between nested sequents and prefixed tableaux [12] we can from our work directly extract *focused tableau systems* for modal logics. Furthermore, even though we spoke in this paper only about classical modal logic, we are confident that the same results can also be obtained for the intuitionistic variant of the modal S5-cube [29], if we start from the non-focused systems in [30].

One extension that would be worth considering would be relaxing the restriction that there can be at most one focus in a KNF or KNS proof. Allowing multiple foci would take us from ordinary focusing to multi-focusing, which is well known to reveal more parallelism in sequent proofs [10]. It has been shown that a certain well chosen multi-focusing system can yield syntactically canonical representatives of equivalence classes of sequent proofs for classical predicate logic [8]. Extending this approach to the modal case seems promising.

References

1. Andreoli, J.-M.: Logic programming with focusing proofs in linear logic. J. Logic Comput. **2**(3), 297–347 (1992)
2. Avron, A.: The method of hypersequents in the proof theory of propositional non-classical logics. In: Logic: From Foundations to Applications: European Logic Colloquium, pp. 1–32. Clarendon Press (1996)
3. Belnap Jr., N.D.: Display logic. J. Philos. Logic **11**, 375–417 (1982)
4. Brock-Nannestad, T., Schürmann, C.: Focused natural deduction. In: Fermüller, C.G., Voronkov, A. (eds.) LPAR-17. LNCS, vol. 6397, pp. 157–171. Springer, Heidelberg (2010)
5. Brünnler, K.: Deep sequent systems for modal logic. Arch. Math. Logic **48**(6), 551–577 (2009)
6. Chaudhuri, K.: Focusing strategies in the sequent calculus of synthetic connectives. In: Cervesato, I., Veith, H., Voronkov, A. (eds.) LPAR 2008. LNCS (LNAI), vol. 5330, pp. 467–481. Springer, Heidelberg (2008)
7. Chaudhuri, K., Guenot, N., Straßburger, L.: The focused calculus of structures. In: Computer Science Logic: 20th Annual Conference of the EACSL. Leibniz International Proceedings in Informatics (LIPIcs), pp. 159–173. Schloss Dagstuhl-Leibniz-Zentrum für Informatik, Sept 2011
8. Chaudhuri, K., Hetzl, S., Miller, D.: A multi-focused proof system isomorphic to expansion proofs. J. Logic Comput., June 2014. doi:10.1093/logcom/exu030
9. Chaudhuri, K., Marin, S., Straßburger, L.: Focused and Synthetic Nested Sequents. Technical report, Inria (2016). https://hal.inria.fr/hal-01251722
10. Chaudhuri, K., Miller, D., Saurin, A.: Canonical sequent proofs via multi-focusing. In: Ausiello, G., Karhumäki, J., Mauri, G., Ong, L. (eds.) IFIP-TCS 2008. IFIP, vol. 273, pp. 383–396. Springer, Heidelberg (2008)
11. Chaudhuri, K., Pfenning, F., Price, G.: A logical characterization of forward and backward chaining in the inverse method. J. Autom. Reasoning **40**(2–3), 133–177 (2008)
12. Fitting, M.: Prefixed tableaus and nested sequents. Ann. Pure Appl. Logic **163**, 291–313 (2012)
13. Garson, J.: Modal logic. Stanford University, In The Stanford Encyclopedia of Philosophy (2008)
14. Kashima, R.: Cut-free sequent calculi for some tense logics. Stud. Logica. **53**(1), 119–136 (1994)
15. Laurent, O.: Étude de la Polarisation en Logique. Ph.D. thesis, Univiversit Aix-Marseille II (2002)
16. Laurent, O.: A proof of the focalization property in linear logic (2004) (Unpublished note)
17. Lellmann, B.: Axioms vs hypersequent rules with context restrictions: theory and applications. In: Demri, S., Kapur, D., Weidenbach, C. (eds.) IJCAR 2014. LNCS, vol. 8562, pp. 307–321. Springer, Heidelberg (2014)
18. Lellmann, B., Pimentel, E.: Proof search in nested sequent calculi. In: Davis, M., Fehnker, A., McIver, A., Voronkov, A. (eds.) LPAR-20 2015. LNCS, vol. 9450, pp. 558–574. Springer, Heidelberg (2015). doi:10.1007/978-3-662-48899-7_39
19. Liang, C., Miller, D.: Focusing and polarization in linear, intuitionistic, and classical logics. Theoret. Comput. Sci. **410**(46), 4747–4768 (2009)
20. Marin, S., Straßburger, L.: Label-free modular systems for classical and intuitionistic modal logics. In: Advances in Modal Logic (AIML-10) (2014)

21. McLaughlin, S., Pfenning, F.: Imogen: focusing the polarized inverse method for intuitionistic propositional logic. In: Cervesato, I., Veith, H., Voronkov, A. (eds.) LPAR 2008. LNCS (LNAI), vol. 5330, pp. 174–181. Springer, Heidelberg (2008)
22. Miller, D., Nadathur, G., Pfenning, F., Scedrov, A.: Uniform proofs as a foundation for logic programming. Ann. Pure Appl. Logic **51**, 125–157 (1991)
23. Miller, D., Volpe, M.: Focused labeled proof systems for modal logic. In: Davis, M., Fehnker, A., McIver, A., Voronkov, A. (eds.) LPAR-20 2015. LNCS, vol. 9450, pp. 266–280. Springer, Heidelberg (2015). doi:10.1007/978-3-662-48899-7_19
24. Negri, S.: Proof analysis in modal logic. J. Philos. Logic **34**(5–6), 507–544 (2005)
25. Pfenning, F., Davies, R.: A judgmental reconstruction of modal logic. Math. Struct. Comput. Sci. **11**, 511–540 (2001). Notes to an invited talk at the Workshop on Intuitionistic Modal Logics and Applications (IMLA 1999)
26. Poggiolesi, F.: The method of tree-hypersequents for modal propositional logic. In: Makinson, D., Malinowski, J., Wansing, H. (eds.) Towards Mathematical Philosophy. Trends in Logic, vol. 28, pp. 31–51. Springer, New York (2009)
27. Reed, J., Pfenning, F.: Focus-preserving embeddings of substructural logics in intuitionistic logic. Draft manuscript, January 2010
28. Simmons, R.J.: Structural focalization. ACM Trans. Comput. Log. **15**(3), 21:1–21:33 (2014)
29. Simpson, A.: The proof theory and semantics of intuitionistic modal logic. Ph.D thesis, University of Edinburgh (1994)
30. Straßburger, L.: Cut elimination in nested sequents for intuitionistic modal logics. In: Pfenning, F. (ed.) FOSSACS 2013 (ETAPS 2013). LNCS, vol. 7794, pp. 209–224. Springer, Heidelberg (2013)
31. Zeilberger, N.: Focusing and higher-order abstract syntax. In: Proceedings of the 35th ACM SIGPLAN-SIGACT Symposium on Principles of Programming Languages, POPL, San Francisco, California, USA, January 7–12, pp. 359–369. ACM (2008)

Strong Normalizability as a Finiteness Structure via the Taylor Expansion of λ-terms

Michele Pagani[1]([⊠]), Christine Tasson[1]([⊠]), and Lionel Vaux[2]([⊠])

[1] Université Paris Diderot, CNRS, IRIF UMR 8243, 75205 Paris, France
{michele.pagani,christine.tasson}@pps.univ-paris-diderot.fr
[2] Aix Marseille Université, CNRS, Centrale Marseille, I2M UMR 7373,
13453 Marseille, France
lionel.vaux@univ-amu.fr

Abstract. In the folklore of linear logic, a common intuition is that the structure of finiteness spaces, introduced by Ehrhard, semantically reflects the strong normalization property of cut-elimination.

We make this intuition formal in the context of the non-deterministic λ-calculus by introducing a finiteness structure on resource terms, which is such that a λ-term is strongly normalizing iff the support of its Taylor expansion is finitary.

An application of our result is the existence of a normal form for the Taylor expansion of any strongly normalizable non-deterministic λ-term.

1 Introduction

It is well-known that sets and relations can be presented as a category of modules and linear functions over the boolean semi-ring, giving one of the simplest semantics of linear logic. In [10] (see also [9]), it is shown how to generalize this construction to any complete[1] semi-ring $\mathcal{R}$ and yet obtain a model of linear logic. In particular, the composition of two matrices $\phi \in \mathcal{R}^{A \times B}$ and $\psi \in \mathcal{R}^{B \times C}$ is given by the usual matrix multiplication:

$$(\phi; \psi)_{a,c} := \sum_{b \in B} \phi_{a,b} \cdot \psi_{b,c} \tag{1}$$

The semi-ring $\mathcal{R}$ must be complete because the above sum might be infinite. This is an issue, because it prevents us from considering standard vector spaces, which are usually constructed over "non-complete" fields like reals or complexes.

In order to overcome this problem, Ehrhard introduced the notion of finiteness space [3]. A *finiteness space* is a pair of a set A and a set $\mathfrak{A}$ (called *finiteness structure* in Definition 7) of subsets of A which is closed under a notion of duality. The point is that, for any field $\mathcal{K}$ (resp. any semi-ring), the set of vectors in $\mathcal{K}^A$ whose support[2] is in $\mathfrak{A}$ constitutes a vector space (resp. a module) over $\mathcal{K}$.

Supported by French ANR Project Coquas (number ANR 12 JS02 006 01).

[1] A semi-ring is complete if any sum, even infinite, is well-defined.

[2] The support of $v \in \mathcal{K}^A$ is the set of those $a \in A$ such that the scalar v_a is non-null.

© Springer-Verlag Berlin Heidelberg 2016
B. Jacobs and C. Löding (Eds.): FOSSACS 2016, LNCS 9634, pp. 408–423, 2016.
DOI: 10.1007/978-3-662-49630-5_24

Moreover, any two matrices $\phi \in \mathcal{K}^{A \times B}$ and $\psi \in \mathcal{K}^{B \times C}$ whose supports are in resp. $\mathfrak{A} \multimap \mathfrak{B}$ and $\mathfrak{B} \multimap \mathfrak{C}$ (the finiteness structures associated with the linear arrow) compose, because the duality condition on the supports makes the terms in the sum of Eq. (1) be zero almost everywhere. This gives rise to a category which is a model of linear logic and its differential extension.

The notion of finiteness space seems strictly related to the property of normalization. Already in [3], it is remarked that the coKleisli category of the exponential comonad is a model of simply typed λ-calculus, but it is not cpo-enriched and thus cannot interpret (at least in a standard way) fixed-point combinators, so neither PCF nor untyped λ-calculus. Moreover, in the setting of differential nets, Pagani showed that the property of having a finitary interpretation corresponds to an acyclicity criterion (called *visible acyclicity* [12]) which entails the normalization property of the cut-elimination procedure [11], while there are examples of visibly cyclic differential nets which do not normalize.

The goal of this paper is to shed further light on the link between finiteness spaces and normalization, this time considering the non-deterministic untyped λ-calculus. Since we deal with λ-terms and not with linear logic proofs (or differential nets), we will speak about formal power series rather than matrices at the semantical level. This corresponds to move from the morphisms of a linear category to those of its coKleisli construction. Moreover, following [7], we describe the monomials of these power series as *resource terms* in normal form. The benefit of this setting is that the interpretation of a λ-term M as a power series $[\![M]\!]$ can be decomposed in two distinct steps: first, the term M is associated with a formal series M^* of resource terms possibly with redexes, called the *Taylor expansion* of M (see Table 1a); second, one reduces each resource term t appearing in the support $\mathcal{T}(M)$ of M^* into a normal form $\mathrm{NF}(t)$ and sum up all the results, that is (M_t^* denotes the coefficient of t in M^*):

$$[\![M]\!] = \sum_{t \in \mathcal{T}(M)} M_t^* \cdot \mathrm{NF}(t) \tag{2}$$

The issue about the convergence of infinite sums appears in Eq. (2) because there might be an infinite number of resource terms in $\mathcal{T}(M)$ reducing to the same normal form and thus possibly giving infinite coefficients to the formal series $[\![M]\!]$. Ehrhard and Regnier proved in [7] that this is not the case for deterministic λ-terms, however the situation gets worse in presence of non-deterministic primitives. If we allow sums $M + N$ representing potential reduction to M or N, then one can construct terms evaluating to a variable y an infinite number of times, like (where Θ denotes Turing's fixed-point combinator):

$$(\Theta)\, \lambda x.(x + y) \to_\beta^* (\Theta)\, \lambda x.(x + y) + y \to_\beta^* (\Theta)\, \lambda x.(x + y) + y + y \to_\beta^* \dots \tag{3}$$

We postpone to Examples 1 and 4 a more detailed discussion of $(\Theta)\, \lambda x.(x + y)$, however we can already guess that this interplay between infinite reductions and non-determinism may produce infinite coefficients.

One can then wonder whether there are interesting classes of terms where the coefficients of the associated power series can be kept finite. Ehrhard proved

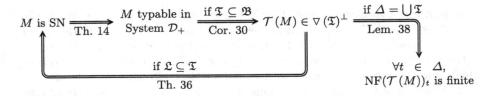

Fig. 1. Main results of the paper

in [4] that the terms typable by a non-deterministic variant of Girard's System $\mathcal{F}$ have always finite coefficients. A by-product of our results is Corollary 39, which is a generalization of Ehrhard's result: every strongly normalizable non-deterministic λ-term can be interpreted by a power series with finite coefficients.

The main focus of our paper is however in the means used for obtaining this result rather than on the result itself. The proof in [4] is based on a finiteness structure $\mathfrak{S}$ over the set of resource terms Δ, such that any term M typable in System $\mathcal{F}$ has the support $\mathcal{T}(M)$ of its Taylor expansion in $\mathfrak{S}$. We show that this method can be both generalized and strengthened in order to characterize strong normalization via finiteness structures. Namely, we give sufficient conditions on a finiteness structure $\mathfrak{S}$ over Δ such that for every non-deterministic λ-term M: (i) if M is strongly normalizable, then $\mathcal{T}(M) \in \mathfrak{S}$ (Corollary 30); (ii) if $\mathcal{T}(M) \in \mathfrak{S}$, then M is strongly normalizable (Theorem 36).

Contents. Section 2 gives the preliminary definitions: the non-deterministic λ-calculus, its Taylor expansion into formal series of resource terms and the notion of finiteness structure. The proof of Item (i) splits into Sects. 3 and 4, using an intersection type system (Table 2) for characterizing strong normalization. Section 5 gives the proof of Item (ii) and Sect. 6 concludes with Corollary 39 about the finiteness of the coefficients of the power series of strongly normalizable terms. Figure 1 sums up the main results of the paper.

2   Preliminaries

2.1   Non-deterministic λ-calculus Λ_+

The non-deterministic λ-calculus is defined by the following grammar[3]:

$$\lambda\text{-terms } \Lambda_+ : \qquad M := x \mid \lambda x.M \mid (M)\,M \mid M + M$$

subject to α-equivalence and to the following identities:

$$M + N = N + M, \qquad (M + N) + P = M + (N + P),$$

$$\lambda x.(M + N) = \lambda x.M + \lambda x.N, (M + N)\,P = (M)\,P + (N)\,P.$$

---

[3] We use Krivine's notation with the standard conventions, see [8] for reference.

The last two equalities state that abstraction is a linear operation (i.e. commutes with sums) while application is linear only in the function but not in the argument (i.e. $(P)(M + N) \neq (P) M + (P) N$). Notice also that the sum is not idempotent: $M + M \neq M$. This is a crucial feature for making a difference between terms reducing to a value once, twice, more times or an infinite number of times (see the discussion about Eq. (3) in the Introduction).

Although this follows an old intuition from linear logic, the first extension of the λ-calculus with (a priori non idempotent) sums subject to these identities was, as far as we know, the differential λ-calculus of Ehrhard and Regnier [5]. This feature is now quite standard in the literature following this revival of quantitative semantics.

The (capture avoiding) substitution of a term for a variable is defined as usual and β-reduction $\to_\beta$ is defined as the context closure of:

$$(\lambda x.M) N \to_\beta M [N/x].$$

We denote as $\to_\beta^*$ the reflexive-transitive closure of $\to_\beta$.

Example 1. Some λ-terms which will be used in the following are:

$$\boldsymbol{\Delta} := \lambda x. (x) x, \qquad \boldsymbol{\Omega} := (\boldsymbol{\Delta}) \boldsymbol{\Delta}, \qquad \boldsymbol{\Delta_3} := \lambda x. (x) xx, \qquad \boldsymbol{\Omega_3} := (\boldsymbol{\Delta_3}) \boldsymbol{\Delta_3},$$

$$\boldsymbol{\Theta} := (\lambda xy. (y) (x) xy) \lambda xy. (y) (x) xy.$$

The term $\boldsymbol{\Omega}$ is the prototypical diverging term, reducing to itself in one single β-step. $\boldsymbol{\Omega_3}$ is another example of diverging term, producing terms of greater and greater size: $\boldsymbol{\Omega_3} \to_\beta (\boldsymbol{\Omega_3}) \boldsymbol{\Delta_3} \to_\beta (\boldsymbol{\Omega_3}) \boldsymbol{\Delta_3}\boldsymbol{\Delta_3} \to_\beta \ldots$ It will be used in Remark 37 to prove the subtlety of characterizing strong normalization with finiteness spaces. The Turing fixed-point combinator $\boldsymbol{\Theta}$ has been used in the Introduction to construct $(\boldsymbol{\Theta}) \lambda x.(x + y)$ as an example of non-deterministic λ-term morally reducing to normal forms with infinite coefficients (Eq. (3)). Notice that, by abstraction linearity, $(\boldsymbol{\Theta}) \lambda x.(x+y) = (\boldsymbol{\Theta}) (\lambda x.x+\lambda x.y)$, however $(\boldsymbol{\Theta}) (\lambda x.x+\lambda x.y) \neq (\boldsymbol{\Theta}) \lambda x.x+(\boldsymbol{\Theta}) \lambda x.y$, because application is not linear in the argument. This distinction is crucial: the latter term reduces to $((\boldsymbol{\Theta}) \lambda x.x) + y$, with $(\boldsymbol{\Theta}) \lambda x.x$ reducing to itself without producing any further occurence of y.

2.2   Resource Calculus $\boldsymbol{\Delta}$ and Taylor Expansion

The syntax. Resource terms and *bags* are given by mutual induction:

resource terms Δ : $s := x \mid \lambda x.s \mid \langle s \rangle \bar{s}$ bags $\Delta^!$: $\bar{s} := 1 \mid s \cdot \bar{s}$

subject to both α-equivalence and permutativity of $(\cdot)$: we most often write $[s_1, \ldots, s_n]$ for $s_1 \cdot (\cdots (s_n \cdot 1) \cdots)$ and then $[s_1, \ldots, s_n] = [s_{\sigma(1)}, \ldots, s_{\sigma(n)}]$ for any permutation σ. In other words, bags are finite multisets of terms.

Linear Extension. Let $\mathcal{R}$ be a rig (a.k.a. semi-ring). Of particular interest are the rigs $\mathbb{B} := (\{0,1\}, \max, \min)$ of booleans, $\mathbb{N} := (\mathbf{N}, +, \times)$ of non-negative

Table 1. Definition of the Taylor expansion ( )* and of its support $\mathcal{T}$ ( )

$$x^* := x \qquad\qquad\qquad \mathcal{T}(x) := \{x\}$$

$$(\lambda x.M)^* := \lambda x.M^* \qquad\qquad \mathcal{T}(\lambda x.M) := \{\lambda x.s; \ s \in \mathcal{T}(M)\}$$

$$((M)\,N)^* := \sum_{n \in \mathbf{N}} \frac{1}{n!} \langle M^* \rangle\,(N^*)^n \qquad \mathcal{T}((M)\,N) := \left\{ \langle s \rangle\,\bar{t}; \ s \in \mathcal{T}(M), \bar{t} \in \mathcal{T}(N)^! \right\}$$

$$(M+N)^* := M^* + N^* \qquad\qquad \mathcal{T}(M+N) := \mathcal{T}(M) \cup \mathcal{T}(N)$$

(a) expansion ( )* $: \Lambda_+ \mapsto \mathbb{Q}[\![\Delta]\!]$	(b) support $\mathcal{T}$ ( ) $: \Lambda_+ \mapsto \mathbb{B}[\![\Delta]\!]$

integers and $\mathbb{Q} := (\mathbf{Q}, +, \times)$ of rational numbers. We denote as $\mathcal{R}[\![\Delta]\!]$ (resp. $\mathcal{R}[\![\Delta^!]\!]$) the set of all formal (finite or infinite) linear combinations of resource terms (resp. bags) with coefficients in $\mathcal{R}$. If $a \in \mathcal{R}[\![\Delta]\!]$ (resp. $\bar{a} \in \mathcal{R}[\![\Delta^!]\!]$) and $s \in \Delta$ (resp. $\bar{s} \in \Delta^!$), then $a_s \in \mathcal{R}$ (resp. $\bar{a}_{\bar{s}} \in \mathcal{R}$) denotes the coefficient of s in a (resp. $\bar{s}$ in $\bar{a}$). As is well-known, $\mathcal{R}[\![\Delta]\!]$ is endowed with a structure of $\mathcal{R}$-module, where addition and scalar multiplication are defined component-wise, i.e. for $a, b \in \mathcal{R}[\![\Delta]\!]$ and $\alpha \in \mathcal{R}$: $(a+b)_s := a_s + b_s$, and $(\alpha a)_s := \alpha a_s$. We will write $|a| \subseteq \Delta$ for the support of a: $|a| = \{s \in \Delta; \ a_s \neq 0\}$.

Moreover, each resource calculus constructor extends to $\mathcal{R}[\![\Delta]\!]$ component-wise, i.e. for any $a, a_1, \ldots, a_n \in \mathcal{R}[\![\Delta]\!]$ and $\bar{a} \in \mathcal{R}[\![\Delta^!]\!]$, we set:

$$\lambda x.a := \textstyle\sum_{s \in \Delta} a_s \lambda x.s, \qquad \langle a \rangle\,\bar{a} := \textstyle\sum_{s \in \Delta, \bar{s} \in \Delta^!} a_s \bar{a}_{\bar{s}} \langle s \rangle\,\bar{s},$$

$$[a_1, \ldots, a_n] := \textstyle\sum_{s_1, \ldots, s_n \in \Delta} (a_1)_{s_1} \cdots (a_n)_{s_n} [s_1, \ldots, s_n].$$

Notice that the last formula is coherent with the notation of the concatenation of bags as a product since it expresses a distributivity law. In particular, we denote $a^n := \underbrace{[a, \ldots, a]}_{n}$ and if $\mathbb{Q} \subseteq \mathcal{R}$, $a^! := \sum_{n \in \mathbf{N}} \frac{1}{n!} a^n$.

In the case $\mathcal{R} = \mathbb{B}$, notice that $\mathbb{B}[\![\Delta]\!]$ is the power-set lattice $\mathfrak{P}(\Delta)$, so that we can use the set-theoretical notation: e.g. writing $s \in a$ instead of $a_s \neq 0$, or $a \cup b$ for $a + b$. Also, in that case the preceding formulas lead to: for $a, b \subseteq \Delta$, $t \in \Delta$, $\bar{a} \subseteq \Delta^!$: $\lambda x.a := \{\lambda x.s; \ s \in a\}$, $a^! := \{[s_1, \cdots, s_n]; \ s_1, \cdots, s_n \in a\}$, $\langle t \rangle\,\bar{a} := \{\langle t \rangle\,\bar{s}; \ \bar{s} \in \bar{a}\}$ and $\langle a \rangle\,\bar{a} := \bigcup \{\langle s \rangle\,\bar{a}; \ s \in a\}$.

Taylor expansion. Ehrhard and Regnier have used in [7] the rig of rational numbers to express the λ-terms as formal combinations in $\mathbb{Q}[\![\Delta]\!]$. We refer to this translation ( )* $: \Lambda_+ \mapsto \mathbb{Q}[\![\Delta]\!]$ as the *Taylor expansion* and we recall it in Table 1a by structural induction. The supports of these expansions can be seen as a map $\mathcal{T}$ ( ) $: \Lambda_+ \mapsto \mathbb{B}[\![\Delta]\!]$ and directly defined by induction as in Table 1b.

Example 2. From the above definitions we have:

$$\Delta^* = \sum_n \frac{1}{n!} \lambda x.\langle x \rangle\,x^n, \qquad \Delta_3{}^* = \sum_{n,m} \frac{1}{n!m!} \lambda x.\langle\langle x \rangle\,x^n \rangle\,x^m.$$

Let us denote as δ_n (resp. $\delta_{n,m}$) the term $\lambda x. \langle x \rangle \, x^n$ (resp. $\lambda x. \langle \langle x \rangle \, x^n \rangle \, x^m$). We can then write:

$$\Omega^* = \sum_k \frac{1}{k!} \sum_{n_0,\ldots,n_k} \frac{1}{n_0! \cdots n_k!} \langle \delta_{n_0} \rangle \, [\delta_{n_1},\ldots,\delta_{n_k}], \tag{4}$$

$$\Omega_3{}^* = \sum_k \frac{1}{k!} \sum_{\substack{n_0,\ldots,n_k \\ m_0,\ldots,m_k}} \frac{1}{n_0! m_0! \cdots n_k! m_k!} \langle \delta_{n_0,m_0} \rangle \, [\delta_{n_1,m_1},\ldots,\delta_{n_k,m_k}]. \tag{5}$$

It is clear that the resource terms appearing with non-zero coefficients in M^* describe the structure of M taking an explicit number of times the argument of each application, and this recursively. The rôle of the rational coefficients will be clearer once defined the reduction rules over Δ (see Example 5).

Operational Semantics. Let us write $\deg_x(t)$ for the number of free occurrences of a variable x in a resource term t. We define the *differential substitution* of a variable x with a bag $[s_1,\ldots,s_n]$ in a resource term t, denoted $\partial_x t \cdot [s_1,\ldots,s_n]$: it is a finite formal sum of resource terms, which is zero whenever $\deg_x(t) \neq n$; otherwise it is the sum of all possible terms obtained by linearly replacing each free occurrence of x with exactly one s_i, for $i = 1,\ldots,n$. Formally,

$$\partial_x t \cdot [s_1,\ldots,s_n] := \begin{cases} \sum_{f \in \mathfrak{S}_n} t \left[s_{f(1)}/x_1,\ldots,s_{f(n)}/x_n \right] & \text{if } \deg_x(t) = n, \\ 0 & \text{otherwise,} \end{cases} \tag{6}$$

where $\mathfrak{S}_n$ is the group of permutations over $n = \{1,\ldots,n\}$ and $x_1,\ldots,x_n$ is any enumeration of the free occurrences of x in t, so that $t \left[s_{f(i)}/x_i \right]$ denotes the term obtained from t by replacing the i-th free occurrence of x with $s_{f(i)}$. Then, we give a linear extension of the differential substitution: if $a \in \mathcal{R}[\![\Delta]\!]$ and $\bar{a} \in \mathcal{R}[\![\Delta^!]\!]$, we set: $\partial_x a \cdot \bar{a} = \sum_{t \in \Delta, \bar{s} \in \Delta^!} a_t \, \bar{a}_{\bar{s}} \partial_x t \cdot \bar{s}$.

The resource reduction $\to_r$ is then the smallest relation satisfying:

$$\langle \lambda x.t \rangle \, [s_1,\ldots,s_n] \to_r \partial_x t \cdot [s_1,\ldots,s_n]$$

and moreover linear and compatible with the resource calculus constructors. Spelling out these two last conditions: for any $t,u \in \Delta$, $\bar{s} \in \Delta^!$, $a,b \in \mathcal{R}[\![\Delta]\!]$, $\alpha \in \mathcal{R} \setminus \{0\}$, whenever $t \to_r a$, we have: (compatibility) $\lambda x.t \to_r \lambda x.a$, $\langle t \rangle \, \bar{s} \to_r \langle a \rangle \, \bar{s}$, $\langle u \rangle \, t \cdot \bar{s} \to_r \langle u \rangle \, a \cdot \bar{s}$, and (linearity) $\alpha t + b \to_r \alpha a + b$.

Proposition 3 ([7]). *Resource reduction $\to_r$ is confluent over the whole $\mathcal{R}[\![\Delta]\!]$ and it is normalizing on the sums in $\mathcal{R}[\![\Delta]\!]$ having a finite support.*

Proposition 3 shows that any single resource term $t \in \Delta$ has a unique normal form that we can denote as $\mathrm{NF}(t)$. What about possibly infinite linear combinations in $\mathcal{R}[\![\Delta]\!]$? We would like to extend the normal form operator component-wise, as follows:

$$\mathrm{NF}(a) := \sum_{t \in \Delta} a_t \cdot \mathrm{NF}(t) \tag{7}$$

Example 4. The sum in Eq. (7) can be undefined for general $a \in \mathcal{R}[\![\Delta]\!]$. Take $a = \lambda x.x + \langle \lambda x.x \rangle \, [\lambda x.x] + \langle \lambda x.x \rangle \, [\langle \lambda x.x \rangle \, [\lambda x.x]] + \ldots$: any single term of this sum reduces to $\lambda x.x$, hence $\mathrm{NF}(a)_{\lambda x.x}$ is infinite.

Another example is given by the Taylor expansion of the term in Eq. (3): one can check that the sum defining $\mathrm{NF}\big(((\boldsymbol{\Theta}) \, \lambda x.(x+y))^*\big)_y$ following Eq. (7) is infinite because, for all $n \in \mathbb{N}$, there is a resource term of the form $\langle t_n \rangle \, [(\lambda x.x)^n, \lambda x.y] \in \mathcal{T}\,((\boldsymbol{\Theta}) \, \lambda x.(x+y))$, reducing to y. A closer inspection of the resulting coefficients (that we do not develop here) moreover shows that this infinite sum has unbounded partial sums in $\mathbb{Q}$, hence it diverges in general.

In fact, Corollary 39 ensures that if a is the Taylor expansion of a strongly normalizing non-deterministic λ-term then Eq. (7) is well-defined.

Example 5. Recall the expansions of Example 2 and consider $((\boldsymbol{\Delta}) \, \lambda x.x)^* = \sum_{n,k} \frac{1}{n!k!} \langle \lambda x. \langle x \rangle \, [x^n] \rangle \, [(\lambda x.x)^k]$. The resource reduction applied to a term of this sum gives zero except for $k = n+1$; in this latter case we get $(n+1)! \, \langle \lambda x.x \rangle \, [(\lambda x.x)^n]$. Hence we have: $((\boldsymbol{\Delta}) \, \lambda x.x)^* \to_r \sum_n \frac{1}{n!} \langle \lambda x.x \rangle \, [(\lambda x.x)^n]$, because the coefficient $(n+1)!$ generated by the reduction step is erased by the fraction $\frac{1}{k!}$ in the definition of Taylor expansion. Then, the term $\langle \lambda x.x \rangle \, [(\lambda x.x)^n]$ reduces to zero but for $n = 1$, in the latter case giving $\lambda x.x$. So we have: $\mathrm{NF}(((\boldsymbol{\Delta}) \, \lambda x.x)^*) = \lambda x.x = (\mathrm{NF}((\boldsymbol{\Delta}) \, \lambda x.x))^*$.

The commutation between computing normal forms and Taylor expansions has been proven in general for deterministic λ-terms [6][4] and witnesses the solidity of the definitions. The general case for Λ_+ is still an open issue.

Example 6. Recall the notation of Eq. (4) from Example 2 expressing the sum $\boldsymbol{\Omega}^*$. All terms with $n_0 \neq k+1$ reduce to zero in one step. For $n_0 = k+1$, we have that a single term rewrites to $\sum_{f \in \mathfrak{S}_k} \langle \delta_{n_{f(1)}} \rangle \, [\delta_{n_{f(2)}}, \ldots, \delta_{n_{f(k)}}]$, which is a sum of terms still in $\mathcal{T}(\boldsymbol{\Omega})$, but with smaller size w.r.t. the redex. Therefore, every term of $\boldsymbol{\Omega}^*$ eventually reduces to zero, after a reduction sequence whose length depends on the initial size of the term, and whose elements are sums with supports in $\mathcal{T}(\boldsymbol{\Omega})$. This is in some sense the way Taylor expansion models the unbounded resource consumption of the loop $\boldsymbol{\Omega} \to_\beta \boldsymbol{\Omega}$ in λ-calculus.

We postpone the discussion of the reduction of $\boldsymbol{\Omega_3}^*$ until Remark 37.

2.3   Finiteness Structures Induced by Antireduction

Let us get back to Eq. (7), and consider it pointwise: for all $s \in \Delta$ in normal form, we want to set $\mathrm{NF}(a)_s = \sum_{t \in \Delta} a_t \cdot \mathrm{NF}(t)_s$. Notice that this series can be obtained as the inner product between a and the vector $\uparrow\!s$ with $(\uparrow\!s)_t = \mathrm{NF}(t)_s$: one can think of s as a test, that a passes whenever the sum converges.

There is one very simple condition that one can impose on a formal series to ensure its convergence: just assume there are finitely many non-zero terms. This seemingly dull remark is in fact the starting point of the definition of finiteness

---

[4] The statement proven in [6] is actually more general, because it considers (possibly infinite) Böhm trees instead of the normal forms.

spaces, introduced by Ehrhard [3] and discussed in the Introduction. The basic construction is that of a finiteness structure:

Definition 7 ([3]). *Let A be a fixed set. A structure on A is any set of subsets $\mathfrak{A} \subseteq \mathfrak{P}(A)$. For all subsets a and $a' \subseteq A$, we write $a \perp a'$ whenever $a \cap a'$ is finite. For all structure $\mathfrak{A} \subseteq \mathfrak{P}(A)$, we define its dual $\mathfrak{A}^{\perp} = \{a \subseteq A; \ \forall a' \in \mathfrak{A}, \ a \perp a'\}$. A finiteness structure on A is any such $\mathfrak{A}^{\perp}$.*

Notice that: $\mathfrak{A} \subseteq \mathfrak{A}^{\perp\perp}$, also $\mathfrak{A} \subseteq \mathfrak{A}'$ entails $\mathfrak{A}'^{\perp} \subseteq \mathfrak{A}^{\perp}$, hence $\mathfrak{A}^{\perp} = \mathfrak{A}^{\perp\perp\perp}$.

Let $\mathfrak{C}_0 = \{ |\!\uparrow\! s| \ ; \ s \in \Delta, \text{ in normal form} \} \subseteq \mathfrak{P}(\Delta)$, we obtain that $|a| \in \mathfrak{C}_0^{\perp}$ iff Eq. (7) involves only pointwise finite sums. So, one is led to focus on support sets only, leaving out coefficients entirely. Henceforth, unless specified otherwise, we will thus stick to the case of $\mathcal{R} = \mathbb{B}$, and use set-theoretical notations only. This approach of ensuring the normalization of Taylor expansion *via* a finiteness structure was first used by Ehrhard [4] for a non-deterministic variant of System $\mathcal{F}$. Our paper strengthens Ehrhard's result in several directions. In order to state them, we introduce a construction of finiteness structures on Δ induced by anticones for the reduction order defined as follows:

Definition 8. *For all $s, t \in \Delta$, we write $t \geq s$ whenever there exists a reduction $t \to_r^* a$ with $s \in a$.*

It should be clear that this defines a partial order relation (in particular we have antisymmetry because $\to_r$ terminates).

Definition 9. *If $a \subseteq \Delta$, $\uparrow a := \{t \in \Delta; \ \exists s \in a, \ t \geq s\}$ is the cone of antireduction over a.[5] For any structure $\mathfrak{T} \subseteq \mathfrak{P}(\Delta)$, we write $\nabla(\mathfrak{T}) = \{\uparrow a \ ; \ a \in \mathfrak{T}\}$.*

We can consider the elements of $\mathfrak{T}$ as tests, and say a set $a \subseteq \Delta$ passes a test $a' \in \mathfrak{T}$ iff $a \perp \uparrow a'$. The structure of sets that pass all tests is exactly $\nabla(\mathfrak{T})^{\perp}$. Then Ehrhard's result can be rephrased as follows:

Theorem 10 ([4]). *If $M \in \Lambda_+$ is typable in System $\mathcal{F}$ then $\mathcal{T}(M) \in \nabla(\mathfrak{S}_{sgl})^{\perp}$ where $\mathfrak{S}_{sgl} := \{\{s\}; \ s \in \Delta\}$.*

Notice that, in contrast with the definition of $\mathfrak{C}_0$, $\mathfrak{S}_{sgl}$ is in fact not restricted to normal forms. Our paper extends this theorem in three directions: first, one can relax the condition that M is typed in System $\mathcal{F}$ and require only that M is strongly normalizable; second, the same result can be established for sets of "tests" larger (hence more demanding) than $\mathfrak{S}_{sgl}$; third, the implication can be reversed for a suitable set of tests $\mathfrak{T}$, i.e. M is strongly normalizable iff $\mathcal{T}(M) \in \nabla(\mathfrak{T})^{\perp}$ (and we do need $\mathfrak{T}$ to provide more tests than just singletons: see Remark 37). In order to state our results precisely, we need to introduce a few more notions.

Definition 11. *We say that a resource term s is* linear *whenever each bag appearing in s has cardinality 1. A set a of resource terms is said* linear *whenever all its elements are* linear. *We say a is* bounded *whenever there exists a number $n \in \mathbf{N}$ bounding the cardinality of all bags in all terms in a. We then write*

---

[5] Observe that $\uparrow\{s\} = \uparrow s$ (up to the identification of $\mathbb{B}[\![\Delta]\!]$ with $\mathfrak{P}(\Delta)$).

Table 2. The intersection type assignment system $\mathcal{D}_+$ for Λ_+

$$A, B := X \mid A \to B \mid A \cap B$$

(a) Grammar of types, X varying over a denumerable set of propositional variables

for $i \in \{1, 2\}$	$A' \preceq A \quad B \preceq B'$	
$\dfrac{}{A_1 \cap A_2 \preceq A_i}$	$\dfrac{}{A \to B \preceq A' \to B'}$	$(A \to B) \cap (A \to C) \preceq A \to (B \cap C)$

(b) Rules generating the subtyping relation $\preceq$

$$\frac{}{\Gamma, x : A \vdash x : A} \ (var) \qquad \frac{\Gamma, x : A \vdash M : B}{\Gamma \vdash \lambda x.M : A \to B} \ (\to_i)$$

$$\frac{\Gamma \vdash M : A \to B \quad \Gamma \vdash N : A}{\Gamma \vdash (M)\, N : B} \ (\to_e) \qquad \frac{\Gamma \vdash M : A \quad \Gamma \vdash M : B}{\Gamma \vdash M : A \cap B} \ (\cap_i)$$

$$\frac{\Gamma \vdash M : A \quad \Gamma \vdash N : A}{\Gamma \vdash M + N : A} \ (+) \qquad \frac{\Gamma \vdash M : A \quad A \preceq A'}{\Gamma \vdash M : A'} \ (\preceq)$$

(c) Derivation rules

$$\mathfrak{L} := \{a \subseteq \Delta; \ a \ linear\} \quad and \quad \mathfrak{B} := \{a \subseteq \Delta; \ a \ bounded\}.$$

We also denote as $\ell(M)$ the subset of the linear resource terms in $\mathcal{T}(M)$. Notice that $\ell(M)$ is always non-empty and can be directly defined by replacing the definition of $\mathcal{T}((M)\,N)$ in Table 1b with: $\ell((M)\,N) := \{\langle s \rangle\,[t]; \ s \in \ell(M), t \in \ell(N)\}$.

Observe that $\mathfrak{S}_{sgl}, \mathfrak{L} \subseteq \mathfrak{B}$.

We can sum up our results Corollary 30 and Theorem 36 as follows:

Theorem 12. *Let $M \in \Lambda_+$:*

- *If M is strongly normalizing, then $\mathcal{T}(M) \in \triangledown(\mathfrak{T})^\perp$ as soon as $\mathfrak{T} \subseteq \mathfrak{B}$.*
- *If $\mathcal{T}(M) \in \triangledown(\mathfrak{T})^\perp$ with $\mathfrak{L} \subseteq \mathfrak{T}$, then M is strongly normalizing.*

3   Strongly Normalizing Terms Are $\mathcal{D}_+$ Typable

Intersection types are well known, as well as their relation with normalizability. We refer to [2] for the original system with subtyping characterizing the set of strongly normalizing λ-terms, and [1,8] for simpler systems. However, as far as we know, the literature about intersection types for non-deterministic λ-calculi is less well established and in fact we could find no previous characterization of strong normalization in a non-deterministic setting. Hence, we give in Table 2 a variant of Krivine's system $\mathcal{D}$ [8], characterizing the set of strongly normalizing terms in Λ_+. In this section, we only prove that strongly normalizing terms are typable (Theorem 14): the reverse implication follows from the rest of the paper (see Fig. 1). These techniques are standard.

Remark 13. Krivine's original System $\mathcal{D}$ does not have $(\preceq)$ and $(+)$, but it has the two usual elimination rules for intersection (here derivable). The rule $(+)$ is necessary to account for non-determinism, however adding just $(+)$ to System $\mathcal{D}$ is misbehaving. We can find terms M and N, and a context Γ such that $(M)\,N$ is typable in System $\mathcal{D}$ with $(+)$ under the context Γ but M is not: take $\Gamma = x : A \to B \cap B', y : A \to B \cap B'', z : A$, observe that $(x + y)\,z = (x)\,z + (y)\,z$, and thus $\Gamma \vdash (x + y)\,z : B$ but $x + y$ is not typable in Γ. This is the reason why we introduce subtyping.

Theorem 14. *For all $M \in \Lambda_+$, if M is strongly normalizable, then there exists a derivable judgement $\Gamma \vdash M : A$ in system $\mathcal{D}_+$.*

Proof (Sketch). For M a strongly normalizable term, let $\mathbf{l}(M)$ be the maximum length of a reduction from M, and $\mathbf{s}(M)$ the number of symbols occurring in M. By well-founded induction on the pair $(\mathbf{l}(M), \mathbf{s}(M))$ we prove that there exists $n_M \in \mathbf{N}$ such that for all type B and all $n \geq n_M$, there is a context Γ and a sequence $(A_1, \ldots, A_n)$ of types such that $\Gamma \vdash M : A_1 \to \cdots \to A_n \to B$.

The proof splits depending on the structure of M. In case $M = M_1 + M_2$, we apply the induction hypothesis on both M_1 and M_2 and conclude by rule $(\preceq)$ and a contravariance property: $\Gamma \vdash M : A$ whenever $\Gamma' \vdash M : A$ and $\Gamma \preceq \Gamma'$.

In case of head-redexes, i.e. $M = ((\lambda x.N)\,P)\,M_1 \cdots M_q$, we apply the induction hypothesis on $M' = (N\,[P/x])\,M_1 \cdots M_q$ and on P. Then, we conclude via a subject expansion lemma stating that: $\Gamma \vdash (\lambda x.N)\,P\,M_1 \cdots M_n : A$, whenever $\Gamma \vdash (N\,[P/x])\,M_1 \cdots M_n : A$ and there exists B such that $\Gamma \vdash P : B$.

The other cases are similar to the first one.   □

4 $\mathcal{D}_+$ Typable Terms Are Finitary

This section proves Corollary 30, giving sufficient conditions (to be dispersed, hereditary and expandable, see resp. Definitions 23, 26 and 27) over a structure $\mathfrak{T}$ in order to have all cones $\uparrow a$ for $a \in \mathfrak{T}$ dual to the Taylor expansion of any strongly normalizing non-deterministic λ-term.

It is easy to check that these conditions are satisfied by the structures $\mathfrak{B}$ of bounded sets and $\mathfrak{L}$ of sets of linear terms (Definition 11). Moreover, as an immediate corollary one gets also that any subset $\mathfrak{T} \subseteq \mathfrak{B}$ is also such that $\mathcal{T}(M) \in \nabla(\mathfrak{T})^\perp$ for any strongly normalizable term $M \in \Lambda_+$, so getting the first Item of Theorem 12.

Thanks to previous Theorem 14 we can prove Corollary 30 by a realizability technique on the intersection type system $\mathcal{D}_+$. For a fixed structure $\mathfrak{S}$, we associate with any type A a realizer $\|A\|_\mathfrak{S}$ (Definition 18). In the case $\mathfrak{S}$ is adapted (Definition 17), we can prove that $\|A\|_\mathfrak{S}$ contains the Taylor expansion of any term of type A and that it is contained in $\mathfrak{S}$ (Theorem 21). These definitions and theorem are adapted from Krivine's proof for System $\mathcal{D}$ [8].

The crucial point is then to find structures $\mathfrak{S}$ which are *adapted*: here is our contribution. The structures that we study have the shape $\nabla(\mathfrak{T})^\perp$, so that we are speaking of the interaction with cones of anti-reducts of tests in a structure $\mathfrak{T}$.

Intuitively, $\mathfrak{T}$ is a set of tests that can be passed by any term typable in System $\mathcal{D}_+$ (hence by any strongly normalizing term). We prove (Lemma 29) that for a structure $\mathfrak{T}$, being dispersed, hereditary and expandable is sufficient to guarantee that the dual structure $\nabla(\mathfrak{T})^{\perp}$ is adapted, then achieving Corollary 30.

Definition 15 (Functional). *Given two structures* $\mathfrak{S}, \mathfrak{S}' \subseteq \mathfrak{P}(\Delta)$, *we define the structure* $\mathfrak{S} \to \mathfrak{S}' := \{f \subseteq \Delta; \ \forall a \in \mathfrak{S}, \langle f \rangle \ a^! \in \mathfrak{S}'\}$.

Definition 16 (Saturation). *Let* $\mathfrak{S}, \mathfrak{S}' \subseteq \mathfrak{P}(\Delta)$. *We say* $\mathfrak{S}'$ *is* $\mathfrak{S}$-*saturated if* $\forall e, f_0, \ldots, f_n \in \mathfrak{S}$, $\left\langle \partial_x e \cdot f_0^! \right\rangle f_1^! \ldots f_n^! \in \mathfrak{S}'$ *implies* $\langle \lambda x.e \rangle \ f_0^! f_1^! \ldots f_n^! \in \mathfrak{S}'$.

Definition 17 (Adaptedness). *For all* $\mathfrak{S} \subseteq \mathfrak{P}(\Delta)$ *we set* $\mathfrak{S}_h := \{\{x\}; \ x \in \mathcal{V}\} \cup \{\langle x \rangle \ a_1^! \cdots a_n^!; \ x \in \mathcal{V}, \ n > 0 \ and \ \forall i, \ a_i \in \mathfrak{S}\}$ *and say* $\mathfrak{S}$ *is adapted if:*

1. $\mathfrak{S}$ *is* $\mathfrak{S}$-*saturated;*
2. $\mathfrak{S}_h \subset (\mathfrak{S} \to \mathfrak{S}_h) \subset (\mathfrak{S}_h \to \mathfrak{S}) \subset \mathfrak{S};$
3. $\mathfrak{S}$ *is closed under finite unions:* $\forall b, b' \in \mathfrak{S}, \ b \cup b' \in \mathfrak{S}$.

Definition 18 (Realizers). *Let* $\mathfrak{S} \subseteq \mathfrak{P}(\Delta)$. *To each type* A *of System* $\mathcal{D}_+$, *we associate a structure* $\|A\|_{\mathfrak{S}}$ *defined inductively (X being a propositional variable):*

$$\|X\|_{\mathfrak{S}} := \mathfrak{S}, \quad \|A \to B\|_{\mathfrak{S}} := \|A\|_{\mathfrak{S}} \to \|B\|_{\mathfrak{S}}, \quad \|A \cap B\|_{\mathfrak{S}} := \|A\|_{\mathfrak{S}} \cap \|B\|_{\mathfrak{S}}.$$

Lemma 19. *Let* $\mathfrak{S}$ *be an adapted structure, then for every type* A, $\|A\|_{\mathfrak{S}}$ *is* $\mathfrak{S}$-*saturated, closed under finite unions and* $\mathfrak{S}_h \subseteq \|A\|_{\mathfrak{S}} \subseteq \mathfrak{S}$.

Lemma 20 (Adequacy). *If* $\mathfrak{S} \subseteq \mathfrak{P}(\Delta)$ *is adapted,* $x_1 : A_1, \ldots, x_n : A_n \vdash M : B$ *and for all* $1 \leq i \leq n$, $a_i \in \|A_i\|_{\mathfrak{S}}$, *then* $\partial_{x_1, \ldots, x_n} \mathcal{T}(M) \cdot a_1^!, \ldots, a_n^! \in \|B\|_{\mathfrak{S}}$.

Proof (Sketch). By structural induction on the derivation of $x_1 : A_1, \ldots, x_n : A_n \vdash M : B$. The cases where the last rule is $(\to_i)$ or $(+)$ use respectively the facts that the realizers are saturated and closed by finite unions. The case where the last rule is $(\preceq)$ is an immediate consequence of the induction hypothesis and of a lemma stating that $A \preceq B$ implies $\|A\|_{\mathfrak{S}} \subseteq \|B\|_{\mathfrak{S}}$. $\qquad\square$

Theorem 21. *If* $\mathfrak{S} \subseteq \mathfrak{P}(\Delta)$ *is adapted and* M *is typable in System* $\mathcal{D}_+$, *then* $\mathcal{T}(M) \in \mathfrak{S}$.

Proof. Let $\Gamma \vdash M : B$. For any $x : A$ in Γ, $\{x\} \in \mathfrak{S}_h \subset \|A\|_{\mathfrak{S}}$ by Lemma 19 and Definition 17. Hence, $\mathcal{T}(M) = \partial_{x_1, \ldots, x_n} \mathcal{T}(M) \cdot \{x_1\}^!, \ldots, \{x_n\}^! \in \|B\|_{\mathfrak{S}}$ by Lemma 20. Again by Lemma 19, $\|B\|_{\mathfrak{S}} \subseteq \mathfrak{S}$, so $\mathcal{T}(M) \in \mathfrak{S}$. $\qquad\square$

Now we look for conditions to ensure that a structure $\mathfrak{S}$ is *adapted*. These conditions (Definitions 23, 26 and 27) are quite technical but they are easy to check, in particular the structures $\mathfrak{B}$ and $\mathfrak{L}$ enjoy them (Remark 28).

Definition 22. *The* height $\mathbf{h}(s)$ *of a resource term* s *is defined inductively:* $\mathbf{h}(x) := 1$, $\mathbf{h}(\lambda x.s) := 1 + \mathbf{h}(s)$ *and* $\mathbf{h}(\langle s_0 \rangle [s_1, \ldots, s_n]) := 1 + \max_i (\mathbf{h}(s_i))$.

Definition 23 (Dispersed). *A set $a \subseteq \Delta$ is dispersed whenever for all $n \in$* **N**, *and all finite set V of variables, the set $\{s \in a;\ \mathbf{h}(s) \leq n \text{ and } \mathsf{fv}(s) \subseteq V\}$ is finite. A structure $\mathfrak{S}$ is dispersed whenever $\forall a \in \mathfrak{S}$, a is dispersed.*

Definition 24. *Let $s \in \Delta$ and $x \notin \mathsf{fv}(s)$. We define immediate subterm projections $\pi_x s \in \mathfrak{P}(\Delta)$, $\pi_0 s \in \mathfrak{P}(\Delta)$, $\overline{\pi}_1 s \in \mathfrak{P}\left(\Delta^!\right)$ and $\pi_1 s \in \mathfrak{P}(\Delta)$ as follows:*

- *if $s = \lambda x.t$ then $\pi_x s = \{t\}$; otherwise $\pi_x s = \emptyset$;*
- *if $s = \langle t \rangle\, \overline{u}$ then $\pi_0 s = \{t\}$, $\overline{\pi}_1 s = \{\overline{u}\}$, $\pi_1 s = |\overline{u}|$; otherwise $\pi_0 s = \overline{\pi}_1 s = \pi_1 s = \emptyset$.*

Observe that up to α-conversion and the hypothesis $x \notin \mathsf{fv}(s)$, the abstraction case is exhaustive. These functions obviously extend to sets of terms, up to some care about free variables. If $V \subseteq \mathcal{V}$ is a set of variables, we write Δ^V for the set of resource λ-terms with free variables in V.

Definition 25. *For all $V \subseteq \mathcal{V}$ and $a \subseteq \Delta^V$, let*

$$\pi_0 a := \bigcup_{s \in a} \pi_0 s \subseteq \Delta^V, \qquad \overline{\pi}_1 a := \bigcup_{s \in a} \overline{\pi}_1 s \subseteq \Delta^{V!}, \qquad \pi_1 a := \bigcup_{s \in a} \pi_1 s \subseteq \Delta^V,$$

and if moreover $x \notin V$, then let $\pi_x a := \bigcup_{s \in a} \pi_x s \subseteq \Delta^{V \cup \{x\}}$.

Definition 26 (Hereditary). *A structure $\mathfrak{S} \subseteq \mathfrak{P}(\Delta)$ is said to be hereditary if, $\mathfrak{S}$ is downwards closed, and for all $a \in \mathfrak{S}$, $\pi_0 a \in \mathfrak{S}$, $\pi_1 a \in \mathfrak{S}$ and for all $x \in \mathcal{V} \setminus \mathsf{fv}(a)$, $\pi_x a \in \mathfrak{S}$.*

Definition 27 (Expandable). *A structure $\mathfrak{S} \subseteq \mathfrak{P}(\Delta)$ is said to be expandable if, for all $x \in \mathcal{V}$ and all $a \in \mathfrak{S}$, we have $\{\langle s \rangle\, [x]\,;\ s \in a\} \in \mathfrak{S}$.*

Remark 28. The structures $\mathfrak{S}_{\mathrm{sgl}}$ (Theorem 10) and $\mathfrak{L}$, $\mathfrak{B}$ (Definition 11) are dispersed and expandable. The last two are also hereditary, while $\mathfrak{S}_{\mathrm{sgl}}$ is not.

Lemma 29. *For any structure $\mathfrak{T}$ which is dispersed, hereditary and expandable, we have that $\nabla(\mathfrak{T})^{\perp}$ is adapted.*

Proof (Sketch). One has to prove the three conditions of Definition 17. Heredity and dispersion are used to obtain saturation (Condition 1). The inclusions of Condition 2 need all hypotheses and an auxiliary lemma proving that $\nabla(\mathfrak{T})^{\perp}{}_h \subseteq \nabla(\mathfrak{T})^{\perp}$, for which dispersion is crucial. Finally, the closure under finite unions (Condition 3) is satisfied by all finiteness structures. □

Corollary 30. *Let $\mathfrak{T} \subseteq \mathfrak{P}(\Delta)$ be dispersed, hereditary and expandable. For every strongly normalizable term M, we have $\mathcal{T}(M) \in \nabla(\mathfrak{T})^{\perp}$. Hence, this holds for $\mathfrak{T} \in \{\mathfrak{L}, \mathfrak{B}\}$ and for any of their subsets, such as $\mathfrak{S}_{\mathrm{sgl}} \subset \mathfrak{B}$.*

Proof. The general statement follows from Theorems 14 and 21 and Lemma 29. Remark 28 implies $\mathcal{T}(M) \in \nabla(\mathfrak{T})^{\perp}$ for $\mathfrak{T} \in \{\mathfrak{B}, \mathfrak{L}\}$. The rest of the statement follows because, for any structures $\mathfrak{S}, \mathfrak{S}'$, $\mathfrak{S} \subseteq \mathfrak{S}'$ implies $\mathfrak{S}'^{\perp} \subseteq \mathfrak{S}^{\perp}$. □

5   Finitary Terms Are Strongly Normalizing

In this section we prove Theorem 36, giving a sufficient condition for a structure $\mathfrak{T}$ to be able to test strong normalization. The condition is that $\mathfrak{T}$ includes at least $\mathfrak{L}$, i.e. the set of all sets of linear terms[6].

The proof is by contraposition, suppose that M is divergent, then $\mathcal{T}(M)$ is not dual to some cone $\uparrow a$, with $a \in \mathfrak{L}$. The proof enlightens two kinds of divergence in λ-calculus: the one generated by looping terms: $\Omega \to_\beta \Omega \to_\beta \cdots$ and the other generated by infinite reduction sequences $(M_i)_{i \in \mathbf{N}}$ with an infinite number of different terms: $\Omega_3 \to_\beta (\Omega_3)\,\Delta_3 \to_\beta ((\Omega_3)\,\Delta_3)\,\Delta_3 \to_\beta \cdots$ (see Example 1).

In the first case, the cone $\uparrow\ell(\Omega)$ of the linear expansion (Definition 11) of the looping term Ω suffices to show up the divergence, since $\mathcal{T}(\Omega) \cap \uparrow\ell(\Omega)$ is infinite. Indeed the Taylor expansion of a looping term, say $\mathcal{T}(\Omega)$, is a kind of "contractible space", where any resource term reduces to a smaller term within the same Taylor expansion or vanishes (see Example 6). In particular, there are unboundedly large resource terms reducing to the linear expansion $\ell(\Omega)$.

In the case of an infinite reduction sequence of different terms, one should take, basically, the cone of all linear expansions of the terms occurring in the sequence: the linear expansion of a single term (or of a finite set of terms) might not suffice to test this kind of divergence. For example, $\mathcal{T}(\Omega_3) \cap \uparrow\ell(\Omega_3)$ is finite, while $\mathcal{T}(\Omega_3) \cap \uparrow\{\ell(\Omega_3), \ell((\Omega_3)\,\Delta_3), \dots\}$ is infinite, so $\mathcal{T}(\Omega_3) \notin \triangledown(\mathfrak{L})^\perp$.

In the presence of the non-deterministic sum $+$, we have a third kind of divergence, which is given by infinite reduction sequences of terms $(M_i)_{i \in \mathbf{N}}$ which are pairwise different but whose Taylor expansion support repeats infinitely many times: consider, e.g., the reducts of $(\Theta)(\lambda x.x + y)$. We prove that this kind of divergence is much more similar to a loop rather than to a sequence of different λ-terms. In particular, there is a single linear resource term (depending on the reduction sequence) whose cone is able to show up the divergence. Indeed, most of the effort in the proof of Theorem 36 is devoted to deal with this kind of "looping Taylor expansion". Namely, Definition 31 gives a notion of non-deterministic reduction $\rightharpoonup$ allowing Lemma 35, which is the key statement used in the proof of Theorem 36 for dealing with both the divergence of looping terms (like Ω) and that of looping Taylor expansions (like $(\Theta)(\lambda x.x + y)$).

We introduce a reduction rule $\rightharpoonup$ on Λ_+ which corresponds to one step of β-reduction and a potential loss of some addenda in a term. For that, we need an order $\unrhd$ on Λ_+ expressing this loss. For instance, $(\Theta)(\lambda x.x + y) + y \unrhd (\Theta)\lambda x.x$, thus $(\Theta)(\lambda x.x + y) \rightharpoonup^* (\Theta)\lambda x.x$, and similarly, $(\Theta)(\lambda x.x + y) \rightharpoonup^* y$.

Definition 31 (Partial reduction). *We write $M \rightharpoonup N$ if there exists P such that $M \to_\beta P$ and $P \unrhd N$, where the partial order $\unlhd$ over Λ_+ is defined as the least order such that $M \unlhd M + N$; $N \unlhd M + N$ and if $M \unlhd N$ then: $M + P \unlhd N + P$, $\lambda x.M \unlhd \lambda x.N$, $(M)\,P \unlhd (N)\,P$, and $(P)\,M \unlhd (P)\,N$.*

---

[6] This condition can be slightly weakened replacing $\mathfrak{L}$ with: $\{a \subseteq \Delta;\ a$ linear and $\mathsf{fv}(a)$ finite$\}$. However, we prefer to stick to the more intuitive definition of $\mathfrak{L}$.

A reduction $M \twoheadrightarrow N$ is at top level if $M = (\lambda x.M')\, M'' \to M'[M''/x] \trianglerighteq N$.

Write $s > t$ whenever $s \geq t$ (Definition 8) and $s \neq t$: this is a strict partial order relation.

Lemma 32. If $M \twoheadrightarrow N$ and $t \in \mathcal{T}(N)$, then there exists $s \in \mathcal{T}(M)$ such that $s \geq t$. If moreover, $M \twoheadrightarrow N$ is at top level, then $s > t$.

Lemma 33. Let $M \twoheadrightarrow N$ and $u \in \Delta$. If $\mathcal{T}(N) \cap {\uparrow}u$ is infinite, then $\mathcal{T}(M) \cap {\uparrow}u$ is also infinite.

Definition 34. The height $\mathbf{h}(M)$ of a term $M \in \Lambda_+$ is defined inductively as follows: $\mathbf{h}(x) := 1$, $\mathbf{h}(\lambda x.M) := 1 + \mathbf{h}(M)$, $\mathbf{h}((M)\,N) := 1 + \max(\mathbf{h}(M), \mathbf{h}(N))$ and $\mathbf{h}(M + N) := \max(\mathbf{h}(M), \mathbf{h}(N))$.

Lemma 35. Let $(M_i)_{i \in \mathbf{N}}$ be a sequence. If $\forall i \in \mathbf{N}$, $M_i \twoheadrightarrow M_{i+1}$ and $(\mathbf{h}(M_i))_{i \in \mathbf{N}}$ is bounded, then there exists a linear term t such that $\mathcal{T}(M_0) \cap {\uparrow}t$ is infinite.

Proof (Sketch). First, it is sufficient to address the case of a sequence $(S_i)_{i \in \mathbf{N}}$ of simple terms (i.e. without $+$ as the top-level constructor) such that $S_i \twoheadrightarrow S_{i+1}$ for all $i \in \mathbf{N}$ and $(\mathbf{h}(S_i))_{i \in \mathbf{N}}$ is bounded. Besides, by Lemma 33, it is sufficient to have $\mathcal{T}(S_{i_0}) \cap {\uparrow}t$ infinite for some $i_0 \in \mathbf{N}$.

Then, by induction on $h = \max\{\mathbf{h}(S_i)\,;\, i \in \mathbf{N}\}$, we show that there exists $i_0 \in \mathbf{N}$ and a sequence $(s_j)_{j \in \mathbf{N}} \in \mathcal{T}(S_{i_0})^{\mathbf{N}}$ such that s_0 is linear and, for all $j \in \mathbf{N}$, $s_{j+1} > s_j$. Since $>$ is a strict order relation, this implies that the set $\{s_j;\, j \in \mathbf{N}\} \subseteq \mathcal{T}(S_{i_0}) \cap {\uparrow}s_0$ is infinite.

First assume that there are infinitely many top level reductions. Observe that, since $\mathbf{h}(S_i) \leq h$ and $\mathsf{fv}(S_i) \subseteq \mathsf{fv}(S_0)$ for all i, the set $\{\mathcal{T}(S_i)\,;\, i \in \mathbf{N}\}$ is finite. Hence there exists an index $i_0 \in \mathbf{N}$ such that $\{i \in \mathbf{N};\, \mathcal{T}(S_i) = \mathcal{T}(S_{i_0})\}$ is infinite. As there are infinitely many top level reductions, there are i_1 and i_2 such that $i_0 < i_1 < i_2$, the reduction i_1 is at top level and $\mathcal{T}(S_{i_2}) = \mathcal{T}(S_{i_0})$. We inductively define the required sequence by choosing arbitrary $s_0 \in \ell(S_{i_0}) \subseteq \mathcal{T}(S_{i_0})$, and by iterating Lemma 32: for $s_j \in \mathcal{T}(S_{i_0}) = \mathcal{T}(S_{i_2})$, we obtain $s_{j+1} \in \mathcal{T}(S_{i_0})$ with $s_{j+1} > s_j$ since the reduction i_1 is at top level.

Now assume that there are only finitely many top level reductions. Let i_1 be such that no reduction $S_i \twoheadrightarrow S_{i+1}$ with $i \geq i_1$ is at top level. Either for all $i \geq i_1$, $S_i = \lambda x.M_i'$ with $M_i' \twoheadrightarrow M_{i+1}'$, and we conclude by applying the induction hypothesis to the sequence $(M_{i+i_1}')_{i \in \mathbf{N}}$; or for all $i \geq i_1$, $S_i = (M_i')\,N_i'$ so that $(M_i')_{i \geq i_1}$ and $(N_i')_{i \geq i_1}$ are sequences of terms, at least one of them involving infinitely many partial reductions. In this case, assume for instance that we can extract from $(M_i')_{i \geq i_1}$ an infinite subsequence $(M_{\phi(i)}')_{i \in \mathbf{N}}$ of partial reductions. It provides i_0' and a sequence $(s_j') \in \mathcal{T}(M_{\phi(i_0')}')^{\mathbf{N}}$ with s_0' linear and, $s_{j+1}' > s_j'$. Fix $t \in \ell(N_{\phi(i_0')}')$ arbitrarily. So we set $i_0 = \phi(i_0')$ and $s_j = \langle s_j' \rangle\,[t]$ for all $j \in \mathbf{N}$. $\square$

Theorem 36. Let $\mathfrak{T}$ be a structure such that $\mathfrak{L} \subseteq \mathfrak{T}$. If $\mathcal{T}(M) \in \nabla(\mathfrak{T})^{\perp}$ then M is strongly normalizable. In particular, this holds for $\mathfrak{T} \in \{\mathfrak{L}, \mathfrak{B}\}$.

Proof. Assume that $(M_i)_{i \in \mathbf{N}}$ is such that $M = M_0$ and for all i, $M_i \to_\beta M_{i+1}$. We prove that $T(M) \notin \nabla(\mathfrak{T})^\perp$ by exhibiting $a \in \mathfrak{T}$ such that $T(M) \not\perp \uparrow a$.

If $(\mathbf{h}(M_i))_{i \in \mathbf{N}}$ is bounded, then fix $a = \{t\}$ with t given by Lemma 35.

Otherwise, $\forall i \in \mathbf{N}$, fix $t_i \in \ell(M_i)$ such that $\mathbf{h}(t_i) = \mathbf{h}(M_i)$. Lemma 32 implies that there is $s_i \in T(M)$ such that $s_i \geq t_i$. Denote by $\mathbf{s}(s)$ the number of symbols occurring in s. Since there is no duplication in reduction $\to_r$ it should be clear that if $s \geq t$ then $\mathbf{s}(s) \geq \mathbf{s}(t)$. Besides, $\mathbf{s}(s) \geq \mathbf{h}(s)$. Therefore, since $\{\mathbf{h}(M_i)\,;\ i \in \mathbf{N}\}$ is unbounded, $\{\mathbf{h}(t_i)\,;\ i \in \mathbf{N}\}$, $\{\mathbf{s}(t_i)\,;\ i \in \mathbf{N}\}$ and $\{\mathbf{s}(s_i)\,;\ i \in \mathbf{N}\}$ are unbounded. Fix $a = \bigcup_{i \in \mathbf{N}} \ell(M_i) \in \mathfrak{T}$, we have proved that $T(M) \cap \uparrow a$ is infinite. $\qquad\square$

Notice that the structure $\mathfrak{S}_{\mathrm{sgl}}$ of singletons used in [4] does not enjoy the hypothesis of Theorem 36 ($\mathfrak{L} \not\subset \mathfrak{S}_{\mathrm{sgl}}$). In fact:

Remark 37. We prove that $T(\mathbf{\Omega_3}) \in \nabla(\mathfrak{S}_{\mathrm{sgl}})^\perp$, although $\mathbf{\Omega_3}$ is not normalizing. Recall from Example 2, that the support of the Taylor expansion of $\mathbf{\Omega_3}$ is made of terms of the form $\langle \delta_{n_0, m_0} \rangle [\delta_{n_1, m_1}, \ldots, \delta_{n_k, m_k}]$ (for $k, n_i, m_i \in \mathbf{N}$). Write $\Delta_h = \{\langle \delta_{-,-} \rangle [\ldots \delta_{-,-} \ldots] \cdots [\ldots \delta_{-,-} \ldots]$ with h bags$\}$: in particular $T(\mathbf{\Omega_3}) = \Delta_1$. One can easily check that if $s \in \Delta_h$ and $s \geq s'$, then $s' \in \Delta_{h'}$ with $h \leq h'$. A careful inspection of such reductions shows that they are moreover reversible: for all $s' \in \Delta_{h'}$ and all $h \leq h'$ there is exactly one $s \in \Delta_h$ such that $s \geq s'$. It follows that $\Delta_1 \cap \uparrow s$ is either empty or a singleton. Therefore $T(\mathbf{\Omega_3}) \in \nabla(\mathfrak{S}_{\mathrm{sgl}})^\perp$.

6   Conclusion

We achieved all implications of Fig. 1, but the rightmost one, concerning the finiteness of the coefficients in the normal form of the Taylor expansion of a strongly normalizing λ-term (recall Eq. (2) in the Introduction).

Thanks to the definition of cones (Definition 9) we immediately have the following lemma, which is the last step to Corollary 39.

Lemma 38. *Let $\mathfrak{T}$ be a structure. If $T(M) \in \nabla(\mathfrak{T})^\perp$, then $\forall t \in \bigcup \mathfrak{T}$, $\mathrm{NF}(T(M))_t$ is finite.*

Applying Corollary 30 and Lemma 38 to a structure like $\mathfrak{B}$ or $\mathfrak{S}_{\mathrm{sgl}}$, we get:

Corollary 39. *Given a non-deterministic λ-term M, if M is strongly normalizable, then $\mathrm{NF}(T(M))_t$ is finite for all $t \in \Delta$.*

References

1. van Bakel, S.: Complete restrictions of the intersection type discipline. Theor. Comput. Sci. **102**(1), 135–163 (1992). http://dx.doi.org/10.1016/0304-3975(92)90297-S
2. Barendregt, H., Coppo, M., Dezani-Ciancaglini, M.: A filter lambda model and the completeness of type assignment. JSL **48**, 931–940 (1983)
3. Ehrhard, T.: Finiteness spaces. Math. Struct. Comput. Sci. **15**(04), 615–646 (2005)

4. Ehrhard, T.: A finiteness structure on resource terms. In: Proceedings of the 25th Annual IEEE Symposium on Logic in Computer Science, LICS 2010, 11–14 July 2010, Edinburgh, United Kingdom, pp. 402–410. IEEE Computer Society (2010). http://dx.doi.org/10.1109/LICS.2010.38

5. Ehrhard, T., Regnier, L.: The differential lambda-calculus. Theor. Comput. Sci. **309**(1), 1–41 (2003)

6. Ehrhard, T., Regnier, L.: Böhm trees, Krivine's Machine and the Taylor expansion of lambda-terms. In: Beckmann, A., Berger, U., Löwe, B., Tucker, J.V. (eds.) CiE 2006. LNCS, vol. 3988, pp. 186–197. Springer, Heidelberg (2006)

7. Ehrhard, T., Regnier, L.: Uniformity and the Taylor expansion of ordinary lambda-terms. Theor. Comput. Sci. **403**(2–3), 347–372 (2008)

8. Krivine, J.L.: Lambda-Calculus, Types and Models. Ellis Horwood, Chichester (1993)

9. Laird, J., Manzonetto, G., McCusker, G., Pagani, M.: Weighted relational models of typed lambda-calculi. In: Proceedings of 28th Annual ACM/IEEE Symposium on Logic in Computer Science (LICS 2013), pp. 25–28, New Orleans, USA, pp. 301–310, June 2013

10. Lamarche, F.: Quantitative domains and infinitary algebras. Theor. Comput. Sci. **1**, 37–62 (1992)

11. Pagani, M.: The cut-elimination theorem for differential nets with promotion. In: Curien, P.-L. (ed.) TLCA 2009. LNCS, vol. 5608, pp. 219–233. Springer, Heidelberg (2009)

12. Pagani, M.: Visible acyclic differential nets, Part I: Semantics. Ann. Pure Appl. Logic **163**(3), 238–265 (2012)

Reasoning About Call-by-need
by Means of Types

Delia Kesner[✉]

Université Paris-Diderot, SPC, IRIF, CNRS, Paris, France
kesner@pps.univ-paris-diderot.fr

Abstract. We first develop a (semantical) characterization of call-by-need normalization by means of typability, *i.e.* we show that a term is normalizing in call-by-need if and only if it is typable in a suitable system with non-idempotent intersection types. This first result is used to derive a new completeness proof of call-by-need w.r.t. call-by-name. Concretely, we show that call-by-need and call-by-name are observationally equivalent, so that in particular, the former turns out to be a correct implementation of the latter.

1 Introduction

There is a real gap between the well-known operational semantics of the *call-by-name* λ-calculus and the actual implementations of *lazy* functional languages such as Miranda or Haskell. Indeed, call-by-name re-evaluates an argument each time it is used – an operation which is quite expensive – while lazy languages store the *value* of an argument the first time it is evaluated, thus avoiding the need for any subsequent re-evaluations. For example, consider the term $t_0 = \Delta(II)$, where $\Delta = \lambda x.xx$ and $I = \lambda z.z$. Call-by-name duplicates the argument II, while lazy languages first reduces II to the value I so that further uses of this argument do not need any more to evaluate it again.

However, lazy languages should not be confused with *call-by-value*: values are only consumed in the former when they are *needed/required*, thus completely ignoring the other arguments. *E.g.* if $t_1 = (\lambda z.I)(II)$, the argument II is evaluated in call-by-value to produce the final answer I, whereas this evaluation does not take place in any lazy language (see *e.g.* [2,3,9,13]). Said differently, lazy languages do not compute unneeded terms, and terms should not be duplicated unless and until they have been reduced to values.

According to the previous paragraphs, lazy languages cannot be modeled by call-by-name, nor by call-by-value; they are indeed specified by *call-by-need*, due to Wadsworth [30], and extensively studied *e.g.* in [1–3,9,13,25].

Despite the fact that the equational theories of call-by-name and call-by-need are not the same [2], call-by-need is observationally equivalent (*i.e.* sound and complete w.r.t.) to call-by-name. The completeness result, operationally developed *e.g.* in [2,25], is quite involved and makes use of different *syntactical* tools such as commutation diagrams, sharing, residual theory and standardization.

© Springer-Verlag Berlin Heidelberg 2016
B. Jacobs and C. Löding (Eds.): FOSSACS 2016, LNCS 9634, pp. 424–441, 2016.
DOI: 10.1007/978-3-662-49630-5_25

In this paper we make use of *typing systems* to provide a *semantical* argument showing that call-by-need and call-by-name are observationally equivalent. More precisely, we develop a new completeness proof of call-by-need w.r.t. call-by-name which follows from two different implications: every term having a normal form in call-by-name is typable and every typable term has a normal form in call-by-need. The second implication is obtained from a stronger characterization property stating that the set of typable terms and the set of call-by-need normalizing terms are the same. This result is completely new, and quite surprising, and constitutes one of the main contributions of this work.

In order to achieve our goal we use intersection types, originally introduced in [11], being able to provide models of the λ-calculus [4], and characterizations of head [10] as well as weakly [8,10] and strongly normalizing λ-terms [22]. Typically, intersection types are *idempotent* [4]. However, in the last years, growing interest has been devoted to *non-idempotent* intersection types [6,19], since they allow for reasoning about *quantitative* properties of terms, both from a syntactical and a semantical point of view. Different assignment systems with non-idempotent intersection types have been studied in the literature for different purposes [5,7,14,15,18,20,21,23,26,27].

Reasoning about call-by-name and call-by-need is achieved in this paper by introducing two (non-idempotent) typing systems, called $\mathcal{V}$ and $\mathcal{A}$ respectively. System $\mathcal{V}$ (resp. $\mathcal{A}$) characterizes the set of **name** (resp. **need**) normalizing terms, *i.e.* a term t is typable in system $\mathcal{V}$ (resp. $\mathcal{A}$) if and only if t is normalizing in call-by-name (resp. call-by-need). While our characterization of call-by-name normalization can be seen as a simple adaptation of the existing one for head-normalization [15], this is, to the best of our knowledge, the first time that call-by-need normalization is characterized by means of semantical/logical tools.

Non-idempotent intersection types provide a full characterizations of call-by-name/need normalizing terms by using very simple combinatorial arguments, no reducibility technique are used. More precisely, there is a measure, defined on type derivations, which *strictly* decreases during name/needed reduction. This gives quantitative information about call-by-name/need reduction sequences.

The following list summarizes the more important points of our work:

1. We provide a characterization of **name**-normalization by adapting an existing one for head-normalization.
2. We develop a completely new characterization of **need**-normalization by means of typability. This characterization, as well as the one for **name**-normalization, is arithmetical, *i.e.* no reducibility arguments are needed.
3. Based on the previous points, we show that call-by-need and call-by-name are observationally equivalent, so that in particular, we obtain a new (semantical) completeness proof of call-by-need w.r.t. call-by-name.

Related Works: Besides all the aforementioned works that use intersection types to characterize operational properties of λ-calculi, two other works make use of typing systems to reason about lazy languages. In [24], the *resource conscious* character of linear logic is used to explain call-by-need in the spirit of the Curry-Howard isomorphism. In [16] non-idempotent intersection types are related to *needed redexes*: a redex r in a term t is *needed* iff r, or some *residual* of r, is reduced in *every* reduction of t to normal form. Despite the use of similar typing techniques to identify needed redexes in well-typed terms, no full characterization of needed normalization is obtained in [16].

Structure of the Paper: Section 2 introduces syntax and operational semantics of call-by-name and call-by-need. Section 3 defines non-idempotent type assignment disciplines for both calculi. Section 4 (resp. Sect. 5) gives a characterization of **name** (resp. **need**)-normalizing terms by means of the intersection type systems introduced in Sect. 3. Section 6 presents the completeness proof by using the semantical/logical arguments developed in the previous sections. Section 7 concludes and suggests some further directions of research.

2   Call-by-name and Call-by-need

This section describes the syntax and the operational semantics of our languages. We start by introducing call-by-name in the setting of the lambda-calculus, as done in the seminal work of Plotkin [28]. Given a countable infinite set of symbols $x, y, z, \ldots$, we define terms, values and name contexts as follows:

Terms	$t, u ::= x \mid tu \mid \lambda x.t$
Values	$v ::= \lambda x.t$
Name contexts	$\mathsf{E} ::= \square \mid \mathsf{E}t$

The set of terms is denoted by $\mathcal{T}_\mathsf{a}$. We write I for the identity function $\lambda x.x$. The sets of **free** and **bound** variables of a term t, written respectively $\mathtt{fv}(t)$ and $\mathtt{bv}(t)$, are defined as usual. We work with the standard notion of α-**conversion** *i.e.* renaming of bound variables for abstractions. **Substitutions** are (finite) functions from variables to terms denoted by $\{x_1/u_1, \ldots, x_n/u_n\}$ $(n \geq 0)$. **Application** of the **substitution** σ to the term t, written $t\sigma$, is defined on α-equivalence classes, as usual, so that capture of free variables cannot hold.

The **call-by-name calculus** is given by the set of terms $\mathcal{T}_\mathsf{a}$ and the **reduction relation** $\rightarrow_\mathsf{name}$, which is the closure by *name* contexts E of the rewriting rule $(\lambda x.t)u \mapsto_\beta t\{x/u\}$. An example of **name**-reduction sequence is

$$(\lambda f.f\mathsf{I}(f\mathsf{I}))(\lambda w.(\mathsf{II})w) \rightarrow_\mathsf{name} (\lambda w.(\mathsf{II})w)\mathsf{I}((\lambda w.(\mathsf{II})w)\mathsf{I}) \rightarrow_\mathsf{name}$$
$$(\mathsf{II})\mathsf{I}((\lambda w.(\mathsf{II})w)\mathsf{I}) \rightarrow_\mathsf{name}^3 (\lambda w.(\mathsf{II})w)\mathsf{I} \rightarrow_\mathsf{name} (\mathsf{II})\mathsf{I} \rightarrow_\mathsf{name} \mathsf{II} \rightarrow_\mathsf{name} \mathsf{I}$$

Remark that $t \rightarrow_\mathsf{name} t'$ implies $\mathtt{fv}(t) \supseteq \mathtt{fv}(t')$, and notice that reduction is *weak*, so that we never reduce under λ-abstractions, which are considered to be values.

The call-by-need calculus we use in this paper was introduced in [1]. It is more concise than previous specifications of call-by-need [2,3,9,25], but it is operationally equivalent to them, so that the results of this paper could also be presented by using other alternative specifications.

Given a countable infinite set of symbols $x, y, z, \ldots$ we define different syntactic categories for terms, values, list contexts, answers and need contexts:

Terms	$t, u ::= x \mid tu \mid \lambda x.t \mid t[x/u]$
Values	$v ::= \lambda x.t$
List contexts	$\text{L} ::= \square \mid \text{L}[x/t]$
Answers	$\text{A} ::= \text{L}[\lambda y.t]$
Need contexts	$\text{M}, \text{N} ::= \square \mid \text{N}t \mid \text{N}[x/t] \mid \text{N}[\![x]\!][x/\text{M}]$

Terms of the form $t[x/u]$ are **closures**, and $[x/u]$ is said to be an **explicit substitution** (ES). The set of all the terms is denoted by $\mathcal{T}_{\text{e}}$; remark that $\mathcal{T}_{\text{a}} \subset \mathcal{T}_{\text{e}}$. The notions of **free** and **bound** variables are defined as expected, in particular, $\text{fv}(t[x/u]) := \text{fv}(t)\backslash\{x\}\cup\text{fv}(u)$, $\text{fv}(\lambda x.t) := \text{fv}(t)\backslash\{x\}$, $\text{bv}(t[x/u]) := \text{bv}(t) \cup \{x\} \cup \text{bv}(u)$ and $\text{bv}(\lambda x.t) := \text{bv}(t) \cup \{x\}$.

We use $\text{N}[t]$ (resp. $\text{L}[t]$) for the term obtained by replacing the hole of N (resp. L) by the term t. We use the special notation $\text{N}[\![u]\!]$ or $\text{L}[\![u]\!]$ when the free variables of u are not captured by the context, *i.e.* there are no abstractions or explicit substitutions in the context that binds the free variables of u. Thus for example, given $\text{N} = (\square x)[x/z]$, we have $(yx)[x/z] = \text{N}[y] = \text{N}[\![y]\!]$, but $(xx)[x/z] = \text{N}[x]$ cannot be written as $\text{N}[\![x]\!]$. Notice the use of this special notation in the last case of needed contexts, an example of such case being $(xy)[y/t][x/\square]$.

The **call-by-need calculus**, introduced in [1], is given by the set of terms $\mathcal{T}_{\text{e}}$ and the **reduction relation** $\rightarrow_{\text{need}}$, the **union** of $\rightarrow_{\text{dB}}$ and $\rightarrow_{\text{lsv}}$, which are, respectively, the closure by *need* contexts N of the following rewriting rules:

$$\text{L}[\lambda x.t]u \quad \mapsto_{\text{dB}} \quad \text{L}[t[x/u]]$$
$$\text{N}[\![x]\!][x/\text{L}[v]] \mapsto_{\text{lsv}} \text{L}[\text{N}[\![v]\!][x/v]]$$

An example of **need**-reduction sequence is

$$
\begin{array}{lll}
(\lambda x_1.\text{I}(x_1\text{I}))(\lambda y.\text{I}y) & \rightarrow_{\text{dB}} (\text{I}(x_1\text{I}))[x_1/\lambda y.\text{I}y] & \rightarrow_{\text{dB}} \\
x_2[x_2/x_1\text{I}][x_1/\lambda y.\text{I}y] & \rightarrow_{\text{lsv}} x_2[x_2/(\lambda x_3.\text{I}x_3)\text{I}][x_1/\lambda y.\text{I}y] & \rightarrow_{\text{dB}} \\
x_2[x_2/(\text{I}x_3)[x_3/\text{I}]][x_1/\lambda y.\text{I}y] & \rightarrow_{\text{dB}} x_2[x_2/x_4[x_4/x_3][x_3/\text{I}]][x_1/\lambda y.\text{I}y] & \rightarrow_{\text{lsv}} \\
x_2[x_2/x_4[x_4/\text{I}][x_3/\text{I}]][x_1/\lambda y.\text{I}y] & \rightarrow_{\text{lsv}} x_2[x_2/\text{I}[x_4/\text{I}][x_3/\text{I}]][x_1/\lambda y.\text{I}y] & \rightarrow_{\text{lsv}} \\
\text{I}[x_2/\text{I}][x_4/\text{I}][x_3/\text{I}][x_1/\lambda y.\text{I}y] & &
\end{array}
$$

As for call-by-name, reduction preserves free variables, *i.e.* $t \rightarrow_{\text{need}} t'$ implies $\text{fv}(t) \supseteq \text{fv}(t')$. Notice that call-by-need reduction is also weak, so that answers are not **need**-reducible. Among the free variables of terms we distinguish the set of **needed free variables**, defined as follows:

$$
\begin{array}{ll}
\text{nv}(x) := \{x\} & \text{nv}(tu) := \text{nv}(t) \\
\text{nv}(\lambda x.t) := \emptyset & \text{nv}(t[y/u]) := \begin{cases} (\text{nv}(t) \backslash \{y\}) \cup \text{nv}(u) & \text{if } y \in \text{nv}(t) \\ \text{nv}(t) \backslash \{y\} & \text{if } y \notin \text{nv}(t) \end{cases}
\end{array}
$$

A useful property about needed free variables can be stated as follows:

Lemma 1. *Let $t \in \mathcal{T}_{\text{e}}$. Then $x \in \text{nv}(t)$ if and only if there exists N s.t. $t = \text{N}[\![x]\!]$.*

Thus for example, for $t = x_1[x_1/x_2y][x_2/x_3y']$, we have $x_3 \in \mathbf{nv}(t)$ and $t = \mathbb{N}[\![x_3]\!]$, for $\mathbb{N} = x_1[x_1/x_2y][x_2/\Box y']$.

We now need some general notions applicable to any reduction system $\mathcal{R}$. We denote by $\twoheadrightarrow_{\mathcal{R}}$ (resp. $\to^+_{\mathcal{R}}$) the **reflexive-transitive** (resp. **transitive**) closure of any given reduction relation $\to_{\mathcal{R}}$. A term t is **in $\mathcal{R}$-normal form**, written $t \in \mathcal{R}\text{-nf}$, if there is no t' s.t. $t \to_{\mathcal{R}} t'$; and t **has an $\mathcal{R}$-normal form** iff there is $t' \in \mathcal{R}\text{-nf}$ such that $t \twoheadrightarrow_{\mathcal{R}} t'$. A term t is said to be **weakly $\mathcal{R}$-normalizing**, or **$\mathcal{R}$-normalizing**, written $t \in \mathcal{WN}(\mathcal{R})$, iff t has an $\mathcal{R}$-nf.

It is well-known that the set of $\mathcal{T}_a$-terms that are in **name**-nf can be characterized by the following grammar:

$$\mathbf{Na} ::= \lambda x.t \mid \mathbf{Nva} \qquad\qquad \mathbf{Nva} ::= x \mid \mathbf{Nva}\ t$$

Similarly, $\mathcal{T}_e$-terms in **need**-nf can be specified by the following grammar:

$$\mathbf{Ne}\ \ ::= \mathsf{L}[\lambda x.t] \mid \mathbf{Nae}$$
$$\mathbf{Nae} ::= x \mid \mathbf{Nae}\ t \mid \mathbf{Nae}[x/u]\ x \notin \mathbf{nv}(\mathbf{Nae}) \mid \mathbf{Nae}[x/\mathbf{Nae}]\ x \in \mathbf{nv}(\mathbf{Nae})$$

Lemma 2. *Let $t \in \mathcal{T}_e$. Then $t \in \mathbf{Ne}$ iff t is in **need**-nf.*

Proof. The proof proceeds by first showing that $t \in \mathbf{Nae}$ iff t is in **need**-nf and t is not an answer. Then the statement of the lemma follows.   ◇

In order to relate **need**-nfs with **name**-nfs we use the following function $\_^{\downarrow}$ defined on $\mathcal{T}_e$-terms.

$$
\begin{aligned}
x^{\downarrow} &:= x & (\lambda x.t)^{\downarrow} &:= \lambda x.t^{\downarrow} \\
(tu)^{\downarrow} &:= t^{\downarrow}u^{\downarrow} & t[x/u]^{\downarrow} &:= t^{\downarrow}\{x/u^{\downarrow}\}
\end{aligned}
$$

Notice that $x \in \mathbf{nv}(t)$ implies $x \in \mathbf{nv}(t^{\downarrow})$.

Lemma 3. *Let $t \in \mathcal{T}_e$. Then t in **need**-nf implies $t^{\downarrow}$ in **name**-nf.*

Proof. We first remark that $t\{x/u\} \in \mathbf{Nva}$ iff $t \in \mathbf{Nva}$ and $x \notin \mathbf{nv}(t)$, or t and u are in $\mathbf{Nva}$ and $x \in \mathbf{nv}(t)$. The proof then proceeds by showing the following two statements by induction on the grammars.

$$1)\ t \in \mathbf{Nae} \text{ implies } t^{\downarrow} \in \mathbf{Nva} \qquad\qquad 2)\ t \in \mathbf{Ne} \text{ implies } t^{\downarrow} \in \mathbf{Na}$$

(1) (a). If $t = x \in \mathbf{Nae}$, then the statement is straightforward. (b). If $t = t_1t_2 \in \mathbf{Nae}$, where $t_1 \in \mathbf{Nae}$, then the *i.h.* gives $t_1{}^{\downarrow} \in \mathbf{Nva}$ so that $t^{\downarrow} = t_1{}^{\downarrow}t_2{}^{\downarrow} \in \mathbf{Nva}$. (c). If $t = t_1[x/t_2] \in \mathbf{Nae}$, where $t_1 \in \mathbf{Nae}$, then the *i.h.* gives $t_1{}^{\downarrow} \in \mathbf{Nva}$. We distinguish two cases. If $x \notin \mathbf{nv}(t_1)$, then $t^{\downarrow} = t_1{}^{\downarrow}\{x/t_2{}^{\downarrow}\} \in \mathbf{Nva}$. If $x \in \mathbf{nv}(t_1)$, then necessarily $t_2 \in \mathbf{Nva}$, so that the *i.h.* gives $t_2{}^{\downarrow} \in \mathbf{Nva}$. Then, $t^{\downarrow} = t_1{}^{\downarrow}\{x/t_2{}^{\downarrow}\} \in \mathbf{Nva}$.

(2) (a). If $t = \mathsf{L}[\lambda x.u] \in \mathbf{Ne}$, then $t^{\downarrow}$ is necessarily an abstraction so that $t^{\downarrow} \in \mathbf{Na}$. (b). If $t \in \mathbf{Ne}$ comes from $t \in \mathbf{Nae}$, then we apply the previous point.   ◇

3   Non-idempotent Intersection Types

Our results rely on typability of terms in suitable systems with non-idempotent intersection types. This section introduces such type systems. The first one, called $\mathcal{V}$ (for values), characterizes the set of name-normalizing terms; it extends the one in [15] which characterizes the set of *head* normalizing terms in λ-calculus. The second one, called $\mathcal{A}$ (for answers), characterizes the set of need-normalizing terms; it extends the one in [18] which characterizes the set of *head-linear* normalizing terms in λ-calculus with explicit substitutions.

In order to introduce the type systems, let us first introduce the notion of type. We denote finite multisets by double curly brackets, so that $\{\!\{\,\}\!\}$ denotes the empty multiset; $\{\!\{a, a, b\}\!\}$ denotes a multiset having two occurrences of the element a and one occurrence of b. We use $\sqcup$ for multiset union. Given a constant type a which denotes *answers*, and a countable infinite set of *base types* $\alpha, \beta, \gamma, \ldots$, we consider **types** and **multiset types** defined by the following grammars:

Types	$\tau, \sigma, \rho ::= \mathsf{a} \mid \alpha \mid \mathcal{M} \rightarrow \tau$	
Multiset types	$\mathcal{M} \quad ::= \{\!\{\tau_i\}\!\}_{i \in I}$	where I is a finite set

The type $\{\!\{\,\}\!\}$ plays the rôle of the universal ω type in [8,10]. Remark that types are *strict* [12,29], *i.e.* the right-hand sides of functional types are never multisets. Moreover, they make use of standard notations for multisets, as in [15], so that $\{\!\{\sigma, \sigma, \tau\}\!\}$ needs to be understood as the intersection type $\sigma \wedge \sigma \wedge \tau$, where the symbol $\wedge$ is commutative and associative but **non-idempotent**, *i.e.* $\sigma \wedge \sigma$ and σ are not equivalent.

Type assignments, written Γ, Δ, are functions from variables to multiset types, assigning the empty multiset to all but a finite set of the variables. The domain of Γ is $\mathrm{dom}(\Gamma) := \{x \mid \Gamma(x) \neq \{\!\{\,\}\!\}\}$. The **union of type assignments**, written $\Gamma + \Delta$, is a type assignment defined by $(\Gamma + \Delta)(x) := \Gamma(x) \sqcup \Delta(x)$, where $\sqcup$ denotes multiset union; thus, $\mathrm{dom}(\Gamma + \Delta) = \mathrm{dom}(\Gamma) \cup \mathrm{dom}(\Delta)$. An example is $\{x : \{\!\{\sigma\}\!\}, y : \{\!\{\tau\}\!\}\} + \{x : \{\!\{\sigma'\}\!\}, z : \{\!\{\tau'\}\!\}\} = \{x : \{\!\{\sigma, \sigma'\}\!\}, y : \{\!\{\tau\}\!\}, z : \{\!\{\tau'\}\!\}\}$. For convenience, we write $+_{i \in I} \Gamma_i$ for a finite union of type assignments (where $I = \emptyset$ gives an empty function), instead of the more traditional notation $\Sigma_{i \in I} \Gamma_i$. When $\mathrm{dom}(\Gamma)$ and $\mathrm{dom}(\Delta)$ are disjoint we use $\Gamma; \Delta$ instead of $\Gamma + \Delta$, and we write $x : \{\!\{\sigma_i\}\!\}_{i \in I}; \Gamma$, even when $I = \emptyset$, for the assignment $(x : \{\!\{\sigma_i\}\!\}_{i \in I}; \Gamma)(x) = \{\!\{\sigma_i\}\!\}_{i \in I}$ and $(x : \{\!\{\sigma_i\}\!\}_{i \in I}; \Gamma)(y) = \Gamma(y)$ if $y \neq x$. We denote by $\Gamma \backslash\!\backslash x$ the assignment $(\Gamma \backslash\!\backslash x)(x) = \{\!\{\,\}\!\}$ and $(\Gamma \backslash\!\backslash x)(y) = \Gamma(y)$ if $y \neq x$. We write $x \# \Gamma$ iff $x \notin \mathrm{dom}(\Gamma)$.

Type judgments have the form $\Gamma \vdash t : \tau$, where Γ is a type assignment, t is a term and τ is a type. The $\mathcal{V}$-**type system** ($\mathcal{V}$ for value) for $\mathcal{T}_{\mathsf{a}}$-terms is given by the typing rules in Fig. 1 and the $\mathcal{A}$-**type system** ($\mathcal{A}$ for answer) for $\mathcal{T}_{\mathsf{e}}$-terms is given by the typing rules in Fig. 2. System $\mathcal{V}$ can be seen as the restriction of system $\mathcal{A}$ to $\mathcal{T}_{\mathsf{a}}$-terms. Given $\mathcal{S} \in \{\mathcal{V}, \mathcal{A}\}$, a **(type) derivation** in $\mathcal{S}$ is a tree obtained by applying the (inductive) rules of the system $\mathcal{S}$. We write $\Phi \rhd_{\mathcal{S}} \Gamma \vdash t : \tau$ if there is a derivation Φ in system $\mathcal{S}$ typing t, *i.e.* ending in the

$$\frac{}{x:\{\!\!\{\tau\}\!\!\} \vdash x:\tau} \ (\mathbf{ax}) \qquad \frac{\Gamma \vdash t:\{\!\!\{\sigma_i\}\!\!\}_{i\in I}\to\tau \qquad (\Delta_i \vdash u:\sigma_i)_{i\in I}}{\Gamma +_{i\in I} \Delta_i \vdash tu:\tau} \ (\to \mathbf{e})$$

$$\frac{\Gamma \vdash t:\tau}{\Gamma \setminus\!\!\setminus x \vdash \lambda x.t:\Gamma(x)\to\tau} \ (\to \mathbf{i}) \qquad \frac{}{\vdash \lambda x.t:\mathbf{a}} \ (\mathbf{val})$$

Fig. 1. The non-idempotent intersection type system $\mathcal{V}$ for terms in $\mathcal{T}_\mathbf{a}$

$$\frac{}{x:\{\!\!\{\tau\}\!\!\} \vdash x:\tau} \ (\mathbf{ax}) \qquad \frac{\Gamma \vdash t:\{\!\!\{\sigma_i\}\!\!\}_{i\in I}\to\tau \qquad (\Delta_i \vdash u:\sigma_i)_{i\in I}}{\Gamma +_{i\in I} \Delta_i \vdash tu:\tau} \ (\to \mathbf{e})$$

$$\frac{\Gamma \vdash t:\tau}{\Gamma \setminus\!\!\setminus x \vdash \lambda x.t:\Gamma(x)\to\tau} \ (\to \mathbf{i}) \qquad \frac{}{\vdash \mathsf{L}[\lambda x.t]:\mathbf{a}} \ (\mathbf{ans})$$

$$\frac{x:\{\!\!\{\sigma_i\}\!\!\}_{i\in I}; \Gamma \vdash t:\tau \qquad (\Delta_i \vdash u:\sigma_i)_{i\in I}}{\Gamma +_{i\in I} \Delta_i \vdash t[x/u]:\tau} \ (\mathbf{cut})$$

Fig. 2. The non-idempotent intersection type system $\mathcal{A}$ for terms in $\mathcal{T}_\mathbf{e}$

type judgment $\Gamma \vdash t:\tau$. A term t is **typable** in $\mathcal{S}$ iff there is a derivation in $\mathcal{S}$ typing t. The **size** of a type derivation Φ is a natural number $\mathbf{sz}(\Phi)$ denoting the number of nodes of the tree Φ.

The constant type $\mathbf{a}$ in rules (**val**) and (**ans**) is used to type values and answers respectively, and rule (**cut**) of system $\mathcal{A}$ may also type answers (when $\tau = \mathbf{a}$ and $t = \mathsf{L}[\lambda x.t']$). The axiom (**ax**) is *relevant* (there is no weakening) and the rules ($\to \mathbf{e}$) and (**cut**) are *multiplicative*; both characteristics being related to the *resource aware* semantics of the underlying calculus. A particular case of rule ($\to \mathbf{e}$) (resp. (**cut**)) is when $I = \emptyset$: the subterm u occurring in the *typed* term tu (resp $t[x/u]$) turns out to be *untyped*. Thus for example, if Ω is the (untypable) non-terminating term $(\lambda z.zz)(\lambda z.zz)$, then from the type derivation of $x:\{\!\!\{\sigma\}\!\!\} \vdash \lambda y.x:\{\!\!\{\ \}\!\!\}\to\sigma$ we can construct one for $x:\{\!\!\{\sigma\}\!\!\} \vdash (\lambda y.x)\Omega:\sigma$, and from the type derivation of $x:\{\!\!\{\sigma\}\!\!\} \vdash x:\sigma$ we can construct one for $x:\{\!\!\{\sigma\}\!\!\} \vdash x[y/\Omega]:\sigma$. A major difference between system $\mathcal{V}$ and the one in [15] is the rule (**val**) which types *any* kind of abstraction. Indeed, given $\Delta = \lambda x.xx$, the abstraction $\lambda x.\Delta\Delta$ –not being head-normalizing in λ-calculus– is typable in our type system (which characterizes **name**-normalizing terms) but is not typable in [15] (which characterizes head-normalizing terms). The same remark applies to the rule (**ans**) in system $\mathcal{A}$ with respect to the one in [18]. Here is an example of typing derivation in system $\mathcal{A}$.

$$\dfrac{\dfrac{z:\{\!\{\{\!\{\sigma\}\!\}\to\sigma\}\!\}\vdash z:\{\!\{\sigma\}\!\}\to\sigma \quad x:\{\!\{\{\!\{\sigma\}\!\}\to\sigma\}\!\}\vdash x:\{\!\{\sigma\}\!\}\to\sigma}{\dfrac{x:\{\!\{\{\!\{\sigma\}\!\}\to\sigma\}\!\}\vdash z[z/x]:\{\!\{\sigma\}\!\}\to\sigma}{\dfrac{x:\{\sigma,\{\!\{\sigma\}\!\}\to\sigma\}\vdash z[z/x]x:\sigma}{\vdash\lambda x.z[z/x]x:\{\sigma,\{\!\{\sigma\}\!\}\to\sigma\}\to\sigma}}} \qquad x:\{\!\{\sigma\}\!\}\vdash x:\sigma}$$

It is worth noticing that system $\mathcal{A}$ is a conservative extension of system $\mathcal{V}$:

Lemma 4. *Let* $t\in\mathcal{T}_a$. *Then* $\varPhi\rhd_{\mathcal{V}}\varGamma\vdash t{:}\sigma$ *iff* $\varPhi\rhd_{\mathcal{A}}\varGamma\vdash t{:}\sigma$.

A last remark of this section concerns relevance. Indeed, given $\varPhi\rhd_{\mathcal{S}}\varGamma\vdash t{:}\sigma$, not every free variable in t necessarily appears in the domain of $\varGamma$. More precisely, both systems enjoy the following property, that can be easily shown by induction on derivations.

Lemma 5. *Let* $\mathcal{S}\in\{\mathcal{V},\mathcal{A}\}$. *If* $\varPhi\rhd_{\mathcal{S}}\varGamma\vdash t{:}\sigma$ *then* $\mathtt{dom}(\varGamma)\subseteq\mathtt{fv}(t)$.

4   Characterization of name-normalizing Terms

In this section we adapt the (standard) characterization of head-normalizing terms of the λ-calculus to our call-by-name calculus, *i.e.* we show that a term t is name-normalizing iff t is typable in system $\mathcal{V}$.

The characterization is split in two parts. The first one shows that typable terms in system $\mathcal{V}$ are name-normalizing, a result which is based on a *weighted subject reduction* property. In contrast to similar results for *idempotent* intersection type systems, which are typically based on *reducibility* arguments, quantitative information of type derivations, obtained by means of *non-idempotent* types, provides a completely *combinatorial* proof. This is exactly the place where the quantitative approach by means of non-idempotent types makes the difference. The second part of the characterization shows that name-normalizing terms are typable in $\mathcal{V}$, and is based on a *subject expansion* property.

We start with the subject reduction property which uses the following lemma.

Lemma 6 (Substitution). *If* $\varPhi_t\rhd_{\mathcal{V}}x{:}\{\!\{\sigma_i\}\!\}_{i\in I};\varGamma\vdash t{:}\tau$ *and* $(\varPhi_u^i\rhd_{\mathcal{V}}\varDelta_i\vdash u{:}\sigma_i)_{i\in I}$ *then there exists a derivation* $\varPhi_{t\{x/u\}}$ *s.t.* $\varPhi_{t\{x/u\}}\rhd_{\mathcal{V}}\varGamma+_{i\in I}\varDelta_i\vdash t\{x/u\}{:}\tau$. *Moreover,* $\mathtt{sz}(\varPhi_{t\{x/u\}})=\mathtt{sz}(\varPhi_t)+_{i\in I}\mathtt{sz}(\varPhi_u^i)-|I|$.

Proof. By induction on $\varPhi_t$. Let $\varPhi_t\rhd_{\mathcal{V}} x{:}\{\!\{\sigma_i\}\!\}_{i\in I};\varGamma\vdash\lambda y.u{:}a$ so that $\varGamma=\emptyset$ and $I=\emptyset$. Since $\varPhi_{t\{x/u\}}\rhd_{\mathcal{V}}\emptyset\vdash\lambda y.u\{x/u\}{:}a$, we conclude because $\emptyset=\varGamma+_{i\in\emptyset}\varDelta_i$. The other cases are similar to those of the λ-calculus (see for example [7]). $\Diamond$

Subject reduction can now be stated in the following form.

Theorem 1 (Weighted Subject Reduction for name). *Let* $\varPhi\rhd_{\mathcal{V}}\varGamma\vdash t{:}\tau$. *If* $t\to_{\mathtt{name}}t'$, *then there exists* $\varPhi'$ *s.t.* $\varPhi'\rhd_{\mathcal{V}}\varGamma\vdash t'{:}\tau$. *Moreover,* $\mathtt{sz}(\varPhi)>\mathtt{sz}(\varPhi')$.

Proof. By induction on Φ. The proof proceeds as that of the λ-calculus [7]. It is worth noticing that when $t = (\lambda x.u)u'$, the subterm $\lambda x.u$ is necessarily typed in Φ using rule $(\to i)$, so that Lemma 6 can be applied to conclude. $\Diamond$

In order to show that **name**-normalizing terms are $\mathcal{V}$-typable we use a subject expansion property, which needs the following lemma.

Lemma 7 (Reverse Substitution). *If* $\Phi_{t\{x/u\}} \rhd_{\mathcal{V}} \Gamma \vdash t\{x/u\}{:}\tau$, *then* $\exists \Gamma_0$, $\exists \Phi_t$, $\exists I$, $\exists (\Delta_i)_{i \in I}$, $\exists (\sigma_i)_{i \in I}$, $\exists (\Phi_u^i)_{i \in I}$ *such that* $\Gamma = \Gamma_0 +_{i \in I} \Delta_i$, *and* $\Phi_t \rhd_{\mathcal{V}}$ $x : \{\!\!\{\sigma_i\}\!\!\}_{i \in I}; \Gamma_0 \vdash t{:}\tau$ *and* $(\Phi_u^i \rhd_{\mathcal{V}} \Delta_i \vdash u{:}\sigma_i)_{i \in I}$.

Proof. By induction on $\Phi_{t\{x/u\}}$. Suppose $\Phi_{t\{x/u\}} \rhd_{\mathcal{V}} \emptyset \vdash \lambda y.u{:}a$ so that $\Gamma = \emptyset$. There are two cases to consider: (1) $t = \lambda y.v$ and $u = v\{x/u\}$. Then $\Phi_t \rhd_{\mathcal{V}}$ $\emptyset \vdash \lambda y.v{:}a$, where $\Gamma_0 = \emptyset$ and $I = \emptyset$ so that the property trivially holds. (2) $t = x$ and $u = \lambda y.v$. Then $\Phi_t \rhd_{\mathcal{V}} x : \{\!\!\{a\}\!\!\} \vdash x{:}a$, $\Phi_u \rhd_{\mathcal{V}} \vdash \lambda y.v{:}a$, so that we let $\Gamma_0 = \emptyset$, $I = \{1\}$, $\sigma_1 = a$ and $\Delta_1 = \emptyset$ and $\Gamma = \emptyset = \Gamma_0 + \Delta_1$.

All the other cases proceed as the one of the λ-calculus [7]. $\Diamond$

Theorem 2 (Subject Expansion for name). *Let* $\Phi' \rhd_{\mathcal{V}} \Gamma \vdash t'{:}\tau$. *If* $t \to_{\text{name}} t'$, *then there exists* Φ *s.t.* $\Phi \rhd_{\mathcal{V}} \Gamma \vdash t{:}\tau$.

Proof. By induction on Φ' using Lemma 7. $\Diamond$

We can now state the following full characterization result of this section:

Theorem 3. *Let* $t \in \mathcal{T}_a$. *Then,* $\Phi \rhd_{\mathcal{V}} \Gamma \vdash t{:}\tau$ *iff* $t \in \mathcal{WN}(\text{name})$.

Proof. Let $\Phi \rhd_{\mathcal{V}} \Gamma \vdash t{:}\tau$. Then **name**-reduction necessarily terminates by Theorem 1 and thus $t \in \mathcal{WN}(\text{name})$.

Let $t \in \mathcal{WN}(\text{name})$ so that $t \twoheadrightarrow_{\text{name}}^k t'$, where $t' \in$ **name**-nf. We proceed by induction on k. If $k = 0$ (*i.e.* $t = t'$), then t is a **name**-nf. We have two cases.

- If $t = \lambda y.v$, then the property trivially holds with $\Gamma = \emptyset$ and $\tau = a$.
- If $t = xt_1 \ldots t_n$ $(n \geq 0)$, let $\Gamma = \{x{:}\{\!\!\{\tau\}\!\!\}\}$, where $\tau = \{\!\!\{\ \}\!\!\} \to \cdots \to \{\!\!\{\ \}\!\!\} \to \alpha$ (α is any base type and τ contains n occurrences of $\{\!\!\{\ \}\!\!\}$). By the rule (ax) and n applications of $(\to e)$ we obtain a derivation in $\mathcal{V}$ ending in $\Gamma \vdash xt_1 \ldots t_n{:}\alpha$.

Otherwise, let $t \to_{\text{name}} u \twoheadrightarrow_{\text{name}}^k t'$. By the *i.h.* we have a derivation in $\mathcal{V}$ ending in $\Gamma \vdash u{:}\tau$. Thus by Theorem 2 the same holds form t. $\Diamond$

5   Characterization of need-normalizing Terms

This section gives a characterization of **need**-normalizing terms by means of $\mathcal{A}$-typability, *i.e.* we show that a term t is **need**-normalizing iff t is typable in system $\mathcal{A}$. At first sight, this result follows the same lines of Sect. 4, however, it is much trickier and requires the development of special tools dealing with need contexts. To the best of our knowledge, this is the first time that call-by-need normalization is characterized by means of typing technology.

Similarly to the call-by-name case, we split the characterization proof in two parts and we use subject reduction and expansion properties to show them. More precisely, the first part of the characterization states that typable terms in system $\mathcal{A}$ are normalizing in call-by-need, a result based on a *weighted subject reduction* property, obtained by using quantitative information of the (non-idempotent) type derivations of system $\mathcal{A}$. The second part of the characterization states that **need**-normalizing terms are typable in system $\mathcal{A}$, a property based on the *subject expansion* property.

In contrast to the call-by-name case, handling **need**-reduction is quite involved, particularly due to the use of contexts in the rewriting rules defining the relation. To deal with this difficulty, we introduce a technical tool which consists in extending system $\mathcal{A}$ (*cf.* Sect. 3) with typing rules for *list contexts* (Fig. 3). The type judgments have the form $\Gamma \Vdash \mathsf{L} \triangleright \Delta$, where Γ, Δ are type assignments and L is a list context. The left-hand side Γ of a judgment $\Gamma \Vdash \mathsf{L} \triangleright \Delta$ is a type assignment for the (typed) free variables of L, while the right-hand side Δ is a type assignment for the term which is supposed to fill in the hole of L. These rules should then be considered modulo α-conversion. Notice the use of two different kinds of assignments in the second type rule: the assignments $(\Delta_i)_{i \in I}$ are used to type the copies of u affecting the free occurrences of x in the list L, while $(\Delta_j)_{j \in J}$ are used to type the copies of u affecting the free occurrences of x in the term which will fill the hole of L.

$$\frac{}{\emptyset \Vdash \square \triangleright \emptyset} \qquad \frac{x : \{\!\!\{\sigma_i\}\!\!\}_{i \in I}; \Gamma \Vdash \mathsf{L} \triangleright \Delta \quad x \# \Delta \quad (\Delta_k \vdash u{:}\sigma_k)_{k \in I \uplus J}}{\Gamma +_{k \in I \uplus J} \Delta_k \Vdash \mathsf{L}[x/u] \triangleright \Delta; x : \{\!\!\{\sigma_j\}\!\!\}_{j \in J}}$$

Fig. 3. Extending the intersection type system $\mathcal{A}$ to list contexts

The following lemma decomposes a type derivation of a term $\mathsf{L}[t]$ into one derivation for the context L and another one for the term t. Reciprocally, context and term derivations can be combined if their types coincide. The proof can be done by induction on L.

Lemma 8. $\Phi_{\mathsf{L}[t]} \triangleright_{\mathcal{A}} \Lambda \vdash \mathsf{L}[t] : \sigma$ *iff* $\exists \Gamma, \exists \Pi, \exists \Delta, \exists \Phi_{\mathsf{L}}, \exists \Phi_t$, *such that* $\Lambda = \Gamma + \Pi$ *and* $\Phi_{\mathsf{L}} \triangleright_{\mathcal{A}} \Gamma \Vdash \mathsf{L} \triangleright \Delta$ *and* $\Phi_t \triangleright_{\mathcal{A}} \Delta; \Pi \vdash t : \sigma$. *Moreover,* $\mathsf{sz}(\Phi_{\mathsf{L}[t]}) = \mathsf{sz}(\Phi_{\mathsf{L}}) + \mathsf{sz}(\Phi_t) - 1$.

Combining different derivable typing judgments of the same list context by means of multiset union yields a derivable typing judgment. Moreover, their sizes can be related using the notion of **height**, defined on list contexts as follows: $\mathsf{height}(\square) := 1$ and $\mathsf{height}(\mathsf{L}'[y/v]) := \mathsf{height}(\mathsf{L}') + 1$.

Lemma 9. *If* $(\Phi_L^j \triangleright_{\mathcal{A}} \Gamma_j \Vdash L \triangleright \Delta_j)_{j \in J}$, *then there exists a derivation* Φ_L *s.t.* $\Phi_L \triangleright_{\mathcal{A}}$ $+_{j \in J} \Gamma_j \Vdash L \triangleright +_{j \in J} \Delta_j$. *Moreover,* $\text{sz}(\Phi_L) = +_{j \in J} \text{sz}(\Phi_L^j) - (\text{height}(L) \cdot (|J| - 1))$.

Proof. Notice that the statement also holds in the case $J = \emptyset$. The proof is by induction on L (see the Appendix for details). ◇

To achieve the proof of the Weighted Subject Reduction property for the need-calculus, we first need to guarantee soundness of the (partial) substitution operation used in our framework, *i.e.* if $N[\![x]\!]$ and u are typable, then $N[\![u]\!]$ is typable too. Moreover, $|K|$ elements of the multiset type $\{\!\{\sigma_i\}\!\}_{i \in I}$ associated to x in the type derivation of $N[\![x]\!]$ are consumed, for some $K \subseteq I$.

Lemma 10 (Partial Substitution). *If* $\Phi_{N[\![x]\!]} \triangleright_{\mathcal{A}} x : \{\!\{\sigma_i\}\!\}_{i \in I}; \Gamma \vdash N[\![x]\!] : \tau$ *and* $(\Phi_u^i \triangleright_{\mathcal{A}} \Delta_i \vdash u : \sigma_i)_{i \in I}$ *then* $\exists \Phi_{N[\![u]\!]}$ *s.t.* $\Phi_{N[\![u]\!]} \triangleright_{\mathcal{A}} x : \{\!\{\sigma_i\}\!\}_{i \in I \setminus K}; \Gamma +_{k \in K} \Delta_k \vdash N[\![u]\!] : \tau$, *for some* $K \subseteq I$ *where* $\text{sz}(\Phi_{N[\![u]\!]}) = \text{sz}(\Phi_{N[\![x]\!]}) +_{k \in K} \text{sz}(\Phi_u^k) - |K|$.

Proof. By induction on typing derivations (a similar proof appears in [17]). ◇

To complete the subject reduction argument we still need to guarantee that every needed variable of a typed term is necessarily typed, a property which is specified by means of the following lemma.

Lemma 11. *If* $\Phi \triangleright_{\mathcal{A}} \Gamma \vdash N[\![x]\!] : \tau$, *then* $\exists \Gamma'$, $\exists I \neq \emptyset$, *and* $\exists (\sigma_i)_{i \in I}$ *such that* $\Gamma = x : \{\!\{\sigma_i\}\!\}_{i \in I}; \Gamma'$.

Proof. By induction on N. The base case $N = \square$ is straightforward. We only show here the interesting inductive case $N[\![x]\!] = N_1[\![y]\!][y/N_2[\![x]\!]]$, for which Φ has necessarily the following form, where $\Gamma = \Pi +_{j \in J} \Delta_j$.

$$\frac{y : \{\!\{\rho_j\}\!\}_{j \in J}; \Pi \vdash N_1[\![y]\!] : \tau \quad (\Delta_j \vdash N_2[\![x]\!] : \rho_j)_{j \in J}}{\Pi +_{j \in J} \Delta_j \vdash N_1[\![y]\!][y/N_2[\![x]\!]] : \tau}$$

By the *i.h.* on the left derivation we have $J \neq \emptyset$. By the *i.h.* on the right derivations $\Delta_j = x : \{\!\{\tau_j^i\}\!\}_{i \in I_j}; \Delta_j'$ and $I_j \neq \emptyset$ for all $j \in J$. Moreover, $\Pi = x : \{\!\{\tau_k\}\!\}_{k \in K}; \Pi'$, where K could be empty. Then

$$\Pi +_{j \in J} \Delta_j = (x : \{\!\{\tau_k\}\!\}_{k \in K}; \Pi') +_{j \in J} (x : \{\!\{\tau_j^i\}\!\}_{i \in I_j}; \Delta_j') =$$
$$x : \{\!\{\tau_k\}\!\}_{k \in K} +_{j \in J} x : \{\!\{\tau_j^i\}\!\}_{i \in I_j}; (\Pi' +_{j \in J} \Delta_j')$$

The property then holds for $\{\!\{\sigma_i\}\!\}_{i \in I} = \{\!\{\tau_k\}\!\}_{k \in K} +_{j \in J} \{\!\{\tau_j^i\}\!\}_{i \in I_j}$ and $\Gamma' = \Pi' +_{j \in J} \Delta_j'$. We have $I \neq \emptyset$ since $J \neq \emptyset$ and $I_j \neq \emptyset$ for all $j \in J$. ◇

Subject reduction can now be stated in a combinatorial way, by using the $\text{sz}(\_)$ measure on derivations defined in Sect. 3.

Theorem 4 (Weighted Subject Reduction for need). *Let* $\Phi \triangleright_{\mathcal{A}} \Gamma \vdash t : \tau$. *If* $t \rightarrow_{\text{need}} t'$, *then there exists* Φ' *s.t.* $\Phi' \triangleright_{\mathcal{A}} \Gamma \vdash t' : \tau$. *Moreover,* $\text{sz}(\Phi) > \text{sz}(\Phi')$.

Proof. By induction on $t \rightarrow_{\text{need}} t'$, using Lemmas 8, 9, 10 and 11. We refer the interested reader to the Appendix for full details of the proof. ◇

To show that **need**-normalizing terms are $\mathcal{A}$-typable we use a subject expansion property, which needs the following lemma.

Lemma 12 (Reverse Partial Substitution). *Let* $\mathtt{N}[\![x]\!], s$ *be terms s.t.* $x \notin \mathtt{fv}(s)$ *and* $\Phi_{\mathtt{N}[\![s]\!]} \rhd_{\mathcal{A}} \Gamma \vdash \mathtt{N}[\![s]\!]{:}\tau$. *Then* $\exists \Gamma_0$, $\exists \Phi_{\mathtt{N}[\![x]\!]}$, $\exists I$, $\exists (\Delta_i)_{i \in I}$, $\exists (\sigma_i)_{i \in I}$, $\exists (\Phi_s^i)_{i \in I}$ *s.t.* $\Gamma = \Gamma_0 +_{i \in I} \Delta_i$ *and* $\Phi_{\mathtt{N}[\![x]\!]} \rhd_{\mathcal{A}} x : \{\!\!\{\sigma_i\}\!\!\}_{i \in I} + \Gamma_0 \vdash \mathtt{N}[\![x]\!]{:}\tau$ *and* $(\Phi_s^i \rhd_{\mathcal{A}} \Delta_i \vdash s{:}\sigma_i)_{i \in I}$.

Proof. By induction on the structure of $\mathtt{N}[\![s]\!]$.

- If $\mathtt{N} = \Box$, then $\mathtt{N}[\![s]\!] = s$ and the result holds, for $\Gamma_0 = \emptyset$, $|I| = 1$ and $\sigma_1 = \tau$.
- If $\mathtt{N} = \lambda y.\mathtt{M}$ then the property is straightforward by the *i.h.* (since $y \notin \mathtt{fv}(s)$ by α-conversion).
- If $\mathtt{N} = \mathtt{M}r$ then $\mathtt{N}[\![s]\!] = \mathtt{M}[\![s]\!]r$ and by construction $\Gamma = \Pi +_{j \in J} \Gamma_j$ and $\Phi_{\mathtt{M}[\![s]\!]} \rhd \Pi \vdash \mathtt{M}[\![s]\!]{:}\{\!\!\{\rho_j\}\!\!\}_{j \in J} \to \tau$ and $(\Phi_r^j \rhd \Gamma_j \vdash r{:}\rho_j)_{j \in J}$. By the *i.h.* $\Pi = \Pi_0 +_{i \in I} \Delta_i$ where $x : \{\!\!\{\sigma_i\}\!\!\}_{i \in I} + \Pi_0 \vdash \mathtt{M}[\![x]\!]{:}\{\!\!\{\rho_j\}\!\!\}_{j \in J} \to \tau$ and $(\Delta_i \vdash s{:}\sigma_i)_{i \in I}$. Then, by the rule $(\to \mathbf{e})$, $x : \{\!\!\{\sigma_i\}\!\!\}_{i \in I} + \Pi_0 +_{j \in J} \Gamma_j \vdash \mathtt{M}[\![x]\!]r{:}\tau$. The result then holds for $\Gamma_0 := \Pi_0 +_{j \in J} \Gamma_j$.
- If $\mathtt{N} = r\mathtt{M}$ then $\mathtt{N}[\![s]\!] = r\mathtt{M}[\![s]\!]$ and by construction $\Gamma = \Pi +_{j \in J} \Gamma_j$ and $\Phi_r \rhd \Pi \vdash r{:}\{\!\!\{\rho_j\}\!\!\}_{j \in J} \to \tau$ and $(\Phi_{\mathtt{M}[\![s]\!]}^j \rhd \Gamma_j \vdash \mathtt{M}[\![s]\!]{:}\rho_j)_{j \in J}$. By the *i.h.* for each $j \in J$, $\Gamma_j = \Gamma_0^j +_{i \in I_j} \Gamma_i^j$ where $x : \{\!\!\{\sigma_i\}\!\!\}_{i \in I_j} + \Gamma_0^j \vdash \mathtt{M}[\![x]\!]{:}\rho_j$ and $(\Gamma_i^j \vdash s{:}\sigma_i)_{i \in I_j}$. Let $I := \cup_{j \in J} I_j$. Then, by the rule $(\to \mathbf{e})$, $\Pi +_{j \in J} (x : \{\!\!\{\sigma_i\}\!\!\}_{i \in I_j} + \Gamma_0^j) \vdash r\mathtt{M}[\![x]\!]{:}\tau$. Note that $\Pi +_{j \in J} (x : \{\!\!\{\sigma_i\}\!\!\}_{i \in I_j} + \Gamma_0^j) = x : \{\!\!\{\sigma_i\}\!\!\}_{i \in I} + \Pi +_{j \in J} \Gamma_0^j$. The result then holds for $\Gamma_0 := \Pi +_{j \in J} \Gamma_0^j$.
- All the remaining cases are similar to the previous ones. $\Diamond$

Theorem 5 (Subject Expansion for need). *Let* $\Phi' \rhd_{\mathcal{A}} \Gamma \vdash t'{:}\tau$. *If* $t \to_{\mathbf{need}} t'$, *then there exists* Φ *s.t.* $\Phi \rhd_{\mathcal{A}} \Gamma \vdash t{:}\tau$.

Proof. By induction on Φ' using Lemmas 8, 9 and 12. $\Diamond$

To state the full characterization result of this section, we still need to relate typing of $\mathcal{T}_\mathbf{e}$-terms in system $\mathcal{A}$ with typing of $\mathcal{T}_\mathbf{a}$-terms in system $\mathcal{V}$.

Lemma 13. *Let* $t \in \mathcal{T}_\mathbf{e}$. *Then* $\Phi \rhd_{\mathcal{V}} \Gamma \vdash t^{\downarrow}{:}\sigma$ *implies* $\Phi' \rhd_{\mathcal{A}} \Gamma \vdash t{:}\sigma$.

Proof. By induction on t.

- If $t = x$, then $t^{\downarrow} = x$. The derivation Φ has the form $x : \{\!\!\{\sigma\}\!\!\} \vdash x{:}\sigma$ so that Φ' has also the form $x : \{\!\!\{\sigma\}\!\!\} \vdash x{:}\sigma$.
- If $t = \lambda x.u$, then $t^{\downarrow} = \lambda x.u^{\downarrow}$. We have $\Gamma = \Delta \setminus\!\setminus x$ and $\sigma = \Delta(x) \to \tau$, where $\Delta \setminus\!\setminus x \vdash \lambda x.u^{\downarrow}{:}\Delta(x) \to \tau$ is necessarily derivable from a derivation $\Phi_u \rhd_{\mathcal{V}} \Delta \vdash u^{\downarrow}{:}\tau$. The *i.h.* gives $\Phi_u' \rhd_{\mathcal{A}} \Delta \vdash u{:}\tau$ so that we construct $\Phi' \rhd_{\mathcal{A}} \Delta \setminus\!\setminus x \vdash \lambda x.u{:}\Delta(x) \to \tau$ which concludes the proof.
- If $t = t_1 t_2$, then the proof proceeds by induction as in the previous case.
- If $t = t_1[x/t_2]$, then $t^{\downarrow} = t_1^{\downarrow}\{x/t_2^{\downarrow}\}$. By Lemma 7 we know that $\Gamma = \Gamma_0 +_{i \in I} \Delta_i$ and $\Phi_{t_1^{\downarrow}} \rhd_{\mathcal{V}} x : \{\!\!\{\sigma_i\}\!\!\}_{i \in I}; \Gamma_0 \vdash t_1^{\downarrow}{:}\tau$ and $(\Phi_{t_2^{\downarrow}}^i \rhd_{\mathcal{V}} \Delta_i \vdash t_2^{\downarrow}{:}\sigma_i)_{i \in I}$. The *i.h.* then gives $\Phi_{t_1}' \rhd_{\mathcal{A}} x : \{\!\!\{\sigma_i\}\!\!\}_{i \in I}; \Gamma_0 \vdash t_1{:}\tau$ and $(\Phi_{t_2}'^i \rhd_{\mathcal{A}} \Delta_i \vdash t_2{:}\sigma_i)_{i \in I}$. We then conclude $\Phi_t' \rhd_{\mathcal{A}} \Gamma \vdash t_1[x/t_2]{:}\tau$ by using rule (**cut**). $\Diamond$

We can now state the full characterization result, which is one of the main results of this paper. The implication "typable terms in system $\mathcal{A}$ are need-normalizing" is obtained through the *weighted subject reduction*, which provides a completely *combinatorial* argument of this property, as in the call-by-name case. This is exactly the advantage provided by the quantitative approach based on non-idempotent types, which makes the difference with a *qualitative* system based on idempotent intersection types.

Theorem 6. *Let $t \in \mathcal{T}_e$. Then, $\Phi \triangleright_{\mathcal{A}} \Gamma \vdash t{:}\tau$ iff $t \in \mathcal{WN}(\mathbf{need})$.*

Proof. Let $\Phi \triangleright \Gamma \vdash t{:}\tau$. Then **need**-reduction necessarily terminates by Theorem 4 so that $t \in \mathcal{WN}(\mathbf{need})$.

Let $t \in \mathcal{WN}(\mathbf{need})$, so that $t \twoheadrightarrow^k_{\mathbf{need}} t'$, where $t' \in \mathbf{need}\text{-nf}$. We proceed by induction on k. If $k = 0$ (*i.e.* $t = t'$), then t is in **need**-nf. By Lemma 3 $t^{\downarrow}$ is in **name**-nf. Then $\Phi \triangleright_{\mathcal{V}} \Gamma \vdash t^{\downarrow}{:}\sigma$ by Theorem 3 and $\Phi \triangleright_{\mathcal{A}} \Gamma \vdash t{:}\sigma$ by Lemma 13.

Otherwise, let $t \to_{\mathbf{need}} u \twoheadrightarrow^k_{\mathbf{need}} t'$. By the *i.h.* we have $\Phi' \triangleright_{\mathcal{A}} \Gamma \vdash u{:}\tau$, thus by Theorem 5 we obtain $\Phi \triangleright_{\mathcal{A}} \Gamma \vdash t{:}\tau$.   ◇

6   Soundness and Completeness

This section uses the two characterization results developed in Sects. 4 and 5 to prove soundness and completeness of call-by-need w.r.t call-by-name. More precisely, a call-by-name interpreter stops in a value if and only if the call-by-need interpreter stops in an answer. This implies that call-by-need and call-by-name are observationally equivalent, so that in particular call-by-need turns out to be a correct implementation of call-by-name.

Lemma 14. *Let $t \in \mathcal{T}_a$. Then $t \in \mathcal{WN}(\mathbf{need}) \Leftrightarrow t \in \mathcal{WN}(\mathbf{name})$.*

Proof. Let $t \in \mathcal{WN}(\mathbf{need})$. Then $\Phi \triangleright_{\mathcal{A}} \Gamma \vdash t{:}\tau$ holds by Theorem 6, and $\Phi \triangleright_{\mathcal{V}} \Gamma \vdash t{:}\tau$ holds by Lemma 4, thus we get $t \in \mathcal{WN}(\mathbf{name})$ by Theorem 3. Conversely, let $t \in \mathcal{WN}(\mathbf{name})$. Then $\Phi \triangleright_{\mathcal{V}} \Gamma \vdash t{:}\tau$ holds by Theorem 3, so that $\Phi \triangleright_{\mathcal{A}} \Gamma \vdash t{:}\tau$ holds by Lemma 4, and thus we get $t \in \mathcal{WN}(\mathbf{need})$ by Theorem 6.   ◇

Given a reduction relation $\mathcal{R}$ on a term language $\mathcal{T}$, and an associated notion of context for the term language $\mathcal{T}$, we define t to be **observationally equivalent** to u, written $t \cong_{\mathcal{R}} u$, if and only if $\mathtt{C}[t] \in \mathcal{WN}(\mathcal{R}) \Leftrightarrow \mathtt{C}[s] \in \mathcal{WN}(\mathcal{R})$ for every context $\mathtt{C}$. Since we work with two different term languages $\mathcal{T}_a$ and $\mathcal{T}_e$, we first need to introduce their associated notions of contexts $\mathtt{C}$ and $\mathtt{C}'$, which represent, respectively, contexts without and with explicit substitutions.

$$\mathtt{C} ::= \Box \mid \lambda x.\mathtt{C} \mid \mathtt{C}\,t \mid t\,\mathtt{C}$$
$$\mathtt{C}' ::= \Box \mid \lambda x.\mathtt{C}' \mid \mathtt{C}'\,t \mid t\,\mathtt{C}' \mid \mathtt{C}'[x/t] \mid t[x/\mathtt{C}']$$

We can thus conclude with the last main result of the paper.

Corollary 1. *For all terms t and u in $\mathcal{T}_a$, $t \cong_{\text{name}} u$ iff $t \cong_{\text{need}} u$.*

Proof. First of all let us consider the relation $=_{\text{B}}$, which is the least equivalence relation generated by the axiom $(\lambda x.t_1)t_2 = t_1[x/t_2]$. We remark that when t is typable in $\mathcal{A}$, and $t =_{\text{B}} t'$, then t' is typable in $\mathcal{A}$. This means that we can indistinctly quantify over the two sort of contexts C and C' previously defined: indeed, from the set of all the contexts C we can construct the set of all the contexts C', and vice-versa. The proof of the corollary then proceeds as follows. Take $t, u \in \mathcal{T}_a$. Then $t \cong_{\text{name}} u$ iff (definition)
$\mathsf{C}[t] \in \mathcal{WN}(\text{name}) \Leftrightarrow \mathsf{C}[u] \in \mathcal{WN}(\text{name})$ for every context C iff (Theorem 3)
$\mathsf{C}[t]$ is typable in $\mathcal{V} \Leftrightarrow \mathsf{C}[u]$ is typable in $\mathcal{V}$ for every context C iff (Lemma 4)
$\mathsf{C}[t]$ is typable in $\mathcal{A} \Leftrightarrow \mathsf{C}[u]$ is typable in $\mathcal{A}$ for every context C iff (Remark)
$\mathsf{C}'[t]$ is typable in $\mathcal{A} \Leftrightarrow \mathsf{C}'[u]$ is typable in $\mathcal{A}$ for every context C' iff (Theorem 6)
$\mathsf{C}'[t] \in \mathcal{WN}(\text{need}) \Leftrightarrow \mathsf{C}'[u] \in \mathcal{WN}(\text{need})$ for every context C' iff (definition)
$t \cong_{\text{need}} u$. $\Diamond$

7   Conclusion

This paper gives the first full characterization of call-by-need normalization by means of intersection types. This result, together with the full characterization of call-by-name normalization, provides a new completeness proof for call-by-need, which is only based on logical arguments and does not make use of any complicated notion of rewriting. The use of non-idempotent types allows us to obtain the result in a combinatorial way, by providing quantitative information about reduction sequences, and without resorting to any reducibility argument.

The paper only considers a core language for call-by-need, but it would be interesting to consider other constructors of lazy languages, *e.g.* data constructors, case-expressions and Haskell's seq operators. Moreover, the results in the paper could be extended to the cyclic call-by-need letrec calculus as well as to full (strong) need normal forms (ongoing work).

Last but not least, we would also like to use the ideas in [16] in order to relate call-by-need and needed reduction by means of intersection types.

A   Appendix

Lemma 9. *If $(\Phi_{\mathsf{L}}^j \triangleright_{\mathcal{A}} \Gamma_j \Vdash \mathsf{L} \triangleright \Delta_j)_{j \in J}$, then $\Phi_{\mathsf{L}} \triangleright_{\mathcal{A}} +_{j \in J} \Gamma_j \Vdash \mathsf{L} \triangleright +_{j \in J} \Delta_j$. Moreover, $\mathsf{sz}(\Phi_{\mathsf{L}}) = +_{j \in J} \mathsf{sz}(\Phi_{\mathsf{L}}^j) - (\mathtt{height}(\mathsf{L}) \cdot (|J| - 1))$.*

Proof. The proof is by induction on L. The case $\mathsf{L} = \square$ is straightforward since $\Gamma_j = \Delta_j = \emptyset$ so that $+_{j \in J} \Gamma_j = +_{j \in J} \Delta_j = \emptyset$. We have $\mathsf{sz}(\Phi_{\square}) = 1 = |J| - |J| + 1 = |J| - [1 \cdot (|J| - 1)] = +_{j \in J} \mathsf{sz}(\Phi_{\square}^j) - (\mathtt{height}(\square) \cdot (|J| - 1))$.

Let $\mathsf{L} = \mathsf{L}'[y/u]$. Then for each $j \in J$, the derivation Φ_{L}^j has the following form, where $\Gamma_j = \Pi_j +_{i \in K_j \uplus H_j} \Lambda_k^j$ and $\Delta_j = \Delta_j'; y : \{\!\{\sigma_h\}\!\}_{h \in H_j}$.

$$\frac{\Phi_{L'}^j \rhd y : \{\!\{\sigma_k\}\!\}_{k \in K_j}; \Pi_j \Vdash L' \rhd \Delta_j' \quad (\Psi_u^{j,i} \rhd \Lambda_i^j \vdash u : \sigma_i)_{i \in K_j \uplus H_j}}{\Pi_j +_{i \in K_j \uplus H_j} \Lambda_i^j \Vdash L'[y/u] \rhd \Delta_j'; y : \{\!\{\sigma_h\}\!\}_{h \in H_j}}$$

By the *i.h.* we have $\Phi_{L'} \rhd +_{j \in J}(y : \{\!\{\sigma_k\}\!\}_{k \in K_j}; \Pi_j) \Vdash L' \rhd +_{j \in J} \Delta_j'$, but $+_{j \in J}(y : \{\!\{\sigma_k\}\!\}_{k \in K_j}; \Pi_j) = y : \{\!\{\sigma_k\}\!\}_{j \in J, k \in K_j}; +_{j \in J} \Pi_j$. We thus construct the derivation Φ_{L}:

$$\frac{\Phi_{L'} \rhd y : \{\!\{\sigma_k\}\!\}_{j \in J, k \in K_j}; +_{j \in J} \Pi_j \Vdash L' \rhd +_{j \in J} \Delta_j' \quad (\Psi_u^{j,i} \rhd \Lambda_i^j \vdash u : \sigma_i)_{j \in J, i \in K_j \uplus H_j}}{+_{j \in J} \Pi_j +_{j \in J, i \in K_j \uplus H_j} \Lambda_i^j \Vdash L'[y/u] \rhd +_{j \in J} \Delta_j'; y : \{\!\{\sigma_h\}\!\}_{j \in J, h \in H_j}}$$

We conclude with the first statement since $+_{j \in J} \Gamma_j = +_{j \in J} \Pi_j +_{j \in J, i \in K_j \uplus H_j} \Lambda_k^j$ and $+_{j \in J} \Delta_j = +_{j \in J} \Delta_j', y : \{\!\{\sigma_h\}\!\}_{j \in J, h \in H_j}$. Moreover:

$$\begin{aligned}
\mathbf{sz}(\Phi_{L}) &= \mathbf{sz}(\Phi_{L'}) +_{j \in J, i \in K_j \uplus H_j} \mathbf{sz}(\Phi_{\Psi_u^{j,i}}) + 1 & =_{i.h.}\\
&+_{j \in J} \mathbf{sz}(\Phi_{L'}) - (\mathbf{height}(L') \cdot (|J| - 1)) +_{j \in J, i \in K_j \uplus H_j} \mathbf{sz}(\Phi_{\Psi_u^{j,i}}) + 1 & =_{i.h.}\\
&+_{j \in J} \mathbf{sz}(\Phi_{L'}) +_{j \in J, i \in K_j \uplus H_j} \mathbf{sz}(\Phi_{\Psi_u^{j,i}}) + |J| - [(\mathbf{height}(L') + 1) \cdot (|J| - 1)] =\\
&+_{j \in J} \mathbf{sz}(\Phi_{L}) - (\mathbf{height}(L) \cdot (|J| - 1)) & \Diamond
\end{aligned}$$

Theorem 4 (Weighted Subject Reduction for need). Let $\Phi \rhd_A \Gamma \vdash t{:}\tau$. If $t \to_{\mathtt{need}} t'$, then there exists Φ' s.t. $\Phi' \rhd_A \Gamma \vdash t'{:}\tau$. Moreover, $\mathbf{sz}(\Phi) > \mathbf{sz}(\Phi')$.

Proof. By induction on $t \to_{\mathtt{need}} t'$.

- If $t = L[\lambda x.u]s \to_{\mathtt{dB}} L[u[x/s]] = t'$, then one shows $\Phi' \rhd \Gamma \vdash t'{:}\tau$ and $\mathbf{sz}(\Phi) > \mathbf{sz}(\Phi')$ by induction on L. See the first case of Lemma 2 in [17] (pp. 19).
- If $t = N[\![x]\!][x/L[u]] \to_{\mathtt{lsv}} L[N[\![u]\!][x/u]] = t'$, then the derivation Φ has the following form, where $\Gamma = \Gamma_0 +_{i \in I} \Delta_i$.

$$\frac{\Phi_{N[\![x]\!]} \rhd x : \{\!\{\sigma_i\}\!\}_{i \in I}; \Gamma_0 \vdash N[\![x]\!] : \sigma \quad \left(\Phi_{L[u]}^i \rhd \Delta_i \vdash L[u] : \sigma_i\right)_{i \in I}}{\Gamma_0 +_{i \in I} \Delta_i \vdash N[\![x]\!][x/L[u]] : \sigma}$$

By Lemma 8, for all $i \in I$, there exist $\Pi_1^i, \Pi_2^i, \Pi_3^i$ such that $\Phi_L^i \rhd \Pi_1^i \Vdash L \rhd \Pi_2^i$, $\Phi_u^i \rhd \Pi_2^i; \Pi_3^i \vdash u : \sigma_i$ and $\Delta_i = \Pi_1^i + \Pi_3^i$.
Then, from the derivations $\Phi_{N[\![x]\!]}$ and $(\Phi_u^i)_{i \in I}$ we get, by Lemma 10, a derivation $\Phi_{N[\![u]\!]} \rhd x : \{\!\{\sigma_i\}\!\}_{i \in I \setminus K}; \Gamma_0 +_{k \in K} (\Pi_2^k; \Pi_3^k) \vdash N[\![u]\!] : \sigma$ for some $K \subseteq I$. Therefore, we can construct the following derivation $\Phi_{N[\![u]\!][x/u]}$.

$$\frac{\Phi_{N[\![u]\!]} \quad \left(\Phi_u^i\right)_{i \in I \setminus K}}{\Gamma_0 +_{k \in K} (\Pi_2^k; \Pi_3^k) +_{i \in I \setminus K} (\Pi_2^i; \Pi_3^i) \vdash N[\![u]\!][x/u] : \sigma}$$

The last sequent can be written $\Gamma_0 + (+_{i \in I} \Pi_2^i; +_{i \in I} \Pi_3^i) \vdash N[\![u]\!][x/u] : \sigma$.

Now, from $\Phi_{N[\![x]\!]}$ and Lemma 11 we know that $I \neq \emptyset$. We can thus apply Lemma 9 to $(\Phi_L^i)_{i \in I}$ and we get $\Phi_L \rhd +_{i \in I} \Pi_1^i \Vdash L \rhd +_{i \in I} \Pi_2^i$. We can thus apply Lemma 8 to Φ_L and $\Phi_{N[\![u]\!][x/u]}$, obtaining $\Phi' \rhd \Gamma_0 +_{i \in I} \Pi_1^i +_{i \in I} \Pi_3^i \vdash L[N[\![u]\!][x/u]] : \sigma$.

We can then conclude with the first statement since $\Gamma_0 +_{i\in I} \Pi_1^1 +_{i\in I} \Pi_3^i = \Gamma_0 +_{i\in I} \Delta_i = \Gamma$ as required. Moreover, for the second one, we have two equalities:

$$\begin{aligned}
\mathtt{sz}(\varPhi) &= \mathtt{sz}(\varPhi_{\mathtt{N}[\![x]\!]}) +_{i\in I} \mathtt{sz}(\varPhi_{\mathtt{L}[u]}^i) + 1 &&=_{L.8}\\
&\mathtt{sz}(\varPhi_{\mathtt{N}[\![x]\!]}) +_{i\in I} (\mathtt{sz}(\varPhi_{\mathtt{L}}^i) + \mathtt{sz}(\varPhi_u^i) - 1) + 1 &&=\\
&\mathtt{sz}(\varPhi_{\mathtt{N}[\![x]\!]}) +_{i\in I} \mathtt{sz}(\varPhi_{\mathtt{L}}^i) +_{i\in I} \mathtt{sz}(\varPhi_u^i) - (|I| - 1) = Z - (|I| - 1)
\end{aligned}$$

and

$$\begin{aligned}
\mathtt{sz}(\varPhi') &=_{L.8} \mathtt{sz}(\varPhi_{\mathtt{L}}) + \mathtt{sz}(\varPhi_{\mathtt{N}[\![u]\!][x/u]}) - 1 &&=\\
&\mathtt{sz}(\varPhi_{\mathtt{L}}) + \mathtt{sz}(\varPhi_{\mathtt{N}[\![u]\!]}) +_{i\in I\setminus K} \mathtt{sz}(\varPhi_u^i) + 1 - 1 &&=\\
&\mathtt{sz}(\varPhi_{\mathtt{L}}) + \mathtt{sz}(\varPhi_{\mathtt{N}[\![u]\!]}) +_{i\in I\setminus K} \mathtt{sz}(\varPhi_u^i) &&=_{L.10}\\
&\mathtt{sz}(\varPhi_{\mathtt{L}}) + \mathtt{sz}(\varPhi_{\mathtt{N}[\![x]\!]}) +_{k\in K} \mathtt{sz}(\varPhi_u^k) - |K| +_{i\in I\setminus K} \mathtt{sz}(\varPhi_u^i) &&=_{L.9}\\
&+_{i\in I}\mathtt{sz}(\varPhi_{\mathtt{L}}^i) - [\mathtt{height}(\mathtt{L}) \cdot (|I| - 1)] + \mathtt{sz}(\varPhi_{\mathtt{N}[\![x]\!]}) +_{i\in I} \mathtt{sz}(\varPhi_u^i) - |K| &&=\\
&\mathtt{sz}(\varPhi_{\mathtt{N}[\![x]\!]}) +_{i\in I} \mathtt{sz}(\varPhi_{\mathtt{L}}^i) +_{i\in I} \mathtt{sz}(\varPhi_u^i) - [\mathtt{height}(\mathtt{L}) \cdot (|I| - 1)] - |K| &&=\\
&Z - [\mathtt{height}(\mathtt{L}) \cdot (|I| - 1)] - |K|
\end{aligned}$$

To conclude, we know by Lemma 10 that $K \neq \emptyset$. Therefore, $|I| - 1 \leq \mathtt{height}(\mathtt{L}) \cdot (|I| - 1)$ so that $Z - (|I| - 1) \geq Z - [\mathtt{height}(\mathtt{L}) \cdot (|I| - 1)] > Z - [\mathtt{height}(\mathtt{L}) \cdot (|I| - 1)] - |K|$. We thus conclude $\mathtt{sz}(\varPhi) > \mathtt{sz}(\varPhi')$ as required.

– If $t = \mathtt{N}_1[\![x]\!][x/\mathtt{N}_2[u]] \to_{\mathtt{need}} \mathtt{N}_1[\![x]\!][x/\mathtt{N}_2[u']] = t'$ comes from $\mathtt{N}[u] \to_{\mathtt{need}} \mathtt{N}[u']$, then $\varPhi$ has the following form, where $\Gamma = \Gamma_0 +_{i\in I} \Delta_i$.

$$\frac{x : \{\!\{\sigma_i\}\!\}_{i\in I}; \Gamma_0 \vdash \mathtt{N}_1[\![x]\!]{:}\tau \quad \left(\varPhi_{\mathtt{N}_2[u]}^i \rhd \Delta_i \vdash \mathtt{N}_2[u]{:}\sigma_i\right)_{i\in I}}{\Gamma_0 +_{i\in I} \Delta_i \vdash \mathtt{N}_1[\![x]\!][x/\mathtt{N}_2[u]]{:}\tau}$$

By the *i.h.* both $\Pi_{\mathtt{N}_2[u]}^i \rhd \Delta_i \vdash \mathtt{N}_2[u']{:}\sigma_i$ and $\mathtt{sz}(\varPhi_{\mathtt{N}_2[u]}^i) > \mathtt{sz}(\Pi_{\mathtt{N}_2[u]}^i)$ hold for all $i \in I$. The first statement gives $\varPhi' \rhd \Gamma_0 +_{i\in I} \Delta_i \vdash \mathtt{N}_1[\![x]\!][x/\mathtt{N}_2[u']]{:}\tau$. The second one gives $\mathtt{sz}(\varPhi) > \mathtt{sz}(\varPhi')$ since $I \neq \emptyset$ holds by Lemma 11.

– The cases $t = \mathtt{N}[u]v \to_{\mathtt{need}} \mathtt{N}[u']v = t'$ and $t = \mathtt{N}[u][x/v] \to_{\mathtt{need}} \mathtt{N}[u'][x/v] = t'$ coming from $\mathtt{N}[u] \to_{\mathtt{need}} \mathtt{N}[u']$ are straightforward inductive cases. $\diamond$

References

1. Accattoli, B., Barenbaum, P., Mazza, D.: Distilling abstract machines. In: ICFP. ACM Press (2014)
2. Ariola, Z.M., Felleisen, M.: The call-by-need lambda calculus. J. Funct. Program. **7**(3), 265–301 (1997)
3. Ariola, Z.M., Felleisen, M., Maraist, J., Odersky, M., Wadler, P.: The call-by-need lambda calculus. In: POPL, pp. 233–246. ACM Press (1995)
4. Barendregt, H., Coppo, M., Dezani-Ciancaglini, M.: A filter lambda model and the completeness of type assignment. Bull. Symbolic Logic **48**, 931–940 (1983)
5. Bernadet, A., Lengrand, S.: Non-idempotent intersection types and strong normalisation. Logical Methods Comput. Sci. **9**(4:3), 1–46 (2013)
6. Boudol, G., Curien, P.-L., Lavatelli, C.: A semantics for lambda calculi with resources. Math. Struct. Comput. Sci. **9**(4), 437–482 (1999)

7. Bucciarelli, A., Kesner, D., Ronchi Della Rocca, S.: The inhabitation problem for non-idempotent intersection types. In: Diaz, J., Lanese, I., Sangiorgi, D. (eds.) TCS 2014. LNCS, vol. 8705, pp. 341–354. Springer, Heidelberg (2014)
8. Cardone, F., Coppo, M.: Two extension of Curry's type inference system. In: Odifreddi, P. (ed.) Logic and Computer Science. APIC Series, vol. 31, pp. 19–75. Academic Press, New York (1990)
9. Chang, S., Felleisen, M.: The call-by-need lambda calculus, revisited. In: Seidl, H. (ed.) ESOP 2012. LNCS, vol. 7211, pp. 128–147. Springer, Heidelberg (2012)
10. Coppo, M., Dezani-Ciancaglini, M., Venneri, B.: Functional characters of solvable terms. Math. Logic Q. 27(2–6), 45–58 (1981)
11. Coppo, M., Dezani-Ciancaglini, M.: A new type-assignment for lambda terms. Archiv für Math. Logik Grundlagenforschung 19, 139–156 (1978)
12. Coppo, M., Dezani-Ciancaglini, M.: An extension of the basic functionality theory for the λ-calculus. Notre Dame J. Formal Logic 21, 685–693 (1980)
13. Danvy, O., Zerny, I.: A synthetic operational account of call-by-need evaluation. In: PPDP, pp. 97–108. ACM Press (2013)
14. De Benedetti, E., Ronchi Della Rocca, S.: Bounding normalization time through intersection types. In: ITRS 2012, EPTCS, pp. 48–57 (2013)
15. de Carvalho, D.: Sémantiques de la logique linéaire et temps de calcul. Thèse de doctorat, Université Aix-Marseille II (2007)
16. Gardner, P.: Discovering needed reductions using type theory. In: Hagiya, M., Mitchell, J.C. (eds.) TACS 1994. LNCS, vol. 789, pp. 555–574. Springer, Heidelberg (1994)
17. Kesner, D., Ventura, D.: Quantitative types for intuitionistic calculi. Technical report (2014). https://hal.archives-ouvertes.fr/hal-00980868
18. Kesner, D., Ventura, D.: Quantitative types for the linear substitution calculus. In: Diaz, J., Lanese, I., Sangiorgi, D. (eds.) TCS 2014. LNCS, vol. 8705, pp. 296–310. Springer, Heidelberg (2014)
19. Kfoury, A.J.: A linearization of the lambda-calculus and consequences. Technical report, Boston Universssity (1996)
20. Kfoury, A.J.: A linearization of the lambda-calculus and consequences. J. Logic Comput. 10(3), 411–436 (2000)
21. Kfoury, A.J., Wells, J.B.: Principality and type inference for intersection types using expansion variables. Theor. Comput. Sci. 311(1–3), 1–70 (2004)
22. Krivine, J.-L.: Lambda-Calculus, Types and Models. Ellis Horwood, Hemel Hempstead (1993)
23. Mairson, H., Neergaard, P.M.: Types, potency, idempotency: why nonlinearity and amnesia make a type system work. In: ICFP, pp. 138–149. ACM (2004)
24. Maraist, J., Odersky, M., Turner, D.N., Wadler, P.: Call-by-name, call-by-value, call-by-need and the linear lambda calculus. Theoret. Comput. Sci. 228(1–2), 175–210 (1999)
25. Maraist, J., Odersky, M., Wadler, P.: The call-by-need lambda calculus. J. Funct. Program. 8(3), 275–317 (1998)
26. Pagani, M., Ronchi Della Rocca, S.: Linearity, non-determinism and solvability. Fundam. Informaticae 103, 358–373 (2010)
27. Pagani, M., della Rocca, S.R.: Solvability in resource lambda-calculus. In: Ong, L. (ed.) FOSSACS 2010. LNCS, vol. 6014, pp. 358–373. Springer, Heidelberg (2010)

28. Plotkin, G.D.: Call-by-Name, call-by-value and the lambda-calculus. Theor. Comput. Sci. **1**(2), 125–159 (1975)
29. van Bakel, S.: Complete restrictions of the intersection type discipline. Theor. Comput. Sci. **102**(1), 135–163 (1992)
30. Wadsworth, C.: Semantics and Pragmatics of the Lambda Calculus. PH.D. thesis, Oxford University (1971)

Algorithms for Infinite Systems

Coverability Trees for Petri Nets
with Unordered Data

Piotr Hofman[1], Sławomir Lasota[2], Ranko Lazić[3], Jérôme Leroux[4],
Sylvain Schmitz[1(✉)], and Patrick Totzke[3]

[1] LSV, ENS Cachan & CNRS, Université Paris-Saclay, Cachan, France
schmitz@lsv.ens-cachan.fr
[2] University of Warsaw, Warsaw, Poland
[3] DIMAP, Department of Computer Science, University of Warwick, Coventry, UK
[4] LaBRI, CNRS, Paris, France

Abstract. We study an extension of classical Petri nets where tokens
carry values from a countable data domain, that can be tested for equality upon firing transitions. These Unordered Data Petri Nets (UDPN) are
well-structured and therefore allow generic decision procedures for several
verification problems including coverability and boundedness.

We show how to construct a finite representation of the coverability set
in terms of its ideal decomposition. This not only provides an alternative
method to decide coverability and boundedness, but is also an important
step towards deciding the reachability problem. This also allows to answer
more precise questions about the reachability set, for instance whether
there is a bound on the number of tokens on a given place (place boundedness), or if such a bound exists for the number of different data values
carried by tokens (place width boundedness).

We provide matching HYPER-ACKERMANN bounds on the size of coverability trees and on the running time of the induced decision procedures.

1 Introduction

Unordered data Petri nets (UDPN [15]) extend Petri nets by decorating tokens
with data values taken from some countable data domain $\mathbb{D}$. These values act as
pure names: they can only be compared for equality or non-equality upon firing
transitions. Such systems can model for instance distributed protocols where
process identities need to be taken into account [21]. UDPNs also coincide with
the natural generalisation of Petri nets in the framework of sets with atoms [3].
In spite of their high expressiveness, UDPNs fit in the large family of Petri net

P. Hofman—Partially funded by the Polish National Science Centre grant
2013/09/B/ST6/01575 and by Labex Digicosme, Université Paris-Saclay, project
VERICONISS.
S. Lasota—Partially funded by the Polish National Science Centre grant
2012/07/B/ST6/01497.
R. Lazić and P. Totzke—Partially supported by the EPSRC grant EP/M011801/1.
S. Schmitz—Partially supported by the ANR grant ANR-14-CE28-0005 PRODAQ and
by the Leverhulme Trust Visiting Professorship VP1-2014-041.

© Springer-Verlag Berlin Heidelberg 2016
B. Jacobs and C. Löding (Eds.): FOSSACS 2016, LNCS 9634, pp. 445–461, 2016.
DOI: 10.1007/978-3-662-49630-5_26

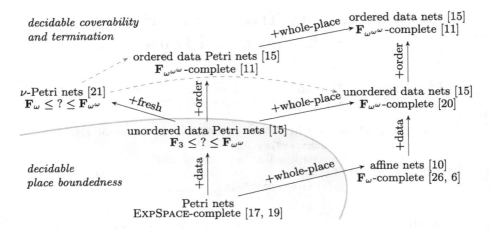

Fig. 1. A short taxonomy of some well-structured extensions of Petri nets. Complexities in violet refer to the coverability and termination problems, and can be taken as proxies for expressiveness; the exact complexities of coverability and termination in ν-Petri nets and UDPNs are unknown at the moment. Place boundedness is decidable below the yellow line and undecidable above. As indicated by the dashed arrows, freshness can be enforced using a dense linear order or whole-place operations (Colour figure online).

extensions among the *well-structured* ones [1,7]. As such, they still enjoy decision procedures for several verification problems, prominently safety (through the *coverability* problem) and termination.

Unordered data Petri nets have an interesting position in the taxonomy of well-structured Petri net extensions (see Fig. 1). Indeed, all their extensions forgo the decidability of the *reachability* problem (whether a target configuration is reachable) and of the *place boundedness* problem (whether the number of tokens in a given place can be bounded along all runs): this is the case of ν-*Petri nets* [21] that allow to create fresh data values, of *ordered data Petri nets* [15] that posit a dense linear ordering on $\mathbb{D}$, and of *unordered data nets* [15] that allow to perform 'whole-place' operations, which move and/or duplicate all the tokens from a place to another. By contrast, it is currently open whether reachability is decidable in UDPNs, and a consequence of our results in this paper is that place boundedness is decidable—which is a significant first step if we wish to adapt to UDPNs some of the known algorithms for reachability in Petri nets [13,18].

Contributions. In this paper, we show how to construct finite *coverability trees* for UDPNs, adapting the existing construction of Karp and Miller [12] for Petri nets. Such trees are constructed forward from an initial configuration like reachability trees, but approximate the latter by *accelerating* sequences of transitions and explicitly manipulating limits of reachable configurations as downwards-closed sets (see Sect. 4.1). We rely for all this on a general theory for representing downwards-closed sets as finite unions of *ideals* developed by Finkel and Goubault-Larrecq [9] for this exact purpose (see Sect. 3).

Coverability trees contain a wealth of information about the system at hand, and allow to answer various coverability and boundedness questions—allowing us to derive a new result: the place boundedness problem is decidable for UDPNs, and so are its variants, like place width- and place depth boundedness (see Sect. 2). We also establish in Sect. 5 matching 'hyper-Ackermannian' lower and upper bounds on the size of UDPNs coverability trees. This yields $\mathbf{F}_{\omega^\omega}$ upper bounds for the already mentioned decidable problems in UDPNs, in terms of the fast-growing complexity classes $(\mathbf{F}_\alpha)_\alpha$ from [23]. These complexity results rely largely on the work of Rosa-Velardo [20] on the complexity of coverability in unordered data nets. Due to space constraints, most proof details are omitted but can be found online in the full version of the paper available from https://hal.inria.fr/hal-01252674.

Related Work. A coverability tree construction has already been undertaken by Rosa-Velardo, Martos-Salgado, and de Frutos-Escrig [22] in the case of ν-Petri nets, and inescapably there are many similarities between their work and ours. Our construction does however not merely remove freshness constraints from theirs: (1) we start a new and rely on a strong invariant on the form of ideals in UDPN coverability trees, which leads to significant simplifications but would be markedly difficult to extract from Rosa-Velardo et al.'s [22] construction, and (2) coverability trees are not necessarily finite for ν-Petri nets (place boundedness is indeed undecidable [21]), which means that our termination argument and complexity bounds are entirely new considerations.

Like Rosa-Velardo et al. [22] we rely on the work of Finkel and Goubault-Larrecq [9] on forward analysis of well-structured systems. Finkel and Goubault-Larrecq provide in particular an abstract generic procedure, but without guarantee of termination in general, and their framework needs to be instantiated for each specific class of systems.

2   Model

Our presentation of unordered data Petri nets differs from the original one [15] on two counts: we work with an equivalent formalism with more of a *vector addition system* [12] flavour, and because we need to work with ideals we define the syntax and the semantics on extended configurations, which allow for infinitely many different data values and infinite counts.

Let $\mathbb{Z}$ and $\mathbb{N}$ denote the sets of integers and non-negative integers respectively, and complete them as $\mathbb{Z}_\omega \overset{\text{def}}{=} \mathbb{Z} \uplus \{\omega\}$ and $\mathbb{N}_\omega \overset{\text{def}}{=} \mathbb{N} \uplus \{\omega\}$ with a new top element ω with $\omega > z$ and $z + \omega = \omega + z = \omega$ for all z in $\mathbb{Z}$. Given a dimension k in $\mathbb{N}$, we denote the projection into the ith component of a vector $\boldsymbol{v} \in \mathbb{Z}_\omega^k$ by $\boldsymbol{v}[i]$ and define the product ordering and sum over $\mathbb{Z}_\omega^k$ componentwise: $\boldsymbol{u} \le \boldsymbol{v}$ if $\boldsymbol{u}[i] \le \boldsymbol{v}[i]$ for all $1 \le i \le k$, and $(\boldsymbol{u} + \boldsymbol{v})[i] \overset{\text{def}}{=} \boldsymbol{u}[i] + \boldsymbol{v}[i]$ for all $1 \le i \le k$. We write $\boldsymbol{0}$ for the vector with 0 on all components.

Data Vectors. Fix some countable domain $\mathbb{D}$ of data values and a dimension k in $\mathbb{N}$. A *data vector* is a function $f \colon \mathbb{D} \to \mathbb{Z}_\omega^k$. Data vectors can be partially ordered and summed pointwise: $f \leq g$ if $f(d) \leq g(d)$ for all d in $\mathbb{D}$, and $(f + g)(d) \overset{\text{def}}{=}$ $f(d) + g(d)$ for all d in $\mathbb{D}$. As usual we write $f < g$ if $f \leq g$ and $f(d) < g(d)$ for some d in $\mathbb{D}$. For a subset $K \subseteq \{1, \ldots, k\}$ we write $f{\restriction}_K$ for the projection of f into components in K: for all d in $\mathbb{D}$, $f{\restriction}_K(d) \overset{\text{def}}{=} (f(d)){\restriction}_K$. The *support* of a data vector f is $Supp_{\mathbf{0}}(f) \overset{\text{def}}{=} \{d \in \mathbb{D} \mid f(d) \neq \mathbf{0}\}$; f is *finitely supported* if $Supp_{\mathbf{0}}(f)$ is finite. We say that a data vector f is *non-negative* if $f(d)$ belongs to $\mathbb{N}_\omega^k$ for all d in $\mathbb{D}$. It is *finite* if $f(d)$ belongs to $\mathbb{Z}^k$ for all d and it is finitely supported.

We call bijections $\sigma : \mathbb{D} \to \mathbb{D}$ *(data) permutations* and write $f\sigma$ for the composition of a permutation σ and a data vector f. If two data vectors f, g satisfy $f = g\sigma$ for some permutation σ, we say f and g are equal *up to permutation* and write $f \equiv g$.

In the sequel we will consider sets of data vectors that are *finite up to permutation*: a set X of data vectors is finite up to permutation if there is a finite subset X' of X such that every $f \in X$ is equal up to permutation to some $f' \in X'$. Note that if X is closed under permutations then X' can be used as its finite presentation; any such finite set X' we call *representative* of X.

Definition 2.1 (UDPN). *An* unordered data Petri net *(UDPN) is a finite set* $\mathcal{T}$ *of finite data vectors. A* transition *is a data vector* $t \overset{\text{def}}{=} f\sigma$*, where* $f \in \mathcal{T}$ *and* σ *is a data permutation. There is a* step $f \overset{t}{\to} g$ *between non-negative data vectors* f, g *if* $g = f + t$ *for some transition* t*. Note that this enforces that* $f(d) + t(d) \geq 0$ *for all* d *in* $\mathbb{D}$ *since* g *is non-negative. We simply write* $f \to g$ *if* $f \overset{t}{\to} g$ *for some transition* t *and let* $\overset{*}{\to}$ *denote the transitive and reflexive closure of* $\to$*.*

A configuration *is a finite non-negative data vector* f*, i.e.* $f(d)$ *belongs to* $\mathbb{N}^k$ *for all* d *in* $\mathbb{D}$*, and* $f(d) = \mathbf{0}$ *for almost all* d *in* $\mathbb{D}$*. We write* Confs *for the set of configurations and note that* Confs *is closed under UDPN steps. The* reachability *set from a given vector* f *is defined as*

$$Reach(f) \overset{\text{def}}{=} \{g \in Confs \mid f \overset{*}{\to} g\}. \tag{1}$$

Observe that UDPNs over any domain with cardinality $|\mathbb{D}| = 1$ are classical vector addition systems [12]. Notice also that, the set of transitions in an UDPN is finite up to permutations of $\mathbb{D}$ and that the step relation is closed under permutations: For every non-negative data vector f, transition t and permutation σ we have that

$$f \overset{t}{\to} g \text{ implies } f\sigma \overset{t\sigma}{\to} g\sigma. \tag{2}$$

Example 2.2. For the domain $\mathbb{D} \overset{\text{def}}{=} \mathbb{N}$ and $k \overset{\text{def}}{=} 2$, consider a 2-dimensional UDPN $\mathcal{T} = \{t_1, t_2\}$, with vectors t_1, t_2 defined as $t_1 : 0 \mapsto (1, 0)$ and $t_1 : n \mapsto (0, 0)$ for all $n > 0$, and $t_2 : 0 \mapsto (-1, -1)$, $t_2 : 1 \mapsto (1, 1)$ and $t_2 : n \mapsto (0, 0)$ for all $n > 1$.

The configuration f_0 with $f_0 : 0 \mapsto (1, 1)$ and $f_0 : n \mapsto (0, 0)$ for $n > 0$, has infinitely many t_1-successors. Namely, $g_i \overset{\text{def}}{=} f_0 + t_1\sigma_i$ for every permutation

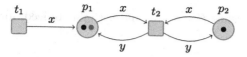

Fig. 2. A place/transition representation of the UDPN of Example 2.2 in the style of [11,21]. Different data values are depicted though differently coloured tokens in places (the circles), and through differently named variables in transitions (the boxes and arrows).

σ_i that swaps 0 and $i \in \mathbb{D}$. However, there are only two such successors up to permutation because $g_i \equiv g_j$ for all $i, j > 0$. The reachability set of f_0 is

$$Reach(f_0) = \left\{ g \;\middle|\; \begin{array}{l} \exists d_1, d_2, \ldots, d_m \in \mathbb{D} \; \exists n_1, n_2, \ldots, n_m \in \mathbb{N} \\ g(d_1) = (n_1, 1) \text{ and } \forall 1 < i \leq m, \; g(d_i) = (n_i, 0), \\ \forall d \in \mathbb{D} \setminus \{d_1, d_2, \ldots, d_m\} \; g(d) = (0,0) \end{array} \right\}. \quad (3)$$

In the sequel, we present UDPNs only up to permutation in matrix form by juxtaposing the vectors from their finite supports: we write $t_1 \stackrel{\text{def}}{=} \left[\begin{smallmatrix} 1 \\ 0 \end{smallmatrix}\right]$, $t_2 \stackrel{\text{def}}{=} \left[\begin{smallmatrix} -1 & 1 \\ -1 & 1 \end{smallmatrix}\right]$ and $f_0 \stackrel{\text{def}}{=} \left[\begin{smallmatrix} 1 \\ 1 \end{smallmatrix}\right]$. The t_1-successors of f_0 are $g_0 = \left[\begin{smallmatrix} 2 \\ 1 \end{smallmatrix}\right]$ and $g_i = \left[\begin{smallmatrix} 1 \\ 1 \end{smallmatrix}\right] + \left[\begin{smallmatrix} 1 \\ 0 \end{smallmatrix}\right] = \left[\begin{smallmatrix} 1 & 1 \\ 1 & 0 \end{smallmatrix}\right]$ for $i \neq 0$. The latter is depicted in Fig. 2 in the style of coloured place/transition nets. The reachability set of f_0 can be written as $Reach(f_0) = \left\{ \left[\begin{smallmatrix} n_0 & n_1 & \cdots & n_m \\ 1 & 0 & \cdots & 0 \end{smallmatrix}\right] \;\middle|\; m \geq 0, n_0, \ldots, n_m \geq 1 \right\}$.

Embeddings. We say that a data vector f *embeds* into a data vector g and write $f \sqsubseteq g$ (resp. $f \sqsubset g$) if there exists an injection $\pi : \mathbb{D} \to \mathbb{D}$ such that $f \leq g\pi$ (resp. $f < g\pi$). The injection π itself is called an *embedding* (of f into g) and a *permutation embedding* in case it is bijective. Given a set of configurations C, its *downward-closure* $\downarrow C$ is $\{ f \in \mathit{Confs} \mid \exists g \in C \,.\, f \sqsubseteq g \}$, and as usual a set C is *downwards-closed* if $\downarrow C = C$.

Finitely supported data vectors are isomorphic to finite multisets of vectors in $\mathbb{Z}_\omega^k$ when working up to data permutation. Moreover, on permutation classes of finitely supported data vectors, the embedding ordering coincides with the usual embedding ordering over finite multisets of vectors; in consequence, UDPN configurations are well-quasi-ordered by the embedding ordering. Thus an UDPN defines a quasi-ordered transition system $(\mathit{Confs}, \to, \sqsubseteq)$, which satisfies a (strong) *compatibility* condition as shown in the following lemma. Together with the fact that $(\mathit{Confs}, \sqsubseteq)$ is a wqo, this entails that it is a *well-structured* transition system in the sense of [1,7].

Lemma 2.3. (Strong Strict Compatibility). *Let f, f', g be configurations. If $f \sqsubseteq f'$ (resp. $f \sqsubset f'$) and $f \to g$, then there exists a configuration g' with $f' \to g'$ and $g \sqsubseteq g'$ (resp. $g \sqsubset g'$).*

Proof. Consider a finite data vector t such that $f \stackrel{t}{\to} g$, and a permutation π of $\mathbb{D}$ such that $f \leq f'\pi$ (recall that, when working with finitely supported data vectors, embeddings can be assumed to be permutations). We claim that

$g' \stackrel{\text{def}}{=} f' + t\pi^{-1}$ satisfies $f' \xrightarrow{t\pi^{-1}} g'$ and $g \leq g'\pi$. Indeed, for all d in $\mathbb{D}$, noting $e \stackrel{\text{def}}{=} \pi(d)$,

$$g(d) = f(d) + t(d) \leq f'(\pi(d)) + t(d) = f'(e) + t(\pi^{-1}(e)) = g'(e) = g'(\pi(d)) .$$

Furthermore, assuming $f < f'\pi$, for at least one d in $\mathbb{D}$ the above inequality is strict. □

Decision Problems. For the purpose of verification, we are interested in standard decision problems for UDPN, including *reachability* (does $f \xrightarrow{*} g$ hold for given configurations f and g?), *coverability* (given configurations f, g, does there exists $g' \sqsupseteq g$ s.t. $f \xrightarrow{*} g'$?), and *boundedness* (is $Reach(f)$ finite up to permutation?).

While the decidability of reachability remains open, well-structuredness of UDPN (and some basic effectiveness assumptions) implies that the coverability and boundedness problems are decidable using the generic algorithms from [1,7]. In fact, decidability holds more generally for ordered data Petri nets [15, Theorm 4.1]. For the coverability problem, Rosa-Velardo [20, Theorem 1] proved an HYPERACKERMANN upper bound ($\mathbf{F}_{\omega^\omega}$ in the hierarchy from [23]; see Sect. 5), while Lazić et al. [15, Theorem 5.2] proved a TOWER lower bound ($\mathbf{F}_3$ in the same hierarchy). The complexity of the boundedness problem has not been studied before. Furthermore, the following, more precise variant of boundedness called *place boundedness* was not known to be decidable:

Input: An UDPN, a configuration f, and a set of coordinates $K \subseteq \{1, \ldots, k\}$.
Question: Is $\{g{\upharpoonright}_K \mid g \in Reach(f)\}$ finite up to permutation?

In the presence of an infinite data domain $\mathbb{D}$, place boundedness can be further refined: even if infinitely many configurations are reachable, the system can still be bounded in the sense that there exists a bound on the number of different data values in reachable configurations; Rosa-Velardo and de Frutos-Escrig [21] call this *bounded width*. Similarly, there may exist some bound on the multiplicities with which any data value occurs, while the number of different data values is unbounded; Rosa-Velardo and de Frutos-Escrig [21] call this *bounded depth*.

We formalise the resulting decision problems in our notation as follows. The *place width boundedness* problem is given as:

Input: An UDPN, a configuration f, and a set of coordinates $K \subseteq \{1, \ldots, k\}$.
Question: Is $\{|Supp_0(g{\upharpoonright}_K)| \mid g \in Reach(f)\}$ finite?

The *place depth boundedness* problem is the following:

Input: An UDPN, a configuration f, and a set of coordinates $K \subseteq \{1, \ldots, k\}$.
Question: Is $\{g{\upharpoonright}_K(d) \mid g \in Reach(f), d \in \mathbb{D}\}$ finite?

If the answer to the depth (width) boundedness problem is positive we call those components $i \in K$ depth (width) bounded.

Example 2.4. From the initial configuration $f_0 = \left[\begin{smallmatrix}1\\1\end{smallmatrix}\right]$, the UDPN from
Example 2.2 can reach any configuration of the form $\left[\begin{smallmatrix}n\\1\end{smallmatrix}\right]$ in n many t_1-steps,
all exercised on the same data value. Similarly, any configuration of the form
$\left[\begin{smallmatrix}1&1&\cdots&1\\1&0&\cdots&0\end{smallmatrix}\right]$ with a support of size $n+1$ can be reached after a sequence of n
transitions t_1, each exercised on a different data value. Consequently, the first
component is neither depth nor width bounded.

However, any reachable configuration g will satisfy $\sum_{d\in\mathbb{D}} g(d)[2] = 1$. In Petri
net parlance, there is always exactly one token in the second place. The system
is thus place bounded for $K \stackrel{\text{def}}{=} \{2\}$.

The main contribution of this paper is the effective computability of a suitable
abstraction of the classical coverability tree construction [12] for UDPNs. This
provides a way to decide all variants of the boundedness problem mentioned
above. We summarise the consequences of our construction below.

Theorem 2.5. *In UDPNs, place depth boundedness implies place width
boundedness. In consequence, place depth boundedness coincides with place
boundedness.*

Theorem 2.6. *The boundedness, place boundedness, and place width boundedness problems for UDPNs are in $\mathbf{F}_{\omega^\omega}$, i.e. in* HYPERACKERMANN.

Let us emphasise the importance of decidability of place boundedness: first,
the problem is undecidable in all the extensions of UDPNs in Fig. 1. Moreover,
in the case of Petri nets, the decidability of place boundedness plays a crucial
role in the decidability proofs for reachability [13,14,16,18], hence Theorem 2.6
provides one of the basic building blocks for future attempts at proving the
decidability of reachability for UDPNs.

3 Simple Ideals

A key observation about all decision problems mentioned in the previous section
is that they do not require computing the reachability set: they can all be solved
given some suitable representation of the *cover* [9], defined as

$$Cover(f) \stackrel{\text{def}}{=} {\downarrow}Reach(f), \tag{4}$$

for f the initial configuration. Indeed, coverability reduces to checking whether
$g \in Cover(f)$, boundedness to checking whether $Cover(f)$ is finite up to permutation of $\mathbb{D}$, and place boundedness to checking whether $\{g{\restriction}_K \mid g \in Cover(f)\}$
is finite up to permutation of $\mathbb{D}$. The main property of the coverability tree we
construct in Sect. 4 is that we can extract a suitable representation of $Cover(f)$.

Ideals and Clovers. We refer the reader to the work of Finkel and Goubault-
Larrecq [8,9] for details; it suffices to say that downwards-closed sets of con-
figurations can be represented as finite unions of so-called *configuration ideals*.
Formally, a configuration ideal J is a non-empty, downwards-closed, and *directed*

set of configurations; this last condition means that, if f and f' are configurations in J, then there exists h in J with $f \sqsubseteq h$ and $f' \sqsubseteq h$. Crucially for algorithmic considerations, a configuration ideal J can in turn be *represented* as the downward-closure

$$J = \downarrow g \overset{\text{def}}{=} \{h \in \mathit{Confs} \mid h \sqsubseteq g\} \tag{5}$$

of a non-negative data vector g having a finite range: $g(\mathbb{D})$ is a finite subset of $\mathbb{N}_\omega^k$. We can check that every such $\downarrow g$ is a configuration ideal (see [8,9] for the converse): it is non-empty and downwards-closed by definition, and we can check it is also directed. Indeed, if f, f' are configurations and π, π' are injections with $f \le g\pi$ and $f' \le g\pi'$, then since f and f' are finitely supported we can assume π and π' to be permutations, and we can define a configuration $h \le g$ such that $f \le h\pi$ and $f' \le h\pi'$: set h as the pointwise least upper bound $h(d)[i] \overset{\text{def}}{=} \max(f(\pi^{-1}(d))[i], f'(\pi'^{-1}(d))[i]) \le g(d)[i]$ for all d and $1 \le i \le k$.

$\mathit{Cover}(f)$, being downwards-closed, is represented by a finite set of representations of configuration ideals, called $\mathit{Clover}(f)$ by Finkel and Goubault-Larrecq:

$$\mathit{Cover}(f) = \bigcup \{\downarrow g \mid g \in \mathit{Clover}(f)\} \,.$$

$\mathit{Clover}(f)$ is determined uniquely up to permutation, and contains $\sqsubseteq$-maximal data vectors g satisfying $\downarrow g \subseteq \mathit{Cover}(f)$; for further details see [8,9]. In the following we identify a configuration ideal $J = \downarrow g$ with its representation g.

Remark 3.1 (Ideals for Petri nets). For readers familiar with Karp and Miller's coverability trees for Petri nets, observe that configuration ideal representations generalise the notion of 'extended markings', which are vectors in $\mathbb{N}_\omega^k$. Also, $\mathit{Clover}(f)$ for a Petri net can be computed as the set of vertex labels in its coverability tree—this will also be our case.

Simple Ideals. Crucially, it turns out that we do not need general configuration ideals for our coverability trees for UDPNs. We only need to consider the downward-closures $\downarrow g$ of non-negative vectors g (cf. (5)), where the set of vectors appearing infinitely often as $g(d)$, when d ranges over $\mathbb{D}$, is a singleton $\{I\}$ for some vector I in $\{0, \omega\}^k$ (instead of a finite subset of $\mathbb{N}_\omega^k$ for general configuration ideals). Put differently, given such a vector I, we define the I-*support* of a data vector f as $\mathit{Supp}_I(f) \overset{\text{def}}{=} \{d \in \mathbb{D} \mid f(d) \ne I\}$, and define an I-*simple ideal (representation)* as a non-negative data vector with finite I-support. In particular, a finitely supported non-negative data vector is a 0-simple ideal. We write M, N, ... to denote simple ideals. A simple ideal M can be represented concretely as a pair $M = \langle m, I \rangle$ where m is the finite multiset of vectors in $\mathbb{N}_\omega^k$ obtained from M by restriction to its I-support.

Example 3.2. We represent simple ideals similarly as configurations, using the additional last column for the I part. Continuing with the UDPN of Example 2.2, its cover is the downward-closure of a single I-simple ideal:

$$\mathit{Clover}(f_0) = \begin{bmatrix} \omega & \omega \\ 1 & 0 \end{bmatrix}, \qquad\qquad \mathit{Cover}(f_0) = \downarrow \begin{bmatrix} \omega & \omega \\ 1 & 0 \end{bmatrix},$$

where $I \overset{\text{def}}{=} (\omega, 0)$. The I-support of the ideal has one element, mapped to $(\omega, 1)$.

Note that UDPN steps map I-simple ideals to I-simple ideals. Lemma 3.3 formally states the relation between steps of ideals and steps of configurations in the downward closures. The next lemma shows that I-simple ideals can only have finitely many successors up to permutation. This property will later be used to define coverability trees of finite branching degree.

Lemma 3.3. *Let M, M' be I-simple ideals such that $M \to M'$. Then for every configuration $c' \in \downarrow M'$ there exist configurations $c \in \downarrow M$ and $c'' \in \downarrow M'$ with $c \to c''$ and $c' \sqsubseteq c''$.*

Proof. Suppose $M \xrightarrow{t} M'$ for a finite data vector t. The data vector $f \stackrel{\text{def}}{=} c' - t$ satisfies $f \leq M$ but $f(d)$ can possibly be negative for some data value d; therefore we can not simply put $c \stackrel{\text{def}}{=} f$. A way to fix this is to define c by

$$c(d)[i] \stackrel{\text{def}}{=} \max(0, x(d)[i]), \quad \text{for all } d \in \mathbb{D} \text{ and all coordinates } i.$$

Thus defined, c satisfies $c \leq M$, and setting $c'' \stackrel{\text{def}}{=} c + t$ satisfies $c' \leq c''$ as required. $\qquad\square$

Lemma 3.4. *Let M be a simple ideal. The set $\{N \mid M \to N\}$ of successors of M is finite up to permutation and has a representative with cardinality bounded by $(|Supp_I(M)| + \max_{t \in T} |Supp_0(t)|)! \cdot |T|^2$.*

Proof. Consider an UDPN defined by the finite set T of data vectors. Fix an I-simple ideal M, and denote by S the I-support of M. We will be now considering S-*permutations*, by which we mean those data permutations π that satisfy $\pi(d) = d$ for all $d \in S$. Equality and finiteness up to S-permutation can be defined exactly as for plain permutations.

A crucial but simple observation is that the set of transitions of the UDPN is finite up to S-permutation. Indeed, assume wlog. that S is disjoint from the supports of all vectors in T. Consider the finite set T' that contains all data vectors $t\sigma$, where $t \in T$ and permutation σ swaps some subset of S with some subset of the support of t. Then every transition of the UDPN is of the form $t'\pi$, where $t' \in T'$ and π is an S-permutation. Regarding the size of this new UDPN, there are at most $\sum_{t \in T}(|S| + |Supp_0(t)|)!$ such permutations σ, hence $|T'| \leq \sum_{t \in T}(|S| + |Supp_0(t)|)! \cdot |T|$.

Now we use the extension, to simple ideals, of the closure of the step relation under permutations, cf. Eq. (2), to derive a strengthening of our claim, namely finiteness of the successors of M up to S-permutations. Consider an arbitrary step $M \xrightarrow{t'\pi} N$ of M; by Eq. (2) we get

$$M = M\pi^{-1} \xrightarrow{t'} N\pi^{-1}$$

(the equality holds as π is an S-permutation). Therefore N is equal up to S-permutation to some T'-successor of M. As T' is finite, the set of T'-successors of M is finite and bounded by $|T'|$, which implies our claim. $\qquad\square$

A consequence of our construction of coverability trees in Sect. 4, and of the complexity analysis conducted in Sect. 5, is the following core result:

Theorem 3.5. *Given an UDPN and an initial configuration f, an ideal representation $Clover(f)$ of $Cover(f)$ is computable in $\mathbf{F}_{\omega^\omega}$. Furthermore, $Clover(f)$ contains only simple ideals.*

Theorem 3.5, together with the following proposition, easily imply Theorems 2.5 and 2.6 (below $Clover(f){\restriction}_K \stackrel{\text{def}}{=} \{g{\restriction}_K \mid g \in Clover(f)\}$):

Proposition 3.6. *Fix $K \subseteq \{1, \dots, k\}$. An UDPN is width-bounded iff $Clover(f){\restriction}_K$ contains only finitely supported vectors. An UDPN is depth-bounded iff $Clover(f){\restriction}_K$ contains only finite vectors.*

Proof. The former equivalence, as well as the if direction of the latter one, follow by finiteness of $Clover(f){\restriction}_K$. It remains to argue that place depth-boundedness forces $Clover(f){\restriction}_K$ to contain only finite vectors. Indeed, a non-finite simple ideal has necessarily ω at some component, which implies depth-unboundedness. $\square$

The remaining part of the paper is devoted to the proof of Theorem 3.5. In Sect. 4, we present an algorithmic construction of the coverability tree, and show its termination and correctness. Then in Sect. 5 we provide upper and lower bounds on the size of the coverability tree.

4   Representing a Cover

We will show that, analogously to the classical construction of Karp and Miller [12] for vector addition systems, the cover set of any UDPN configuration can be effectively represented in the form of a finite *coverability tree*, where nodes are labelled by simple ideals.

For a given initial ideal the construction of a coverability tree amounts to iteratively computing successors (up to permutation), applying symbolic *acceleration* steps when a strictly dominating pair $M \sqsubset M'$ appears on a branch, and terminating a branch if a label embeds into one of its ancestors.

4.1   Accelerations

The idea behind acceleration steps is that due to monotonicity (Lemma 2.3), any finite sequence of steps

$$M_0 \xrightarrow{t_1} M_1 \xrightarrow{t_2} \dots \xrightarrow{t_k} M_k \tag{6}$$

such that $M_0 \sqsubset M_k$ can be extended indefinitely. Such an unfolding may have two distinct kinds of effect: Firstly, it may unboundedly increase components in data values already contained in the initial I-support (we call this effect *depth acceleration*). Secondly, it may increase an unbounded number of 'fresh' data values, outside of the initial I-support (we call this effect *width acceleration*).

Our construction only accelerates increasing sequences as above when there is a permutation (i.e. bijective) embedding of M_0 into M_k.

As a building block we shall use the usual vector acceleration: for two non-negative vectors $v, v' \in \mathbb{N}_\omega^k$ with $v' \leq v$, define a new vector $\mathrm{acc}(v', v)$, for $1 \leq i \leq k$ by:

$$\mathrm{acc}(v', v)[i] \stackrel{\mathrm{def}}{=} \begin{cases} v[i], & \text{if } v'[i] = v[i], \\ \omega, & \text{if } v'[i] < v[i]. \end{cases}$$

Definition 4.1 (Depth and Width Acceleration). *For I-simple ideals M', M and a permutation π with $M' < M\pi$, or equivalently $M'\pi^{-1} < M$, the* depth *acceleration of M', M, π is the I-simple ideal defined by*

$$M_{depth}(d) \stackrel{\mathrm{def}}{=} \mathrm{acc}(M'(\pi^{-1}(d)), M(d)), \qquad \text{for all data values } d \in \mathbb{D}.$$

For $d \in \mathbb{D}$ such that $M'(\pi^{-1}(d)) = I < M(d)$, put $I_d \stackrel{\mathrm{def}}{=} \mathrm{acc}(M'(\pi^{-1}(d)), M(d))$; the width *acceleration of M', M, π, d is the I_d-simple ideal defined by*

$$M_{width}(d) \stackrel{\mathrm{def}}{=} \begin{cases} I_d, & \text{if } M(d) = I \\ M(d), & \text{otherwise,} \end{cases}$$

By definition, $M < M_{depth}, M_{width}$.

4.2   Coverability Trees

By Lemma 3.4 we can compute for any I-simple ideal M a *successor representative*, namely a finite set such that every successor of M is equal up to permutation to some element of this set.

For the sake of simplicity, we choose a conservative policy of application of accelerations: first, a proper nesting is imposed, in the sense that two different accelerated paths are either disjoint, or contained one in the other; second, a depth-accelerated path can not contain another accelerated path, while a width-accelerated path can. However, as width accelerations strictly increase the I part, a width-accelerated path is never contained in another accelerated path. Therefore the only allowed inclusion is when a depth-accelerated path is included in a width-accelerated one.

Definition 4.2 (Coverability Tree). *A coverability tree is a tree with nodes labelled by simple ideals such that the following criteria are satisfied.*

1. *A node with label N is a leaf iff it has an ancestor with label $N' \sqsupseteq N$.*
2. *Otherwise, suppose an interior node N has an ancestor N' such that both N', N are I-simple and $N' \sqsubset N$. Let $\mathcal{P}$ denote the path from N' to N in the tree, including N' and N.*
   (a) *Suppose $N'(\pi^{-1}(d)) = I < N(d)$ for some permutation π with $N'\pi < N$ and $d \in \mathbb{D}$; and for every node in $\mathcal{P}$ that is a depth acceleration of some nodes M', M, both M' and M belong to $\mathcal{P}$. Then N has exactly one child labelled by the width acceleration of N', N, π, d.*

(b) *Otherwise, if $\mathcal{P}$ contains no acceleration then N has exactly one child labelled by the depth acceleration of N', N, π, for some permutation π with $N'\pi < N$.*

3. *Otherwise, if a node N satisfies none of the above criteria then its set of children is the successor representative of N.*

Remark 4.3. Note that Definition 4.2 does not determine the coverability tree unambiguously: the choice of a permutation π in points 2(a) and 2(b) is not unique.

Remark 4.4. The condition in point 1 in Definition 4.2 implies that no branch of a coverability tree contains two different nodes with the same label. We identify a node with its label in the sequel.

Example 4.5. We pick some coverability tree for the UDPN from Example 2.2 rooted in the configuration f_0. There is a branch with labels (up to permutation)

$$f_0 = \begin{bmatrix} 1 & | & 0 \\ 1 & | & 0 \end{bmatrix},\ f_1 = \begin{bmatrix} 2 & | & 0 \\ 1 & | & 0 \end{bmatrix},\ f_2 = \begin{bmatrix} \omega & | & 0 \\ 1 & | & 0 \end{bmatrix},\ f_3 = \begin{bmatrix} \omega & 1 & | & 0 \\ 0 & 1 & | & 0 \end{bmatrix},\ f_4 = \begin{bmatrix} \omega & 1 & | & \omega \\ 0 & 1 & | & 0 \end{bmatrix},\ f_5 = \begin{bmatrix} \omega & 1 & 1 & | & \omega \\ 0 & 1 & 0 & | & 0 \end{bmatrix},$$

where f_2 is a depth acceleration (of f_0, f_1), f_4 is a width acceleration (of f_0, f_3), and all other nodes are the result of successor steps from their parent. The node f_5 is a leaf because $f_5 \sqsubseteq f_4$.

Correctness. A coverability tree is finite (termination), and represents the cover of its root node (completeness and soundness). These required properties are proven in detail in the full paper:

- *Finiteness* is proven by first exhibiting a wqo for the specific type of I-simple ideals that appears on coverability trees. This wqo depends on the existence of permutation embeddings, a property that on its own does *not* induce a well-quasi-ordering over the set of all I-simple ideals. Our termination argument is further refined to derive complexity bounds; see Sect. 5.2.
- The *completeness* proof relies on the monotonicity of steps over simple ideals, and shows that all the elements in $Cover(f)$ are covered by some simple ideal in any coverability tree.
- *Soundness* is the most delicate property to establish. Its crux is that neither width nor depth accelerations may take us outside the cover of the initial configuration.

5   Complexity Bounds

In the section, we prove lower and upper bounds on the resources needed by the construction of the coverability tree. We refer the reader to [24,25] for gentle introductions to the techniques employed to prove these results. The enormous complexities involved in our construction require to use *fast-growing complexity classes* [23], which we present succinctly in Sect. 5.1 and in more details in the full paper, before showing hyper-Ackermannian upper and lower bounds in Sects. 5.2 and 5.3.

5.1   Fast-Growing Complexity

In order to express the non-elementary functions required for our complexity statements, we shall employ a family of subrecursive functions $(h^\alpha)_\alpha$ indexed by ordinals α known as the *Hardy hierarchy*.

Ordinal Terms. We use ordinal terms α in *Cantor Normal Form* (CNF), which can be written as terms $\alpha = \omega^{\alpha_1} + \cdots + \omega^{\alpha_n}$ where $\alpha_1 \geq \cdots \geq \alpha_n$ are themselves written in CNF. Using such notations, we can express any ordinal below ε_0, the minimal fixpoint of $x = \omega^x$. The ordinal 0 is obtained when $n = 0$; otherwise if $\alpha_n = 0$ the ordinal α is a *successor* ordinal $\omega^{\alpha_1} + \cdots + \omega^{\alpha_{n-1}} + 1$, and if $\alpha_n > 0$ the ordinal α is a *limit* ordinal. We usually write λ to denote limit ordinals.

Fundamental Sequences. For all x in $\mathbb{N}$ and limit ordinals λ, we use a standard assignment of fundamental sequences $\lambda(0) < \lambda(1) < \cdots < \lambda(x) < \cdots < \lambda$ with supremum λ. Fundamental sequences are defined by transfinite induction by:

$$(\gamma + \omega^{\beta+1})(x) \stackrel{\text{def}}{=} \gamma + \omega^\beta \cdot (x+1) , \qquad (\gamma + \omega^{\lambda'})(x) \stackrel{\text{def}}{=} \gamma + \omega^{\lambda'(x)} . \qquad (7)$$

For instance, $\omega(x) = x + 1$, $\omega^2(x) = \omega \cdot (x+1)$, $\omega^\omega(x) = \omega^{x+1}$, etc.

The Hardy Hierarchy. Let $h\colon \mathbb{N} \to \mathbb{N}$ be a strictly increasing function. The Hardy functions $(h^\alpha\colon \mathbb{N} \to \mathbb{N})_\alpha$ are defined by transfinite induction on their ordinal indices by

$$h^0(x) \stackrel{\text{def}}{=} x , \qquad h^{\alpha+1}(x) \stackrel{\text{def}}{=} h^\alpha(h(x)) , \qquad h^\lambda(x) \stackrel{\text{def}}{=} h^{\lambda(x)}(x) . \qquad (8)$$

Observe that $h^k(x)$ for a finite k is simply the kth iterate of h. For limit ordinals λ, $h^\lambda(x)$ performs a form of diagonalisation: for instance, setting $H(x) \stackrel{\text{def}}{=} x + 1$ the successor function, $H^\omega(x) = H^{x+1}(x) = 2x + 1$, $H^{\omega^2}(x) = 2^{x+1}(x+1) - 1$ is a function of exponential growth, while H^{ω^3} is a non elementary function akin to a tower of exponentials of height x, H^{ω^ω} is a non primitive-recursive function with growth similar to the Ackermann function, and $H^{\omega^{\omega^\omega}}$ is a non multiply-recursive function characteristic of hyper-Ackermannian complexity.

Complexity Classes. Following [23], we can define complexity classes for computations with time or space resources bounded by Hardy functions of the size of the input. We concentrate in this paper on the HYPERACKERMANN complexity class. Let FMR denote the set of multiply-recursive functions and let h be any multiply-recursive strictly increasing function, then [23, Theorem 4.2]:

$$\text{HYPERACKERMANN} \stackrel{\text{def}}{=} \mathbf{F}_{\omega^\omega} = \bigcup_{m \in \text{FMR}} \text{DTIME}(h^{\omega^{\omega^\omega}}(m(n))) \qquad (9)$$

is the set of decision problems solvable with resources bounded by an hyper-Ackermannian function applied to a multiply-recursive function m of the size of the input. This class is closed under multiply-recursive reductions, and several problems are known to be complete for it (see Sect. 6.2 of [23] for a survey), including coverability in unordered data nets [20].

5.2   Upper Bounds

We focus on the worst-case *norm* of the constructed simple ideals, from which bounds on the total size of the coverability tree and the complexity upper bound in Theorem 3.5 can both be derived.

Norms of Simple Ideals. For a vector $\boldsymbol{u}$ in $\mathbb{Z}_\omega^k$, its *norm* is its maximal finite absolute value: $\|\boldsymbol{v}\| \overset{\text{def}}{=} \max\{|\boldsymbol{v}[i]| \mid 1 \le i \le k \wedge \boldsymbol{v}[i] \ne \omega\}$. Observe that, if $\boldsymbol{I}$ is in $\{0, \omega\}^k$, then $\|\boldsymbol{I}\| = 0$. For an $\boldsymbol{I}$-simple ideal M, and thus for finitely supported ones in particular, we define its norm as the maximum between the cardinality of its support and the maximal norm of its vectors: $\|M\| \overset{\text{def}}{=} \max\{|Supp_{\boldsymbol{I}}(M)|, \|M(d)\| \mid d \in \mathbb{D}\}$. Note that the vectors for data d outside the support have all norm 0. In the full paper, we exhibit a bound $B \overset{\text{def}}{=} h^{\omega^{\omega^{k+3}}}(\|f_0\|)$ on the norms of all the simple ideals constructed in a coverability tree rooted by f_0 as defined in Definition 4.2, where h also depends on the UDPN:

Theorem 5.1. *The norms of the simple ideals in a coverability tree rooted in a configuration f_0 for a k-dimensional UDPN $\mathcal{T}$ are bounded by $h^{\omega^{\omega^{k+3}}}(\|f_0\|)$, where $h(x)$ is an elementary function of x, k, and $\|\mathcal{T}\|$.*

The main technical ingredients for Theorem 5.1 are combinatorial statements on the lengths of so-called *controlled bad sequences* proven by Rosa-Velardo [20, Appendix A] for finite multisets of vectors of natural numbers. Our proofs require however a substantial amount of work on top of that of Rosa-Velardo's for two reasons: we work with extended vectors in $\mathbb{N}_\omega^k$, and use permutation embeddings rather than just plain embeddings.

Relating Norms with Sizes and Complexity. The norm $\|M\| \le B$ of a simple ideal M is directly related to the size of its concrete binary representation: the latter needs at most $\|M\| \cdot k \cdot (\lceil \log\|M\| \rceil + 1)$ bits for the $\boldsymbol{I}$ supported part of the ideal and k bits for the $\boldsymbol{I}$ vector itself. We can also bound the length of the branches in our coverability trees: there are indeed at most $(B + 2)^{kB} \cdot 2^k$ different simple ideals with norm $\le B$, and no two interior nodes on a branch are labelled by the same ideal due to condition 1 in Definition 4.2 (see Remark 4.4). Finally, by Lemma 3.4, the branching degree of the coverability tree is bounded by an exponential function $(B + \|\mathcal{T}\|)! \cdot |\mathcal{T}|^2$ in B and the size of $\mathcal{T}$. These three observations combined allow to bound the size of the coverability tree:

Theorem 5.2 (Size of Coverability Trees). *The size of a coverability tree built from an initial configuration f_0 for a k-dimensional UDPN $\mathcal{T}$ is bounded by an elementary function of B, k, and the size of $\mathcal{T}$.*

Theorem 5.2 along with Eq. (9) and the completeness and soundness of coverability trees yields the proof of Theorem 3.5, using the fact that $\mathbf{F}_{\omega^\omega}$ is closed under elementary reductions [23, Theorem 4.7].

5.3   Lower Bounds

The sheer complexity bounds we just obtained on the size of coverability trees beg the question whether they are the best possible. We show in Theorem 5.3 that, indeed, the size of coverability trees for a family of UDPNs is provably non multiply-recursive, matching essentially the statement of Theorem 5.2:

Theorem 5.3 (Hyper-Ackermannian Coverability Trees). *There exists families of $O(k)$-sized UDPNs $(T_k)_k$ and $O(k + \log n)$-sized initial configurations $(f_{k,n})_{k,n}$, whose coverability trees are of size at least $H^{\omega^{\omega^k}}(n)$.*

Hardy Computations. As detailed in the full paper, we prove Theorem 5.3 by 'implementing' the computation of Hardy functions $H^{\omega^{\omega^k}}$ in nets T_k. The main idea, first developed in [11,24], is to see the equations in (8) for $0 < \alpha$ as rewriting rules operating on pairs (α, n):

$$(\alpha + 1, n) \to (\alpha, n + 1), \qquad\qquad (\lambda, n) \to (\lambda(n), n). \qquad (10)$$

Note that a sequence $(\alpha_0, n_0) \to (\alpha_1, n_1) \to \cdots \to (\alpha_i, n_i) \to \cdots$ of rewriting steps maintains $H^{\alpha_i}(n_i) = H^{\alpha_0}(n_0)$ for all i, and must eventually terminate at some rank ℓ with $\alpha_\ell = 0$ since $\alpha_i > \alpha_{i+1}$ for all i, and then $n_\ell = H^{\alpha_0}(n_0)$.

Using a natural representation of ordinals $\alpha < \omega^{\omega^k}$ as finite multisets of vectors also employed by Rosa-Velardo [20], a pair (α, n) can be encoded as a configuration of T_k, and the rewriting rules of (10) can be implemented on such codes by steps of T_k. This is however not a perfect implementation: many incorrect computations yielding results different from $H^{\omega^{\omega^k}}(n) = H^{\omega^{\omega^{k-1} \cdot (n+1)}}(n)$ are possible. The crucial point is that there exists a *perfect* computation in T_k, of length at least $H^{\omega^{\omega^k}}(n)$. Furthermore, this computation does not allow any acceleration step, and has therefore to occur as such in any coverability tree.

6   Concluding Remarks

In this paper, we have presented a procedure to construct coverability trees for UDPNs in the style of Karp and Miller [12]. This yields decision procedures for coverability and several variants of the boundedness problem including place-boundedness, depth- and width place-boundedness. Besides its interest for the formal verification of UDPNs, this paves the way towards future attempts at proving the decidability of reachability along the lines developed for Petri nets in [13,14,16,18].

We have derived hyper-Ackermannian upper bounds on the complexity of our construction, and shown that such enormous complexities are actually attained on some UDPNs. Note that this however does *not* provide a lower bound

– on the size of $Clover(f)$, for which the best known bound is an Ackermannian lower bound adapted from the case of Petri nets [4], nor

– on the complexity of the various boundedness problems on UDPNs, for which the best lower bound is hardness for TOWER $= \mathbf{F}_3$, adapted from the coverability problem [15].

We actually suspect that much lower complexities that HYPERACKERMANN could be obtained for the coverability and boundedness problems. For instance, in the case of Petri nets, coverability trees have a worst-case Ackermannian size [4,6], but coverability, boundedness, and place-boundedness are all EXP-SPACE-complete [2,5,17,19].

References

1. Abdulla, P.A., Čerāns, K., Jonsson, B., Tsay, Y.K.: Algorithmic analysis of programs with well quasi-ordered domains. Inform. and Comput. **160**(1–2), 109–127 (2000)
2. Blockelet, M., Schmitz, S.: Model checking coverability graphs of vector addition systems. In: Murlak, F., Sankowski, P. (eds.) MFCS 2011. LNCS, vol. 6907, pp. 108–119. Springer, Heidelberg (2011)
3. Bojańczyk, M., Klin, B., Lasota, S.: Automata theory in nominal sets. Logic. Meth. Comput. Sci. **10**(3:4), 1–44 (2014)
4. Cardoza, E., Lipton, R.J., Meyer, A.R.: Exponential space complete problems for Petri nets and commutative semigroups: preliminary report. In: STOC 1976, pp. 50–54. ACM (1976)
5. Demri, S.: On selective unboundedness of VASS. J. Comput. Syst. Sci. **79**(5), 689–713 (2013)
6. Figueira, D., Figueira, S., Schmitz, S., Schnoebelen, P.: Ackermannian and primitive-recursive bounds with Dickson's Lemma. In: LICS 2011, pp. 269–278. IEEE Press (2011)
7. Finkel, A., Schnoebelen, P.: Well-structured transition systems everywhere!. Theor. Comput. Sci. **256**(1–2), 63–92 (2001)
8. Finkel, A., Goubault-Larrecq, J.: Forward analysis for WSTS, part I: completions. In: STACS 2009. LIPIcs, vol. 3, pp. 433–444. LZI (2009)
9. Finkel, A., Goubault-Larrecq, J.: Forward analysis for WSTS, part II: complete WSTS. Logic. Meth. Comput. Sci. **8**(3:28), 1–35 (2012)
10. Finkel, A., McKenzie, P., Picaronny, C.: A well-structured framework for analysing Petri net extensions. Inform. and Comput. **195**(1–2), 1–29 (2004)
11. Haddad, S., Schmitz, S., Schnoebelen, P.: The ordinal recursive complexity of timed-arc Petri nets, data nets, and other enriched nets. In: LICS 2012, pp. 355–364. IEEE Press (2012)
12. Karp, R.M., Miller, R.E.: Parallel program schemata. J. Comput. Syst. Sci. **3**(2), 147–195 (1969)
13. Kosaraju, S.R.: Decidability of reachability in vector addition systems. In: Proceedings STOC 1982, pp. 267–281. ACM (1982)
14. Lambert, J.L.: A structure to decide reachability in Petri nets. Theor. Comput. Sci. **99**(1), 79–104 (1992)
15. Lazić, R., Newcomb, T., Ouaknine, J., Roscoe, A., Worrell, J.: Nets with tokens which carry data. Fund. Inform. **88**(3), 251–274 (2008)
16. Leroux, J., Schmitz, S.: Demystifying reachability in vector addition systems. In: LICS 2015, pp. 56–67. IEEE Press (2015)

17. Lipton, R.: The reachability problem requires exponential space. Technical Report 62, Yale University (1976)
18. Mayr, E.W.: An algorithm for the general Petri net reachability problem. In: Proceedings STOC 1981, pp. 238–246. ACM (1981)
19. Rackoff, C.: The covering and boundedness problems for vector addition systems. Theor. Comput. Sci. 6(2), 223–231 (1978)
20. Rosa-Velardo, F.: Ordinal recursive complexity of unordered data nets. Technical Report TR-4-14, Departamento de Sistemas Informáticos y Computación, Universidad Complutense de Madrid (2014). http://antares.sip.ucm.es/frosa/docs/complexityUDN.pdf
21. Rosa-Velardo, F., de Frutos-Escrig, D.: Decidability and complexity of Petri nets with unordered data. Theor. Comput. Sci. 412(34), 4439–4451 (2011)
22. Rosa-Velardo, F., Martos-Salgado, M., de Frutos-Escrig, D.: Accelerations for the coverability set of Petri nets with names. Fund. Inform. 113(3–4), 313–341 (2011)
23. Schmitz, S.: Complexity hierarchies beyond elementary. ACM Trans. Comput. Theor. (2016) (to appear). http://arxiv.org/abs/1312.5686
24. Schmitz, S., Schnoebelen, P.: Algorithmic aspects of WQO theory. Lecture notes (2012).http://cel.archives-ouvertes.fr/cel-00727025
25. Schmitz, S., Schnoebelen, P.: The power of well-structured systems. In: D'Argenio, P.R., Melgratti, H. (eds.) CONCUR 2013 – Concurrency Theory. LNCS, vol. 8052, pp. 5–24. Springer, Heidelberg (2013)
26. Schnoebelen, P.: Revisiting Ackermann-hardness for lossy counter machines and reset Petri nets. In: Hliněný, P., Kučera, A. (eds.) MFCS 2010. LNCS, vol. 6281, pp. 616–628. Springer, Heidelberg (2010)

Shortest Paths in One-Counter Systems

Dmitry Chistikov[1]([✉]), Wojciech Czerwiński[2], Piotr Hofman[3],
Michał Pilipczuk[2], and Michael Wehar[4]

[1] Max Planck Institute for Software Systems (MPI-SWS),
Kaiserslautern and Saarbrücken, Germany
dch@mpi-sws.org
[2] Institute of Informatics, University of Warsaw, Warsaw, Poland
{wczerwin,michal.pilipczuk}@mimuw.edu.pl
[3] Laboratoire Spécification et Vérification (LSV),
ENS Cachan & CNRS, Paris, France
piotr.hofman@lsv.ens-cachan.fr
[4] Department of Computer Science and Engineering,
University at Buffalo, Buffalo, USA
mwehar@buffalo.edu

Abstract. We show that any one-counter automaton with n states, if its language is non-empty, accepts some word of length at most $O(n^2)$. This closes the gap between the previously known upper bound of $O(n^3)$ and lower bound of $\Omega(n^2)$. More generally, we prove a tight upper bound on the length of shortest paths between arbitrary configurations in one-counter transition systems (weaker bounds have previously appeared in the literature).

1 Introduction

Extremal combinatorial questions are ubiquitous in today's theory of computing: How many steps does an algorithm take in the worst case when traversing a data structure? How large is the most compact automaton for a formal language? While some specific questions of this form are best seen as standalone puzzles, only interesting for their own sake, others can be used as basic building blocks for more involved arguments.

We look into the following extremal problem: Given a one-counter automaton $\mathcal{A}$ with n states, how long can the shortest word accepted by $\mathcal{A}$ be? It is folklore that, unless the language of $\mathcal{A}$ is empty, $\mathcal{A}$ accepts some word of length at most polynomial in n. This fact and a number of related results of similar form have

The main part of these results was obtained during Autobóz'15, the annual research camp of Warsaw automata group. During the work on these results, Mi. Pilipczuk held a post-doc position at Warsaw Centre of Mathematics and Computer Science and was supported by the Foundation for Polish Science via the START stipend programme. P. Hofman was supported by Labex Digicosme, Univ. Paris-Saclay, project VERICONISS. W. Czerwiński acknowledges a partial support by the Polish National Science Centre grant 2013/09/B/ST6/01575.

© Springer-Verlag Berlin Heidelberg 2016
B. Jacobs and C. Löding (Eds.): FOSSACS 2016, LNCS 9634, pp. 462–478, 2016.
DOI: 10.1007/978-3-662-49630-5_27

appeared as auxiliary lemmas in the literature on formal languages, analysis of infinite-state systems, and applications of formal methods [12, Lemma 6], [11, Sect. 8.1], [8, Lemma 5], [1, Lemma 11], [9, Lemmas 28 and 29], [7, Sect. 5].

A closer inspection reveals that the arguments behind these results deliver (or can deliver) an upper bound of $O(n^3)$, while the best known lower bound comes from examples of one-counter automata with shortest accepted words of length $\Theta(n^2)$. In other words, the true value is at least quadratic and at most cubic.

The main result of this paper is that we close this gap by showing a quadratic upper bound, $O(n^2)$. We also extend this result to a more general reachability setting: in any one-counter (transition) system with n control states, whenever there is a path from a configuration α to a configuration β—recall that configurations are pairs of the form (q, c) where $q \in Q$ is the control state, $|Q| = n$, and c is a counter value, a nonnegative integer—there is also a path from α to β that has length at most $O(n^2 + n \cdot \max(c_\alpha, c_\beta))$ where c_α and c_β are the counter values of α and β. We discuss our contribution in more detail in Sect. 2.

Related Work and Motivation. Reachability is a fundamental problem in theoretical computer science and in its applications in verification, notably via analysis of infinite-state systems [2,4,14,17]. Among such systems, counter-based models of computation are a standard abstraction that has attracted a lot of attention [3]; machines with a single counter are, of course, the most basic. Nevertheless, while our main motivation has been purely theoretical, we note that bounds on the length of shortest paths in one-counter systems have appeared as building blocks in the literature on rather diverse topics.

More specifically, a polynomial upper bound is used by Etessami et al. [8] in an analysis of *probabilistic* one-counter systems (which are equivalent to so-called discrete-time quasi-birth-death processes, QBDs). They prove that in the $(q, 1) \rightsquigarrow (q', 0)$-reachability setting the counter does not need to grow higher than n^2 and provide examples showing that this bound is tight. However, they only deduce upper bounds of n^3 and n^4 on the length of shortest paths without and with zero tests, respectively. A simple corollary shows that if a state q can eventually reach a state q' with a non-zero probability, then this probability is lower-bounded by $p^{\text{poly}(n)}$ where p is the smallest among positive probabilities associated with transitions. This becomes a step in the proof that a (decomposed) Newton's method approximates *termination probabilities* of the system in time polynomial in its size, n; the results of the present paper reduce the (theoretical) worst-case upper bounds on the number of steps roughly by a factor of n.

In a subsequent work, Hofman et al. [9] reuse the auxiliary lemmas on the length of shortest paths from [8] and show that (strong and weak) trace inclusion for a one-counter system and a finite-state process is decidable in PSPACE (and is, in fact, PSPACE-complete).

One may note that a stronger upper bound of $O(n^3)$ on the length of shortest paths can be derived from the above bound on the largest needed counter value even in the presence of zero tests. This value, $O(n^3)$, seems to be a recurring theme in the literature on one-counter systems; it already appears in the pumping lemma for one-counter languages due to Latteux [13] as the *pumping constant*: a number N such that any accepted word longer than N can be pumped. In fact, the formulation in [13] does not permit *removals* of factors from an accepted word, but even such a version would only yield the same upper bound of $O(n^3)$ on the length of shortest paths. While the arguments of the present paper do not lead to an improvement in the pumping constant for one-counter languages, we nevertheless show that in the reachability setting the optimal value (the length of the shortest path) is actually $O(n^2)$.

A cubic upper bound on the largest needed counter value (for the reachability setting) in one-counter systems without zero tests, also known as one-counter nets, appears in the work of Lafourcade et al. [11,12]. This result is applied in the context of the Dolev-Yao intruder model, where the question of whether a passive eavesdropper (an intruder) can obtain a piece of information is reduced to the decision problem for a deduction system. For several such systems, Lafourcade et al. show that, under certain assumptions, the problem is decidable in polynomial time. They construct a one-counter system where states represent terms from a finite set and the counter value corresponds to the number of applications of a free unary function symbol to a term. After this, the upper bound on counter values along shortest paths is extended to an upper bound on the size of terms that can be used in a minimal deductive proof; needless to say, an improvement in the upper bound extends in a natural way.

Finally, we would like to mention the work of Alur and Černý [1], who use a related model of one-counter systems with counter values in $\mathbb{Z}$ and without zero tests. They reduce the equivalence problem for so-called streaming data-string transducers to $(q, 0) \rightsquigarrow (q', 0)$-reachability in such counter systems: the transducers produce output at the end of the computation, and the counter is used to track the accumulated distance between a distinguished pair of symbols in the output. Since these transducers are designed to model list-manipulating programs (in two syntactically restricted models), decision procedures for equivalence of such programs can rely on the upper bounds for shortest paths to efficiently prune the search space. In [1], the upper bound on the path length is the familiar $O(n^3)$; this gives an upper bound on the length of smallest counterexamples to equivalence. Our upper bound of $O(n^2)$ extends to this model of counter systems too; because of space constraints, details are only given in the full version of the paper. The reduction to reachability in one-counter systems was recently implemented by Thakkar et al. [16] on top of ARMC, an abstraction-refinement model checker [15], for the purpose of verifying retransmission protocols over noisy channels.

2   Summary

One-Counter Systems. In this paper we work in the framework of one-counter systems, which are an abstract version of one-counter automata. More precisely, they are one-counter automata without input alphabet (see below).

Formally, a *one-counter system (OCS)* $\mathcal{O}$ consists of a finite set of states Q, a set of non-zero transitions $T_{>0} \subseteq Q \times \{-1, 0, 1\} \times Q$, and a set of zero tests

$T_{=0} \subseteq Q \times \{0,1\} \times Q$. A *configuration* of the OCS $\mathcal{O}$ is a pair in $Q \times \mathbb{N}$. We define a binary relation $\longrightarrow$ on the set $Q \times \mathbb{N}$ as follows: $(p,c) \longrightarrow (q,c+d)$ whenever (i) $c \geq 1$ and $(p,d,q) \in T_{>0}$ or (ii) $c = 0$ and $(p,d,q) \in T_{=0}$. The reflexive transitive closure of $\longrightarrow$ is denoted by $\longrightarrow^*$; we say that a configuration β is *reachable* from α if $\alpha \longrightarrow^* \beta$. This reachability is witnessed by a *path* in OCS $\mathcal{O}$, which is simply a path in the infinite directed graph with vertices $Q \times \mathbb{N}$ and edge relation $\longrightarrow$; vertices and edges along the path can be repeated. The *length* of the path is the number of (not necessarily distinct) edges that occur on it.

Our Contribution. We first formulate our results in terms of one-counter systems. Our first result is on paths between configurations with zero counter values.

Theorem 1. *Let $\mathcal{O}$ be a one-counter system with n states. Suppose a configuration $\beta = (p_\beta, 0)$ is reachable from a configuration $\alpha = (p_\alpha, 0)$ in $\mathcal{O}$. Then $\mathcal{O}$ has a path from α to β of length at most $14n^2$.*

We then generalize the result to arbitrary source and target configurations.

Theorem 2. *Let $\mathcal{O}$ be a one-counter system with n states. Suppose a configuration $\beta = (p_\beta, c_\beta)$ is reachable from a configuration $\alpha = (p_\alpha, c_\alpha)$ in $\mathcal{O}$. Then $\mathcal{O}$ has a path from α to β of length at most $14n^2 + n \cdot \max(c_\alpha, c_\beta)$.*

The proof of Theorem 1 is the main technical contribution of this work. For this reason, in this extended abstract we focus on proving Theorem 1, while the reasoning leading to Theorem 2, as well as an extension to OCS with negative counter values, can be found in the full version of the paper. The full version contains also the proofs of all the statements marked with ♠.

One-Counter Automata. We now restate our contribution in terms of one-counter automata (which are the original motivation for this work).

Take any finite set Σ. The set of all finite words over Σ is denoted by Σ^*, and the empty word by ε. A (*nondeterministic*) *one-counter automaton* $\mathcal{A}$ over Σ is a one-counter system where every transition $t \in T_{>0} \cup T_{=0}$ is associated with a label, $\lambda(t) \in \Sigma \cup \{\varepsilon\}$, and where some subsets $I \subseteq Q$ and $F \subseteq Q$ are distinguished as sets of initial and final states respectively. The labeling function λ is extended from transitions to edges $\longrightarrow$ and to paths in a natural way; the automaton *accepts* all words that are labels of paths from $I \times \{0\}$ to $F \times \mathbb{N}$. The *language* of a one-counter automaton $\mathcal{A}$ is the set of all words accepted by $\mathcal{A}$.

Corollary 1 (♠). *Let $\mathcal{A}$ be a nondeterministic one-counter automaton with n states. If the language of $\mathcal{A}$ is non-empty, then $\mathcal{A}$ accepts some word of length at most $14n^2$.*

As a concrete example, from Corollary 1 it follows that any nondeterministic one-counter automaton that accepts the singleton unary language $\{a^n\}$ —a basic version of counting to n— must have at least $\Omega(\sqrt{n})$ states. This lower bound is tight and shows that nondeterminism does not help to "count to n", because *deterministic* one-counter automata can also do this using $\Theta(\sqrt{n})$ states [5].

Lower Bounds. As we already said, the lower bound on the length of the shortest path is $\Omega(n^2)$. We present constructions of OCS that match the upper bounds of Theorems 1 and 2. Note that Examples 1 and 2 seem to use different phenomena.

Example 1. [5,8] Consider an OCS $\mathcal{O}_1$ with $2n$ states: $p_1, \ldots, p_n$ and $q_1, \ldots, q_n$. Let $\mathcal{O}_1$ have, for $1 \le i < n$, transitions $(p_i, +1, p_{i+1})$ and $(q_i, 0, q_{i+1})$, as well as $(q_n, -1, q_1)$ and $(p_n, 0, q_1)$. All the transitions are non-zero, except for transition $(p_1, +1, p_2)$, which is a zero test. This OCS is deterministic: every configuration has at most one outgoing transition. The only path from $(p_1, 0)$ to $(q_1, 0)$ has length n^2.

Example 2. [8] Let k and m be coprime and let OCS $\mathcal{O}_2'$ have states $p_0, \ldots, p_{k-1}$, $q_0, \ldots, q_{m-1}$, and s_1, s_2. Let $\mathcal{O}_2'$ have, for all $0 \le i < k$ and $0 \le j < m$, non-zero transitions $(p_i, +1, p_{i+1 \bmod k})$ and $(q_j, -1, q_{j+1 \bmod m})$, a non-zero $(p_0, -1, q_1)$, and zero tests $(s_1, +1, p_1)$, $(q_0, 0, s_2)$. Now paths from $(s_1, 0)$ to $(s_2, 0)$ correspond to solutions of $x \cdot k - y \cdot m = 0$; the shortest path takes the first cycle $x = m$ times and the second cycle $y = k$ times. Exiting the second cycle uses an additional transition, making the length $2km + 1$. Setting $k = n$ and $m = n - 1$ gives an OCS $\mathcal{O}_2$ with $2n+1$ states where not only does the shortest path have quadratic length, but all such paths also need to use quadratic counter values.

Example 3. This example justifies the need for the term $n \cdot \max(c_\alpha, c_\beta)$ in Theorem 2. Modify $\mathcal{O}_1$ from Example 1 as follows. Add states $a_1, \ldots, a_n$, $b_1, \ldots, b_n$ and the following non-zero transitions: $(a_n, -1, a_1)$, $(b_n, +1, b_1)$, and, for all $0 \le i < n$, $(a_i, 0, a_{i+1})$ and $(b_i, 0, b_{i+1})$. For each of these non-zero transition, apart from $(a_n, -1, a_1)$, introduce also the same transition as a zero test. Finally, add two more zero tests: $(a_n, 0, p_1)$ and $(q_1, 0, b_1)$. Thus, the obtained OCS $\mathcal{O}_3$ has $4n$ states. Observe that every path in $\mathcal{O}_3$ from (a_1, c_α) to (b_n, c_β) has to go through $(a_n, 0)$ and $(b_1, 0)$ and thus has length at least $n^2 + n(c_\alpha + c_\beta + 2)$.

3   Challenges and Techniques

We now discuss shortly the intuition behind our approach to proving Theorem 1, and where the main challenges lie.

The first, obvious observation is as follows: if some configuration appears more than once on a path, then the segment between any two appearances of this configuration can safely be removed. If we apply this modification exhaustively, then on each "level" — a set of configurations with the same counter value — we cannot see more than n configurations. If the maximum counter value observed on some path were bounded by $O(n)$, then we would immediately obtain a quadratic upper bound on its length. Unfortunately, this is not the case: as Example 2 shows, the counter values in the shortest accepting path can be as large as quadratic. Hence, applying this observation in a straightforward manner cannot lead to any upper bound better than cubic.

Instead, we perform an involved surgery on the path. The first idea is to start with a path ρ_o that is not the shortest, but uses the fewest zero tests;

the observation above shows that their number is bounded by n. Each subpath between two consecutive zero tests is called an *arc*, and we aim at modifying each arc separately to make it short. An arc is called *low* if it contains only configurations with counter values at most $5n$, and *high* otherwise. The total length of low arcs can again be bounded by $O(n^2)$ by just excluding repeated configurations, so it suffices to focus on high arcs.

Suppose ρ is a high arc. Since we observe high counter values on ρ, one can easily find a *positive cycle* σ^+ in the early parts of ρ, and a *negative cycle* σ^- in the late parts of ρ. Here by a cycle we mean a sequence of transitions that starts and ends in the same state, and the cycle is positive/negative if the total effect it has on the counter during its traversal is positive/negative. Let A be the (positive) effect of σ^+ on the counter, and $-B$ be the (negative) effect of σ^-.

Now comes the crucial idea of the proof: we can modify ρ by pumping σ^+ and σ^- up many times, thus effectively "lifting" the central part of the path (called *cap*) to counter levels where there is no threat of hitting counter value zero while performing modifications (see Fig. 1, p. 11). More importantly, the cap can now be unpumped "modulo $\gcd(A, B)$" in the following sense: we can exhaustively remove subpaths between configurations that have the same state and whose counter values are congruent modulo $\gcd(A, B)$. The reason is that any change in the total effect of the cap on the counter that is divisible by $\gcd(A, B)$ can be compensated by adjusting the number of times we pump cycles σ^+ and σ^-. In particular, the length of the cap becomes reduced to at most $\gcd(A, B) \cdot n$, at the cost of pumping σ^+ and σ^- several times.

By performing this operation (we call it *normalization*) on all high arcs, we make them *normal*. After this, we apply an involved amortization scheme to show that the total length of normal arcs is at most quadratic in n. This requires very delicate arguments for bounding (i) the total length of the caps and (ii) the total length of the pumped cycles σ^+ and σ^- throughout all the normal arcs. In particular, for this part of the proof to work we need to assert a number of technical properties of normal arcs; we ensure that these properties hold when we perform the normalization. Most importantly, whenever for two arcs the corresponding cycles σ^+ (or σ^-) lie in the same strongly connected component of the system (looking at the graph induced only by non-zero transitions), we stipulate that in both arcs σ^+ (or σ^-) actually refer to the same cycle. The final amortization is based on the analysis of pairs of strongly connected components to which σ^+ and σ^- belong, for all normal arcs.

At least as of now, arguments of this flavor (inspired by *amortized analysis* reasoning) are not typical for formal language theory and are more characteristic of the body of work on algorithms and data structures; see, e.g., [6, 10].

4   Preliminaries

In this paper $\mathbb{N}$ stands for the set of nonnegative integers. For any set X and a word $w \in X^*$, the *length* of $w = x_1 \ldots x_n$, denoted LEN(w), is the number n of symbols in w. For $k \in \mathbb{N}$ and a word w, by w^k we denote the word w repeated

k times. For two positive integers x, y, by $\gcd(x, y)$ and $\operatorname{lcm}(x, y)$ we denote the greatest common divisor and the least common multiple of x and y, respectively. Recall that $x \cdot y = \gcd(x, y) \cdot \operatorname{lcm}(x, y)$.

We now give all definitions related to one-counter systems that we need later. For the reader's convenience, concepts from Sect. 2 are defined anew.

A *one-counter system* (OCS) $\mathcal{O}$ consists of a finite set of *states* Q, a set of *non-zero transitions* $T_{>0} \subseteq Q \times \{-1, 0, 1\} \times Q$, and a set of *zero tests* $T_{=0} \subseteq Q \times \{0, 1\} \times Q$. The set of *transitions* is $T = T_{>0} \cup T_{=0}$. For a transition $t = (q, d, q') \in T$, by $\operatorname{SRC}(t)$ and $\operatorname{TARG}(t)$ we denote q and q', i.e., the source and the target state of t respectively. Further, the *effect* of the transition $t = (q, d, q')$ is the number d; we write $\operatorname{EFF}(t) = d$. We extend this notion to sequences of transitions: $\operatorname{EFF}(t_1 \ldots t_m) = \sum_{i=1}^{m} \operatorname{EFF}(t_i)$. A *configuration* of the OCS $\mathcal{O}$ is a pair in $Q \times \mathbb{N}$. The *state of a configuration* (q, c) is the state q; we also say that configuration (q, c) *has state* q, and write $\operatorname{ST}((q, c)) = q$. The *counter value* of configuration (q, c) is the number c; we write $\operatorname{CNT}((q, c)) = c$.

A transition $t = (q, d, q') \in T$ can be *fired* in a configuration $\gamma = (q, c)$ if either $t \in T_{>0}$ and $c > 0$ or $t \in T_{=0}$ and $c = 0$. In other words, zero tests can be fired only if the counter value is zero, and non-zero transitions can be fired only if the counter value is positive. The *result* of firing (q, d, q') in (q, c) is the configuration $\gamma' = (q', c + d)$. We then write $\gamma \xrightarrow{t} \gamma'$.

A *path* ρ of the OCS $\mathcal{O}$ is a sequence of pairs

$$(\gamma_1, t_1)(\gamma_2, t_2) \ldots (\gamma_m, t_m) \in ((Q \times \mathbb{N}) \times T)^*$$

such that for every $i \in \{1, \ldots, m-1\}$ we have $\gamma_i \xrightarrow{t_i} \gamma_{i+1}$ and there exists a configuration γ_{m+1} such that $\gamma_m \xrightarrow{t_m} \gamma_{m+1}$. The *length* of this path is m. The *source* of ρ, denoted by $\operatorname{SRC}(\rho)$, is γ_1; we also say that ρ *starts* in its source. Similarly, the *target* of ρ, denoted by $\operatorname{TARG}(\rho)$, is γ_{m+1}; we say that ρ *finishes* in its target. Note that now the source and target are configurations, rather than individual states; the path is *from* its source *to* its target. All $\gamma_2, \ldots, \gamma_m$ are called *intermediate configurations*. We also say that configurations $\gamma_1, \gamma_2, \ldots, \gamma_{m+1}$ *appear* on ρ; note that the target of ρ also appears on ρ. Finally, when such a path exists, the configuration γ_{m+1} is said to be *reachable* from the configuration γ_1.

The *projection* of a path ρ is the sequence of its transitions $t_1 t_2 \ldots t_m$; we write $\operatorname{PROJ}(\rho) = t_1 t_2 \ldots t_m$. We follow the convention of denoting paths by ρ and sequences of transitions by σ. The *effect* of a path ρ is $\operatorname{EFF}(\rho) = \operatorname{EFF}(\operatorname{PROJ}(\rho))$. A sequence of transitions $\sigma = t_1 t_2 \ldots t_m$ is *fireable* in a configuration γ_1 if there exists a path $\rho = (\gamma_1, t_1)(\gamma_2, t_2) \ldots (\gamma_m, t_m)$. This path ρ is called the *fastening* of σ at γ_1, denoted $\rho = \operatorname{FASTEN}(\gamma_1, \sigma)$. Note that in particular $\operatorname{PROJ}(\operatorname{FASTEN}(\gamma, \sigma)) = \sigma$ for every γ in which σ is fireable.

A sequence of transitions $t_1 t_2 \ldots t_m$ is *consistent* if for all $i \in \{1, \ldots, m-1\}$ it holds that $\operatorname{TARG}(t_i) = \operatorname{SRC}(t_{i+1})$. Note that a sequence of transitions fireable in some configuration is always consistent, but the other implication does not hold in general. We extend the notation $\operatorname{SRC}(\cdot)$ and $\operatorname{TARG}(\cdot)$ to consistent sequences of transitions: $\operatorname{SRC}(t_1 t_2 \ldots t_m) = \operatorname{SRC}(t_1)$ and $\operatorname{TARG}(t_1 t_2 \ldots t_m) = \operatorname{TARG}(t_m)$. The sources and targets of the transitions of $t_1 t_2 \ldots t_m$ are *visited* on $t_1 t_2 \ldots t_m$.

A *cycle* σ is a consistent sequence of non-zero transitions that starts and finishes in the same state q. This q is called the *base state of the cycle* σ. If the effect of σ is positive (resp. negative), then it is a *positive* (resp. *negative*) cycle. A cycle σ is called *simple* if every state is visited at most once on σ, except for the base of σ, which is visited only at the start and at the end.

5 Proof of Theorem 1

5.1 Proof Overview and Notation

Let us fix the OCS $\mathcal{O}$ we work with; let Q be its state set and let $n = |Q|$. Suppose ρ_0 is a path from α to β, and let ρ_0 be chosen such that it has the smallest possible number of configurations with counter value zero. Note that ρ_0 does not have to be the shortest path between α and β. The first step is to divide ρ_0 into subpaths, called *arcs*, between consecutive configurations with counter value zero. Then we modify the arcs separately. If a counter value in an arc does not exceed $5n$, then we say that the arc is *low*, otherwise it is *high*. The low arcs will not be changed at all, and the reason is that we can bound quadratically the total number of configurations with counter value at most $5n$ using the following straightforward proposition. It is similar, in the spirit, to pumping lemmas, but simply removes a part of the path.

Proposition 1. *Suppose* $\rho = (\gamma_1, t_1)(\gamma_2, t_2) \ldots (\gamma_m, t_m)$ *is a path from* α *to* β. *Suppose further that for some* i *and* j *with* $1 \le i < j \le m + 1$ *it holds that* $\gamma_i = \gamma_j$, *where* γ_{m+1} *is such that* $\gamma_m \xrightarrow{t_m} \gamma_{m+1}$. *Consider*

$$\rho' = (\gamma_1, t_1)(\gamma_2, t_2) \ldots (\gamma_{i-1}, t_{i-1})(\gamma_j, t_j)(\gamma_{j+1}, t_{j+1}) \ldots (\gamma_m, t_m).$$

Then ρ' *is also a path from* α *to* β.

However, the high arcs will be heavily modified. Roughly speaking, if an arc is high, then it contains both a positive cycle near its beginning and a negative cycle near its end. We can use these cycles to pump the middle part of the path as much up as we like. Thus, the modified path will consist of a short prefix; then several iterations of a positive cycle pumping it up; then a so called *cap*: a part of the path with only high counter values; then several iterations of a negative cycle pumping it down; and finally a short suffix. We show in the sequel how to perform this construction in such a way that the total length of pumping cycles, short prefixes and suffixes, and caps is quadratic. The construction itself (with arc-level length estimates) is presented in the following Subsect. 5.2, and the upper bound on the length of the entire path is given in Subsect. 5.3.

Transition multigraph. One can view a transition $(p, c, q) \in Q \times \{-1, 0, 1\} \times Q$ also as an edge $(p, q) \in Q \times Q$ labelled by a number $c \in \{-1, 0, 1\}$. In the proof we will many times switch back and forth between these two perspectives. In order to keep the mathematical precision we introduce a bit of notation.

The *transition multigraph* $G = (V, E, \ell)$ of an OCS consists of a set of nodes V, a multiset of directed edges E, and a labeling $\ell : E \to \{-1, 0, 1\}$. Set V equals the set of states Q. Every non-zero transition $t = (p, c, q) \in T_{>0}$ in $\mathcal{O}$ gives rise to an edge $e = (u, v) \in E$ with $\ell(e) = c$. Note that the definition of the transition multigraph does not take into account the zero transitions.

In the proof we pay a special attention to strongly connected components (SCCs) of G. Recall that two vertices $p, q \in V$ are said to *communicate* if G has a walk from p to q and a walk from q to p. Communication is an equivalence relation, and its equivalence classes are called the *strongly connected components* of G. Let $\mathfrak{S}$ be the set of all strongly connected components of G. For a strongly connected component $S \in \mathfrak{S}$, by n_S we denote the number of vertices in S. We say that a cycle σ is *contained* in S if each state appearing on σ belongs to S. Note that every cycle is contained in some SCC, and a simple cycle contained in S has length at most n_S. We say that an SCC S is *positively enabled* if it contains a cycle that has a positive effect. Similarly, S is *negatively enabled* if it contains a cycle that has a negative effect. Note that an SCC S can be both positively and negatively enabled.

Lemma 1 (♠). *Let G be a transition multigraph of an OCS and S a positively (respectively, negatively) enabled SCC. Then there exists a positive (respectively, negative) cycle σ contained in S that is simple.*

For every positively enabled SCC S we distinguish one, arbitrarily chosen, simple cycle with positive effect contained in S; we denote it by σ_S^+. Its existence is guaranteed by Lemma 1. Similarly, for every negatively enabled S we distinguish one simple cycle with negative effect contained in S, and we denote it by σ_S^-. The base states of these cycles are chosen arbitrarily.

5.2   Normal Paths

A path is an *arc* if both its source and target have counter value zero, but all its intermediate configurations have counter values strictly larger than zero. An arc (or a path) is *low* if all its configurations (including the target) have counter values strictly smaller than $5n$. An arc ρ is (S, T)-*normal*, where S and T are some SCCs of the transition multigraph, if it admits the following *normal decomposition* (see Fig. 1, p. 11):

$$\rho = \rho_{\text{PREF}} \, \rho_{\text{UP}} \, \rho_{\text{CAP}} \, \rho_{\text{DOWN}} \, \rho_{\text{SUFF}},$$

where

- ρ_{PREF} and ρ_{SUFF} are low;
- $\text{PROJ}(\rho_{\text{UP}}) = (\sigma_{\text{UP}})^k$ for some $k \in \mathbb{N}$, where $\sigma_{\text{UP}} = \sigma_S^+$;
- $\text{PROJ}(\rho_{\text{DOWN}}) = (\sigma_{\text{DOWN}})^\ell$ for some $\ell \in \mathbb{N}$, where $\sigma_{\text{DOWN}} = \sigma_T^-$;
- $\text{ST}(\text{SRC}(\rho_{\text{CAP}}))$ is the base state of σ_{UP}; and
- $\text{ST}(\text{TARG}(\rho_{\text{CAP}}))$ is the base state of σ_{DOWN}.

We say that an arc ρ is *normal* if it is (S,T)-normal for some $S, T \in \mathfrak{S}$. See Fig. 1 for an illustration. Then a path ρ' is *normal* if it is a concatenation of normal arcs (possibly for different pairs (S,T)) and low arcs.

In the remaining part of the proof we will show that if β is reachable from α, where $\mathrm{CNT}(\alpha) = \mathrm{CNT}(\beta) = 0$, then there exists a short normal path from α to β. We start by analyzing a single arc. The following lemma, which is the most technically involved step in this paper, shows that we can restrict ourselves to normal arcs that have a very special structure.

Lemma 2 ($\spadesuit$). *If* $\mathrm{CNT}(\alpha) = \mathrm{CNT}(\beta) = 0$ *and there exists an arc from* α *to* β, *then there exists an arc* ρ *from* α *to* β *which is either low or normal. Moreover, in the case when* ρ *is normal, a normal decomposition* $\rho = \rho_{\mathrm{PREF}}\, \rho_{\mathrm{UP}}\, \rho_{\mathrm{CAP}}\, \rho_{\mathrm{DOWN}}\, \rho_{\mathrm{SUFF}}$ *can be chosen such that:*

(i) $\mathrm{PROJ}(\rho_{\mathrm{UP}}) = (\sigma_{\mathrm{UP}})^a$, $\mathrm{EFF}(\sigma_{\mathrm{UP}}) = A$ *for some* $a, A \in \mathbb{N}$;
(ii) $\mathrm{PROJ}(\rho_{\mathrm{DOWN}}) = (\sigma_{\mathrm{DOWN}})^b$, $\mathrm{EFF}(\sigma_{\mathrm{DOWN}}) = -B$ *for some* $b, B \in \mathbb{N}$;
(iii) $a \cdot A \le 2 \cdot \mathrm{LEN}(\rho_{\mathrm{CAP}}) + 2 \cdot \mathrm{lcm}(A, B)$;
(iv) $b \cdot B \le 2 \cdot \mathrm{LEN}(\rho_{\mathrm{CAP}}) + 2 \cdot \mathrm{lcm}(A, B)$;
(v) *no infix of* $\mathrm{PROJ}(\rho_{\mathrm{CAP}})$ *is a cycle with effect divisible by* $\gcd(A, B)$;
(vi) $\mathrm{CNT}(\mathrm{TARG}(\rho_{\mathrm{UP}})), \mathrm{CNT}(\mathrm{SRC}(\rho_{\mathrm{DOWN}})) > n$; *and*
(vii) *all configurations appearing on* ρ_{PREF} *and* ρ_{SUFF} *are pairwise different.*

We now explain some intuition behind this statement. First note that, by condition (vii), the total number of configurations appearing on ρ_{PREF} and ρ_{SUFF} is at most $5n \cdot n$, since n is the number of states of the OCS $\mathcal{O}$ and both of these paths are low (so counter values $5n$ and above do not occur). Thus, $\mathrm{LEN}(\rho_{\mathrm{PREF}}) + \mathrm{LEN}(\rho_{\mathrm{SUFF}}) \le 5n^2$. Second, we can conclude from condition (v) that every state $q \in Q$ can occur in configurations appearing in ρ_{CAP} at most $\gcd(A, B)$ times; hence, $\mathrm{LEN}(\rho_{\mathrm{CAP}}) \le n \cdot \gcd(A, B) \le n^2$. Finally, condition (i) implies $\mathrm{LEN}(\rho_{\mathrm{UP}}) \le a \cdot n$; if, for instance, $a \le \mathrm{const} \cdot n$, then $\mathrm{LEN}(\rho_{\mathrm{UP}}) \le \mathrm{const} \cdot n^2$; similarly, $\mathrm{LEN}(\rho_{\mathrm{DOWN}}) \le \mathrm{const} \cdot n^2$. Combined together, these bounds would in this case show that $\mathrm{LEN}(\rho)$ is at most quadratic in n.

However, this reasoning would be insufficient for our purposes, since the number of normal arcs itself can be linear in n. This motivates more subtle upper bounds (iii) and (iv) and the fine-grained choice of parameter in (v). We show how to use Lemma 2 to obtain a quadratic upper bound on the size of the *entire* path in the following Subsect. 5.3; the remainder of the present subsection provides an intuitive sketch of the proof of Lemma 2.

Fix configurations α and β such that $\mathrm{CNT}(\alpha) = \mathrm{CNT}(\beta) = 0$ and there exists an arc from α to β. If there is a low arc from α to β, then there is nothing to prove, so assume that all the arcs from α to β are not low. Let ρ_0 be such an arc of the shortest possible length; then ρ_0 is not low. Let

$$\rho_0 = (\gamma_1, t_1) \ldots (\gamma_m, t_m),$$

where $\alpha = \gamma_1$ and $\gamma_m \xrightarrow{t_m} \gamma_{m+1} = \beta$. Since ρ_0 is shortest possible, from Proposition 1 we infer that configurations $\gamma_1, \gamma_2, \ldots, \gamma_{m+1}$ are pairwise different.

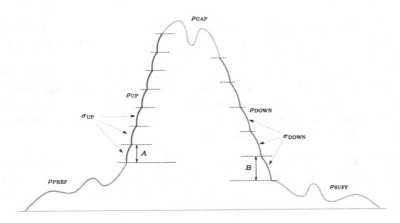

Fig. 1. A normal decomposition of an arc

Since $\rho_\circ$ is not low, for each $k = 0, 1, 2, \ldots, 5n$ we can distinguish the first configuration γ_{i_k} on $\rho_\circ$ that has counter value k. Consider configurations γ_{i_k} for $2n \leq k \leq 3n$. Among these configurations, some state p repeats in two configurations γ_{i_k} and $\gamma_{i_{k'}}$, for some $2n \leq k < k' \leq 3n$. This means that the part of $\rho_\circ$ between γ_{i_k} and $\gamma_{i_{k'}}$ corresponds to a cycle σ in the transition multigraph. This cycle has a positive effect on the counter, and hence it is contained in a positively enabled strongly connected component $S \in \mathfrak{S}$. Recall that we cannot simply pump the cycle σ in order to create ρ_{UP}, because by the definition of a normal arc, the cycle that creates ρ_{UP} has to be the pre-chosen cycle σ_S^+ assigned to S. This, however, poses no real difficulty for the following reason. Since p is contained in the same strongly connected component as σ_S^+, we can travel through S from p to the base of σ_S^+, then pump it arbitrarily many times, and then go back to p. The part ρ_{DOWN} is defined in a symmetric manner.

More precisely, the consecutive parts ρ_{PREF}, ρ_{UP}, ρ_{CAP}, ρ_{DOWN} and ρ_{SUFF} are defined as follows; the reader is advised to check the description against Fig. 2 while reading. First, ρ_{PREF} is constructed by taking the prefix of $\rho_\circ$ up to configuration γ_{i_k}, and then traveling along a path σ_{pq} within S from p to q, the base state of σ_S^+. Then we repeat cycle σ_S^+ a number of times, say a, thus creating ρ_{UP}. The reader should think of a as of a variable, because the possibility of changing this number will be essential for the constructions to follow. Note that we chose k so that $k \geq 2n$ in order to make sure that during these manipulations we never hit nonpositive counter values.

In a symmetrical manner we define ρ_{SUFF} and ρ_{DOWN}. First, we find a configuration $\gamma_{j_{\bar{k}}}$ on $\rho_\circ$ such that it has some counter value $\bar{k}$ with $2n \leq \bar{k} \leq 3n$, all the configurations later on $\rho_\circ$ have smaller counter values, and its state $\bar{p}$ belongs to a negatively enabled strongly connected component T. Let $\bar{q}$ be the base state of σ_T^-. Then ρ_{SUFF} is the suffix of $\rho_\circ$ starting from $\gamma_{j_{\bar{k}}}$, with a path $\sigma_{\bar{q}\bar{p}}$ appended in the front, where $\sigma_{\bar{q}\bar{p}}$ leads from $\bar{q}$ to $\bar{p}$ within T. Also, ρ_{DOWN} is constructed by repeating σ_T^- a number of times, say b. We denote $A = \text{EFF}(\sigma_S^+)$ and $-B = \text{EFF}(\sigma_T^-)$.

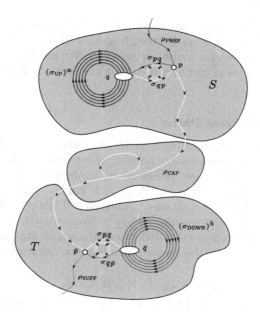

Fig. 2. The normalization procedure applied to an arc. Parts ρ_{PREF}, ρ_{UP}, ρ_{CAP}, ρ_{DOWN}, ρ_{SUFF} are depicted in green, blue, grey, red, and orange, respectively, as in Fig. 1 (Color figure online)

The middle part of the path, i.e. ρ_{CAP}, is constructed as follows. First, we follow a path σ_{qp} from q to p within T in order to get back to the original path. Then we repeat the cycle $(\sigma_{pq}\sigma_{qp})$ exactly $\gcd(A, B) - 1$ times, so that the total number of times paths σ_{pq} and σ_{qp} are traversed is $\gcd(A, B)$. It is necessary that the total effect on the counter value from traversing these paths is divisible by $\gcd(A, B)$, so that this effect can be compensated for by selecting a and b appropriately. Then we follow the infix of the original path up to configuration γ_{j_k}. Afterwards, a symmetric construction follows: we repeat the cycle $(\sigma_{\bar{p}\bar{q}}\sigma_{\bar{q}\bar{p}})$ exactly $\gcd(A, B) - 1$ times, and then travel from $\bar{p}$ to $\bar{q}$ using $\sigma_{\bar{p}\bar{q}}$. It can be easily seen that one can choose numbers a and b so that the whole construction indeed yields a path from α to β. Here we use the fact that all numbers divisible by $\gcd(A, B)$ can be represented as nonnegative combinations of A and $-B$, i.e., $a \cdot A - b \cdot B$ for some $a, b \in \mathbb{N}$.

Finally, we modify ρ_{CAP} by unpumping it "modulo $\gcd(A, B)$" exhaustively: as long as there are two configurations that have the same state, and their counter values are congruent modulo $\gcd(A, B)$, we remove the whole subpath between these configurations. When performing such an operation, the total effect of ρ_{CAP} on the counter changes by a number divisible by $\gcd(A, B)$. Hence, by adjusting once more the numbers a and b we can compensate for this change.

From the description above, it should be relatively clear that the construction yields a normal path satisfying all the conditions apart from the quantitative ones: (iii) and (iv). For this, some arithmetic calculations are needed to ensure that we can choose a and b small enough so that (iii) and (iv) hold, while all the necessary properties of a and b are satisfied. We remark that in this sketch we have glossed over some technicalities that are used to satisfy conditions (iii) and (iv).

5.3   Length of Shortest Paths

Let α and β be such as in the statement of Theorem 1. Let ρ_o be a path from α to β that has the minimum possible number of intermediate configurations with counter value zero. Let all these intermediate configurations with counter value zero be $\gamma_2, \ldots, \gamma_k$, where $\gamma_1 = \alpha$ and $\gamma_{k+1} = \beta$. For $i = 1, 2, \ldots, k$, let ρ_o^i be the subpath of ρ_o between configurations γ_i and γ_{i+1}. Then ρ_o^i is an arc from γ_i to γ_{i+1}. By Lemma 2, there exists also an arc ρ^i from γ_i to γ_{i+1} that is either low or is normal and admits a normal decomposition satisfying properties (i)–(vii). If ρ^i is low, choose ρ^i to be the shortest possible low arc from γ_i to γ_{i+1}. If ρ^i is normal, let

$$\rho^i = \rho^i_{\text{PREF}} \, \rho^i_{\text{UP}} \, \rho^i_{\text{CAP}} \, \rho^i_{\text{DOWN}} \, \rho^i_{\text{SUFF}}$$

be its normal decomposition. Our goal for the rest of the proof is to show that $\rho = \rho^1 \ldots \rho^k$, which is clearly a path from α to β, has length at most $14n^2$. Note that ρ has the same number of configurations with counter value zero as ρ_o. Let $\mathcal{N} \subseteq \{1, 2, \ldots, k\}$ be the set of indices i for which ρ^i is normal, and let $\mathcal{L} = \{1, 2, \ldots, k\} \setminus \mathcal{N}$ be the set of indices i for which ρ^i is low.

First we show that the sum of the lengths of low parts of ρ (more precisely, of low arcs, of ρ^i_{PREF} and ρ^i_{SUFF}) is small. The following claim follows from a simple application of Proposition 1.

Lemma 3 (♠). *The following inequality holds:*

$$\sum_{i \in \mathcal{L}} \text{LEN}(\rho^i) + \sum_{i \in \mathcal{N}} \left(\text{LEN}(\rho^i_{\text{PREF}}) + \text{LEN}(\rho^i_{\text{SUFF}}) \right) \leq 5n^2.$$

Now we will estimate the length of the rest of the path ρ. First, however, we have to prepare a toolbox of lemmas. We introduce the following notation. For $S, T \in \mathfrak{S}$, let $\mathcal{N}_{(S,T)} \subseteq \mathcal{N}$ be the set of all those indices i for which ρ^i is (S, T)-normal. Moreover, let $\mathcal{N}_{(S, \cdot)} = \bigcup_{T' \in \mathfrak{S}} \mathcal{N}_{(S,T')}$ and $\mathcal{N}_{(\cdot, T)} = \bigcup_{S' \in \mathfrak{S}} \mathcal{N}_{(S',T)}$.

Lemma 4 (♠). *Let $S, T \in \mathfrak{S}$. Suppose $i \in \mathcal{N}_{(S, \cdot)}$ and $j \in \mathcal{N}_{(\cdot, T)}$ for some i, j with $1 \leq i < j \leq k$. Then there are no two configurations δ_i and δ_j appearing on ρ^i_{CAP} and ρ^j_{CAP} respectively such that $\text{ST}(\delta_i) = \text{ST}(\delta_j)$ and $\text{CNT}(\delta_i) - \text{CNT}(\delta_j)$ is divisible by $\gcd(\text{EFF}(\sigma_S^+), -\text{EFF}(\sigma_T^-))$.*

In the proof of Lemma 4 we observe that if such configurations δ_i and δ_j existed, then one could repeat σ_S^+ on ρ^i and σ_T^- on ρ_j more times so that the "lifted" configurations δ_i and δ_j would have the same counter value. Then we could cut the whole part of the path between them, thus reducing the number of configurations with counter value zero; this would be a contradiction with the choice of ρ_o. The following lemma is a simple corollary of Lemma 4.

Lemma 5 (♠). *Let $S, T \in \mathfrak{S}$. Then $|\mathcal{N}_{(S,T)}| \leq \gcd(\mathrm{EFF}(\sigma_S^+), -\mathrm{EFF}(\sigma_T^-))$.*

Total length of caps. We have now all the necessary ingredients to establish the desired upper bounds on the lengths of caps. Recall that for a strongly connected component $S \in \mathfrak{S}$ we denote by n_S the number of vertices in S.

Lemma 6. *Let $S, T \in \mathfrak{S}$, let $A_S = \mathrm{EFF}(\sigma_S^+)$ and let $B_T = -\mathrm{EFF}(\sigma_T^-)$. Then:*

$$\sum_{i \in \mathcal{N}_{(S,\cdot)}} \mathrm{LEN}(\rho_{\mathrm{CAP}}^i) \leq A_S \cdot n; \tag{1}$$

$$\sum_{i \in \mathcal{N}_{(\cdot,T)}} \mathrm{LEN}(\rho_{\mathrm{CAP}}^i) \leq n \cdot B_T; \tag{2}$$

moreover, $\quad \displaystyle\sum_{i \in \mathcal{N}} \mathrm{LEN}(\rho_{\mathrm{CAP}}^i) \leq n^2. \tag{3}$

Proof. For (1), assume towards a contradiction that $\sum_{i \in \mathcal{N}_{(S,\cdot)}} \mathrm{LEN}(\rho_{\mathrm{CAP}}^i) > A_S \cdot n$. Then by the pigeonhole principle there exists two configurations δ and δ' on the paths ρ_{CAP}^i for $i \in \mathcal{N}_{(S,\cdot)}$ which have the same state and the same counter value modulo A_S. Assume w.l.o.g. that δ is earlier in the path than δ'. By property (v) of Lemma 2, configurations δ and δ' cannot appear in the same path ρ_{CAP}^i. Indeed, otherwise the projection of the part of ρ_{CAP}^i between δ to δ' would be a cycle with effect divisible by A_S, so also by $\gcd(A_S, -\mathrm{EFF}(\sigma_T^-))$, where T is the SCC for which ρ^i is (S,T)-normal. Therefore they have to belong to different arcs. Let δ belong to ρ^i and δ' belong to ρ^j, where $j \in \mathcal{N}_{(S,T)}$ for some $T \in \mathfrak{S}$. However, by Lemma 4, there are no two configurations δ and δ' on ρ^i and ρ^j, respectively, such that their states are the same and the difference in counter values is divisible by $\gcd(A_S, -\mathrm{EFF}(\sigma_T^-))$. Contradiction, as δ and δ' are such configurations: the difference of its counter values is divisible by A_S, so also by $\gcd(A_S, -\mathrm{EFF}(\sigma_T^-))$. Thus (1) is proved, and (2) follows from a symmetric reasoning. The bound (3) follows by summing (1) through all $S \in \mathfrak{S}$ and using the facts that $\mathrm{EFF}(\sigma_S^+) \leq n_S$ and $\sum_{S \in \mathfrak{S}} n_S = n$. $\qquad\square$

Total length of positive and negative cycles. We now show that the total sum of the lengths of ρ_{UP}^i and ρ_{DOWN}^i is at most $8n^2$. This is the case where we need the key estimations (iii) and (iv) in Lemma 2.

Lemma 7. *The following inequalities hold:*

$$\sum_{i \in \mathcal{N}} \mathrm{LEN}(\rho_{\mathrm{UP}}^i) \leq 4n^2, \qquad\qquad \sum_{i \in \mathcal{N}} \mathrm{LEN}(\rho_{\mathrm{DOWN}}^i) \leq 4n^2.$$

Proof. We show how to bound the sum of lengths of paths ρ_{UP}^i. For any $S \in \mathfrak{S}$, let us denote $A_S = \mathrm{EFF}(\sigma_S^+)$ and $B_S = -\mathrm{EFF}(\sigma_S^-)$. For each $i \in \mathcal{N}$, let $S_i, T_i \in \mathfrak{S}$ be such that ρ^i is (S_i, T_i)-normal, and let $L_i = \mathrm{LEN}(\rho_{\mathrm{CAP}}^i)$. By Lemma 2 we know that $\text{EFF}(\rho_{\text{UP}}^i) \leq 2L_i + 2 \cdot \text{lcm}(A_{S_i}, B_{T_i})$. Since $\text{PROJ}(\rho_{\text{UP}}^i) = (\sigma_{S_i}^+)^a$ for some integer a, we have

$$\text{LEN}(\rho_{\text{UP}}^i) = \text{EFF}(\rho_{\text{UP}}^i) \cdot \frac{\text{LEN}(\sigma_{S_i}^+)}{\text{EFF}(\sigma_{S_i}^+)} \leq \text{EFF}(\rho_{\text{UP}}^i) \cdot \frac{n_{S_i}}{A_{S_i}} \leq (2L_i + 2 \cdot \text{lcm}(A_{S_i}, B_{T_i})) \cdot \frac{n_{S_i}}{A_{S_i}}.$$

Hence,

$$\sum_{i \in \mathcal{N}} \text{LEN}(\rho_{\text{UP}}^i) \leq 2 \sum_{i \in \mathcal{N}} \frac{L_i \, n_{S_i}}{A_{S_i}} + 2 \sum_{i \in \mathcal{N}} \frac{\text{lcm}(A_{S_i}, B_{T_i}) \cdot n_{S_i}}{A_{S_i}}. \tag{4}$$

We will separately estimate the first and the second term. First we focus on $\sum_{i \in \mathcal{N}} \frac{L_i \, n_{S_i}}{A_{S_i}}$. Let us fix some specific $S \in \mathfrak{S}$. We have

$$\sum_{i \in \mathcal{N}_{(S, \cdot)}} \frac{L_i \, n_{S_i}}{A_{S_i}} = \frac{n_S}{A_S} \cdot \sum_{i \in \mathcal{N}_{(S, \cdot)}} L_i \leq \frac{n_S}{A_S} \cdot A_S \cdot n = n_S \cdot n,$$

where the inequality follows from Lemma 6(1). Thus

$$\sum_{i \in \mathcal{N}} \frac{L_i \, n_{S_i}}{A_{S_i}} = \sum_{S \in \mathfrak{S}} \sum_{i \in \mathcal{N}_{(S, \cdot)}} \frac{L_i \, n_{S_i}}{A_{S_i}} \leq \sum_{S \in \mathfrak{S}} n_S \cdot n = n^2. \tag{5}$$

In order to estimate the second term, fix some $S, T \in \mathfrak{S}$. Note that $\frac{\text{lcm}(x,y)}{x} = \frac{xy}{\gcd(x,y) \cdot x} = \frac{y}{\gcd(x,y)}$ for all positive integers x, y. Now we have

$$\sum_{i \in \mathcal{N}_{(S,T)}} \frac{B_{T_i} \cdot n_{S_i}}{\gcd(A_{S_i}, B_{T_i})} = \sum_{i \in \mathcal{N}_{(S,T)}} \frac{B_T \cdot n_S}{\gcd(A_S, B_T)} = |\mathcal{N}_{(S,T)}| \cdot \frac{B_T \cdot n_S}{\gcd(A_S, B_T)}$$

$$\leq \gcd(A_S, B_T) \cdot \frac{B_T \cdot n_S}{\gcd(A_S, B_T)} = B_T \cdot n_S \leq n_T \cdot n_S,$$

where the first inequality follows from Lemma 5 and the second one from the fact that the effect of a path is bounded by its length. Therefore,

$$\sum_{i \in \mathcal{N}} \frac{B_{T_i} \cdot n_{S_i}}{\gcd(A_{S_i}, B_{T_i})} = \sum_{S, T \in \mathfrak{S}} \sum_{i \in \mathcal{N}_{(S,T)}} \frac{B_{T_i} \cdot n_{S_i}}{\gcd(A_{S_i}, B_{T_i})}$$

$$\leq \sum_{S, T \in \mathfrak{S}} n_T \cdot n_S = \sum_{S \in \mathfrak{S}} n_S \cdot \sum_{T \in \mathfrak{S}} n_T = n^2. \tag{6}$$

By connecting equations (4), (5) and (6) we obtain

$$\sum_{i \in \mathcal{N}} \text{LEN}(\rho_{\text{UP}}^i) \leq 2n^2 + 2n^2 = 4n^2.$$

The upper bound on the sum of lengths of paths ρ_{DOWN}^i is obtained analogously, using Lemma 6(2) instead of Lemma 6(1). □

Combining bounds of Lemma 3, Lemma 6(3), and Lemma 7, we conclude that

$$\text{LEN}(\rho) \leq 5n^2 + n^2 + 4n^2 + 4n^2 \leq 14n^2,$$

which completes the proof of Theorem 1.

Acknowledgements. The authors are grateful to Christoph Haase and Aditya Kanade for discussions and comments.

References

1. Alur, R., Černý, P.: Streaming transducers for algorithmic verification of single-pass list-processing programs. In: Proceedings of the 38th ACM SIGPLAN-SIGACT Symposium on Principles of Programming Languages, POPL 2011, Austin, TX, USA, 26–28 January 2011, pp. 599–610 (2011)
2. Atig, M.F., Bouajjani, A., Kumar, K.N., Saivasan, P.: On bounded reachability analysis of shared memory systems. In: 34th International Conference on Foundation of Software Technology and Theoretical Computer Science, FSTTCS 2014, 15–17 December 2014, New Delhi, India, pp. 611–623 (2014)
3. Barrett, C., Demri, S., Deters, M.: Witness runs for counter machines. In: Fontaine, P., Ringeissen, C., Schmidt, R.A. (eds.) FroCoS 2013. LNCS, vol. 8152, pp. 120–150. Springer, Heidelberg (2013)
4. Bouajjani, A., Esparza, J., Maler, O.: Reachability analysis of pushdown automata: application to model-checking. In: Mazurkiewicz, A., Winkowski, J. (eds.) CONCUR 1997. LNCS, vol. 1243, pp. 135–150. Springer, Heidelberg (1997)
5. Chistikov, D.: Notes on counting with finite machines. In: 34th International Conference on Foundation of Software Technology and Theoretical Computer Science, FSTTCS 2014, 15–17 December 2014, New Delhi, India, pp. 339–350 (2014)
6. Cormen, T.H., Leiserson, C.E., Rivest, R.L., Stein, C.: Introduction to Algorithms 2nd (edn.) The MIT Press and McGraw-Hill Book Company. ISBN 0-262-03293-7 (2001)
7. Demri, S., Gascon, R.: The effects of bounding syntactic resources on Presburger LTL. J. Log. Comput. **19**(6), 1541–1575 (2009)
8. Etessami, K., Wojtczak, D., Yannakakis, M.: Quasi-birth-death processes, tree-like QBDs, probabilistic 1-counter automata, and pushdown systems. Perform. Eval. **67**(9), 837–857 (2010)
9. Hofman, P., Mayr, R., Totzke, P.: Decidability of weak simulation on one-counter nets. In: 28th Annual ACM/IEEE Symposium on Logic in Computer Science. LICS 2013, New Orleans, LA, USA, 25–28 June 2013, pp. 203–212 (2013)
10. Kozen, D.C.: Design and Analysis of Algorithms. Texts and Monographs in Computer Science. Springer, New York (1992). ISBN: 978-3-540-97687-5
11. Lafourcade, P., Lugiez, D., Treinen, R.: Intruder deduction for AC-like equational theories with homomorphisms. Research report LSV-04-16, Laboratoire Spécification et Vérification, ENS Cachan, France, p. 69, November 2004. http://www.lsv.ens-cachan.fr/Publis/RAPPORTS_LSV/PS/rr-lsv-2004-16.rr.ps
12. Lafourcade, P., Lugiez, D., Treinen, R.: Intruder deduction for AC-like equational theories with homomorphisms. In: Giesl, J. (ed.) RTA 2005. LNCS, vol. 3467, pp. 308–322. Springer, Heidelberg (2005)

13. Latteux, M.: Langages à un compteur. J. Comput. Syst. Sci. **26**(1), 14–33 (1983)
14. Leroux, J., Schmitz, S.: Demystifying reachability in vector addition systems. In: 30th Annual ACM/IEEE Symposium on Logic in Computer Science. LICS 2015, 6–10 July 2015, Kyoto, Japan, pp. 56–67 (2015)
15. Podelski, A., Rybalchenko, A.: ARMC: the logical choice for software model checking with abstraction refinement. In: Hanus, M. (ed.) PADL 2007. LNCS, vol. 4354, pp. 245–259. Springer, Heidelberg (2007)
16. Thakkar, J., Kanade, A., Alur, R.: Transducer-based algorithmic verification of retransmission protocols over noisy channels. In: Beyer, D., Boreale, M. (eds.) FORTE 2013 and FMOODS 2013. LNCS, vol. 7892, pp. 209–224. Springer, Heidelberg (2013)
17. Thomas, W.: The reachability problem over infinite graphs. In: Frid, A., Morozov, A., Rybalchenko, A., Wagner, K.W. (eds.) CSR 2009. LNCS, vol. 5675, pp. 12–18. Springer, Heidelberg (2009)

The Invariance Problem for Matrix Semigroups

Klaus Dräger[(✉)]

EECS, Queen Mary University of London, London, UK
klaus.draeger@gmail.com

Abstract. The question of whether a given subspace of $\mathbb{Q}^d$ can be reached from a starting vector using linear transformations from a given finite set is well known to be undecidable in dimension 3 and above. We show that, in contrast, the *invariance* problem, i.e. the question of whether it is possible to remain inside a given subspace indefinitely using linear transformations from a given finite set, is decidable.

1 Introduction

The classic subspace reachability problem for matrix semigroups is the following.

- Given: A finite set $A \subseteq M_d(\mathbb{Q})$ of matrices, a linear subspace $U \subseteq \mathbb{Q}^d$, and a vector $x_0 \in \mathbb{Q}^d$.
- Question: Starting from x_0, can we reach U by applying a finite sequence of matrices from A? That is, do there exist $M_1, \ldots, M_k \in A$ such that $M_k \cdots M_1 x_0 \in U$?

This problem is known to be undecidable for $d \geq 3$ [11]. In this paper, we consider a temporal dual, the *invariance* problem:

- Given: A finite set $A \subseteq M_d(\mathbb{Q})$ of matrices, a linear subspace $U \subseteq \mathbb{Q}^d$, and a vector $x_0 \in \mathbb{Q}^d$.
- Question: Starting from x_0, can we remain in U indefinitely, using matrices from A? That is, does there exist a sequence $M_1, M_2, \ldots$ such that, for all $k \in \mathbb{N}$, $M_k \in A$ and $M_k \cdots M_1 x_0 \in U$?

The main result of this paper is that, unlike the reachability problem, the invariance problem is decidable.

The temporal duality becomes clearer when thinking about the negation of the properties: Consider the infinite-state transition system $S = (\mathbb{Q}^d, x_0, A)$ with transitions $\mathbb{Q}^d \rightarrow \mathbb{Q}^d$ defined by the given set A of matrices, and the formula $\varphi_U \equiv r_1 \cdot x = \ldots = r_k \cdot x = 0$ defining the subspace U in terms of a basis $(r_1, \ldots, r_k)$ of its orthogonal complement, then a solution to the reachability problem is a counterexample to the LTL assertion $S \vDash \Box \neg \varphi_U$ (stating that S will *always* be outside U), while a solution to the invariance problem is a counterexample to the LTL assertion $S \vDash \Diamond \neg \varphi_U$ (stating that S will *eventually* be outside U). Note the existential character of the problem: we are asking about *satisfiability* of the invariant. The universal version (the question of *validity*) can easily be shown to be also decidable; see Sect. 4.3.

© Springer-Verlag Berlin Heidelberg 2016
B. Jacobs and C. Löding (Eds.): FOSSACS 2016, LNCS 9634, pp. 479–492, 2016.
DOI: 10.1007/978-3-662-49630-5_28

As a technical aside, when we talk about a matrix semigroup in this paper, we mean a sub-semigroup G of $M_n(\mathbb{Q})$ *equipped with a particular generating set* A. For the reachability problem, this detail is irrelevant (all that is required is the existence of some $M \in G$ with $Mx_0 \in U$), but it matters for the invariance problem. Consider the case $x_0 = (1,1,0)^T$, $U = \{(x,y,0)^T \mid x,y \in \mathbb{Q}\}$, and $A_1 = \{M_1, M_3\}$, $A_2 = \{M_2, M_3\}$, where

$$M_1 = \begin{pmatrix} 0 & 1 & 0 \\ 1 & 0 & 0 \\ 0 & 0 & 1 \end{pmatrix}, M_2 = \begin{pmatrix} 0 & 0 & 1 \\ 0 & 1 & 0 \\ 1 & 0 & 0 \end{pmatrix}, M_3 = \begin{pmatrix} 1 & 0 & 0 \\ 0 & 0 & 1 \\ 0 & 1 & 0 \end{pmatrix}.$$

Both A_1 and A_2 generate the natural permutation representation of the symmetric group S_3, but the invariance problem for x_0, U, A_1 has a solution $M_1^\omega \in A_1^\omega$, while there is no solution for x_0, U, A_2.

1.1   Attacking the Invariance Problem

There is an intuitively obvious approach to the invariance problem, which proceeds as follows:

- Expand the tree of words $w \in A^*$.
- Abort any branch $M_1 \ldots M_k$ with $M_k \cdots M_1 x_0 \notin U$; if there are no more branches left, then there is no solution.
- If for some branch $M_1 \ldots M_k$ we have $M_k \cdots M_1 x_0 = 0$, we have a solution, since $0 \in U$ is fixed by any $M \in A$ (i.e. $M_1 \ldots M_k w$ will do for any $w \in A^\omega$).

However, this method is not complete. The result which allows us to fix it is a pumping lemma for solution prefixes: there is a bound N depending only on $|A|$ and $\dim U$ such that any word $w \in A^\omega$ has a prefix $uv \trianglelefteq w$ with

- $|uv| \le N$, and
- (u, v) is *dominating* in a sense defined below, which in particular implies that v is nonempty and if w is a solution to the invariance problem, then so is uv^ω.

Once we have this, the decision problem reduces to checking finitely many pairs (u, v), as in the algorithm in Fig. 1.

Example 1. Let $x_0 = (1,0,0,0)^T \in \mathbb{Q}^4$, $U = \{(x,y,z,0)^T \mid x,y,z \in \mathbb{Q}\}$, and $A = \{P, Q, R\}$ with

$$P = \begin{pmatrix} 1 & 2 & 0 & 0 \\ 0 & 0 & 1 & 2 \\ 2 & 1 & 0 & 0 \\ 0 & 0 & 2 & 1 \end{pmatrix}, Q = \begin{pmatrix} 0 & -1 & 0 & 2 \\ -1 & 0 & 2 & 0 \\ 2 & 0 & -1 & 0 \\ 0 & 2 & 0 & -1 \end{pmatrix}, R = \begin{pmatrix} 0 & 0 & -1 & 2 \\ -1 & 0 & 2 & 0 \\ 0 & 1 & 0 & 0 \\ 2 & 0 & 0 & -1 \end{pmatrix}.$$

Figure 2 shows the beginning of a breadth-first exploration for this example; one solution to the invariance problem is the periodic sequence $PQR(RPPQPQ)^\omega$, corresponding to the dominating prefix $(PQR, RPPQPQ)$.

Data: finite set $A \subseteq M_d(\mathbb{Q})$ of matrices,
initial vector $x_0 \in \mathbb{Q}^d$,
invariant subspace $U \subseteq \mathbb{Q}^d$
Result: A pair $(u, v) \in A^* \times A^*$ such that uv^ω solves the invariance problem for
$\quad\quad A, x_0, U$, or FAIL if no such pair exists
if $A = \emptyset$ *or* $x_0 \notin U$ **then return** FAIL;
branches := $\{\epsilon\}$;
while *branches not empty* **do**
$\quad$ pop first w from branches;
$\quad$ **if** $w(x_0) = 0$ **then**
$\quad\quad$ pick $M \in A$;
$\quad\quad$ **return** (w, M) ;   /* wM^ω is solution for any M */
$\quad$ **if** $w(x_0) \in U$ **then**
$\quad\quad$ **foreach** *split* $w = uv$ *with* $v \neq \epsilon$ **do**
$\quad\quad\quad$ **if** v *is pumpable* **then**
$\quad\quad\quad\quad$ **return** (u, v) ; /* w is dominating prefix for all wM */
$\quad\quad$ **foreach** $M \in A$ **do**
$\quad\quad\quad$ append wM to branches;
return FAIL;

Fig. 1. Finding a trace remaining inside U, starting from x_0. Exploration follows a breadth-first strategy in order to find a minimal-length solution. The details of the notions of *pumpability* and *dominating prefix*, and proof that such a prefix exists for any sufficiently long branch, are given in Sects. 2 and 3.

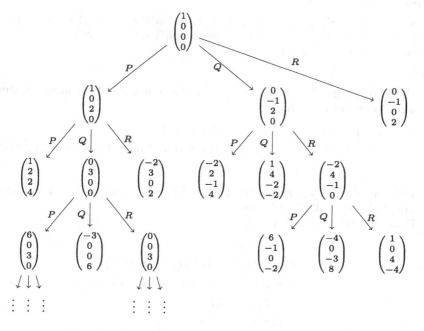

Fig. 2. The first few layers of the running example

2 Preliminaries

2.1 Setting

Throughout this paper, we work within $\mathbb{Q}^d$ for some $d \in \mathbb{N}$. We assume the linear subspace $U \subseteq \mathbb{Q}^d$, starting vector $x_0 \in U$, and finite non-empty set of matrices $A \subseteq M_d(\mathbb{Q})$ to be arbitrary but fixed, subject to the non-triviality condition

$$MU \nsubseteq U \text{ for all } M \in A.$$

If there is some M violating this condition, then M^ω is a trivial solution to the invariance problem.

We use A^* and A^ω for the sets of finite and infinite words over A, respectively, and ϵ for the empty word. For $x \in \mathbb{Q}^n, S \subseteq \mathbb{Q}^n$, and $w = M_1 \ldots M_k \in A^*$, $w(x) := M_k \cdots M_1 x$ and $w(S) := \{w(x) \mid x \in S\}$. A word $p \in A^*$ is a prefix of $w = M_1 \ldots M_k \in A^*$ (resp. $w = M_1 M_2 \ldots \in A^\omega$), denoted by $p \trianglelefteq w$, iff $p = M_1 \ldots M_j$ for some $j \leq k$ (resp. some $j \in \mathbb{N}$).

Definition 1. *Let* $w = M_1 \ldots M_k \in A^*$. *Associated with* w *are the following subspaces of* $\mathbb{Q}^n$:

– *the* source space $S(w) = \{x \in \mathbb{Q}^n \mid p(x) \in U \text{ for each prefix } p \trianglelefteq w\}$, *and*
– *the* target space $T(w) = w(S(w))$.

The following elementary properties of $S(\_), T(\_)$ are used throughout the proof of the main result:

Lemma 1. *For all* $u, v, w \in A^*$,

(i) $S(uv) = \{x \in S(u) \mid u(x) \in S(v)\} \subseteq S(u)$, *with equality iff* $T(u) \subseteq S(v)$,
(ii) $T(uv) = v(T(u) \cap S(v)) \subseteq T(v)$, *with equality if* $T(u) \supseteq S(v)$,
(iii) $\dim T(uvw) \leq \dim T(v)$.

Proof

(i) Since any prefix of uv is either a prefix of u or a word of the form up, where p is a prefix of v, we have

$$
\begin{aligned}
S(uv) &= \{x \in \mathbb{Q}^n \mid p(x) \in U \text{ for all } p \trianglelefteq uv\} \\
&= \{x \in \mathbb{Q}^n \mid p(x) \in U \text{ for all } p \trianglelefteq u \text{ and } p(u(x)) \in U \text{ for all } p \trianglelefteq v\} \\
&= \{x \in \mathbb{Q}^n \mid x \in S(u) \text{ and } u(x) \in S(v)\},
\end{aligned}
$$

which is obviously a subspace of $S(u)$. Equality holds iff for all $x \in S(u)$, $u(x)$ is in $S(v)$, iff $T(u) \subseteq S(v)$.
(ii) Using $uv(x) = v(u(x))$, we get

$$
\begin{aligned}
T(uv) &= v(u(S(uv))) \\
&= v(u(\{x \in S(u) \mid u(x) \in S(v)\})) \\
&= v(\{u(x) \mid x \in S(u) \text{ and } u(x) \in S(v)\}) \\
&= v(T(u) \cap S(v)) \\
&\subseteq v(S(v)) = T(v).
\end{aligned}
$$

If $T(u) \supseteq S(v)$, the inclusion in the last line holds with equality.

(iii) By (ii), $T(uvw) \subseteq T(vw)$, and we have

$$\dim T(uvw) \leq \dim T(vw)$$
$$= \dim w(T(v) \cap S(w))$$
$$\leq \dim w(T(v))$$
$$\leq \dim T(v),$$

where in the last step we use that $\dim f(V) \leq \dim V$ for any linear map f and vector space V. □

If $w = M_1 M_2 \ldots \in A^\omega$ is an infinite word, then due to Lemma 1(i), the source spaces of its prefixes form a descending chain $S(\epsilon) \supseteq S(M_1) \supseteq \ldots$; since the lattice of subspaces satisfies the descending chain condition, this chain has a limit, $S(w)$, the space of all vectors whose w-orbit remains in U. The invariance problem obviously amounts to checking the existence of an infinite word w with $x_0 \in S(w)$.

Definition 2. *A word $q \in A^*$ is* pumpable *if $q \neq \epsilon$ and $T(q) \subseteq S(q)$.*

A dominating prefix *of a (finite or infinite) word w is a pair (p, q) such that pq is a proper prefix of w and q is pumpable.*

Any word which has a dominating prefix can then be disregarded due to the following lemma.

Lemma 2. *Let $p, q \in A^*$. If q is pumpable, then*

(i) $S(q^k) = S(q)$ *for all $k \geq 1$,*
(ii) $S(pq^k) = S(pq)$ *for all $k \geq 1$, and*
(iii) *if pq is a prefix of a word $w \in A^\omega$, and w is a solution to the invariance problem for x_0, U, A, then so is pq^ω.*

Proof

(i) We use induction on k. The assertions holds trivially for $k = 1$; for the step $k \to k + 1$, from $T(q) \subseteq S(q) = S(q^k)$ we get, using Lemma 1(i), that $S(q) = S(qq^k) = S(q^{k+1})$.
(ii) From (i) and Lemma 1(i) we have
$S(pq) = \{x \in S(p) \mid p(x) \in S(q)\} = \{x \in S(p) \mid p(x) \in S(q^k)\} = S(pq^k)$.
(iii) $S(pq^\omega)$ is the limit of $(S(pq^k))_{k \geq 1}$, which by (ii) equals the constant sequence $(S(pq))_{k \geq 1}$, and therefore $S(pq^\omega) = S(pq)$. Since pq is a prefix of w, and $x_0 \in S(w)$, we get
$x_0 \in S(w) \subseteq S(pq) = S(pq^\omega)$. □

Our goal now is to show that there is a bound N such that any word w with $|w| > N$ has a dominating prefix (p, q) with $|pq| \leq N$.

Definition 3. *A word $w \in A^*$ is*

– essential *if it has no dominating prefix,*
– S-minimal *of dimension k if $S(w) \subsetneq S(p)$ for each proper prefix $p \triangleleft w$ and $\dim S(w) = k$,*

– *T-minimal of dimension k if $k = \dim T(w) < \dim T(p)$ for each proper prefix $p \triangleleft w$,*
– *S-essential (resp. T-essential) of dimension k if it is both essential and S-minimal (resp. T-minimal) of dimension k.*

We will omit the dimension for the last three properties when it is irrelevant.

Example. Continuing from the partial exploration shown in Fig. 2, Table 1 contains the source and target spaces for some selected words occurring in the tree, and whether or not they are S-minimal. All the words in the figure are essential.

Table 1. Some source and target spaces occurring in the running example

w	$S(w)$	$T(w)$	S-minimal
ϵ	$\{(x,y,z,0)^T\}$	$\{(x,y,z,0)^T\}$	yes, dimension 3
P	$\{(x,y,0,0)^T\}$	$\{(x+2y,0,2x+y,0)^T\}$	yes, dimension 2
Q	$\{(x,0,z,0)^T\}$	$\{(0,2z-x,2x-z,0)^T\}$	yes, dimension 2
R	$\{(0,y,z,0)^T\}$	$\{(-z,2z,y,0)^T\}$	yes, dimension 2
PQ	$\{(x,y,0,0)^T\}$	$\{(0,3x,3y,0)^T\}$	no
QR	$\{(x,0,z,0)^T\}$	$\{(z-2x,4x-2z,2z-x,0)^T\}$	no
PQP	$\{(x,0,0,0)^T\}$	$\{(6x,0,3x,0)^T\}$	yes, dimension 1
PQR	$\{(x,y,0,0)^T\}$	$\{(-3y,6y,3x,0)^T\}$	no
$PQRQ$	$\{(x,0,0,0)^T\}$	$\{(0,6y,-3x,0)^T\}$	yes, dimension 1

The plan now is to prove that there are only finitely many essential words, using the following *factorization*.

Definition 4. *The S-factorization $F(w)$ of a word $w \in A^*$ is a finite sequence of nonempty finite words defined as follows. If $w = \epsilon$, then $F(w) = ()$. For $w \neq \epsilon$, let $p \trianglelefteq w$ be the shortest prefix of w for which $S(p) = S(w)$, and $(q_1, \ldots, q_k) = F(q)$, where q is the suffix with $w = pq$; then $F(w) = (p, q_1, \ldots, q_k)$. Note that since we require $MU \nsubseteq U$ for all $M \in A$, we have $U = S(\epsilon) \supsetneq S(w)$ for all $w \neq \epsilon$, which ensures that $p \neq \epsilon$.*

For infinite $w \in A^\omega$, we get an infinite version of this factorization by corecursively defining $F(w) = (p_1, p_2, \ldots)$, where p_1 is the shortest prefix of w with $S(p_1) = S(w)$, and $(p_2, \ldots) = F(q)$ for the infinite suffix q with $w = pq$.

Note that actually computing the infinite factorization (even incrementally) would generally not be feasible (since a decrease in dimension $S(uM) \subsetneq S(u)$ could occur after an arbitrarily long prefix u, we could not determine p_1 based on any finite prefix u, unless $S(u)$ happens to be $\{0\}$), but we will just need its existence and some of its properties. However, in case w is periodic, we can compute $F(w)$:

Example 2. Consider the word $w = uv^\omega$ with $u = PQR, v = RPPQPQ$ from Example 1. A quick calculation gives that $S(v) = T(v) = S(v^\omega) = \{(0,0,z,0)^T \mid z \in \mathbb{Q}\}$. Since $u(x_0) \in S(v)$, we get that $x_0 \in S(p)$, and therefore $\dim S(p) \geq 1$, for any prefix $p \trianglelefteq w$.

On the other hand, since P, Q, R are invertible, we have that $\dim S(pv) = \dim T(pv) \leq \dim T(v) = 1$ for any word p, so that the dimension of each factor in $F(w)$ must be 1. Since w is periodic, the same will be true for the factorization. In fact, we get

$$F(PQR(RPPQPQ)^\omega) = (PQR, RP, PQ, PQR, PPQ, PQR, \ldots)$$

3   Deciding Satisfiability

We now show that there are only finitely many essential words, and derive upper bounds on their number and length, from which the main result follows.

3.1   Finiteness of the Set of Essential Words

Lemma 3. *If $w \in A^*$ is S-minimal of dimension k, then it is also T-minimal of some dimension $j \leq k$. As a direct corollary, if w is S-essential of dimension k, then it is also T-essential of some dimension $j \leq k$.*

Proof. That $\dim T(w) \leq \dim S(w)$ follows directly from $T(w) = w(S(w))$. If $w = \epsilon$, then it is trivially T-minimal.

Otherwise, $w = vM$ for some $v \in A^*$ and $M \in A$. By Lemma 1(iii), it suffices to show $\dim T(w) < \dim T(v)$. Since w is S-minimal, $S(w) = S(vM) \subsetneq S(v)$, and thus $T(v) \not\subseteq S(M)$ by Lemma 1(i). Therefore

$$\begin{aligned}
\dim T(vM) &= \dim M(T(v) \cap S(M)) \qquad \text{by Lemma 1(ii)} \\
&\leq \dim \, (T(v) \cap S(M)) \\
&< \dim T(v),
\end{aligned}$$

i.e. w is T-minimal.

The corollary follows by just adding non-existence of dominating prefixes of w to both the assumption and conclusion.   □

Theorem 1. *Let $w = vM$ be a non-empty essential word, where $v \in A^*$ and $M \in A$. Let the S-factorization of v be $F(v) = (p_1, \ldots, p_m)$. Then*

(i) *each p_i is T-essential,*
(ii) *if w is T-minimal of dimension k, then each p_i is T-minimal of some dimension $d_i > k$, and*
(iii) *$p_i \neq p_j$ for $i \neq j$.*

Proof

(i) By construction of the S-factorization, each p_i is S-minimal. By Lemma 3, it is also T-minimal.

   Suppose p_i is not essential, then it has a dominating prefix (r, s). This implies that $(p_1 \ldots p_{i-1}r, s)$ is a dominating prefix for the essential word w, contradiction.

(ii) We already have that each p_i is S-minimal and thus T-minimal by Lemma 3; it remains to show $\dim T(p_i) > \dim T(w)$. This follows because p_i is a factor of v, so $\dim T(p_i) \geq \dim T(v)$ by Lemma 1(iii), and $\dim T(v) > \dim T(w)$ due to T-minimality of w.

(iii) Suppose $p_i = p_j$ for some $i < j$. By the definition of $F(v)$ we then have $S(p_i \ldots p_m) = S(p_i) = S(p_j) = S(p_j \ldots p_m)$; furthermore, since the spaces $(S(p_i \ldots p_k))$ form a descending chain, we have in fact $S(p_i) = S(p_i \ldots p_k)$ for all $i \leq k \leq m$, and in particular $S(p_i) = S(p_i \ldots p_{j-1}) = S(p_i \ldots p_m)$. This implies

$$
\begin{aligned}
T(p_i \ldots p_{j-1}) \subsetneq S(p_j \ldots p_m) \qquad & \text{by Lemma 1(i)} \\
= S(p_j) & \\
= S(p_i) & \\
= S(p_i \ldots p_{j-1}). &
\end{aligned}
$$

Therefore $(p_1 \ldots p_{i-1}, p_i \ldots p_{j-1})$ is a dominating prefix for w, contradiction. □

This theorem allows us to prove finiteness of the set of essential words by induction on the *codimension* $c(w) := \dim U - \dim T(w)$. It also enables us to derive upper bounds on their number and length, for which we need the following definition.

Definition 5

– *The* arrangement function $a : \mathbb{N} \to \mathbb{N}$ *is given by*

$$
a(n) = \sum_{i=0}^{n} \frac{n!}{i!};
$$

it is the number of sequences from a set of n elements with no repeated element. Note that $a(n)/n!$ converges to Euler's number e from below, in particular $a(n) \leq 3n!$ for all n.

– *The numbers N_i for $i \in \mathbb{N}$ are defined by* $N_i = \begin{cases} 1 & \text{for } i = 0 \\ |A| \cdot a(N_{i-1}) & \text{otherwise.} \end{cases}$

– *The numbers L_i for $i \in \mathbb{N}$ are defined by* $L_i = \begin{cases} 0 & \text{for } i = 0 \\ N_{i-1}L_{i-1} + 1 & \text{otherwise.} \end{cases}$

Theorem 2. *We have the following bounds on the numbers and lengths of essential words w, based on their codimension $c(w) = \dim U - \dim T(w)$.*

(i) There are at most N_i T-essential words w of codimension $c(w) \leq i$.

(ii) A T-essential word of codimension i has length $\leq L_i$.

(iii) There at most $N_{1+\dim U}$ essential words, and none of them is longer than $L_{1+\dim U}$.

Proof

(i) We proceed by induction on i. For $i = 0$, the empty word ϵ is trivially T-essential. Since $T(\epsilon) = U$ and $\epsilon \trianglelefteq w$ for all $w \in A^*$, it is the only T-essential word of dimension $\dim U$, i.e. codimension 0.

For $i \to i + 1$, by the induction hypothesis there are at most N_i T-essential words of codimension $c(w) \leq i$. By Theorem 1, any T-essential word w of codimension $i + 1$ has a factorization $w = p_1 \ldots p_n M$ in which the p_j are pairwise distinct and T-essential of codimension $\leq i$, and $M \in A$. The number of such factorizations is at most $|A| \cdot a(N_i) = N_{i+1}$, and they include the ones for words of codimension $\leq i$, giving the upper bound N_{i+1} for the number of T-essential words w of codimension $c(w) \leq i + 1$.

(ii) As in (i), we argue inductively using Theorem 1. For $i = 0$, the only T-essential word ϵ of codimension 0 has length $0 = L_0$.

For $i \to i+1$, the decomposition in Theorem 1 consists of at most N_i words, each of length at most L_i, plus the final letter, giving a total length of at most $N_i L_i + 1 = L_{i+1}$.

(iii) As in (i) and (ii), we get from Theorem 1 that any non-empty essential word has a factorization into (at most $N_{\dim U}$) pairwise T-essential words of length at most $L_{\dim U}$ and a single trailing $M \in A$. The number of such factorizations is at most $N_{1+\dim U}$, and their length is bounded by $L_{1+\dim U}$, by the same argument as before.   □

3.2   Decidability of the Invariance Problem

The main result now follows immediately from the bounds established in the previous section.

Theorem 3. *Algorithm 1 terminates. It returns FAIL if and only if there is no solution to the invariance problem.*

Proof. Let $w = M_1 M_2 \ldots \in A^\omega$ be any infinite word. By Theorem 2, w has an essential prefix $m(w) = M_1 \ldots M_k$ of maximal length $|m(w)| \leq L_{1+\dim U}$ (note that the empty word is always essential, so $m(w)$ exists). Then $M_1 \ldots M_{k+1}$ has a dominating prefix (p, q). We must have that $pq = m(w)$ and there is no shorter dominating prefix, since otherwise $m(w)$ would also fail to be essential. Due to the properties of dominating prefixes, $x_0 \in S(m(w))$ if and only if pq^ω is a solution to the invariance problem. Therefore we have two cases.

If there is no solution to the invariance problem, then for any branch w, x_0 cannot be in $S(m(w))$, i.e. the branch will be discarded before reaching depth $|m(w)| \leq L_{1+\dim U}$. By König's lemma, only finitely many words are explored, and the algorithm returns FAIL.

If there is a solution w, then $x_0 \in S(p)$ for every prefix $p \trianglelefteq w$, and the algorithm keep exploring until it reaches depth $|m(w)|$ for one such w, at which point the dominating prefix is discovered and returned.   □

4   Further Remarks and Variations

4.1   Computing All Possible Initial Vectors

The algorithm we gave can be easily adapted to solve the following, more general problem:

- Given: A finite set $A \subseteq M_d(\mathbb{Q})$ of matrices, and a subspace $U \subseteq \mathbb{Q}^d$.
- Question: From which starting vectors x_0 can we remain in U indefinitely, using matrices from A? That is, for which $x_0 \in \mathbb{Q}^d$ does there exist a sequence $M_1, M_2, \ldots$ such that, for all $k \in \mathbb{N}$, $M_k \in A$ and $M_k \cdots M_1 x_0 \in U$?

Essentially, all that has to be changed is to remove the special treatment of x_0 and collect all the pairs which would have been returned into a set P, as in Fig. 3.

Data: finite set $A \subseteq M_d(\mathbb{Q})$ of matrices, invariant subspace $U \subseteq \mathbb{Q}^d$
Result: A set P of pairs $(u, v) \in A^* \times A^*$ such that $\bigcup_{(u,v) \in P} S(uv^\omega)$ contains
      exactly the initial vectors x_0 from which the invariance problem for
      A, x_0, U has a solution
if $A = \emptyset$ **then return** $\emptyset$;
branches := $\{\epsilon\}$;
while *branches not empty* **do**
| pop first w from branches;
| **foreach** *split $w = uv$ with $v \neq \epsilon$* **do**
| | **if** *v is pumpable* **then**
| | | Add (u, v) to P;
| **if** *no split for w was added* **then**
| | **foreach** $M \in A$ **do**
| | | append wM to branches;
return P;

Fig. 3. Finding all starting vectors from which the invariance problem has a solution.

4.2   Locations

The transition system $(\mathbb{Q}^d, x_0, A)$ can be extended using a finite set L of control locations, giving $(L \times \mathbb{Q}^d, (l_0, x_0), T)$ for a finite set $T \subseteq L \times M_n(\mathbb{Q}) \times L$. The main properties of words $w \in A^*$ can still be used as before, the main difference being that a pumpable word q is now additionally required to label a cycle in the location graph.

The algorithm then proceeds as before, except that nodes are labeled with states $(l, x) \in L \times \mathbb{Q}^d$, and only successors using matrices which are available in l are considered.

4.3 The Universal Version

The question whether the invariant given by U is *valid*, i.e. whether $w(x_0) \in U$ for *all* $w \in A^*$, is also decidable, and is in fact easier than the problem we have dealt with in the previous sections. Again, the basic idea is to expand the tree of words $w \in A^*$ in a breadth-first order. While doing so, we can

(i) as soon as we encounter a counterexample $w(x_0) \notin U$, return w;
(ii) cut any branch v if $v(x_0)$ is a linear combination of vectors we have previously explored.

The reason for (ii) is that, if $y := v(x_0) = \lambda_1 x_1 + \cdots + \lambda_n x_n$, then due to linearity for any $w \in A^*$, $w(y) = \lambda_1 w(x_1) + \cdots + \lambda_n w(x_n)$; in particular, if $w(y) \notin U$ for some $w \in A^*$, then there is some i for which $w(x_i)$ is also not in U. Since we use breadth-first search, $x_i = u_i(x_0)$ for some word u_i which is smaller than v in the length-lexicographic order. Thus for any counterexample which we lose by discarding y, there is a length-lexicographically shorter one. In particular, if there are any counterexamples, then the length-lexicographically minimal one among them cannot be lost and will be found by the search.

Data: finite set $A \subseteq M_d(\mathbb{Q})$ of matrices,
initial vector $x_0 \in \mathbb{Q}^d$,
invariant subspace $U \subseteq \mathbb{Q}^d$
Result: A $w \in A^*$ such that $w(x_0) \notin U$, or SUCCESS if no such pair exists
if $A = \emptyset$ **then return** SUCCESS;
branches $:= \{\epsilon\}$;
basis $:= \{x_0\}$;
while *branches not empty* **do**
    pick and remove w from branches;
    if $w(x_0) \notin U$ **then return** w;
    foreach $M \in A$ **do**
        $y := wM(x)$;
        if y *linearly independent of basis* **then**
            add wM to branches;
            add y to basis
return SUCCESS;

Fig. 4. Checking validity of the invariant U, starting from x_0.

---

5 Summary and Future Work

5.1 Summary

We presented a solution to the invariance problem for matrix semigroups, i.e. the question of an infinite sequence of matrices satisfying a given linear invariant.

We gave an algorithm to find a solution if one exists, and proved its termination. The latter relied on the analysis of various properties of words in matrix semigroups and their interaction. In particular, we showed that for any finite set A of matrices and subspace U, there is a bound N such that any word of length $> N$ has a *dominating prefix*, reducing the problem to a finite one (Fig. 4).

5.2   Related Work

Matrix semigroups are a rich source of problems [3,11], including many surprisingly complicated decision problems. Among these are the *scalar reachability problem* (undecidable in dimension 3 and above [3]), which is the problem of reaching a subspace of codimension 1 from a starting vector using matrices from a given semigroup, and the *vector reachability problem*, in which the target is a single vector. A special case of the latter, for a single generating matrix, is the *orbit problem* which was shown to be decidable by Kannan and Lipton [5]. A closely related problem to the universal version of the invariance problem (Sect. 4.3) is the question of *boundedness*, which is undecidable [1].

One source of the complexity of such problems is that, in contrast to similar models like *vector addition systems* [4,6,9], the behaviour of matrix semigroups has inherently nonlinear aspects; for example, the simple 3-dimensional matrix $\begin{pmatrix} 1 & 2 & 1 \\ 0 & 1 & 1 \\ 0 & 0 & 1 \end{pmatrix}$ has the orbit $\{(n^2, n, 1)^T \mid n \in \mathbb{N}\}$. This ability to reflect polynomial relationships connects problems like scalar reachability to known undecidable ones, like solvability of diophantine equations [10].

This complexity extends to various related models. Polynomial Register Machines [2] generalize vector addition systems with polynomial update functions (with integer coefficients); while this leads to undecidability in most cases, in dimension 1 reachability turns out to be decidable (in fact PSPACE-complete). Iteration of piecewise affine maps [7,8], similarly to matrix semigroups, involves a choice between affine-linear transformations, but this choice is deterministic based on the current variable values; the (vector) reachability problem is undecidable in general, but decidability is still open in dimension 1.

5.3   Future Work

There are a number of interesting ways to extend these results. Among them are:

Complexity Bounds. From the proof of decidability we get the upper bound $L_\infty \leq 1 + N_{\dim U}(1 + N_{\dim U - 1}(\ldots (1 + N_0) \ldots)$ for the exploration depth, where $N_0 = 1$ and $N_{i+1} \leq 3 \cdot |A| \cdot N_i!$, for a total of $\dim U$ nested factorials. This implies a complexity upper bound of $O(2^{L_\infty})$ for the algorithm. It would be interesting to see how much this can be improved, and what lower bounds can be found.

Polyhedral Invariants. The invariant in this paper was given as a linear subspace U, corresponding to a conjunction of linear equations. Generalizing this to linear inequalities leads to the question of whether we can find a sequence of matrices from A which allows us to remain inside a given polyhedron. This adds significant complications; in particular, it is not the case that a descending sequence of polyhedra $P_0 \supseteq P_1 \supseteq \ldots$ stabilizes after finitely many steps, so notions like the S-factorization cannot simply be translated to this setting. It is not clear at all whether this more general question is decidable.

Guards. The control structure of the transition system $(\mathbb{Q}^d, x_0, A)$ is relatively simple in that any transition is enabled at any time. Adding control location already changes this, but the values of the vector x in a state (l, x) still have no influence on the control flow. This changes with the introduction of application conditions or *guards*: linear equations or inequalities which have to be satisfied before the associated transition can be taken. Note that equation guards can be translated into extra dimensions in such a way that guard violations translate into (extended) invariance violations, so that they don't increase expressivity; inequalities on the other hand make for an interesting addition.

Games. Since both the existential and (as seen in Sect. 4.3) the universal version of the invariance problem are decidable, it is natural to ask what can be done about an alternating version. This would amount to considering games in which two players $\Box, \Diamond$ take turns applying matrices from given sets $A_\Box, A_\Diamond$ to the current vector x, with the goal of preserving and violating the invariant U, respectively.

Acknowledgements. The author is part supported by EPSRC project EP/K032011/1.

References

1. Blondel, V.D., Tsitsiklis, J.N.: The boundedness of all products of a pair of matrices is undecidable. Syst. Control Lett. **41**(2), 135–140 (2000)
2. Finkel, A., Göller, S., Haase, C.: Reachability in register machines with polynomial updates. In: Chatterjee, K., Sgall, J. (eds.) MFCS 2013. LNCS, vol. 8087, pp. 409–420. Springer, Heidelberg (2013)
3. Halava, V., Harju, T., Hirvensalo, M.: Undecidability bounds for integer matrices using claus instances. Technical report 766 (2006)
4. Hopcroft, J., Pansiot, J.-J.: On the reachability problem for 5-dimensional vector addition systems. Theor. Comput. Sci. **8**(2), 135–159 (1979)
5. Kannan, R., Lipton, R.J.: Polynomial-time algorithm for the orbit problem. J. ACM **33**(4), 808–821 (1986)
6. Karp, R.M., Miller, R.E.: Parallel program schemata. J. Comput. Syst. Sci. **3**(2), 147–195 (1969)
7. Kurganskyy, O., Potapov, I.: Reachability problems for pams. CoRR, abs/1510.04121 (2015)

8. Kurganskyy, O., Potapov, I., Sancho-Caparrini, F.: Reachability problems in low-dimensional iterative maps. Int. J. Found. Comput. Sci. **19**(04), 935–951 (2008)
9. Leroux, J.: Vector addition systems reachability problem (a simpler solution). In: Voronkov, A. (ed.)Turing-100. The Alan Turing Centenary. EasyChair Proceedings in Computing, vol. 10, pp. 214–228. EasyChair (2012)
10. Matiyasevich, Y.: Hilbert's Tenth Problem. With a foreword by Martin Davis. MIT Press, Cambridge (1993)
11. Potapov, I.: From post systems to the reachability problems for matrix semigroups and multicounter automata. In: Calude, C.S., Calude, E., Dinneen, M.J. (eds.) DLT 2004. LNCS, vol. 3340, pp. 345–356. Springer, Heidelberg (2004)

Order-Sorted Rewriting and Congruence Closure

José Meseguer[(⊠)]

Department of Computer Science,
University of Illinois at Urbana-Champaign, Urbana, USA
meseguer@illinois.edu

Abstract. Order-sorted type systems supporting inheritance hierarchies and subtype polymorphism are used in theorem proving, AI, and declarative programming. The satisfiability problems for the theories of: (i) order-sorted uninterpreted function symbols, and (ii) of such symbols *modulo* a subset Δ of associative-commutative ones are *reduced* to the *unsorted* versions of such problems at no extra computational cost. New results on order-sorted rewriting are needed to achieve this reduction.

Keywords: Order-sorted rewriting · Congruence closure · Satisfiability

1 Introduction

For greater expressiveness and efficiency, type systems supporting inheritance hierarchies and subtype polymorphism are used in many areas such as resolution theorem proving, e.g., [26,32], declarative logic and rule-based languages, e.g., [4,9,10,29], and artificial intelligence, e.g., [8,29]. Order-sorted (OS) equational logic, e.g., [15,21], is a logical framework supporting inheritance hierarchies and subtype polymorphism widely used for these purposes. Therefore, the development of *decision procedures* for OS theories is of interest in all these areas. I focus here on decision procedures for the OS theory of *uninterpreted function symbols*, which in an unsorted setting is decided by congruence closure algorithms [7,24,27]. However, for greater expressiveness one can allow some of the function symbols, say in a subsignature $\Delta \subseteq \Sigma$, to be *interpreted* by some axioms B_Δ. For example, for an unsorted subsignature $\Delta \subseteq \Sigma$ of binary function symbols, congruence closure algorithms *modulo* the axioms AC_Δ, asserting the associativity and commutativity of all symbols in Δ have been given in [2,19,22]. Therefore, I also study satisfiability in the OS theory (Σ, AC_Δ) of *uninterpreted function symbols* Σ *modulo* AC_Δ.

The most obvious approach would be to develop an *order-sorted* congruence closure algorithm along the lines of [11] and then extended it to the modulo AC case. However, the main, somewhat surprising message of this paper is that such OS congruence closure algorithms *are not needed at all*: the already existing and efficient *unsorted* congruence closure algorithms in [7,24,27] and congruence closure modulo AC_Δ in [2,19,22] and tools supporting them can be reused *without change* and *at no extra cost* to solve the corresponding OS satisfiability problems.

© Springer-Verlag Berlin Heidelberg 2016
B. Jacobs and C. Löding (Eds.): FOSSACS 2016, LNCS 9634, pp. 493–509, 2016.
DOI: 10.1007/978-3-662-49630-5_29

A Simple Example. Consider the following order-sorted signature Σ

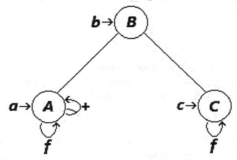

with sorts A, B, C, subsorts $A, C < B$, f subsort-polymorphic with typings $f : A \to A$ and $f : C \to C$, and a binary $+$ with typing $+ : AA \to A$. Its so-called *theory of uninterpreted function symbols* is just the order-sorted equational theory $(\Sigma, \emptyset)$ with empty set of equations, whose class of models, **OSAlg**$_\Sigma$, is that of *all* order-sorted Σ-algebras detailed in Sect. 2. Is the formula

$$(b) \qquad a = b \wedge b = c \wedge f(f(a)) = f(a) \wedge a + f(f(a)) \neq f(a) + a$$

$(\Sigma, \emptyset)$-*satisfiable*? The standard way to answer this question if Σ were unsorted would be to: (1) compute the congruence closure of the first three equations; and (2) test the last inequality using such a congruence closure. Since, as pointed out in [2,12,16], unsorted congruence closure algorithms are *ground Knuth-Bendix* completion algorithms [18], an obvious way to try to answer this question would be to try to *complete* the first three equations into an equivalent set of confluent and terminating rewrite rules. But this runs into serious trouble. An order-sorted Knuth-Bendix completion algorithm such as [13] will orient $a = b$ and $b = c$ as $b \to a$ and $b \to c$ because rules must be *sort-decreasing*, i.e., rewrite to a term of equal or lower sort. This then generates the critical pair $a = c$, which is *unorientable*, so completion fails. Notice also that *replacement of equals by equals* does not hold in an order-sorted setting: from $a = b$ we *cannot* derive $f(a) = f(b)$, because $f(b)$ doesn't type. These difficulties were clearly felt by the authors of [11], the only order-sorted congruence closure algorithm I am aware of, which is quite complex and is *not* a Knuth-Bendix completion. They say:

> *An approach using rewriting [...] fails due to the well-known problem that rewriting with order-sorted rewrite rules may create ill-typed terms.*

Let us now widen the problem into one of *satisfiability modulo AC* by making the $+$ symbol associative-commutative. That is, we consider the axioms $AC_+ = \{x + y = y + x, (x + y) + z = x + (y + z)\}$, with x, y, z of sort A, and ask: is the formula (b) (Σ, AC_+)-*satisfiable*? For this case, I am not aware of any order-sorted AC-congruence closure algorithm, but unsorted, ground-AC-completion-based ones exist [2,19,22]. The trouble, again, is that *order-sorted AC-completion* as in [13] fails miserably in the *same* way ($a = c$ cannot be oriented).

Wouldn't it be nice if we could *completely ignore* all sort information in the above two OS satisfiability problems and solve them as *unsorted* problems using standard (and efficient!) congruence closure [7,24,27] and congruence closure modulo AC [2,19,22] algorithms? If this reduction method were *sound*, we could easily settle the $(\Sigma, \emptyset)$- and (Σ, AC_+)-satisfiability of $(\flat)$: the confluent and terminating rules $R = \{a \to b, c \to b, f(f(b)) \to f(b)\}$ play the role of a "congruence closure" for the first three equations, and also of an AC_+-congruence closure. Since the disequality $a + f(f(a)) \neq f(a) + a$ reduces to $b + f(b) \neq f(b) + b$, the formula $(\flat)$ is $(\Sigma, \emptyset)$-satisfiable. However, since $b + f(b) =_{AC_+} f(b) + b$, $(\flat)$ is (Σ, AC_+)-*unsatisfiable*. But is this *reduction* to unsorted satisfiability *sound*?

Initial Algebra Semantics of Uninterpreted Satisfiability. Ignoring the sort information of an OS signature Σ is captured by a signature map $u : \Sigma \ni (f : s_1 \ldots s_n \to s) \mapsto (f : U .^n. U \to U) \in \Sigma^u$, where U is the single "universe" sort in the unsorted signature Σ^u. As further detailed at the end of Sect. 2, u induces a *reduct* map of algebras in the opposite direction, $\_|_u : \mathbf{Alg}_{\Sigma^u} \ni A \mapsto A|_u \in \mathbf{OSAlg}_\Sigma$, making each unsorted algebra A into and order-sorted one $A|_u$, and such that for a set of ground OS Σ-equations E we have the equivalence: $A|_u \models E \Leftrightarrow A \models E$. In particular, the E-initial unsorted Σ^u-algebra $T_{\Sigma^u/E}$ is mapped to the OS Σ-algebra $T_{\Sigma^u/E}|_u$ and, since $T_{\Sigma^u/E}|_u \models E$, there is a unique OS homomorphism $h : T_{\Sigma/E} \to T_{\Sigma^u/E}|_u$ from the E-initial OS Σ-algebra $T_{\Sigma/E}$.

But the proof of Theorem 5 shows that, for equations E and disequations D, the conjunction $\bigwedge E \wedge \bigwedge D$ is satisfiable iff $T_{\Sigma(C)/E} \models \bigwedge E \wedge \bigwedge D$, where the variables C of $E \cup D$ are seen as *fresh new constants* added to Σ to get a supersignature $\Sigma(C) \supseteq \Sigma$, so that $\bigwedge E \wedge \bigwedge D$ becomes a *ground* formula. This gives us, in model-theoretic terms, the key to verify the soundness of the hoped-for *reduction* of the satisfiability for the theory of OS uninterpreted function symbols to that of the unsorted theory of uninterpreted function symbols: this reduction method will be *sound* if and only if the OS homomorphism $h : T_{\Sigma(C)/E} \to T_{\Sigma(C)^u/E}|_u$ is *injective*. In proof-theoretic terms this injectivity will hold if and only if for all ground Σ-equation $u = v$ we have the equivalence: $(\Sigma, E) \vdash u = v \Leftrightarrow (\Sigma^u, E) \vdash u = v$. The $(\Rightarrow)$ direction is obvious, but the $(\Leftarrow)$ direction is a non-trivial new result that follows from several *conservativity theorems* that I prove in Sects. 3.2 and 4.1 by factoring the signature map $u : \Sigma \to \Sigma^u$ through a sequence $\Sigma \hookrightarrow \Sigma^\square \to \widehat{\Sigma} \to \Sigma^u$ of increasingly simpler order-sorted, many-sorted and finally unsorted signatures and relating equational and rewriting deductions at all these levels.

The Plot Thickens. The soundness of the hoped-for reduction to the unsorted case for satisfiability modulo AC_Δ is a thornier issue. As before, the reduction will be sound if and only if for ground Σ-equations E the unique Σ-homomorphism $h : T_{\Sigma/E \cup AC_\Delta} \to T_{\Sigma^u/E \cup AC_{\Delta^u}}|_u$ from the initial $E \cup AC_\Delta$-algebra $T_{\Sigma/E \cup AC_\Delta}$ is *injective*. But some of the conservativity theorems along the above sequence of signature maps $\Sigma \hookrightarrow \Sigma^\square \to \widehat{\Sigma} \to \Sigma^u$ needed to make h injective actually *break down* in the AC_Δ case. The problem has to do with the translation of the equations AC_Δ along these signature maps. At the unsorted level of Σ^u the translated equations AC_{Δ^u}, are *more general* and therefore *identify more terms* than the original OS equations AC_Δ. Consider a simple example: the equation $a + b = b + a$ does not type in our example signature Σ, but it types in the supersignature $\Sigma^\square \supseteq \Sigma$, which for our running example is depicted in Sect. 3.1. The AC equations AC_Δ in our example are just associativity and commutativity of $+ : A\ A \to A$ and therefore *apply only* to terms of sort A. Instead, the AC equations AC_{Δ^u} are unsorted, and *apply to all terms*. This means that $a + b =_{AC_{\Delta^u}} b + a$, but since b does not have sort A, we have $a + b \neq_{AC_\Delta} b + a$. It also means that the homomorphism $h' : T_{\Sigma^\square/E\cup AC_\Delta} \to T_{\Sigma^u/E\cup AC_{\Delta^u}}|_u$ in general is *not* injective. However, all hope is not lost. As a direct consequence of Corollary 2 in Sect. 3.2, there is an isomorphism $\alpha : T_{\Sigma/E\cup AC_\Delta} \cong T_{\Sigma^\square/E\cup AC_\Delta}|_\Sigma$ to the Σ-*reduct* of $T_{\Sigma^\square/E\cup AC_\Delta}$ and this shows that the homomorphism $h : T_{\Sigma/E\cup AC_\Delta} \to T_{\Sigma^u/E\cup AC_{\Delta^u}}|_u$ that we need to prove injective for the reduction to be sound is up to isomorphism a *restriction* of h' to $T_{\Sigma/E\cup AC_\Delta}$, which *could* be injective even if h' is not. Lemma 3 in Sect. 4.1 and the highly non-trivial Theorem 8 in Sect. 5 save the day: it follows from them that h is indeed injective and the reduction is also sound for the AC case. To the best of my knowledge the results on reducing order-sorted to unsorted satisfiability and on order-sorted rewriting and equality are new.

The paper is organized as follows. After some preliminaries in Sect. 2, the new results on order-rewriting and equality are given in Sect. 3. The reductions of satisfiability in the theory of OS uninterpreted function symbols (resp. OS uninterpreted function symbols modulo AC) to satisfiability in their respective unsorted theories is given in Sect. 4 (resp. Sect. 5). Related work and conclusions are discussed in Sect. 6. Due to space limitations no proofs are given; they can be found in the Technical Report [20].

2   Preliminaries on Order-Sorted Algebra

The following material is adapted from [21], which generalizes [15]. It summarizes the basic notions of order-sorted algebra needed in the rest of the paper.

Definition 1. *A many-sorted signature is a pair* $\Sigma = (S, \Sigma)$, *with* S *a set of sorts, and* Σ *and* $S^* \times S$-*indexed set* $\Sigma = \{\Sigma_{w,s}\}_{w,s\in S^*\times S}$ *of operation symbols, where* S^* *denotes the free monoid generated by* S. *We denote each* $f \in \Sigma_{w,s}$ *as* $f : w \to s$. *In particular, a* constant *of sort* s *is an operation* $a : \epsilon \to s$, *with* ϵ *the empty word.*

An order-sorted (OS) signature *is a triple* $\Sigma = (S, \leq, \Sigma)$ *with* $(S, \leq)$ *a poset and* (S, Σ) *a many-sorted signature.* $\widehat{S} = S/\equiv_\leq$, *the quotient of* S *under the equivalence relation* $\equiv_\leq = (\leq \cup \geq)^+$, *is called the set of* connected components *of* $(S, \leq)$. *Note that a many-sorted signature* Σ *is the special case where the poset* $(S, \leq)$ *is discrete, i.e.,* $s \leq s'$ *iff* $s = s'$.

The order $\leq$ *and equivalence* $\equiv_\leq$ *are extended to sequences of same length in the usual way, e.g.,* $s'_1 \ldots s'_n \leq s_1 \ldots s_n$ *iff* $s'_i \leq s_i$, $1 \leq i \leq n$. Σ *is called* sensible[1] *if for any two* $f : w \to s, f : w' \to s' \in \Sigma$, *with* w *and* w' *of same length, we have* $w \equiv_{\leq} w' \Rightarrow s \equiv_{\leq} s'$.

For connected components $[s_1], \ldots, [s_n], [s] \in \widehat{S}$

$$f^{[s_1]\cdots[s_n]}_{[s]} = \{f : s'_1 \ldots s'_n \to s' \in \Sigma \mid s'_i \in [s_i],\ 1 \leq i \leq n,\ s' \in [s]\}$$

denotes the family of "subsort polymorphic" operators f.   □

Definition 2. *For* $\Sigma = (S, \Sigma)$ *a many-sorted signature, a* Σ-*algebra is an* S-*indexed set* $A = \{A_s\}_{s \in S}$ *together with an assignment of: (i) to each constant* $a : \epsilon \to s$ *of sort* s *an element* $A_a \in A_s$, *and (ii) to each operation* $f : w \to s$, *with* $w = s_1 \ldots s_n$, $n \geq 1$, *a function* $A_{f:w \to s} : A^w \to A_s$, *where, by convention,* $A^{s_1 \ldots s_n} = A_{s_1} \times \ldots \times A_{s_n}$.

For $\Sigma = (S, \leq, \Sigma)$ *an OS signature, an* order-sorted Σ-*algebra* A *is a many-sorted* (S, Σ)-*algebra* A *such that:*

– *whenever* $s \leq s'$, *then we have* $A_s \subseteq A_{s'}$, *and*
– *whenever* $f : w \to s, f : w' \to s' \in f^{[s_1]\cdots[s_n]}_{[s]}$ *and* $\overline{a} \in A^w \cap A^{w'}$, *then we have* $A_{f:w \to s}(\overline{a}) = A_{f:w' \to s'}(\overline{a})$.

A many-sorted Σ-*homomorphism* $h : A \to B$ *is an* S-*indexed family of functions* $h = \{h_s : A_s \to B_s\}_{s \in S}$ *such that: (i) for* $a : \epsilon \to s$, $h_s(A_a) = B_a$, *and (ii) for* $f : w \to s$ *with* $w \neq \epsilon$, $A_f; h_s = h^w; B_f$.

An order-sorted Σ-*homomorphism* $h : A \to B$ *is a many-sorted* (S, Σ)-*homomorphism such that whenever* $[s] = [s']$ *and* $a \in A_s \cap A_{s'}$, *then we have* $h_s(a) = h_{s'}(a)$. *We call* h injective, *resp.* surjective, *resp.* bijective, *iff for each* $s \in S$ h_s *is injective, resp. surjective, resp. bijective. We call* h *an* isomorphism *if there is another order-sorted* Σ-*homomorphism* $g : B \to A$ *such that for each* $s \in S$, $h_s; g_s = 1_{A_s}$, *and* $g_s; h_s = 1_{B_s}$, *with* $1_{A_s}, 1_{B_s}$ *the identity functions on* A_s, B_s. *This defines a category* **OSAlg**$_\Sigma$. □

Theorem 1 [21]. *The category* **OSAlg**$_\Sigma$ *has an initial algebra. Furthermore, if* Σ *is sensible, then the term algebra* T_Σ *with:*

– *if* $a : \epsilon \to s$ *then* $a \in T_{\Sigma,s}$ (ϵ *denotes the empty string*),
– *if* $t \in T_{\Sigma,s}$ *and* $s \leq s'$ *then* $t \in T_{\Sigma,s'}$,
– *if* $f : s_1 \ldots s_n \to s$ *and* $t_i \in T_{\Sigma,s_i}$ $1 \leq i \leq n$, *then* $f(t_1, \ldots, t_n) \in T_{\Sigma,s}$,

is initial, *i.e., there is a unique* Σ-*homomorphism to each* Σ-*algebra.*

For $[s] \in \widehat{S}$, $T_{\Sigma,[s]}$ denotes the set $T_{\Sigma,[s]} = \bigcup_{s' \in [s]} T_{\Sigma,s'}$. Similarly, T_Σ will (ambiguously) denote both the above-defined S-sorted set and the set $T_\Sigma =$

---

[1] The notion of a sensible signature is a *minimal syntactic requirement* to avoid excessive ambiguity. For example, a many-sorted signature Σ with sorts A, B and C, constant $a : \epsilon \to A$ and operations $f : A \to B$ and $f : A \to C$ is not sensible and therefore is intrinsically ambiguous: the term $f(a)$ has both sorts B and C, which are completely different sorts.

$\bigcup_{s \in S} T_{\Sigma,s}$. We say that an OS signature Σ *has non-empty sorts* iff for each $s \in S$, $T_{\Sigma,s} \neq \emptyset$. *We will assume throughout that* Σ has non-empty sorts.

An S-sorted set $X = \{X_s\}_{s \in S}$ of *variables*, satisfies $s \neq s' \Rightarrow X_s \cap X_{s'} = \emptyset$, and the variables in X are always assumed disjoint from all constants in Σ. The Σ-*term algebra* on variables X, $T_\Sigma(X)$, is the *initial algebra* for the signature $\Sigma(X)$ obtained by adding to Σ the variables X *as extra constants*. Since a $\Sigma(X)$-algebra is just a pair (A, α), with A a Σ-algebra, and α an *interpretation of the constants* in X, i.e., an S-sorted function $\alpha \in [X \to A]$, the $\Sigma(X)$-initiality of $T_\Sigma(X)$ can be expressed as the following corollary of Theorem 1:

Theorem 2 *(Freeness Theorem). If* Σ *is sensible, for each* $A \in \mathbf{OSAlg}_\Sigma$ *and* $\alpha \in [X \to A]$, *there exists a unique* Σ-*homomorphim,* $\_\alpha : T_\Sigma(X) \longrightarrow A$ *extending* α, *i.e., such that for each* $s \in S$ *and* $x \in X_s$ *we have* $x\alpha_s = \alpha_s(x)$.

The first-order language of *equational* Σ-*formulas*[2] is defined in the usual way: its atoms are Σ-*equations* $t = t'$, where $t, t' \in T_\Sigma(X)_{[s]}$ for some $[s] \in \widehat{S}$ and each X_s is assumed countably infinite. The set $Form(\Sigma)$ of *equational* Σ-*formulas* is then inductively built from atoms by: conjunction ($\wedge$), disjunction ($\vee$) negation ($\neg$), and universal ($\forall x{:}s$) and existential ($\exists x{:}s$) quantification with sorted variables $x{:}s \in X_s$ for some $s \in S$. The literal $\neg(t = t')$ is denoted $t \neq t'$.

Given a Σ-algebra A, a formula $\varphi \in Form(\Sigma)$, and an assignment $\alpha \in [Y \to A]$, with $Y = fvars(\varphi)$ the free variables of φ, we define the *satisfaction relation* $A, \alpha \models \varphi$ inductively as usual: for atoms, $A, \alpha \models t = t'$ iff $t\alpha = t'\alpha$; for Boolean connectives it is the corresponding Boolean combination of the satisfaction relations for subformulas; and for quantifiers: $A, \alpha \models (\forall x{:}s) \varphi$ (resp. $A, \alpha \models (\exists x : s) \varphi$) holds iff for all $a \in A_s$ (resp. some $a \in A_s$) we have $A, \alpha \uplus \{(x{:}s, a)\} \models \varphi$, where the assignment $\alpha \uplus \{(x{:}s, a)\}$ extends α by mapping $x{:}s$ to a. Finally, $A \models \varphi$ holds iff $A, \alpha \models \varphi$ holds for each $\alpha \in [Y \to A]$, where $Y = fvars(\varphi)$. We say that φ is *valid* (or *true*) in A iff $A \models \varphi$. We say that φ is *satisfiable* in A iff $\exists \alpha \in [Y \to A]$ such that $A, \alpha \models \varphi$, where $Y = fvars(\varphi)$.

An *order-sorted equational theory* is a pair $T = (\Sigma, E)$, with E a set of Σ-equations. $\mathbf{OSAlg}_{(\Sigma,E)}$ denotes the full subcategory of $\mathbf{OSAlg}_\Sigma$ with objects those $A \in \mathbf{OSAlg}_\Sigma$ such that $A \models E$, called the (Σ, E)-*algebras*. $\mathbf{OSAlg}_{(\Sigma,E)}$ has an *initial algebra* $T_{\Sigma/E}$ [21], further discussed in Sect. 3. Given $T = (\Sigma, E)$ and $\varphi \in Form(\Sigma)$, we call φ T-*valid*, written $E \models \varphi$, iff $A \models \varphi$ for each $A \in \mathbf{OSAlg}_{(\Sigma,E)}$. We call φ T-*satisfiable* iff there exists $A \in \mathbf{OSAlg}_{(\Sigma,E)}$ with φ satisfiable in A. Note that φ is T-*valid* iff $\neg\varphi$ is T-*unsatisfiable*.

$\Sigma = ((S, \leq), \Sigma)$ is a *subsignature* of $\Sigma' = ((S', \leq'), \Sigma')$, denoted $\Sigma \subseteq \Sigma'$, iff $(S, \leq) \subseteq (S', \leq')$ is a subposet inclusion, and $\Sigma \subseteq \Sigma'$. A *signature map* $H : \Sigma \to \Sigma'$ is a monotonic function $H : (S, \leq) \to (S', \leq')$ of the underlying posets of sorts together with a mapping $H : \Sigma \ni (f : s_1 \dots s_n \to s) \mapsto (H(f) :$

---

[2] There is only an apparent lack of predicate symbols. To express a predicate $p(x_1: s_1, \dots, x_n{:}s_n)$, add a new sort *Truth* with a constant *tt*, and with $\{Truth\}$ a separate connected component, and view p as a function symbol $p : s_1, \dots, s_n \to Truth$. An atomic formula $p(t_1, \dots, t_n)$ is then expressed as the equation $p(t_1, \dots, t_n) = tt$.

$H(s_1)\dots H(s_n) \to H(s)) \in \Sigma'$. H induces a map $H : Form(\Sigma) \to Form(\Sigma')$. A signature inclusion $\Sigma \subseteq \Sigma'$ defines a signature map $\Sigma \hookrightarrow \Sigma' : f \mapsto f$.

A signature map $H : \Sigma \to \Sigma'$ induces a functor in the *opposite* direction $\_|_H\colon \mathbf{OSAlg}_{\Sigma'} \ni B \mapsto B|_H \in \mathbf{OSAlg}_{\Sigma}$, where the H-*reduct* $B|_H$ has: (i) for each $s \in S$, $(B|_H)_s = B_{H(s)}$; and (ii) for each $f : s_1 \dots s_n \to s$ in Σ, $(B|_H)_f = B_{H(f)}$. For $H : \Sigma \hookrightarrow \Sigma'$ a signature inclusion, $B|_H$ is denoted $B|_\Sigma$. For $B \in \mathbf{OSAlg}_{\Sigma'}$ and $\varphi \in Form(\Sigma)$ with $fvars(\varphi) = \emptyset$ we have [21]:

$$(\dagger) \quad B \models H(\varphi) \quad \Leftrightarrow \quad B|_H \models \varphi.$$

3 Order-Sorted Rewriting and Equality

Given an OS signature $\Sigma = ((S, \leq), \Sigma)$, a Σ-*rewrite rule*[3] is a sequent $l \to r$ with $l, r \in T_\Sigma(X)_{[s]}$ for some $[s] \in \widehat{S}$. An *order-sorted term rewriting system* (OSTRS) is then a pair (Σ, R) with R a set of Σ-rewrite rules.

Since, as shown in the Introduction, replacement of equals for equals and standard rewriting break down in the order-sorted case, we should define rewriting deductions with an OSTRS not by means of the reflexive-transitive closure $\to_R^*$ of the rewrite relation $\to_R$, but by means of an *inference system* with two kinds of *sequents*: sequents $t \to t'$, where $t, t' \in T_\Sigma(X)_{[s]}$, $[s] \in \widehat{S}$, corresponding to *one-step* application of rules, and sequents $t \to^\circledast t'$, where $t, t' \in T_\Sigma(X)_{[s]}$, $[s] \in \widehat{S}$, corresponding to more complex rewriting deductions. The symbol $\to^\circledast$ is close enough to $\to^*$ to suggest that: (i) it plays a role similar to a reflexive transitive-closure in the unsorted case, but (ii) in general it is *different* from such a closure. For example, for Σ the signature in the Introduction and $R = \{a \to b, b \to c\}$, we can derive $f(a) \to^\circledast f(c)$, but there is no sequence of one-step rewrites from $f(a)$ to $f(c)$. We then define two kinds of *rewriting deductions*: $(\Sigma, R) \vdash t \to t'$ and $(\Sigma, R) \vdash t \to^\circledast t'$, as those sequents derivable from (Σ, R) by a finite application of the following inference rules, where σ denotes an S-sorted *substitution*, i.e., an S-sorted function $\sigma \in [X \to T_\Sigma(X)]$:

Reflexivity	$t \to^\circledast t$
Subsumption	$\dfrac{t \to t'}{t \to^\circledast t'}$
Transitivity	$\dfrac{t \to^\circledast t' \quad t' \to^\circledast t''}{t \to^\circledast t''}$
Congruence	$\dfrac{u_1 \to^\circledast u_1' \quad \dots \quad u_n \to^\circledast u_n'}{f(u_1, \dots, u_n) \to^\circledast f(u_1', \dots, u_n')}$ where $f(u_1, \dots, u_n), f(u_1', \dots, u_n') \in T_\Sigma(X)$
Replacement	$\dfrac{}{t\sigma \to t'\sigma}$ where $t \to t' \in R$

---

[3] For greater generality no restriction is placed on the variables of l and r.

The first three and the last inference rule are standard, but the **Congruence** rule is more subtle. We can better understand these rules by means of our running example (Σ, R). The sequent $f(a) \to^{\circledast} f(b)$ is *not* derivable: the attempt to obtain it by applying **Replacement** with rule $a \to b$, **Subsumption** to get $a \to^{\circledast} b$, and then **Congruence** fails, because of the side condition, since $f(b) \notin T_{\Sigma}(X)$. To see what *can* be derived, consider the derivation of the sequent $f(a) \to^{\circledast} f(c)$. Since we have rules $a \to b$ and $b \to c$, we can derive $a \to^{\circledast} c$ by two applications of **Replacement** followed by **Subsumption** and one application of **Transitivity**. Then **Congruence** gives us:

$$\frac{a \to^{\circledast} c}{f(a) \to^{\circledast} f(c)}$$

Note the interesting fact that $f(a)$ is typed with $f : A \to A$, and $f(c)$ is typed with $f : C \to C$. We can think of **Congruence** as a "tunneling rule." $f(a) \to^{\circledast} f(c)$ *cannot* be obtained by composing one-step rewrites: failed attempts such as that for deriving $f(a) \to^{\circledast} f(b)$ make it impossible; but we can "tunnel through" such failed attempts and obtain a more complex sequent like $f(a) \to^{\circledast} f(c)$ when the left- and right-hand sides are well-formed terms in $T_{\Sigma}(X)$.

The above inference system yields as a *special case* a sound and complete inference system for *order-sorted equational logic*: we just view an order-sorted equational theory (Σ, E) as the OSTRS $(\Sigma, R(E))$, where $R(E) = \{t \to t' \mid t = t' \in E \ \lor \ t' = t \in E\}$. That is, equality steps are viewed as either left-to-right or right-to-left rewrite steps. We then have:

Definition 3. *Given an order-sorted equational theory (Σ, E) with Σ sensible, its equational deduction relation, denoted $(\Sigma, E) \vdash u = v$, or just $E \vdash u = v$, is defined by the equivalence:*

$$(\Sigma, E) \vdash u = v \quad \Leftrightarrow \quad (\Sigma, R(E)) \vdash u \to^{\circledast} v.$$

Theorem 3 *(Soundness and Completeness) [21] Theorem 24. For Σ sensible and $E \cup \{u = v\}$ a set of Σ-equations we have the equivalence:*

$$(\Sigma, E) \vdash u = v \quad \Leftrightarrow \quad (\Sigma, E) \models u = v$$

The above theorem has as a corollary the construction of the *initial algebra* $T_{\Sigma/E}$ for the category **OSAlg**$_{(\Sigma,E)}$ of (Σ, E)-algebras. Assuming Σ sensible, $T_{\Sigma/E}$, has an easy definition. Note that the relation $E \vdash u = v$ induces an equivalence relation $=_E$ on each set $T_{\Sigma,[s]}$, $[s] \in \widehat{S}$. We then define $T_{\Sigma/E,s'} = \{[t]_{=_E} \in T_{\Sigma,[s]}/=_E \mid [t]_{=_E} \cap T_{\Sigma,s'} \neq \emptyset\}$ for each $s' \in [s]$, and define each operation $f : s_1 \ldots s_n \to s \in \Sigma$ by the map $([t_1]_{=_E}, \ldots, [t_1]_{=_E}) \mapsto [f(t'_1, \ldots, t'_n)]_{=_E}$, where $t'_i \in [t_i]_{=_E} \cap T_{\Sigma,s_i}$, $1 \leq i \leq n$, showing it does not depend on the choice of t'_i's.

3.1   Kind-Complete OS-Rewriting and Equational Deduction

The order-sorted rewrite relation $t \to^{\circledast} t'$ is obviously quite impractical and hard to implement. For this reason, given an OSTRS (Σ, R) several conditions on either Σ or R have been sought to be able to perform rewriting computations in essentially the standard and efficient way in which it is performed in an unsorted or many-sorted TRS. Two such conditions, going back to [14], are to either: (i) require that the rules R are *sort-decreasing*, i.e., for each $l \to r \in R$ and S-sorted substitution σ, if $l\sigma \in T_{\Sigma,s}$ then $r\sigma \in T_{\Sigma,s}$ (this can be checked by the method explained in [17]); or (ii) if R is not sort-decreasing, extend Σ with new "retract operators" $r_{s,s'} : s \to s'$, $s, s' \in [s]$, $s \nleq s'$, to catch typing errors, add to R "error recovery" rules of the form $r_{s,s'}(x{:}s') \to x{:}s'$, and force sort-decreasingness of R by replacing each not sort-decreasing $u \to v \in R$ by suitable rules of the form $u\sigma \to r_{s,s'}(v\sigma)$, where σ may lower the sorts of some variables.

Conditions (i) or in its defect (ii) work and can be shown to be conservative in a certain sense [14]. However, they have serious limitations. Sort decreasingness is a strong condition that may be impossible to achieve for some OSTRS arising in practice; and if the solution with retracts is adopted, an unpleasant consequence is that we *change the models*, including the initial ones, since retracts add new operations and new error terms *to the original sorts*.

All these limitations can be avoided —while allowing rewriting with rules R and equational deduction with equations E to be performed in the *standard* way— by using a *faithful embedding* of order-sorted equational logic into *membership equational logic* (MEL) [3,21]. MEL introduces a typing distinction between *sorts* $s \in S$, which may be related by subsort relations just as in the order-sorted way, and the *kind* $\top_{[s]}$ associated to each connected component $[s] \in \widehat{S}$, which is above all sorts in $[s]$. An ill-formed term like $f(b)$ in the OS signature of the Introduction has no sort, but has kind $\top_{[B]}$. In this way, the earlier side condition in the **Congruence** rule in Sect. 3 can be avoided.

The faithfulness of this embedding of logics means in particular that *both* initial models and equational deduction are preserved ([21], Corollary 28). However: (i) the proof in [21] is model-theoretic; (ii) it focuses on the equational logic level, and does not deal with the more general rewriting logic level; and (iii) it assumes that the entire MEL framework is adopted. Can the essential advantages of this embedding be still obtained *while remaining at the order-sorted level*? The answer is *yes!* Since: (i) this solution plays a key role in the treatment of satisfiability for the theory of OS uninterpreted function symbols in Sect. 4, and (ii) having a much simpler theory of OS rewriting is useful in its own right, I give a detailed treatment of it below. The key idea is to use a signature transformation $\Sigma \mapsto \Sigma^{\square}$ extending any OS signature Σ into one whose components have a top sort, understood as the kind of that component. The essential point is that $\Sigma^{\square}$ belongs to a class of order-sorted signatures called *kind complete* where both rewriting and equational deduction can be performed in the standard way.

Definition 4. *An OS signature* $\Sigma = ((S, \leq), \Sigma)$ *is called* kind-complete *iff each connected component* $[s] \in \widehat{S}$ *has a top sort* $\top_{[s]}$, *called its* kind, *with* $\top_{[s]} \geq s'$ *for each* $s' \in [s]$, *and any non-empty subsort-polymorphic family* $f_{[s]}^{[s_1]\ldots[s_n]} \subseteq \Sigma$

includes the typing $f : \top_{[s_1]}, \ldots, \top_{[s_n]} \to \top_{[s]}$. *Note that any many-sorted* Σ — *and in particular any unsorted (i.e., single-sorted)* Σ— *is trivially kind-complete.*

Any OS signature Σ can be extended to a kind-complete one by a transformation $\Sigma \mapsto \Sigma^{\square}$. $\Sigma^{\square}$ is constructed in two-steps: (i) we first associate to the order-sorted signature $((S, \leq), \Sigma)$ the many-sorted signature $\widehat{\Sigma} = (\widehat{S}_\top, \widehat{\Sigma})$, where $\widehat{S}_\top = \{\top_{[s]} \mid [s] \in \widehat{S}\}$, and with $f : \top_{[s_1]} \cdots \top_{[s_n]} \to \top_{[s]} \in \widehat{\Sigma}$ iff $f_{[s]}^{[s_1]\ldots[s_n]} \neq \emptyset$; and (ii) we then define $\Sigma^{\square} = ((S \uplus \widehat{S}_\top, \leq_{\square}), \Sigma \uplus \widehat{\Sigma})$, where $\leq_{\square} \cap S^2 = \leq$, and for each $\top_{[s]} \in \widehat{S}_\top$ we have $s' <_{\square} \top_{[s]}$ for each $s' \in [s]$. That is, we add $\top_{[s]}$ as a top sort above each $s' \in [s]$ and add the new typing $f : \top_{[s_1]} \cdots \top_{[s_n]} \to \top_{[s]}$ for each $f_{[s]}^{[s_1]\ldots[s_n]} \neq \emptyset$.

For Σ the signature in the Introduction, $\Sigma^{\square}$ is as follows:

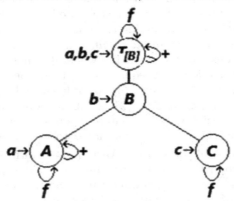

Instead, the many-sorted signature $\widehat{\Sigma}$ in this example happens to be unsorted, and is obtained by keeping only the sort $\top_{[B]}$ in the above figure, with the operations f and $+$ and constants a, b, c of of sort $\top_{[B]}$, and removing all other sorts and operations in the figure. In summary, $\Sigma^{\square}$ is the signature obtained by adding a new top sort $\top_{[s]}$ on top of each connected component $[s]$ and "lifting" to those top sorts all operations and constants, whereas $\widehat{\Sigma}$ is the many sorted signature obtained when we remove from $\Sigma^{\square}$ all sorts except the newly added top sorts of the form $\top_{[s]}$ for each $[s]$.

We then have subsignature inclusions: $\Sigma \subseteq \Sigma^{\square}$ and $\widehat{\Sigma} \subseteq \Sigma^{\square}$. Note that, by construction, if Σ is sensible, both $\widehat{\Sigma}$ and $\Sigma^{\square}$ are also sensible; and that the initial algebra $T_{\Sigma^{\square}}$ is *preserved by reducts*, i.e., we have:

$$T_{\Sigma^{\square}}|_{\Sigma} = T_{\Sigma} \quad and \quad T_{\Sigma^{\square}}|_{\widehat{\Sigma}} = T_{\widehat{\Sigma}}.$$

For kind-complete signatures, rewriting, and in particular equational deduction, can be performed in the standard, sorted way. Recall the usual notation to denote term positions, subterms, decompositions and term replacement from [6]: (i) positions in a term viewed as a tree are marked by strings $p \in \mathbb{N}^*$ specifying a path from the root, (ii) $t|_p$ denotes the subterm of term t at position p, (iii)

$t = t[t|_p]_p$ denotes a *decomposition* of t into a context $t[]_p$ and its subterm $t|_p$, and (iv) $t[u]_p$ denotes the result of *replacing* subterm $t|_p$ at position p by u.

Definition 5. *Let (Σ, R) be an OSTRS with Σ sensible and kind-complete. The one-step R-rewrite relation $u \to_R v$ holds between $u, v \in T_\Sigma(X)_{[s]}$, $[s] \in \widehat{S}$, iff there is a rewrite rule $t \to t' \in R$, a substitution $\sigma \in [X \to T_\Sigma(X)]$, and a term position p in u such that $u = u[t\sigma]_p$ and $v = u[t'\sigma]_p$.*

We denote by $\to_R^+$ the transitive closure of $\to_R$, and by $\to_R^*$ the reflexive-transitive closure of $\to_R$, and write $(\Sigma, R) \vdash u \to_R^* v$ to make Σ explicit.

(Σ, R) is called terminating iff $\to_R$ is a well-founded relation; and is called confluent iff whenever $t \to_R^* u$ and $t \to_R^* v$ there exists w such that $u \to_R^* w$ and $v \to_R^* w$. (Σ, R) is called convergent iff it is both confluent and terminating. If (Σ, R) is convergent, each Σ-term t rewrites by some $t \to_R^* t!_R$ to a unique term $t!_R$, called its R-canonical form, that cannot be further rewritten.

When Σ is kind-complete, if $u \in T_\Sigma(X)_{[s]}$, $t \to t' \in R$, and $u = u[t\sigma]_p \in T_\Sigma(X)_{[s]}$, then we always have $u[t'\sigma]_p \in T_\Sigma(X)_{[s]}$. That is, $\to_R$ *never produces ill-formed terms*, so that in the above definition of $\to_R$ the requirement the $v \in T_\Sigma(X)_{[s]}$ is unnecessary and does not have to be checked. Indeed, for kind-complete signatures order-sorted rewriting *becomes standard sorted rewriting*:

Lemma 1. *Let (Σ, R) be an OSTRS with Σ sensible and kind-complete. Then we have the equivalence:*

$$(\Sigma, R) \vdash u \to^\circledast v \quad \Leftrightarrow \quad (\Sigma, R) \vdash u \to_R^* v.$$

Corollary 1. *Let Σ be a sensible and kind-complete OS signature, and $E \cup \{u = v\}$ a set of Σ-equations. Then we have the equivalence:*

$$(\Sigma, E) \vdash u = v \quad \Leftrightarrow \quad (\Sigma, R(E)) \vdash u \to_{R(E)}^* v.$$

3.2   Conservativity Results

The whole point of the signature transformation $\Sigma \mapsto \Sigma^\square$ is to replace complex deductions of the form $(\Sigma, R) \vdash u \to^\circledast v$ by simple rewrite sequences $u \to_R^* v$ in the *extended* OSTRS $(\Sigma^\square, R)$. But is this sound?

Theorem 4. *Let (Σ, R) be an OSTRS with Σ sensible. Then for any $u, v \in T_\Sigma(X)_{[s]}$, $[s] \in \widehat{S}$ we have the equivalence:*

$$(\Sigma, R) \vdash u \to^\circledast v \quad \Leftrightarrow \quad (\Sigma^\square, R) \vdash u \to_R^* v.$$

Corollary 2. *Let Σ be a sensible OS signature and $E \cup \{u = v\}$ a set of Σ-equations. Then we have the equivalences:*

$$(\Sigma, E) \vdash u = v \quad \Leftrightarrow \quad (\Sigma^\square, E) \vdash u = v \quad \Leftrightarrow \quad (\Sigma^\square, R(E)) \vdash u \to_{R(E)}^* v.$$

Since, besides the subsignature inclusion $\Sigma \subseteq \Sigma^\square$, we also have the inclusion $\widehat{\Sigma} \subseteq \Sigma^\square$, we have a further conservativity result:

Lemma 2. *Let Σ be a sensible OS signature and $(\widehat{\Sigma}, R)$ a many-sorted TRS. Then for any $u, v \in T_{\widehat{\Sigma}}(X)_{\top_{[s]}}$, $\top_{[s]} \in \widehat{S}_\top$, where $X = \{X_{\top_{[s]}}\}_{\top_{[s]} \in \widehat{S}_\top}$, we have $(\widehat{\Sigma}, R) \vdash u \rightarrow^*_R v$ iff $(\Sigma^\square, R) \vdash u \rightarrow^*_R v$. As an immediate consequence, for $E \cup \{u = v\}$ a set of $\widehat{\Sigma}$-equations, we have the equivalence:*

$$(\widehat{\Sigma}, E) \vdash u = v \quad \Leftrightarrow \quad (\Sigma^\square, E) \vdash u = v.$$

4   Order-Sorted $(\Sigma, \emptyset)$-QF-Satisfiability

In theorem proving the theory $(\Sigma, \emptyset)$, whose category of algebras is $\mathbf{OSAlg}_\Sigma$, is called the theory of *uninterpreted function symbols* Σ. As remarked in Definition 1, a *many-sorted* signature Σ is a special case of an order-sorted signature, and an *unsorted* signature is a many-sorted signature where $S = \{U\}$ is a singleton set. Let $QFForm(\Sigma) \subseteq Form(\Sigma)$ denote the set of *quantifier-free* Σ-formulas, i.e., formulas with no quantifiers. When Σ is unsorted, $(\Sigma, \emptyset)$-*QF-satisfiability*, i.e., $(\Sigma, \emptyset)$-satisfiability for any $\varphi \in QFForm(\Sigma)$ is *decidable* [1]. The goal of this section is to show that the same holds for any sensible OS signature Σ by a *reduction* method. This can be done by two reductions. The first reduces this decidability problem to that of the *OS word problem*, which is the problem of whether, given a sensible OS signature Σ and a finite set $E \cup \{u = v\}$ of *ground* Σ-equations, $E \vdash u = v$ holds or not. The desired first reduction is as follows:

Theorem 5. $(\Sigma, \emptyset)$-*QF-satisfiability is decidable for any sensible order-sorted signature* Σ *iff the OS word problem is decidable.*

The proof follows from the more general Theorem 7 in Sect. 5, which deals with the OS word problem *modulo* equations B. The theorem's algorithmic content mirrors its proof: $\varphi = \bigvee_{1 \leq i \leq n} (\bigwedge E_i \wedge \bigwedge D_i)$ in DNF with the E_i equalities and the D_i disequalities is satisfiable iff, when we view the variables in φ as fresh new constants C, there is an i, $1 \leq i \leq n$, such that $E_i \not\vdash u = v$ for each $u \neq v \in D_i$. Furthermore, $\bigwedge E_i \wedge \bigwedge D_i$ is satisfiable iff $T_{\Sigma(C)/E_i} \models \bigwedge E_i \wedge \bigwedge D_i$.

The second reduction is from the OS word problem to the *unsorted* word problem. This is broken into *two* reductions: (i) of the many-sorted word problem to the unsorted word problem in Sect. 4.1, and (ii) of the OS word problem to the many-sorted word problem in Sect. 4.2.

For Σ *unsorted* and $E \cup \{u = v\}$ a finite set of ground Σ-equations it is well-known that the word problem $E \vdash u = v$ can be decided by a *congruence closure* algorithm [7,24,27]. What the various such algorithms have in common is that they are all instances (by applying difference strategies) of the same *abstract congruence closure* algorithm in the sense of [2], which is summarized below.

4.1   Abstract Congruence Closure

What the abstract congruence closure algorithm in [2] captures is what all concrete congruence closure algorithms have in common: they all are efficient, specialized *ground Knuth-Bendix* completion algorithms [2,12,16,18]: they all begin with a set E of ground equations, and return a set R of *convergent* ground rewrite rules R equivalent to E (on a possibly extended signature). We can then decide the word problem $E \vdash u = v$ by checking the syntactic equality $u!_R = v!_R$.

The key notion of *abstract congruence closure* in [2] is then as follows:

Definition 6. *[2] For Σ an unsorted signature and E a finite set of ground Σ-equations, an* abstract congruence closure *for E is a set R of ground convergent $\Sigma(K)$-rewrite rules, where K is a finite set of new constants, such that: (i) they are either of the form $c \to c'$, with $c, c' \in K$, or of the form $f(c_1, \ldots, c_n) \to c$, with $c_1, \ldots, c_n, c \in K$, $f \in \Sigma$ with $n \geq 0$ arguments; (ii) for each $c \in K$ there is a ground Σ-term t such that $t!_R = c!_R$; and (iii) for any ground Σ-equation $u = v$ we have $E \vdash u = v$ iff we have the syntactic equality $u!_R = v!_R$.*

The paper [2] then gives an *abstract congruence closure algorithm* described by six inference rules, with an optional seventh, such that: (i) takes as input a triple $(\emptyset, E, \emptyset)$ with E is a set of ground Σ-equations; (ii) operates on triples of the form (K', E', R') with E' (resp. R') the current $\Sigma(K')$-equations (resp. $\Sigma(K')$-rules); and (iii) terminates with a triple of the form $(K, \emptyset, R)$ such that R is a congruence closure for E. The name *abstract congruence closure* is well-deserved: the algorithms in [7, 24, 27], and two other ones, are all shown to be *instantiations* of the abstract algorithm by applying the inference rules with different *strategies*, so that both the operation of each algorithm and its actual complexity are faithfully captured by the corresponding instantiation [2].

We need to decide *the many-sorted* word problem as a step for deciding the more general order-sorted one. But the many-sorted word problem can be easily *reduced* to the unsorted one by means of the signature transformation $\Sigma \ni (f : s_1 \ldots s_n \to s) \mapsto (f : U \ldots^n \ldots U \to U) \in \Sigma^u$, where $\Sigma = (S, \Sigma)$ is a many-sorted signature. Then all boils down to the following lemma:

Lemma 3. *For Σ a sensible many-sorted signature and E a set of* regular *Σ-equations —i.e., t and t' have the same variables for each $t = t' \in E$— we have $(\Sigma, E) \vdash u = v$ iff $(\Sigma^u, E^u) \vdash (u = v)^u$, where for any Σ-equation $t = t'$, $(t = t')^u$ leaves the terms unchanged but regards all variables as unsorted.*

This lemma has a very practical consequence: we can use an unsorted congruence closure algorithm to solve the many-sorted word problem *at no extra cost*: no changes are needed either to the input E or to the unsorted algorithm.

4.2 Deciding OS $(\Sigma, \emptyset)$-QF-Satisfiability

For any sensible OS signature Σ we have reduced the decidability of the $(\Sigma, \emptyset)$-QF-satisfiability problem to that of the OS word problem in Theorem 5. And in Lemma 3 we have reduced the many-sorted word problem to the unsorted word problem, which is decidable by a congruence closure algorithm. To prove the decidability of the OS $(\Sigma, \emptyset)$-QF-satisfiability problem and obtain a correct algorithm for it we just need to reduce the OS word problem to the many-sorted word problem. For this, the conservativity results in Sect. 3.2 are crucial:

Theorem 6. *Let Σ be a sensible OS signature and $E \cup \{u = v\}$ a set of ground Σ-equations. Then we have the equivalence:*

$$(\Sigma, E) \vdash u = v \quad \Leftrightarrow \quad (\widehat{\Sigma}, E) \vdash u = v.$$

The decidability of the OS $(\Sigma, \emptyset)$-QF-satisfiability problem goes back to [11]; but the reduction achieved by Theorem 5, Lemma 3 and Theorem 6 yields a new, very simple algorithm. Either by already having φ in DNF or by using a DPLL$(\Sigma, \emptyset)$ solver, deciding the satisfiability of φ boils down to finding a satisfiable conjunction $\bigwedge E \wedge \bigwedge D$, with E (resp. D) a finite sets of equations (resp. disquations), which can be viewed as a *ground* $\Sigma(C)$-formula by adding $C = fvars(\varphi)$ as *new constants*. Then, satisfiability of $\bigwedge E \wedge \bigwedge D$ is decided by:

1. regarding at no cost $\bigwedge E \wedge \bigwedge D$ as a ground $\Sigma(C)^u$-formula,
2. computing a congruence closure R for E in the usual way [7,24,27], and
3. checking the syntactic inequality $u!_R \not\equiv v!_R$ for each $u \neq v \in D$.

Therefore we can *reuse* the same algorithms and tools used in the *unsorted case at no extra cost*: the input to such algorithms and the algorithms or tools themselves need no changes, and the complexity is that of the unsorted case.

5   Order-Sorted (Σ, AC_Δ)-QF-Satisfiability

Let Σ be a sensible OS signature with $\Delta \subseteq \Sigma$ made exclusively of binary function symbols, say, $g, h, \ldots$, each of the form $g : s\,s \to s$ for some sorts $s \in S$, and with any typing of any such g in Σ necessarily a typing in Δ, i.e., Δ and $(\Sigma - \Delta)$ share no symbols. Assume that each non-empty subsort-polymorphic family $g_{[s]}^{[s]\,[s]} \subseteq \Delta$ has always a biggest possible typing $g : s_g\,s_g \to s_g$ such that for any other typing $g : s\,s \to s$ in $g_{[s]}^{[s]\,[s]}$ we have $s \leq s_g$. The equations: $AC_g = \{g(x, y) = g(y, x), g(x, g(y, z)) = g(g(x, y), z)\}$, with x, y, z of sort s_g, express the *associativity-commutativity* (AC) of the subsort-polymorphic family $g_{[s]}^{[s]\,[s]}$. We require that the axioms AC_g are *sort-preserving*, that is, that for each S-sorted substitution σ and each sort $s \in S$ we have: $g(x, y)\sigma \in T_\Sigma(X)_s \Leftrightarrow g(y, x)\sigma \in T_\Sigma(X)_s$, and $g(x, g(y, z))\sigma \in T_\Sigma(X)_s \Leftrightarrow g(g(x, y), z)\sigma \in T_\Sigma(X)_s$, which can be easily checked by the method explained in [17]. Let AC_Δ denote the set $AC_\Delta = \bigcup_{g \in \Delta} AC_g$ making all symbols in Δ AC. Call (Σ, AC_Δ) the OS theory of Σ *uninterpreted function symbols* Σ modulo AC_Δ. When $\Sigma = \Delta$ is unsorted and has a single symbol $+$, this is called the *theory of commutative semigroups*.

We can generalize the above setting by replacing (Δ, AC_Δ) by any OS theory (Δ, B) with Δ sensible and considering any sensible supersignature $\Sigma \supseteq \Delta$ with Δ and $\Sigma - \Delta$ not sharing any symbols. Call (Σ, B) the theory of *uninterpreted function symbols* Σ modulo B. We can then reduce the decidability of the (Σ, B)-QF-satisfiabilty problem to that of the *OS word problem modulo B*, defined as the problem of whether given any $\Sigma \supseteq \Delta$ as above, and a set $E \cup \{u = v\}$ of ground Σ-equations, $E \cup B \vdash u = v$ holds or not. The reduction is as follows:

Theorem 7. *For any (Δ, B) and $\Sigma \supseteq \Delta$ as above, (Σ, B)-QF-satisfiability is decidable iff the OS word problem modulo B is decidable.*

For $\Sigma \supseteq \Delta$ unsorted, there are *AC congruence closure* algorithms for the theory (Σ, AC_Δ) [2,19,22] that decide the word problem modulo AC_Δ and therefore, by above Theorem 7, the unsorted (Σ, AC_Δ)-QF-satisfiability problem. In the spirit of Sect. 4, the main goal of this section is to *reduce* the decidability of the OS (Σ, AC_Δ)-QF-satisfiability problem to that of its unsorted version, and to furthermore *reuse* the *same* unsorted AC congruence closure algorithms in [2,19,22] to decide *at no extra cost* and with the *same complexity* the OS (Σ, AC_Δ)-QF-satisfiability problem.

The decidability of OS (Σ, AC_Δ)-QF-satisfiability has already been reduced to that of the OS word problem modulo AC_Δ, now we just need to reduce the OS word problem modulo AC_Δ to the unsorted word problem modulo AC_{Δ^u}.

This is achieved in two steps. First, we reduce the many-sorted word problem modulo $AC_{\widehat{\Delta}}$ to the unsorted word problem modulo AC_{Δ^u} using the $\widehat{\Sigma} \mapsto \Sigma^u$ transformation of Sect. 4.1. This first reduction is easy: the equations $AC_{\widehat{\Delta}}$ are *regular*. Therefore, if $E \cup \{u = v\}$ is a finite set of ground many-sorted $\widehat{\Sigma}$-equations, the equations $E \cup AC_{\widehat{\Delta}}$ are also regular and the conditions of Lemma 3 apply. We then reduce the OS word problem modulo AC_Δ to the many-sorted word problem modulo $AC_{\widehat{\Delta}}$. The $\widehat{\Delta}$-equations $AC_{\widehat{\Delta}}$ are obtained from the OS Δ-equations in AC_Δ by replacing each variable $x{:}s$ by the variable $x{:}\top_{[s]}$. That is, for $E \cup \{u = v\}$ a finite set of *ground* Σ-equations must show the equivalence:

$$(\Sigma, E \cup AC_\Delta) \vdash u = v \quad \Leftrightarrow \quad (\widehat{\Sigma}, E \cup AC_{\widehat{\Delta}}) \vdash u = v$$

which, by Corollary 2, reduces to proving the equivalence:

$$(\Sigma^\square, E \cup AC_\Delta) \vdash u = v \quad \Leftrightarrow \quad (\widehat{\Sigma}, E \cup AC_{\widehat{\Delta}}) \vdash u = v$$

which, by Lemma 2, follows as a special case from the more general theorem:

Theorem 8. *Let $\Sigma \supseteq \Delta$ be a sensible OS supersignature, R a set of Σ-rewrite rules, and $u, v \in T_\Sigma(X)$. Then we have the equivalence:*

$$(\Sigma^\square, R \cup R(AC_\Delta)) \vdash u \rightarrow^*_{R \cup R(AC_\Delta)} v \quad \Leftrightarrow \quad (\Sigma^\square, R \cup R(AC_{\widehat{\Delta}})) \vdash u \rightarrow^*_{R \cup R(AC_{\widehat{\Delta}})} v.$$

6   Related Work and Conclusions

[11] presents the only *order-sorted* congruence closure algorithm I am aware of. It provides a good solution under some extra assumptions on Σ, but it requires a quite complex congruence generation method and has worse complexity, $O(n^2)$, than the best $O(n \ log(n))$ unsorted algorithms. The papers [2,12,16,19,22] present the view of congruence closure as completion. In particular, I have used *abstract congruence closure* [2] and *AC-congruence closure* [2,19,22]. The modular combination of congruence closure, AC congruence, and

polynomial ring congruence closure algorithms for different symbols and its relation to the Nelson-Oppen combination method [23, 25] is studied in [31]. Likewise, the combination of AC congruence closure with other satisfiability algorithms using the Shostak combination method [28] is studied in [5] The first general study I know of satisfiability modulo theories in an order-sorted setting is [30].

The above-mentioned work has influenced and motivated the present one. The good news is that we get all the benefits of order-sorted $(\Sigma, \emptyset)$- and (Σ, AC_Δ)-satisfiability *for free*, with no added computational cost and being able to reuse unsorted tools. At a more theoretical level, the order-sorted rewriting and equality results presented here are also good news and belong to the foundations of such an area. Future work will focus on exploiting these results at the tool level.

Acknowledgements. Partially supported by NSF Grant CNS 13-19109. I thank Maria Paola Bonacina for suggested improvements.

References

1. Ackermann, W.: Solvable Cases of the Decision Problem. North-Holland Publishing Company, Amsterdam (1954)
2. Bachmair, L., Tiwari, A., Vigneron, L.: Abstract congruence closure. J. Autom. Reasoning **31**(2), 129–168 (2003)
3. Bouhoula, A., Jouannaud, J.P., Meseguer, J.: Specification and proof in membership equational logic. Theoret. Comput. Sci. **236**, 35–132 (2000)
4. Clavel, M., Durán, F., Eker, S., Meseguer, J., Lincoln, P., Martí-Oliet, N., Talcott, C.: All About Maude. LNCS, vol. 4350. Springer, Heidelberg (2007)
5. Conchon, S., Contejean, E., Iguernelala, M.: Canonized rewriting and ground AC completion modulo Shostak theories : design and implementation. Logical Methods Comput. Sci. **8**(3), 1–29 (2012)
6. Dershowitz, N., Jouannaud, J.P.: Rewrite systems. In: van Leeuwen, J. (ed.) Handbook of Theoretical Computer Science, vol. B, pp. 243–320. North-Holland Publishing Company, Amsterdam (1990)
7. Downey, P.J., Sethi, R., Tarjan, R.E.: Variations on the common subexpressions problem. J. ACM **27**(4), 758–771 (1980)
8. Frisch, A.M.: The substitutional framework for sorted deduction: fundamental results on hybrid reasoning. Artif. Intell. **49**(1–3), 161–198 (1991)
9. Futatsugi, K., Diaconescu, R.: CafeOBJ Report. World Scientific, Singapore (1998)
10. Futatsugi, K., Goguen, J., Jouannaud, J.P., Meseguer, J.: Principles of OBJ2. In: Proceedings of POPL 1985, pp. 52–66. ACM (1985)
11. Gallier, J., Isakowitz, T.: Order-sorted congruence closure. Technical report CIS-686, UPenn (1988). http://repository.upenn.edu/cis_reports/686
12. Gallier, J.H., Narendran, P., Plaisted, D.A., Raatz, S., Snyder, W.: An algorithm for finding canonical sets of ground rewrite rules in polynomial time. J. ACM **40**(1), 1–16 (1993)
13. Gnaedig, I., Kirchner, C., Kirchner, H.: Equational completion in order-sorted algebras. Theoret. Comput. Sci. **72**(2–3), 169–202 (1990)

14. Goguen, J., Jouannaud, J.P., Meseguer, J.: Operational semantics of order-sorted algebra. In: Brauer, W. (ed.) Automata, Languages and Programming. LNCS, vol. 194, pp. 221–231. Springer, Heidelberg (1985)

15. Goguen, J., Meseguer, J.: Order-sorted algebra I. Theoret. Comput. Sci. **105**, 217–273 (1992)

16. Kapur, D.: Shostak's congruence closure as completion. In: Comon, H. (ed.) RTA 1997. LNCS, vol. 1232, pp. 23–37. Springer, Heidelberg (1997)

17. Kirchner, C., Kirchner, H., Meseguer, J.: Operational semantics of OBJ3. In: Lepistö, T., Salomaa, A. (eds.) Automata, Languages and Programming. LNCS, vol. 317, pp. 287–301. Springer, Heidelberg (1988)

18. Knuth, D., Bendix, P.: Simple word problems in universal algebra. In: Leech, J. (ed.) Computational Problems in Abstract Algebra. Pergamon Press, Oxford (1970)

19. Marché, C.: On ground AC-completion. In: Book, R.V. (ed.) RTA 1991. LNCS, vol. 488, pp. 411–422. Springer, Heidelberg (1991)

20. Meseguer, J.: Order-sorted rewriting and congruence closure. Technical report, C.S. Department, University of Illinois at Urbana-Champaign, June 2015. http://hdl.handle.net/2142/78008

21. Meseguer, J.: Membership algebra as a logical framework for equational specification. In: Parisi-Presicce, F. (ed.) WADT 1997. LNCS, vol. 1376, pp. 18–61. Springer, Heidelberg (1998)

22. Narendran, P., Rusinowitch, M.: Any ground associative-commutative theory has a finite canonical system. In: Book, R.V. (ed.) RTA 1991. LNCS, vol. 488, pp. 423–434. Springer, Heidelberg (1991)

23. Nelson, G., Oppen, D.C.: Simplification by cooperating decision procedures. ACM Trans. Program. Lang. Syst. **1**(2), 245–257 (1979)

24. Nelson, G., Oppen, D.C.: Fast decision procedures based on congruence closure. J. ACM **27**(2), 356–364 (1980)

25. Oppen, D.C.: Complexity, convexity and combinations of theories. Theoret. Comput. Sci. **12**, 291–302 (1980)

26. Schmidt-Schauss, M.: Computational Aspects of Order-Sorted Logic with Term Declarations. LNCS (LNAI), vol. 395. Springer, Heidelberg (1989)

27. Shostak, R.E.: An algorithm for reasoning about equality. Commun. ACM **21**(7), 583–585 (1978)

28. Shostak, R.E.: Deciding combinations of theories. J. ACM **31**(1), 1–12 (1984)

29. Smolka, G., Aït-Kaci, H.: Inheritance hierarchies: semantics and unification. J. Symb. Comput. **7**(3/4), 343–370 (1989)

30. Tinelli, C., Zarba, C.G.: Combining decision procedures for sorted theories. In: Alferes, J.J., Leite, J. (eds.) JELIA 2004. LNCS (LNAI), vol. 3229, pp. 641–653. Springer, Heidelberg (2004)

31. Tiwari, A.: Combining equational reasoning. In: Ghilardi, S., Sebastiani, R. (eds.) FroCoS 2009. LNCS, vol. 5749, pp. 68–83. Springer, Heidelberg (2009)

32. Walther, C.: A mechanical solution of Schubert's steamroller by many-sorted resolution. Artif. Intell. **26**(2), 217–224 (1985)

Monads

Towards a Formal Theory of Graded Monads

Soichiro Fujii[1], Shin-ya Katsumata[2(✉)], and Paul-André Melliès[3]

[1] Department of Computer Science, The University of Tokyo, Tokyo, Japan
[2] RIMS, Kyoto University, Kyoto, Japan
sinya@kurims.kyoto-u.ac.jp
[3] Laboratoire PPS, CNRS, Univ. Paris Diderot, Sorbonne Paris Cité, Paris, France

Abstract. We initiate a formal theory of graded monads whose purpose is to adapt and to extend the formal theory of monads developed by Street in the early 1970's. We establish in particular that every graded monad can be factored in two different ways as a strict action transported along a left adjoint functor. We also explain in what sense the first construction generalizes the Eilenberg-Moore construction while the second construction generalizes the Kleisli construction. Finally, we illustrate the Eilenberg-Moore construction on the graded state monad induced by any object V in a symmetric monoidal closed category $\mathscr{C}$.

1 Introduction

An important principle in categorical semantics is that *lax algebraic structures* are transported along left adjoint functors. This principle is a bit abstract and not so well known, so let us explain what it means. Suppose that we pick a 2-monad T on the 2-category Cat of categories and a category $\mathscr{B}$ equipped with a lax algebra structure of the 2-monad T, provided by the functor

$$*_{\mathscr{B}} \quad : \quad T\mathscr{B} \longrightarrow \mathscr{B}$$

Suppose moreover that the category $\mathscr{B}$ is related to a category $\mathscr{A}$ by adjunction where the functor $L : \mathscr{A} \to \mathscr{B}$ is left adjoint to the functor $R : \mathscr{B} \to \mathscr{A}$, in the following way:

$$\mathscr{A} \underset{R}{\overset{L}{\rightleftarrows}} \mathscr{B} \qquad \perp$$

In that case, the composite functor

$$*_{\mathscr{A}} \quad := \quad R \circ *_{\mathscr{B}} \circ TL \quad : \quad T\mathscr{A} \longrightarrow \mathscr{A}$$

provides a lax algebra structure on the category $\mathscr{A}$ inherited from the lax algebra structure of the category $\mathscr{B}$. This basic observation was inspired by homotopy theory and played a central rôle in the early development by Melliès of tensorial

© Springer-Verlag Berlin Heidelberg 2016
B. Jacobs and C. Löding (Eds.): FOSSACS 2016, LNCS 9634, pp. 513–530, 2016.
DOI: 10.1007/978-3-662-49630-5_30

logic [9,10,15]. A particularly important instance is the following one. Every monoidal category $(\mathcal{M}, \otimes, I)$ induces a 2-monad

$$T \;=\; \mathcal{A} \;\mapsto\; \mathcal{M} \times \mathcal{A} \;:\; Cat \longrightarrow Cat$$

on the category Cat. An algebra (in the strict sense) of the 2-monad T is a functor

$$* \;:\; \mathcal{M} \times \mathscr{C} \longrightarrow \mathscr{C} \tag{1}$$

which satisfies the equations:

$$m * (n * A) = (m \otimes n) * A \qquad A = I * A \tag{2}$$

for all objects m, n of the category $\mathcal{M}$ and every object A of the category $\mathscr{C}$. As such, a strict T-algebra is the same thing as an *action* of the monoidal category $(\mathcal{M}, \otimes, I)$ over the category $\mathscr{C}$. By way of comparison, a lax T-algebra structure on a category $\mathscr{C}$ is a functor (1) where the equalities (2) are replaced by a family of morphisms

$$\mu_{m,n,A} : m * (n * A) \to (m \otimes n) * A \qquad \eta_A : A \to I * A$$

natural in objects m, n of the category $\mathcal{M}$ and in the object A of the category $\mathscr{C}$, and making the three coherence diagrams commute for all objects m, n, p of the category $\mathcal{M}$ and all objects A of the category $\mathscr{C}$:

$$
\begin{array}{ccc}
m * (n * (p * A)) & \xrightarrow{\;m*\mu_{n,p}\;} & m * ((n \otimes p) * A) \\
{\scriptstyle \mu_{m,n}}\downarrow & & \downarrow{\scriptstyle \mu_{m,n\otimes p}} \\
(m \otimes n) * (p * A) & \xrightarrow[\;\mu_{m\otimes n,p}\;]{} & (m \otimes n \otimes p) * A
\end{array}
$$

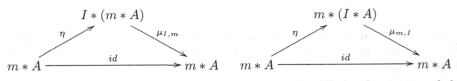

So, a lax T-algebra defines what is traditionally called a *lax action* of the monoidal category $\mathcal{M}$ on the category $\mathscr{C}$. Now, suppose that the category $\mathscr{B}$ is equipped with an action

$$\circledast \;:\; \mathcal{M} \times \mathscr{B} \longrightarrow \mathscr{B}.$$

In that case, the category $\mathscr{A}$ inherits a lax action

$$* \;:\; \mathcal{M} \times \mathscr{A} \longrightarrow \mathscr{A}$$

along the left adjoint functor L, defined as the composite

$$m * A \;:=\; R(m \circledast LA).$$

Since adjunctions $L \dashv R$ and actions $\circledast : \mathscr{M} \times \mathscr{B} \to \mathscr{B}$ are ubiquitous in programming language semantics, this inheritance property implies that the notion of *lax action* is just as central in the theory.

Note that in the particular case when the monoidal category $\mathscr{M}$ coincides with the terminal category 1, a lax action of $\mathscr{M}$ on a category $\mathscr{C}$ is the same thing as a monad S on the category $\mathscr{C}$, with (S, μ', η') defined as

$$SA := I * A \qquad \mu'_A := \mu_{I,I,A} : SSA \to SA \qquad \eta'_A := \eta_A : A \to SA$$

For that reason, Melliès found convenient to introduce the terminology of *parametric monad* in his work on tensorial logic [10,13]. One additional reason for choosing that terminology was that the dual notion of *parametric comonad* appeared at about the same time in his work with Grellois on higher-order model-checking [6]. The idea of developing a general theory of parametric monads for effect systems and of parametric comonads for resource systems emerged at this point and was announced in [12] as an algebraic counterpart to the works on implicit complexity [4] and on linear dependent types [5]. At about the same time, Petricek, Orchard and Mycroft designed the syntax and semantics of a calculus which can explicitly manage resource usage based on the structure of graded comonads [17]. The concept and terminology of *parametric monad* was then taken up and popularised by Katsumata [8] with a series of new applications to the semantics of effect systems. Milius, Pattinson and Schröder applied graded monads to extend the trace semantics of coalgebras with the concept of trace length [16].

The combination of these works raised a lot of interest in the community and established the notion of *parametric monad* as an important concept of the discipline. We thus feel useful and timely to join forces and to develop a formal theory of parametric monads inspired by the seminal work by Street [21] on formal monads in 2-categories. However, before doing that, we will explain in Sect. 2 why we decided to revise the original terminology and to call *graded monad* what we used to call *parametric monad*. As we will see, the change of terminology is justified mathematically, and the terminology seems to be convenient in itself[1].

Using the new terminology, one of the main contributions of the paper will be to establish that given a monoidal category $(\mathscr{M}, \otimes, I)$, every *graded monad*

$$* \; : \; \mathscr{M} \times \mathscr{A} \; \longrightarrow \; \mathscr{A}$$

is the graded monad

$$m * A \quad := \quad R(m \circledast LA) \tag{3}$$

---

[1] It should be noted that the notion of $\mathscr{M}$-graded monad is the same thing as a lax 2-functor $\Sigma \mathscr{M} \to \mathbf{Cat}$ from the bicategory $\Sigma \mathscr{M}$ with one object $*$ obtained by "suspending" the monoidal category $\mathscr{M}$, to the 2-category $\mathbf{Cat}$. For that reason, we consider that the notion of lax action and of graded monad (in its full generality) deserves to be traced back to the seminal work by Bénabou on bicategories [2].

associated to an adjunction

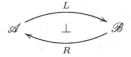

and to a *strict* action

$$\circledast \quad : \quad \mathcal{M} \times \mathcal{B} \quad \longrightarrow \quad \mathcal{B}.$$

of the monoidal category $(\mathcal{M}, \otimes, I)$ on the category $\mathcal{B}$. Following an original idea by Street [20], we will establish that the factorisation (3) can be performed in two different ways. One recovers in the particular case $\mathcal{M} = 1$ the factorisation of a monad $S = R \circ L$ as an adjunction $L \dashv R$ using either the category $\mathcal{B}$ of Eilenberg-Moore algebras, or the Kleisli category $\mathcal{B}$ associated to the monad S. As we will see in Sects. 3.1 and 3.2, the constructions of the Eilenberg-Moore category and of the Kleisli category are more involved in the case of a graded monad. In particular, in order to recover the expected universal characterizations of Eilenberg-Moore and Kleisli objects in the more general case of graded monads, the category $\mathcal{B}$ has to be considered as an object of the 2-category of $\mathcal{M}$-categories, where by $\mathcal{M}$-category, we mean a category $\mathcal{C}$ equipped with a strict action of $\mathcal{M}$.

Since the Eilenberg-Moore and Kleisli constructions are a bit formal, we find it instructive to illustrate them with a specific example. Besides the original example of the continuation monad treated in [15], an original motivation for the notion of graded monad emerged in the study of the local state monad [14,18]. As we will see in Sect. 3.1, an interesting aspect of the theory is that an Eilenberg-Moore algebra of a graded monad $* : \mathcal{M} \times \mathcal{A} \to \mathcal{A}$, which we call a *graded algebra*, is defined as a functor $A : \mathcal{M} \to \mathcal{A}$ equipped with a family of morphisms

$$h_{m,n} \quad : \quad m * A_n \to A_{m \otimes n}$$

natural in $m, n \in \mathcal{M}$ and making the diagrams below commute

$$
\begin{array}{ccc}
& I * A_m & \\
{}^{\mu_I}\nearrow & & \searrow^{h_{I,m}} \\
A_m \xrightarrow{\quad id \quad} & & A_m
\end{array}
\qquad
\begin{array}{ccc}
m * (n * A_p) & \xrightarrow{m * h_{n,p}} & m * A_{n \otimes p} \\
{}^{\mu_{m,n}}\downarrow & & \downarrow^{h_{m,n \otimes p}} \\
(m \otimes n) * A_p & \xrightarrow{h_{m \otimes n,p}} & A_{m \otimes n \otimes p}
\end{array}
$$

for all objects m, n, p of the monoidal category $(\mathcal{M}, \otimes, I)$. In particular, in the case $\mathcal{A} = Set$, the category $\mathcal{B}$ of Eilenberg-Moore algebras of the graded monad $*$ can be seen as a category of covariant presheaves over $\mathcal{M}$ with an extra structure provided by the family of morphisms $h_{m,n}$.

We will illustrate the construction with an example: suppose given a symmetric monoidal closed category $(\mathcal{C}, \otimes, \multimap, I)$ equipped with an object V, where V stands for *values*. The category $\mathcal{C}$ is then equipped with a parametric monad

$$* \quad : \quad Inj \times \mathcal{C} \quad \longrightarrow \quad \mathcal{C}$$

where $(Inj, +, 0)$ denotes the monoidal category with natural numbers

$$[m] \quad = \quad \{0, \ldots, m - 1\}$$

seen as finite sets as objects, and injections $f : [m] \to [n]$ as morphisms. We will often write m for the object $[m]$. The lax action of the monoidal category $(Inj, +, 0)$ over the category $\mathscr{C}$ is defined as

$$n * A \quad := \quad V^{\otimes n} \multimap (V^{\otimes n} \otimes A)$$

where we write $V^{\otimes n}$ for the object V to the tensorial power n:

$$V^{\otimes n} \quad := \quad V \otimes \cdots \otimes V.$$

We show that, in the particular case when $\mathscr{C} = Set$, the category $\mathscr{B}$ of algebras of the graded monad $* : Inj \times Set \to Set$ coincides with the category of S-algebras for a monad S on the presheaf category $[Inj, Set]$. The monad S is moreover described by a Lawvere theory with arities $\mathscr{L}$ in the sense of [14] which is presented by generators and relations in the Appendix.

We believe that these constructions are interesting in themselves. They also contribute to the general theory of graded monads, and more generally, of parametric notions of effects and resources.

Plan of the Paper. We start by explaining in Sect. 2 why it makes sense to call graded monads what we used to call parametric monads. Then, we describe in Sect. 3 the Eilenberg-Moore construction (see Sect. 3.1) and the Kleisli construction (see Sect. 3.2) for graded monads. After that, in Sect. 4 we provide a 2-categorical perspective on our construction, by proving that we indeed defined the Eilenberg-Moore and Kleisli objects in the sense of Street. We illustrate the construction by applying it in Sect. 5 to the Inj-graded state monad $\mathbf{S}$ on the category Set. In particular, we present by generators and relations the Lawvere theory characterizing the graded $\mathbf{S}$-algebras of the graded state monad $\mathbf{S}$ as covariant presheaves over Inj with an extra structure.

2   Parametric Monads Are Graded Monads

Quite obviously, the terminology "graded" comes from the ring-theoretic concept of "graded ring". Let $(R, +, 0, \times, 1)$ be a ring and $\mathbf{N}$ be the additive monoid on natural numbers. An $\mathbf{N}$-*grading* on R is an $\mathbf{N}$-indexed family $(A_m)_{m \in \mathbf{N}}$ of abelian groups such that $R = \bigoplus_{m \in \mathbf{N}} A_m$ and such that the following holds for all $m, n \in \mathbf{N}$:

$$\{x \times y \mid x \in A_m, y \in A_n\} \subseteq A_{m+n}. \tag{4}$$

From these conditions, it follows that $1 \in A_0$ and A_0 is a subring of R. An $\mathbf{N}$-*graded ring* is a pair of a ring R and an $\mathbf{N}$-grading $(A_m)_{m \in \mathbf{N}}$ on it.

An $\mathbf{N}$-grading $(A_m)_{m \in \mathbf{N}}$ on R, which is the primary data of the $\mathbf{N}$-graded ring, depicts a monoid-like structure in $\mathbf{Ab}$. It consists of (1) multiple carrier objects A_m given for each grade $m \in \mathbf{N}$, (2) a unit group homomorphism $r_0 :$ $\mathbf{Z} \to A_0$ at grade 0, which corresponds to $1 \in A_0$, and (3) a family of grade-respecting multiplications $r_{m,n} : A_m \otimes A_n \to A_{m+n}$, which are restrictions of the multiplication $(\times) : R \otimes R \to R$ by the condition (4). These morphisms satisfy the usual unit and associativity laws. We thus call such a structure an $\mathbf{N}$-*graded monoid* in $\mathbf{Ab}$ [19], and identify it with a lax monoidal functor of type $(\mathbf{N}, +, 0) \to (\mathbf{Ab}, \otimes, \mathbf{Z})$, because both structures carry exactly the same data. More generally, for $\mathscr{M}$ a monoidal category, we define an $\mathscr{M}$-*graded monoid* in a monoidal category $\mathscr{C}$ to be a lax monoidal functor of type $\mathscr{M} \to \mathscr{C}$. Of course, ordinary monoids coincide with 1-graded monoids.

A $\mathscr{M}$-*graded monad on* $\mathscr{A}$ may be then defined as an $\mathscr{M}$-graded monoid in the strict monoidal category $([\mathscr{A}, \mathscr{A}], \circ, Id)$ of endofunctors on $\mathscr{A}$, in the style of [19, Sect. 1.1]. An easy calculation shows that $\mathscr{M}$-graded monads on $\mathscr{A}$ bijectively correspond to lax $\mathscr{M}$-actions on $\mathscr{A}$ in the previous section, and to $\mathscr{M}$-parametric monads on $\mathscr{A}$ as they are called in [8,10,13]. Following this correspondence, in the rest of the paper we use the terminology "graded monad" instead of "parametric monad". The main reason for this change is that it makes it easy to relate categorical concepts around graded monads and algebraic concepts around graded rings. For instance, one easily sees that the concept of *graded algebra* of a graded monad, introduced in the previous section, is a categorical analogue of the concept of *graded module* over a graded ring.

3   Adjunction Pairs Induced from Graded Monads

Throughout this section we fix a monoidal category $(\mathscr{M}, \otimes, I)$, which we will consider strict for convenience, together with an $\mathscr{M}$-graded monad $\mathbf{T} = (*, \mu, \eta)$ on a given category $\mathscr{A}$. We have explained in the introduction that every adjunction $L \dashv R : \mathscr{B} \to \mathscr{A}$ combined with a strict $\mathscr{M}$-action $\circledast$ on the category $\mathscr{B}$ induces an $\mathscr{M}$-graded monad $m * a = R(m \circledast La)$ on the category $\mathscr{A}$. Especially, when $\mathscr{M} = 1$, this reduces to the well-known fact that the adjunction $L \dashv R$ induces a monad $R \circ L$. Conversely, a natural question is whether one can derive *any* $\mathscr{M}$-graded monad $\mathbf{T} = (*, \mu, \eta)$ on a category $\mathscr{A}$ as the result of "deforming" a strict $\mathscr{M}$-action $\circledast$ on a category $\mathscr{B}$ along a suitable adjunction $L \dashv R$ with $L : \mathscr{A} \to \mathscr{B}$. Just as in the case of monads, we provide two answers, each of them corresponding to a different construction of the category $\mathscr{B}$ as the category $\mathscr{A}^{\mathbf{T}}$ of Eilenberg-Moore algebras, or as the Kleisli category $\mathscr{A}_{\mathbf{T}}$ associated to the graded monad $\mathbf{T}$. The constructions require that the category $\mathscr{M}$ is small, and we thus make this hypothesis from now on. A pair of very similar constructions have been studied by Street in a nice but not sufficiently known paper [20] where two ordinary functors $\hat{F}, \tilde{F} : \mathscr{M} \to Cat$ are associated to a given *lax functor* $F : \mathscr{M} \to Cat$ starting from a category $\mathscr{M}$. As we will see, the two constructions adapt Street's original constructions and mildly extend it to allow $\mathscr{M}$ to be any monoidal category (seen as a one-object 2-category).

3.1   The Eilenberg-Moore Construction

Given an $\mathcal{M}$-graded monad $\mathbf{T} = (*, \mu, \eta)$ over a category $\mathcal{A}$, the category $\mathcal{A}^{\mathbf{T}}$ of its Eilenberg-Moore algebras is defined in the following way.

Definition 1 (graded T-algebras). *A graded $\mathbf{T}$-algebra is a pair (A, h) that consists of a functor $A : \mathcal{M} \to \mathcal{A}$ and of a family h of morphisms*

$$h_{m,n} : m * A_n \to A_{m \otimes n}$$

natural in m, n and making the diagrams below commute for all objects m, n, p of $\mathcal{M}$:

$$
\begin{array}{ccc}
& I * A_m & \\
\eta \nearrow & & \searrow h_{I,m} \\
A_m \xrightarrow{\quad id \quad} & & A_m
\end{array}
\qquad
\begin{array}{ccc}
m * (n * A_p) & \xrightarrow{m * h_{n,p}} & m * A_{n \otimes p} \\
\mu_{m,n} \downarrow & & \downarrow h_{m, n \otimes p} \\
(m \otimes n) * A_p & \xrightarrow{h_{m \otimes n, p}} & A_{m \otimes n \otimes p}
\end{array}
\qquad (5)
$$

Definition 2 (homomorphisms). *Given two graded $\mathbf{T}$-algebras (A, h) and (A', h'), a homomorphism*

$$\varphi \;\; : \;\; (A, h) \;\; \longrightarrow \;\; (A', h')$$

is defined as a natural transformation $\varphi : A \Rightarrow A'$ making the diagram below commute for all objects m, n of $\mathcal{M}$:

$$
\begin{array}{ccc}
m * A_n & \xrightarrow{m * \varphi_n} & m * A'_n \\
h_{m,n} \downarrow & \cdot & \downarrow h'_{m,n} \\
A_{m \otimes n} & \xrightarrow{\varphi_{m \otimes n}} & A'_{m \otimes n}
\end{array}
\qquad (6)
$$

Definition 3 (Eilenberg-Moore construction). *The category $\mathcal{A}^{\mathbf{T}}$ has graded $\mathbf{T}$-algebras as objects and homomorphisms between them as morphisms.*

One important observation is that the category $\mathcal{A}^{\mathbf{T}}$ admits the following strict $\mathcal{M}$-action.

Definition 4 (strict action). *The strict $\mathcal{M}$-action*

$$\circledast \;\; : \;\; \mathcal{M} \times \mathcal{A}^{\mathbf{T}} \;\; \longrightarrow \;\; \mathcal{A}^{\mathbf{T}}$$

of an object $p \in \mathcal{M}$ is defined as follows: it transports a graded $\mathbf{T}$-algebra (A, h) to the graded $\mathbf{T}$-algebra defined by right translation:

$$p \circledast (A, h) \;\; := \;\; \left((A_{m \otimes p})_{m \in \mathcal{M}}, (h_{m, n \otimes p})_{m, n \in \mathcal{M}} \right)$$

and it transports a homomorphism $\varphi : (A, h) \to (A', h')$ into the homomorphism

$$p \circledast \varphi \;\; : \;\; p \circledast (A, h) \;\; \longrightarrow \;\; p \circledast (A', h')$$

defined by the natural transformation:

$$(p \circledast \varphi)_n \;\; := \;\; \varphi_{n \otimes p} \;\; : \;\; A_{n \otimes p} \to A'_{n \otimes p}$$

It is worth observing that the definition of the action of p and of q on a graded $\mathbf{T}$-algebra (A, h) ensures that the equality below (expected by the definition of an $\mathcal{M}$-action) is satisfied:

$$p \circledast (q \circledast (A, h)) \quad = \quad (p \otimes q) \circledast (A, h)$$

for all objects p, q of the monoidal category $\mathcal{M}$.

Theorem 5. *The functor* $u^{\mathbf{T}} : \mathscr{A}^{\mathbf{T}} \to \mathscr{A}$ *defined by* $(A, h) \mapsto A_I$ *has a left adjoint* $f^{\mathbf{T}}$ *such that the graded monad* $\mathbf{T} = (*, \mu, \eta)$ *coincides with the graded monad*

$$(m, a) \quad \mapsto \quad u^{\mathbf{T}}(m \circledast (f^{\mathbf{T}}(a))) \quad : \quad \mathscr{M} \times \mathscr{A} \quad \longrightarrow \quad \mathscr{A}$$

derived from the adjunction $f^{\mathbf{T}} \dashv u^{\mathbf{T}}$ *and from the* $\mathscr{M}$-action $\circledast$ *on* $\mathscr{A}^{\mathbf{T}}$.

The functor $f^{\mathbf{T}}$ is constructed in the following way: to any object a of the category $\mathscr{A}$, it associates the graded $\mathbf{T}$-algebra $f^{\mathbf{T}}(a)$ defined by the functor

$$f^{\mathbf{T}}(a) \quad := \quad m \quad \mapsto \quad m * a \quad : \quad \mathscr{M} \quad \longrightarrow \quad \mathscr{A}$$

together with the family of morphisms

$$h_{m,n} \quad := \quad \mu_{m,n,a} \quad : \quad m * (n * a) \quad \longrightarrow \quad (m \otimes n) * a.$$

3.2   The Kleisli Construction

Given an $\mathcal{M}$-graded monad $\mathbf{T} = (*, \mu, \eta)$ over a category $\mathscr{A}$, the Kleisli category $\mathscr{A}_{\mathbf{T}}$ is defined in the following way.

Definition 6 (Kleisli construction). *The category* $\mathscr{A}_{\mathbf{T}}$ *has objects the pairs* (m, a) *where* m *is an object of* $\mathcal{M}$ *and* a *is an object of* $\mathscr{A}$, *and each hom-set is defined by the coend formula*

$$\mathscr{A}_{\mathbf{T}}((m, a), (m', a')) \quad := \quad \int^{n \in \mathcal{M}} \mathscr{A}(a, n * a') \times \mathscr{M}(m \otimes n, m').$$

In other words, a morphism is an equivalence class of triples of the form

$$[\, n, a \xrightarrow{f} n * a', m \otimes n \xrightarrow{w} m' \,]$$

modulo the equivalence relation defined by the coend formula. The identity morphism on (m, a) *is defined as*

$$[\, I, a \xrightarrow{\eta} I * a, m \otimes I \xrightarrow{\mathrm{id}} m \,]$$

and the composition of morphisms is defined as

$$[\, n', a' \xrightarrow{f'} n' * a'', m' \otimes n' \xrightarrow{w'} m'' \,] \circ n, a \xrightarrow{f} n * a', m \otimes n \xrightarrow{w} m' \,]$$

$$:= \quad [\, n \otimes n', a \xrightarrow{f} n * a' \xrightarrow{n*f'} n * n' * a'' \xrightarrow{\mu_{n,n'}} (n \otimes n') * a'',$$

$$m \otimes n \otimes n' \xrightarrow{w \otimes n'} m' \otimes n' \xrightarrow{w'} m'' \,].$$

Definition 7. *We define a strict $\mathcal{M}$-action $\circledast$ on $\mathscr{A}_\mathbf{T}$ by*

$$l \circledast (m, a) := (l \otimes m, a)$$
$$v \circledast [n, f, w] := [n, f, v \otimes w] \quad (v : l \to l', [n, f, w] : (m, a) \to (m', a'))$$

Theorem 8. *The functor $v_\mathbf{T} : \mathscr{A} \to \mathscr{A}_\mathbf{T}$ defined by $a \mapsto (I, a)$ has a right adjoint $g_\mathbf{T}$ such that the graded monad $\mathbf{T} = (*, \mu, \eta)$ coincides with the graded monad*

$$(m, a) \quad \mapsto \quad g_\mathbf{T}(m \circledast (v_\mathbf{T}(a))) \quad : \quad \mathcal{M} \times \mathscr{A} \quad \longrightarrow \quad \mathscr{A}$$

derived from the adjunction $v_\mathbf{T} \dashv g_\mathbf{T}$ and from the $\mathcal{M}$-action $\circledast$ on $\mathscr{A}_\mathbf{T}$.

The right adjoint functor $g_\mathbf{T} : \mathscr{A}_\mathbf{T} \to \mathscr{A}$ is defined as $g_\mathbf{T}(m, a) := m * a$ on objects and

$$g_\mathbf{T}([n, a \xrightarrow{f} n * a', m \otimes n \xrightarrow{w} m'])$$
$$:= \quad m * a \xrightarrow{m*f} m * n * a' \xrightarrow{\mu_{m,n}} (m \otimes n) * a' \xrightarrow{w*a'} n' * a'$$

on morphisms $[n, a \xrightarrow{f} n * a', m \otimes n \xrightarrow{w} m'] : (m, a) \to (m', a')$.

3.3   Resolutions of Graded Monads

What are special about the Eilenberg-Moore and Kleisli resolutions of a graded monad? To answer this question, we introduce a suitable category consisting of resolutions of a graded monad, and show that Eilenberg-Moore and Kleisli resolutions are *terminal* and *initial* objects in this category. This is an extension of the theory of resolutions of monads to graded monads.

The key ingredient of a resolution of an $\mathcal{M}$-graded monad is a category with strict $\mathcal{M}$-actions. For the categorical treatment of such categories, we introduce the 2-category $\mathcal{M}$-Cat of categories with strict $\mathcal{M}$-actions. It is the Eilenberg-Moore 2-category of the 2-monad $\mathcal{M} \times (-)$ on Cat. We associate to it the 2-adjunction $F^{\mathcal{M}} \dashv U^{\mathcal{M}} : \mathcal{M}$-$Cat \to Cat$ that behaves as follows on 0-cells:

$$F^{\mathcal{M}}(\mathscr{A}) := (\mathcal{M} \times \mathscr{A}, (\otimes) \times \mathscr{A} : \mathcal{M} \times \mathcal{M} \times \mathscr{A} \to \mathcal{M} \times \mathscr{A}), \quad U^{\mathcal{M}}(\mathscr{A}, \circledast) := \mathscr{A}.$$

Definition 9. *Let $\mathbf{T} = (*, \mu, \eta)$ be an $\mathcal{M}$-graded monad on $\mathscr{A}$.*

- *A resolution of $\mathbf{T}$ is a tuple of a 0-cell $(\mathscr{B}, \circledast)$ in $\mathcal{M}$-Cat and an adjunction $l \dashv r : \mathscr{B} \to \mathscr{A}$ in Cat such that $\mathbf{T}$ coincides with the graded monad $r(-\circledast(l-))$ derived from the adjunction $l \dashv r$ and the strict $\mathcal{M}$-action $\circledast$.*
- *Given two resolutions $((\mathscr{B}, \circledast), l \dashv r)$ and $((\mathscr{B}', \circledast'), l' \dashv r')$ of $\mathbf{T}$, a morphism from the former to the latter is a 1-cell $h : (\mathscr{B}, \circledast) \to (\mathscr{B}', \circledast')$ in $\mathcal{M}$-Cat such that $h \circ l = l'$ and $r = r' \circ h$ (here $U^{\mathcal{M}}$ is implicitly applied to h).*
- *We define the category $Res(\mathbf{T})$ of resolutions of $\mathbf{T}$ by the above data.*

4   Towards a Formal Theory of Graded Monads

We explain how Street's formal theory of monads can be adapted in order to characterize the two constructions of $\mathscr{A}^{\mathbf{T}}$ and of $\mathscr{A}_{\mathbf{T}}$ described in Sect. 3 as *universal constructions*. In his seminal paper [21], Street developed a general theory of monads relative to an arbitrary 2-category K, so that the usual theory of monads is regained by instantiating K by Cat, the 2-category of categories, functors, and natural transformations.

Definition 10. *A monad $\mathbf{T}$ in K is given by a 0-cell k, a 1-cell $T : k \to k$, and 2-cells $\mu : T \circ T \Rightarrow T$ of K and $\eta : \mathrm{id}_k \Rightarrow T$, satisfying the usual axioms $\mu \circ \eta T = \mathrm{id}_T = \mu \circ T\eta$ and $\mu \circ T\mu = \mu \circ \mu T$.*

Among his various abstract developments of the theory, the notions of *Eilenberg-Moore object* and *Kleisli object* for a monad in a 2-category will be the most important ones to our current work. We adopt the following definition, which appears for instance in [20]:

Definition 11. *The* Eilenberg-Moore object *of* $\mathbf{T}$ *is a 0-cell $k^{\mathbf{T}}$ such that there is a family of isomorphisms of categories*

$$K(x, k^{\mathbf{T}}) \quad \cong \quad K(x, k)^{K(x, \mathbf{T})}$$

2-natural in $x \in K$. Here the category on the right hand side is the (usual) Eilenberg-Moore category of the monad $K(x, \mathbf{T})$ on the category $K(x, k)$.

Definition 12. *The* Kleisli object *of* $\mathbf{T}$ *is a 0-cell $k_{\mathbf{T}}$ such that there is a family of isomorphisms of categories*

$$K(k_{\mathbf{T}}, x) \quad \cong \quad K(k, x)^{K(\mathbf{T}, x)}$$

2-natural in $x \in K$. Here the category on the right hand side is the (usual) Eilenberg-Moore category of the monad $K(\mathbf{T}, x)$ on the category $K(k, x)$.

Now a remarkable point is that from this simple and abstract definition, one can reconstruct a fair amount of the well-known properties of Eilenberg-Moore or Kleisli categories, including the existence of adjunctions which generate the monads, and the existence and uniqueness of comparison 1-cells. The interested reader should consult [21] for an ingenious 2-categorical manipulation achieving this reconstruction. In what follows, however, we choose to describe the adjunctions explicitly, for the sake of concreteness. As we did in Sect. 3, we suppose here that the category $\mathscr{M}$ is small, a necessary condition in order to perform the constructions of the Eilenberg-Moore and Kleisli objects.

4.1   A 2-Category for Eilenberg-Moore Objects

We introduce the 2-category E^{++} where the category $\mathscr{A}^{\mathbf{T}}$ of graded algebras (Definition 1) arises as an Eilenberg-Moore object in it. This 2-category is obtained by a suitable lax comma construction for the 3-category 2-Cat of 2-categories, 2-functors, 2-natural transformations and modifications. We denote the terminal 2-category by $\mathbf{1}$.

Definition 13. *We define the 2-category E^{++} by the following data.*

- *A 0-cell of E^{++} is a 2-functor $a : 1 \to A$ where A is a 2-category; equivalently, it is a pair (A, a) where a is a 0-cell of A.*
- *A 1-cell of E^{++} from (A, a) to (A', a') is a diagram in 2-Cat*

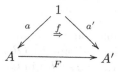

filled with a 2-natural transformation f; equivalently, it is a pair (F, f) where $f : Fa \to a'$ is a 1-cell of A'.

- *A 2-cell of E^{++} from (F, f) to (F', f') is a pair (Θ, α) where $\Theta : F \to F'$ is a 2-natural transformation and α is a modification of the following type:*

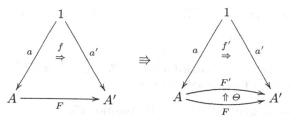

Equivalently, α is a 2-cell of A' of the following type:

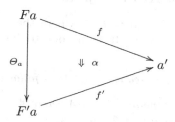

The first projection of the data defines a 2-functor $p^{++} : E^{++} \to 2\text{-}Cat_2$, where $2\text{-}Cat_2$ is the 2-category of 2-categories, 2-functors, and 2-natural transformations. We take a fibrational viewpoint [1,7] and say a notion X is *above I* if $p^{++}(X) = I$. A first key observation is the following:

Proposition 14. *Let $(\mathcal{M}, \otimes, I)$ be a strict monoidal category and $\mathscr{A}$ a category. Then, an $\mathcal{M}$-graded monad on $\mathscr{A}$ is the same thing as a monad in E^{++} on $(Cat, \mathscr{A})$, above the 2-monad $\mathcal{M} \times (-)$ on Cat.*

Thanks to this proposition, it makes sense to speculate on the Eilenberg-Moore objects (in the sense of Street) of graded monads in this 2-category E^{++}. Indeed, E^{++} turns out to admit Eilenberg-Moore objects of graded monads, and moreover the Eilenberg-Moore adjunction for an $\mathcal{M}$-graded monad lies above that for the 2-monad $\mathcal{M} \times (-)$.

Proposition 15. *The following is an adjunction in the 2-category E^{++}:*

$$(Cat, \mathscr{A}) \underset{(U^{\mathscr{M}}, u^{\mathbf{T}})}{\overset{(F^{\mathscr{M}}, -\circledast f^{\mathbf{T}}-)}{\rightleftarrows}} \perp \quad (\mathscr{M}\text{-}Cat, (\mathscr{A}^{\mathbf{T}}, \circledast))$$

Proof. In general, for an adjunction $L \dashv R$ in 2-Cat_2 and a morphism (R, r) : $(D, d) \to (C, c)$ in E^{++}, a left adjoint to (R, r) above L in E^{++} bijectively corresponds to a left adjoint to $r : c \to Rd$ in C. By letting (R, r) be $(U^{\mathscr{M}}, u^{\mathbf{T}})$, where $u^{\mathbf{T}}$ is a right adjoint, we obtain the above left adjoint, lying above $F^{\mathscr{M}}$.

A long, but straightforward calculation establishes the announced result:

Theorem 16. *There is a family of isomorphisms of categories*

$$E^{++}((X, x), (\mathscr{M}\text{-}Cat, \mathscr{A}^{\mathbf{T}})) \;\cong\; E^{++}((X, x), (Cat, \mathscr{A}))^{E^{++}((X,x),\mathbf{T})}$$

2-natural in $(X, x) \in E^{++}$.

Corollary 17. *Let $\mathbf{T}$ be a graded monad. Then $((\mathscr{A}^{\mathbf{T}}, \circledast), f^{\mathbf{T}} \dashv u^{\mathbf{T}})$ is terminal in the category $Res(\mathbf{T})$ of resolutions of $\mathbf{T}$.*

Proof. The idea is similar to that of Proposition 15.

4.2 A 2-Category for Kleisli Objects

We next introduce the 2-category E^{--} where the category $\mathscr{A}_{\mathbf{T}}$ (Definition 6) arises as a Kleisli object in it. It turns out to be a certain dual of the 2-category E^{++}:

Definition 18. *Define the 2-category E^{--} as follows.*

- *A 0-cell of E^{--} is a 2-functor $a : 1 \to A$ where A is a 2-category; equivalently, it is a pair (A, a) where a is a 0-cell of A.*
- *A 1-cell of E^{--} from (A, a) to (A', a') is a diagram in 2-Cat*

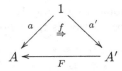

filled with a 2-natural transformation f; equivalently, it is a pair (F, f) where $f : a \to Fa'$ is a 1-cell of A.
- *A 2-cell of E^{--} from (F, f) to (F', f') is a pair (Θ, α) where $\Theta : F' \to F$ is a 2-natural transformation and α is a modification of the following type:*

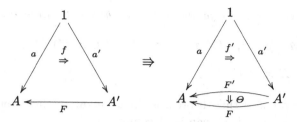

Equivalently, α *is a 2-cell of A of the following type:*

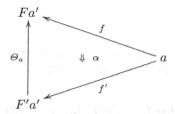

Again the first projection of the data defines a 2-functor $p^{--} : E^{--} \to$ $2\text{-}Cat_2^{op(1,2)}$, where $2\text{-}Cat_2^{op(1,2)}$ is the 2-category obtained by reversing both 1-cells and 2-cells of $2\text{-}Cat_2$.

Proposition 19. *Let* $(\mathscr{M}, \otimes, I)$ *be a strict monoidal category and* $\mathscr{A}$ *a category. Then, an* $\mathscr{M}$-*graded monad on* $\mathscr{A}$ *is the same thing as a monad in* E^{--} *on* $(Cat, \mathscr{A})$, *above the 2-comonad* $[\mathscr{M}, -]$ *on* Cat.

The 2-category E^{--} admits Kleisli objects of graded monads, and the Kleisli adjunction for an $\mathscr{M}$-graded monad lies above the *co-Eilenberg-Moore adjunction* for the 2-comonad $[\mathscr{M}, -]$. Observe that the 2-comonad $[\mathscr{M}, -]$, being right adjoint to the 2-monad $\mathscr{M} \times (-)$, has as its co-Eilenberg-Moore 2-category again the 2-category $\mathscr{M}\text{-}Cat$. Let us denote $V_{\mathscr{M}} \dashv G_{\mathscr{M}}$ for the associated 2-adjunction. Their behaviour on 0-cells are given as follows:

$$G_{\mathscr{M}}(\mathscr{C}) := ([\mathscr{M}, \mathscr{C}], \otimes^{\wedge} : \mathscr{M} \times [\mathscr{M}, \mathscr{C}] \to [\mathscr{M}, \mathscr{C}]), \quad V_{\mathscr{M}}(\mathscr{C}, \circledast) := \mathscr{C},$$

where $\otimes^{\wedge}(m, C) = C(- \otimes m)$.

Proposition 20. *The following is an adjunction in the 2-category* E^{--}:

$$(Cat, \mathscr{A}) \underset{(G_{\mathscr{M}}, g_{\mathbf{T}}(-\circledast -))}{\overset{(V_{\mathscr{M}}, v_{\mathbf{T}})}{\rightleftarrows}} \bot \quad (\mathscr{M}\text{-}Cat, (\mathscr{A}_{\mathbf{T}}, \circledast))$$

Proof. We give a proof similar to Proposition 15. This time we use the following fact: for an adjunction $L \dashv R$ in $2\text{-}Cat_2$ and a 1-cell $(L, l) : (C, c) \to (D, d)$ in E^{--}, a right adjoint to (L, l) above R in E^{--} bijectively corresponds to a right adjoint to $l : c \to Ld$ in C.

Theorem 21. *There is a family of isomorphisms of categories*

$$E^{--}((\mathscr{M}\text{-}Cat, \mathscr{A}_{\mathbf{T}}), (X, x)) \;\cong\; E^{--}((Cat, \mathscr{A}), (X, x))^{E^{--}(\mathbf{T}, (X, x))}$$

2-natural in $(X, x) \in E^{--}$.

A key to the proof of this theorem is the observation that every 1-cell $[n, a \xrightarrow{f} n * a', m \otimes n \xrightarrow{w} m']$ of $\mathscr{A}_{\mathbf{T}}$ can be decomposed as

$$[n, a \xrightarrow{f} n * a', m \otimes n \xrightarrow{w} m']$$
$$= \; (w \circledast v_{\mathbf{T}}(a')) \circ (m \circledast [n, n * a' \xrightarrow{\mathrm{id}} n * a', I \otimes n \xrightarrow{\mathrm{id}} n]) \circ (m \circledast v_{\mathbf{T}}(f)).$$

Corollary 22. *Let* $\mathbf{T}$ *be an* $\mathscr{M}$*-graded monad. Then* $((\mathscr{A}_{\mathbf{T}}, \circledast), v_{\mathbf{T}} \dashv g_{\mathbf{T}})$ *is initial in the category* $Res(\mathbf{T})$ *of resolutions of* $\mathbf{T}$.

5   Illustration: The Graded State Monad

Suppose given an object V in a symmetric monoidal closed category $\mathscr{C}$. We start by describing the graded state monad

$$\mathbf{S} = (*, \mu, \eta) \quad : \quad Inj \times \mathscr{C} \;\longrightarrow\; \mathscr{C}$$

mentioned at the end of the introduction, and defined as

$$n * A \quad := \quad V^{\otimes n} \multimap (V^{\otimes n} \otimes A).$$

One simple way to define the graded monad $\mathbf{S}$ is to start from the observation that the formula $A \mapsto n * A$ defines an Inj-indexed monad, defined as a functor

$$* \quad : Inj \;\longrightarrow\; \mathbf{Mnd}(\mathscr{C})$$

from the category Inj to the category $\mathbf{Mnd}(\mathscr{C})$ of monads over the category $\mathscr{C}$, and monad homomorphisms between them. We write

$$\mu_{m,A} \; : \; m * (m * A) \;\longrightarrow\; m * A \qquad \eta_{m,A} \; : \; A \;\longrightarrow\; m * A$$

for the multiplication and unit of the monad $A \mapsto m * A$. The multiplication $\mu_{m,n,A}$ of the graded state monad $\mathbf{S}$ may be then defined as the composite

$$m * (n * A) \xrightarrow{\;\mathrm{inl}*(\mathrm{inr}*A)\;} (m + n) * ((m + n) * A) \xrightarrow{\;\mu_{m+n,A}\;} (m + n) * A$$

where the lefthand side morphism is defined by the injection morphisms $\mathbf{inl}$: $m \to m + n$ and $\mathbf{inr}$: $n \to m + n$ and where $\mu_{m+n,A}$ is the multiplication of the monad $A \mapsto (m + n) * A$. Similarly, the unit $\eta_A : A \to 0 * A$ of the graded monad $\mathbf{S}$ is defined as $\eta_{0,A}$ which is an isomorphism. This defines the graded monad $\mathbf{S} = (*, \mu, \eta)$. More generally, one observes that every $\mathscr{M}$-indexed monad induces an $\mathscr{M}$-graded monad in this way, when the unit I of the monoidal category $(\mathscr{M}, \otimes, I)$ is initial, as in the case of the category Inj.

We find instructive to explicate the notion of graded $\mathbf{S}$-algebra introduced in Sect. 3.1 in the particular case when $\mathscr{C} = Set$ and where V is a finite set. As in the case of any such cartesian closed category $\mathscr{C}$, the action can be rewritten as

$$n * A \;\; = \;\; (V^n \Rightarrow V^n) \times (V^n \Rightarrow A).$$

Now, a graded $\mathbf{S}$-algebra (A, h) is given by a functor $A : Inj \to Set$, together with a family h of functions

$$h_{m,n} \;\; : \;\; (V^m \Rightarrow V^m) \times (V^m \Rightarrow A_n) \;\; \longrightarrow \;\; A_{m+n}$$

subject to the axioms (5) of graded algebras. Since

$$(V^m \Rightarrow V^m) \times (V^m \Rightarrow A_n) \;\; = \;\; \coprod_{f \in (V^m \Rightarrow V^m)} (V^m \Rightarrow A_n),$$

one can see the family h as a family of operations

$$\langle f, n \rangle \;\; : \;\; V^m \Rightarrow A_n \;\; \longrightarrow \;\; A_{m+n}.$$

indexed by the functions $f : V^m \to V^m$ and the natural numbers n. Note that each such operation $\langle f, n \rangle$ transports V^m elements of grade n into an element of grade $m + n$. As such, a graded $\mathbf{S}$-algebra (A, h) can be seen in terms of multisorted universal algebra as a family $(A_m)_{m \in \mathbf{N}}$ of sets with sorts provided by natural numbers $m \in \mathbb{N}$. Following [3,11,14], the algebraic theory can be presented by extending with the operations $\langle f, n \rangle$ the trivial Lawvere theory with arities

$$\Sigma(Inj)^{op} \longrightarrow [Inj, Set]$$

whose models are the covariant presheaves over $[Inj, Set]$ with the generators $\langle f, n \rangle$ together with a number of equations expressing that

– the family $h_{m,n} : m * A_n \to A_{m \otimes n}$ is natural in m and n,
– h satisfies the Eq. (5) of a graded $\mathbf{S}$-algebra.

The equations are given in the Appendix. The resulting algebraic presentation of graded $\mathbf{S}$-algebras by operations and equations enables one to establish that

Theorem 23. *The canonical forgetful functor* $U : Set^{\mathbf{S}} \to [Inj, Set]$ *given by* $(A, h) \mapsto A$ *is monadic.*

One main reason for studying the Inj-graded monad $\mathbf{S}$ is that it induces in this way a monad on $[Inj, Set]$ with arities $\Theta : \Sigma Inj^{op} \to [Inj, Set]$ whose Lawvere theory $\mathfrak{L}(\mathbf{S})$ with arities Θ is a sub-theory of the Lawvere theory $\mathfrak{L}$ (with same arities) of the local state monad L presented by generators and relations in [14]. Interestingly, the resulting algebraic theory $\mathfrak{L}(\mathbf{S})$ captures only a restricted part of the original algebraic theory $\mathfrak{L}$ since the multiplication $\mu_{m,n,A}$ does not enable the graded algebra $(A_m)_{m \in Inj}$ to pass states from one layer of application $(m*-)$ of the graded state monad to the next layer $(n*-)$. This limitation should not be seen as a defect but rather as a feature of the graded state monad $\mathbf{S}$ since it enables us to delineate a natural fragment of the local state monad L.

Acknowledgments. The authors are grateful to the anonymous reviewer for suggesting an alternative and more elegant construction of the graded state monad. The authors are also grateful to Marco Gaboardi and to Dominic Orchard for a number of useful discussions about this work. The authors were supported by the JSPS-INRIA Bilateral Joint Research Project CRECOGI, the second author was supported by Grant-in-Aid No.15K00014 while the third author was partly supported by the ANR Project Recre.

Appendix: An Algebraic Presentation of Graded S-Algebras

Formulated in the language of multisorted universal algebra, a graded $\mathbf{S}$-algebra (A, h) is completely determined by a family $(A_m)_{m \in \mathbf{N}}$ of sets equipped with an operation $A_v : A_m \to A_n$ for each injection $v : m \to n$ and with an operation $\langle f, n \rangle : A_n^{V^m} \to A_{m+n}$ for each pair of natural numbers m, n and each function $f : V^m \to V^m$. These operations should moreover satisfy the equations below. First of all, the two *functoriality* equations below:

$$A_{\mathrm{id}_m} = \mathrm{id}_{A_m} \qquad\qquad A_{w \circ v} = A_w \circ A_v.$$

Then, the *naturality* equation, for all injections $v : m \to m'$ and $w : n \to n'$,

$$A_{v+w}(\langle f, n \rangle (a_i)_{i \in V^m}) = \langle v \bullet f, n' \rangle (A_w(a_{i' \circ v}))_{i' \in V^{m'}},$$

where the function $v \bullet f : V^{m'} \to V^{m'}$ is defined as

$$((v \bullet f)(val_{k'})_{k' \in m'})_{l'} = \begin{cases} \big(f(val_{v(k)})_{k \in m}\big)_l & \text{if } l' = v(l) \text{ for some } l \in m; \\ val_{l'} & \text{otherwise.} \end{cases}$$

Then, the *unit* equation

$$\langle \mathrm{id}_{V^0}, m \rangle = \mathrm{id}_{A_m},$$

for a function $f : V^m \to V^m$ and an injection $v : m \to m'$; and finally the *associativity* equation

$$\langle f \rangle_{n+p}(\langle g_i, p \rangle (a_{i,j})_{j \in V^n})_{i \in V^m} = \langle f \star (g_i)_{i \in V^m}, p \rangle (a_{i,j})_{i,j \in V^{m+n}},$$

where the function

$$f \star (g_i)_{i \in V^m} : \quad V^{m+n} \longrightarrow V^{m+n}$$

is defined as follows, for a function $f : V^m \to V^m$ and for a family of functions $(g_i : V^n \to V^n)_{i \in V^m}$:

$$\left((f \star (g_i)_{i \in V^m})(val_k, wal_{k'})_{k \in m, k' \in n}\right)_l = \begin{cases} \left(f(val_k)_{k \in m}\right)_l & \text{if } l \in m, \\ \left(g_{(val_k)_{k \in m}}(wal_{k'})_{k' \in n}\right)_l & \text{if } l \in n. \end{cases}$$

Homomorphisms of graded **S**-algebras are just families of maps $\varphi_m : A_m \to A'_m$ commuting with the operations introduced above.

References

1. Baković, I.: Fibrations of bicategories. Available on the ArXiV
2. Bénabou, J.: Introduction to bicategories. In: Reports of the Midwest Category Seminar. Lecture Notes in Mathematics, vol. 47, pp. 1–77. Springer, Heidelberg (1967)
3. Berger, C., Melliès, P.-A., Weber, M.: Monads with arities and their associated theories. J. Pure Appl. Algebra **216**, 2029–2048 (2012)
4. Dal Lago, U.: A short introduction to implicit computational complexity. In: Bezhanishvili, N., Goranko, V. (eds.) ESSLLI 2010 and ESSLLI 2011. LNCS, vol. 7388, pp. 89–109. Springer, Heidelberg (2012)
5. Dal Lago, U., Gaboardi, M.: Linear dependent types and relative completeness. Log. Meth. Comput. Sci. **8**(4), 12 (2012)
6. Grellois, C., Melliès, P.-A.: Relational semantics of linear logic, higher-order model checking. In: Proceedings of CSL 2015, pp. 260–276 (2015)
7. Hermida, C.: Descent on 2-fibrations and strongly 2-regular 2-categories. Appl. Categorical Struct. **12**(5–6), 427–459 (2004)
8. Katsumata, S.-y.: Parametric effect monads and semantics of effect systems. In: Proceedings of POPL 2014, pp. 633–645. ACM (2014)
9. Melliès, P.-A.: Towards an algebra of duality. Talk given during the workshop Linear Logic, Ludics, Implicit Complexity, Operator Algebras, dedicated to Jean-Yves Girard on the occasion of his 60th birthday, May 2007
10. Melliès, P.-A.: Game semantics in string diagrams. In: Proceedings of Logic In Computer Science, LICS, Dubrovnik (2012)
11. Melliès, P.-A.: Segal condition meets computational effects. LICS (2010)
12. Melliès, P.-A.: Sharing and duplication in tensorial logic. Invited talk at the 4th International workshop on Developments in Implicit Computational complexity (DICE), Rome, March 2013
13. Melliès, P.-A.: Parametric monads and enriched adjunctions. Syntax and Semantics of Low Level Languages, LOLA, Dubrovnik. Manuscript available on the author's webpage (2012)
14. Melliès, P.-A.: Local states in string diagrams. In: Dowek, G. (ed.) RTA-TLCA 2014. LNCS, vol. 8560, pp. 334–348. Springer, Heidelberg (2014)
15. Melliés, P.-A.: The parametric continuation monad. Festschrift in honor of Corrado Böhm for his 90th birthday. Mathematical Structures in Computer Science (2016)
16. Milius, S., Pattinson, D., Schröder, L.: Generic trace semantics and graded monads. Calco (2015)
17. Petricek, T., Orchard, D., Mycroft, A.: Coeffects: unified static analysis of context-dependence. In: Fomin, F.V., Freivalds, R., Kwiatkowska, M., Peleg, D. (eds.) ICALP 2013, Part II. LNCS, vol. 7966, pp. 385–397. Springer, Heidelberg (2013)

18. Plotkin, G., Power, J.: Computational effects determine monads. In: Proceedings of FoSSaCS, Grenoble (2002)
19. Smirnov, A.: Graded monads and rings of polynomials. J. Math. Sci. **151**(3), 3032–3051 (2008)
20. Street, R.: Two constructions on lax functors. Cahiers de topologie et géométrie différentielle **13**, 217–264 (1972)
21. Street, R.: The formal theory of monads. J. Pure Appl. Algebra **2**(2), 149–168 (1972)

Profinite Monads, Profinite Equations, and Reiterman's Theorem

Liang-Ting Chen[1]([✉]), Jiří Adámek[1], Stefan Milius[2], and Henning Urbat[1]

[1] Institut für Theoretische Informatik,
Technische Universität Braunschweig, Braunschweig, Germany
l.chen@iti.cs.tu-bs.de
[2] Lehrstuhl für Theoretische Informatik,
Friedrich-Alexander Universität Erlangen-Nürnberg, Erlangen, Germany

Abstract. Profinite equations are an indispensable tool for the algebraic classification of formal languages. Reiterman's theorem states that they precisely specify pseudovarieties, i.e. classes of finite algebras closed under finite products, subalgebras and quotients. In this paper Reiterman's theorem is generalised to finite Eilenberg-Moore algebras for a monad $\mathbf{T}$ on a variety $\mathscr{D}$ of (ordered) algebras: a class of finite $\mathbf{T}$-algebras is a pseudovariety iff it is presentable by profinite (in-)equations. As an application, quasivarieties of finite algebras are shown to be presentable by profinite implications. Other examples include finite ordered algebras, finite categories, finite ∞-monoids, etc.

1 Introduction

Algebraic automata theory investigates the relationship between the behaviour of finite machines and descriptions of these behaviours in terms of finite algebraic structures. For example, regular languages of finite words are precisely the languages recognised by finite monoids. And Schützenberger's theorem [26] shows that star-free regular languages correspond to aperiodic finite monoids, which easily leads to the decidability of star-freeness. A generic correspondence result of this kind is Eilenberg's variety theorem [11]. It gives a bijective correspondence between *varieties of languages* (classes of regular languages closed under boolean operations, derivatives and homomorphic preimages) and *pseudovarieties of monoids* (classes of finite monoids closed under finite products, submonoids and quotients). Another, more syntactic, characterisation of pseudovarieties follows from Reiterman's theorem [23] (see also Banaschewski [6]): they are precisely the classes of finite monoids specified by *profinite equations*.

In the meantime Eilenberg-type correspondences have been discovered for other kinds of algebraic structures, including ordered monoids [19], idempotent

Liang-Ting Chen acknowledges gratefully partial support from AFOSR.
Stefan Milius acknowledges support by the Deutsche Forschungsgemeinschaft (DFG) under project MI 717/5-1.
Jiří Adámek and Henning Urbat acknowledge support by the Deutsche Forschungsgemeinschaft (DFG) under project AD 187/2-1.

© Springer-Verlag Berlin Heidelberg 2016
B. Jacobs and C. Löding (Eds.): FOSSACS 2016, LNCS 9634, pp. 531–547, 2016.
DOI: 10.1007/978-3-662-49630-5_31

semirings [21], associative algebras over a field [24] and Wilke algebras [27], always with rather similar proofs. This has spurred recent interest in generic approaches to algebraic language theory that can produce such correspondences as instances of a single result. Bojańczyk [9] extends the classical notion of language recognition by monoids (viewed as algebraic structures over the category of sets) to algebras for an arbitrary monad on many-sorted sets. He also presents an Eilenberg-type theorem at this level of generality, interpreting a result of Almeida [5] in categorical terms. Our previous work in [1–3,10] takes an orthogonal approach: one keeps monoids but considers them in categories $\mathscr{D}$ of (ordered) algebras such as posets, semilattices and vector spaces. Analysing the latter work it becomes clear that the step from sets to more general categories $\mathscr{D}$ is necessary to obtain the right notion of language recognition by finite monoids; e.g. to cover Polák's Eilenberg-type theorem for idempotent semirings [21], one needs to take the base category $\mathscr{D}$ of semilattices. On the other hand, from Bojańczyk's work it is clear that one also has to generalise from monoids to other algebraic structures if one wants to capture such examples as Wilke algebras.

The present paper is the first step in a line of work that considers a common roof for both approaches, working with algebras for a monad $\mathbf{T}$ on an arbitrary variety $\mathscr{D}$ of many-sorted, possibly ordered algebras.

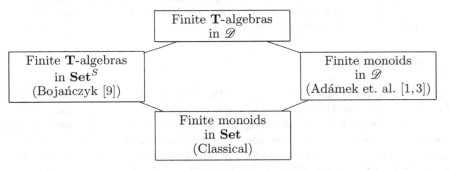

Our main contribution is a generalisation of Reiterman's theorem, stating that pseudovarieties of finite algebras are presentable by profinite equations, to the more general situation of algebras for a monad. Starting with a variety $\mathscr{D}$, we form the pro-completion of the full subcategory $\mathscr{D}_f$ of finite algebras,

$$\widehat{\mathscr{D}} := \mathrm{Pro}\text{-}\mathscr{D}_f .$$

For example, for $\mathscr{D} =$ sets, posets and monoids we get $\widehat{\mathscr{D}} =$ Stone spaces, Priestley spaces and profinite monoids. Next, we consider a monad $\mathbf{T}$ on $\mathscr{D}$ and associate to it a monad $\widehat{\mathbf{T}}$ on $\widehat{\mathscr{D}}$, called the *profinite monad* of $\mathbf{T}$. For example, if $\mathscr{D} = \mathbf{Set}$ and $\mathbf{T}$ is the finite word monad (whose algebras are precisely monoids), then $\widehat{\mathbf{T}}$ is the monad of profinite monoids on the category of Stone spaces; that is, $\widehat{\mathbf{T}}$ associates to each finite Stone space (= finite set) X the space X^* of profinite words on X. Similarly, for the monad $\mathbf{T}$ of finite and infinite words on $\mathbf{Set}$

(whose algebras we call ∞-*monoids*) the profinite monad $\widehat{\mathbf{T}}$ constructs the space of *profinite ∞-words*.

The classical profinite equations for monoids, used for presenting pseudovarieties of monoids, are generalised to *profinite equations* $u = v$ that are pairs of elements of $\widehat{\mathbf{T}}\hat{\varPhi}_X$, where $\hat{\varPhi}_X$ is the free profinite $\mathscr{D}$-algebra on a finite set X of variables. Our main result is that profinite equations present precisely classes of finite $\mathbf{T}$-algebras closed under finite products, subalgebras, and quotients.

We will additionally study a somewhat unusual concept of profinite equation where in lieu of finite *sets* X of variables we use finite *algebras* $X \in \mathscr{D}_f$ of variables. The classes of finite $\mathbf{T}$-algebras presented by such profinite equations are then precisely those closed under finite products, subalgebras, and split quotients. These two variants are actually instances of a general result (Theorem 4.12) that is parametric in a class $\mathscr{X}$ of "algebras of variables" in $\mathscr{D}$.

The above results hold if $\mathscr{D}$ is a variety of algebras. In case that $\mathscr{D}$ is a variety of ordered algebras, we obtain the analogous two results, working with *profinite inequations* $u \leq v$ instead of equations. As instances we recover Reiterman's original theorem [23] and its version for ordered algebras due to Pin and Weil [20]. Another consequence of our theorem is the observation that *quasivarieties of finite algebras in* $\mathscr{D}$, i.e. subclasses of $\mathscr{D}_f$ closed under finite products and subalgebras, are presentable by *profinite implications*. Moreover, we obtain a number of new Reiterman-type results. For example, for the monad of finite and infinite words on **Set**, our Reiterman theorem shows that a class of finite ∞-monoids is a pseudovariety iff it can be presented by equations between profinite ∞-words. Finally, we can also treat categories of $\mathbf{T}$-algebras that are not varieties. E.g. by taking for $\mathscr{D}$ the category of graphs and $\mathbf{T}$ the free-category monad we essentially recover a result of Jones on pseudovarieties of finite categories [15].

2 Preliminaries

In this section we review the necessary concepts from category theory, universal algebra and topology we will use throughout the paper. Recall that for a finitary many-sorted signature Γ a *variety of Γ-algebras* is a full subcategory of Alg_Γ, the category of Γ-algebras, specified by equations $s = t$ between Γ-terms. By Birkhoff's HSP theorem varieties are precisely the classes of algebras closed under products, subalgebras, and quotients (= homomorphic images). Similarly, *ordered Γ-algebras* are posets equipped with order-preserving Γ-operations, and their morphisms are order-preserving Γ-homomorphisms. A *quotient* of an ordered algebra B is represented by a surjective morphism $e \colon B \twoheadrightarrow A$, and a *subalgebra* of B is represented by an *order-reflecting* morphism $m \colon A \rightarrowtail B$, i.e. $mx \leq my$ iff $x \leq y$. A *variety of ordered Γ-algebras* is a full subcategory of $\mathsf{Alg}_{\leq\Gamma}$, the category of ordered Γ-algebras, specified by inequations $s \leq t$ between Γ-terms. By Bloom's HSP theorem [8], varieties of ordered algebras are precisely the classes of ordered algebras closed under products, subalgebras and quotients.

Remark 2.1. For notational simplicity we restrict our attention to single-sorted varieties. However, all definitions, theorems and proofs that follow are easily adapted to a many-sorted setting. See also Remark 5.7 and Example 5.8.

Definition 2.2. Let $\mathscr{D}$ be a variety of algebras or ordered algebras.

(a) A *topological $\mathscr{D}$-algebra* is a topological space endowed with a $\mathscr{D}$-algebraic structure such that every operation is continuous with respect to the product topology. *Morphisms* of topological $\mathscr{D}$-algebras are continuous $\mathscr{D}$-morphisms.
(b) A topological $\mathscr{D}$-algebra is *profinite* if it is a cofiltered limit of finite $\mathscr{D}$-algebras with discrete topology.

Notation 2.3. Throughout this paper we fix a variety $\mathscr{D}$ of algebras or ordered algebras, equipped with the factorisation system of quotients and subalgebras. We denote by $\widehat{\mathscr{D}}$ the category of profinite $\mathscr{D}$-algebras. We use the forgetful functors

$$\mathscr{D}_f \overset{\hat{J}}{\rightarrowtail} \widehat{\mathscr{D}} \overset{V}{\longrightarrow} \mathscr{D}$$

where V forgets the topology and $\hat{J}$ views a finite $\mathscr{D}$-algebra as a profinite $\mathscr{D}$-algebra with discrete topology. We will often identify $A \in \mathscr{D}_f$ with $\hat{J}A$.

Example 2.4. 1. $\widehat{\mathbf{Set}}$ is the category $\mathbf{Stone}$ of Stone spaces, i.e. compact spaces such that any two distinct elements can be separated by a clopen set.
2. Let $\mathbf{Pos}$ be the category of posets and monotone maps, viewed as the variety of ordered algebras over the empty signature. Then $\widehat{\mathbf{Pos}}$ is the category $\mathbf{Priest}$ of Priestley spaces [22], i.e. ordered compact spaces such that for any two elements u, v with $u \not\leq v$ there is a clopen upper set containing u but not v.
3. For the variety $\mathbf{Mon}$ of monoids, the category $\widehat{\mathbf{Mon}}$ consists of all monoids in $\mathbf{Stone}$; that is, a topological monoid is profinite iff it carries a Stone topology. Analogous descriptions of $\widehat{\mathscr{D}}$ hold for most familiar varieties $\mathscr{D}$ over a finite signature, e.g. groups, semilattices, vector spaces over a finite field; see [14].

Remark 2.5. By [14, Remark VI.2.4] the category $\widehat{\mathscr{D}}$ is the *pro-completion*, i.e. the free completion under cofiltered limits, of $\mathscr{D}_f$. Hence $\widehat{\mathscr{D}}$ is dual to a *locally finitely presentable* category [4], which entails the following properties:

(i) Every object A of $\widehat{\mathscr{D}}$ is the cofiltered limit of all morphisms $h \colon A \to A'$ with finite codomain. More precisely, if $(A \downarrow \mathscr{D}_f)$ denotes the comma category of all such morphisms h, the diagram

$$(A \downarrow \mathscr{D}_f) \to \widehat{\mathscr{D}}, \quad h \mapsto A',$$

has the limit A with limit projections h.
(ii) Given a cofiltered limit cone $\pi_i \colon A \to A_i$ ($i \in I$) in $\widehat{\mathscr{D}}$, any morphism $f \colon A \to B$ with finite codomain factors through some π_i.

Lemma 2.6. $\widehat{\mathscr{D}}$ *has the factorisation system of surjective morphisms and injective (resp. order-reflecting) morphisms.*

Definition 2.7. The *profinite completion* of an object $D \in \mathscr{D}$ is the limit $\hat{D} \in \widehat{\mathscr{D}}$ of the cofiltered diagram

$$(D \downarrow \mathscr{D}_f) \to \widehat{\mathscr{D}}, \quad (h \colon D \to D') \mapsto D'$$

We denote the limit projection corresponding to $h : D \to D'$ by $\hat{h} \colon \hat{D} \to D'$. Observe that $\hat{D} = D$ for any $D \in \mathscr{D}_f$, and $\hat{h} = h$ for any morphism h in $\mathscr{D}_f$.

Proposition 2.8. *The maps $D \mapsto \hat{D}$ and $h \mapsto \hat{h}$ extend to a left adjoint for the forgetful functor V, denoted by*

$$\hat{} \colon \mathscr{D} \to \widehat{\mathscr{D}}.$$

Remark 2.9. We will frequently use the following facts:

(a) *Homomorphism theorem.* Given morphisms $e \colon A \twoheadrightarrow B$ and $f \colon A \to C$ in $\mathscr{D}$ with e surjective, there exists a morphism f' with $f' \cdot e = f$ iff $e(a) = e(a')$ implies $f(a) = f(a')$ (resp. $e(a) \leq e(a')$ implies $f(a) \leq f(a')$) for all $a, a' \in A$. Moreover, if A, B, C are topological $\mathscr{D}$-algebras with a compact Hausdorff topology and e and f are continuous $\mathscr{D}$-morphisms, then f' is continuous.

(b) The forgetful functor $|-| \colon \mathscr{D} \to \mathbf{Set}$ has a left adjoint assigning to each set X the free $\mathscr{D}$-algebra Φ_X on X.

(c) Free $\mathscr{D}$-algebras are projective: for any morphism $f \colon \Phi_X \to B$ and any surjective morphism $e \colon A \twoheadrightarrow B$ in $\mathscr{D}$ there exists a morphism $f' \colon \Phi_X \to A$ with $e \cdot f' = f$. Indeed, choose a function $m \colon |B| \to |A|$ with $e \cdot m = \mathrm{id}$. Then the restriction of $m \cdot f$ to X extends to a morphism $f' \colon \Phi_X \to A$ of $\mathscr{D}$ with $f = f' \cdot e$, since the morphisms on both sides agree on the generators X.

Notation 2.10. For a monad $\mathbf{T} = (T, \eta, \mu)$ on $\mathscr{D}$, we write $\mathscr{D}^{\mathbf{T}}$ for the category of $\mathbf{T}$-algebras and $\mathbf{T}$-homomorphisms, and $\mathscr{D}_f^{\mathbf{T}}$ for the full subcategory of finite $\mathbf{T}$-algebras. The forgetful functors are denoted by

$$U \colon \mathscr{D}_f^{\mathbf{T}} \to \mathscr{D}_f \quad \text{and} \quad U^{\mathbf{T}} \colon \mathscr{D}^{\mathbf{T}} \to \mathscr{D}.$$

Recall that $U^{\mathbf{T}}$ has a left adjoint mapping $D \in \mathscr{D}$ to its free $\mathbf{T}$-algebra (TD, μ_D).

Remark 2.11. If T preserves surjective morphisms, the homomorphism theorem applies to $\mathbf{T}$-algebras. That is, if A, B, C in Remark 2.9(a) are $\mathbf{T}$-algebras and e and f are $\mathbf{T}$-homomorphisms, so is f'. Moreover the factorisation system of $\mathscr{D}$ lifts to $\mathscr{D}^{\mathbf{T}}$: every $\mathbf{T}$-homomorphism $h \colon (A, \alpha) \to (B, \beta)$ can be factorised into a surjective $\mathbf{T}$-homomorphism followed by an injective (resp. order-reflecting) one. *Quotients* and *subalgebras* of $\mathbf{T}$-algebras are taken w.r.t. this factorisation system.

Example 2.12. We are mainly interested in monads representing structures in algebraic language theory.

(a) *Finite words.* The classical example is the free-monoid monad $\mathbf{T}$ on $\mathscr{D} = \mathbf{Set}$,

$$TX = X^* = \coprod_{n<\omega} X^n.$$

The importance of the monad $\mathbf{T}$ is that functions $TX \to \{0, 1\}$ correspond to languages of finite words over the alphabet X, and regular languages are precisely the languages recognized by finite $\mathbf{T}$-algebras (= finite monoids). Bojańczyk [9] recently gave a generalisation of the classical Eilenberg theorem to arbitrary monads $\mathbf{T}$ on $\mathbf{Set}$, relating pseudovarieties of finite $\mathbf{T}$-algebras to varieties of $\mathbf{T}$-recognisable languages.

(b) *Finite words over semilattices.* From the perspective of algebraic language theory it is natural to study monoids in algebraic categories beyond $\mathbf{Set}$. For example, let $\mathscr{D} = \mathbf{JSL}$ be the variety of join-semilattices with 0, considered as a monoidal category w.r.t. the usual tensor product. The free-monoid monad on $\mathbf{JSL}$ is given by

$$TX = X^{\circledast} = \coprod_{n<\omega} X^{\otimes n},$$

the coproduct of all finite tensor powers of X, and $\mathbf{T}$-algebras are precisely idempotent semirings. In case $X = \mathcal{P}_f X_0$ is the free semilattice on a set X_0 one has $TX = \mathcal{P}_f X_0^*$, the semilattice of all finite languages over X_0. Hence semilattice morphisms from TX into the two-chain $0 < 1$ correspond again to formal languages over X_0. This setting allows one to study *disjunctive* varieties of languages in the sense of Polák [21], see [1–3]. Note that although the variety of idempotent semirings can also be represented by the free idempotent semiring monad $T'X = \mathcal{P}_f X^*$ on $\mathbf{Set}$, *functions* from $T'X = \mathcal{P}_f X^*$ to $\{0, 1\}$ do not correpond to formal languages over X.

(c) *Infinite words.* The monad

$$TX = X^\infty = X^* + X^\omega$$

on $\mathscr{D} = \mathbf{Set}$ represents languages of finite and infinite words. The unit $\eta_X \colon X \to X^*$ is given by inclusion, and the multiplication $\mu_X \colon (X^\infty)^\infty \to X^\infty$ is concatentation: $\mu_X(w_0 w_1 w_2 \ldots) = w_0 w_1 w_2 \ldots$ if all words w_i are finite, and otherwise $\mu_X(w_0 w_1 w_2 \ldots) = w_0 w_1 w_2 \ldots w_j$ for the smallest j with w_j infinite. $\mathbf{T}$-algebras are ∞-*monoids*, i.e. monoids with an additional ω-ary multiplication and the expected mixed associative laws. Again, functions from TX to $\{0, 1\}$ correspond to languages (of finite and infinite words), and ω-regular languages are precisely the languages recognised by finite ∞-monoids. This was observed by Bojańczyk [9], who also derived an Eilenberg-type theorem for varieties of ω-regular languages and pseudovarieties of ∞-monoids along the lines of Wilke [27]. As in (b) one can replace ∞-monoids in $\mathbf{Set}$ by "idempotent ∞-semirings", viewed as algebras for a suitable monad on $\mathbf{JSL}$, and thus extend Polák's theorem [21] from finite word languages to ω-regular languages. We leave the details for future work.

(d) In contrast to the previous examples, the category $\mathscr{D}^{\mathbf{T}}$ is not always monadic over **Set** resp. **Pos**. To see this, let $\mathscr{D} = \mathbf{Set}_{0,1}$ be the variety of sets with two constants, that is, the category of all algebras over the signature with two constant symbols $0, 1$. The full subcategory $\mathbf{Set}_{0 \neq 1}$, consisting of singletons and sets with distinct constants $0 \neq 1$, is reflective and hence monadic over $\mathbf{Set}_{0,1}$. However, it is not monadic over **Set**.

3   Profinite Monads

In this section we introduce profinite monads, our main tool for the investigation of profinite equations and Reiterman's theorem for **T**-algebras in Sect. 4.

Assumption 3.1. As in the previous section let $\mathscr{D}$ be a variety of algebras or ordered algebras. Moreover, let $\mathbf{T} = (T, \eta, \mu)$ be a monad on $\mathscr{D}$ such that T preserves surjective morphisms.

Recall that the *right Kan extension* of a functor $F \colon \mathscr{A} \to \mathscr{C}$ along $K \colon \mathscr{A} \to \mathscr{B}$ is a functor $R \colon \mathscr{B} \to \mathscr{C}$ with a universal natural transformation $\epsilon \colon RK \to F$, i.e. for every functor $G \colon \mathscr{B} \to \mathscr{C}$ and every natural transformation $\gamma \colon GK \to F$ there exists a unique natural transformation $\gamma^\dagger \colon G \to R$ with $\gamma = \epsilon \cdot \gamma^\dagger K$. In case $F = K$, the functor R carries a natural monad structure: the unit is given by $\hat{\eta} = (id_K)^\dagger \colon \mathsf{Id} \to R$ and the multiplication by $\hat{\mu} = (\epsilon \cdot R\epsilon)^\dagger \colon RR \to R$. The monad $(R, \hat{\eta}, \hat{\mu})$ is called the *codensity monad* of K, see e.g., [17].

Definition 3.2. The *profinite monad* of $\mathbf{T}$ is the codensity monad $\widehat{\mathbf{T}} = (\hat{T}, \hat{\eta}, \hat{\mu})$ of the functor

$$K = \hat{J}U \colon \mathscr{D}_f^{\mathbf{T}} \to \mathscr{D}_f \to \widehat{\mathscr{D}}.$$

Remark 3.3. A related concept was recently studied by Bojańczyk [9] who associates to every monad $\mathbf{T}$ on **Set** a monad $\overline{\mathbf{T}}$ on **Set** (rather than $\widehat{\mathbf{Set}} = $ **Stone** as in our setting!). Specifically, $\overline{\mathbf{T}}$ is the monad induced by the composite right adjoint $\mathbf{Stone}^{\widehat{\mathbf{T}}} \to \mathbf{Stone} \xrightarrow{V} \mathbf{Set}$. Its construction also appears in the work of Kennison and Gildenhuys [16] who investigated codensity monads for **Set**-valued functors and their connection with profinite algebras.

Remark 3.4.(a) One can compute $\hat{T}X$ for $X \in \widehat{\mathscr{D}}$ via the limit formula for right Kan extensions, see e.g. [18, Theorem X.3.1]. Letting $(X \downarrow \hat{J}U)$ denote the comma category of all arrows $f \colon X \to A$ with $(A, \alpha) \in \mathscr{D}_f^{\mathbf{T}}$, the object $\hat{T}X$ is the limit of the diagram

$$(X \downarrow \hat{J}U) \to \widehat{\mathscr{D}}, \quad f \mapsto A.$$

(b) For $D \in \mathscr{D}$ a morphism $f \colon \hat{D} \to A$ with $(A, \alpha) \in \mathscr{D}_f^{\mathbf{T}}$ corresponds to a **T**-homomorphism $h \colon (TD, \mu_D) \to (A, \alpha)$, since (TD, μ_D) is the free **T**-algebra on D. Hence to compute $\hat{T}\hat{D}$ one can replace $(\hat{D} \downarrow \hat{J}U)$ by the category of all $h \colon (TD, \mu_D) \to (A, \alpha)$ with $(A, \alpha) \in \mathscr{D}_f^{\mathbf{T}}$. We denote the limit cone by

$$h^+ \colon \hat{T}\hat{D} \to \hat{A}. \tag{3.1}$$

One can restrict the diagram defining $\hat{T}\hat{D}$ to surjective **T**-homomorphisms:

Proposition 3.5. *For all $D \in \mathscr{D}$ the object $\hat{T}D$ is the cofiltered limit of all finite $\mathbf{T}$-algebra quotients $e \colon (TD, \mu_D) \twoheadrightarrow (A, \alpha)$.*

Example 3.6 (Profinite words). For the monad $TX = X^*$ on $\mathscr{D} = \mathbf{Set}$ the profinite monad $\hat{\mathbf{T}}$ assigns to every finite set (= finite Stone space) X the space $\hat{T}X = \widehat{X^*}$ of profinite words over X. This is the limit in $\mathbf{Stone}$ of all finite (discrete) quotient monoids of X^*. Similarly, for $TX = X^\infty$ the profinite monad $\hat{\mathbf{T}}$ constructs the space $\hat{T}X$ of "profinite ∞-words" over X.

Lemma 3.7. *(a) $\hat{T}$ preserves cofiltered limits and surjections.*

(b) Given a cofiltered limit cone $h_i \colon A \rightarrow A_i$ $(i \in I)$ in $\widehat{\mathscr{D}}^{\hat{\mathbf{T}}}$, any $\hat{\mathbf{T}}$-homomorphism $h \colon A \rightarrow B$ with finite codomain factors through some h_i.

Remark 3.8. (a) Since $\hat{T}$ preserves surjections, the factorisation system of $\widehat{\mathscr{D}}$ lifts to $\widehat{\mathscr{D}}^{\hat{\mathbf{T}}}$, so we can speak about *quotients* and *subalgebras* of $\hat{\mathbf{T}}$-algebras. Moreover, the homomorphism theorem holds for $\hat{\mathbf{T}}$-algebras, cf. Remark 2.11.

(b) Lemma 3.7(b) exhibits a crucial technical difference between our profinite monad $\hat{\mathbf{T}}$ and Bojańczyk's $\overline{\mathbf{T}}$, see Remark 3.3. For example, for the identity monad $\mathbf{T}$ on $\mathbf{Set}$, the monad $\overline{\mathbf{T}}$ is the ultrafilter monad whose algebras are compact Hausdorff spaces, and the factorisation property in the lemma fails.

Remark 3.9. For each finite $\mathbf{T}$-algebra (A, α) the morphism α is itself a $\mathbf{T}$-homomorphism $\alpha \colon (TA, \mu_A) \twoheadrightarrow (A, \alpha)$, and thus yields the limit projection

$$\alpha^+ \colon \hat{T}\hat{A} \rightarrow \hat{A}$$

of (3.1). The unit $\hat{\eta}_{\hat{D}}$ and multiplication $\hat{\mu}_{\hat{D}}$ of $\hat{\mathbf{T}}$ are determined by the following commutative diagrams for all $\mathbf{T}$-homomorphisms $h \colon (TD, \mu_D) \rightarrow (A, \alpha)$:

$$
\begin{array}{ccc}
\hat{D} \xrightarrow{\hat{\eta}_{\hat{D}}} \hat{T}\hat{D} & \qquad & \hat{T}\hat{T}\hat{D} \xrightarrow{\hat{\mu}_{\hat{D}}} \hat{T}\hat{D} \\
\end{array}
\tag{3.2}
$$

Hence $(\hat{A}, \alpha^+)$ is a $\hat{\mathbf{T}}$-algebra: the unit and associative law for $\hat{\mathbf{T}}$-algebras follow by putting $D = A$ and $h = \alpha$ in (3.2). Moreover, (3.2) states precisely that $h^+ \colon (\hat{T}\hat{D}, \hat{\mu}_{\hat{D}}) \rightarrow (A, \alpha^+)$ is the unique $\hat{\mathbf{T}}$-homomorphism extending the map $\widehat{h\eta_D}$ for every h as above.

Proposition 3.10. *The maps $(A, \alpha) \mapsto (\hat{A}, \alpha^+)$ and $h \mapsto \hat{h}$ define an isomorphism between the categories of finite $\mathbf{T}$-algebras and finite $\hat{\mathbf{T}}$-algebras:*

$$\mathscr{D}_f^{\mathbf{T}} \cong \widehat{\mathscr{D}}_f^{\hat{\mathbf{T}}}.$$

4   Reiterman's Theorem for T-Algebras

Reiterman's theorem [6,23] states that, for any variety $\mathscr{D}$ of algebras, a class of finite algebras in $\mathscr{D}$ is a *pseudovariety*, i.e. closed under finite products, subobjects and quotients, iff it is presented by *profinite equations*. Later Pin and Weil [20] proved the corresponding result for varieties $\mathscr{D}$ of ordered algebras: pseudovarieties are precisely the classes of finite algebras in $\mathscr{D}$ presented by *profinite inequations*. In our categorical setting these two theorems represent the case where $\mathbf{T}$ is chosen to be the identity monad on $\mathscr{D}$. In Sect. 4.1 we introduce pseudovarieties and profinite (in-)equations for arbitrary monads $\mathbf{T}$ on $\mathscr{D}$, a straightforward extension of the original notions. In Sect. 4.2 we present a further generalisation and prove the main result of this paper, Reiterman's theorem for finite $\mathbf{T}$-algebras.

4.1   Pseudovarieties and Profinite (In-)equations

Let us start with extending the classical concept of a pseudovariety to $\mathbf{T}$-algebras.

Definition 4.1. A *pseudovariety of* $\mathbf{T}$-*algebras* is a class of finite $\mathbf{T}$-algebras closed under finite products, subalgebras and quotients.

Notation 4.2. Recall from Remark 2.9 the forgetful functor $|-| : \mathscr{D} \to \mathbf{Set}$ and its left adjoint $X \mapsto \Phi_X$. For any finite $\mathbf{T}$-algebra (A, α) to interpret variables from a finite set X in A means to give a morphism $h_0 : \Phi_X \to A$ in $\mathscr{D}$, or equivalently a $\mathbf{T}$-homomorphism $h : (T\Phi_X, \mu_{\Phi_X}) \to (A, \alpha)$. The corresponding $\widehat{\mathbf{T}}$-homomorphism is denoted $h^+ : \hat{T}\hat{\Phi}_X \to A$, see Remarks 3.4 and 3.9.

Definition 4.3.   1. Let $\mathscr{D}$ be a variety of unordered algebras. By a *profinite equation* over a finite set X of variables is meant a pair $u, v \in \hat{T}\hat{\Phi}_X$, denoted $u = v$. A finite $\mathbf{T}$-algebra (A, α) *satisfies* $u = v$ provided that

$$h^+(u) = h^+(v) \quad \text{for all } \mathbf{T}\text{-homomorphisms } h : T\Phi_X \to A.$$

2 Let $\mathscr{D}$ be a variety of ordered algebras. A *profinite inequation* over a finite set X of variables is again a pair $u, v \in \hat{T}\hat{\Phi}_X$, denoted $u \leq v$. A finite $\mathbf{T}$-algebra (A, α) *satisfies* $u \leq v$ provided that

$$h^+(u) \leq h^+(v) \quad \text{for all— } \mathbf{T}\text{-homomorphisms } h : T\Phi_X \to A.$$

A class E of profinite (in-)equations *presents* the class of all finite $\mathbf{T}$-algebras that satisfy all (in-)equations in E.

Lemma 4.4. *Every class of finite* $\mathbf{T}$-*algebras presented by profinite (in-) equations forms a pseudovariety.*

The proof is an easy verification. In the following subsection we show the converse of the lemma: every pseudovariety is presented by profinite equations.

4.2   Reiterman's Theorem for T-algebras

The concept of profinite (in-)equation as introduced above only considers the free finitely generated objects Φ_X of $\mathscr{D}$ as objects of variables. A natural variation is to admit any finite object $X \in \mathscr{D}_f$ as an object of variables. That is, we define a *profinite equation over* X as a pair $u, v \in \hat{T}\hat{X}$, and say that a finite **T**-algebra (A, α) *satisfies* $u = v$ if for every **T**-homomorphism $h \colon (TX, \mu_X) \to (A, \alpha)$ the $\widehat{\mathbf{T}}$-homomorphism $h^+ \colon \hat{T}\hat{X} \to A$ merges u, v; analogously for inequations. A class of finite **T**-algebras presented by such profinite equations is still closed under finite products and subalgebras, but not necessarily under quotients. However, it is closed under U-*split quotients* for the forgetful functor $U \colon \mathscr{D}_f^{\mathbf{T}} \to \mathscr{D}_f$, where a surjective morphism e in $\mathscr{D}_f^{\mathbf{T}}$ is called U-*split* if there is a morphism m in $\mathscr{D}_f$ with $Ue \cdot m = id$.

More generally, we introduce below for a class $\mathscr{X}$ of objects in $\mathscr{D}$ the concept of *profinite (in-)equation* over $\mathscr{X}$: a pair of elements of $\hat{T}\hat{X}$ with $X \in \mathscr{X}$. This subsumes both of the above situations: by taking as $\mathscr{X}$ all free finitely generated objects of $\mathscr{D}$ we recover the concept of Sect. 4.1. And the choice $\mathscr{X} = \mathscr{D}_f$ leads to a new variant of Reiterman's theorem: a characterisation of classes of finite **T**-algebras closed under finite products, subalgebras and U-split quotients. The latter can be understood as a finite analogue of Barr's result [7], which states that classes of **T**-algebras closed under products, subalgebras and U-split quotients are in bijective correspondence with quotient monads of **T**.

Notation 4.5.   For a class $\mathscr{X}$ of objects in $\mathscr{D}$ we denote by $\mathcal{E}_{\mathscr{X}}$ the class of all surjective morphisms $e \colon A \twoheadrightarrow B$ with finite codomain such that all objects X of $\mathscr{X}$ are projective w.r.t. e. That is, every morphism $f \colon X \to B$ factors through e.

Assumption 4.6.   We assume that a class $\mathscr{X}$ of objects in $\mathscr{D}$ is given that forms a *projective presentation* of $\mathscr{D}_f$, i.e. for every finite object $A \in \mathscr{D}_f$ there exists an object $X \in \mathscr{X}$ and a quotient $e \colon X \twoheadrightarrow A$ in $\mathcal{E}_{\mathscr{X}}$.

Definition 4.7.   An $\mathscr{X}$-*pseudovariety of* **T**-*algebras* is a class of finite **T**-algebras closed under finite products, subalgebras and $\mathcal{E}_{\mathscr{X}}$-quotients, i.e. quotients carried by a morphism in $\mathcal{E}_{\mathscr{X}}$.

Example 4.8.   (a) For the choice of Sect. 4.1,

$$\mathscr{X} = \text{ free finitely generated objects of } \mathscr{D},$$

the class $\mathcal{E}_{\mathscr{X}}$ consists of all surjective morphisms with finite codomain, see Remark 2.9(c). Clearly Assumption 4.6 is fulfilled since every finite object in a variety $\mathscr{D}$ is a quotient of a free finitely generated one. Thus an $\mathscr{X}$-pseudovariety is simply a pseudovariety in the sense of Definition 4.1.

(b) If we choose

$$\mathscr{X} = \mathscr{D}_f$$

then $\mathcal{E}_{\mathscr{X}}$ consists precisely of the split surjections with finite codomain. Indeed, clearly every split surjection lies in $\mathcal{E}_{\mathscr{X}}$. Conversely, given $e \colon A \twoheadrightarrow B$

in $\mathcal{E}_{\mathscr{X}}$, apply the definition of $\mathcal{E}_{\mathscr{X}}$ to $X = B$ and $f = id$. Assumption 4.6 is fulfilled because every object in $\mathscr{D}_f$ is a split quotient of itself. A $\mathscr{D}_f$-pseudovariety is a class of finite **T**-algebras closed under finite products, subalgebras and U-split quotients.

Definition 4.9. 1. Let $\mathscr{D}$ be a variety of unordered algebras. A *profinite equation over* $\mathscr{X}$ is an expression of the form $u = v$ with $u, v \in \hat{T}\hat{X}$ and $X \in \mathscr{X}$. A finite **T**-algebra (A, α) *satisfies* $u = v$ if

$$h^+(u) = h^+(v) \quad \text{for all } \mathbf{T}\text{-homomorphisms } h \colon TX \to A.$$

2. Let $\mathscr{D}$ be a variety of ordered algebras. A *profinite inequation over* $\mathscr{X}$ is an expression of the form $u \leq v$ with $u, v \in \hat{T}\hat{X}$ and $X \in \mathscr{X}$. A finite **T**-algebra (A, α) *satisfies* $u \leq v$ if

$$h^+(u) \leq h^+(v) \quad \text{for all } \mathbf{T}\text{-homomorphisms } h \colon TX \to A.$$

A class E of profinite (in-)equations over $\mathscr{X}$ *presents* the class of all finite **T**-algebras that satisfy all (in-)equations in E.

Remark 4.10. For any full subcategory $\mathcal{V} \subseteq \mathscr{D}_f^{\mathbf{T}}$ closed under finite products and subalgebras, the *pro-$\mathcal{V}$ monad* of **T** is the monad $\widehat{\mathbf{T}}_{\mathcal{V}} = (\hat{T}_{\mathcal{V}}, \hat{\mu}^{\mathcal{V}}, \hat{\eta}^{\mathcal{V}})$ on $\widehat{\mathscr{D}}$ defined by replacing in Definition 3.2 the functor $U \colon \mathscr{D}_f^{\mathbf{T}} \to \mathscr{D}_f$ by its restriction $U_{\mathcal{V}} \colon \mathcal{V} \to \mathscr{D}_f$. That is, $\hat{T}_{\mathcal{V}}$ is the right Kan extension of $\hat{J} U_{\mathcal{V}}$ along itself. In analogy to Remark 3.4, one can describe $\hat{T}_{\mathcal{V}}\hat{X}$ with $X \in \mathscr{D}$ as the cofiltered limit of the diagram of all homomorphisms $h \colon (TX, \mu_X) \to (A, \alpha)$ with $(A, \alpha) \in \mathcal{V}$. The limit projections are denoted $h_{\mathcal{V}}^+ \colon \hat{T}_{\mathcal{V}}\hat{X} \to A$. The universal property of $\hat{T}_{\mathcal{V}}$ as a right Kan extension yields a monad morphism $\varphi^{\mathcal{V}} \colon \widehat{\mathbf{T}} \to \widehat{\mathbf{T}}_{\mathcal{V}}$; its component $\varphi_{\hat{X}}^{\mathcal{V}}$ for $X \in \mathscr{D}$ is the unique $\widehat{\mathscr{D}}$-morphism making the triangle below commute for all $h \colon (TX, \mu_X) \to (A, \alpha)$ with $(A, \alpha) \in \mathcal{V}$.

$$
\begin{array}{ccc}
\hat{T}\hat{X} & \xrightarrow{\;\varphi_{\hat{X}}^{\mathcal{V}}\;} & \hat{T}_{\mathcal{V}}\hat{X} \\
{\scriptstyle h^+}\big\downarrow & \swarrow {\scriptstyle h_{\mathcal{V}}^+} & \\
A & &
\end{array}
\tag{4.1}
$$

Lemma 4.11. *Let $\mathcal{V}$ be a class of finite **T**-algebras closed under finite products and subalgebras and $u, v \in \hat{T}\hat{X}$ with $X \in \mathscr{D}$.*

1. *Unordered case:* $\varphi_{\hat{X}}^{\mathcal{V}}(u) = \varphi_{\hat{X}}^{\mathcal{V}}(v)$ *iff every algebra in $\mathcal{V}$ satisfies $u = v$.*
2. *Ordered case:* $\varphi_{\hat{X}}^{\mathcal{V}}(u) \leq \varphi_{\hat{X}}^{\mathcal{V}}(v)$ *iff every algebra in $\mathcal{V}$ satisfies $u \leq v$.*

Theorem 4.12 (Reiterman's Theorem for T-algebras). *A class of finite **T**-algebras is an $\mathscr{X}$-pseudovariety iff it is presented by profinite equations over $\mathscr{X}$ (unordered case) resp. profinite inequations over $\mathscr{X}$ (ordered case).*

Proof. Consider first the unordered case. The "if" direction is a straightforward verification. For the "only if" direction let $\mathcal{V}$ be an $\mathscr{X}$-pseudovariety.

(a) In analogy to Proposition 3.5 one can restrict the cofiltered diagram defining $\hat{T}_\mathcal{V}\hat{X}$ to surjective homomorphisms $h\colon TX \twoheadrightarrow A$. Then the limit projections $h_\mathcal{V}^+$ and the mediating map $\varphi_{\hat{X}}^\mathcal{V}$ in (4.1) are also surjective, see [25, Corollary 1.1.6]. Moreover, since $\varphi^\mathcal{V}$ is a monad morphism, the free $\hat{T}_\mathcal{V}$-algebra $(\hat{T}_\mathcal{V}\hat{X}, \hat{\mu}_{\hat{X}}^\mathcal{V})$ on $\hat{X}$ can be turned into a $\hat{T}$-algebra $(\hat{T}_\mathcal{V}\hat{X}, \hat{\mu}_{\hat{X}}^\mathcal{V} \cdot \varphi_{\hat{T}_\mathcal{V}\hat{X}}^\mathcal{V})$, and $\varphi_{\hat{X}}^\mathcal{V}\colon (\hat{T}\hat{X}, \hat{\mu}_{\hat{X}}) \to (\hat{T}_\mathcal{V}\hat{X}, \hat{\mu}_{\hat{X}}^\mathcal{V} \cdot \varphi_{\hat{T}_\mathcal{V}\hat{X}}^\mathcal{V})$ is a $\hat{T}$-homomorphism.

(b) Let E the class of all profinite equations over $\mathscr{X}$ satisfied by all algebras in $\mathcal{V}$. We prove that $\mathcal{V}$ is presented by E, which only requires to show that every finite $\mathbf{T}$-algebra (A, α) satisfying all equations in E lies in $\mathcal{V}$.

By Assumption 4.6 choose $X \in \mathscr{X}$ and a quotient $e_0\colon X \twoheadrightarrow A$ in $\mathcal{E}_\mathscr{X}$, and freely extend e_0 to a (necessarily surjective) $\mathbf{T}$-homomorphism $e\colon TX \twoheadrightarrow A$. We first show that the corresponding $\hat{\mathbf{T}}$-homomorphism $e^+\colon \hat{T}\hat{X} \to \hat{A}$ factors through $\varphi_{\hat{X}}^\mathcal{V}$. Indeed, whenever $\varphi_{\hat{X}}^\mathcal{V}$ merges $u, v \in \hat{T}\hat{X}$ then the profinite equation $u = v$ lies in E by Lemma 4.11, so e^+ merges u, v since (A, α) satisfies all equations in E. Since $\varphi_{\hat{X}}^\mathcal{V}$ is surjective by (a), the homomorphism theorem (see Remark 3.8) yields a $\hat{\mathbf{T}}$-homomorphism $g\colon \hat{T}_\mathcal{V}\hat{X} \to A$ in $\hat{\mathcal{D}}$ with $g \cdot \varphi_{\hat{X}}^\mathcal{V} = e^+$.

(c) By Lemma 3.7(b) the $\hat{\mathbf{T}}$-homomorphism g factors through the limit cone defining $\hat{T}_\mathcal{V}\hat{X}$: there is a $\mathbf{T}$-homomorphism $h\colon TX \to B$ with $(B, \beta) \in \mathcal{V}$ and a $\hat{\mathbf{T}}$-homomorphism $q\colon B \to A$ with $q \cdot h_\mathcal{V}^+ = g$. By Proposition 3.10 the morphism q is also a $\mathbf{T}$-homomorphism, and is surjective because g is.

(d) To conclude the proof it suffices to verify that q lies in $\mathcal{E}_\mathscr{X}$ (then $(B, \beta) \in \mathcal{V}$ implies $(A, \alpha) \in \mathcal{V}$ because $\mathcal{V}$ is closed under $\mathcal{E}_\mathscr{X}$-quotients). Indeed: every morphism $f\colon Y \to A$ with $Y \in \mathscr{X}$ factors through e_0 because $e_0 \in \mathcal{E}_\mathscr{X}$, i.e.

$$f = e_0 \cdot k \quad \text{for some } k\colon Y \to X \text{ in } \mathcal{D}.$$

Then the diagram below commutes (for the second triangle see (3.2)) and shows that $\hat{f}$ factors through $\hat{q} = q$ in $\hat{\mathcal{D}}$, so f factors through q in $\mathcal{D}$. We conclude that $q \in \mathcal{E}_\mathscr{X}$, as desired.

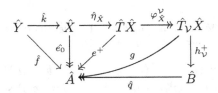

This proves the theorem for the unordered case. The proof for the ordered case is analogous: replace profinite equations by inequations, and use the homomorphism theorem for ordered algebras to construct the morphism g.

5   Applications and Examples

Let us consider some examples and applications. First note that the original Reiterman theorem and its ordered version emerge from Theorem 4.12 by taking the identity monad $\mathbf{T} = \mathsf{Id}$ and $\mathscr{X} = $ free finitely generated objects of $\mathscr{D}$, see Example 4.8(a). In this case we have $\widehat{\mathbf{T}} = \mathsf{Id}$, $\mathscr{D}^{\mathbf{T}} = \mathscr{D}$, $\widehat{\mathscr{D}}^{\widehat{\mathbf{T}}} = \widehat{\mathscr{D}}$, and a profinite equation $u = v$ (resp. a profinite inequation $u \leq v$) is a pair $u, v \in \hat{\Phi}_X$ for a finite set X. We conclude:

Corollary 5.1 (Reiterman [23], Banaschewski [6]). *Let $\mathscr{D}$ be a variety of algebras. A class $\mathcal{V} \subseteq \mathscr{D}_f$ is a pseudovariety iff it is presented by profinite equations over finite sets of variables.*

Corollary 5.2 (Pin and Weil [20]). *Let $\mathscr{D}$ be a variety of ordered algebras. A class $\mathcal{V} \subseteq \mathscr{D}_f$ is a pseudovariety iff it is presented by profinite inequations over finite sets of variables.*

Recall from Isbell [13] that a class $\mathcal{V} \subseteq \mathscr{D}$ is closed under products and subalgebras iff it is presented by implications

$$\bigwedge_{i \in I} s_i = t_i \;\Rightarrow\; s = t$$

where s_i, t_i, s, t are terms and I is a set. Choosing $\mathbf{T}$ to be the identity monad and $\mathscr{X} = \mathscr{D}_f$ gives us the counterpart for finite algebras: by Example 4.8(b) a $\mathscr{D}_f$-pseudovariety is precisely a class $\mathcal{V} \subseteq \mathscr{D}_f$ closed under finite products and subalgebras, since the closure under split quotients is implied by closure under subalgebras. Such a class could be called "quasi-pseudovariety", but to avoid this clumsy terminology we prefer "quasivariety of finite algebras".

Definition 5.3. A *quasivariety of finite algebras of $\mathscr{D}$* is a class $\mathcal{V} \subseteq \mathscr{D}_f$ closed under finite products and subalgebras.

In analogy to Isbell's result we show that quasivarieties of finite algebras are precisely the classes of finite algebras of $\mathscr{D}$ presented by *profinite implications*.

Definition 5.4. Let X be a finite set of variables.

1. Unordered case: a *profinite implication* over X is an expression

$$\bigwedge_{i \in I} u_i = v_i \;\Rightarrow\; u = v \tag{5.1}$$

where I is a set and $u_i, v_i, u, v \in \hat{\Phi}_X$. An object $A \in \mathscr{D}_f$ satisfies (5.1) if for every $h \colon \Phi_X \to A$ with $\hat{h}(u_i) = \hat{h}(v_i)$ for all $i \in I$ one has $\hat{h}(u) = \hat{h}(v)$.
2. Ordered case: a *profinite implication* over X is an expression

$$\bigwedge_{i \in I} u_i \leq v_i \;\Rightarrow\; u \leq v \tag{5.2}$$

where I is a set and $u_i, v_i, u, v \in \hat{\Phi}_X$. An object $A \in \mathscr{D}_f$ satisfies (5.2) if for every $h \colon \Phi_X \to A$ with $\hat{h}(u_i) = \hat{h}(v_i)$ for all $i \in I$ one has $\hat{h}(u) \leq \hat{h}(v)$.

A class P of profinite implications *presents* the class of all finite algebras in $\mathscr{D}$ satisfying all implications in P.

Theorem 5.5. *For any class $\mathcal{V} \subseteq \mathscr{D}_f$ the following statements are equivalent:*

1. $\mathcal{V}$ *is a quasivariety of finite algebras.*
2. $\mathcal{V}$ *is presented by profinite (in-)equations over $\mathscr{D}_f$.*
3. $\mathcal{V}$ *is presented by profinite implications.*

Proof Sketch. 3⇒1 requires a routine verification, and 1⇒2 is Theorem 4.12. For 2⇒3 assume w.l.o.g. that $\mathcal{V}$ is presented by a single profinite equation $u = v$ with u, v elements of some $X \in \mathscr{D}_f$. Express X as a quotient $q \colon \varPhi_Y \twoheadrightarrow X$ for some finite set Y. Let $\{ (u_i, v_i) : i \in I \}$ be the kernel of $\hat{q} \colon \hat{\varPhi}_Y \twoheadrightarrow X$ (consisting of all pairs $(u_i, v_i) \in \hat{\varPhi}_Y \times \hat{\varPhi}_Y$ with $\hat{q}(u_i) = \hat{q}(v_i)$), and choose $u', v' \in \hat{\varPhi}_Y$ with $\hat{q}(u') = u$ and $\hat{q}(v') = v$. Then a finite object $A \in \mathscr{D}_f$ satisfies the profinite equation $u = v$ iff it satisfies the profinite implication

$$\bigwedge_{i \in I} u_i = v_i \;\Rightarrow\; u' = v', \tag{5.3}$$

which proves that $\mathcal{V}$ is presented (5.3). Analogously for the ordered case.

Example 5.6. 1. Let $\mathcal{V} \subseteq \mathbf{Mon}_f$ be the quasivariety of all finite monoids whose only invertible element is the unit. It is presented by the profinite implication $x^\omega = 1 \Rightarrow x = 1$ over the set of variables $X = \{x\}$. Here the profinite word $x^\omega \in \widehat{X^*}$ is interpreted, for every finite monoid M with x interpreted as $m \in M$, as the unique idempotent power of m. Indeed, if M has no nontrivial invertible elements, it satisfies the implication: given $m \neq 1$ and m^k idempotent, then $m^k \neq 1$ (otherwise m has the inverse m^{k-1}). Conversely, if M satisfies the implication and m is invertible, then so is its idempotent power m^k. Hence $m^k \cdot m^k = m^k$ implies $m^k = 1$, so $m = 1$.

2. Let **Pos** be the variety of posets (i.e. the variety of all ordered algebras over the empty signature). The quasivariety $\mathcal{V} \subseteq \mathbf{Pos}_f$ of finite discrete posets is presented by the profinite implication $v \leq u \Rightarrow u \leq v$ over the set $X = \{u, v\}$.

Remark 5.7. As indicated before all concepts in this paper also apply to a setting where $\mathscr{D}$ is a many-sorted variety of algebras or ordered algebras. In this case an algebra is *finite* if the disjoint union of the underlying sets of all sorts is a finite set. By a *profinite equation* over $X \in \mathscr{D}$ is a meant pair of elements u, v in some sort s of $\hat{T}\hat{X}$, and it is *satisfied* by a finite **T**-algebra A if for every **T**-homomorphism $h \colon TX \to A$ the s-component of $h^+ \colon \hat{T}\hat{X} \to A$ merges u, v. Similarly for profinite inequations and profinite implications.

Example 5.8. Consider the variety $\mathscr{D}$ of directed graphs, i.e. algebras for the two-sorted signature consisting of a sort Ob (objects), a sort Mor (morphisms) and two unary operations $s, t \colon$ Mor $\to$ Ob specifying the source and target of a morphism. Then **Cat**, the category of small categories and functors, is isomorphic to $\mathscr{D}^{\mathbf{T}}$ for the monad **T** constructing the free category on a graph. Choosing

$\mathscr{X}$ = free finitely generated graphs, Theorem 4.12 shows that every pseudovariety of categories, i.e. every class of finite categories closed under finite products, subcategories (represented by injective functors) and quotient categories (represented by surjective functors), can be specified by profinite equations over a two-sorted set of variables. This result was essentially proved by Jones [15]. The difference is that he restricts to quotients represented by surjective functors which are bijective on objects, and replaces subcategories by faithful functors. Moreover, profinite equations are restricted to the sort of morphisms.

6   Conclusions and Future Work

Motivated by recent developments in algebraic language theory, we generalised Reiterman's theorem to finite algebras for an arbitrary monad $\mathbf{T}$ on a base category $\mathscr{D}$. Here $\mathscr{D}$ is a variety of (possibly ordered, many-sorted) algebras. The core concept of our paper is the profinite monad $\widehat{\mathbf{T}}$ of $\mathbf{T}$, which makes it possible to introduce profinite (in-)equations at the level of monads and prove that they precisely present pseudovarieties of $\mathbf{T}$-algebras.

Referring to the diagram in the Introduction, our Reiterman theorem is presented in a setting that unifies the two categorical approaches to algebraic language theory of Bojańczyk [9] and in our work [1–3,10]. The next step is to also derive an Eilenberg theorem in this setting. For each monad $\mathbf{T}$ on a category of sorted sets, Bojańczyk [9] proved an Eilenberg-type characterisation of pseudovarieties of $\mathbf{T}$-algebras: they correspond to *varieties of* $\mathbf{T}$-*recognisable languages*. Here by a "language" is meant a function from TX to $\{0,1\}$ for some alphabet X, and a variety of languages is a class of such languages closed under boolean operations, homomorphic preimages and a suitably generalised notion of derivatives. On the other hand, as indicated in Example 2.12, one needs to consider monoids on algebraic categories beyond **Set** in order to study varieties of languages with relaxed closure properties, e.g. dropping closure under complement or intersection. The aim is thus to prove an Eilenberg theorem parametric in a monad $\mathbf{T}$ on an algebraic category $\mathscr{D}$. Observing that e.g. for $\mathscr{D} = \mathbf{Set}$ the monad $\widehat{\mathbf{T}}$ on **Stone** dualises to a *comonad* on the category of boolean algebras, we expect this can be achieved in a duality-based setting along the lines of Gehrke, Grigorieff and Pin [12] and our work [1,3].

Throughout this paper we presented the case of ordered and unordered algebras as separated but analogous developments. Pin and Weil [20] gave a uniform treatment of ordered and unordered algebras by generalising Reiterman's theorem from finite algebras to finite first-order structures. A similar approach should also work in our categorical framework: replace $\mathscr{D}$ by a variety of relational algebras over a quasivariety $\mathcal{Q}$ of relational first-order structures, with $\mathcal{Q} = \mathbf{Set}$ and $\mathcal{Q} = \mathbf{Pos}$ covering the case of algebras and ordered algebras.

Finally, observe that categories of the form $\mathscr{D}^{\mathbf{T}}$, where $\mathscr{D}$ is a many-sorted variety of algebras and $\mathbf{T}$ is an accessible monad, correspond precisely to locally presentable categories. This opens the door towards an abstract treatment, and further generalisation, of Reiterman's theorem in purely categorical terms.

References

1. Adámek, J., Milius, S., Myers, R.S.R., Urbat, H.: Generalized Eilenberg theorem I: local varieties of languages. In: Muscholl, A. (ed.) FOSSACS 2014 (ETAPS). LNCS, vol. 8412, pp. 366–380. Springer, Heidelberg (2014)
2. Adámek, J., Milius, S., Urbat, H.: Syntactic monoids in a category. In: Moss, L.S., Sobocinski, P. (eds.) Proceedings of CALCO 2015 (2015)
3. Adámek, J., Myers, R.S.R., Urbat, H., Milius, S.: Varieties of languages in a category. In: Proceedings LICS 2015. IEEE (2015)
4. Adámek, J., Rosický, J.: Locally Presentable and Accessible Categories. Cambridge University Press, Cambridge (1994)
5. Almeida, J.: On pseudovarieties, varieties of languages, filters of congruences, pseudoidentities and related topics. Algebra Universalis 27(3), 333–350 (1990)
6. Banaschewski, B.: The Birkhoff theorem for varieties of finite algebras. Algebra Universalis 17(1), 360–368 (1983)
7. Barr, M.: HSP subcategories of Eilenberg-Moore algebras. Theory Appl. Categ. 10(18), 461–468 (2002)
8. Bloom, S.L.: Varieties of ordered algebras. J. Comput. Syst. Sci. 13(2), 200–212 (1976)
9. Bojańczyk, M.: Recognisable languages over monads. In: Potapov, I. (ed.) DLT 2015. LNCS, vol. 9168, pp. 1–13. Springer, Heidelberg (2015). Full version: http://arxiv.org/abs/1502.04898
10. Chen, L.T., Urbat, H.: A fibrational approach to automata theory. In: Moss, L.S., Sobocinski, P. (eds.) Proceedings of CALCO 2015 (2015)
11. Eilenberg, S.: Automata, Languages, and Machines, vol. 2. Academic Press, New York (1976)
12. Gehrke, M., Grigorieff, S., Pin, J.É.: Duality and equational theory of regular languages. In: Aceto, L., Damgård, I., Goldberg, L.A., Halldórsson, M.M., Ingólfsdóttir, A., Walukiewicz, I. (eds.) ICALP 2008, Part II. LNCS, vol. 5126, pp. 246–257. Springer, Heidelberg (2008)
13. Isbell, J.R.: Subobjects, Adequacy, Completeness and Categories of Algebras. Instytut Matematyczny Polskiej Akademi Nauk, Warsaw (1964)
14. Johnstone, P.T.: Stone Spaces. Cambridge University Press, Cambridge (1982)
15. Jones, P.R.: Profinite categories, implicit operations and pseudovarieties of categories. J. Pure Appl. Algebr. 109(1), 61–95 (1996)
16. Kennison, J.F., Gildenhuys, D.: Equational completion, model induced triples and pro-objects. J. Pure Appl. Algebr. 1(4), 317–346 (1971)
17. Linton, F.E.J.: An outline of functorial semantics. In: Eckmann, B. (ed.) Seminor on Triples and Categorical Homology Theory. LNM, vol. 80, pp. 7–52. Springer, Heidelberg (1969)
18. Lane, S.M.: Categories for the Working Mathematician, 2nd edn. Springer, New York (1998)
19. Pin, J.E.: A variety theorem without complementation. Russ. Math. (Izvestija vuzov.Matematika) 39, 80–90 (1995)
20. Pin, J.E., Weil, P.: A Reiterman theorem for pseudovarieties of finite first-order structures. Algebra Universalis 35, 577–595 (1996)
21. Polák, L.: Syntactic semiring of a language. In: Sgall, J., Pultr, A., Kolman, P. (eds.) MFCS 2001. LNCS, vol. 2136, p. 611. Springer, Heidelberg (2001)
22. Priestley, H.A.: Ordered topological spaces and the representation of distributive lattices. Proc. London Math. Soc. 3(3), 507 (1972)

23. Reiterman, J.: The Birkhoff theorem for finite algebras. Algebra Universalis **14**(1), 1–10 (1982)
24. Reutenauer, C.: Séries formelles et algèbres syntactiques. J. Algebra **66**, 448–483 (1980)
25. Ribes, L., Zalesskii, P.: Profinite Groups. A Series of Modern Surveys in Mathematics. Springer, Berlin (2010)
26. Schützenberger, M.P.: On finite monoids having only trivial subgroups. Inf. Control **8**, 190–194 (1965)
27. Wilke, T.: An Eilenberg theorem for infinity-languages. In: Proceedings of ICALP 1991, pp. 588–599 (1991)

Author Index

Printed in the United States
by Bookmasters

Printed in the United States
By Bookmasters